Tony Peetoom

Law for
Estate Management Students

D1495094

Law for
Estate Management Students

Fifth edition

Richard Card LLB LLM FRSA

Professor of Law
De Montfort University, Leicester

John Murdoch LLB ACIArb

Professor of Law
University of Reading

Sandi Murdoch LLB LLM

Senior Lecturer in Law
University of Reading

Butterworths
London Edinburgh & Dublin
1998

United Kingdom	Butterworths, a Division of Reed Elsevier (UK) Ltd, Halsbury House, 35 Chancery Lane, LONDON WC2A 1EL and 4 Hill Street, EDINBURGH EH2 3JZ
Australia	Butterworths, a Division of Reed International Books Australia Pty Ltd, CHATSWOOD, New South Wales
Canada	Butterworths Canada Ltd, MARKHAM, Ontario
Hong Kong	Butterworths Asia (Hong Kong), HONG KONG
India	Butterworths Asia, NEW DELHI
Ireland	Butterworth (Ireland) Ltd, DUBLIN
Malaysia	Malayan Law Journal Sdn Bhd, KUALA LUMPUR
New Zealand	Butterworths of New Zealand Ltd, WELLINGTON
Singapore	Butterworths Asia, SINGAPORE
South Africa	Butterworths Publishers (Pty) Ltd, DURBAN
USA	Lexis Law Publishing, CHARLOTTESVILLE, Virginia

© Reed Elsevier (UK) Ltd 1998

All rights reserved. No part of this publication may be reproduced in any material form (including photocopying or storing it in any medium by electronic means and whether or not transiently or incidentally to some other use of this publication) without the written permission of the copyright owner except in accordance with the provisions of the Copyright, Designs and Patents Act 1988 or under the terms of a licence issued by the Copyright Licensing Agency Ltd, 90 Tottenham Court Road, London, England W1P 0LP. Applications for the copyright owner's written permission to reproduce any part of this publication should be addressed to the publisher.

Warning: The doing of an unauthorised act in relation to a copyright work may result in both a civil claim for damages and criminal prosecution.

Any Crown copyright material is reproduced with the permission of the Controller of Her Majesty's Stationery Office.

A CIP Catalogue record for this book is available from the British Library.

ISBN 0 406 90187 2

Printed by The Bath Press, Somerset

Preface

Like its previous editions, this book is intended to serve as a comprehensive textbook for estate management students studying courses in basic legal topics, particularly ones which treat the subject matter in some depth.

We have had in mind the syllabuses for examinations in basic legal subjects for degrees and diplomas in estate management, land management and allied fields, as well as those for the comparable examinations of the relevant professional bodies. Despite its title, this book should also prove useful for those following similar courses in law for other types of qualifications.

This book is divided into four parts. Part I outlines the English legal system. Parts II, III and IV deal with the law of contract, the law of tort and land law, respectively. The need to produce a book of manageable size has meant that we have not dealt with what may be regarded as the more specialist legal subjects studied by estate management students, such as planning law, local government law, or the law of landlord and tenant.

In addition to the usual flood of case law, we have also had to deal with a number of pieces of new legislation, in particular the Landlord and Tenant (Covenants) Act 1995, the Trusts of Land and Appointment of Trustees Act 1996, the Arbitration Act 1996, the Housing Act 1996, the Land Registration Act 1997 and the Unfair Terms in Consumer Contracts Regulations 1994.

Besides the inevitable updating and associated rewriting, this edition sees a substantial restructuring of Parts I and II so as to reflect changes in the needs of our readership.

We have tried to summarise and explain the law as it has been reported on 1 April 1998.

1 June 1998

RICHARD CARD
JOHN MURDOCH
SANDI MURDOCH

Contents

PART I

Outline of the English legal system

CHAPTER I

Introduction   3

CHAPTER 2

Administration of the law   11

CHAPTER 3

Sources of English law   38

PART II

The law of contract

CHAPTER 4

Introduction   71

PART III

The law of tort

CHAPTER 17

Introduction   255

CHAPTER 18

Negligence – duty of care   265

CHAPTER **37**

Easements   556

CHAPTER **38**

Restrictive covenants   577

Table of statutes

References in the right-hand column are to paragraph numbers.

Table of cases

F

l

Part I

Outline of the English legal system

Chapter 1

Introduction

1.1 This book is concerned with aspects of *English* law. The laws and legal systems of Scotland and, to a lesser extent, Northern Ireland are distinct from those of England and Wales and, while Scots and Northern Irish law may coincide with English law in certain fields it cannot be assumed that this is always the case.

In this chapter we examine the following issues:

- the different areas of law, classified by reference to the subject matter of a dispute;
- the distinction between common law and legislation, and between the common law and equity, as sources of English law;
- the elements of the law of civil evidence which will apply to any court proceedings involving the areas of law described in Parts II to IV of this book.

It is usual to divide English law into categories. These categories are not laid down by any statute but have been devised as aids to exposition. They are by no means hard and fast.

One set of facts may involve more than one category of law. If A, a taxi driver, collides with another car while driving you to the station, the law of contract, the law of tort and criminal law may all be applicable. A has certainly broken his contract to drive you to the station, and if his driving was careless this may occasion not only criminal liability but also tortious liability for the damage caused to the other car. This example illustrates classification of law by reference to the subject matter of the dispute.

Classification by reference to the subject matter of a dispute

1.2 When using this method of classification, a major distinction can be drawn between civil and criminal law. It is criminal law which occupies most of the attention of non-lawyers, but lawyers are frequently more concerned with non-criminal, ie civil law. Civil law can be subdivided into categories, for example contract and tort. These categories of civil law are no less important than criminal law.

1.3 It is surprisingly difficult in theory, though not in practice, to distinguish between civil and criminal law. Criminal cases, which are called prosecutions, are normally initiated by the state, but they may be brought by a private citizen, although this is rare. If a prosecution is successful the accused, or defendant, is liable to punishment. This affords no direct benefit to the victim of the crime since he does not receive fines payable or the fruits of a criminal's labours in prison. The victims of some crimes, such as an attempted theft or blackmail, may have suffered no loss from the commission of the crime anyway. Some crimes can be committed without there being a victim, for example homosexual offences involving consenting adults and offences involving obscene publications. Although punishment does not compensate victims, it is possible for the criminal courts to order the criminal to make reparation directly to his victim. The victim of a criminal offence cannot prevent a prosecution nor order its discontinuance, however much he may wish to avoid a criminal trial.

In contrast, civil actions are brought by an individual (the plaintiff) who is seeking to obtain compensation for the loss he has suffered or to establish his legal rights. If damages are awarded as the result of a successful civil action, they are payable to the plaintiff and are generally assessed on the basis that they should compensate him and not on the basis of punishing the defendant. In certain restricted circumstances the courts may award punitive damages, over and above what is necessary to compensate the plaintiff, for the specific purpose of punishing the defendant,[1] but in such cases all the damages are payable to the plaintiff and not merely the compensatory element. A victim is not required to commence a civil action, and the plaintiff can discontinue it at any time before judgment.

Facts which disclose a criminal offence may also form the basis of a civil action but the victim cannot have both claims adjudicated by the same court. It is necessary to bring a separate civil action as well as any prosecution which the state may initiate.

1   See para 29.3 below.

1.4   In Parts II to IV of this book we concentrate on three of the principal categories of civil law: the law of contract, the law of tort and land law. There are many other generally accepted categories of civil law, some of which involve elements of one or more of those three, such as:

* *Commercial law* This is concerned with special contractual situations– agency, sale of goods, consumer credit and other matters relating to business transactions.
* *Employment law* This again involves special and general rules of contract but it also embraces statutory rights and obligations between employer and employee. It includes such topics as health and safety at work (much of which is also covered by the law of tort) and unfair dismissal.
* *Company law* Companies are legal persons and are subject to special rules both common law and statutory, partly because they are artificial legal persons and partly because of the need to regulate their dealings with shareholders, employees and creditors.
* *Constitutional law* This is a slightly different category of law in that it is that branch of the law which regulates the principal organs of government and their impact on the individual citizen, as opposed to providing rules which regulate the relationship between one member of society and another.
* *The law of evidence* This determines how facts are proved in a case, by whom and to what standard. Certain aspects may be relevant to those in the surveying and related professions. Consequently, we consider elements of the law of civil evidence at the end of this chapter.

Classification by reference to the source of the legal rule

1.5   It is also possible to classify law by reference to its source. Common law and legislation are sources of law.

Common law and legislation[1]

1.6 Common law means judge-made law. It is contained in the decisions or judgments made by the English judiciary over many centuries. Legislation comprises Acts of Parliament, subordinate legislation (examples of which are byelaws and statutory instruments deriving their authority from Acts of Parliament) and the legislation of the European Community. Legislation can change the common law, but judges cannot change or ignore legislation, although their interpretation of it may occasionally stultify or modify the wishes of Parliament. Some categories of law, the law of contract and the law of tort for example, are almost entirely based on judicial decisions, and such legislation as amends them is narrow in its scope, whereas much of the law relating to land has a statutory basis. Sometimes, Acts of Parliament seek merely to clarify and codify existing law. In other cases, they may create a body of rights and duties where none existed before, as has occurred, for example, in relation to employment law and company law.

1   Chapter 3 below.

Common law and equity

1.7 The common law can be further subdivided into common law and equity. If both are branches of the common law and therefore both judge-made law, wherein lies the difference between them? The difference between them is that of their origins. Prior to the Judicature Acts of 1873–1875 there were two systems of courts in England, the common law courts and the Court of Chancery.

1.8 The common law courts had evolved from the centralised system for the administration of justice developed by a powerful monarchy between the eleventh and thirteenth centuries, which had gradually ousted the jurisdiction of the local courts. Therefore, common law is that body of law developed by the common law courts, such as the Court of Exchequer (whose judges were called Barons), the Court of Common Pleas and the Court of King's Bench, prior to the fusion of the administration of justice in 1875, and modifications and extensions effected since 1875. The common law is not static but subject to constant affirmation, revision and development by modern judges.

It is generally accepted that it was only the administration of the law, and not the law itself, which was fused in 1875 and thus it is still possible to speak of common law and equity as distinct bodies of law. Since 1875 a case involving both common law and equitable principles can be heard in one court which can, where necessary, apply both sets of rules. Prior to 1875 the unfortunate litigant might have had to bring two actions – one to establish his common law rights and another before the Court of Chancery to establish his equitable rights. An even more unfortunate party might have succeeded at common law, but have had the efficacy of the common law court's judgment nullified in equitable proceedings.

1.9 Equity is that body of law developed in the Court of Chancery prior to 1875 and its subsequent amendments and developments. The Court of Chancery developed later than the common law courts because of defects in those courts and in the law which they administered; the common law courts had entangled themselves in an extremely rigid procedure which made it difficult to initiate actions and severely limited the development of the common law, and the remedies available in the common law courts for the successful litigant were inadequate. Thus, the habit arose in the fourteenth and fifteenth centuries of petitioning the King to remedy injustice. After a while, the King delegated the task of determining these petitions to his Chancellor. Initially, the

Chancellor decided cases in the name of the King but in 1474 he began to do so in his own name, and this marked the beginning of the Court of Chancery presided over by the Lord Chancellor. Until 1529 the Lord Chancellor was an ecclesiastic whose decisions were supposedly guided by conscience but thereafter he was a lawyer. The procedure in the Court of Chancery was originally less rigid than that of the common law courts; and the basis of decisions was supposed to be the merits of each action and what was just between the parties, with little reference to previous cases. Subsequently, both procedure and substantive law became more rigid; the notion of creating a remedy to fit the particular case before the court disappeared and the Court of Chancery became as much influenced by previous cases as the common law courts. By the nineteenth century the Court of Chancery had a well-deserved reputation for tardiness. This was due to the fact that until 1813 all cases were heard by the Lord Chancellor, quite apart from the innate conservatism and caution of some Lord Chancellors.

The rules of equity developed by the Court of Chancery were concerned either with entirely new rights totally unknown to the common law or with remedies (such as injunctions and specific performance[1]) designed to counter the inefficacy or injustice of the common law. Equity did not amend the common law but enabled a litigant who had failed to establish a claim at common law, or been disappointed by the remedies available there, to seek an equitable remedy which made good the defects of the common law in a particular case. For example, if the parties to a contract agree to vary their agreement the common law provides that the variation cannot take effect unless it is supported by consideration, whereas equity may prevent the agreement being enforced in its unvaried form, for a time at least.[2]

1   Paras 12.28 and 12.31 below.
2   Para 6.17 below.

1.10   Even modern courts, which administer both common law and equity, will tend to consider the common law first and then see if it is affected by equity. This process is reversed where a case is concerned with a body of rules developed almost entirely by equity, for example the law of trusts. If there is a conflict between the rules of the common law and those of equity, the rules of equity prevail.[1] It cannot be emphasised too much that the remedies developed by equity cannot be demanded as of right (unlike common law remedies) but, reflecting the origins of equity in conscience, are discretionary and may or may not be awarded by the court. A litigant who has acted unfairly or inequitably may find that the court will decline to award an equitable remedy and that he must be content with common law remedies. If, for example, a purchaser delays completing the purchase of a house, the vendor has a right to the common law remedy of damages for breach of the contract of sale but no right to have the completion enforced by an order for the equitable remedy of specific performance of the contract (although he may be awarded it at the court's discretion).

1   Now enacted in the Supreme Court Act 1981, s 49.

Elements of civil evidence

1.11   When a civil case comes to court,[1] the judge (or jury, in those rare cases where one is used) is required to decide what happened in fact and then apply the law to those facts and any agreed facts. The rules of law determine what facts are relevant to a particular issue; the rules of evidence determine which party is required to prove (or disprove) those facts, and to what standard, and also what material can be tendered in evidence.

1   Most legal claims are, in practice, settled out of court.

The burden and standard of proof
The burden of proof
1.12   The burden of proof is the requirement placed upon a party to proceedings to prove, to the requisite standard, a material fact which has not been admitted by the other party. Failure by such a party to adduce sufficient evidence on an issue results in it being lost. For example, a party bringing an action for breach of contract must prove the existence of the contract and breach by the defendant. Failure to prove the existence of the contract is fatal to the plaintiff's case for then there can be no issue of breach.

In civil cases the burden of proof generally rests upon the party making a claim: he is alleging that he has a cause of action so he must prove all the facts necessary in law to establish that cause of action. Similarly, a party defending an action bears the burden of proving any defence on which he proposes to rely. It must be stressed that this is a general rule and there are exceptions in most areas of civil litigation. Generally, the allocation of the burden of proof on a particular issue is well established by previous cases.

1.13   A party who prima facie bears the burden of proof on an issue may be able to rely upon a presumption of law (an assumption which must be drawn on his behalf by the judge, in the absence of evidence to the contrary) to satisfy the burden of proof cast upon him. For an illustration of a presumption of law and its operation see paras 19.17 to 19.20 below, in which *res ipsa loquitur* is discussed.

The standard of proof
1.14   A party bearing a burden of proof on an issue in a civil case will be required to prove that issue on 'a balance of probabilities'. He is not required to produce absolute proof, nor prove the issue beyond reasonable doubt; instead, he must convince the court that it is more probable than not that the facts which he is asserting are true. The balance of probabilities is a remarkably flexible standard and in some cases, eg when a party to a civil action alleges fraud or some other criminal offence on the part of his opponent, the court, while still holding that the standard of proof is the balance of probabilities, will in practice require more convincing than is usual before it will hold that the burden of proof is satisfied.

Any single piece of cogent evidence (perhaps the testimony of a single witness or even that of the plaintiff himself) can be sufficient to satisfy the burden of proof cast upon a party. One good witness may convince a judge and the case be won despite a plethora of witnesses supporting the opposing case, if they are less than convincing. Of course, the more credible the evidence that can be gathered by a party the more likely the balance of probabilities will be held to have tipped in his favour.

Admissibility of evidence
1.15   Material will be considered by a court only if it is both relevant to an issue before the court and admissible as evidence.

Provided that material is admissible as evidence it can be oral, documentary or 'real'. Real evidence consists of material objects, other than certain documents which are capable of inspection by the court. Printouts from breath/alcohol testing machines, an automatic radar trace of a ship's course, and even a dog, which was the subject of the action in that it was alleged to be dangerous, have been produced in court. The dog was kept on a chain. The court can draw inferences from real evidence.

1.16 Essentially anyone is a competent witness (ie can give evidence) in a civil case and can be asked by either party to the action questions on any relevant issue and be compelled (ie required) to answer them, provided that the answers are admissible as evidence.

A competent and compellable witness may be permitted to refuse to answer questions about matters which are the subject of a privilege. For example, communications between a lawyer and his client are privileged, with the result that a lawyer cannot reveal information about his client or his affairs without the client's permission. This privilege is accepted because it is thought to encourage honesty between lawyer and client, and thereby to improve the quality of justice. Communications between a surveyor or estate agent and a client are not similarly privileged.

The principal case where material will not be admitted as evidence in a civil case is when it constitutes an opinion.

Opinion

1.17 A non-expert witness must state facts and not give his opinion on or draw inferences from those facts. However, it is frequently impossible to distinguish absolutely between fact and opinion and a witness is allowed to give his opinion in so far as it constitutes a means of conveying relevant facts. Subject to this, the court does not permit a non-expert to give his opinion because it is for the court, and not the witness, to decide the significance of evidence. Thus, a non-expert witness is entitled to say that a vehicle seemed to be travelling very fast, giving reasons for this view, but could not say that the driver was driving negligently because negligence is the issue of law on which the court must adjudicate.

1.18 *Expert witnesses* A witness who is an expert on a particular area can state facts and give his opinion on those facts, provided that the issue about which the opinion is being given requires expert analysis.[1] A witness is an expert if the judge rules him to be qualified in the relevant area either formally or by appropriate experience.

It must be stressed that merely because a witness is an expert he cannot give his opinions on anything and everything. Expert opinion evidence is admitted only when the issue falls within the area of expertise of the witness (surveyors are experts but not on medical matters) *and* the judge needs assistance in drawing inferences from the facts before the court. In *Alchemy (International) Ltd v Tattersalls Ltd*,[2] the judge permitted several experts to testify as to what was, in their opinion, the appropriate procedure to follow in the event of a disputed bid at an auction. Having ruled that this was a case where an auctioneer could not be negligent if he followed sound commercial practice, ie a practice regarded as appropriate by a body of competent professionals, the judge considered the expert opinion evidence on what was sound commercial practice. On the facts he found no negligence on the part of the defendant auctioneers.

An expert witness should give independent testimony and not tailor his evidence simply to meet the needs of the party calling him.[3]

A party wishing to call an expert witness should seek leave to do so from the court. The court can order advance disclosure of any expert's report to the opposing party.[4]

1   Areas calling for expert analysis are constantly expanding; recent cases have allowed expert evidence in voice identification, DNA testing and the abilities of tracker dogs.
2   [1985] 2 EGLR 17.
3   *Whitehouse v Jordan* [1981] 1 All ER 267, HL.

4   See the Rules of the Supreme Court, Ord 38. For a summary of the duties of an expert witness see
     National Justice Cia Naviera SA v Prudential Assurance Co Ltd, The Ikarian Reefer [1993] 2 Lloyd's
     Rep 68.

Hearsay

1.19   A statement, made otherwise than by a person while giving oral evidence in
the proceedings, which is tendered as evidence of the fact stated, is hearsay evidence.
Thus, the evidence of a witness as to what X, who is not a witness, said to him is hearsay,
and so is evidence of what the witness said out of court to X. However, not all out of
court statements are hearsay; if a statement is produced merely to prove the fact that
it was made, as opposed to the truth of what was stated in it, it is not hearsay evidence.
For example, if it was an issue in proceedings whether X had died at or after a particular
time, a witness could testify that he heard X (who is patently not a witness) call for
medical aid after the time in issue to prove that he could speak after that time (so that
he must then have been alive).

At common law, hearsay evidence was inadmissible in civil cases. However, the
position has been changed by statute. The general position is now governed by the
Civil Evidence Act 1995.

1.20   *Civil Evidence Act 1995, s 1*   This section provides that in civil proceedings
to which the rules of evidence apply (in law or by agreement of the parties) a statement
shall not be excluded on the ground that it is hearsay. Hence, subject to certain
safeguards in later sections, hearsay evidence is now admitted in civil cases.

A statement is defined as 'any representation of fact or opinion however made'.[1]
Thus, s 1 applies to statements made orally or in writing or in some other form and it
allows the admission of out-of-court statements made by the witness currently testifying
or some other person.

Section 1 does not limit its application to 'first-hand' hearsay, that is an out-of-
court statement made by X, heard by Y, which Y is proposing to give in evidence, but
can apply to any out-of-court statement no matter how remote the relationship between
the maker of the statement and the witness. Thus, if A were to give an out-of-court
opinion, based on observations made by B, which he dictates to C who writes it down
and then shows it to D who relates its contents to E, E could testify as to the contents
of A's opinion in court. Obviously in cases of multiple hearsay the chances of error
are magnified and the Act addresses this in later sections to which we now turn.

1   Section 13.

1.21   *Safeguards applicable to s 1*   Section 1 does not give a party to a civil action
an unfettered right to introduce hearsay evidence in proceedings. In particular, a
statement is not admissible at all if the maker of it (not the witness but the person whose
words it is sought to admit) would not have been a competent witness. In addition a
number of sections provide specific safeguards.

* *Section 2* of the Act provides that a party proposing to adduce hearsay evidence
  must give notice to that effect and provide further details if requested to do so by
  the other party to the action. Failure to give notice (or provide further details if
  requested) does not affect the admissibility of the evidence but may affect the
  weight that is given to it.
* *Section 4* of the Act provides that in estimating the degree of weight which is given
  to the statement the court 'shall have regard to any circumstances from which any
  inference can reasonably be drawn as to the reliability or otherwise of the
  evidence.' Section 4(2) lists a number of factors to which the court should have

regard in assessing weight but does not restrict the court to these factors. Factors listed include whether it would have been reasonable and practicable to call the maker of the statement, whether the statement was contemporaneous with events narrated in it and whether the statement involved multiple hearsay. Thus, in cases of multiple hearsay, a court may well give little credence to evidence which is many steps removed from the maker of the statement since each transmission of a statement increases the scope for inaccuracy to arise.

- *Section 5* of the Act allows the credibility of the maker of the statement to be impeached and also allows the admission of inconsistent statements made by the maker of the statement. With the leave of the court the maker of the statement, if available, may be called as a witness. Thus, if it was suggested that a party was seeking to call X to testify as to an out-of-court statement made by Y because Y might have proved to be a less than convincing witness who would have broken down under cross-examination, the court might allow.

1.22   *Civil Evidence Act 1995, s 9*   This section, which complements s 1, permits the admission of certain documents[1] in evidence. While documents admissible under this section would also be admissible under s 1 the advantage of using s 9 is that the safeguards outlined in para 1.21 above do not apply, although a court may direct that s 9 shall not apply having regard to the circumstances of the case. Thus, if there was doubt as to the authenticity of the document or as to whether it was genuinely contemporaneous with the information it purported to record, a court might reject it wholly or in part.

1   A document is defined in s 13 as 'anything in which information of any description is recorded'. Consequently, it includes tapes, computer disks and CDs as well as paper records.

1.23   Section 9 can be used to admit a document when it forms part of the records of a business or public authority.[1]

1   A document forms part of such a record if it is certified as such by an officer of the business or authority.

Chapter 2

Administration of the law

2.1 In this chapter we examine:

- the system of courts with a fairly wide jurisdiction;
- specialist courts and tribunals;
- arbitration as a mode of dispute resolution;
- alternative methods of dispute resolution;
- the role of the jury in those courts where it is used.

The courts

2.2 The first thing to be noted in any discussion of the court system is that not every type of court exercises both a civil and a criminal jurisdiction. Moreover, within the sphere of either of these jurisdictions, the particular type of court which will try the case (or hear an appeal) will depend on a number of disparate factors. Overleaf is a chart which shows the outline of the court structure.

Magistrates' courts[1]

2.3 A magistrates' court is constituted by justices of the peace. The terms 'justice of the peace' and 'magistrate' are synonymous and henceforth to avoid confusion we shall use the word 'magistrate'.

Magistrates are appointed by the Lord Chancellor (or by the Chancellor of the Duchy of Lancaster) in the name of the Queen as magistrates for a particular area (normally a county). Each county is divided into a number of petty sessional divisions (ie magistrates' courts districts). There are about 30,000 magistrates; all but some 90 of them are 'lay' magistrates. Lay magistrates are unpaid but get an allowance for loss of earnings and for expenses. They are not required to possess any legal qualifications: for legal advice they rely on their clerk, but even though the clerk to the magistrates is legally qualified an individual court may be served by an unadmitted assistant. In the inner London area, and in some other places, jurisdiction is exercised both by lay magistrates and by stipendiary (ie salaried) magistrates. To be appointed as a stipendiary magistrate, a person must for seven years have had a right of audience in relation to any class of case in the Supreme Court,[2] or all proceedings in county courts or magistrates' courts. Currently, only barristers and solicitors can satisfy this requirement.

THE COURT STRUCTURE

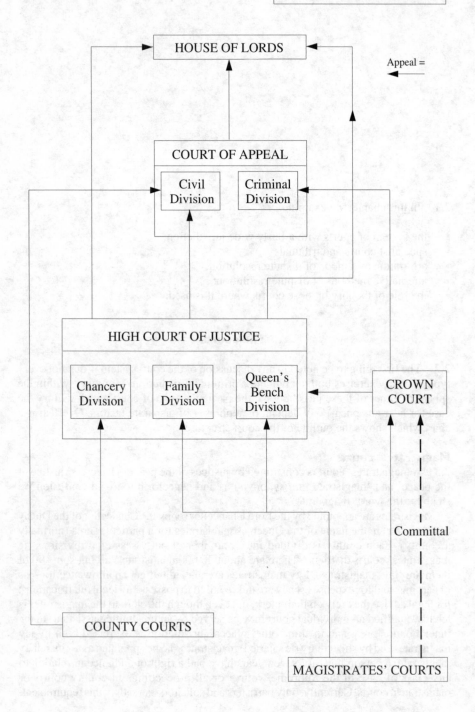

COURT OF JUSTICE OF
EUROPEAN COMMUNITIES

HOUSE OF LORDS

Appeal =

COURT OF APPEAL

Civil
Division

Criminal
Division

HIGH COURT OF JUSTICE

Chancery
Division

Family
Division

Queen's
Bench
Division

CROWN
COURT

Committal

COUNTY COURTS

MAGISTRATES' COURTS

The Lord Chancellor can dismiss a magistrate without showing cause. Magistrates are put on the supplemental list at the age of 70, which is de facto retirement in that they cease to be entitled to exercise judicial functions. Magistrates may be put on the supplemental list before that age either at their own request or on the ground of 'age, infirmity or other like cause' or neglect of judicial duties.

Normally a magistrates' court is composed of three lay magistrates. The normal minimum number of lay magistrates who must comprise the bench is two. The most important exception is that one magistrate can conduct committal proceedings in his capacity of examining magistrate. Stipendiary magistrates sit alone and have all the powers of two lay magistrates in a magistrates' court. Some of the powers of a single lay magistrate may be exercised by the clerk to the magistrates.

There are over 500 magistrates' courts in England and Wales. Magistrates' courts have jurisdiction in both criminal and civil matters. Their summary procedure is inexpensive and speedy but their jurisdiction only extends to matters of minor importance compared with that of the other courts of trial in the court system.

1   The principal statute governing the constitution and jurisdiction of magistrates' courts is the Magistrates'
    Courts Act 1980.
2   Para 2.15 below.

Criminal jurisdiction

2.4   There are two methods of trying persons accused of criminal offences. One is by judge and jury in the Crown Court after committal for trial on a written accusation of crime called an indictment; the other is summary trial by a magistrates' court without a jury. Over 95% of criminal cases are tried summarily. Magistrates' courts have two functions:

•   That of a court of summary jurisdiction or petty sessions, which hears and determines cases, subject to appeal. Not only do magistrates' courts deal summarily with those minor offences which are defined in the statute creating them as summary offences (offences which are only triable in a magistrates' court) but they may also try offences which are 'triable either way' (either in a magistrates' court or on indictment in the Crown Court if the accused intends to plead not guilty) with the consent of the accused. Whether the accused consents or not, a magistrates court will deal with a person accused of an either way offence who intends to plead guilty. Magistrates cannot impose a sentence in excess of six months' imprisonment, except that they may impose consecutive sentences up to a total of 12 months' imprisonment if the accused has been convicted of more than one offence triable either way. In the case of an either way offence, they can commit an offender for sentence to the Crown Court if these powers are inadequate.

•   That of examining magistrates by whom committal proceedings are held as a necessary preliminary, in almost all cases, to a trial by jury in the Crown Court. The function of examining magistrates is different from that when they sit to hear and determine a case. The question in committal proceedings is whether there is evidence upon which a reasonable jury properly directed could convict. It matters not that the magistrates themselves would not have convicted on the evidence before them. The system acts as a filter so that persons against whom there is no evidence upon which a reasonable jury could convict are spared the anxiety and expense of a trial. If the magistrates decide that there is no prima facie case against the accused, they decline to commit him for trial and discharge him.

2.5   A person convicted by a magistrates' court may appeal to the Crown Court against conviction, or against sentence, or against both, except that if he pleaded guilty he may appeal to the Crown Court against sentence only. An alternative avenue of appeal is to appeal to a divisional court of the Queen's Bench Division. This is open to the prosecution or the defence, or to any other party to a proceeding before a magistrates' court, if aggrieved with the determination of the magistrates as being wrong in law or in excess of jurisdiction. This type of appeal is solely concerned with questions of law or jurisdiction, but is usually the preferable course to adopt when the appeal is founded on such questions alone.

Civil jurisdiction
2.6 This is very varied. It extends over the recovery of certain civil debts, such as income tax; the grant and renewal of licences; and 'family proceedings'.

'Family proceedings' are the most important aspect of the civil jurisdiction of magistrates' courts. They are dealt with by magistrates sitting as a 'family proceedings court'. Magistrates sitting in these courts are drawn from special 'family proceedings panels'. Family proceedings heard by magistrates in a family proceedings court include proceedings for maintenance orders for the complainant spouse on proof that the defendant spouse has failed to provide reasonable maintenance for the complainant spouse or a child of the family. In such proceedings the magistrates may also make orders concerning the separation of the spouses. Family proceedings courts also have powers under a number of statutes to make orders as to whom a child should live with and as to the care and supervision of a child under 17. They may also make adoption orders.

When hearing family proceedings, a magistrates' court must include, so far as practicable, both a man and a woman. Unless the court otherwise directs, only the officers of the court, and parties to the case and their legal representatives, witnesses, and news reporters may attend. There are strict limitations on the particulars which may be published in a news report of family proceedings.

2.7 Appeals in civil proceedings in magistrates' courts generally lie to the Crown Court with a further (or alternative) appeal on a point of law to the Queen's Bench Division of the High Court by case stated, except that in family proceedings appeal is to the Family Division and there is no alternative of appeal to the Crown Court.

Youth courts
2.8 Generally, someone aged under 18 who is charged with a criminal offence must be tried in a youth court.

The bench in a youth court consists of magistrates from a special panel. The bench must consist of three magistrates, of whom at least one must be female and one male. There are restrictions similar to those which apply in a family proceedings court in relation to attendance and news reporting.

Appeal from a youth court lies to the Crown Court with a further (or alternative) appeal by case stated on a point of law to a divisional court of the Queen's Bench Division.

County courts
2.9 The jurisdiction of the county courts is exclusively civil. There are some 270 county courts in England and Wales, of which about 75 are trial centres providing facilities for the continuous hearing of cases lasting more than a day. Each trial centre takes in the more substantial cases from a number of satellite courts.

The full jurisdiction of the county courts is typically exercised by circuit judges. Circuit judges are appointed by the Queen on the recommendation of the Lord Chancellor to serve in the Crown Court[1] and in the county courts, and to carry out such other judicial functions as may be conferred on them. There are about 420 circuit judges. Generally, only circuit judges specifically assigned for the purpose sit in county courts. Those qualified to be a circuit judge are:

- people who for 10 years have had rights of audience in relation to all proceedings in the Crown Court or to all proceedings in county courts;
- recorders; and
- provided that they have held appointment on a full-time basis for three years, district judges, stipendiary magistrates and certain other people exercising a judicial function.[2]

Circuit judges retire at 72, or 70 if appointed on or after 31 March 1995, although in either case the Lord Chancellor can extend a circuit judge's appointment by one year at a time until he is 75 if the Lord Chancellor thinks that this is in the public interest. A circuit judge can be dismissed by the Lord Chancellor on grounds of incapacity or misbehaviour.[3]

To reduce delay in the administration of justice, the Lord Chancellor can appoint deputy circuit judges on a temporary basis. Deputy circuit judges can exercise the full jurisdiction of a county court judge, and so can two other types of judge, recorders and assistant recorders. Recorders and assistant recorders are part-time judges appointed by the Lord Chancellor. The duration of their appointment and the grounds on which they may be dismissed are similar to those for a circuit judge. The only people who can be appointed as a recorder or assistant recorder are those who for 10 years have had rights of audience in relation to all proceedings in the Crown Court or all proceedings in county courts. There are over 750 recorders and 420 assistant recorders.

Currently, only barristers and solicitors can satisfy any of the requirements for appointment as a circuit judge, recorder or assistant recorder.

There are also some 230 district judges, appointed and removable by the Lord Chancellor and a substantial number of part-time deputy district judges.[4] To be appointed as a district judge (or a deputy district judge, hereafter the term 'district judge' includes a deputy), a person must for seven years have had a right of audience in relation to any class of proceedings in the Supreme Court,[5] or all proceedings in county courts or magistrates' courts. Currently, only barristers and solicitors can satisfy this requirement. District judges deal with the interlocutory work of the county courts and also have jurisdiction to try claims not exceeding £5,000 in value (although normally a claim for less than £3,000 will be referred to arbitration, as we show in para 2.14 below). In addition, by leave of a judge of the court and with the consent of the parties, a district judge may try any other action. A district judge has the full jurisdiction of a circuit judge in all undefended actions. An appeal lies from a district judge to the judge.

1   Paras 2.22–2.24 below.
2   In practice, a person will not be appointed a circuit judge unless he is a recorder.
3   Courts Act 1971, ss 16 and 17; Judicial Pensions and Retirement Act 1993, s 26.
4   In practice, a person will not be appointed a district judge unless he is a deputy district judge.
5   Para 2.15 below.

Jurisdiction

2.10   Under the provision of the County Courts Act 1984, county courts have jurisdiction over a wide range of civil matters. This jurisdiction includes:

Jurisdiction over actions in contract or tort, except defamation, or for money recoverable by statute. A county court has jurisdiction over defamation if the parties agree to accept its jurisdiction or if the High Court transfers the case to it.

An action in contract or tort may be *commenced* in a county court or in the High Court, save that a personal injury claim must be commenced in a county court unless the value of the action is £50,000 or more.

An action of which the value is less than £25,000 must be *tried* in a county court unless:

- where the action was commenced in a county court, the county court considers that it ought to be transferred to the High Court (and the High Court agrees), having regard to–
  - the importance of the action and, in particular, whether it raises questions of importance to people who are not parties or questions of public importance;
  - the complexity of the action;
  - the financial substance of the action, including the value of the counterclaim; and
  - whether a transfer will result in a speedier trial (although a transfer will not be ordered on this ground alone); or
- the case commenced in the High Court and the High Court, having regard to the above criteria, considers that it ought to try the action.

An action whose value is £50,000[1] or more must be tried in the High Court unless:

- it is commenced in a county court and the county court, having regard to the above criteria, considers that the action ought not to be transferred to the High Court; or
- where it is commenced in the High Court, the High Court, having regard to the same criteria as above, considers that it ought to transfer the action to a county court for trial.

In other words, there is a rebuttable presumption that actions whose value is less than £25,000 will be tried in a county court, and those whose value is £50,000[1] or more in the High Court.

Jurisdiction over actions for the recovery of land.

An equity jurisdiction, eg in cases of administration of estates, foreclosure of mortgages and specific performance of contracts for the sale of land, where the amount of the estate, the amount owing under the mortgage or purchase price, as the case may be, does not exceed £30,000.

1   £200,000 in respect of a case listed in the Business List at the Central London County Court: County Court Rules 1981, Ord 48C. Cases in this list are more complex commercial cases transferred from county courts in the south east of England.

2.11   Types of county court jurisdiction under other statutes include:

- (In designated courts) divorce, separation and annulment of marriage cases, proceedings (eg for financial relief) ancillary to them, domestic violence and adoption.
- Bankruptcy and winding up of companies.
- Matters under the Rent, Landlord and Tenant, Housing and Consumer Credit Acts.

2.12   The procedure in the county courts is simpler, speedier and less costly, than in the High Court. To discourage the conduct of minor litigation in the High Court which could have been brought in a county court, the fact that a party has commenced proceedings in the High Court on a matter falling within the county courts' jurisdiction may be taken into account when the amount of his costs (if he has succeeded in his action) is determined and may lead to a lower award of costs than otherwise.[1]

1   Supreme Court Act 1981, s 51.

2.13   Appeal from a county court judge lies to the Court of Appeal (subject to certain conditions), except in bankruptcy where appeals are heard by a single judge of the High Court.

Small claims[1]

2.14   A defended action[2] in the county court must be referred to arbitration if the sum claimed or amount involved is not in excess of £3,000 (or £1,000 in the case of a personal injury claim). If referral to arbitration occurs the hearing takes place before an arbitrator, generally in private, without the formalities associated with a trial. The arbitrator will usually be a district judge, but a party may apply for the appointment of any other suitable person. A referral to arbitration of a claim not in excess of the relevant limit may be rescinded by a district judge on the application of a party, if the parties are agreed that the case should be tried in court, or if the case involves a difficult question of law or of fact or an allegation of fraud, or if it would otherwise be unreasonable for the claim to proceed to arbitration, having regard to its subject matter, the size of any counterclaim, the parties' circumstances or the interests of any party likely to be affected by the award.

If the amount in dispute exceeds the relevant limit the matter can still be referred to arbitration if the parties agree to this or one of the parties does not object to a district judge deciding the application for arbitration. If a party does object, a judge of the court can decide whether the case should be dealt with by arbitration.

The award of the arbitrator is entered as a judgment in the court proceedings, and is binding as such. A judge of the court has power, on application, to set the award aside.

The advantage of the arbitration procedure is that it is eminently suitable for the litigant in person in small claims cases, which are mainly 'consumer disputes', since it is even more informal and inexpensive than trial in the county court. The arbitration may take place round a table and the oath may not be administered. Legal representation is discouraged by the fact that, contrary to the usual rule, a successful party cannot normally recover the costs of legal representation from his opponent. Formality is kept to the minimum necessary to protect the interests of each party.

1   County Courts Act 1984, s 64; County Court Rules 1981.
2   Actions for possession of land are excluded from the automatic referral to arbitration regime.

The High Court of Justice

2.15   The High Court is part of the Supreme Court of Judicature: the Crown Court and Court of Appeal are the other two constituent parts. The High Court was established by the Judicature Acts 1873–1875, replacing the separate Courts of Chancery, Queen's Bench, Common Pleas, and Exchequer, and also the Courts of Admiralty, Probate, and Matrimonial Causes.

For historical reasons, and to ensure the resolution of disputes by judges with the relevant expertise,[1] the High Court consists of three divisions, each of which has a separate jurisdiction. Although High Court judges are assigned to a particular division according to their expertise, they are judges of the High Court and can exercise any jurisdiction appertaining to a High Court judge, irrespective of the division to which they have been assigned.[2]

High Court judges are appointed by the Queen on the recommendation of the Lord Chancellor. Those qualified for appointment are persons who have for ten years had a right of audience in relation to all proceedings in the High Court (currently only barristers and a few solicitors have this right) or who have been a circuit judge for at least two years.[3] To reduce delay, the Lord Chancellor can appoint deputy High Court judges on a temporary basis. Because of the shortage of High Court judges, a significant number of cases, mainly in the Queen's Bench Division, are heard by deputy High Court judges.

A High Court judge has greater security of tenure than a circuit judge since he is only removable on an address presented by both Houses of Parliament to the Queen, except that the Lord Chancellor may, with the concurrence of senior judges, declare vacant the office of a judge who is subject to permanent medical incapacity and is unable to tender his resignation.[4] High Court judges appointed before 31 March 1995 must retire on attaining the age of 75. Those first appointed to judicial office on or after that date must retire on reaching 70. Like any other retired judge, a retired High Court judge can be invited to sit as a judge on an ad hoc basis, in the courts in which he could have sat before retirement, up to the age of 75.[5]

Some cases in the High Court are heard by an official referee or an 'official referee recorder'. An official referee is a circuit judge specially assigned to official referee work. Official referee's business includes any Chancery or Queen's Bench cause or matter:

- which involves a prolonged examination of documents or accounts, or technical, scientific or local investigation, such as could more conveniently be conducted by an official referee; or
- for which trial by an official referee is desirable in the interests of one or more of the parties on grounds of expedition, economy or convenience or otherwise.

The majority of official referee cases come from the construction industry and concern architects, engineers, surveyors, contractors, house builders, developers and others involved in that industry.

1   This latter reason was doubted by the Court of Appeal in *Barclays Bank plc v Bemister* [1989] 1 All ER 10, on the ground that nowadays judges have acquired sufficient expertise before appointment to enable them to handle a wide range of High Court work across divisional boundaries.
2   See *Re Hastings (No 3)* [1959] 1 All ER 698; *Re Kray* [1965] 1 All ER 710; *Re L (Infant)* [1968] 1 All ER 20, CA.
3   Supreme Court Act 1981, s 10.
4   Supreme Court Act 1981, s 11.
5   Ibid; Judicial Pensions and Retirement Act 1993, s 26.

Chancery Division
2.16   The Chancery Division consists of the Lord Chancellor, as its nominal head, although he never sits at first instance, a Vice-Chancellor and, at present, 14 judges. The jurisdiction of the Chancery Division is exercised in London and seven provincial towns.

There are six masters of the Chancery Division. To be appointed as a Chancery master, a person must have had for seven years a right of audience in relation to any class of proceedings in the Supreme Court, or all proceedings in county courts or magistrates' courts. Currently, only barristers and solicitors can satisfy this requirement. Applications are made to the masters in chambers in the preliminary stages of litigation, and they make orders thereon in the name of the judge to whom they are assigned. Complicated accounts and inquiries are also referred to them. If a party is not satisfied with the master's ruling, he may adjourn the matter to the judge.

Masters of the Chancery Division are based at the Royal Courts of Justice in London. Elsewhere district judges at designated county courts which also operate as district registries of the High Court perform similar functions to those performed by a master in the Chancery Division.

2.17 The jurisdiction of the Chancery Division is entirely civil and can be split into original and appellate jurisdictions.

Original jurisdiction By virtue of the Supreme Court Act 1981, s 61 and Sch 1, jurisdiction over a number of matters is assigned to the Chancery Division. These include:

- the administration of estates of deceased persons;
- the execution of trusts;
- the redemption and foreclosure of mortgages;
- the rectification and cancellation of deeds;
- partnership actions;
- bankruptcy;
- the sale, exchange or partition of land, or the raising of charges on land; and
- all causes and matters under enactments relating to companies.

As can be seen, there is some concurrence between the Chancery Division's original jurisdiction and some of the heads of jurisdiction possessed by the county courts (save for the financial limits which apply, for example, to their equity jurisdiction).

Appellate jurisdiction This is much more limited. Certain statutes empower a single judge to hear appeals of various kinds, eg income tax appeals from the Commissioners of Inland Revenue and bankruptcy appeals from a county court. A divisional court of the Chancery Division (which normally consists of two judges) hears appeals from county courts in land registration matters.

Queen's Bench Division

2.18 This division is the largest of the three divisions and has the most varied jurisdiction. Its head is the Lord Chief Justice. At present, 57 judges are assigned to it. The original civil jurisdiction of this division is exercised in first-tier Crown Court centres,[1] as well as in London.

There are nine masters of the Queen's Bench Division. The qualification for appointment is the same as for a Chancery master. Masters of the Queen's Bench Division supervise the Central Office of the Supreme Court in which official documents are issued and registered. Applications are made to a master in chambers in the preliminary stages of litigation in the Queen's Bench Division, appeal lying from his order to a judge. Masters of the Queen's Bench Division are based in London. Outside London, their functions are carried out by district judges at district registries.

1   Para 2.22 below.

2.19 The jurisdiction of the Queen's Bench Division can be divided into four heads, the first of which is the busiest:

Original civil jurisdiction The principal aspects of this are actions in contract and tort. Commercial matters are dealt with by specialist judges in the Commercial Court which sits in London, and whose procedure is more flexible than the normal High Court procedure. Traditionally, cases in the Commercial Court were dealt with more speedily than elsewhere in the High Court. The success of the Commercial Court has meant that it has become inundated with work. Because of this, cases can take as long to get to trial as elsewhere, or even longer. To avoid the cost and inconvenience of advocates having to travel to the Commercial Court, commercial cases are also heard by specialist circuit judges in the Mercantile Courts which sit in Birmingham, Bristol, Leeds, Liverpool, Manchester and Newcastle and can hear any commercial dispute – other than one relating to land and certain company regulatory matters.

Appellate civil jurisdiction A single judge (or, if the High Court's decision is final, a divisional court) has jurisdiction to hear appeals from certain tribunals and certain other appeals. In addition, a single judge (or, if the court so directs, a divisional court) hears appeals by way of case stated on a miscellaneous collection of civil matters from magistrates' courts (excluding family proceedings), the Crown Court and certain other bodies. A divisional court consists of two or more judges, increasingly two, of whom one will normally be the Lord Chief Justice or a Lord Justice of Appeal (a member of the Court of Appeal). An appeal by case stated must be on the ground that the determination or decision is wrong in law or is in excess of jurisdiction. The case is not re-heard, the judge or court merely hearing legal argument.

Appellate criminal jurisdiction A divisional court hears appeals in criminal matters by case stated from magistrates' courts and the Crown Court (in that court's appellate capacity).[1] The appeal must be on the same ground, and is conducted in the same way, as described for civil jurisdiction above.

Supervisory jurisdiction The most important aspects of this are the jurisdiction to issue the writ of habeas corpus and the jurisdiction, on an application for judicial review, to make 'prerogative orders' against magistrates' courts, county courts, the Crown Court (except in respect of trials on indictment[1]), tribunals and other decision-making bodies of a public nature, such as local authorities.[2]

The prerogative orders are mandamus, prohibition and certiorari. An order of mandamus is used to compel the body to whom it is directed to carry out a definite public duty imposed on it by law. The order cannot be used to compel the body to exercise its discretion in a particular way, but it may be used to compel it to hear and determine a case, or to state a case for the opinion of the High Court.[3] An order of prohibition or certiorari will issue only in relation to an order or decision of a body which is under a public duty to 'act judicially' or 'act fairly' in making that decision, as opposed to purely administratively. This does not mean that prohibition and certiorari issue only to courts or tribunals, for many other bodies, such as local authorities, may sometimes be required to act judicially, and in other cases are required to act fairly. The order of prohibition is issued to *prevent* such a body from acting in excess of jurisdiction or otherwise acting improperly. The order of certiorari covers much the same area but after such a body has done something and it is desired to review it and, if necessary, quash it on the ground of excess of jurisdiction, denial of natural justice, or error of law on the face of the record. The latter ground is the most common now, partly because the Tribunals and Inquiries Act 1992, s 10, requires many tribunals and ministers, after statutory inquiries, to give their reasons for their decisions if requested.

Applications for judicial review in civil cases are heard by a single judge unless the court directs a hearing by a divisional court. Applications for judicial review in criminal cases are always heard by a divisional court, as are applications for habeas corpus.

1   Supreme Court Act 1981, s 29(3); para 2.23 below.

2   In contrast, the supervisory jurisdiction does not extend to arbitrations in pursuance of an agreement
     out of court, which we discuss in paras 2.41–2.50 below: *Bremer Vulkan Schiffbau und Maschinenfabrik
     v South India Shipping Corpn* [1981] 1 All ER 289, HL.
3   Magistrates' Court Act 1980, s 111(6).

Family Division

2.20   The Family Division consists of the President of the Division and, at present,
16 judges. The jurisdiction of this division is entirely civil, and is exercised in London
and at first-tier Crown Court centres. It can be divided into original and appellate
jurisdictions:

Original jurisdiction The Division deals with all aspects of family law; the following
are the most important examples:

*   on transfer from a county court, proceedings for divorce, separation or annulment
    of marriage and ancillary relief (eg financial provision) connected therewith;
*   proceedings for the determination of title to property in dispute between spouses;
*   proceedings concerning the occupation of the matrimonial home and/or the
    exclusion of a violent spouse; and
*   wardship of court, guardianship and adoption proceedings.

Appellate jurisdiction This is principally concerned with appeals from the decisions
of magistrates' courts sitting as family proceedings courts.[1] Some such appeals, eg
against the making of a maintenance order, must be heard by a divisional court (which
must be composed of two or more judges), but others, for example appeals against the
making of a care order, will be heard by a single judge unless the court directs a hearing
by a divisional court. Appeals of the second type are by case stated.

1   Para 2.6 above.

2.21   Appeals from the original jurisdiction of any division of the High Court lies to
the Court of Appeal (Civil Division), as do appeals from the appellate jurisdiction of
any Division,[1] save that appeals from the criminal appellate jurisdiction of a divisional
court of the Queen's Bench Division go straight to the House of Lords.

1   But note the 'leap-frogging' exception mentioned at para 2.29 below.

The Crown Court

2.22   The jurisdiction and powers of the Crown Court are exercised by:

*   any judge of the High Court;
*   any circuit judge;
*   any recorder;[1] and
*   in some circumstances any judge of the High Court, circuit judge or recorder sitting
    with lay magistrates.

In this paragraph, references to circuit judges and recorders include deputy circuit
judges and assistant recorders.

   The Crown Court in England and Wales is divided into six circuits, in which there
are a total of 90 court centres. The court centres in each circuit are divided into first-
tier, second-tier and third-tier centres. The first- and second-tier centres are served by
High Court and circuit judges and by recorders; the distinction between the two centres
is that in the former sittings of the High Court are held for civil cases[2] as well as of the
Crown Court for criminal cases. Like the second-tier centres, third-tier centres are

limited to Crown Court work but they are only served by circuit judges and recorders with the result that a few very serious offences, such as murder, cannot be tried at them.

Lay magistrates cannot act as judges of the Crown Court by themselves but only with a High Court or circuit judge or with a recorder. They must form part of the Crown Court when it hears appeals from magistrates' courts and also when it is sentencing persons who have been committed for sentence by magistrates' courts, but the Lord Chancellor has power to dispense with this requirement. The number of magistrates so sitting must be not less than two nor more than four.[3] Rulings on questions of law are for the judge but decisions on other questions, eg sentence, are the product of all members of the court.

1   See para 2.9 above in relation to these appointments.
2   Paras 2.18 and 2.20 above.
3   Supreme Court Act 1981, s 74.

Criminal jurisdiction

2.23   The Crown Court has exclusive jurisdiction over all offences tried by jury on indictment, an appeal by a convicted person lying to the Court of Appeal.

The Crown Court also has jurisdiction:

*   to deal with convicted persons committed for sentence by magistrates' courts because their sentencing powers are inadequate; and
*   to hear appeals from magistrates' courts, including youth courts, against conviction or sentence. An appeal against conviction takes the form of a full re-hearing of the case, ie the case is tried all over again, witnesses being called, etc. Where the Crown Court has given its decision on an appeal from a magistrates' court against conviction or sentence, either the prosecution or the defence, if dissatisfied with the determination of the Crown Court as being wrong in law or in excess of jurisdiction, may appeal to a divisional court of the Queen's Bench Division by way of case stated.

Juries are not used in the Crown Court when it deals with persons committed for sentence or with appeals.

Civil jurisdiction

2.24   The civil jurisdiction of the Crown Court is far less important. It is principally concerned with betting, gaming and liquor licensing appeals, but other appeals within its jurisdiction are appeals from various administrative decisions made by local authorities.

The Court of Appeal

2.25   The Court of Appeal is composed of the Master of the Rolls, the Lord Chief Justice, the President of the Family Division and, at present, 35 Lords Justice of Appeal (which is the permitted maximum). Lords Justice are appointed by the Queen on the advice of the Prime Minister who acts on the recommendation of the Lord Chancellor. They must have been judges of the High Court or for 10 years have had a right of audience in relation to all proceedings in the High Court.[1] The tenure of their office by Lords Justice is the same as for High Court judges.[2] A High Court judge may be required to sit in the Court of Appeal if this is necessary.[3] The Court of Appeal is divided into a civil and a criminal division. The Master of the Rolls is the President of the Civil Division, and the Lord Chief Justice is the President of the Criminal Divison.[4]

1   Supreme Court Act 1981, s 10. See para 2.15 in relation to this requirement.

2   Para 2.15 above.
3   Supreme Court Act 1981, s 9.
4   Ibid, s 3.

Court of Appeal (Civil Division)
2.26   This hears appeals from:

- the decisions in civil matters of all three divisions of the High Court. In some cases, leave to appeal is required from the court appealed from or the Court of Appeal. An example is an appeal from the determination of an appeal by a divisional court;[1]
- the decisions of a county court judge, save for a few exceptions (such as bankruptcy) where appeal lies to the High Court. In actions in contract or tort, and in certain other cases, the leave of the county court judge or of the Court of Appeal is required if the amount of the claim does not exceed a prescribed limit (£5,000 in the case of contract or tort);[2]
- the decisions of the Employment Appeal Tribunal, the Lands Tribunal and certain other tribunals.[3] In some cases, leave is required.

Except in the case of appeals from the Lands Tribunal and certain other tribunals[4] (which are by case stated), the method of appeal is by way of re-hearing. This means that the court reviews the whole case from the shorthand notes of the trial and the judge's notes and in the light of legal argument: it does not mean that the witnesses heard in the trial court are re-called, nor that fresh evidence will normally be admitted. Since the Court of Appeal does not have the advantage of seeing the trial witnesses and observing their demeanour, it does not normally upset direct findings of fact (as opposed to inferences from the facts).

Generally, a civil appeal must be heard by three members of the Court of Appeal. However, in certain cases, such as appeals from a county court, an appeal may be heard by two members. A single judge may (and generally does) determine an application for leave to appeal and deal with other matters arising incidentally. The Division may be sitting simultaneously in as many as 10 courts. While most appeals are on points of law, an appeal may be against a finding of fact or the exercise of a discretion by the trial judge or against the damages which have been awarded, except in the case of appeals by case stated.

1   In a few cases the High Court's decision on a procedural point is final, which means that it cannot be appealed to the Court of Appeal.
2   County Courts Act 1984, s 77; County Courts Appeal Order 1991.
3   Paras 2.36 and 2.38 below.
4   Paras 2.37 and 2.38 below.

Court of Appeal (Criminal Division)
2.27   The Criminal Division hears appeals from persons convicted by the Crown Court on indictment. The convicted person may appeal against conviction or against sentence, unless the sentence is one fixed by law.[1] An appeal requires the leave of the Court of Appeal or a certificate from the trial judge that the case is fit to appeal.[1]

In the case of an appeal against conviction, the court must allow the appeal if it thinks that the conviction was unsafe, otherwise it will dismiss the appeal.[2] On appeal against sentence, the Court may reduce it or vary it, provided that in the result the appellant is not dealt with more severely than he was in the court below.[3]

Although the prosecution has no right of appeal against an acquittal on indictment, the Attorney-General may refer to the Court of Appeal a point of law arising at a trial on indictment where the accused was acquitted.[4] The Court's opinion does not affect the acquittal but provides authoritative guidance on the point for the future. Likewise, although the prosecution cannot appeal against a sentence imposed by the Crown Court, in certain cases the Attorney-General may refer a sentence imposed by the Crown Court to the Court of Appeal with its leave if it appears to him to be unduly lenient.[5] On such a reference, the Court may impose a more severe sentence.

The Criminal Division normally sits in at least three, and on occasions as many as six, courts: one composed of the Lord Chief Justice and two judges of the Queen's Bench Division, and the others of a Lord Justice and two Queen's Bench judges. A circuit judge, especially approved for this purpose by the Lord Chancellor, may also sit as a judge of the Criminal Division in most cases.[6] Very occasionally, when it is necessary to resolve a conflict between Court of Appeal decisions, a five-judge court will hear the case. By way of exception to the general requirement that criminal appeals must be heard by three judges, a two-judge court may hear an appeal against sentence.[7] A single judge (other than an approved circuit judge)[7] may deal with applications for leave to appeal and may perform certain other incidental functions.

1 Criminal Appeal Act 1968, ss 1, 9–11.
2 Ibid, s 2.
3 Ibid, s 11.
4 Criminal Justice Act 1972, s 36.
5 Criminal Justice Act 1988, s 36.
6 Supreme Court Act 1981, s 9.
7 Supreme Court Act 1981, s 55.

The House of Lords

2.28   While the House of Lords has original jurisdiction over disputed claims to peerages and breaches of privilege, such as contempt of the House or wrongs committed within its precincts, this is of minor importance compared with its appellate jurisdiction. The House of Lords' appellate jurisdiction is discharged by its Appellate Committee. The Appellate Jurisdiction Act 1876 provides that at the hearing of an appeal there must be present at least three of the following – the Lord Chancellor, the Lords of Appeal in Ordinary and such peers who hold or have held high judicial office (for example, ex-Lord Chancellors). Normally, five Lords of Appeal in Ordinary hear an appeal and by convention peers other than the above do not attend meetings of the Appellate Committee. Lords of Appeal in Ordinary (commonly called 'Law Lords', and not to be confused with Lords Justice of Appeal[1]), must have held high judicial office for two years or for 15 years have had rights of audience in the Supreme Court (ie the Court of Appeal, the High Court and the Crown Court).[2] They are appointed by the Queen on the advice of the Prime Minister who acts on the recommendation of the Lord Chancellor and have the same security of tenure and retirement age as High Court judges.[3] At present there are 12 Lords of Appeal in Ordinary (which is the permitted maximum). Normally, one or two of the Lords of Appeal are appointed from Scotland. Unless the Lord Chancellor is sitting, the proceedings of the Appellate Committee are presided over by one or other of two senior Lords of Appeal nominated for this purpose by him. The House of Lords has both a civil and a criminal appellate jurisdiction.

1 Para 2.25 above.
2 Appellate Jurisdiction Act 1876, s 6.
3 Para 2.15 above.

Civil appellate jurisdiction

2.29   The House of Lords hears:

• Appeals from the Court of Appeal (Civil Division), provided that leave has been granted by that Court or by the House.

- 'Leap-frog' appeals from the High Court. To save cost and delay, the Administration of Justice Act 1970 provides that in most civil cases appeal may be made direct from the High Court to the House of Lords. This procedure may only be used where:
  - the parties agree to it;
  - the High Court judge grants a certificate to sanction it (which he may only do if he is satisfied that a point of law is involved which is of general public importance and which either relates to a matter of construction of an Act – or of a statutory instrument – or else is one in respect of which he considers that he is 'bound' by a decision of the Court of Appeal or of the House of Lords); and
  - the House of Lords gives leave to appeal.

  The 'leap-frog' procedure is used in comparatively few cases.

The House of Lords will not generally interfere with findings of fact on which the trial judge and appellate court are agreed, unless it can be shown that both courts were clearly wrong.[1]

1   *Hicks v Chief Constable of the South Yorkshire Police* [1992] 2 All ER 65, HL.

Criminal appellate jurisdiction

2.30   The House of Lords can hear an appeal by either the prosecution or the accused from the determination of an appeal by the Court of Appeal (Criminal Division) or by a divisional court of the Queen's Bench Division provided:

- the court below (ie the Court of Appeal or a divisional court) has certified that a point of law of general public importance is involved and that court or the House of Lords is satisfied that the point of law is one which ought to be considered by the House; and
- either the court or the House of Lords has granted leave to appeal.[1]

As can be seen, an appeal on a question of fact is not possible to the House of Lords in a criminal case.

1   Criminal Appeal Act 1968, s 33.

The Court of Justice of the European Communities (European Court)

2.31   The European Court operates under the Treaties establishing the European Communities (ie the European Economic Community (EEC), the European Coal and Steel Community (ECSC) and the European Atomic Energy Community (EURATOM)) which make up the European Union. The EEC has now changed its name to the European Community (EC). The European Community is, of course, the pre-eminent one. How many readers have heard of the other two Communities? It is the European Community and its legislation which have an increasing impact on everyday business and society. The Court consists of 15 judges and is assisted by nine Advocates-General, a type of official unknown to English law. The duty of an Advocate-General is, with complete impartiality and independence, to make reasoned submissions in open court on cases brought before the Court in order to assist in the performance of its functions. The Court sits in plenary session, ie as a 'court' (generally consisting of 11 judges), unless the decision has been made to hear the case in a 'chamber' of three or five judges.

Judges and Advocates-General are appointed for six-year periods by the governments of member states acting in agreement and are eligible for re-appointment.

They are chosen from those who fulfil the conditions required for the holding of the highest judicial office in their respective countries or who are jurisconsults (persons learned in the law) of recognised competence.

Before 1973 the House of Lords was the final court of appeal in all cases in this country but the accession of the United Kingdom to membership of the European Community meant that the European Court became the ultimate court (ie its decisions are binding on the House of Lords and other United Kingdom courts[1]) in matters within its jurisdiction. Nevertheless, in the great majority of cases arising within the United Kingdom the House of Lords remains the ultimate court. The fundamental point that the treaties under which the European Court operates are concerned only with those matters which have a European element must be firmly grasped in order to understand the relationship of the European Court to the rest of our legal system.[2]

1   *Litster v Forth Dry Dock and Engineering Co Ltd* [1989] 1 All ER 1134.
2   See *H P Bulmer Ltd v J Bollinger SA* [1974] 2 All ER 1226, CA.

Jurisdiction

2.32   The jurisdiction of the European Court can be divided into the following principal categories:

- Matters concerning the conduct of member states or of the institutions of the Community, such as
  - the hearing of complaints brought by member states or by the Commission of the European Community that a member state has failed to fulfil its obligations under the Treaties;
  - the review of the legality of the regulations, directives and decisions of the Council (of Ministers) of the European Union and of the Commission; and
  - the hearing of disputes between member states which relate to the subject matter of the Treaties, provided the states in question agree.
- Matters of direct concern to litigants or prospective litigants in a member state, which have been referred for a preliminary ruling by the European Court under art 177 of the European Economic Community Treaty. Under art 177, the European Court may give preliminary rulings on three matters
  - on the interpretation of the treaties establishing the EEC anfd Euratom;
  - on the validity and interpretation of the regulations, directives, decisions and other acts of the institutions of the Community or the European Central Bank; and
  - on the interpretation of certain statutes of bodies established by an act of the Council.

  The essence of a preliminary ruling is that it should precede the judgment of the referring court. Accordingly, once the domestic court has given judgment, it cannot make a reference under art 177.[1]

  Where a question of the above types of interpretation is raised before any court or tribunal of a member state, the court or tribunal *may*, if it considers that a decision on the question is necessary to enable it to give judgment, refer the matter to the European Court for a ruling. However, where any such question is raised in a case pending before a court or tribunal of a member state, against whose decisions there is no judicial remedy under national law, that court or tribunal *must* generally refer the matter to the European Court for a ruling. This provision refers to the House of Lords where an appeal lies to the House of Lords, despite the fact that its leave to appeal is required if the necessary leave has not been given by the court below.[1] On the other hand, it appears that, where there is no right of appeal at all from a lower court to a higher court in respect of the matter in issue, that court is the court of 'last resort'.[1] The obligation to refer just mentioned does not apply if the question raised is not relevant to the outcome of the proceedings, or if it has already been answered in a previous ruling of the European Court, or if the correct interpretation of the Community law is so obvious as to leave no reasonable doubt.[2]

Where a matter is referred to the European Court for a preliminary ruling, only the request for interpretation or decision on validity is referred. The case itself is not transferred. Consequently, the court making the reference remains seised of it, although its procedure is suspended until the European Court has given its ruling on the reference.[3] The European Court will only give a ruling on a question material to the outcome of the proceedings from which the reference comes. It will not give an opinion on a question merely of a general or hypothetical nature.[4]

In terms of the relationship between the European Court and English courts it is important to distinguish between the task of interpreting the Treaties, regulations etc – to see what they mean – and the task of applying them to the case in hand.

The English judges have the final say in applying the Treaties etc: only they are empowered to find the facts and give judgment for one side or the other. However, before they can apply the Treaties, etc they have to see what they mean, and in this task of interpretation English judges are not the final authority: the European Court is.[5]

The purpose of the preliminary rulings procedure is to ensure uniform interpretation of Community law throughout the Community, without which the Community could not function effectively.

- The European Court also hears appeals from the European Court of First Instance.

1   *Chiron Corpn v Murex Diagnostics Ltd (No 8)* [1995] All ER (EC) 88, CA.
2   *CILFIT Srl v Ministry of Health* [1982] ECR 3415, [1983] 1 CMLR 472, ECJ; *Magnavision NV SA v General Optical Council (No 2)* [1987] 2 CMLR 262, DC; *Zabala Erasun v Instituto Nacional de Empleo* [1995] All ER (EC) 758, ECJ.
3   *Zabala Erasun v Instituto Nacional de Empleo* [1995] All ER (EC) 758, ECJ.
4   *Société d'Importation Édouard Leclere-Siplac v TFI Publicité SA* [1995] All ER (EC) 343, ECJ.
5   See *H P Bulmer Ltd v J Bollinger SA* [1974] 2 All ER 1226, CA.

European Court of First Instance

2.33   Because of the increasing workload of the European Court, and its increasing inability to deal expeditiously with it, the European Court of First Instance (the Court of First Instance) came into being in the autumn of 1989. The Court of First Instance has five judges. It normally sits in chambers of three or five judges.

The Court of First Instance's jurisdiction was designed to relieve the European Court of types of cases, many quite minor, which were taking up an inordinate amount of that Court's time. The main areas of the Court of First Instance's jurisdiction are:

- over disputes between the Community institutions and their employees (or ex-employees);
- over actions for review by the court, and in some cases for compensation, brought against Community measures taken in implementation of competition rules applicable to undertakings.

Appeal on a point of law against decisions of the Court of First Instance may be made to the European Court on grounds of lack of jurisdiction, infringement of Community law by the Court of First Instance or breach of procedure before it. If the European Court allows the appeal, it may give final judgment or it may remit the case to the

Court of First Instance, which will be bound by the European Court's decision on points of law.

Specialist courts and tribunals

The Judicial Committee of the Privy Council

2.34   The Judicial Committee of the Privy Council is the final court of appeal from the courts of some Commonwealth countries. It also entertains appeals against 'striking-off' from the disciplinary committees of the medical, dental and related professions, and certain other appeals. The Committee is normally composed of five Lords of Appeal, but Privy Councillors who are holders or past holders of high judicial office in this country or a Commonwealth country may, and do occasionally, sit.

The Court of Protection

2.35   This court, which is an 'office' of the Supreme Court, can assume jurisdiction over the management and administration of the property and affairs of a person who it is satisfied is incapable of managing his property or affairs by reason of mental disorder. Its jurisdiction is conferred by Part VII of the Mental Health Act 1983. Certain orders (eg those authorising proceedings for divorce or the making of a will on the patient's behalf) can only be made by the Lord Chancellor or one of the Chancery judges whom he has nominated to the court. Otherwise, the jurisdiction (including the assumption of responsibility) is, in practice, exercised by the master, deputy master and other officers of the court, subject to appeal to a judge.

The Employment Appeal Tribunal

2.36   This tribunal, established in 1975, is now governed by the Industrial Tribunals Act 1996. It consists of judges from the High Court and Court of Appeal (one of whom is president) nominated by the Lord Chancellor, at least one judge nominated from the Scots Court of Session and lay members with specialised knowledge of industrial relations. The lay members may be removed by the Lord Chancellor, after consultation with the Secretary of State for Education and Employment, on specified grounds, eg incapacity or misbehaviour. The tribunal has a central office in London but can sit anywhere in Great Britain, in any number of divisions. It is duly constituted when sitting with a judge and two or (or, exceptionally, four) lay members; a judge and one lay member will suffice if the parties consent.

The tribunal's jurisdiction is entirely appellate. It can hear appeals on points of law from Industrial Tribunals under legislation relating to the following matters: unfair dismissal; redundancy payments; equal pay; sex discrimination; racial discrimination; disability discrimination; contracts of employment; trade unions, and employment protection. In addition, the tribunal can hear appeals on questions of law or fact concerning the certification of a trade union as independent. The tribunal's procedure is designed to be as speedy, informal and simple as possible.

The Lands Tribunal

2.37   The Lands Tribunal was established by the Lands Tribunal Act 1949. Its offices are in London but it also sits at various places in the provinces to determine cases. Its membership is appointed by the Lord Chancellor. Lawyers, certain other people with a right of audience in the courts (currently no one else is so qualified) and qualified surveyors are eligible for appointment. Its jurisdiction may be exercised by any one or more of its members, the composition of a tribunal in a particular case depending on the nature of the issues involved. The procedure at the hearing is less formal than in court proceedings.

The Lands Tribunal has jurisdiction over the following matters:

- appeals from local valuation courts (which are largely composed of local councillors and magistrates and which themselves hear appeals against assessments of the rateable value of land by local valuation officers);
- assessment of compensation for the compulsory purchase of land, where this has not been agreed between the acquiring authority and the property owner, or of compensation for certain other matters, such as compensation for planning restrictions restricting new development; and
- applications for the variation, modification or discharge of restrictive covenants under the Law of Property Act 1925, s 84, as amended,[1] and applications for certificates as to notice under the Rights of Light Act 1959.[2]

1 Paras 38.35–38.40 below.
2 Para 37.48 below.

Other tribunals

2.38 A large number of different tribunals have been created to deal with particular matters arising under modern legislation, especially social welfare legislation. The function of most administrative tribunals is to enable individual citizens to challenge the administrative decisions of a government department. For example, the Social Security Appeals Tribunal hears appeals against social security decisions. Some tribunals, however, adjudicate disputes between individuals; Industrial Tribunals are an example. Tribunals are usually composed of a legally qualified chairman and lay members. Their hallmarks have traditionally been said to be speed, accessibility, informality, cheapness and freedom from technicality. For these reasons they have been compared favourably with courts. However, there has been concern recently that tribunal procedures can often no longer be described as speedy or free from technicality.

The nature and powers of tribunals vary but they have the common function of determining the facts of a case and deciding it according to law rather than the dictates of policy. In the case of some 'first instance' tribunals there is a right to appeal to an appellate tribunal or to a minister. In addition, there is generally a right of appeal to the High Court, on a question of law only, from the decision of an appellate tribunal or (if there is not such a tribunal) a 'first instance' tribunal. Whether or not there is the possibility of an appeal, a tribunal's decision may be challenged by applying to the High Court for judicial review (which we mentioned in para 2.19 above).

2.39 In addition, a number of 'domestic tribunals' have been established by private or professional associations to resolve disputes between their own members or to exercise disciplinary powers over them. The jurisdiction of these tribunals is sometimes derived from statute. In other cases it rests solely on contract, in that, by joining the association, a member contracts to accept the jurisdiction of its domestic tribunal.

Arbitration

2.40 Where it is used as an alternative to proceedings in court or as part of such proceedings, arbitration is a method for the settlement of civil disputes, other than those affecting status (such as divorce and bankruptcy). Arbitration is generally more informal, private, cheaper and quicker than a trial in a court. However, where the main issues are questions of commercial law (as opposed to the facts or commercial practice), trial in the Commercial Court or a Mercantile Court[1] may be as cheap and quick, and certainly more appropriate.

A dispute may be referred to arbitration in three ways: by agreement out of court, by statute or by order of the court.

1   Para 2.19 above.

Reference by agreement out of court

2.41   Particularly in commercial and consumer matters, the parties to a dispute may prefer to go straight to arbitration rather than become involved in court proceedings. Hence, they may voluntarily agree before or after the dispute to refer it to arbitration. Many construction contracts provide for such a reference, as do various codes of practice initiated by trade associations which are incorporated in their standard form contracts used by members.

A growing tendency for arbitration clauses to be inserted in standard form contracts made with consumers has caused concern in recent years since consumers have less choice than business organisations over the terms on which they contract and such a clause may be to their prejudice (as where a consumer's claim would otherwise have been dealt with much more cheaply under the 'small claims procedure' described in para 2.14, above, or, in a case involving a larger claim, where the consumer would have received legal aid for a court case). For this reason, an arbitration agreement which has not been individually negotiated is unfair for the purposes of the Unfair Terms in Consumer Contracts Regulations 1994, and therefore not enforceable against a consumer, so far as it relates to a pecuniary claim not exceeding £3,000.[1]

1   The Regulations were extended in the way indicated by the Arbitration Act 1996, ss 89–91; paras 14.61–14.65 below.

2.42   If an arbitration agreement is in writing, as is usually the case, it, and the arbitration under it is governed by the Arbitration Act 1996,[1] provided that the seat (ie place) of arbitration is designated or determined as being in England and Wales or Northern Ireland under the agreement or in accordance with it.[2] We set out below the position under that Act.

Normally, if a party to an arbitration agreement brings court proceedings in respect of a dispute covered by the agreement without referring it to arbitration, the court has jurisdiction to try the case. However, if such proceedings are instituted the other party to an arbitration agreement may apply to the court for an order staying the proceedings. On such an application, the court must stay the proceedings, unless satisfied that the arbitration agreement is null and void, inoperative or incapable of being performed.[3]

The normal position outlined above does not apply if the arbitration agreement contains a *Scott v Avery*[4] clause, which is an agreement to refer a dispute to arbitration as a condition precedent to an action in the courts. Since no right of action accrues until the arbitration has taken place, non-observance of the clause will afford a complete defence to a court action.

1   Arbitration Act 1996, s 5 'Agreement in writing' is given an extended meaning by s 5. It includes, for example, an agreement made by exchange of communications in writing.
2   Arbitration Act 1996, ss 2 and 3.
3   Arbitration Act 1996, s 9. If the Arbitration Act 1996, s 86, is ever brought into force, the court will also be able to refuse to stay a domestic arbitration agreement, if satisfied that there are other sufficient grounds for not requiring the parties to abide by the arbitration agreement. A 'domestic arbitration agreement' is one under which the seat of arbitration is not designated or determined or is in the United Kingdom, and to which neither an individual who is a national of, or habitually resident in, a foreign state, nor a corporation incorporated in, or centrally managed in, a foreign state, is a party (Arbitration Act 1996, s 85).
4   (1856) 5 HL Cas 811.

Appointment of arbitrators and umpires

2.43   The parties are free to agree on the number of persons whom they wish to act as arbitrators and whether there is to be a chairman or umpire. Subject to any agreement to the contrary, an agreement that there shall be two or any other even number of arbitrators requires the appointment of an additional arbitrator as chairman. If there is no agreement as to the number of arbitrators, a sole arbitrator will be appointed.[1]

The parties are also free to agree on the procedure for appointing the arbitrator or arbitrators, including the chairman or umpire. They may, for example, provide that the appointment shall be made by the President of a relevant professional society. If there is no agreement as to the procedure for appointment, and the agreed number of arbitrators is one, that person must be appointed by the parties jointly. Where the agreed number is two, each party must appoint one arbitrator. The same is the case where the agreed number is three; the third arbitrator is then appointed as chairman by the two arbitrators so appointed. The like procedure applies where there are to be two arbitrators and an umpire. In any other case, the same rules apply as in the case of a failure of the appointment procedure (see below).[2] Lawyers are appointed quite frequently as arbitrators, but in some cases a person with the relevant technical expertise, eg an accountant or surveyor, is appointed.

Where a party who is to make an appointment fails to do so within a specified time, the other party, if he has made his appointment, can then appoint his arbitrator as sole arbitrator if he gives the other party seven days' notice and that party still does not appoint his arbitrator.[3]

If there is a failure in an agreed procedure for appointment, the situation is governed by any further agreed provision or, failing that, a party to the arbitration agreement can apply to the High Court or a county court, which may give directions as to what should happen or make any necessary appointment itself.[4]

The parties can agree on the functions of a chairman or umpire. If they do not, the position is as follows:

- in the case of a chairman, decisions, orders and awards are made by all or a majority of the arbitrators (including the chairman, whose view prevails if the views of the arbitrators are equally divided);
- in the case of an umpire, decisions, orders and awards are made by the other arbitrators unless and until they cannot agree on a matter relating to the arbitration, in which case the umpire shall replace them and act as if he were the sole arbitrator.[5]

A judge of the Commercial Court (or an official referee) may, if in all the circumstances he thinks fit, accept appointment as sole arbitrator or umpire by or by virtue of an arbitration agreement, provided that the Lord Chief Justice has informed him that the state of business in the High Court (or the state of official referee's business) permits him to be made available.[6]

1   Arbitration Act 1996, s 15.
2   Ibid, s 16.
3   Ibid, s 17.
4   Ibid, s 18.
5   Ibid, ss 20 and 21.
6   Arbitration Act 1996, s 93. Official referees are described in para 2.15 above.

Conduct of the proceedings

2.44   In reaching a decision (called 'the award') arbitrators must do so in accordance with the law (eg English law) chosen by the parties or, if the parties agree, in accordance with non-legal considerations agreed by them or determined by the arbitrator(s). If the parties do not make a choice of the applicable law, the arbitrator(s) must decide which body of law is applicable under the rules of the conflict of laws.[1]

1 Arbitration Act 1996, s 46.

2.45 The award may provide for the payment of money, direct costs to be paid,[1] order the specific performance of a contract (other than one relating to land or an interest in land), order a party to do or not to do something, or order rectification of a document, [1] unless the arbitration agreement is to the contrary.

The award is final and binding on the parties and persons claiming through them, unless the arbitration agreement otherwise provides,[2] and there is no right of appeal to the courts except on a point of law. However, the High Court or a county court has power, on application by a party, to intervene where an award is challenged on the ground that there was no valid arbitration agreement, or that the arbitral tribunal was not properly constituted, or that a matter has been considered which was not submitted for arbitration in accordance with the arbitration agreement. In such a case, the court may confirm the award, vary it or set it aside. An appeal from its decision lies to the Court of Appeal, but only with the court's leave.[3]

In addition, the High Court or a county court, on application by a party, has power to set aside an award, or declare it to be of no effect, or remit it for reconsideration, on the ground of a serious irregularity affecting the arbitral tribunal, the proceedings or the award. An appeal from the court's decision lies to the Court of Appeal, but only with the court's leave.[4] Lastly, the High Court or a county court has power to remove an arbitrator whose impartiality is doubtful, or who lacks the qualifications required by the arbitration agreement, or whose capability to conduct the proceedings is doubtful, or who has improperly conducted the proceedings.[5] Examples of misconduct for these purposes are the receipt by the arbitrator of evidence from one party in the absence of the other, and the failure by him to deal with some of the matters submitted or to put to the parties certain matters on which he relies. On the other hand, a mere error of law or fact is not misconduct for these purposes.[6] A decision about the removal of an arbitrator can be appealed to the Court of Appeal, but only with the court's leave.[5]

1 Arbitration Act 1996, s 48.
2 Ibid, s 58.
3 Ibid, s 67.
4 Ibid, s 68.
5 Ibid, s 24.
6 *Blexen v G Percy Trentham Ltd* [1990] 2 EGLR 9, CA.

Enforcement of an award
2.46 An award may, by leave of the High Court or a county court, be enforced in the same manner as a judgment or order of that court.[1] Otherwise, the award is enforced by bringing a court action on the award as a contractual debt.

1 Arbitration Act 1996, s 66.

Resort to the courts on a point of law
2.47 There are two procedures whereby the courts may intervene in arbitration cases on a point of law:

- an appeal on a point of law after an award has been made; and
- an application for the determination of a preliminary point of law in the course of a reference.

2.48 Unless otherwise agreed by the parties, appeals lie to the High Court or a county court on any question of law[1] arising out of an award made in arbitral proceedings. Such appeal may be brought by any of the parties to the reference, but, unless all the other parties consent, the leave of the court must be obtained. Leave can only be granted if the court is satisfied that:

- the determination of the question of law could substantially affect the rights of one or more parties;
- the question of law is one which the arbitrators were asked to determine;
- the arbitrators' decision is obviously wrong or that the question is one of general public importance and the decision is at least open to serious doubt; and
- it is just and proper in the circumstances for the court to determine the question, despite the parties' agreement to resolve the matter by arbitration.[2]

An appeal against a decision to grant or refuse leave itself requires the court's leave.[2] Leave cannot be granted if the parties to the reference in question have effectively agreed to exclude the right of appeal.

The philosophy behind the requirement for leave is to avoid delay and expense in arbitrations arising out of commercial or shipping contracts by giving primacy to finality over questions concerning the correctness of awards. Consequently, it was not surprising that, in *Pioneer Shipping Ltd v BTP Tioxide Ltd, The Nema*,[3] the House of Lords took a restrictive view concerning the exercise by judges of their discretion to grant leave. It held that, generally, leave to appeal should not be granted unless it is shown either that the arbitrator has misdirected himself in point of law or that the decision is such that no reasonable person could have reached it. Where the question of law concerns the construction of a contract or contractual clause in standard terms, leave should only be granted if the judge considers that a strong prima facie case has been made out that the arbitrator was wrong in his construction.[4] The test is even stricter here the question of law concerns the construction of a 'one-off' contract or ntractual clause (ie one which is not of a standard term nature). Here, leave to appeal uld not be granted unless it is apparent to the judge, on a mere perusal of the arbitrator's reasoned award without hearing argument from counsel, that the meaning ascribed to the clause by the arbitrator is obviously wrong. The guidelines laid down in *Pioneer Shipping Ltd v BTP Tioxide Ltd* by the House of Lords are not applicable in all cases. It has been held that they do not apply where complex questions of European Community law arise.[5] In such cases, the approach of the court to the granting of leave is less strict.

On the determination of an appeal the High Court may confirm, vary or set aside the award, or remit it for consideration in the light of its determination on the question of law which was the subject of the appeal.[6] In order that an appeal, if it takes place, may be effective, the court has power to order an arbitrator to give reasons for his decision.[7] An appeal to the Court of Appeal from the court's determination of an appeal is possible; but only if the court gives leave, which it cannot do unless it considers that the question of law is one of general public importance or is one which for some other special reason should be considered by the Court of Appeal.[6]

A further appeal from the Court of Appeal to the House of Lords is only possible with the leave of that Court or of the House.

1   An appeal cannot be brought on a question of fact. It is normally obvious whether a question is one of fact or of law but it should be noted that a question concerning the construction or frustration of a contract is a question of law: *Tsakiroglou & Co Ltd v Noblee Thorl GmbH* [1961] 2 All ER 179, HL; *Pioneer Shipping Ltd v BTP Tioxide Ltd, The Nema* [1981] 2 All ER 1030, HL.
2   Arbitration Act 1996, s 69. An appeal cannot be brought if any further recourse within the arbitral

proceedings (eg a review) has not been exhausted: ibid, s 70. As to the parties' ability to exclude an appeal, see para 2.50 below.

3   [1981] 2 All ER 1030, HL.
4   *Antaios Cia Naviera SA v Salen Rederierna AB, The Antaios* [1984] 3 All ER 229, HL; *Ipswich Borough Council v Fisons plc* [1990] 1 All ER 730, CA.
5   *Bulk Oil (Zug) AG v Sun International Ltd* [1984] 1 All ER 386, CA.
6   Arbitration Act 1996, s 69.
7   Arbitration Act 1996, s 70.

2.49   Unless otherwise agreed by the parties, the High Court may determine any question of law arising in the course of a reference to arbitration (a preliminary point of law) on the application of a party. However, unless all the other parties agree to the application, the court must not entertain it unless it has the permission of the arbitrators (including the umpire, if there is one) *and* it is satisfied that the determination of the question is likely substantially to reduce costs and that the application was made without delay.[1] Notwithstanding any agreement of the parties, the court is not bound to entertain the application. Instead, the court should only entertain it in exceptional circumstances; for example, where the preliminary point of law, if rightly decided, would determine the whole dispute.[2]

Unless the court gives leave, no appeal lies from a decision of the court whether the conditions described above are met.[1]

Subject to the same restrictions as apply to an appeal from the court's determination of an appeal on a point of law after an award, an appeal lies to the Court of Appeal from a decision on a preliminary point of law.[1]

A further appeal from the Court of Appeal to the House of Lords is only possible with the leave of that Court or of the House.

1   Arbitration Act 1996, s 45.
2   *Babanaft International Co SA v Avant Petroleum Inc, The Oltenia* [1982] 3 All ER 244, CA.

Exclusion agreements
2.50   At common law an agreement, whether contained in the arbitration agreement or made thereafter, which excludes the courts' power to give a final decision on a question of law is void on grounds of public policy and thus of no effect.[1] However, this rule has been severely curtailed by statute, since the parties to an arbitration agreement, by 'otherwise agreeing', can exclude the jurisdiction of the courts to determine a point of law after an award or to make a determination on a preliminary point of law.

1   *Czarnikow v Roth, Schmidt & Co* [1922] 2 KB 478, CA.
2   If ever the Arbitration Act 1996, s 87 is brought into force, the parties' power to 'otherwise agree' will be limited in the case of a 'domestic arbitration agreement' (as defined in para 2.42 above) because an exclusion agreement in such a case is only effective under that section if it was entered into after commencement of the relevant arbitral proceedings.

Reference by statute
2.51   Numerous statutes provide for the reference of certain types of dispute to arbitration. In some cases, eg disputes involving building societies, the parties have an option to refer; in others reference is compulsory, eg disputes involving street works. The provisions of the Arbitration Act 1996 apply to statutory references, with minor exceptions, unless the particular statute otherwise provides.[1]

1   Arbitration Act 1996, ss 94–98.

Reference by order of the court
2.52   The High Court may refer any case within its jurisdiction, or any particular issue

in such a case, to be tried by an official referee,[1] by a senior officer of the court, such as a master, or, where the issue is of a technical nature requiring specialist knowledge, by a special referee. A reference to such an arbitrator can be made even against the wishes of the parties and is particularly likely to be made if:

- the prolonged examination of documents, or scientific or local examination, is required; or
- the examination of accounts is involved.

The award of the arbitrator is entered as a judgment in the court proceedings, and is binding as such. In certain circumstances an appeal lies to the Court of Appeal (Civil Division).

In addition, the High Court has a similar power to refer to the same persons as above any question in a cause or matter before it for inquiry and report. The report may be adopted wholly or partially by the court, and if so adopted is as binding as a judgment to the same effect.[2]

The power of a county court to refer a case to arbitration has been discussed in para 2.14 above. In addition, any question in a case before a county court judge may be referred to a district judge or a referee for inquiry and report.[3]

1   Para 2.15 above.
2   Supreme Court Act 1981, s 84; Rules of the Supreme Court, Ord 36.
3   County Courts Act, 1984, s 65; County Court Rules 1981.

2.53   References to arbitration by the courts must be distinguished from references to arbitration by agreement or under a statutory provision because they operate in the context of court proceedings rather than as an alternative to them.

Alternative Dispute Resolution

2.54   Alternative dispute resolution (ADR) refers to any method of resolving an issue capable of resolution by litigation in the courts or by arbitration without resorting to that type of process.

Normally, the results of ADR are not binding, although the parties can agree otherwise. In the normal type of case, ADR is concerned with aiding the parties to reach a solution, as opposed to imposing one. It follows that ADR is only worth pursuing if the parties are likely to be voluntarily co-operative or there is a contractual obligation to pursue it.

ADR is a quicker and cheaper method than litigation in the courts or, even, arbitration. It is therefore of interest both to consumers and to businesses involved in commercial disputes. In addition to speeding up settlement, ADR has the advantage of making it possible to reach settlements reflecting commercial or personal interests as well as strict rights. It also has the advantage of focusing on the issues rather than on the combat involved in the courts or in arbitration. It is, therefore, less destructive of relationships between the parties.

These benefits have been recognised by legislation, in respect of matrimonial disputes, and by the Commercial Court which has issued a *Practice Note*[1] encouraging judges in that court to consider adjourning appropriate cases to enable the parties to give thought to, and set in motion, ADR procedures.

1   [1996] 3 All ER 383.

2.55   A number of organisations offer ADR services, for example the Centre for

Dispute Resolution (CEDR), the City Disputes Panel, the Chartered Institute of Arbitrators, and Mediation UK. Lawyers are often involved in conducting the ADR process, but this is not essential.

Negotiation could be described as a form of ADR but the term is normally used to refer to mediation, to conciliation and to a formalised settlement conference.

Mediation

2.56 In mediation a neutral mediator helps the parties to reach a common position. It can be 'facilitative' or 'evaluative'. It is 'facilitative' if the mediator does not advise the parties of his own opinion of the merits of the dispute. It is 'evaluative' if he is expected to express his own opinion.

Mediation is particularly appropriate where the claim is small or not complex, or both. It is also appropriate where it is particularly important to reduce conflict and bitterness between the parties.

Mediation can take place in the context of the courts' organisation whereby a case before the courts is referred to mediation or some other form of ADR, as in the Commercial Court or (in a pilot project) in a county court.

Conciliation

2.57 This is similar to mediation but differs in that the conciliator moves from one party to the other, discussing the merits of each side's case and the risks in litigation. Sometimes, if the conciliation does not lead to a settlement, the conciliator's role may extend to advising the parties of his assessment of the likely result of a trial. Of course, this is not binding, but it often leads to a settlement.

Formalised settlement conference

2.58 At a formalised settlement conference, advocates present their client's best case to a panel composed of one executive decision-maker representing each party, often assisted by a neutral person to assist the panel in assessing representations. This method of ADR is sometimes called a 'mini-trial'.

The jury

2.59 The only courts mentioned above in which juries are found are the Crown Court and the High Court (12 jurors) and the county courts (eight jurors). The use of juries in civil cases is rare and the parties generally have no right to demand a jury; except that a jury must be ordered on the application of either party in cases of defamation, malicious prosecution and false imprisonment, or on the application of a party against whom fraud is charged, unless the case requires a prolonged examination of accounts or documents, or a scientific or local investigation which cannot conveniently be made with a jury.[1] The only civil cases where a jury is common are defamation cases.

Provided the accused has pleaded not guilty, a jury is always empanelled in trials on indictment in the Crown Court.

1 Supreme Court Act 1981, s 69.

2.60 A person is eligible for jury service if he or she is between the ages of 18 and 70, is included on the electoral register for parliamentary or local government elections, and has been resident in the United Kingdom, the Channel Islands or the Isle of Man for five years since the age of 13. There are certain exceptions. Some persons are ineligible for jury service, including judges, barristers and solicitors, police officers, clergymen and the mentally ill. Certain ex-prisoners and certain other people who have received non-custodial sentences are disqualified and persons such as peers, people aged more than 65, soldiers and doctors are excusable as of right.[1]

1   Juries Act 1974, ss 1 and 3, and Sch 1.

2.61   The division of labour between judge and jury is that the judge rules on law, the jury on fact. In criminal cases, the judge directs the jury as to the law and they apply it to the facts and then return their verdict of guilty or not guilty. In civil cases, the judge directs the jury on the relevant law and leaves the jury to make specific findings of fact on the various issues raised in the case to enable the judge to make the final finding of liability.[1] These specific findings are referred to as a special verdict (to distinguish them from the general verdict delivered in a criminal case). It will be noted that in criminal cases the decision on liability is taken by the jury, whereas in civil cases involving a jury it is ultimately taken by the judge.

A jury's discussions are in secret, they choose their own foreman and they give no reasons for their decisions. Their verdict in a civil case can be overturned by the Court of Appeal but only if no reasonable jury properly directed could have reached it. In his summing-up the judge may comment on the plausibility of the evidence and may give guidance as to what inferences may be drawn. Generally, the jury must reach a unanimous verdict but a majority of 10 (seven in the county courts) may be accepted after the jury have had a reasonable time in all the circumstances for deliberation; there is a minimum time of two hours in the Crown Court.[2] In civil cases the parties can always consent to accept any majority verdict.[3]

1   See *West v Chief Constable of West Midlands Police* (1997) Times, 15 December, CA.
2   Juries Act 1974, s 17.
3   Recognised in the Juries Act 1974, s 17(5).

Chapter 3

Sources of English law

3.1   In this chapter we explain two things:

- The direct means by which English law and, since it impacts on English law, European Community law are made. These are otherwise known as *legal sources*. In the case of English law, they are
  - legislation
  - judicial precedent
  - custom (which is now of very little relevance);
- the written material in which a legal source is recorded.

Legislation

3.2   Unlike many continental countries where, the law having been codified, most legal rules are derived from legislation, our law is predominantly derived from judicial precedent. Leaving aside certain areas which have been codified, such as the law relating to partnership (by the Partnership Act 1890), the body of law concerning private rights is essentially derived from judicial precedent with relatively few alterations made by statute. Normally, the purpose of statutory alteration of this area of the law is to revise a legal rule which has become inappropriate in changing social circumstances and which, because of the operation of the doctrine of judicial precedent, is incapable of adaptation by the courts.

The generation of law reform proposals has been greatly assisted since 1965 by the existence of the Law Commission, consisting of full-time commissioners, assisted by a research staff. Under the Law Commissions Act 1965, it is the duty of the Law Commission to keep under review all the law with a view to its systematic development and reform, including in particular the codification of such law, the elimination of anomalies, the repeal of obsolete and unnecessary enactments, the reduction in the number of separate enactments, and generally the simplification and modernisation of the law. A large number of the 250 Law Commission reports and draft Bills have been implemented by Act of Parliament.

Legislation plays an important part in criminal law, mainly in defining most offences, and in the spheres of company law and employment law. Another notable example is legislation concerning the revenue, for instance the Finance Acts which implement the budget proposals. The great majority of modern statutes can be put into the category of 'social legislation'. Such legislation is concerned essentially with regulating the day-to-day running of the social system rather than with creating criminal offences or rights and duties between individuals. In this area, in particular, much of the flesh is put on the bones of the relevant Act by delegated legislation. Examples of 'social legislation' are the Health and Safety at Work etc Act 1974, the Landlord and Tenant Acts, the Rent Act 1977 and the Housing Act 1988.

3.3 Sometimes a statute is described as a consolidating or codifying statute. Where a branch of statute law has evolved piecemeal, a consolidating statute may be passed, for the purpose of clarification, containing substantially the existing law in a consolidated form. Two examples of a modern consolidation Act are the Income and Corporation Taxes Act 1988 and the Trade Union and Labour Relations (Consolidation) Act 1992. A consolidation Act only consolidates statute law: a codifying Act may codify both case law and statute law, a notable example being the Sale of Goods Act 1893 (which has now been consolidated with subsequent amending statutes in the Sale of Goods Act 1979). However, the object of both consolidation and codification is to simplify and clarify the existing law rather than to effect substantial alterations to it.

3.4 There are essentially three types of legislation: Acts of Parliament; subordinate legislation, which mainly consists of delegated legislation made by government ministers, local authorities and other bodies under powers derived from parliament; and the legislation of the European Community. Subject to an exception which we discuss in para 3.36 below, Parliament (which consists of the Queen, House of Lords and House of Commons) is sovereign, which means that it is not subject to any legal limits on its power to create, alter and repeal English law. It also means that an Act of Parliament cannot be questioned in, or by, the courts: it has to be applied by them. In certain cases the validity of subordinate legislation and of most types of legislation of the European Community can be challenged.

Acts of Parliament

3.5 It is a fundamental common law rule that to be an Act of Parliament a measure requires the assent of the Queen, the House of Lords and the House of Commons. However, this rule has been modified by the Parliament Acts 1911 and 1949 whereby, in the circumstances outlined in para 3.8 below, a measure can be an Act of Parliament without the assent of the House of Lords. [3]

While it is going through the parliamentary process, and before it receives the royal assent, an Act is known as a Bill. Most Bills originate from government departments, having been drafted by parliamentary draftsmen, and are introduced into either House of Parliament by a government minister. By a constitutional convention, Finance Bills (ie Bills authorising taxation) and Consolidated Fund Bills and Appropriation Bills (ie Bills authorising national expenditure) must be introduced in the House of Commons by a government minister. Apart from these types of Bill, a Public Bill may be introduced by an ordinary member of the House of Commons or House of Lords, although the opportunities for doing so are rather limited. Private members' Bills are unlikely to succeed in becoming law because of the limited time available for them, unless they are adopted by the government and accorded extra parliamentary time. A further limitation is that it is a constitutional convention that every Bill whose effect will be to increase taxation or central government expenditure must be supported by a financial resolution moved by a government minister. It follows that if a private member's Bill has such an effect it cannot succeed unless the member can persuade a minister to move a financial resolution.

So far we have concentrated on Public Bills, ie Bills which when enacted will be general in their application. In addition, Private Bills – Bills of a local or personal nature – may be presented to Parliament. Most private Bills are promoted by local authorities seeking special powers; a few are promoted by companies and other corporate bodies for similar reasons. Private Bills are subject to a different parliamentary procedure. A third type of Bill is the Hybrid Bill. A Hybrid Bill is one which is introduced as a Public Bill but which affects the private interests of particular bodies or individuals. Part of the parliamentary procedure for a Hybrid Bill is similar to that for a Private Bill.

The passage of a Bill

3.6   In the case of a Public Bill the normal procedure is as follows, assuming that it is first introduced into the House of Commons.

A Bill is introduced by a First Reading, a purely formal stage at which one of the clerks reads out the Bill's title. The Bill is then ordered to be printed and published, and a date is fixed for its Second Reading.

At the Second Reading the general principles of the Bill are debated by the House. Amendments to specific clauses may not be moved. Normally, the Second Reading is taken 'on the floor of the House', ie it is debated by the whole House. However, it is possible for the Bill to be referred to a Second Reading Committee, in which case that Committee will consider the Bill and recommend to the House that it should be read a second time. Such a referral is only likely if the Bill is uncontroversial. Referral can only take place if a minister moves for it and fewer than 20 members of Parliament object.

Assuming that it is not successfully opposed on Second Reading, the Bill proceeds (after a financial resolution, if one is necessary) to the Committee stage. This stage involves a clause by clause consideration of the Bill, during which clauses may be amended and new clauses added provided that they are relevant to the subject matter of the Bill. Most routine Bills go to a Standing Committee, a group of around 18 members of Parliament reflecting party strength in the House. There are a number of Standing Committees and their sole function is to deal with Bills as and when necessary. The Committee Stage may be dealt with by two other types of committee: a Select Committee (which enables the committee to question witnesses and require the submission of evidence) and a Special Standing Committee (which, unlike the ordinary Standing Committee, may use up to four of its sessions as a Select Committee). If a Bill is of constitutional importance, or is straightforward and uncontroversial, or requires a very rapid passage, it may be considered by a Committee of the Whole House. The annual Bills authorising public expenditure must be considered by a Committee of the Whole House and the annual Finance Bill is partly considered by such a Committee and partly by a Standing Committee. When the House sits as a Committee the Speaker, who is its normal chairman, vacates the chair, and the Chairman of Ways and Means or his deputy chairs the meeting.

The next stage is the Report Stage, which constitutes a detailed review of the Bill as amended in Committee. Further amendments, alteration of amendments made by the Committee, and new clauses, may be made at this stage.

The final stage in the House of Commons is the Third Reading, which normally takes place immediately after the Report Stage. This enables the House to take an overall consideration of the Bill, as amended, and to permit it to proceed, or otherwise, as it thinks appropriate. The Third Reading debate is brief and general in nature. Substantive amendments cannot be made at this stage, but minor verbal ones may.

A Bill which has passed all its stages in the Commons then goes to the House of Lords, where it undergoes a similar procedure except that there is never a financial resolution and the Committee Stage is nearly always taken on the floor of the House;

if it is not it is dealt with by a Select Committee or by a Special Standing Committee. If the Lords amend the Bill it is returned to the Commons for their consideration. If the Commons agree to the amendments this is the end of the matter, but if they disagree the Bill is returned to the Lords with the Commons' reasons for the disagreement and the Lords consider the matter further. On further consideration in such a case it is most exceptional in modern times for the Lords not to give way. However, in the event of an impasse between the Houses, the Parliament Acts 1911 and 1949 provide that ultimately the wishes of the Commons can prevail. We discuss this matter in para 3.8 below.

Once a Bill has passed through the above stages it is submitted for royal assent by the Queen, after which it becomes an Act.

3.7   The procedure for Private Bills does not call for extensive description. Normally, they must have satisfied various strict requirements, such as their purpose being advertised, before they can be laid before Parliament and given a First Reading. At the Committee Stage in the House of Commons, Private Bills are examined by small committees of four or five members who, unlike committees dealing with Public Bills, conduct an enquiry into the merits of the Bill. The promoters and any opposers of the Bill may appear before the committee and they will usually be represented by counsel; evidence may be called and submissions made. In short, the Committee Stage in the House of Commons resembles a judicial inquiry. Otherwise, however, the parliamentary procedure is very similar to that for a Public Bill, except that there is no Report stage. A Private Bill, with any amendment, goes straight from the Committee stage to the Third Reading. The procedure is similar in the House of Lords, save that that the Committee Stage of unopposed private Bills is dealt with by the whole House and only opposed ones by a Select Committee.

3.8   The 'official' copies of Acts of Parliament are printed by the Queen's Printer and published by the Stationery Office which also publishes annual volumes of Public Acts. The Incorporated Council of Law Reporting publishes texts of Acts taken from the Queen's Printer's copies, as do certain commercial publishers who publish annual volumes of Acts of Parliament verbatim, as well as in unbound parts soon after the Act is passed; a leading series is *Halsbury's Statutes of England.* Acts of Parliament are also included in the LEXIS electronic database and the official statute law database. In the last few years, new Acts of Parliament have been available free on the Internet on the UK Parliament home page at http://www.parliament.uk.

Parliament Acts 1911 and 1949

3.9   At one time the House of Lords had a general power to reject Bills from the House of Commons and thereby prevent them being enacted, but this power has been severely restricted in relation to Public Bills by the Parliament Act 1911, as amended by the Parliament Act 1949.

The Parliament Act 1911, s 1 provides that any Public Bill which has been passed by the House of Commons and has been certified by the Speaker as a 'Money Bill', ie a Bill whose provisions exclusively relate to central government taxation, expenditure or loans, may be presented for the royal assent even though the House of Lords has failed to pass it without amendment after it has been with that House for one month. This means that the Lords must pass a 'Money Bill' unamended within one month of receiving it, otherwise the royal assent can be given without their assent.

In addition, the Parliament Act 1911, s 2, as amended by the Parliament Act 1949, provides that any other Public Bill, with the important exception mentioned below, which has been passed by the House of Commons in two successive sessions and been rejected in each session by the House of Lords, may be presented for the royal assent without the concurrence of the Lords, provided that one year has elapsed between the Second Reading in the Commons in the first session and the Third Reading there in the second session and that in both sessions the Bill had been submitted to the Lords at least one month before the end of the session. The result is that the House of Lords may delay a Public Bill, other than a 'Money Bill', for a maximum of one year. Section 2 of the Act of 1911 provides an important exception to the basic rule which it lays down: that rule does not apply to Bills to prolong the maximum duration of a Parliament beyond five years. Here the House of Lords retains an unfettered right of veto.

Citation
3.10   Until 1963, statutes were cited by the date of the regnal year or years of the parliamentary session in which the Act was passed, the regnal year being assessed from the monarch's accession, together with a chapter number which denoted the order in which it received the royal assent. Thus, the Law of Property Act 1925 is cited '15 and 16 Geo 5, c 20'. Acts passed after 1962 are cited by reference to the calendar year, not the regnal year, in which they were passed. Thus, the Misrepresentation Act 1967 is cited '1967, c 7'.

Of course, the more usual way to cite an Act is by its short title.

Commencement and repeal
3.11   An Act of Parliament comes into operation on the date on which it receives the royal assent unless, as frequently occurs, some other date is specified in the Act or it is to be appointed by a commencement order made either by Order in Council[1] or by a government minister by way of statutory instrument.[2] Sometimes, a commencement order is not made for a considerable time. An extreme example concerns the Easter Act 1928, which provides a fixed date for Easter but for which a commencement order has not yet been made.

A commencement order may only relate to certain parts of an Act, so that the legislation is brought into force in a piecemeal fashion. For example, while most of the Estate Agents Act 1979 has been brought into force, a commencement order has not yet been made in relation to the requirement for bonding and the provisions on standards of competence.

An Act of Parliament may be repealed expressly by a subsequent statute, or impliedly by being inconsistent with it (although there is a presumption against implied repeal).[3] Unless the contrary intention appears, repeal does not:

* revive a previously repealed rule of law; or
* affect existing rights and liabilities, or legal proceedings, civil or criminal.[4]

No statute becomes obsolete through the passing of time, except for certain Acts, usually of an experimental or transitional nature, which are expressed to be operative only for a limited period.

One way of finding out whether a statute has been wholly or partly repealed or amended is to look it up in the *Chronological Table of the Statutes* published biennially by the Stationery Office. This covers the period from 1235 to the end of the year preceding publication. Other ways are to consult LEXIS or to look at the index to *The Statutes in Force*, which is published annually by the Stationery Office.

1   Para 3.12 below.
2   Interpretation Act 1978, s 4.
3   Para 3.30 below.
4   Interpretation Act 1978, ss 15 and 16.

Subordinate legislation

3.12 Various institutions, such as the Crown, ministers, public corporations and local authorities, have legislative powers. Such legislation is subordinate since it is made by bodies with limited powers and it is always subject to abrogation or amendment by Act of Parliament. Moreover, it may be required to be subject to parliamentary scrutiny and, unlike an Act of Parliament, it may be held invalid in certain cases by the courts. Subordinate legislation can be of two types: delegated legislation and autonomic legislation.

Delegated legislation

3.13 Delegated legislation comprises the great bulk of subordinate legislation. Delegated legislation is legislation made by some executive body under powers delegated to it by Act of Parliament. An Act of Parliament often gives powers to some bodies, such as the Queen in Council (in effect the government), a minister or a local authority or public corporation, to make regulations and prescribe for their breach. Delegated legislation includes sub-delegated legislation which may validly be made where it is authorised by an Act of Parliament, as where an Act provides that the Queen in Council may make regulations empowering a particular minister to make further regulations.

There is a vast amount of delegated legislation – the number of pieces made annually being numbered in thousands, whereas the number of Public and Private Acts of Parliament a year rarely exceeds 90. Examples of Acts giving very wide powers of delegated legislation are the European Communities Act 1972[1] and the Consumer Credit Act 1974. Delegated legislation made by the central executive may be required to be made by Order in Council made by the Queen in Council, otherwise it takes the form of regulations, rules or orders made by a minister or government department. Generally, delegated legislation of these types must be made by statutory instrument (formerly Statutory Rules and Orders).

1 Para 3.44, below.

3.14 Statutory instruments are printed by the Queen's Printer and are published by the Stationery Office. They are also included in the LEXIS database and other electronic media. They are cited by calendar year and number and by a short title. For instance, the Land Registration (Official Searches) Rules are cited SI 1993 No 3276. A statutory instrument comes into effect when made unless, as is usual, it specifies a later date.[1] Unlike an Act of Parliament, it is a defence for a person charged with contravening a statutory instrument to prove that it had not been issued by the Stationery Office at the date of the alleged offence, unless it is proved that at that date reasonable steps had been taken to bring the purport of the instrument to the notice of the public, or of persons likely to be affected by it, or of the person charged.[2]

1 *Johnson v Sargant & Sons* [1918] 1 KB 101.
2 Statutory Instruments Act 1946, s 3.

3.15 Parliamentary control over statutory instruments is secured to some extent by requirements of 'laying' and of publication. Often the enabling statute will require the instrument to be laid before Parliament, in which case it must be so laid before it comes into operation. In addition, an affirmative resolution by Parliament may be required to give it effect or it may be made subject to cancellation by a negative resolution of either House within 40 'sitting' days.[1] Closer parliamentary scrutiny of new statutory instruments is provided by the Joint Select Committee on Statutory

Instruments, which is composed of members of both Houses and reports to Parliament. Its terms of reference include consideration of every statutory instrument laid or laid in draft before Parliament, with a view to seeing whether the special attention of Parliament should be drawn to the instrument on one of a number of grounds, eg that it is obscurely worded, or appears to impose charges on the subject or on the public revenue, or purports to have a retrospective effect unauthorised by the parent statute. The Select Committee is not concerned with the merits of delegated legislation.

1   Statutory Instruments Act 1946, ss 4 and 5, as clarified by the Laying of Documents before Parliament (Interpretation) Act 1948.

3.16   Another type of delegated legislation is the byelaw. Byelaws are made by local authorities, public corporations and certain other bodies authorised by statute. Although general in operation, they are restricted to the locality or undertaking to which they apply. They are not made by statutory instrument.

3.17   All forms of delegated legislation are invalid if they are ultra vires. Delegated legislation is ultra vires if it is in excess of the powers conferred by the enabling statute on the rule-making body (substantive ultra vires); or if it is made in breach of a mandatory part of the procedure concerning its making prescribed by that statute (procedural ultra vires); or, in the case of byelaws only, if it is patently unreasonable, or so uncertain as to have no ascertainable meaning, or so unclear in its effect as to be incapable of certain application in any given situation, or repugnant to the general law (in which cases it is regarded as substantively ultra vires).[1]

If delegated legislation is partly ultra vires and partly not, because it purports (or its effect is) to deal with matters outside the delegated powers as well as matters within them, it may be valid and enforceable to the extent that it is not ultra vires. It will be valid to that extent if the ultra vires part can be severed. Severance is always possible if the ultra vires part can be removed simply by cutting out the relevant words. If this is not possible, severance may be effected by modifying the text so as to omit the ultra vires aspect of it, provided that this does not change the substantial purpose and effect of the provision as a whole.[2]

The invalidity of delegated legislation is either challenged directly before the courts on an application for judicial review or raised as a defence to a court action which concerns the application of the delegated legislation. The latter course is not possible if there is a clear Parliamentary intention to the contrary in the Act of Parliament under which the delegated legislation was made.[2]

1   *Nash v Finlay* (1901) 85 LT 682, DC; *Powell v May* [1946] 1 All ER 444, DC; *Percy v Hall* [1996] 4 All ER 523, CA.
2   *Boddington v British Transport Police* [1998] 2 All ER 203, HL.

3.18   The principal advantages of delegated legislation are:

• Parliament has insufficient time to deal with details. The availability of delegated legislation enables Parliament to limit itself to settling the general policy of a measure, such as the Consumer Credit Act 1974, leaving a minister to supply the detailed provisions in the form of regulations and orders.
• Delegated legislation is eminently suitable in the case of provisions on technical matters which would be inappropriate for parliamentary discussion.
• In some cases, the power to make delegated legislation enables a minister to deal speedily with urgent situations, such as an economic crisis or a strike in an essential industry.

- The power to make delegated legislation is also useful in that, within the terms of the parent Act, it enables the application of an Act to be tailored to deal with contingencies which were not foreseen when the Act was passed.

On the other hand, delegated legislation is open to the following criticisms:

- Parliament has neither the time nor the opportunity to supervise all delegated legislation effectively.
- The detail which delegated legislation provides may be just as important as the general policy of the parent Act, yet Parliament cannot discuss its merits.

Autonomic legislation

3.19 Autonomic legislation is legislation made by the Queen by Order in Council, or by autonomous associations within the state, under powers which are not delegated by Parliament but which are recognised by the courts. Trade unions and professional associations are examples of autonomous associations in this context. The legislation of such autonomous associations is directly binding only on their members, though negatively it binds everyone since interference with it is wrongful; it is invalid if ultra vires. Autonomic legislation made by the Queen in Council is made under the royal prerogative. There is no power under the prerogative to alter the general law of the land[1] but there is a limited prerogative power to legislate for the dependent territories, the armed forces and the civil service. The prerogative comprises those independent powers left to the Crown by Parliament, and legislation outside the prerogative powers of the Crown will be held invalid by the courts if it is not delegated legislation (ie made with statutory authority).

1   *Proclamations' Case* (1611) 12 Co Rep 74.

European Convention on Human Rights

3.20 The European Convention on Human Rights and the First Protocol to it, to both of which the United Kingdom is a party, are not part of English law. Although English courts are increasingly being influenced by it in their interpretation and development of the law, the provisions of the Convention cannot prevail over a rule of English law in the event of any inconsistency. A judge may seek to interpret English law so as to accord with a right in the Convention, but if he cannot do so he must apply the rule of English law.

When the Human Rights Bill, before Parliament at the time of writing, is enacted, English and Welsh courts will be legally obliged, so far as possible, to read, and give effect to, Acts of Parliament, Orders in Council, and subordinate legislation in general in a way which is compatible with the rights and fundamental freedoms set out in the Convention and the First Protocol ('the Convention rights').

This obligation, however, will not affect the validity or enforcement of any incompatible Act of Parliament or Order in Council made under the royal prerogative, nor of any incompatible Order in Council, regulation, byelaw or the like made under statutory powers if primary legislation prevents removal of the incompatibility.

The Bill goes on to provide that, where a court determines that a provision in an Act of Parliament or Order in Council made under the royal prerogative is incompatible with one or more of the Convention rights, it may make a declaration of that incompatibility. In addition, if a court determines that a provision of subordinate legislation made under statutory powers is incompatible with one or more of the Convention rights, and it is satisfied that the primary legislation concerned prevents removal of the incompatibility, it may make a declaration of that incompatibility. The effect of such a declaration will be that a Government minister may, by order, amend the legislation, as he thinks appropriate, to remove the incompatibility. Such an amendment will also be possible without a declaration of incompatibility if a Government minister or the Queen in Council thinks that a piece of legislation is, in the light of a finding of the European Convention on Human Rights, incompatible with the United Kingdom's obligations under the Convention.

The Bill also makes it unlawful for a public authority, including a court, to act in a way which is incompatible with one or more Convention rights, unless it was compelled to do so by an Act of Parliament, an Order in Council or other subordinate legislation. A person who claims that a public authority has acted (or proposes to act) unlawfully in the above way may bring court proceedings against the authority, or rely on the Convention right or rights in any legal proceedings, if he is (or would be) a victim of the unlawful act. Where the public authority is a court, proceedings against it may be brought only by way of an appeal or (where the court is subject to it) judicial review, and damages may not be awarded against the court.

Interpretation
3.21   Language being inherently capable of ambiguity and human affairs being capable of great diversity, the courts are often faced with the question whether a particular matter or piece of conduct falls within the wording of a particular legislative provision. The exposition which follows is concerned with the interpretation of Public Acts of Parliament but, essentially, the same rules apply to the interpretation of other Acts of Parliament and of subordinate legislation. In interpreting statutes, the courts are trying to discover Parliament's intentions from the words. There are two, radically different, approaches to this task: the 'literal approach' and the 'purposive approach'. It is impossible to know in advance which approach the court will adopt in a particular case. We shall consider them in turn, and then deal with various rules of interpretation which apply whichever of the two approaches is adopted.

The two approaches to interpretation
The literal approach
3.22   The literal approach to statutory interpretation is otherwise known as the literal rule. This states that Parliament's intention must be found by interpreting the words used in their ordinary, literal and grammatical sense. If the words can be so interpreted a judge must give effect to that interpretation, unless the statute or the legal context in which the words are used compels him to give the word a special meaning, even though he considers that it produces an undesirable, inexpedient or unjust result or that Parliament cannot have intended it or that the situation is one which was not contemplated when the statute was enacted.[1] In *IRC v Hinchy*,[2] the House of Lords had to interpret the Income Tax Act 1952, s 25(3), which provided that a person who failed to deliver a correct income tax return should forfeit 'the sum of twenty pounds and treble the tax which he ought to be charged under this Act'. The House of Lords held that, in addition to the penalty of £20, a taxpayer who had declared only part of his Post Office interest was liable to pay treble the whole tax chargeable for the year, and not merely treble the tax on the undeclared income.

1   *Duport Steels Ltd v Sirs* [1980] 1 All ER 529, HL; *Leedale v Lewis* [1982] 3 All ER 808, HL; *Comdel Commodities Ltd v Siporex Trade SA (No 2)* [1990] 2 All ER 552, HL.
2   [1960] 1 All ER 505, HL. The actual decision in this case was overruled by the Finance Act 1960, s 44, which amended the wording of the provision in question.

3.23   It may happen that to interpret statutory words according to their ordinary, literal and grammatical sense in their context would give rise to manifest absurdity, repugnancy or inconsistency *with the rest of the statute*. In such a case, the so-called 'golden rule' permits a judge to modify the literal interpretation so as to avoid such a result. The classical exposition of the golden rule was given by Lord Wensleydale in *Grey v Pearson*.[1]

> 'in construing... statutes ..., the grammatical and ordinary sense of the words is to be adhered to, unless that would lead to some absurdity or some repugnance or inconsistency with the rest of the instrument, in which case the grammatical and ordinary sense of the words may be modified so as to avoid that absurdity or inconsistency, but no further.'

A modern example is provided by the House of Lords' decision in *McMonagle v Westminster City Council*.[2] M was charged with the offence of using premises as a 'sex encounter establishment' without a licence, contrary to the Local Government (Miscellaneous Provisions) Act 1982. The definition of such an establishment was 'premises at which performances which are *not* unlawful are given, which ... comprise the sexual stimulation of persons admitted to the premises ...'. M's defence was that it had not been proved that the performances in question were *not* unlawful and that, if they were unlawful, a licence was not required under the plain words of the Act. The House of Lords rejected this interpretation, as being absurd, and held that the words 'which are not unlawful' were mere surplusage which had been introduced by an incompetent draftsman solely to emphasise that a licence conferred no immunity from the ordinary criminal law. Thus, the prosecution did not have to prove that the performances were not unlawful and it was no defence that they were unlawful.

1   (1857) 6 HL Cas 61 at 106.
2   [1990] 1 All ER 993, HL.

Purposive approach

3.24   Under this approach to statutory interpretation, the words in a statute are interpreted not only in their ordinary, literal and grammatical sense but also with reference to their context and purpose. If the judge thinks that the interpretation of the words in their ordinary, literal and grammatical sense would produce a result contrary to the purpose of the statute as he understands it to be, the judge may construe them in any other way consistent with that purpose which the words are capable of bearing. This approach differs from the literal approach in that, while the court starts with a consideration of the ordinary, literal and grammatical meaning of the words, it can depart from that meaning not only in cases covered by the golden rule but also where that meaning would give rise to a result contrary to the purpose of the statute. In *Richard Thomas and Baldwins Ltd v Cummings*,[1] for example, a provision in the Factories Act 1937, which required the fencing of dangerous parts of a machine while it was in motion, was held not to apply where a worker turned the machine by hand. The machine could not have been repaired while it was fenced, and the purpose of the statute was to protect workers operating machines with dangerous parts.

1   [1955] 1 All ER 285, HL.

3.25   As part of the purposive approach, judges can imply or substitute words where the words are 'necessarily implied' by words already in the statute. For example, in *Federal Steam Navigation Co Ltd v Department of Trade and Industry*,[1] where the Oil in Navigable Waters Act 1955 provided that, where oil was discharged from a British ship in a prohibited area, 'the owner or master of the ship' committed an offence, it was held that, if the owner or master were separate people, both could be convicted, the words being construed as if they read 'the owner *and/or* master of the ship'. On the other hand, if a court is faced with a factual situation for which the statute has not provided, even the purposive approach does not permit the court to fill the gap. To do so would be to attribute to Parliament an intention which it never had. Like the literal approach, the purposive approach is limited to giving effects to the words of the statute. It does not extend to reading words into it to rectify an anomaly or absurdity, *unless clear reason is found within the body* of the Act itself;[2] a judge cannot attribute to Parliament an intention which Parliament never had. For a judge to do so was condemned by Lord Simonds in *Magor and St Mellons RDC v Newport Corpn*,[3] as a 'naked usurpation of the legislative function under the thin disguise of interpretation'. His Lordship added that if a gap is disclosed the remedy lies in an amending Act.

1   [1974] 2 All ER 97, HL.
2   *Stock v Frank Jones (Tipton) Ltd* [1978] 1 All ER 948, HL.
3   [1951] 2 All ER 839 at 841.

General rules of interpretation
3.26   Whichever of the two approaches to interpretation is adopted, the court will be assisted by various general rules of interpretation. Indeed, if the provision proves to be uncertain or ambiguous, one or more of these rules may be determinative of the court's interpretation.

Consideration of the whole enactment
3.27   Consideration of the whole enactment assists in resolving apparent ambiguities, inconsistencies or redundancies in a particular provision. A statute must be read as a whole. Every section must be read in the light of every other section,[1] including its interpretation section (if any) normally found towards the end of a statute. The definitions in an interpretation section apply throughout the Act, unless a contrary intention, express or implied, appears in a particular context.

1   *Beswick v Beswick* [1967] 2 All ER 1197, HL.

The mischief rule
3.28   The literal approach breaks down, in particular, in the case of an ambiguity. In such a case, a judge may apply the mischief rule, which is often called the rule in *Heydon's Case* since it was formulated there.[1] The rule is best paraphrased by the statement by Lord Halsbury in *Eastman Photographic Materials Co v Comptroller-General of Patents, Designs and Trade Marks.* 'We are to see what was the law before the Act was passed, and what was the mischief or defect for which the law had not provided, what remedy Parliament appointed, and the reason of the remedy'.[2] An example of the application of the mischief rule is *Gorris v Scott*.[3] The plaintiff claimed in respect of the loss of his sheep which were washed overboard and drowned while the defendant was engaged in carrying them by sea. The loss was due to the fact that, in breach of a statutory duty to do so, no pens had been provided. The plaintiff based his claim on the fact that the loss had been caused by the breach of the statutory duty. However, it was held that the purpose of the relevant provision was not to prevent loss overboard but to minimise the spread of contagious diseases, and that therefore the claim did not fall within the 'mischief' of the Act.

1   (1584) 3 Co Rep 7a.
2   [1898] AC 571 at 573.
3   (1874) LR 9 Exch 125.

Other rules

3.29 The rule that the whole enactment must be considered is really part of the principle that words must be taken in their context. A word in itself does not have an absolute meaning: its meaning is relevant to its context (this statement is often described by the Latin tag *noscitur a sociis*). Another important example of this principle is the *ejusdem generis* (of the same class) rule. Enactments often list things which are so similar as to form a class to which a provision is to apply, following the list with some general words implying that some other similar things are intended to fall within the class. Whether something which is not specified in the list of things falls within the general words depends upon whether or not it is ejusdem generis as the specified things. In *Powell v Kempton Park Racecourse Co Ltd*,[1] an Act prohibited the keeping of a 'house, office, room or other place' for betting with persons resorting thereto. The House of Lords held that Tattersall's Ring (an uncovered enclosure of a superior sort) at a racecourse was not ejusdem generis as the specified things, and was not therefore an 'other place' within the meaning of the Act, since the specific words 'house, office, room' created a *genus* (class) of indoor places. There cannot be a *genus* for the purposes of the present rule unless the 'other' thing is preceded by a list of at least two or more specific things which share the same common characteristics.[2]

1   [1899] AC 143, HL. Also see *Brownsea Haven Properties Ltd v Poole Corpn* [1958] Ch 574, [1958] 1 All ER 205, CA.
2   *Quazi v Quazi* [1979] 3 All ER 897, HL.

Presumptions

3.30 There are a number of presumptions as to the intentions of Parliament, which may be rebutted by the express words of the Act or by necessary implication from the subject matter of the Act itself.

An Act applies to the United Kingdom   There is a presumption that an Act applies to the whole of the United Kingdom but not elsewhere. Acts frequently reveal a contrary intention by containing a section restricting their operation to one or more of the four home countries, or, in the case of a local Act,[1] to a particular locality: on the other hand, an extension of the application of an Act outside the United Kingdom is rarely provided for.

Against retrospective effect of legislation   This presumption is not concerned with when a statute comes into operation but with whether it affects factual situations which arose before that date. Parliament is presumed not to have intended to alter the law applicable to past events and transactions in a manner which is unfair to those concerned in them, unless a contrary intention appears.[2] The presumption is particularly strong where the statute creates offences or tax obligations. The greater the degree of unfairness, the stronger will have to be the evidence that Parliament intended the legislation to have retrospective effect.[2]

Against alteration of the law   Parliament is presumed to know the common law and not to intend to change it, with the result that, unless the words of the statute unmistakably indicate that the common law is changed, they must be interpreted so as not to alter it.[3] As part of the presumption against alteration in the law there are certain more specific presumptions: against the restriction of individual liberty; against compulsory deprivation of property, at least without compensation; and that there should be no criminal liability without fault. The presumption against alteration of the law also applies in relation to statute law. In particular, a consolidating Act is presumed not to introduce a change in the law by a change of words.[4]

Against the Crown being bound The Crown is not bound by a statute unless there can be gathered from it an intention that it should be bound.[5] The presumption also extends to employees of the Crown, in the course of their duties, and to Crown property. However, statutes frequently provide that they are to bind the Crown. Even if a statute does not expressly bind the Crown, a statute may construe it as doing so by necessary implication.

Other presumptions made in construing a statute are those against implied repeal of earlier legislation by later, apparently inconsistent, legislation (the earlier only being impliedly repealed if reconciliation is logically impossible); against ousting the jurisdiction of the courts; and against inconsistency with European Community law or international law.

We deal with the presumption against inconsistency with European Community Law in para 3.43, below.

1   See para 3.5 above.
2   *L'Office Cherifien des Phosphates Unitramp SA v Yamashita-Shinnihon Steamship Co Ltd* [1994] 1 All ER 20, HL.
3   *Leach v R* [1912] AC 305, HL.
4   *Beswick v Beswick* [1967] 2 All ER 1197, HL.
5   *Tamlin v Hannaford* [1950] 1 KB 18, CA; *Lord Advocate v Dumbarton District Council* [1990] 1 All ER 1, HL.

Aids to interpretation
Intrinsic aids
3.31   The rule that the whole enactment must be considered makes it of obvious importance to know what parts of an Act may be regarded as intrinsic aids to interpretation.

Long title and short title   These are part of the Act, but, in practice, the courts do not refer to the short title and only refer to the long title to resolve an ambiguity; in other words the long title is not allowed to restrict the clear meaning of a provision. In *Re Groos*,[1] it was held that the Wills Act 1861, s 3, applied to the will of an alien, even though the long title read: 'An Act to amend the law with respect to wills of personal estates made by British subjects.'

A preamble is part of the Act. It appears at the beginning and sets out the background and purpose of the enactment. Modern statutes very rarely contain a preamble and the best-known examples appear in earlier statutes. The preamble can only be looked at for guidance if the body of the Act is not clear and unambiguous.[2]

Punctuation, marginal notes and headings to a section or group of sections are inserted into a Bill by the parliamentary draftsmen and can be altered any time up to royal assent. They are not debated by parliament and are therefore not part of the Act. The result is that they may only be looked at to determine the purpose, as opposed to the scope, of the section,[3] although it may be that headings have a wider use.[4] Even in their limited sphere of operation, punctuation and marginal notes in particular carry little weight and cannot oust a meaning indicated by some part of the Act itself.

Schedules which are used, for instance, to list repeals and set out transitional or more detailed provisions, are part of the Act, but they cannot affect the interpretation of a word in the body of the Act unless it is ambiguous or uncertain.[5]

1   [1904] P 269. Also see *R v Gelvin* [1987] 2 All ER 851, CA.
2   *Powell v Kempton Park Racecourse Co Ltd* [1899] AC 143 at 157.

3   *DPP v Schildkamp* [1969] 3 All ER 1640, HL; *R v Kelt* [1977] 3 All ER 1099, CA.
4   *DPP v Schildkamp* [1969] 3 All ER 1640 at 1656.
5   *Ellerman Lines Ltd v Murray* [1931] AC 126, HL.

Extrinsic aids

3.32   While a court may look at the enactment as a whole, unlike most continental courts, it may not generally look at material outside the four walls of the Act to find Parliament's intention. It cannot, for instance, generally look at reports of the parliamentary debates on the Bill which became the Act.[1] This may appear to fly in the face of common sense but it must be admitted that it might be difficult in some cases to determine a legislative intent from a two, or more, sided parliamentary debate, especially where the Bill has been subject to amendment in Parliament. However, the following extrinsic aids (including parliamentary debates) can be looked at for limited purposes:

Dictionaries can be consulted to ascertain the ordinary and natural meaning, for the purpose of the literal rule, of words which have no particular legal meaning.[2]

Parliamentary debates   In 1992, the majority of the House of Lords in *Pepper v Hart*[3] held that the courts can refer to reports of debates or proceedings in Parliament relating to the provision in question[4] as an aid to interpreting a statute if it is ambiguous or absurd or if its literal meaning would lead to absurdity. Even in such cases, it held, reference to parliamentary reports is only possible if:

- it discloses the mischief aimed at or the legislative intention behind the ambiguous or obscure words;
- the statements relied on were by a minister or other promoter of the Bill; and
- those statements are clear.

In *Pepper v Hart* a public school operated a concessionary fees scheme for members of staff. The education of the children at a reduced rate was a taxable benefit under s 61(1) of the Finance Act 1976, which provided that an amount equal to the cash equivalent of the benefit was chargeable to tax. By s 63(1) the cash equivalent of the benefit was 'an amount equal to the cost of the benefit' and by s 63(2) the cost of the benefit was 'the amount of any expense incurred in or in connection with its provision'. Although the concessionary fees more than covered the marginal cost to the school of educating the employees' children, the employees were assessed to income tax on the basis that they were liable for a rateable proportion of the expenses in running the school, which proportion was roughly equal to the ordinary school fee. The employees appealed, claiming that since all the costs of running the school would have had to be incurred in any event the only expense incurred by the school 'in or in connection with' the education of their children was the small marginal cost to the school caused by the presence of their children, which was covered by the concessionary fees paid, and so the 'cash equivalent of the benefit' was nil.

The majority of the House of Lords held that s 63(2) was clearly ambiguous because the 'expense incurred in or in connection with' the provision of in-house benefits could be interpreted either as the marginal cost caused by the provision of the benefit or as a proportion of the total cost incurred in providing the service for all parents of pupils (the average cost). Allowing the employees' appeal, the majority of the House held that the requirements set out above were satisfied and that reference to a statement made by the Financial Secretary to the Treasury at the Committee stage of the Bill made it clear that Parliament had intended to assess the expense incurred in the provision of in-house benefits, particularly concessionary fees, on the basis of the marginal cost to the employer, and not on the average cost of the benefit. Most of the majority would have reached the contrary conclusion if they had had to interpret s 63 without reference to the parliamentary report.

There is authority at first instance that, where the purpose of the legislation is to introduce into English law the provisions of an international convention or of a European directive, the strict criteria for admissibility of parliamentary materials set out above do not apply, so that recourse to them can be made on a wider basis.[5]

The admissibility of parliamentary materials is of obvious importance where a purposive approach is being taken to the interpretation of a statute.

Reports of committees containing proposals for legislation which have been presented to Parliament and resulted in the enactment in question can be looked at, for the purpose of the mischief rule, to discover the state of the pre-existing law and the mischief which the enactment was passed to remedy. An example is provided by the House of Lords' decision in *Black-Clawson International Ltd v Papierwerke Waldhof-Aschaffenburg AG,*[6] where their Lordships, in order to interpret the Foreign Judgments (Reciprocal Enforcement) Act 1933, s 8, referred to the report of a committee, which had resulted in the passing of the Act, to discover what the pre-existing law was understood to be and what its mischief was. Two of the five Lords of Appeal, Viscount Dilhorne and Lord Simon, went further and stated that it was permissible to look at such a report for a direct statement of what the resulting enactment meant. This minority statement went further than our courts have been prepared to go in the past. Lord Reid and Lord Wilberforce disagreed with it expressly in *Black-Clawson,* and subsequent House of Lords' decisions have indicated that it is not correct.[7]

Government White Papers which have resulted in legislation may, like the reports of committees just mentioned, be referred to in order to ascertain the mischief which Parliament intended to remedy.[8]

Judicial precedent   The interpretation given by a court to a statutory provision or word may be binding in relation to *that* provision or word in *that* Act, in accordance with the principles of the doctrine of judicial precedent (paras 3.46 to 3.62 below). Moreover, a judicial interpretation of a particular provision in one Act will be a similarly binding precedent in a subsequent one if they both deal with the same subject matter, as where the latter is a consolidating Act.

Interpretation Act 1978 The Act lays down various definitions which apply unless there is a contrary intention, express or implied, in a particular statute. For example, 'unless the contrary intention appears, (a) words importing the masculine gender shall include females; and (b) words in the singular shall include the plural and words in the plural shall include the singular.[9] Again, 'person' includes any body of persons corporate or unincorporate.[10]

1   *Assam Railways and Trading Co Ltd v IRC* [1935] AC 445, HL; *Davis v Johnson* [1978] 1 All ER 1132, HL; *Hadmor Productions Ltd v Hamilton* [1982] 1 All ER 1042, HL.
2   *Re Ripon (Highfield) Housing Confirmation Order* 1938 [1939] 3 All ER 548, CA.
3   [1993] 1 All ER 42, HL. See also *R v Warwickshire County Council, ex p Johnson* [1993] 2 WLR 1, HL.
4   But not other provisions: *Melluish (Inspector of Taxes) v BMI (No 3) Ltd* [1995] 4 All ER 453, HL.
5   *Three Rivers District Council v Governor of the Bank of England (No 2)* [1996] 2 All ER 363. The statement was only an obiter dictum, a term defined and explained in paras 3.46 - 3.48 below .
6   [1975] 1 All ER 810, HL. Also see *Davis v Johnson* [1978] 1 All ER 1132, HL.
7   *R v Ayres* [1984] 1 All ER 619, HL; *R v Allen* [1985] 2 All ER 641, HL. For views in support of the minority statement, see *R v Shivpuri* [1986] 2 All ER 334 at 343; *Aswan Engineering Establishment Co v Lupdine Ltd* [1987] 1 All ER 135 at 146–147; *R v Gomez* [1993] 1 All ER 1 at 24.

8   *Black-Clawson International Ltd v Papierwerke Waldof-Aschaffenberg AG* [1975] AC 591 at 638; *A-G's Reference (No 1 of 1988)* [1989] 1 All ER 321 at 324.
9   Section 6.
10   Schedule 1.

Acts giving effect to international conventions

3.33   Increasingly, the purpose of an Act of Parliament is to put into domestic effect an international convention. In such a case recourse may be had to the terms of the convention if a provision of the Act is ambiguous or vague.[1]

Sometimes, an Act actually incorporates the convention. In such a case there are no limits on recourse to the terms of the convention because they have been made provisions of the Act. Conventions are apt to be more loosely worded than Acts of Parliament, and in *James Buchanan & Co Ltd v Babco Forwarding and Shipping (UK) Ltd*[2] the House of Lords held that a court must interpret the English text of an incorporated convention in a broad and sensible manner unconstrained by the technical rules of English law. Moreover, the majority of their Lordships held, if there is doubt about the true construction of the English text the court can look at an authorised text in a foreign language to resolve it. In the event of ambiguity or obscurity in the convention, the court can look at material in the public records of the international conference at which it was drafted provided that that material was intended to clear up the ambiguity or obscurity.[3]

1   *Post Office v Estuary Radio* [1967] 3 All ER 663, CA.
2   [1977] 3 All ER 1048, HL. Also see *Rothmans of Pall Mall (Overseas) Ltd v Saudi Arabian Airlines Corpn* [1980] 3 All ER 359, CA.
3   *Fothergill v Monarch Airlines Ltd* [1980] 2 All ER 696, HL.

Legislation of the European Community

3.34   The fundamental legislation of the European Community is to be found in the treaties, including amending treaties, which established the three Communities - the European Economic Community (EEC), the European Coal and Steel Community (ECSC) and the European Atomic Energy Community (EURATOM). The EEC, now known as the European Community (EC) is easily the most important of the three. Although in strict law there are three distinct Communities, in practice they are administered as one, sharing a single Council and Commission.

The three Communities' structures and law are one of the three areas which make up the European Union established under the Treaty of Maastricht which came into force in 1993. The other two areas are inter-governmental co-ordination on matters of foreign policy and common external defence, and political inter-governmental co-operation on internal affairs such as policing, criminal justice and immigration.

Since 'European Union' is a wider concept than the legal order of the three Communities it is common to refer to that legal order as 'the Community' or 'the European Community', and this is the course adopted in this book. The singular, rather than plural, of the term is used because this reflects the practical reality of the situation.

The overwhelming mass of the Community legislation is found not in the treaties referred to above but in regulations, directives and decisions of the Community's organs. It is largely concerned with economic matters, such as agriculture, free trade and fair competition, but it also deals with other matters, such as immigration, employment and other social matters.

Regulations, directives and decisions

3.35   Regulations have general application and are made by the Council of Ministers of the European Union (a political body composed normally of foreign ministers) or the Commission (a supranational body composed of the highest officials) under the treaties.

Directives can be issued or decisions made by the Council or the Commission. Directives are directed to member states, who are obliged to implement them although they have a choice as to the form and methods of implementation. Decisions are addressed either to a member state or to an individual or institution. They are a formal method of enunciating administrative decisions effecting the policy of the Community and are binding on the addressee.

Regulations, directives and decisions are published in the *Official Journal of the European Communities*. The current forms of numerical citation can be exemplified as follows: Reg (EC) 2094 [1]/96[2]; Dec 96[2]/2[1]/EC; Dir 93[2]/13[1]/EEC.

1   Number in series for year made.
2   Year made.

Direct applicability and direct effect

3.36   In discussing the types of legislation of the Community, a fundamental point must be emphasised at the outset: regulations are *'directly applicable'* in the sense that they confer rights and duties on individuals and institutions which are enforceable in the courts of member states without being re-enacted by legislation in those states. This is provided by the treaties establishing the Community. However, although the treaties conclude the matter according to *Community law*, they do not in themselves give the concept of 'direct applicability' legal effect in the *law of the United Kingdom*. The reason is that treaty provisions do not become part of our law unless they have been incorporated into it by legislation. Such incorporation has been achieved by the European Communities Act 1972, s 2(1), which provides that those rights and duties which are, as a matter of Community law, 'directly applicable' or 'directly effective' are to have legal effect in the UK.

Section 2(4) of the Act goes on to provide that Acts of Parliament passed or to be passed shall have effect subject to the rules of Community law which are directly applicable or of direct effect. According to the decisions of the House of Lords in *R v Secretary of State for Transport, ex p Factortame Ltd*[1] and *R v Secretary of State for Transport, ex p Factortame Ltd (No 2)*,[2] the effect of s 2(4) seems to be to imply into every piece of United Kingdom legislation a term that it takes effect subject to directly applicable or directly effective Community law and to require the United Kingdom courts to override a piece of United Kingdom legislation to the extent that it is inconsistent with Community law which is directly applicable or of direct effect.

It is inconceivable that a UK court would so act without first seeking a preliminary ruling from the European Court confirming the inconsistency.[3] Pending the preliminary ruling, a UK court may suspend the operation of the Act of Parliament by granting an interlocutory injunction.[4] Whether or not a court will grant an interlocutory injunction in such a case against a public authority seeking to enforce the Act of Parliament depends on the balance of convenience, whether damages would be an appropriate remedy, the importance of upholding the law and the obligation of certain authorities to enforce the law, and whether the challenge to the Act is prima facie so firmly based as to justify so exceptional a course.[5]

To the extent that directly applicable or directly effective Community law prevails over an Act of Parliament under United Kingdom law, the sovereignty of Parliament has been limited.

1   [1989] 2 All ER 692, HL.
2   [1991] 1 All ER 70, ECJ and HL.
3   Para 2.32, above.
4   *R v Secretary of State for Transport, ex p Factortame Ltd* [1989] 2 All ER 692, HL.

5   *R v Secretary of State for Transport, ex p Factortame Ltd (No 2)* [1991] 1 All ER 70, ECJ and HL.

3.37   No other form of Community legislation is expressly stated in the treaties establishing the Community to be directly applicable. It was once thought that these other forms could only take effect in member states if they were implemented by them. However, in 1963 it was established by the European Court of Justice that the provisions of treaties of the Community could directly confer rights or impose obligations on individuals without implementation in national law.[1] This concept of *direct effect* has subsequently been extended to directives[2] and decisions.[3] In *Van Duyn v Home Office*,[4] for example, the European Court held that a directive was of binding effect so as to confer rights on the plaintiff against the United Kingdom government even though the UK had not implemented that directive.

In order to have direct effect, a treaty provision, directive or decision must be unconditional and sufficiently precise. Not surprisingly, it cannot be directly effective if details remain to be resolved by a member state before it can be implemented.[5]

Where it exists, the direct effect of a directive is narrower than the direct applicability of a regulation or the direct effect of a treaty provision. The reason is that directives can only have 'vertical' direct effect (ie in favour of an individual against the state or an arm of the state) and not, unlike regulations and treaty provisions, 'horizontal' effect (ie as between individuals in the state or in favour of the state or an arm of the state against an individual). In other words, they can only confer rights on individuals, and not obligations on them. This was held by the European Court in *Marshall v Southampton and South West Hampshire Area Health Authority*,[6] where a woman who had been dismissed by an area health authority on reaching the retirement age for women (60, as opposed to 65 for men) succeeded in her claim that this constituted sexual discrimination contrary to a directive. The directive had not been incorporated into English law by United Kingdom legislation but the European Court held that it was directly effective vis-à-vis the employer, the area health authority, because it was an arm of the state. The European Court has held that the concept of direct effect can be relied on against any organisation or body providing a public service, which is subject to the authority or control of the state and which has for that purpose special powers beyond those which result from the normal rules applicable to relations between individuals; these can all be regarded as an arm of the state. Accordingly, directives have been held directly effective against local or regional authorities, police authorities and nationalised industries, and the governors of a voluntarily aided school,[7] as well as public authorities providing public health services.

Whether or not a directive is directly effective depends on an examination of the nature, general scheme and wording of its provisions to see whether they are capable of producing direct effects.[3] In practice, very few directives are likely to be regarded as having direct effect.

1   *Algemene Transport-en Expedite Onderneming Van Gend en Loos v Nederlands Administratie Der Belastingadministratie* [1963] ECR 1, ECJ.
2   *Van Duyn v Home Office* [1975] 3 All ER 190, ECJ.
3   *Grad v Finanzamt Traunstein* [1970] ECR 825, [1971] CMLR 1, ECJ.
4   [1975] 3 All ER 190, ECJ.
5   *Becker v Finanzamt Münster-Innenstadt* [1982] ECR 53, [1982] 1 CMLR 499, ECJ.
6   [1986] 2 All ER 584, ECJ. In *Faccini Dori v Recreb Srl* [1994] ECR I-3325, [1995] All ER (EC) 1, ECI, the European Court affirmed its view in *Marshall* that a directive cannot have horizontal effect.
7   See, respectively, *Fratelli Costanzo SpA v Comune di Milano* [1989] ECR 1839, [1990] 3 CMLR 239, ECJ; *Johnston v Chief Constable of the Royal Ulster Constabulary* [1986] 3 All ER 135, ECJ; and *Foster v British Gas plc* [1991] 2 All ER 705, HL, where it was held that the British Gas Corporation, a public corporation (and not to be confused with the subsequent privatised public limited company), under the ultimate control of the state which could dictate its policies and retain its surplus revenue, was a body against whom a directive could be directly applicable; *National Union of Teachers v*

Governing Body of St Mary's C of E Aided Junior School [1997] ICR 334, CA. Contrast *Doughty v Rolls-Royce plc* [1992] 1 CMLR 1045, CA, where a directive was held not to be directly effective against a commercial undertaking notwithstanding that all its shares were held by nominees of the government.

Unimplemented directives: any effect in English law?

3.38 A directive which has not been implemented into the law of a member state and is not of direct effect in the circumstances is not devoid of all effect under that law. It may have effect in two ways, according to the European Court of Justice. First, a national court can have regard to an unimplemented directive in interpreting national regulations. Second, the failure of a member state to implement a directive may give rise to a liability in damages.

3.39 As the Court held in *Marleasing SA v La Comercial Internacional de Alimentación SA*,[1] national law, whenever passed, must be interpreted by a national court in such a way as to give effect to Community directives so far as possible. In this case, there was a dispute in a Spanish court between two Spanish companies. One sought to have the memorandum and articles of association of the other (company A) set aside on a ground prescribed by Spanish legislation. Company A argued in reply that its memorandum and articles were in accordance with a directive of the EC Commission, the First Company Law Directive. That directive had not been enacted into Spanish law. The European Court held that company A could not rely directly on the unenacted directive in an action with a private entity, but went on to state that the Spanish court was obliged to interpret the Spanish legislation 'in every way possible in the light of the text and aim of the directive to achieve the result envisaged by it'. This, the European Court held, required that in the particular case the Spanish court should ignore a specific provision of Spanish law which was inconsistent with the aim of the directive.

The ruling in *Marleasing* only requires a national court interpreting national law to do so *so far as possible* in such a way as to give effect to a directive which has not been implemented nationally. The words italicised led the European Court of Justice in *Criminal proceedings against Arcaro*[2] to hold that the ruling in *Marleasing* did not extend to permitting a national court to interpret a national law so as to impose on an individual an obligation laid down by a directive which has not been implemented in national law or, more especially, so as to impose or increase the criminal liability of persons who act in breach of a directive. In other words, a national court cannot eliminate national provisions contrary to a provision of a directive which has not been implemented nationally and substitute the terms of the directive. To do so would be to introduce direct effect between individuals under the guise of interpretation.

The correct approach of an English court to the interpretation of unimplemented directives has been stated in similar terms in our courts. It has been said that it is for an English court to construe an Act of Parliament so as to accord with a directive, if this can be done without distorting the meaning of the Act, whether the Act came after or before the directive.[3] This has been explained as consistent with the statement in *Marleasing* that a national court must construe a domestic law to accord with a relevant directive if it is possible to do so, which it will not be if the domestic law is not open to an interpretation consistent with the directive.[4]

1   [1990] ECR I-4135, [1992] 1 CMLR 305, ECJ.
2   [1997] All ER (EC) 82, ECJ.
3   *Webb v EMO Air Cargo (UK) Ltd* [1992] 4 All ER 929 at 939–940; *Duke v GEC Reliance Ltd* [1988] 1 All ER 626, HL.
4   *Webb v EMO Air Cargo (UK) Ltd*, ibid.

3.40 The European Court's decision in *Francovich v Italy*[1] indicates that a person may be able to claim from a member state in the courts of that state damages for loss suffered as a result of its failure to implement nationally a directive. In this case, the Italian government had failed to implement a directive requiring a national institution to be established to ensure that employees of insolvent employers received arrears of salary. Employees of companies which had become insolvent owing substantial arrears of salaries brought proceedings in an Italian court against the Italian Republic, seeking payments under the directive. The European Court held that the directive was not of direct effect because it was insufficiently precise, in that it did not specify which organ of state was to bear the liability. Consequently, the employees could not rely on it in an action in an Italian court. However, the European Court held that the employees could succeed in their claim against the Italian Republic for damages for loss resulting from its failure to implement the directive in breach of its obligation to do so under Community law. The court stated that three conditions must be fulfilled before such a claim could succeed:

- the objective of the directive must include the conferment of rights on individuals;
- the content of those rights must be ascertainable from the directive itself; and
- there must be a causal link between the state's failure to fulfil its obligations and the loss sustained by the individual.

1   [1991] ECR I-5357, [1993] 2 CMLR 66, ECJ.

3.41 *Francovich* concerned non-implementation of a directive. It left unclear the extent to which a member state might be liable for damages where it was otherwise in breach of its obligations under Community law. A relevant example, in the present context, would be where the state had tried to implement its obligations but had done so inadequately or erroneously. The issue was addressed by the European Court in the joined cases of *Brasserie du Pêcheur SA v Germany* and *R v Secretary of State for Transport, ex p Factortame Ltd (No 4)*.[1] In *Brasserie du Pêcheur* a French brewery, which had been forced to discontinue exports to Germany because its beer did not comply with a German purity law which was contrary to art 30 of the EC Treaty (a provision not directly effective), claimed damages against Germany. In *Factortame Ltd (No 4)* Spanish fishermen, who had suffered loss as a result of British legislation which had imposed strict conditions on eligibility to fish under the British flag in breach of non-directly effective articles in the Treaty, claimed damages against the United Kingdom. The cases were referred to the European Court under art 177 of the EEC Treaty for preliminary rulings.

The Court held that the principle of state liability established in *Francovich* applied to all acts or omissions in a state, whether legislative, executive or judicial, in breach of Community law, whether or not directly effective. This does not mean that a member state will always be liable if, for example, it fails to implement by legislation its obligations under Community law, or does so inadequately or erroneously. This is because the conditions for liability laid down in *Brasserie du Pêcheur* and *Factortame Ltd (No 4)* introduce an important restriction. The European Court held that, where a member state is faced with a situation involving legislative choices comparable to those made by Community institutions when they adopt Community measures (legislation), as it is in respect of legislating to implement Community law, the state will only be liable to individuals who have suffered loss for breach of the Community law if three conditions are met:

- the rule of law infringed must be intended to confer rights on the individuals;

- the breach must be sufficiently serious, in that the state or institution concerned has manifestly and gravely disregarded the limits on its discretion; and
- there must be a direct causal link between the breach of the state's obligation and the loss sustained by the injured individuals.

To some extent these conditions say no more than expressly said in *Francovich*, but the second condition (breach must be sufficiently serious) is an addition to what was said in *Francovich*.

Further consideration to the 'sufficiently serious' condition was given by the European Court in *R v HM Treasury, ex p British Telecommunications plc*,[2] which concerned a claim for damages by BT for loss suffered as a result of the alleged improper implementation by the United Kingdom of a Council directive. The Court found that the United Kingdom's implementing legislation had incorrectly transposed the directive, but it held that the breach of Community law was not sufficiently serious to confer a right to damages. Its reason was that one of the factors to be taken into consideration in determining whether there was a manifest and grave disregard by a state or institution of the limits of its legislative discretion, and therefore whether there was a sufficiently serious breach, was the clarity and precision of the Community law breached. Here the article of the Treaty in question was imprecisely worded and the United Kingdom's interpretation made in good faith was one which the provision was reasonably capable of bearing, although it was not the interpretation given by the Court.

The three conditions laid down in *Brasserie du Pêcheur* and *Factortame Ltd (No 4)* were applied by the Court of Appeal in *R v Secretary for Transport, ex p Factortame Ltd (No 5)*.[3] The Court held that the conditions were satisfied and that the United Kingdom was therefore liable in damages for any loss which had been caused to these fishermen by the British legislation in breach of Community law. It reached this decision despite a finding that the United Kingdom government had acted in good faith and did not intend to break Community law. It held that a breach of Community law could be manifest and grave, so as to make it sufficiently serious, without being intentional or negligent. Seriousness had to be judged objectively, taking into account all the relevant circumstances. The lack of intention to commit the breach or negligence or fault were relevant circumstances but their presence was not a condition precedent to a breach being sufficiently grave or manifest.

1 [1996] All ER (EC) 301, ECJ.
2 [1996] All ER (EC) 411, ECJ.
3 (1998) Times, 28 April, CA.

3.42 The conditions laid down in *Brasserie du Pêcheur* and *Factortame Ltd (No 4)* were laid down in the context of the situation where the member state has legislative choices comparable to those made by Community institutions when they adopt measures. It has now been established that they also apply where the state has no legislative choices (as where it is obliged to legislate along certain lines by a set date) and has considerably reduced discretion, or even no discretion. In this type of case, the condition of a sufficiently serious breach is much more easily established. The mere infringement may in itself be enough to establish it.[1]

1 *R v Ministry of Agriculture, Fisheries and Food, ex p Hedley Lomas (Ireland) Ltd* [1996] All ER (EC) 493, ECJ; *Dillenkofer v Germany* [1996] All ER (EC) 917, ECJ.

Supremacy of European Community law
3.43 In Community law, where there is a conflict between binding Community law and a national law of a member state, Community law takes precedence over that

national law, whether the latter was enacted before or after the Community law in question.[1]

The position in English law, which is the law that an English court must apply, is more complicated.

Where a provision in an Act of Parliament is *followed* by an inconsistent directly applicable or directly effective provision[2] of Community law, the latter has precedence.[3]

The same is true if the inconsistent directly applicable or directly effective Community law provision *preceded* the provision in the Act if both were made before the European Communities Act 1972.[2] However, if the subsequent Act was made after the 1972 Act the position is as follows. If the Act of Parliament is unclear, an English court will seek to interpret it so as to be consistent with the directly applicable or directly effective Community law provision.[3] The reason is that, as already stated, a statute is presumed to be consistent with Community law. On the other hand, if the Act clearly conflicts with the prior Community law, then, unless the wording of the Act unambiguously compels the court to do otherwise, an Act of Parliament must be construed so as to be consistent with directly applicable or directly effective Community law, and if the Act is unintentionally inconsistent, precedence must be given to Community law.[4]

1   *Costa v ENEL* [1964] ECR 585, ECJ.
2   As to these terms, see paras 3.36 and 3.37 above.
3   European Communities Act 1972, s 2.
4   *Macarthys Ltd v Smith* [1979] 3 All ER 325, CA.

Validity of legislation of European Community

3.44   Regulations, directives and decisions are subject to review by the European Court. They can be held invalid by it (but not by a court of a member state[1]) on the grounds of lack of competence, or infringement of any essential procedural requirement, or infringement of the treaties or of any rule of law concerning their application, or misuse of power.[2] Where the validity of a piece of Community legislation is referred to the European Court under art 177 of the European Economic Community Treaty, the referring court may adopt interim measures suspending the application of that law.[3]

Directives and decisions are implemented in the United Kingdom by delegated legislation made under powers given by the European Communities Act 1972, s 2(2), which also governs the implementation in further detail of regulations made by the Council or Commission. Orders in Council and departmental regulations made under these powers can include any provision which might be made in an Act of Parliament.[4] This power to make delegated legislation is the widest given to the executive in modern times apart from times of war. The power must be exercised by way of statutory instrument and presumably such an instrument will be ultra vires if it is not related to the affairs of the Communities. There are a number of limits on this power of delegated legislation; for instance, it cannot be used to impose taxation.

1   *Foto-Frost v Hauptzollamt Lûbeck-Ost* [1987] ECR 4199, [1987] 3 CMLR 57, ECJ.
2   EEC Treaty, art 173; Euratom Treaty, art 146. Also see ECSC Treaty, art 33.
3   *Atlanta Fruchthandelsgesellschaft mbH v Bundesant fûr Ernâhrung and Forswirtschaft* [1995] ECR I-3761, ECJ.
4   European Communities Act 1972, s 2(4). Also see Sch 2.

Interpretation of the legislation of the European Community

3.45   The drafting of the legislation of the Community is quite unlike that of English legislation but, like the legislation of other European countries, is drafted in terms of broad principle, leaving the courts to supply the detail by giving effect to the general intention of the legislature. As an essential aid to this process, the regulations, directives and decisions mentioned above are required to state the reasons on which they are based and to refer to any proposals or opinions which were required to be obtained pursuant to the Treaties. These are usually incorporated in a preamble.

The result of this difference in drafting is that the interpretation of the legislation of the Community, whether by the European Court or by an English court,[1] is not based on a slavish interpretation of the words or the grammatical structure of the sentences but on the purpose or intent of the legislation;[2] in other words, a purposive approach is taken to the interpretation of such legislation.

1   *HP Bulmer Ltd v J Bollinger SA* [1974] 2 All ER 1226 at 1237–1238.
2   *HP Bulmer Ltd v J Bollinger SA; Van Duyn v Home Office* [1975] 3 All ER 190, ECJ; *Litster v Forth Dry Dock and Engineering Co Ltd* [1989] 1 All ER 1134, HL.

Judicial precedent

3.46   This is the other important legal source and consists of the 'decisions' of courts made in the course of litigation. As will be seen, the 'decisions' of certain courts are more than just authoritative statements of the law since they can be binding (ie must be applied) in subsequent cases where the legally material facts are the same, whether or not the later court considers them to be correct or appropriate. Whether a particular statement of law made by a judge in one case is binding in a subsequent case depends partly on whether the statement formed the *ratio decidendi* (the reason of the decision) of the case or was merely an *obiter dictum* (something said by the way), and partly on the relative position of the two courts. Even if it is not binding, a judicial statement of the law has a persuasive effect in subsequent cases, the strength of its persuasiveness being a matter of degree, as we explain in para 3.58 below.

Ratio decidendi and obiter dictum
3.47   Only the ratio decidendi of a case can have binding effect. A judgment usually contains the following elements:

a.   A statement of the facts found with an indication, express or implied, of which of them are material facts. In reading the report of a judgment, great care must be taken to ascertain what facts were found to be material.
b.   Statements by the judge of the legal principles which apply to the legal issues raised by the material facts and are the reason for his decision. Normally these statements are only made after a review of existing precedents and general legal principles.
c.   The actual judgment, decree or order delivered by the judge after application of b. to a., eg that the defendant is liable coupled with an award of damages.

Part c. is binding only on the parties to the case and is not a precedent for the future, nor is part a. in itself. It is part b. of this process which constitutes the ratio decidendi.

3.48   Sometimes the statements of the applicable principles made by the judge may be wider than the material facts necessitate. In such a case the ratio of the decision will be limited to that part of it which applies to the material facts and, to the extent that the statement is wider, it will be obiter dictum.[1] Apart from that just mentioned, there are two other types of obiter dictum.

First, a statement of legal principle is obiter if it relates to facts which were not found to exist in the case or, if found, were not material. Two famous cases provide good examples. In *Central London Property Trust Ltd v High Trees House Ltd*, which we discuss later in this book,[2] Denning J's principal statement about promissory estoppel was obiter since it applied to a set of facts which were not found to exist in the case. Similarly, in *Rondel v Worsley*,[3] the House of Lords expressed opinions that a barrister who was negligent when acting other than in connection with litigation might be held liable in tort and that a solicitor, when acting as an advocate, might be immune from liability. Both statements were obiter since the case concerned the tortious liability of a barrister when acting as an advocate, so that these statements were not necessary to the court's decision.

Second, a statement of legal principle which relates to some or all of the material facts but is not the basis of the court's decision, eg because it is given in a dissenting judgment or because another material fact prevents the principle applying, is also obiter. A leading example is *Hedley Byrne & Co Ltd v Heller & Partners Ltd*.[4] The House of Lords expressed the opinion that the maker of a statement owes a duty of care, in certain circumstances, to persons who suffer loss in reliance on it. This opinion was obiter because, although it was based on material facts found to exist in the case, the actual decision – that there was no breach of such a duty – was based on another material fact, that the maker of the statement had made it subject to an effective disclaimer of responsibility.

1   *Cassidy v Ministry of Health* [1951] 2 KB 343, CA.
2   Para 6.17 below.
3   [1967] 3 All ER 993, HL; para 18.36 below.
4   [1963] 2 All ER 575, HL; para 18.28 below.

The hierarchy of the courts and judicial precedent

3.49   We saw in the previous chapter that the system of courts is a hierarchy. Essentially, one court is bound by the ratio decidendi of a case decided by another court if it is lower in the hierarchy than the latter and will not be bound by it if it is higher. Magistrates' courts and county courts are bound by the rationes decidendi in cases decided by a High Court judge or the courts above such judges. A High Court judge is bound by the rationes decidendi of cases decided by the Court of Appeal and the House of Lords, and the Court of Appeal is bound by those of the House of Lords. This basic statement will be expanded by taking courts in turn, starting from the top of the hierarchy. For convenience, the word 'decision' will be used to indicate 'ratio decidendi'.

The Court of Justice of the European Communities

3.50   As we said in para 2.32 above, the European Court is now the ultimate court in the following matters:

- the interpretation of the treaties establishing the EEC and Euratom;
- the validity and interpretation of the acts of the institutions of the Community and of the European Central Bank; and
- the interpretation of the statutes of bodies established by an act of the Council of the European Union.

Consequently, in these limited areas of jurisdiction the decisions of the European Court bind all English courts. Indeed, the European Communities Act 1972, s 3(1) provides that any question as to the meaning or effect of any of the Treaties, or as to the validity, meaning or effect of any Community instrument, shall be treated as a question of law (and, if not referred to the European Court, be for determination in accordance with the principles laid down by, and any relevant decision of, the European Court or any court attached thereto).

The European Court does not observe a doctrine of binding precedent and does not regard itself as bound by its previous decisions,[1] although it leans in favour of consistency with its previous decisions.

1   *Da Costa en Schaake NV v Nederlandse Belastingadministratie:* [1963] ECR 31, [1963] CMLR 224, ECJ.

The House of Lords

3.51   A decision of the House of Lords binds all courts inferior to it. Until 1966, a decision of the House of Lords also bound that House, a principle which was finally established at the end of the 19th century in *London Tramways Co Ltd v LCC*.[1] This meant that a legal principle might become unalterable by the House of Lords, in which case legislation was the only remedy if a change in the law was desired. In 1966, the House of Lords reversed this principle in an extra-judicial statement made by the Lord Chancellor (which has been regarded as having the force of law) declaring that it would not be bound by its own decisions where it appeared right to depart from them.[2] The declaration added that in this connection the House would bear in mind the danger of disturbing retrospectively the basis on which contracts, settlements of property and fiscal arrangements have been entered into and also the special need for certainty as to the criminal law. The declaration emphasised that it was not intended to apply elsewhere than in the House of Lords.

So far their Lordships have not made much use of their rediscovered freedom and have held that it is not enough that they should consider their previous decision was wrong; there must be an additional factor, such as a change of circumstances on which the decision was based or that it is productive of manifest injustice.[3] In addition, they have held that they should not embark upon a review of a previous decision of theirs unless they felt free, if necessary, to depart both from the reasoning and the decision in the previous case and, in addition, were satisfied that the review would be of relevance to the resolution of the dispute in the case before them.[4] One of the few cases in which the House of Lords has overruled one of its previous decisions is *Murphy v Brentwood District Council*[5] where it overruled its decision in *Anns v London Borough Council of Merton*[6] that a local authority, exercising its statutory function of controlling building works, was under a common law duty to take reasonable care to ensure that the building complied with building regulations.[7]

1   [1898] AC 375, HL.
2   [1966] 3 All ER 77.
3   *Fitzleet Estates Ltd v Cherry* [1977] 3 All ER 996, HL.
4   *Food Corpn of India v Antclizo Shipping Corpn, The Antclizo* [1988] 2 All ER 513, HL.
5   [1990] 2 All ER 908, HL.
6   [1977] 2 All ER 492, HL.
7   See paras 22.26–22.27 below.

The Court of Appeal

3.52   The Civil Division of the Court of Appeal is bound by the previous decisions of the House of Lords. It is also bound by the previous decisions of either division of the Court of Appeal.[1] This was settled by the Court of Appeal in *Young v Bristol Aeroplane Co Ltd*.[2] The Court, however, recognised three exceptional situations where an earlier Court of Appeal decision is not binding on the Civil Division:

•   where two of its previous decisions conflict. The decision not followed will be deemed to be overruled;[3]

- the Court must refuse to follow a previous decision of its own which, though not expressly overruled, is inconsistent with a later House of Lords decision;
- the Court is not bound to follow its previous decision if that decision was given per incuriam (ie through lack of care). A decision is regarded as having been given per incuriam where some relevant statute or binding precedent, which would have affected the decision, was overlooked by the court making it.[4] Only in very rare instances can a case not strictly within this formulation be held to have been decided per incuriam, since such a case must involve a manifest slip or error and it must be likely to cause serious inconvenience in the administration of justice or serious injustice or some equally serious consequence.[5] The Court is not bound to follow another of its decisions (decision B) if, although not itself per incuriam, decision B was based solely on another Court of Appeal decision (decision A) which, unknown to the Court of Appeal when it made decision B, was per incuriam.[6]

While the per incuriam doctrine is also open to the House of Lords as a basis for rejecting one of its own previous decisions, the refusal of the Court of Appeal to follow the House of Lords decision in *Rookes v Barnard*,[7] on the basis that it had been reached per incuriam because of two previous House of Lords decisions, was rejected in strong terms by the House of Lords on appeal in *Cassell & Co Ltd v Broome*.[8]

In addition to the exceptions mentioned in *Young v Bristol Aeroplane*, three other exceptions have been indicated by subsequent cases: a decision by a two-judge Court of Appeal hearing an interlocutory appeal does not bind a court of three;[9] a Court of Appeal decision subsequently disapproved by the Privy Council need not be followed by the Court of Appeal,[10] and, if a Court of Appeal decision goes to the House of Lords and the House decides the appeal on a different ground from that argued in the Court of Appeal, being of the opinion that the issue decided in the Court of Appeal did not arise, the Court of Appeal's decision is not binding on a subsequent Court of Appeal.[11]

1 And those of its predecessors: the Court of Exchequer Chamber and the Court of Appeal in Chancery, but not by the decisions of the now defunct Court of Criminal Appeal.
2 [1944] 2 All ER 293, CA. The rule in *Young v Bristol Aeroplane* was reaffirmed by the House of Lords in *Davis v Johnson* [1978] 1 All ER 1132.
3 As happened in *Fisher v Ruislip-Northwood UDC and Middlesex County Council* [1945] 2 All ER 458, CA.
4 See, for example, *Miliangos v George Frank (Textiles) Ltd* [1976] AC 443 at 477; *Duke v Reliance Systems Ltd* [1987] 2 All ER 858, CA (affirmed without adverting to this point: [1988] 1 All ER 626, HL).
5 *Williams v Fawcett* [1985] 1 All ER 787, CA; *Rickards v Rickards* [1989] 3 All ER 193, CA; *Re Probe Data Systems (No 3)* [1992] BCC 110, CA.
6 *Rakhit v Carty* [1990] 2 All ER 202, HL.
7 [1964] 1 All ER 367, HL.
8 [1972] 1 All ER 801, HL.
9 *Boys v Chaplin* [1968] 1 All ER 283, CA. A *final* decision of a two-judge Court of Appeal has the same binding effect as that of a court of three: *Langley v N W Water Authority* [1991] 3 All ER 610, CA.
10 *Doughty v Turner Manufacturing Co Ltd* [1964] 1 All ER 98, CA; *Worcester Works Finance Ltd v Cooden Engineering Co Ltd* [1971] 3 All ER 708, CA.
11 *R v Secretary of State for the Home Department, ex p Al-Mehdawi* [1989] 1 All ER 777, CA; reversed on appeal on another point [1989] 3 All ER 843, HL.

3.53 The Criminal Division of the Court of Appeal is bound not only by the decisions of the House of Lords and Court of Appeal but also by those of its predecessor, the Court of Criminal Appeal.[1] However, in the case of decisions of the last two named courts there are exceptions:

- the three exceptions mentioned in *Young v Bristol Aeroplane*[2] and the other exceptions mentioned in the previous paragraph;
- the Criminal Division has power to overrule a previous decision of itself or the Court of Criminal Appeal, on the grounds that the law has been 'misapplied or misunderstood'[3] but only if this is necessary in the interests of the appellant.[4]

1 *Hoskyn v Metropolitan Police Comr* [1978] 2 All ER 136, HL.
2 *R v Taylor* [1950] 2 All ER 170 at 172; *R v Ewing* [1983] QB 1039 at 1047.
3 *R v Taylor* [1950] 2 All ER 170; *R v Newsome; R v Browne* [1970] 3 All ER 455, CA.
4 *R v Spencer; R v Smails* [1985] 1 All ER 673, CA.

Divisional courts
3.54 Divisional courts are bound by decisions of the House of Lords and of the Court of Appeal, except, apparently, a Court of Appeal decision which is per incuriam, in that a relevant decision of the House of Lords was not cited.[1] A divisional court is bound by one of its own previous decisions unless the *Young v Bristol Aeroplane* principles apply[2] or, in criminal cases and cases where it is exercising the supervisory jurisdiction of the High Court,[3] unless that previous decision was clearly wrong.[4]

1 *R v Northumberland Compensation Appeal Tribunal, ex p Shaw* [1952] 1 All ER 122, CA.
2 *Huddersfield Police Authority v Watson* [1947] 2 All ER 193, DC.
3 Para 2.19 above.
4 *R v Greater Manchester Coroner, ex p Tal* [1984] 3 All ER 240, DC: *Hornigold v Chief Constable of Lancashire* [1985] Crim LR 792, DC; *Wakeley v Hyams* [1987] RTR 49, DC.

High Court judges
3.55 A High Court judge is bound by the decisions of the courts mentioned above (other than a divisional court exercising the supervisory jurisdiction of the High Court), but he is not bound by decisions of another High Court judge although he will treat such a decision as strong persuasive authority and will only refuse to follow it if he is convinced that it is wrong, and with a clear statement of the reason for doing so.[1] Where a High Court judge is faced with two conflicting decisions of other High Court judges, he should normally treat the legal point at issue as settled by the second decision, provided the judge in that case has reached his decision after full consideration of the first decision. The only, rare, exception is where the third judge is convinced that the second judge was wrong in not following the first, as, for example, where a binding or persuasive precedent had not been cited in either of the first two cases.[2]

Although, strictly, a High Court judge is not bound by a decision of a divisional court exercising the supervisory jurisdiction of the High Court, he will follow that decision unless convinced that it is wrong.[3]

1 *Re Hillas-Drake, National Provincial Bank v Liddell* [1944] 1 All ER 375.
2 *Colchester Estates (Cardiff) v Carlton Industries plc* [1984] 2 All ER 601.
3 *R v Greater Manchester Coroner, ex p Tal* [1984] 3 All ER 240 at 248.

Other courts
3.56 County courts, magistrates' courts and other inferior tribunals are bound by the decisions of all the courts mentioned in the previous paragraphs, and by those of High Court judges sitting alone. The decisions of one of these courts are not binding on another mainly because they are not reported.

Although it is part of the Supreme Court a judge in the Crown Court is similarly bound, even – it seems – by a decision of a High Court judge sitting alone. A legal ruling by a judge in the Crown Court is never a binding precedent but is merely a persuasive authority.

Application of judicial precedents

3.57 The fact that a judicial precedent may be binding or merely persuasive in a subsequent case has already been touched on. It may also be noticed that a judicial precedent will become devoid of effect if it is overruled by a court competent to do so (normally, one higher in the hierarchy). As opposed to overruling by statute,[1] judicial overruling operates retrospectively, which may have the effect of disturbing financial interests or vested rights generally. For this reason the courts are reluctant to overrule a previous decision unless they consider it is clearly wrong.

Where a precedent is binding on a court, that court must follow it unless that court can distinguish it on the facts. Suppose that the House of Lords has held that if facts A and B exist, principle X applies, and that a case is heard by a High Court judge at first instance where facts A and B exist as well as fact E, which did not exist in the House of Lords' case. The judge may distinguish the House of Lords' case on its material facts and consequently, since that decision will not be binding in relation to the case before him, decide to apply some other principle or to apply principle X by analogy. Since the facts are never identical in any two cases there is wide scope for 'distinguishing'. However, a court inferior to that which gave the previous decision will not normally distinguish it on strained grounds.

1   Para 3.10 above.

3.58 There are various types of persuasive precedents:

- those decisions of courts inferior in the hierarchy to a court which subsequently hears a similar case. Into this category one can also put decisions of the Judicial Committee of the Privy Council on appeals from Commonwealth states, which do not bind English courts or the Privy Council itself. However, the decisions of the Privy Council are particularly persuasive (since the Judicial Committee normally consists of Lords of Appeal in Ordinary), and the Court of Appeal has held that if one of its previous decisions in respect of a matter of civil law has been disapproved by the Privy Council it is at liberty to depart from it and apply the Privy Council decision;[1]
- where an otherwise binding precedent is distinguishable; it will nevertheless have persuasive authority;[2]
- obiter dicta, the persuasiveness of which depends on the seniority of the court or prestige of the judge by whom the words were uttered and the relative position of that court and a subsequent court. One of the most significant examples is the 'neighbour principle' expounded by Lord Atkin in 1932 in *Donoghue v Stevenson*,[3] which was much wider than the actual case required but has become the basis of the modern tort of negligence and has been applied in numerous cases since;
- decisions of Irish, Scottish, Commonwealth and US courts, which are being referred to increasingly by our courts.

1   *Doughty v Turner Manufacturing Co Ltd* [1964] 1 All ER 98, CA; para 20.19 below; *Worcester Works Finance Ltd v Cooden Engineering Co Ltd* [1971] 3 All ER 708, CA; para 3.52 above. For no apparent reason, the Court of Appeal regards itself as bound by its previous decisions in respect of a matter of criminal law, despite their disapproval by the Privy Council: *Campbell (No 2)* [1997] 1 Cr App Rep 199, CA.
2   Especially if it is a House of Lords decision: *Re House Property and Investment Co* [1953] 2 All ER 1525.
3   [1932] AC 562, HL.

General comments

3.59 Essentially, judicial decisions are declarative of the common law, merely applying existing law to new fact situations. However, where there is no relevant statute or judicial precedent on a particular point, as still happens occasionally, a judge has to decide the case in accordance with general principles and his decision becomes the original source of a new rule since he is making law rather than applying it.

3.60 The advantages of the system of judicial precedent are its precision and detail, and consequent certainty of application, and in these respects it is far superior to a code or statute which cannot hope to anticipate the innumerable factual situations which can arise in a given area of law. It is sometimes said that the system also has the advantage of flexibility in that outmoded or unsound decisions can be overruled or distinguished. Too much should not be made of this since overruling may be difficult, if not impossible, given the relationship of the courts in question. There is also the danger of illogical or over-subtle distinctions being drawn to avoid hardship in a particular case, but increasing the complexity of the law. Moreover, the vast mass of reported cases can make discovering the law an arduous task and cause a precedent to be overlooked.

Literary sources of judicial precedent

3.61 The most important of these are, of course, the law reports. A law report must be differentiated from a court record which simply contains the name of the parties, the pleadings, the main facts and the decision, decree or order of the court. Apart from containing most of these things, a law report also contains the judgment of the court, which includes the reasoning on which the result was based.

It may appear surprising that there is no official series of law reports. By no means all cases in the superior courts are reported in the law reports: only those of legal interest. Law reports may be divided roughly into those published from the time of Henry VIII to 1865, and those published subsequently. Before Henry VIII's time there were the year books dating from the time of Edward I, which contained notes on the argument, exchanges between bench and bar and rulings on points of law in cases. The publication of law reports began in about 1535. They were usually published under the names of the reporter and initially were very little more detailed than the year books. Gradually, they developed until they came to resemble the modern law report. Altogether there were some hundreds of different series. Most of them have been reprinted in a series known as the English Reports. These 'nominate reports', as they are sometimes called, vary a good deal in quality. However, the reports of Coke, often simply referred to as 'The Reports', Dyer, Plowden, Burroughs and certain others are regarded as particularly outstanding and authoritative. The name of the reporters or reports is traditionally cited in abbreviated form in footnote references, eg Co Rep (Coke), Burr (Burroughs), B & Ald (Barnewell and Alderson) and Term Rep (Term Reports).

In 1865, the semi-official 'Law Reports' commenced. One or more volumes is published annually under each of the following titles 'Queen's Bench' ('QB') (covering cases decided in the Queen's Bench Division or by the Court of Appeal on appeal therefrom or from a county court), 'Chancery' ('Ch') (covering cases decided in the Chancery Division or by the Court of Appeal on appeal therefrom), 'Family' ('Fam')[1] (covering cases decided in the Family Division or by the Court of Appeal on appeal therefrom or from a county court in family matters) and 'Appeals Cases' ('AC') (covering decisions of the House of Lords and Privy Council). Since 1952, many cases appearing in the Law Reports have appeared previously, soon after judgment has been given, in the Weekly Law Reports (WLR) published by the same organisation, the Incorporated Council of Law Reporting, as do some cases not subsequently published in the Law Reports. The difference between the two series is that the Law Reports contain a summary of the arguments of counsel.

Although the Law Reports superseded most of the series of private reports, there are still a number of commercially owned reports. The All England Reports (All ER), a weekly publication, are a general series of reports, while others, such as Lloyd's Law Reports (Lloyd's Rep), which deal with commercial cases, are more specialised. The All England Reports commenced publication in 1936 and subsequently superseded two other series, the Law Times Reports and the Law Journal Reports. Mention may also be made of the Estates Gazette, in which cases of special interest to the landed professions are reported.

Cases decided by the European Court of Justice and the European Court of First Instance may be found in the Official Reports of the Court and in the Common Market Law Reports (CMLR). Since 1996, they have also been reported in a separate volume of the All England Law Reports (All ER (EC)). They are occasionally reported in the series of reports referred to in the previous two paragraphs.

Cases before the European Court are referenced both by name and number; for example, Case C-213/89: *R v Secretary of State for Transport, ex p Factortame*. 'C-' indicates that the case was before the European Court, 'T-' being used for cases before the Court of First Instance. The first figure is a serial number; the second is the year in which the action was brought.

A judgment can be cited to a court even though it has not been published in any series of law reports but is merely contained in a transcript. The transcripts of many recent judgments are now available on LEXIS, a computerised legal database. In addition, transcripts of appeals to the Court of Appeal for the period 1951–1980 have been published by Her Majesty's Stationery Office. For reasons which are unconvincing, the House of Lords has held that transcripts of unreported judgments of the Court of Appeal (Civil Division) should not be cited on appeals to the House, except with its leave (which will only be given if counsel gives an assurance that the transcript contains a statement of a relevant principle of law whose substance is not to be found in any reported judgment of the Court of Appeal).[2] Likewise, the Court of Appeal has directed that it will only give leave for transcripts of unreported cases to be cited if the transcript in question contains a relevant statement of legal principle not found in a reported case.[3]

Since November 1996, all decisions of the House of Lords have been available on the Internet on the UK Parliament home page on http://www.parliament.uk.

1   Until 1972 the citation was 'P' since what is now the Family Division was known as the Probate, Divorce and Admiralty Division until its name, and jurisdiction, were changed.
2   *Roberts Petroleum Ltd v Bernard Kenny Ltd* [1983] 1 All ER 564, HL.
3   *Practice Note* [1996] 3 All ER 382, CA.

3.62   Mention can be conveniently made at this stage of a secondary literary source, certain 'books of authority'. On the Continent the writings of legal authors form an important source of law. In England, in accordance with the traditional approach that the common law is to be found in judicial decisions, the works of writers are of no official effect, except for books of authority. These are books of some antiquity by authors of great eminence which are regarded as being persuasive authority on the common law as it was when they were written and on the present law if it is not shown to have changed. Generally, these do not contain reports of cases but state principles instead. Perhaps the best known books of authority are Coke's *Institutes*, written in the 17th century, and Blackstone's *Commentaries* of the 18th century. While the works of modern authors are not in the above sense authoritative, the courts are increasingly being referred to them for guidance on the correct interpretation of the law.

Custom

3.63 In Anglo-Saxon times, custom, in the sense of patterns of behaviour recognised and enforced by the courts, was the principal source of law. However, general customs, ie customs universally observed throughout the land, have either fallen into desuetude or become absorbed into judicial precedent or statute.

A process of absorption has also occurred in relation to the general customs of merchants, which were assimilated by our courts in the 17th and 18th centuries and developed into commercial law as we now know it.

On the other hand, local customs, ie customs operative in a particular locality or among a particular group of people in a particular locality, are even now occasionally recognised by the courts as establishing a local 'law' for the locality in question at variance with the general law of the land, although they must not be contrary to statute or to a fundamental principle of the common law.

Local customs are largely to be found in rights of way and common. Recognition of a local custom depends on a number of conditions being satisfied, the most important of which are that the alleged custom must:

- have existed since 'time immemorial', which, theoretically, it will only do if it goes back to 1189 (for reasons of historical accident);
- have been continuous. The custom must have been in existence continuously. This means that the right to exercise it must not have been interrupted; but the fact that the right has not actually been exercised for a period of time, even 100 years in one case,[1] does not negative the existence of a local custom (although if the evidence of custom is dubious it will go far to negative any customary right);
- not be unreasonable;[2]
- be certain; in other words the right claimed must be certain in nature and scope and prove to adhere to a defined locality or group of people;
- be recognised as compulsory.[3]

The first condition is not as strict as may appear since the plaintiff can succeed in proving it if he can prove that the practice in question has existed in the locality for a substantial time: the oldest local inhabitant is often called as a witness in this context. If the plaintiff proves this, existence since 1189 will be presumed,[4] provided, of course, that such a practice was possible in 1189. In *Simpson v Wells*,[5] a person who was charged with obstructing a public footway with his refreshment stall pleaded that he did so by virtue of a custom existing at a 'statute session', a fair held for hiring servants. His defence failed because statute sessions were first introduced by a 14th-century statute, so that the custom could not have existed before then.

1 *New Windsor Corpn v Mellor* [1975] 3 All ER 44, CA.
2 *Wolstanton Ltd v Newcastle-under-Lyme Borough Council* [1940] 3 All ER 101, HL.
3 Blackstone's *Commentaries*: 'a custom that all the inhabitants shall be rated towards the maintenance of a bridge will be good, but a custom that every man is to contribute thereto at his own pleasure is idle and absurd, and indeed not custom at all'.
4 *Mercer v Denne* [1905] 2 Ch 538 at 577.
5 (1872) LR 7 QB 214.

Part II

The law of contract

Chapter 4

Introduction

4.1 In this part of the book we adopt the following order:

- in this chapter and the next three we outline those basic elements of the law of contract which relate to the existence and enforcement of a valid contract;
- in the following five chapters (8–12) we deal with contractual obligations, with how they are discharged, and with the remedies available if they are broken;
- in chapters 13–15 we deal with factors such as mistake and misrepresentation which may affect the validity of what would otherwise be a valid contract;
- the last chapter in this part is concerned with the law relating to agency.

Sometimes a contract may be tainted with illegality, either because it is prohibited by statute, or because it is performed in a way prohibited by statute, or because it involves an unlawful or immoral element. In such cases, one or both parties may be unable to enforce it. The relevant rules are outside the scope of this book, as are the rules whereby a wagering or gaming contract is void and unenforceable.

The essential elements of a contract

4.2 For there to be a contract (ie a binding agreement):

- there must be an agreement;
- the parties must have intended their agreement to be legally binding; and
- the contract must be supported by consideration or be made by deed.

Although it is usual to talk about enforcing a contract, it must not be forgotten that what is being enforced is a promise by one party to an agreement by the other party to it. A mere statement of present fact to which another person agrees cannot be enforced, even if it relates to the fact of the present intentions of the party making the statement. Thus, if a company says 'it is our policy to ensure that any of our subsidiaries is always in a position to meet its liabilities in respect of a loan made to it', there is not a breach of contract if one of the subsidiaries becomes unable to meet its liabilities in respect of a loan.[1]

Another point which must be made at the outset is that contracts may be either bilateral or unilateral. A bilateral contract is one in which a party (A) promises to do something if the other party (B) promises to do something in return and B makes that counter-promise. In such a case, the mere exchange of promises normally renders them both enforceable. A unilateral contract, on the other hand, arises where A promises to do something in return for an act by B, rather than a counter-promise, as where A promises to pay B a reward if he finds some lost property or where A promises to pay B £10 if he completes a 'sponsored walk', and B responds by doing the requested act. In such a case B is not bound to do anything at all; only if he does the act will A's promise become enforceable. A less obvious example of a unilateral contract, though one which is of great commercial importance, is the normal type of commission agreement entered into by estate agents, mortgage brokers and the like. According to the decision of the House of Lords in *Luxor (Eastbourne) Ltd v Cooper*,[2] an estate agent instructed to find a purchaser is under no obligation to take any action at all; only when he complies with the client's instructions does the client's promise of commission become enforceable.

Before discussing the basic requirement of any contract, agreement between the parties, something must be said about contractual capacity and about whether or not an agreement must be in writing in order to be a valid and enforceable contract.

1   *Kleinwort Benson Ltd v Malaysia Mining Corpn Bhd* [1989] 1 All ER 785, [1989] 1 WLR 379, CA.
2   [1941] 1 All ER 33, HL.

Form

4.3   With the exceptions mentioned hereafter, English law does not require an agreement to be in writing in order to be a valid and enforceable contract, but there are obvious advantages in reducing it into writing.

Contracts which must be made by deed
Leases for three years or more
4.4   These are void at law and pass no legal estate unless made by deed. However, such a lease not made by deed can take effect as a contract to grant a lease, which can be specifically enforced provided it complies with the provisions of the Law of Property (Miscellaneous Provisions) Act 1989, s 2, and will create the same rights between the parties for many purposes.[1]

1   See further, paras 32.3–32.5 below.

Contracts in which there is no consideration
4.5   If there is no consideration for the promise made by one party to the other the contract is invalid unless made by deed.[1] A common example of such a contract made by deed is a covenant for the gratuitous payment of a sum to a charity over a period of more than three years, whereby the charity is enabled to claim the income tax paid by the donor in addition to the covenanted sum.

1   *Rann v Hughes* (1778) 7 Term Rep 350n, HL.

4.6   A contract is not made by deed unless the instrument in which it is written:

• makes it clear on its face that it is intended to be a deed by the person making it or, as the case may be, by the parties to it either because it describes itself as such or because it expresses itself to be executed or signed as such; and

- it is validly executed as a deed by that person or, as the case may be, by one or more of those parties.[1]

An instrument is validly executed as a deed by an individual only if:

- it is signed–
  - by him in the presence of a witness who attests the signature, or
  - at his direction and in his presence and the presence of two witnesses who attest the signature; and
- it is delivered as a deed by him or a person authorised to do so on his behalf.[2]

A deed is no longer required to be sealed.

A deed is regarded as delivered as soon as there are acts which show that the person making it intends unconditionally to be bound by it: physical delivery of it to the other party is no longer required and a deed may be delivered even though it remains in the custody of its maker.[3]

There are special statutory provisions governing the execution of a deed by a company.

A contract made by deed is known as a contract of specialty: all other contracts, whether written or not, are known as simple contracts.

1 Law of Property (Miscellaneous Provisions) Act 1989, s 1(2).
2 Ibid, s 1(3).
3 *Vincent v Premo Enterprises (Voucher Sales) Ltd* [1969] 2 All ER 941, CA.

Contracts which must be in writing

4.7 Some contracts are invalid or unenforceable unless they are in writing. For example, an agreement for the sale or other disposition of land or an interest in land is generally invalid unless it is made in writing, as we explain in para 31.2 below. By way of further example, consumer credit agreements and consumer hire agreements which are not executed in writing in the manner required by the Consumer Credit Act 1974 are enforceable against the debtor or hirer only on an order of the court.[1]

1 Consumer Credit Act 1974, s 65.

Contracts which must be evidenced in writing

4.8 Contracts of guarantee do not have to be written but merely to be evidenced in writing before they can be enforced in legal proceedings.[1]

1 Statute of Frauds 1677, s 4.

Capacity

4.9 There are special rules about the capacity of the following to make contracts:

- minors (ie people under 18);
- mentally disordered and intoxicated persons;
- companies; and
- partnerships.

Those who are engaged in estate management are most unlikely to make contracts with people in the first two categories. Consequently, the contractual capacity of such people is not dealt with in this book. On the other hand, the contractual capacity of companies and partnerships is of importance to estate managers.

Companies

Legal status
4.10   Under British law, a company (which is an artificial legal person) may be formed in any one of three ways:

* by registration under the Companies Act 1985 (registered companies); or
* by Private Act of Parliament (statutory companies); or
* by Royal Charter (chartered companies).

It is extremely rare (as well as difficult and expensive) to form a company other than under the Companies Act 1985. The Companies Act 1985 permits the formation of private companies and public companies. Only public companies can apply for listing on the Stock Exchange or the Alternative Investment Market (AIM). Although company law usually applies equally to both types of registered company, there are important differences. One concerns company formation. A public limited company must reveal its status and its name, by using the words 'public limited company' (plc), or their Welsh equivalent, and must have a specified minimum amount of capital on its formation. A private limited company must use the word 'limited' (ltd) in its name (or the Welsh equivalent) and need not have capital exceeding two pence on its formation. Both types of registered company are easy to form and the costs of formation are modest, although flotation of a public company on the Stock Exchange or AIM is expensive.

Companies may be formed for any purpose which their progenitors or promoters choose but trading bodies will usually be in registered form. Statutory companies are often specialised trading bodies, for example building societies, friendly societies and insurance companies. Chartered companies are typically charitable or quasi-charitable associations or non-trading bodies, such as the Royal Institution of Chartered Surveyors. However, in the past some famous trading companies have been incorporated by Royal Charter, for example the East India Co and the Hudson Bay Co.

4.11   Other associations of people may pursue some common purpose, such as trade unions, clubs and partnerships, but companies can be distinguished from other associations in that a company is itself a legal person totally distinct from its shareholders (who are also called members) and employees. Companies are artificial legal persons and when a statute refers to a person then prima facie it means human beings and companies. Even if a company is totally dominated by one shareholder, the company and that shareholder are distinct legal persons.[1] An example is provided by *Lee v Lee's Air Farming Ltd*,[2] where Lee, who was founder, principal shareholder, managing director, and chief pilot of a company, had been killed while engaged on the business of the company. The Privy Council held that Lee and the company were distinct legal persons. Consequently, Lee could enter into a contract of employment with the company and his widow could therefore claim compensation under a government scheme which was limited to widows of employees.

Two consequences of the separate legal identities of a company and its members are:

* a company can sue and be sued in its own name;

- a company can make contracts on its own behalf (and its members cannot claim the benefit nor be subject to the burden of such contracts[3]).

1   *Salomon v Salomon & Co Ltd* [1897] AC 22, HL.
2   [1960] 3 All ER 420, PC.
3   This is merely the effect of the doctrine of privity, ch 7.

Contractual capacity

4.12   Although a company is a legal person, it does not – except in the case of a chartered company[1] – have the contractual capacity of a natural person. The contractual capacity of registered and statutory companies is limited by the memorandum of association and the creating statute respectively.

1   *Sutton's Hospital Case* (1612) 10 Co Rep 23a; *Pharmaceutical Society of Great Britain v Dickson* [1970] AC 403, [1968] 2 All ER 686, HL.

4.13   When a registered company is created, the people forming the company are required to lodge with the Registrar of Companies at Companies House in Cardiff the memorandum of association of the company. In addition, they may or, in some cases, must lodge articles of association. These documents are available for public inspection.[1] The memorandum of association can be described as the constitution of the company and the articles of association as the rulebook governing the relations of the participants in the company. The memorandum of association must state certain specific things including the objects of the company[2] (ie the purposes for which the company was formed and the aims and business it intends to pursue). The provision setting out the company's objects is known as the objects clause. A company can register its own specially drafted objects clause but the objects clauses of many companies created in the last few years adopt the wording of the Companies Act 1985, s 3A which permits a company 'to carry on business as a general commercial company'.

1   Companies Act 1985, ss 1, 7 and 10.
2   Ibid, s 2.

4.14   The Companies Act 1985, s 35(1), states that the validity of an act done by a company cannot be called into question on the ground of lack of capacity by reason of the fact that it is beyond the objects of the company stated in the memorandum. Consequently if a company enters into a contract with another person (X), which is not authorised by its objects clause, the contract binds the company and X.

By s 35(2), a shareholder (who has a right to have the memorandum enforced) can bring proceedings to restrain the company entering into a contract outside the scope of its objects clause. However, a shareholder cannot stop the carrying out of a contract which has already been made by a company, nor can a shareholder impugn its validity.

4.15   Although it is a person in law, a company obviously cannot negotiate contracts personally; it must act through agents. An agent, such as a director of the company, is subject to the usual rules of agency described in chapter 16. Hence, a contract entered into by an agent of a company is only binding on the company if he had actual, implied or ostensible authority to enter into it.

The authority which an agent of a company appears to possess may be restricted and that restriction may be capable of discovery. For example, the board of directors has actual, implied or ostensible authority to enter into almost any transaction on behalf of the company but the company's memorandum may say, for example, that transactions in excess of £500,000 in value must be approved by the shareholders. Can the board bind the company by a transaction which is in breach of such a restriction?

The Companies Act 1985, s 35A provides that, in favour of a person dealing with the company, the power of the board to bind the company (or to authorise others to do so) is deemed to be free of any limitations contained in the company's memorandum or articles, provided that that person dealt with the company in good faith. Thus, a company cannot enforce a contract which was entered into by an unauthorised agent but the other party may be able to do so. A person does not manifest bad faith simply by knowing that there is a restriction on the powers of the directors or by failing to inquire whether their powers are limited.

Partnerships

4.16   A partnership will usually be governed by the rules laid down in the Partnership Act 1890, but it is possible to create limited partnerships and they are governed by the Limited Partnerships Act 1907. The limited partnership, which is a partnership with some of the characteristics of a limited liability company, is not very popular in the United Kingdom, although much used in continental Europe.

Although a partnership and its partners are not separate legal entities, a partnership can usually sue and be sued in its own name.

The Partnership Act 1890, s 1 defines a partnership as 'the relation existing between two or more persons carrying on a business in common with a view to profit'. Because the partners and the partnership are not separate legal entities, unlike the shareholders and the company in which they hold shares, there are important differences between being a partner and being a shareholder. For example:

- a partner is liable for the debts and liabilities of the partnership: a shareholder is not liable for the debts and liabilities of the company;
- a partner has a legal interest in the assets of the partnership: a shareholder does not have any legally recognised interest in the assets of the company;
- shares in a partnership are not transferable: shares in a company are; and
- the death of a partner technically terminates the partnership, although the remaining partners may agree to carry on the partnership: the death of a shareholder leaves the company unaffected.

The maximum number of partners permissible for a partnership is 20, except that some types of partnership of professional people may exceed this number.[1] For example, a partnership formed to carry on one or more of the following activities, viz surveying, auctioneering, valuing, estate agency, land agency, or estate management, is permitted to have more than 20 partners, provided that not less than three-quarters of them are members of the Royal Institution of Chartered Surveyors or of the Incorporated Society of Valuers and Auctioneers.[2]

A limited partnership is a partnership where one or more partners has only a limited liability for the debts of the partnership. Every limited partnership must have at least one general partner[3] (ie with full liability for debts) and any limited partner who is active in the affairs of the partnership becomes a general partner.[4] The limited partnership is only suitable for those who wish to invest money in a partnership but take no part in its running; their lack of popularity seems hardly surprising .

It is unusual to find large businesses run as partnerships and, while there are advantages over companies in that there is less publicity for the affairs of the partnership, and perhaps less tax to be paid, these benefits will probably be outweighed by the advantages enjoyed by a company of limited liability and tax saving once profits reach a certain size.

In making contracts, a partnership has to work through agents, usually the partners. In theory, a partnership can make any contract it wishes. Whether a contract entered into by a partner binds his fellow partners depends on the usual rules of agency,[5] with the additional rule that any contract entered into by a partner which would be within the usual practice of the partnership will bind his fellow partners.[6]

1   Companies Act 1985, s 716.
2   Partnership (Unrestricted Size) No 1 Regulations 1968.
3   Limited Partnerships Act 1907, s 4.
4   Ibid, s 6.
5   Ch 16.
6   Partnership Act 1890, s 5.

Chapter 5

Agreement

5.1 An 'agreement' is often said to require a meeting of the minds of the parties to it, but this is rather misleading. The reason is that the law tends to take an objective, rather than a subjective, approach to an agreement. It is concerned not so much with what is actually in the minds of the parties, but with what a reasonable person would infer, from their conduct and the circumstances, as being in their minds (ie did they agree and, if so, on what terms?). This approach is not surprising: when the question of whether or not there is agreement is raised it is not possible to look back into the actual minds of the parties.

The following quotation indicates the approach of the courts:

'In contracts you do not look into the actual intent in a man's mind. You look at what he said and did. A contract is formed when there is, to all outward appearances, a contract.'[1]

In this chapter we examine:

- the way in which an agreement is normally proved by proof that one person made an offer to another which the latter accepted;
- what constitutes an offer;
- what constitutes an effective acceptance of an offer;
- how offers may be terminated before acceptance;
- what the legal position is if an agreement is uncertain in its terms, or is inconclusive, or is subject to the operation of a condition.

1   *Storer v Manchester City Council* [1974] 3 All ER 824 at 828.

5.2 The agreement involved in most contracts can be reduced to an offer by one party which has been accepted by the other. However, not all agreements can easily be so reduced. This is the case, for example, where two parties agree to terms suggested by a third person. It may also be the case where several parties agree independently with X that they will be bound by terms stipulated by him. In such an event the parties may have entered into a contract not merely with X but with each other. In *Clarke v Dunraven*,[1] yachtsmen wrote to the secretary of a yacht club agreeing to be bound by certain rules during a yacht race. The House of Lords held that a contract containing those rules existed between the yachtsmen with the result that a yachtsman whose yacht was damaged was able to recover damages in accordance with the rules. While there was agreement between the yachtsmen to be bound by the rules, it cannot be analysed in terms of offer and acceptance between them.

Despite exceptional cases such as these, it is the law that generally, for there to be an agreement, what has occurred must be capable of analysis into an offer by one party accepted by the other. Some judges have taken a more liberal approach. For example, in *Gibson v Manchester City Council*,[2] Lord Denning MR said: 'To my mind it is a mistake to think that all contracts can be analysed into the form of offer and acceptance... You should look at the correspondence as a whole and at the conduct of the parties... and see therefore whether the parties have come to an agreement on everything that was material'. However, on appeal in that case, Lord Denning's approach was disapproved by the House of Lords. For example, Lord Diplock said: 'My Lords there may be certain types of contract, *though I think they are exceptional*, which do not fit easily into the normal analysis of a contract as constituted by offer and acceptance; but a contract alleged to have been made by an exchange of correspondence between the parties in which the successive communications other than the first are in reply to one another is not one of these... I venture to think that it was in departing from this conventional approach that the majority of the Court of Appeal was led into error'.[3] Lord Diplock's statement represents the weight of judicial opinion, although Lord Denning's approach is a more appropriate reflection of what happens in business than a strict 'offer and acceptance approach'.

Since the agreement in most contracts is formed by an offer being made by one party which is accepted by the other, we must now consider what constitutes an offer, what constitutes an acceptance, whether an acceptance must be conveyed to the offeror, and how an offer can be terminated.

1   [1897] AC 59, HL.
2   [1978] 2 All ER 583. Also see *New Zealand Shipping Co Ltd v A M Satterthwaite & Co Ltd, The Eurymedon* [1974] 1 All ER 1015, PC, and *G Percy Trentham Ltd v Archital Luxfer Ltd* [1993] 1 Lloyd's Rep 25 at 29–30.
3   [1979] 1 All ER 972 at 974.

Offer

5.3   An offer is made where a person (the offeror) unequivocally expresses to another (the offeree) his willingness to make a binding agreement on the terms specified by him if they are accepted by the offeree.

An offer may be made to a specific person, to a group of people, or to the world at large.[1] An offer to a specific person cannot be accepted by anyone else.[2]

The fact that an offer requires an expression of unequivocal willingness to contract means that quotations of rates or prices are not offers.[3] It also means that inquiries and replies to inquiries are not offers, although sometimes they may resemble them. In *Harvey v Facey*,[4] one party inquired as to the lowest acceptable price for certain land, and the other party telegraphed his lowest acceptable price. This was held not to be an offer but merely a reply to the inquiry. Likewise, in *Gibson v Manchester City Council*,[5] where a letter had been sent saying that the council 'may be prepared to sell the house to you', it was held by the House of Lords that the letter did not constitute an offer to sell but merely an invitation to treat.

'An offer must be distinguished from an 'invitation to treat' (ie an invitation to enter into negotiations which may lead to the making of an offer). In certain situations, what may appear to be an offer by X to Y will be regarded by a court merely as an invitation to treat, unless there is clear evidence that X was willing to be bound as soon as Y indicated his assent or satisfied a particular condition. The following examples of these situations can be given.

1   *Carlill v Carbolic Smoke Ball Co* [1893] 1 QB 256, CA.
2   *Cundy v Lindsay* (1878) 3 App Cas 459, HL.
3   *Scancarriers A/S v Aotearoa International Ltd* [1985] 2 Lloyd's Rep 419, PC.
4   [1893] AC 552, PC.
5   [1979] 1 All ER 972, HL.

Invitation to treat

5.4   An invitation to treat is a starting point for contractual negotiations and precedes the making of an offer. In *Fisher v Bell*,[1] a shopkeeper was charged with offering for sale a flick knife which was on display in his shop window.[2] A divisional court held that the display of goods in a shop window was not an offer to sell but an invitation to treat; it was for customers to make the offer. The rationale behind this decision is that a shop is a place for negotiation over the terms of a contract, including the price, and that the shopkeeper invites customers to make him an offer which he can accept or reject as he pleases. This is an unrealistic view of how shops operate today. Circulars sent to potential customers are also invitations to treat for the supply of goods, and not offers.[3]

Like the display of goods in shop windows, the display of goods in self-service shops is an invitation to treat. In *Pharmaceutical Society of Great Britain v Boots Cash Chemists (Southern) Ltd*,[4] statute required certain drugs to be sold only under the supervision of a qualified pharmacist. A pharmacist was at the cash desk but, if the sale of drugs had been made before a customer reached it, the statute would have been infringed. The Court of Appeal had no hesitation in finding that the display of goods was only an invitation to treat, that the offer to buy was made by the customer at the cash desk, and that the contract was concluded when the offer was accepted. Consequently, Boots were not in breach of the statute. It was not necessary to decide precisely when a customer's offer is accepted at the cash desk, but one member of the Court of Appeal agreed with the view that acceptance occurs when the price is accepted.[5]

1   [1960] 3 All ER 731, DC.
2   Contrary to the Restriction of Offensive Weapons Act 1959. The Restriction of Offensive Weapons Act 1961 reverses the actual decision in the case.
3   *Grainger & Son v Gough* [1896] AC 325, HL.
4   [1953] 1 All ER 482, CA.
5   Ibid, at 484.

Advertisements

5.5   Whether an advertisement is an offer or an invitation to treat depends on the intention with which it is made. Advertisements of rewards and the like are normally offers since the advertiser does not intend any further negotiation to take place. An example is provided by *Carlill v Carbolic Smoke Ball Co*,[1] where the defendants advertised that they would pay £100 to anyone catching influenza after using their product in a specified manner. The Court of Appeal held that, since no further negotiations on the defendants' part were intended, the advertisement constituted an offer made to all the world which would ripen into a contract with anyone who came forward and fulfilled the conditions.

On the other hand, an advertisement of goods for sale is presumptively an invitation to treat, and not an offer,[2] because otherwise the advertiser might find himself contractually obliged to supply the advertised goods to a greater number of people (those who had responded positively to the advertisement) than the number of specified goods which had been advertised.[3] Similarly, the advertising of an auction is not an offer; instead, those who bid at auction make an offer which the auctioneer is free to accept or reject, and an offer can be withdrawn at any time before the auctioneer accepts.[4] Because the advertisement of an auction is merely a declaration of an intention to hold the auction, potential buyers have no claim against the auctioneers if they fail to hold the auction.[5] Although these rules even apply where an auctioneer advertises an auction as 'without reserve' (ie that the bid of the highest bona fide bidder will be accepted and that the property will not be withdrawn if a reserve price is not reached), so that there is no contract *of sale* if the auctioneer refuses to accept the highest bid and withdraws the property, the auctioneer is liable in such circumstances for breach of a contract *that the sale would be without reserve.* This contract comes into existence as follows: by advertising the sale as without reserve the auctioneer makes an offer to this effect to whoever is the highest bona fide bidder, which is accepted by the person who makes the highest bona fide bid before the property is withdrawn.[6]

1   [1893] 1 QB 256, CA.
2   *Partridge v Crittenden* [1968] 2 All ER 421, DC.
3   This reason would not apply if the advertiser was the manufacturer of the goods advertised, because he could make more. In *Partridge v Crittenden* [1968] 2 All ER 421 at 424, Lord Parker CJ suggested that an advertisement or circular for the sale of goods by a manufacturer could be interpreted as an offer.
4   *Payne v Cave* (1789) 3 Term Rep 148; Sale of Goods Act 1979, s 57(2).
5   *Harris v Nickerson* (1873) LR 8 QB 286.
6   *Warlow v Harrison* (1859) 1 E & E 309.

Tenders

5.6   Normally, an announcement that the provision of goods or services (or the purchase of goods or services) is open to tender is not an offer but only an invitation to treat. Consequently, a person who submits a tender normally makes an offer, which may be accepted or rejected by the person seeking tenders.[1] In *Spencer v Harding,*[2] for example, the defendant issued a circular offering by tender the stock in trade of X. This was held not to be an offer. Thus, the defendant was not required to sell the goods to the plaintiff who had submitted the highest tender.

A person seeking tenders who indicates that he will accept the highest or lowest tender, as the case may be, will be contractually bound to do so. The reason is that, in accompanying his request for tenders with such an indication, he thereby accompanies his invitation to treat with an offer of a unilateral contract to accept the highest or lowest tender, as the case may be. The highest or lowest tender, as the case may be, will constitute an acceptance of that offer, and the person seeking tenders will be contractually obliged to accept that tender.[3]

Where an invitation to tender is made only to a small, selected group of persons, it will be held to be accompanied by an offer to consider all conforming tenders submitted by the stipulated deadline, which offer is accepted by so submitting such a tender. Consequently, in such a case, it will be a breach of contract (a contract to consider a conforming tender submitted in time) to fail to consider such a tender.[4] It will not, of course, be a breach of contract to fail to accept a conforming tender after considering it.

1   For acceptance of tenders see para 5.11 below.
2   (1870) LR 5 CP 561..
3   *Harvela Investments Ltd v Royal Trust Co of Canada (CI) Ltd* [1985] 2 All ER 966, HL.
4   *Blackpool and Fylde Aero Club Ltd v Blackpool Borough Council* [1990] 3 All ER 25, CA.

Acceptance

Requirements

5.7 To convert an offer into a contract the offeree must unequivocally and unconditionally accept the offer; if, for example, A offers to sell B a computer for £5,000, payable in advance, B does not accept the offer if he replies purporting to accept the offer but saying that he will pay the £5,000 on delivery.[1] In addition, the offeree is normally required to communicate his acceptance to the offeror.

1 *Hyde v Wrench* (1840) 3 Beav 334.

5.8 It should come as no surprise to anyone to learn that one cannot accept an offer of which one is ignorant. This is important in the case where B offers a reward for the performance of a particular action, eg finding his lost dog. If A, who is ignorant of the offer, finds the dog, his action cannot constitute an acceptance of the offer and he cannot claim the reward successfully.[1] Moreover, if someone who knows of the offer performs the specified action for reasons entirely unconnected with that offer, there is no acceptance.[1] But, if his conduct is motivated partly by the offer and partly by other reasons there is a valid acceptance.[2]

A related point is that, if two offers which are identical in terms cross in the post, there can be no contract. The courts will not construe one offer as the offer and the other offer as the acceptance.[3] The practical basis for such a view would seem to be that neither party would know if he was bound, although if the terms of the offers were identical the parties would surely have no objection to being bound.

1 *R v Clarke* (1927) 40 CLR 227.
2 *Williams v Carwardine* (1833) 5 C & P 566.
3 *Tinn v Hoffmann & Co* (1873) 29 LT 271.

Counter-offers distinguished

5.9 As stated in para 5.7 above, for an acceptance there must be an unequivocal agreement to the terms proposed in the offer. If an offeree who purports to accept the offer seeks to introduce an entirely new term in his acceptance, eg as to the amount of goods to be delivered or the time of payment, this is not an acceptance. Instead, it is a counter-offer which may or may not be accepted by the original offeror.

A counter-offer puts an end to the original offer, so that it cannot subsequently be accepted by the offeree. In *Hyde v Wrench*,[1] for instance, the defendant offered to sell property to the plaintiff for £1,000. The plaintiff 'agreed' to buy the property for £950. This was rejected and the plaintiff then purported to accept the original offer of the property for £1,000. The Master of the Rolls held that the plaintiff's purported acceptance for £950 was a counter-offer which destroyed the original offer, so that it was no longer capable of acceptance when the plaintiff purported to accept it.

A counter-offer must be distinguished from an inquiry or request for information by an offeree. Such an inquiry or request, even if answered negatively by the offeror, does not destroy the offer. An example is *Stevenson, Jacques & Co v McLean*.[2] The defendant offered to sell iron to the plaintiffs at 40 shillings a ton with immediate delivery. The plaintiffs asked the defendant by telegram if he would sell at the same price if delivery was staggered over two months. On receiving no reply, the plaintiffs accepted the original offer but the defendant failed to deliver and claimed the telegram was a counter-offer. The court rejected the defendant's claim and held that the telegram was a mere request for information, and not a counter-offer, so that the original offer could still be accepted.

A contract may arise during the course of long and complicated negotiations, during which one party offers to contract on certain terms (eg terms A, B and C contained in a document sent by him) and the other agrees to contract, but on different terms (eg terms A, B and D contained in a document sent by him), and so on. Even if it is expressed to be an acceptance, such a response will in law be a counter-offer and not an acceptance. If neither party expressly accepts the other's terms, what is the legal situation? The orthodox view is that if, after the communication of the last set of terms, the recipient does something which indicates a relevant agreement with the sender, for example by delivering the goods which the sender has ordered, the recipient will be held to have accepted[3] the sender's counter-offer and thus contracted on the sender's terms.[4] Of course, this approach does not produce a contract at all if the last set of terms are not followed by anything on the recipient's part which can be described as acceptance. An alternative approach, taken by Lord Denning MR in *Butler Machine Tool Corpn (England) Ltd v Ex-Cell-O Ltd*,[5] which does not yet represent the law, is that in such a case a 'compromise' contract can be constructed by the court on reasonable terms.

1   (1840) 3 Beav 334.
2   (1880) 5 QBD 346.
3   Acceptance can be by conduct; see para 5.10 below.
4   *BRS Ltd v AV Crutchley Ltd* [1968] 1 All ER 811, CA; *Butler Machine Tool Co Ltd v Ex-Cell-O Corpn (England) Ltd* [1979] 1 All ER 965, CA.
5   [1979] 1 All ER 965 at 968–969.

Acceptance by conduct

5.10   An acceptance may be express, as where the offeree accepts the offer by a written or oral statement intended to constitute an acceptance,[1] or it may be manifested by the offeree's conduct. For instance, a cover note issued by an insurance company is an offer to insure which would be accepted by using a car in reliance on it.[2] A more complicated case of acceptance by conduct is that of *Brogden v Metropolitan Rly Co*,[3] in which Brogden was sued for failing to deliver coal. Brogden regularly supplied the company with coal and they decided to draw up a contract for such supply. A draft contract was submitted to Brogden with a blank space for the name of a mutually agreeable arbitrator. This constituted an offer. Brogden filled in the name of an arbitrator, marked the draft 'approved', and returned it to the agent of the company (who put it in a drawer where it remained). Brogden's action was not an acceptance but a counter-offer,[4] because the company had to consider whether to accept his choice of arbitrator. Nevertheless, the parties bought and sold coal in accordance with the terms of the draft contract. Subsequently, Brogden refused to supply more coal and claimed that there was no binding contract for its supply. The House of Lords inferred from the conduct of the parties, the buying and selling of coal on terms exactly the same as those in the draft contract, that a contract had been concluded on the terms of the final draft, which came into effect either with the first order of coal by the company on the terms of the draft (since this conduct could be said to have manifested the company's acceptance of Brogden's counter-offer) or, at least, when Brogden supplied the coal. The first explanation is the more acceptable. The House of Lords stressed that mere mental acquiescence by the parties that the contract should exist would not have sufficed.

1   See, for example, *Wilson Smithett & Cape (Sugar) Ltd v Bangladesh Sugar and Food Industries Corpn* [1986] 1 Lloyd's Rep 378 (letter of intent to supply materials as per terms of offer held to constitute an acceptance, because it was found to have been intended to constitute an acceptance).
2   *Taylor v Allon* [1965] 1 All ER 557 at 559.
3   (1877) 2 App Cas 666, HL.
4   Para 5.9 above.

Acceptance of tenders

5.11   The acceptance of tenders illustrates another aspect of acceptance. Tenders can be in two forms:

- Where people are invited to tender, for example by a local authority, for the supply of specified goods or services over a given period, a contract for the supply of those goods or services is constituted when a person's tender (offer) is accepted.
- However, if people are invited to tender for the supply of such goods and services as may be required over a given period, a contract is not immediately concluded with the successful tenderer. Instead, his offer is treated as a standing offer and each time an order is placed this constitutes acceptance of the standing offer and there is a contract for the goods or services ordered. Because the person making the successful tender has no definite contract, he can revoke his offer before any particular order is placed, and the person who invited tenders need never place an order.[1]

1   *Great Northern Rly Co v Witham* (1873) LR 9 CP 16.

Communication of acceptance

5.12   If an offer has been made and the offeree has decided to accept, there is normally no completed agreement until he (or his agent) has communicated his acceptance to the offeror (or his agent), by words or conduct which manifest his acceptance.[1] The reason for this is practical: if the offeror is not told that his offer has been accepted he does not know whether he has made a contract or can make offers to others.

Communication of acceptance usually requires actual communication. Consequently, an oral acceptance which is drowned by a passing aeroplane or is inaudible because of interference on the telephone is not effectively communicated.[2] Telex messages (and presumably fax messages) sent during office hours are regarded as instantaneous communications and are subject to the same principles as oral acceptances; they take effect when printed out on the offeror's telex (or fax) machine.[3] This rule would not apply where the communication was not instantaneous, as where a telex message is sent out of office hours; the time of acceptance in such a case would depend on the parties' intentions and sound business practice, and in some cases on a judgment as to where the risk should lie.

If an oral acceptance or one by telex or fax does not completely reach the offeror and the party accepting does not realise this, there may be a valid communication of acceptance. But this will only be the case where the offeror realises he has missed some of what the offeree is seeking to communicate and does not attempt to discover what he has missed.[4]

It remains to be seen what rule applies to an acceptance by e-mail. An e-mail message is stored on a network database until it is communicated to its addressee as a result of the addressee logging into the network. It is clearly not an instantaneous communication. An e-mail acceptance may be held by a court – when the occasion arises – to be subject to the same approach as the non-instantaneous communication of an acceptance by telex or fax. Alternatively, the court may consider that committing the message to the network is akin to committing a letter of acceptance to the post office by posting and that the rules relating to postal acceptance, described in para 5.16, are applicable.

1   Para 5.10 above.
2   *Entores v Miles Far East Corpn* [1955] 2 All ER 493, CA; *Brinkibon v Stahag Stahl GmbH* [1982] 1 All ER 293, HL.
3   *Brinkibon v Stahag Stahl GmbH* [1982] 1 All ER 293, HL.
4   *Entores v Miles Far East Corpn* [1955] 2 QB 327 at 333.

Dispensation from need for communication of acceptance
5.13   The offeror may by the terms of the offer expressly or impliedly dispense with the need to communicate acceptance. In particular, dispensation with the need for communication will normally be implied where the alleged contract is of the unilateral variety. An example is provided by *Carlill v Carbolic Smoke Ball Co*,[1] where the vendors of a product argued that a user of it, who claimed a reward which they had offered to anyone catching influenza after using the product, should have told them of her acceptance of their offer of a reward. The vendors' claim was rejected, since it was clear they had not intended every purchaser of the product to write to them formally accepting the offer of a reward if illness was not avoided; consequently, they had impliedly dispensed with the need for communication of acceptance.

1   [1893] 1 QB 256, CA.

5.14   If the offeror does expressly or impliedly dispense with the need for communication of acceptance, the offeree's non-communication of acceptance does not enable the offeror successfully to deny that there is a contract enforceable against him.[1] In addition, there will be a contract enforceable against the offeree if he has unambiguously manifested his acceptance, as by driving a car in reliance on an offer of motor insurance.[2] On the other hand, an offeree is not bound simply because an offeror has framed his offer in such terms that a contract is presumed to exist unless non-acceptance is communicated. Contractual liability cannot be imposed on the offeree in this way; as against the offeree, silence is not assent. In *Felthouse v Bindley*,[3] the plaintiff offered to buy X's horse and said that he would presume his offer to be accepted unless he heard to the contrary. X did not reply. The horse was sold by the defendant, an auctioneer, to another. It was held that no contract binding on X had been formed: the plaintiff was not entitled to presume acceptance unless he heard to the contrary.

1   This is certainly the case in a unilateral contract, as *Carlill v Carbolic Smoke Ball Co*, para 5.5 above, shows.
2   *Taylor v Allon* [1965] 1 All ER 557 at 559.
3   (1862) 11 CBNS 869.

5.15   While some offers dispense with the need for communication of acceptance, others require a particular form of acceptance to be employed (as where the offer states: 'Please send acceptance in writing by first class post to our Liverpool branch'). If the offer states that the acceptance may only be made in the specified manner, an acceptance in any other way cannot be effective (unless the offeror waives the requirement).[1] On the other hand, if the offer does not state that only the specified method may be used, an acceptance made in some other way (eg by telex to the Liverpool branch in the above example) can be effective as long as it is no less disadvantageous to the offeror than the prescribed method;[2] but if it is not, it is ineffective[3] (unless the offeror waives the specified mode).

1   *Compagnie de Commerce et Commission SARL v Parkinson Stove Co* [1953] 2 Lloyd's Rep 487, CA.
2   *Tinn v Hoffmann* (1873) 29 LT 271; *Yates Building Co Ltd v RJ Pulleyn & Sons (York) Ltd* (1975) 119 Sol Jo 370, CA.
3   *Financings Ltd v Stimson* [1962] 3 All ER 386, CA.

Postal acceptances
5.16   There is another exception to the general rule that acceptance must be actually communicated to be effective. It is that, subject to the qualifications referred to below, a posted acceptance is effective when it is posted, and this is so even if that acceptance is delivered late or is never delivered. This was first established in *Adams v Lindsell*,[1]

where a letter of acceptance was posted the day that a postal offer to sell wool was received. The acceptance arrived two days later than expected and, after it had been posted but before it arrived, the offeror sold the wool to another. It was held that a contract had been formed as soon as the letter of acceptance had been posted. A letter is 'posted' when it is placed, correctly stamped, in an official box or into the hands of a Post Office employee or agent authorised to receive letters;[2] most postmen who deliver letters are not so authorised.

The offeror can exclude the special postal acceptance rule by specifying in his offer that acceptance must be actually communicated to him.[3] In addition, the postal acceptance rule will be disregarded, and the general rule requiring communication prevail, if it is not reasonable to accept by post[4] or if the special rule would give rise to 'manifest inconvenience or absurdity'.[5] For example, it would not be reasonable to accept by post an offer by fax to sell highly perishable goods.

The justification for the special rule for postal acceptances seems to be that the offeror, by expressly or impliedly (eg by making the offer by post) allowing an acceptance to be made by post, must stand the risk of failures of the postal system. However, if a postal acceptance is delayed in the post because of the negligence of the offeree, as where he wrongly addresses the letter, there seems no reason why the court should not decide the acceptance to have been effective at whatever time is least advantageous to the negligent offeree.

1   (1818) 1 B & Ald 681.
2   *Re London & Northern Bank, ex p Jones* [1900] 1 Ch 220.
3   For an example see *Holwell Securities Ltd v Hughes* [1974] 1 All ER 161, CA.
4   *Henthorn v Fraser* [1892] 2 Ch 27, 61 LJ Ch 373, CA.
5   *Holwell Securities Ltd v Hughes* [1974] 1 All ER 161, CA.

5.17   If an acceptance made by letter is effective when it is posted, then, logically, an attempt to withdraw the acceptance after the letter has been posted should be ineffective since the contract has been concluded. There are no English cases which support this view, although the principle stated is consistent with decisions in New Zealand and South Africa.[1] On the other hand, the Scottish case of *Countess of Dunmore v Alexander*[2] has been cited as authority for the view that, if a revocation of an acceptance is communicated before a postal acceptance arrives, the revocation is effective. However, the facts of this case are somewhat obscure and it is by no means certain that this is what the case decided.

1   *Wenkheim v Arndt* (1861–1902) 1 JR 73; *A to Z Bazaars (Pty) Ltd v Minister of Agriculture* 1974 (4) SA 392.
2   (1830) 9 Sh (Ct of Sess) 190.

Termination of offers

5.18   An offer may be terminated in several ways: by rejection (including a counter-offer[1]), by revocation, by lapse of time and by death.

1   Para 5.9 above.

Revocation

5.19   At any time until acceptance by the offeree, the offeror can withdraw his offer. The fact that the offeror has given the offeree time to make up his mind does not mean that the offeror is required to keep the offer open for that length of time. In *Routledge v Grant*,[1] a reply to an offer was required within six weeks; it was held that nevertheless the offer could be withdrawn within that period.

There is an exception to the rule that the offer need not be kept open for a specified period. This is where there is a separate contract whereby the offeror contracts to keep the offer open for a given time. It there is such a contract the offer can be accepted at any time within the specified period. An example of such a contract is the granting of an option.

The revocation of an offer only becomes effective when it is communicated to the offeree. In *Byrne v Van Tienhoven*,[2] the defendants in Cardiff wrote on 1 October to the plaintiffs in New York, offering to sell them goods. The plaintiff received the offer on 11 October and accepted it by telegram on the same day. Meanwhile, on 8 October the defendants had sent a letter to the plaintiffs revoking their offer; this letter reached the plaintiffs on 20 October. It was held that the revocation was ineffective because the plaintiffs' acceptance had taken effect on 11 October (acceptance by telegram being treated in the same way as acceptance by letter) and therefore the defendants' offer was no longer capable of being revoked when their letter of revocation reached the plaintiffs. Consequently, there was a contract between the plaintiffs and defendants for the sale of the goods. There is no parallel rule to that which treats a posted acceptance as a communicated acceptance; a revocation must always be actually communicated.

This raises a question which has yet to be authoritatively determined: does communication by letter, telex or fax require that the revocation is actually read by the offeror[3] or does it occur when the letter is delivered, or the telex or fax is printed out, at his premises, regardless of whether it comes to the attention of the offeror[3] at that time? In the case of a business, the latter is probably the answer provided that the delivery or print-out is during normal business hours.[4] The answer in other cases is less certain.

Communication of revocation may be indirect, in that, if the offeree hears from a reliable source that the offer has been withdrawn (and thereby knows beyond all question of the withdrawal), the courts will regard this as an effective revocation.[5] The difficulty inherent in this is that it is difficult to know what constitutes a reliable source.

1   (1828) 4 Bing 653.
2   (1880) 5 CPD 344.
3   Or his agent.
4   Suggested by the decision in another context in *The Brimnes* [1974] 3 All ER 88, CA.
5   *Dickinson v Dodds* (1876) 2 Ch D 463, CA.

5.20   Special rules apply in the case of unilateral contracts, where A does something (eg returning lost property) in response to B's offer (promise) to do something (eg to pay a reward) if he does it. The general rule is that once the offeree has embarked on the performance of the stipulated act or acts necessary for acceptance, as where B has found lost property and is en route to return it in response to the offer of a reward, the offer cannot be withdrawn.[1] The reason is that, when the offer is made which will mature into a unilateral contract when accepted, there is alongside that principal offer a collateral offer to keep the principal offer open once performance in relation to it has begun, which is accepted by the offeree starting to perform the stipulated act or acts.[2] In *Errington v Errington and Woods*,[3] a father purchased a house, partially by means of a mortgage, and allowed his daughter and her husband to live in it. The daughter and her husband paid the mortgage instalments in response to the father's offer that, if they did so, he would give them the house when it was paid for. The Court of Appeal held that this offer could not be revoked once the daughter and her husband had begun performance of the conduct specified in the offer. Of course, in the present type of case the offeror is not bound unless and until the offeree has fully performed the act or acts specified in the offer. This is subject to the important qualification that, if the offeror prevents performance of the necessary act or acts being completed, he cannot rely on the offeree's failure fully to perform as a defence to a breach of contract action by the offeree, because there is an implied obligation on the part of the offeror (which arises as soon as the offeree starts to perform) not to prevent performance by the offeree.[4]

What we have just said will not apply if the terms of the offer, or its surrounding circumstances, indicate that it was not intended to become irrevocable before the offeree had completely performed the envisaged act. A good example is the kind of commission agreement commonly used by estate agents. Although this is a unilateral contract (as we explained in para 4.2 above) it is well settled that the client may revoke his instructions at any time, notwithstanding that the agent may have expended time and money in attempting to find a purchaser.[5] The courts take the view that a change of mind by a client is simply one of the business risks which an estate agent must bear, and his fees for successful negotiations should be at a level sufficient to cover other abortive work.

1   *Offord v Davies* (1862) 12 CBNS 748; *Errington v Errington and Woods* [1952] 1 All ER 149, CA; *Daulia Ltd v Four Millbank Nominees Ltd* [1978] 2 All ER 557 at 561.
2   *Daulia Ltd v Four Millbank Nominees Ltd* [1978] 2 All ER 557 at 561.
3   [1952] 1 All ER 149, CA.
4   *Daulia Ltd v Four Millbank Nominees Ltd* [1978] 2 All ER 557 at 561.
5   *Luxor (Eastbourne) Ltd v Cooper* [1941] 1 All ER 33, HL.

Lapse of time
5.21   Obviously, an offer which is to remain open for a set time lapses at the end of that time and cannot thereafter be accepted. If no time limit is expressly set for the offer, it will normally lapse after a reasonable period.[1] In *Ramsgate Victoria Hotel v Montefiore*,[2] for example, it was held that an offer to buy shares, which was made in June, could not be accepted in November since the offer had lapsed by then. What is a reasonable period varies, depending on the facts of the case.

1   *Chemco Leasing SpA v Rediffusion* [1987] 1 FTLR 201, CA.
2   (1866) LR 1 Ex Ch 109.

Death
5.22   Death after an offer has been accepted cannot affect the validity of a contract.[1] There are, however, cases where either the offeror or the offeree dies before the offer is accepted. If the offeror dies the offer does not seem to terminate automatically (except where the offer is clearly of such a type that it must end on death, eg an offer to work for X). However, the offeree cannot accept the offer once he knows of the death of the offeror.[2]

The effects of the death of the offeree have not been decided conclusively but uncontradicted dicta suggest that the offer lapses. In *Reynolds v Atherton*,[3] it was suggested that an offer, being made to a living person, cannot survive his death and be accepted by someone else. This may be an illustration of the basic rule that an offer made to A cannot be accepted by B. On the other hand, if an offer is made to A or B there seems no reason why the death of B should prevent A accepting it.

1   But it may discharge the contract: see para 11.6 below.
2   *Bradbury v Morgan* (1862) 1 H & C 249; *Coulthart v Clementson* (1879) 5 QBD 42.
3   (1921) 125 LT 690, CA; affd by the House of Lords who did not comment on this point.

Uncertain, inconclusive and conditional agreements

5.23   Here we are concerned with cases where, although there is an agreement, there may not be a legally binding contract because the agreement is uncertain in its terms, or is merely an agreement to agree in the future, or is subject to the operation of a condition.

Uncertainty

5.24   Where particular terms in an agreement are vague or unclear, the courts will try to divine the intention of the parties and find a contract, but if such intention cannot be discovered the agreement is not a legally binding contract and cannot be enforced.[1] In *Bushwall Properties Ltd v Vortex Properties Ltd*,[2] for instance, A agreed to buy from B 51$\frac{1}{2}$ acres of land for £500,000. Under the terms of the agreement the price was to be paid in three instalments and on each payment a 'proportionate part' of the land was to be conveyed to A. The Court of Appeal held that the agreement was void for uncertainty because it did not provide the machinery for identifying the proportionate part to be conveyed in each phase, nor could a term (based on the parties' presumed intention) be implied as to how each proportionate part was to be identified. Another agreement which has been held not to be binding because of lack of certainty is an agreement to continue to negotiate in good faith for an unspecified period, since a party would never know whether he was entitled to withdraw from the negotiations and the court could not be expected to decide whether a proper reason existed for him to do so.[3] For similar reasons an agreement of unspecified duration not to negotiate with anyone else is void for uncertainty. We return to this type of agreement in para 5.29.

On the other hand, a court can supply the details of an apparently vague term, so that the agreement is a valid contract, if the parties have provided the machinery to ascertain its precise nature, as where there is an agreement for the sale of land at 'market price' (in which case the court can fix that price after making an inquiry),[4] or if the details which the parties must have intended can be implied by reference to the practices of a particular trade to which they belong or by reference to their previous dealings. In *Hillas & Co Ltd v Arcos Ltd*,[5] the parties had entered into an agreement for the sale and purchase of timber in 1930. The agreement contained an option to buy 100,000 standards of timber in 1931 but the size and quality of the timber were not specified. The House of Lords refused to find the agreement unenforceable, clarifying any uncertainties by reference to the previous dealings of the parties and usual practice in the timber trade. The judgment of the House is permeated by the view that the courts ought to strive to give effect to business arrangements and not zealously demand absolute certainty of all terms.

Another case where there can be a valid contract despite the apparent uncertainty of a term is where the parties have provided the machinery for one of them, or for a third party or third parties, to fix the precise nature of that term. This was recognised in *Sudbrook Trading Estate Ltd v Eggleton*,[6] where the House of Lords dealt with the situation where the price of a piece of property was left to be decided by two valuers, one to be appointed by each party. It held that if the task of the valuers, expressly or impliedly, was to fix a fair and reasonable price and that method proved ineffective, either because a party refused to appoint a valuer or because the valuers failed to agree, a court could substitute its own machinery to ascertain the price, eg by appointing its own valuers. On the other hand, it held, if the price was to be fixed by a named valuer or valuers, it could not be implied that the price was to be a fair and reasonable one because the implication was that the price was to be fixed by a specified means, the use of the named valuer or valuers. In such a case, it held, a court could not substitute its own machinery if for some reason the named valuer or valuers failed to fix the price, and there would not be an enforceable contract for the sale of the property.

There can be a valid contract for the sale of goods or the supply of a service, even though the price is not fixed, or left to be fixed in an agreed manner, and cannot be determined by a course of dealings between the parties. Statute provides that, in such a case, a reasonable price must be paid.[7]

Where an apparently uncertain term can be determined in one of the above ways, the contract is complete on the agreement of the parties even though the precise nature of that term remains to be fixed.[8]

If a transaction has been performed on both sides, it will be difficult for a party to submit successfully that there is no agreement or that there is not a legally binding contract on grounds of uncertainty or vagueness.[9]

1   *Scammell and Nephew Ltd v Ouston* [1941] 1 All ER 14, HL.
2   [1976] 2 All ER 283, CA.
3   *Walford v Miles* [1992] 1 All ER 453, HL.
4   *Bushwall Properties Ltd v Vortex Properties Ltd* [1976] 2 All ER 283 at 289.
5   (1932) 147 LT 503, HL.
6   [1982] 3 All ER 1, HL.
7   Sale of Goods Act 1979, s 8; Supply of Goods and Services Act 1982, s 15.
8   *Sudbrook Trading Estate Ltd v Eggleton* [1982] 3 All ER 1, HL.
9   *G Percy Trentham Ltd v Archital Luxfer Ltd* [1993] 1 Lloyd's Rep 25 at 27.

5.25   Sometimes it may be possible to ignore uncertainty in an agreement. This can be done, for instance, where the uncertainty relates to what is a meaningless term. In *Nicolene Ltd v Simmonds*,[1] the agreement contained the phrase 'I assume the usual conditions of acceptance apply'. There were no usual conditions of acceptance, but the Court of Appeal said the phrase was meaningless and, since it did not relate to an important term or part of the contract, it could be ignored. A distinction must be drawn between meaningless phrases and phrases which denote that terms are still to be agreed. A phrase is unlikely to be considered meaningless, and thus capable of being ignored, if it concerns an important term of the contract.

1   [1953] 1 All ER 822, CA.

Agreement to agree
5.26   If the parties have agreed the vital terms of an agreement and agreed to be bound immediately, there is a concluded agreement despite the fact that further terms must be negotiated.[1] On the other hand, if a vital term of an agreement is open to further negotiation, or if the parties have not agreed to be bound immediately because further negotiation is necessary before a binding agreement can be concluded, there is no concluded agreement, but merely an agreement to agree. An example is where an agreement for the sale of goods leaves the price to be fixed by agreement between the parties. In *May and Butcher Ltd v R*,[2] the price of surplus tentage which was being sold by a government department to the plaintiffs was such as 'shall be agreed upon from time to time between the government department and the purchasers'. The House of Lords found that, because a vital term was left open for future negotiation, the agreement was not a legally binding contract.

However, if the agreement expressly or impliedly provides a method for resolving the lack of agreement, there will be a valid contract. An example is provided by *Foley v Classique Coaches Ltd*,[3] the Court of Appeal held that an agreement containing the words 'price to be agreed by the parties' was a binding contract. The court felt able to distinguish *May and Butcher Ltd v R* on two grounds. First, on the basis that the parties had acted on the agreement for three years and their implied belief that they had been contractually bound during that period must be given effect, and, second, because the contract provided that in the absence of agreement on price it was to be determined by arbitration. *Beer v Bowden*[4] provides another example. Premises were let for 10 years (later extended to 14) at a fixed rent for the first five years, but at a rent 'to be agreed' thereafter. The Court of Appeal implied a term that in the absence of agreement a reasonable rent determined by the court should be paid.

1   *Pagnan SpA v Feed Products* [1987] 2 Lloyd's Rep 601, CA.
2   [1934] 2 KB 17n, HL.
3   [1934] 2 KB 1, CA.
4   [1981] 1 All ER 1070, CA.

Operation of a condition
Condition precedent
5.27   An agreement which appears to be a binding contract may never come into operation because it is subject to a condition precedent which is not satisfied. An example is afforded by *Pym v Campbell*.[1] In this case an agreement to purchase a share in an invention was subject to the condition precedent that the invention be approved by X. X failed to approve and thus no binding contract to buy came into existence.[2]

An agreement subject to a condition precedent is not necessarily devoid of all effect. It all depends on the interpretation which the court gives to it.

On its true construction, the effect of an agreement subject to a condition precedent may be that, although the agreement containing it is not binding before the condition is satisfied, neither party can withdraw until it is clear whether or not the condition will be satisfied.[3]

Alternatively, or in addition, the effect of such an agreement may be that one party must do his best to fulfil the condition[4] or, at least, not obstruct its fulfilment.[5] For example, the phrase 'subject to survey' in an agreement for the sale of land has been construed as meaning that the purchaser must proceed with due diligence to obtain a surveyor's report and, having received it, consider it, and must act in good faith. If, in good faith, he is not satisfied with the report he is not obliged to proceed with the purchase, but in the meantime neither party can withdraw.[6]

Lastly, a condition precedent may be construed as imposing no obligation on either party. This is the prima facie construction[7] given to 'subject to contract' and similar conditions. We deal with these further in para 5.28.

A condition precedent may be void for uncertainty, in which case the agreement in which it is contained is also void. An example is an agreement for the sale of land 'subject to the purchaser obtaining a satisfactory mortgage', since such a condition is too vague for the courts to enforce.[8]

1   (1856) 6 E & B 370.
2   In fact, it was held that there was no agreement at all.
3   *Smith v Butler* [1900] 1 QB 694, CA. In *Smallman v Smallman* [1971] 3 All ER 717, CA, a buyer, who withdrew from an agreement to purchase which was subject to a condition precedent before it was clear whether the condition was satisfied, was unable to recover the deposit he had paid.
4   *Marten v Whale* [1917] 2 KB 480, CA.
5   *Mackay v Dick* (1881) 6 App Cas 251, HL.
6   *Ee v Kakar* (1979) 40 P & CR 223.
7   *Alpenstow Ltd v Regalian Properties plc* [1985] 2 All ER 545.
8   *Lee-Parker v Izzet (No 2)* [1972] 2 All ER 800.

'Subject to contract' and similar conditions
5.28   A 'subject to contract' condition is usually inserted initially in an agreement to buy land which is for sale by private treaty. Unless there are very exceptional circumstances which oust the prima facie meaning of the phrase,[1] such agreements are simply 'agreements to agree' and are not binding, nor are the parties required to try to ensure that a contract is concluded.[2] Phrases similar to 'subject to contract' have the same effect, except that where an agreement for the sale of land is made 'subject to the purchaser obtaining a mortgage on terms satisfactory to himself' a further term

is implied that such satisfaction must not be unreasonably withheld.[3]

Because an agreement to buy land 'subject to contract' is not binding, it is legally permissible for the vendor to agree to sell the property to someone else offering a higher price. This is particularly common when property prices are rising; it is called 'gazumping'.

1   *Alpenstow Ltd v Regalian Properties plc* [1985] 2 All ER 545.
2   *Winn v Bull* (1877) 7 Ch D 29.
3   *Janmohamed v Hassam* (1976) 241 Estates Gazette 609.

5.29   The precarious position of a party to an agreement to buy property 'subject to contract' has led such parties, and their legal advisers, to seek ways of protecting their legal position by the use of 'lock-out agreements', with varying success. A lock-out agreement is one where, in return for consideration by the other party, one party agrees to give the other party an exclusive opportunity to conclude a contract with him, ie he agrees not to negotiate with anyone else. A lock-out agreement whose duration is unlimited in time is not binding, but one which is subject to such a limit is.

This was held by the House of Lords in *Walford v Miles*.[1] In this case the plaintiffs agreed in March 1987 'subject to contract' to buy a business from the defendants. Later that month there was a further agreement between one of the plaintiffs and one of the defendants that, if the plaintiffs obtained a 'comfort letter' from their bank that it was prepared to provide the finance for the purchase, the defendants would terminate negotiations with any third party. The comfort letter was provided, but at the end of March the defendants notified the plaintiffs that they had decided to sell the business to a third party.

The plaintiffs claimed that, although there was no binding contract for the sale of the business, their lock-out agreement with the defendants was binding, since they had provided consideration for the defendants' lock-out promise by providing the comfort letter and by promising to continue negotiations with the defendants.

The House of Lords held that, although it was possible for a lock-out agreement to be binding, the agreement in question was not binding because it was indefinite in duration.[2]

Walford v Miles can be contrasted with *Pitt v PHH Asset Management Ltd*[3] where a lock-out agreement for a specified period was held to be binding. In this case the defendant company had put on the market a property which attracted the interest of the plaintiff and of another person, Miss B. The plaintiff and Miss B made a number of offers, in which in effect they bid each other up. At one point the defendant company agreed subject to contract to sell the property to the plaintiff for £200,000. Miss B then increased her offer to £210,000 and the next day the defendant company's acceptance of the plaintiff's offer was withdrawn. The plaintiff then threatened to seek an injunction to prevent the sale to Miss B and to tell Miss B that he was withdrawing so that she should withdraw her offer. The plaintiff then entered an agreement through the defendant company's estate agents that the defendant company would sell the property to the plaintiff for £200,000 and would not consider any other offer provided that the plaintiff exchanged contracts within two weeks of receipt of a draft contract.

The defendant company sent a draft contract to the plaintiff. Eight days later the plaintiff indicated that he was ready to exchange contracts. However, on the same day, the plaintiff was notified that it had been decided to go ahead with a sale to Miss B at £210,000 unless the plaintiff was prepared to exchange contracts that day at £210,000. The plaintiffs refused to do so and the property was sold to Miss B.

The plaintiff's action for breach of its lock-out agreement with the defendant company succeeded since it was of a specified duration (two weeks) and the defendant company was in breach of it. Of course, the defendant company was not bound by the lock-out agreement to sell to the plaintiff; it was only bound not to negotiate during the specified period. If it had waited for the two weeks to elapse, and not exchanged during that period, it would have been perfectly entitled thereafter to sell to Miss B.

Walford v Miles can also be contrasted with *Global Container Lines Ltd v Black Sea Shipping Co*[4] where it was held that a lock-out agreement containing an express or implied term for termination on reasonable notice is not of indefinite duration and therefore can be binding.

The appropriate remedy for breach of a lock-out agreement is an award of damages, and not an injunction, since the purpose of such an agreement is to protect a potential purchaser from wasting expenses incurred in getting ready to complete when the vendor elects to sell to another. The potential purchaser can recover as damages his costs which have been wasted.[5]

1   [1992] 1 All ER 453, HL.
2   The plaintiffs had argued that the lock-out agreement was subject to an implied term that the defendants would continue to negotiate in good faith with the plaintiffs. The House of Lords held that, even if such a term could be implied, it would not assist the plaintiffs because an agreement to such an effect was void for uncertainty, as stated in para 5.24 above.
3   [1993] 4 All ER 961, CA.
4   [1997] 9 CL 554. A *commercial* contract without an express term as to its duration normally has such a term implied into it (*Global Container Lines v Black Sea Shipping Co*), but the same is not normally the case in relation to other types of contract.
5   *Tye v House* [1997] 41 EG 160.

Condition subsequent

5.30   An agreement may also be subject to the operation of a condition subsequent. In such cases an agreement will be a binding contract unless and until the condition occurs. If it does occur, either the contract will automatically cease to bind or one party will have the right to cancel it, depending on the construction of the condition. In *Head v Tattersall*,[1] a contract for the sale of a horse was subject to the condition subsequent that, if the purchaser found within a given time that the horse did not meet its contractual description, the horse could be returned and the contract terminated. During that period, the purchaser found that the horse did not correspond with its description. It was held that he could return it and recover the price, even though it had been injured in the meanwhile.

1   (1871) LR 7 Exch 7.

Chapter 6

Binding agreement

6.1 An agreement which complies with the rules specified in the previous chapter will constitute a legally binding contract, provided

- it is supported by consideration; and
- the parties intend to enter into a legally binding contract.

Alternatively, it will constitute a legally binding contract if it is made by deed. We defined the requirements for a deed in para 4.6 above

Intention to create legal relations

6.2 If an agreement is supported by consideration there is usually an intention to create legal relations, although the parties to an agreement rarely state this intention expressly. If the parties do not wish their agreement to be legally binding, they may expressly state this and the courts will give effect to their intention. In the absence of an express indication of intention, the courts rely on two presumptions in deciding whether there was an intention to create legal relations, both of which can be rebutted expressly or impliedly by the parties:

- parties to social, domestic and family arrangements do not intend to be legally bound;[1] *and*
- parties to business and commercial agreements expect their agreements to be legally binding.[2]

An example of the first type of arrangement is an agreement to give lifts to work, even if it is on an organised basis and involves payment to the car owners for their petrol.[3] While arrangements made within the family or household are presumed not to be intended to be legally binding, the nature of the agreement may clearly indicate that the parties intended a particular arrangement to be legally binding. In *Ward v Warnke*,[4] X and Y allowed their daughter and her husband to occupy their holiday home. The daughter and her husband paid a modest rent (£3.50, later £6.00, per week) which was paid into a building society account in their names, as well as the outgoings resulting from occupation of the premises. The Court of Appeal held that the agreement constituted a legally binding tenancy agreement between the parties.

If there is a business arrangement it is extremely difficult to rebut the presumption that the arrangement is to be legally binding, other than by clear words. A case where clear words led to the presumption being rebutted is *Rose and Frank Co v J R Crompton & Bros Ltd*,[5] in which the defendants appointed the plaintiffs their agents to sell their products in America under an agreement which contained an 'honour clause', ie a clause which said the agreement was merely recording the intention of the parties and was binding in honour only and not in law. The plaintiffs sued for alleged breach of contract. The Court of Appeal and the House of Lords held that the honour clause constituted a clearly expressed intention that the agency agreement was not to be legally binding and that effect had to be given to this intention.

Even where the presumption is rebutted by clear words, this does not prevent the subsequent conduct of the parties to the agreement constituting a legally binding contract. In *Rose and Frank Co v J R Crompton & Bros Ltd*, the parties to the agency agreement ordered and supplied goods for sale in America. It was held that these orders and acceptances gave rise to binding contracts, even though the agency agreement was not legally binding.

An important statutory exception to the presumption that business and commercial dealings are intended to be legally binding is contained in the Trade Union and Labour Relations (Consolidation) Act 1992, s 179, which provides that collective agreements between employers and trade unions are presumed not to be legally enforceable unless they are made in writing and expressly state that the agreement is to be legally enforceable. However, if terms in a collective agreement are incorporated in an individual employee's contract of employment, they are presumed to be intended to be binding.[6]

1 *Balfour v Balfour* [1919] 2 KB 571, CA.
2 *Edwards v Skyways Ltd* [1964] 1 All ER 494.
3 *Coward v Motor Insurers' Bureau* [1962] 1 All ER 531, CA.
4 (1990) 22 HLR 496, CA.
5 [1925] AC 445, HL.
6 *Robertson v British Gas Corpn* [1983] ICR 351, CA; *Marley v Forward Trust Group Ltd* [1986] ICR 891, CA.

Consideration

6.3 Agreements not made by deed[1] must be supported by consideration if they are to be legally binding, and a person who wishes to enforce a contract must show that he provided consideration for the promise which he is seeking to enforce.[2] It is in the requirement of consideration that English law recognises the idea that a contract is a bargain.

In order to provide consideration for a promise, the promisee (the person to whom the promise was made) must have made a promise or done an act:

- in return for that promise; and
- at the express or implied request of the promisor (the person making that promise).

It follows from the requirement that the promisee's act or promise must have been requested by the promisor that a 'gratuitous' act or promise by a promisee is not consideration. This is shown by *Re Cory*.[3] The YMCA wished to build a hall. It needed £150,000 to do so. £85,000 had been promised or was available. However, the YMCA decided not to commit itself to going on with the project until it saw that its efforts to raise the whole sum were likely to succeed. C then promised a donation of 1,000 guineas (£1,050) for the purpose of building the hall. The YMCA subsequently entered into a building contract for the hall, which they alleged they were largely induced to do by C's promise. C then died and the question arose whether his promise to pay was legally binding, in which case his estate would be bound by it. It was held that C's promise was not binding; the YMCA had not provided any consideration for C's promise because C had not expressly or impliedly requested the YMCA to do (or promise to do) anything in return.

It also follows from the definition of consideration that a promise (not made by deed) to give property on condition that something occurs is not legally binding if the promisee is not expressly or impliedly requested by the promisor to do or promise anything in return. In *Dickinson v Abel*,[4] A told B that he was willing to pay £100,000 for a farm which was vested in a bank as trustees. B had no proprietary interest in the farm but had previously passed on to the bank offers for the farm. B asked: 'What's in it for me?' and was told that he would be paid £10,000 if A bought the farm for £100,000 or less. A did not ask B to perform any specific services, but B telephoned the bank and told them that an offer of £100,000 was on its way and that he personally would accept it. The farm was sold to A for less than £100,000 and B was paid the £10,000. The question later arose as to whether the £10,000 was taxable, which it would be if paid under a contract. It was somewhat surprisingly found as a fact that A had not expressly or impliedly requested B to do anything. Consequently, it was held, what B had done was not consideration for A's promise and there was therefore no legally binding agreement (ie contract) between A and B but merely a conditional gift. While the finding on the facts is hard to accept, the important legal point is the judge's application of the law to those facts.

1   Para 4.6 above.
2   See, further, para 7.1 – 7.3 below.
3   (1912) 29 TLR 18. For a recent example of the requirement of a request, see *Southwark London Borough Council v Logan* [1995] EGCS 165, CA.
4   [1969] 1 All ER 484.

6.4   In a number of cases, particularly in the 19th century,[1] consideration has been defined as follows: that X provides consideration for Y's promise if he confers a benefit on Y, in return for which Y's promise is given, or if he incurs a detriment, in compensation for which Y's promise is given. Certainly if there is either a benefit or a detriment to the appropriate party that is good consideration, but this definition has been criticised and some cases cannot be explained in terms of benefit and detriment. A more modern view of consideration is that if one party's action or forbearance, promised or actual, is the price for which the other's promise is bought, and without that price there would be no bargain,[2] the former party has provided consideration for the latter's promise.

1   See, for example, *Currie v Misa* (1875) LR 10 Exch 153. For a more recent reference to this type of definition, see *Midland Bank Trust Co Ltd v Green* [1981] AC 513 at 531, [1981] 1 All ER 153; *Johnsey Estates Ltd v Lewis & Manley (Engineering) Ltd* (1987) 54 P & CR 296, CA.
2   *Dunlop Pneumatic Tyre Co Ltd v Selfridge & Co Ltd* [1915] AC 847 at 855.

Executed and executory consideration

6.5   In the case of a unilateral contract, ie where a person does something at the request of another, such as finding a lost dog, in return for the promise of a reward, the person doing the requested act thereby provides consideration for the other's promise. In a unilateral contract, consideration is only given by one party and only the other party is bound (hence the description 'unilateral contract'). The consideration provided in a unilateral contract is said to be 'executed' because it consists of the actual doing of something in response to a promise by the other party and at his request.

In the case of a bilateral contract, ie where a party to an agreement promises to do something in response to a promise by the other and at his request, as where X promises to pay for goods to be supplied by Y, a party provides consideration by giving his promise. Thus, in the above example, X provides consideration for Y's promise to supply the goods. In a bilateral contract, consideration is given by both parties and both parties are bound (hence the description 'bilateral contract'). The consideration here is said to be 'executory' because it consists of a promise by each party which need not be executed (ie the promise need not be carried out) in order for the promise of the other party, for which it is exchanged, to be binding. The concept of executory consideration illustrates the difficulty of the benefit or detriment theory of consideration. When no one has done anything and there are merely promises there is no benefit or detriment to anyone, but it is possible to say that the price of one party's promise was the promise made by the other party.

Both executed and executory consideration are good consideration in law, unlike 'past consideration'.

Past consideration

6.6 'Past consideration' is said to have been given by a person when, only *after* he has done something, a promise (eg to reward him) is made in return by another person. 'Past consideration' is an inaccurate expression, since it is not consideration at all and a person who has given it cannot enforce another's promise made in return for it.

The fact that past consideration is not good consideration illustrates the idea that consideration is the price of a promise. In *Re McArdle*,[1] work was done by X on a house which had been left to her and other members of her family. The other members then promised to reimburse the cost to her of the work but failed to keep their promise. X sued on the promise to pay but failed because she had provided no consideration for it, since her acts (doing the work on the house), which she alleged constituted consideration, pre-dated the promise by the relatives.

It would be wrong to think that all actions which are not preceded by an express promise constitute past consideration. If an act is done by X at the request of Y in circumstances where X and Y must have understood that the act was to be remunerated (so that a prior promise of remuneration by Y can be *implied*), the act by X is good consideration.[2] An act done in response to a request accompanied by an implied promise of remuneration may be followed by an express promise to pay a particular sum or confer a particular benefit. If this is so, the promise quantifies the amount due to the party who performed the requested act. If there is no subsequent promise, the amount due is determined on the basis of reasonable remuneration for the services provided or the things supplied. What transforms apparently past consideration into good consideration is the fact that the action is in response to a request which raises an implied promise of payment. The requested action is the price of the implied promise to pay. In *Re McArdle* there was no prior request or expectation of payment. However, in *Re Casey's Patents, Stewart v Casey*,[3] the plaintiffs wrote to Casey saying that 'in consideration of your [past] services as practical manager' they would give him a one-third share in certain patents. This promise was fulfilled but subsequently the plaintiffs sought to recover the patents, claiming that Casey had given no consideration for their promise. The Court of Appeal rejected this argument, saying that Casey's services as manager clearly raised an implication that they would be remunerated and thus Casey had provided consideration, the subsequent express promise merely fixing the amount of that remuneration.

1   [1951] 1 All ER 905, CA.
2   *Lampleigh v Brathwait* (1615) Hob 105; *Kennedy v Broun* (1863) 13 CBNS 677; *Re Casey's Patents, Stewart v Casey* [1892] 1 Ch 104, CA; *Pao On v Lau Yiu Long* [1979] 3 All ER 65, PC.
3   [1892] 1 Ch 104, CA.

6.7 In determining whether a contract is supported by consideration, the courts have regard to two factors:

* consideration must have some value but need not be adequate; and
* consideration must be real and sufficient, ie what is alleged to be consideration must be an action or promise which the law recognises as capable of being consideration.

Adequacy

6.8 Provided that the alleged consideration has some economic value in the eyes of the law, the courts will not question its adequacy, even though one party is apparently making a very good bargain and the other is not. In *Mountford v Scott*,[1] £1, paid for an option to purchase a house, was found to be good consideration. Money is always considered to have an economic value and the fact that the amount was small was irrelevant.

Although the courts will not question the adequacy of consideration, the fact that the consideration is clearly inadequate may indicate that the contract has been procured by fraudulent misrepresentation, undue influence or duress on the part of the party benefiting from the inadequacy, in which case the contract may be set aside if the rules described in Chapter 14 are satisfied.

The next paragraph provides another illustration that the courts will not question the adequacy of consideration which has some value.

1   [1975] 1 All ER 198, CA.

Forbearance to sue

6.9 If a person who could sue another promises not to pursue his claim, that constitutes good consideration for a promise by the other person to pay a sum of money as a final settlement of the claim. In addition, the person promising to pay that sum thereby provides consideration for the other's promise not to pursue his claim. In such a case, the amount of the acknowledged liability is the sum agreed to be paid. It is important to distinguish this situation from that where the acknowledged liability is greater than the sum promised or actually paid;[1] a promise to accept part payment in such a case is not binding, as explained in para 6.15 below. It might be thought that promising to abandon an invalid claim[2] cannot be good consideration. However, the abandonment of an invalid claim will be good consideration if the party abandoning it can show that the claim was reasonable in itself, that he genuinely believed the claim had some chance of success and intended to pursue it, and that he was not concealing from the other party facts which would constitute a defence to the claim.[3] The argument is that abandoning a doubtful claim saves the parties from the uncertainties of litigation and its attendant expense.

1   The dividing line between the two can be fine: see *Ferguson v Davies* [1997] 1 All ER 315, CA.
2   For example, in *Poteliakhoff v Teakle* [1938] 2 KB 816, [1938] 3 All ER 686, CA, a creditor's promise not to sue on unenforceable gaming debts was not good consideration for a promise by the debtor because the creditor knew that the claim was invalid.
3   *Horton v Horton (No 2)* [1960] 3 All ER 649, CA; *Miles v New Zealand Alford Estate Co* (1886) 32 Ch D 266; *Syros Shipping Co SA v Elaghill Trading Co, The Proodos C* [1981] 3 All ER 189.

Sufficiency

6.10 The law refuses to recognise certain types of action or promise as capable of constituting consideration, with the result that a person making such an action or promise cannot enforce another's promise given in return for it. Such an action or promise is said not to be sufficient consideration, which is rather confusing since in law it is not consideration at all.

Performance of an existing duty imposed by law

6.11 The law imposes obligations on all people, and it is necessary to discuss whether performing or promising to perform such an obligation can also be good consideration for the contractual promise of another. The basic position was stated in *Collins v Godefroy*,[1] in which the plaintiff gave evidence at the defendant's trial in response to a promise of payment. When he sued for the payment, it was held that he could not succeed because he had provided no consideration since he was obliged by law to give evidence. It is now clear that the principle in *Collins v Godefroy* has been refined by the principle in *Williams v Roffey Bros & Nicholls (Contractors) Ltd*, referred to in para 6.13 below. The result is that, except where the existing duty is to pay money,[2] where A makes a promise to B in return for B's promise to perform his existing duty imposed by law to do something (other than to pay money), B will provide consideration for A's promise if, as a result of B's promise, A obtains a practical benefit (or avoids a 'disbenefit').

1   (1831) 1 B & Ad 950.
2   *Re Selectmove Ltd* [1995] 2 All ER 531, CA.

6.12 The principle in *Collins v Godefroy* does not apply if the party seeking to show that he provided consideration promised to do, or did, more than was required by law, as where he promises to pay (or pays) more than he is legally obliged, because that is good consideration. In *Glasbrook Bros Ltd v Glamorgan County Council*,[1] the company requested greater protection for its mine during a strike than the police thought necessary and offered to pay for the increased police presence. The company later refused to pay, claiming that, since the police were under a legal duty to protect property, they had provided no consideration for the company's promise of payment. The House of Lords held that the company was obliged to pay because the duty of the police was to take such steps as they reasonably thought necessary and, by providing protection beyond that level, they had done more than they were legally obliged to do and thus had provided consideration for the company's promise.

1   [1925] AC 270, HL. Also see *Ward v Byham* [1956] 2 All ER 318, CA.

Performance of an existing contractual duty owed to the other party

6.13 If a person is under a contractual duty to do something, a mere promise to perform it (or mere performance of it) cannot be good consideration for another promise by the person to whom the contractual duty is already owed. In *Stilk v Myrick*,[1] the crew of a ship were paid a lump sum for a voyage including all normal emergencies. During the voyage two of the crew deserted and the captain promised to pay the wages of the deserters to the rest of the crew if they would continue the voyage short-handed. Once returned to England, the extra wages were not paid and the seamen sued. Their claim failed, the court finding that they had provided no consideration since they were required to cope with normal emergencies by their existing contracts. Desertion or death of fellow crew members was a normal emergency so they had done no more than they had contracted to do. But the court stressed that, if they had promised to do more than they were obliged to do by their existing contracts, they would have provided good consideration. For example, if they had promised to face exceptional hazards that would have been good consideration for their employer's promise.[2]

In *Williams v Roffey Bros & Nicholls (Contractors) Ltd*[3] the Court of Appeal propounded a major limitation on the principle in *Stilk v Myrick*. It held that, where A makes a further promise to B in return for B's promise to perform his contractual obligations already owed to A, and as a result of B's promise (or performance) A obtains a practical benefit (or avoids a 'disbenefit'), B provides good consideration for A's further promise. The facts of this case were that the plaintiff had been engaged by the defendants, who were the main contractors in refurbishing a block of flats, to carry out carpentry work for £20,000 which turned out to be unprofitable for him. The main contract contained a 'time penalty' clause and, fearful that the plaintiff would not complete the work on time, the defendants promised him an extra £10,300, payable at the rate of £575 per flat, if he carried out the work on time. The plaintiff promised to do so and completed the work in a number of flats, but was not paid the amount promised. The Court of Appeal held that the plaintiff could recover the unpaid amount; the defendants' promise was binding, consideration having been given for it by the plaintiff, since his promise benefited the defendants (apparently by avoiding the penalty for delay and avoiding the trouble and expense of engaging other people to complete the carpentry work). The Court of Appeal added that, if the defendant's promise had been obtained by duress or fraud, the contract could have been set aside on that ground.[4]

Since it is unlikely that A will make a further promise to B if he is not going to obtain some benefit from B's promise to perform (or performance of) his contractual obligations owed to A, the decision appeared to refine the principle in *Stilk v Myrick* almost out of existence. However, in the subsequent case of *Re Selectmove Ltd*[5] the Court of Appeal took a restrictive approach to its decision in *Williams v Roffey Bros*, saying that it did not apply where the existing obligation was one to pay money. It held that a promise to pay (or the payment of) money already due could not be consideration for the promise of another. The Court emphasised that the existing obligation in *Williams v Roffey Bros* was to do work and supply materials and distinguished that case on that ground.

1   (1809) 2 Camp 317. For an affirmation of this rule, see *Syros Shipping Co SA v Elaghill Trading Co, The Proodos C* [1981] 3 All ER 189.
2   *Hartley v Ponsonby* (1857) 7 E & B 872; *North Ocean Shipping Co Ltd v Hyundai Construction Co, The Atlantic Baron* [1978] 3 All ER 1170.
3   [1990] 1 All ER 512, CA.
4   Ch 14 below.
5   [1995] 2 All ER 531, CA.

Performance of an existing contractual duty owed to a third party

6.14   If a party to a contract with X (the 'third party') is obliged by it to perform some action, a subsequent promise by him to perform that action (or his performance of it) can be good consideration for a promise by another person, whether or not there is any benefit to that person. The principle in *Stilk v Myrick*[1] has never applied to this situation. In *Scotson v Pegg*,[2] for example, the plaintiffs had contracted to deliver coal to X, or wherever X ordered it to be delivered. X sold the coal to the defendant and told the plaintiffs to deliver it to him. The defendant then promised the plaintiffs that if they delivered the coal he would unload it at a given rate. The defendant failed to unload at this rate and, when sued, argued that the plaintiffs had not provided consideration for his promise by delivering the coal, because they were obliged to do so under their contracts with X. The court held that the plaintiffs had provided consideration.

In two modern cases, *New Zealand Shipping Co Ltd v A M Satterthwaite & Co Ltd, The Eurymedon*[3] and *Pao On v Lau Yiu Long*,[4] the Privy Council has affirmed that a promise to discharge, or the discharge of, a pre-existing contractual obligation to a third party can be valid consideration for another's promise. In the former case, consideration for the promise consisted of unloading a ship which the promisee was already bound to unload under a contract with a third party.

1   See para 6.13 above.
2   (1861) 6 H & N 295.
3   [1974] 1 All ER 1015, PC.
4   [1979] 3 All ER 65, PC.

Part payment of debts

6.15   *Position at common law* It is not surprising that, if A is under a contractual obligation to pay B and B agrees to forego part of the debt, A's payment of the rest of the debt (ie his partial performance of his existing obligation to B) is not consideration for B's promise and, according to the common law, B can subsequently recover the remainder of the debt. In *Foakes v Beer*,[1] Mrs Beer was owed money under a judgment debt by Dr Foakes. She agreed to accept payment by instalments but the agreement did not refer to the question of interest, which is payable on a judgment debt. Dr Foakes paid the debt. Mrs Beer then sued for the interest. In reply, Dr Foakes pleaded the agreement between them, in which Mrs Beer had agreed to bring no further action on the judgment. Mrs Beer contended successfully that there was no consideration for her promise and that, therefore, it was not binding. Dr Foakes' payment by instalments of the judgment debts could not be consideration for a promise by her to take no further action. He was merely paying less than what he was obliged to do. The House of Lords regretted that this decision had to be reached, but considered itself bound by previous cases.

There are exceptions to the rule that part payment of a debt is no consideration for a promise to remit the rest of the debt. In *Pinnel's Case*,[2] for instance, it was said that, provided it was done at the creditor's request, early payment of part of a debt, or part payment at another place than that specified for payment, or payment in kind, even if the value of the goods is less than the debt, is good consideration for a promise by the creditor to forego the remainder of the debt. Thus, if A owes B £100 payable on 1 January 2001 at Reading and, at B's request, A pays £1 on 31 December (or pays £1 at Leicester on the correct day, or gives B a rose or a scarf on the correct day), the debt is validly discharged. It used to be thought that a part payment by cheque was good consideration for a promise to remit a debt payable in cash. This has been rejected by the Court of Appeal who decided that nowadays there is no effective difference between cash and a cheque which is honoured.[3]

1   (1884) 9 App Cas 605, HL.
2   (1602) 5 Co Rep 117a.
3   *D & C Builders Ltd v Rees* [1965] 3 All ER 837, CA.

6.16   There are two somewhat anomalous areas where partial payment of a debt discharges it. Both areas concern debts. First, where a debtor makes an arrangement with all his creditors that they will all be paid a given percentage of what they are owed, no creditor who has been paid it can recover more than that given percentage.[1] Second, when a third party pays part of a debt in full settlement, that is a valid discharge of the whole debt, and the creditor cannot recover the balance from the debtor.[2] The reason which has been given is that it would be a fraud on the third party if the creditor could do so.[3]

Neither of these areas can satisfactorily be explained in terms of principle (ie consideration by the debtor for the creditor's promise) and are best explained as based on grounds of public policy.

1   *Good v Cheesman* (1831) 2 B & Ad 328.
2   *Welby v Drake* (1825) 1 C & P 557; *Hirachand Punamchand v Temple* [1911] 2 KB 330, CA.
3   *Hirachand Punamchand v Temple* [1911] 2 KB 330, CA.

6.17   *Position in equity* Apart from these exceptions it appeared that a debtor who paid part of a debt, believing that the creditor had agreed to remit the remainder of the debt, had no defence if the creditor sought to recover the amount foregone. However, in 1947 Denning J (as he was then) called upon equity to aid the debtor. In *Central London Property Trust Ltd v High Trees House Ltd*,[1] the plaintiffs let a block of flats to the defendants in 1937 for 99 years at a rent of £2,500 per year. The defendants intended to sub-let the flats but, because of the war, found they had many vacant flats and could not pay the rent out of profits. The plaintiffs agreed to accept a reduced rent of £1,250, which was paid quarterly from 1941 until September 1945, by which time all the flats were let. The plaintiffs demanded full rent from September 1945 and claimed the amount of rent underpaid during the previous quarter. The defendants had provided no consideration for the promise by the plaintiffs to remit the rent, but Denning J found that, while the common law could provide no defence in such a case, equity could. The judge, drawing on two little-known cases decided in the 19th century, said that where one party gave a promise which he intended to be binding and to be acted on, and which was acted on, that promise could be raised as a defence by the promisee if the promisor sought to enforce his strict legal rights. In this case the plaintiffs had promised to reduce the rent; they intended their promise to be binding, they knew the defendants would act on it and the defendants did so act; therefore the rent underpaid in the past could not be demanded by the plaintiffs since this would be inequitable. However, the judge found that the promise was understood by the parties only to apply under the conditions prevailing at the time it was made, namely when the flats were only partially let, and that when the flats became fully let, early in 1945, the promise to remit part of the rent ceased to bind the plaintiffs. The judge also suggested that a promise of this type might be terminated by notice. This case illustrates the equitable doctrine known as promissory estoppel,[2] which applies to promises to remit debts (in whole or part) and also to promises not to enforce other contractual rights.

1   [1956] 1 All ER 256n.
2   Estoppel (as opposed to promissory estoppel) is a legal doctrine whereby if a person misrepresents to another an existing fact and intends this misrepresentation to be acted on, and it is acted on by the other who suffers detriment in consequence, he cannot subsequently deny the truth of that fact. The doctrine was inapplicable in the *High Trees* case because the representation was as to the future and not to an existing fact.

Promissory estoppel
6.18   Under the doctrine of promissory estoppel a promise not to enforce a contractual right is given some effect, despite the absence of consideration for it, where it would be inequitable for the promisor simply to go back on his promise and enforce that right. There is authority that the doctrine can even apply where the promise is made before the contract is entered into, as where a person who is negotiating to lease property to another promises not to enforce a repairing covenant in the draft lease.[1] This goes beyond the previous authorities, which required or assumed that there must be an existing relationship between promisor and promisee when the promise was made, and its compatibility with certain other rules of the law of contract is as yet explained.[2]

1   *Brikom Investments Ltd v Carr* [1979] 2 All ER 753 at 758.
2   Such as the law relating to pre-contractual misrepresentations: ch 14.

6.19   The precise scope of promissory estoppel is still not entirely clear; indeed, in *Woodhouse A C Israel Cocoa Ltd SA v Nigerian Produce Marketing Co Ltd*,[1] Lord Hailsham LC said that it may need to be reviewed and reduced to a coherent body of doctrine by the courts. Nevertheless, its requirements appear to be as follows:

Unequivocal promise   There must be an unequivocal promise[2] by one party that he will not, at least for the time being, enforce his strict contractual rights against the other. The promise may be either express or implied from conduct.[3] Silence and inaction cannot by themselves give rise to a promissory estoppel because they are by their nature equivocal, since there can be more than one reason why the party concerned is silent and inactive.[4]

Alteration of position   The promisor must have intended that his promise should be acted on by the promisee, and the promisee must have acted on it in the sense of altering his position in reliance on the promise.[5] This requirement was satisfied in *Hughes v Metropolitan Rly Co*,[6] where a tenant, who had been given six months' notice to repair the premises in accordance with a repairing covenant but who had been induced by the landlord's conduct soon afterwards to believe that the lease would not be forfeited for failure to repair, failed to repair in reliance on this belief. It is not so easy to discern an alteration of position in the *High Trees* case, but the requirement has been said to be satisfied by the fact that the lessees elected to pay a lower rent and to continue liable as lessees in reliance on the lessor's promise that a lower rent would be accepted in satisfaction.[7]

The present requirement means that promissory estoppel cannot arise if the promisee does nothing, by action or inaction, in reliance on the promise but simply does what he was going to do anyway regardless of whether or not the promise was made.[8] This is illustrated by *Fontana NV v Mautner*.[9] T, the tenant of a flat which was not subject to the Rent Act, refused to leave when his tenancy expired, on the grounds that he had been a model tenant for many years and that a move would be disastrous for the health of his chronically-ill wife. At a meeting with a representative of the landlord, T was assured by the representative that he could stay on in the flat as long as he wished, but he subsequently received a notice to quit. In proceedings for possession, Balcombe J rejected T's claim that the assurance gave rise to a promissory estoppel, and made an order for possession. The judge held that this was not a case of promissory estoppel because T had done nothing, by action or inaction, in reliance on the assurance but had simply done what he was going to do anyway (and that was to sit tight for as long as he possibly could).

Inequitable for promisor to resile   It must be inequitable for the promisor to go back on his promise, having regard to the course of dealings which has taken place between the parties.[10] Normally, the present requirement will be satisfied if the promisee has altered his position in reliance on the promise. However, this will not always be the case, as is shown by *The Post Chaser*,[11] where the promisors resiled from their promise not to enforce their strict rights only two days after making it. It was held that this was not inequitable because, in this short period, the promisees had not suffered any prejudice, despite having relied on the promise.

The present requirement has another aspect; even if it can be said that the promisee has suffered 'detriment', it is not inequitable for the promisor to go back on his promise, and the promisee is therefore not protected by promissory estoppel, if the promise has been procured by improper pressure or fraud on the part of the promisee or an associate (or by other similar conduct which would render it unfair to the promisor to hold him to his promise). In *D & C Builders Ltd v Rees*,[12] the plaintiffs were owed £482 by the defendant who knew that they were in desperate need of money to stave off bankruptcy. The defendant's wife offered the plaintiffs £300 in settlement of the debt, saying in effect that if they refused they would get nothing. The plaintiffs accepted the £300 reluctantly in settlement of the debt but later sued successfully for the balance. Lord Denning MR refused to allow the defendant to rely on promissory estoppel; his wife's conduct had been improper and therefore it was not inequitable for the plaintiffs to go back on their promise and insist on their strict contractual right to payment of the balance.

1   [1972] 2 All ER 271 at 282.
2   *Woodhouse A C Israel Cocoa Ltd SA v Nigerian Produce Marketing Co Ltd* [1972] 2 All ER 271, HL; *China Pacific SA v Food Corpn of India, The Winson* [1980] 3 All ER 556, CA (revsd on other grounds [1981] 3 All ER 688, HL); *Scandinavian Trading Tanker Co AB v Flota Petrolera Ecuatoriana, The Scaptrade* [1983] 1 All ER 301, CA (affd [1983] 2 All ER 763, HL).
3   *Hughes v Metropolitan Rly Co* (1877) 2 App Cas 439, HL; *B P Exploration Co (Libya) Ltd v Hunt (No 2)* [1979] 1 WLR 783 at 810.
4   *Allied Maritime Transport Ltd v Vale do Rio Doce Navegaeao SA, The Leonidas D* [1985] 2 All ER 796, CA.
5   *Hughes v Metropolitan Rly Co* (1877) 2 App Cas 439, HL; *Central London Property Trust Ltd v High Trees House Ltd* [1947] KB 130, [1956] 1 All ER 256n; *Tool Metal Manufacturing Co Ltd v Tungsten Electric Co Ltd* [1955] 2 All ER 657, HL; *Ajayi v R T Briscoe (Nigeria) Ltd* [1964] 3 All ER 556, PC. Cf. *Brikom Investments Ltd v Carr* [1979] 2 All ER 753 at 758–759.
6   (1877) 2 App Cas 439, HL.
7   Spencer Bower and Turner *Estoppel by Misrepresentation* (3rd edn) p 393.
8   *Fontana NV v Mautner* (1979) 254 Estates Gazette 199; *Scandinavian Trading Tanker Co AB v Flota Petrolera Ecuatoriana, The Scaptrade* [1983] 1 All ER 301, CA (affd [1983] 2 All ER 763, HL).
9   (1979) 254 Estates Gazette 199.
10 *Hughes v Metropolitan Railway* (1877) 2 App Cas 439, HL; *Birmingham and District Land Co v London and North Western Rly Co* (1888) 40 Ch D 268 at 286; *Tool Metal Manufacturing Co Ltd v Tungsten Electric Co Ltd* [1955] 2 All ER 657, HL; *Ajayi v R T Briscoe (Nigeria) Ltd* [1964] 3 All ER 556, PC.
11 *Société Italo-Belge pour le Commerce et l'Industrie SA v Palm and Vegetable Oils (Malaysian) Sdn Bhd* [1982] 1 All ER 19.
12 [1965] 3 All ER 837, CA.

6.20   *Effect of promissory estoppel* Generally, promissory estoppel only suspends, and does not discharge (ie does not wholly extinguish), an obligation. Where promissory estoppel operates to suspend an obligation, the promisor may, by giving reasonable notice to the promisee, revert to his strict contractual rights thereafter.[1] If a promise not to enforce a strict contractual right was clearly intended to be operative only for a certain period, as in the *High Trees* case, the promisor automatically reverts to that right on the expiry of the period, if he has not previously determined his promise by giving reasonable notice.[2]

Where an obligation has been suspended, the effect of the promisor's reversion to the strict contractual position varies. If the obligation is to pay a lump sum or to perform some other act, such as to repair under a repairing covenant in a lease, the effect of a reversion is that after the period of reasonable notice the promisee must then perform his strict contractual obligation. An example is provided by *Hughes v Metropolitan Rly Co*,[3] discussed above, where the House of Lords held that the six months' notice to repair which had been suspended ran from the time of the landlord's reversion to his strict contractual rights. On the other hand, where the obligation in question is to make periodic payments (such as the payment of rent) or to make some other performance by instalments, a reversion to the strict contractual position, after a promise to accept part payment (or part performance) in lieu or to waive it entirely, results in the promisee being liable to make future payments (or other performance) in full in respect of instalments due after the period of reasonable notice, but (unless the promise otherwise provides) does not render him liable to pay (or perform) what was due, and unpaid (or unperformed), during the currency of the estoppel.[4]

Exceptionally, the effect of promissory estoppel may be to make a promise irrevocable, and thereby to discharge, and not just suspend, the promisee's obligations. A promise subject to promissory estoppel becomes irrevocable if the promisee cannot revert to his strict contractual position.[5]

1   *Tool Metal Manufacturing Co Ltd v Tungsten Electric Co Ltd* [1955] 2 All ER 657, HL; *Ajayi v R T Briscoe (Nigeria) Ltd* [1964] 3 All ER 556, PC. Cf *D & C Builders Ltd v Rees* [1965] 3 All ER 837 at 841; *Brikom Investments Ltd v Carr* [1979] 2 All ER 753 at 758.

2   *Birmingham and District Land Co Ltd v London and North Western Rly Co* (1888) 40 Ch D 268 at 288.

3   (1877) 2 App Cas 439, HL.

4   *Central London Property Trust Ltd v High Trees House Ltd* [1947] KB 130, [1956] 1 All ER 256n; *Tungsten Electric Co Ltd v Tool Metal Manufacturing Co Ltd* (1950) 69 RPC 108, CA; *Tool Metal Manufacturing Co Ltd v Tungsten Electric Co Ltd* [1955] 2 All ER 657, HL.

5   *Ajayi v R T Briscoe (Nigeria) Ltd* [1964] 3 All ER 556, PC.

6.21   *A shield, not a sword* Promissory estoppel only prevents the promisor from enforcing his strict rights (at least, without reasonable notice) despite the absence of consideration from the promisee for the promise; it cannot be used to found a cause of action. In *Combe v Combe*,[1] an ex-husband promised, informally, to pay his divorced wife maintenance. In reliance on his promise she did not bring court proceedings for financial provision. He failed to pay and she sued him. She had provided no consideration for his promise because he had not requested her not to bring proceedings for financial provision. Consequently, she alleged that he was estopped from going back on his promise (so that it was binding on him) because she had relied on his promise. The Court of Appeal rejected her claim, on the ground that promissory estoppel was a shield and not a sword.

1   [1951] 1 All ER 767, CA. Also see *Argy Trading Development Co Ltd v Lapid Developments Ltd* [1977] 3 All ER 785; *Syros Shipping Co SA v Elaghill Trading Co, The Proodos C* [1981] 3 All ER 189.

Consideration: discharge and variation

6.22   We have seen that consideration is necessary for the formation of contracts which are not made by deed, and that a promise by the creditor to remit a debt is not binding at common law without the provision of consideration by the debtor.[1] Consideration is also necessary when the parties agree (otherwise than by deed) to discharge (ie end) or to vary their contract before it is completely performed. Otherwise, the agreement is not binding at common law.

1   For two cases which are probable exceptions, see para 6.16 above.

6.23   The discharge of a contract by agreement may be either mutual or unilateral. It will be mutual, subject to the rules discussed later, where both parties still have contractual obligations to perform, ie there is executory consideration on both sides; it will be unilateral, subject to what we say in para 6.25 below, where one party still has contractual obligations to perform but the other party has completed his performance of the contract.

Mutual discharge

6.24   An agreement to discharge a contract must be supported by consideration. However, if both parties still have contractual obligations to perform, any agreement to discharge the contract relieves both parties from further performance of it. In such a case, both parties have provided consideration, for each party promises not to require further performance of contractual obligations by the other party in return for being absolved himself from further performance.

Unilateral discharge

6.25 A unilateral discharge by agreement is only effective if the party to be absolved has provided separate consideration for the other's promise to absolve him. In other words, where one party has performed all his contractual obligations prior to the agreement, his promise to release the other party from further performance does not bind him unless that other party provides separate consideration. Unilateral discharge by agreement is also known as accord (agreement to discharge) and satisfaction (consideration for that agreement). In relation to whether simply performing (or promising) to perform the existing contractual obligation (in whole or part) in response to a promise of release can constitute consideration, the reader is referred to paras 6.13 and 6.15 above, in particular.

Accord without satisfaction is ineffective to discharge a contract. Satisfaction usually consists of doing something in return for the promise to discharge, but the satisfaction which is offered may be a promise to do something. If so, it is necessary to decide whether the original contract is discharged from the moment of the accord or only when the promise, which is the alleged satisfaction, has been translated into action. It is a question of construction. If the accord can be construed to mean that the promise to do something was intended to be satisfaction, the original contract is discharged from the making of the accord.[1] However, if, on its true construction, the accord means that *performance* of a promise to do something was intended to be satisfaction, the original contract can only be discharged when the promise is performed.

Promissory estoppel[2] may be available as a defence to a person who has been promised a release from further performance in circumstances where his obligation has not been discharged by accord and satisfaction because he has not provided consideration for the promise.

1   See, for example, *Elton Cop Dyeing Co Ltd v Robert Broadbent & Son Ltd* (1919) 89 LJKB 186, CA.
2   Paras 6.17–6.21 above.

Variation

6.26 If the variation of a contract benefits both parties (or could benefit one or other of them[1] depending on the outcome of a contingency) it will have contractual effect because each party will provide consideration for the other's variation promise, but it will have no effect (because of lack of consideration) if it can only be of benefit to one party. Suppose that a contract between A and B requires A to deliver 100 tons of copper to B in Leicester on 1 June. If A and B agree that A should, instead, deliver 95 tons on 1 May (or 100 tons on 1 July in Reading) the variation has contractual effect because it benefits both parties; in contrast, a variation whereby B agreed to accept the delivery of 95 tons in Leicester on 1 June would have no contractual effect, because it could only be of benefit to A, except that it might have a limited effect by virtue of the doctrine of promissory estoppel.

1   As where the variation consists of the alteration of the currency of payment, whose exchange rate against the original currency of payment may go up or down by the time payment is due: *W J Alan & Co Ltd v El Nasr Export and Import Co* [1972] 2 All ER 127, CA.

Chapter 7

Privity of contract

7.1   In order to enforce a contractual promise by another, the promisee must show:

* unless the contract was made by deed, that he (or an agent on his behalf) has provided consideration for the other's promise; and
* that he is a party to the contract in question.

Subject to certain recognised exceptions, a person who does not satisfy these requirements is not entitled to enforce the contract, even if it was intended to benefit him and he has provided consideration. Suggested reasons are:

* that mere donees should not be able to enforce a contract; and
* that the parties to the contract should not have their freedom to vary it restricted by the existence of third-party rights.

7.2   Another aspect of the doctrine of privity of contract is that, subject to exceptions, a contract cannot impose obligations (burdens) on a third party to it.

Benefits

Enforcement by the party intended to benefit
7.3   Prior to *Tweddle v Atkinson*,[1] a benefit enforceable by a third person could be conferred on him if there was some family relationship between him and one of the contracting parties. However, in *Tweddle v Atkinson*, a contract between the plaintiff's father and X for the benefit of the plaintiff was regarded as unenforceable by the plaintiff because he was not a party to the contract and had not provided consideration.

It may be possible to confer a benefit which he can enforce on someone not really involved in a contract by making him a party to it, even if in name only. However, that party will only be able to enforce the promised benefit if he has provided consideration for the promise. This is subject to the following possible exception. Suppose that a contract is made in which A on the one part and B and C, on the other, are named as parties, and that in response to A's promise B promises 'on behalf of [himself] and C' to do something. Can B's promise, expressed as it is, constitute consideration on C's part, so that C can enforce A's promise? The answer 'yes' is persuasively provided in the Australian case of *Coulls v Bagot's Executor and Trustee Co Ltd*,[2] where a contract for the right to quarry a mine made all royalties payable to the owner of the land, who had granted the right, and his wife, jointly. The High Court of Australia was not unanimous about the meaning of the contract but a majority was agreed that, if she was a party to the contract, the wife was entitled to the royalties after her husband's death, even though she had personally provided no consideration for it, because the promise to pay her and her husband was supported by consideration furnished by the husband expressly on behalf of himself and his wife. The basis of the wife's entitlement was that joint consideration had been provided by the husband and wife through the husband's promise expressed to be on behalf of both of them. The concept of joint consideration may be acceptable if there is a *genuine* joint consideration (ie where A looks to C to honour the promise if B does not). However, there cannot be a genuine joint consideration when, as in *Coulls*, it is clear that C is not able (legally or physically) to honour the promise made by B on his behalf, as where C does not own the subject matter which B has promised to sell to A. For this reason, it is submitted that *Coulls* goes further than is legitimate.

1   (1861) 1 B & S 393.
2   [1967] ALR 385.

7.4   The fact that, under the doctrine of privity, a third party to a contract is not entitled by virtue of the contract itself to enforce a benefit arising under it does not mean that a contract can never indirectly benefit him. For example, if it is foreseeable that negligent performance of a contract by a party to it will cause physical injury to a third party, that party may owe a duty of care to the third party and be liable to him in the tort of negligence if he is in breach of that duty. By way of another example, surveyors, accountants and other professional people may be held liable in tort to people who are not their clients if they cause them foreseeable economic loss in negligently carrying out a contract made with a client. However, it is exceptional for a person to be held liable in tort for negligently causing foreseeable economic loss. We discuss liability in tort in Part III; chapter 18 is particularly relevant in the present context.

Exceptions and qualifications

7.5   There are certain established exceptions and qualifications to the doctrine of privity of contract. If an agent enters into an authorised contract with a third party on behalf of his principal, there is a contract between the principal and the third party.[1] It is possible to assign rights under a contract.[2] A third party can sue on a bill of exchange or cheque.[3] Beneficiaries under certain types of contract of insurance have a statutory right to claim the benefit of the contract even if they are not parties to it. An example is where one spouse has made a life insurance contract which is expressed to be for the benefit of the other.[4] In certain circumstances, a third party to a contract can take the benefit of a clause in it excluding or restricting liability.[5]

The requirements of land law have also necessitated some modifications of the strict rules of privity. The benefits of covenants in leases are transferred to successors in title of the landlord and tenant, despite the absence of privity, if the covenants affect the land.[6]

1   Ch 16.
2   See Card and James *Law for Accountancy Students* (6th edn), Ch 22.
3   Bills of Exchange Act 1882, s 29.
4   Married Women's Property Act 1882, s 11.
5   Paras 10.15 and 10.16, below.
6   Law of Property Act 1925, ss 78, 141 and 142. See paras 36.45-36.47 and 38.23-38.24 below.

7.6 The above situations are exceptions or qualifications to the doctrine of privity. It may also be possible to outflank the rule. For example, if a collateral contract can be found, a person not a party to the principal contract can sue on the collateral contract instead. In *Shanklin Pier Ltd v Detel Products Ltd,*[1] the plaintiffs employed contractors to paint their pier and instructed them to buy and use the defendants' paint. The defendants had told the plaintiffs the paint would last for seven to ten years, but it lasted for only three months. It was held that, while the plaintiffs could not sue on the contract of sale of the paint, to which they were not parties, they could sue on a collateral contract between them and the defendants which contained a promise by the defendants that the paint would last seven to ten years. The plaintiffs had provided consideration for the collateral contract by requiring their contractors to use the defendants' paint.

1   [1951] 2 All ER 471.

7.7 Another method of evasion of the privity doctrine is the use of a trust. The subject matter of a trust is normally tangible property, but when used in this context the subject matter of the trust is the right to sue on the promise given by one party to a contract to the other party that he will benefit a third party; a right to sue on a contract is an intangible piece of property. In equity, if a trust of a right to sue on a promise can be discovered, the courts will enforce an agreement for the benefit of the third party; he is regarded as a beneficiary and the party contracting for his benefit as a trustee. In *Lloyd's v Harper,*[1] Lush LJ said that, 'when a contract is made with A for the benefit of B, A can sue on the contract for the benefit of B and recover all that B could have recovered if the contract had been made by B himself'. The case concerned a contract which guaranteed that the creditors of a Lloyd's underwriter would be paid. The contract was with Lloyd's, not the creditors, but the Court of Appeal held that Lloyd's could recover on behalf of the creditors, and not merely for their own loss. The difficulty with using the trust concept to defeat the doctrine of privity is that it is not certain when it will apply, and the type of trust recognised by these cases cannot be regarded as the usual type of trust which is subject to strict rules clearly inapplicable here. The decision in *Lloyd's v Harper* allowed the trustee-party to recover for the third party beneficiary (the creditors in that case); it did not give a right to sue to the third party beneficiary. However, it seems that if the third party beneficiary wishes to sue he can do so by joining as co-plaintiff the trustee-party.[2] If the trustee-party pursues a claim for the third party beneficiary any damages are payable to the third party beneficiary. If the trustee-party refuses to sue either alone or as co-plaintiff, there seems no reason why he should not be joined as co-defendant in an action by the third party beneficiary.

1   (1880) 16 Ch D 290, CA.
2   *Les Affréteurs Réunis SA v Leopold Walford (London) Ltd* [1919] AC 801, HL.

7.8 The difficulty with using the trust concept to defeat the doctrine of privity is that it is not certain when it will apply. Although no formal words are required, an intention to create a trust, not merely an intention to benefit a third party, must exist, and this is the principal reason why the application of the trust concept is uncertain. In modern times, the courts generally seem reluctant to impute such an intention, in the absence of clear words. For example, in *Re Schebsman,*[1] decided in 1943, a contract between Schebsman and X Ltd, which provided that in certain circumstances his wife and daughter should be paid a lump sum, was held not to create a trust. The Court of Appeal was influenced by the fact that Schebsman and the company might have wished to vary the agreement, which would have been impossible had the contract created a trust.

Beswick v Beswick,[2] the most important modern case on privity of contract, does not discuss trusts and so this attempt to outflank privity seems to have been limited by the courts.

1   [1943] 2 All ER 768, CA.
2   [1967] 2 All ER 1197, HL.

Enforcement by a party to the contract

7.9   The party who was promised that the benefit would be conferred on the third party may be prepared to sue if the other party to the agreement does not carry out his contractual obligations. Damages, the usual remedy for failure to perform contractual obligations, are available, but, unless the contracting party is suing as agent or trustee for the third party, he cannot recover any damages on behalf of the third party in respect of his loss[1]. The reason is that generally[2] a plaintiff can only recover damages for the loss which he has suffered.[3] If the contract was intended solely to benefit the third party, so that the contracting party has suffered no loss, only nominal damages (usually in the region of £2 to £20) will be recoverable by the contracting party.[4]

This being so, it is preferable for the contracting party to seek the enforcement of the contract by means of the equitable remedy of specific performance. The advantages of this remedy are illustrated by *Beswick v Beswick*.[5] In this case, in consideration of Peter Beswick transferring his business to his nephew, the nephew agreed to pay his uncle a pension and, after his death, a weekly annuity to his widow. The nephew paid his uncle the pension but only one payment of the annuity was made. The widow, an administratrix of her husband's estate, successfully sued her nephew for specific performance of the contract to pay the annuity, although the House of Lords held that she would not have succeeded if she had sued merely as the intended recipient. Thus, if specific performance of a contract can be ordered, a party to a contract or his personal representative can ensure enforcement of the contract for the benefit of a third party. However, it would be wrong to think that specific performance will always be ordered in the present type of case. It is a discretionary remedy and is subject to a number of other limits described in paras 12.29 and 12.30 below.

1   If the contracting party sues for, and recovers, damages for the third party as agent or trustee, he will be obliged as trustee or agent to hand over the damages to the third party. Although there is no binding authority on this point, it seems that, in any other case where the contracting party can, and does, recover damages in respect of the third party's loss, the third party may recover any damages obtained by the contracting party in respect of it, either under the law of restitution (*Jackson v Horizon Holidays Ltd* [1975] 3 All ER 92 at 96) or on the basis that the contracting party holds the damages in trust for the third party (*Darlington Borough Council v Wiltshier Northern Ltd* [1995] 3 All ER 895 at 902–903 and 908).
2   For exceptional cases where a contracting party can recover damages for loss suffered by another, see para 12.2 below.
3   If the contract is one to provide a contracting party with a benefit which others will also enjoy, such as a contract for a family holiday or a group coach trip, he is entitled to substantial damages for his loss (the family holiday or group coach trip) if the other party breaks the contract by failing to provide the benefit: *Jackson v Horizon Holidays Ltd* [1975] 3 All ER 92, CA, as explained in *Woodar Investment Development Ltd v Wimpey Construction UK Ltd* [1980] 1 All ER 571, HL.
4   *Beswick v Beswick* [1967] 2 All ER 1197, HL.
5   [1967] 2 All ER 1197, HL.

Burdens

7.10   As we have already indicated, the general rule is that only a person who is a party to a contract can be subject to any obligations contained in it; consequently, a third party cannot generally be sued for contravening a provision in a contract made between others.[1]

The principal exceptions or qualifications to this general rule can be summarised as follows:

- the burdens of a contract apply to a person on whose behalf the contract was made by an agent;[2]
- the burdens of covenants in leases are transferred to the successors in title of the landlord and tenant, despite the absence of privity of contract, but in the case of leases created before 1 January 1996 only if the covenants affect the land; we discuss this further in paras 36.40 to 36.56 below;
- the burdens of negative covenants affecting the use of land (ie covenants *not* to do specified things on the land), inserted in a contract of sale of land, bind subsequent purchasers of the land, provided certain conditions are satisfied; we discuss this further in paras 38.8 to 38.12 below;
- where someone hands over goods to another for repair, cleaning, carriage, loading or the like, the transaction gives rise to what is called a 'bailment', the transferor being the 'bailor' and the recipient the 'bailee'. If the bailee sub-contracts the work to someone else, the terms of the contract between the bailee and that person will bind the bailor (a third party to the contract, which involves a 'sub-bailment') if the bailee had the bailor's authority to make the sub-bailment and the bailor had expressly or impliedly authorised him to make the sub-bailment on the terms in question;[3]
- in certain cases, the right of a person, by virtue of a contract to which he is party, to make use of a chattel is enforceable against a third party; and
- in certain cases, a third party can be bound by a provision as to the resale price of goods contained in a contract between others.

The last item in this list merits further explanation at this point.

1   For an authority, see *McGruther v Pitcher* [1904] 2 Ch 306, CA. The actual decision in this case would now be governed by the Resale Prices Act 1976, s 9; para 7.11, below.
2   Ch 16.
3   *K H Enterprise (Cargo Owners) v Pioneer Container (Owners), The Pioneer Container* [1994] 2 All ER 250, PC; see further, in respect of exemption clauses, para 10.18.

Restrictions on price

7.11   At common law, a contract of sale which fixed the resale price of goods could not, because of the doctrine of privity, bind a third party who could sell any goods he acquired for whatever price he desired.

The matter is now governed by statute. Under the Resale Prices Act 1976, s 26, a supplier who sells goods under a contract which provides a maximum resale price can enforce that price against anyone not party to the contract who acquires the goods for resale with notice of that maximum resale price. Any attempt to fix a *minimum* price is void by virtue of the Resale Prices Act 1976, s 9, unless the goods are exempt from the operation of the 1976 Act, in which case s 26 of the Act applies and a minimum resale price provision in a contract can be enforced by the supplier against a third party who acquires the goods for resale with notice of the provision.

Chapter 8

Contractual terms

8.1 The terms of a contract may be:

- express; or
- implied.

Express terms

8.2 Clearly, the ascertainment of its express terms is facilitated when the contract has been reduced into writing, particularly because under the 'parol evidence'[1] rule oral or other evidence extrinsic to the document is not admissible generally to add to, vary, or contradict, the terms of the written agreement.[2] However, this rule is not as harsh as might be supposed, since in a number of cases extrinsic evidence is admissible, either as an exception to the parol evidence rule or because the circumstances fall outside its bounds. The following can be mentioned as examples.

1   Parol evidence of a written document means extrinsic evidence, whether oral or otherwise: Jowitt's *Dictionary of English Law.*
2   *Jacobs v Batavia and General Plantations Trust Ltd* [1924] 1 Ch 287 at 295.

Implied terms
8.3 The fact that a contract has been reduced into writing does not prevent extrinsic evidence being given to support or rebut the implication of a term into it[1] under rules which are discussed shortly.

1   *Burges v Wickham* (1863) 3 B & S 669; *Gillespie Bros & Co v Cheney, Eggar & Co* [1896] 2 QB 59.

Conditions precedent
8.4 Extrinsic evidence is admissible to show that, although a written contract appears absolute on its face, it was not intended that a binding contract should be created (or that, although there was an immediate binding contract, a party's obligation to perform would not arise) until the occurrence of a particular event, such as a surveyor's report or the availability of finance.[1]

1   *Pym v Campbell* (1856) 6 E & B 370; para 5.27 above.

Invalidating factors
8.5 Extrinsic evidence of a factor, such as mistake or misrepresentation, which invalidates the written contract is, of course, admissible.

Written contract not the whole contract
8.6 While a document which looks like a contract is presumed to include all the terms of the contract, this presumption may be rebutted by evidence that the parties did not intend all the terms of their contract to be contained in the document.[1] If the presumption is rebutted, extrinsic evidence is admissible to prove the other terms of the contract. An example is provided by the case of *J Evans & Son (Portsmouth) Ltd v Andrea Merzario Ltd,* which is discussed in para 8.12 below.

1   *Gillespie Bros & Co v Cheney, Eggar & Co* [1896] 2 QB 59 at 62.

Collateral contracts
8.7 The parol evidence rule will also be circumvented if the court finds that the parties have made two contracts, the main written one and an oral one collateral to it. An example is provided by *Birch v Paramount Estates Ltd*[1] where the defendants, who were developing a housing estate, offered a house they were then building to the plaintiff, stating orally that it would be as good as the show house. Subsequently, the plaintiff agreed to buy the house but the written contract of sale made no reference to this statement. The completed house was not as good as the show house. The Court of Appeal held that there was an oral contract, to the effect that the house would be as good as the show house, collateral to the contract of sale and upheld the award of damages for its breach.

In essence, a collateral contract exists where A promises B something certain[2] in return for B making the main contract. A's promise must have been intended by the parties to be legally binding and to take effect as a collateral contract, and not merely as a term of the main contract, and it must be supported by separate consideration, although this may simply be B's making of the main contract.[3] Provided these requirements are satisfied, a collateral contract will be valid and enforceable by B, even though it conflicts with a term in the main contract. This is shown by *City and Westminster Properties (1934) Ltd v Mudd.*[4] In 1941, the defendant became the tenant of a lock-up shop for three years. He was allowed by the landlords, the plaintiffs, to sleep in the shop. In 1944, a second lease for three years was granted to the defendant. In 1947, during negotiations for a new lease, the plaintiffs inserted in the draft lease a clause restricting the use of the premises to trade purposes only. The defendant objected and was told by the plaintiffs' agent that, if he accepted the new lease as it stood, the plaintiffs would not object to him residing on the premises. In consequence, the defendant signed the lease. Later, the plaintiffs sought to forfeit the lease for breach of the covenant only to use the premises for trade purposes. It was held that the defendant could plead the collateral contract as a defence to a charge of breach of the main contract, the lease.

1   (1956) 167 Estates Gazette 396, CA.
2   *Wake v Renault (UK) Ltd* (1996) Times, 1 August, CA.
3   *Heilbut, Symons & Co v Buckleton* [1913] AC 30, HL.
4   [1958] 2 All ER 733.

Determination of whether a written term is a term of contract
8.8 The determination of whether what purports to be a term of the contract is indeed a term of the contract can sometimes give rise to nice questions. It depends very much on whether or not the term is contained in a signed contractual document. If it is, the

general rule is that it is a contractual term binding on a party who signed the document, even though he was unaware of it because he had not read the document.[1] This is so even though that party is, to the other's knowledge, illiterate or unfamiliar with the English language.[2] An exception is where the party seeking to rely on a term has misrepresented to the other its contents or effect. In such a case, the term is rendered ineffective to the extent that it differs from the misrepresentation.[3]

Where the term is not contained in a contractual document signed by the party against whom it is being relied, eg where it is printed on a ticket or an order form or a notice, the term will only be a contractual term if adequate notice of it is given. The law in this respect has largely been developed in relation to a particular type of term, an exemption clause, and we deal with it in relation to such a clause in paras 10.4 - 10.7 below.

1   *L'Estrange v F Graucob Ltd* [1934] 2 KB 394, DC.
2   *Barclays Bank plc v Schwartz* (1995) Times, 2 August, CA.
3   *Curtis v Chemical Cleaning and Dyeing Co Ltd* [1951] 1 All ER 631, CA.

Contractual terms and mere representations

8.9   Where contractual terms are oral they must be proved by the evidence of the parties and other witnesses in the event of a dispute.

Problems can sometimes arise concerning whether a written or oral statement, which is made in contractual negotiations and not explicitly referred to at the time the contract is made, is nevertheless a term of the contract instead of being a mere representation. The present issue can be exemplified as follows. At the time the contract was made A may simply have said to B: 'I offer you £3,000 for the car' to which B replied 'I accept'. These two sentences will probably be the culmination of previous, and perhaps lengthy, negotiations between the parties during which B will have given A a number of assurances as to the condition of the car, its mileage and so on. Whether these pre-contractual statements are contractual terms or undertakings, or simply mere representations, is of importance for the following reason. Breach of a contractual term results in liability in damages, and certain other remedies for breach of contract may also be available to the 'injured party'. On the other hand, if a mere representation turns out to be false there can be no liability for breach of contract, although it *may* be possible for the misrepresentee to have the contract set aside (rescinded) for misrepresentation; and in certain circumstances he can recover damages for misrepresentation. Generally speaking, the remedies for misrepresentation are inferior to those for breach of contract. We discuss the subjects of breach of contract, remedies for breach and misrepresentation in chapters 9, 12 and 14, and for the present we are concerned with the question of how it is ascertained whether a pre-contractual statement has become a contractual term.

8.10   A representation will be a contractual term if the parties intended that the representor was making a binding promise as to it.[1] Whether the parties did so intend can only be deduced from all the evidence. Of course, it is always possible for the parties actually to state that a particular representation is or is not a term of their contract. If they do not, then, if an intelligent bystander would infer from the words and behaviour of the parties that a binding promise was intended, that will suffice.[2] In approaching the question of the parties' intentions, the courts take into account factors such as the following.

1   *Oscar Chess Ltd v Williams* [1957] 1 All ER 325 at 327–328.
2   Ibid. See also *Howard Marine and Dredging Co Ltd v A Ogden & Sons (Excavations) Ltd* [1978] 2 All ER 1134 at 1140.

Execution of a written contract

8.11 If the representation was followed by a written contract in which it does not appear, it will probably (but not necessarily) be regarded as a mere representation[1] since, because of the parol evidence rule, it can only take effect as a contractual term if the court finds that the parties intended that the contract should not be contained wholly in the written document or that the representation should form part of a collateral contract. An example of a case where a pre-contractual representation was found to be a contractual term despite the subsequent execution of a written contract is *J Evans & Son (Portsmouth) Ltd v Andrea Merzario Ltd*, which is discussed in the next paragraph.

1   *Heilbut, Symons & Co v Buckleton* [1913] AC 30 at 50; *Oscar Chess Ltd v Williams* [1957] 1 All ER 325 at 329.

The importance of the representation

8.12 The more important the subject matter of the representation the more likely it is that the parties intended a binding promise concerning it. In particular, if the representation was so important that without it the representee would not have made the contract, the court is very likely to hold that it is a contractual term. In *J Evans & Son (Portsmouth) Ltd v Andrea Merzario Ltd*,[1] the plaintiffs bought some machines from an Italian company. They had previously employed the defendants to arrange transport, and the machinery had always been packed in crates or trailers and carried below deck. On this occasion the defendants' representative told the plaintiffs' that it was proposed that the machinery should be packed in containers. The plaintiffs' representative replied that if containers were used they must be stowed below, and not on, deck in case the machinery rusted. He was assured by the defendants' representative that this would be done but this oral assurance was not included in the written agreement subsequently made between the plaintiffs and the defendants. In fact, the containers were carried on deck and two fell into the sea. In the Court of Appeal, Roskill and Geoffrey Lane LJJ held that the oral assurance had become a term of the contract between the parties, which was not wholly written, and that the plaintiff could recover damages for its breach. Roskill LJ stated that in the light of the totality of the evidence it was clear that the plaintiffs had only agreed to contract with the defendants on the basis that the containers were stowed below deck, and therefore the defendants' assurance concerning this had become a contractual term. Similarly, in *Bannerman v White*,[2] a representation that sulphur had not been used in the treatment of hops was found to have become a term of the subsequent contract. It related to a matter of great importance and the buyer would not have made the contract without it.

1   [1976] 2 All ER 930, CA.
2   (1861) 10 CBNS 844.

Invitation to verify

8.13 If a seller invites the buyer to check his representation it is very unlikely to be regarded as a contractual term. In *Ecay v Godfrey*,[1] for instance, the seller of a boat said that it was sound but advised a survey. It was held that this advice negatived any intention that the representation should be a contractual term. Conversely, if the seller assures the buyer that it is not necessary to verify the representation since he can take the seller's word for it, the representation is likely to be found to be intended to be a term of the resulting contract if the buyer contracts in reliance on it. In *Schawel v Reade*,[2] the plaintiff, who required a stallion for stud purposes, went to the defendant's stables to inspect a horse. While he was inspecting it, the defendant said: 'You need not look for anything: the horse is perfectly sound. If there was anything the matter with the horse I would tell you.' The plaintiff thereupon ended his inspection and a price was agreed three weeks later, the plaintiff relying on the defendant's statement. The House of Lords held that the jury's finding that the defendant's statement was a contractual term was correct.

1   (1947) 80 L1 L Rep 286.
2   (1913) 2 IR 64, HL. Cf *Hopkins v Tanqueray* (1854) 15 CB 130.

Statements of fact, of opinion or as to the future
8.14   A statement of fact is more likely to be construed as intended to have contractual effect than a statement of opinion or as to future facts (eg a forecast).[1] A statement about something which is, or should be, within the promisor's control is very likely to be construed as a contractual term.[2]

1   *Esso Petroleum Co Ltd v Mardon* [1976] 2 All ER 5 at 20.
2   *Oscar Chess Ltd v Williams* [1957] 1 All ER 325 at 329.

Ability of the parties to ascertain the accuracy of the statement
8.15   If the representor had a special skill or knowledge, or was otherwise in a better position than the representee to ascertain the truth of the representation, this strongly suggests that the representation was intended to be a contractual term, and vice versa. An example is provided by *Dick Bentley (Productions) Ltd v Harold Smith (Motors) Ltd*.[1] The plaintiff purchased a Bentley car from the defendants in reliance on their statement that the car had been fitted with a new engine and gear box and had done only 20,000 miles since then. The representation as to mileage, although honestly made, was untrue. The Court of Appeal held that the representation had become one of the terms of the contract because it had been made by a dealer who was in a position to know or find out the car's history, and it could therefore be inferred that the representation was intended to have contractual effect. The Court distinguished its previous decision in *Oscar Chess Ltd v Williams*.[2] There, Williams, a private person, represented in negotiations for the part-exchange of his Morris car that it was a 1948 model. This representation was based on the logbook which had been falsified by a person unknown. The representation was held not to have become a contractual term on the ground that Williams had no special knowledge as to the car's age, while the other party, who were car dealers, were in at least as good a position to ascertain whether the representation was true.

1   [1965] 2 All ER 65, CA. Cf *Gilchester Properties Ltd v Gomm* [1948] 1 All ER 493.
2   [1957] 1 All ER 325, CA.

8.16   It must be emphasised that the factors mentioned above are only guides, not decisive tests or the only factors, to determining the parties' intentions.[1] Sometimes, they can point in different directions.

On many occasions, judges, having found that the parties intended a pre-contractual representation to have contractual effect, have found that it has taken effect under a collateral contract rather than as a term of the main contract.

1   *Heilbut, Symons & Co v Buckleton* [1913] AC 30, HL.

Implied terms

8.17   In addition to its express terms, the contract may contain certain terms implied by custom or by statute or by the courts.

Terms implied by custom or usage

8.18 Terms may be implied by the custom of a particular locality, as in *Hutton v Warren*,[1] or by the usage of a particular trade, as in *Harley & Co v Nagata*.[2] Although the terms are often used interchangeably, 'usage' differs from 'custom' in that it need not be ancient, but like custom it must be reasonable and certain in the sense that it is clearly established.[3] In *Hutton v Warren*, where a local custom was proved that a tenant was obliged to farm according to a certain course of husbandry for the whole of his tenancy and, on quitting, was entitled to a fair allowance for seeds and labour on the arable land, it was held that a term to this effect was implied in the lease. In *Harley & Co v Nagata*, it was held that, in the case of a time charterparty, a usage that the commission of a broker who negotiated the charterparty should be paid out of the hire which was earned, and should not be payable unless hire was in fact earned, was an implied term of the charterparty.

A term cannot be implied by custom or usage if the express wording of the contract shows that the parties had a contrary intention. This is shown by *Les Affréteurs Réunis SA v Leopold Walford (London) Ltd*.[4] Walford acted as a broker in effecting the time charter of a ship. The charterparty provided that commission should be payable to Walford 'on signing this charter (ship lost or not lost)'. Before the charterparty could be operated, and therefore before any hire could be earned, the French government requisitioned the ship. The House of Lords held that Walford could recover his commission because the commercial usage referred to above (commission payable only in respect of hire earned) could have no application since it was inconsistent with the express terms of the charterparty.

1   (1836) 1 M & W 466. For the requirements of a valid local custom, see para 3.63 above.
2   (1917) 23 Com Cas 121.
3   *Cunliffe-Owen v Teather and Greenwood* [1967] 3 All ER 561 at 572.
4   [1919] AC 801, HL.

Terms implied by statute

8.19 The best-known examples of such terms are those implied into contracts for the sale of goods by the Sale of Goods Act 1979 (which consolidated the Sale of Goods Act 1893 and amendments thereto).

Section 12(1) of the Act of 1979 provides that there is an implied condition[1] on the part of a seller of goods that he has a right to sell them. Section 12(2) provides, inter alia, that there is an implied warranty[1] that the goods are free, and will remain free until the property passes, from any charge or encumbrance not known or disclosed to the buyer before the contract is made.

Section 13(1) provides that, where there is a contract for the sale of goods by description, there is an implied condition[2] that the goods will correspond with the description.

Section 14(2)[3] provides that, where the seller sells goods in the course of a business, there is generally an implied condition[2] that the goods supplied under the contract are of satisfactory quality (ie of the standard that any reasonable person would regard as satisfactory). Section 14(3) provides that, where the seller sells goods in the course of a business and the buyer expressly or impliedly makes known to him any particular purpose for which the goods are being bought, there is generally an implied condition[2] that the goods supplied are reasonably fit for that purpose, whether or not that is a purpose for which such goods are commonly supplied. Unlike ss 12 and 13, sub-ss (2) and (3) of s 14 only apply where goods are sold *in the course of a business*. 'Business' is not limited to commercial activities in the ordinary sense because it is defined by s 61 to include 'a profession and the activities of any governmental department, or local or public authority'. If a private individual sells goods through an agent, such as an auctioneer, acting in the course of a business, the two subsections apply to the sale, unless the buyer knows that the seller is a private individual or reasonable steps have been taken to bring that fact to the buyer's attention before the contract is made.[4] It follows that it is extremely important that an auctioneer acting on behalf of a private client should notify prospective bidders for the goods of this fact, so as to avoid exposing his client to the risk of liability under the two subsections.

Finally, s 15 provides that where goods are sold by sample there is an implied condition[2] that the bulk will correspond with the sample in quality, and an implied condition that the goods will be free from any defect, rendering them unsatisfactory, which would not be apparent on reasonable examination of the sample.

1   This classification is made by the Sale of Goods Act 1979, s 12(5A).
2   By the Sale of Goods Act 1979, the term is classified as a condition.
3   As substituted by the Sale and Supply of Goods Act 1994.
4   Sale of Goods Act 1979, s 14(5).

8.20   Terms modelled on those implied into sale of goods contracts are implied:

•   into contracts of hire purchase, by the Supply of Goods (Implied Terms) Act 1973, ss 8 to 11;
•   into contracts of hire, by the Supply of Goods and Services Act 1982, ss 7 to 10; and
•   into contracts analogous to sale under which a person transfers or agrees to transfer to another the property (ie ownership) in goods, by the Supply of Goods and Services Act 1982, ss 2 to 5. One example of a contract analogous to sale is a contract for work and materials, such as a contract for double glazing; another is a contract of exchange or part exchange.

Although the exclusion or restriction by the contract of one of the implied terms referred to in para 8.19 and this paragraph, or of liability for its breach, is permissible,[1] there are strict limitations on this under the Unfair Contract Terms Act 1977 (paras 10.25 to 10.28 below).

1   Sale of Goods Act 1979, s 55; Supply of Goods and Services Act 1982, s 11.

8.21   By way of a further example, it may be noted that in a 'contract for the supply of a service' certain terms are implied by the Supply of Goods and Services Act 1982. Such a contract includes, for example, a contract between a surveyor and his client (but does not include a contract of employment or apprenticeship[1]). The fact that goods are transferred or hired under the contract does not prevent it being a contract for the supply of a service.[2] Consequently, for example, while a contract for work and materials will be subject to the implied terms under ss 2 to 5 of the 1982 Act in relation to the materials element, the work element will be subject to the terms implied into a contract of service by that Act.

The following terms are implied by the Act of 1982 into a contract for the supply of a service:

•   by s 13, where the supplier of the service is acting in the course of a business, there is an implied term that he will carry out the service with reasonable care and skill;[3]
•   by ss 14 and 15, where the time for the service to be carried out (s 14), or the consideration for the service (s 15), is not stated by the contract, or left to be determined in a manner agreed by the contract, or determined by the course of

dealings between the parties, there is an implied term that the service will be carried out within a reasonable time or, as the case may be, that a reasonable charge will be paid. The implied term as to the time of performance only applies where the contract is for the supply of a service by a supplier acting *in the course of a business*.[4]

Section 16 of the Act of 1982 permits the rights, duties and liabilities which may arise by virtue of ss 13 to 15 to be negatived or varied, subject to the relevant provisions of the Unfair Contract Terms Act 1977 (paras 10.19 to 10.30 below) and to any other legislation relating to the particular contract which defines or restricts rights, duties or liabilities.

1   Supply of Goods and Services Act 1982, s 12(2).
2   Ibid, s 12(3).
3   There are very limited exceptions under the Supply of Services (Exclusion of Implied Terms) Orders 1982, 1983 and 1985, the most notable being that the implied term under s 13 does not apply to the services rendered by an advocate in court or before any tribunal, inquiry or arbitrator or in carrying out certain preliminary work, nor to the services rendered by an arbitrator, nor to the services rendered by a company director to his company.
4   Business includes a profession and the activities of any government department or local or public authority: Supply of Goods and Services Act 1982, s 18.

8.22   Under the Landlord and Tenant Act 1985 terms as to fitness for habitation and as to repairs are implied into certain types of leases. We discuss this in para 36.22 below.

Terms implied by the courts
8.23   In *Liverpool City Council v Irwin*,[1] the House of Lords recognised that terms could be implied by the courts in two distinct situations:

*   where the term was a necessary incident of the kind of contract in question, and
*   where it was necessary to give 'business efficacy' to the particular contract.

1   [1976] 2 All ER 39, HL.

Implication of a term which is a necessary incident of the type of contract in question
8.24   When a court implies this type of term for the first time it lays down a general rule for contracts of the same type, eg employment contracts or leases, so that the term will be implied in subsequent cases concerning that type of contract,[1] subject to the rules of precedent, unless it is inconsistent with the express terms of the contract[2] or the contract validly excludes it.[3] In implying a term of the present type, the court is not trying to put the parties' intentions, actual or presumed, into effect but is implying it as a necessary incident of the type of contractual relationship in question.[4] In deciding whether to make such an implication, the courts take into account the reasonableness of the suggested term and whether it is called for by the nature of the subject matter of the type of contract in question.[5]

1   *Lister v Romford Ice and Cold Storage Co Ltd* [1957] AC 555 at 576; *Liverpool City Council v Irwin* [1976] 2 All ER 39 at 46; *Shell UK Ltd v Lostock Garage Ltd* [1977] 1 All ER 481 at 487.
2   The Unfair Contract Terms Act 1977 (paras 10.19–10.29 below) may have the effect of invalidating an inconsistent express term, in which case the implication can be made: *Johnstone v Bloomsbury Health Authority* [1991] 2 All ER 293, CA.
3   *Lynch v Thorne* [1956] 1 All ER 744, CA.
4   *Shell UK Ltd v Lostock Garage Ltd* [1977] 1 All ER 481 at 487; *Tai Hing Cotton Mill Ltd v Liu Chong Bank Ltd* [1985] 2 All ER 947, PC.
5   *Liverpool City Council v Irwin* [1976] 2 All ER 39, HL.

8.25 It is only possible here to refer to a few of the terms implied into contracts under the present heading.

In contracts of employment a number of obligations on the employee are implied. The fundamental implied duty is that the employee will faithfully serve his employer (the implied duty of fidelity).[1] A number of more specific implied duties to which an employee is subject are merely instances of the duty of fidelity, for instance:

- not to use or disclose confidential information relating to his employer's business contrary to his employer's interests;[2]
- not to copy or memorise such information for use after his employment has ceased;[2]
- not to act against his employer's interests;[3]
- to use reasonable care and skill in performing his duties;[4] and
- to indemnify his employer against any liability incurred by the employer as a result of his wrongful acts.[5]

There is a separate implied duty whereby an ex-employee must not use or disclose a trade secret or information relating to the former employer's business which is so confidential that it requires the same protection as a trade secret.[6]

Reciprocal terms are implied in the employee's favour, the employer being obliged, for instance:

- not to require the employee to do any unlawful act;[7]
- to use reasonable care to provide safe premises, to provide a safe system of work and not to injure the employee's health;[8] and
- not, without reasonable and proper cause, to conduct his business in a manner likely to destroy or damage seriously the relationship of trust and confidence between employer and employee.[9]

Another example of an implied term of the present type is provided by *Liverpool City Council v Irwin*.[10] In that case, the House of Lords held that, where parts of a building have been let to different tenants (the case concerned a high-rise block of flats) and essential rights of access over parts of the building, such as stairs, retained by the landlord have been granted to the individual tenants, a term could be implied into the tenancy agreements that the landlord would take reasonable care to keep them reasonably safe and reasonably fit for use by tenants, their families and their visitors. Likewise, it has been held that, where a tenant has a right of way over a path which is an essential means of access to his premises, the landlord having retained control of the path, there is implied in the tenancy agreement a term that the landlord will take reasonable steps to keep the path in good repair.[11] In a lease of furnished premises there is an implied term that they are fit for human habitation when let,[12] but for some obscure reason such a term is not implied by the courts in a contract for the sale of land with a house on it or for the letting of land with unfurnished premises on it[13] (although if the vendor or lessor is the builder he may be liable in tort to the purchaser, lessee, or even a visitor, who is injured as a result of his negligent building[14]). Lastly, where a builder contracts to construct a dwelling there is a term implied by the courts that the dwelling, when completed, will be reasonably fit for human habitation.[15] However, this implication may be rebutted where the contract expressly specifies the way in which the work is to be done and the work is completed according to that specification.[16]

1   *Hivac Ltd v Park Royal Scientific Instruments Ltd* [1946] 1 All ER 350, CA.
2   *Faccenda Chicken Ltd v Fowler* [1986] 1 All ER 617, CA. This duty of non-disclosure of confidential information does not extend so as to bar disclosures to the Inland Revenue or a regulatory body of

confidential matters which it is in the province of such an authority to investigate: *Re a Company's Application* [1989] 2 All ER 248.

3   *Wessex Dairies Ltd v Smith* [1935] 2 KB 80, CA.
4   *Lister v Romford Ice and Cold Storage Co Ltd* [1957] 1 All ER 125, HL.
5   Ibid.
6   *Faccenda Chicken Ltd v Fowler*, above.
7   *Gregory v Ford* [1951] 1 All ER 121.
8   *Lister v Romford Ice and Cold Storage Co Ltd*, above.
9   *Malik v Bank of Credit and Commerce International SA* [1997] 3 All ER 1, HL.
10 [1976] 2 All ER 39, HL.
11 *King v South Northamptonshire District Council* [1992] 1 EGLR 53, CA.
12 Para 36.22 below. For other examples of terms implied into leases as a necessary incident, see paras 36.20, 36.21 and 36.23-36.25 below.
13 *Hart v Windsor* (1843) 12 M & W 68. For possible liability for breach of statutory duty see para 22.28 below.
14 Para 22.27 below.
15 *Hancock v BW Brazier (Anerley) Ltd* [1966] 2 All ER 901, CA; *Basildon District Council v JE Lesser (Properties) Ltd* [1985] 1 All ER 20.
16 *Lynch v Thorne* [1956] 1 All ER 744, CA.

Implication to give business efficacy

8.26   The implication of a term under this heading is less common and can only be made when it is necessary in the particular circumstances to imply a term to fill an obvious gap in a contract[1] and thereby to give it business efficacy and make it a workable agreement in such manner as the parties would clearly have done if they had applied their minds to what has occurred. This power of judicial implication was recognised in *The Moorcock*,[2] which concerned a contract permitting the plaintiff to unload his ship at the defendants' jetty. A warranty on the part of the defendants was implied into the contract that the river bed was, so far as reasonable care could provide, in a condition which would not damage the ship when she grounded at low tide, as both parties realised she would. Bowen LJ stated that, where the parties had not dealt with the burden of a particular peril, a court could imply a term which would give such efficacy to the contract as both parties must have intended it to have.

The test which the courts apply in deciding whether to imply a term to give the contract business efficacy is a strict one. A term cannot be implied unless it is *necessary* to give business efficacy to the contract and it can be formulated with a *sufficient degree of precision*; it is not enough that it is reasonable in all the circumstances to imply the term,[3] nor that that the contract would be more efficient or effective if the term was implied.[4] A classic statement of the test is that of Scrutton LJ in *Reigate v Union Manufacturing Co (Ramsbottom) Ltd*:[5] 'A term can only be implied if it is necessary in the business sense to give efficacy to the contract, ie if it is such a term that it can confidently be said that if at the time the contract was being negotiated someone had said to the parties: "What will happen in such a case?" they would both have replied: "Of course, so and so will happen; we did not trouble to say that; it is too clear".'

1   *Adams Holden & Pearson Ltd v Trent Regional Health Authority* (1989) 47 BLR 34 and 39, CA.
2   (1889) 14 PD 64, CA.
3   *Liverpool City Council v Irwin* [1976] 2 All ER 39, HL; *Shell UK Ltd v Lostock Garage Ltd* [1977] 1 All ER 481, CA.
4   *Express Newspapers v Silverstone Circuits* (1989) Independent, 16 June, CA.
5   [1918] 1 KB 592 at 605. Also see *Shirlaw v Southern Foundries (1926) Ltd* [1939] 2 All ER 113 at 124.

8.27   Pursuant to these principles, the courts have, for instance, refused to imply terms in the following cases: where tariff booklets were supplied free to a hotel in consideration of its proprietors undertaking to circulate or display them for a specified period, a term to the effect that the proprietors' obligation should cease if the business was sold was not implied;[1] where a petrol company subsidised two neighbouring filling stations during a price cutting war, a term to the effect that it would not abnormally discriminate against the plaintiff's filling station in favour of competitors was not implied into a contract for the exclusive supply of petrol by the petrol company to the plaintiff;[2] where a contract between an estate agent and a vendor of property did not provide that the commission payable on completion of the sale should be paid out of the proceeds of sale, a term to that effect was not implied into the contract because it was held not to be necessary to give it business efficacy to provide any particular way in which the debt should be discharged.[3]

In contrast, the courts have, for example, implied a term: into a statutory tenancy containing an express term that the tenant would repair the interior of the premises, that the landlord would repair the exterior;[4] into a contractual licence, that the premises were of sound construction and reasonably suitable for the purpose required by the licensees;[5] into a contract of transfer of a footballer, which provided that an additional sum be paid when he had scored 20 goals for the first team, that he was entitled to a reasonable opportunity to score the goals;[6] and into a contract for the sale of land, where the vendor undertook to give the purchaser 'first refusal' of adjacent land, that the vendor should not defeat the purchaser's right of 'first refusal' by disposing of the adjacent land to a third party by way of *gift* without first offering it to the purchaser.[7] In addition, the courts have held that generally a term is necessarily implied in any contract that neither party shall prevent the other from performing it.[8]

Since the implication of a term under *The Moorcock* principle is always dependent on the particular circumstances of the case, the implication of a term under it does not lay down a general rule for the future.

1   *General Publicity Services Ltd v Best's Brewery Co Ltd* [1951] 2 TLR 875, CA.
2   *Shell UK Ltd v Lostock Garage Ltd* [1977] 1 All ER 481, CA.
3   *W A Ellis Services Ltd v Wood* [1993] 31 EG 78.
4   *Barrett v Lounova (1982) Ltd* [1989] 1 All ER 351, CA.
5   *Wettern Electric Ltd v Welsh Development Agency* [1983] 2 All ER 629.
6   *Bournemouth and Boscombe Athletic Football Club Co Ltd v Manchester United Football Club Ltd* (1980) Times, 22 May, CA.
7   *Gardner v Coutts & Co* [1967] 3 All ER 1064.
8   *William Cory & Son Ltd v London Corpn* [1951] 2 All ER 85 at 88.

Unfair contract terms

8.28   Under the Unfair Contract Terms Act 1977 and the Unfair Terms in Consumer Contracts Regulations 1994, which implement the EC Directive on unfair terms in consumer contracts, Directive 93/13/EEC, there are special provisions relating to contract terms which are unfair. In some cases, these provisions render an unfair term of no effect. We deal with these provisions later.[1]

1   Paras 10.19–10.30 and 14.61–14.67 below.

Chapter 9

Performance and breach

9.1 In this chapter we examine the following issues:

- how a party to a contract can be discharged from his obligations under it by performing them;
- the legal effect of a tender of performance by a party;
- the legal effect of a breach of contract by the party.

Performance

9.2 A contract may be discharged by agreement between the parties, by being broken by one of them, or by being frustrated, if the rules described elsewhere in this book[1] are satisfied. However, a contract is most frequently discharged by both parties performing their obligations under it, both parties being released from further liability thereby. If only one party performs his contractual obligations he alone is discharged and he acquires a right of action against the other for breach of contract. Special rules govern the discharge of a party who has unsuccessfully tendered performance.

1 Paras 6.22–6.25 above; 9.12–9.31 and 11.3–11.12 below.

9.3 For a party to be discharged by performance he must have precisely performed all his obligations under the contract. Thus, to decide whether a party is discharged by performance, one must first ascertain and construe the terms of the contract, express and implied, to see what his contractual obligations were, and then look at what has happened to see whether what he has done precisely corresponds with those obligations. The requirement of precise performance is a strict one and, if it is not met, it is irrelevant that the performance effected is commercially no less valuable than that which was promised. In *Arcos Ltd v E A Ronaasen & Sons*,[1] the plaintiffs contracted to supply the defendants with a certain quantity of timber which, as they knew, was to be used for constructing cement barrels. The contract specified that the timber should be half an inch thick but when it was delivered the defendants discovered that 95% of it was over half an inch thick, although none of it exceeded three-quarters of an inch in thickness. It was still perfectly possible for the defendants to use all the wood, as it had been delivered, for the construction of cement barrels but the House of Lords held that they were entitled to reject the whole consignment since the plaintiffs had not performed a contractual obligation which was a condition of the contract.[2] Lord Atkin stated, obiter, that only if a deviation from the terms of the contract was 'microscopic' could the contract be taken to have been correctly performed. An example of this is provided by *Shipton, Anderson & Co v Weil Bros & Co*,[3] where a contract requiring the delivery of 4,950 tons of wheat was held to have been performed by the seller although he had delivered 4,950 tons 55 lbs.

Generally, no demand for performance is necessary to render an obligation to perform operative.[4] Thus, a debtor is bound to seek out his creditor and pay him.[5]

1 [1933] AC 470, HL.
2 The contractual obligation broken was the condition implied by the Sale of Goods Act 1979, s 13(1), viz, that in a sale of goods by description the goods must correspond with the description. See paras 8.19 above and 9.24–9.27 below.
3 [1912] 1 KB 574.
4 A demand will be necessary if there is an express agreement or trade usage requiring it.
5 *Walton v Mascall* (1844) 13 M & W 452.

Payment

9.4 Where the obligation of one party to the other consists of the payment of a sum of money, the contract is discharged by the payment of that sum. Payment should, primarily, be made in legal tender but may, with the consent of the creditor, be made by cheque.

Legal tender is as follows:

* Bank of England notes, to any amount;
* gold coins of the Mint, to any amount;
* silver and cupro-nickel coins of the Mint of more than 10p, up to £10;
* silver and cupro-nickel coins of the Mint of not more than 10p, up to £5;
* bronze coins, up to 20p.

Where a cheque is given, and accepted,[1] in payment, its effect may be absolutely to discharge or only conditionally to discharge the debtor. The discharge will be *absolute* if the creditor promises expressly or impliedly, in accepting the cheque, to discharge the debtor from his existing obligations. If this occurs the creditor loses his right of action on the original contract but can sue on his rights under the cheque if it is dishonoured.[2] However, the presumption is that the creditor only accepts a cheque as a *conditional* discharge, in which case the debtor is not discharged unless, and until, the cheque is honoured; if it is dishonoured, the debtor may be sued on the original contract or on the dishonoured cheque.[3]

1 *Official Solicitor to the Supreme Court v Thomas* [1986] 2 EGLR 1, CA.
2 *Sard v Rhodes* (1836) 1 M & W 153.
3 *Sayer v Wagstaff* (1844) 5 Beav 415:*Re Romer and Haslam* [1893] 2 QB 286, CA.

Tender of performance

9.5 If a party makes a valid tender (ie offer) of performance of his contractual obligations and the other party refuses to accept performance, the party making the tender is freed from liability for non-performance of those obligations, provided that the tender is made under such circumstances that the other party has a reasonable opportunity of examining the performance tendered, eg the goods tendered, in order to ascertain that it conforms with the contract.[1]

1 *Startup v Macdonald* (1843) 6 Man & G 593 at 610. Also see Sale of Goods Act 1979, s 29.

Tender of payment

9.6 If a party makes a valid tender of payment of money which he owes by producing the amount owed in legal tender but the other party refuses to accept it, this does not discharge his debt but there is no obligation to make a further tender. If an action is brought for non-payment against a party who has tendered unsuccessfully, all he has to do is to pay the money into court.

Tender of acts

9.7 Where a party is obliged to perform some act, other than the payment of something, he will make a valid tender of performance if he attempts to perform the act in precise accordance with the terms of the contract. In the case of a contract for the sale of goods, the tender of them must be made at a reasonable hour.[1]

1 Sale of Goods Act 1979, s 29.

Time of performance

9.8 When a contract does not stipulate a time within which a party's contractual obligations must be performed, they must be performed within a reasonable time.[1]

1 *Postlethwaite v Freeland* (1880) 5 App Cas 599, HL. The Sale of Goods Act 1979, s 29 gives this rule statutory effect in relation to a seller's obligation to send goods to a buyer. The Supply of Goods and Services Act 1982, s 14, has the like effect in relation to the provision of services by a supplier acting in the course of a business: see para 8.21, above.

9.9 Whether a time is stipulated for performance of a party's obligations by the contract or whether it is implied that they must be performed within a reasonable time, the question arises whether time is 'of the essence of the contract'. If it is, the stipulation or implied obligation as to time will be classified as a condition[1] and a party's failure to perform in that time will not only constitute a breach of contract entitling the other party to maintain an action for damages but also a repudiatory breach of the contract, which the other party can accept as discharging him from his contractual obligations.[2] The rule is a strict one; it applies even though the party in default tenders performance shortly after a stipulated time for performance. This was re-affirmed by the Privy Council in *Union Eagle Ltd v Golden Achievement Ltd*,[3] where a purchaser of a flat was required to complete by 5 pm on a specified day, time being of the essence. The purchaser failed to complete by that time. The purchaser's vendor declared that the contract was terminated and the purchaser's deposit forfeited. Ten minutes after the time for completion, the purchaser tendered the purchase price. The Privy Council refused to intervene by ordering the specific performance of the contract of sale on the ground that it had no power to do so.

If time is not of the essence but a party delays in performing the contract, it may be possible to infer that he does not intend to carry out his obligations under it. In such a case the other party will be entitled to accept this implied renunciation as discharging him from his contractual obligation (ie entitled to terminate the contract for repudiatory breach).[4]

1 This point was made by the majority of the Court of Appeal in *Bunge Corpn v Tradax SA* [1981] 2 All ER 513 at 523, 536 and 539 and is implicit in the leading speeches in the House of Lords in that case: [1981] 2 All ER 513. With regard to conditions, see para 9.24 below.
2 See, in particular, *Bunge Corpn v Tradax SA* [1981] 2 All ER 513, HL. See also paras 9.14–9.19, below.
3 [1997] 2 All ER 215, PC.
4 *Graham v Pitkin* [1992] 2 All ER 235, PC. See para 9.21 below.

9.10 Whether time is of the essence of a contract, other than a contract which is specifically enforceable (see para 9.11 below), depends on the parties' intentions when the contract is made. If they are not expressed in the contract, they must be inferred from the nature of the subject matter of the contract and of the obligation which has not been performed in time. In this context certain presumptions have been established. For instance, a stipulation as to time in a commercial contract is presumptively of the essence of the contract.[1] However, the Sale of Goods Act 1979, s 10 provides that a term as to the time of payment for goods is deemed not to be of the essence of the contract, unless the contrary intention appears from the contract.

1   *Bunge Corpn v Tradax SA* [1981] 2 All ER 513, HL.

9.11 Before the Judicature Act 1873, common law and equity had different rules about when the time for completion was of the essence in a contract which was specifically enforceable,[1] such as a contract for the sale of an interest in land or for the sale of a unique chattel, but since that Act the equitable rules prevail.[2] The result is that time is not of the essence in such a contract unless it falls within one of the following three categories where equity treated it as of the essence:

* where the contract expressly states that obligations as to time must be strictly complied with. In *Harold Wood Brick Co Ltd v Ferris*[3] for instance, a stipulation that the purchase of a brickfield should be completed by 31 August which added that 'the purchase shall in any event be completed not later than 15 September' was held to make time (15 September) of the essence of the contract;
* where the contract does not expressly make time of the essence of the contract, but the stipulated or impliedly required time has passed by, the party who has been subjected to delay can make time of the essence by invoking a period of notice for performance (eg completion in the case of a contract for the sale of land) if one is specified in the contract or, if one is not specified, by giving a notice fixing a reasonable time for performance;[4]
* where the subject matter of the contract, or the circumstances surrounding it, makes punctual compliance with an obligation as to time imperative, time must be taken to be of the essence of the contract. For example, under this heading time has been held to be of the essence of a contract for the sale of business premises as a going concern.[5]

Even if time is not of the essence of a contract for the sale of an interest in land or of some other specifically enforceable contract, a party who fails to complete within the required time is, of course, in breach of that term and liable in damages, provided that the failure was not due to some conveyancing difficulty or some difficulty with regard to title.[6] Inability to raise the necessary finance is no defence.[6]

1   Para 12.29 below.
2   Law of Property Act 1925, s 41.
3   [1935] 2 KB 198, CA.
4   *Stickney v Keeble* [1915] AC 386, HL; *Behzadi v Shaftesbury Hotels Ltd* [1991] 2 All ER 477, CA.
5   *Lock v Bell* [1931] 1 Ch 35. Also see *Harold Wood Brick Co Ltd v Ferris* [1935] 2 KB 198, CA.
6   *Raineri v Miles* [1980] 2 All ER 145, HL.

Breach

9.12 Breach of contract occurs where a party does not perform one or more of his contractual obligations precisely, in the sense discussed in para 9.3 above, and this failure is without lawful excuse. Thus, a breach will occur where a party without lawful excuse refuses to perform one or more of his contractual obligations, or simply fails to perform them, or incapacitates himself from performing them, or performs them defectively. Consequently, to decide whether a party is in breach of contract, one must first ascertain and construe the terms of the contract, express and implied, to see what his contractual obligations were, and then look at what has happened to see whether he has failed without lawful excuse to perform one or more of them precisely.

A person has a lawful excuse for failing to perform his contractual obligations precisely in the following cases:

- if the contract has been discharged by frustration, a matter which we discuss in chapter 11;
- if there is impossibility of performance less than frustration; for instance, a temporary illness preventing an employee working provides a lawful excuse for his failure to work during the period of the illness;[1]
- if he has validly tendered performance of his obligations in accordance with the rules set out in paras 9.5 to 9.7 above, but this has been rejected by the other party;
- if the other party has made it impossible for him to perform his obligations.

1   *Poussard v Spicers and Pond* (1876) 1 QBD 410.

9.13   Subject to a valid exemption clause to the contrary, whenever a party to the contract is in breach of contract, he is legally liable to pay compensation (ie damages) to the other party (the 'injured party') for the loss sustained by him in consequence of that breach but, unless the breach can be classified as a repudiatory breach and the injured party elects to terminate the contract, the contractual obligations of the parties so far as they have not been fully performed remain unchanged. The injured party may claim damages for breach either by an action of his own or by way of a counter-claim in an action brought against him by the defaulting party, and even where no actual loss or damage to the injured party can be proved nominal damages (usually in the region of £2 to £20) will be awarded. Quite apart from damages, the injured party may be entitled, additionally or alternatively, to claim an order of specific performance of the contract or an injunction or to recover an agreed sum. We consider the question of remedies in chapter 12.

In the case of certain serious breaches of contract, which are commonly described as repudiatory breaches, the injured party can elect to treat the contract as repudiated by the other, accept the repudiation, and recover damages for breach, both parties being discharged from performance of their primary obligations under the contract which would have been due thereafter. If the injured party does this, he is said to terminate (or rescind[1]) the contract for repudiatory breach.

1   Termination for repudiatory breach should not be confused with rescission for misrepresentation (discussed in chapter 14), the effects of which (and the rules concerning which) are different.

Repudiatory breach

Option to terminate or affirm
9.14   A repudiatory breach does not automatically discharge the contract. Instead, the injured party has an option to terminate the contract or to affirm it.[1] We shall see in para 9.27 below that in one type of case an injured party can lose the option to terminate, even though he has not affirmed the contract.

1   *Heyman v Darwins Ltd* [1942] 1 All ER 337 at 340.

Termination

9.15   The injured party will terminate the contract if he indicates to the defaulting party that he regards himself as discharged by the repudiatory breach. No particular form of indication is required.[1] It is sufficient that by words or conduct the injured party clearly and unequivocally conveys to the repudiating party that he is treating the contract as at an end.[1] Thus, the contract will be terminated if the injured party refuses to accept defective performance, or refuses to accept further performance, or simply refuses to perform his own contractual obligations. Moreover, termination can be inferred if the injured party simply does something incompatible with his own continued performance of the contract, or simply fails to perform his side of the contract, provided that this unequivocally points to the fact that he is treating the contract as at an end.[1] Suppose, for example, that an employer at the end of a day tells a contractor that he, the employer, is renouncing the contract and that the contractor need not return the next day. This would constitute a repudiatory breach of contract by the employer.[2] The contractor does not return the next day or at all. The contractor's failure to return may, in the absence of any other explanation, convey a decision to terminate the contract.[3] The injured party need not personally, or by an agent, notify the guilty party of his election to terminate. It is sufficient that the election comes to the guilty party's attention. For example, notification by an unauthorised intermediary can suffice.[3]

1   *Vitol SA v Norelf Ltd* [1996] 3 All ER 193, HL.
2   Para 9.21 below.
3   *Vitol SA v Norelf Ltd* [1996] 3 All ER 193 at 200.

9.16   If the injured party elects to terminate the contract, he is discharged for the future from his obligations under the contract which would otherwise have been due or continuing thereafter. One result is that he is not obliged to accept or pay for further performance. Another result is that an injured party who has terminated a contract for breach can resist successfully any action for failing thereafter to observe or perform a continuing obligation or an obligation due thereafter, even if the contract purports to make the obligation applicable after a repudiatory breach by the defaulting party.[1] Consequently, for example, a wrongfully dismissed employee who has indicated that he regards himself as discharged by the repudiatory breach from his employment contract is no longer bound by terms in that contract restraining his future employment, even if his employment contract purports to make those terms applicable after a repudiatory breach by the employer.[2]

On the other hand, an injured party who has terminated is not generally discharged from his obligations which are already due at the time of termination, since rights and obligations which arise from the partial execution of the contract – as well as causes of action which have accrued from its breach – continue unaffected.[3]

1   *General Billposting Co Ltd v Atkinson* [1909] AC 118, HL; *Rock Refrigeration Ltd v Jones* [1997] 1 All ER 1, CA.
2   *Rock Refrigeration Ltd v Jones* [1997] 1 All ER 1, CA.
3   *Damon Cia Naviera SA v Hapag-Lloyd International S A, The Blankenstein* [1985] 1 All ER 475, [1985] 1 WLR 435, CA.

9.17   An injured party who has terminated may be entitled to refuse to pay for partial or defective performance already received by him if complete and precise performance of the broken obligation by the defaulting party is a pre-condition of his right to be paid. However, if the injured party is in a position to return the partial or defective performance (eg faulty goods), and does not do so, he must pay a reasonable sum or pro rata for the work done or goods supplied. It was held in *Sumpter v Hedges*[1] that, on the other hand, there is no such obligation where the acceptance of the partial or defective performance was not voluntary, ie the injured party had no choice. In that case A agreed to build two houses and a stable, for a lump sum payable on completion, on B's land. A did part of the work to the value of about three-fifths of the contract price but then abandoned the contract (a repudiatory breach) because of lack of money. It was held that A could not recover a reasonable sum for his work because B had no option but to accept the partial performance, viz the partly erected buildings.

In addition, an injured party who has terminated can recover back under the law of restitution any money which he has deposited or paid to the defaulting party under the contract if there has been a total failure of consideration on the part of the latter.[2] There will be a total failure of consideration on the part of the defaulting party if he has not performed any part of his contractual duties in respect of which the payment is due under the contract.[3]

Thus, if P pays D £500 as a deposit on a car but D fails to supply the car, P can terminate the contract and recover back the £500 which he paid. If the failure of consideration is not total but only partial, the action for the recovery of money paid is not available, so that, whether the contract is terminated or not, the appropriate remedy is an action for damages for breach of contract. Thus, if P employs D to build a house for him and pays in advance, and D starts the work but abandons it before it is finished, P cannot recover any part of his payment and must claim damages for breach of contract.[4] However, if:

- the partial performance is such as to entitle the plaintiff to terminate the contract, and he elects to do so; and
- he is able to restore what he has received under the contract, and does so before he has derived any benefit from it,[5]

he is said to bring about a total failure of consideration and is entitled to recover back any money which he has paid.[6] A common example of this is where the buyer of defective goods rejects them immediately and claims back his payment.

As a final point, it should be noted that, if the injured party has started to perform his contractual obligations but is unjustifiably prevented from completing them by the other party, he can bring an action for reasonable remuneration. This is called suing on a quantum meruit.[7]

1 [1898] 1 QB 673.
2 *Wilkinson v Lloyd* (1845) 7 QB 27.
3 *Stocznia Gdanska SA v Latvian Shipping Co* [1998] 1 All ER 883, HL.
4 *Whincup v Hughes* (1871) LR 6 CP 78.
5 *Hunt v Silk* (1804) 5 East 449.
6 *Baldry v Marshall* [1925] 1 KB 260, CA.
7 Para 12.27 below.

9.18 After termination by the injured party, the defaulting party's position is as follows:

- he is not discharged from his contractual obligations which are due at the time of the termination and have not been performed (so that, for instance, he is still obliged to pay a sum of money then due[1]); and he is also liable to pay damages to the injured party for loss sustained by him in consequence of the breach of any such obligations;[2]
- his contractual obligations, so far as they are due or continuing after the termination, are discharged and there is substituted for them an obligation arising from the contract to pay damages to the injured party for the loss sustained by him in consequence of their non-performance in the future.[2]

1   *McDonald v Dennys Lascelles Ltd* (1933) 48 CLR 457 at 476–477; *Hyundai Heavy Industries Co Ltd v Papodopolous* [1980] 2 All ER 29, HL.
2   *R V Ward Ltd v Bignall* [1967] 2 All ER 449, CA; *Moschi v LEP Air Services Ltd* [1972] 2 All ER 393, HL; *Photo Production Ltd v Securicor Transport Ltd* [1980] 1 All ER 556, HL.

9.19   Termination for repudiatory breach does not necessarily extinguish the contract completely in relation to obligations whose performance is due after the time of the election to terminate, since obligations relating to matters such as arbitration or jurisdiction may continue in existence if it was the intention of the parties, when they made the contract, that this should be so.[1] In addition, terms which validly 'liquidate' damages or which validly exclude or restrict liability remain in force.[2]

1   *Heyman v Darwins Ltd* [1942] 1 All ER 337, HL; *Photo Production Ltd v Securicor Transport Ltd* [1980] 1 All ER 556 at 567.
2   *Photo Production Ltd v Securicor Transport Ltd* [1980] 1 All ER 556, HL; *Port Jackson Stevedoring Pty Ltd v Salmond & Spraggon (Australia) Pty Ltd, The New York Star* [1980] 3 All ER 257, PC. For liquidated damages provisions, see para 12.19 below, and for exemption clauses, see ch 10. The proposition in the text has been given statutory force in relation to exemption clauses which must satisfy the requirement of reasonableness under the Unfair Contract Terms Act 1977 (see paras 10.20 to 10.28 below) by s 9 of that Act.

Affirmation
9.20   The injured party will affirm the contract if, with full knowledge of the facts and of his right to terminate the contract,[1] he decides to treat it as still in existence, as where he decides to keep the defective goods delivered or, if the defaulting party has not completed performance, where he calls on him to perform. The injured party does not affirm a contract simply because he does not immediately terminate the contract but delays while he considers whether or not to terminate it.[2]

If the injured party elects to affirm, the contract remains in force, so that both parties are bound to continue performing any outstanding contractual obligations. Each party retains the right to sue for past or future breaches. Thus, if a seller of goods affirms the contract after a repudiatory breach by the buyer, the seller remains liable to deliver possession of the goods to the buyer and the buyer remains liable to accept delivery of the goods and pay the contract price.[3] Another example is provided by *Bentsen v Taylor, Sons & Co (No 2)*,[4] where a charterparty described the ship as 'now sailed or about to sail' from a port to the United Kingdom. In fact, she did not sail for another month. This constituted a repudiatory breach of contract by the shipowner[5] but, instead of electing to terminate the contract, the charterers intimated to the shipowner that he was still bound to send the ship to the port of loading and that they, the charterers, would load her there, thereby affirming the contract. When the ship arrived, the charterers refused to load her. The Court of Appeal held that, since the contract had been affirmed, the shipowner was entitled to payment of freight, subject to a set-off for the charterers for damages for breach of contract by the shipowner referred to above.

1   *Peyman v Lanjani* [1984] 3 All ER 703, CA.
2   *Bliss v South East Thames Regional Health Authority* [1987] ICR 700, CA.
3   *R V Ward Ltd v Bignall* [1967] 2 All ER 449, CA; *Segap Garages Ltd v Gulf Oil (Great Britain) Ltd* (1988) Times, 24 October, CA.
4   [1893] 2 QB 274, CA.
5   Because the term broken was a condition: see paras 9.24 and 9.25 below.

Types of repudiatory breach
Renunciation
9.21   Where one party renounces his contractual obligations the other party is entitled to terminate the contract. A party is said to renounce his contractual obligations if he has evinced an unconditional intention not to perform them or otherwise no longer to

be bound by the contract or one of its essential terms.[1] Such an intention is easily established where there has been an express and unequivocal refusal to perform. Thus, if an employee unqualifiedly refuses to carry out his contractual duties (or to carry out a duty which is an essential contractual term), his employer is entitled to dismiss him (ie terminate the contract of employment).[2] However, express refusal is not necessary; an intent no longer to be bound by the contract (or one of its essential terms) can also be implied by the words or conduct of a party. The actual intention of the party is not the crucial issue in such a case; the test is whether his words and conduct were such as to lead a reasonable person to believe that he did not intend to be bound by the contract.[3]

1   *Mersey Steel and Iron Co v Naylor Benzon and Co* (1884) 9 App Cas 434, HL.
2   *Gorse v Durham County Council* [1971] 2 All ER 666.
3   *Woodar Investment Development Ltd v Wimpey Construction UK Ltd* [1980] 1 All ER 571, HL; *André et Cie SA v Marine Transocean Ltd, The Splendid Sun* [1981] 2 All ER 993, CA.

Incapacitation

9.22   Even though he has not evinced an intention not to be bound by the contract, a party who, *by his own act or default*, incapacitates himself from performing his contractual obligations is treated as if he had refused to perform them.[1] As Devlin J said in *Universal Cargo Carriers Corpn v Citati*,[2] 'To say "I would like to but cannot" negatives intent to perform as much as "I will not"'. Where a party has incapacitated himself from performing, it is no defence to show that he might be able to recover the capacity to perform.[3] One example of a case where a party has made performance of his obligations impossible is where A has contracted to sell a specific thing to B but then sells it to C.

1   *Torvald Klaveness A/S v Arni Maritime Corpn, The Gregos* [1994] 4 All ER 998, HL.
2   [1957] 2 All ER 70.
3   *Omnium D'Enterprises v Sutherland* [1919] 1 KB 618, CA.

Defective performance

9.23   Unless the party in default has a lawful excuse the injured party can, of course, recover damages for breach of contract but, leaving aside termination for renunciation[1] or incapacitation,[2] he can only terminate for failure to perform an obligation in two cases:

- where it involves breach of a term of the contract which is a condition;
- where it involves breach of an 'intermediate term' and the effect of the breach deprives the injured party of substantially the whole of his intended benefit under the contract.

1   Para 9.21 above.
2   Para 9.22 above.

9.24   *Breach of condition* Some contractual terms can be classified as conditions, others as intermediate terms, and others as warranties. A condition is an essential term of the contract,[1] or, as it is sometimes put, one which goes to the root of the contract. If it is broken, the injured party may[2] terminate the contract for breach of condition, as well as claiming damages, whether the effect of the breach is serious or trivial.[3] In this context the word 'condition' is used in yet another sense. It does not bear its orthodox meaning, discussed in paras 5.27, 5.28 and 5.30 above, of an event by which an obligation is suspended or cancelled but is used to describe a particular type of contractual term. It is certainly an odd word to use for this purpose.

An intermediate term is one whose breach may entitle the injured party to terminate the contract, depending on how serious the effect of the breach is. We explain this further in para 9.28 below.

A warranty is a contractual term concerning a less important or subsidiary statement of fact or promise.[4] If a warranty is broken this does not entitle the other party to terminate the contract. It simply entitles him to sue for damages or make a set-off and the party in breach is entitled to the contractual price less the damages or set-off.[5]

1   *Heyworth v Hutchinson* (1867) LR 2 QB 447 at 451.
2   Unless the failure in performance is microscopic: para 9.3 above.
3   In relation to contracts for sale of goods this rule is given statutory effect by the Sale of Goods Act 1979, s 11(3).
4   *Oscar Chess Ltd v Williams* [1957] 1 All ER 325 at 328; Sale of Goods Act 1979, s 11(3).
5   *Gilbert Ash (Northern) Ltd v Modern Engineering (Bristol) Ltd* [1973] 3 All ER 195, HL; Sale of Goods Act 1979, s 53(1)(a).

9.25   The classification of a term as a condition depends on the following considerations:

*   Sometimes statute provides that particular terms are conditions, eg the implied conditions in sale of goods contracts, hire purchase contracts, contracts analogous to contracts for the sale of goods and hire contracts under ss 12 to 15 of the Sale of Goods Act 1979, ss 8 to 11 of the Supply of Goods (Implied Terms) Act 1973 and ss 7 to10 of the Supply of Goods and Services Act 1982, respectively.[1]
*   In other cases, a term which has been classified as a condition in judicial decisions will be so classified thereafter, subject to the rules of judicial precedent.[2] An example is a stipulation as to time (other than the time for payment) in a commercial contract.[3]
*   In the absence of classification by statute or case authority, a court has to decide whether the broken term is a condition by ascertaining the intention of the parties as at the time the contract was made.[3] The parties' intentions are particularly important and it is open to them to agree that what is a condition according to a previous judicial decision shall not be so treated in their contract, and vice versa. Because of the drastic consequences, the courts lean against construing a term as a condition: in fact, they are increasingly reluctant so to construe a term unless compelled by clear evidence of the parties' intentions.[4]

    The approach of the courts is as follows:

    First, the court must seek to ascertain the intention of the parties as expressed in the contract. If the wording clearly reveals that the parties intended that any breach of the term should give rise to a right to terminate, that term will be regarded as a condition. But if the parties clearly did not so intend, the term will not be regarded as a condition even though it is described as a 'condition' in the contract. This is shown by *Schuler AG v Wickman Machine Tool Sales Ltd.*[5] A four-year distributorship agreement provided that the distributor should visit six named customers every week. The agreement described this provision as a 'condition'. The House of Lords held that the contract could not be terminated simply because of breach of this 'condition'. Its reasoning was that the parties could not have intended a mere failure to make one visit to result in a right to terminate. It thought that more probably 'condition' had been used simply to mean 'term'.

    Second, if the wording of the contract does not indicate the parties' intentions, the court must ascertain them by inference from the nature, purpose and circumstances of the contract. If, in the context of the whole contract, it is clear that the term was so important that a party would always want to be entitled to terminate if it was broken it will be regarded as a condition. An example is *Behn v Burness*,[6] where one term of a charterparty was that the ship was 'now in the port of Amsterdam': the ship was not then there. The statement was held to be a condition because of the commercial importance attached to such a statement. On the other hand, a term in a charterparty that a ship is seaworthy has not been construed as a condition because it can be broken in a number of ways, in some of which the parties would clearly not intend that the charterer should be entitled to terminate.[7] As this decision indicates, if a term can be broken in a variety of ways it is unlikely that it will be inferred that the parties intended that the injured party should always be entitled to terminate the contract for breach of that term, since where a variety of breaches occur it is likely that some of them may not be serious. This can be compared with the situation where the term can only be broken in one way and that breach will always be serious.

1 Paras 8.19 and 8.20 above.
2 *Maredelante Cia Naviera SA v Bergbau-Handel GmbH, The Mihalis Angelos* [1970] 3 All ER 125, CA.
3 *Bunge Corpn v Tradax SA* [1981] 2 All ER 513, HL; para 9.10 above.
4 *Cehave NV v Bremer Handelsgesellschaft mbH, The Hansa Nord* [1975] 3 All ER 739 at 755; *Bunge Corpn v Tradax SA* [1981] 2 All ER 513 at 542, 551.
5 [1973] 2 All ER 39, HL.
6 (1863) 3 B & S 751.
7 *Hong Kong Fir Shipping Co Ltd v Kawasaki Kisen Kaisha Ltd* [1962] 1 All ER 474, CA.

9.26 In the case of a contract for the sale or supply of goods, the right to terminate for breach of condition is subject to statutory limitations.

First, s 15A of the Sale of Goods Act 1979 provides that, where in the case of a contract of sale:

- the buyer would otherwise have the right to reject goods (ie terminate the contract) by reason of a breach by the seller of one of the terms implied by ss 12 to 15 of the Act; but
- the seller proves that the breach is so slight that it would be unreasonable for him to do so,

then, if the buyer does not deal as consumer, the breach is not to be treated as a breach of condition but only as a breach of warranty (with the result that there is no right to reject the goods).

Similar provision is made by s 11A of the Supply of Goods (Implied Terms) Act 1973 and s 5A of the Supply of Goods and Services Act 1982 in relation to hire purchase contracts and contracts analogous to contracts for the sale of goods, respectively.

9.27 Second, there is a special rule which (where it is applicable) prevents a buyer of goods terminating the contract of sale for breach of a condition of it, even though he has not affirmed it because he lacks the knowledge of the breach necessary for affirmation. This rule – which only applies to contracts for the sale of goods – is provided by s 11(4) of the Sale of Goods Act 1979. This states that, where a contract for the sale of goods is not severable and the buyer has accepted the goods or part of them, he can only treat a breach of condition as a breach of warranty, 'and not as a ground for rejecting the goods and treating the contract as repudiated', unless there is a term of the contract, express or implied, to that effect.

Section 11(4) only applies where the contract of sale is not severable, so that it is inapplicable to a contract under which goods are to be delivered by instalments, each of which is to be separately paid for, because this is a severable contract. On the other hand, a contract for a lump sum price payable after the completion of delivery is not severable where the seller has an option to fulfil his obligations by one delivery or two or more,[1] unless the seller exercises that option (whereupon the contract becomes a severable one).

By s 35(1) of the Sale of Goods Act 1979, a buyer is deemed to have accepted goods:

- when he intimates to the seller that he has accepted them; or
- when the goods have been delivered to him and he does any act in relation to them which is inconsistent with the ownership of the seller.

However, by s 35(2), where goods are delivered to the buyer and he has not previously examined them, he is not deemed to have accepted them under s 35(1) until he has had a reasonable opportunity of examining them to see whether they conform with the contract or, in the case of a contract for sale by sample, to compare the bulk with the sample.

Section 35(4) of the 1979 Act provides that a buyer is also deemed to have accepted the goods when, after a lapse of a reasonable time, he retains the goods without intimating to the seller that he has rejected them. In determining whether a reasonable time has elapsed, account must be taken of whether the buyer had a reasonable opportunity to examine the goods.[2]

What constitutes a reasonable time varies according to the nature of the goods: 'What is a reasonable time for a bicycle would scarcely be adequate for a nuclear submarine'.[3]

A buyer may be deemed to have accepted goods under this heading even though the defect has not manifested itself during the 'reasonable time' and even though he has not had a reasonable time to discover the defect.[3]

By s 35(6) of the 1979 Act, a buyer is not deemed to have accepted the goods merely because:

- he asks for, or agrees to, their repair by or under an arrangement with the seller; or
- the goods are delivered to another under a sub-sale or other disposition.

If there has been a breach of the implied condition under s 12(1) of the Sale of Goods Act 1979 that the seller has the right to sell the goods,[4] the buyer who is forced to hand them over to the true owner is entitled to recover back the price he has paid, on the grounds that there has been a total failure of consideration,[5] notwithstanding that he has used the goods for some time. Section 11(4) has no application to a breach of s 12(1) because there is not really a contract of sale at all if the seller has no right to sell the goods.[6]

1 *J Rosenthal & Sons Ltd v Esmail* [1965] 2 All ER 860, HL.
2 Sale of Goods Act 1979, s 35(5).
3 *Bernstein v Pamson Motors (Golders Green) Ltd* [1987] 2 All ER 220 at 230.
4 Para 8.19 above.
5 Para 9.17 above.
6 *Rowland v Divall* [1923] 2 KB 500, CA.

9.28 *Breach of an intermediate term* If the term broken is not a condition, it must not be assumed that it is a warranty for which the only remedy is damages, unless statute or a judicial decision compels such a classification.[1] Instead, the contract must be construed and, unless the contract makes it clear (either by express provision or by necessary implication from its nature, purpose and circumstances) that the parties intended that no breach of the term should entitle the injured party to terminate the contract, the term will be classified as an intermediate (or innominate) term and not as a warranty. If it is so classified one must then ask whether the nature and effect of its breach is such as to deprive the injured party of substantially the whole benefit which it was intended that he should obtain under the contract.[2] If it is, the injured party is entitled to terminate the contract, as well as claiming damages. In applying this test, account must be taken not only of the actual consequences of the breach but also of those whose occurrence is reasonably foreseeable.[3] There is high judicial authority in a number of cases that the present doctrine, whereby termination for breach of a term depends on the effects of the breach, is preferable to making termination dependent on whether the term itself is classified as a condition or a warranty, since it is far more likely to ensure that termination is possible when it is appropriate.[4]

A leading authority for the present doctrine is *Hong Kong Fir Shipping Co Ltd v Kawasaki Kisen Kaisha Ltd*.[5] The plaintiffs chartered a ship to the defendants for 24 months. The ship was old and needed to be maintained by an adequate and competent engine room crew but the plaintiffs did not provide such a crew and thereby were in breach of a term of the charterparty to provide a ship 'in every way fitted for ordinary cargo service' (otherwise called a 'seaworthiness clause'). Because of the incompetence and inadequacy of the engine room crew and the age of the engines, the ship was held up for repairs for five weeks on her first voyage, and when she reached her destination it was found that further repairs, which would take 15 weeks, were necessary to make her seaworthy. The defendants purported to terminate the charterparty and the plaintiffs sued for breach of contract on the ground that termination was wrongful. The defendants pleaded that the seaworthiness clause was a condition of the contract, and that therefore they could terminate the contract for breach of it. Having held that the clause was not a condition for the reason set out towards the end of para 9.25 above, the Court of Appeal held that the effect of the plaintiffs' breach of the clause was not sufficiently serious to justify the defendants in terminating the charterparty. One reason which it particularly relied on was the fact that after the repairs the ship was still available for 17 of the original 24 months. The defendants' termination had therefore been wrongful.

The same decision was reached in *The Hansa Nord*.[6] Citrus pulp pellets were sold by a German company to a Dutch company, delivery to be made in Rotterdam. The contract included a term that shipment was to be made in good condition. Some of the pellets arrived damaged. The buyers rejected the whole consignment (ie terminated the contract) and the goods were sold by the order of a Dutch court to a third person. Subsequently, they were re-sold at one-third the original contract price to the original buyers who then used the whole consignment for a purpose (cattle food) similar to that for which they had originally bought it (animal feed) – though at a lower rate of inclusion in the case of the damaged pellets. The Court of Appeal held that the 'shipment in good condition' term was not a condition of the contract because it could not have been intended that any breach of it should entitle the buyers to terminate the contract.[7] The Court then turned to the present doctrine and held that the buyers were not entitled to terminate under it because, particularly in the light of the subsequent events, the effect of the breach was not sufficiently serious to justify termination. Thus, the buyers were only entitled to damages and could not treat themselves as discharged from their obligation to accept the pellets and pay the contract price.

1   *Hong Kong Fir Shipping Co Ltd v Kawasaki Kisen Kaisha Ltd* [1962] 2 QB 26 at 63–64; *Reardon Smith Line Ltd v Hansen-Tangen* [1976] 3 All ER 570 at 573–573.
2   *Hong Kong Fir Shipping Co Ltd v Kawasaki Kisen Kaisha Ltd* [1962] 2 QB 26 at 70.
3   Ibid, at 64.
4   Eg *Reardon Smith Line Ltd v Hansen-Tangen* [1976] 3 All ER 570 at 577.
5   [1962] 1 All ER 474, CA.
6   *Cehave NV v Bremer Handelsgesellschaft mbH* [1975] 3 All ER 739, CA.

7   The Court also held that there was no breach of the implied condition as to quality under the Sale of
Goods Act 1979, s 14(2); see para 8.19 above.

9.29   These two cases can be contrasted with *Aerial Advertising Co v Batchelors Peas
Ltd (Manchester)*.[1] The plaintiffs agreed to conduct an aerial advertising campaign
for the defendants. One term of the contract was that the pilot of the aeroplane should
telephone the defendants each day and obtain their approval for what he proposed to
do. On Armistice Day 1937, the pilot, in breach of this term, failed to contact the
defendants and flew over Salford during the two minutes' silence. The aeroplane was
towing a banner saying 'Eat Batchelors Peas'. Of course, the term broken was not a
condition since breach of it might well only have had trivial consequences, so that the
parties could not have intended that its breach should always entitle the defendants to
terminate the contract. However, the effect of the particular breach was disastrous since
it aroused public hostility towards the defendants and their products. It was held that
the defendants were entitled to terminate the contract.

1   [1938] 2 All ER 788.

Anticipatory breach

9.30   So far we have been concerned with actual breaches of contract, ie breaches of
contractual obligations whose performance is due at the time of the breach. An
anticipatory breach of contract occurs where a party renounces[1] his contractual
obligations, or incapacitates himself[2] from performing them, *before the time fixed for
their performance*. If a party commits such an anticipatory breach, the injured party
can accept the breach as discharging the contract (ie terminate it) and immediately
bring an action for damages for breach of contract or a quantum meruit action: he does
not have to wait for the time of performance to become due. An example is provided
by *Lovelock v Franklyn*,[3] where the defendant agreed to assign his interest in a lease
to the plaintiff for £140. Before the agreed date of performance arrived, the defendant
assigned his interest to another person. It was held that the plaintiff could bring an
action for damages immediately: he did not have to wait for the time of performance
to arrive.

   If the injured party validly terminates the contract for anticipatory breach, the other
party is not permitted to change his mind and seek to perform his contractual
obligations,[4] but he may do so at any time before there is a valid termination by the
injured party.[5]

1   Para 9.21 above.
2   Para 9.22 above.
3   (1846) 8 QB 371.
4   *Xenos v Danube and Black Sea Rly Co* (1863) 13 CBNS 825.
5   *Norwest Holst Group Administration Ltd v Harrison* [1985] ICR 668, CA.

9.31   As in the other situations where a party can terminate a contract for the other's
failure to perform, a contract is never automatically discharged by anticipatory breach;
instead, the injured party has an election to terminate or affirm the contract. If he refuses
to accept the anticipatory breach as discharging the contract and continues to insist on
performance, he will affirm it. When a contract is affirmed after anticipatory breach
the effects are as follows:

•   the injured party loses his right to bring an action for damages for anticipatory
     breach;
•   the contract remains in force. Each party remains liable to perform his obligations
     when they become due and will be liable if he fails to perform them then. Thus,

the party who committed the anticipatory breach is given an opportunity to perform his obligations, and only if he fails to do so will he be liable. The contract remains in existence at the risk of both parties; consequently, if the party who has affirmed after anticipatory breach subsequently commits a breach of contract he will be liable,[1] and either party can take advantage of any supervening circumstance which would justify him in declining to perform;[2]

- as opposed to the case where the injured party immediately sues for damages for anticipatory breach, a party who affirms is under no duty to mitigate his loss before performance is due.[3] This may result in the recovery of larger damages in the event of ultimate non-performance by the other.[4]

1   *Fercometal SARL v Mediterranean Shipping Co SA, The Simona* [1988] 2 All ER 742, HL.
2   *Avery v Bowden* (1855) 5 E & B 714.
3   *Tredegar Iron and Coal Co Ltd v Hawthorn Bros & Co* (1902) 18 TLR 716, CA.
4   Para 12.17 below.

Chapter 10

Exemption clauses

10.1 A contract may contain an exemption clause. An exemption clause may:

- purport to exclude or restrict one of the parties' liability for breach of contract, or some other liability, such as for misrepresentation or for the tort of negligence, or both; or
- purport to exclude or modify the obligations of a party which would normally be implied by law from the legal nature of the contract.

Because exemption clauses can operate very unfairly in the case of standard form contracts, where one party has no real option but to accept the terms offered by the other, a number of restrictive rules have been introduced by the courts and by legislation, as explained below'.

10.2 In this chapter we consider:

- the requirements that a person who wishes to rely on an exemption clause must prove that it is a term of a contract to which he is a party and that, as a matter of construction, it covers the liability in question;
- various limitations on the operation of exemption clauses, which have been introduced by the courts;
- various legislative limitations on the validity of exemption clauses.

Term of the contract

10.3 As in the case of any purported contractual term, the determination of whether what purports to be an exemption clause is a term of the contract depends very much on whether or not the clause is contained in a signed contractual document or not. If it is, it is a contractual term, binding on the party who signed the document, even though he was unaware of it (eg because he had not read it).[1]

1 *L'Estrange v Graucob* [1934] 2 KB 394, DC. For an exception, see para 10.12 below.

10.4 In other cases, eg where the clause is printed on a ticket or an order form or a notice, the clause will only be a contractual term if reasonable notice of it is given. If reasonable notice of it is given, it is irrelevant that the party affected by the term is unaware of it. The following rules apply in this connection.

Notice must be given before or at the time of the contract

10.5 The exemption clause is ineffective unless it was brought to the party's notice before or at the time the contract was made. This is shown by *Olley v Marlborough Court Ltd.*[1] The plaintiff and her husband were accepted as guests at a hotel. They paid for a week in advance and went to their room, on the wall of which was a notice exempting the hotel proprietors from liability for the loss or theft of property. Due to the negligence of the hotel staff, property was stolen from the plaintiff's room. The Court of Appeal held that the hotel was not protected by the exemption clause because the contract had been made before the exemption clause was communicated so that it formed no part of the contract.

There are two exceptions to the present rule. The first is that, if there has been a course of dealings between the parties on the basis of documents incorporating similar terms exempting liability, then, provided those dealings have been of a consistent nature,[2] the court may imply the exemption clause into a particular contract where express notice is given too late. In *J Spurling Ltd v Bradshaw,*[3] the defendant had dealt with the plaintiff warehousemen for many years. He delivered barrels of orange juice to them for storage. Later, he received a document from them which acknowledged receipt and referred to clauses on its back, one of which excluded the plaintiffs from any liability for loss or damage occasioned by their negligence. Subsequently, the defendant refused to pay the storage charges because the barrels were empty on collection. He was sued for these charges and counter-claimed for negligence. The Court of Appeal held that the exemption clause was incorporated into the contract, and the defendant was therefore bound by it, because in previous dealings he had received a document containing the clause, although he had never read it. Since incorporation of an exemption clause in this way depends on a previous consistent course of dealings between the parties it is less likely to occur in the case of contracts to which a private individual is a party, because normally he will have had insufficient dealings with the other party to constitute a course of dealings; three or four dealings over a five-year period, for instance, have been held insufficient to constitute a course of dealing.[4]

The second exception to the rule that an exemption clause is ineffective unless brought to the notice of the party affected before or at the time the contract was made is as follows. An exemption clause may be implied into a contract if both parties are in a particular trade and the clause is used so frequently in dealings in that trade that the party affected must (as a reasonable person in that trade) have known that it would be included in the contract.[5]

1   [1949] 1 All ER 127, CA.
2   *McCutcheon v David MacBrayne Ltd* [1964] 1 All ER 430, HL.
3   [1956] 2 All ER 121, CA.
4   *Hollier v Rambler Motors (AMC) Ltd* [1972] 1 All ER 399, CA.
5   *British Crane Hire Corpn Ltd v Ipswich Plant Hire Ltd* [1974] 1 All ER 1059, CA.

The notice must be contained in a contractual document

10.6 An exemption clause is ineffective if it, or notice of it, is contained in a document which a reasonable person would not assume to contain contractual terms. Thus, in *Chapelton v Barry UDC,*[1] it was held that an exemption clause contained in a ticket for a deck chair on a beach was ineffective because no reasonable person would expect the ticket to be more than a receipt whose object was to enable a hirer to show that he had paid: he would not assume it contained contractual terms.

1   [1940] 1 All ER 356, CA.

Reasonable notice of the exemption clause must be given

10.7   A leading authority is *Parker v South Eastern Rly Co.*[1] The plaintiff left his bag at a station cloakroom. He received a ticket which said on its face: 'See back'. On the back were a number of terms, one of which limited the railway company's liability to £10 per package. The plaintiff's bag was lost and he claimed its value of £24 10s (£24.50). It was held that the plaintiff would be bound by the exemption clause, even though he had not read it, if the railway company had given reasonable notice of its terms. Notice can be reasonable even though it involves reference to other documents or to a notice.[2] The test laid down in *Parker v South Eastern Rly Co* is objective, and if reasonable notice has been given, it is irrelevant that the party affected by the exemption clause was blind or illiterate or otherwise unable to comprehend its meaning.[3]

What amounts to reasonable notice depends in part on the nature of the exemption clause. If it is particularly onerous or unusual and would not generally be known to the other party, more will be required (eg that the clause be printed in different type or colour from the other terms) in order that the notice be held to be reasonable[4] than would be required in a clause of a less onerous or unusual type.

1   (1877) 2 CPD 416, CA.
2   *Watkins v Rymill* (1883) 10 QBD 178; *Thompson v London, Midland and Scottish Rly Co* [1930] 1 KB 41, CA.
3   *Thompson v London, Midland and Scottish Rly Co* [1930] 1 KB 41, CA.
4   *Thornton v Shoe Lane Parking Ltd* [1971] 1 All ER 686, CA; *Interfoto Picture Library Ltd v Stiletto Ltd* [1988] 1 All ER 348, CA.

Interpretation

10.8   If an exemption clause is a term of the contract the next question is whether it applies to the liability in question.

It must be emphasised that there is no rule of law that an exemption clause is eliminated, or deprived of effect, regardless of its terms by a breach of contract, however fundamental that breach may be. The question whether, and to what extent, an exemption clause applies in the event of any breach of contract is answered by construing the contract to see whether the parties intended that the clause should apply to the loss or damage which has occurred in the circumstances in which it has occurred. This was stated by the House of Lords in *Photo Production Ltd v Securicor Transport Ltd.*[1]

In the *Photo Production* case, the plaintiff company employed the defendant company to check against burglaries and fires at their factory at night. One night, the defendant's patrolman deliberately started a fire in the factory. It got out of control and a large part of the premises was burnt down. The loss and damage suffered amounted to £615,000. By way of defence to the plaintiff's action to recover this amount as damages, the defendant relied principally on an exemption clause in its contract with the plaintiff which purported to exempt the defendant from liability for any injurious act by an employee unless it could have been foreseen and avoided by due diligence on its part. The clause added that the defendant was not to be liable for any loss suffered by the plaintiff through fire, except in so far as such loss was solely attributable to the negligence of the defendant's employees acting within the scope of their employment. The House of Lords held that, although the defendant would otherwise have been liable to the plaintiff, on its true construction the exemption clause clearly and unambiguously applied to what had occurred, and protected the defendant from liability.[2]

In case it should be thought that the rule that the application of an exemption clause depends on the construction of the contract is liable to cause injustice in consumer contracts and other contracts based on standard terms, we would point out that exemption clauses in such a contract made nowadays are rendered either totally invalid or invalid unless fair and reasonable by the Unfair Contract Terms Act 1977, as we explain in paras 10.19 to 10.29 below, even though on their true construction they were intended to apply to what has occurred. It follows that the construction of an exemption clause is now generally of crucial importance only where the contract has been negotiated between businessmen capable of looking after their own interests and of deciding how the risks inherent in the performance of the contract can most economically be borne, which is usually by one or other party insuring against such risks.

We set out below certain rules of construction which are applied to exemption clauses by the courts and which tend to favour the party affected by such a clause.

1   [1980] 1 All ER 556, HL. See also *George Mitchell (Chesterhall) Ltd v Finney Lock Seeds Ltd* [1983] 2 All ER 737, HL.
2   The contract in this case was a standard form contract, but, since it was entered into before the Unfair Contract Terms Act 1977, the House of Lords was not concerned with the validity of the exemption clause under that Act.

Liability can only be excluded or restricted by clear words

10.9   The liability in question must be precisely covered by the exemption clause relied on. In *Andrews Bros (Bournemouth) Ltd v Singer & Co Ltd*,[1] the plaintiffs entered into a contract to buy 'new Singer cars' from the defendants. One of the cars delivered by the defendants was not a new car, having run a considerable mileage. A clause in the contract exempted the defendants from liability for breach of all 'conditions, warranties and liabilities *implied* by common law, statute or otherwise' but the Court of Appeal held that this did not protect the defendants against liability for breach of an express term. A similar decision was reached in *Wallis Son and Wells v Pratt and Haynes*.[2] The defendants sold by sample to the plaintiffs seed described as 'common English sainfoin'. The contract stated that the defendants gave 'no *warranty* express or implied' as to any matter concerning the seed. The seed turned out to be the inferior and cheaper 'giant sainfoin'. The House of Lords held that the exemption clause did not apply because there had been a breach of the *condition* implied by the Sale of Goods Act 1979, s 13 (that goods sold by description correspond with it) and the clause did not purport to exclude liability for breach of condition.

This rule of construction is applied more rigorously in the case of clauses purporting to exclude liability than in the case of those purporting to restrict it.[3]

1   [1934] 1 KB 17, CA.
2   [1911] AC 394, HL.
3   *Ailsa Craig Fishing Co Ltd v Malvern Fishing Co Ltd* [1983] 1 All ER 101, HL; *George Mitchell (Chesterhall) Ltd v Finney Lock Seeds Ltd* [1983] 2 All ER 737, HL.

All ambiguities in the exemption clause are construed against the party relying on it

10.10   This is in accordance with the *contra proferentem* rule normally applied in the construction of contracts.[1]

1   *Houghton v Trafalgar Insurance Co* [1953] 2 All ER 1409, CA.

Exclusion of liability for negligence

10.11   The nature of liability for a breach of contract depends on the term broken. In the case of most terms, liability for their breach is strict (ie a party who does not comply with the term is liable despite the absence of any negligence on his part); in the case of others, liability for their breach only arises if the party in question has been negligent (ie he has failed to show reasonable care). This distinction depends upon whether the term broken simply imposes an obligation to do something or that something be of a certain standard, or whether it imposes an obligation *to take reasonable care* (or the like) in relation to something. It should also be borne in mind that, where contractual liability for the breach in question is strict, the guilty party may also be liable in tort if he can be proved to have been negligent.

If an exemption clause clearly purports to exclude *all* liability, effect must be given to it[1] (subject to the general rules as to the validity of exemption clauses), but if the clause is not so clearly drafted the law is as follows:

Where contractual liability for the breach in question is strict, the clause is normally construed as being confined to that contractual liability, and not as extending to any tortious liability for negligence, with the result that the guilty party is not protected by it if he is proved to have been negligent.[2] A leading example is *White v John Warrick & Co Ltd.*[3] The plaintiff hired a tricycle from the defendants. While he was riding it the saddle tilted forward and he was injured. The contract of hire stated: 'nothing in this agreement shall render the owners liable for any personal injury'. The Court of Appeal held that the exemption clause would not protect the defendants from liability in tort if they were found to have been negligent. Its reason was that, in the absence of the exemption clause, the defendants could have been liable for breach of contract in supplying a defective tricycle[4] irrespective of negligence and the operation of the clause had to be restricted to that strict liability.

Where liability can be based on negligence and nothing else, the exemption clause will normally be construed as extending to that head of damage, because if it were not so construed it would lack subject matter.[5] This is shown by *Alderslade v Hendon Laundry Ltd.*[6] The defendants contracted to launder the plaintiff's handkerchiefs, the contract limiting their liability 'for lost or damaged articles' to 20 times the laundering charge. The handkerchiefs were lost through the defendants' negligence. The Court of Appeal held that the only way in which the defendants could be made liable for the loss of the handkerchiefs would be if they could be shown to have been guilty of negligence. It held that the exemption clause applied to limit the defendants' liability for negligence because otherwise the clause would be left without any content at all.

Both these rules are only rules of construction and, although they will normally be adopted, the court is free to construe the clause in another way if, on its wording or other evidence, it considers that the parties had some other intention.[7]

1   *Joseph Travers & Sons Ltd v Cooper* [1915] 1 KB 73, CA.
2   *Alderslade v Hendon Laundry Ltd* [1945] KB 189, CA.
3   [1953] 2 All ER 1021, CA.
4   The term broken would have been an implied term that the tricycle was reasonably fit for the purpose for which it was hired: paras 8.19–8.20 above.
5   *Alderslade v Hendon Laundry Ltd* [1945] KB 189 at 192; *Hollier v Rambler Motors (AMC) Ltd* [1972] 1 All ER 399, CA.
6   [1945] 1 All ER 244, CA.
7   *J Archdale Ltd v Comservices Ltd* [1954] 1 All ER 210, CA; *Hollier v Rambler Motors (AMC) Ltd* [1972] 1 All ER 399, CA; *Mineralimportexport v Eastern Mediterranean Maritime,The Golden Leader* [1980] 2 Lloyds Rep 573.

General limitations on the application of an exemption clause

Misrepresentation

10.12   If the party favoured by an exemption clause induced the other party to accept it by misrepresenting its contents or effect, the clause is rendered ineffective to the extent that it is wider than the misrepresentation, even though the contract was signed by the other party and even though the misrepresentation was innocent. In *Curtis v Chemical Cleaning and Dyeing Co Ltd*,[1] the plaintiff took a dress to the defendants' shop for cleaning. The dress was trimmed with beads and sequins. The plaintiff was asked to sign a receipt exempting the defendants from all liability for any damage to articles cleaned. The plaintiff asked why her signature was required and was told that the receipt exempted the defendants from liability for damage to the sequins and beads. When the dress was returned it was badly stained. It was held that the defendants were not protected by the clause because through their employee they had innocently induced the plaintiff to believe that the clause only referred to damage to the beads and sequins and therefore the clause only protected them against liability for such damage.

1   [1951] 1 All ER 631, CA.

Inconsistent undertakings

10.13   If, at or before the time the contract was made, the party favoured by an exemption clause gives an undertaking which is inconsistent with it, the exemption clause is rendered ineffective to the extent that it is inconsistent with the undertaking, even though the undertaking does not form part of the contract or of a contract collateral to it. In *Mendelssohn v Normand Ltd*,[1] the plaintiff left his car in the defendants' garage on terms contained in a ticket, one of which was that the defendants would not accept any responsibility for any loss sustained by the vehicle or its contents, however caused. The car contained valuables and the plaintiff wanted to lock it, but the attendant told him that this was not permissible. The plaintiff told the attendant about the valuables and the attendant promised to lock the car after he had moved it. On his return, the plaintiff discovered that the valuables had been stolen. The Court of Appeal held that the defendants were not protected by the exemption clause because their employee had in effect promised to see that the valuables were safe, and this oral undertaking took priority over the exemption clause.

1   [1969] 2 All ER 1215, CA.

Third party generally not protected by an exemption clause

10.14   As part of the doctrine of privity of contract,[1] a person who is not a party to a contract containing an exemption clause is generally not protected by the clause, even though it purports to have this effect. In *Cosgrove v Horsfall*,[2] the Court of Appeal held that a clause in a bus pass, exempting the London Passenger Transport Board and its employees from liability for injury, was ineffective to protect the employees from liability in tort for negligence since they were not parties to the contract between the Board and the pass-holder. This decision was approved by the House of Lords in *Scruttons Ltd v Midland Silicones Ltd*,[3] although the clause in that case did not expressly purport to exclude or restrict the liability of the third parties in question. A drum containing chemicals was shipped from New York to London. It was consigned to the plaintiffs under a bill of lading which restricted the carriers' liability to $500 (then about £180). While the drum was being handled by the defendants, who were stevedores employed by the carriers, it was damaged through the defendants' negligence; the damage amounted to £593. The contract between the carriers and the defendants stated that the defendants should have the benefit of the exemption clause in the bill of lading, but the majority of the House of Lords held that the defendants could not limit their liability to the plaintiffs for negligence by relying on the exemption clause because they were not parties to the bill of lading. These two decisions show that it will sometimes be possible to circumvent an exemption clause by bringing proceedings against an employee or sub-contractor on the ground of his negligence. This may be desirable in the case of a standard form contract, particularly because the employee will usually be reimbursed by his employer for, and a sub-contractor insured against, any damages awarded. However, the reliance on the technical rule of privity of contract is harder to justify in the case of a freely negotiated contract in which one party has agreed to assume the risk of damage, particularly where the contract purports to exempt an employee or sub-contractor of the other party.

1   Para 7.1 above.
2   (1945) 175 LT 334, CA.
3   [1962] 1 All ER 1, HL.

10.15   The position may be different where a party to the main contract (A) contracts with the other (B) as agent for the third person on terms that the third person shall have the benefit of the exemption clause. In such a case, the third person may be brought into contractual relations with B and be protected by the clause. This was recognised by the Privy Council in *New Zealand Shipping Co Ltd v A M Satterthwaite & Co Ltd, The Eurymedon*,[1] which showed that there are four prerequisites for the validity of a contract between a third party and B:

- the main contract must make it clear that the third person is intended to be protected by the exemption clause;
- the main contract must make it clear that A, in addition to contracting for the exemption clause on his own behalf, is also contracting as agent for the third person that these provisions should apply to the third person;
- A must have authority from the third person to do that (or the third person can subsequently ratify the agency contract provided he was identifiable at the time it was made[2]); and
- the third person must have provided consideration for the promise as to exemption made to him, through A as his agent, by B.

In the *New Zealand Shipping Co* case the Privy Council explained how the third person can provide consideration for B's promise as to exemption. The main contract brings into existence a bargain initially unilateral but capable of becoming mutual, between B and the third person, made through A as agent. This will become a full contract when the third person performs services under the main contract. The performance of these services for the benefit of B is the consideration for the agreement by B that the third person should have the benefit of the exemption clause contained in the main contract.

The *New Zealand Shipping Co* case is of limited effect because:

- consideration can only be furnished if the third person does something after the main contract has been made. If he has already performed his services, there can be no unilateral contract of the above type and he will not have furnished the consideration necessary to make enforceable any promise as to exemption;
- the third person cannot be said to accept the offer of a unilateral contract unless he knows of the main contract.

1   [1974] 1 All ER 1015, PC.
2   Para 16.9 below.

10.16   Although a party cannot directly take the benefit of an exemption clause if he is not a party to a contract entitling him to do so, he may indirectly benefit from it in some cases. The reason is that an exemption clause may limit his duty of care to one of the contracting parties, and hence his liability in tort for negligence. For example, in two cases where an exemption clause in a building contract placed the risk of damage by fire on the employer, rather than the building contractor, it was held that it would not be just and reasonable to impose on a sub-contractor hired by the building contractor a duty of care to avoid causing damage by fire.[1]

1   *Southern Water Authority v Carey* [1985] 2 All ER 1077; *Norwich City Council v Harvey* [1989] 1 All ER 1180, CA. See, further, para 18.25 below.

Third party not bound by an exemption clause

10.17   Because of the doctrine of privity of contract a third party cannot be deprived of his right to sue in tort by an exemption clause contained in a contract between others, even though it purports to have that effect. An authority is *Haseldine v CA Daw & Son Ltd.*[1] The owners of a block of flats employed the defendants to repair a lift in the block. The defendants repaired the lift negligently and the plaintiff was injured when the lift fell to the bottom of the lift shaft. The defendants were held liable to the plaintiff, it being irrelevant that the contract between the defendants and the owners of the block purported to exempt the defendants from liability for personal injury. Likewise, in *Leigh and Sillivan Ltd v Aliakmon Shipping Co Ltd, The Aliakmon*,[2] where a contract of carriage of goods by sea contained an exemption clause, the buyers of the goods were not bound by it because they were not parties to that contract (whose only parties were the sellers and the shipowners).

1   [1941] 3 All ER 156, CA.
2   [1986] 2 All ER 145, HL.

10.18   The above rule can be avoided in the following cases:

*   If one of the parties to a contract containing an exemption clause in favour of the other contracted as agent for a third person, that person is bound by the clause.
*   It sometimes happens, where T has handed goods to X for repair, cleaning, carriage, loading or the like, that X sub-contracts the work to Y. If the contract between X and Y contains an exemption clause in favour of Y it will not bind T under the law of contract, as we have just seen, and T will normally be able to recover damages from Y for the tort of negligence should Y carry out the sub-contracted work negligently. However, T will not have the right to sue Y for the tort of negligence if he has expressly or impliedly authorised X to make the sub-contract on terms including the exemption clause in question.[1]

1   *Morris v C W Martin & Sons Ltd* [1966] 1 QB 716 at 728; *Singer Co (UK) Ltd v Tees and Hartlepool Port Authority* [1988] 1 FTLR 442.

Validity

10.19   The Unfair Contract Terms Act 1977 contains a number of provisions greatly limiting the extent to which it is possible to 'exclude or restrict liability'. Generally these provisions only apply to the clauses seeking to exclude or restrict 'business liability', which is defined as liability (whether in tort or for breach of contract) which arises *from things done or to be done in the course of a business or from the occupation of premises used for business purposes of the occupier*.[1] In the 1977 Act, *'business'* includes a profession and the activities of any government department or public or local authority.[2] The phrase 'in the course of a business' is discussed in para 10.21 below. The main impact of the 'business liability limitation' on the effect of the Act is that its provisions do not generally apply to exemption clauses in contracts made between private individuals. The exceptions are indicated at the appropriate points below.

Although the Act uses the words 'contract term', we propose generally to use the more familiar expression 'exemption clause'.

1　Unfair Contract Terms Act 1977, s 1(3). The liability of an occupier of premises for breach of an obligation or duty towards a person obtaining access to them for recreational or educational purposes, being liability based on the dangerous state of the premises, is not a business liability of the occupier unless granting that person such access for the purposes concerned falls within the business purposes of the occupier: ibid. Thus, the potential liability of a farmer in the Pennines who grants free access to potholers is not a 'business liability', in so far as it relates to the dangerous state of the potholes and the rest of his premises.

2　Ibid, s 14.

Avoidance of liability for negligence

10.20　Section 2(1) of the Act provides that a person cannot, by reference to an exemption clause or notice, exclude or restrict his liability for death or personal injury (including any disease or impairment of physical or mental condition) resulting from negligence.

In the case of other loss or damage, s 2(2) provides that a person cannot, by reference to an exemption clause or notice, exclude or restrict his liability for negligence, *except in so far as the clause or notice satisfies the 'requirement of reasonableness'*.

These provisions do not extend to a contract of employment, except in favour of the employee.[1]

'Negligence' in this context means the breach:

- of any obligation, arising from the express or implied terms of a contract, to take reasonable care or exercise reasonable skill in the performance of the contract; or
- of any common law duty to take reasonable care or exercise reasonable skill; or
- of the common duty of care imposed by the Occupiers' Liability Act 1957.[2]

Section 2 does not prevent the parties to a contract (eg for the hire of industrial plant) agreeing between themselves which of them should bear liability in negligence for any injury to a third party (eg injury arising from the negligent use of the plant) since this merely *allocates* liability (as opposed to excluding or restricting it).[3]

1　Unfair Contract Terms Act 1977, Sch 1.

2　Ibid, s 1(1). The duty at common law to take reasonable care or exercise reasonable skill, and the duty under the 1957 Act, are discussed in chs 18 and 22 below.

3　*Thompson v T Lohan (Plant Hire) Ltd* [1987] 2 All ER 631, CA.

Avoidance of liability for breach of contract

10.21　Section 3 lays down special rules which apply *as between the contracting parties where one of them deals as consumer or on the other's written standard terms of business*.[1] In the present context, a party to a contract 'deals as consumer' in relation to another party if he neither makes the contract in the course of a business nor holds himself out as doing so, and the other party does make the contract in the course of a business.[2] A dictum by Dillon LJ in *R & B Customs Brokers Co Ltd v United Dominions Trust*[3] provides an explanation of the meaning of the phrase 'in the course of a business':

'There are some transactions which are *clearly integral parts of the business* concerned, and these should be held to have been carried out in the course of those businesses; this would cover, apart from much else, the instance of a one-off adventure in the nature of trade where the transaction itself would constitute a trade or business. There are other transactions, however, ... which are at the highest *only* incidental to the carrying on of the relevant business; *here* a degree of *regularity* is *required* before it can be said that they are an integral part of the business carried on and so entered into in the course of that business.'

In *R & B Customs Brokers* the Court of Appeal held that a company operating as a freight forwarding agent, which had bought a car for the business and personal use of its two directors and sole shareholder, a husband and wife, had not made the purchase in the course of a business. The purchase was *not clearly* an *integral* part of the freight forwarding agency business. It was *only incidental* to it and there was *no regularity* of purchases of the type in question.

In the case of contracts for the sale, hire purchase or other supply[4] of goods there is an additional requirement in order for a party to be 'dealing as consumer', viz that the goods are of a type ordinarily supplied for private use or consumption.[2]

A buyer at an auction or by competitive tender is never regarded as dealing as a consumer.[2]

It is for those claiming that a party does not deal as consumer to show that he does not.[2]

Section 3 provides that, *as against the party dealing as consumer or on the other's written standard terms of business*, the other party cannot by reference to any contract term:

* exclude or restrict his liability for breach of contract; or
* claim to be entitled
  - to render a contractual performance substantially different from that which was reasonably expected of him, or
  - in respect of the whole or any part of his contractual obligation, to render no performance at all,

except in so far as the contract term satisfies the 'requirement of reasonableness'. This provision is widely drawn; for example, a term permitting a holiday company to provide accommodation in a different hotel from that specified in the contract may be held invalid, and so may a term entitling a theatre company to cancel a performance without a refund.

1 Unfair Contract Terms Act 1977, s 3(1).
2 Ibid, s 12.
3 [1988] 1 All ER 847, CA. See also *Davies v Sumner* [1984] 3 All ER 831, HL; *Devlin v Hall* [1990] RTR 320, DC.
4 Ie those described in para 10.27 below.

Matters common to sections 2 and 3
Excepted agreements[1]
10.22 Sections 2 and 3 do not extend to:

* any contract of insurance;
* any contract *so far* as it relates to the creation, transfer or termination of an interest in land[2] or of any right or interest in any patent, trade mark, copyright or the like;
* any contract *so far* as it relates—
  - to the formation or dissolution of a company (which in this context means any body corporate or unincorporated association and includes a partnership), or
  - to its constitution or the rights or obligations of its corporators or members;
* any contract *so far* as it relates to the creation or transfer of securities or of any right or interest in securities.

Contracts of insurance are totally excepted from the Act, but the other contracts are only excepted *so far* as they relate to the specified matters. Presumably, only those parts of such a contract which relate to the specified matters (such as the transfer of an interest in land) are excepted from ss 2 and 3 and the rest of the contract is subject to those sections.

Other exceptions relate to charterparties and the like, and are outside the scope of this book.

1   Unfair Contract Terms Act 1977, Sch 1.
2   A mere contractual licence does not create or transfer an interest in land (see para 30.40 below) and therefore an exemption clause contained in it is subject to ss 2 and 3.

The 'requirement of reasonableness'

10.23   In relation to an exemption clause, the requirement of reasonableness is that the clause itself must have been a fair and reasonable one to be included having regard to the circumstances which were, or ought reasonably to have been, known or in the contemplation of the parties when the contract was made.[1]

Where a party seeks to restrict liability to a specified sum in reliance on an exemption clause, then, in determining whether the clause satisfies the requirement of reasonableness, regard must be had in particular to:

- the resources which that party could expect to be available to him for the purpose of meeting the liability should it arise; and
- how far it was open to him to cover himself by insurance.[2]

It is for the party claiming that an exemption clause satisfies the requirement of reasonableness to show on the balance of probabilities that it does.[3]

In *Smith v Eric S Bush; Harris v Wyre Forest District Council*,[4] Lord Griffiths was of the opinion that the following matters should always be considered in relation to the requirement of reasonableness:

- Were the parties of equal bargaining power? If they were the requirement of reasonableness is more easily discharged than if they were not.
- How difficult is the task being undertaken to which the exemption clause applies? If the task is very difficult or dangerous there may be a high risk of failure, which would be a pointer to the requirement of reasonableness being satisfied.
- What are the practical consequences of the decision on the requirement of reasonableness? This involves the amount of money potentially at stake and the ability of the parties to bear the loss involved, which in turn raises the question of insurance.

It cannot be over-emphasised that it is the clause which must be reasonable in relation to the particular contract; the question is not whether its particular application in the particular case is reasonable. If a clause is drawn so widely as to be capable of applying in unreasonable circumstances it will not be held to be reasonable, even though in the actual situation which has arisen its application would not be unreasonable.[5] A clause may well have various parts to it but, because the whole clause must be subjected to the test of reasonableness, it is not permissible to look only at that part of it which is relied on.[6] A court will be particularly unwilling to find a clause reasonable if it purports to exclude all potential liability.[7]

1   Unfair Contract Terms Act 1977, s 11(1).
2   Ibid, s 11(4).
3   Ibid, s 11(5); *Phillips Products Ltd v Hyland* [1987] 2 All ER 620, CA.

4   [1989] 2 All ER 514, HL.
5   *Walker v Boyle* [1982] 1 All ER 634; *Phillips Products Ltd v Hyland Ltd* [1987] 2 All ER 620 at 628.
6   *Stewart Gill Ltd v Horatio Myer & Co Ltd* [1992] 2 All ER 257, CA.
7   *Lease Management Services Ltd v Purnell Secretarial Services Ltd* (1994) 13 Tr LR 337.

Avoidance of liability arising from sale or supply of goods

10.24   Sections 6 and 7 of the Act of 1977 contain additional provisions dealing with attempts to avoid liability where the ownership or possession of goods has passed.

Sale and hire purchase

10.25   By s 6(1), liability for breach of the obligations arising from:

- the Sale of Goods Act 1979, s 12 (seller's implied undertakings as to title etc);[1]
- the Supply of Goods (Implied Terms) Act 1973, s 8 (the corresponding things in relation to hire purchase),

cannot be excluded or restricted by reference to an exemption clause.

1   These terms are described in para 8.19 above.

10.26   Section 6(2) provides that, *as against a person dealing as consumer,* liability for breach of the obligations arising from:

- the Sale of Goods Act 1979, ss 13, 14 or 15 (seller's implied undertakings as to conformity of goods with description or sample, or as to their quality or fitness for a particular purpose);[1]
- the Supply of Goods (Implied Terms) Act 1973, ss 9, 10 or 11 (the corresponding things in relation to hire purchase),

cannot be excluded or restricted by reference to an exemption clause. It must be emphasised that this provision is limited to the implied terms specified. The validity of a clause excluding or restricting liability for breach of any express term will depend on the application of the principles which we have mentioned in para 10.21 above.

Unlike s 6(1), s 6(2) only vitiates the exemption clause as against a person dealing as consumer. In the present context, a party to a contract 'deals as consumer' in relation to another party if:

- he neither makes the contract in the course of a business nor holds himself out as doing so; and
- the other party does make the contract in the course of a business; and
- the goods passing under or in pursuance of the contract are of a type ordinarily supplied for private use or consumption.[2]

We dealt with the meaning of 'in the course of a business' in para 10.21 above. The upshot of the above provision is that, if a company buys from a dealer a Rolls Royce or a yacht for its chairman, it will 'deal as consumer' and liability for breach of the implied terms just mentioned cannot be excluded or restricted. A buyer at an auction or by competitive tender is never regarded as dealing as consumer.[2] It is for those claiming that a party does not deal as consumer to show that he does not.[2]

Where a party does not deal as consumer, s 6(3) is the operative provision. Section 6(3) provides that, *as against a person dealing otherwise than as consumer,* liability for breach of the obligations arising from the Sale of Goods Act 1979, ss 13–15, or the Supply of Goods (Implied Terms) Act 1973, ss 9–11, can be excluded or restricted by an exemption clause, but *only in so far as the clause satisfies the 'requirement of reasonableness'*.

The provisions of s 6(1) and (3) are exceptional in that they are not limited to liabilities arising in the course of business. Section 6 replaces substantially similar provisions introduced by the Supply of Goods (Implied Terms) Act 1973.

1   These terms are described in para 8.19 above.
2   Unfair Contract Terms Act 1977, s 12.

Miscellaneous contracts under which the ownership or possession of goods passes

10.27   Section 7 of the Act of 1977 deals with exemption clauses purporting to exclude or restrict liability for breach of obligations implied by law[1] into contracts such as those of hire or exchange or for work and materials. Section 7 applies to these contracts a regime which is broadly similar to that just mentioned in relation to sale of goods and hire purchase.

Section 7(2) provides that, *as against a person dealing as consumer* (in the same sense as in sale of goods and hire purchase), liability in respect of the goods' correspondence with description or sample, or their quality or fitness for any particular purpose, cannot be excluded or restricted by reference to an exemption clause.

On the other hand, as against a person dealing otherwise than as consumer, s 7(3) provides that such liability can be excluded or restricted by reference to such a clause, but *only in so far as the clause satisfies the 'requirement of reasonableness'*.

In relation to an exemption clause purporting to exclude or restrict liability for breach of the various terms as to title which are implied by s 2 of the Supply of Goods and Services Act 1982, the position is as follows. Section 7(3A) provides that, where the contract is one by which a person transfers or agrees to transfer to another the property (ie ownership) in the goods, liability for breach of these terms cannot be excluded or restricted by reference to an exemption clause. A contract for work and materials is an example of such a contract. Section 7(3A) does not apply in the case of a contract for the transfer of goods in the case of which there is an intention that the transferor should transfer only such title as he or a third party may have.

On the other hand, by s 7(4), liability in respect of breach of the various terms as to title etc which are implied into other contracts under which ownership or possession passes cannot be excluded or restricted by such a clause, *in so far as the clause satisfies the 'requirement of reasonableness'*. Thus, a different rule applies where such a clause appears in a contract of hire or of pledge from that which applies where it appears in a contract for, say, work and materials.

1   Supply of Goods and Services Act 1982, ss 2–5 and 7–10; see paras 8.19 and 8.20 above.

The 'requirement of reasonableness' in relation to ss 6 and 7

10.28   The provisions which we mentioned in para 10.23 concerning the requirement of reasonableness also apply where that requirement is relevant under ss 6 and 7. However, in addition, in determining for the purposes of these two sections whether a contract term satisfies the requirement of reasonableness, regard must be had in particular to the guidelines specified in Sch 2 to the Act,[1] viz:

•   the strength of the bargaining positions of the parties relative to each other;
•   whether the customer received an inducement to agree to the term, or in accepting it had an opportunity of entering into a similar contract with other persons, but without having to accept a similar term;

- where the term excludes or restricts any relevant liability if some condition is not complied with, whether it was reasonable at the time of the contract to expect that compliance with that condition would be practicable;
- whether the goods were manufactured, processed or adapted to the special order of the customer;
- whether the customer knew or ought reasonably to have known of the existence and extent of the term (eg because it was in small print or was unlikely to be read in full by the customer). We saw in paras 10.3 to 10.7 above that an exemption clause may be a term of the contract even though the customer was unaware of it, especially if he has signed a contractual document containing it. This provision enables the court to hold an exemption clause which is undoubtedly a term of the contract unreasonable, and therefore invalid, because, for instance, the customer could not reasonably have known of its existence.

Although Sch 2 does not apply to the requirement of reasonableness as it applies to ss 2 or 3, it is clear that the courts rely on similar factors to those in Sch 2 when considering the requirement of reasonableness in relation to those sections.[2]

1   Unfair Contract Terms Act 1977, s 11(2).
2   *Phillips Products Ltd v Hyland* [1987] 2 All ER 620, CA; *Stewart Gill Ltd v Horatio Myer & Co Ltd* [1992] 2 All ER 257, CA.

Varieties of exemption clauses

10.29   As we have shown, the Act repeatedly refers to the 'exclusion or restriction of liability'. These words are given a wide interpretation by s 13(1) which provides that, to the extent that the provisions mentioned above prevent the exclusion or restriction of any liability, they also prevent:

- making the liability or its enforcement subject to restrictive or onerous conditions (eg a term requiring 14 days' notice of loss);
- excluding or restricting rules of evidence or procedure (eg a term that failure to complain within 14 days is deemed to be conclusive evidence of proper performance of the contract); or
- excluding or restricting any right or remedy in respect of the liability,[1] or subjecting a person to any prejudice in consequence of his pursuing any such right or remedy.

Section 13(1) also provides that, to the extent that ss 2, 6 and 7 prevent the exclusion or restriction of liability, they also prevent excluding or restricting liability by reference to terms which exclude or restrict the relevant obligation or duty. It follows that a clause purporting to disclaim any potential liability is caught by this provision, even though it purports to prevent a duty arising in the first place (as opposed simply to disclaiming liability for breach of an acknowledged duty).[2]

Whether or not a contract term has the effect of excluding or restricting liability within the above formulation is determined by looking at its effect and substance, and not at its form.[3]

1   Eg a term which allows recovery of damages but which purports to remove any right to terminate the contract for repudiatory breach, or a term which excludes a right to set-off a claim by a buyer for damages for breach against a claim for the price by a seller: *Stewart Gill Ltd v Horatio Myer & Co Ltd* [1992] 2 All ER 257, CA.
2   *Smith v Eric S Bush; Harris v Wyre Forest District Council* [1989] 2 All ER 514, HL.
3   *Phillips Products Ltd v Hyland* [1987] 2 All ER 620, CA; *Smith v Eric S Bush; Harris v Wyre Forest District Council* [1989] 2 All ER 514 at 530; *Johnstone v Bloomsbury Health Authority* [1991] 2 All ER 293, CA.

Unfair Terms in Consumer Contracts Regulations 1994

10.30   These Regulations, which give effect to the EC Directive on Unfair Terms in Consumer Contracts, Directive 93/13/EEC, are intended to harmonise the law relating to unfair terms in contracts between a seller or supplier and a consumer.

We deal in more detail with the regulations in chapter 14; but it should be noted here that they cover matters already covered by the Unfair Contract Terms Act 1977. However, as will be seen, in some respects the Act is wider than the Regulations since:

- the Regulations are limited to contracts made by a 'consumer', whereas the Act is not;
- to the extent that the Act has special provisions relating to 'consumers', 'consumer' has a wider meaning under the Act, since under the Regulations a 'consumer' means 'any natural person who ... is acting for purposes outside his business' (so that, for example, a company entering into a one-off contract which was not integral to its business would not be a 'consumer' under the Regulations, although it would be under the Act);[1]
- in the case of consumer contracts for the sale or supply of goods, liability for breach of statutorily implied terms as to description or quality cannot be excluded under the Act regardless of whether they are reasonable or not, nor can liability for breach of the implied term as to title in any sale or supply contract, whereas under the Regulations an exemption clause of such a type in a consumer contract will only be invalid if it is unfair.

As will be seen in chapter 14, in some respects the Regulations are wider than the Unfair Contract Terms Act, since they are not limited to exemption clauses, but extend to any 'unfair term' (as defined by the Regulations).

Despite these differences, there is a substantial area of overlap between the Act and the Regulations. It follows that, in many cases involving exemption clauses, the application of the Act and of the Regulations must be considered.

1   Para 10.21 above.

Chapter 11

Discharge by frustration

11.1 Under the doctrine of frustration a contract is automatically discharged 'whenever the law recognises that, without default of either party,[1] a contractual obligation has become incapable of being performed because the circumstances in which performance is called for would render it a thing radically different from that which was undertaken by the contract'.[2] This classic statement has been approved in a substantial number of cases.[3]

1 For a qualification see para 11.13 below.
2 *Davis Contractors Ltd v Fareham UDC* [1956] 2 All ER 145.
3 See, for example, *National Carriers Ltd v Panalpina (Northern) Ltd* [1981] 1 All ER 161, HL; *Pioneer Shipping Ltd v BTP Tioxide Ltd*, *The Nema* [1981] 2 All ER 1030, HL; *Paal Wilson & Co A/S v Partenreederei Hannah Blumenthal*, *The Hannah Blumenthal* [1983] 1 All ER 34, HL.

11.2 In this chapter we consider:

- the scope of the doctrine of frustration;
- certain limits on its application;
- the legal effect of the frustration of a contract.

Scope

11.3 A contract may be frustrated if, for example, *subsequent to its formation*:

- a thing essential to its performance is destroyed or becomes unavailable; or
- a fundamental change of circumstances occurs; or
- a party to a contract of a personal nature dies or is otherwise incapacitated from performing it; or
- performance of it is rendered illegal; or
- a basic assumption on which the parties contracted is destroyed.

The doctrine of frustration does not apply to cases where one of these circumstances existed at the time the contract was made: there the legal position must be answered by reference to the law relating to mistake[1] and illegal contracts.[2]

In addition, a contract is not discharged by frustration simply because a subsequent event makes its performance more costly or difficult than envisaged when the contract was made. This is shown by *Davis Contractors Ltd v Fareham UDC*.[3] In 1946, the contractors entered into a contract with the council to build 78 houses for the fixed sum of £94,000. Owing to an unexpected shortage of skilled labour and of certain materials, the contract took 22 months to complete instead of the anticipated eight months and cost £115,000. The contractors contended that the contract had been frustrated by the long delay and that they were entitled to a sum in excess of the contract price on a restitutionary basis (ie reasonable recompense for the benefit which they had conferred). The House of Lords disagreed, holding that the mere fact that unforeseen circumstances had delayed the performance of the contract and made it more costly to perform did not discharge the contract.

1   Paras 13.3–13.13 below.
2   Para 4.1 above.
3   [1956] 2 All ER 145, HL.

Supervening destruction or unavailability

11.4   A contract is discharged by frustration if performance of it is rendered impossible by the subsequent destruction or unavailability of a specific thing contemplated by the contract as essential to its performance. A leading authority is *Taylor v Caldwell*.[1] The defendants agreed to hire a music hall and gardens to the plaintiffs on specified days for the purpose of concerts. Before the first of the specified days, the music hall was destroyed by fire without the fault of either party. The defendants were held not liable for breach of contract because performance of the contract had become impossible through the destruction of the hall and they were not at fault. The contract was therefore frustrated and both parties discharged from their contractual obligations.

The subsequent unavailability of a thing will frustrate a contract if it renders performance of the contract in accordance with its terms impossible. This is shown by *Nickoll and Knight v Ashton Edridge & Co*.[2] The defendants sold the plaintiffs a cargo of cotton seed to be shipped 'per steamship *Orlando* during the month of January'. Before the time for shipping arrived, the ship was so damaged by stranding as to be unable to load in January. It was held that the contract was discharged by frustration.

In order that a contract be frustrated under the present heading, the thing which has been destroyed or is otherwise unavailable must have been expressly or impliedly required by the contract for its performance. This point is well illustrated by *Tsakiroglou & Co Ltd v Noblee Thorl GmbH*,[3] which concerned a contract for the sale of groundnuts which were to be shipped from the Sudan to Hamburg during November or December 1956. Both parties contemplated that the ship would proceed via the Suez Canal but this was not stated in the contract. On 2 November 1956, the Canal was closed (and remained so for five months). The House of Lords held that the unavailability of the Canal did not frustrate the contract, one of its reasons being that there was no express provision in the contract for shipping via the Canal, nor could a provision be implied to that effect, because the route was immaterial to the buyers.

A fortiori, unavailability of a thing does not frustrate the contract if it merely affects the method of performance contemplated by one of the parties.[4] In *Nickoll and Knight v Ashton Edridge & Co*, for instance, the contract would not have been frustrated if, instead of the name of the ship on which the cargo was to be loaded being stated in the contract, the defendant sellers had merely intended to load on that ship.

1   (1863) 3 B & S 826.
2   [1901] 2 KB 126, CA.
3   [1961] 2 All ER 179, HL.
4   *Blackburn Bobbin Co v T W Allen & Sons* [1918] 2 KB 467, CA.

Fundamental change of circumstances

11.5   A contract is frustrated if an event occurs of such gravity that, although technically the contract could still be performed, it would be the performance of a radically different contract from that contemplated.

In *Metropolitan Water Board v Dick Kerr & Co Ltd,*[1] the company contracted with the Board to construct a reservoir within six years, subject to a proviso that time could be extended if delay was caused by difficulties, impediments or obstructions. After two years had elapsed the Minister of Munitions, acting under statutory powers, required the company to stop work on the contract and remove and sell their plant. The House of Lords held that the interruption created by the prohibition was of such a nature and duration that the contract, if resumed, would in effect be radically different from that originally made. Therefore it was frustrated.

This case can be contrasted with *Tsakiroglou & Co Ltd v Noblee Thorl GmbH.* In that case, the House of Lords held that the contract was not frustrated by the closure of the Suez Canal because a voyage round the Cape of Good Hope would not be commercially or fundamentally different from shipping via the Canal, albeit it was more expensive for the sellers.

1   [1918] AC 119, HL.

Death or other personal incapacity

11.6   A contract of employment, or any other contract which can only be performed by a party personally, eg a contract to paint a portrait, is discharged by frustration if that party dies[1] or is otherwise rendered *permanently* incapable of performing it.[2]

If a person becomes *temporarily* incapable of performing such a contract, it may be discharged. Whether or not the temporary incapacity frustrates a contract depends on whether, in the light of the probable duration of the incapacity at its inception, performance after it has ceased would be radically different from what was envisaged by the contract and in effect be the substitution of a new contract. In *Morgan v Manser,*[3] the defendant, a comedian, entered into a contract with the plaintiff in 1938 whereby he engaged the plaintiff's services as manager for 10 years. In 1940, the defendant was called up and was not demobilised until 1946. It was held that the contract was discharged by frustration in 1940 since it was then likely that the defendant would have to remain in the forces for a very long time. Similarly, if the duration of an employee's illness is likely to be so lengthy as to make performance of a contract of employment radically different from that undertaken by him and accepted by his employer, the contract will be discharged by frustration, and so will a contract to perform at a concert on a specified day by an illness of short duration.[4] Conversely, a contract of a personal nature is not frustrated by the illness of a party where this is likely to last for only a small part of the period of the contract: further performance after the party becomes available again will not be the performance of a radically different contract.

1   *Stubbs v Holywell Rly Co Ltd* (1867) LR 2 Exch 311.
2   *Notcutt v Universal Equipment Co (London) Ltd* [1986] 3 All ER 582, CA.
3   [1947] 2 All ER 666.
4   *Robinson v Davison* (1871) LR 6 Exch 269.

Supervening illegality

11.7   A change in the law or in the circumstances may make performance of the contract illegal. If the change is such as to make it impossible to perform the contract legally it is discharged by frustration. In *White and Carter Ltd v Carbis Bay Garage Ltd,*[1] for instance, it was held that a contract made in 1939 to display advertisements for three years was frustrated by wartime Defence Regulations prohibiting advertisements of the type in question. On the other hand, in *Cricklewood Property and Investment Trust Ltd v Leighton's Investment Trust Ltd*,[2] the House of Lords held that a 99-year building lease was not frustrated by Defence Regulations prohibiting building for only a small part of that term: performance had merely been suspended, not made impossible.

1   [1941] 2 All ER 633, CA.
2   [1945] 1 All ER 252, HL.

Supervening destruction of a basic assumption on which the parties contracted

11.8   A contract is discharged by frustration if, although it is physically and legally possible for each party to perform his obligations under the contract, a change of circumstances has destroyed a basic assumption on which the parties contracted. In *Krell v Henry*,[1] the defendant agreed to hire a flat in Pall Mall from the plaintiff for 26 and 27 June 1902, on one of which days Edward VII was to be crowned. To the plaintiff's knowledge, the defendant hired the flat in order to view the Coronation processions, but this was not mentioned in their written contract. The processions were postponed because of the King's illness.

The Court of Appeal held that a view of the processions was not simply the purpose of the defendant in hiring the flat but the basis of the contract for both parties, and that since the postponement of the processions prevented this being achieved the contract was frustrated.

It is not enough that the purpose of one party in making the contract cannot be fulfilled; the basis on which both parties contracted must have been destroyed. This is shown by *Herne Bay Steam Boat Co v Hutton*,[2] which also reveals the difficulty in drawing the distinction. The defendant chartered a ship from the plaintiffs for 28 and 29 June 1902, for the express purpose of taking fare-paying passengers to see the Coronation naval review at Spithead and to cruise round the fleet. The review was cancelled, but the fleet remained.

The Court of Appeal held that the charterparty was not frustrated because the holding of the review was not the basis on which both parties had contracted and it was irrelevant that the purpose of the defendant was defeated.

1   [1903] 2 KB 740, CA.
2   [1903] 2 KB 683, CA.

Limits

11.9   There are no limits on the type of contract to which, as a matter of law, the doctrine of frustration can apply. In relation to most types of contract, the applicability of the doctrine is long-established; but it was only in 1980 in *National Carriers Ltd v Panalpina (Northern) Ltd*[1] that the House of Lords finally decided, with one dissentient, that the doctrine of frustration is applicable to a lease, although on the facts the particular lease was not frustrated. Their Lordships stated that cases where a lease would be frustrated would be extremely rare. In the case of a long lease, and it must be remembered that a lease may often be for 99 years or 999 years, a prime reason is that, if the lessee is only deprived temporarily of the use of the premises, the interruption of use will almost never be for long enough to frustrate the contract. Moreover, in the case of the destruction, or the like, of the premises, the lease will normally expressly provide for that event by covenants as to insurance and rebuilding, and thereby exclude the doctrine of frustration.

A contract for a lease and a contract for the sale of land can, of course, be discharged by frustration.[2] However, it is clear that such a contract will only be frustrated in the most extreme cases, since it has been held, for example, that a contract for the sale of premises is not frustrated simply because, before completion of the contract by conveyance, they are destroyed[3] or made subject to a compulsory purchase order.[4] In these cases, at least, the purchaser will be compensated by the payment of insurance monies or compulsory purchase compensation. Much greater hardship will be suffered by the person who has contracted to lease or buy land for redevelopment but before completion the buildings on it are listed as being of special architectural interest, so that re-development becomes difficult or impossible and the land loses most of its value. It has been held that the contract is not frustrated in such a case,[5] and consequently the person who has contracted to lease or buy remains bound to go ahead with a venture which is financially disastrous.

1   [1981] 1 All ER 161, HL.
2   Contract for a lease: *Rom Securities Ltd v Rogers (Holdings) Ltd* (1967) 205 Estates Gazette 427; contract for sale of land: assumed in *Amalgamated Investment and Property Co Ltd v John Walker & Sons Ltd* [1976] 3 All ER 509, CA.
3   *Paine v Meller* (1801) 6 Ves 349.
4   *Hillingdon Estates Co v Stonefield Estates Ltd* [1952] 1 All ER 853.
5   *Amalgamated Investment and Property Co Ltd v John Walker & Sons Ltd* [1976] 3 All ER 509, CA,

Express provision for frustrating event

11.10   The doctrine of frustration does not apply if the parties have made provision to deal with the frustrating event which has occurred. There is one exception: a contract is frustrated by supervening illegality despite an express provision to the contrary.[1]

A provision concerned with the effect of a possible future event is narrowly construed and, unless on its true construction it covers the frustrating event in question, the doctrine of frustration is not ousted. This is shown by *Metropolitan Water Board v Dick Kerr & Co Ltd*,[2] discussed above, where the contract for the reservoir provided that in the event of delays 'however caused' the contractors were to be given an extension of time. The House of Lords held that this provision did not prevent the doctrine of frustration applying because it did not cover the particular event which had occurred. Although the event was literally within the provision, the provision could be construed as limited to temporary difficulties, such as shortage of supplies, and not as extending to events which fundamentally altered the nature of the contract and which could not have been in the parties' contemplation when they made the contract.

1   *Ertel Bieber & Co v Rio Tinto Co Ltd* [1918] AC 260, HL.
2   [1918] AC 119, HL.

Foreseen and foreseeable events

11.11   If, by reason of special knowledge, the risk of the particular frustrating event was foreseen or foreseeable by only *one* party the doctrine of frustration cannot apply. It is up to that party to provide against the risk of that event and, if he fails to do so and cannot perform the contract, he is liable for breach.[1]

On the other hand, where the risk of the frustrating event was foreseen or foreseeable by both parties, but they did not make provision to deal with it, the doctrine of frustration can apply.[2] In each case, however, it is a question of construction whether the failure to make provision for the event means that each party took the risk of it rendering contractual performance impossible or whether, in the absence of any such intention, the doctrine of frustration should apply to discharge the contract.[3]

1   *Walton Harvey Ltd v Walker and Homfrays Ltd* [1931] 1 Ch 274, CA.
2   *Ocean Tramp Tankers Corpn v V/O Sovfracht, The Eugenia* [1964] 1 All ER 161, CA.

3   *Chandler Bros Ltd v Boswell* [1936] 3 All ER 179, CA; *Ocean Tramp Tankers Corpn v V/O Sovfracht, The Eugenia* [1964] 1 All ER 161, CA.

Fault of a party

11.12   A party cannot rely on the doctrine of frustration if it is proved that the frustrating event was brought about by his fault, but (assuming that he has not also contributed to the event by his fault) the other party can.[1]

A deliberate election to pursue a course of conduct which renders performance of the contract impossible or illegal is clearly established as fault in this context; that conduct may in itself be a breach of contract,[2] but it is not necessary that it should be.[3] In *Maritime National Fish Ltd v Ocean Trawlers Ltd*,[4] the plaintiffs chartered to the defendants a trawler fitted with an otter trawl. Both parties knew that the use of an otter trawl without a licence from a minister was illegal. Later, the defendants applied for licences for five trawlers which they were operating, including the plaintiffs'. They were only granted three licences and were asked to specify the three trawlers which they wished to have licensed. The defendants named three trawlers other than the plaintiffs'. They then claimed that they were no longer bound by the charterparty because it had been frustrated. The Privy Council held that the frustration was due to the defendants' deliberate act in not specifying the plaintiffs' trawler for a licence and that therefore they could not rely on the doctrine of frustration. Consequently, the plaintiffs could recover the hire under the charterparty.

Any deliberate choice of conduct which renders performance of the contract impossible or illegal suffices for present purposes, however reasonable it is to make that choice.[5]

It would seem that a negligent act by a party, as opposed to a deliberate choice of conduct, which renders performance of the contract impossible or illegal prevents him relying on the doctrine of frustration.[6]

The onus of proof where fault is alleged is on the party alleging it.[7]

1   *FC Shepherd & Co Ltd v Jerrom* [1986] 3 All ER 589, CA.
2   As in *Ocean Tramp Tankers Corpn v V/O Sovfracht, The Eugenia* [1964] 1 All ER 161, CA. In fact, the deliberate conduct in question may constitute a breach by both parties: *Paal Wilson & Co A/S v Partenreederei Hannah Blumenthal, The Hannah Blumenthal* [1983] 1 All ER 34, HL.
3   *Denmark Productions Ltd v Boscobel Productions Ltd* [1968] 3 All ER 513, CA; *J Lauritzen AS v Wijsmuller BV, The Super Servant Two* [1990] 1 Lloyd's Rep 1, CA.
4   [1935] AC 524, PC.
5   *J Lauritzen AS v Wijsmuller BV, The Super Servant Two* [1990] 1 Lloyd's Rep 1, CA.
6   Ibid.
7   *Joseph Constantine SS Line Ltd v Imperial Smelting Corpn Ltd* [1941] 2 All ER 165, HL.

Effect

11.13   Frustration does not merely make the contract terminable at the election of a party: the frustrating event *automatically* discharges the contract at the time that it is frustrated[1] (except that provisions intended by the parties to apply in the event of frustration, such as one dealing with its consequences, remain in force).[2]

As explained in the previous paragraph, where the frustrating event is brought about by the fault of one party, the other party may rely on it as discharging the contract but the party at fault cannot.[3]

Leaving aside the complicated question of the effect of frustration on money paid or payable under the contract, the effect of frustration on other obligations under the contract is governed by the common law and is as follows: the discharge of a contract by frustration releases both parties from further performance of any such obligations due after the frustrating event[4] but not from any such obligations due before that time, which remain enforceable.[4]

Turning to the effect of frustration on money paid or payable under the contract, the position is as follows.

1   *Hirji Mulji v Cheong Yue SS Co Ltd* [1926] AC 497, PC.
2   *Heyman v Darwins Ltd* [1942] 1 All ER 337, HL; *B P Exploration Co (Libya) Ltd v Hunt (No 2)* [1982] 1 All ER 925, CA; affd ibid, 986, HL.
3   *F C Shepherd & Co Ltd v Jerrom* [1986] 3 All ER 589, CA.
4   *Chandler v Webster* [1904] 1 KB 493, CA.

Money paid or payable under the contract before the occurrence of the frustrating event

11.14   At common law, the original position was that an obligation to pay money due before the frustrating event remained enforceable and money paid under the contract before that event was irrecoverable.[1] However, in 1942, in *Fibrosa Spolka Akcyjna v Fairbairn Lawson Combe Barbour Ltd*,[2] a case where money payable in advance for machinery had been paid but the contract had been frustrated before any of the machinery had been delivered, the House of Lords held that the money could be recovered back on the ground of a total failure of consideration, in the sense that the sellers had not performed any part of their contractual duties in respect of which payment was due.[3]

The decision in the *Fibrosa* case left the law unjust in two ways:

*   The decision only permitted recovery if there had been a total failure of consideration. This could be unjust to the payer of the money because, if the payee had performed any part of his contractual duties, however small, in respect of which the money was due, the payer could not recover a penny of what he had paid.
*   The decision could also be unjust to a payee who was ordered to return a pre-payment because he might have incurred expenses in preparing to perform his contractual duties in respect of which the money was due.

1   *Chandler v Webster* [1904] 1 KB 493, CA.
2   [1942] 2 All ER 122, HL.
3   *Stocznia Gdanska SA v Latvian Shipping Co* [1998] 1 All ER 883, HL.

11.15   These injustices were removed by the Law Reform (Frustrated Contracts) Act 1943. Section 1(2) of the Act provides:

*   all sums *payable* under the contract *before* the frustrating event *cease to be payable* whether or not there has been a total failure of consideration;
*   all sums *paid* under the contract *before* the frustrating event are *recoverable* whether or not there has been a total failure of consideration;
*   the court has a discretionary power to allow the payee to set off against the sums so paid or payable a sum not exceeding the value of the expenses he has incurred before the frustrating event in, or for the purpose of, the performance of the contract.

If the court exercises this power, the last point above, it allows the payee to retain the amount stipulated by it (if he has been paid) or to recover the stipulated amount (if money was payable but not paid). The stipulated amount, which may include an element in respect of overhead expenses and of any work or services performed personally by the payee,[1] cannot exceed the sums paid or payable to him. The following illustrates the operation of these provisions. X contracts with Y to manufacture and deliver certain machinery by 1 March for £5,000, £1,000 to be paid on 1 January and the balance of £4,000 on delivery. The contract is discharged by frustration on 1 February before the machinery is delivered but after X has incurred expenses of £500 in making the machinery. Pursuant to s 1(2), Y need not pay the £1,000 if he has not paid it before 1 February or, if he has, he can recover the £1,000, but the court may order Y to pay X up to £500 for his expenses or may allow X to retain up to £500, as the case may be.

1   Law Reform (Frustrated Contracts) Act 1943, s 1(4).

Money payable under the contract after the occurrence of the frustrating event

11.16   Such money is not recoverable by the party to whom it was due, in accordance with the rule that frustration releases both parties from performing any contractual obligation due after the frustrating event. Thus, in *Krell v Henry*,[1] it was held that the owner of the flat could not recover a sum payable for the hire of the flat because it was not due until a time after the processions had been postponed (the frustrating event). Likewise, the balance of £4,000 referred to in the example in the previous paragraph is not recoverable by X because it was not due until after the frustrating event. In further contrast to the rules outlined in para 11.15 above, the courts do not have power to allow a claim in respect of his expenses by a party to whom money was payable only after the frustrating event, because the Act of 1943 does not apply in such a case.

1   [1903] 2 KB 740, CA; para 11.8 above.

Award for valuable benefit obtained

11.17   At common law, a party who had benefited another by partly performing the contract before it was frustrated could not recover any sum of money for this.[1] This rule was particularly harsh where payment was not due to him until after the occurrence of the frustrating event because where money was paid or payable before that time he could retain or recover it, as the case might be.

The Law Reform (Frustrated Contracts) Act 1943, s 1(3), now makes a monetary award available to either party for a valuable benefit conferred on the other. It provides that where a party to a frustrated contract has, by reason of anything done by any other party in, or for the purpose of, the performance of the contract, obtained a valuable benefit before the frustrating event (other than the payment of money to which s 1(2) applies), that other party may recover from him such sum, if any, as the court considers just, having regard to all the circumstances of the case.

In assessing the amount of an award under s 1(3), the court must first identify and value the benefit obtained by the benefited party (whom we will call B). Where services rendered by the other party (whom we will call A) have an end-product, B's benefit is the end-product of those services.[2] It follows, for example, that, in the case of a building contract which is frustrated when the building is partially completed, the benefit to be valued is the uncompleted building, not the work put in by the builder. This is important because occasionally a relatively small service performed under a contract may confer a substantial benefit, and vice versa. Sometimes services will have no end-product, as where they consist of transporting goods. In such a case the benefit is the value of the services.[2] Generally speaking, valuation of the benefit must be made as at the date of the frustration and not at an earlier time when the benefit was received.[2] In particular, the court must take into account the effect in relation to the benefit of the circumstances giving rise to the frustration,[3] so that if a builder (A) contracts to do building work on B's house and, when he has nearly finished, the house (including A's work) is seriously damaged by fire, and the building contract is thereby frustrated, the valuation of the benefit relates to the value of what remains of A's work as at the date of frustration. From the benefit valued in the above way there must be deducted any expenses incurred by the benefited party (B) before the contract was frustrated, including any sums paid or payable by him to A under the contract and retained or recoverable by A under s 1(2).[3]

The value of the benefit assessed by the court under the above principles forms the upper limit of an award under s 1(3) but not the award itself. This is because the court, having identified and valued the benefit, must then decide on a 'just sum' within that upper limit to award to A in respect of his performance. Here, the court should take into particular account the contract consideration, since in many cases it will be unjust to award more than that consideration or a rateable part of it. The fact that A has broken the contract in some way before the frustration has no bearing on the just sum to be awarded to him, although B's claim to damages for the breach may be the subject of a counter-claim or set-off if not statute-barred.[2]

1   *Appleby v Myers* (1867) LR 2 CP 651.
2   *BP Exploration Co (Libya) Ltd v Hunt (No 2)* [1982] 1 All ER 925; affd ibid, 986, HL.
3   Law Reform (Frustrated Contracts) Act 1943, s 1(3).

11.18   The operation of the Act of 1943 can be illustrated as follows: A, a jobbing decorator, contracts with B to paint the outside of B's house for £900, £300 to be paid on 1 September and the rest on completion. B pays A the £300 on 1 September. After A has painted most of the house the contract is frustrated, A having been seriously incapacitated in a car crash. Under s 1(2), A must return the £300 to B, unless and to the extent that the court exercises its discretion to allow A to retain some or all of it. Suppose that A's expenses were £50 and the court allows him to retain this, only £250 will be recoverable by B. The obligation as to the further £600 is, of course, discharged by frustration and A cannot claim this from B. However, as A has conferred a valuable benefit on B before the frustrating event, s 1(3) comes into play. Suppose that the value of the paintwork completed by A is £525 as at the date of the frustration, the court must then deduct what it has allowed A to retain under s 1(2) and the resulting sum (ie £475) will be the upper limit of the 'just sum' awarded by the court under s 1(3).

Scope of the Act of 1943

11.19   Where a contract to which the Act applies is severable,[1] eg a contract to work for a year at £900 a month, and a severable part of it is wholly performed before the frustrating event, or wholly performed except in respect of payment of sums which are or can be ascertained under the contract, that part is to be treated as if it were a separate contract and had not been frustrated, and the Act is only applicable to the remainder of the contract.[2] The result is that, if the employee under the above contract works for two months and two weeks and then dies before any salary has been paid, his executors can recover the two months' salary owing to him (each month being treated as a separate contract) plus an award under s 1(3) of the Act for any valuable benefit conferred by the deceased on the employer during the remaining two weeks.

1   Ie complete performance by one party is not a condition of the other party's obligations becoming due.
2   Section 2(4).

11.20   Where a contract contains a provision (such as one precluding any recovery of any award under the Act or one limiting such an award) which is intended to have effect in the event of circumstances arising which operate, or would but for the provision operate, to frustrate the contract, or is intended to have effect whether such circumstances arise or not, the court must give effect to that provision and only give effect to s 1(2) and (3) of the Act to such extent, if any, as is consistent with that provision.[1]

1   Section 2(3). See, further, *BP Exploration Co (Libya) Ltd v Hunt (No 2)* [1982] 1 All ER 925; affd ibid, 986, HL.

11.21   The Act does not apply to the following types of contract:

- a contract of insurance.[1] Generally, a premium is not returnable once the risk has attached;
- a contract to which the Sale of Goods Act 1979, s 7 applies.[1] Section 7 provides that where there is an agreement to sell specific goods, and subsequently, without any fault on the part of the seller or buyer, the goods *perish before the risk passes to the buyer*, the agreement is thereby avoided. Where a contract is avoided under s 7, the principles laid down by the House of Lords in the *Fibrosa* case[2] apply. Under these a buyer who has paid for the goods before they perished can recover his payment only if there has been a total failure of consideration, in which case the seller has no right of set-off for any expenses he may have incurred in seeking to perform the contract before the goods perished.

1   Section 2(5).
2   Para 11.14 above.

Chapter 12

Remedies for breach of contract

12.1 In the event of a breach of contract, the injured party may have one or more of the following remedies:

- He may, subject to any applicable and effective exemption clause,[1] and to the rules discussed in paras 12.2 to 12.23 below, recover damages for any loss suffered as a result of the breach by bringing an action for damages for breach of contract.
- If a breach consists of the other party's failure to pay a debt, ie the contractually agreed price or other remuneration, due under the contract, the appropriate course for the injured party is to bring an action for the agreed sum to recover that amount, rather than an action for damages. We discuss this further in paras 12.24 to 12.26 below. A person who recovers an agreed sum may also recover damages for any further loss which he has suffered.
- In the case of a repudiatory breach, the injured party may terminate the contract for breach, ie accept the breach as discharging the contract, thereby discharging himself from any obligation to perform the contract further. If the injured party elects to terminate for repudiatory breach, he may also bring an action for damages for any loss suffered. We have already discussed termination for repudiatory breach in detail in paras 9.14 to 9.31 above.
- Where the injured party has performed part of his own obligations, but is unjustifiably prevented from completing them by the other party, he may sue under the law of restitution for the value of what he has done *if he terminates the contract for breach.* We discuss this further in para 12.27 below.
- Where he has paid the contractual price, but the other party has not performed any part of his contractual duties in respect of which the payment is due under the contract, the injured party may sue under the law of restitution for the return of the money paid *if he terminates the contract for breach.* If the failure of consideration is not total but only partial, an action for the return of money paid is not available. However, if–
  - the partial performance is such as to entitle the plaintiff to terminate the contract, and he elects to do so, and
  - he is able to restore what he has received under the contract, and does so before he has derived any benefit from it,

  he is said to bring about a total failure of consideration and is entitled to recover back what he has paid. A common example of this is where the buyer of defective goods rejects them immediately and claims back his payment. We dealt with these matters in slightly more detail in para 9.17 above.

• In appropriate cases, the injured party may seek a decree of specific performance or an injunction in addition to, or instead of, damages. We discuss this further in paras 12.28 to 12.35 below.

1   Ch 10.

Damages

12.2   Damages for breach of contract are not awarded to punish the defendant (with the result that the amount awarded is not affected by the manner of the breach or the motive behind it[1]) but to compensate the plaintiff for the loss or damage which he has suffered as a result of the breach of contract.[2]

This means that, where he has not suffered any loss or damage as a result of the breach, the damages recoverable by him will as a general rule be purely nominal (usually in the region of £2 to £20). However, in a few exceptional cases, a plaintiff can recover substantial damages for a loss which he has not suffered. One exception is where the plaintiff made the contract as agent or trustee for another.[3] If the contract is broken in such a case and the plaintiff sues for damages on the other's behalf he can recover substantial damages for the loss suffered by the other as a result of the breach.[4]

Judicial awareness that the general rule can have unfortunate results has led to the creation of further exceptions to it in a number of modern decisions. One of these was established by the decision in *St Albans City and District Council v International Computers Ltd,*[5] where the Court of Appeal held that a plaintiff could recover substantial damages in respect of loss suffered by a third party if the plaintiff was under a duty to act in the best interests of the third party, although not strictly a trustee. In this case, the plaintiff council purchased from the defendant company a computer program for its collection of community charge payments. The program was defective. As a result of this breach of contract the number of chargepayers was overstated when the program was used to extract the number of chargepayers. One result was that the plaintiff council had to pay £685,000 to the county council by way of increased precept payments. It could not recover it from the county council, but it was obliged to recover it from chargepayers by setting a higher community charge for the following year. When sued for the £685,000, the defendant company argued that the plaintiff council had not itself suffered any loss as a result of its breach of contract because the council had recouped its loss, and the only loss remaining was that of the chargepayers. The Court of Appeal upheld an award of £685,000 on the ground that, although not strictly a trustee, the plaintiff council had no less a capacity than a trustee to recover damage for breach of contract for the chargepayers' benefit. Otherwise the chargepayers would be out of pocket.

Another modern exception relates to a contract concerning land or goods where the parties contemplated when they contracted that the proprietary interest in the property might be transferred, before the time for contractual performance, by one party to a third party who would not have a right of action for breach of the contract. Here, unless they had some other intention, the parties are treated as having made the contract on the footing that the party who subsequently transfers his interest would be entitled to enforce his contractual rights for the benefit of the third party transferee.[6] Thus, if A makes a contract with B for B to do some repair work to a building, which (as B knows) A may transfer to a third party before the time the contract is to be performed, and B in breach of contract does the work defectively after the property has been transferred to C, A can sue B for substantial damages for the loss caused to C by the defective work, since A and B are treated as having contracted on the basis that A would be entitled to enforce his contractual rights for the benefit of the third party transferee who has no contractual right of action.[6]

In a recent case the Court of Appeal[7] derived a broad principle from the case law on the above exception. It held that the general rule can be modified by an agreement, express or implied, between the parties so as to permit recovery of substantial damages by a party where the actual financial loss has been borne by a third party.

1   *Addis v Gramophone Co Ltd* [1909] AC 488, HL.
2   For a recent authority for this well-established rule, see *Surrey County Council v Bredero Homes Ltd* [1993] 3 All ER 705, CA.
3   *Lloyd's v Harper* (1880) 16 Ch D 290, CA.
4   *Lloyd's v Harper* (1880) 16 Ch D 290, CA; *Woodar Investment Development Ltd v Wimpey Construction (UK) Ltd* [1980] 1 All ER 571, HL.
5   [1996] 4 All ER 481, CA.
6   *Linden Gardens Trust Ltd v Lenesta Sludge Disposal Ltd* [1993] 3 All ER 417, HL; *Darlington Borough Council v Wiltshier Northern Ltd* [1995] 3 All ER 895, CA.
7   *Alfred McAlpine Construction Ltd v Panatown Ltd* (1998) Times, 11 February, CA.

Loss of expectations

12.3   The principal function of damages for breach of contract is to put the plaintiff into the same position, so far as money can, *as if the contract had been performed* as agreed.[1] In achieving this, damages are awarded to compensate the plaintiff for the loss of his expectations under the contract.

1   *Wertheim v Chicoutimi Pulp Co* [1911] AC 301, PC.

12.4   Lost expectations may consist of a loss of profit which the plaintiff expected to make if the contract had been properly performed but which has been lost as a result of the breach. Suppose, for example, that X agrees to sell some machinery to Y, a manufacturer, who intends to use it to make goods for sale at a profit, and that X does not deliver the machinery on time. X's loss as a result of Y's breach is the profit he would have made from selling the goods if the machinery had been delivered on time.

Where the plaintiff did not contract with any expectation of making a profit, his loss of expectation in a case where the subject matter of the contract involved property will be quantified either by reference to the diminished value of what he has received (ie the difference between what the thing would have been worth if the contract had been properly performed and its actual value) or by the cost of cure/repair/reinstatement of the thing so as to make it as it would have been if the contract had been properly performed.

In the case of many contracts there is no significant (if any) difference in the amount quantified by the 'diminution in value' measure and the 'cost of cure' measure. However, in some contracts, the two measures may produce significantly different sums. This is particularly likely to happen in the case of building contracts. Normally, the plaintiff's loss of expectations in respect of defective or incomplete workmanship is assessed by the cost of cure, but the choice between the two measures is essentially based on whether or not it is reasonable to use the cost of reinstatement measure. This was affirmed by the House of Lords in *Ruxley Electronics and Construction Ltd v Forsyth*.[1] The defendant contracted with the plaintiffs for the construction by the defendant of a swimming pool at the plaintiff's house. A term of the contract specifically required the pool to be 7'6" deep at its deepest point. However, the defendant constructed a pool which was, at most, 6' deep. More importantly, at a point where the diving board was situated, the pool was less than 6' deep. As indicated above, the House of Lords was faced with a choice of two options as to the quantification of damages in respect of the defect:

- capital value of pool in a non-defective state minus its value in its defective state ('diminution in value' measure). This was favoured by the trial judge, who found that there had been no diminution in value because, despite its defects, the pool still enhanced the value of the plaintiff's property;
- cost of repair/reinstatement ('cost of cure' measure). This was favoured by the Court of Appeal and involved an award of damages in line with the expensive cost of digging up and extensively reconstructing the pool (£21,650).

The House of Lords took the same view as the trial judge who had simply awarded the plaintiff £2,500 for loss of amenity and nothing as damages in respect of the defect to the pool itself. It held that the cost of cure could only be recovered if it was reasonable to allow this. In assessing this, it was appropriate to consider the personal preferences of the plaintiff and whether or not he intended to cure the defect (since if the plaintiff did not intend to rebuild he would have lost nothing except the diminution in value). Moreover, the House held that, where the cost of reinstatement was *less* than the difference in value, the measure should be the cost of reinstatement. On the other hand, where the cost of reinstatement was *out of all proportion* to the good to be obtained, the appropriate measure was the diminution in value measure, and if there was no diminution in value substantial damages could not be awarded in respect of the defect in the pool itself.

Loss of expectations can vary from contract to contract. The above has concerned contracts relating to property. In the other contracts there are no special rules about the quantification of lost expectations, and the court must quantify adequate compensation for the plaintiff's loss as best it can.

1   [1995] 3 All ER 268, HL.

12.5   The fact that the precise assessment of the value of a lost expectation is difficult does not prevent an award being made, as is shown by *Chaplin v Hicks*.[1] The defendant advertised that he would employ, as actresses, 12 women to be selected by him out of 50 chosen as the most beautiful by the readers of various newspapers, in which the candidates' photographs appeared. The plaintiff was one of the 50 chosen by the readers but the defendant made an unreasonable appointment for an interview with her, and selected 12 out of the 49 who were able to keep the appointment. In an action for breach of contract, the defendant contended that only nominal damages were payable, since the plaintiff would only have had a one in four chance of being selected. Nevertheless, the Court of Appeal refused to disturb an award of £100 damages for the loss of her chance of being selected. Where damages are claimed for a lost chance, the plaintiff must prove that the chance was a real or substantial, and not merely speculative, one. The value of the lost chance will depend on where the chance lay on a range between a real or substantial one and a virtually certain one.[2]

1   [1911] 2 KB 786, CA.
2   *Allied Maples Group Ltd v Simmons & Simmons* [1995] 4 All ER 907, CA; *Stovold v Barlows* [1995] EGCS 155, CA.

12.6   Where damages are awarded to compensate the plaintiff for loss of his expectations, they are normally assessed as at the date of the breach. However, this is not an absolute rule since, if its observance would give rise to injustice, the court has power to fix such other date as may be appropriate in the circumstances.[1] For example, where the plaintiff could only reasonably have been expected to mitigate his loss at a point of time after the breach, damages should be assessed as at that point of time, or, if that point of time is not earlier, at the date of the judgment.[2] By way of further example, if, as has happened with house prices in the recent past, there has been a rapid and dramatic rise in the value of the subject matter of the contract, it may be more appropriate for damages to be assessed at the date of the judgment rather than the date of the breach.[3]

In the case of an anticipatory breach of contract, damages for loss of bargain or expectations are assessed by reference to the time when performance ought to have been made, and not by reference to the time of the anticipatory breach.[4]

1　*Johnson v Agnew* [1979] 1 All ER 883 at 896.
2　*Radford v de Froberville* [1978] 1 All ER 33; *William Cory & Son Ltd v Wingate Investments (London Colney) Ltd* (1978) 17 BLR 104, CA. For mitigation of loss, see paras 12.16 and 12.17 below.
3　*Suleman v Shahsavari* [1989] 2 All ER 460.
4　*Tai Hing Cotton Mill Ltd v Kamsing Knitting Factory* [1978] 1 All ER 515, PC; *Gebruder Metelmann GmbH & Co KG v NBR (London) Ltd* [1984] 1 Lloyd's Rep 614, CA.

Reliance loss

12.7　In some cases, damages are awarded to compensate the plaintiff for expenditure which he has incurred in reliance on the contract and which has been wasted as a result of its breach. Damages of this type are called damages for reliance loss. By way of an extension, damages can even be recovered for expenses incurred prior to, and in anticipation of, the contract and wasted as a result of the breach. In *Lloyd v Stanbury*,[1] for instance, the plaintiff, who had made a contract to buy a farm, which was broken by the defendant's failure to complete, was awarded damages for (inter alia) the following losses incurred before there was a binding contract of sale: legal expenses incurred in carrying out pre-contract searches and drafting the contract, and the cost of moving a caravan to the farm, as a temporary home for the defendant, prior to and in anticipation of the contract.

Because they compensate for expenditure which has been incurred in reliance on the contract and wasted *as a result of its breach*, damages for reliance loss cannot be awarded if this would make the plaintiff better off than if the contract had been performed, as where the plaintiff has made a bad bargain by agreeing to pay more for something than it was worth. *C and P Haulage v Middleton*[2] provides an example of the operation of this limitation. A was granted by B a contractual licence (on a six-month renewable basis) to occupy premises as a workshop. A spent money in making the premises suitable, although the contract provided that fixtures installed by him were not to be removed. Ten weeks before the end of a six-month term, A was ejected in breach of the contractual licence. As a temporary measure, A was permitted by his local authority to use his own home as a workshop, which he did until well after the six-month term had expired. The Court of Appeal held that A could only recover nominal damages. He could not recover, as reliance loss, his expenditure in equipping the premises, because, it was held, if the contract had been lawfully terminated at the end of the six-month term, there would have been no question of him recovering that expenditure and, therefore, to award him such damages would leave him better off than if the contract had been wholly performed. His ability to use his home as a workshop meant that he suffered no loss in terms of the deprivation of his licence. In order to defeat a plaintiff's claim for wasted expenditure, the onus is on the defendant to prove that the expenditure would not have been recovered if the contract had been performed.[3]

1　[1971] 2 All ER 267. Also see *Anglia Television Ltd v Reed* [1971] 3 All ER 690, CA.
2　[1983] 3 All ER 94, CA.
3　*CCC Films (London) Ltd v Impact Quadrant Films Ltd* [1984] 3 All ER 298.

12.8　A plaintiff has an unfettered right to frame his claim as one for loss of expectations or as one for reliance loss resulting from the breach. Although a claim for reliance loss is particularly appropriate where a plaintiff cannot prove any loss of expectations or can only prove a small loss of this type or where the contract is aborted too early for the value of the eventual loss of bargain properly to be assessed, a claim for reliance loss is not limited to such cases.[1]

Damages for loss of expectations and damages for reliance loss are not mutually exclusive since claims for both can be combined if this does not have the effect of compensating the plaintiff twice over for the same loss. For example, in *Cullinane v British Rema Manufacturing Co Ltd*,[2] the defendants sold to the plaintiffs a machine. A term of the contract related to the machine's output rate. The plaintiffs claimed damages for breach of this term under two headings:

* loss of profits (loss of expectations), and
* the capital cost of the machine and its installation (reliance loss).

It was held that the plaintiffs could not recover damages for both types of loss, as a claim for loss of profits could only be based on the fact that money had been spent on acquiring and installing the machine.

1   *CCC Films (London) Ltd v Impact Films Ltd* [1984] 3 All ER 298.
2   [1953] 2 All ER 1257, CA.

Other loss

12.9   Subject to the rules of remoteness, a plaintiff can recover not merely for the above types of economic loss resulting from the breach of contract, but also for personal injury (including pain and suffering), injury to property, or inconvenience or discomfort,[1] resulting from the breach.

Damages for disappointment or distress brought about by breach of contract may also be awarded, but only:

* where it is a consequence of physical inconvenience or discomfort caused by the breach;[2] or
* where an object of the contract was the giving of pleasure or enjoyment or the prevention of disturbed peace of mind or of distress.

In *Jarvis v Swans Tours Ltd*,[3] for instance, the plaintiff booked a 15-day winter sports holiday with the defendants. He did so on the faith of the defendants' brochure, which described the holiday as a house party and promised a number of entertainments, including excellent skiing, a yodeller evening, a bar, and afternoon tea and cakes. In the first week there were 13 guests; in the second the plaintiff was entirely alone. The entertainments fell far short of the promised standard. The Court of Appeal held that the plaintiff was entitled to damages for mental distress and disappointment due to loss of enjoyment caused by the breach of contract. A similar decision was reached in *Heywood v Wellers*,[4] where a solicitor's client suffered distress as a result of the solicitor's incompetent handling of an injunction designed to prevent molestation of the client. In *Ruxley Electronics and Construction Ltd v Forsyth*, referred to in para 12.4 above, the award of damages for loss of amenity was held by the House of Lords to be justified on the basis that the object of the contract was the provision of a pleasurable amenity and that the plaintiff's pleasure was not as great as it would have been if the pool had been 7'6" deep. The trial judge had awarded £2,500 for loss of amenity, and this amount had not been attacked in the House of Lords, who were consequently reluctant to interfere with it. The one Law Lord who considered the matter further justified an award for loss of amenity on the basis that it was a logical adaptation or application of the existing exceptions to the rule that generally damages for distress or disappointment cannot be awarded.

In contrast, unless it is caused by physical discomfort or inconvenience resulting from the breach, damages for emotional distress cannot be awarded where the breach is of an employment contract (eg wrongful dismissal)[5] or of a contract of survey or of a covenant for quiet enjoyment[6] in a lease, since the giving of pleasure or peace of mind or the like is not an object of such a contract or covenant.[7] For example, in *Hayes v James & Charles Dodd (a firm)*,[8] a married couple, who suffered anxiety and distress when their car repair business failed because their solicitors had incorrectly advised them (in breach of contract) that there was a right of access to the rear of the workshop they were purchasing, were held by the Court of Appeal not to be entitled to damages for that distress (although they recovered damages for the financial loss which they had suffered). This case makes an interesting contrast to *Heywood v Wellers* where the object of the contract was to prevent the client suffering distress.

Damages for injury to reputation are not as a general rule recoverable in a breach of contract action[9] but, where the loss of reputation leads to financial loss, damages are recoverable for that loss. This was held by the House of Lords in *Malik v Bank of Credit and Commerce International SA*,[10] where the plaintiffs had been employees of the defendant bank which, unknown to them, had been engaged in a massive fraud. The bank collapsed and went into liquidation. The plaintiffs were made redundant by the liquidator. Their association with the bank made it difficult to obtain employment in the banking field, and they suffered financial loss in consequence. The House of Lords held that the defendant bank was in breach of its implied obligation not, without reasonable cause, to conduct its business in a manner likely to destroy or seriously damage the relationship of confidence between employer and employee,[11] that this breach had caused financial loss as a result of the injury which it had done to the plaintiff's reputation, and that therefore the plaintiffs could recover damages for that loss. In addition, where damages for distress are recoverable, that distress (and therefore the amount recoverable for it) may be increased by the mental anguish suffered by the plaintiff as a result of the loss of his reputation.[12]

1   *Hobbs v London and South Western Rly Co* (1875) LR 10 QB 111; *Bailey v Bullock* [1950] 2 All ER 1167.
2   *Perry v Sidney Phillips & Son* [1982] 3 All ER 705, CA; *Watts v Morrow* [1991] 4 All ER 937, CA.
3   [1973] 1 All ER 71, CA.
4   [1976] 1 All ER 300, CA.
5   *Addis v Gramophone Co Ltd* [1909] AC 488, HL.
6   Para 36.20 below.
7   *Bliss v South East Thames Regional Health Authority* [1987] ICR 700, CA (breach of employment contract); *Hayes v James & Charles Dodd (a firm)* [1990] 2 All ER 815, CA; *Watts v Morrow* [1991] 4 All ER 937, CA (breach of surveying contract); *Branchett v Beaney, Coster and Swale Borough Council* (1992) 24 HLR 348, CA (breach of covenant for quiet enjoyment in a lease; for a description of this type of covenant, see para 36.20 below).
8   [1990] 2 All ER 815, CA.
9   *Addis v Gramophone Co Ltd* [1909] AC 488, HL.
10 [1997] 3 All ER 1, HL.
11 Para 8.25 above.
12 *McLeish v Amoco-Gottfried & Co* (1993) 10 PN 102.

Remoteness of damage

12.10   In order to succeed in his action for damages, the plaintiff must, of course, prove that the loss or damage (hereafter simply referred to as 'loss') which he has suffered resulted from the defendant's breach of contract.[1] This requires that the plaintiff's loss would not have occurred but for the defendant's breach. The defendant's breach need not be the only cause of the loss, since the conduct of others or the occurrence of extraneous events may also contribute to it, but it must be an effective or dominant cause of the loss.[2]

Proof of a causal link between breach and loss is not in itself enough to entitle the plaintiff to damages for that loss, because a defendant will only be liable for it if it was not too 'remote'. Whether or not loss suffered is too remote is determined by applying the rule in *Hadley v Baxendale*[3] (as explained in *Victoria Laundry (Windsor) Ltd v Newman Industries Ltd*[4] and *Koufos v C Czarnikow Ltd, The Heron II*[5]).

The rule, as explained, provides that damage is not too remote if one of the two following sub-rules is satisfied:

* if the loss arises naturally, ie according to the usual course of things, from the breach of contract as a seriously possible result of it; or
* if the loss could reasonably be supposed to have been in the contemplation of the parties, when they made the contract, as a seriously possible result of the breach of it.

The first sub-rule deals with 'normal' damage which arises in the ordinary course of events, while the second sub-rule deals with 'abnormal' damage which arises from special circumstances.

1   *Weld-Blundell v Stephens* [1920] AC 956, HL.
2   See, for example, *Galoo Ltd v Bright Grahame Murray* [1995] 1 All ER 16, CA; *County Ltd v Girozentrale Securities* [1996] 3 All ER 834, CA.
3   (1854) 23 LJ Ex 179.
4   [1949] 1 All ER 997, CA.
5   [1967] 3 All ER 686, HL.

12.11   In the light of subsequent cases, a number of things can be said about both sub-rules.

First, the plaintiff can only recover for such loss as would, *at the time of the contract*, have been within the reasonable contemplation of the parties as a serious possibility as a result of its breach, *had they had their attention drawn to the possibility of the breach which has in fact occurred*.[1] It must be emphasised that the particular breach itself need not have been contemplated. Suppose that the loss has been caused by some defect in the subject matter of the contract which was unknown, or even unknowable, when the contract was made. The court has to assume, even though it is contrary to the facts, that the parties had in mind the breach which has occurred when it considers whether the plaintiff's loss was within their reasonable contemplation.[1]

Second, what was within the parties' reasonable contemplation depends on the knowledge 'possessed' by them at that time. For this purpose, knowledge 'possessed' is of two kinds: one imputed, the other actual. Under the first sub-rule, everyone is taken to know (ie knowledge is imputed) the 'ordinary course of things' and, consequently, what loss is a seriously possible result of a breach of contract in that ordinary course. In addition, 'knowledge possessed' may, in a particular case, include knowledge which the guilty party (and the other party) actually possess of special circumstances, outside the ordinary course of things, of such a kind that the breach in these special circumstances would as a serious possibility be liable to cause more loss. Such a case attracts the second sub-rule so as to make the additional loss recoverable.[2]

Third, provided the *type* of loss caused by a breach of contract was within the reasonable contemplation of the parties when the contract was made, the loss is not too remote, and damages can therefore be recovered for it, even though its extent was much greater than could have been reasonably contemplated[3] and even though it occurred in a way which could not have been reasonably contemplated as a serious possibility.[4] An example is provided by *H Parsons (Livestock) Ltd v Uttley Ingham & Co Ltd*.[5] The defendants supplied the plaintiffs with a hopper in which to store pig nuts. The hopper was not properly ventilated, and this constituted a breach of contract by the defendants; as a result, the pig nuts became mouldy and many of the plaintiffs' pigs suffered a rare intestinal disease (E coli) from which 254 of them died. The plaintiffs were awarded damages by the Court of Appeal for the loss sustained by the death and sickness of the pigs. The reasoning of the majority of the Court of Appeal was that, if the breach had been brought to the parties' attention and they had asked themselves what was likely to happen as a result, they would have contemplated the serious possibility that the pigs would become ill, and that, since the type of loss caused (physical harm) was within the parties' reasonable contemplation, it was irrelevant that its extent and the way in which it occurred were not.

1 *H Parsons (Livestock) Ltd v Uttley Ingham & Co Ltd* [1978] 1 All ER 525, CA.
2 *Victoria Laundry (Windsor) Ltd v Newman Industries Ltd* [1949] 1 All ER 997, CA.
3 *Wroth v Tyler* [1973] 1 All ER 897; *H Parsons (Livestock) Ltd v Uttley Ingham & Co Ltd* [1978] 1 All ER 525, CA.
4 *H Parsons (Livestock) Ltd v Uttley Ingham & Co Ltd* [1978] 1 All ER 525, CA.
5 [1978] 1 All ER 525, CA.

12.12 The degree of risk which is required to have been within the parties' reasonable contemplation in order to satisfy the test of remoteness has been variously described in the cases. In *Koufos v C Czarnikow Ltd, The Heron II*,[1] which can be taken as settling the point, the House of Lords made it clear that the degree of risk is more than mere possibility or a risk that is 'on the cards'. However, they were not unanimous in their terminology as to the degree of risk required. Lords Pearce and Upjohn favoured 'serious possibility' or 'real danger'; Lord Reid favoured 'not unlikely' (ie 'considerably less than even chance, but nevertheless not very unusual and easily foreseeable'). With the exception of Lord Reid, the House was prepared to accept the phrase 'liable to result', a rather colourless and vague term which two of them thought was a convenient term to describe 'serious possibility' or 'real danger'. We have used 'serious possibility' in this book on the basis that it best conveys the degree of risk required which emerges from the speeches in the House of Lords.

1 [1967] 3 All ER 686, HL.

12.13 The application of the contractual rule of remoteness can best be illustrated by reference to past decisions. In *Hadley v Baxendale*,[1] the plaintiff's mill at Gloucester was brought to a halt when a crankshaft broke. The shaft had to be sent to its makers in Greenwich as a pattern for a new one. The defendant carriers undertook to deliver it at Greenwich the following day, but in breach of contract delayed its delivery so that the duration of the stoppage at the mill was extended. The plaintiff's claim to recover damages for loss of profits caused by the defendants' delay was unsuccessful since this loss was held to be too remote. The basis of the court's decision was that the defendants only knew that they were transporting a broken shaft owned by the plaintiffs. The court applied the two sub-rules in turn, and held:

• the plaintiffs might have had a spare shaft or been able to borrow one, and therefore the loss of profits did not arise in the usual course of events from the defendants' breach; and
• on the facts known to the defendants (they were unaware of the lack of a substitute shaft), the loss of profits could not be supposed to have been within the reasonable

contemplation of the parties at the time they made the contract as the probable result of the breach.

1   (1854) 23 LJ Ex 179.

12.14   In *Victoria Laundry (Windsor) Ltd v Newman Industries Ltd*,[1] the defendants agreed to sell to the plaintiffs, who were launderers and dyers, a boiler to be delivered on a certain date. The boiler was damaged in a fall and was not delivered until five months after the agreed delivery date. The plaintiffs claimed damages for loss of profits that would have been earned during the five-month period through the extension of their business, and also for loss of several highly lucrative dyeing contracts which they would have obtained with the Ministry of Supply. The Court of Appeal held that the plaintiffs could recover for the loss of 'normal' profits (ie those which would have been earned through an extension of the business) but not for the loss of 'exceptional' profits (ie loss of the highly lucrative contracts), which it treated as a different type of loss. This decision was based on the following application of the two sub-rules:

• the defendants knew at the time of the contract that the plaintiffs were laundrymen and dyers and required the boiler for immediate use in their business and, with their technical experience and knowledge of the facts, it could be presumed that loss of 'normal' profits was foreseeable by them, and therefore within both parties' reasonable contemplation, as liable to result from the breach; but
• in the absence of special knowledge, the defendants could not reasonably foresee the loss of the 'exceptional' profits under the highly lucrative contracts as liable to result from the breach.

The case was, therefore, remitted to an official referee for a decision as to the amount of 'normal' profits which had been lost in the circumstances.

1   [1949] 1 All ER 997, CA.

12.15   In *Koufos v C Czarnikow Ltd, The Heron II*,[1] the plaintiff sugar merchants chartered a ship from the defendant to carry a cargo of sugar from Constanza to Basrah. The ship deviated in breach of contract and arrived in Basrah nine days later than expected. Because of a fall in the market price of sugar, the plaintiffs obtained £3,800 less for the cargo than would have been obtained if it had arrived on time. The defendant did not know of the plaintiffs' intention to sell the sugar in Basrah, but he did know that there was a market for sugar at Basrah and that the plaintiffs were sugar merchants. The House of Lords held that the plaintiffs' loss of profits (£3,800) was not too remote under the first sub-rule, since knowledge could be imputed to the defendant that the goods might be sold at market price on their arrival in Basrah and that market prices were apt to fluctuate daily, and therefore the loss of profits was within the reasonable contemplation of the parties at the time of the contract as a serious possibility in the event of the breach in question.

1   [1967] 3 All ER 686, HL.

Mitigation
12.16   The plaintiff cannot recover for loss which he could reasonably have avoided. Thus, the seller of goods which have been wrongly rejected by the buyer must not unreasonably refuse another's offer to buy them. Similarly, an employee who has been wrongfully dismissed must not unreasonably refuse an offer of employment from another.[1] If such refusals occur, the plaintiff is said to be in breach of his duty to mitigate

his loss and cannot recover his unmitigated loss but only the loss which he would have suffered if the damage had been mitigated. If he would have suffered no loss at all, only nominal damages are recoverable.[1]

A leading case on the duty to mitigate is *Payzu Ltd v Saunders.*[2] A contract for the sale of goods by the defendant to the plaintiffs provided that delivery should be as required over a nine-month period and that payment should be made within one month of delivery. The plaintiffs failed to make prompt payment for the first instalment and the defendant, in breach of contract, refused to deliver any more instalments under the contract. He did, however, offer to deliver goods at the contract price if the plaintiffs would pay cash with each order. The plaintiffs refused to do so and brought an action for breach of contract, claiming the difference between the contract price and the market price (which had risen). The Court of Appeal held that the plaintiffs should have mitigated their loss by accepting the defendant's offer; consequently, the damages which they could recover were to be measured by the loss which they would have suffered if the offer had been accepted, not by the difference between the contract and market prices.

The following points may be noted about the duty to mitigate:

- The phrase 'duty to mitigate' is somewhat misleading because the plaintiff is not legally obliged to do so. He is free to act as he judges to be in his best interest, but if he does so he cannot recover for loss which he could reasonably have avoided.[3]
- The duty to mitigate may require the plaintiff to do something positive. In the examples given earlier in this paragraph, the seller and the employee would equally have been in breach of their duty to mitigate if they had not made reasonable efforts to seek other offers to buy the goods or alternative equivalent employment: it would not necessarily excuse them that no one had spontaneously made them an offer. Damages cannot be recovered for any loss which would have been avoided if such reasonable steps had been taken.[4]
- The duty to mitigate only requires the plaintiff to take reasonable steps to minimise his loss. He is not required to act with lightning speed, nor to accept the first or, indeed, any offer that is made (unless it is a reasonable one). For example, a wrongfully dismissed managing director is not expected to mitigate his loss by taking a job sweeping floors. Indeed, in one case it was held that it was reasonable for a person who had wrongfully been dismissed as managing director in an arbitrary and high-handed fashion to refuse the company's offer of a slightly lower post at the same salary.[5]

1   *Brace v Calder* [1895] 2 QB 253, CA.
2   [1919] 2 KB 581, CA.
3   *Sotiros Shipping Inc v Sameit Solholt, The Solholt* [1983] 1 Lloyd's Rep 605 at 608.
4   *British Westinghouse Co v Underground Electric Rlys Co of London* [1912] AC 673 at 689.
5   *Yetton v Eastwood Froy Ltd* [1966] 3 All ER 353.

12.17   Where there is an anticipatory breach of contract, the injured party has an option either to terminate the contract and sue immediately for damages or to affirm the contract and await the time fixed for performance, in which case he can then bring an action for damages if the other party is still in breach. If the injured party elects to terminate he is under a duty to mitigate his loss.[1] On the other hand, the injured party is under no duty to mitigate his loss before performance is due if he affirms the contract.[2]

1   *Roth & Co v Taysen Townsend & Co* (1895) 1 Com Cas 240; *Gebruder Metelmann GmbH & Co KG v NBR (London) Ltd* [1984] 1 Lloyd's Rep 614, CA.
2   Para 9.29 above.

Contributory negligence

12.18   Where a plaintiff has by his own fault contributed to his loss or the event causing it, his damages for breach of contract are not generally reduced in proportion to his degree of responsibility for that loss or event.[1] The doctrine of contributory negligence, under which a plaintiff in a tort action may have his damages reduced where he is partly at fault,[2] does not generally apply to an action for breach of contract.[3] There is one exception. If the defendant is liable in tort for negligence independently of the contract and also for breach of a contractual obligation to take reasonable care which was the same as the common law duty in the tort of negligence,[4] a court may apportion the blame and reduce the damages awarded to the plaintiff for breach of contract by reason of his contributory negligence.[5] Suppose that a surveyor's client is negligently given incorrect information by the surveyor, and relies on it when he should know better (ie is negligent in doing so), and suppose that, as a result of his and the surveyor's negligence, the client suffers economic loss. The doctrine of contributory negligence would apply to an action by the client for breach of contract because the surveyor's liability to the client in the tort of negligence and for breach of contract would be based on the same obligation to take reasonable care.

Of course, in any breach of contract case, if the plaintiff's contribution to his loss is so great as to prevent the defendant's breach of contract being an effective cause of the plaintiff's loss, the plaintiff will not be able to recover any damages at all for it.[6] Moreover, if the defendant successfully brings a counter-claim to a successful claim by the plaintiff, the effect on the damages awarded to each party may be the same as if there was an apportionment of liability on grounds of contributory negligence. In *Tennant Radiant Heat Ltd v Warrington Development Corpn*,[7] for instance, the plaintiffs leased a unit in a warehouse owned by the defendants. Goods stored there by the plaintiffs were damaged when the roof collapsed under an accumulation of rainwater. The roof would not have collapsed but for the facts that that the plaintiffs in breach of covenant had failed to repair the roof over their unit and that the defendants had failed to keep clear the water outlets on the roof as a whole (and were therefore liable in tort for negligence and nuisance).[8] The Court of Appeal held that the damages recoverable on the claim and the counter-claim should be assessed on the basis of the extent to which the damage to the goods (plaintiffs' claim) and to the roof (defendants' counter-claim) were caused, respectively, by the defendants' tortious behaviour and by the plaintiffs' breach of covenant.

1   *Basildon District Council v J E Lesser (Properties) Ltd* [1985] 1 All ER 20.
2   Law Reform (Contributory Negligence) Act 1945. See para 21.12 below.
3   *Basildon District Council v J E Lesser (Properties) Ltd* [1985] 1 All ER 20; *Marintrans AB v Comet Shipping Co Ltd* [1985] 3 All ER 442; *Barclays Bank plc v Fairclough Building Ltd* [1995] 1 All ER 289, CA.
4   As to when there may be concurrent liability in tort and in contract, see para 18.24 below.
5   *Forsikringsaktieselskapet Vesta v Butcher* [1988] 2 All ER 43, CA; affd on other grounds [1989] 1 All ER 402, HL.
6   Para 12.10 above; *Marintrans AB v Comet Shipping Co Ltd,* above.
7   [1988] 1 EGLR 41, CA.
8   See chs 18 and 25.

Liquidated damages and penalties

12.19   So far we have been concerned with unliquidated damages, ie damages which are assessed by the court and not by the agreement of the parties. It is, however, possible for the parties to agree in their contract that in the event of a breach of it the damages shall be a fixed sum or be calculated in a specific way. Such damages are called liquidated damages. Liquidated damages have the obvious advantage that the amount recoverable as damages is always certain, whereas in the case of unliquidated damages it is uncertain until the court has decided the matter. Provision for liquidated damages is often found in contracts which have to be completed within a certain time. Thus, contracts for building or civil engineering work normally provide for a specified sum to be paid for every day or week of delay.

It is customary to refer to penalty clauses and liquidated damages clauses as involving the payment of a sum of money, and for convenience we shall discuss them mainly in that context. However, it should not be forgotten that penalty clauses and liquidated damages clauses may involve the transfer of property, and not the payment of money.[1]

If a contract containing a liquidated damages provision is broken, the injured party can recover the specified sum, whether this is greater or less than the actual loss suffered. This rule may benefit a plaintiff who has suffered little or no loss but can be to his disadvantage if the loss suffered greatly exceeds the specified sum. In *Cellulose Acetate Silk Co Ltd v Widnes Foundry (1925) Ltd*,[2] the defendants agreed to build machinery for the plaintiffs in 18 weeks and, in the event of taking longer, to pay 'by way of penalty £20 per working week'. The machinery was completed 30 weeks late and the plaintiffs lost £5,850 in consequence. The House of Lords held that the provision for payment was one for liquidated damages and that the plaintiffs could only recover 30 weeks at £20, ie £600.

1   *Jobson v Johnson* [1989] 1 All ER 621, CA.
2   [1933] AC 20, HL.

12.20   Liquidated damages provisions must be distinguished from two other provisions:

Exemption clauses restricting liability   A liquidated damages clause is not an exemption clause limiting liability because it fixes the sum payable for breach whether the actual loss is greater or less, whereas (assuming it is valid) such an exemption clause merely fixes the maximum sum recoverable and, if the actual loss is less than that sum, only the actual loss can be recovered.

Penalty clauses   Where the sum fixed by the contract is a genuine pre-estimate of the loss which will be caused by its breach, the provision is one for liquidated damages, but if instead the sum is intended to operate as a threat to hold a potential defaulter to his bargain it is a penalty.[1] The distinction between a penalty and liquidated damages is crucial because their effects are different.

1   *Law v Redditch Local Board* [1892] 1 QB 127 at 132.

Penalty
12.21   If the actual loss by a plaintiff is less than the sum specified in a penalty clause, he can only recover his actual loss.[1] Suppose that a broken contract contains a penalty clause providing for a £1,000 penalty but the plaintiff's actual loss is only £100, the plaintiff can only recover £100 (whereas if the clause had been one for liquidated damages the plaintiff could have recovered £1,000). On the other hand, if the penalty is less than the actual loss suffered by the plaintiff, eg because of inflation since the contract was made, he cannot recover more than the penalty if he sues for it, although if he sues instead for (unliquidated) damages he can recover the whole of his loss.[2] This option is not, of course, open in the case of a liquidated damages provision.

1   *Wilbeam v Ashton* (1807) 1 Camp 78. A similar principle applies where the penalty involves the transfer of property whose value exceeds the plaintiff's actual loss: *Jobson v Johnson* [1989] 1 All ER 621, CA.
2   *Wall v Rederiaktiebolaget Luggude* [1915] 3 KB 66.

Parties' intention

12.22 Whether an agreed sum is liquidated damages or a penalty depends on the parties' intention and, as is shown by the *Cellulose Acetate* case,[1] the use of the words 'penalty' or 'liquidated damages' in the contract is not conclusive. The crucial question is whether the parties intended the specified sum to be a genuine pre-estimate of the damage likely to be caused by the breach or to operate as a fine or penalty for breach. This intention is to be gathered from the terms and inherent circumstances of the contract at the time it was made, not at the time of its breach.[2] This does not mean that what has happened subsequently is irrelevant, since it can provide valuable evidence as to what could reasonably have been expected to be the loss when the contract was made.[3]

The determination of the parties' intention is aided by a number of rebuttable presumptions of intention summarised by Lord Dunedin in *Dunlop Pneumatic Tyre Co Ltd v New Garage and Motor Co Ltd:*[4]

- 'It will be held to be a penalty if the sum stipulated for is extravagant and unconscionable in amount in comparison with the greatest loss that could conceivably be proved to have followed from the breach.'
- 'It will be held to be a penalty if the breach consists only in not paying a sum of money, and the sum stipulated is a sum greater than the sum which ought to have been paid.'
- 'There is a presumption (but no more) that it is a penalty when a single lump sum is made payable by way of compensation, on the occurrence of one or more or all of several events, some of which may occasion serious and others but trifling damage.' In *Kemble v Farren*,[5] for example, the defendant agreed with the plaintiff to appear at Covent Garden for four seasons at £3.6s.8d (£3.33) a night. The contract provided that if either party refused to fulfil the agreement, or any part of it, he should pay the other £1,000 as 'liquidated damages'. The defendant refused to act during the second season. It was held that the stipulation was a penalty. The obligation to pay £1,000 might have arisen simply on the plaintiff's failure to pay £3.6s.8d and was therefore quite obviously a penalty. It has been held that the court should be careful not to set too stringent a standard and should bear in mind that what the parties have agreed should normally be upheld, since any other approach would lead to undesirable uncertainty, especially in commercial contracts.[3]
- 'It is no obstacle to the sum stipulated being a genuine pre-estimate of damage, that the consequences of the breach are such as to make precise pre-estimation almost an impossibility.' This is illustrated by the *Dunlop* case itself. The plaintiffs supplied tyres to the defendants subject to an agreement that the defendants would not sell below the list price and would pay £5 by way of liquidated damages for every tyre sold in breach of the agreement. The House of Lords held that the stipulated sum was one for liquidated damages. (The agreement would now be void under the Resale Prices Act 1976.) Clearly, the figure of £5 was, at most, only a rough and ready estimate of the possible loss which the plaintiffs might suffer if their price list was undercut.

1   Para 12.19 above.
2   *Dunlop Pneumatic Tyre Co Ltd v New Garage and Motor Co Ltd* [1915] AC 79 at 868–7.
3   *Philips Hong Kong Ltd v A-G of Hong Kong* (1993) 61 BLR 41, PC.
4   [1915] AC 79 at 86.
5   (1829) 6 Bing 141.

12.23 In *Jobson v Johnson*,[1] a similar approach was taken to a clause providing for the re-transfer of property at a fixed price in the event of a breach. The plaintiff contracted to sell to the defendant 45% of the shares in Southend United Football Club for a total of £350,000, £311,000 of which was payable by six instalments. The contract contained a clause providing for the re-transfer of the shares at a fixed price (£340,000) if the defendant defaulted in payment of the second or any subsequent instalment. It was held that this was a penalty clause since it was equally applicable if the defendant defaulted on the second instalment (when the plaintiff's loss would be great) or on the last (when his loss would be relatively small); the provision that in the event of default the defendant should re-transfer to the plaintiff the shares at a fixed price could therefore not be regarded as a genuine pre-estimate of the plaintiff's loss.

1   [1989] 1 All ER 621, CA.

Action for price or other agreed sum

12.24   If a breach consists of a party's failure to pay a debt, ie the contractually agreed price or other remuneration, which is due under the contract, the appropriate course for the injured party is to bring an action for the agreed sum to recover that amount.

Limitation: sale of goods contracts
12.25   There is an important limitation on an action for the agreed sum in the case of a contract for the sale of goods. The Sale of Goods Act 1979, s 49 provides that, unless the agreed price is payable on a specified date irrespective of delivery, an action for it only lies if the property (ie ownership) in the goods has passed to the buyer.

Limitation: repudiatory breach
12.26   Where a repudiatory breach is committed, the injured party may, of course, recover an agreed sum already due at the time of the breach, whether he terminates or affirms the contract.

The position is more complicated where the agreed sum is not due at the time of the repudiatory breach but may become due subsequently:

*   If the injured party elects to terminate the contract, he cannot claim an agreed sum which might have become due to him subsequently.[1]
*   If the injured party elects to affirm the contract, then, as we have already said,[2] the contract remains in force, so that both parties are bound to perform any outstanding contractual obligations. Consequently, if the injured party affirms the contract, he may be able to recover the agreed sum when it becomes due in the future. Whether or not he will be able to recover that sum depends on the rules discussed in the rest of this paragraph.

    It was recognised by the majority of the House of Lords in *White and Carter (Councils) Ltd v McGregor*[3] that, if further performance on the part of the injured party is required in order for the sum to become due, he will be unable to recover the agreed sum if his further performance depends on the co-operation of the other party and it is withheld. It is for this reason that a wrongfully dismissed employee cannot sue for his wages payable thereafter, even though he has subsequently indicated his willingness to go on working under the employment contract.[4] Instead he must sue for damages for breach of contract (in respect of which he must take reasonable steps to mitigate his loss by obtaining other employment) or seek payment under the law of restitution on a quantum meruit basis (see below) for the value of work already done.

It will not be often that the injured party can perform his side of the contract without the co-operation of the other party, although it was possible in *White and Carter (Councils) Ltd v McGregor.*[3] The plaintiffs were advertising contractors. They carried on a business of supplying free litter bins to local authorities, the bins being paid for by businesses which hired advertising space on them. The plaintiffs agreed with the defendant garage proprietor to display advertisements for his garage on bins for three years. On the same day, the defendant renounced the contract and asked the plaintiffs to cancel it. They refused, thereby affirming the contract, and proceeded to prepare advertisement plates which they attached to bins and displayed. When the defendant failed to pay at the appropriate time, the plaintiffs sued for the full contract price. The House of Lords held that they could recover the full contract price despite the fact that they had made no effort to mitigate their loss by getting other advertisers in substitution for the defendant and had increased their loss after the renunciation by performing their side of the contract.

Even if he can perform his side of the contract without the co-operation of the other party, and does so, an injured party cannot recover an agreed sum when it becomes due in the future (as opposed to such damages as would be available) if it is shown that he had no legitimate interest, financial or otherwise, in performing the contract rather than claiming damages. This was stated by one of the Law Lords in the *White and Carter* case,[5] where a lack of a legitimate interest was not shown, and has subsequently been adopted in other cases.[6] What is a 'legitimate interest' in this context remains to be fully determined, although it has been held that a commitment to a third party is such an interest.[7] The term is difficult to define since it is arguable that most injured parties have a legitimate interest in seeing their contract performed. Some judges have stated a corresponding, substitute limitation in terms of whether the injured party's conduct in performing the contract was wholly unreasonable (which would prevent him recovering an agreed sum), as opposed to merely unreasonable (which would not).[8] This test would seem to be easier to apply than that of 'legitimate interest'.

1 Para 9.18 above.
2 Paras 9.20 and 9.29 above.
3 [1961] 3 All ER 1178, HL.
4 *Denmark Productions Ltd v Boscobel Productions Ltd* [1968] 3 All ER 513, CA; *Gunton v Richmond-upon-Thames London Borough Council* [1980] 3 All ER 577, CA.
5 [1962] AC 413 at 431.
6 *Attica Sea Carriers Corpn v Ferrostaal Poseidon Bulk Reederei GmbH, The Puerto Buitrago* [1976] 1 Lloyd's Rep 250, CA; *Gator Shipping Corpn v Trans-Asiatic Oil Ltd SA, The Odenfeld* [1978] 2 Lloyd's Rep 357; *Clea Shipping Corpn v Bulk Oil International Ltd, The Alaskan Trader* [1984] 1 All ER 129.
7 *Gator Shipping Corpn v Trans-Asiatic Oil Ltd SA, The Odenfeld* [1978] 2 Lloyd's Rep 357.
8 *Attica Sea Carriers Corpn v Ferrostaal Poseidon Bulk Reederei GmbH, The Puerto Buitrago* [1976] 1 Lloyd's Rep 250 at 255; *Gator Shipping Corpn v Trans-Asiatic Oil Ltd SA, The Odenfeld* [1978] 2 Lloyd's Rep 357 at 374; *Clea Shipping Corpn v Bulk Oil International Ltd, The Alaskan Trader* [1984] 1 All ER 129 at 136.

Restitutionary claim: quantum meruit

12.27 In a particular situation, set out below, a claim on what is called a quantum meruit basis is available to a plaintiff as an *alternative* to a claim for damages for breach of contract.

If a party to a contract unjustifiably prevents the other party performing his contractual obligations, as where he states that he will not accept performance, or renders performance impossible, his conduct will normally constitute a repudiatory breach of contract and the injured party can recover damages for breach of contract, whether he elects to terminate or to affirm the contract. Alternatively, if the injured party has partly performed his obligations under the contract he can claim under the law of restitution the reasonable value of the work done, provided he has elected to terminate the contract.[1] *Lusty v Finsbury Securities Ltd*[2] provides an example of the rules. The defendant company contracted with the plaintiff for the plaintiff to act as its architect for an office block development. After the plaintiff had done some work under the contract, the defendant company decided to use the land for residential development instead and cancelled future performance by the plaintiff of his contract. This was clearly a repudiatory breach of contract. It was held that the plaintiff could recover reasonable remuneration for his work on a quantum meruit basis.

It must be emphasised that an award of damages and quantum meruit award are distinct remedies. As we have already stated, damages are compensatory, their object generally being to put the plaintiff into the same position, so far as money can do it, as if the contract had been performed. Thus, if the injured party in a case like *Lusty v Finsbury Securities* decides to sue for damages, the damages awarded will be equivalent to the sum payable to him on completion of his work, less any savings (eg on labour and materials) made through not completing performance. However, if it is shown that the plaintiff would in any event have been unable to perform his entire obligation, he will at most be entitled to nominal damages.[3] On the other hand, a quantum meruit award is restitutory, its object being to restore the plaintiff to the position in which he would have been if the contract had never been made by awarding him an amount equivalent to the value of the work which he has done. Generally, an award of damages will be more generous than a quantum meruit award, but the converse may be true if the plaintiff originally made a bad bargain or if only nominal damages would be awarded.

1   *Planché v Colburn* (1831) 8 Bing 14; *Lusty v Finsbury Securities* (1993) 58 BLR 66, CA.
2   (1993) 58 BLR 66, CA.
3   *Maredelanto Cia Naviera SA v Bergbau-Handel GmbH, The Mihalis Angelos* [1970] 3 All ER 125, CA.

Specific performance

12.28   The court may grant a decree of specific performance to the injured party, instead of, or in addition to, awarding him damages. Such a decree orders the defaulting party to carry out his contractual obligations.

12.29   Specific performance will not be granted in the following cases:

Where damages are an adequate remedy   It is for this reason that specific performance of a contract to sell goods is not normally ordered; the payment of damages enables the plaintiff to go out into the market and buy the equivalent goods.[1] However, in exceptional cases, eg where the contract is for the sale of specific goods of a unique character or of special value or interest, the contract is specifically enforceable.[2] By way of contrast, every plot of land is unique, with the result that contracts for the sale or lease of land are always specifically enforceable. This has produced the rule that, since the contract is specifically enforceable in favour of the purchaser or lessee, a vendor or lessor of land can obtain an order of specific performance even though, in the particular case, damages would be an adequate remedy.[3]

It is because damages are normally adequate that a contractual obligation to pay money is not normally specifically enforceable. However, in addition to the exception just mentioned, there are other exceptions. For instance, as the House of Lords held in *Beswick v Beswick:*[4]

- a contract to pay money to a third party can be specifically enforced where, as is normally the case, any damages awarded would be nominal; and
- where the contract is for an annuity or other periodical payment it can be specifically enforced (thereby avoiding the need to sue for damages every time a payment is not made).

Where consideration has not been provided   The remedy of specific performance is an equitable one and, since equity does not recognise the making of a contract by deed as an effective substitute for consideration, specific performance cannot be awarded in favour of a person who has not provided consideration ('equity will not assist a volunteer') and he is left to his common law remedy of damages.[5]

Where the court's constant supervision would be necessary to secure compliance with the order   An example is provided by *Ryan v Mutual Tontine Westminster Chambers Association.*[6] In the lease of a flat in a block of flats the lessors agreed to keep a resident porter, who should be in constant attendance and perform specified duties. The person appointed got his duties done by deputies and was absent for hours at a time at another job. The court refused to order against the lessors specific performance of the agreement relating to the performance of the specified duties by the porter because such an order would have required its constant supervision. On the other hand, in *Posner v Scott-Lewis*,[7] specific performance was ordered against a lessor of a covenant to appoint a porter because what had to be done to comply with the order (appointing a porter) could be defined with sufficient certainty and enforcement of the order would not require the constant supervision of the course.

In *Co-operative Insurance Society Ltd v Argyll Stores (Holdings) Ltd*,[8] where the House of Lords allowed an appeal against the Court of Appeal's order for specific performance of a covenant in a lease of a supermarket which required it to be kept open for trade, the House of Lords held that specific performance should not be ordered if it would require a defendant to run a business (save in exceptional circumstances). One of the House's reasons was that to order someone to carry on a business would require the court's constant supervision.

Where the contract is for services of a personal nature   The obvious example of such a contract is one of employment. The Trade Union and Labour Relations (Consolidation) Act 1992, s 236 prohibits an order of specific performance against an employee to compel him to do any work or to attend at any place for the doing of any work. It is well established by the cases that contracts for personal services not covered by the Act (for example an agency contract)[9] cannot be specifically enforced either, nor can an order of specific performance be made against an employer (except, possibly, in very exceptional circumstances). Reasons given are that such contracts would require constant supervision and that it is contrary to public policy to force one person to submit to the orders of another.

Lack of mutuality   There is a rule that a plaintiff who has not performed his contractual obligations cannot obtain specific performance against the defendant if, in the circumstances, it would not be available to the defendant against the plaintiff. In *Flight v Bolland*,[10] for instance, it was held that a minor could not be awarded specific performance of the contract in question because such an order could not be made against him in the circumstances. While there is no doubting the present rule, its extent is uncertain.

1   Apart from its inherent jurisdiction to order specific recovery of goods, the court has power under the Sale of Goods Act 1979 to order the specific performance of contracts for the sale of specific or ascertained goods. This power has not been used more liberally than the inherent power.
2   *Behnke v Bede Shipping Co Ltd* [1927] 1 KB 649; *Phillips v Lamdin* [1949] 1 All ER 770; *Sky Petroleum Ltd v VIP Petroleum Ltd* [1974] 1 All ER 954. Cf *Cohen v Roche* [1927] 1 KB 169.
3   *Cogent v Gibson* (1864) 33 Beav 557.
4   [1967] 2 All ER 1197, HL; para 7.9 above.
5   *Cannon v Hartley* [1949] 1 All ER 50.
6   [1893] 1 Ch 116.
7   [1987] Ch 25.
8   [1997] 3 All ER 297, HL.
9   *Clarke v Price* (1819) 2 Wils Ch 157.
10 (1828) 4 Russ 298.

12.30   If the case does not fall within one of the above cases, specific performance may be ordered, but it must not be forgotten that, since specific performance is an equitable remedy, its award does not lie as of right (unlike the common law remedy of damages) but lies in the court's discretion.

Factors which make it unlikely that the court will exercise its discretion in favour of specific performance include:

- a mistake on the part of the defendant such that it would be unjust specifically to enforce the contract against him;[1]
- delay in bringing an action for specific performance which resulted in the defendant so changing his position that it would be unjust specifically to enforce the contract against him;[2]
- exceptional severity of the hardship to the defendant if the contract is specifically enforced against him;[3]
- breach by the plaintiff of his contractual obligations in circumstances where the grant of specific performance would be unjust to the defendant.[4]

Lastly, it is clearly established that the court will refuse specific performance of a contract for the sale of land in favour of a plaintiff who is in breach of a contractual stipulation concerning the time of completion where time is of 'the essence of the contract',[5] although it will normally grant it to such a plaintiff (subject to a condition that the plaintiff pays damages for his delay) where time is not 'of the essence' since this will not cause injustice to the defendant.

1   Paras 13.12 and 13.21 below.
2   *Stuart v London and North Western Rly Co* (1852) 1 De GM & G 721; *Lazard Bros & Co Ltd v Fairfield Properties Co (Mayfair) Ltd* (1977) 121 Sol Jo 793.
3   *Patel v Ali* [1984] 1 All ER 978.
4   *Walsh v Lonsdale* (1882) 21 Ch D 9.
5   *Stickney v Keeble* [1915] AC 386 at 415–416.

Injunction

12.31   An injunction is a court order restraining a party to a contract from acting in breach of a negative stipulation contained in it. By way of comparison, specific performance is concerned with the enforcement of positive contractual stipulations.

12.32   While it is correct to say that injunctions are concerned with restraining breaches of negative contractual stipulations, it would be erroneous to assume that only an express negative stipulation can be remedied by an injunction. Generally, a breach of a positive stipulation can be enjoined if the stipulation can properly be construed as impliedly being a negative stipulation. Thus, in *Manchester Ship Canal Co v Manchester Racecourse Co*,[1] a stipulation for the grant of a 'first refusal' was construed as a stipulation, enforceable by injunction, not to sell to anyone else in breach of the stipulation. Similarly, in *Metropolitan Electric Supply Co Ltd v Ginder*,[2] where the defendant had undertaken to take all the electricity required for his premises from the plaintiffs, it was held that this was impliedly an undertaking not to take electricity from any other person, which could be enforced by an injunction.

1   [1901] 2 Ch 37.
2   [1901] 2 Ch 799.

12.33   Although the courts are prepared to enforce negative stipulations in a contract for personal services, consistency with the rule that such a contract cannot normally be the subject of a decree of specific performance means that an injunction will not be issued to restrain an employee or the like from breaking a promise not to work for any other person, if this would indirectly amount to compelling him to perform his contract with his employer.[1] This is given statutory force in relation to contracts of employment by the Trade Union and Labour Relations (Consolidation) Act 1992, s 236, which provides that no court may, by an injunction restraining a breach or threatened breach of a contract of employment, compel an employee to do any work or to attend at any place of work.

On the other hand, a negative promise by an employee or the like will be enforced against him by injunction if it does not indirectly force him to work for his employer. For example, in *Lumley v Wagner*,[2] the defendant, an opera star, agreed to sing at the plaintiff's theatre for three months and in no other theatre during that time. An injunction was granted restraining her from singing for another theatre owner during the three-month period. The approach taken in *Lumley v Wagner* was followed in *Warner Bros Pictures Inc v Nelson*.[3] The defendant, whose stage name was Bette Davis, agreed with the plaintiff company not to work in a film or stage production for any other company for a year nor to be engaged in any other occupation. During the year she contracted to work for another film company. The judge stated that, while an injunction enforcing all the negative stipulations in the contract could not be granted (because it would force Bette Davis either to be idle or to perform her contract with the plaintiff company), the injunction requested would be granted because it was limited to prohibiting her from working in a film or stage production for anyone other than the plaintiff company; she would still be free to earn her living in some other less remunerative way. The judge was unimpressed by the argument that the difference between what the plaintiff could earn acting and what she could earn in any other capacity would be so substantial that the injunction would drive her to work for the plaintiff company. An argument of this type did, however, persuade the judge in *Page One Records Ltd v Britton*,[4] an employee against employer case referred to in para 12.34 below. In *Warren v Mendy*,[5] the Court of Appeal was also persuaded by such an argument on grounds of realism and practicality. Consequently, it is now the law that, contrary to the view of the judge in *Warner Bros v Nelson*, the question of whether an injunction against him would compel the defendant to work for the plaintiff is not answered in the negative simply because the defendant is not debarred from doing other work. If the nature of, or remuneration for, that work is so different that effectively the defendant would be driven to work for the plaintiff, it will be held that an injunction would so compel him and an injunction will not be ordered. Thus, if the facts of *Warner Bros v Nelson* arose today the decision on them would no doubt be against an injunction being ordered.

1   *Rely-a-Bell Burglar and Fire Alarm Co Ltd v Eisler* [1926] Ch 609.
2   (1852) 1 De GM & G 604.
3   [1936] 3 All ER 160.
4   [1967] 3 All ER 822.
5   [1989] 3 All ER 103, CA.

12.34   The law is similar where an employee seeks to enforce a negative stipulation against his employer. Thus, generally, an injunction will not be issued if its effect is to compel the employer to continue employment. But an injunction may be granted in exceptional cases where employer and employee retain their mutual confidence.

In *Page One Records Ltd v Britton*,[1] The Troggs, a pop group, appointed the plaintiff as their manager for five years, agreeing not to let anyone else act as their manager during that time. After a year, The Troggs dismissed the plaintiff, who sought an injunction restraining them from appointing anyone else as their manager. It was held that an injunction would indirectly compel The Troggs to continue to employ the plaintiff because pop groups could not operate successfully without a manager, and it would be bad to pressure The Troggs into continuing to employ a person in whom they had lost confidence. Therefore the injunction sought was not granted. In comparison, one may note the exceptional case of *Hill v C A Parsons & Co Ltd*.[2] The defendant employers were forced by union pressure to dismiss the plaintiff in breach of contract. An injunction was granted to restrain this breach, even though its effect was to compel the reinstatement of the plaintiff. As the Court of Appeal pointed out, the circumstances were special, in particular because the parties retained their mutual confidence. Mutual confidence has been stressed as a pre-condition in other cases; it can be shown either by evidence that the employer and employee have expressed confidence in each other or by inference from evidence of an established and satisfactory employment relationship.[3]

Despite the general reluctance of the courts to grant specific performance or an injunction in respect of a contract of employment, there are increasing signs that, in cases where the employee's contract requires a specified procedure to be followed before dismissal can take place, the courts will grant an injunction to restrain a proposed dismissal in breach of that procedure.[4]

1   [1967] 3 All ER 822.
2   [1971] 3 All ER 1345, CA.
3   *Powell v Brent London Borough Council* [1987] IRLR 466, CA; *Wishart v National Association of Citizens Advice Bureaux* [1990] IRLR 393, CA.
4   *Irani v Southampton and South West Hampshire Health Authority* [1985] ICR 590; *R v BBC, ex p Lavelle* [1983] 1 All ER 241; *Jones v Lee* [1980] ICR 310, CA.

12.35   An injunction is like specific performance in that:

*   it may be granted with or without an order for damages;
*   where it is applicable, the grant of an injunction is discretionary (since it is an equitable remedy) and is likely to be refused where, for example, the plaintiff is guilty of delay or is in breach of his own obligations under the contract. In particular, an injunction will normally be refused if damages would be an adequate remedy.

On the other hand, an injunction is a much wider remedy than specific performance, partly because it can be ordered in many situations other than contractual situations, and partly because it can be ordered in contractual situations where specific performance could not, eg where enforcement of the contract would require the court's constant superintendence or where the contract is one for personal services.

Limitation of actions

12.36 An action will be barred if it is not brought within the relevant limitation period. The rules relating to these periods are statutory, the relevant Act being the Limitation Act 1980. If an action is statute-barred this does not extinguish the plaintiff's substantive right but simply bars the procedural remedies available to him. Two consequences of this are that if a debtor pays a statute-barred debt, he cannot recover the money as money not due,[1] and that if a debtor who owes a creditor two or more debts, one of which is statute-barred, pays money to the creditor without appropriating it to a debt which is not statute-barred, the creditor is entitled to appropriate it to the statute-barred debt.[2]

1 *Bize v Dickason* (1786) 1 Term Rep 285 at 287.
2 *Mills v Fowkes* (1839) 5 Bing NC 455.

Limitation periods
12.37 Under the Limitation Act 1980:

- Actions founded on a simple contract (ie one not made by deed) cannot be brought after the expiry of six years from the date on which the cause of action accrued,[1] which is normally when the breach of contract occurs and never when the damage is suffered.[2] However, if the damages claimed consist of or include damages for personal injuries caused by a breach of contract, the time limit is reduced to three years,[3] although this period may be extended in certain circumstances.[4]
- Actions founded on a contract made by deed cannot be brought after the expiration of 12 years from the date on which the cause of action accrued.[5] The special rules mentioned above concerning personal injuries claims also apply here.

1 In a few exceptional situations the limitation period begins to run from a later point of time. For example, if the cause of action is based on fraud or is for relief from the consequences of mistake, the period does not begin to run until the plaintiff has discovered the fraud or mistake or could with reasonable diligence have discovered it: Limitation Act 1980, s 32.
2 Limitation Act 1980, s 5. For a special rule in relation to actions on certain contracts of loan, see Limitation Act 1980, s 6. If the plaintiff can establish a cause of action in tort for negligence, that cause of action accrues (and time runs from) when the damage is suffered, although there are numerous exceptions (eg in personal injury cases and claims based on the negligent construction of buildings; paras 29.23 and 29.24 below).
3 Limitation Act 1980, s 11(4).
4 Para 29.25 below.
5 Limitation Act 1980, s 8.

Extending the limitation period
12.38 An acknowledgment or part payment of *a debt or other agreed pecuniary claim* may start time running again, provided that the right of action has not previously become statute-barred (ie the acknowledgment or part payment must be made during the currency of the relevant limitation period).[1] A cause of action for unliquidated damages cannot be extended by an acknowledgment or part payment. The basic provision is the Limitation Act 1980, s 29(5), which provides that where any right of action has accrued to recover any debt or other liquidated pecuniary claim and the person (or his agent) liable or accountable therefor acknowledges the claim or makes any payment in respect thereof, the right of action is deemed to have accrued on the date of the acknowledgment or the payment. Such an extension of a current limitation period may be continually repeated by further acknowledgments or part payments.[1]

An acknowledgment must be in writing and signed by the person making it (or his agent), and must be made to the person (or his agent) whose claim is acknowledged.[2]

An acknowledgment is only sufficient to start time running again if it amounts to an admission of legal liability to pay the debt in question.[3]

1 Limitation Act 1980, s 29(7).
2 Limitation Act 1980, s 30.
3 *Surrendra Overseas Ltd v Government of Sri Lanka* [1977] 2 All ER 481.

Equitable relief

12.39 The provisions of the Limitation Act do not apply to claims for equitable relief.[1] However, in cases where, before the Judicature Act 1873, the claim for relief could have been entertained in either the common law courts or in the Court of Chancery, the limitation periods under the Limitation Act 1980 are applied to equitable claims by analogy.[2] The position is different in the case of purely equitable claims, ie claims which could only have been entertained by the Court of Chancery before the Act of 1873, such as claims for specific performance or an injunction. Here, the claim may fail under the equitable doctrine of laches, which enables a court to hold a claim barred for delay. Under the doctrine there are not pre-determined periods of delay. The avoidance of fixed limitation periods in this area is obviously more appropriate to the discretionary nature of equitable remedies.

1 Limitation Act 1980, s 36(1).
2 Ibid; *Knox v Gye* (1872) LR 5 HL 656 at 674.

Chapter 13

Mistake

13.1   In this chapter we consider:

- the types of mistake by a contracting party which can render the contract void;
- the availability, or otherwise, of equitable remedies where a party contracts under a mistake;
- the rectification of a written contract which does not accord with a prior oral agreement;
- the validity of a written contract which a party has signed under a mistake as to its contents, character or effect;
- the legal situation where money is paid under a mistake.

13.2   In certain cases a contract[1] is void if it is made in circumstances where one or both parties are labouring under a mistake as to the facts existing at the time of their agreement. If a contract is void for mistake it has no legal effect; consequently, it is unenforceable by either party, money paid under it is recoverable back[2] and title to property cannot pass under it. A party who has received goods under a void contract will be liable to the transferor in tort if he wrongfully interferes with them, and so will a third party who has bought them from him.

Because of the serious consequences of finding a contract void for mistake, the law defines the situations in which a mistake will render a contract void very narrowly. It follows from this that a mistake made by a party in concluding a contract does not normally render it void. Even mistakes which are induced by the other contracting party rarely render the contract void, although there may be a remedy for misrepresentation (which we discuss in the next chapter).

A contract may be void for mistake:

- if the parties have reached an agreement, but have done so on the basis of some fundamental mistake which they share; or
- if, because of a mistake which the parties do not share, they are fundamentally at cross-purposes.

1   It is traditional, although perhaps inaccurate, to describe agreements void for mistake as contracts.
2   *Griffith v Brymer* (1903) 19 TLR 434.

Shared mistake

Common law
Construction

13.3 If the parties have reached an agreement on the basis of a misapprehension as to the facts, which is shared by both of them, the contract may be void for mistake. Whether the rules relating to mistake come into play depends on whether or not the general law relating to the type of contract in question allocates the risk as between the parties in relation to a particular fact or event, or whether or not the contract, on its true construction, expressly or impliedly does so or provides some other solution.[1] If the risk is allocated in one of these ways or the contract provides some other solution, the court will give effect to this. In such a case, the contract is not void but enforceable, and the rules relating to mistake do not come into play. In either case, the position is as follows: if, to take as an example the case of a contract for the sale of specific goods which it turns out have never existed, the buyer assumed the risk of the goods' existence, he must pay the contractual price; but if the seller assumed that risk he will be liable in damages for breach of contract.

In the Australian case of *McRae v Commonwealth Disposals Commission*,[2] the Commission sold to McRae the right to salvage a tanker which was, they claimed, lying on a specified reef. There was no reef of that name at the map reference given, nor was there any tanker. The court found as a matter of construction that the Commission had impliedly undertaken that the tanker existed and thus McRae could claim damages for breach of this undertaking. This case can be contrasted with *Clark v Lindsay*,[3] which shows that a contract may also provide a solution, other than placing the risk on one of the parties, should a jointly assumed fact not exist. In *Clark v Lindsay*, A had agreed with B to hire a room along the route of Edward VII's coronation procession. When they made the contract both parties were unaware that the coronation had been postponed because of the King's illness, but the contract expressly provided that, if the procession was postponed, A should have the use of the room on any later day on which it took place. Consequently, it was held that the contract was not void for mistake and both parties were bound to perform their obligations on the re-arranged day.

The approach of first construing the contract to see whether it allocates the risk in, or otherwise provides a solution for, the matter about which the parties shared a mistake was adopted also by the House of Lords in *Couturier v Hastie*.[4] Here, a cargo of grain being shipped to the UK was sold after, unknown to the parties, it had 'perished' in the legal sense, in that it had deteriorated and had already been sold by the ship's captain. The seller demanded payment for the cargo. The House of Lords held that on a true construction of the contract the risk that the cargo did not exist had not been placed on the buyer and therefore he did not have to pay for the goods. It was not necessary for the House to decide whether the risk was placed on the seller, who could thus have been sued for non-delivery, or whether the contract was void.

1   *Associated Japanese Bank (International) Ltd v Credit du Nord* SA [1988] 3 All ER 902; *William Sindall plc v Cambridgeshire County Council* [1994] 3 All ER 932, CA.
2   (1950) 84 CLR 377.
3   (1903) 88 LT 198.
4   (1856) 5 HL Cas 673, HL. For a more recent case where this approach was adopted, see *Associated Japanese Bank (International) Ltd v Credit du Nord SA* [1988] 3 All ER 902.

Rules relating to shared mistake

13.4 If the law or, on its true construction, the contract does not allocate the risk in, or otherwise provide a solution for, the matter concerning which the parties shared a mistake, the rules relating to mistake must be looked at. Under them, not every shared mistake renders a contract void: the mistake must be fundamental. If it is not fundamental the contract is enforceable at common law.

13.5 *Shared mistake as to existence of subject matter* One example of a fundamental mistake in this context is a shared mistake as to the existence of the subject matter of the contract. In *Galloway v Galloway*,[1] for instance, a separation agreement based on a marriage which, unknown to the parties, was invalid (and therefore non-existent) was held void. Clearly, in such a case, the separation agreement would not attempt to throw the risk of the marriage being invalid on either party and so it is not surprising that the court did not first consider the question of construction.

1   (1914) 30 TLR 531, DC.

13.6   If the facts in *Couturier v Hastie* occurred today, the basis of the decision would almost certainly be different (although the buyer would still not be liable) because there is now a special statutory provision dealing with the perishing of specific goods unknown to the seller before a contract for their sale is made. The Sale of Goods Act 1979, s 6 provides that in such a case the contract is void. Presumably, this provision can be displaced if the contract expressly places the risk as to the goods' continued existence on one of the parties or provides some other solution. Section 6 does not apply to specific goods which, unknown to the parties, have never existed. In such cases, the contract is first construed. If the risk is placed on either party, expressly or impliedly, or some other solution is provided by the contract, the contract governs; but if the risk is not allocated the contract is void.

13.7   *Shared mistake as to possibility of performing contract* A contract is void if it is made under a shared mistaken belief that it is possible to perform it, unless the risk of impossibility of performance is allocated to a party or the contract provides some other solution to deal with the problem. Thus, a contract, whereby X agrees to lease land to Y, which Y already owns, is void at common law,[1] and so is a contract whereby X agrees with Y to cut and process a certain tonnage of a particular crop on land, when there is not that tonnage to be cropped.[2] It would be different, however, if X had warranted (as a seller normally does) that he had title to the land or had guaranteed the yield (in that case, X would be liable for breach of contract) or if Y had agreed to run the risk (ie to pay in any event).

Another example is provided by *Griffith v Brymer*.[3] As in *Clark v Lindsay,* this case concerned an agreement for the hire of a room along the route of Edward VII's coronation procession, which had been made by the parties in ignorance of the postponement of the procession. The court did not specifically deal with the construction of the contract, but presumably the contract had not provided for the risk of the postponement. It held that the contract was void for mistake and that the plaintiff could recover back money he had paid under it.

1   *Bell v Lever Bros Ltd* [1932] AC 161 at 218; *Norwich Union Fire Insurance Society Ltd v Price* [1934] AC 455 at 463.
2   *Sheikh Bros v Ochsner* [1957] AC 136, PC.
3   (1903) 19 TLR 434.

13.8   *Shared mistake as to a fundamental assumption* A contract is void if the parties have made their agreement on the basis of a particular assumption which turns out to be untrue, provided the assumption was fundamental to the continued validity of the contract, or was a foundation essential to its existence. This was accepted by the House of Lords in *Bell v Lever Bros Ltd*,[1] whose facts are set out in para 13.9 below, although their Lordships were divided on whether or not the assumption in question was sufficiently fundamental and did not find the contract in that case void for mistake on this or any other ground.

There is an element of overlap between this type of shared mistake and the two just mentioned. *Galloway v Galloway*[2] and *Griffith v Brymer*,[3] for example, are both cases where the requirements of the present ground were satisfied.

The present ground was applied recently at first instance in *Grains & Fourrages SA v Huyton*.[4] The parties to two contracts concerning two different cargoes mistakenly believed that analytical certificates issued in respect of them related to the wrong cargo, whereas each certificate did relate to the cargo actually named in it. They agreed to rectify the matter themselves. The judge held that the rectification agreement was void, and therefore not binding on the parties, because of their shared mistake as to a fundamental assumption, viz the inaccuracy of the certificates.

1   [1932] AC 161, HL.
2   (1903) 19 TLR 434.
3   (1914) 30 TLR 531, DC.
4   [1997] 1 Lloyd's Rep 628.

13.9   *Shared mistake as to quality* A vexed question is whether a shared mistake as to the quality (as opposed to the existence) of the subject matter of the contract can ever be sufficiently fundamental to render it void. Frequently, of course, the risk that the goods etc lack that quality is borne by the seller because the supposed quality of the goods is a term, express or implied, of the contract. If this occurs, the law of mistake is irrelevant because the contract provides that the seller shall be liable for breach of contract if the quality is absent. But if the risk that the quality is lacking is not allocated, is the contract *ever* void for mistake? Dicta in *Bell v Lever Bros Ltd*[1] suggest that in some cases a contract can be void for a shared mistake as to quality. In that case, Bell was employed by Lever Bros under a contract of employment for five years at £8,000 per annum. Lever Bros agreed to pay Bell £30,000 to relinquish this contract. Subsequently, they discovered that they could have terminated the contract without compensation because of breaches of it by Bell. Bell had forgotten about these breaches and he and Lever Bros were treated as being under a shared mistake as to the *quality* of the contract of employment, in that they had believed it was only determinable with Bell's agreement when in truth it was immediately determinable by Lever Bros without his agreement. Lever Bros' claim to recover back the compensation paid, as money paid under a void contract, failed before the House of Lords, who held the contract of compensation valid despite the shared mistake, although three of their Lordships stated that a sufficiently fundamental mistake as to quality might render a contract void. Lords Atkin and Thankerton stated that, to be sufficiently fundamental, the mistake would have to be as to a quality which made the thing essentially different from the thing which it was believed to be. The reader may think that, if the mistake as to quality in *Bell v Lever Bros* was not sufficiently fundamental, it is hard to imagine when a mistake as to quality will be.[2]

No case has actually been decided on the basis that a contract was void because of a fundamental mistake as to quality. However, it has been held, obiter, in two first instance cases, that the contract in issue was, or could have been held, void for mistake on this ground.

The first case was *Nicholson and Venn v Smith Marriott*,[3] where a set of linen napkins and table cloths was put up for sale, described as dating from the 17th century. Unknown to both the buyers and the sellers, it was in fact Georgian, and the buyers were able to recover for breach of contract since the sellers were in breach of the implied condition under the Sale of Goods Act 1979, s 13(1) that the goods corresponded with their description. Strangely, the judge added as an obiter dictum that, had the buyers sought to recover the whole of the price paid as money paid under a void contract,[4] he would have been disposed to hold the contract void for mistake as to quality. The judge did not enlarge on this view.

Associated Japanese Bank (International) Ltd v Credit du Nord SA[5] is a more impressive authority since the judge discussed the rules relating to mistake at some length. X made two contracts with the plaintiffs. The first was for the sale by X to the plaintiffs of four specified machines. The second was for the lease of the four machines by the plaintiffs to X. By these two contracts the plaintiffs effected in favour of X what is called a leaseback arrangement. X's obligations under the leasing contract were guaranteed by the defendants under a contract of guarantee between them and the plaintiffs. In fact, the specified machines did not exist and the arrangement was a fraud perpetrated by X. The plaintiffs claimed from X the outstanding balance under the leasing contract but X was made bankrupt and the plaintiffs were not paid. They sued the defendants on the contract of guarantee.

The judge held that, on the construction of the contract of guarantee, the defendants were excused from liability under it by the non-fulfilment of a condition precedent of it, viz the existence of the machines. However, he went on to consider whether, alternatively, the contract of guarantee was void for shared mistake. By his own admission, the judge's views on this matter were obiter because, as he pointed out himself, if the contract itself resolves the matter, the rules relating to mistake do not come into play.

Relying on the speeches of Lords Atkin and Thankerton in *Bell v Lever Bros Ltd*, the judge held that, to render a contract void, a shared mistake as to quality must render the subject matter of the contract essentially different from the subject matter which the parties believed to exist. Applying this test to the particular facts, the judge held that, for both parties, the guarantee of obligations under a lease with four non-existent machines was essentially different from a guarantee of a lease with four machines which both parties reasonably believed to exist. Thus, since the parties had a shared mistake as to an essential quality of the subject matter (the leasing contract) of the contract of guarantee, the contract of guarantee was void.

Although the judge did not base his conclusion in respect of mistake on it, it would seem that he could have reached the same conclusion on the basis that there was a shared mistake as to a fundamental assumption underlying the contract since the existence of the machines was a fundamental assumption of the guarantee contract.

1   [1932] AC 161, HL.
2   An unconvincing attempt was made to rationalise the statement of principle in *Bell's* case with the decision in *Associated Japanese Bank (International) Ltd v Credit du Nord SA* [1988] 3 All ER 902.
3   (1947) 177 LT 189.
4   Para 13.2 above.
5   [1988] 3 All ER 902.

13.10   The dicta in support of the proposition that a contract can be void for a fundamental mistake as to quality can be contrasted with the actual decisions in a number of cases. In *Solle v Butcher*,[1] a Court of Appeal decision, the fact that both parties to a lease mistakenly believed that the premises were free from rent control did not render the contract void. Similarly, in *Magee v Pennine Insurance Co Ltd*,[2] another Court of Appeal decision, compromise of a claim under an insurance policy which both parties mistakenly believed to be valid, when in fact the policy was voidable, was held not to be void for mistake. Again, we are prompted to ask, if these mistakes were not fundamental, what sort of mistake as to quality would have been?

Our conclusion is that, despite the dicta to the contrary, a contract can never be void at law simply because of a mistake as to quality, however fundamental.

1   [1950] 1 KB 671, [1949] 2 All ER 1107, CA.
2   [1969] 2 All ER 891, CA.

13.11   *Effect of unreasonable mistake* According to the judge in *Associated Japanese Bank (International) Ltd v Credit du Nord SA*,[1] a party to a contract cannot rely on a shared mistake which would otherwise render the contract void against him if he had no reasonable ground for his mistaken belief. The judge gave as an extreme example of a case falling within this exception that of the person who makes a contract with minimal knowledge of the facts to which the mistake relates but who is content that it is a good speculative risk. This qualification is part of the obiter dictum, which has already been referred to. If it is subsequently held to represent the law it will correspond to the approach under the equitable rules on shared mistake, whereby fault on the part of a mistaken party precludes the granting to him of relief.[2]

1   [1988] 3 All ER 902.
2   Para 13.12 below.

Equity

13.12   If a contract is void at law for mistake, it is of no legal effect and no damages can be awarded for non-performance or faulty performance. Further, equity, following the law, will not grant specific performance.

Moreover, to put the matter beyond doubt, the equitable remedy of rescission (ie setting aside) of the contract can be obtained. Since the contract is void this is not necessary, but it is a useful remedy where there is a formal contractual document, such as a lease.

Even though the shared mistake in question, such as one as to quality, does not make the contract void at common law, equitable relief may be available. This relief, which lies in the court's discretion,[1] may take the form of refusing specific performance (which will not affect liability in damages), or of awarding specific performance on terms which do justice, or of rescinding the contract for *mistake*.

1   Equitable relief will not be granted, for example, in favour of a party who has been at fault in making the mistake: *Solle v Butcher* [1950] 1 KB 671 at 693.

13.13   Where a contract which is not void for mistake is rescinded, the rescission sets aside a contract which previously existed, and the parties are restored to their former positions. In addition, the court may impose terms on the parties in the interests of justice and equity. Thus, if a contract of sale of goods is rescinded for mistake, this may be done on terms that the buyer is compensated for any improvements which he has made to the goods. Rescission for mistake is not possible if the law or the contract allocates the risk in respect of the 'mistaken matter'.[1]

It is not certain what mistakes are sufficient to enable a contract to be rescinded under the equitable power. Certainly, all mistakes which the law considers sufficient will suffice in equity and so will other types of mistake, although the limits are not clearly established.

Solle v Butcher[2] is an example of a case where equity has set aside a contract for mistake; the mistake was one as to quality. In this case, a lease was granted at a specified rent in the shared mistaken belief that the nature of the flat had been so changed as not to be a rent-controlled property. As we have said, the Court of Appeal refused to hold the contract void but it set it aside in equity. At the time there was a housing shortage and rescission was ordered on terms that the tenant should have an option either to surrender the lease or to stay in the premises under a new lease at the maximum rent which the landlord could charge under the statutory provisions then in force.

By way of further example, the contract in *Magee v Pennine Insurance Co Ltd*[3] was rescinded.

The rescission of a contract for shared mistake is subject to similar bars to those which apply to rescission for misrepresentation and which we outline in para 14.17 below.

1   *William Sindall plc v Cambridgeshire County Council* [1994] 3 All ER 932, CA.
2   [1950] 1 KB 671, [1949] 2 All ER 1107, CA. For a similar example, see *Grist v Bailey* [1966] 2 All ER 875.
3   [1969] 2 All ER 891, CA, para 13.10 above.

Mistake not shared by the parties

Common law
13.14   The fact that one party entered into an apparent contract under a mistake does not normally render the contract void, and the same is true if both parties were labouring under different mistaken beliefs. However, a contract will be void if a mistake which is not shared by the parties relates to:

- the identity of the other party; or
- the essence of the subject matter of the contract; or
- whether a particular matter is a term of the contract,

and the mistake is an operative mistake in the sense discussed in para 13.20 below.

Mistake as to identity
13.15   A mistake as to identity can make an apparent contract void; a mistake which merely relates to an attribute, eg creditworthiness, of the other party can never do so.

In *Cundy v Lindsay*,[1] a rogue, Blenkarn, who had hired premises at 37 Wood Street, wrote to the plaintiffs, offering to buy some goods. Blenkarn deliberately signed his letter 'A Blenkarn & Co' in such a way that the signature appeared to be that of A. Blenkiron & Co. A. Blenkiron & Co were a well-known firm which had traded for many years at 123 Wood Street. The plaintiffs accepted the offer and sent their letter of acceptance to 'Messrs Blenkiron, 37 Wood Street'. Later, goods were delivered under the contract to the same address. The House of Lords held that the plaintiffs had purported to accept an offer made by Blenkiron and had never intended to contract with Blenkarn at all. In consequence, the apparent contract with Blenkarn was void and the innocent party to whom Blenkarn had resold the goods was held liable to the plaintiffs for the tort of conversion. The plaintiffs could, of course, have sued Blenkarn for the torts of conversion and deceit[2] if they could have traced him.

In *Cundy v Lindsay*, the plaintiffs were able to establish that they meant to deal only with Blenkiron and not with the writer of the letter; there was thus a mistake as to identity. On the other hand, in *King's Norton Metal Co Ltd v Edridge, Merrett & Co Ltd*,[3] the mistake made by the plaintiffs who sold goods to a rogue who resold them to the defendants before the plaintiffs discovered the truth was one as to attribute, not identity. In this case, a rogue, one Wallis, offered to buy goods in a letter written on paper headed 'Hallam & Co' and embellished with references to depots and a picture of a factory. The plaintiffs mistakenly believed Hallam & Co to be a respectable firm but they did not think that they were dealing with someone other than the writer of the letter. Their mistake was as to the credit and reliability of the writer of the letter, and not as to the identity of the other party. Thus, their contract with the rogue was not void and he had passed title to the defendants. Consequently, the defendants were not liable to the plaintiffs for conversion of the goods.

The important distinguishing feature between these two cases is that in *Cundy v Lindsay* there was an actual separate entity, 'A. Blenkiron & Co', with whom the plaintiffs wished to contract, whereas in *King's Norton* there was not.

1   (1878) 3 App Cas 459, HL.
2   Para 14.21 below.
3   (1897) 14 TLR 98, CA.

13.16   When the parties contract face to face, it is much more difficult to establish that a mistake relates to the identity, as opposed to attributes, of the other party, and it can normally be presumed that a party intended to deal with the person in front of him. However, every case turns on its facts and it may be possible to establish a mistake as to identity if the identity of one party was of vital importance to the other.

In *Phillips v Brooks Ltd*,[1] a rogue, named North, entered the plaintiff's shop and selected some jewellery, including a ring. He then wrote out a cheque for the full amount. As he did so, he announced that he was Sir George Bullough of St James' Square. The plaintiff had heard of Sir George Bullough; he consulted a directory and found that Sir George Bullough did live at the address given. He therefore allowed North to take away the ring without first having the cheque cleared. North pledged the ring with the defendant, who was wholly innocent.

The cheque was dishonoured and the plaintiff sued the defendant in tort for the conversion of the ring. He could only succeed if the contract was void for mistake. The judge held that it was not; his reason was that he found that the plaintiff had intended to contract with the person in the shop. The plaintiff's mistaken belief related to an attribute of the customer (his creditworthiness), not his identity. It would have been different if the plaintiff had established that the identity of his customer was of vital importance to him. He had, it is true, consulted a directory to see whether there was a Sir George Bullough of St James' Square, but this was not sufficient to rebut the presumption that he intended to deal with the customer before him, whoever he was.

A similar case is that of *Lewis v Averay*,[2] where a rogue, claiming to be Richard Greene, a well-known actor, bought from the plaintiff a car which he then sold to the defendant, who was innocent. The plaintiff sued the defendant for the conversion of his car but failed to establish that he had made a mistake as to the identity of the other party to the agreement. He had to be presumed to intend to deal with the person in front of him, said the Court of Appeal, unless he could establish that the identity of the buyer was of vital importance to him. In this case, the only attempt to check whether the rogue was Richard Greene was the perusal of a Pinewood Studio pass in the name of Richard Green, which was produced by the rogue, and this was insufficient to establish that he intended to deal only with Richard Greene, the actor.

1   [1919] 2 KB 243.
2   [1971] 3 All ER 907, CA.

13.17   *Ingram v Little*[1] is a case where the plaintiff was able to establish a mistake as to the identity of the other party. In *Ingram v Little*, the plaintiffs, two elderly sisters, were confronted by a rogue who called himself Hutchinson. They agreed to sell him their car, but refused to continue the sale when the rogue proposed to pay by cheque. He then announced himself to be PGM Hutchinson of Stanstead House, Caterham. One sister slipped out to the Post Office, consulted the telephone directory and found that there was a PGM Hutchinson of Stanstead House, while the other sister plied the rogue with conversation. They accepted the cheque, which was dishonoured, and the rogue sold the car to the defendant, whom the sisters sued in conversion. The Court of Appeal found that on the facts of the case the plaintiffs had done sufficient to establish that they intended to deal only with PGM Hutchinson of Stanstead House, and not with the person in front of them. This decision has been greatly criticised but, since all cases turn on their own facts, it may have been correctly decided.

1   [1960] 3 All ER 332, CA. For another case where mistake of identity was established, see *Sowler v Potter* [1939] 4 All ER 478.

Mistake as to the essence of the subject matter
13.18   A mistake as to the essence of the subject matter of a contract renders it void. An example of such a mistake would be where A agrees to buy a computer from B, mistakenly believing that it is a Viglen computer when, in fact, it is an IBM computer. In such a case, there would be no genuine agreement for the parties are at cross-purposes. Similarly, if X agrees to buy a consignment of wheat from Y, thinking that it is a consignment of oats, his mistake is as to the essence of the subject matter.[1] In both cases, of course, the contract would only be void if A or X's mistake was operative in the sense explained in para 13.20 below.

On the other hand, a mistake which simply relates to a quality, but not the essence of the thing, is not sufficiently fundamental to render the contract void. Thus, if X agrees to buy oats from Y, mistakenly believing that they are old oats, the contract cannot be void for mistake.[2]

1   *Scriven Bros v Hindley & Co* [1913] 3 KB 564; *Raffles v Wichelhaus* (1864) 2 H & C 906.
2   *Smith v Hughes* (1871) LR 6 QB 597.

Mistake as to the terms of the contract
13.19   A contract may be void if a party mistakenly believes that a particular matter is a term of the contract, even though the mistake does not relate to the identity of the other party or the essence of the subject matter. Thus, if X mistakenly believes that Y warrants that the oats which he is selling him are old oats, the contract may be void for mistake.[1] Whether or not it is depends on whether or not the mistake is operative.

In *Hartog v Colin and Shields*,[2] the sellers mistakenly offered to sell goods at a given price per pound when they had intended to offer to sell at that given price per piece, there being about three pieces to the pound. The buyer accepted the offer. The contract was apparently held void because of the sellers' mistake as to the price (a term of the contract). All the preliminary negotiations had been on the basis of price per piece and trade custom also related to price per piece. The effect of this was that the court found that the buyer must have realised that the sellers had made a mistake and could not rush in and accept what would have been a most advantageous offer.

1   *Smith v Hughes* (1871) LR 6 QB 597.
2   [1939] 3 All ER 566.

Operative mistake
13.20   It is not enough that a party was mistaken as to the identity of the other party, or as to the essence of the subject matter, or as to a term of the contract. Such a mistake must be operative to render the contract void and it will only be so if:

- The other party knew of the mistake, as in *Cundy v Lindsay, Ingram v Little, Sowler v Potter* and *Hartog v Colin & Shields*; or
- The circumstances are so ambiguous that a reasonable person could not say whether the contract meant what one party thought it meant or what the other party

thought it meant. It is only in exceptional cases that the circumstances are so ambiguous. The approach taken by the courts is that if, whatever A's real intention may be, A so conducts himself that a reasonable person would believe that A was assenting to the contract proposed by the other party (B), and B contracts with A in that belief, there is a contract with the meaning and terms understood by B.[1] In *Wood v Scarth*,[2] the defendant wrote to the plaintiff, offering to let him a public house at £63 a year. After an interview with the defendant's clerk, the plaintiff accepted the offer by letter. The defendant had intended also to take a premium for the tenancy and thought that the clerk had made it clear to the plaintiff that this was a term of the contract. The plaintiff accepted the offer, thinking that his only financial obligation was to pay the rent. It was held that there was a contract in the sense understood by the plaintiff. *Wood v Scarth* can be contrasted with *Scriven Bros v Hindley*,[3] where the defendants successfully bid at an auction sale for a lot which consisted of tow, thinking that they were bidding for hemp, an infinitely superior product. Both tow and hemp were sold at the auction and samples of each were on display, although the defendants had not inspected them because they had already seen samples of hemp at the plaintiff's showroom. However, the lot in question was misleadingly described in the auctioneer's catalogue and the samples were confusingly marked. It was held that the contract was void. Clearly, in the special circumstances a reasonable person could not say whether there was a contract for the sale of hemp or for the sale of tow.

1   *Smith v Hughes* (1871) LR 6 QB 597 at 607; *Centrovincial Estates plc v Merchant Investors Assurance Co Ltd* [1983] Com LR 158, CA.
2   (1855) 2 K & J 33; (1858) 1 F & F 293.
3   [1913] 3 KB 564.

Equity

13.21   Where a contract is void at common law because of an operative mistake not shared by the parties, equity follows the law and will not grant specific performance[1] of the contract and may, to put the matter beyond doubt, rescind the contract.

In addition, the equitable remedy of specific performance may be refused if justice so demands, and it is reasonable to do so, even though the contract is not void for mistake at common law. It was refused, for instance, in *Wood v Scarth*,[2] although the plaintiff was able to obtain the common law remedy of damages. On the other hand, in *Tamplin v James*,[3] where the defendant had successfully bid for a property under the mistaken belief as to its extent, specific performance was ordered: the defendant's mistake was his own fault since he had failed to check the plans to which the auctioneer had drawn attention.

1   *Webster v Cecil* (1861) 30 Beav 62.
2   (1855) 2 K & J 33; (1858) 1 F & F 293; para 13.20 above.
3   (1880) 15 Ch D 215.

Mistake and documents

Rectification

13.22   We are concerned here with the case where the parties have made a perfectly valid oral agreement but it is later embodied in a document which *records their agreement inaccurately.* In such a case, the equitable remedy of rectification is available. This enables a court to rectify the document so that it embodies the agreement of the parties accurately. Oral evidence is admissible to show that the written document does not represent the agreement of the parties even if the contract at issue is one which must be made or evidenced in writing.

Rectification will normally only be ordered if the document does not represent the intentions of both parties up to the time of the written agreement. However, rectification can be ordered where one party (A) mistakenly believed that a particular term was (or was not) included in the document to give effect to that intention, if:

- the other party (B) knew of[1] that mistake but nevertheless failed to draw the mistake to A's notice and allowed the document to be executed,[2] or conducted himself as to divert A from discovering the mistake,[3] and
- the mistake would inequitably benefit B or be detrimental to A.[4]

On the other hand, if the document simply fails to mention an obligation which one party, but not the other, had intended to be a term of the contract rectification cannot be ordered.[5]

There is no right to rectification; it will only be ordered where it is just and equitable to do so. For example, the existence of third-party rights dependent on the written contract will bar rectification unless the third party knows of the mistake. Lapse of time may also prevent rectification.

1 Knowledge here includes wilfully shutting one's eyes to the obvious or wilfully and recklessly failing to make reasonable enquiries: *Commission for the New Towns v Cooper (Great Britain) Ltd* [1995] 2 All ER 929 at 947. Cf *J J Huber (Investment) Ltd v Private DIY Co Ltd* [1995] EGCS 112 (mere suspicion not enough).
2 *A Roberts & Co v Leicestershire County Council* [1961] 2 All ER 545; *Thomas Bates & Son Ltd v Wyndham's (Lingerie) Ltd* [1981] 1 All ER 1077, CA.
3 *Commission for the New Towns v Cooper (Great Britain) Ltd* [1995] 2 All ER 929 at 946.
4 *Thomas Bates & Son Ltd v Wyndham's (Lingerie) Ltd* [1981] 1 All ER 1077, CA.
5 *Riverlate Properties Ltd v Paul* [1974] 2 All ER 656, CA.

Documents mistakenly signed

13.23 Where a person signs a document which contains a contract he is bound by that contract. This is so even if it is not the contract which he expected and whether or not he has read or understood the document. An example of the potential harshness of this rule is provided by *Pilkington v Flack*.[1] The defendant wished to sell her shop. She signed a document produced by the plaintiff, a business broker. She did so without reading it because she was serving customers. The document, which was described by the court as 'scandalous', provided that the plaintiff should have for 26 weeks the sole rights to sell the business for £500 and that he should have his commission even if the business was sold by someone else. The commission stipulated was more than double the usual rate and, in addition, the plaintiff was to be entitled to any part of the price over £500. The plaintiff was held to be bound by the document.

There is an exception to the above rule; it is the plea of *non est factum* (it is not my deed), which, if proved, renders the contract void and permits the signatory of a written contract to deny liability under it.

To succeed in his plea of *non est factum*, the signatory must prove:

- that the signed document was radically different in character or effect from that which he thought he was signing; and
- that he was not careless in signing the document.

It will be rare that both requirements can be proved.

The leading case is the House of Lords' decision in *Saunders v Anglia Building Society*.[2] Mrs Gallie, an elderly widow, occupied a house under a lease. Her nephew, Parkin, wished to raise money using the house as security. Mrs Gallie was happy for this to happen, provided she could live in the house rent-free until her death.[3] Because Parkin did not want to pay maintenance to his estranged wife, he adopted a circuitous method of raising money so as to appear not to have any funds. The scheme was to induce Mrs Gallie to assign the property by way of sale to a friend of Parkin, Lee, who would mortgage it and pay the money to Parkin. A document which assigned the property to Lee by way of sale was drawn up and Mrs Gallie signed it without reading it; she had, in fact, broken her glasses. She thought the document was a deed of gift transferring the house to Parkin so that he could mortgage it. Lee mortgaged the property to the building society but paid Parkin nothing. Mrs Gallie, pleading *non est factum*, subsequently sought a declaration that the assignment to Lee was void, so that the building society could not enforce the mortgage.

The House of Lords rejected Mrs Gallie's plea of *non est factum*. They found that the document she had signed was not radically different in effect from what she had intended to sign. Legally, there may be a great difference between an assignment by way of sale and a deed of gift, but the effect in this case was the same – to enable Parkin to raise money on the security of the house. Even if the signed document had been radically different from what was intended, Mrs Gallie had failed to establish that she had not been careless. She had not read the document nor asked for it to be read to her; she had consulted no professional advisers and she had not acted sensibly.

In deciding whether a party has established that he was not careless, the standard of the reasonable man applies to those of full age and understanding. On the other hand, the House of Lords' decision suggests that, if the party is illiterate or is mentally handicapped or is blind, that characteristic should be taken into account in deciding whether it has been established that he was not careless. On this basis, a court dealing with a case involving an 'incapable' signatory would have to consider whether he used such care as a reasonable man with his incapacity would have used. If a blind man is proposing to sign a document, he should ask for it to be read to him by a trustworthy person, and, if he fails to do so, he cannot rely on *non est factum*.

1   (1948) 152 Estates Gazette 366, CA.
2   [1970] 3 All ER 961, HL.
3   Mrs Gallie died before the case was heard by the House of Lords. Saunders was her executrix.

13.24   The above principles apply where a person signs a document, knowing that it contains blanks which the other party will fill in. In *United Dominions Trust Ltd v Western*,[1] the defendant agreed to buy a car on hire purchase. He signed a document which was in fact a loan agreement with the plaintiffs and which did not specify the price of the car or the deposit paid. Incorrect figures were subsequently inserted by the sellers of the car, as the defendant later learned. He failed to pay any instalments under the loan agreement and was sued. The Court of Appeal refused to allow the defendant to rely on the doctrine of *non est factum* because neither of its two requirements had been proved by him. First, the document signed was not radically different from that which he thought he was signing. Second, since the same legal principles as to carelessness applied to documents signed in blank as they applied to other cases of erroneously signed documents, the defendant had not proved that he had exercised due care in signing in blank.

1   [1975] 3 All ER 1017, CA.

Money paid under a mistake of fact

13.25   This aspect of the law of restitution is dealt with here for convenience, since it is not limited to a situation of actual or supposed contractual relationship. It is for this reason that the relevant rules are part of the law of restitution, and not of the law of contract. Money paid under a mistaken belief in the truth of a fact which, if true, would have entitled the payee to payment is recoverable back by the payer, subject to the exceptions set out later. In *Kelly v Solari*,[1] for example, the plaintiff was the director of a life insurance company which had paid out insurance money to the defendant under her husband's life insurance policy. The policy had, in fact, lapsed because the last premium had not been paid. The company had noted this, but the lapse had been overlooked when the defendant claimed the money. It was held that the plaintiff could recover back the money because it had been paid under a mistaken belief in facts which, if true, would have entitled the defendant to payment.

A vexed question is whether, as in *Kelly v Solari*, the mistake must have led the plaintiff to believe a fact which, if true, would have meant that he was *legally* obliged to pay. Although this requirement has been reiterated in a number of cases,[2] the Court of Appeal in *Larner v LCC*[3] held that money paid under a mistake of fact which, if true, would have morally (but not legally) obliged its payment was recoverable back. The LCC passed a resolution to make up the pay of their employees who were on war service to the amount of their civil salaries. L was one of their employees and he joined the RAF. Although he had agreed to inform the LCC of any increase in his service wages, he failed to do so and, consequently, was overpaid by the LCC. If the facts had been as supposed, the LCC would only have been morally, not legally,[4] obliged to make the payments, but the mistake was held to be sufficient to entitle the Council to recover back the amount of the overpayment. It may be that the decision in this case can be justified on its special facts and goes no further than holding that a mistake as to moral liability to honour a promise to pay made for reasons of *national policy* (a matter emphasised by the Court of Appeal) is to be equated with mistakes as to legal liability to pay. On this view, the Court of Appeal did not lay down a wider rule that, whenever a person pays money to another under a mistake of fact which causes him to make the payment, he is entitled to recover it back as money paid under a mistake of fact. However, in *Barclays Bank Ltd v W J Simms, Son and Cooke (Southern) Ltd*,[5] the judge stated the law in these broad terms, relying on an impressive list of authorities; but an examination of them suggests that he misinterpreted them, so that his statement of the law must be viewed with suspicion and cannot be regarded with confidence as representing the current state of the law in the light of the authority to the contrary.

Subject to what we have just said, a payment can be recovered back from the payee even though the mistake was not shared by the payer and payee,[6] and even though the mistake was induced by a third person.[7]

1   (1841) 9 M & W 54.
2   Eg *Aiken v Short* (1856) 1 H & N 210 at 215; *Maskell v Horner* [1915] 3 KB 106, CA.
3   [1949] 1 All ER 964, CA.
4   Para 6.3 above.
5   [1979] 3 All ER 522.
6   *Barclays Bank Ltd v W J Simms, Son and Cooke (Southern) Ltd* [1979] 3 All ER 522.
7   *R E Jones Ltd v Waring and Gillow Ltd* [1926] AC 670, HL.

13.26   The mistake must be one of fact: money paid under a mistake of law is not recoverable, generally. A mistake as to the construction of a statute,[1] or of regulations,[2] or of a contract,[3] is one of law. On the other hand, a mistake as to the existence of a private right, such as a person's title to property, is, oddly enough, regarded as a mistake of fact.[4]

The recovery back of money paid under a mistake of fact is subject to the following limits:

- Where the money was paid under a contract which had been induced under a mistake on the payer's part, there can be no recovery back of the money on the ground that it was paid under a mistake of fact, unless the contract itself is void for mistake or is rescinded by the payer.[5]
- Where the payer intends that the payee should have the money at all events, whether the fact be true or false,[6] or is deemed in law so to intend (which is the case where a bookmaker pays or overpays a betting debt by mistake), he cannot recover it back.[7]
- Where the payee has altered his position in good faith, as where an agent without notice of the payer's mistake hands the money (or part of it) over to his principal, so that it would be inequitable in all the circumstances to require him to make restitution (or to make restitution in full), the payer cannot recover it back from him (or cannot recover it back in full, as the case may be).[8]

1 *National Pari-Mutuel Association Ltd v R* (1930) 47 TLR 110, CA.
2 *Holt v Markham* [1923] 1 KB 504, CA.
3 *Ord v Ord* [1923] 2 KB 432.
4 *Cooper v Phibbs* (1867) LR 2 HL 149, HL.
5 *Norwich Union Fire Insurance Society Ltd v William H Price Ltd* [1934] AC 455, PC; *Barclays Bank Ltd v W J Simms, Son and Cooke (Southern) Ltd* [1979] 3 All ER 522 at 535.
6 *Kelly v Solari* (1841) 9 M & W 54 at 58.
7 *Morgan v Ashcroft* [1937] 3 All ER 92, CA, as explained in *Barclays Bank Ltd v W J Simms, Son and Cooke (Southern) Ltd* [1979] 3 All ER 522.
8 *Lipkin Gorman v Karpnale Ltd* [1992] 4 All ER 512, HL.

Chapter 14

Misrepresentation, duress and undue influence

14.1 In this chapter we consider:

- when a contract can be set aside by one party because of a misrepresentation by the other party;
- when damages can be recovered for misrepresentation;
- when a contract can be set aside for non-disclosure of a material fact by a party;
- when a contract can be set aside for duress or undue influence;
- the effect of an unfair term in a consumer contract for the sale or supply of goods or the supply of a service.

Misrepresentation

14.2 A misrepresentation is a false or misleading statement. In certain circumstances, a misrepresentation can give rise to criminal liability. For example, an estate agent or property developer (or an employee of such a person) commits an offence, contrary to the Property Misdescriptions Act 1991, if he makes a misrepresentation about certain prescribed matters such as the aspect of a property, or its view or environment, its proximity to any services, facilities or amenities, its physical or structural characteristics, or its accommodation or measurements. It is a defence to such a charge for a defendant to prove that he took all reasonable steps and exercised all due diligence to avoid committing the offence.

We are not concerned in this chapter with criminal liability for misrepresentation. Instead, we are concerned with the validity of a contract which has been induced by a misrepresentation by one of the parties to it (or his agent). Unless, as rarely happens, a mistake induced by a misrepresentation is such as to render the contract void under the rules discussed in the previous chapter, it is the rules which follow which govern the situation. These rules are somewhat involved, and different rules apply depending on whether there has been an active misrepresentation or a misrepresentation through non-disclosure.

Active misrepresentation

14.3 When one is faced with a situation involving an 'active misrepresentation' one must first ask whether the representation has become a term of the contract or not, applying the rules set out in paras 8.9 to 8.16 above. The division between active misrepresentations which have remained precontractual representations (mere representations) and those which have become terms of a resulting contract is fundamental since the remedies are different.

Active misrepresentations which have remained mere representations

14.4   If the misrepresentation has not become a contractual term, and provided certain requirements are satisfied, two remedies may be available to the misrepresentee: rescission of the contract (unless this is barred) and (in many cases) damages. The requirements mentioned above are that:

- the misrepresentation must be one of fact;
- it must have been addressed to the person misled; and
- it must have induced the contract.

Misrepresentation of fact

14.5   There must be a misrepresentation by words or conduct of a past or existing fact. An example of a misrepresentation by conduct would be where the vendor of a house covered up dry rot in it.[1] It follows from the requirement that there must be a misrepresentation of a past or existing fact that there are many misrepresentations for which no relief is available. The following must be distinguished from misrepresentation of fact.

1   See *Gordon v Selico Co Ltd* [1986] 1 EGLR 71, CA.

14.6   *Mere puffs* A representation which is mere vague sales talk is not regarded as a representation of fact, as is shown by *Dimmock v Hallett*.[1] At a sale of land by auction, it was said to be 'fertile and improvable'; in fact it was partly abandoned and useless. The representation was held to be a 'mere flourishing description by an auctioneer' affording no ground for relief. It is a question of fact whether a particular statement is merely vague sales talk or the assertion of some verifiable fact.

1   (1866) 2 Ch App 21.

14.7   *Statements of opinion* A statement which merely expresses an opinion or belief does not give grounds for relief if the opinion or belief turns out to be wrong. In *Bisset v Wilkinson*,[1] the vendor of a farm which had never been used as a sheep farm, told a prospective purchaser that in his judgment the land would support 2,000 sheep. It was held that this statement was one of opinion, given that the farm had never been used for sheep, and that, since it was an honest statement, no relief was available. It would have been different if there had been a misrepresentation of its actual capacity since this would have been a misrepresentation of fact.

What has been said in the last paragraph must be qualified by pointing out that in two cases statements of opinion can involve an implied misrepresentation of fact and so give rise to relief:

- Where a person represents an opinion which he does not honestly hold he will at the same time make a misrepresentation of fact, viz that he holds the opinion.[2]
- Where a person represents an opinion for which he does not have reasonable grounds, he will at the same time make a misrepresentation of fact if he impliedly represents that he has reasonable grounds for his opinion. A classic example is *Smith v Land and House Property Corpn*.[3] The vendor of a hotel described it as

let to 'Mr Frederick Fleck (a most desirable tenant)... for an unexpired term of 27 plus years, thus offering a first-class investment'. Fleck had not paid the last quarter's rent and had paid the previous one by instalments and under pressure. The Court of Appeal held that the above statement was not merely of opinion but also involved a misrepresentation of fact because the vendor impliedly stated that he had reasonable grounds for his opinion. Too much should not be read into this decision because the court will only find such an implied representation where the facts on which the opinion is based are particularly within the knowledge of the person stating the opinion, and not when the facts are equally known to both parties.[4]

1   [1927] AC 177, PC.
2   *Brown v Raphael* [1958] 2 All ER 79 at 81.
3   (1884) 28 Ch D 7, CA.
4   *Smith v Land and House Property Corpn* (1884) 28 Ch D 7 at 15.

14.8   *Statements as to the future* Such statements, the best example of which is a statement of intention, are obviously not statements of fact in themselves and no remedy is available if the future event does not occur. However, a statement as to the future will involve a misrepresentation of fact if its maker does not honestly believe in its truth. In the case of a misrepresentation of intention this rule is well summarised by the statement of Bowen LJ in *Edgington v Fitzmaurice*[1] that the state of a man's mind is as much a fact as the state of his digestion. In this case the plaintiff was induced to lend money to a company by representations made in a prospectus by the directors that the money would be used to improve the company's buildings and to expand its business. The directors' true intention was to use the money to pay off the company's debts. They were held liable in deceit (fraudulent misrepresentation) on the basis that their misrepresentation of present intentions was a misrepresentation of fact.

1   (1885) 29 Ch D 459, CA.

14.9   *Statements of law* A person who is induced to contract by a misrepresentation of law has no remedy.[1] The only exceptions are:

*   where, as in the case of a statement of opinion or intention, the representor wilfully misrepresents the fact that he does not believe his statement of the law;[2] and
*   where the misrepresentation relates to the existence or meaning of a foreign law, since such a misrepresentation is regarded by our courts as one of fact.[3]

A difficulty in this area is distinguishing a statement of law from a statement of fact. Clearly, a representation as to the meaning of a statute is one of law. However, in *West London Commercial Bank v Kitson*,[4] it was held that a misrepresentation of the contents of a Private Act was one of fact. The directors of a company represented that the company had power to accept bills of exchange and that they had authority to accept on its behalf. There was a misrepresentation since, under the Private Act which incorporated it, the company had no power to accept bills or authorise anyone to do so. It was held that the misrepresentation was one of fact since it related to the contents of a Private Act. It is doubtful whether this decision would be extended to a misrepresentation as to the contents of a Public Act because such a misrepresentation seems clearly to be one as to the general law.

A misrepresentation as to the contents or meaning of a document is one of fact. One authority is *Wauton v Coppard*.[5] The plaintiff contracted to buy a house from the defendant for use as a preparatory school. He made the contract after the defendant's agent had told him that there was nothing in the deed of restrictive covenants to prevent the running of a school. When the plaintiff received the deed he discovered that it prohibited any business or occupation whereby disagreeable noise or nuisance might be caused and he sought to rescind the contract. Romer J held that the misrepresentation made by the defendant's agent was one of fact, and that the contract would be set aside, because it concerned the contents of the deed. Likewise, in *Horry v Tate and Lyle Refineries Ltd*,[6] it was held that a misrepresentation as to the nature and effect of a contract for the settlement of a claim for compensation for personal injuries was one of fact.

1   *Beattie v Lord Ebury* (1872) 7 Ch App 777.
2   The point has not yet been decided by a court. It was left open for future decision in *West London Commercial Bank v Kitson* (1884) 13 QBD 360 at 362–363.
3   *André & Ce SA v Ets Michel Blanc & Fils* [1979] 2 Lloyd's Rep 427, CA.
4   (1884) 13 QBD 360, CA.
5   [1899] 1 Ch 92.
6   [1982] 2 Lloyd's Rep 416.

14.10   *Silence* Not surprisingly, silence cannot generally constitute an active misrepresentation.[1] However, there are two exceptions:

*   Where silence distorts a positive assertion of fact there will be an active misrepresentation of fact. Thus, in *Dimmock v Hallett*,[2] it was said that if a vendor of land states that farms on it are let, but omits to say that the tenants have given notice to quit, his statement will be a misrepresentation of fact.
*   Where a representation of fact is falsified by later events, before the conclusion of the contract, there will be an active misrepresentation if the representor fails to notify the other of the change. This is shown by *With v O'Flanagan*.[3] Negotiations for the sale of a medical practice were begun in January 1934. The defendant vendor represented to the plaintiff that the practice was producing £2,000 per annum, which was then true. Between January and May, the defendant was seriously ill and the practice was looked after by a number of substitutes with the result that the receipts had fallen to £5 per week by 1 May 1934. On 1 May 1934, the plaintiff, who had not been informed of the change of circumstances, signed a contract to purchase the practice. The Court of Appeal rescinded the contract on the ground that the defendant ought to have communicated the change of circumstances to the plaintiff. It said that the representation made to induce the contract must be treated as continuing until the contract was signed and what was initially a true representation had turned into a misrepresentation.

1   See further paras 14.40–14.44 below.
2   (1866) 2 Ch App 21.
3   [1936] 1 All ER 727, CA.

The misrepresentation must have been addressed by the misrepresentor to the person misled[1]

14.11   The present requirement is not as stringent as may appear at first sight because:

*   It is possible for a representation to be made to the public in general, as in the case of an advertisement.
*   A representation need not be made directly to the person misled, or his agent, in order to satisfy the present requirement. It suffices that the representor knew that the person to whom he made the misrepresentation would pass it on to the plaintiff. This is shown by *Pilmore v Hood*.[2] The defendant wished to sell a public house

to X and fraudulently misrepresented that the annual takings were £180. X was unable to buy and with the defendant's knowledge persuaded the plaintiff to buy by repeating the defendant's misrepresentation. The defendant was held liable in damages to the plaintiff for his fraudulent misrepresentation. An important limit on the rule in *Pilmore v Hood* is that, if the person (A) to whom the misrepresentation is originally made by the defendant (D) contracts with D as a result, the misrepresentation is deemed to be exhausted. Thus, if A then contracts to sell the property to B, repeating D's misrepresentation, as D knew he would, B has no redress against D because D's misrepresentation, being exhausted, is not regarded as addressed to B.[3] Of course, in such a case B is not remediless because he can pursue the normal remedies for misrepresentation against A who passed on the misrepresentation.

1   *Peek v Gurney* (1873) LR 6 HL 377, HL.
2   (1838) 5 Bing NC 97.
3   *Gross v Lewis Hillman Ltd* [1969] 3 All ER 1476, CA.

The misrepresentation must have induced the misrepresentee to make the contract
14.12 The question of inducement is one of fact but, if the misrepresentor made a statement of a nature likely to induce a person to contract and with a view to inducing this, it will normally be inferred that it did induce the misrepresentee to contract. However, this inference is rebuttable and will, for example, be rebutted in the following three cases:

- if the misrepresentee actually knew the truth,[1] or if an agent acting for him in the transaction knew the truth as a result of information received in the course of it (since such knowledge is imputed to the misrepresentee). *Strover v Harrington*[2] provides an example. In the course of pre-contractual inquiries the solicitors of purchasers of land learned that, contrary to the representations of the vendors, the property was not connected to main drainage; the solicitors' knowledge was imputed to the purchasers;
- if the misrepresentee was ignorant of the misrepresentation when the contract was made. In *Re Northumberland and Durham District Banking Co, ex p Bigge*,[3] the plaintiff, who had bought some shares in a company, sought to have the purchase rescinded on the ground that the company had published false reports of its financial state. He failed; one of the reasons was because he was unable to prove that he had read any of the reports or that anyone had told him of their contents;
- if the misrepresentee did not allow the representation to affect his judgment. Thus, if the misrepresentee investigates the truth of the representation (as where a prospective purchaser has a house surveyed) and relies on his investigation, rather than the representation, in making the contract the inference of inducement is rebutted, except in the case of fraud. In *Attwood v Small*,[4] the appellant offered to sell a mine, making exaggerated representations as to its earning capacity. The respondent agreed to buy if the appellant could verify his representations and appointed agents to investigate the matter. The agents, who were experienced, visited the mine and were given every facility. They reported that the representations were true and the contract was made. The House of Lords held that the contract could not be rescinded for misrepresentation because the respondents had not relied on the misrepresentations but on their own independent investigations. By way of contrast, the inference of inducement is not rebutted where the misrepresentee could have investigated and discovered the falsity of the representation but chose not to do so.[5]

1   *Begbie v Phosphate Sewage Co* (1875) LR 10 QB 491; *Redgrave v Hurd* (1881) 20 Ch D 1, CA.
2   [1988] 1 All ER 769.
3   (1858) 28 LJ Ch 50.
4   (1838) 6 Cl & Fin 232, HL.
5   *Redgrave v Hurd* (1881) 20 Ch D 1, CA; *Laurence v Lexcourt Holdings Ltd* [1978] 2 All ER 810.

14.13   Before leaving the requirement of inducement two general points must be noted. First, provided that it was one of the inducements, the misrepresentation need not be the sole inducement. This is shown by *Edgington v Fitzmaurice*,[1] where the plaintiff was induced to take debentures in a company partly by a misrepresentation in the prospectus and partly by his own mistaken belief that debenture holders would have a charge on the company's property. He was held entitled to rescission.

Second, the misrepresentation must not only have induced the misrepresentee to contract but it must also have been material, in that it related to a matter which would have influenced the judgment of a reasonable person.[2] It is uncertain whether there is a similar requirement in other types of contract. The point is not an important one because an immaterial misrepresentation is unlikely to cause substantial loss with the result that any damages awarded are likely to be nominal and rescission is likely to be refused under the court's discretion to do so (which is described in para 14.30 below).

1   (1885) 29 Ch D 459, CA.
2   *Container Transport International Inc v Oceanus Mutual Underwriting Association (Bermuda) Ltd* [1984] 1 Lloyd's Rep 476, CA; *Pan Atlantic Insurance Co Ltd v Pine Top Insurance Co Ltd* [1994] 3 All ER 581, HL (see especially pp 600–610); Marine Insurance Act 1906, s 20(1) and (2).

Remedies for active misrepresentations which have remained mere representations

14.14   Provided the above requirements are satisfied, one or more of the remedies set out below is or are available to the misrepresentee. Alternatively, the misrepresentee can refuse to carry out the contract and, provided (generally) that he returns what he obtained under it, successfully resist any claim for damages or specific performance.

Rescission

14.15   The effect of a misrepresentation is to make the contract voidable – not void so that it remains valid unless and until the misrepresentee elects to rescind it on discovering the misrepresentation. Rescission entails setting the contract aside as if it had never been made, the misrepresentee recovering what he transferred under the contract but having to restore what he obtained under it. The effect of misrepresentation is important in relation to the rights of third parties. If A sells a car to B under a contract which is voidable for B's misrepresentation, a voidable title passes to B and, if C (an innocent purchaser) buys the car from B before A has decided to rescind, A loses the right to rescind and C obtains a valid title.[1] This must be distinguished from the situation where the contract is void for mistake. There, title to the goods never passes and they can always be recovered, or damages obtained in lieu, from the other party or a third person to whom they have been transferred.[2]

1   *White v Garden* (1851) 10 CB 919.
2   *Cundy v Lindsay* (1878) 3 App Cas 459, HL.

14.16   Rescission can be effected in two ways. First, by bringing legal proceedings for an order for rescission. This may be necessary where a formal document or transaction, such as a lease, has to be set aside by a court order. In other cases a court order is not essential but may be advantageous if the misrepresentor is likely to prove unwilling to return what he has obtained under the contract.

Second, rescission can be effected by the misrepresentee making it clear that he refuses to be bound by the contract. Normally, communication of this decision to the misrepresentor is required, but there is an exception. If a fraudulent misrepresentor absconds, it suffices that the misrepresentee records his intention to rescind the contract by some overt act that is reasonable in the circumstances. This was decided by the Court of Appeal in *Car and Universal Finance Co Ltd v Caldwell.*[1] The defendant sold his car to N in return for a cheque which was dishonoured when he presented it the next day.[2] The defendant immediately informed the police and the Automobile Association of the fraudulent transaction. Subsequently, N sold the car to X who sold it to Y who sold it to Z who sold it to the plaintiffs who bought it in good faith. It was held that in the circumstances the defendant had done enough to rescind the contract before the plaintiffs bought the car, title had therefore re-vested in him and the plaintiffs had not got title.

1 [1964] 1 All ER 290, CA.
2 By his conduct in drawing the cheque, N had fraudulently misrepresented that the existing state of facts was such that in the ordinary course of events the cheque would be honoured: *R v Hazelton* (1874) LR 2 CCR 134 at 140.

14.17 There are four bars to the right to rescind:

Affirmation of contract by misrepresentee This occurs if, after discovering that the misrepresentation is untrue and knowing of his right to rescind,[1] the misrepresentee declares his intention to waive his right to rescission or acts in a way that such an intention can be inferred. An inference of such an intention was drawn in *Long v Lloyd.*[2] The plaintiff bought a lorry as the result of the defendant's misrepresentation that it was in excellent condition. On the plaintiff's first business journey the dynamo broke and he noticed several other serious defects. On the next business journey the lorry broke down and the plaintiff, realising that it was in a very bad condition, sought to rescind the contract. The Court of Appeal held that the second journey constituted an affirmation because the plaintiff knew by then that the representation was untrue.

Lapse of time This can provide evidence of affirmation where the misrepresentee fails to rescind for a considerable time after discovering the falsity. In addition, lapse of time can operate as a separate bar to rescission in cases where the misrepresentee has not delayed after discovering the falsity. This is shown by *Leaf v International Galleries,*[3] where the plaintiff bought from the defendant a picture of Salisbury Cathedral which the latter had innocently represented to be by Constable. Five years later, the plaintiff discovered that this was a misrepresentation and immediately sought to rescind the contract. The Court of Appeal held that his right to rescind had been lost through lapse of a reasonable time to discover the falsity.

This bar does not apply in the case of a fraudulent misrepresentation.

Inability to restore The main objects of rescission are to restore the parties to their former position and to prevent unjust enrichment.[4] Thus, if either party has so changed or otherwise dealt with what he has obtained under the contract that he cannot restore it, rescission is barred.[5] So, for example, the purchaser of a cake cannot rescind the contract if he has eaten the cake.

There are three qualifications on the present bar:

• A fraudulent misrepresentor cannot rely on his own dealings with what he has obtained as a bar to rescission by the misrepresentee.[6]

- The fact that a seller has spent the money which he has received does not make restitution impossible since one bank note is as good as another and the seller can restore what he obtained under the contract by handing over other notes.
- Precise restitution is not required for rescission. Provided the property obtained under the contract can substantially be restored, rescission can be enforced even though the property has deteriorated, declined in value or otherwise changed. For example, in *Armstrong v Jackson*,[7] a broker fraudulently sold shares to the plaintiff. Later, when the shares had fallen to one-twelfth of their value at the time of sale, the plaintiff claimed rescission. It was held that, since the plaintiff could return the actual shares, rescission would be ordered, subject to the defendant's repayment of the purchase price being credited with the dividends received by the plaintiff. Likewise, in *Cheese v Thomas*,[8] where the contract had involved the plaintiff contributing £43,000 to the purchase of a house at a price of £83,000 but, because of a fall in property values, the house had subsequently been sold for only £55,400, rescission of the contract was ordered on the basis that the plaintiff and defendant should share the loss brought about by the fall in value in the same proportions (43:40) as they had contributed to the price, and not on the basis of the plaintiff's contribution of £43,000 being repaid.

The Court of Appeal emphasised that the basic object of rescission was to restore each party as near as possible to his original position. Where a deterioration or loss of value results from the voluntary dealings with it by the person who obtained it under the contract, he must not only account for any profits derived from it but also pay compensation for such deterioration or loss of value.[9]

Bona fide purchaser for value   As has been indicated in para 14.15 above, if, before the misrepresentee elects to rescind, a third party has innocently purchased the property, or an interest in it, for value from the misrepresentor, his rights are valid against the misrepresentee, who loses the chance to rescind. This is illustrated by *White v Garden*,[10] where a rogue bought 50 tons of iron from Garden by persuading him to take in payment a fraudulent bill of exchange. The rogue then sold the iron for value to White who acted in good faith (ie was unaware of the rogue's fraudulent misrepresentation) and Garden delivered the iron to White. The bill of exchange was subsequently dishonoured and Garden seized and removed some of the iron. Garden was held liable for what is now the tort of conversion; he had purported to rescind the contract with the rogue too late, the rogue's voidable title having been made unavoidable when White innocently bought the iron from him.

In *Car and Universal Finance Co Ltd v Caldwell*,[11] on the other hand, rescission was not barred because it occurred before the intervention of a bona fide purchaser for value.

1 *Peyman v Lanjani* [1984] 3 All ER 703, CA.
2 [1958] 2 All ER 402, CA.
3 [1950] 1 All ER 693, CA.
4 *Spence v Crawford* [1939] 3 All ER 271 at 288–289.
5 *Clarke v Dickson* (1858) EB & E 148; *MacKenzie v Royal Bank of Canada* [1934] AC 468, PC.
6 *Spence v Crawford* [1939] 3 All ER 271 at 280–282.
7 [1917] 2 KB 822.
8 [1994] 1 All ER 35, CA.
9 *Erlanger v New Sombrero Phosphate Co* (1878) 3 App Cas 1218 at 1278–1279.
10 (1851) 10 CB 919.
11 Para 14.16 above.

14.18   Before leaving the bars to rescission it should be noted that the courts have power, in the case of non-fraudulent misrepresentations, to refuse rescission, or to refuse to recognise a purported rescission, and to award damages in lieu. This power is discussed in para 14.30 below.

Damages

14.19 We are concerned here with damages for misrepresentation and not with damages for breach of contract, discussed in chapter 12, which are a different species. Sometimes damages for misrepresentation can be recovered under the common law rules of tort: sometimes under the Misrepresentation Act 1967. Rescission and damages are alternative remedies in many cases, but if the victim of a fraudulent or negligent misrepresentation has suffered consequential loss he may rescind and sue for damages.

The duty to mitigate loss referred to in para 12.16 above, in respect of the assessment of damages from breach of contract also applies to damages for misrepresentation; the duty arises when the misrepresentee discovers the truth.[1] The same provisions as to limitation periods apply as in the case of an action for breach of contract;[2] the cause of action for damages for misrepresentation accrues (and the limitation period begins to run) when the misrepresentation is made, except in the case of the tort of negligent misrepresentation where it accrues when loss results from the misrepresentation.

1 *Smith New Court Securities Ltd v Scrimgeour Vickers (Asset Management) Ltd* [1996] 4 All ER 769, HL.
2 Para 12.36 above.

14.20 The discussion of the rules of assessment of damages for misrepresentation requires the division of the relevant law into five classes:

14.21 *Fraudulent misrepresentation* Fraudulent misrepresentation gives rise to an action for damages for the tort of deceit. The classic definition of fraud in this context was given by Lord Herschell in *Derry v Peek*.[1] Lord Herschell stated that fraud is proved where it is shown that a misrepresentation has been made:

* knowingly; or
* without belief in its truth; or
* recklessly, careless whether it be true or false.

A misrepresentation is not fraudulent if there is an honest belief in its truth when it is made, even though there are no reasonable grounds for that belief[2]. Motive is irrelevant: an intention to cheat or injure is not required.

1 (1889) 14 App Cas 337, HL.
2 Ibid. See also *Thomas Witter Ltd v TBP Industries Ltd* [1996] 2 All ER 573.

14.22 *Negligent misrepresentation under the Misrepresentation Act 1967* Section 2(1) of the Act of 1967 provides that where a person has entered into a contract after a misrepresentation has been made to him by another party thereto and as a result of it has suffered loss, then, if the misrepresentor would be liable to damages for misrepresentation if it had been made fraudulently, he is to be so liable notwithstanding that the misrepresentation was not made fraudulently, unless he proves that he had reasonable grounds to believe and did believe up to the time the contract was made that the facts represented were true. In other words, the misrepresentor is deemed negligent, and liable to pay damages, unless he proves in the stated way that he was not negligent. Whether the misrepresentor can prove this will depend, for instance, on whether he was an expert or not, the length of the negotiations and whether he himself had been misled by another. The representor's burden of proof is a difficult one to discharge. This is shown by *Howard Marine and Dredging Co Ltd v A Ogden & Sons*

(Excavations) Ltd.[1] During negotiations for the hire of two barges, Howard's agent misrepresented their capacity in reliance on an error in Lloyd's Register. The Court of Appeal held that the burden of proof had not been discharged, since a file in Howard's possession disclosed the real capacity.

Section 2(1) applies where the misrepresentation was made on behalf of a party to the subsequent contract by his agent,[2] but in such a case the misrepresentee only has an action under s 2(1) against that party and not against his agent.[3]

1   [1978] 2 All ER 1134, CA.
2   *Gosling v Anderson* (1972) 223 Estates Gazette 1743, CA.
3   *Resolute Maritime Inc v Nippon Kaiji Kyokai* [1983] 2 All ER 1; an agent may be liable for a fraudulent misrepresentation or for negligent misrepresentation at common law.

14.23   *Remoteness and measure of damages*   In the tort of deceit and under s 2(1) of the 1967 Act the rule of remoteness of damage is that the defendant is liable for all actual damage or loss directly flowing from the misrepresentation.[1] This is a more liberal rule than that of reasonable foreseeability of the possibility of the damage which applies in other torts, and also more liberal than the rule of remoteness which applies in the case of damages for breach of contract, where damages are limited to compensation for loss which was within the parties' reasonable contemplation, when the contract was made, as a seriously possible result of its breach.[2]

1   *Doyle v Olby (Ironmongers) Ltd* [1969] 2 All ER 119, CA; *East v Maurer* [1991] 2 All ER 733, CA; *Smith New Court Securities Ltd v Scrimgeour Vickers (Asset Management) Ltd* [1996] 4 All ER 769, HL (action for deceit); *Royscot Trust Ltd v Rogerson* [1991] 3 All ER 294, CA (action under Misrepresentation Act 1967, s 2(1)).
2   See paras 20.17–20.20 below (other torts) and paras 12.10–12.12, above (breach of contract).

14.24   Damages for deceit or under s 2(1) of the 1967 Act are assessed according to the 'out of pocket rule',[1] ie an amount is awarded which puts the misrepresentee into the position in which he would have been had the misrepresentation never been made.

Where he has been induced to buy something by a misrepresentation, the plaintiff is entitled to recover as damages the full price paid by him, but he must give credit for any benefits which he has received as a direct result of the transaction.[2] As a general rule, the benefits received by him include the market value of the property acquired as at the date of acquisition, with the result that the damages awarded will be the difference between the price paid and the real value of the property at the date of the acquisition by the plaintiff.[2] However, this general rule is not inflexibly applied; it will not be applied where to do so would prevent the misrepresentee obtaining full compensation for the wrong suffered.[2] Examples of cases where the general rule will not apply are where:

* the misrepresentation has continued to operate after the date of the acquisition of the asset so as to cause the misrepresentee to retain the asset; or
* the circumstances are such that the plaintiff is, by reason of the fraud, locked into the property.[2]

One case where the general rule did not apply is *Smith New Court Securities Ltd v Scrimgeour Vickers (Asset Management) Ltd*,[3] where the plaintiffs were induced to buy some shares in company X for £23m by the defendants' fraudulent misrepresentation. Because a fraud had been practised on company X before the plaintiffs acquired the shares, the shares were doomed to tumble in value and were therefore a flawed asset. There was a slump in their value and the plaintiffs were only able to sell them by degrees and only received £11m for them in total. The plaintiffs were awarded as damages the difference between what they had paid for the shares and what they had obtained by their sale of the shares, since the latter amount was to be regarded as the benefit received by them as a result of the transaction, because they could not have sold the shares at the value they had when they acquired them.

The principles set out above were stated in *Smith New Court* in relation to damages for fraudulent misrepresentation, but they are of equal application to damages under s 2(1) of the Misrepresentation Act 1967. In *Royscot Trust Ltd v Rogerson*[4] the Court of Appeal held that damages under s 2(1) should be assessed as if the misrepresentation had been made fraudulently.

The 'out of pocket rule' should be contrasted with the measure of damages for breach of contract. Here the 'loss of expectations rule' normally applies, as has been explained in para 12.3, above, and the injured party recovers an amount which puts him into the position in which he would have been if the representation had been true. Where the breach relates to the thing's quality, this amount is the difference between the 'represented value' and the actual value. The application of the 'out of pocket rule' does not mean that recovery as damages for deceit or under s 2(1) can never be made in respect of loss of profits. This is shown by *East v Maurer*,[5] where the seller of a hairdressing salon fraudulently represented that he would no longer be working at another salon in the area, in order to induce the plaintiff to contract to buy the salon. The plaintiff was induced by the representation to buy the salon. As a result of the untruth of the representation, the plaintiff was unable to run a successful business at the salon. He was unable to sell it for three years. The Court of Appeal held that the damages for deceit were to be assessed on the basis that the plaintiff should be compensated for all losses which he had suffered, including his loss on the resale *and his loss of profits*. The profits lost were assessed not on the basis of the profits which would have been earned if the representation had been true (which would have been the amount under the 'loss of expectations' rule) but on the basis of the profits which the misrepresentee would have made if he had not been induced into buying the salon but had bought a different one in the area (because this was the amount by which he was out of pocket as a result of the defendant's deceit).

1 *Smith New Court Securities Ltd v Scrimgeour Vickers (Asset Management) Ltd* [1996] 4 All ER 769, HL (action for deceit); *Royscot Trust Ltd v Rogerson* [1991] 3 All ER 294, CA (action under Misrepresentation Act 1967, s 2(1)).
2 *Smith New Court Securities Ltd v Scrimgeour Vickers (Asset Management) Ltd* [1996] 4 All ER 769, HL.
3 [1996] 4 All ER 769, HL.
4 [1991] 3 All ER 294, CA.
5 [1991] 2 All ER 733, CA.

14.25 A person who has been induced into a contract by a misrepresentation which is fraudulent or which is negligent under s 2(1) of the Misrepresentation Act may also recover damages for any consequential loss or damage, such as expenses, personal injury, damage to his property,[1] which he may have suffered, provided it is not too remote.

1 Damages for distress or disappointment are also recoverable in an action in deceit: *Archer v Brown* [1985] QB 401.

14.26 The contributory negligence of the misrepresentee is not a ground for reducing damages awarded for deceit,[1] but it is such a ground if damages are awarded under s 2(1) of the Misrepresentation Act, provided that the defendant is also liable in tort for negligence, since the Law Reform (Contributory Negligence) Act 1945[2] applies in such a case.[3]

1   *Alliance and Leicester Building Society v Edgestop* [1994] 2 All ER 38; affd on another point [1995] CLY 2828, CA.
2   Para 21.12 below.
3   *Gran Gelato Ltd v Richcliff (Group) Ltd* [1992] 1 All ER 865.

14.27   Given that, where a fraudulent misrepresentation has been made, an action may normally be brought for the same amount of damages under s 2(1) of the Misrepresentation Act 1967 without the need to prove fraud, or indeed negligence, it makes sense in many cases of suspected fraudulent misrepresentation for an action to be brought under s 2(1) rather than for deceit.

14.28   *Negligent misrepresentation at common law* The victim of a negligent misrepresentation may be able to sue the misrepresentor under the principles of the tort of negligence, particularly those enunciated in *Hedley Byrne v Heller & Partners*[1] which we discuss in paras 18.28 to 18.30 below. If the misrepresentee sues under the *Hedley Byrne* principles, he must prove:

- that the misrepresentor owed him a duty to take reasonable care in making representation, which duty only arises if there is an 'appropriate (or special) relationship';
- that the misrepresentor was in breach of that duty; and
- that damage resulted from that breach.

The circumstances in which a court may find an 'appropriate relationship' are the subject of a certain amount of dispute, as we explain in paras 18.28 and 18.29 below.

The *Hedley Byrne* principles were applied to a representation made in pre-contractual negotiations by the Court of Appeal in *Esso Petroleum Co Ltd v Mardon.*[2] In negotiations in 1963 for the tenancy of a filling station, Esso negligently told Mr Mardon that the station had an estimated annual throughput of 200,000 gallons. Mr Mardon was induced to take the tenancy but the actual annual throughput never exceeded 86,000 gallons and Mr Mardon was awarded damages against Esso. One reason for its decision given by the Court of Appeal was that Esso were under the duty of care imposed by *Hedley Byrne* – which applied to pre-contractual statements – and were in breach of that duty. In this case, Mr Mardon could not have relied on the Misrepresentation Act 1967, s 2(1) because the misrepresentation had occurred before the Act came into force.

In practice, it is normally better to rely on s 2(1) in the case of a negligent misrepresentation because the onus of disproving negligence is placed on the defendant under that section, whereas if he relies on the *Hedley Byrne* principles the plaintiff must prove that they are satisfied. In addition, no appropriate relationship need be proved under s 2(1). However, the *Hedley Byrne* principles are still important in cases of pre-contractual misrepresentation in three situations: where the misrepresentation is made by a third party to the contract; where the contractual negotiations do not result in a contract between the defendant and the plaintiff but the plaintiff nevertheless suffers loss in reliance on the misrepresentation; and where the limitation period for an action under s 2(1) has expired but that for negligence at common law (which runs from the suffering of loss, and not the misrepresentation) has not. In these cases, assuming their requirements are satisfied, there can be tortious liability under the principles in *Hedley Byrne*, although there can be no rescission for misrepresentation nor damages under the Act of 1967.

The measure of damages under *Hedley Byrne* is governed by the 'out of pocket' rule[3] and questions of remoteness of damage by the test of reasonable foreseeability at the time of the breach of duty.[4] This is a narrower test of remoteness than that under the Misrepresentation Act 1967, s 2(1), which is another reason for an action under s 2(1) being preferable to a claim based on negligent misrepresentation at common law when both actions are available.

1   [1963] 2 All ER 575, HL.
2   [1976] 2 All ER 5, CA.
3   See, for example, *JEB Fasteners Ltd v Marks, Bloom & Co Ltd* [1983] 1 All ER 583 at 587.
4   Paras 20.17–20.20 below.

14.29   *Innocent misrepresentation* Subject to what is said in para 14.30 below, damages cannot be awarded for a misrepresentation which is not fraudulent or negligent, as defined above. However, an indemnity – which is different from damages – may be awarded.

14.30   *Damages in lieu of rescission* The Misrepresentation Act 1967, s 2(2) provides that, where a person has entered into a contract after a non-fraudulent misrepresentation has been made to him which would entitle him to rescind the contract, then, if it is claimed in proceedings arising out of the contract that the contract ought to be or has been rescinded, the court or arbitrator may declare the contract subsisting and award damages in lieu of rescission, if of the opinion that it would be equitable to do so. The rationale for this power is that rescission may be too drastic in some cases, eg where the misrepresentation was trifling. An award of damages under s 2(2) is discretionary. In exercising his discretion, a judge or arbitrator is required by s 2(2) to have regard to the nature of the misrepresentation and the loss that would be caused by it if the contract was upheld, as well as the loss that rescission would cause to the other party.

A literal interpretation of s 2(2) might be thought to suggest that the power to award damages in lieu of rescission can only be exercised if rescission has not been barred, eg by affirmation of the contract. However, it has been held by a judge in the Chancery Division that this is not so and that the power to award damages under s 2(2) does not depend on an extant right to rescind, but only on a right having existed at some time after the contract was made.[1]

Important distinctions between s 2(1) and s 2(2) are that damages cannot be awarded under s 2(1) if lack of negligence is proved, whereas they can be awarded in such a case under s 2(2); that damages under s 2(1) can be awarded in addition to rescission; that an award of damages under s 2(1) is not discretionary; and that s 2(3), described below, contemplates that the measure of damages under s 2(1) is different from, and more generous than, an award under s 2(2).[2]

In the light of this, obiter dicta in the Court of Appeal that, unlike damages under s 2(1), damages under s 2(2) cannot include damages for consequential loss, is not surprising, although the other part of the obiter dicta, that damages under s 2(2) in respect of the value of the thing are assessed on the basis of 'loss of expectations' is surprising and doubtful in the light of the generally less generous rule which applies to damages under s 2(1).[3]

Where a person has been held liable to pay damages under s 2(1) of the 1967 Act, the judge or arbitrator, in assessing damages thereunder, is required by s 2(3) to take into account any damages in lieu of rescission under s 2(2).

1   *Thomas Witter Ltd v TBP Industries Ltd* [1996] 2 All ER 573; cf *The Lucy* [1983] 1 Lloyd's Rep 188 at 202.
2   *William Sindall plc v Cambridgeshire County Council* [1994] 3 All ER 932 at 954; *Thomas Witter Ltd v TBP Industries Ltd* [1996] 2 All ER 573 at 591.
3   *William Sindall plc v Cambridgeshire County Council* [1994] 3 All ER 932 at 954 and 961.

Indemnity

14.31   It has already been noted that the object of rescission is to restore the contracting parties to their former position as if the contract had never been made. As part of this restoration the misrepresentee can claim an indemnity against any *obligations necessarily created by the contract.*[1] The italicised words must be emphasised since they indicate that an indemnity is far less extensive than damages, as was recognised by the Court of Appeal in *Newbigging v Adam.*[2] A classic example of this distinction is provided by *Whittington v Scale-Hayne.*[3] The plaintiffs, breeders of prize poultry, were induced to take a lease of the defendant's premises by his innocent misrepresentation that the premises were in a thoroughly sanitary condition. Under the lease, the plaintiffs covenanted to execute all works required by any local or public authority. Owing to the insanitary condition of the premises the water supply was poisoned, the plaintiffs' manager and his family became very ill, and the poultry became valueless for breeding purposes or died. In addition, the local authority required the drains to be renewed. The plaintiffs sought an indemnity for the following losses: the value of the stock lost; loss of profit on sales; loss of breeding season; rent, and medical expenses on behalf of the manager. The trial judge rescinded the lease and held that the plaintiffs could recover an indemnity for what they had spent on rent, rates and repairs under the covenants in the lease, because these expenses arose necessarily out of the occupation of the premises or were incurred under the covenants in the lease and were thus obligations necessarily created by the contract. However, the judge refused to award an indemnity for the loss of stock, loss of profits, loss of breeding season or the medical expenses, since to do so would be to award damages, not an indemnity, there being no obligation created by the contract to carry on a poultry farm on the premises or to employ a manager, etc.

1   *Whittington v Scale-Hayne* (1900) 82 LT 49, adopting the view of Bowen LJ in *Newbigging v Adam* (1886) 34 Ch D 582, CA.
2   (1886) 34 Ch D 582, CA.
3   (1900) 82 LT 49.

14.32   Two further points may be made concerning the award of an indemnity:

*   Being ancillary to rescission, an indemnity cannot be awarded if rescission is barred.
*   The remedy of an indemnity is redundant where the court can, and does, award damages for misrepresentation. However, where there has merely been an innocent misrepresentation and the court decides not to award damages in lieu of rescission, the availability of an award of an indemnity is very important.

Active misrepresentations which have become contractual terms

14.33   Whether a misrepresentation made during pre-contractual negotiations has become a term of the resulting contract, or of a contract collateral to it, is determined in accordance with the rules set out in paras 8.9 to 8.16 above.

If the misrepresentation has become a contractual term the misrepresentee has a choice between two courses of action.

Breach of contract

14.34   As in the case of the breach of any other contractual term, the misrepresentee can sue for breach of contract. If he does so, he can recover damages for breach of contract (as opposed to damages for misrepresentation). Where the misrepresentation relates to the subject matter of the contract, damages will be assessed according to the normal contractual rule, the 'loss of expectations' rule, and recovery can also be had

213

for all consequential loss, provided the loss was within the parties' reasonable contemplation, at the time the contract was made, as a seriously possible result of the breach. The relevant law has already been discussed in detail in chapter 12. In addition, if the misrepresentation has become a condition of the contract, or an 'intermediate term' and there has been a sufficiently serious breach of it, the misrepresentee can also terminate the contract for breach, a matter which we discussed in paras 9.14 to 9.31 above.

Misrepresentation Act 1967, s 1(a)
14.35 The misrepresentee's alternative course of action is to make use of the Misrepresentation Act 1967, s 1(a). Under this provision a person who is induced to enter into a contract by a misrepresentation of fact, which has become a term of the contract, can elect to rescind the contract for misrepresentation subject to the bars to rescission mentioned in para 14.17 above.

However, if he does so rescind he cannot recover damages for breach of contract since rescission for misrepresentation sets the contract aside for all purposes, including his right to claim damages for its breach, although he may be able to claim damages for misrepresentation, depending on the circumstances, in accordance with the rules set out in paras 14.19 to 14.28 above.

14.36 The choice of a particular course of action will depend very much on whether greater damages will be obtained for breach of contract or for misrepresentation and on whether the plaintiff wishes, and is able, to rescind for misrepresentation.

Avoidance of provision excluding or limiting liability for misrepresentation
14.37 The Misrepresentation Act 1967, s 3 provides that if a contract contains a term which would exclude or restrict:

- any liability to which a party to a contract may be subject by reason of any misrepresentation made by him before the contract was made; or
- any remedy available to another party to the contract by reason of such a misrepresentation,

that term is of no effect, except in so far as it satisfies the requirement of reasonableness. It is for the person claiming that it satisfies that requirement to show that it does. The requirement of reasonableness is that the term must have been a fair and reasonable one to be included having regard to the circumstances which were, or ought reasonably to have been, known to or in the contemplation of the parties when the contract was made.[1]

It is important to note that what must be considered under the requirement of reasonableness is the term itself and its potential effect in respect of any liability for any misrepresentation covered by it, as opposed to its effect in respect of the particular liability for the actual misrepresentation made.[2]

1 Unfair Contract Terms Act 1977, s 11(1). See, further, para 10.23 above.
2 *Thomas Witter Ltd v TBP Industries Ltd* [1996] 2 All ER 573.

14.38 Section 3 is of great importance in relation to the purported exclusion or restriction of liability for misrepresentations made by estate agents. Where an estate agent makes a misrepresentation in respect of a property which he has been instructed to sell and thereby induces another to enter into a contract to buy it, it is his client who becomes liable for misrepresentation to the other party,[1] although the client may seek to recover an indemnity for his loss from the agent[2] and the agent himself may be held liable to the other party in tort if deceit or negligence can be proved. Not surprisingly, in an attempt to exclude or restrict a client's liability for a misrepresentation made by his estate agent, auction conditions, conditions of sale by tender and the like often contain a contract term (exemption clause) purporting so to exclude or restrict. Such a term is caught by the Misrepresentation Act 1967, s 3 and is of no effect except in so far as it satisfies the requirement of reasonableness. In this context, a 'contract term' is not limited to one which expressly excludes or restricts liability, since it has been held that it also includes a term of the contract purporting to nullify any representation altogether so as to bring about a situation in law as if there was no representation, such as a term that 'although the particulars are believed to be correct their accuracy is not guaranteed and any intending purchaser must satisfy himself by inspection or otherwise as to their correctness'.[3] Similarly, even if a contract term which states that, notwithstanding any statement of fact included in the particulars, the vendor shall conclusively be presumed to have made no representation is capable of excluding liability for any misrepresentation actually made,[4] s 3 applies to that term.[5] On the other hand, a contract term which denies that an estate agent has any authority at all to make representations is not caught by s 3 and may therefore prevent the client from incurring liability for a misrepresentation by the estate agent.[6]

It must be emphasised that s 3 is solely concerned with 'contract terms' (ie exemption clauses contained in a contract), and has no application to non-contractual clauses of the type commonly found in estate agents' particulars. Although it has been held that such a non-contractual clause denying that an estate agent has any authority to make representations is effective to prevent the client incurring liability for a misrepresentation by the estate agent,[7] it has been suggested that other non-contractual clauses purporting to exclude or restrict the client's liability for misrepresentation are ineffective to do so.[8]

1 Para 16.30 below.
2 Para 16.16 below.
3 *Cremdean Properties Ltd v Nash* (1977) 244 Estates Gazette 547, CA; *Walker v Boyle* [1982] 1 All ER 634, [1982] 1 WLR 495; *South Western General Property Co Ltd v Marton* (1982) 263 Estates Gazette 1090.
4 In *Thomas Witter Ltd v TBP Industries Ltd* [1996] 2 All ER 573 it was held by a judge in the Chancery Division that such a term was not capable of excluding liability for misrepresentation but a contrary view was taken obiter by a judge in the Court of Appeal in *Cremdean Properties Ltd v Nash* (1977) 244 Estates Gazette 547 at 551.
5 *Cremdean Properties Ltd v Nash* (1977) 244 Estates Gazette 547 at 551; *Thomas Witter Ltd v TBP Industries Ltd* [1996] 2 All ER 573.
6 *Overbrooke Estates Ltd v Glencombe Properties Ltd* [1974] 3 All ER 511; cf *South Western General Property Co Ltd v Marton* (1982) 263 Estates Gazette 1090 (where s 3 was applied to such a term but without any consideration or mention of whether s 3 applied to an authority-denying term).
7 *Collins v Howell-Jones* (1980) 259 Estates Gazette 331, CA.
8 *Cremdean Properties Ltd v Nash* (1977) 244 Estates Gazette 547 at 551.

14.39 Section 3 not only applies where the relevant misrepresentation has remained a mere representation but also where it has become a contractual term, at least as far as rescission for misrepresentation and damages for misrepresentation are concerned, although it is uncertain whether it applies if the misrepresentee elects to treat it as a breach of contract.

Misrepresentation through non-disclosure

14.40 Generally, mere silence as to a material fact or tacit acquiescence in another's erroneous belief concerning such a fact does not constitute a misrepresentation. Thus, in *Turner v Green*,[1] where two solicitors arranged a compromise of certain legal proceedings, the failure of the plaintiff's solicitor to inform the defendant's of a material fact was held not to be a ground for relief, even though the defendant would not have made the compromise if he had known of that fact.

1   [1895] 2 Ch 205.

14.41   However, in certain situations there is a duty to disclose material facts, breach of which gives rise to relief. Two of these situations have been referred to already: where silence distorts a positive assertion and where a positive assertion is falsified by later events (see para 14.10 above). In these cases silence is deemed to be an active misrepresentation. In addition, in the case of contracts *uberrimae fidei* – of the utmost good faith – a duty to disclose fully all material facts is imposed, breach of which is regarded as a misrepresentation through non-disclosure for which relief is available.

Contracts uberrimae fidei can be divided into two main types:

* insurance contracts; and
* contracts where one party is in a fiduciary relationship with the other.

Insurance contracts

14.42   An intending insurer or insured is under a duty to disclose all material facts known to him.[1] In the case of an intending insured, a material fact is one which would have an effect, not necessarily a decisive influence, on the mind of a prudent insurer in deciding whether to accept the risk or as to the premium to be charged.[2] In the case of an intending insurer, a material fact is one relating to the nature of the risk to be covered or the recoverability of a claim, which a prudent insured would take into account in deciding whether or not to place the risk in question with that insurer.[3] The duty of disclosure only extends to those material facts which are actually known to an intending insurer or insured.[4] If a material fact is not disclosed as required, the other party cannot rely on it as a ground to avoid the contract if it did not induce him to make the contract.[5]

1   *Carter v Boehm* (1766) 3 Burr 1905; *Banque Financière de la Cité SA v Westgate Insurance Co Ltd* [1989] 2 All ER 952, CA; affd [1990] 2 All ER 947, HL.
2   *Lambert v Co-operative Insurance Society* [1975] 2 Lloyd's Rep 485, CA; *Container Transport International Inc v Oceanus Mutual Underwriting Association (Bermuda) Ltd* [1984] 1 Lloyd's Rep 476, CA; *Pan Atlantic Insurance Co Ltd v Pine Top Insurance Co Ltd* [1994] 3 All ER 581, HL; Marine Insurance Act 1906, s, 18(2).
3   *Banque Financière de la Cité SA v Westgate Insurance Co Ltd* [1989] 2 All ER 952, CA; affd [1990] 2 All ER 947, HL.
4   *Joel v Law Union and Crown Insurance Co* [1908] 2 KB 863, CA.
5   See, for example *Pan Atlantic Insurance Co Ltd v Pine Top Insurance Co Ltd* [1994] 3 All ER 581, HL (marine insurance contract).

Contracts where one party is in a confidential or fiduciary relationship with the other

14.43   Where one prospective contracting party stands in a confidential relationship with the other (such as parent and child; solicitor or accountant and client; trustee and beneficiary; partner and partner and principal and agent)[1] he is under a duty to disclose any material fact known to him. The same duty of disclosure applies where one person has placed himself in such a position that he becomes obliged to act fairly and with due regard to the interests of the other party.[2]

1   See paras 14.50–14.52 below.
2   *Tate v Williamson* (1866) 2 Ch App 55.

14.44   The effect of a breach of the duty of disclosure in contracts uberrimae fidei is that the person to whom the duty was owed can have the contract rescinded, in which case an indemnity can be awarded where appropriate. The same bars to rescission apply as described above. Alternatively, the person to whom the duty was owed can refuse to carry out the contract and, provided (generally) that he returns what he obtained under it, successfully resist any claim for damages for breach of duty.[1] The Misrepresentation Act 1967 does not apply to misrepresentation through non-disclosure in contracts uberrimae fidei, nor do the common law rules relating to liability for negligent misrepresentation.

1   *Banque Financière de la Cité SA v Westgate Insurance Co Ltd* [1989] 2 All ER 952, CA; affd [1990] 2 All ER 947, HL.

Duress and undue influence

14.45   In some situations a contract can be avoided on the ground that it has been procured by illegitimate pressure or that unfair influence over a contracting party has been proved or may be presumed. The first case is governed by the common law of duress, and the second by principles of equity relating to undue influence and to what may be called 'unconscionable bargains'.

Duress
14.46   At one time only duress to the person, ie actual or threatened personal violence or imprisonment, sufficed for duress at common law.[1] In recent times, however, it has been held that economic duress, eg a threat to goods or to a person's business or a threat to break a contract, can also constitute duress at common law.[2]

To constitute duress at common law, the pressure must be 'illegitimate'. Legitimate commercial pressure cannot constitute duress.[3] Pressure will be illegitimate if what is threatened is unlawful (ie a breach of contract, tort or crime).[4] Pressure can also be illegitimate, even though the threat is of lawful action, because of the nature of the pressure and of the demand to which it relates. Consequently, a threat to assault someone can amount to duress (because what is threatened is unlawful) and so can a threat to report a crime to the police unless a demand is complied with (because the pressure is illegitimate on the second ground).[5] Cases where a threat of lawful action amounts to illegitimate pressure will be rare in commercial dealings. The Court of Appeal has held that where parties are traders dealing at arm's length and one threatens lawful action (eg not to grant credit) thinking in good faith that his demand is valid, it will be particularly difficult to establish illegitimate pressure, and relatively rare if he did not consider his demand valid.[6]

Even if there is illegitimate pressure, it will not constitute duress unless the victim has been coerced by that pressure into doing something because he had no practical alternative to submission to the pressure, so that he cannot be regarded as having given his true consent to that act.[3]

If duress is proved, it is irrelevant that that was not the sole or predominant cause inducing the contract, provided that it was a cause.[7]

It appears that duress renders a contract voidable, so that it is valid unless and until rescinded by the coerced party,[8] not void.

1   Co Litt 353b; *Cumming v Ince* (1847) 11 QB 112 at 120.
2   *Occidental Worldwide Investment Corpn v Skibs A/S Avanti, The Siboen and The Sibotre;* [1976] 1 Lloyd's Rep 293; *Pao On v Lau Yiu Long* [1980] AC 614, [1979] 3 All ER 65, PC; *B & S Contracts and Designs Ltd v Victor Green Publications Ltd* [1984] ICR 419, CA; *Atlas Express Ltd v Kafco (Importers and Distributors) Ltd* [1989] 1 All ER 641.

3 *Occidental Worldwide Investment Corpn v Skibs A/S Avanti, The Siboen and The Sibotre; Pao On v Lau Yiu Long; Hennessy v Craigmyle & Co Ltd* [1986] ICR 461, CA.
4 *Barton v Armstrong* [1976] AC 104 at 121; *Universe Tankships Inc of Monrovia v International Transport Workers Federation, The Universe Sentinel* [1982] 2 All ER 67, HL.
5 *Universe Tankships Inc of Monrovia v International Transport Workers Federation, The Universe Sentinel; B & S Contracts and Designs Ltd v Victor Green Publications Ltd; Atlas Express Ltd v Kafco (Importers and Distributors) Ltd.*
6 *CTN Cash and Carry Ltd v Gallaher Ltd* [1994] 4 All ER 714, CA.
7 *Barton v Armstrong* [1975] 2 All ER 465, PC.
8 *Pao On v Lau Yiu Long* [1980] AC 614 at 634; *Universe Tankships Inc of Monrovia v International Transport Workers Federation, The Universe Sentinel.*

Undue influence

14.47 A contract which falls within the equitable doctrine of undue influence is voidable at the instance of the party influenced. Two types of case fall within the equitable doctrine:

- where actual undue influence is proved;
- where there is a confidential relationship between the parties, in which case undue influence is presumed provided that the contract is manifestly disadvantageous to the weaker party.

Actual undue influence

14.48 The party alleging undue influence must prove that the other party actually exerted unfair or improper influence over him and thereby procured a contract that would not otherwise have been made, as where a bank procured a mortgage from a father by a threat to prosecute his son for forgery otherwise.[1] There is no need for him to prove that the contract is manifestly disadvantageous to him.[2]

Developments in the common law rules of duress mean that there is now little difference in coverage between those rules and the equitable rules on actual undue influence.

1 *Williams v Bayley* (1866) LR 1 HL 200, HL.
2 *CIBC Mortgages plc v Pitt* [1993] 4 All ER 433, HL.

Presumed undue influence

14.49 A presumption of undue influence arises if the party alleging undue influence proves:

- that there was a confidential relationship between him and the other party to the contract, in which the other was the dominant party; *and*
- that the contract is manifestly disadvantageous to him.

Once the presumption of undue influence has arisen, the contract can be set aside at the instance of the weaker party, unless the presumption is rebutted by the dominant one.

14.50 *Confidential relationship* What is required here is a relationship in which one party places confidence in the other who thereby has the opportunity to exercise overt or subtle influence over him: undue influence cannot be presumed where the parties are in an ordinary, everyday business relationship.

14.51 In the case of some relationships, it is presumed that the relationship is a confidential one. Examples are the relationships of: parent and child;[1] solicitor or accountant and client;[2] and trustee and beneficiary;[3] in each of which the first-named party is presumed to be in a position to influence the other. While the list of relationships which can be presumed to be confidential is not closed, it has been held that the relationships between husband and wife[4] and between employer and employee[5] are not presumed to be confidential.

1   *Bainbrigge v Browne* (1881) 18 Ch D 188.
2   *Wright v Carter* [1903] 1 Ch 27, CA.
3   *Beningfield v Baxter* (1886) 12 App Cas 167, PC.
4   *Howes v Bishop* [1909] 2 KB 390, CA; *Kingsnorth Trust Ltd v Bell* [1986] 1 All ER 423, CA.
5   *Mathew v Bobbins* (1980) 41 P & CR 1, CA.

14.52   Where a confidential relationship cannot be presumed, undue influence may be presumed if it is positively proved that one party actually had a position of personal ascendancy[1] and influence over the other at the material time. For example, although the relationships of banker and customer and of creditor and debtor are not normally confidential,[2] they will be held to be so if special facts exist which justify such a finding. This is shown by *Lloyds Bank v Bundy*.[3] The defendant was an elderly farmer. A company which was run by his son got into difficulties and the defendant guaranteed its overdraft with the plaintiff bank, mortgaging his farmhouse, which was his home and only asset, to the bank as security for the guarantee. In relation to this transaction he had placed himself entirely in the hands of the assistant bank manager who not only explained the legal effects of the transaction *but also advised on more general matters germane to the wisdom of the transaction*. In the light of this special fact it is not surprising that the Court of Appeal held that there was a confidential relationship between the bank and the defendant and that not only could the mortgage not be enforced but it, and the guarantee, should be set aside.

1   Domination is not required; a relationship of trust will do: *Goldsworthy v Brickell* [1987] 1 All ER 853, CA.
2   *National Westminster Bank plc v Morgan* [1985] 1 All ER 821, HL.
3   [1974] 3 All ER 757, CA.

14.53   *Manifestly disadvantageous contract* Even if a confidential relationship is presumed or proved, this is not in itself enough to give rise to the presumption that the dominant party actually exercised undue influence over the other. That presumption can only be drawn if the contract between them is manifestly disadvantageous to the weaker party.

This was held by the House of Lords in *National Westminster Bank plc v Morgan*.[1] Mr and Mrs M got into difficulties with the repayments to a building society of the mortgage on their house. Consequently, Mr M sought a bank rescue operation, asking the bank to refinance the building society loan. The bank agreed and Mr M executed a legal charge in favour of the bank to secure a loan from it sufficient to redeem the mortgage. Because the house was in joint names, the bank required Mrs M's signature to the legal charge, and the bank manager called on Mrs M to obtain it. She told him that she did not wish the legal charge to extend to the husband's business liabilities. The bank manager assured her in good faith, but incorrectly, that the charge did not extend to those liabilities but was limited to securing the amount financed for the refinancing of the mortgage. Without taking any independent legal advice, Mrs M signed the legal charge. Subsequently, Mr and Mrs M fell into arrears with their repayments to the bank, which obtained a possession order on the house. Mr M died soon afterwards without any business debts owing to the bank. Mrs M appealed against the possession order, contending that she had signed the legal charge because of undue influence from the bank via its manager.

The House of Lords rejected this. It held that the case was not one in which there was a presumption of undue influence, not only because the relationship between the parties was merely that of bank and customer, and not a confidential relationship, but also because the legal charge was not manifestly disadvantageous to Mr and Mrs M; in fact, it provided a desperately urgent rescue of their house from the building society.

1   [1985] AC 686, [1985] 1 All ER 821, HL.

14.54   *Rebutting the presumption* The presumption that undue influence has been exercised can only be rebutted by proof that the party presumed to have been influenced has been placed in such a position as will enable him to form an entirely free and unfettered judgment, independent altogether of any sort of control.[1] The onus of proving this is on the party presumed to have exercised undue influence. The best, but not the only,[2] way of doing so is by proving that the other party received independent and informed advice, particularly legal advice, before making the contract.[3]

1   *Archer v Hudson* (1844) 7 Beav 551 at 560.
2   *Inche Noriah v Shaik Allie Bin Omar* [1929] AC 127, PC.
3   See *Credit Lyonnais Bank Nederland NV v Burch* [1997] 1 All ER 144, CA. One member of the Court of Appeal went further, obiter, and held that taking independent legal advice is not in itself enough to rebut the presumption. It must also be proved that the party concerned has acted on that legal advice, that the legal adviser was satisfied that the transaction was one that that party could sensibly enter into, and that the legal adviser advised the party concerned that he was under no obligation to enter into the transaction: ibid, at 155–156.

Where the other party to the contract was not the person who exercised undue influence, actual or presumed

14.55   It can happen that a person under the undue influence of a third party (or of a co-contracting party) makes a contract with another person who is not involved in that undue influence. An example would be where a person under the domination of a third party contracts with a bank to guarantee a loan by the bank to the third party. The unduly influenced person can have the contract rescinded if:

•   the third party was an agent of the other party to the contract, which is normally unlikely; or
•   when making the contract, the other party had actual notice (ie actually knew) or constructive notice that there had been undue influence.[1]

Whether or not there was constructive notice depends on whether the other contracting party knew of facts (for example, that the contract was manifestly disadvantageous to the person concerned) which should have put him on enquiry. If he did, he will have constructive notice unless he took reasonable steps to satisfy himself that the agreement of the party in question has been properly obtained. For example, suppose that a wife agrees with a bank to act as surety for her husband's debt to the bank. The bank will have constructive notice of any undue influence (because the transaction is not of financial benefit to the wife and is of a type where there is a substantial risk that the husband has procured the wife's agreement by undue influence) unless it takes reasonable steps to bring home to the wife the risk she was running by standing as surety and to advise her to take independent advice.[1]

The same rules apply where a dominant person in a relationship has by misrepresentation induced the weaker one to contract with another.[1]

1   *Barclays Bank plc v O'Brien* [1993] 4 All ER 417, HL; *CIBC Mortgages plc v Pitt* [1993] 4 All ER

433, HL. Also see *Banco Exterior Internacional SA v Thomas* [1997] 1 All ER 46, CA; *Credit Lyonnais Bank Nederland NV v Burch* [1997] 1 All ER 144, CA.

Unconscionable bargains
14.56   Acting under equitable principles, a court will rescind a contract on the basis that unfair advantage has been taken by one party (or his agent) of the other party who was poor, ignorant, weak-minded, illiterate, unfamiliar with the English language, or otherwise in need of special protection.[1] Unfair advantage will have been taken if the party at risk has not received independent legal advice.[2]

The law on unconscionable bargains has the same basis as the other areas of equitable intervention which have just been mentioned: inequality of bargaining power. Although there are dicta in some cases that this 'common thread' permits the courts to intervene in contractual situations other than those involving pressure or influence, or the taking of an unfair advantage of a poor, ignorant or weak-minded party or one otherwise in need of special protection, fairly recent decisions have rejected the argument that inequality of bargaining power is in itself a ground for rescinding a contract.[3]

1   *Evans v Llewellin* (1787) 1 Cox Eq Cas 333; *Barclays Bank plc v Schwartz* (1995) Times, 2 August, CA.
2   *Fry v Lane* (1888) 40 Ch D 312.
3   *Pao On v Lau Yiu Long* [1979] 3 All ER 65, PC; *Alec Lobb (Garages) Ltd v Total Oil GB Ltd* [1985] 1 All ER 303, CA.

Bars to rescission
14.57   Where a contract is voidable for duress or undue influence, or because it is an unconscionable bargain, it is valid unless and until it is rescinded. Rescission will be barred in three cases.

Affirmation
14.58   Rescission is barred if, after the pressure or influence, or relationship giving rise to a presumption of undue influence, has ceased, the party influenced expressly or impliedly affirms the contract.[1] An unreasonable lapse of time after removal of the influence before seeking rescission of the contract is a particularly important evidential factor suggesting affirmation,[2] and so is the fact that the party influenced performs obligations under the contract without protest.[3] A person can be held to have affirmed even though he has not had independent advice after the removal of the influence[4] and did not know that he could have the contract rescinded, provided he was aware that he might have rights and deliberately refrained from finding out.[5]

1   *Allcard v Skinner* (1887) 36 Ch D 145, CA; *Fry v Lane* (1888) 40 Ch D 312.
2   *Allcard v Skinner*.
3   *The Atlantic Baron* [1978] 3 All ER 1170.
4   *Mitchell v Homfray* (1881) 8 QBD 587, CA.
5   *Allcard v Skinner* (1887) 36 Ch D 145 at 192.

Inability to restore
14.59   Since, as in the case of misrepresentation, the party seeking to rescind must restore what he obtained under the contract, an inability to do so is a bar to rescission.[1]

However, precise restitution is not necessary; where precise restitution is not possible the same principles apply as in the case of rescission for misrepresentation.[2]

If restitution is not possible under the above principles, the court may order that the party influenced be paid compensation by the other party to the value of what the party influenced surrendered under the contract, less anything which he received under it.[3]

1   *O'Sullivan v Management Agency and Music Ltd* [1985] QB 428, [1985] 3 All ER 351, CA.
2   Para 14.17 above.
3   *Mahoney v Purnell* [1996] 3 All ER 61.

Purchasers without notice

14.60   The right to rescission is lost if a third party acquires an interest for value in the property transferred by the party influenced, without notice of the pressure or influence, or of the facts giving rise to a presumption of undue influence, in question.[1]

1   *Bainbrigge v Browne* (1881) 18 Ch D 188; *O'Sullivan v Management Agency and Music Ltd* [1985] 3 All ER 351, CA.

Unfair terms in consumer contracts

14.61   We saw in para 10.30 above, that the Unfair Terms in Consumer Contracts Regulations 1994, which give domestic effect to an EC directive on unfair terms in consumer contracts, Directive 93/13/EEC, are concerned not only with exemption clauses but with unfair terms in general in *consumer* contracts relating to the sale or supply of goods or the supply of a service. In para 10.30 above, we contrasted the coverage of the Unfair Contract Terms Act 1977 with that of the directive in relation to exemption clauses.

The Regulations deal with two separate issues:

•   unfair terms in consumer contracts; and
•   interpretation of written terms in consumer contracts,

provided in each case that the term is one to which the Regulations apply.

Terms to which the Regulations apply

14.62   Regulation 3(1) provides that the Regulations apply to any term in a contract, whether written or oral, between a *seller of goods or supplier of goods or services* and a *consumer* where the term has *not been individually negotiated*, with the exception of the following types of contract excluded by Sch 1 to the Regulations:

•   any contract relating to employment;
•   any contract relating to succession rights;
•   any contract relating to rights under family law;
•   any contract relating to the incorporation and organisation of companies or partnerships; and
•   any term incorporated in order to comply with or which reflects -
     -    statutory or regulatory provisions of the United Kingdom; or
     -    the provisions or principles of international conventions to which the member states or the Community are party.

14.63   Regulation 2(1) provides the following important definitions for the purposes of the Regulations:

A *'seller'* is defined as meaning a person who sells goods and who, in making a contract to which the Regulations apply, is acting for purposes relating to his *business*.

A *'supplier'* is defined as meaning a person who supplies goods or services and who, in making a contract to which the Regulations apply, is acting for purposes relating to his *business*.

A *'person'* in both definitions includes a company or other corporate body.

A *'consumer'* is defined as meaning a natural person who, in making a contract to which the Regulations apply, is acting for purposes which are *outside* his business. As this definition indicates, a 'legal person' (ie a company or other corporate body) cannot be a 'consumer' for the purposes of the Regulations.[1]

Lastly, a 'business' includes a trade or profession and the activities of any government department or local or public authority.

As reg 3(1) indicates, the Regulations only apply to a term which has not been individually negotiated. By reg 3(3), a term is always to be regarded as not having been individually negotiated where it has been *drafted in advance and the consumer has not been able to influence the substance of the term*. Regulation 3(4) adds that, notwithstanding that a specific term or certain aspects of it in a contract has been individually negotiated, the Regulations apply to the rest of a contract if an overall assessment of the contract indicates that it is a pre-formulated standard contract.

If a *seller or supplier* claims that a term was *individually negotiated*, he has the burden of proving this.[2]

1   There is one exception. Where the term constitutes an 'arbitration agreement', the Regulations apply where the 'consumer' is a legal person as they apply where the consumer is a natural person: Arbitration Act 1996, s 90.
2   Reg 3(5).

Unfair terms

14.64   The Regulations subject any term to which they apply to a test of fairness, save for an exception set out in reg 3(2). This provides that, *in so far as it is in plain, intelligible language*, no assessment shall be made of the fairness of any term which:

*   defines the main subject matter of the contract; or
*   concerns the adequacy of the price or remuneration, as against the goods or services sold or supplied.

The meaning of these exceptions, especially the first is obscure. If they are given a liberal interpretation by the courts, the efficacy of the Regulations as a consumer-protection measure will be limited.

14.65   *The test of fairness* Regulation 4(1) sets out the test of fairness. It provides that, subject to reg 4(2) and (3), 'unfair term' means any term which contrary to the requirement of good faith causes a significant imbalance in the parties' rights and obligations under the contract to the detriment of the consumer.

From these two elements of unfairness can be derived:

*   the term must cause significant imbalance to the parties' rights and obligations to the detriment of the consumer; and
*   this 'significant imbalance' must be 'contrary to the requirement of good faith'.

Regulation 4(3) provides that, in determining whether a term satisfies the requirement of good faith, regard must be had in particular to the matters specified in Sch 2, viz:

*   the strength of the bargaining positions of the parties;
*   whether the consumer had an inducement to agree to the term;
*   whether the goods or services were sold or supplied to the special order of the consumer, and

- the extent to which the seller or supplier has dealt fairly and equitably with the consumer.

The first three of these factors are similar to those in Sch 2 to the Unfair Contract Terms Act 1977.[1]

As with the test of reasonableness under the Unfair Contract Terms Act, the test of fairness is assessed as at the time of the conclusion of the contract. Regulation 4(2) provides an assessment of the unfair nature of a term and must take into account the nature of the goods or services for which the contract was concluded and refer, as at the time of the conclusion of the contract, to all circumstances attending the conclusion of the contract and to all the other terms of the contract or of another contract on which it is dependent.

The application of the test of fairness is greatly assisted by Sch 3 which contains an indicative, non-exhaustive and lengthy list of terms which may be regarded as unfair.

1   Para 10.28 above.

14.66   *Consequence of inclusion of unfair term* An unfair term under the provisions of the Regulations is not binding on the consumer.[1] However, the rest of the contract continues to bind the parties if it is capable of continuing in existence without the unfair term.[1]

1   Reg 5.

Interpretation of written terms in consumer contracts

14.67   By reg 6, a seller or supplier must ensure that any written contractual term to which the Regulations apply is expressed in plain, intelligible language. The only effect of a breach of this requirement is that, where there is doubt about the meaning of a written term, the interpretation most favourable to the consumer prevails, a rule akin to the *contra proferentem* rule;[1] the term is not rendered ineffective.

1   Para 10.10 above.

Chapter 15

Contracts in restraint of trade

15.1 Contracts in restraint of trade may be void at common law or, in some cases (which are outside the scope of this book), by statute.

In this chapter we describe:

- the principal types of restraints of trade caught by the common law rules;
- the effect where a restraint is void under those rules.

Contracts (or more commonly covenants, ie promises in them) in restraint of trade which are void at common law include:

- agreements restricting the subsequent occupation of an employee;
- agreements restricting the subsequent occupation of a partner;
- agreements between the vendor and purchaser of the goodwill of a business restricting competition by the vendor.

Tests of validity

15.2 The general tests of validity applicable to contracts falling within the restraint of trade doctrine are as follows:

- A contract in restraint of trade is prima facie void; but
- Such a contract will be valid and enforceable if–
  - the person seeking to enforce it shows that the restraint is reasonable between the parties to the contract; *and,*
  - the other party does not show that the restraint is unreasonable in the public interest.[1]

The tests of reasonableness must be applied as at the date the contract was made and in the light of the then existing facts and of what might possibly happen in the future. Anything else which has occurred subsequently must be ignored.[2] The test must also be applied by reference to what the terms of the restraint entitle or require the parties to do, and not by reference to what they have actually done or intend to do.[3]

A restraint of trade which is not void is most commonly enforced by an injunction restraining the defendant from breaking it.

1   These tests have their foundation in *Nordenfelt's* case [1894] AC 535, HL and *Herbert Morris Ltd v Saxelby* [1916] 1 AC 688, HL.
2   *Putsman v Taylor* [1927] 1 KB 637 at 643; *Gledhow Autoparts Ltd v Delaney* [1965] 3 All ER 288 at 295.
3   *Watson v Prager* [1991] 3 All ER 487, CA.

Agreements restricting the subsequent occupation of an employee

15.3   A contract between employer and employee, normally the contract of employment, may contain a covenant (promise) by the employee that he will not be employed in, or conduct, a business competing with his employer's after leaving his employment. Although this is the common form of a covenant restricting subsequent occupation, such a covenant need not be formed in these terms. A covenant is also in restraint of trade where it contains a restriction which provides that after leaving his employer's employment an employee shall be paid a pension or arrears of commission provided that he does not take employment with a competitor of the employer.[1] A covenant restricting the subsequent employment of an employee will normally be limited in duration and area. Being in restraint of trade, it is prima facie void and will only be valid and enforceable if the tests of reasonableness referred to above are satisfied.

1   *Wyatt v Kreglinger and Fernau* [1933] 1 KB 793, CA (facts set out in para 15.7 below); *Sadler v Imperial Life Assurance Co of Canada* [1988] IRLR 388.

Reasonable between the parties

15.4   Two things must be proved to satisfy this test:

15.5   *The restriction must protect a legally recognised interest of the employer* Only two types of interest are so recognised:

*   *Protection of employer's trade secrets or other confidential information equivalent to a trade secret concerning employer's affairs*   An example of a case involving the protection of trade secrets is provided by *Forster & Sons Ltd v Suggett*.[1] The defendant was the plaintiff company's works manager. He was instructed in secret methods relating to the production of glass which the plaintiff company produced. He agreed that, during the five years after the end of his employment with the plaintiff company, he would not carry on in the United Kingdom, or be interested in, glass bottle manufacturing or any other business connected with glass making as carried on by the company. It was held that this restriction was reasonable to protect the plaintiff company's trade secrets and an injunction was ordered to restrain breach of it. Examples of information equivalent to a trade secret concerning the employer's affairs are detailed information on costing, customer accounts, profit margins and development plans.[2]
*   *Protection of employer's business connections*   An employer is entitled to prevent an employee misusing influence which he has obtained over the employer's customers and thereby enticing them away.[3] Thus, in *Fitch v Dewes*,[4] where the contract provided that a Tamworth solicitor's managing clerk (who was himself a solicitor) should never practice within seven miles of Tamworth Town Hall, the House of Lords held that the restriction was valid because it constituted a reasonable protection of the employer's business connections against an employee who could gain influence over his clients.

It is not enough merely to show that the restriction purports to protect trade secrets or connections: it must also be shown that they require protection against the particular employee. Thus, the restriction will be invalid if the employee did not know enough about a trade secret to be able to use it or was insufficiently acquainted with customers to be able to influence them. This is shown, for example, by *S W Strange Ltd v Mann*,[5] where a restriction imposed on a bookmaker's manager was held to be void because the business was mostly conducted by telephone and the manager had no chance to get to know his employer's customers or to influence them.

No other interests can be protected validly by the present type of restriction;[6] consequently, a restriction whose object is simply to protect the employer against competition is invalid.[6]

1   (1918) 35 TLR 87.
2   *Poly Lina Ltd v Finch* [1995] FSR 751.
3   *Herbert Morris Ltd v Saxelby* [1916] 1 AC 688 at 709.
4   [1921] 2 AC 158, HL.
5   [1965] 1 All ER 1069.
6   *Herbert Morris Ltd v Saxelby* [1916] 1 AC 688 at 710.

15.6   *Reasonableness* To be reasonable between the parties, the restriction must be no wider than is reasonably necessary to protect the employer's trade secrets (or other equivalent information) or business connections. Reasonableness is a matter of degree: the terms of the restriction must be measured against the degree of knowledge or influence which the employee has gained in his employment. A fortiori, a restriction will be void if it relates to a wider range of occupations than is reasonably necessary to protect the relevant protectable interests. Two other factors which are particularly important are the duration and area of restriction.

*   *Duration* In *M and S Drapers v Reynolds*,[1] a collector-salesman of a credit drapery firm convenanted not to canvass his employers' customers for a period of five years after leaving their employment. The restriction was held to be void: in view of the lowly position of a collector-salesman it was for a longer period than was reasonably necessary to protect the employers' business connections. On the other hand, the restriction in *Fitch v Dewes* was upheld, even though it was to last for life, because of the degree of influence which the solicitor's managing clerk would gain over his employer's clients.
*   *Area*   In *Mason v Provident Clothing and Supply Co Ltd*,[2] a canvasser in the plaintiff company's Islington branch district covenanted not to work in any similar business for three years within 25 miles of London. The restriction was held to be void because it extended further than was reasonably necessary to protect the plaintiff company's business connections. On the other hand, a covenant by a sales representative employed by a small company that, for two years after leaving his employment, he would not canvass (in the same goods) people who had been customers of his employer during his employment, was upheld in *G W Plowman & Son v Ash*,[3] even though it was unlimited in area.

1   [1956] 3 All ER 814, CA.
2   [1913] AC 724, HL. Also see *Marley Tile Co Ltd v Johnson* [1982] IRLR 75, CA.
3   [1964] 2 All ER 10.

Reasonable in the public interest
15.7   The operation of this test is demonstrated by *Wyatt v Kreglinger and Fernau*.[1] The employers of a wool broker promised to pay him a pension on his retirement provided he did not re-enter the wool trade and did nothing to their detriment (fair competition excepted). The broker subsequently sued for arrears of pension but the

Court of Appeal held that he could not succeed since the contract was void for two reasons:

- the restriction was unreasonable as between the parties;
- the contract was unreasonable in the public interest because the permanent restriction on the broker working anywhere in the wool trade deprived the community of services from which it might benefit.

Provided the restriction is reasonable between the parties, employer-employee restrictions will rarely be invalidated on the ground that they are unreasonable in the public interest. However, where the employee has a special skill of particular value to the community, the restriction may well be found unreasonable in the public interest, even though it affords reasonable protection for the employer's trade secrets or business connections.[2]

1 [1933] 1 KB 793, CA.
2 *Bull v Pitney-Bowes Ltd* [1966] 3 All ER 384.

15.8 It may be noted in passing that, even in the absence of an express restraint, where an employee uses or discloses an employer's trade secrets or confidential information concerning his employer's affairs, or where an employee solicits an employer's customers, the employer can obtain an injunction to restrain this.[1] An employer can also obtain an injunction, even in the absence of an express restraint, to restrain an ex-employee from using or disclosing a trade secret of the employer or confidential information relating to the employer's business equivalent to a trade secret.[2]

The basis on which such conduct is restrained is that there has been a breach of an implied term of the contract of employment whereby the employee is obliged not to engage in such conduct.[3]

1 *Wessex Dairies Ltd v Smith* [1935] 2 KB 80; *Faccenda Chicken Ltd v Fowler* [1986] 1 All ER 617, CA.
2 *Printers and Finishers Ltd v Holloway* [1964] 3 All ER 731; *Faccenda Chicken Ltd v Fowler* [1986] 1 All ER 617, CA; *Roger Bullivant Ltd v Ellis* [1987] ICR 464, CA; *Johnson & Bloy (Holdings) Ltd v Wolstenholme Rink plc* [1987] IRLR 499, CA.
3 Para 8.25 above.

Agreements restricting the subsequent occupation of a partner

15.9 Partnership agreements commonly provide that a partner who ceases to be a partner shall not, for a specified period, act or deal with any client of the firm in the professional capacity in which he was a partner. Such a restraint is valid and enforceable only if it is reasonable as between the parties to protect some legitimate interest of the firm and is not unreasonable in the public interest.[1] What is a legitimate interest of the firm depends largely on the nature of its business and on the ex-partner's position in the firm, but an example of such an interest is a firm's connections with its clients. This was held in *Bridge v Deacons*,[2] which was concerned with a covenant in a Hong Kong solicitors' partnership agreement whereby a partner who ceased to be a partner was restricted for five years thereafter from acting as a solicitor in Hong Kong for anyone who had been a client of the firm when he ceased to be a partner or during the preceding three years. The Privy Council held that the covenant, which applied to all the partners, was reasonable as between the parties, since it went no further in extent or time than was reasonable to protect the firm's connections with its clients, and was not unreasonable in the public interest; the covenant was therefore held enforceable against an ex-partner.

1   *Bridge v Deacons* [1984] 2 All ER 19, PC; *Edwards v Worboys* [1984] AC 724n, CA.
2   [1984] 2 All ER 19, PC.

Agreements between the vendor and purchaser of the goodwill of a business restricting competition by the vendor

15.10   The goodwill of a business means its commercial reputation, its customer connections and its potential customers through referrals by existing customers.[1] An agreement of the present type is prima facie void for restraint of trade but will be valid and enforceable if it is reasonable between the parties and not unreasonable in the public interest. The following can be said concerning the requirements of reasonableness between the parties.

1   *Allied Dunbar (Frank Weisinger) Ltd v Weisinger* [1988] IRLR 60.

The restriction must protect the goodwill of the business sold

15.11   An agreement whereby one business surrenders its liberty to trade in a particular field is void since mere competition is not a protectable interest.[1] The restriction must relate to an actual business which has been sold. Thus, even though it is contained in what purports to be a contract for the sale of a business, a restriction will be void if there is no actual business to protect. This is shown by *Vancouver Malt and Sake Brewing Co Ltd v Vancouver Breweries Ltd.*[2] The appellants held a licence to brew beer and other liquors but the only trade actually carried on by them under the licence was brewing sake. They purported to sell the goodwill of their licence, so far as it related to brewing beer, to the respondents and covenanted not to brew beer for 15 years thereafter. The Privy Council held that the covenant was void because, if there was a sale, it was merely a sale of the appellants' liberty to brew beer since there was no goodwill of a beer-brewing business to be transferred and the covenant was simply a bare restriction on competition.

Other aspects of the rule that the covenant must protect the goodwill of the business actually sold are demonstrated by *British Reinforced Concrete Engineering Co Ltd v Schelff.*[3] The defendant, who ran a small business for the sale of 'Loop' road reinforcements, sold it to the plaintiff company, a large company which manufactured and sold 'BRC' road reinforcements. In the contract of sale the defendant covenanted that, for three years after the end of the First World War, he would not 'either alone or jointly or in partnership with any other person or persons whomsoever and either directly or indirectly carry on or manage or be concerned or interested in or act as servant of any person concerned or interested in the business of the manufacture or sale of road reinforcements in any part of the UK'. It was held that this covenant was too wide because it extended to the manufacture of road reinforcements as well as their sale, and thus it sought to protect more than the actual business sold (the sale of road reinforcements) in that it sought to protect the purchaser's existing business (the sale and manufacture of road reinforcements).

1   *Vancouver Malt and Sake Brewing Co Ltd v Vancouver Breweries Ltd* [1934] AC 181, PC.
2   [1934] AC 181, PC.
3   [1921] 2 Ch 563.

The restriction must go no further than is reasonably necessary to protect the business sold

15.12   As was pointed out in the *Schelff* case, the reasonableness of the restriction must be judged by reference to the extent and circumstances of the business sold, and not by the extent and range of any business already run by the purchaser. Reasonableness is judged from the standpoint of both parties. For example, in the

Schelff case it was held that the 'servant clause' was unreasonable because it would preclude the defendant from becoming the servant of a trust company which, as part of its investments, held shares in a company manufacturing or selling road reinforcements.

The amount of the consideration for the agreement is a relevant factor in assessing the reasonableness of the restriction.[1] In addition, the duration and area of the restriction are particularly important factors to be taken into account in assessing its reasonableness. The approach of the courts is more liberal here than in the case of employer-employee restrictions because buyers and sellers of businesses are more obviously equal bargaining partners. A good example of this liberality is provided by *Nordenfelt v Maxim Nordenfelt Guns and Ammunition Co Ltd*.[2] The appellant, who had obtained patents for improving quick-firing guns, carried on, among other things, business as a maker of such guns and ammunition. He sold the goodwill and assets of the business to a company, entering into a covenant which restricted his future activities. The company later merged with another to become the respondent company and the appellant's earlier covenant was substantially repeated with it. This covenant provided that for 25 years the appellant would not engage, except on behalf of the company, directly or indirectly in the trade or business of a manufacturer of guns, gun mountings or carriages, gunpowder, explosives or ammunition, or in any business competing or liable to compete in any way with that for the time being carried on by the respondent company. The first part of the covenant, relating to engaging in a business manufacturing guns, etc was held by the House of Lords to provide reasonable protection for the business acquired by the company, even though the restriction was worldwide and was to last 25 years, and was therefore valid. It was recognised, however, that the second part of the covenant, relating to engaging in any business competing with that carried on by the company, was void because it went further than was reasonable to protect the business acquired by the company. Similarly, the restriction in the *Schelff* case, even in so far as it related to the management, etc of a business selling reinforcements, was held void because it applied to the whole of the United Kingdom, which was regarded as a wider area than was necessary to protect the actual business sold.

1   *Nordenfelt v Maxim Nordenfelt Guns and Ammunition Co Ltd* [1894] AC 535 at 565.
2   [1894] AC 535, HL.

Effect

15.13   Provided that the part of the contract which is void on grounds of public policy can be severed from the rest of the contract, the latter, as opposed to the void part, is enforceable. However, if the void part cannot be severed the whole contract is void and unenforceable. Severance can operate in two ways.

Severance of the whole of an objectionable promise

15.14   If this can be done the rest of the contract is valid and enforceable by the party subject to the clause. Severance of a whole promise is not possible if it is the whole or substantially the whole of the consideration furnished by the plaintiff for the promise by the defendant which the plaintiff wishes to enforce. Thus, in *Wyatt v Kreglinger and Fernau*, which we discussed in para 15.7 above, it was held that the ex-employee could not enforce the promise to pay him a pension since he had given no valid consideration for it, his only promise – not to compete – being void under the restraint of trade doctrine. This can be contrasted with *Marshall v N M Financial Management Ltd*,[1] where the plaintiff's contract of employment stated that commission should be payable to him after the termination of his employment, provided that he did not compete with his former employer. This proviso was void under the restraint of trade doctrine. It was held, however, that the plaintiff could enforce his right to commission because his promise not to compete was not the whole or substantially the whole of the consideration given by him for the former employer's promise to pay it; the main consideration given by him for that promise was his provision of services during the period of his employment.

1   [1997] 1 WLR 1527, CA.

Severance of the objectionable part of a promise

15.15   If severance of part of a promise is possible, the rest of the contract, including the unsevered part of the promise, can be enforced against the party subject to it. Severance of this type is only possible if two tests are satisfied:

The 'blue pencil' test

15.16   This test is only satisfied if the objectionable words can be struck out of the promise as it stands. This was possible in relation to the offending part of the promise in the *Nordenfelt* case, which has been discussed in para 15.12 above. Another example is provided by *Goldsoll v Goldman*.[1] The defendant sold his imitation jewellery business in Old Bond Street to the plaintiff, another jeweller. The defendant covenanted that for two years he would not 'either solely or jointly with or as agent or employee for any person or company… carry on or be interested in the business of a vendor of or dealer in real or imitation jewellery in the county of London, England, Scotland, Ireland, Wales or any part of the UK and the Isle of Man or in France, the USA, Russia or Spain, or within 25 miles of Potsdamerstrasse, Berlin, or St Stephan's Kirche, Vienna'. The defendant joined a rival jeweller's in New Bond Street within two years and the plaintiff sought an injunction to restrain breach of the covenant. The Court of Appeal held that the covenant was unreasonably wide in respect of subject matter (for the defendant had not dealt in real jewellery) and also in respect of area (because the defendant had not traded abroad), but that the references to foreign places and real jewellery could be severed because it was possible to delete them from the covenant as it stood. After severance, the covenant merely prohibited dealing in imitation jewellery in the United Kingdom and the Isle of Man, and an injunction was granted to prevent such dealing. A more recent example is provided by *Anscombe & Ringland v Butchoff*.[2] A & R, a firm of estate agents carrying on business in London, employed B under a contract containing a clause that, for one year after the termination of the contract, B would not undertake 'either alone or in partnership or as a member of a company nor be interested directly or indirectly in the business of an auctioneer, valuer, surveyor or estate agent within a radius of one mile of the firm's office'. B left the firm and soon afterwards set up in business as an estate agent only 150 yards away from A & R's office. It was held:

- that the clause was unreasonable in so far as it forbade B to be interested in the business of a surveyor or valuer, for he had never been a suveyor or valuer, and that part of the clause would be severed; but
- that part of the clause relating to the carrying on of business as an estate agent within the specified area was reasonable and would be enforced.

If the unreasonable part of the promise cannot be deleted from the promise as it stands, severance of it is not possible. The court cannot rewrite the promise by adding or altering even one word so as to make it reasonable. Thus, in *Mason v Provident Clothing and Supply Co Ltd,*[3] which has already been referred to,[4] where the contract in question contained a promise that the employee would not work within 25 miles of London after leaving his employment, the House of Lords held that the promise was too wide in area, and therefore unreasonable, and refused to re-draft the clause so as to make it reasonable and enforceable. The whole promise was therefore held void and unenforceable.

1   [1915] 1 Ch 292, CA.
2   (1984) 134 NLJ 37.
3   [1913] AC 724, HL.
4   Para 15.6 above.

Severance of the objectionable part must not alter the nature (as opposed to the extent) of the original contract

15.17   This means that severance of part of a promise is impossible unless it can be construed as being divisible into a number of separate and independent parts. This rule is sensible – otherwise the mechanical deletion of the objectionable part of the promise could radically change the whole contract – but difficult to apply.

The application of this test can be illustrated by two cases. In *Attwood v Lamont,*[1] the plaintiffs owned a general outfitter's business in Kidderminster. The business was divided into a number of departments. The defendant was the head of the tailoring department but had no concern with any other department. In his contract of employment the defendant had undertaken that, after the termination of his employment, he would not 'be concerned in any of the following trades or businesses, that is to say, the trade or business of a tailor, dressmaker, general draper, milliner, hatter, haberdasher, gentlemen's, ladies' or children's outfitter' within 10 miles of Kidderminster. Later the plaintiffs sought to enforce this covenant. They admitted that it was too wide in terms of the trades covered but argued that the references to aspects of the business other than tailoring could be severed, leaving the tailoring restraint enforceable. The Court of Appeal rejected this course because such severance would have altered the whole nature of the covenant: the covenant as it stood was one indivisible covenant (or promise) for the protection of the whole of the plaintiffs' business, not several covenants for the protection of the plaintiffs' several departments, and to alter it would be to alter its nature.

This case can be contrasted with *Scorer v Seymour v Johns.*[2] The defendant was in sole charge of the plaintiff's estate agency in Kingsbridge, Devon; the main office was in Dartmouth, Devon. He contracted that, for three years after the end of his contract of employment, he would not 'undertake or carry on either alone or in partnership or be employed or interested directly or indirectly in any capacity whatsoever in the business of an auctioneer surveyor or estate agent or in any ancillary business carried on by [the plaintiff] at 85, Fore Street, Kingsbridge or Duke Street, Dartmouth aforesaid within a radius of five miles thereof.' After the end of his employment with the plaintiff, the defendant set up his own estate agency business within five miles of the Kingsbridge office. The covenant in respect of Kingsbridge was held reasonable, but not the covenant in respect of Dartmouth. The latter was severed, and the plaintiffs granted an injunction in relation to the Kingsbridge covenant.

1   [1920] 3 KB 571, CA.
2   [1966] 3 All ER 347.

Chapter 16

Agency

16.1 Agency is the relationship between two legal persons, whereby one person, the principal, appoints another, the agent, to act on his behalf. The relationship is usually, though not necessarily, contractual.[1] The major importance of agency lies in the fact that an authorised agent[2] may affect the legal position of his principal vis-à-vis third parties. In most cases, the agent does this by making a contract on his principal's behalf, or by disposing of property which the principal owns. However, he may also bind his principal in other ways, for example by signing a document,[3] receiving notice,[4] or committing a tort.[5] With certain exceptions,[6] mostly statutory, a principal may do anything through the medium of an agent which he could lawfully do in person.

1   *Yasuda Fire and Marine Insurance Co of Europe Ltd v Orion Marine Insurance Underwriting Agency Ltd* [1995] 3 All ER 211.
2   Including one who, though not actually appointed, is given the appearance of authority by his principal: paras 16.32–16.36 below.
3   *LCC v Agricultural Food Products Ltd* [1955] 2 QB 218, [1955] 2 All ER 229, CA.
4   *Proudfoot v Montefiore* (1867) LR 2 QB 511.
5   Paras 28.18–28.20 below.
6   See *Clauss v Pir* [1987] 2 All ER 752.

Three issues

16.2 The three issues with which we are concerned in this chapter are:

- the relationship of principal and agent (ie the creation of agency, the duties and rights of agents and the termination of agency);
- the changes in the legal relationship of the principal and third parties which may be effected by an agent; and
- the legal relationship, if any, between the agent and third parties.

Principal and agent

Creation of agency

16.3 Agency may be created by agreement, express or implied, by ratification or by virtue of necessity. In determining whether a principal (P) has appointed another person to act as his agent (A), it is necessary to decide whether P had the capacity to appoint an agent and whether A had the capacity to act as an agent, before considering how an agent is appointed.

Capacity

16.4   An agent can be appointed to effect any transaction for which the principal has capacity.[1] However, an agent who lacks full contractual capacity can only be made personally liable on those contracts which he would have had capacity to make on his own behalf.[2] Further, the agent may well not be liable on the contract of agency itself. Companies, no less than natural legal persons, can be appointed as agents.

1   For the law relating to capacity to contract, see paras 4.9–4.15 above.
2   *Smally v Smally* (1700) 1 Eq Cas Abr 6; for when an agent is personally liable on contracts see paras 16.41–16.46 below.

Appointment by express agreement

16.5   An agent may be appointed by express agreement between principal and agent. This agreement is frequently, but not necessarily, a contract. If the appointment is by contract, the usual rules for the formation of contracts must be complied with. Normally, the appointment can be made informally, even if the agent is to transact contracts which must be made or evidenced in writing. All that is necessary is a desire to appoint A as agent and A's consent to act as such. However, in some cases certain formalities are necessary to create agency. For instance, if an agent has to execute a deed, his appointment must be by deed, and is known as a power of attorney.[1]

The agreement which appoints an agent will usually specify the authority which the principal bestows upon him, though this may be extended by implication.[2] The authority of an agent to bind the principal to a contract with a third party may also be extended by ostensible authority.[3]

1   *Steiglitz v Egginton* (1815) Holt NP 141, and see also the Powers of Attorney Act 1971, ss 1 and 7.
2   Para 16.31 below.
3   Paras 16.32–16.36 below.

Appointment by implied agreement

16.6   If the parties have not expressly agreed to become principal and agent, it may be possible to find an implied agreement based on their conduct or relationship. If the parties have so conducted themselves towards one another that it would be reasonable for them to assume that they have consented to act as principal and agent, then they are principal and agent.[1] For example, the agent of a finance company or of an insurance company may also be held to be the agent of the party seeking finance or insurance if the circumstances warrant an implication of agreement to such an agency relationship.[2] Factors which have been found relevant in determining whether agency has been created by implied agreement are whether one party acts for the other at the other's request and whether commission is payable.

An implied agreement to agency by virtue of the relationship of the parties arises in the case of husband and wife. A wife has authority to pledge her husband's credit for household necessaries even if he has not expressly appointed her his agent.[3]

Since there is no express appointment in the present type of case, the authority which the principal bestows upon the agent is implied authority;[4] but, as with agents expressly appointed, agents impliedly appointed may have the power to bind the principal to contracts with third parties by virtue of ostensible authority.[5]

1   *Ashford Shire Council v Dependable Motors Pty Ltd* [1961] AC 336, [1961] 1 All ER 96, PC.
2   *Newsholme Bros v Road Transport and General Insurance Co Ltd* [1929] 2 KB 356, CA.
3   *Debenham v Mellon* (1880) 6 App Cas 24, HL.

4   Para 16.31 below.
5   Paras 16.32–16.36 below.

Ratification

16.7   In certain circumstances, the relationship of principal and agent can be created or extended retrospectively under the doctrine of ratification. What this means is that, if A purports to act as agent for B in a particular transaction (although he is not authorised to do so), B may subsequently 'ratify' or adopt what A has done. In such a case, A is deemed to have been acting as an authorised agent when he effected the transaction.[1] However, ratification only validates past acts of the 'agent' and gives no authority for the future,[2] although frequent acts of ratification by an alleged principal may create agency by implied agreement or confer ostensible authority on the agent.[3]

1   *Bolton Partners v Lambert* (1889) 41 Ch D 295, CA.
2   *Irvine v Union Bank of Australia* (1877) 2 App Cas 366, PC.
3   *Midland Bank Ltd v Reckitt* [1933] AC 1, HL.

16.8   *Effects of ratification*   If a person ratifies a transaction entered into on his behalf he must be taken to have ratified the whole transaction, and not merely those parts which are to his advantage.[1] The effect of ratification is to make the transaction (which is usually a contract) binding on the principal from the moment it was made by the agent.[2] Since the acts of the agent are retrospectively validated, the agent cannot be liable to a third party for breach of warranty of authority, nor to his principal for acting outside the scope of his authority,[3] and can claim commission and an indemnity.[4] Once a contract is ratified, the agent generally ceases to be liable on the contract, but ratification cannot vary rights in property which had vested before ratification.[5]

Perhaps the most controversial effect of ratification is that it allows the alleged principal to decide whether to accept a contract or reject it. The third party may wish to repudiate an agreement with the agent because of the agent's lack of authority, but find himself bound by the contract if the alleged principal subsequently ratifies.[6] However, if a contract is explicitly made 'subject to ratification' the third party can withdraw prior to ratification and, if he does so, ratification cannot bind him.[7] Because the effects of ratification are at least potentially unfair to third parties, ratification is only possible in some circumstances.

1   *Cornwal v Wilson* (1750) 1 Ves Sen 509.
2   *Bolton Partners v Lambert* (1889) 41 Ch D 295, CA.
3   *Smith v Cologan* (1788) 2 Term Rep 188n. For breach of warranty of authority see para 16.47 below.
4   *Hartas v Ribbons* (1889) 22 QBD 254, CA. For indemnities see para 16.21 below.
5   *Bird v Brown* (1850) 4 Exch 786.
6   *Bolton Partners v Lambert* (1889) 41 Ch D 295, CA.
7   *Warehousing and Forwarding Co of East Africa Ltd v Jafferali & Sons Ltd* [1964] AC 1, [1963] 3 All ER 571, PC.

16.9   *Who can ratify*   Only the alleged principal can ratify the actions of his alleged agent and then only if the latter purported to act on his behalf.[2] Therefore, if an agent has not revealed he was acting as an agent, ie he has an undisclosed principal, the undisclosed principal cannot ratify.[2] A leading illustration of this is the case of *Keighley, Maxsted & Co v Durant*.[3] In this case an agent purchased wheat at a price which was higher than he had been authorised to pay. The agent had not revealed that he was acting as an agent when he bought the grain. Because of this the House of Lords found the defendant principal was not liable for breach of contract when he refused to accept delivery of the grain, even though he had purported to ratify the contract of sale.

Provided that an agent reveals that he is acting as agent, his principal, even though unnamed, can ratify his unauthorised actions.[4] However, an unnamed principal should be identifiable,[4] unless, perhaps, the third party has shown that he is uninterested in the identity of the principal. Further, there is a strange rule by which unnamed, and possibly unidentifiable, principals can ratify contracts of marine insurance.[5]

A company which is a disclosed principal can only ratify if it is in existence at the time the agent enters into any contract.[6] Even if a company takes the benefit of a pre-incorporation contract it is not liable on it, although it will be liable if it makes a new contract post-incorporation on the same subject matter.[7] Such a new contract will not be implied merely because the company takes the benefit of the pre-incorporation contract[8] and any new contract is of course only prospective in effect. An agent who makes a pre-incorporation contract on behalf of a non-existent company is personally liable on it unless personal liability has been excluded 'by contract or otherwise'.[9]

To be able to ratify, the disclosed principal must have had the capacity to make the contract himself at the date when his 'agent' contracted.[10]

1   *Wilson v Tumman* (1843) 6 Man & G 236.
2   However, an alleged principal who acts towards the third party as if his agent's act was authorised may become liable for it on the basis of estoppel: *Spiro v Lintern* [1973] 3 All ER 319, CA; *Worboys v Carter* [1987] 2 EGLR 1, CA.
3   [1901] AC 240, HL.
4   *Watson v Swann* [1862] 11 CBNS 756; *Southern Water Authority v Carey* [1985] 2 All ER 1077.
5   *Boston Fruit Co v British and Foreign Marine Insurance Co* [1906] AC 336, HL.
6   *Kelner v Baxter* (1866) LR 2 CP 174. However, a company may claim damages in tort for a negligent act committed before its incorporation: *Miro Properties Ltd v J Trevor & Sons* [1989] 1 EGLR 151.
7   *Howard v Patent Ivory Manufacturing Co* (1888) 38 Ch D 156.
8   *Touche v Metropolitan Railway Warehousing Co* (1871) 6 Ch App 671.
9   Companies Act 1985, s 36C.
10 *Boston Deep Sea Fishing and Ice Co Ltd v Farnham* (Inspector of Taxes) [1957] 3 All ER 204, [1957] 1 WLR 1051.

16.10   *What can be ratified*   Apparently any action can be ratified (even where the purported agent was seeking to benefit himself[1]) except those which are illegal[2] or otherwise void. Early cases treated a forgery as an act which was void and which could not therefore be ratified. However, subsequent interpretation of the leading case, *Brook v Hook*,[3] has suggested that, while forgeries are generally regarded as unratifiable, it is for a different reason. Current opinion is that a forgery is not ratifiable because an 'agent' who forges the principal's signature does not purport to be an agent, but rather to be the principal.

1   *Re Tiedemann and Ledermann Frères* [1899] 2 QB 66.
2   *Bedford Insurance Co Ltd v Instituto de Resseguros do Brasil* [1985] QB 966, [1984] 3 All ER 766.
3   (1871) LR 6 Exch 89.

16.11   *How to ratify*   Ratification may be made by express affirmation of the unauthorised actions of the agent by the principal.[1] It need not, as a rule, take any special form, except that, where the agent has without authority executed a deed, ratification too must be by deed.[2] Ratification must take place within a reasonable time.[3] What is reasonable is a question of fact in every case but, if the time for performance of a contract has passed, ratification is impossible.[4] However, where an agent without authority commences legal proceedings, the client may ratify the agent's act even after the expiry of the limitation period within which proceedings must be commenced.[5]

Ratification may also be effected by conduct,[6] although mere passive acceptance of the benefit of a contract may be insufficient,[7] but if the conduct of the alleged principal amounts to ratification he cannot repudiate the actions of his agent.[8] Examples of ratification are provided by the following cases. In *Lyell v Kennedy*,[9] A received rent from property for many years, although not authorised to do so. When the owner sued him for an account of the rents, it was held that the owner's action constituted ratification of A's receipt of the rents. Similarly, in *Cornwal v Wilson*,[10] A bought some goods in excess of the price authorised by P. P objected to the purchase but sold some of the goods; it was held that he had ratified the unauthorised act by selling the goods. An action by the alleged principal will only be implied ratification if he had a choice of whether or not to act. If the alleged principal had no real choice, other than to accept the benefit of the unauthorised actions of his agent, accepting such benefit is not ratification. For example, if an agent has had unauthorised repairs done on a ship, merely retaking the ship with these repairs is not ratification by the alleged principal. This is because if he wished to recover his property he had to have it with the unauthorised repairs.[11]

Ratification will, generally, only be implied from conduct if the alleged principal has acted with full knowledge of the facts.[12] However, if the alleged principal is prepared to take the risk of what his agent has done, he can choose to ratify without full knowledge. For instance, in *Fitzmaurice v Bayley*[13] an agent entered into an unauthorised contract for the purchase of property. The alleged principal wrote a letter saying he did not know what his agent had done but would stand by all that he had done. This was an express ratification by him; he had agreed to bear the risk of being bound by the unauthorised acts of his agent, whatever they were.

1   *Soames v Spencer* (1822) 1 Dow & Ry KB 32.
2   *Hunter v Parker* (1840) 7 M & W 322.
3   *Re Portuguese Consolidated Copper Mines Ltd* (1890) 45 Ch D 16, CA.
4   *Metropolitan Asylums Board (Managers) v Kingham & Sons* (1890) 6 TLR 217.
5   *Presentaciones Musicales SA v Secunda* [1994] 2 All ER 737, CA.
6   *Lyell v Kennedy* (1889) 14 App Cas 437, HL.
7   *Hughes v Hughes* (1971) 221 Estates Gazette 145, CA.
8   *Cornwal v Wilson* (1750) 1 Ves Sen 509.
9   (1889) 14 App Cas 437, HL.
10 (1750) 1 Ves Sen 509.
11 *Forman & Co Pty Ltd v The Liddesdale* [1900] AC 190, PC.
12 *The Bonita, The Charlotte* (1861) 1 Lush 252.
13 (1856) 6 E & B 868.

Agency of necessity

16.12   Agency of necessity is a limited exception to the concept that agency is based on a consensual relationship between the parties. When certain emergencies occur, immediate action may be necessary and the courts may be prepared to find that the person taking such action was thereby acting as an agent of necessity. A common example of agency of necessity is that masters of ships faced with an emergency are agents of the shipowner, and have authority to enter into contracts with third parties on behalf of him.[1]

Frequently, agency of necessity will merely extend the authority of existing agents but in other cases it may create agency where none existed previously – for example, between masters of ships and cargo owners. In other cases, if a person claims to be an agent of necessity, such agency will only affect the relationship of the alleged principal and agent, and will confer no power on the 'agent' to deal with third parties on behalf of the 'principal'. This type of agency of necessity is more likely than the former if the parties were not already principal and agent; for example, someone who salvages a ship cannot make contracts on behalf of the shipowner.

Agency of necessity will only arise if the 'agent' has no practical way of communicating with the 'principal',[2] if the action of the 'agent' is reasonably necessary to benefit the principal[3] and if the agent has acted bona fide.

1   *The Gratitudine* (1801) 3 Ch Rob 240.

2   *Springer v Great Western Rly Co* [1921] 1 KB 257, CA.
3   *Prager v Blatspiel, Stamp and Heacock Ltd* [1924] 1 KB 566.

A postscript

16.13   In some cases a person will be held to have authority to affect the legal
relationship of an apparent principal and third parties, even if the person whose actions
thereby bind the apparent principal is not technically an agent. This is not a method of
creating agency between principal and agent but it may result in an alleged principal
being unable to deny that his apparent agent was authorised to act on his behalf.[1] The
doctrine is sometimes called agency by estoppel.

1   Paras 16.32–16.36 below

Duties of an agent

Duty to act

16.14   A paid agent is under a duty to act, and any loss suffered by the principal
because of failure to act is recoverable by the principal.[1] If the agent does not intend
to act he should inform his principal of this fact, but the agent cannot be made liable
for failure to perform acts which are illegal or void.[2] A gratuitous agent does not appear
to be under any positive duty to act, although if he chooses to act and does so negligently
he is liable.[3]

1   *Turpin v Bilton* (1843) 5 Man & G 455.
2   *Cohen v Kittell* (1889) 22 QBD 680, DC.
3   *Wilkinson v Coverdale* (1793) 1 Esp 74, CA.

Duty to obey instructions

16.15   The primary obligation imposed on an agent is to act strictly in accordance
with the instructions of his principal in so far as they are lawful and reasonable. An
agent has no discretion to disobey his instructions, even in what he honestly and
reasonably regards to be his principal's best interests.[1] If an agent carries out his
instructions he cannot be liable for loss suffered by the principal because the instructions
were at fault.[2] If the instructions which an agent receives are not complied with he
will be responsible to his principal for any loss thereby suffered, even if the loss is not
occasioned by any fault on his part.[3] However, if the instructions received by an agent
are ambiguous, he is not in breach of his duty if he makes a reasonable but incorrect
interpretation of them.[4] If instructions confer a discretion on the agent, he will not be
liable for failure to obey instructions if he exercises the discretion reasonably.[5]

The instructions which an agent should obey may be clarified or extended by virtue
of custom or trade usage applying in the trade or profession which the agent follows.

1   *Bertram, Armstrong & Co v Godfray* (1830) 1 Knapp 381.
2   *Overend Gurney and Co v Gibb* (1872) LR 5 HL 480, HL.
3   *Lilley v Doubleday* (1881) 7 QBD 510.
4   *Weigall & Co v Runciman & Co* (1916) 85 LJKB 1187, CA.
5   *Boden v French* (1851) 10 CB 886.

Duty to exercise care and skill

16.16   An agent, whether paid or gratuitous,[1] is required to display reasonable care
in carrying out his instructions and also, where appropriate, such skill as may reasonably
be expected from a member of his profession.[2] If he fails to do so, the agent will be
liable for any loss which his principal suffers thereby. A negligent agent may also forfeit
the right to remuneration where his negligence renders his services to the principal
worthless.[3]

1   *Chaudhry v Prabhakar* [1988] 3 All ER 718, CA; see para 18.29 below.

2   Supply of Goods and Services Act 1982, s 13. For examples, see paras 19.8 and 19.9 below.
3   *Nye Saunders v Bristow* (1987) 37 BLR 92, CA.

Fiduciary duties

16.17   Every agent owes fiduciary duties, ie duties of good faith, to his principal. These duties are based on the confidential nature of the agency relationship. However, it is important to appreciate that an agent may be in breach of these duties, and liable for the consequences, even where he acts innocently.[1] There are two main fiduciary duties – a duty to disclose any conflict of interest and a duty not to take secret profits or bribes.

a. *Conflict of interest*   Wherever an agent's own interests, or the interests of a third party, come into conflict with those of the principal, the agent must make a full disclosure to the principal of all relevant facts, so that the latter may decide whether to continue with the transaction. It is this rule which prevents an agent, in the absence of disclosure, from selling his own property to the principal,[2] purchasing the principal's property for himself[3] or acting as agent for both vendor and purchaser[4] or for two competing would-be purchasers.[5] Similarly, an estate agent instructed to sell property must not favour one potential purchaser at the expense of others, in the hope of reward from that purchaser.[6] If the agent is in breach of this duty, the principal may have any resulting transaction set aside, claim any profit accruing to the agent and refuse to pay commission.[7]

b. *Secret profits and bribes*   If an agent, in the course of his agency and without his principal's knowledge and consent, makes a profit for himself out of his position, or out of property or information with which he is entrusted, he must account for this property to the principal.[8] Thus, an agent may not accept commission from both parties to a transaction,[9] nor keep for himself the benefit of a trade discount while charging his principal the full price.[10] It makes no difference that the agent has acted honestly throughout, nor even that his actions have conferred substantial benefit upon the principal.[11] However, an agent who has his principal's informed consent may keep whatever profit he makes.[12]

Where the secret profit takes the form of a payment from a third party who is aware that he is dealing with an agent, it is called a bribe, even if the payment is not made with any evil motive and even if the principal suffers no loss thereby.[13] The taking of a bribe entitles the principal to dismiss the agent,[14] recover either the amount of the bribe or his actual loss (if greater) from the agent or third party,[15] repudiate any transaction in respect of which the bribe was given[16] and refuse to pay commission.[17]

1   *Keppel v Wheeler* [1927] 1 KB 577, CA.
2   *Gillett v Peppercorne* (1840) 3 Beav 78.
3   *McPherson v Watt* (1877) 3 App Cas 254, HL.
4   *Harrods Ltd v Lemon* [1931] 2 KB 157, CA.
5   *Eric V Stansfield v South East Nursing Home Services Ltd* [1986] EGLR 29. An estate agent can of course act for more than one vendor, but must not disclose to one of them information which is confidential to another: *Brent Kelly v Cooper Associates* [1993] AC 205, PC.
6   *Henry Smith & Son v Muskett* (1977) 246 Estates Gazette 655.
7   Para 16.20 below.
8   *Regal (Hastings) Ltd v Gulliver* [1967] 2 AC 134n, [1942] 1 All ER 378, HL.
9   *Andrews v Ramsay & Co* [1903] 2 KB 635, CA.
10   *Hippisley v Knee Bros* [1905] 1 KB 1, DC.
11   *Boardman v Phipps* [1967] 2 AC 46, [1966] 3 All ER 721, HL.
12   See *Anangel Atlas Compania Naviera SA v Ishikawajima-Harima Heavy Industries Co* [1990] 1 Lloyd's Rep 167.
13   *Industries and General Mortgage Co Ltd v Lewis* [1949] 2 All ER 573.

14   *Boston Deep Sea Fishing and Ice Co v Ansell* (1888) 39 Ch D 339, CA.
15   *Mahesan S/O Thambiah v Malaysia Government Officers' Co-operative Housing Society Ltd* [1979] AC 374, [1978] 2 All ER 405, PC.
16   *Shipway v Broadwood* [1899] 1 QB 369; *Logicrose v Southend United Football Club* [1988] 1 WLR 1256.
17   Para 16.20 below.

Other duties

16.18   An agent has a duty not to delegate his responsibilities to a sub-agent without the authority of the principal.[1] An agent must pay over to the principal any money received for the use of the principal in the course of the agency, even if it is claimed by third parties,[2] and must keep proper accounts. An agent must allow the principal to inspect his accounts and all documents and records relating to acts done by the agent on the principal's behalf.[3]

1   *De Bussche v Alt* (1878) 8 Ch D 286, CA.
2   *Blaustein v Maltz, Mitchell & Co* [1937] 2 KB 142, [1937] 1 All ER 497, CA.
3   *Yasuda Fire and Marine Insurance Co of Europe Ltd v Orion Marine Insurance Underwriting Agency Ltd* [1995] 3 All ER 211.

Rights of agents
Remuneration

16.19   Where there is a contract of agency, an agent may be entitled thereunder to be paid for his services. The right to be paid may be an express term of the contract of agency or, in the absence of such a term, may be implied if it was clearly the intention of the parties that the agent was to be paid.[1] The agent will only be entitled to remuneration where he has performed, precisely and completely, the obligations in the agency agreement. If an agent does less than he is contractually required to do he can recover nothing, unless the contract provides for payment for partial services.

If the contract of agency expressly provides the amount of remuneration for a given task, this is the amount payable. If the contract merely provides that the agent is to be paid without specifying an amount, he is entitled to recover a reasonable amount.[2] If the contract mentions remuneration, but on its true construction does not entitle the agent to payment, he can recover nothing. For instance, in *Kofi Sunkersette Obu v Strauss & Co Ltd*,[3] the Privy Council refused to allow an agent to recover any commission in a case where the contract of agency provided that the amount of commission, if any, was to be fixed by the principal. If there is an implied term providing for payment, the amount of such payment must be determined by the courts. Usually it will be on the basis of what is reasonable, but it may be possible to imply the fixed scale costs of professional men.[4]

In the absence of a contract of agency, an agent may be entitled to be paid on a *quantum meruit* ('reasonable sum') basis. However, where an agent is to be paid on the occurrence of a certain event, such as a commission on sale, there can be no claim for a quantum meruit if the event does not occur.[5]

1   *Reeve v Reeve* (1858) 1 F & F 280. Also see the Supply of Goods and Services Act 1982, s 15 and the Commercial Agents (Council Directive) Regulations 1993.
2   *Way v Latilla* [1937] 3 All ER 759, HL.
3   [1951] AC 243, PC.
4   For when the courts will imply terms into contracts see paras 8.23–8.27 above.
5   *Howard Houlder & Partners Ltd v Manx Isles SS Co Ltd* [1923] 1 KB 110.

16.20   The mere occurrence of the transaction which the agent is commissioned to effect does not entitle the agent to remuneration; the occurrence must be brought about by the agent[1] unless the contract provides that he is to be paid however the desired result occurs.[2]

If the principal hinders the earning of commission by the agent, the agent cannot recover any commission thereby lost or sue the principal, unless the latter's action amounts to a breach of contract. The contract of agency may contain a term that the principal will not hinder the agent in his efforts to earn his commission,[3] but if it is not an express term the courts are reluctant to imply such a term into the contract of agency.[4]

Even if an agent complies with his instructions, he cannot recover any commission in respect of a transaction rendered void or illegal by statute.[5] An agent who is in breach of his duties towards his principal normally forfeits his right to commission,[6] unless the breach is a technical one and the agent has acted honestly.[7]

1   *Millar, Son & Co v Radford* (1903) 19 TLR 575, CA.
2   See *Brian Cooper & Co v Fairview Estates (Investments) Ltd* (1987) 282 Estates Gazette 1131, CA; *Barnard Marcus & Co v Ashraf* [1988] 1 EGLR 7, CA.
3   A 'sole agency' is a good example of this.
4   *Luxor (Eastbourne) Ltd v Cooper* [1941] AC 108, [1941] 1 All ER 33, HL; *Marcan Shipping (London) v Polish Steamship Co* [1989] 2 Lloyd's Rep 138, CA. See also para 16.25 below.
5   Ch 14 above.
6   *Salomons v Pender* (1865) 3 H & C 639.
7   *Keppel v Wheeler* [1927] 1 KB 577, CA.

Indemnity

16.21   An agent who has suffered loss or incurred liabilities in the course of carrying out authorised actions for his principal is entitled to be reimbursed or indemnified by the principal.[1] However, he has no right to reimbursement or an indemnity for losses or liabilities arising because of breaches of duty (eg failing to comply with his instructions) or in carrying out an illegal transaction or a transaction rendered void by statute.[2] In *ex p Mather*,[3] a principal employed an agent to purchase smuggled goods. The agent was not entitled to recover the cost of these goods from the principal, even though the principal had obtained possession of them.

1   *Hooper v Treffry* (1847) 1 Exch 17.
2   *Capp v Topham* (1805) 6 East 392; *Gasson v Cole* (1910) 26 TLR 468.
3   (1797) 3 Ves 373.

Sub-agents

16.22   Even where an agent is authorised to appoint a sub-agent to carry out his instructions, it is presumed that the person appointed is merely an agent of the agent; he does not, in the absence of clear evidence, become an agent of the principal.[1] As a result, the sub-agent has no claim against the principal for remuneration or indemnity, nor does he owe the principal any duty to act or to obey instructions. It has further been held, somewhat controversially, that the sub-agent owes the principal no duty of care in tort, unless he is also a bailee of the principal's goods.[2] Whether the sub-agent owes fiduciary duties to the principal is unclear, for there are conflicting decisions of the Court of Appeal.[3]

1   *Calico Printers' Association Ltd v Barclays Bank* (1931) 145 LT 51.
2   *Balsamo v Medici* [1984] 2 All ER 304, [1984] 1 WLR 951.
3   *Powell and Thomas v Evan Jones & Co* [1905] 1 KB 11, CA; cf *New Zealand and Australian Land Co v Watson* (1881) 7 QBD 374, CA.

Termination of agency

16.23   A contract of agency may be terminated, like any other contract, by agreement,[1] by performance,[2] by breach[3] or by frustration,[4] although it is important to remember that termination of agency between principal and agent need not terminate the agent's ostensible authority (which we discuss in paras 16.32 to 16.36 below). In addition, there are certain special rules applicable to agency, which we now discuss.

1   Paras 6.23–6.26 above.
2   Paras 9.2–9.11 above.
3   Paras 9.12–9.31 above.
4   Ch 10 above.

Act of parties

16.24 A contract of agency will not be specifically enforced, because it is a contract for personal services.[1] As a corollary, either party may terminate the relationship at will. This may amount to a breach of contract, as where the agency was for a fixed period which has not expired, or where a required period of notice has not been given. If so, the innocent party is entitled to damages, but the agency itself is nonetheless determined.[2]

As to whether termination of an agency relationship without notice amounts to a breach of contract, we have already seen that, if an agent accepts a bribe, his contract of agency can be terminated without notice.[3] There are other contracts which on their true construction allow either principal or agent to terminate the agreement without any notice.[4] If an agent is employed on a commission basis, so that he is only entitled to remuneration when he does the act required by the agency agreement (eg sells a house), it would seem that such contracts can be terminated without notice.[5] Agency contracts which resemble contracts of employment, in that the agent is paid merely for being an agent, rather than for facilitating a particular transaction, require notice.[6]

There are some cases where the authority of an agent is irrevocable.[7] Under the Powers of Attorney Act 1971, s 4, a power of attorney expressed to be irrevocable, and given to secure a proprietary interest of the donee of the power, can be revoked neither by the donor of that power without the consent of the donee nor by the death, mental incapacity or bankruptcy of the donor. This is essentially a restatement of the common law rule that, if the agent is given authority by deed, or for valuable consideration, to effect a security or to protect an interest of the agent, that authority is irrevocable while the security or interest subsists.[8] Again, an authority coupled with an interest is not revoked by the death, mental incapacity or bankruptcy of the donor.

1   *Chinnock v Sainsbury* (1860) 30 LJ Ch 409; para 12.29 above.
2   *Page One Records Ltd v Britton* [1967] 3 All ER 822, [1968] 1 WLR 157.
3   Para 16.17b above.
4   *Atkinson v Cotesworth* (1825) 3 B & C 647.
5   *Motion v Michaud* (1892) 8 TLR 253, affd by the Court of Appeal (1892) 8 TLR 447, CA.
6   *Parker v Ibbetson* (1858) 4 CBNS 346. Also see the Commercial Agents (Council Directive) Regulations 1993.
7   See the Enduring Powers of Attorney Act 1985 (para 16.27 below).
8   *Gaussen v Morton* (1830) 10 B & C 731.

16.25 A problem may arise where a principal, without actually revoking his agent's authority, effectively brings the agency to an end, for example by closing down the business to which it relates. In order to recover damages for loss of earnings, the agent must be able to prove that the principal's action amounts to a breach either of an express term of the contract of agency, or of one necessarily implied to give business efficacy.[1] The courts are slow to imply such terms. In *Rhodes v Forwood*,[2] a colliery owner appointed brokers as sole agents for the sale of his coal in Liverpool for seven years or as long as he did business there. After four years the colliery was sold. It was held that the owner had not contracted, either expressly or impliedly, to keep the brokers supplied with coal for sale, and he was therefore not liable for breach of contract. On the other hand, in *Turner v Goldsmith*,[3] a shirt manufacturer expressly agreed to employ a travelling salesman for five years, but his factory was destroyed by fire after only two years. It was held that the manufacturer was not released from his obligation, so that the agent was entitled to damages.

1   Paras 8.26, 8.27 above.
2   (1876) 1 App Cas 256, HL.
3   [1891] 1 QB 544, CA.

Death

16.26   The death of a principal or of an agent determines the agency.[1] An agent's right to remuneration ceases with the death of his principal, as does his right of indemnity.[2] Most importantly, the actual authority of an agent (and, probably, his ostensible authority) ceases on the death of his principal and any transactions entered into thereafter bind the agent, but not the principal's estate, even if the agent does not know of the death.[3]

1   *Blades v Free* (1829) 9 B & C 167; *Friend v Young* [1897] 2 Ch 421.
2   *Farrow v Wilson* (1869) LR 4 CP 744; *Pool v Pool* (1889) 58 LJP 67.
3   *Blades v Free* (1829) 9 B & C 167.

Mental incapacity

16.27   If a principal becomes mentally incapable the agency is terminated, and the agent can presumably claim no commission in relation to transactions entered into after his actual authority is determined. Where the agent has ostensible authority, this survives his principal's mental incapacity, and any contract entered into by him is binding upon the principal, unless the third party knew of the principal's incapacity.[1] Somewhat inconsistently, however, it has also been held that, provided that the third party did not know of the incapacity, the agent can be liable for breach of warranty of authority even if he was unaware of his principal's mental incapacity.[2]

Under the Enduring Powers of Attorney Act 1985, it is now possible for a principal to execute a power of attorney, the authority of which will survive his subsequent mental incapacity.[3] To achieve this effect, various prescribed formalities must be complied with and the agent, on realising that the principal is becoming mentally incapable, must register the power of attorney with the Court of Protection, having first given notice to certain of the principal's relatives.

1   *Drew v Nunn* (1879) 4 QBD 661, CA.
2   *Yonge v Toynbee* [1910] 1 KB 215, CA.
3   For the mental capacity required to execute such a power, see *Re K; Re F* [1988] 1 All ER 358.

Bankruptcy

16.28   The bankruptcy of a principal terminates a contract of agency.[1] On the other hand, the bankruptcy of an agent does not automatically determine the agency, unless it effectively prevents the agent from doing what he was appointed to do.[2]

1   *Elliott v Turquand* (1881) 7 App Cas 79, HL.
2   *McCall v Australian Meat Co Ltd* (1870) 19 WR 188.

Effects of termination

16.29   While the termination of agency cannot deprive the agent of any rights to commission or indemnity which have already accrued,[1] it prevents him from acquiring such rights in the future.[2] Furthermore, an agent who continues to act may become liable to a third party for breach of warranty of authority, even if he is unaware that his actual authority has been determined.[3]

In the absence of ostensible authority, a principal is not usually bound by anything which his agent does after termination of the agency. However, where the agency is created by deed, both an agent and a third party are given statutory protection in respect of transactions effected after termination, provided that they were unaware of this.[4]

1   *Chappell v Bray* (1860) 6 H & N 145.

2   *Farrow v Wilson* (1869) LR 4 CP 744; *Pool v Pool* (1889) 58 LJP 67.
3   *Yonge v Toynbee* [1910] 1 KB 215, CA.
4   Powers of Attorney Act 1971, s 5. See also the Enduring Powers of Attorney Act 1985 (para 16.27 above).

Principal and third parties

16.30   If an agent makes an authorised contract on behalf of his principal, then the principal is deemed to have made the contract. Indeed, if a principal is a disclosed principal, he alone is deemed to have entered into the contract, except in certain limited circumstances.[1] A principal may sue and be sued on authorised contracts made by his agent, and he may be sued for a pre-contractual misrepresentation made by his agent. If a principal is undisclosed then both principal and agent can sue or be sued on the authorised contract. If a contract or other transaction, such as a disposition of property, is not authorised then it does not bind the principal but the agent may incur personal liability in respect thereof. An agent's authority may take various forms.

1   See paras 16.41–16.46 below.

The authority of agents
Actual authority
16.31   An agent who has been expressly appointed may have both express and implied actual authority. An agent appointed by implied agreement has implied actual authority.

Express authority is the authority conferred by the agreement (which is usually a contract) creating agency. Implied authority consists of those terms which will be implied into the contract of agency by applying the usual rules for the implication of terms into contracts.[1] Certain types of implied actual authority are well recognised, for instance incidental and customary authority.

Incidental authority is implied authority to do all subordinate acts incident to and necessary for the execution of the agent's express authority.[2] Thus, incidental authority supplements the express authority of the agent and gives the agent authority to undertake tasks which are incidental to his expressly authorised task. It is a question of fact in every case whether a particular action is incidental to the authorised purpose of the agent.

Customary authority means that an agent operating in a particular market or business has the authority which an agent operating in that market or business usually has.[3] If an agent has a particular position in his principal's business, such as company secretary or foreman, or in his own right, such as stockbroker or auctioneer, he has a type of customary authority commonly called usual authority, which confers on him the authority to undertake any tasks which an agent in that position usually has authority to undertake.[4] In *Panorama Developments Ltd v Fidelis Furnishing Fabrics Ltd*,[5] a company appointed X their company secretary. As such he was an agent of the company, and the company was liable to pay for cars hired by X, even though he used them for his own and not the company's purposes, because hiring cars was within the customary or usual authority of an agent holding the position of company secretary.

It should be noted that, as between principal and agent, express authority is paramount. An agent who disobeys an express instruction cannot avoid liability on the ground that his actions lay within, for example, his usual authority. However, as far as third parties are concerned, they are entitled to assume, until they have notice to the contrary, that the agent has whatever authority would usually be implied in the circumstances.

1   Paras 8.23–8.27 above.

2   *Collen v Gardner* (1856) 21 Beav 540.
3   *Bayliffe v Butterworth* (1847) 1 Exch 425.
4   *Hely-Hutchinson v Brayhead Ltd* [1968] 1 QB 549, [1967] 3 All ER 98; affd on other grounds by the
    Court of Appeal.
5   [1971] 2 QB 711, [1971] 3 All ER 16, CA.

Ostensible authority
16.32   Ostensible authority may result (for the benefit of a third party) in:

*   a person who is not an agent being regarded as an agent of a person for whom he
    acts or appears to act in a particular transaction; or
*   the extension of the authority of an agent.[1]

It does not create a real agency relationship, nor does it extend the actual authority
of the agent in relation to his principal, but merely allows the third party to deal with
someone as if he were an authorised agent. Thus, if a bank promises unequivocally
and without qualification to honour cheques backed by a cheque guarantee card, a
person (even a thief) in possession of both a cheque and a guarantee card has
ostensible authority to bind the bank by forging a signature on the cheque, provided
that a third party had no reason to believe that the signatory was not the genuine
card-holder.[2]

1   The important case of *Freeman and Lockyer v Buckhurst Park Properties (Mangal) Ltd* [1964] 2 QB
    480, [1964] 1 All ER 630, CA, reaffirmed that ostensible authority operates in these two ways.
2   *First Sport Ltd v Barclays Bank plc* [1993] 3 All ER 789, CA.

16.33   Ostensible authority can arise when the alleged principal makes to a third party
a representation of fact, usually by conduct, which the third party relies on, that another
person is authorised to act as his agent.[1] If the third party can show that such was the
case, the principal cannot deny the authority of the person whom he has held out as
being his agent. Thus, a person who permits someone to act on his behalf may find
himself unable to deny that the other person is his agent. Ostensible authority can
operate in a single transaction. For instance, if a person stands by and watches someone
acting for him, he conveys the impression to a third party that the person is authorised
to act for him.[1] However, ostensible authority can also operate in a series of transactions;
if a person has frequently allowed an unauthorised person to act for him, he may be
unable to deny that the person had ostensible authority to act for him in future
transactions of a similar type. For example, if a company allows X to act as managing
director, even though he has not been appointed as such, third parties are entitled to
assume that he is managing director.

If there is a single transaction, the ostensible authority of the agent is to effect that
transaction and no more. That is all the 'principal' has represented to the world that
the agent has authority to undertake. If the 'principal' has allowed a person to act on
his behalf more than once, that person has ostensible authority to effect such
transactions and similar transactions in the future, and may also have ostensible usual
authority. Ostensible usual authority means that where a person is held out as occupying
a particular position, for example managing director, then he will have all the usual
authority that a person would have if properly appointed to that position.[2] If a person
has invested an agent with ostensible authority, it is not necessarily limited to exactly
the same transactions as those from which the ostensible authority arose. In *Swiss Air
Transport Co Ltd v Palmer*,[3] an agent who was held out as having authority to ship
wigs was held to have ostensible authority to arrange the shipment of wigs and other
items over the same route, but not to buy himself an air ticket.

1   See *Egyptian International Foreign Trade Co v Soplex Wholesale Supplies and Refson (PS) & Co* [1985] 2 Lloyd's Rep 36.
2   *Freeman and Lockyer v Buckhurst Park Properties (Mangal) Ltd* [1964] 2 QB 480, [1964] 1 All ER 630, CA.
3   [1976] 2 Lloyd's Rep 604.

16.34   Ostensible authority is of great importance where a principal has restricted or terminated the actual authority of his validly appointed agent. As between principal and agent, the restriction or termination is binding, and the agent will be liable to his principal if he acts without actual authority. However, third parties are not bound by any restriction, provided that they are unaware of the restriction or termination.[1]

Acts within the ostensible authority of an agent bind the principal even if they are entered into for the agent's own purposes or are fraudulent, provided the fraud occurs while the agent is purporting to carry out what he is ostensibly authorised to do.[2]

1   *Trickett v Tomlinson* (1863) 13 CBNS 663.
2   *Lloyd v Grace, Smith & Co* [1912] AC 716, HL.

16.35   Ostensible authority is based on the belief raised in the mind of the third party by the representation of the alleged principal that a particular person is his agent or that a properly appointed agent has authority in excess of his actual authority. It follows that a third party, who knows, or ought to know, that the principal has not invested with authority the person whom he appears to hold out as his agent, cannot rely on the doctrine of ostensible authority – because he cannot say that he was led to believe that that person was the principal's authorised agent.[1]

1   See, for example, *Overbrooke Estates Ltd v Glencombe Properties Ltd* [1974] 3 All ER 511, [1974] 1 WLR 1355; para 14.38 above.

16.36   It must be emphasised that ostensible authority depends upon a representation of fact made by the alleged principal. A statement by the 'agent' that he is authorised to carry out a particular transaction does not in itself give him ostensible authority to do so.[1] However, in exceptional circumstances an agent may have ostensible authority to describe his own authority (eg by assuring the third party that his actions have been approved by head office).[2]

1   *British Bank of the Middle East Ltd v Sun Life Assurance Co of Canada (UK) Ltd* [1983] 2 Lloyd's Rep 9, HL; *Armagas v Mundogas SA* [1986] AC 717, HL.
2   See *First Energy (UK) Ltd v Hungarian International Bank Ltd* [1993] BCLC 1409, [1993] 2 Lloyd's Rep 194, CA.

The disclosed principal

16.37   A disclosed principal is one whose existence, though not necessarily his identity, is known to the third party at the time of contracting. To put it another way, a principal is disclosed wherever the third party is aware that he is dealing with an agent.

If the agent of a disclosed principal makes an authorised contract, the principal can almost invariably sue and be sued upon it.[1] Whether the agent also can sue or be sued on the contract is a question which we discuss in paras 16.41 to 16.46 below.

Contracts made by deed form an exception to the general rule. At common law, the principal could not sue or be sued unless he was named as a party to the deed and it was executed in his name.[2] In equity, the principal could sue on a deed if the agent contracted as trustee for the principal and the agent was made co-plaintiff.[3]

Statute now provides that, if an agent executes a contract made by deed on behalf of the principal, the principal can sue on it,[4] although there is authority to suggest that he must still be named in the deed.[5]

1   *Montgomerie v United Kingdom Mutual SS Association* [1891] 1 QB 370.
2   *Schack v Anthony* (1813) 1 M & S 573.
3   *Harmer v Armstrong* [1934] Ch 65, CA.
4   Powers of Attorney Act 1971, s 7.
5   *Harmer v Armstrong* [1934] Ch 65, CA.

The undisclosed principal

16.38   If the third party is unaware that he is dealing with an agent, the principal is called an undisclosed principal. An undisclosed principal can sue and be sued on authorised contracts entered into on his behalf.[1] The agent can also sue and be sued on such contracts.[2] It may seem odd that the third party can be sued by someone with whom he did not know he was contracting and with whom he may not have wished to contract. To protect the third party certain limitations have been placed on the right of the undisclosed principal to sue.

1   *Scrimshire v Alderton* (1743) 2 Stra 1182; *Thomson v Davenport* (1829) 9 B & C 78.
2   *Saxon v Blake* (1861) 29 Beav 438.

Limitations on the right of the undisclosed principal to sue
16.39   An undisclosed principal cannot sue in the following circumstances:

- where he did not exist or lacked capacity at the time the agent contracted;[1]
- where the contract expressly prohibits the intervention of an undisclosed principal;[2]
- where the contract impliedly excludes the intervention of an undisclosed principal. For example, if the contract 'shows' the agent to be contracting as principal. In *Humble v Hunter*,[3] the agent of an undisclosed principal signed a charterparty as 'owner' of the ship. This contract was found impliedly to regard the agent as owner, and the true owner (the principal) could not sue on the contract. The logic of this decision may be questioned, for it might be said that the agent is 'shown' to be the principal in every case where the principal is undisclosed;[4]
- where the third party can establish that he had some reason for wishing to deal with the agent personally. For example, if the agent was a man of fine reputation and acknowledged skill, and the contract involved reliance on such integrity and skill;[5]
- where the third party would have a defence to an action by the agent. This most commonly arises where the third party has paid the agent what is due under the contract (for example, by setting-off money which the agent owes the third party). However, this only prevents the undisclosed principal from suing where it is his conduct which has enabled the agent to appear to be dealing on his own account;[6]
- where the third party's legal position would be materially worse as a result of the principal's intervention.[7] For example, where two persons became protected tenants of a flat, it was held that evidence could not be brought to show that they had taken the lease as agents for an undisclosed principal (consisting of themselves and a third person), since this would increase the number of people who would be entitled to security of tenure under the Rent Act.[8]

Apart from these cases, an undisclosed principal can intervene on the contract, even where it is clear that the third party would have refused for personal reasons to deal with him, provided that there has been no positive misrepresentation.[9]

1   Para 16.4 above.
2   *United Kingdom Mutual SS Assurance Ltd v Nevill* (1887) 19 QBD 110, CA.
3   (1848) 12 QB 310.
4   See *Siu Yin Kwan v Eastern Insurance Co Ltd* [1994] 1 All ER 213, PC.
5   *Greer v Downs Supply Co* [1927] 2 KB 28, CA.

6   *Cooke v Eshelby* (1887) 12 App Cas 271, HL.
7   *Collins v Associated Greyhound Racecourses Ltd* [1930] 1 Ch 1.
8   *Hanstown Properties Ltd v Green* (1977) 246 Estates Gazette 917, CA.
9   *Dyster v Randall & Sons* [1926] Ch 932.

Election

16.40   Where the third party is in a position to sue either the agent or the principal
(eg where the agent has acted on behalf of an undisclosed principal), the third party
may, if he takes action against one party, be deemed to have elected to pursue that
party exclusively. In such a case, even if the third party fails to obtain satisfaction, he
cannot turn to the other party.[1] 'Election' in this sense may be express or implied. An
implied election will only occur if a third party with full knowledge of all the relevant
facts indicates clearly which party he intends to hold liable on the contract.[2] What
constitutes implied election is a question of fact – beginning legal proceedings,[3]
demanding payment, and debiting an account[4] are all relevant but not conclusive factors.
Where principal and agent are jointly liable, the third party may even obtain judgment
against one of them without forfeiting his right to sue the other.[5]

1   *Paterson v Gandasequi* (1812) 15 East 62.
2   *Thomson v Davenport* (1829) 9 B & C 78; *Chestertons v Barone* [1987] 1 EGLR 15, CA.
3   *Clarkson, Booker Ltd v Andjel* [1964] 2 QB 775, [1964] 3 All ER 260, CA.
4   *Young & Co Ltd v White* (1911) 28 TLR 87.
5   Civil Liability (Contribution) Act 1978, s 3: para 29.15 below.

Agents and third parties

16.41   As we have seen, where an agent makes an authorised contract on behalf of
an undisclosed principal, the agent can sue and be sued upon the contract.[1] Where an
agent makes an authorised contract on behalf of a disclosed principal, the general rule
is that the agent cannot sue or be sued on the contract.[2] However, in certain cases the
agent is liable and entitled on the contract, either alone or jointly with the principal.

1   *Saxon v Blake* (1861) 29 Beav 438.
2   See, for example, *Foalquest Ltd v Roberts* [1990] 1 EGLR 50.

Contracts made by deed
16.42   An agent who enters into a contract made by deed is liable on it, even if he is
known to be contracting as an agent.[1]

1   *Schack v Anthony* (1813) 1 M & S 573.

Trade usage
16.43   If a trade custom, not inconsistent with the contract, makes an agent liable on
a contract the courts will give effect to that custom.[1]

1   *Barrow & Bros v Dyster, Nalder & Co* (1884) 13 QBD 635, DC.

Where the agent is in fact principal
16.44   If an agent contracts on behalf of a non-existent principal then the agent must
be contracting on his own behalf.[1] If someone purports to contract as agent but is in
fact the principal, he can sue and be sued on the contract.[2] But, if X, a purported
agent who is in fact a principal, appears to contract on behalf of a named principal,
he cannot sue or be sued on the contract[3] (though he can be sued for breach of
warranty of authority[4]). The agent can sue if he contracts on his own behalf and the
contract indicates, but does not name, a principal and shows that the identity of the

principal is not relevant.[5] The cases in this area are generally considered to be unsatisfactory.

1   See in relation to unformed companies, the Companies Act 1985, s 36C.
2   *Gardiner v Heading* [1928] 2 KB 284, CA.
3   *Fairlie v Fenton* (1870) LR 5 Exch 169; *Hector v Lyons* (1988) 58 P & CR 156, CA.
4   Para 16.47 below.
5   *Schmaltz v Avery* (1851) 16 QB 655.

Other cases

16.45   Apart from these special cases, an agent may be jointly or solely liable on the contract entered into on behalf of his disclosed principal, if the contract expressly or impliedly reveals this to be the intention of the parties.[1] Under the Partnership Act 1890, s 5, a partner who contracts on behalf of the partnership is jointly liable with the rest of the partners on that contract. In other cases, whether there is an implied intention that an agent shall be jointly or solely liable on the contract is a question of construction.

Particular note is taken of the description of the agent in a written contract and of how the agent signed a written contract. If either the description of the agent in the document or the form of his signature makes it clear that he is acting merely as an agent, he is not usually liable on the contract.[2] If neither the document nor the signature describes him as an agent, he is liable on the contract,[3] even if he is known to be acting as an agent. If the contract is oral and the agent is known to be an agent, the above rules for written contracts do not apply and every case is determined by reference to its particular facts.[4] If an agent is liable on a contract he will probably also have the benefit of that contract, unless, as a matter of construction, the contract reveals that the agent is to be liable without having the benefit of the contract.

1   See, for example, *Savills v Scott* [1988] 1 EGLR 20.
2   *Lucas v Beale* (1851) 10 CB 739. Cf *Punjab National Bank v de Boinville* [1992] 3 All ER 104, CA.
3   *Basma v Weekes* [1950] AC 441, [1950] 2 All ER 146, PC.
4   *N and J Vlassopulos Ltd v Ney Shipping Ltd* [1977] 1 Lloyd's Rep 478, CA.

Rights of third parties against agents
On the contract
16.46   If the agent is jointly or solely liable on the contract, the third party can, subject to the doctrine of election,[1] sue the agent.

1   Para 16.40 above.

For breach of warranty of authority
16.47   If a person acts as agent, knowing that he has no authority, he is liable to the third party for breach of warranty of authority if he has represented to the third party that he had authority.[1] Purporting to act as agent constitutes a representation of authority, unless the third party knew or ought to have known of the lack of authority.[2]

Even if the agent genuinely and reasonably believes he has authority, when he has not, he may be liable to the third party.[3] In *Yonge v Toynbee*,[4] an agent acting on behalf of his principal was held liable for breach of warranty of authority when, entirely unknown to him, his authority had been terminated by the mental incapacity of his principal. The third party can sue even if he has not entered into a contract, provided he has altered his position in reliance on the representation.

If the representation made by the agent is one of law, not fact, he is not liable if it is untrue.[5] An action for breach of warranty cannot lie if the principal ratifies the unauthorised act.

The amount of damages which may be awarded under this head is the amount which would put the third party in the same position as if the representation (of authority) had been true.[6] Therefore, if the third party could have recovered nothing from the principal, even if the agent had had authority (for example because the principal is insolvent), he can recover only nominal damages for breach of warranty of authority.

1   *Collen v Wright* (1857) 8 E & B 647.
2   *Halbot v Lens* [1901] 1 Ch 344.
3   *Penn v Bristol & West Building Society* [1997] 3 All ER 470, CA.
4   *Yonge v Toynbee* [1910] 1 KB 215, CA.
5   *Beattie v Ebury* (1872) 7 Ch App 777, HL.
6   *Richardson v Williamson and Lawson* (1871) LR 6 QB 276; *Suleman v Shahsavari* [1988] 1 WLR 1181.

In tort

16.48   An agent may be liable even if his principal is also vicariously liable. Therefore, an agent may be liable in deceit, or under the rules in *Hedley Byrne & Co Ltd v Heller & Partners Ltd*[1] or, of course, for such actions as knocking down a third party by negligent driving. However, an agent may not be personally liable under the Misrepresentation Act 1967 unless he is a party to the contract which he makes on behalf of his principal.[2]

1   [1964] AC 465, [1963] 2 All ER 575, HL; para 18.28 below.
2   *Resolute Maritime Inc v Nippon Kaiji Kyokai* [1983] 2 All ER 1, [1983] 1 WLR 857; para 14.22 above.

Types of agent

Estate agent

16.49   The primary function of an estate agent is to effect an introduction between persons who wish to buy and sell land. His implied or ostensible authority, and thus the extent to which he can bind his principal, is very restricted. Unless expressly authorised, an estate agent cannot make a binding contract for the sale of his principal's property,[1] accept a pre-contract deposit,[2] or appoint a sub-agent.[3] In fact, his implied authority is limited to the making of statements about the property. If a third party relies on a misrepresentation made to him by an estate agent, the principal cannot enforce the contract[4] and may be liable in damages.[5]

The relationship between an estate agent and his client is a unilateral contract.[6] The agent is under no positive duty to act (except, perhaps, where he is a 'sole agent'[7]) but, if he does act, he must display reasonable care and skill.[8] In order to be entitled to his commission, the estate agent must fulfil precisely the terms of his instructions, which may vary from the mere introduction of a person who is willing to purchase the principal's property to the completion of a sale. The law on this matter is complex, but it may be said that the courts seldom award an estate agent his commission unless there is an actual sale.[9]

1   *Chadburn v Moore* (1892) 61 LJ Ch 674.
2   *Sorrell v Finch* [1977] AC 728, [1976] 2 All ER 371, HL.
3   *John McCann & Co v Pow* [1975] 1 All ER 129. [1974] 1 WLR 1643, CA.
4   *Mullens v Miller* (1882) 22 Ch D 194.
5   *Gosling v Anderson* (1972) 223 Estates Gazette 1743, CA.
6   *Luxor (Eastbourne) Ltd v Cooper* [1941] AC 108, [1941] All ER 33, HL; para 4.2 above.
7   *E Christopher & Co v Essig* [1948] WN 461.
8   *Prebble & Co v West* (1969) 211 Estates Gazette 831, CA.
9   For further discussion, see Murdoch *The Law of Estate Agency and Auctions* (3rd edn, 1994), ch 5.

Auctioneer

16.50   Unlike an estate agent, an auctioneer has implied authority to effect an actual sale of his principal's land or goods,[1] as well as to make statements about the property.[2]

1   *Pickering v Busk* (1812) 15 East 38 at 43.
2   *Smith v Land and House Property Corpn* (1884) 28 Ch D 7, CA.

Mercantile agent or factor

16.51   A mercantile agent or factor is an agent 'having in the customary course of his business as such agent authority either to sell goods, or to consign goods for the purpose of sale, or to buy goods, or to raise money on the security of goods'.[1] Such an agent has ostensible authority to dispose of his principal's goods in the ordinary course of business.

1   Factors Act 1889, s 1.

Commercial agent

16.52   Statutory regulations[1] enacted to give effect to a 1986 EC Directive[2] define a 'commercial agent' as a self-employed intermediary who has continuing authority to negotiate, or to negotiate and conclude, the sale or purchase of goods on behalf of another person (the principal). The regulations lay down the basic rights and obligations of commercial agents and their principals, and provide that these cannot be contracted out of. Particular provision is made as to the circumstances in which a commercial agent becomes entitled to commission from the principal, the period of notice which must be given by either party to terminate their agency relationship and the entitlement of the commercial agent to compensation on such termination.

1   Commercial Agents (Council Directive) Regulations 1993.
2   Council Directive 86/653/EEC.

Part III

The law of tort

Chapter 17

Introduction

Aims and functions of the law of tort

17.1   The main purpose of this chapter is to describe the subject matter of the law of tort and to distinguish it from other fields of legal liability. This is a matter of formal definition. However, a mere definition of a tort gives little or no indication as to *why* certain conduct is treated as wrongful. Because of this, we shall begin with a brief description of the law of tort, in terms of its function within the legal system and within society as a whole.

In this chapter we examine the following issues:

- the main aims of the law of tort in providing a source of compensation for loss suffered, while at the same time seeking to strike a fair balance between the victim and the cause of harm;
- the essential elements of a tort, and how it differs from other kinds of legal liability;
- the various interests which are protected within the law of tort;
- the difficulty of relating the various torts to any general underlying principle;
- the extent to which liability in tort should be and is dependent upon proof of fault on the part of the defendant;
- the alternative sources of financial compensation which exist for injury, damage or loss.

17.2   Wherever people live together, the acts, activities or omissions of one may cause losses of various kinds to another. Compensation for such losses may take a variety of forms; unemployment benefit from the state, sick pay from one's employer, the proceeds of a private insurance policy and so on. Apart from these sources, it is the law of tort which decides whether the primary loss should remain where it has fallen (on the plaintiff) or be transferred to the person who caused it (the defendant). It is important to appreciate that this is all that the law of tort can do; the loss which has occurred cannot be repaired but only allocated. In reaching a decision on this question, the law takes into account both the kind and the severity of the plaintiff's loss, and the defendant's reason for causing it: in short, it is for the law of tort to implement social policy by laying down the circumstances in which the loss *ought* to be transferred from one party to the other.

If a single main function can be ascribed to the law of tort, therefore, it is the provision of *compensation* for loss suffered, within the general confines of attempting to strike a fair balance between plaintiff and defendant. This is not to say, however, that there are no other aims to be fulfilled. The very fact that a defendant is not usually liable unless he is 'at fault' (in the sense of having deliberately or carelessly caused harm to the plaintiff) indicates an element of *punishment* for misconduct. The same principle, by enabling a careful defendant to avoid liability, also has a *deterrent* effect which plays a part in helping to prevent accidents. On a very different note, some parts of the law of tort reflect the preoccupation of former centuries with *preserving the peace*, and encouraging people to settle their disputes in court instead of by acts of private vengeance. This perhaps explains why any form of trespass automatically gives rise to a right of action, whether or not any real damage has been done.

Balance of interests

17.3 Compensation may be described as the keynote of the law of tort. But compensation is not an end in itself (although a surprising number of laymen assume that an injured person will automatically be entitled to recover damages). What the law of tort seeks to achieve is, in truth, a just balance between the many conflicting interests which are inevitably found in any society. These conflicts are sometimes obvious. For example, where the tort of private nuisance is concerned, the courts are asked to reconcile A's right to use his land as he pleases with B's right not to be interfered with in the enjoyment of his own land. Similarly, the tort of defamation seeks to balance C's interest in his reputation with D's freedom of speech.

Other situations commonly dealt with by the law of tort do not raise the question of conflict of interests in quite such an obvious fashion. It might, for example, be thought that the *careless* causing of harm would always be actionable, on the basis that nobody has a legitimate interest in acting unreasonably. However, even here, the familiar balance is in operation; the court may regard the particular interest of the plaintiff which has been infringed as too trivial to merit protection against merely careless invasions. Indeed, to take this to its logical conclusion, certain types of harm are not actionable even when *deliberately* inflicted, for society is simply not prepared to give protection to the interests involved. For example, there is nothing tortious in our opening a supermarket next door to your established but uncompetitive grocer's shop, even if it is our earnest hope that this will quickly put you out of business.

If the balancing approach leads, on occasion, to exemption from liability for those who cause loss carelessly or deliberately, it may equally bring about the imposition of liability upon a defendant who, far from wishing to harm the plaintiff, has in fact taken all reasonable steps to avoid doing so. Suppose, for example, that there is an explosion at a chemical plant (a highly dangerous and highly profitable enterprise) which causes severe damage in the neighbourhood. The law might well say that, provided all due care has been used in running the plant, the victims of the explosions will have no grounds on which to claim damages. But might it not say instead, and with equal justification, that the risk of such losses should lie upon those who run chemical plants for profit, rather than upon those who merely happen to live in their vicinity? If the latter view is taken, then it would be for the law of tort to impose strict liability upon those responsible for operating the plant.

Definition of a tort

17.4 A tort may be defined as the breach of a legal duty owed, independent of contract, by one person to another, for which a common law action for unliquidated damages may be brought. Such a definition is, however, of fairly limited value, since it does not help us to recognise the circumstances in which a legal duty will be imposed. Its major purpose, as we shall see in the next few paragraphs, is the formal one of excluding other types of liability.

If this definition contains one *positive* identifying feature, it is that of the 'common law action for unliquidated damages': unless this particular remedy is available, the defendant's liability (if any) does not lie within the law of tort. However, this is not to say that an action for damages is the only remedy available to a plaintiff in tort, nor even that it is necessarily always the most important. Some torts, such as nuisance, lend themselves readily to control by the grant of an injunction. A person who has been wrongfully dispossessed of land or goods may obtain an order for their return, and a limited amount of self-help (eg ejecting a trespasser) is tolerated by the courts in the interest of avoiding unnecessary litigation. Nonetheless, the possibility of damages on a common law basis must always be there and, further, these must be unliquidated, in the sense of being subject to assessment by the court rather than by prior agreement between the parties.[1]

1   As to liquidated damages, see para 12.19 above.

Tort and crime

17.5   A tort is the breach of a legal duty which is owed by one person to another; a crime, on the other hand, is the breach of a legal duty which is owed to, and enforceable by, society as a whole. Thus, the true distinction between these two fields of law lies, not in their subject matter (for such things as assault, theft and careless driving may be both crimes and torts), but in the purpose of the legal proceedings to which each gives rise. The main object of a criminal prosecution (which is usually instigated by the state) is to vindicate the rights of society against the offender by punishing him. Such compensation as he may be ordered to pay to his victim[1] is an afterthought; the court's attention is focused primarily upon the question of what should be done with the defendant. The usual aim of a tort action, on the other hand, is to secure compensation for harm suffered by an individual plaintiff. It is true that, in very limited circumstances, a court is empowered to punish a defendant by ordering him to pay an extra sum as 'exemplary damages', over and above what is needed to compensate the plaintiff,[2] but this is subsidiary to the main object of the proceedings.

1   Under the Powers of Criminal Courts Act 1973.
2   See para 29.3 below.

Tort and contract

17.6   It is sometimes said that duties in tort are automatically imposed upon a person by law, while contractual duties arise only out of his voluntary acceptance. Both sides of this distinction, however, require some qualification. In the first place, there are many tortious duties which come into effect only as a result of some voluntary act by the defendant (eg permitting another person to enter his land, or offering him some advice). Second, while the existence of a contract depends upon the parties' agreement (although even this may be a question of interpreting their conduct rather than their secret thoughts), much of its content may be decided on by the general law, as in hire-purchase or sales of goods, which we discuss in chapter 8.[1] Thus, any attempt to differentiate between the law of contract and the law of tort in terms of their sources is of little value.

A better distinction, perhaps, lies in the purpose of each field of law. Tort, as we have seen, aims to compensate the plaintiff for harm done to him; it does this by awarding as damages a sum which will, as far as possible, restore him to his original position. In actions for breach of contract, by contrast, the plaintiff's basic complaint is that he has not received some benefit which he was promised, and damages are generally designed to fulfil the plaintiff's expectation, by putting him into the position in which he would have been had the contract been performed.[2]

Theory apart, there are some significant practical distinctions between a breach of contract and a tort, with regard to such matters as the liability of minors, the awarding of exemplary damages (available in tort alone) and claims against bankrupt defendants. Most important, the rules as to limitation of actions are different. The time within which a plaintiff must serve his writ (or automatically lose his case) generally runs, in contract, from the date of the breach, while in tort the relevant date is usually that on which damage is suffered.[3]

It sometimes happens that a defendant's conduct is capable of constituting both a tort and a breach of contract. For instance, a taxi driver who drives negligently and thereby injures his passenger is guilty of both a breach of contract (an implied term that he will convey the passenger with due skill and care) and the tort of negligence, as well as of a criminal offence. In such circumstances, the law allows a plaintiff to frame his case in whatever way he chooses (usually in tort, so as to gain the advantage of more generous limitation rules).[4]

1   Paras 8.19–8.21 above.
2   Para 12.3 above.
3   Paras 12.36–12.39 above, and 29.22–29.24 below.
4   *Henderson v Merrett Syndicates Ltd* [1994] 3 All ER 506, HL; see para 18.24 below.

Tort and restitution

17.7   In some circumstances, a person who has been unjustly enriched at the expense of another may be compelled by law to make restitution. For instance, if A pays money to B under certain mistakes of fact, B may be ordered to return it. This area of law falls outside the definition of a tort because A is not claiming unliquidated damages; nor, indeed, can it meaningfully be said that B has broken any legal duty in merely receiving the money.

Tort and breach of trust

17.8   The obligations which a trustee owes to a beneficiary arise out of the trust relationship and may, if broken, lead to an award of damages. The whole matter, however (including the principles on which these damages are assessed) is governed by equity, rather than by common law, and the administration of trusts is today a function of the Chancery Division of the High Court; tort, by contrast, is normally regarded as within the province of the Queen's Bench Division.[1]

1   Paras 2.15–2.18 above.

Scope of the law of tort

Interests protected

17.9   The kinds of harm which come within the law of tort are extremely diverse and, since the interests of the plaintiff which may be infringed vary greatly in importance, so does the degree of protection which the law affords them. Thus, for example, an interest which is regarded as relatively trivial may be protected only against intentional invasions, whereas more important interests may give rise to actions against a defendant whose conduct is merely negligent or even accidental.

The most important interest to be recognised by any legal system is that of personal security which, broadly speaking, involves freedom from both physical injury[1] and wrongful deprivation of liberty. This particular interest also finds expression in other less obvious ways, such as the protection of a person's reputation and of certain status-based rights, eg the right to vote. Of rather less importance, though still well protected, are interests in the ownership and possession of land and goods.

As a general rule, since no person has a proprietary interest in another person, A is not allowed to sue in respect of an injury to B. However, an important statutory exception to this principle permits the dependants of a deceased person to sue the person responsible for his death for the loss of their breadwinner.[2]

It takes a fairly sophisticated legal system to recognise the possibility of compensating a plaintiff for those effects of the defendant's conduct which are purely financial. Even where protection is given to such economic interests (eg by the torts of conspiracy, intimidation and interference with contract) it is usually limited to cases where the defendant's conduct is deliberate. By and large, as we shall see, the causing of financial loss through mere carelessness is not actionable.[3]

1 Including psychiatric damage; para 18.38 below.
2 Fatal Accidents Act 1976; see para 29.12 below.
3 Paras 18.18–18.22 below.

The relevance of damage

17.10 Unless the plaintiff suffers an invasion of a recognised interest, he cannot claim compensation for his losses under the law of tort. There is, for example, no right of privacy as such; consequently, a person who wishes to protect himself against unwanted intrusions must, in order to succeed, show that the defendant has committed some recognised tort such as trespass or nuisance. Similarly, while injury to the plaintiff's feelings may aggravate the damages to which he is entitled in respect of a known tort, as where the defendant trespasses on the plaintiff's land in order to hurl abuse at him, it is not of itself an interest which the law will protect.

Examples of loss falling outside the scope of the law of tort are not difficult to find. In *Day v Brownrigg*,[1] the defendant, wishing to spite the plaintiff, his next-door neighbour, changed the name of his house to match that of the plaintiff's. It was held that, since there was no interference with any trading interest of the plaintiff, this conduct was not actionable. In *Bradford Corpn v Pickles*,[2] the defendant, irritated by the plaintiff's refusal to buy his land, excavated in such a way that water which would otherwise have percolated into the plaintiff's reservoir instead collected on the defendant's property. The House of Lords held that, since the defendant was absolutely entitled to this water (unlike water flowing in a defined channel), the plaintiffs could not complain when he intercepted it. Finally, in *Perera v Vandiyar*,[3] a landlord harassed his tenant by cutting off the supply of gas and electricity to the flat. This was undoubtedly a breach of contract, but it was held by the Court of Appeal that, since the landlord did not actually enter the premises, he was not guilty of any tort.[4]

The other side of the coin consists of circumstances in which the defendant's conduct may be actionable as a tort, notwithstanding that it has caused no actual damage to the plaintiff. The torts which come within this principle are said to be actionable per se; they are trespass in all its forms and libel (but not usually slander). The reasons for treating these torts differently and imposing liability are purely historical.

1 (1878) 10 Ch D 294.
2 [1895] AC 587, HL.
3 [1953] 1 All ER 1109, [1953] 1 WLR 672, CA.
4 A tort claim may now arise in such circumstances, under the Housing Act 1988, s 27.

General principle of liability

Tort or torts?

17.11   An argument on which much has been written over the years is whether the whole field of tortious liability rests upon any general principle, or whether it consists simply of a random collection of civil wrongs, each with its own elements of liability. The dispute may be summed up by asking whether there is a 'law of tort' or merely a 'law of torts', and the fact that among the leading textbooks both titles are to be found indicates that there is something at least to be said for both approaches.

The law of tort theory suggests that the law will presume any causing of injury or damage to be actionable, unless there is some legal justification for it. This, of course, provokes the obvious criticism that it gives no indication as to what is a sufficient justification. However, there are signs that modern courts do adopt this approach, albeit in a somewhat modified form; it is probably true to say that, where a defendant intentionally or negligently inflicts physical damage on the plaintiff or his possessions, he can expect to be liable unless there is some good reason (eg self-defence) for his action.

The law of torts theory, which compels every plaintiff to find an appropriate pigeonhole for his complaint, is perhaps attractive if the law is considered at any given moment, without any reference to its past or future development. In its extreme form, however, it fails to allow for what undoubtedly occurs, namely the creation by judges from time to time of new torts. Outstanding among these are *Lumley v Gye*,[1] in which the courts for the first time recognised that, if A induces B to break his contract with C, an action *in tort* will lie against A, and *Rylands v Fletcher*,[2] where liability even in the absence of negligence was imposed upon a landowner for the escape of dangerous objects from his property. In more recent times, the rapid development of the tort of negligence is far better explained as the coherent exposition of a general principle than as the arbitrary creation of new pigeonholes.

The law of tort theory may have some merits, but these should not be over-stressed; the very existence of different torts, each with its own elements of liability, serves to indicate that no simple principle can be found to underlie the whole field of law. Nor is this surprising; as we have already seen, the function of the law of tort is to resolve the conflicts of interest which necessarily arise between members of society and, since these interests may vary greatly in importance, so the appropriate balance to be struck between them will alter. Any attempt to reduce to a single sentence all the policy factors which may play a part in judicial decisions would result in a proposition so generalised as to be practically meaningless.

1   (1853) 2 E & B 216.
2   (1866) LR 1 Ex Ch 265.

Mental element

17.12   A major obstacle in the way of any attempt to deduce a general principle of liability from the law of tort is the fact that different torts depend upon different mental elements on the part of the defendant. Three levels are involved. In the first place, some torts (such as assault, false imprisonment and deceit) depend upon proof of intention, that is to say that the defendant was aware of the likely consequences of his act and in fact desired those consequences. It is of course impossible to be absolutely certain of what a person wants but this, like so much else, can be proved to the satisfaction of a court by evidence as to what he says and does. Further, for the purposes of the law of tort 'recklessness' is equivalent to intention. This covers cases where the defendant is well aware of the risks inherent in what he is doing and those where, while not actually wanting to injure the plaintiff, he is totally indifferent to the possibility that he will do so.

The second mental element which may be relevant to the law of tort is negligence, which normally signifies a blameworthy failure to appreciate and guard against the likely consequences of one's acts or omissions.[1] This concept, which today governs liability in the great majority of cases, involves testing the defendant's conduct against the objective yardstick of the hypothetical reasonable man; if it falls short of that standard, the defendant is liable, whatever his subjective state of mind.

Third, certain torts are based upon what is termed strict liability. This means that a defendant is liable for the consequences of his actions, even though he neither desired nor ought reasonably to have foreseen and avoided them. Naturally, the law requires fairly strong reasons for imposing this type of liability; these may lie in the importance of the plaintiff's interest which is to be protected, the inherently risky nature of the defendant's activity or (in modern times) perhaps the ease with which the defendant may absorb the loss (eg by insuring against it and passing on the cost to his customers). This kind of liability includes the rule in *Rylands v Fletcher*,[2] liability for animals[3] and breach of statutory duty;[4] the vicarious liability of an employer for torts committed by his employees is also strict.[5]

1   Ch 19 below.
2   Paras 26.2–26.13 below.
3   Ch 27 below.
4   Ch 23 below.
5   Paras 28.4–28.16 below.

Motive

17.13 'Intention' signifies a person's desire for certain consequences; his 'motive', on the other hand, tells us why he wants them to occur. Broadly speaking, the law of torts is not concerned with motive; it asks only what the defendant has done, not why. Occasionally, however, a good motive will excuse acts which would otherwise be unlawful. This is of particular relevance in relation to torts such as conspiracy and inducement to break a contract, which protect the plaintiff's economic interests.

As a general rule, a bad motive is no more relevant than a good one; if A is exercising a legal right, the law does not enquire why he chooses to do so. This principle, which helps to explain the case of *Bradford Corpn v Pickles*,[1] was also applied by a majority of the Court of Appeal in *Chapman v Honig*.[2] The defendant in that case was a landlord who, incensed that the plaintiff, his tenant, had given evidence against him on behalf of another tenant, served the plaintiff with a valid notice to quit. This, it was held, could not be regarded as wrongful, even though the defendant had clearly acted out of spite.

It is important to appreciate that bad motives are ignored only where the defendant is exercising an absolute legal right. In other cases, where his rights are qualified or limited, a bad motive may be the factor which tips his conduct over the line into what is unlawful. The tort of nuisance, for instance, permits a landowner to make some noise on his own land, provided that the interference which is thereby caused to his neighbours is not unreasonable; in deciding what noise level is acceptable, it is legitimate to ask why the noise is being made. In *Hollywood Silver Fox Farm Ltd v Emmett*,[3] the defendant fired guns near where his land adjoined that of the plaintiffs, frightening the plaintiff's silver foxes and ruining their breeding season. A landowner is of course usually entitled to shoot over his own land; here, however, the defendant's actions were motivated by malice, and he was therefore held liable in nuisance.

1   [1895] AC 587, HL; para 17.10 above.
2   [1963] 2 QB 502, [1963] 2 All ER 513, CA.
3   [1936] 2 KB 468, [1936] 1 All ER 825.

Fault liability

17.14   Although, as we have said, it is impossible to reduce the law of tort to a single principle, one particular idea has, over the last century, come to occupy a dominant position. This is the notion that a person's liability should be related to his 'fault', in the sense of intentional or negligent causing of harm. This principle, and its important corollary, that a person should not be liable *unless* he is at fault, became prominent at the time of the Industrial Revolution, when its moral appeal coincided with important vested interests. The vast increase in both traffic and industrial activity which occurred at this time were bound to lead to more accidents and, if liability for these were strict, development would thereby be retarded. Accordingly, 'no liability without fault' became the popular cry, and casualties were regarded merely as an unfortunate but inevitable price of progress.

Today, 'fault' is established as the major, though not the only, criterion of liability in the law of tort. However, at least where personal injuries are concerned, the requirement for a victim to prove fault has not passed without criticism. We now examine briefly the main arguments for and against fault liability in this context.

Arguments for fault liability
17.15   Apart from the rather cynical view described above, that strict liability is undesirable because it impedes industrial progress, attempts to justify fault liability are usually based upon the moral argument that a wrongdoer should pay for the consequences of his misconduct. There is no doubt that ideas of personal responsibility and justice strike a strong chord with the public in general although, as we shall see, damages in practice are not paid from the funds of the individual defendant in all, or even most, tort cases.

One aspect of the personal responsibility argument is the notion that making a person responsible for his fault has a valuable deterrent effect; if the defendant knows that by taking care he can avoid liability, he is more likely to do so than if he would be strictly liable in any case. Thus, the argument goes, the punitive effect of an award of damages operates as a useful means of moulding people's conduct in areas where accidents are likely to occur.

The twin goals of fairness and deterrence might seem of overwhelming importance in assessing the value of fault liability. In practice, however, it is extremely doubtful whether the operation of the law in its present form comes near to achieving either aim. One reason for this is that, since the vast majority of tort cases arise out of accidents on the roads or at work, it is only rarely that the person who is actually at fault will have to meet the damages awarded out of his own pocket. If he drives a car negligently, his liability in tort for causing death or personal injury (or property damage up to £250,000) is required by law to be covered by insurance. If he causes damage in the course of his employment, the doctrine of vicarious liability enables the plaintiff to claim directly against the tortfeasor's employer (who will frequently be insured against this very contingency). If, then, the actual tortfeasor does not have to pay, how is he deterred? And, in any case, why should the plaintiff's ability to obtain compensation from an insurance company depend upon whether or not the defendant (a third party) is 'at fault'?

The effectiveness of this so-called deterrent may be further questioned upon other grounds. First, since damages are assessed on the basis of the plaintiff's loss, rather than the seriousness of the defendant's conduct, it may be objected that the 'punishment' does not fit the 'crime'. Second, the idea of fault itself bears an unreal air, for the courts, well aware of any insurance fund standing behind the defendant, are more likely to convict him of negligence in order to secure compensation for the plaintiff. This is done by demanding from the 'reasonable man' a standard of conduct so high that the defendant may well fail to achieve it even whether no moral blame attaches to him. Indeed, this distortion of the meaning of fault is accentuated by the courts' refusal to take account of the fact that a defendant is accident-prone, notwithstanding that the existence of such a condition is medically well established. The question which this raises is whether, if a defendant is genuinely prone to accidents, it is likely that civil liability will deter him? For that matter, can it even be said that such a person is, in any meaningful sense, at fault?

Criticisms of fault liability

17.16   If the main argument in favour of fault liability, that it does justice as between plaintiff and defendant, can thus be exposed as fallacious, then the whole concept falls to be judged simply as a method of compensating the victims of accidents. As such, it is susceptible to a number of severe criticisms. In the first place, it is estimated that the cost of administering the system (legal fees, the whole apparatus of insurance and so on) is greater than the compensation actually paid out; that is to say that, out of every pound paid by motorists for liability insurance, for example, only some 45p reaches accident victims as compensation. By comparison, a system of direct benefits, such as social security, has an administrative cost of approximately 10% of its turnover.

If fault liability is expensive, it is also highly inefficient, in that it depends upon a detailed investigation of facts (either by lawyers or by insurers), which usually takes place long after the event. Human memory being what it is, researchers have suggested that one out of every two tort cases is decided on 'facts' which never actually occurred. If this is true, it deprives 'fault' of much of its meaning.

In social terms, perhaps the most telling criticism of fault liability is that it leaves totally uncompensated those accident victims who are unable to make out a case in tort. Where it is genuinely a question of whether or not an individual defendant shall pay an individual plaintiff, this is of course perfectly reasonable. As we have said, however, this is seldom the case today, and it can be strongly argued therefore that fault liability merely serves to create an artificial and arbitrary distinction between two classes of victim. After all, a pedestrian who is run over suffers exactly the same injuries whether or not the driver took reasonable care to avoid him. It might therefore seem somewhat capricious, at least when one considers accidents as a whole, that the pedestrian's ability to obtain compensation from the driver's insurance company should depend upon such an elusive and unreliable concept as 'fault'.

Tort in context

Other compensation systems

17.17   This part of the book is concerned with the law of tort, rather than with compensation as a whole. Nevertheless, the role of tort cannot be fully understood without at least a mention of other actual or potential methods of compensation for losses of various kinds. In this connection it should be noted that liability insurance, such as is carried by all drivers of motor vehicles, is not an alternative compensation system, but simply a method of ensuring that tort damages, once awarded, are actually paid; a plaintiff's recovery of compensation by this route depends upon his ability to make out a case in tort against the defendant.

Apart from the law of tort, there are two obvious sources of monetary compensation. In the first place, almost any kind of potential damage, from death to loss of business through bad weather, may be the subject of private (loss) insurance. Such insurance policies may be taken out privately by individuals, but they are often found (in the guise of sick pay or disablement benefits) as part of the benefits offered to an employee under his contract of employment.

The second major source of compensation is the social security system; this contains a large number of different benefits, most of which are designed to cover the financial consequences of accident or disease. The system is extremely complex and is constantly under review. However, an important general point is that injuries (including certain diseases) contracted at work are more generously compensated than the rest, which are simply dealt with in the same way as sickness.

A mixed system in operation

17.18   Of the compensation which is paid in the United Kingdom in respect of accidents causing personal injury or death, approximately one-half comes from the social security system, one-quarter from private insurance and one-quarter from the law of tort. Interestingly, however, the tort damages are shared among a mere 6% of accident victims, which means that these victims are a privileged minority. The discrepancy arises because tort, unlike social security, places no fixed monetary ceiling on awards, and also because tort damages on a generous scale may be awarded for such non-financial losses as pain and suffering. The favoured position of tort victims is accentuated by the fact that, broadly speaking, their damages are not reduced to take account of any private insurance benefits (except occupational sick pay) which accrue to them as a result of their injuries; some reduction in damages is made on account of social security benefits, but the overall position is nonetheless that, in financial terms at least, the victim of a tort may receive far more than he has lost.

In most people's scale of values, property damage ranks well below personal injury, and the case of the uncompensated victim is not regarded as such a pressing social problem. This has two practical consequences: little or no state aid is available to those whose goods or land are damaged, and liability insurance in respect of causing such loss is in general not compulsory.[1] It might be thought that these factors would render the law of tort vitally important in this area; in fact, however, its significance is greatly reduced by the widespread use of private loss insurance, such as 'comprehensive' motor cover and 'house and contents' policies, and by the fact that many liability insurance policies in fact cover property damage.

1   It is now compulsory for the user of a motor vehicle to be insured against liability of up to £250,000 for damage to property (including that belonging to his passengers): Road Traffic Act 1988, s 145.

Chapter 18

Negligence – duty of care

18.1 Negligence is by far the most important ground of liability in tort. Indeed, the idea that careless conduct should in itself be a ground of legal liability seems today almost self-evident. Surprisingly, however, the emergence of negligence as a tort in its own right is a comparatively recent development; it is only in the last 150 years or so that the attention of the law has been focussed upon the *standard* of a defendant's conduct rather than its *type*, and attempts to deduce general principles in this area are largely confined to an even shorter period, namely the last 60 or so years.

Many dictionary definitions of negligence concentrate on 'lack of proper care and attention' or 'carelessness', thus stressing the mental element involved. As we shall see, however, the law of tort is concerned with negligence *as conduct*. A person is considered to be negligent whenever his conduct falls below the standard which is set by the law, usually that of the 'reasonable man'. Thus a person may be held guilty of negligence in circumstances where he personally could not possibly have avoided causing the damage in question, for example, because he was not sufficiently intelligent to appreciate the risks inherent in his conduct, or because he could not afford to take the necessary steps to avert the danger. In this sense of conduct which is not up to the required standard, negligence may be either a tort in itself or an element in various other torts, such as trespass or nuisance, which do not require a plaintiff to establish that the defendant positively intended to cause him harm.

18.2 As an independent tort, negligence may be defined as the breach of a legal duty to take care, owed by the defendant to the plaintiff, which results in damage to the plaintiff. There are thus three elements of liability, each of which must be proved by the plaintiff if his action is to succeed:

- a duty of care owed by the defendant to the plaintiff;
- breach by the defendant of his duty;
- damage to the plaintiff which is caused by the defendant's breach.

At first sight, this definition appears almost limitless in scope, at least in comparison with other torts, which tend to be restricted to a particular factual situation, such as *Rylands v Fletcher*,[1] or to protect only one interest of the plaintiff, such as defamation, which protects his reputation. However, the law does not suggest that a person should always and in all circumstances be liable for all the consequences of his carelessness;

such a burden would, it is thought, be an intolerably heavy one. The problem, therefore, is one of exclusion, and two of the elements of liability mentioned above are used by the courts to keep the tort of negligence within reasonable bounds. In the first place, however careless a defendant may have been, he is not legally liable to the plaintiff unless he owed him a legal duty to be careful. Second, even where the defendant is in breach of a duty of care, certain of the consequences of his breach are regarded by the courts as too remote to be actionable in law.[2]

1   Paras 26.2–26.13 below
2   Remoteness of damage is dealt with in ch 20 below.

18.3   In this chapter we examine the following issues:

- the principles used by the courts in deciding whether a particular situation gives rise to a duty of care;
- the extent to which the law imposes liability on one person for failing to protect another, for example against harm deliberately caused by a third party;
- the reluctance of the courts to permit a claim in respect of losses which are purely financial;
- the way in which liability in the tort of negligence may be shaped by the existence of a contract;
- the extent to which liability for negligent words is different from liability for negligent acts;
- the problems involved in claims against a public authority for negligence in the exercise of its statutory powers;
- the extent to which judges, arbitrators, advocates and others are immune from liability in negligence;
- the extent to which damages may be claimed for injuries which are purely psychological.

Duty of care

18.4   We have already noted that a defendant is liable, not for all his careless conduct, but only for that which occurs when the defendant is under a duty to take care. This emphasis on the idea of duty may be best understood from a historical perspective. Most legal systems find it easier to prohibit persons from causing harm than to make them take positive steps to prevent it from occurring. In its early days, the common law had quite enough to contend with in the field of intentional wrongdoing; its excursions into areas of unintended harm concerned mainly the subject matter of existing torts, such as trespass or nuisance. Later, when the law began to create positive obligations to take care, it did so in the context of certain easily recognisable relationships, whose common feature was that one party reasonably relied on the other to exercise the care and skill appropriate to his trade or profession. In this way liability for negligence was imposed upon the 'common callings' such as innkeepers, surgeons and attorneys, all of whom were said to owe a duty of care to those with whom they dealt in the way of their business or profession.

At about the time of the Industrial Revolution, the scope of negligence as a basis of legal liability increased dramatically, and it spread into areas where the relationship between the parties was far more tenuous than in the case of the common callings, for example between one highway user and another. No doubt there was a general underlying feeling that a person *ought* to be liable simply because he unreasonably caused harm to another; the language of the law, however, continued to be that of 'duty'.

A plaintiff who wished to sue in negligence was required either to show that his case fell within an existing category of duty, or to persuade the court that a new duty should be recognised to cover it. As a result, it has been said, this area of law was built up in disconnected slabs, as new duties were created to cover more situations.

A general principle

Donoghue v Stevenson

18.5 The requirement of a duty of care served a very useful practical purpose in the formative period of negligence as a tort, for it enabled the courts to exclude certain classes of plaintiff who were regarded as lacking merit, such as trespassers, and certain types of injury which were not thought important enough to deserve protection, such as losses which were purely financial. Conceptually, however, it was unsatisfactory, since there appeared to be no general principle underlying a judge's decision as to whether or not a duty of care existed. An attempt to deduce such a general principle was eventually made in 1932 in the leading case of *Donoghue v Stevenson*.[1] The facts of that case were that the appellant was treated by a friend, in a café, to a bottle of ginger beer manufactured by the respondents. Having poured out and drunk part of the contents, the appellant discovered that the bottle contained a partially decomposed snail; this discovery, she claimed, caused her severe nervous shock and, later, an attack of gastro-enteritis. Since the appellant had no contract with the proprietor of the café, she sued the manufacturers of the ginger beer, who argued that their duty in respect of products was owed only to those to whom they sold them. In rejecting this argument, a majority of the House of Lords laid down that, in normal circumstances, a manufacturer owes a duty of care to the ultimate consumer of his products, notwithstanding the absence of any contractual relationship between them. In short, whatever else it may have done, *Donoghue v Stevenson* undoubtedly added a new duty to the existing list.

1   [1932] AC 562, HL.

18.6 The main importance of *Donoghue v Stevenson* for present purposes, however, lies in the speech of Lord Atkin, in which an attempt was made to formulate a general test for ascertaining whether or not a relationship is sufficient to found a duty of care. Having pointed out that 'the rule that you are to love your neighbour becomes, in law, you must not injure your neighbour', Lord Atkin went on to consider the question of duty in these terms: 'Who, then, in law is my neighbour? The answer seems to be – persons who are so closely and directly affected by my act that I ought reasonably to have them in contemplation as being so affected when I am directing my mind to the acts or omissions which are called in question.'

If taken at face value, this approach would impose a duty of care upon a defendant whenever he ought reasonably to have foreseen injury, loss or damage to the plaintiff. This is manifestly not the real position for, as was recognised by Lord Reid in *Home Office v Dorset Yacht Co Ltd*,[1] there are a number of areas in which the question whether or not there is a duty depends, not upon some purely mechanical test, but upon wider considerations of public policy. Nonetheless, foreseeability is always relevant in an exclusionary sense for, if it is not foreseeable to the defendant that the plaintiff may suffer damage, then no considerations of policy can justify a court in imposing a duty of care upon him. Thus in *Bourhill v Young*,[2] where a motor cyclist carelessly collided with a car and was killed, an action by a woman who suffered nervous shock as a result of hearing the crash failed, since it was not foreseeable that she would suffer injury of any kind, either by impact or through shock alone. Similarly, in *Hewett v Alf Brown's Transport*,[3] where a worker's clothing became coated with lead oxide powder, his employers were held not liable to his wife, since it was not foreseeable that she would contract lead poisoning from washing the clothes.

Apart from its relevance in this exclusionary sense, the foreseeability principle referred to by Lord Atkin has a wider part to play in determining whether or not a duty of care exists, as we now explain.

1   [1970] AC 1004 at 1027, [1970] 2 All ER 294 at 297.
2   [1943] AC 92, [1942] 2 All ER 396, HL.
3   [1992] ICR 530, CA.

Anns v Merton London Borough Council

18.7   An important and, for a time, very influential judicial analysis of the duty of care question was carried out by Lord Wilberforce in *Anns v Merton London Borough Council*.[1] In his speech in this case, the learned judge made it clear that there was no closed list of duty-situations, so that the success of a plaintiff's action would not necessarily depend upon proof that it fell within the facts of a previous case. The task of the judge faced with a novel type of claim had instead to be tackled in two stages. 'First one has to ask whether, as between the alleged wrongdoer and the person who has suffered damage there is a sufficient relationship of proximity or neighbourhood such that, in the reasonable contemplation of the former, carelessness on his part may be likely to cause damage to the latter, in which case a prima facie duty of care arises. Second, if the first question is answered affirmatively, it is necessary to consider whether there are any considerations which ought to negative, or to reduce or limit the scope of the duty or the class of persons to whom it is owed or the damages to which a breach of it may give rise.'

1   [1978] AC 728 at 751, [1977] 2 All ER 492 at 498.

A period of expansion

18.8   For a few years after the decision in *Anns*, the two-stage approach suggested by Lord Wilberforce was the conventional tool of analysis for trial judges faced with arguments about the duty of care. The result was undoubtedly to enlarge the scope of the tort of negligence, as legal duties were claimed and recognised in a number of novel circumstances. Nor was this enlargement surprising, since the courts tended to emphasise the first stage of Lord Wilberforce's test rather than the second. After all, once it was shown that a defendant ought to have foreseen some injury to the plaintiff (the first stage), it would naturally be difficult to convince a court that policy considerations justified not imposing a duty of care upon the defendant (the second stage).

The pendulum swings

18.9   Following this expansive period in the law of negligence, a quite remarkable change of direction took place in decisions on the scope of the duty of care. With hindsight, this sudden about-turn can be traced to the decision of the House of Lords in *Peabody Donation Fund Governors v Sir Lindsay Parkinson & Co Ltd*.[1] It was there held that, while a local authority building inspector might owe a duty of care to future owners or occupiers of the premises which he was inspecting,[2] he most certainly did not owe any duty to the property developer concerned to see that the latter did not suffer financial loss as a result of being allowed to build in a way which contravened the building regulations. That the developer might suffer loss in such circumstances was undoubtedly foreseeable; but to impose a duty on the local authority to prevent it would not be 'just and reasonable'.

1   [1985] AC 210, [1984] 3 All ER 529, HL.

2   As established in *Anns v Merton London Borough Council* [1978] AC 728, [1977] 2 All ER 492, HL.

18.10   Lord Keith in *Peabody* strongly criticised the two-stage approach laid down in *Anns v Merton London Borough Council*, mainly because he felt that it might lead a judge to fail to 'have regard to, and to analyse and weigh, all the relevant considerations in considering whether it is appropriate that a duty of care should be imposed'. His lordship was especially concerned that such considerations should be given equal weight with questions of foreseeability, and should not be relegated to the status of possible 'excuses' at the second stage of the enquiry. Such misgivings about the *Anns* test were echoed on numerous occasions in both the Court of Appeal and the House of Lords, notably by Lord Bridge in *Curran v Northern Ireland Co-ownership Housing Association Ltd*[1] and by Lord Brandon in *Leigh & Sillivan Ltd v Aliakmon Shipping Co Ltd*.[2] The latter speech is of particular importance, since Lord Brandon suggested strongly that Lord Wilberforce had never intended the *Anns* test to be used as a means of overturning established legal principles, but only as a guide in wholly novel circumstances. This remark, more than any other, exemplifies the restrictive attitude which the courts have consistently shown since the *Peabody* case was decided.

1   [1987] 2 All ER 13, HL.
2   [1986] 2 All ER 145 at 153.

The current position
18.11   The duty of care issue has been debated by both the House of Lords and the Court of Appeal on numerous occasions in the past few years.[1] Not surprisingly, judges have expressed a range of opinions as to the current state of the law. The most extreme view is that the situations in which a duty of care exists cannot be explained by reference to any general principle at all, and that the question which a judge should ask, when faced with a novel type of claim, is simply whether it is sufficiently similar to a situation in which a duty of care has previously been held to exist. In this way, it is said, the law can expand 'incrementally and by analogy with established categories of liability'.

If correct, this view would effectively return the law to its position prior to *Donoghue v Stevenson*.[2] However, we believe that it is not correct, and that in truth there remains a general principle, albeit one which is vague and flexible. This principle is that a duty of care in tort will be recognised where:

•   it is foreseeable to the defendant that negligence on his part will cause injury, damage or loss to the plaintiff; and
•   there is a relationship of sufficient 'proximity' between the parties; and
•   it would be 'just and reasonable' to impose liability.

This three-fold test has been adopted and applied by the courts in a wide range of recent cases, dealing for example with negligent statements,[3] the causing of nervous shock,[4] the responsibilities of public authorities[5] and the liability of builders.[6] Moreover, despite suggestions that 'foreseeability' in itself is sufficient to found a duty of care in cases of physical damage,[7] it appears that the threefold test is equally applicable to such cases.[8]

1   The most important House of Lords discussions are found in *Caparo Industries plc v Dickman* [1990] 2 AC 605, [1990] 1 All ER 568, HL, *Murphy v Brentwood District Council* [1990] 2 All ER 908, HL and *Alcock v Chief Constable of the South Yorkshire Police* [1991] 4 All ER 907, HL.
2   [1932] AC 562, HL.
3   *Smith v Eric S Bush; Harris v Wyre Forest DC* [1990] 1 AC 831, [1989] 2 All ER 514, HL; *Caparo Industries plc v Dickman* [1990] 2 AC 605, [1990] 1 All ER 568, HL.
4   *Alcock v Chief Constable of the South Yorkshire Police* [1992] 1 AC 310, [1991] 4 All ER 907, HL.
5   *Hill v Chief Constable of West Yorkshire* [1989] AC 53, [1988] 2 All ER 238, HL.

6   _Murphy v Brentwood District Council_ [1991] 1 AC 398, [1990] 2 All ER 908, HL.
7   See _Caparo Industries plc v Dickman_ [1990] 1 All ER 568 at 585.
8   _Marc Rich & Co AG v Bishop Rock Marine Co Ltd_ [1995] 3 All ER 307, HL.

18.12   In considering the three-fold test described above, it is important to understand that it cannot be, and is not intended to be, applied in a mechanical way. Even the element of 'foreseeability', which might appear to be a question of fact, involves a judge in evaluating what a reasonable person could be expected to foresee. As for 'proximity' and 'justice and reasonableness', the courts themselves have emphasised that these are not capable of precise definition, but are merely convenient labels used to describe the features of a particular situation which call for the imposition of a duty of care.[1] In effect, it appears that a court uses these labels to justify a decision which it has reached on pragmatic, even instinctive, grounds.

In the remainder of this chapter we consider a number of areas in which the existence or scope of a duty of care is subject to important and difficult issues of policy. In such cases the courts, while applying the general principle described above (and especially the second and third elements), have also attempted to lay down guidelines more specifically relevant to the type of case under consideration.

1   See, for example, _Caparo Industries plc v Dickman_ [1990] 1 All ER 568 at 574, 582, 585.

Omissions

18.13   Most simple definitions of negligence draw no distinction between a defendant's acts and his omissions; in either case, it is said, he is responsible for the foreseeable consequences. This is true in the sense that, where a duty of care clearly exists, this is as frequently breached by omission as by positive conduct, as where a motorist fails to give a signal or a valuer does not check his figures. However, cases in which the duty of care itself consists of an obligation to take positive action are highly infrequent. It has, for example, often been said that, in the absence of a prior legal relationship, there will be no liability involved in watching a blind man walk over a cliff edge, or a child drown in shallow water. Thus in _Ancell v McDermott_,[1] where police officers discovered an oil spillage on a main road which was an obvious danger to traffic, it was held that they owed no duty of care to road users to remain at the scene and warn them of the danger.

So reluctant, indeed, is the common law to impose positive duties where there is not already a legal relationship between the parties that it has also taken the position that a person who would not be liable for failing to act at all is equally not liable for acting negligently, provided that he does nothing which makes the plaintiff's position worse. In _East Suffolk Rivers Catchment Board v Kent_,[2] the plaintiff's farm was flooded by the bursting of a sea wall. The defendants, who had a statutory power but no statutory duty to repair the wall, adopted such inefficient methods of doing so that the land remained under water for an unnecessarily long time. Despite a strong dissent from Lord Atkin, the House of Lords held that the defendants were not liable in negligence, for they had not created any new source of loss to the plaintiff, but had simply failed to reduce a loss which had already occurred and for which they were not themselves responsible.

The principle laid down in _East Suffolk Rivers Catchment Board v Kent_ (that, if there is no duty to act at all, there can be no duty to act carefully) was criticised by Lord Wilberforce in _Anns v Merton London Borough Council_.[3] However, it was strongly endorsed in _Capital and Counties plc v Hampshire County Council_,[4] which concerned the liability of fire brigades. The Court of Appeal there held that a fire brigade would be liable if, in the course of fighting a fire at the plaintiff's premises, it negligently increased the risk of damage (eg by turning off a sprinkler system). However, the fire brigade owed no positive duty either to turn up at the scene of the fire or, once there, to exercise care and skill in fighting the fire.

1 [1993] 4 All ER 355, CA.
2 [1941] AC 74, [1940] 1 All ER 527, HL.
3 [1978] AC 728, [1977] 2 All ER 492, HL.
4 [1997] 2 All ER 865, CA.

18.14 Lying at the root of the law's refusal to impose liability for pure omissions is the view that, while everyone may reasonably expect his neighbour not positively to cause him harm, he should not be entitled to demand any benefits (including protection from harm) from that neighbour unless he has given something in return for those benefits. As a consequence of this view, affirmative obligations, or duties of protection, have traditionally been excluded from the sphere of tort and assigned to that of contract, where there is a requirement of consideration.[1]

Judicial reluctance to impose obligations in this area is at its strongest in cases where the plaintiff is effectively demanding to be protected from harm which is purely financial. Thus it has been held that an employer who sends an employee to work in a country where there is no compulsory insurance in respect of road accidents is under no duty to advise him to take out his own personal insurance policy.[2] Similarly, a school is under no legal obligation to warn its pupils or their parents of the desirability of taking out personal accident insurance to cover the risk of being injured during sporting activities at the school.[3]

1 Paras 6.3–6.22 above.
2 *Reid v Rush & Tompkins Group plc* [1989] 3 All ER 228, CA.
3 *Van Oppen v Clerk to the Bedford Charity Trustees* [1989] 3 All ER 389, CA.

Duties of protection

18.15 What was said in the previous two paragraphs does not mean that an affirmative duty to protect the plaintiff can never be established. In cases where there is an existing relationship between plaintiff and defendant, a different conclusion may be justified. Thus an employer may owe a duty to prevent a mentally disturbed seaman from throwing himself overboard,[1] or to protect an employee (a naval airman) from dying in a drunken stupor following a heavy drinking session on a naval base.[2] Similarly, where a patient is known to have suicidal tendencies, a duty of care to prevent him from harming himself may be imposed upon those who have care of him, whether it be the police[3] or a hospital.[4]

A duty of protection may occasionally be found in cases where the existing relationship is less obvious. In *Goldman v Hargrave*,[5] for example, a tall redgum tree on the defendant's land caught fire after being struck by lightning. The defendant could not of course be blamed for this, but he was held liable in negligence for leaving the fire to burn itself out, with the result that it spread to the plaintiff's land. Similarly, in *Barnett v Chelsea and Kensington Hospital Management Committee*,[6] the plaintiff's husband went to the casualty department of a hospital, complaining of vomiting and violent stomach pains, but the doctor on duty, who was himself feeling unwell, refused to examine him. In an action against the hospital authority for negligence,[7] it was held that on the facts a duty of care was owed, although the court left open the question of what the position would have been if the hospital had closed its doors altogether. Again, in *Smoldon v Whitworth*,[8] it was held that a referee in charge of an under-19 rugby match owed a duty of care to ensure the players' safety, and was accordingly liable to a player who suffered serious injuries when a scrum collapsed.

1 *Ali v Furness Withy (Shipping) Ltd* [1988] 2 Lloyd's Rep 379.
2 *Barrett v Ministry of Defence* [1995] 3 All ER 87, CA.

3   *Kirkham v Chief Constable of the Greater Manchester Police* [1990] 2 QB 283, [1990] 3 All ER 246, CA.
4   *Knight v Home Office* [1990] 3 All ER 237.
5   [1967] 1 AC 645, [1966] 2 All ER 989, PC.
6   [1969] 1 QB 428, [1968] 1 All ER 1068.
7   Which failed on the ground of causation; see para 20.3 below.
8   [1997] ELR 249, CA.

Damage caused by third parties

18.16   The general principle of non-liability for omissions also underpins the specific rule that, in the absence of special circumstances, the defendant is not to be held responsible for harm to the plaintiff which results from the unlawful (usually criminal) conduct of an independent third party, even where such harm is foreseeable. Thus a bus company is not liable if one of its vehicles, left unattended with its keys in the ignition, is stolen and then negligently driven so as to cause a fatal accident;[1] the management of a theatre owes no duty to actors to safeguard their belongings against theft from the dressing-room;[2] and the owner of an empty and dilapidated building cannot be held responsible if neighbours suffer when it is used as a means of access by thieves[3] or as a playground by vandals[4] or fire-raising children.[5] Moreover, this approach serves to exclude actions by the victims of crime which allege negligence on the part of the police in failing to arrest a suspected murderer[6] or failing properly to investigate a burglary.[7]

Given that there is no duty to prevent physical injury and damage, it is hardly surprising that there is no duty to prevent financial loss resulting from fraud. Thus, where a finance company carelessly failed to register a hire purchase agreement concerning a car, it was held by a majority of the House of Lords that the company owed no duty of care to future purchasers; they were accordingly not liable when the hire purchaser, fraudulently concealing the existence of the agreement, 'sold' the vehicle to a dealer.[8] Even more extreme, it has been held that an insurance company is under no duty to inform a client that his broker is deliberately deceiving him as to the extent of his insurance cover,[9] nor to tell the assignee of a policy that the insured person is dishonestly jeopardising the cover.[10]

1   *Topp v London Country Bus (South West) Ltd* [1993] 3 All ER 448, CA.
2   *Deyong v Shenburn* [1946] KB 227, [1946] 1 All ER 226.
3   *Perl (P) (Exporters) Ltd v Camden London Borough Council* [1984] QB 342, [1983] 3 All ER 161, CA.
4   *King v Liverpool City Council* [1986] 3 All ER 544, CA.
5   *Smith v Littlewoods Organisation Ltd* [1987] AC 241, HL.
6   *Hill v Chief Constable of West Yorkshire* [1988] 2 All ER 238, HL.
7   *Alexandrou v Oxford* [1993] 4 All ER 328, CA.
8   *Moorgate Mercantile Co Ltd v Twitchings* [1977] AC 890, [1976] 2 All ER 641, HL.
9   *Banque Financière de la Cité, SA v Westgate Insurance Co Ltd* [1989] 2 All ER 952, CA.
10   *Bank of Nova Scotia v Hellenic Mutual War Risks Association (Bermuda) Ltd* [1989] 3 All ER 628, CA.

18.17   The scope of this area of non-liability, and the principles on which exceptions to it may be based, was carefully considered by the House of Lords in *Smith v Littlewoods Organisation Ltd*.[1] The defendants there owned a disused cinema which they intended to demolish in order to redevelop the site. While the building was empty and unguarded, children broke in and caused damage in various ways, including the attempted lighting of fires. However, neither the defendants nor the police were told of these attempts, and eventually a serious fire was started which got out of control and damaged neighbouring property.

In holding the defendants not liable for this fire, a majority of the House of Lords took the view that a landowner's responsibility for the deliberate actions of a third party can be determined on the basis of 'foreseeability', albeit by using that term in a special sense. It will not, it appears, be enough that the third party's intervention is foreseeable as a mere possibility or even on the balance of probabilities; it must be 'highly likely' to occur.

The view taken by Lord Goff in *Smith v Littlewoods*, although failing to attract support from the majority of the House of Lords, nonetheless offers a convincing rationalisation of the cases in this area of law. This suggests that a duty of care can only arise in special circumstances, of which the most important concern the defendant's relationship with either the plaintiff or the third party.[2] As to the relationships with the plaintiff which may be sufficient to create a duty of protection, it seems that an employer owes a duty not to expose his employee to a foreseeable wages snatch;[3] a decorator working alone in a client's house may be answerable for a theft which occurs when he leaves it empty and unlocked;[4] and the prison authorities may be liable for negligently revealing a sex offender's record to other prisoners, resulting in a foreseeable attack upon him.[5] As to relationships which are sufficient to create a duty to control the third party, it seems that an institution which assumes control of a potentially dangerous person such as a violent lunatic[6] or a borstal inmate[7] may be liable for negligently permitting its charge to escape and cause damage.

1 [1987] AC 241, HL.
2 Others mentioned are the negligent creation of a source of danger which might foreseeably be sparked off by other persons, and failure to take reasonable steps to create a known danger created on his land by other persons.
3 *Charlton v Forrest Printing Ink Co Ltd* [1980] IRLR 331, CA (on the facts, employers not negligent). However, the police authorities owe no duty to individual officers in deciding on the policing of a potential riot: *Hughes v National Union of Mineworkers* [1991] 4 All ER 278.
4 *Stansbie v Troman* [1948] 2 KB 48, [1948] 1 All ER 599, CA. As to possible liability under the Occupiers' Liability Act 1957, see *Cunningham v Reading Football Club* [1992] 1 PIQR P141: para 22.13 below.
5 *Steele v Northern Ireland Office* [1988] 12 NIJB 1.
6 *Holgate v Lancashire Mental Hospitals Board* [1937] 4 All ER 19.
7 *Home Office v Dorset Yacht Co Ltd* [1970] AC 1004, [1970] 2 All ER 294, HL.

Economic loss

18.18 Where a person suffers physical injury, or where property in which he has an interest is damaged, any action in negligence which he brings will, if successful, entitle him to damages for the financial consequences (eg loss of earnings if he is unable to work through injury, or the cost of repairing damaged goods). As a general rule, however, no damages may be recovered for pure economic or financial loss which results from the defendant's negligence, even where this is foreseeable. In *Cattle v Stockton Waterworks Co*,[1] the plaintiff was employed under a fixed-price contract to build a tunnel through an embankment. His costs were greatly increased by water which escaped from the defendants' negligently laid main, and he sued in negligence to recover this loss. It was held that the claim must fail, since no damage had been done to any property of the plaintiff; to allow his action would, the court pointed out, mean opening the door to every employee who had lost wages as a result of the flooding.

The principle that no damages are awarded for the negligent causing of pure economic loss, which was approved by the House of Lords in *Simpson v Thomson*,[2] has been accused of tending to produce results which are both harsh and illogical. Particular criticism has been levelled at the fine distinction drawn between pure economic loss and that which is consequential upon property damage, a distinction illustrated by the case of *Spartan Steel and Alloys Ltd v Martin & Co (Contractors) Ltd*.[3] The defendants there negligently severed an electricity cable laid under the highway, thus cutting off power to the plaintiffs' foundry. Molten metal which was passing through a furnace threatened to solidify, which would have damaged both the metal and the furnace, and so the plaintiffs had to incur expense (and damage the metal) in removing it. Furthermore, the loss of power meant that four more 'melts' which were planned could not be carried out, so that the plaintiffs lost their expected profits on these. The Court of Appeal by a majority held that, while the defendants were liable for the physical damage and consequential loss of profit on the melt which had already been in progress, the inability to go ahead with the other four melts was pure economic loss and was therefore irrecoverable. It should be noted however that, if the metal had solidified in the furnace and production had been held up while it was cleaned out, the loss of profits would then have been classed as consequential economic loss and would thus have been recoverable.[4]

Perhaps the most telling criticism of the pure economic loss rule is that it focuses the attention of the courts upon a question of form: 'is it more accurate to describe the plaintiff's loss as physical or economic?', rather than one of substance: 'are there good reasons of policy for not imposing a duty of care in these circumstances?'. The reality is that the cases on pure economic loss fall into different categories and raise different problems and, while there may be good reasons for denying recovery, these reasons are not always the same. Some of the most important categories of case we now consider.

1   (1875) LR 10 QB 453.
2   (1877) 3 App Cas 279, HL.
3   [1973] QB 27, [1972] 3 All ER 557, CA.
4   *SCM (UK) Ltd v WJ Whittall & Son Ltd* [1971] 1 QB 337, [1970] 3 All ER 245, CA.

Dependent interests

18.19   The *Cattle* and *Spartan Steel* cases mentioned above represent the classic type of pure economic loss case; that in which physical damage to the property of A causes financial loss to B, who was in some way dependent upon it. The main reason why damages are not available in such cases is the judicial fear of opening the floodgates; the financial consequences of a single incident may be felt by a great number of people and may produce a total liability out of all proportion to the defendant's wrong. Such fears were expressed in *Weller & Co v Foot and Mouth Disease Research Institute*,[1] where it was held that, while a person whose negligence caused an outbreak of cattle disease would be liable to farmers who owned the affected cattle, he would not be liable to auctioneers who lost business when the local cattle markets were closed.

Most cases of the present type concern damage to property, but the same principle applies to cases of personal injury. If injury to A causes financial loss to B, who is dependent upon him, then that loss will not be recoverable in the tort of negligence.[2] This is demonstrated by the case of *Kirkham v Boughey*,[3] where the plaintiff and his wife were both injured in an accident caused by the negligence of the defendant. After the plaintiff had recovered from his injuries, he gave up his highly-paid job in order to be near his wife, who was still in hospital. It was held that, since this part of the plaintiff's loss of earnings resulted from his wife's injuries and not from his own, it was a purely financial loss; hence, even though it could be regarded as foreseeable, he could not claim for it.

Apart from the 'floodgates' argument, the line drawn in *Spartan Steel* also makes some sense in terms of economic efficiency. It is assumed that an industrialist who knows that, if the defendant negligently cuts off the power to his factory, he will be unable to sue for lost production, will insure against the possibility of that loss and pass on the cost of the premium to his customers. Conversely, if the plaintiff were allowed to sue, the defendant would have to take out liability insurance against the possibility of causing the harm. In terms of efficiency within the insurance market, it is better for the risk to be borne by the factory owner's insurance, since it is easier to quantify. After all, the loss of a day's production may be fairly accurately assessed, but how does one begin to measure the losses which might be caused by a single excavator cutting off power to an industrial estate, or even to a whole town?

The principle that the tort of negligence does not extend to the protection of dependent interests against financial loss has been applied with a high degree of consistency throughout the common law world. This makes all the more remarkable two decisions, by the highest courts in Australia and Canada respectively, in which damages were awarded in apparent contravention of that principle. In the Australian case,[4] the defendants' dredger negligently damaged a submarine pipeline which was used to transport oil belonging to the plaintiffs from the refinery to their depot. In the Canadian case,[5] the defendants' ship negligently damaged a railway bridge which carried the plaintiffs' trains. In neither case did the plaintiffs have any proprietary interest in the damaged property but the respective courts, emphasising that the plaintiffs were the only users of the property in each case, found sufficient special factors to justify the imposition of a duty of care upon the defendants for the plaintiffs' benefit.

1   [1966] 1 QB 569, [1965] 3 All ER 560.
2   The position is different if B's loss results from A's death, but only by virtue of a statutory right to claim: see the Fatal Accidents Act 1976, para 29.12 below.
3   [1958] 2 QB 338, [1957] 3 All ER 153. Also see *Buckley v Farrow* [1997] 4 CL 216, CA.
4   *Caltex Oil (Australia) Pty Ltd v The Dredge 'Willemstad'* (1976) 136 CLR 529, High Court of Australia.
5   *Canadian National Railway Co v Norsk Pacific Steamship Co Ltd* (1992) 91 DLR (4th) 289, Supreme Court of Canada.

18.20   The floodgates problem appears clearly in these classic dependent interest cases, and it is easy to see why judges have adopted a simple rule of non-recovery. However, pure economic loss may arise in more subtle ways and, in some at least of these situations, the reasons for protecting the defendant are not at all obvious. For instance, the damages payable to the owner of a negligently damaged ship would normally include, not only the cost of repairing the vessel, but also those other losses (such as loss of profit on her expected use) which are foreseeable and thus not too remote. However, it has been held by the Privy Council[1] that, if the owner has at the time of damage chartered the ship to a time charterer (ie someone who has no interest in the vessel, but merely a contractual right to use it), the latter cannot sue for being deprived of the ship, even though he must continue paying under the charterparty for something which he cannot now use. The effect of this decision is that the defendant will pay less in damages when ownership and use are divided between two persons than when the owner is using the vessel himself, which seems a wholly unjustifiable application of the economic loss principle.

Similar arguments arise where, for example, the plaintiff is an insurer who has to compensate an owner for his damaged property, or an employer who has to continue paying an employee's wages while the latter is injured and unable to work. Again, the law has generally denied recovery in such cases.[2]

1   *Candlewood Navigation Corp Ltd v Mitsui OSK Lines Ltd* [1986] AC 1, PC.
2   *Simpson v Thomson* (1877) 3 App Cas 279.

18.21   The cases discussed in the previous paragraph might be described as 'wrong plaintiff' cases; what happens is that, because of some contractual arrangement, damage caused to the property of B results in financial loss to C instead of to B. This appears in an acute form where A negligently damages property which belongs to B at the time that the damage occurs, but which is thereafter transferred to C. Assuming that C has paid a price for the property which is based upon its undamaged value, he is the obvious loser in this situation; however, problems arise due to the fact that his loss is classified as economic. In some, though not all, cases of this kind the law will allow B (despite the fact that he has suffered no loss) to recover damages which must then be handed over to C;[1] however, C cannot recover damages from A in his own right.

This problem has tended in practice to arise in slightly different forms in relation to land and goods. In relation to land (which usually means a building), damage may occur in an undiscoverable form during the ownership of B, only to be revealed after he has sold the building to C. In such a case, it was held by the House of Lords that, since a person's right to sue in negligence arises as soon as the damage occurs,[2] it is B and not C who can recover damages in respect of the defect.[3] The apparent injustice of this result has now been alleviated by the Latent Damage Act 1986, s 3, which effectively allows C to 'inherit' B's right of action against A, together with whatever remains of its limitation period.[4]

In relation to goods, cases have arisen in which cargo in the process of being sold is damaged by negligence for which the carrier is responsible, at a time when that cargo is still owned by the seller but is at the risk of the buyer in the sense that he must nevertheless pay the full price for it. In *Leigh & Sillivan Ltd v Aliakmon Shipping Co Ltd*,[5] the House of Lords held that the buyer cannot recover damages in tort from the carrier unless he has either legal ownership of or a possessory title to the goods. The decision was based, not on any fear of opening the floodgates, but rather on the feeling that the carrier should not be made liable beyond what he has positively undertaken. Contracts of carriage usually incorporate exemption and limitation clauses, and it was felt that it would be unjust to allow the buyer to circumvent these by bringing an action in tort.[6]

1 *The Albazero* [1977] AC 774, [1976] 3 All ER 129, HL; *Linden Gardens Trust Ltd v Lenesta Sludge Disposals Ltd* [1993] 3 All ER 417, HL.
2 *Pirelli General Cable Works Ltd v Oscar Faber & Partners* [1983] 2 AC 1, [1983] 1 All ER 65, HL.
3 *GUS Property Management v Littlewoods Mail Order Stores* [1982] SLT 533, HL.
4 See para 29.24 below.
5 [1986] AC 785, HL.
6 See further para 18.25 below.

Defects of quality

18.22 In *Donoghue v Stevenson*,[1] it was clearly laid down that a manufacturer of defective goods, who was guilty of a breach of contract vis-à-vis the person to whom he supplied those goods, could at the same time be liable in the tort of negligence to a third party (the consumer) who suffered injury or whose property was damaged. What the House of Lords did not consider, far less decide, was whether a consumer could recover damages from the manufacturer where the goods in question did no actual harm to persons or property but were simply defective, in the sense of not being of the quality one would normally expect. In such a case, what the consumer had suffered would be perceived by the courts as pure economic loss, since he would not have received value for money.

It has now been clearly established that a manufacturer[2] owes no duty of care to a consumer to avoid causing pure economic loss of this kind.[3] Moreover, it makes no difference that the defect has caused physical damage to the product itself, nor even that it has rendered the product dangerous.[4] The manufacturer can, however, be made liable where a defective product causes damage to other property, although there may be some difficulty in deciding what constitutes 'other property' for this purpose.[5]

There remains the possibility that, in certain circumstances, the relationship between a particular manufacturer and a particular consumer may be of sufficient 'proximity' to create a duty of care to avoid the causing of pure economic loss. In *Junior Books*

Ltd v Veitchi Co Ltd,[6] the House of Lords held that such a relationship existed between a client who commissioned the building of a factory and the specialist sub-contractor nominated by the client to construct the floor in the main production area. The House of Lords' decision (which enabled the client to recover damages from the sub-contractor for work which was defective though not dangerous) has been repeatedly distinguished or simply ignored by subsequent courts. However, it has not yet been overruled and, indeed, it was suggested in *Murphy v Brentwood District Council*[7] that the decision remains good law.

1   [1932] AC 562, HL; para 18.5 above.
2   Most of the cases have in fact concerned defective buildings, but the relevant legal principles appear identical.
3   *Muirhead v Industrial Tank Specialities Ltd* [1985] 3 All ER 705, [1985] 3 WLR 993, CA.
4   *Murphy v Brentwood District Council* [1990] 2 All ER 908, HL.
5   Eg where defective packaging results in damage to what is inside it: see *Aswan Engineering Establishment Co v Lupdine Ltd* [1987] 1 All ER 135, CA.
6   [1983] 1 AC 520, [1982] 3 All ER 201, HL.
7   [1990] 2 All ER 908, HL.

The interaction of contract and tort

18.23   A feature of many of the economic loss cases considered above is the contractual relationships which are involved. In recent years the courts have begun to consider the significance of this, and to question openly whether the tort of negligence should be permitted to create rights where a contractual analysis of the situation would suggest that none exist.

The problem arises in two ways. First, where plaintiff and defendant are themselves linked by a contractual relationship, the question is whether a parallel claim in tort should be allowed to avoid the restrictions of that contract (exemption clauses, limitation periods and the like). Secondly, where both plaintiff and defendant have contracts with a third party, the question is whether a direct claim in tort for pure economic loss should be allowed to outflank the principle of privity of contract, under which contractual rights and duties do not affect third parties.[1]

These two situations we now consider.

1   Ch 7 above.

Contracts between plaintiff and defendant

18.24   For many years, the question whether English law would permit 'concurrent liability' (that is, liability in tort between the parties to a contract) was one of considerable uncertainty. There was authority from the Privy Council for the view that, where parties had entered into a contract, their mutual rights and obligations were governed exclusively by that contract, so that it was not open to one of them to gain some advantage by bringing an action in the tort of negligence.[1] Similarly, where parties had entered into a relationship of mortgagor and mortgagee, which is governed by clearly defined equitable rights and duties, it was held that a party could not superimpose a claim in negligence on that relationship.[2] On the other hand, in *Midland Bank Trust Co Ltd v Hett, Stubbs and Kemp*[3] it was held that a solicitor's client was entitled to bring an action for negligence in tort, at a time when his right to sue for breach of contract was barred by lapse of time under the Limitation Act 1980.[4]

The issue has now been authoritatively settled by the decision of the House of Lords in *Henderson v Merrett Syndicates Ltd*,[5] which makes clear that concurrent liability is in principle available. Provided that the relationship between the contracting parties is of sufficient proximity to found a duty of care in tort, the plaintiff is entitled to frame his action in whichever way he chooses.[6] However, this is subject to the important qualification that the contractual context must be closely examined, and may be found to exclude or restrict a potential duty of care in tort. Thus, where the contract lays down clear limitations upon the scope of a party's obligation, it will not be just and reasonable to imply a duty of care in tort which is of wider scope.[7]

Apart from the possibility of contract terms which clearly exclude or limit a duty of care, the terms of a contract may have a more subtle effect. This may be illustrated by the decision of the Court of Appeal in *Greater Nottingham Co-operative Society Ltd v Cementation Piling & Foundations Ltd.*[8] The defendants there were the nominated sub-contractors for piling work on a large construction project in which the plaintiffs were the clients. The defendants entered into a collateral contract with the plaintiffs, by which they undertook to use skill and care in the design of the work and the selection of material; however, this contract was silent as to the execution of the work. When, due to the negligent execution of the piling work by the defendants, the plaintiffs suffered economic loss, the Court of Appeal held that this loss could not be recovered from the defendants by an action in tort. The parties, it was held, had set out their rights and duties in a contract which must be presumed to be exhaustive.

1   *Tai Hing Cotton Mill Ltd v Liu Chong Hing Bank Ltd* [1985] 2 All ER 947 at 957, PC.
2   *China and South Seas Bank Ltd v Tan* [1989] 3 All ER 839, PC.
3   [1978] 3 All ER 571.
4   See para 29.22 below.
5   [1994] 3 All ER 506, HL.
6   In most cases, the only advantage to be gained by claiming in tort is that of the longer limitation period which applies.
7   *William Hill Organisation v Bernard Sunley & Sons* (1982) 22 BLR 8, CA.
8   [1988] 2 All ER 971, CA.

Contracts with third parties

18.25   Cases such as *White v Jones*[1] (where a disappointed beneficiary claimed against a solicitor for negligence in the execution of a client's will) and *Junior Books Ltd v Veitchi Co Ltd*[2] (where a client sued a sub-contractor in tort in respect of a defective floor) raise formidable problems, both theoretical and practical, for the law. The theoretical problem arises from the fact that, in such cases, the test of whether the defendant is guilty of negligence toward A is whether he is in breach of contract with B. For practical purposes, therefore, it is as if A is suing for the breach of a contract to which he is not a party. This would be contrary to the doctrine of privity of contract,[3] a point expressly acknowledged by Walton J in *Balsamo v Medici.*[4] The client of an agent there sought to sue a sub-agent in negligence for having lost a sum of money with which he had been entrusted. The sub-agent was clearly guilty of negligence and would have been liable to the main agent; however, the learned judge held that to permit the principal to sue would abrogate the doctrine of privity altogether, something which he was not prepared to allow.

In practical terms, difficulties arise where the plaintiff and defendant both have contracts with a third party, and one of those contracts contains an exemption clause. To take a common example from the construction industry, a client and a sub-contractor will both be linked by contract to the main contractor. A well-established rule of contract law states that a person cannot take the benefit of an exemption clause in a contract to which he is not party,[5] but it would surely seem harsh to allow the client in such circumstances to outflank a clearly intended restriction on liability by bringing a direct action against the sub-contractor in the tort of negligence. An argument to this effect has led the Court of Appeal to rule that, where a sub-contractor negligently causes a fire which damages the contract works, it would not be 'just and reasonable' to hold the sub-contractor liable if the main contract states clearly that the risk of damage by fire lies on the employer rather than on the main contractor.[6] Similarly, in holding that an engineer in charge of a major construction project owed no duty of care to the contractor in issuing certificates, the Court of Appeal gave very detailed consideration to the terms of the main contract (to which of course the engineer was not party).[7]

As these examples demonstrate, the courts today are increasingly willing to use the terms of a relevant contract in shaping duties in tort. However, this process is not without its critics. In *Leigh & Sillivan Ltd v Aliakmon Shipping Co Ltd*,[8] for example, where it was suggested that a carrier of goods might owe a duty of care in tort to the consignee, which would be based on the terms of his contract with the consignor, the House of Lords held that this was not possible; indeed, their Lordships' refusal to use contract to shape tort was the main reason for their decision that no duty at all was owed.

1   [1995] 1 All ER 691, HL.
2   [1983] 1 AC 520, HL.
3   See ch 7 above.
4   [1984] 2 All ER 304, [1984] 1 WLR 951.
5   See para 10.14 above.
6   *Norwich City Council v Harvey* [1989] 1 All ER 1180, CA. Unless the main contract clearly allocates the risk in this way, the sub-contractor will of course be liable for his negligence: *National Trust for Places of Historic Interest or Natural Beauty v Haden Young Ltd* (1994) 72 BLR 1, CA.
7   *Pacific Associates Inc v Baxter* [1989] 2 All ER 159, CA.
8   [1986] AC 785, HL.

Negligent statements
Physical damage and financial loss
18.26   Where a person causes physical damage, there seems in principle no reason for the law to distinguish between negligent acts and negligent words. A doctor's liability to a patient who is treated with the wrong drug should surely be the same, whether the doctor injects it himself or merely prescribes it. Accordingly, and despite occasional expressions of concern at the enormous liability which might arise in this way (for example by negligently misstating the position of a submerged rock in a marine chart), the law has found little difficulty in imposing liability where a person suffers injury as a result of relying on negligent advice. In *Sharp v Avery*,[1] for example, the defendant motor cyclist offered to lead a second motor cycle, on which the plaintiff was a passenger, along a road which the defendant claimed to know. When the defendant went off the road at a bend and drove on to a piece of waste ground, the second motor cycle followed, and the plaintiff fell off and was injured. The Court of Appeal held that the defendant had assumed a duty of care towards the plaintiff, by his assurance that he knew the way and might safely be followed.

1   [1938] 4 All ER 85, CA.

18.27   Where the effect of a defendant's negligent words is simply to cause *financial* loss to the plaintiff, the legal position is more complicated; two factors in particular have restricted the development of the tort of negligence in this area, so as to prevent the imposition of a test based purely on foreseeability. In the first place, the realisation that words may be used over and over again, reaching unsuspected audiences without losing their power, has led to fears that a single slip might expose a defendant to unlimited liability. Second, there has undoubtedly been a feeling underlying many of the decisions that the right to complain of financial loss suffered through following a person's advice should be restricted to those who have paid for the advice, so that a professional man should be liable to his client but to no-one else. By contrast, it is generally accepted that a person may expect not to be physically injured by others, whether or not he has paid them.

For some three-quarters of a century, the possibility of development in this field was overshadowed by the decision of the House of Lords in *Derry v Peek*,[1] in which it was held that, in the absence of fraud, company directors were not liable for false statements made in a prospectus.[2] In *Candler v Crane, Christmas & Co*,[3] a majority of the Court of Appeal held that the neighbour principle laid down by *Donoghue v Stevenson*[4] made no difference to this situation, so that a duty of care in respect of words was restricted to cases of physical damage, contractual relationships and certain fiduciary relationships (eg that between trustee and beneficiary) which were recognised by equity.[5]

1   (1889) 14 App Cas 337, HL.
2   The actual decision was immediately reversed by statute; see now Companies Act 1985, ss 67 and 68.
3   [1951] 2 KB 164, [1951] 1 All ER 426, CA.
4   Para 18.6 above.
5   *Nocton v Lord Ashburton* [1914] AC 932, HL.

Hedley Byrne v Heller

18.28   The breakthrough, in the sense of recognition by the courts that the law of tort might give a remedy in the case of negligent statements causing financial loss, finally came with the decision of the House of Lords in the leading case of *Hedley Byrne & Co Ltd v Heller & Partners Ltd*.[1] The plaintiffs, a firm of advertising agents, were asked to arrange advertising space on behalf of Easipower, a client. Since, in accordance with trade practice, the plaintiffs would incur personal responsibility for paying for this space, they asked their bankers to check on Easipower's credit-worthiness. An enquiry was made of the defendants, who were Easipower's bankers and financial backers, and they replied 'without responsibility' that Easipower was 'a respectably constituted company, considered good for its ordinary business engagements'. Relying on this reference, the plaintiffs went ahead with the contracts; when, shortly afterwards Easipower became insolvent, the plaintiffs lost some £17,000. It was held, at first instance and in the Court of Appeal, that the defendants were not liable because, although they had been careless, they did not owe the plaintiffs any duty of care.

On appeal, the House of Lords held that the disclaimer ('without responsibility') prevented a duty from arising in the present case.[2] However, after an exhaustive review of the authorities, it was laid down that in an appropriate case a duty could arise. As to what would be an appropriate case, the test could not, it was said, be simply that of foreseeability, for this would impose an unacceptably heavy burden upon professional advisers. What was required was evidence of a special relationship between the parties, arising out of a *voluntary assumption of responsibility* by the defendant.

The circumstances in which a court might expect to find a special relationship and, with it, a duty of care were the subject of a wide range of opinions in the House of Lords; Lord Devlin, for example, took the narrow view that only a relationship which was 'equivalent to contract' would suffice. This apparently meant that all the elements of a valid contract, with the exception of consideration, must be present in the relationship. On the other hand, the decision may support a wider principle, namely, that a duty of care will arise whenever the defendant realises or ought to realise that his skill and care are being relied upon, provided both that there is such reliance and that the reliance is reasonable in the circumstances. However, even if this wider approach were adopted, it is highly unlikely that a person would be held liable in respect of words casually uttered on a social occasion. It may also be necessary to show that the defendant gave the advice with a particular transaction in mind.[3] Thus a person who issues a prospectus inviting shareholders to take up a special 'rights issue' of shares is not liable if they decide, on the basis of misleading information in the prospectus, to purchase more shares on the open market,[4] unless the prospectus was clearly intended to encourage such further purchases.[5]

The House of Lords in *Hedley Byrne v Heller* spoke in terms of a voluntary assumption of responsibility by the defendant, and a similar approach may be seen in many subsequent cases, including recent decisions of the House of Lords.[6] In *Hood v National Farmers Union*,[7] for example, the defendants were sued by one of their members for failing to warn him of the strict time limits within which he must act if he wished to challenge the decision of a Milk Quota Tribunal. The reason they were held liable was specifically that they had taken upon themselves the role of adviser to their member in respect of such a challenge. Again, in *Verity and Spindler v Lloyds Bank*,[8] where the plaintiff sought a loan from the defendants in respect of a business venture, her bank manager took it upon himself to advise her as to the prudence of the venture. The advice was negligent and the bank was held liable for it.

Despite the attention paid to the need for an assumption of responsibility, it has been suggested in several cases that the idea is really a fiction. The important question, it is said, is not: 'did the defendant undertake, expressly or impliedly, to be responsible for his advice?' but rather 'in what circumstances will the law impose a duty of care upon him?'. In *Smith v Eric S Bush; Harris v Wyre Forest DC*,[9] Lord Griffiths, having described the voluntary assumption of responsibility test as neither helpful nor realistic, suggested that the courts should approach this question as it would any other duty of care inquiry, by using a composite test involving foreseeability, proximity and 'justice and reasonableness'.[10] Nevertheless, it is only in rare cases that a duty of care in respect of financial loss will exist in the absence of a voluntary assumption of responsibility and/or reliance by the plaintiff on such an assumption.[11] All in all, the concept of assumption of responsibility remains a significant one.

In *James McNaughton Papers Group Ltd v Hicks Anderson & Co*,[12] an attempt was made in the Court of Appeal to identify those matters likely to be of importance when considering whether a duty of care arises in respect of an allegedly negligent statement. These are the purpose for which the statement was made; the purpose for which it was communicated; the relationship between the adviser, the advisee and any relevant third party; the size of any class to which the advisee belongs; the state of knowledge of the adviser; and reliance by the advisee.

1 [1964] AC 465, [1963] 2 All ER 575, HL.
2 Such a disclaimer would now, at least in business circumstances, be subject to a test of 'reasonableness' under the Unfair Contract Terms Act 1977 (paras 10.19–10.29 above): *Smith v Eric S Bush; Harris v Wyre Forest DC* [1989] 2 All ER 514, HL.
3 *Candler v Crane, Christmas & Co* [1951] 2 KB 164 at 183–184, [1951] All ER 426 at 435.
4 *Al-Nakib Investments (Jersey) Ltd v Longcroft* [1990] 3 All ER 321.
5 *Possfund Custodian Trustee Ltd v Diamond* [1996] 2 All ER 774.
6 See, for example, *Spring v Guardian Assurance plc* [1994] 3 All ER 129, HL; *Henderson v Merrett Syndicates Ltd* [1994] 3 All ER 506, HL.
7 [1994] 1 EGLR 1, CA.
8 [1996] Fam Law 213.
9 [1989] 2 All ER 514 at 536.
10 See para 18.11 above.
11 *Banque Financière de la Cité SA v Westgate Insurance Co Ltd* [1989] 2 All ER 952 at 1009, CA; *Reid v Rush & Tompkins Group plc* [1989] 3 All ER 228 at 239, CA.
12 [1991] 1 All ER 134 at 144.

18.29 *Hedley Byrne v Heller* was undoubtedly a decision of major importance in expanding the frontiers of negligence, and subsequent courts have by and large adopted a liberal approach in basing new duties upon this broad principle. A striking exception, however, is the decision of the Privy Council in *Mutual Life and Citizens Assurance Co Ltd v Evatt*,[1] in which a policyholder in the defendant company asked for advice as to the financial stability of an associated company, in which he had invested money. The Australian courts regarded this as a 'special relationship', but a bare majority of the Privy Council held that, in the absence of an express undertaking to use care, a duty of care would only arise if either the defendant had a direct financial interest in the transaction on which he was advising[2] or the advice given was of a type which the defendant was in business to give. It should be noted, however, that, in a strong dissent, Lords Reid and Morris (both of whom had sat in *Hedley Byrne v Heller*) thought that a person giving advice outside the scope of his business or profession should still owe a duty of care, although the standard demanded of him might well be lower.

It is not easy to see why a person giving advice outside his normal field should owe no duty of care at all, and it is perhaps not surprising that the Court of Appeal has twice expressed a preference for the reasoning of the minority in *Evatt's* case.[3] Indeed, a car enthusiast who advised a friend on the purchase of a second-hand vehicle has been held liable in negligence,[4] although the case is not of great authority, since the defendant there actually conceded that he owed the plaintiff a duty of care.

1   [1971] AC 793, [1971] 1 All ER 150, PC.
2   As in *Anderson (WB) & Sons Ltd v Rhodes (Liverpool) Ltd* [1967] 2 All ER 850.
3   *Esso Petroleum Co Ltd v Mardon* [1976] QB 801, [1976] 2 All ER 5, CA: *Howard Marine and Dredging Co Ltd v A Ogden & Sons (Excavations) Ltd* [1978] QB 574, [1978] 2 All ER 1134, CA.
4   *Chaudhry v Prabhakar* [1988] 3 All ER 718, CA.

18.30   The limits of the *Hedley Byrne* doctrine have been explored in a number of subsequent cases, and the courts have resisted attempts to use it as a basis for a positive duty to advise or warn of some danger.[1] Furthermore, the case of *Argy Trading Development Co Ltd v Lapid Developments Ltd*[2] suggests that, even for those who choose to speak, the duty of care is subject to strict limits. In that case a lease of part of a warehouse placed the obligation to insure against fire upon the tenants. In fact, however, the landlords had a block policy which covered the whole building and so the tenants, at the landlords' suggestion, simply paid the landlords a proportionate part of the premiums. Some time later the landlords allowed the policy to lapse without telling the tenants, who consequently found themselves uninsured when fire gutted the building. In an action for negligence it was held that, although the relationship between the parties was such that the landlords owed the tenants a duty of care, this merely meant that they must not give inaccurate information as to the insurance position at the time; they were under no positive duty to notify the tenants if circumstances changed.

Another controversial issue is whether liability is limited to circumstances in which information or advice is specifically requested by and given to the plaintiff. It appears that the lack of an enquiry *from the plaintiff* is not an absolute barrier to the imposition of a duty of care, so that an employer who gives a reference for an ex-employee may owe him a duty of care, notwithstanding that the reference is requested by and given to a third party.[3] Indeed, a duty may occasionally arise without any request at all, so that a bank manager who takes it upon himself to explain to a customer the legal significance of a mortgage which she is about to execute in the bank's favour must do so with care and skill.[4] However, success in such cases is rare; the Court of Appeal has held that, where information had not been requested at all (it was contained in advertisements published by a manufacturer), the mere fact that a person might be expected to rely on it was not sufficient to establish a 'special relationship'.[5] Similarly, where a medical charity advised a man that, following a vasectomy operation, he need no longer use contraception, the charity was held to owe no duty of care to a future sexual partner who became pregnant when, most unexpectedly, the vasectomy spontaneously reversed itself.[6]

1   Para 18.14 above.
2   [1977] 3 All ER 785, [1977] WLR 444.
3   *Spring v Guardian Assurance plc* [1994] 3 All ER 129, HL.
4   *Cornish v Midland Bank plc* [1985] 3 All ER 513, CA.
5   *Lexmead (Basingstoke) Ltd v Lewis* [1982] AC 225 sub nom *Lambert v Lewis* [1980] All ER 978, CA.
6   *Goodwill v British Pregnancy Advisory Service* [1996] 2 All ER 161, CA.

Professional liability

18.31   We suggested above that the Privy Council's attempt in *Mutual Life* to restrict liability to professional advisers is incorrect. Nonetheless, there is no doubt that the greatest impact of *Hedley Byrne v Heller* has been felt in the professional sphere, mainly because it is in this context that reliance by a person upon advice given to him by another is most likely to he judged reasonable.

Of the various advisers who have been sued by persons other than their clients, a number of examples may help to show what the courts regard as a 'special relationship' for this purpose. In *Shankie-Williams v Heavey*[1] a surveyor, who was instructed by the vendor of three flats in a converted house to investigate the ground floor flat, reported that it was free from dry rot. It was held by the Court of Appeal that the surveyor, although instructed and paid by the vendor, owed a duty of care to a purchaser of that flat, but not to the purchaser of one of the other flats, who saw his report and jumped to the conclusion that the whole property must be rot-free.

Where a valuer carries out a valuation of commercial property for a potential borrower, knowing that it will be shown to and relied upon by a lender, the valuer will owe a duty of care to the lender.[2] However, if the valuer in such circumstances makes it clear that the valuation is for the use only of a named lender, he will owe no duty of care to any other lender to whom it is passed on without his consent.[3] In residential cases, a valuer who is instructed by a building society or other lender to value a house for mortgage purposes will owe a duty of care to the purchaser and, moreover, any attempt to disclaim liability is likely to be held unreasonable and thus invalid under the Unfair Contract Terms Act 1977.[4]

It appears in principle that an estate agent acting for a vendor owes a duty of care to a prospective purchaser in respect of information about the property which the agent passes on,[5] unless the agent is protected by an effective disclaimer.[6]

Turning to the legal profession, it appears that a vendor's solicitor owes no duty to the purchaser in answering preliminary enquiries before the conclusion of a contract for the sale of land.[7] However, a solicitor who, on behalf of his client, gives an express or implied undertaking to take certain measures for the protection of a known third party, will owe a duty of care to that third party to fulfil his undertaking.[8] Of more far-reaching effect, it has been held that a solicitor instructed to draft a client's will owes a duty of care to those who are intended to benefit under it.[9] This ruling is especially interesting in that liability may be imposed upon the solicitor, even though it cannot be said that the beneficiaries have 'relied' upon any 'advice' which he gives. However, the duty imposed upon a solicitor in such circumstances appears limited to ensuring that the will achieves the testator's purpose; he is under no duty towards a beneficiary to warn the testator that subsequent dealings with his property are likely to affect that beneficiary's interest,[10] nor to advise the testator of further steps which may be required if the gift to the beneficiary is to be effective.[11] Nor can this duty of care be extended beyond wills to a badly drafted and thus ineffective deed of gift, where the donor (the client's solicitor) refused to execute another deed.[12]

As for other professions, it has been held that accountants instructed by a company to audit its accounts owe a duty of care to its existing shareholders as a group, but not to an individual existing or potential investor[13] or a creditor,[14] unless they make a specific representation to an identified individual which is intended to be relied upon.[15]

An architect or engineer undoubtedly owes a duty to his client in issuing certificates under a construction contract,[16] but it appears that he owes no comparable duty of care in tort to the contractor.[17] Finally, it has been held that a surveyor who certifies a ship as seaworthy[18] or an aircraft as airworthy[19] owes no duty of care to a prospective purchaser, nor to the owner of cargo lost when the ship subsequently sinks.[20]

1   [1986] 2 EGLR 139, CA.
2   *Cann v Willson* (1888) 39 ChD 39.
3   *Omega Trust Co Ltd v Wright Son & Pepper* [1997] 1 EGLR 120, CA.
4   *Smith v Eric S Bush; Harris v Wyre Forest DC* [1989] 2 All ER 514, HL.
5   *Computastaff Ltd v Ingledew, Brown, Bennison and Garrett* (1983) 268 Estates Gazette 906. Likewise an auctioneer: *McAnarney v Hanraham* [1993] IR 492.
6   *McCullagh v Lane Fox & Partners Ltd* [1996] 1 EGLR 35, CA.
7   *Cemp Properties (UK) Ltd v Dentsply Research and Development Corporation* [1991] 2 EGLR 197, CA; *Gran Gelato Ltd v Richcliff (Group) Ltd* [1992] 1 All ER 865.
8   *Al-Kandari v JR Brown & Co* [1988] QB 665, CA.
9   *White v Jones* [1995] 1 All ER 691, HL.
10   *Clarke v Bruce Lance & Co* [1988] 1 All ER 364, CA.
11   *Carr-Glynn v Frearsons* [1997] 2 All ER 614.
12   *Hemmens v Wilson Browne* [1993] 4 All ER 826.
13   *Caparo Industries plc v Dickman* [1990] 2 AC 605, [1990] 1 All ER 568, HL; *James McNaughton Papers Group Ltd v Hicks Anderson & Co* [1991] 1 All ER 134, CA.
14   *Al Saudi Banque v Clark Pixley* [1989] 3 All ER 361.
15   *Morgan Crucible Co plc v Hill Samuel Bank Ltd* [1991] 1 All ER 148, CA.
16   *Sutcliffe v Thackrah* [1974] AC 727, [1974] All ER 859, HL: para 18.35 below.
17   *Pacific Associates Inc v Baxter* [1989] 2 All ER 159, CA.
18   *Reeman v Department of Transport* [1997] 2 Lloyd's Rep 648, CA.
19   *Philcox v Civil Aviation Authority* [1995] 27 LS Gaz R 33, CA.
20   *Marc Rich & Co AG v Bishop Rock Marine Co Ltd* [1995] 3 All ER 307, HL.

Public authorities

18.32   Public bodies such as local authorities operate against the background of detailed and complex statutory provisions. Parts of these statutory codes impose positive duties on the bodies in question, others confer discretionary powers. Where, in the exercise of its statutory functions, a public body causes injury, damage or loss to an individual, a question which arises is whether an action by the victim may lead to the recovery of damages.

The general principles of law governing such actions were subjected to detailed examination by the House of Lords in the cases of *X v Bedfordshire County Council*[1] and *Stovin v Wise*,[2] where the following propositions were put forward:

•   In certain limited circumstances, an action may lie for the breach by a public authority of a statutory duty, independent of any question of negligence. However, this requires the plaintiff to convince the court that Parliament intended the statute in question to create a civil right of action for damages.[3]
•   The mere fact of carelessness by a public authority in the exercise of a statutory power or duty does not lead to liability. In order to succeed in an action for negligence, the plaintiff must establish a common law duty of care in accordance with the general principles described earlier.[4]
•   Although a public authority may in principle owe a common law duty of care as to the manner in which it performs its statutory functions, it owes no such duty of care as to the way in which it exercises a statutory discretion; anything within the ambit of its discretion is a matter for the authority, not for the courts. Furthermore, if the factors relevant to the exercise of the discretion include matters of policy, the courts will not even consider whether or not the decision was within the ambit of the statutory discretion.[5]

- Where the plaintiff's complaint is that the public authority negligently failed to exercise a statutory power, the plaintiff can only succeed by showing that:
  - any rational public authority would have exercised the power in question (so that there was in effect a public law duty to act); and
  - the policy of the statute requires compensation to be paid to persons who suffer loss because the power was not exercised.

The way in which these principles have been applied by the courts in recent years renders it unlikely that there will be many successful actions for negligence against public authorities. The courts have shown considerable reluctance to deal with the kind of claims put forward in *X v Bedfordshire County Council*[1] (inadequate handling of potential child abuse cases, and failure to cater sufficiently for children with special educational needs). This is perhaps not altogether surprising, in view of the delicate decision-making processes involved, but a similar judicial attitude may be found in other less delicate areas. *Stovin v Wise*,[2] for example, concerned a claim by a motor-cyclist who was seriously injured when struck by a car emerging from a road junction. The junction was known to be dangerous, and the plaintiff claimed that the highway authority should have exercised its statutory power to remove a bank of earth which obstructed visibility. However, this claim was rejected by the House of Lords (albeit by a bare 3–2 majority).

In adopting such a restrictive approach (of which *Stovin v Wise* is just one example) to claims against public authorities, the courts clearly recognise that such actions raise a number of difficult issues which are not present in other cases of negligence. For example, it is always necessary to examine the particular statute under which the public body was acting at the time of its alleged negligence, to see whether its purpose was to protect the plaintiff from the type of harm which he has suffered.[6] So too, the courts have shown an increasing awareness of the fact that, in many of these cases, the defendant has not positively caused harm to the plaintiff, but has merely failed to offer him protection against harm arising naturally or from the acts of some third party. The law is slow to impose affirmative duties of protection,[7] and actions of this kind have failed against financial regulators,[8] a local authority responsible for vetting nursing homes,[9] the Law Society in its function of controlling solicitors,[10] the police in their function of investigating and suppressing crime,[11] the fire brigade[12] and the coastguard.[13]

In a number of cases, plaintiffs have sought to use the tort of negligence as a means in effect of challenging decisions reached by various officials or public bodies. In rejecting these claims, the policy grounds relied upon by the courts have included the availability of alternative remedies such as statutory appeal procedures, the need to avoid putting undue pressure on public decision-makers and the undesirability of attempts by the courts to 'second-guess' the valid exercise of a discretion specifically conferred upon some other person or body. A combination of these factors has proved fatal to actions brought against an adjudicating officer deciding on a social security claim,[14] an immigration officer dealing with an asylum seeker,[15] a government minister exercising a discretionary power over foreign investment,[16] a police authority conducting disciplinary proceedings against a constable,[17] the charity commissioners[18] and university examiners.[19]

In contrast to the generally restrictive approach described above, the courts have shown much greater willingness to impose a duty of care on a public authority where it offers specific advice to someone in such circumstances as to indicate that it assumes responsibility for the accuracy of that advice.[20] A duty of care has accordingly been imposed upon an environmental health officer who advised the owners of a guest house that expensive building work was necessary to meet statutory requirements,[21] and on local authorities which offered specific psychological advice to children with special educational needs,[22] recommended a child minder who then mistreated children in her care[23] and assured prospective foster parents that they would not be sent any child suspected of committing sexual abuse.[24]

1   [1995] 3 All ER 353, HL.
2   [1996] 3 All ER 801, HL.
3   See ch 23.
4   Paras 18.11–18.12 above.
5   The distinction between 'policy' and 'operational' decisions was given detailed consideration in *Anns v Merton London Borough Council* [1977] 2 All ER 492, HL.
6   See *Curran v Northern Ireland Co-ownership Housing Association Ltd* [1987] 2 All ER 13, HL.
7   See paras 18.13–18.17 above.
8   *Yuen Kun-yeu v A-G of Hong Kong* [1987] 2 All ER 705, PC.
9   *Martine v South East Kent Health Authority* (1993) 20 BMLR 51, CA.
10 *Wood v Law Society* [1993] NLJR 1475.
11 *Hill v Chief Constable of West Yorkshire* [1988] 2 All ER 238, HL; para 18.16 below.
12 *Capital and Counties plc v Hampshire County Council* [1997] 2 All ER 865, CA.
13 *OLL Ltd v Secretary of State for Transport* [1997] 3 All ER 897.
14 *Jones v Department of Employment* [1988] 1 All ER 725, CA.
15 *W v Home Office* [1997] Imm AR 302, CA.
16 *Rowling v Takaro Properties Ltd* [1988] 1 All ER 163, PC.
17 *Calveley v Chief Constable of Merseyside* [1989] 1 All ER 1025, HL.
18 *Mills v Winchester Diocesan Board of Finance* [1989] 2 All ER 317.
19 *Thorne v University of London* [1966] 2 QB 237, [1966] 2 All ER 338, CA.
20 See para 18.28 above
21 *Welton v North Cornwall District Council* [1997] 1 WLR 570 108, CA.
22 *X v Bedfordshire County Council* [1995] 3 All ER 353, HL.
23 *T (a minor) v Surrey County Council* [1994] 4 All ER 577.
24 *W v Essex County Council* [1998] 3 All ER 111.

Judicial process

18.33   Despite the tremendous expansion in liability for negligent statements which has taken place since 1964, certain areas remain unaffected. For example, it has been said that judges, barristers, solicitors, jurors and witnesses enjoy an absolute immunity from any form of civil action being brought against them in respect of anything they say or do in court during the course of a trial. Indeed, it has been held that neither a party to an action[1] nor his solicitor[2] owes any duty of care to an opposing party as to the way in which proceedings are conducted, so that there is no liability for causing loss to another party by negligently serving a notice upon him at the wrong address. However, immunity is not conferred upon everyone connected with legal proceedings. A sequestrator, for example, owes a duty of care to the owner of property which he administers, notwithstanding that he is acting as an officer of the court.[3]

We now consider the most important effects of this rule.

1   *Business Computers International Ltd v Registrar of Companies* [1987] 3 All ER 465. This includes the Crown Prosecution Service: *Elguzouli-Daf v Metropolitan Police Comr* [1995] 1 All ER 833, CA.
2   *Al-Kandari v JR Brown & Co* [1988] QB 665 at 672, [1988] 1 All ER 833 at 835, CA.
3   *IRC v Hoogstraten* [1985] QB 1077, [1984] 3 All ER 25, CA.

Judges and magistrates

18.34   A judge (at least one who sits in a superior court of record)[1] has total immunity from any form of civil action in respect of anything which he says or does within his jurisdiction.[2] Even if he exceeds his jurisdiction, it seems that he is still immune from civil action, provided that he acts in good faith.[2] Statute has now in effect brought the legal position of magistrates into line with that of judges.[3]

1　The Crown Court, High Court and higher courts.
2　*Sirros v Moore* [1975] QB 118, [1974] 3 All ER 776. CA.
3　Courts and Legal Services Act 1990, s 108.

Arbitrators and valuers

18.35　The immunity of judges has been extended to certain other persons who exercise a judicial or quasi-judicial function. In particular, an arbitrator is not liable for anything which he does or fails to do unless the act or omission is shown to have been in bad faith.[1]

It was for a long time thought that a similar immunity was enjoyed by 'quasi-arbitrators', ie persons who occupied a similar position to arbitrators but who were not formally appointed. Indeed, it was even said that any person determining a question which compelled him to hold the scales fairly between two other persons would be immune from an action in negligence. If correct, this would include any case in which the parties agree to be bound by the decision of a valuer appointed jointly by them both.

Two decisions of the House of Lords indicate that the immunity of quasi-arbitrators is not as wide-ranging as had previously been thought, although the present limits are not altogether clear. In *Sutcliffe v Thackrah*,[2] the defendant, an architect, was employed to supervise the construction of a house which was being built for the plaintiff. The defendant negligently certified certain work as having been properly executed, whereupon the plaintiff paid the builder. The work had not in fact been properly done, but the plaintiff was unable to recover his money as the builder had become insolvent, whereupon the plaintiff sued the defendant in negligence. The defendant claimed to be entitled to immunity as a quasi-arbitrator, on the basis that he was deciding a question which affected the parties' rights, but the House of Lords held that this immunity exists only where a person is engaged in settling a specific dispute, present or future. Nor did it matter that, in issuing certificates, the architect owed a duty to the builder to act honestly; this duty, said the House of Lords, in no way conflicted with the duty of care which he owed to his client.

In *Arenson v Casson, Beckman, Rutley & Co*,[3] the plaintiff, on entering his uncle's business, was given a number of shares in the private company which operated it. It was agreed that, if the plaintiff left the business, he would sell the shares to his uncle at whatever the defendants, who were the company's auditors, decided was a fair value. This eventually fell to be done, but the plaintiff subsequently complained that the true value of his shares was six times the fair value placed on them by the defendants. The Court of Appeal by a majority held that the defendants owed no duty of care in making this valuation, but their decision was unanimously reversed by the House of Lords, who took the opportunity to consider the general question of 'quasi-arbitrators'. Their Lordships agreed that immunity in this area does not depend simply on whether or not the defendant is formally appointed as an arbitrator. What matters, according to the majority, is whether the defendant is appointed to settle an existing dispute by judicial means, so as to bind the parties by his decision.[4]

In principle, there is much to be said in theory for linking immunity to function, rather than to the formal question of whether the defendant is an arbitrator or not. However, it should not be overlooked that a party who is dissatisfied with the result of an arbitration has a limited right of appeal to the courts,[5] and it might therefore be argued that he does not need to be able to sue the arbitrator in negligence. A valuation, on the other hand, cannot be challenged, even where the valuer gives reasons for his decision which are demonstrably wrong, provided only that the valuer has at least addressed the correct question.[6] In consequence, if the valuer were personally immune from liability this would leave a dissatisfied party without any effective legal remedy.

1   Arbitration Act 1996, s 29.
2   [1974] AC 727, [1974] All ER 859, HL.
3   [1977] AC 405, [1975] 3 All ER 901, HL.
4   A surveyor appointed as an independent expert under a rent review provision owes a duty of care to both parties: *Zubaida v Hargreaves* [1995] 1 EGLR 127, CA.
5   Para 2.47 above.
6   *Campbell v Edwards* [1976] 1 All ER 785, [1976] 1 WLR 403, CA; *Jones v Sherwood Computer Services plc* [1992] 2 All ER 170, CA.

Advocates

18.36   When professional advisers were liable for negligence in contract alone, it was not possible for an action to be brought against a barrister, for it had long been established that there was no contractual relationship between a barrister and a person whom he represented in court. Once *Hedley Byrne v Heller* had opened up the possibility of an action in tort, therefore, the position of barristers called for re-examination, and this was carried out by the House of Lords in *Rondel v Worsley*.[1] The plaintiff in that case, who had been sentenced to 18 months' imprisonment for causing grievous bodily harm, sought to claim damages for negligence from the barrister who had unsuccessfully defended him on that occasion. The House of Lords unanimously held that, on grounds of public policy, no action would lie against a barrister for negligence in the conduct of a case in court. The reasons given for this immunity (which were said to be unconnected with the absence of a contractual relationship) were that a barrister's primary duty lies, not to his client, but to the court to secure the true administration of justice, which may compel him, on occasion, to disclose matters unfavourable to his case; that a barrister, unlike a solicitor, cannot pick and choose his clients, but must act for anyone, however offensive, who pays his fee; and that there must at some point be an end to litigation (whereas an action against one's barrister would always necessitate to some extent a retrial of the original case).

The immunity which covers a barrister's work as an advocate does not stop short at the door of the courtroom; it applies also to certain pre-trial work. The test, according to a majority of the House of Lords in *Saif Ali v Sydney Mitchell & Co*,[2] is whether the particular work is so intimately connected with the conduct of the case in court that it can fairly be said to be a preliminary decision affecting the way that case is to be conducted when it comes to a hearing. Applying this test, courts have rejected claims for negligence in respect of advice on what evidence to use in a forthcoming trial[3] and advice on the settlement of a case immediately prior to trial.[4]

The immunity of barristers has now been confirmed by s 62 of the Courts and Legal Services Act 1990, which provides that the same immunity will apply where (as is now possible) a barrister performs advocacy services under a contract with the client. The statute also confers equivalent immunity on any person other than a barrister who lawfully provides legal services in relation to litigation proceedings.

It should be noted that the House of Lords in *Hunter v Chief Constable of West Midlands*[5] provided a completely different justification for the immunity of an advocate from those contained in the above cases, by ruling that no negligence action can be permitted which would amount to a collateral attack upon a previous decision of a court of competent jurisdiction. An action by a disappointed litigant against his lawyer would very commonly fall foul of this principle, since the essence of the plaintiff's claim is that he should have won the previous case. The *Hunter* principle has subsequently been applied on several occasions by the Court of Appeal, but its precise relationship to the advocate's immunity remains unclear.

1   [1969] 1 AC 191, [1967] 3 All ER 993, HL.
2   [1980] AC 198, [1978] 3 All ER 1033, HL.
3   *Bateman v Owen White* [1996] 1 PNLR 1, CA.

4   *Kelley v Corston* [1997] 4 All ER 466, CA.
5   [1981] 3 All ER 727, HL.

18.37   It is important to appreciate that the immunity conferred by *Rondel v Worsley* is limited to advocacy. In relation to their other work, barristers and solicitors are like other professional advisers in owing a duty of care to both their clients and third parties.

Psychiatric damage

18.38   Where a person recovers damages for physical injury, some compensation in respect of any accompanying psychological trauma is normally recoverable under the heading of pain and suffering.[1] Where, however, there is no 'impact injury', the courts have proved much less sympathetic to a claim in respect of purely mental harm. The most difficult cases are those in which the defendant negligently causes an accident in which someone is injured or killed, and the plaintiff suffers psychiatric injury as a consequence of witnessing or being told about the accident.

In *Alcock v Chief Constable of the South Yorkshire Police*[2] (a case arising out of the Hillsborough disaster, in which 95 Liverpool football supporters were crushed to death), the House of Lords stressed the importance of three criteria by which such cases were to be judged: the class of persons whose claims should be recognised; the proximity of such persons to the accident; and the means by which the shock is caused. Applying these criteria to the facts of *Alcock*, the House of Lords held:

- there is no arbitrary list of relationships which are close enough to render it foreseeable that injury to or death of one partner may result in shock to the other. However, the only relationships close enough to raise a presumption that shock may be suffered are those of husband-wife and parent-child. In order for other relatives or friends to recover damages, they must positively prove an equivalent emotional tie.
- as a general rule, proximity requires a plaintiff to be physically close to the accident in time and space.
- as a general rule, proximity also requires the plaintiff to witness the accident or its immediate aftermath personally. It is not enough to be told of the accident by a third party, to see a televised recording of it or to read about it in a newspaper.

1   Para 29.6 below.
2   [1991] 4 All ER 907, HL.

Chapter 19

Negligence – breach of duty

19.1   Once a court has decided that a particular defendant owed a duty of care to a particular plaintiff, the next question is whether or not that duty was broken. The test to be applied is this: did the defendant act reasonably in all the circumstances of the case? It should be noted from the outset that, while the concept of 'reasonableness' is of course capable of great flexibility, so that subtle differences of fact between one case and another may lead the court to apparently conflicting conclusions, the legal standard itself is always the same. Furthermore, this standard of reasonableness is the only one recognised by the English law of negligence; such concepts as 'gross negligence' have no part to play.

An important point, and one which is all too frequently overlooked, is that decisions on breach of duty are matters of fact; consequently, they are not of binding authority for the future. Thus, the fact that a driver in one case is held to have been negligent in turning right without giving a signal does not mean that such conduct will automatically amount to negligence in another case. Indeed, it has even been held that, in extreme circumstances, a person may be driving a vehicle with reasonable care, despite the fact that he is exceeding the speed limit.[1]

We have already remarked that the tort of negligence imposes an objective standard of conduct. What is required of a person, if he is to avoid liability, is not that he does his best, but that he does what is reasonable. At first glance, this may appear rather harsh, in that a defendant is sometimes held liable in circumstances where no moral blame attaches to him. However, it may be pointed out that a court which sympathised with such a defendant to the extent of acquitting him of negligence would, in effect, be condemning an equally innocent plaintiff to shoulder his own loss. When it is also recognised that the majority of modern defendants are either insured against liability or backed by employers who are so insured, the courts' insistence upon the objective standard is easy to understand.

The prevalence of liability insurance is one of the factors which have led the courts to impose, under the guise of reasonableness, standards of conduct which are rather higher than most people can consistently achieve. Another is undoubtedly the feeling that, while to set an impossibly high standard would be self-defeating, the aim of the law should always be an overall improvement in performance, since the reduction of accidents is to everyone's benefit. Interestingly, however, the courts are more lenient when considering the conduct of a plaintiff for the purpose of deciding whether his damages should be reduced on the ground of contributory negligence.[2] In theory, the test to be applied is again that of reasonableness, but here the imposition of too high a standard would restrict the availability of compensation rather than increasing it, and this would run counter to modern trends.

1   *Barna v Hudes Merchandising Corpn* (1962) 106 Sol Jo 194, CA.
2   See para 21.11–21.16 below, especially para 21.13.

19.2   In this chapter we examine the following issues:

•   the extent to which the courts, in deciding whether a person has been guilty of a breach of his duty of care, make allowance for disabilities or age;
•   the standards of skill and care which the law demands from members of established professions;
•   the modern 'risk/benefit' approach which is often used to determine negligence;
•   the way in which a breach of duty is proved, and the circumstances in which it may be presumed.

The reasonable man

19.3   When civil actions were tried by a judge and jury, the reasonableness or otherwise of the defendant's conduct was one of the matters which fell to the jury to decide. In order to assist these laymen in reaching their verdict, which required them to set a legal standard, judges would refer to such hypothetical creatures as 'the man in the street', 'the man of ordinary prudence' and, most famously, 'the man on the Clapham omnibus'. The jury would then be asked to measure the conduct of the actual defendant against what might have been expected of his mythical counterpart. As Alderson B put it in *Blyth v Birmingham Waterworks Co:*[1] 'Negligence is the omission to do something which a reasonable man guided upon those considerations which ordinarily regulate the conduct of human affairs, would do, or doing something which a prudent and reasonable man would not do.'

Negligence actions are no longer tried by jury, but the judge has to carry out exactly the same process of evaluation, and the idea of the reasonable man therefore remains relevant. In considering whether the defendant's conduct has reached the requisite standard, various personal attributes of the defendant will be taken into account, and these we consider below. Further, modern courts frequently evaluate a person's conduct by reference to the risk which it creates, and this we discuss under the heading of 'The principle of risk'.

1   (1856) 11 Exch 781 at 784.

Intellectual and emotional characteristics
19.4   As a general rule, no allowance is made in law for any lack of intelligence or emotional restraint on the part of a particular defendant. Indeed, both judges and academic writers have expressed the view that, in an appropriate case, liability in negligence may be imposed upon a person who is mentally incapable, notwithstanding his obvious personal inability to reach the standard of reasonableness. This is on the ground that to excuse such a defendant would be unfair to the victims of his actions. Similar reasoning (supported in this instance by the comforting presence of compulsory insurance) has been used where the defendant is merely inexperienced, rather than mentally incapable; it was held by the Court of Appeal in *Nettleship v Weston*[1] that a learner-driver is negligent if he or she does not achieve the standard of an ordinarily competent and experienced driver.

1   [1971] 2 QB 691, [1971] 3 All ER 581, CA.

Physical defects

19.5   Although a person's psychological make-up is thus irrelevant to his liability in negligence, the courts are more prepared to make allowances in the case of a defendant who suffers from some recognisable physical impediment. This may be simply because of the comparative ease with which such a disability may be proved to exist, but, whatever the reason, there is no doubt that a person who is blind or who has only one leg will be judged by what may reasonably be expected from someone in that condition. However, it may be noted that this is two-edged. While a disabled person may not be held negligent for failing to achieve the same standard of agility or awareness as a person with no disability, he must recognise his own limitations and refrain from activities which, because of his condition, are fraught with special risk. The law does not recognise the concept of the reasonable blind car driver!

A particular problem arises where a person is unaware of his disability. In *Mansfield v Weetabix Ltd*[1] a lorry belonging to the defendants crashed into the plaintiff's shop and caused extensive damage. It appeared that the driver was suffering from a medical condition, of which he was unaware, which rendered him incapable of driving safely. The Court of Appeal, having found that the driver would not have continued to drive had he known the truth, held that he could not be regarded as negligent. However, if the driver had ignored clear symptoms of possible danger, the decision might well have been different.

1   [1997] 6 CL 425, CA.

Age

19.6   Children are very seldom sued in negligence, for the practical reason that it would be difficult for the plaintiff in such a case to obtain satisfaction; children normally have neither personal funds nor insurance to pay any damages, and the law does not make parents vicariously responsible for the torts of their children. Nevertheless, the courts are not infrequently called upon to consider the reasonableness or otherwise of a child's conduct, when an injured child's claim is met with a defence of contributory negligence.[1] In *Morales v Eccleston*,[2] for example, where an 11-year-old boy ran into the road without looking and was struck by a negligently driven car, the boy was held 75% responsible for his own injuries.

The *Morales* case shows that even 11-year-olds are expected to have some road sense, and yet it is clear that the courts take full account of a plaintiff's age in assessing the standard of care which they must reach. In the very similar case of *Foskett v Mistry*,[3] for example, the plaintiff who ran into the road was 16 years old. The Court of Appeal stated that an adult pedestrian would have been totally responsible for this accident; however, in view of his age, the plaintiff was only 75% responsible. Likewise, in *Gough v Thorne*,[4] a 13-year-old girl was beckoned across the road by the driver of a stationary lorry. Relying entirely upon this signal, she stepped out past the lorry and was knocked down by a negligently driven car. The trial judge held that her failure to look out for vehicles overtaking the lorry amounted to contributory negligence, but the Court of Appeal, while accepting that this would be true in the case of a more experienced adult, held that a child of this age could not be faulted for trusting her elders.

In contributory negligence cases, a lenient approach to children has the desirable effect of enlarging the overall scope of compensation. To give similar latitude in the rare cases where a child's conduct has caused injury or damage to others would, of course, have the opposite effect. Nevertheless, it is clear that this is the correct approach to adopt. In *Mullin v Richards*,[5] two 15-year-old schoolgirls were fencing with plastic rulers when one of the rulers snapped, causing a serious eye injury to one of the girls. The Court of Appeal held that, when age was properly taken into account, it could not be said that a reasonable 15-year-old ought to have foreseen the likelihood of injury from what was nothing more than a children's game.

Of course, even a child is expected to achieve certain standards. In *Watkins v Birmingham City Council*,[6] a 10-year-old boy, while distributing school milk to various classrooms, left his tricycle in a position where a teacher fell over it. This was held to constitute negligence, a finding which was not challenged in the Court of Appeal, where the decision was reversed on another ground.[7]

Although there is less authority than in respect of children, it seems that an elderly litigant is also to be judged in the light of his age. In *Daly v Liverpool Corpn*,[8] where a collision occurred between the plaintiff, a 69-year-old pedestrian, and the defendants' bus, it was held that a charge of contributory negligence against the plaintiff must take her age into account. As Stable J remarked: 'I cannot believe that the law is quite so absurd as to say that, if a pedestrian happens to be old and slow and a little stupid, he or she can only walk about his or her native country at his or her own risk.'

1   Paras 21.11–21.16 below.
2   [1991] RTR 151, CA.
3   [1984] RTR 1, CA.
4   [1966] 3 All ER 398, CA.
5   [1998] 1 All ER 920, CA.
6   (1976) 126 NLJ 442.
7   See para 28.7 below.
8   [1939] 2 All ER 142.

Knowledge of other people

19.7 In order to attain the standard which the law demands of the reasonable man, the defendant must take into account, and make due allowance for, those shortcomings of others which are reasonably to be foreseen. Thus, for example, if it is foreseeable that blind persons will use a city pavement, the reasonable man who excavates there will erect a barrier sufficient to protect them, and not merely one which is sufficient to safeguard those who can see it.[1]

Similarly, the reasonable man may have to recognise that others do not always act reasonably towards him, and must thus take such precautions against their negligence as experience shows to be necessary. For example, while one pedestrian was held not to have been negligent in assuming that a driver would stop at a red light[2]), another pedestrian was held negligent for stepping out on to a zebra crossing without looking, relying blindly on drivers to give way to him.[3]

There may even be extreme cases in which a defendant ought to foresee and guard against even the criminal misconduct of others, although, as we have seen,[4] the law is reluctant to impose a duty of care in such circumstances.

1   *Haley v London Electricity Board* [1965] AC 778, [1964] 3 All ER 185, HL.
2   *Tremayne v Hill* [1987] RTR 131, CA.
3   *London Passenger Transport Board v Upson* [1949] AC 155, [1949] 1 All ER 60, HL.
4   Paras 18.16–18.17 above.

Professional status

19.8 Unlike most of the factors so far considered, which may lead a court to expect rather less of a defendant than of other people, a person's status within a trade or profession may mean that he has to achieve a higher standard than others, in the sense of displaying skill as well as care. As to the degree of skill which must be shown, this is whatever may be expected of a reasonably competent practitioner, rather than a leading specialist (although a defendant who sets himself up as a specialist will probably be judged accordingly[1]). In *Roe v Minister of Health*,[2] the plaintiff underwent minor surgery in 1947, during which he became partially paralysed as a result of being injected with a contaminated anaesthetic. The danger of such contamination was appreciated by very few doctors until about 1951, after which the profession in general took action to prevent it from happening again. In acquitting the hospital staff of negligence, Denning LJ pointed out that: 'We must not look at the 1947 accident with 1954 spectacles.'

Where a person acts in accordance with what is the generally accepted practice of his profession, he is unlikely to be found negligent,[3] although there have been occasions on which a court has declared such common practice to be unreasonable.[4] Conversely, a practitioner who ignores the usual procedures runs an increased risk of being judged negligent,[5] although failure to adhere to a professional institution's guidance notes is not conclusive evidence of negligence.[6] What, then, of the case in which professional opinion is split? In *Bolam v Friern Hospital Management Committee*,[7] McNair J made it clear that it was not for the court to select one body of opinion as correct and to discount all others; the question was simply whether it could be said that no reasonably competent practitioner could possibly hold the view which the defendant preferred. This statement of principle was approved by the House of Lords in *Maynard v West Midlands Regional Health Authority*.[8]

It should always be remembered that a professional man's duty is to be skilful and careful, not necessarily to be correct. Nevertheless, it is not true to say that an error of judgment cannot amount to negligence; the vital question is whether the error is one which a reasonably competent practitioner would not have made.[9]

In deciding whether or not a charge of professional negligence has been established, the courts rely heavily upon evidence from expert witnesses as to what might reasonably be expected of a competent member of the profession. Such expert witnesses should be drawn from the same profession as the defendant; thus a structural engineer is not qualified to give evidence as to what a building surveyor should have seen or done.[10] Expert witnesses are almost always called by the parties, although a court has a power (which is seldom exercised) to appoint its own expert.[11]

1   *Duchess of Argyll v Beuselinck* [1972] 2 Lloyd's Rep 172; cf *Wimpey Construction UK Ltd v Poole* (1984) 27 BLR 58.
2   [1954] 2 QB 66, [1954] 2 All ER 131, CA.
3   *Morton v William Dixon Ltd* 1909 SC 807 at 809; *Beaumont v Humberts* [1990] 2 EGLR 166, CA.
4   See, for example, *Edward Wong Finance Co v Johnson, Stokes and Master* [1984] AC 296, PC.
5   See, for example, *Clark v MacLennan* [1983] 1 All ER 416.
6   See *PK Finans International (UK) Ltd v Andrew Downs & Co Ltd* [1992] 1 EGLR 172.
7   [1957] 2 All ER 118, [1957] 1 WLR 582.
8   [1985] 1 All ER 635, [1984] 1 WLR 635, HL.
9   *Whitehouse v Jordan* [1981] 1 All ER 267, [1981] 1 WLR 246, HL. See also para 19.9 below.
10 *Sansom v Metcalfe Hambleton & Co* [1998] 05 LS Gaz R 28, CA.
11 Under Ord 40 of the Rules of the Supreme Court: see *Abbey National Mortgages plc v Key Surveyors Nationwide Ltd* [1996] 2 EGLR 99, CA.

19.9   *Valuers and surveyors* Although it was not until the decision of the House of Lords in *Hedley, Byrne & Co Ltd v Heller & Partners Ltd*[1] that it became possible for a negligent valuer to be sued in tort, it had long been settled that a claim in contract would lie at the suit of a dissatisfied client. Consequently, in seeking guidance as to how a valuer's legal duty to use such care and skill as is reasonable should be translated into practical terms, decisions of the courts both before and after 1964 are of equal relevance.

In the first place, it must be stressed that valuation is not an exact science, and that to be wrong is not necessarily to be negligent:

'The law does not require any man, valuer of public-houses or any other expert agent, to be perfect. The law does not say that in any branch of intelligent operation, intelligent skill, there is necessarily one defined path which must be strictly followed, and that if one departs by an inch from that defined path one were necessarily at fault.'[2]

Even more in point are the words of Goddard LJ, in *Baxter v F W Gapp & Co Ltd:*[3]

'Valuation is very much a matter of opinion. We are all liable to make mistakes, and a valuer is certainly not to be found guilty of negligence merely because his valuation turns out to be wrong. He may have taken too optimistic or too pessimistic a view of a particular property. One has to bear in mind that, in matters of valuation, matters of opinion must come very largely into account.'

Notwithstanding such comments, a sizeable error in a valuation will normally require some explanation and justification from the valuer who made it. Indeed, it was said in one case that a valuation which departs from the 'correct' figure (as found by the judge with the help of expert witnesses) by more than 10% or 15% 'brings into question the competence of the valuer and the sort of care he gave to the task of valuation'.[4] However, it has subsequently been doubted whether a single 'correct' value really exists, and it has been suggested that a better approach is to ask whether the defendant's figure lies within the 'bracket' of values which competent practitioners might reasonably have arrived at for the property in question.[5]

Even assuming that a valuer has reached a wrong conclusion, in the sense described above, damages for negligence can only be recovered if it is established that his error was due to a lack of reasonable care and skill. This has been found in such matters as failure to keep up to date with the principles of law which affect the type of valuation in question,[6] and, where the complaint was of an under-valuation, the overlooking of a potential market.[7] As far as the actual valuation process is concerned, the courts are careful not to lay down restrictive rules, since it is appreciated that an experienced valuer may often operate intuitively. Hence, the absence of comparables or detailed calculations does not of itself indicate negligence.[8] On the other hand, a valuer who does not trouble to visit the site which he is to value,[9] who clearly ignores the price at which the property has recently changed hands[10] or who (after only three months' experience, all of it limited to property worth less than £33,000) nonchalantly values a house at £100,000 without seeking confirmation from a more experienced colleague,[11] is unlikely to attract the sympathy of a judge when it is alleged that he was lacking in reasonable care and skill.

In relation to surveys and other inspections of property, the crucial question is normally whether the survey was too superficial to reveal obvious defects in the property.[12] This naturally depends, to some extent at least, on the type of survey carried out, although it has been held that the standard of skill and care required in carrying a House Buyers Report and Valuation is identical to that for a structural survey.[13] In the case of a mortgage valuation ('a walking inspection by someone with a knowledgeable eye, experienced in practice, who knows where to look'[14]), a surveyor is not expected to move furniture or to lift floor coverings; however, if his limited inspection reveals clear evidence of a defect, it is then his duty to 'follow the trail'.[15]

1   [1964] AC 465, [1963] 2 All ER 575, HL; para 18.28 above.
2   *Love v Mack* (1905) 92 LT 345 at 349.
3   [1938] 4 All ER 457 at 459.
4   *Singer and Friedlander Ltd v John D Wood & Co* (1977) 243 Estates Gazette 212 at 213.
5   See *Mount Banking Corporation Ltd v Brian Cooper & Co* [1992] 2 EGLR 142.
6   *Weedon v Hindwood, Clarke and Esplin* (1974) 234 Estates Gazette 121.
7   *Bell Hotels (1935) Ltd v Motion* (1952) 159 Estates Gazette 496.
8   *Corisand Investments Ltd v Druce & Co* (1978) 248 EG 315 at 319.

9   *Singer and Friedlander Ltd v John D Wood & Co* (1977) 243 Estates Gazette 212.
10 *Banque Bruxelles Lambert SA v Eagle Star* [1995] 2 All ER 769.
11 *Kenney v Hall Pain and Foster* (1976) 239 EG 355.
12 As it was in *Philips v Ward* [1956] 1 All ER 874, [1956] 1 WLR 471, CA.
13 *Cross v David Martin & Mortimer* [1989] 1 EGLR 154.
14 *Lloyd v Butler* [1990] 2 EGLR 155.
15 *Roberts v J Hampson & Co* [1989] 2 All ER 504; *Sneesby v Goldings* [1995] 2 EGLR 102, CA.

19.10   An obligation to display professional skill as well as reasonable care is imposed, not only upon those who are actually members of that profession, but also on those who attempt to take on work which requires professional skill.[1] Indeed, some jobs so obviously require an expert that a defendant who attempts to carry them out himself is almost bound to be regarded as negligent.[2] In *Freeman v Marshall & Co*,[3] the plaintiff complained of a survey carried out for him by the defendant, which failed to diagnose rising damp. The defendant argued that, since he was unqualified and had little knowledge of structures, he had done all that could be reasonably expected of him. It was held, however, that, by advertising himself as an estate agent, valuer and surveyor, and by undertaking a structural survey, he had laid claim to the necessary expertise and must be judged accordingly.

Many jobs may as reasonably be undertaken by semi-skilled or unskilled persons as by professionals. Where this is so, the courts will not necessarily judge the defendant by the standard of the most skilled person who might be expected to do the work. In *Philips v William Whiteley Ltd*,[4] for example, a jeweller pierced a woman's ears. The instruments used were disinfected, although not to the standard which a surgeon would be expected to achieve, and she developed an abscess. It was held that, since this operation was frequently performed by jewellers, the defendants fell to be judged by the standards of a reasonable jeweller, and not those of a reasonable surgeon. A similar decision was reached in the case of *Wells v Cooper*,[5] where a door handle fitted by the defendant householder, who was an amateur carpenter of some experience, came off, with the result that the plaintiff was injured. The Court of Appeal held that, since this was the sort of job which the reasonable householder might be expected to do for himself the defendant was to be judged by amateur, and not professional, standards.

Some doubt is thrown on the latitude given to defendants in these two cases by the later decision in *Nettleship v Weston*.[6] There the Court of Appeal, no doubt influenced by their awareness of available insurance, held that the standard which a learner-driver must achieve, if he is not to be held negligent, is not that of a reasonable learner, but that of a reasonable experienced driver.

1   However, there is no concept of 'team negligence' under which all members of, say, a medical unit would be judged by the standard of the unit as a whole: *Wilsher v Essex AHA* [1986] 3 All ER 801, CA.
2   Eg lift maintenance: *Haseldine v C A Daw & Son Ltd* [1941] 2 KB 343, [1941] 3 All ER 156, CA.
3   (1966) 200 Estates Gazette 777.
4   [1938] 1 All ER 566.
5   [1958] 2 QB 265, [1958] 2 All ER 527, CA.
6   [1971] 2 QB 691, [1971] 3 All ER 581, CA.

The principle of risk

19.11   The traditional way of approaching the question of negligence was to envisage the hypothetical reasonable man and ask what he ought to have foreseen. More recently, courts have tended to look at the situation as a whole and to consider whether the risks inherent in the defendant's activity are such as to outweigh any value it may have or the cost and difficulty of rendering it safe. In conducting this balancing operation a court will take into account one or both of the following matters:

- the likelihood that the activity in question will cause injury or damage; and
- the seriousness of the injury that may result if the risk materialises.

Against these factors may be set:

- the value, social utility or other desirability of the activity; and
- the cost and practicability of taking steps to reduce or eliminate the danger.

Likelihood of injury

19.12   As Lord Dunedin remarked in *Fardon v Harcourt-Rivington:*[1] 'People must guard against reasonable probabilities, but they are not bound to guard against fantastic possibilities'. This means that a risk may be so remote that the reasonable man is quite justified in ignoring it altogether. Perhaps the most famous example of this is the case of *Bolton v Stone*,[2] where the plaintiff was injured by a cricket ball which a visiting batsman had struck more than 100 yards, clearing a high fence on the way. The evidence indicated that shots of this kind had occurred on the ground no more than six times in 28 years. The House of Lords held that, while the risk was clearly foreseeable, from the very fact that there had been such shots in the past, it was sufficiently remote that the defendants might reasonably ignore it. While this principle has subsequently been accepted, it should not be overlooked that the conduct of the defendants in that case (playing cricket) was considered by the House of Lords to be socially valuable; hence, there was a second reason for holding the defendants not liable.

1   (1932) 146 LT 391 at 392.
2   [1951] AC 850, [1951] 1 All ER 1078, HL.

Seriousness of consequences

19.13   Quite apart from the probability or improbability that a particular type of accident will occur, a court assessing a defendant's conduct may justifiably consider the gravity of the potential consequences. This principle was laid down by the House of Lords in *Paris v Stepney Borough Council*,[1] where a one-eyed garage hand was struck in his remaining eye by a metal chip and became completely blind. It was not the practice of the employers to supply their workmen with safety spectacles, since they regarded the risk of eye injury as extremely remote. The House of Lords held that, although this approach was justifiable in relation to the other employees, special precautions should have been taken in the plaintiff's case, since he had so much more to lose.

1   [1951] AC 367, [1951] 1 All ER 42, HL.

Value of conduct

19.14   The number of accidents which occur every day could be drastically reduced if certain steps were taken. To take a simple example, it is obvious that road accidents would be far less likely to happen if everyone drove at no more than 10 mph. Can it then be said that anyone who exceeds that speed is automatically guilty of negligence, since he thereby increases the risk of injury to other road users? The answer to this question is, of course, that the reasonable man would regard the increased risk as justified, in view of the enormous inconvenience which would be caused to the general public if all traffic were to move at a snail's pace.

The principle that important ends may be held to justify risky means was invoked in *Daborn v Bath Tramways Motor Co Ltd*,[1] where it was held that the use of a left-hand drive vehicle as an ambulance in wartime was reasonable in view of the shortage of suitable transport, notwithstanding the dangers which it created to other road users when turning right without giving any signal. In *Watt v Hertfordshire County Council*,[2] a heavy jack, which was needed to rescue a woman trapped under a bus, was carried on a lorry not suited to the purpose. During the journey the jack shifted, injuring the plaintiff, a fireman. The Court of Appeal held that the fire brigade's decision to use this unsuitable vehicle was a reasonable one, having regard to the emergency.

1   [1946] 2 All ER 333, CA.
2   [1954] 2 All ER 368, [1954] 1 WLR 835, CA.

Cost of precautions

19.15   In deciding whether a defendant has dealt adequately with a particular risk, the courts will have regard to the ease with which that risk could have been reduced or eliminated. This is not simply a matter of money, although financial considerations are undoubtedly of importance; it also covers questions of convenience and practicability. In extreme cases, where the risk is a very serious one, it may be that the only course of action open to the reasonable man is to cease altogether the dangerous activity, although the courts are reluctant to impose such a heavy burden.[1] In *Withers v Perry Chain Co Ltd*,[2] for example, a woman who was susceptible to dermatitis (a skin complaint caused by contact with grease) was given the driest work which her employers had available; nevertheless, she again contracted the disease. Her argument that the defendants should have dismissed her for her own protection was rejected by the Court of Appeal, who held that such a drastic step could not possibly be justified by the relatively minor risk to which she was exposed.

At the other end of the scale, a person may be held liable for failing to eliminate even a small risk, if he could have done so with ease. As Lord Reid put it:[3] 'It does not follow that, no matter what the circumstances may be, it is justifiable to neglect a risk of such a small magnitude. A reasonable man ... would not neglect such a risk if action to eliminate it presented no difficulty, involved no disadvantage, and required no expense.'

By and large, the objective standard of reasonable care applies to questions of cost and inconvenience as it does to other factors in the assessment of negligence. Thus, once a court decides that a reasonable man would have taken certain precautions (ie that they were not too costly in relation to the risk) a defendant who did not do so is liable, even if he personally could not afford them. However, a degree of subjectivity has been introduced for the benefit of an occupier upon whose land a danger arises through natural causes (and for which he naturally cannot be blamed). Where this happens, it has been held that the occupier may avoid liability to a neighbour by establishing that the actions necessary to eliminate the danger would have been beyond his personal means.[4]

1   See *Bolton v Stone* [1951] AC 850, [1951] 1 All ER 1078, HL; para 19.12 above.
2   [1961] 3 All ER 676, [1961] WLR 1314, CA.
3   *The Wagon Mound (No 2)* [1967] 1 AC 617 at 642, [1966] 2 All ER 709 at 718.
4   *Goldman v Hargrave* [1967] 1 AC 645, [1966] 2 All ER 989.

The proof of negligence

19.16   The burden of proof in negligence actions, as in civil cases generally,[1] lies on the plaintiff. This means that it is for the plaintiff to bring evidence which establishes on the balance of probabilities that the defendant has been careless. If he cannot do this, the plaintiff's claim fails. Thus in *Carter v Sheath*,[2] a 13-year-old pedestrian struck by a car failed in his action against the driver, since there was simply no evidence as to where the plaintiff was when he was hit.

In seeking to establish negligence, a plaintiff may be able to rely on the Civil Evidence Act 1968, s 11 which provides that a criminal conviction for an offence which involves negligence (eg driving without due care and attention) is to be regarded in subsequent civil proceedings as sufficient evidence of negligence. This means that, in subsequent civil proceedings, the defendant's negligence will be presumed, although it is still open to him to rebut this presumption.

1   Para 1.12 above.
2   [1990] RTR 12, CA.

Res ipsa loquitur

19.17 In attempting to prove negligence against the defendant, a plaintiff is entitled to rely on circumstantial evidence. Indeed, in many of the situations in which allegations of negligence are most common, the plaintiff will be forced into this position, since the details of the accident will be known only to the defendant. Where this occurs, the plaintiff may gain assistance from the maxim *res ipsa loquitur* ('the thing speaks for itself'). The operation of this maxim is illustrated by the leading case of *Scott v London and St Katherine Docks Co*,[1] in which the plaintiff, who was walking past the defendant's warehouse, was injured when six bags of sugar fell on him. Neither party could offer any explanation of this occurrence, and the trial judge held that there was not enough evidence to allow the case to go to the jury. However, on appeal, this decision was held to be incorrect, and the following principle was laid down by Erle CJ:

> 'There must be reasonable evidence of negligence. But where the thing is shown to be under the management of the defendant or his servants, and the accident is such as in the ordinary course of things does not happen if those who have the management use proper care, it affords reasonable evidence, in the absence of explanation by the defendants, that the accident arose from want of care.'

It is clear, then, that for *res ipsa loquitur* to apply, it must be shown that:

- the thing which did the damage was under the management and control of the defendant or someone for whom the defendant was responsible; and
- the occurrence was such as would ordinarily indicate negligence.

1   (1865) 3 H & C 596.

Control by the defendant

19.18 The mere fact that an unauthorised person *could* have tampered with the thing which causes injury to the plaintiff will not preclude reliance on *res ipsa loquitur*, provided that such intervention is improbable. Thus, where a railway passenger fell from a moving train immediately after leaving the station, it was held that the carriage doors could be regarded as under the control of the railway company.[1] However, the opposite conclusion was reached in the case of a child falling from the corridor of a train which had travelled a considerable distance since its last stop.[2]

1   *Gee v Metropolitan Rly Co* (1873) LR 8 QB 161.
2   *Easson v London North Eastern Rly Co* [1944] KB 421, [1944] 2 All ER 425, CA.

Inference of negligence

19.19   The facts from which an inference of negligence may be drawn are extremely varied. Apart from the obvious case of objects falling from the upper floors of buildings,[1] the doctrine has been invoked in cases of railway collisions,[2] an aircraft which crashed on taking off,[3] the sudden and violent skid of a motor vehicle[4] and the running down of a pedestrian at night on a dual carriageway road.[5] In *Ward v Tesco Stores Ltd*,[6] where a supermarket customer slipped on some yoghurt which had been spilled on the floor, a majority of the Court of Appeal reached the somewhat doubtful conclusion that, in the absence of further evidence as to how the yoghurt came to be on the floor, its presence there could be attributed to negligence on the part of the defendants.

In practical terms, *res ipsa loquitur* is of most benefit to a plaintiff who is injured by a process the details of which he does not understand, or who cannot show which of the defendant's employees has been guilty of negligence. Common cases include consumers injured by defective products[7] and patients whose condition is rendered worse rather than better by the medical treatment which they receive, as in *Cassidy v Ministry of Health*,[8] where hospital treatment of the plaintiff's two stiff fingers left him with four stiff fingers.

1   *Scott v London and St Katherine Docks Co* (1865) 3 H & C 596; para 19.17 above.
2   *Skinner v London, Brighton and South Coast Rly Co* (1850) 5 Exch 787.
3   *Fosbroke-Hobbes v Airwork Ltd and British American Air Services Ltd* [1937] 1 All ER 108.
4   *Richley v Faull* [1965] 3 All ER 109, [1965] 1 WLR 1454.
5   *Widdowson v Newgate Meat Co* [1997] 47 LS Gaz R 31, CA, where it was said that *res ipsa loquitur* would seldom apply in traffic accident cases.
6   [1976] 1 All ER 219, [1976] 1 WLR 810, CA.
7   Such victims may now hold the manufacturer strictly liable under the Consumer Protection Act 1987.
8   [1951] 2 KB 343, [1951] 1 All ER 574, CA. Also see *Saunders v Leeds Western Health Authority* [1993] 4 Med LR 355 (*res ipsa loquitor* where heart of fit child stopped under anaesthetic).

Effect of the maxim

19.20   The precise effect of *res ipsa loquitur* upon a negligence action is a matter of some controversy. As originally conceived, it entitled a plaintiff to have the case considered by the jury but in no way compelled the jury to find in his favour. However, the removal of the jury from civil actions, leaving them to be tried by the judge alone, has resulted in the position becoming less clear. The courts have appeared on several occasions to treat the maxim as raising a legal presumption, and thus shifting the burden of disproving negligence on to the defendant.[1]

The practical significance of this theoretical controversy is shown by cases in which, after an initial finding that something speaks for itself, the defendant is able to identify the true cause of the accident. The crucial question then becomes whether the defendant must go on to prove that he was not to blame for this cause, or whether the onus of proving negligence reverts to the plaintiff. In *Henderson v Henry E Jenkins & Sons*,[2] where a man was killed by a runaway lorry, the defendants, who were the owners of the lorry, proved that concealed corrosion in a pipe had caused the brakes to fail. The defendants also showed that they had complied with the recommended maintenance schedules in respect of this vehicle. But the House of Lords held that even this was not sufficient to preclude a finding that they were guilty of negligence. In order to do this, they would have had to establish that nothing had happened to the lorry throughout its history which would call for extra precautions to be taken.[3]

The decision in *Henderson v Henry E Jenkins & Sons* is thought by some writers to mean that the legal burden of proof in *res ipsa loquitur* cases is indeed shifted to the defendant. However, this was strongly denied by the Privy Council in *Ng Chun Pui v Lee Chuen Tat*.[4] The defendants there were the owners of a coach which suddenly went out of control, crossing the central reservation of a dual carriageway and colliding with a bus. The Privy Council held that such an occurrence would normally speak for itself; however, once the defendants had shown that their driver had swerved to avoid an unidentified car which had suddenly cut in front of him, the onus of proving negligence was back on the plaintiffs and they had failed to discharge it.

Even where the cause of an accident remains unknown, the defendant may avoid liability by showing that he has not been in any way guilty of negligence. Of course the burden of proof on the defendant in such a case is an extremely heavy one, especially where the evidence consists of little more than his word.[5]

1 The most important cases are *Moore v R Fox & Sons* [1956] 1 QB 596, [1956] 1 All ER 182, CA; *Henderson v Henry E Jenkins & Sons* [1970] AC 282, [1969] 3 All ER 756, HL and *Colvilles Ltd v Devine* [1969] 2 All ER 53, [1969] WLR 475, HL. Authority for the opposite view (ie that the legal burden of proof remains throughout on the plaintiff) is to be found in *Lloyde v West Midlands Gas Board* [1971] 2 All ER 1240, CA; *Turner v Mansfield Corpn* (1975) 119 Sol Jo 629, CA; and *Ng Chun Pui v Lee Chuen Tat* [1988] RTR 298, PC.
2 [1970] AC 282, [1969] 3 All ER 756, HL.
3 Rather less is expected of a private motorist: *Rees v Saville* [1983] RTR 332, CA.
4 [1988] RTR 298, PC.
5 See, for example, *Ludgate v Lovett* [1969] 2 All ER 1275, [1969] 1 WLR 1016, CA.

Chapter 20

Negligence – the causing of damage

20.1 The mere fact that a defendant acts carelessly towards a plaintiff is not enough to render him liable in tort. In order to succeed in an action, the plaintiff must prove that he has suffered damage of a kind which is actionable in the tort in question. For example, a plaintiff who brings an action for negligence must establish that he has suffered personal injury, damage to property or (in certain circumstances) pure financial loss. A plaintiff who complains that, because of negligence by prison officers, he has been segregated from his fellow-prisoners, has therefore not suffered the kind of damage which will support an action in negligence.[1] Less obviously, where negligence on the part of auditors enables a company to continue trading, the company cannot hold the auditors responsible for loans which it thereafter receives, nor for the further losses which it then suffers.[2]

It was held by the House of Lords in *South Australia Asset Management Corpn v York Montague Ltd*[3] that, in order to recover damages, a plaintiff must show that his loss falls within the scope of the defendant's duty. Thus, where a valuer is commissioned to provide a valuation of property, on the basis of which the plaintiff will decide how much to lend, the valuer's duty is merely to take reasonable care to provide accurate information. If he is negligent and thus inaccurate, he will be liable for the consequences of the information being wrong, but not for losses which the lender would have suffered even if the property had been worth as much as the valuer said.

In addition to proving that he has suffered damage, the plaintiff must show that the damage was caused by the defendant's breach of duty. In this connection it must be appreciated that 'causation' in legal terms has a rather more restricted meaning than that given to it in a purely factual sense. To take a simple example: A is walking past some scaffolding when a brick falls on his head. From the *factual* point of view, we might say that A's injuries are caused by his presence there; by the act of a workman who leaned against the stack of bricks; by the action of a labourer who placed the stack in that position; by the decision of the owners to have their building repaired at that time; and so on. Add to these such passive causes (no less essential to the accident) as the law of gravity, without which the brick would have floated safely away, and the regrettable truth that bricks are harder than skulls, and the complexity of factual causation is apparent.

Fortunately perhaps, the lawyer is not concerned to identify all the causes of an accident, but merely to consider whether any or all of a small number of identified conditions (normally the acts or omissions of the parties to a lawsuit) may be regarded as sufficiently important to rank as *legal* causes and thus to attract responsibility. This task, clearly, is one of selection in which the judge, aided by common sense and human experience, arrives at what in the end is a value judgement.

1   *H v Secretary of State for the Home Department* [1992] 22 LS Gaz R 36, CA.
2   *Galoo Ltd v Bright Grahame Murray* [1995] 1 All ER 16, CA.
3   [1996] 3 All ER 365, HL.

20.2   Causation in law is really two problems in one. In the first place, there must be a factual enquiry in order to ascertain whether the conduct of the defendant *can* be regarded as a cause of loss; if it cannot be so regarded, there could be no justification for holding the defendant liable for the plaintiff's misfortune. Second, assuming that the first question receives an affirmative answer, the law must decide whether the defendant's conduct and the plaintiff's damage are sufficiently closely connected that liability *ought* to be imposed. The reason for this second enquiry is that if human activity is not to grind to a complete halt, a line has to be drawn beyond which a wrongdoer is not to be held liable; where that line is drawn depends upon public policy and the good sense of the judge.

An example may make this clear. Suppose that A negligently breaks B's arm. Obviously A is liable for such consequences as B's loss of earnings and medical expenses, and also for the pain which B suffers. What is the position, however, if B is run over by a car on his way to hospital to have the arm set? Or if a post-operative infection causes the arm to be amputated? Or if a boat in which B is travelling a month later sinks, and B is drowned because he cannot swim to safety? Or if, in a fit of depression at being unable to play cricket for his country, B commits suicide? All these catastrophes can in factual terms be traced back to A's original negligence, but should he be legally responsible for them?

Where a court concludes that a particular consequence of the defendant's breach of duty is not sufficiently connected to it to found liability, it may express this by stating that the conduct is not a legal cause or, as is more common today, that the item of damage is too remote.

In this chapter we examine the following issues:

- the way in which the law seeks to decide whether or not a defendant's breach of duty has 'caused' the plaintiff's loss;
- the situations in which the 'chain of causation' is broken, either by the plaintiff himself or by a third party;
- the legal rules which govern 'remoteness of damage', that is, the range of consequences for which a defendant can be held responsible.

Causation in fact

The 'but for' test
20.3   In order to establish whether or not the defendant's act was a factual cause of the plaintiff's injury, a court will normally apply the 'but for' test. According to this test (which, as we show later, is subject to some important exceptions), the question to be asked is whether the damage would have happened but for the defendant's breach of duty. If the answer is that it would not, then that breach may be said, at least in a factual sense, to have been a cause of it.[1] If, however, it would have happened anyway, then the defendant's breach is not a cause.

The operation of the 'but for' test is strikingly shown by the case of *McWilliams v Sir William Arrol & Co Ltd*,[2] in which a steel erector fell to his death from a tower on which he was working. His employers had failed in their statutory obligation to provide him with a safety belt. Nevertheless, his widow's action was successfully answered by showing to a high degree of probability that, even if a belt had been provided, the deceased would not have worn it and would therefore in any event have fallen.[3] Similarly, in *Barnett v Chelsea and Kensington Hospital Management Committee*,[4] a casualty doctor's negligent refusal to examine a poisoned night-watchman was held not to be a cause of his death, since the evidence established that accurate diagnosis would have been too late to save him.

In deciding what would have happened but for the defendant's intervention, the court is of course entering the realm of conjecture. Nevertheless, it appears that a finding on the balance of probabilities is decisive. In *Cutler v Vauxhall Motors Ltd*,[5] the plaintiff, who suffered from an unsuspected varicose condition, grazed an ankle in circumstances which rendered the defendants liable. The graze led to an ulcer, and the plaintiff was forced to undergo an operation to strip the veins. A majority of the Court of Appeal held that, since the plaintiff would probably have required this operation anyway at a later date, the defendants were not liable for it; they had merely accelerated it, rather than caused it to happen. However, the third judge dissented on the ground that the defendants had turned into a certainty what was previously a mere possibility.

It should be remembered that the 'but for' test is essentially exclusive in nature. A cause which does not satisfy this requirement cannot be a legal cause; one which does satisfy it may be treated as legally operative, but only if a court regards it as sufficiently important. In *Rouse v Squires*,[6] for example, a negligently driven lorry jack-knifed and blocked two lanes of a motorway. In trying to avoid it, a second lorry, also negligently driven, skidded and killed a bystander. The accident would obviously not have happened but for the presence of both lorries, and the Court of Appeal held that both drivers were liable.[7] In *Dymond v Pearce*,[8] by contrast, where a motor cyclist injured his pillion passenger by negligently driving into a parked lorry, it was held that the lorry's presence, although again a necessary condition for the accident, was not a legal cause of it; responsibility here was attributed solely to the motor cyclist.

1   Note that the defendant is in no way excused merely because other factors were also necessary.
2   [1962] 1 All ER 623, [1962] 1 WLR 295, HL.
3   Where a defendant is admittedly in breach of a safety regulation, such an argument is unlikely to succeed unless the evidence is overwhelming.
4   [1969] 1 QB 428, [1968] 1 All ER 1068.
5   [1971] 1 QB 418, [1970] 2 All ER 56, CA.
6   [1973] QB 889, [1973] 2 All ER 903, CA.
7   Liability was apportioned at 25% to the first driver and 75% to the second.
8   [1972] 1 QB 496, [1972] 1 All ER 1142, CA.

Proof

20.4   There is sometimes a tendency to assume that causation in the factual sense is an absolute; that it is either definitely present or definitely absent. This assumption, however, is erroneous; in matters of causation, as in all other elements of liability, it is for the plaintiff to prove his case on the balance of probabilities. In *Metropolitan Rly Co v Jackson*,[1] for example, a railway passenger's hand was crushed when a porter, without negligence, slammed the door of the compartment. The plaintiff's hand was in that position because he was standing up to prevent more people from entering the compartment, which the defendants had negligently permitted to become overcrowded. The plaintiff claimed that his injury could be attributed to this original negligence, but the House of Lords held that the evidence did not justify this conclusion.

Where the attempt to prove causation reveals an 'evidential gap', the courts in a number of cases have shown a willingness to resolve the causal doubts in favour of the plaintiff. A striking example of this is the decision of the House of Lords in *McGhee v National Coal Board*,[2] where the plaintiff's job exposed him to abrasive brick dust. The plaintiff contracted dermatitis and claimed that this was due to the defendants' failure to provide washing facilities on site, as a result of which he had to cycle home each day still caked with dust and sweat. It was held that, although a positive connection could not be established between the defendants' failure and the plaintiff's injury (since his exposure to the brick dust might have been enough to cause dermatitis even if washing facilities had been provided), it was sufficient to impose liability upon the defendants that they had materially increased the risk.

The *McGhee* principle might appear to be a powerful weapon for plaintiffs, but it has subsequently been treated in a very restrictive way by the House of Lords. In *Hotson v East Berkshire Health Authority*,[3] the plaintiff, who was injured in a fall, claimed that the defendants' negligent failure to make a correct diagnosis of his injuries had allowed a more serious medical condition to develop. The evidence established that, when the plaintiff was first examined by the defendants, there was already a 75% likelihood that this condition would develop. The trial judge and the Court of Appeal awarded the plaintiff 25% of the damages claimed, on the basis that the defendants' negligence had turned a 75% risk into an inevitability. However, this approach was rejected by the House of Lords, which ruled that the plaintiff in these circumstances could only recover by showing that the defendants were responsible for his medical condition, something which, on the balance of probabilities, he was clearly unable to do.

It should not be thought, on the basis of *Hotson v East Berkshire Health Authority*, that damages can never be awarded for loss of a chance. In *Allied Maples Group Ltd v Simmons & Simmons*,[4] the plaintiff company entered into a contract to purchase certain business property on the basis of advice from its solicitors, the defendants. The advice was negligent and, as a result, the plaintiffs incurred liabilities. The plaintiffs alleged that, had they been given the correct advice, they would have taken steps to protect themselves against these liabilities, but the defendants pointed out that the success of those steps would have depended upon negotiations with a third party. The Court of Appeal held that, once the plaintiffs had proved that they would have taken the necessary steps, it was not necessary for them also to prove on the balance of probabilities that the negotiations with the third party would have succeeded; they were entitled to damages based on the chance that this would have been so.

1   (1877) 3 App Cas 193, HL.
2   [1972] 3 All ER 1008, HL. See also *Fitzgerald v Lane* [1987] QB 781, CA.
3   [1987] 2 All ER 909, HL. See also *Wilsher v Essex AHA* [1988] 1 All ER 871, HL, where the defendants' negligence was only one of six possible causes of the infant plaintiff's blindness.
4   [1995] 4 All ER 907, CA.

Multiple causes

20.5   Unfortunately, the 'but for' test is apt to lose its potency in the very situations in which causation becomes most difficult. Suppose, for example, that two independent fires, negligently lit by A and B, together destroy C's house. Can A and B each evade liability by claiming that the house would in any event have been destroyed by the other fire? Clearly, no legal system could tolerate such an absurdity, and so both A and B are liable in full. Of course, this does not mean that the plaintiff can recover double damages. He may take his compensation as he chooses (all from one defendant, or some from each) and, once he has done so, the defendants may seek contribution from each other in proportions assessed by the court.[1]

In the example of the two fires, either cause would have sufficed to bring about the damage in question. The same applies, however, where both are necessary, for instance where a passenger is injured in a collision caused by two negligent drivers. Thus, the defendants in *Bonnington Castings Ltd v Wardlaw*[2] were held liable in full when their employee contracted silicosis after inhaling noxious dust over a long period, notwithstanding that part of the noxious dust came from a source for which the defendants were not responsible.

1 Paras 29.15–29.16 below.
2 [1956] AC 613, [1956] 1 All ER 615, HL.

Overlapping injuries
20.6 In the last paragraph we were concerned with the plaintiff who suffers one item of loss as a result of two or more independent causes. Slightly different is the case where the same injuries, or injuries which overlap each other, are 'caused' on separate occasions. The rule here is that the first cause in time is treated as the legally operative one, to the exclusion of all others. This may be illustrated by *Performance Cars Ltd v Abraham*,[1] where the defendant damaged the plaintiffs' car in such a way that it required a repaint. In fact, however, as the result of a previous accident, the car already required a repaint, and it was accordingly held that the defendant could not be said to have caused this item of damage.

The principle of this case is that the second tortfeasor takes his victim as he finds him (ie in a damaged state). The effect which this has upon the liability of the first tortfeasor was considered in the important case of *Baker v Willoughby*,[2] in which the defendant was responsible for negligently injuring the plaintiff's leg and thereby reducing his earning capacity. Some time later, but before the case came to trial, the plaintiff was shot by robbers and his injured leg had to be amputated. The question was whether the defendant's liability for loss of earnings ceased at the time of the amputation. The Court of Appeal held that it did, on the ground that the second injury effectively 'swallowed up' the first. The House of Lords, however, pointed out that since the robbers, if sued, would be liable only for depriving the plaintiff of an already damaged leg, this solution would leave him out of pocket. It was accordingly held that, in assessing the defendant's liability, the second injury was to be ignored.

It should be noted that the approach adopted in *Baker v Willoughby* does not apply where the other cause of injury is natural, rather than tortious. In *Jobling v Associated Dairies Ltd*,[3] it was held that a plaintiff's damages for loss of earnings should only compensate him up to the date on which an earlier injury would in any case have rendered him totally disabled. The House of Lords there pointed out that any other result would over-compensate the plaintiff, and suggested that the *Baker v Willoughby* approach can only be justified by the need to prevent the plaintiff from falling between two tortfeasors, in the sense of being unable to obtain compensation from either of them.

1 [1962] 1 QB 33, [1961] 3 All ER 413, CA.
2 [1970] AC 467, [1969] 3 All ER 1528, HL.
3 [1982] AC 794, [1981] 2 All ER 752, HL.

Intervening causes

20.7 Particular problems arise in cases where the injury or damage to the plaintiff is separated from the defendant's wrongful act by what has been called 'the conscious act of another volition'. The question for the court to decide is whether such an act, which may be carried out by a third party or by the plaintiff himself, is sufficient to 'break the chain of causation' and thus to free the defendant from liability.

It should be understood that a decision on this question cannot be made upon factual or scientific grounds, since the defendant's conduct is undoubtedly a cause of the plaintiff's injury in the factual sense. It is in truth a value judgement; the judge must evaluate the intervening conduct in order to decide whether responsibility, whether partial or total, should still attach to the defendant. A good example of this evaluation is provided by the case of *Wright v Lodge*,[1] in which a lorry, travelling at an excessive speed on a foggy night, crashed into a car which had broken down and was stationary on a dual carriageway road. The lorry then veered out of control on to the opposite carriageway and caused a fatal accident. The Court of Appeal held that, although the negligence of the car driver in failing to push her car off the road was a partial (10%) cause of the original collision, it was not a cause of the subsequent accident, for which the lorry driver was wholly responsible.

We now examine a number of examples of intervening acts, by both third parties and plaintiffs, drawn from decided cases, before considering whether it is possible to reduce the question of intervening cause to a statement of legal principle.

1   [1993] 4 All ER 299, CA.

Conduct of a third party
'Innocent' conduct
20.8   The chain of causation will seldom, if ever, be held to have been broken by the act of a third party who, for one reason or another, cannot be regarded as fully responsible for his actions. Where, for example, the defendant's negligence consists of leaving his horse untethered in the street, he cannot avoid liability by pointing out that it was stampeded by mischievous children.[1] Similarly, the unthinking action of a person in an emergency will not be regarded as the conscious act of another volition. In *Scott v Shepherd*,[2] the defendant threw a lighted squib in a crowded market. Two people in turn, seeking to protect themselves and their goods, picked up the squib and threw it away; it finally exploded in the plaintiff's eye. The defendant was held liable.

The emergency principle can on occasion be extended beyond the instinctive reactions of an endangered person to cover also his reasonable, albeit mistaken, decisions. In *The Oropesa*,[3] one of the many maritime collision cases to have raised this point, the master of a badly damaged ship launched a boat in heavy seas towards the *Oropesa*, which had been responsible for the collision, in order to discuss salvage. The boat overturned and a seaman was drowned. It was held that the seaman's death could be attributed to the negligence of the *Oropesa*; the decision of the other ship's master, at a time when the hand of the casualty lay heavily upon him, could not be said to break the chain of causation.

It should not be thought from what has been said above that a decision taken in an emergency can never be challenged on the ground of negligence. In *Knightley v Johns*[4] a police inspector, who was in control following an accident in a one-way road tunnel, ordered a police motor cyclist to ride through the tunnel against the traffic flow, in order to stop cars from entering the tunnel. When the motor cyclist was struck by a car and injured, it was held by the Court of Appeal that the inspector's order was negligent; moreover, this broke the chain of causation between the injury to the plaintiff and the negligence of the motorist who had caused the original accident.

1   *Haynes v Harwood* [1935] 1 KB 146, CA.
2   (1773) 2 Wm Bl 892.
3   [1943] P 32, [1943] 1 All ER 211, CA.
4   [1982] 1 All ER 851, [1982] 1 WLR 349, CA.

'Guilty' conduct
20.9   As *Knightley v Johns*[1] shows, a negligent act of a third party may be sufficient to exempt the defendant from liability. However, it must again be emphasised that such decisions represent judicial value judgements, and it cannot be assumed that this

will always be the case. In *Prendergast v Sam and Dee*,[2] for example, where a doctor's bad handwriting led a pharmacist negligently to dispense the wrong drug, both the doctor and the pharmacist were held liable in negligence to the plaintiff.

A negligent intervention by a third party may or may not break the chain of causation, but it might be thought that any deliberate, conscious act by a person of full capacity, in circumstances where there is no emergency, would always do so. However, even here the courts are occasionally prepared to trace liability back to the defendant. In *Philco Radio Ltd v J Spurling Ltd*,[3] the defendants negligently misdelivered cases of highly inflammable material to the plaintiffs' premises. A typist employed by the plaintiffs (intending to do minor damage, although unaware of the true contents) touched a case with a lighted cigarette and a serious explosion and fire resulted. The defendants were held liable, notwithstanding the typist's act. Indeed, in extreme cases it has been held that even a deliberate criminal act may not break the chain of causation. This is shown by *Stansbie v Troman*,[4] where a decorator, who was working alone in the plaintiff's house, left it unlocked and unoccupied for two hours. He was held liable for a theft of jewellery which occurred during his absence.

1   [1982] 1 All ER 851, [1982] 1 WLR 349, CA; para 20.8 above.
2   [1989] 1 Med LR 36, CA.
3   [1949] 2 All ER 882, CA.
4   [1948] 2 KB 48, [1948] 1 All ER 599, CA.

Conduct of the plaintiff

20.10   Principles similar to those which govern the conduct of a third party may also apply to an intervening act of the plaintiff himself, which may be held by the court to be so unreasonable that the effect of the defendant's original wrongdoing is entirely wiped out. In *McKew v Holland and Hannen and Cubitts (Scotland) Ltd*,[1] for example, an accident for which the defendants were responsible left the plaintiff's leg with a tendency to collapse suddenly and without warning. When, a few days later, knowing of this tendency, the plaintiff attempted to descend a steep staircase without assistance, it was held that he was entirely to blame for his resulting fall. On the other hand, in *Pigney v Pointers Transport Services Ltd*,[2] the defendants were held liable when serious head injuries, for which they were responsible, led the injured person several months later to commit suicide.

A decision upon the effect of the plaintiff's conduct is frequently treated as a question of *volenti non fit injuria* (ie by asking whether the plaintiff has assumed the risk of injury)[3] rather than as one of causation. In modern times, however, an even more common tendency is to treat the case as one of contributory negligence,[4] so as to enable a more flexible decision to be reached. Using this approach, a court can hold that the plaintiff's conduct, while not so outrageous as to exonerate the defendant entirely, is nevertheless a sufficiently significant cause of his injury that he should, by suffering a reduction in the damages awarded, be made to bear a proportion of his own loss.

In a number of cases, it can safely be said that the plaintiff's conduct will not affect causation, nor indeed amount to contributory negligence; these are considered below.

1   [1969] 3 All ER 1621, HL.
2   [1957] 2 All ER 807, [1957] 1 WLR 1121.
3   Paras 21.2–21.10 below.
4   Paras 21.11–21.16 below.

Rescue cases

20.11   The act of a person who knowingly courts danger in attempting to rescue persons or even property[1] will not normally break the chain of causation. In *Haynes v Harwood*,[2] for example, the owner of a runaway horse was held liable to a policeman, who was injured in attempting to stop it in a crowded street. However, where the rescue attempt is unreasonable, for example because the danger outweighs the value of what is threatened, the chain of causation may be broken. In *Cutler v United Dairies (London) Ltd*,[3] the plaintiff was injured in helping the driver of a milk float whose runaway horse had come to rest safely in a field. The Court of Appeal held that, since the danger was over at the time of the plaintiff's intervention, he must be regarded as having caused his own injury. A rescuer has also been held to be a partial cause of his own injury and thus to be guilty of contributory negligence,[4] although this related to the manner in which he went about the rescue rather than his initial decision to attempt it.[5]

1   *Hyett v Great Western Rly Co* [1948] 1 KB 345, [1947] 2 All ER 264, CA.
2   [1935] 1 KB 146, CA.
3   [1933] 2 KB 297, CA.
4   Paras 21.11–21.16 below.
5   *Harrison v British Railway's Board* [1981] 3 All ER 679.

Emergencies

20.12   Like third parties, whom we discussed in para 20.8 above, plaintiffs who are faced with an emergency are given considerable latitude by the courts, in the sense that an instinctive decision, albeit one which turns out to be wrong, will not break the chain of causation unless it is totally unreasonable. In *Jones v Boyce*,[1] the defendant's negligence led the plaintiff to believe that his stagecoach, in which the plaintiff was a passenger, was about to overturn. The coach did not in fact overturn but the plaintiff, in jumping to safety, broke his leg. The defendant was held liable.

1   (1816) 1 Stark 493. See also *Colvilles Ltd v Devine* [1969] 2 All ER 53, [1969] 1 WLR 475, HL.

Legal rights

20.13   The generous treatment which is given by the courts to plaintiffs in an emergency is also reflected in their attitude towards those who act in defence of their legal rights, where these are infringed by the defendant. In *Clayards v Dethick and Davis*,[1] for example, the defendant unlawfully dug a trench in such a way that the sole access to the plaintiff's stables became dangerous. When a horse which the plaintiff attempted to lead out was injured, the defendant was held liable; it could not be said that the plaintiff had caused his own loss, since this was a risk which he was perfectly entitled to take in exercising his right of way.

In the celebrated case of *Sayers v Harlow UDC*,[2] the Court of Appeal reached a compromise solution. The plaintiff there was trapped in a public toilet by the negligence of the defendant local authority, who were responsible for the fact that there was no handle on the inside of the toilet door. In trying to climb out in order to catch a bus, the plaintiff fell and was injured. It was held that, since the plaintiff's predicament was one of inconvenience rather than danger, her attempt to escape was unreasonable; she should, it was held, have endured her loss of liberty rather than run this risk. Nonetheless, her negligence could not be said to have wiped out altogether the effects of the defendants' negligence, and so the plaintiff was held to be 25% responsible for her injuries.

1   (1848) 12 QB 439.
2   [1958] 2 All ER 342, [1958] 1 WLR 623, CA.

Test of intervening cause

20.14   It is clear, from the cases mentioned above, that the question whether or not an intervening act breaks the chain of causation and so exculpates the defendant cannot be answered simply by asking whether or not that act was 'the conscious act of another volition'. It must indeed be regarded as highly doubtful whether a single satisfactory test can be devised; most of the judicial attempts to do so have concentrated either upon the foreseeability of the intervening act or upon its reasonableness. In so far as these tests are designed to show what is an intervening cause, rather than what is not, they are patently inadequate. The conduct of the typist, for example, in *Philco Radio Ltd v J Spurling Ltd*[1] must, by any rational standards, be regarded as both unreasonable and unforeseeable; yet the chain of causation remained unbroken.

The converse proposition, that a foreseeable or reasonable act does not exonerate the defendant, is much closer to the truth. Even here, however, there are exceptions. In *Quinn v Burch Bros (Builders) Ltd*,[2] the plaintiff fell from an unstable trestle, which he was using because the defendants had failed in their contractual duty to provide him with a stepladder. The Court of Appeal held that the plaintiff's unreasonable decision to adopt this dangerous practice was the sole cause of his injury, even though it was foreseeable. It should be noted that it was not open to the court in this case to reduce the damages on the ground of contributory negligence by the plaintiff; the action was one for breach of a contract term not involving an obligation to take reasonable care, so that the Law Reform (Contributory Negligence) Act 1945 did not apply.[3]

In truth it seems that no single legal test can be devised which will accurately predict the outcome of what is essentially a practical, common sense enquiry. The question is whether, in the opinion of the judge, the intervening cause can be regarded as arising in the ordinary course of things out of the risks created by the defendant's breach of duty, or whether it is so powerful and overwhelming that it relegates the defendant's conduct from the status of 'cause' to being merely part of the surrounding circumstances.

1   [1949] 2 KB 33, [1949] 2 All ER 882, CA; para 20.9 above.
2   [1966] 2 QB 370, [1966] 2 All ER 283, CA.
3   See paras 12.18 above and 21.12 below.

Remoteness of damage

20.15   Even where it can be shown that the defendant's breach of duty is a factual cause of the plaintiff's injury, and that no intervening cause has deprived it of relevance, it is still not certain that the defendant will be held responsible for a particular consequence. In attempting to keep liability for a single act of negligence within bounds, the law treats certain results as too remote from the original tort to found an action.[1] The principle on which a decision as to remoteness is based is somewhat elusive; English law has wavered between two different tests.

1   The same principle applies to actions for breach of contract, although the detailed rules are different; paras 12.10–12.15 above.

The 'directness' test

20.16   In 1921 the Court of Appeal laid down the rule that, once a defendant was shown to have committed an act of negligence against a plaintiff, he was liable for all the *direct* consequences of that act, whether or not they were *foreseeable*. It is important to realise that this test did not render the question of foreseeability totally irrelevant for, unless the circumstances were such that the defendant ought to have foreseen some kind of injury or damage to the plaintiff, he could not be said to have been negligent at all. What the test meant was that, once it could be shown that some damage to the plaintiff was foreseeable, whether or not this actually materialised,[1] the defendant was liable for all the damage caused by him, however unforeseeable this might be in kind or extent, or in the manner of its infliction.

The operation of the directness test is exemplified by the case of *Re Polemis and Furness, Withy & Co*,[2] in which it was established. The defendants in that case, having chartered the plaintiffs' ship, used it to carry tins of petrol. Unknown to anyone, petrol vapour leaked from these tins, so that, when the defendants' employees carelessly caused a plank to fall into the hold, and this struck a spark, the ship was completely destroyed by fire. It was found as a fact that the reasonable man would not have foreseen the possibility of fire, although he would have foreseen the possibility of other forms of damage from the plank's impact. The Court of Appeal held that the possibility of this relatively minor damage was enough to render the employees, and through them the defendants, guilty of negligence in dropping the plank. Given this, the defendants were liable in full for the ship's loss, notwithstanding the unforeseeable way in which this occurred.

An important limitation was placed upon the *Re Polemis* principle in *Liesbosch Dredger v SS Edison*,[3] where the plaintiffs' dredger was sunk by the negligence of the defendants. The plaintiffs were at that time engaged in performing contract work which, on pain of heavy penalty clauses, they had to complete within a given time. Consequently, they required a substitute dredger immediately and, lacking the financial resources necessary to buy one, had to hire one at exorbitant rates. The House of Lords held that, while the plaintiffs were entitled to claim from the defendants the cost of buying a suitable replacement dredger, the hire charges were too remote, since these resulted from the plaintiffs' own lack of funds. The plaintiffs' argument based on *Re Polemis* was rejected; this principle, it was said, applied only to the direct *physical* consequences of a negligent act.

1   *Thurogood v Van Den Berghs and Jurgens Ltd* [1951] 2 KB 537, [1951] 1 All ER 682, CA.
2   [1921] 3 KB 560, CA.
3   [1933] AC 449, HL.

The 'foreseeability' test

20.17   Despite criticisms of it as being both unjust and illogical, the directness test was applied by the courts for 40 years until, in the case of *Overseas Tankship (UK) v Morts Dock and Engineering Co*[1] (commonly known as *The Wagon Mound*), the Privy Council declared it to be wrong. The facts of that case were that the defendants negligently spilled large quantities of fuel oil into Sydney Harbour while their ship was being bunkered. Wind and tide carried this oil to the plaintiffs' wharf, where two ships were being repaired by means of oxy-acetylene welding. The plaintiffs ceased welding because of the fire risk but, on being assured by experts that fuel oil spread thus thinly on cool water would not ignite, recommenced; as a result a catastrophic fire badly damaged both the wharf and the ships. The Australian courts held that, since some damage to the plaintiffs' wharf was foreseeable, viz the fouling of the slipways, the defendants were also responsible (on the basis of *Re Polemis*) for the damage done by fire, notwithstanding that this was unforeseeable. However, on appeal, the Privy Council held that foreseeability must embrace, not only the fact of injury, but also its kind; therefore, in this case, the defendants were not liable for the damage done by fire, since it was unforeseeable.

In *Overseas Tankship (UK) v Miller SS Co Pty*,[2] (commonly known as *The Wagon Mound (No 2)*), a second action arose out of the same incident, this time brought by the owners of the damaged ships. The evidence which was put before the trial judge on this occasion[3] indicated that a reasonable ship's officer would have regarded fire as a possibility, albeit a slight one. The Privy Council held that, so long as the risk was not so remote that a reasonable man would brush it aside as far-fetched, it was foreseeable enough; accordingly, the defendants were held liable.

Two claims have been made for the *Wagon Mound* doctrine. In the first place, it has been said to be logically superior to *Re Polemis* in that it applies the same test to remoteness of damage as that which governs the initial question of breach of duty. On close examination, however, it may be doubted whether the foreseeability test is applied in quite the same way in these two areas. Where breach of duty is concerned, a court is concerned to assess how foreseeable the damage was, and to balance the degree of foreseeability against other factors.[4] Where remoteness of damage is concerned, the principle appears to be that the defendant is liable if the damage in question was foreseeable to any degree at all.

Apart from being arguably more logical than *Re Polemis,* the *Wagon Mound* principle is also said to be more just, since it is unfair to expose a defendant who is guilty of a trivial act of negligence to liability for the serious unforeseeable consequences of that act. This, however, prompts the question: given that the unforeseeable loss must fall on someone, is it more just to place it on the defendant, who is at least guilty of some negligence, or on the plaintiff, who is guilty of none at all? In truth, the answer is a matter of policy, and depends upon whether plaintiffs or defendants are to be favoured.

The practical effects of the change from directness to foreseeability can best be measured by considering separately the three identifying characteristics of any particular consequence in respect of which damages may be claimed. These are the kind of damage, the manner of its infliction and its extent. As we shall see, the interpretation which since 1961 has been given to foreseeability in this area means that the change brought about by the *Wagon Mound* principle is less fundamental than might have been expected.

1   [1961] AC 388, [1961] 1 All ER 404, PC.
2   [1967] 1 AC 617, [1966] 2 All ER 709, PC.
3   Why the evidence in the two cases was different is not easy to see. It may be, however, that the plaintiffs in *Wagon Mound (No 1)* did not really want to establish that the fire was foreseeable, lest they be held contributorily negligent for continuing with their welding.
4   Paras 19.11–19.15 above.

Kind of damage

20.18   Under *Re Polemis,* the requirement of foreseeability extended to the kind of damage in issue only in the very broad sense that the law distinguished between injury to the person and to property. Since *Wagon Mound,* however, it is clear that the categories are narrower (foreseeability of damage by fouling, for example, will not render a defendant liable for damage by fire). The extent to which this represents a change in the law depends upon how precisely these classes are defined, and the general trend of decisions since 1961 has undoubtedly been against the drawing of over nice distinctions. In *Bradford v Robinson Rentals Ltd,*[1] for example, a van driver, sent by his employers on a long journey in exceptionally cold weather in an unheated vehicle, suffered frostbite. It was held that, even if frostbite itself was unforeseeable, it was insufficiently akin to other foreseeable injuries from cold and fatigue to permit recovery.

1   [1967] 1 All ER 267, [1967] WLR 337.

Manner of infliction of damage

20.19   The approach of judges to the question of how damage is caused has, by and large, shown the same generosity as that which characterises their treatment of 'kind of damage'. Once again, foreseeability of the general outline, rather than of precise details, is all that is required. For example, where the defendant negligently causes a ship to collide with a quay, the true test of remoteness is whether it is foreseeable that the ship will suffer damage to its hull, not whether it is foreseeable that its hull will be holed by a badly designed fender on the side of the quay.[1] Furthermore, there has been a readiness to impose liability upon the defendant where an injury which he has caused to the plaintiff leads to a second accident,[2] to medical treatment with adverse effects,[3] or to even more unlikely consequences.[4]

The general attitude of the courts is well illustrated by the case of *Hughes v Lord Advocate*,[5] where employees of the Post Office left an open manhole covered by a canvas shelter and surrounded by paraffin warning lamps. An eight-year-old boy took one of these lamps into the shelter, where he accidentally knocked it down the hole; there was a violent explosion and the boy was severely burned. The Scottish courts held that the defendants were not liable, on the ground that, while injury by burning was foreseeable, the explosion was not. The House of Lords, however, held that such a distinction was too fine to be accepted, and that the accident fell within the area of risk which the defendants had created.

Occasionally, a decision stands out as taking a much narrower line, although it may for that very reason be regarded with some doubt. One such is *Doughty v Turner Manufacturing Co Ltd*,[6] where the defendants' employee negligently dropped an asbestos cement cover into a cauldron of molten liquid. There was no splash, but two minutes later, due to an unforeseeable chemical reaction, the liquid erupted and the plaintiff was burned. The Court of Appeal held that, even if injury by splashing were foreseeable, this eruption was not; nor could it be treated as a mere variant of the foreseeable risk. The defendants were accordingly not liable.

1 *Prekookeanska Plovidba v Felstar Shipping Corpn, The Carnival* [1994] 2 Lloyd's Rep 14, CA.
2 *Wieland v Cyril Lord Carpets Ltd* [1969] 3 All ER 1006.
3 *Robinson v Post Office* [1974] 2 All ER 737, [1974] 1 WLR 1176, CA.
4 See the cases discussed in para 20.21 below.
5 [1963] AC 837, [1963] 1 All ER 705, HL.
6 [1964] 1 QB 518, [1964] 1 All ER 98, CA.

Extent of damage

20.20 While the kind of damage and the manner in which it is caused must both be reasonably foreseeable, albeit in only a general sense, it appears that the extent of the damage need not be foreseeable at all. In *Vacwell Engineering Co Ltd v BDH Chemicals Ltd*,[1] for example, the defendants negligently failed to warn the plaintiffs that a chemical which they had supplied was liable to explode on contact with water. An employee of the plaintiffs placed a large quantity of this substance in a sink. This resulted in a violent explosion, which extensively damaged the plaintiffs' premises. It was found that, while a minor explosion was foreseeable, one of this magnitude was not; nevertheless, the defendants were held liable for all the damage.

The best-known illustrations of the principle that the extent of damage is not subject to the requirement of foreseeability are the so-called 'egg-shell skull' cases, in which the defendant is held fully liable when the plaintiff's injuries are aggravated by some inherent defect such as haemophilia, notwithstanding that the defendant could not possibly have foreseen this. The basis for these decisions is the rule that a tortfeasor takes his victim as he finds him, a rule which was held, in *Smith v Leech Brain & Co Ltd*,[2] to have survived *The Wagon Mound*. The defendants in that case negligently caused an employee's lip to be burned by molten metal. This burn activated an unsuspected pre-malignant cancerous condition which, three years later, led to the man's death. The defendants were held liable, not only for the initial burn, but also for the death.

Although the egg-shell skull principle has been applied to plaintiffs with a weak heart,[3] an allergy to certain vaccine[4] and even an 'egg-shell personality',[5] the House of Lords ruled in 1933 that it could not be extended to a plaintiff's financial state.[6]

Consequently, if the loss caused to a plaintiff was aggravated due to his lack of means, the additional loss could not be treated as having been caused by the defendant. More recently, the courts have retreated somewhat from this position;[7] on several occasions, the Court of Appeal has distinguished *Liesbosch Dredger v SS Edison* on grounds which are unconvincing. For example, in *Dodd Properties (Kent) Ltd v Canterbury City Council*,[8] the plaintiffs sued the defendants for the cost of repairing their garage, which the defendants had negligently damaged. By the time the case came to court, the cost of repairs had escalated and the defendants claimed that they were liable only for what the repairs would have cost if put in hand at an earlier date. The Court of Appeal held that, while pure lack of funds would have given the plaintiffs no excuse to delay, and would thus have restricted their claim to the lower figure, their decision to delay until they had recovered damages (based upon principles of cash flow) was a reasonable one. The defendants were therefore liable in full.

1 [1971] 1 QB 111n, [1970] 3 All ER 553n, CA.
2 [1962] 2 QB 405, [1961] 2 All ER 1159.
3 *Love v Port of London Authority* [1959] 2 Lloyd's Rep 541.
4 *Robinson v Post Office* [1974] 2 All ER 737, [1974] 1 WLR 1176, CA.
5 *Malcolm v Broadhurst* [1970] 3 All ER 508.
6 *Liesbosch Dredger v SS Edison* [1933] AC 449, HL; para 20.16 above.
7 But see *Ramwade v WJ Emson & Co* [1987] RTR 72, CA.
8 [1980] 1 All ER 928, [1980] 1 WLR 433, CA; para 29.14 below.

Policy considerations

20.21 Decisions on both legal causation and remoteness of damage are, in truth, value judgments in which a judge's personal experience, common sense and notions of public policy all play their part. Notwithstanding the lip service which is habitually paid to the test of reasonable foreseeability, it must be all too obvious that many problems arise which no legal system can possibly answer by the mechanical application of such a principle. Among such difficult issues of policy which have troubled the Court of Appeal are whether a person should be held liable for negligently failing to prevent another from attempting or committing suicide[1] and whether a defendant who causes the plaintiff severe head injuries leading to a personality change can be held responsible when the plaintiff's wife divorces him.[2]

In *Clunis v Camden and Islington Health Authority*[3] the plaintiff, a mentally disordered person, was in the care of the defendants when he killed a stranger in an unprovoked attack, for which he was convicted of manslaughter. He sued the defendants for negligently failing to control him, but this claim was rejected by the Court of Appeal, which ruled that a person could not recover damages on the basis of his own criminal act, unless he either did not know the nature and quality of that act or did not know that it was wrong.

The court in *Clunis* was not faced in that case by a claim on behalf of the victim, but such a claim was rejected in the earlier case of *Meah v McCreamer (No 2)*.[4] The plaintiff in that case, who had suffered serious head injuries in a road accident for which the defendant was responsible, subsequently carried out a series of sexual assaults for which he was sentenced to life imprisonment. When the plaintiff was successfully sued by two of his rape victims,[5] it was held that public policy would not allow him to reclaim from the driver the damages which he had to pay, nor would it permit those victims to sue the driver directly.

1 See *Hyde v Tameside Area Health Authority* (1981) Times, 16 April, CA (no); *Kirkham v Chief Constable of the Greater Manchester Police* [1990] 2 QB 283, [1990] 3 All ER 246, CA (yes); *Reeves v Metropolitan Police Comr* [1998] 2 All ER 381, CA (yes).
2 *Jones v Jones* [1984] 3 All ER 1003, [1984] 3 WLR 862, CA (yes); *Pritchard v JH Cobden Ltd* [1987] 1 All ER 300, CA (no).

3 [1998] 3 All ER 180, CA.
4 [1986] 1 All ER 943.
5 *W v Meah* [1986] 1 All ER 935.

Chapter 21

Defences to negligence

21.1 A defendant in a negligence action may seek to defeat the plaintiff's claim by arguing that one of the essential elements of liability is missing. He may, for example, be able to show the court that no duty of care was owed, or that his carelessness did not cause the plaintiff's loss. In so doing, the defendant does not in truth establish a defence; rather the plaintiff has failed to make out his case.

Apart from producing arguments of the kind outlined above, the defendant may seek to rely on either or both of two specific defences. These are, first, *volenti non fit injuria,* the rule that a person cannot complain of harm to which he has expressly or impliedly consented, or of which he has assumed the legal risk; and, second, contributory negligence, which applies where the plaintiff is partly responsible for his own injury. A significant difference between these defences is that a plea of *volenti,* if successful, defeats the plaintiff's action altogether. Contributory negligence, on the other hand, is no longer a complete answer but, since 1945, has led only to a reduction in the damages awarded. The added flexibility which contributory negligence thus gives the courts has led them to prefer this defence, and it has consequently become most unusual to find *volenti* successfully pleaded. However, in *Morris v Murray*,[1] where the plaintiff accepted a flight in the defendant's light aircraft in bad weather when both parties were drunk, the Court of Appeal held that the plaintiff's claim for injuries received in the ensuing crash must fail altogether. The court was asked merely to reduce the plaintiff's damages for contributory negligence but refused to do so, stating that 'the wild irresponsibility of the venture is such that the law should not intervene to award damages and should leave the loss where it falls'.

In this chapter we examine the following issues:

- the extent to which a person is debarred from claiming damages in respect of harm to which he has consented, or of which he has voluntarily assumed the risk;
- the problems involved in applying the concept of 'assumption of risk' to cases of negligence;
- the power of the courts to divide responsibility between plaintiff and defendant where both are partly responsible for causing the plaintiff's loss.

1   [1990] 3 All ER 801, CA.

Volenti non fit injuria

Consent

21.2 The defence of *volenti non fit injuria* is the plaintiff's consent (albeit that this may be fictitious). This is most straightforward in relation to intentional torts such as trespass to the person; a boxer cannot complain of a fair punch, for example, nor a patient of the invasion of his body which is inherent in a surgical operation.[1] Consent, however, has its limits; even a participant in a fist fight may not be precluded from claiming damages if his antagonist inflicts serious injury with a savage blow which is quite out of proportion to the occasion.[2]

Volenti is also a relatively simple matter in relation to torts of strict liability, although the terminology here is different; the plaintiff will lose his case wherever it can fairly be said that he has assumed the legal risk of being injured. Thus, a person who keeps a dog which he knows to be vicious takes the legal risk that it will bite someone; but that legal risk will be transferred to the shoulders of anyone who ignores a clear 'Beware of the Dog' notice.[3]

1 See para 21.3 below.
2 *Lane v Holloway* [1968] 1 QB 379, [1967] 3 All ER 129, CA.
3 *Cummings v Granger* [1977] QB 397, [1977] 1 All ER 104, CA.

Knowledge

21.3 A person will not be treated as having consented to run a risk unless he is fully aware of the nature and extent of that risk. In this context, actual knowledge is what counts; thus in *Sarch v Blackburn*,[1] where the plaintiff was bitten by the defendant's dog, his right to recover damages was held to be unaffected by a large 'Beware of the Dog' notice, since he could not read.

The law in many American states contains a doctrine of 'informed consent' whereby, if a patient is not given full information about the risks involved in a proposed operation, his or her consent is vitiated; the operation then becomes actionable as a trespass to the person, even if it is carried out with all due care and skill. In *Sidaway v Board of Governors of the Bethlem Royal Hospital and the Maudsley Hospital*,[2] the House of Lords held that this doctrine has no place in English law and that a doctor's duty to warn of risks is merely part of the general duty of care which he owes to his patient. As a result, a patient who seeks legal redress for a failure to warn must bring an action for negligence; whether the failure is negligence is judged in the same way as any other aspect of the doctor's duty.

Where a person's consent is obtained by fraud, it is usually said to be no defence, since he will lack the necessary knowledge. However, in the Irish case of *Hegarty v Shine*,[3] where the plaintiff sued her lover for trespass to the person after he had infected her with venereal disease, it was held that the defendant's concealment of his condition was not enough to vitiate her consent to intercourse; the fraud did not go to the nature of the act, but concerned a collateral detail.[4]

Knowledge is a necessary condition of this defence, but knowledge alone is not sufficient to show consent. A plaintiff may be fully entitled to undertake a risk of which he is aware, for example to keep his job,[5] effect a rescue[6] or exercise his legal right which the defendant has infringed.[7]

1 (1830) 4 C & P 297.
2 [1985] 1 All ER 643, [1985] 2 WLR 480, HL.
3 (1878) 4 LR Ir 288, 14 Cox CC 124.
4 This refinement, introduced from the criminal law, seems wholly out of place as between the parties to a civil action; we think that any fraud should suffice to defeat consent.
5 Para 21.8 below.

6   Para 21.9 below.
7   See *Clayards v Dethick and Davis* (1848) 12 QB 439; para 20.13 above.

Voluntariness

21.4   To be of legal effect, a person's consent to assume a risk must be fully and freely given. This means that the plaintiff must not be under such pressure as to override his free will. For example, in cases of employer and employee,[1] it is usually said that economic pressure on the employee not to lose his job prevents the implication that he assumes the risks inherent in it. Similarly, in rescue cases,[2] the defence of *volenti* is ruled out by the moral obligation on the plaintiff to go to the aid of someone in danger.

1   Para 21.8 below.
2   Paras 21.9 and 21.10 below.

Consent in negligence cases

21.5   *Express consent*   It is in relation to negligence, and those other torts where liability is based upon lack of care, that most difficulties are found. Nor is this surprising. A finding of *volenti* means, in effect, that the plaintiff has agreed to allow the defendant to commit a tort against him, and the very idea of the plaintiff agreeing to allow the defendant to be negligent seems highly unrealistic.

Where the plaintiff is alleged to have consented expressly to negligence on the part of the defendant, the case is usually concerned with an exemption clause, although a non-contractual waiver is in principle also effective.[1] However, statute has now deprived the latter of one of its most important practical applications, namely, 'Ride at your own risk' as regards passengers in motor vehicles.[2] Further, the extent to which liability for negligence may be excluded by a contract term or notice is heavily restricted,[3] and the Unfair Contract Terms Act 1977, s 2(3) makes it clear that a person's agreement to or awareness of a purported exemption clause does not in itself lead to the conclusion that he assumes any risk.

1   *Buckpitt v Oates* [1968] 1 All ER 1145.
2   Road Traffic Act 1988, s 149(3).
3   Paras 10.11 and 10.20 above.

21.6   *Implied consent*   Attempts in negligence cases to base a defence of *volenti* on the plaintiff's conduct are seldom successful. If a defendant is to escape liability on this ground, it will almost certainly be where the defendant's negligence takes place first, so that its full effects are visible to the plaintiff before he puts himself in danger. In *Cutler v United Dairies (London) Ltd*,[1] due to negligence for which the defendants were responsible, a horse ran away into a field. There was no danger, but the driver called for assistance in pacifying the animal, and the plaintiff was injured in helping him. The Court of Appeal held that the plaintiff had obviously assumed the risk and that he could not, therefore, recover damages.

The very idea of a plaintiff taking on the risk that the defendant will in future act negligently towards him is one which judges dislike; it has even been suggested that *volenti* can never apply to negligence in the simple sense of a duty of care based upon foreseeability.[2] This may overstate the case, but it is worth remembering that the vital question is not whether the plaintiff foolishly risked injury, but whether he agreed in effect that the legal risk of loss should be upon him and not upon the defendant. It may be that a court will only come to such a conclusion in cases where the parties are engaged on a thoroughly irresponsible (and possibly illegal) joint venture.[3]

1   [1933] 2 KB 297, CA; para 20.11 above.

2   *Dann v Hamilton* [1939] 1 KB 509 at 512, [1939] 1 All ER 59 at 60; *Wooldridge v Sumner* [1963] 2
     QB 43 at 69, [1962] 2 All ER 978 at 990.
3   See, for example, *Morris v Murray* [1990] 3 All ER 801, CA; para. 21.1 above.

21.7 *Variable duties* Notwithstanding the reluctance of the courts to permit a
negligent defendant to avoid liability altogether on the ground of the plaintiff's
assumption of risk, there is undoubtedly some judicial sympathy for the view that the
plaintiff's carelessness for his own safety should not go entirely unmarked. Nowadays,
of course, this can be achieved through the medium of apportionment for contributory
negligence. Quite apart from this, however, the courts have flirted with the idea that
the relationship between the parties, and their appreciation of the risks involved in a
particular enterprise, may make it fair to impose something less than a full duty of
care upon the defendant. In *Wooldridge v Sumner*,[1] for example, a competitor at the
National Horse Show took a corner too fast, injuring a photographer who was standing
in the arena. In holding the defendant not liable, a majority of the Court of Appeal laid
down that no duty of reasonable care was owed, and that, since neither the photographer
nor any other spectator would expect a competitor to consider his interests, liability
could only be imposed if the defendant had shown reckless disregard of the spectator's
safety.

The reckless disregard test has been applied subsequently, but its limits should be
noted. In *Harrison v Vincent*,[2] a sidecar passenger was injured when a mechanical defect
caused the defendant to lose control of his motor cycle combination during a race.
The Court of Appeal held that, while the actual riding of the machine should be judged
on the *Wooldridge v Sumner* principle, since it was done in the flurry and excitement
of the sport, the mechanical preparations were done in the calm of the workshop and
accordingly fell within the normal rules of negligence. Defects in course design or
safety are also subject to the normal rules of negligence.[3]

Supporters of the 'variable duty' idea claim that, although it raises theoretical
problems for the law of negligence, it achieves a fair result. Nevertheless, the courts
have not universally accepted this approach as correct. In *Wilks v Cheltenham Home
Guard Motor Cycle and Light Car Club*,[4] where a spectator at a motor cycle scramble
was injured when a machine inexplicably jumped over a safety rope, it was said that
even a competitor must exercise reasonable care, although what is reasonable depends
upon all the circumstances, including the fact that he is expected to go all out to win.
Similarly, in *Nettleship v Weston*,[5] where a learner driver crashed into a lamp-post and
injured her instructor, the Court of Appeal rejected the argument that the instructor
must necessarily be taken to accept a lower standard of skill from his pupil than from
an experienced driver. Here, the instructor, by requiring an assurance that his pupil
had passenger insurance, had shown that he did not accept any legal risk of injury.
Indeed, the court held that, in assessing the defendant's conduct, no allowance at all
was to be made for the fact that she was only learning to drive.

1   [1963] 2 QB 43, [1962] 2 All ER 978, CA.
2   [1982] RTR 8.
3   *Harrison v Vincent* [1982] RTR 8.
4   [1971] 2 All ER 369, [1971] 1 WLR 668, CA. See also *Condon v Basi* [1985] 2 All ER 453, CA
     (footballer's duty of care to opponent).
5   [1971] 2 QB 691, [1971] 3 All ER 581, CA; paras 19.4 and 19.10 above.

Employment cases
21.8 If the mere awareness of a risk signified consent to run it, *volenti* would seem
particularly applicable to cases of injuries sustained in the course of employment.
Indeed in the early 19th century, when society regarded the growth of industry as
more important than the safety of the workforce, the view was often taken that a

workman who continued to do his job in the face of clear danger could not recover damages for either negligence or breach of statutory duty if he was subsequently injured. A more humane era, however, was ushered in by the leading case of *Smith v Baker & Sons*,[1] where the plaintiff, who was working in a cutting, was injured when a crane dropped a stone on him. For several months this crane had swung its loads over the plaintiff's head, and at no time had any warning been given that it was about to do so. The House of Lords held that the plaintiff could not be said to have accepted the risk merely by virtue of continuing to work for the defendant with knowledge of it.

The principle of *Smith v Baker* was extended beyond the strict field of employer and employee in *Burnett v British Waterways Board*,[2] where the plaintiff was compelled in the course of his employment to make use of the defendants' facilities. The defendants had put up a notice disclaiming responsibility for any injury sustained, and the plaintiff was aware of this; however, the Court of Appeal held that the notice was not binding on the plaintiff, since he had no free choice in the matter.

The desire of the courts to protect employees from being forced by economic pressures to submit to risks means that an employer who is guilty of negligence will today find it almost impossible to plead *volenti*. Further, one who is personally in breach of a statutory duty will certainly not be allowed to do so, since it would be totally opposed to public policy to permit someone to contract out of a duty imposed upon him by statute.[3] Even in this enlightened age, however, there may be extreme cases in which the use of the defence against an employee would not offend public policy, and one such was *ICI Ltd v Shatwell*.[4] That case concerned two shot-firers who, in flagrant breach of statutory duties which were imposed upon them personally, tested a firing circuit without taking cover. When an explosion injured one of the men, he claimed that his employers were vicariously liable for his colleague's breach of statutory duty. The House of Lords held that the employers, who were morally innocent in this matter (having done everything in their power to see that these regulations were obeyed) and who were personally not guilty of any tort, were entitled to avoid liability by raising the defence of *volenti*.

1   [1891] AC 325, HL.
2   [1973] 2 All ER 631, [1973] 1 WLR 700, CA.
3   *Baddeley v Earl of Granville* (1887) 19 QBD 423, DC.
4   [1965] AC 656, [1964] 2 All ER 999, HL.

Rescue cases

21.9   At first sight, *volenti* would seem highly applicable to the case of someone who is injured in attempting to rescue another person[1] from danger. However, such a rule would hardly seem destined to encourage humanitarian conduct and, not surprisingly, the law does not apply it. In *Haynes v Harwood*,[2] for example, where a policeman was injured in stopping a runaway horse in a crowded street, it was held that the defendant, whose negligence had permitted the horse to run away, could not avoid liability by claiming that the policeman had voluntarily incurred the risk.

The theoretical basis on which a rescuer is allowed to recover damages is that, because he acts under some form of moral compulsion, he lacks the necessary free will to assume the risk. It has been suggested that the plaintiff in *Haynes v Harwood* was under a legal obligation to act as he did, by virtue of his status as a policeman. This, however, does not seem crucial; in *Chadwick v British Transport Commission*,[3] a person who volunteered to help in the wreckage of a disastrous train crash was awarded damages for nervous shock, although it could not be said that he owed anyone a legal duty to act in this way.

1 Or property; *Hyett v Great Western Rly Co* [1948] 1 KB 345, [1947] 2 All ER 264, CA.
2 [1935] 1 KB 146, CA; para 20.11 above.
3 [1967] 2 All ER 945, [1967] 1 WLR 912.

21.10 It is now settled that an action brought by an injured rescuer is quite independent of any claim by the person rescued. It rests on a separate duty of care which is owed to the rescuer personally by whoever causes the danger and hence also causes the need for rescue. As a result, a rescuer is not adversely affected by any defect in the claim of the person rescued, such as contributory negligence, or the fact that the person is a trespasser.[1]

The legal independence of the rescuer's claim has further consequences. For instance, a person who negligently endangers himself may be liable to a rescuer, if the circumstances are such as to render a rescue attempt foreseeable.[2] Moreover, the Supreme Court of Canada has held that a rescuer who so bungles the job that someone is induced to make a second attempt may be liable to the second rescuer if the latter is injured.[3]

1 *Videan v British Transport Commission* [1963] 2 QB 650, [1963] 2 All ER 860, CA.
2 *Harrison v British Railways Board* [1981] 3 All ER 679.
3 *Horsley v Maclaren, The Ogopogo* [1971] 2 Lloyd's Rep 410.

Contributory negligence

21.11 At common law a plaintiff who, by failing to take reasonable care of himself, contributed to his own injury could recover nothing at all from the defendant whose tort would otherwise have been regarded as the legal cause. The obvious harshness of this rule led the courts in a number of cases to deny that plaintiffs were contributorily negligent, in the face of clear evidence that they were. These decisions must be regarded as doubtful, now that the rule itself has been removed by statute.

The 1945 Act

21.12 The present law on contributory negligence is governed by the Law Reform (Contributory Negligence) Act 1945, s 1(1) of which provides that where a person suffers damage as the result partly of his own fault and partly of the fault of another person, the damages recoverable by him shall be reduced to such extent as the court thinks just and equitable having regard to the claimant's share in the responsibility for the damage.

Interestingly, the Act speaks not of negligence but of *fault*. According to s 4, this means 'negligence, breach of statutory duty or other act or omission which gives rise to a liability in tort or would, apart from this Act, give rise to the defence of contributory negligence'. Clearly, then, this defence is available not only in cases of negligence, but also in a number of other torts. It has no application, however, to those torts based upon the intentional causing of harm, such as assault and battery[1] or deceit.[2]

The 1945 Act is inapplicable to actions based purely on a breach of contract,[3] so that, if the plaintiff in such a case is also at fault, the court must either hold him entirely responsible and thus deny him compensation altogether, or ignore his share of the blame and award him damages in full.[4] Where, however, a defendant's liability in contract is identical to what his liability would be in the tort of negligence, the plaintiff will not be able to avoid the operation of the 1945 Act by framing his action in contract; the court has the power to reduce the plaintiff's damages, whatever the action is called.[5]

1 *Lane v Holloway* [1968] 1 QB 379, [1967] 3 All ER 129, CA.
2 *Alliance & Leicester Building Society v Edgestop Ltd* [1994] 2 All ER 38.

3 *Barclays Bank v Fairclough Building Ltd* [1995] QB 214, CA; see para 12.18 above.
4 In *Tennant Radiant Heat Ltd v Warrington Development Corpn* [1988] 11 EG 71, CA, the Court of Appeal managed to award partial compensation in such a case, by ruling that the defendant had only caused part of the plaintiff's loss, but this seems wrong.
5 *Forsikringsaktieselskapet Vesta v Butcher* [1988] 2 All ER 43, CA; para 12.18 above.

Standard of care

21.13 When a defendant alleges that the plaintiff was contributorily negligent, he is not called upon to show that the plaintiff owed him a legal duty; contributory negligence consists simply of failing to take such care of oneself as is reasonable in all the circumstances of the case. Thus, a mortgage lender who claims damages from a negligent valuer may suffer a reduction in those damages if either it was unreasonable for the lender to rely on the valuation[1] or the decision to lend was negligent for other reasons.[2]

As to the standard which the plaintiff is required to reach, this is evaluated in much the same way as is a defendant's for the purpose of establishing a breach of a duty of care.[3] Indeed, many of the factors which we considered in that context, such as the standard of care demanded of children, and the extent to which the reasonable man must foresee negligence in others, are of special relevance here. So too, those cases where the plaintiff's conduct tends not be regarded as an intervening cause,[4] such as rescue attempts, or the plaintiff's instinctive reactions to an emergency, may well today give rise to a finding of contributory negligence.[5] In such cases, the plaintiff's lack of care does not overwhelm the defendant's breach in causative terms, but instead operates alongside it.

In considering the defence of *volenti non fit injuria* we noted that knowledge of a risk does not necessarily imply acceptance of it.[6] Such knowledge may, however, lead a court to the conclusion that the plaintiff was contributorily negligent in failing to take avoiding action. In *Owens v Brimmell*,[7] for example, a passenger in a car who knew that his driver had been drinking heavily lost 20% of his damages when the driver negligently crashed the car and the passenger was injured. So too, in *Gregory v Kelly*,[8] the plaintiff was held to be contributorily negligent in travelling in a car when he knew that the footbrake did not work.

Theoretically, at least, the standard to which the plaintiff must conform is identical to that which is demanded of the defendant. In practice, however, this is not strictly true, for plaintiffs are treated rather more leniently. As to why this should be so, various reasons have been suggested. In the first place, it seems legitimate to argue that conduct which endangers others is more serious than conduct which only endangers oneself, and that consequently a defendant must take greater steps to keep the risk within bounds. Second, there is no doubt that the modern trend is towards increasing the availability of compensation, and that both the raising of standards for defendants and the lowering of those for plaintiffs lead in this direction. Third, in the specific case of industrial safety regulations, the courts feel that it would be wrong to use apportionment so as to deprive a workman of his intended benefit, especially where his fault consists of inattention to a job which is boring, tiring and repetitious.[9]

1 *Banque Bruxelles Lambert SA v Eagle Star* [1995] 2 All ER 769.
2 *Platform Home Loans Ltd v Oyston Shipways Ltd* [1998] 13 EG 148, CA.
3 Ch 19 above.
4 Paras 20.10–20.14 above.
5 See *Harrison v British Railways Board* [1981] 3 All ER 679; para 20.11 above.
6 Para 21.3 above.
7 [1977] QB 859, [1976] 3 All ER 765.
8 [1978] RTR 426.
9 See, for example, *Mullard v Ben Line Steamers Ltd* [1971] 2 All ER 424 at 428.

Causation

21.14 It is not enough for a defendant to show that the plaintiff failed to take reasonable care of himself; the lack of care must also be shown to have contributed, at least in part, to the plaintiff's damage. This is simply a matter of causation, although it is worth mentioning that modern courts, secure in the knowledge that they can dispense justice through the medium of apportionment, are more ready to regard the plaintiff's conduct as a legal cause than were their predecessors when such a finding would have defeated the action altogether.

It should be noted that the plaintiff's fault need not contribute to the accident, but only to the damage. Thus, a moped rider who is in no way responsible for a collision may nevertheless lose part of his damages if his injuries are increased by the fact that he was not wearing a helmet[1] or that his chin strap was not fastened.[2] The same principle applies to seat belts in motor vehicles;[3] failure by a driver or front-seat passenger to wear a seat belt normally leads to a reduction in damages of between 15% and 25%, depending on whether the injuries would have been substantially or even totally avoided but ignoring the question of what other injuries the seat belt itself might have caused.[4]

Since the attribution of legal cause is really, as we have seen,[5] a matter in which the judge exercises a choice, no hard and fast rules can be laid down. An important factor, however, is that of risk; if the plaintiff's damage does not fall within the scope of the risk to which he unreasonably exposed himself, then his negligence is not contributory. In *Jones v Livox Quarries Ltd*,[6] an employee who stood, contrary to instructions, on the back of a moving traxcavator was injured when another vehicle collided with it. The plaintiff argued that his negligence did not contribute to his injuries, since the only risk he had undertaken was that of falling off. The Court of Appeal, while accepting that he would not have been in any way to blame if, during his unauthorised ride, he had been shot by a negligent sportsman, nevertheless felt that the actual accident was within the risk. Accordingly damages were reduced by 20%. A similar problem arose in *Westwood v Post Office*,[7] where an employee was killed when he ignored a notice which read: 'Authorised personnel only', entered a lift motor room and fell through a defective trapdoor. A bare (3–2) majority of the House of Lords held that, since the notice gave no indication of danger, let alone of the specific danger, the trespasser's only fault was disobedience, and not contributory negligence.

1   *O'Connell v Jackson* [1972] 1 QB 270, [1971] 3 All ER 129, CA.
2   *Capps v Miller* [1989] 2 All ER 333, CA.
3   *Froom v Butcher* [1976] QB 286, [1975] 3 All ER 520, CA.
4   *Patience v Andrews* [1983] RTR 447.
5   Paras 20.7–20.14 above.
6   [1952] 2 QB 608, CA.
7   [1974] AC 1, [1973] 3 All ER 184, HL.

Identification

21.15 In some circumstances, A may be 'identified' with B for the purposes of contributory negligence. Where this is so, it means that any damages which are awarded to A in an action against a third party may be reduced because of the contributory negligence of B. For example, if a lorry is involved in a collision with another vehicle due to the negligence of both drivers, any damages which the lorry driver's employers claim as owners of the lorry from the other driver may be reduced on the ground of their employee's contributory negligence.

This doctrine of identification applies wherever there is a relationship sufficient to impose vicarious liability.[1] It also applies to a claim by dependants under the Fatal Accidents Act 1976, where the deceased was partly to blame for his own death.[2]

1   Ch 29 below.
2   Para 29.12 below.

Apportionment

21.16 Section 1(1) of the 1945 Act instructs the court to reduce the plaintiff's damages to such an extent as is just and equitable in view of the plaintiff's share in the responsibility for the damage. No statutory guidance is given for this process, but two factors are clearly regarded by the courts as relevant. The first of these, naturally, is the degree of fault which may be attributed to each party. This, however, cannot be the sole criterion for, in a case where the defendant is strictly liable, such as for a breach of statutory duty, it would lead to the absurd conclusion that a slightly negligent plaintiff receives nothing at all. Thus a second factor, that of 'causative importance', must also be considered.[1]

It should not be thought that equal carelessness compels equal division. For example, it is not unreasonable to place a greater burden upon a negligent motorist than upon an equally negligent pedestrian, since the conduct of the former entails grave risks to others as well as to himself. All that can be said is that the courts make full use of the discretion which they are given; reductions have ranged from a mere 5% in the case of a passenger injured by negligent driving, whose failure to wear a seat-belt was itself partly the driver's fault,[2] to 80% where safety regulations were deliberately flouted by a workman and his colleague.[3] In one case the Court of Appeal even held an injured workman 100% contributorily negligent,[4] although a differently constituted Court of Appeal described such a conclusion as 'logically unsupportable'.[5] It would be preferable in such a case to regard the plaintiff as the sole cause of his injuries.

Where an action is brought against more than one defendant, any contributory negligence by the plaintiff must be measured against the totality of the defendants' conduct, rather than against each of them separately. Thus, for example, if the plaintiff, defendant A and defendant B are all equally to blame, the plaintiff should be awarded two-thirds of his damages against each defendant rather than one-half.[6]

1   *Stapley v Gypsum Mines Ltd* [1953] AC 663 at 682, [1953] 2 All ER 478 at 486.
2   *Pasternack v Poulton* [1973] 2 All ER 74, [1973] 1 WLR 476. However, a passenger failed in her claim against a *non-negligent* driver for merely failing to advise her to wear a seat belt: *Eastman v South West Thames Area Health Authority* [1991] RTR 389, CA.
3   *Stapley v Gypsum Mines Ltd* [1953] AC 663, [1953] 2 All ER 478, HL.
4   *Jayes v IMI* (Kynoch) Ltd [1985] ICR 155, CA.
5   *Pitts v Hunt* [1990] 3 All ER 344, CA.
6   *Fitzgerald v Lane* [1988] 2 All ER 961, HL.

Chapter 22

Liability for dangerous premises

22.1 A person whose land, buildings or other structures are in a dangerous condition may incur liability for this under a number of different torts. For example, where damage is caused to adjoining property, or to the highway or its users, a claim in respect of that damage may be made under the heading of nuisance. Such claims will be considered later;[1] for present purposes we are concerned with injury or damage which results on the land itself.

In this chapter we accordingly examine the following issues:

- the statutory duty which is owed by the occupier of premises to his lawful visitors;
- the lesser statutory duty which the occupier owes to those who are not lawful visitors (mainly trespassers);
- the liability which the law of tort imposes upon those who are negligent in the design or construction of buildings;
- the extent to which a person who sells or lets dangerous property can be held responsible for the consequences.

1   Ch 25 below.

Lawful visitors

Scope of the duty
22.2   Prior to 1957, the law which governed the liability of occupiers to their lawful visitors was extremely technical and complex. Fine distinctions were drawn between various categories of visitor, such as those in whose visit the occupier had a material interest, and those whose presence was merely permitted, and the duty owed by the occupier to each category was slightly different. Fortunately, most of these distinctions may now be forgotten, for the law has been restated on a simpler and more rational basis by the Occupiers' Liability Act 1957.

Section 2(1) of that Act provides: 'An occupier of premises owes the same duty, the "common duty of care", to all his visitors, except in so far as he is free to and does extend, restrict, modify or exclude his duty to any visitor or visitors by agreement or otherwise.'

Most of the litigation in this area concerns personal injury or death, but the Act of 1957 makes it clear that the occupier's duty is not restricted in law to this; s 1(3) provides that the statutory rules also apply to the obligations of a person occupying or having control over any premises or structure in respect of damage to property, including the property of persons who are not themselves his visitors. Further, where damage to property is proved, the occupier's liability extends also to consequential financial loss, such as the expense of salvaging damaged goods.[1]

1   *AMF International Ltd v Magnet Bowling Ltd* [1968] 2 All ER 789, [1968] 1 WLR 1028.

Exclusion of liability by contract

22.3   Section 2(1) clearly envisages that an occupier may exclude or restrict the duty which he would otherwise owe to a visitor. However, the qualification 'in so far as he is free to' indicates that there are circumstances in which the occupier is denied this freedom. It seems, for instance, that an innkeeper is not permitted to exclude his liability for damage to the property of guests.[1] Further, while s 5 of the 1957 Act makes a contract between the occupier and a visitor decisive as to the rights of the latter, s 3 provides that a person entering premises under a contract to which he is not a party may not be adversely affected by the terms of that contract.[2]

Any attempt by an occupier to exclude or restrict his duty by means of a contractual term is subject to the rules which govern exemption clauses.[3] Of fundamental importance is the Unfair Contract Terms Act 1977. This, when it applies, prohibits the exclusion or restriction of liability for personal injury or death altogether, and makes the exclusion or restriction of liability for other kinds of damage subject to a test of reasonableness. The provisions of this Act are considered in detail elsewhere;[4] for present purposes it is sufficient to state that its operation is limited to duties which arise 'from the occupation of premises used for business purposes of the occupier'. However, a relaxation of the rules, which was introduced by the Occupiers' Liability Act 1984, s 2, permits a business occupier to exclude or restrict liability to those whom he permits to enter his land for recreational or educational purposes which do not themselves form part of his business. A private occupier is not affected by the Unfair Contract Terms Act, but any attempt which he makes to exclude or restrict his liability by means of a contract term must still satisfy the stringent requirements of common law.

1   *Williams v Linnit* [1951] 1 KB 565, [1951] 1 All ER 278, CA; see now the Hotel Proprietors Act 1956, s 2(3).
2   Para 22.12 below.
3   Ch 9.
4   Paras 10.19–10.29 above.

Exclusion of liability by notice

22.4   Occupiers not infrequently seek to exclude or restrict their liability by displaying prominently on their premises notices which state, for example: 'Entry at Own Risk' or 'No Liability is Accepted for any Injury or Damage'. It appears that, in principle, such notices can be effective. The leading case is *Ashdown v Samuel Williams & Sons Ltd*,[1] in which the defendants, who owned and occupied a dockyard estate containing railway sidings, erected notices around their land, stating that persons entering did so at their own risk. The plaintiff (who was held to be a lawful visitor) took a short cut to work across the land and was injured by the shunting of trucks, which was negligently carried on by the defendants' employees. It was held by the Court of Appeal that the notices were effective to exclude the defendants' liability.

Ashdown v Williams was decided before the Occupiers' Liability Act 1957 became law, and doubts were expressed as to whether it had survived the Act. In *White v Blackmore*,[2] however, it was followed by a majority of the Court of Appeal, who held that the Act's reference to exclusion of liability 'by agreement or otherwise' clearly covered this situation.

The principle which underlies both *Ashdown v Williams* and *White v Blackmore* is that, since an occupier is entitled to say: 'Keep Out', he is equally entitled to impose conditions upon which persons may enter.[3] This principle is quite distinct, therefore, from two other defences which may be available to an occupier, namely that he gave a visitor a sufficient warning of a danger to make him reasonably safe,[4] and that the visitor voluntarily accepted the risk of injury.[5] Nevertheless, a desire to limit the effectiveness of 'Own Risk' notices led Lord Denning to blur these concepts. In *White v Blackmore*, for instance, Lord Denning held that a notice was insufficient to exclude liability because it did not adequately warn of the danger in question. And in *Burnett v British Waterways Board*,[6] where a lighterman had to enter the defendants' dock in the course of his employment, Lord Denning said (by analogy with the rules of *volenti non fit injuria*[7]) that he was not bound by a notice excluding the defendants' liability. We do not think that these dicta represent the law in its present state.

It should be noted that the rules stated above have now been altered by the Unfair Contract Terms Act, at least in so far as they relate to business premises.[8] As a result, *Ashdown v Williams* would be decided differently today.[9] The effect of the Act on *White v Blackmore* is less certain, since it is not clear whether the land in that case was being occupied for business purposes (it was being used for racing old cars to raise money for charity).

1   [1957] 1 QB 409, [1957] 1 All ER 35, CA.
2   [1972] 2 QB 651, [1972] 3 All ER 158, CA.
3   For this reason it seems that a notice excluding liability will be of no effect against a person who enters the premises by some legal right.
4   S 2(4)(a): para 22.16 below.
5   S 2(5): para 22.18 below.
6   [1973] 2 All ER 631, [1973] 1 WLR 700, CA.
7   Paras 21.2–21.10 above, especially para 21.8.
8   Paras 10.19, 10.20 and 22.3 above.
9   It may also be that a visitor's rights would today be restricted, rather than totally excluded; see para 22.24 below.

Occupier

22.5   The Occupiers' Liability Act 1957 contains no definition of 'occupier', indeed, the common law position is expressly preserved by s 1(3). Traditionally, this question has been approached by the courts on a commonsense basis, looking to the practicalities of the situation rather than to the technicalities of land law. Thus, for example, on a large-scale building project, the main contractor may well be held to be the occupier of the site (either alone or jointly with the owner).[1] Similarly, in a Canadian case where an auction was conducted on a farm, both the farmer and the auctioneer were held to be occupiers of the barn in which it took place.[2]

The most important single factor used in deciding who is an occupier is that of *control*. This need be neither entire nor exclusive but, unless a person is sufficiently in control of premises to realise that carelessness on his part may lead to a visitor being injured, he cannot be regarded as an occupier.[3] It is on the basis of control that liability has been imposed upon a fairground concessionaire (who had no interest in the property)[4] and upon a local authority which, having acquired a house by compulsory purchase, ordered the resident to leave by serving a notice of intention to enter.[5] In the latter case, the local authority did not actually take possession, but the Court of Appeal held that their statement of intention to do so showed sufficient control, so that their responsibility began as soon as the previous resident left. Similarly, where the owner of premises licenses another to use them, it may well be that he retains sufficient control to be treated as an occupier,[6] and it is then a question of fact whether the licensee is an occupier as well. On the other hand, where property is leased,[7] it is the tenant, and not the landlord, who is the occupier, although a landlord who is in breach of his repairing obligations may incur liability under a separate provision.[8] The landlord will also be regarded as the occupier of the common parts of premises, such as lifts and staircases in a block of flats, notwithstanding that he cannot deny access to these areas to his tenants' families or guests.[9]

1   *AMF International Ltd v Magnet Bowling Ltd* [1968] 2 All ER 789, [1968] 1 WLR 1028.
2   *Couch v McCann* (1977) 77 DLR (3d) 387.
3   See *Cavalier v Pope* [1906] AC 428 at 433.
4   *Humphreys v Dreamland (Margate) Ltd* (1930) 144 LT 529, HL.
5   *Harris v Birkenhead Corpn* [1976] 1 All ER 341, [1976] 1 WLR 279, CA.
6   *Wheat v E Lacon & Co Ltd* [1966] AC 552, [1966] 1 All ER 582, HL.
7   For the distinction between a lease and a licence, see para 36.9 below.
8   Para 22.29 below.
9   *Moloney v Lambeth London Borough Council* (1966) 64 LGR 440.

Multiple occupation

22.6   The courts have repeatedly held that neither occupation, nor the control on which it is based, need be exclusive, and that consequently there may be more than one occupier of the same premises. In *Fisher v CRT Ltd (No 2)*,[1] for example, X owned a gaming club; a restaurant on the premises was held under licence by Y, who ran it as a separate business. Although detailed control over the restaurant was in the hands of Y, its sole entrance was through X's premises, and X had a right of entry. When a workman was injured in the restaurant, both X and Y were held liable as occupiers.

The leading case on the subject of multiple occupation, *Wheat v E Lacon & Co Ltd*,[2] concerned a public house with a resident manager. The brewery company which owned the public house permitted the manager and his wife (who occupied part of the premises as licensees) to take in paying guests, and one of these guests was killed when he fell down the unlighted back stairs. In an action by the guest's widow (which failed because she was unable to prove negligence), the House of Lords obiter made some important comments on the question of occupation. The brewery, it was held, was to be regarded as occupying the residential part of the premises, either vicariously (through its employee, the manager) or because it retained sufficient control. The manager, too, was an occupier of the relevant part. Both occupiers therefore owed visitors a duty of care; the content of their duties, however, might well differ. For example, the structure of the property would probably be the responsibility of the brewery, while liability for such matters as defective carpeting in the manager's flat would more appropriately be imposed upon the manager himself.

1   [1966] 2 QB 475, [1966] 1 All ER 88, CA.
2   [1966] AC 552, [1966] 1 All ER 582, HL.

Premises

22.7   The Occupiers' Liability Act 1957 does not define what is meant by 'premises', although these clearly include land and buildings. In addition, it is provided by s 1(3)(a) that the statutory rules shall regulate 'the obligations of a person occupying or having control over any fixed or moveable structure, including any vessel, vehicle or aircraft', a list which seems apt to include both such permanent structures as grandstands[1] or pylons,[2] and more temporary erections such as scaffolding[3] or ladders.[4] However, in *Wheeler v Copas*,[5] it was held that the Act did not apply to a farmer who lent an unsuitable ladder to a bricklayer; the farmer could not be said to remain in occupation of the ladder once it was lent. As far as 'vessels, vehicles or aircraft' are concerned, it appears that the Act covers only damage caused by defective structure and not that which results from, say, negligent driving.

1   *Francis v Cockrell* (1870) LR 5 QB 501.
2   *Kenny v Electricity Supply Board* [1932] IR 73.
3   *Pratt v Richards* [1951] 2 KB 208, [1951] 1 All ER 90n.
4   *Woodman v Richardson* [1937] 3 All ER 866, CA.
5   [1981] 3 All ER 405.

Visitor

22.8   The simplification of occupiers' liability by the Act of 1957 leaves untouched one vital distinction, namely that between a lawful visitor and a trespasser; the statutory duty of care is owed only to the former. The most frequently cited definition of a trespasser is 'he who goes on the land without invitation of any sort and whose presence is either unknown to the proprietor or, if known, is practically objected to'.[1] This category embraces a wide variety of entrants, from the burglar or poacher to the lost rambler or wandering child. However, where bee-keepers complained that their bees had been killed by the chemical spray used by a neighbouring farmer on his crops, the judge refused to categorise the bees as either visitors or trespassers; he held nonetheless that a duty of care was owed.[2]

Whether or not a person is *expressly* permitted to enter premises is simply a question of fact. However, more difficulties arise where it is alleged that the occupier has *impliedly* given permission. As a general rule, the courts are reluctant to reach such a conclusion, as is illustrated by the case of *Great Central Rly Co v Bates*,[3] in which a policeman, seeing a warehouse door open at night and going in to investigate, was held to be a trespasser. On the other hand, the mere existence of a path across one's front garden is regarded as a tacit invitation to members of the public wishing to conduct lawful business with the occupier, although this licence extends no further than the front door.[4] Further, even this implication can be excluded, for example by a clearly displayed notice stating: 'No salesmen'. In the entertaining case of *Snook v Mannion*,[5] however, a householder's instruction to two police officers to 'F—— off' was held to constitute mere vulgar abuse, rather than a valid revocation of their implied permission to be on the premises.

Particular problems are caused by cases of repeated trespass, for instance where the occupier's land is frequently used by members of the public as a short cut, or for picnicking. No permission can be inferred if the occupier takes reasonable steps to keep such people out.[6] Even if he takes no steps, however, it seems that acquiescence, rather than mere knowledge, is what must be proved; as Lord Goddard put it: 'How is it to be said that he had licensed what he cannot prevent?'[7] Nonetheless, in extreme cases, failure to take action may amount to permission, as it did in *Lowery v Walker*,[8] where a farmer's field had been used as a short cut to the local railway station for some 35 years. The farmer occasionally turned people back but otherwise took no action until, without warning, he put a savage horse in the field. The plaintiff, who was attacked and injured by this horse, was held by the House of Lords to be a lawful visitor and therefore entitled to sue the farmer for damages.

Now that trespassers themselves receive a much greater measure of protection in law,[9] it may well be that the courts will no longer strain to infer a licence as they did in *Lowery v Walker*. The same may also be true of the old doctrine of 'allurement', under which a child enticed on to the defendant's land by something dangerous and attractive might be regarded in law as a licensee rather than as a trespasser. An example of this doctrine may be seen in *Cooke v Midland Great Western Rly of Ireland*,[10] where it was well known that children frequently played on the defendants' turntable; indeed, a well-worn track led to it through a gap in the hedge which bordered a nearby road. When the turntable, which was kept unlocked, moved and crushed a four-year-old boy, the House of Lords held that he was not to be regarded as a trespasser.

1   *R Addie & Sons (Collieries) Ltd v Dumbreck* [1929] AC 358 at 371.
2   *Tutton v AD Walter Ltd* [1985] 3 All ER 757.
3   [1921] 3 KB 578.
4   *Robson v Hallett* [1967] 2 QB 939, [1967] 2 All ER 407, DC.
5   [1982] RTR 321, DC.
6   *Hardy v Central London Rly Co* [1920] 3 KB 459, CA.
7   *Edwards v Railway Executive* [1952] AC 737 at 746, [1952] 2 All ER 430.
8   [1911] AC 10, HL.
9   Paras 22.21–22.24 below.
10   [1909] AC 229, HL.

Limited permission

22.9   The permission, whether express or implied, by which a person enters premises may be limited in scope. If this is so, and the permission is exceeded, that person ceases to be a lawful visitor and becomes a trespasser.

The limitations which may be placed upon a licence to enter take various forms, of which the most common relates to area. A hotel guest, for example, becomes a trespasser if he chooses to go through a door marked 'Private'. In *Westwood v Post Office*,[1] an employee who disregarded a notice on a door which stated: 'Authorised personnel only' was held to be a trespasser when he fell through a defective trapdoor in the room and was killed. On the other hand, where a limitation is not clearly shown, a visitor is given a certain amount of leeway. Thus, in *Pearson v Coleman Bros*,[2] a little girl was held to be a licensee when, in searching for a lavatory at a circus, she strayed into the zoo area and was mauled by a lion.

Permission may also be limited as to time, in which case it seems that, to be effective, the limitation must be brought to the entrant's notice. In *Stone v Taffe*,[3] where the manager of a public house gave an unauthorised after-hours party, it was held that the brewers were not entitled to treat a guest as a trespasser, as he did not know that they objected to this practice. This seems surprising since, as a general rule, a person may be a trespasser without being aware of it.[4]

The third limitation which may be placed upon permission to enter premises relates to the purpose of entry; a person may become a trespasser by abusing his licence. This rule, which Scrutton LJ summarised by saying: 'When you invite a person into your house to use the staircase, you do not invite him to slide down the banisters',[5] was applied by the Court of Appeal in *R v Jones and R v Smith*.[6] The two defendants in that case, who were accused of stealing two television sets from the house of Smith's father, could only be convicted of burglary under the Theft Act 1968 if they had entered the house 'as trespassers'. Smith's father gave evidence that his son had unrestricted permission to enter it; it was held, however, that the father's general permission had been exceeded in this case, so that both defendants were trespassers.

1   [1973] QB 591, [1973] 1 All ER 283, CA; revsd on other grounds [1974] AC 1, [1973] 3 All ER 184, HL.
2   [1948] 2 KB 359, [1948] 2 All ER 274, CA.
3   [1974] 3 All ER 1016, [1974] 1 WLR 1575, CA.
4   Para 24.1 below.
5   *The Carlgarth* [1927] P 93 at 110.
6   [1976] 3 All ER 54, [1976] 1 WLR 672, CA.

Entry as of right

22.10   It is provided by the Occupiers' Liability Act 1957, s 2(6) that 'persons who enter premises for any purpose in the exercise of a right conferred by law are to be treated as permitted by the occupier to be there for that purpose, whether they in fact have his permission or not'. As a result, the occupier owes the common duty of care to any of a host of officials who have statutory powers of entry (eg police, firemen, inspectors of the Health and Safety Executive, electricity board officials, etc). Similarly, where a local authority provides such facilities as parks, playgrounds, lavatories or libraries, it seems that persons using these are lawful visitors.

An exception to the above rule is contained in s 1(4) of the 1957 Act. Persons who enter property by virtue of an access agreement or order made under the National Parks and Access to the Countryside Act 1949 may not be sued for trespass but, if injured, they may not claim the rights of a visitor.[1] This is presumably because few landowners would make access agreements if they were thereby subjected to undue legal risks.

1   They will now come within the Occupiers' Liability Act 1984: see para 22.21 below.

Rights of way

22.11   Where a person uses a public right of way across land, he is, of course, not guilty of the tort of trespass. However, the common law did not regard him as a visitor to the land, with the result that the occupier owed him no positive duty to make the way safe. In *Greenhalgh v British Railways Board*,[1] it was held by the Court of Appeal that this rule had not been altered by the Occupiers' Liability Act 1957, so that a woman who was injured when she tripped in a pothole on a railway bridge could not recover damages from the owners of the bridge, notwithstanding that it was crossed by a public footpath. Furthermore, the user of a public right of way cannot even take advantage of the statutory duty which an occupier of land owes to trespassers and other uninvited entrants,[2] for the Occupiers' Liability Act 1984, s 1(7) specifically provides that that duty is not owed to persons using the highway.

The occupier's immunity in such cases is subject to two qualifications. In the first place there may be liability where the danger arises, not from the condition of the way itself, but from activities which are carried on by the occupier on the same or adjoining land. In *Thomas v British Railways Board*,[3] for example, the defendants were held liable when their failure to repair a stile allowed a two-year-old girl to stray on to a railway line, where she was struck by a train. Second, where a right of way is maintainable at the public expense, the relevant highway authority is now under a positive statutory duty to repair and maintain the way, and can be liable for damages to anyone injured by its failure to do so.[4]

A person using a private right of way across land is likewise not treated, either by the common law or under the Occupiers' Liability Act 1957, as a visitor to the land.[5] However, he is now entitled to the more limited protection which is afforded to trespassers and other uninvited entrants by the Occupiers' Liability Act 1984.[2]

1   [1969] 2 QB 286, [1969] 2 All ER 114, CA; affd in *McGeown v Northern Ireland Housing Executive* [1994] 3 All ER 53, HL.
2   See para 22.21 below.
3   [1976] QB 912, [1976] 3 All ER 15, CA.
4   Highways Act 1980, Part IV.
5   *Holden v White* [1982] QB 679, [1982] 2 All ER 328, CA.

Visitors under contract

22.12   Persons who enter premises by virtue of a contract are subject to two specific provisions of the 1957 Act. First, where the contract is made between the occupier and the visitor (eg where entry is by ticket), s 5 provides in effect that the visitor's rights depend upon the terms of that contract; if the contract is silent on this point, the common duty of care will apply. However, this provision must now be read subject to the Unfair Contract Terms Act 1977, which contains severe restrictions on the use of exemption clauses where premises are 'business premises'.[1]

The Law Reform (Contributory Negligence) Act 1945 (which empowers a court to reduce the damages of a plaintiff who is partly to blame for his injuries, rather than to reject his claim altogether) does not apply to actions for pure breach of contract.[2] This would appear to mean that a contractual visitor who is guilty of contributory negligence will fail altogether, but it has been held that a person whose claim is jeopardised on this ground may, if he prefers, base his action on the Occupiers' Liability Act 1957, s 2.[3]

Section 3 of the Act of 1957 deals with persons who enter premises under some contract to which they are not party. For instance, where an occupier employs a firm of builders to work on his house, the actual workmen are not normally parties to the contract under which the work is done. So too, a lease may grant access to 'common parts' of the landlord's building, such as staircases and lifts, not only to tenants, but also their families and guests. In all such cases, it is provided that, while the visitor may take the benefit of any additional obligations which the contract imposes upon the occupier, his rights may not be reduced below the level which is imposed by the common duty of care.

1   Paras 10.20 and 22.3 above.
2   Paras 12.18 and 21.12 above.
3   *Sole v WJ Hallt Ltd* [1973] QB 574, [1973] 1 All ER 1032.

The common duty of care

22.13   The duty which an occupier owes to his lawful visitors is defined by the Occupiers' Liability Act 1957, s 2(2) as 'a duty to take such care as in all the circumstances of the case is reasonable to see that the visitor will be reasonably safe in using the premises for the purpose for which he is invited or permitted by the occupier to be there'. This definition is a straightforward application of the rules of negligence and, in deciding whether or not an occupier's duty has been breached, a court will consider all the circumstances of the case. To take a few examples, liability was imposed upon a local authority for allowing a school path which was swept free of snow to remain in a dangerously slippery condition[1] and upon a hotel whose balconies had balustrades several inches lower than the height recommended by the British Standards Institution.[2] On the other hand, there was held to be no duty on a local authority to put up warning notices in respect of obvious dangers such as a cliff path[3] or seaweed-covered rocks;[4] nor on the owners of a disused gravel pit to erect a 'no swimming' sign.[5]

A crucial issue in many cases is the extent to which an occupier should predict what people will do on his premises. In *Wheeler v Trustees of St Mary's Hall, Chislehurst*,[6] it was held that the trustees of a church hall, who hired it out for a martial arts training session, could not be expected to ensure that the experienced hirer had supplied mats to cover the concrete floor. The trustees were accordingly not liable to a participant who suffered serious head injuries when he fell on the floor. By contrast, in *Bell v Department of Health and Social Security*,[7] employers who knew that their employees frequently carried tea and coffee from the kitchen back to their offices in a four-storey building were held liable for a danger created by the spillage of drinks on pseudo-marble floors. It has even been held that a football club can be liable to visitors if, knowing of the risk, it fails to prevent visiting hooligans from tearing pieces of concrete from the terracing to use as missiles.[8]

The 1957 Act might well have left the courts to work out the details of the common duty of care; however, certain areas which had caused problems before 1957 are specifically dealt with, and these we consider in the next five paragraphs.

1   *Murphy v City of Bradford Metropolitan Council* [1992] PIQR P68, CA.
2   *Ward v Ritz Hotel (London)* [1992] PIQR P315, CA.
3   *Cotton v Derbyshire Dales District Council* (1994) Times, 20 June, CA.
4   *Staples v West Dorset District Council* (1995) 93 LGR 536, CA.

5   *Whyte v Redland Aggregates Ltd* [1998] 2 CL 485, CA.
6   (1989) Times, 10 October.
7   (1989) Times, 13 June.
8   *Cunningham v Reading Football Club* [1992] 1 PIQR P141.

Children

22.14   In pointing out that the carefulness or otherwise which may be expected of a visitor is relevant to the occupier's duty towards him, s 2(3)(a) provides that 'an occupier must be prepared for children to be less careful than adults'. That children are especially at risk is obvious. For example, in *Moloney v Lambeth London Borough Council*,[1] the defendants were held liable to a four-year-old who fell through a gap in a staircase balustrade which was too small to have endangered an adult.

A particular problem with children is that, even when on premises lawfully, they may be tempted by some dangerous and attractive object to exceed the scope of their permission. If this leads to injury, it is well established that the occupier may not use the child's technical trespass as a ground for avoiding liability. Thus in *Glasgow Corpn v Taylor*,[2] where a seven-year-old boy stole some attractive berries from an unfenced bush in a public park, it was held that his death by poisoning disclosed a good cause of action.

In relation to very young children, to whom almost anything is dangerous but who cannot understand warnings, the law seeks to balance the duty of the occupier with that of the parent. The courts take the view that an occupier, in taking precautions for the safety of small children, is entitled to assume that their parents will also take care. This approach was adopted by Devlin J in *Phipps v Rochester Corpn*,[3] where a five-year-old boy went blackberrying with his sister, aged seven, on a large grassy space forming part of the defendants' building site. The defendants were well aware that children frequently played in this place, so that they were to be regarded as lawful visitors.[4] When the boy fell into a trench and broke his leg, it was held that the defendants were not liable, since this was the kind of danger from which the occupier might expect a reasonable parent to protect his child.

1   (1966) 64 LGR 440.
2   [1922] 1 AC 44, HL.
3   [1955] 1 QB 450, [1955] 1 All ER 129. See also *Simkiss v Rhondda Borough Council* (1982) 81 LGR 460, CA.
4   See para 22.8 above.

Specialists

22.15   It is provided by s 2(3)(b) that 'an occupier may expect that a person, in the exercise of his calling, will appreciate and guard against any special risks ordinarily incident to it, so far as the occupier leaves him free to do so'. One important effect of this is that an occupier whose property becomes dangerous will not normally be liable to persons who come for the very purpose of repairing it. It might be thought that this would apply to the case of a fireman who is injured in fighting a fire which is caused by the occupier's negligence, but it has twice been held that such a person may recover damages from the occupier, provided that his presence at the fire was foreseeable and that he would be at risk despite exercising all the skill of his calling. Unfortunately, the first ruling to this effect[1] did not mention s 2(3)(b) of the Occupiers' Liability Act; the second[2] did not mention the Act at all but dealt with the case on the basis of common law negligence.

Whether or not a risk is 'incident to a person's calling' is a question of fact, but some guidance may be obtained from a comparison of two decisions. In *Howitt v Alfred Bagnall & Sons Ltd*,[3] a clerk of works fell from scaffolding on which he was standing to inspect roof repairs. The occupiers were held not liable, for the scaffolding was not

333

defective; the only risk lay in using it at all, and this was inherent in the man's job. In *Woollins v British Celanese Ltd*,[4] on the other hand, a post office engineer fell through some hardboard roofing at the defendants' factory. It was held by the Court of Appeal that, while he could be expected to guard against live wires, the structure of the building was not connected with his job; he was therefore able to recover damages.

1   *Salmon v Seafarer Restaurants Ltd* [1983] 3 All ER 729, [1983] 1 WLR 1264.
2   *Ogwo v Taylor* [1987] 3 All ER 961, HL.
3   [1967] 2 Lloyd's Rep 370.
4   (1966) 1 KIR 438, CA.

Warnings

22.16   A reminder that an occupier's duty is to render the *visitor* safe, rather than the *premises,* is given by s 2(4)(a), which provides: 'Where damage is caused to a visitor by a danger of which he had been warned by the occupier, the warning is not to be treated without more as absolving the occupier from liability, unless in all the circumstances it was enough to enable the visitor to be reasonably safe'. The legal effect of compliance with this provision is that the common duty of care is fulfilled, which has two important consequences in deciding whether or not a warning is valid. First, the warning must come from the occupier himself,[1] although a warning from another source may lead to the conclusion that a visitor either assumes the risk of injury or is contributorily negligent. Second, it must be adequate, in the sense of both specifying the particular danger sufficiently clearly that the visitor can avoid it and being visible. In *Woollins v British Celanese Ltd*,[2] a warning hidden behind a door was held to be inadequate.[3]

1   *Bunker v Charles Brand & Son Ltd* [1969] 2 QB 480, [1969] 2 All ER 59.
2   (1966) 1 KIR 438, CA.
3   In *Rae v Mars (UK) Ltd* [1990] 1 EGLR 161, it was held that no sufficient warning of danger had been
     given to a surveyor who, in inspecting an unlighted storehouse in a factory, fell on to the sunken floor
     and was injured.

Independent contractors

22.17   Prior to 1957 there was some doubt as to whether an occupier was liable in respect of dangers on his land which were attributable to the fault of an independent contractor. In order to clarify this point, s 2(4)(b) provides:

'Where damage is caused to a visitor by a danger due to the faulty execution of any work of construction, maintenance or repair by an independent contractor employed by the occupier, the occupier is not to be treated without more as answerable for the danger if in all the circumstances he had acted reasonably in entrusting the work to an independent contractor and had taken such steps (if any) as he reasonably ought in order to satisfy himself that the contractor was competent and that the work had been properly done.'

This, in effect, gives statutory approval to two earlier decisions of the Court of Appeal. In *Haseldine v CA Daw & Son Ltd*,[1] the plaintiff was injured when a lift in the defendants' block of flats fell to the bottom of the shaft. The accident resulted from negligent work by the firm of specialist engineers employed by the defendants to service the lift and it was held that, since the defendants had no reason to doubt the competence of their contractors, they had in no way failed in their duty towards the plaintiff.

The wording of s 2(4)(b) also endorses the principle laid down in *Woodward v Hastings Corpn*[2] that, if an occupier chooses to leave to an independent contractor jobs which he could and should do for himself, he remains personally responsible for their proper execution. In that case a school cleaner (who was assumed to be an independent contractor) swept the snow from a step and carelessly left it in a dangerously icy condition. It was held that the local authority were liable in negligence to a person who slipped on the step, since this was not a specialist task.

Even where it is reasonable to entrust the work to an independent contractor, the occupier must take reasonable steps to see that the work is properly done. It has been held that on a large-scale construction job, for instance, the occupier may be obliged to appoint a qualified architect or surveyor (who would himself be an independent contractor of the occupier) to supervise the work.[3] However, the courts do not demand very much from an occupier in this connection where he cannot be expected to understand the intricacies of the job, so that where a demolition contractor adopted an unsafe method of working and one of his employees was injured as a result, it was held that the occupier, who was unaware of what was happening, could not be liable.[4]

1   [1941] 2 KB 343, [1941] 3 All ER 156, CA.
2   [1945] KB 174, [1944] 2 All ER 565, CA.
3   *AMF International Ltd v Magnet Bowling Ltd* [1968] 2 All ER 789, [1968] WLR 1028.
4   *Ferguson v Welsh* [1987] 3 All ER 777, HL.

Volenti non fit injuria
22.18   Section 2(5) makes it clear that an occupier is not liable to a visitor in respect of risks which the latter willingly assumes. Thus, in *Simms v Leigh Rugby Football Club Ltd*,[1] where a professional Rugby League player was thrown against a concrete wall which surrounded the defendants' pitch, it was held that he could not recover damages for the injuries received; since the ground satisfied the League rules, it had to be assumed that players had accepted the risks inherent in playing on it.

Since s 2(5), in effect, applies the common law defence of *volenti non fit injuria,* the rules which govern that defence are applicable.[2] In particular, it will not protect an occupier if the visitor has no real choice in the matter; for example, where his employer orders him to enter the premises[3] or to incur the risk.[4]

It should also be noted that, although the Act is silent on the point, it has frequently been held that the defence of contributory negligence is available to an occupier.[5]

1   [1969] 2 All ER 923. Cf *Harrison v Vincent* [1982] RTR 8, CA; para 21.7 above.
2   Paras 21.2–21.10 above.
3   *Burnett v British Waterways Board* [1973] 2 All ER 631, [1973] 1 WLR 700, CA.
4   *Bunker v Charles Brand & Son Ltd* [1969] 2 QB 480, [1969] 2 All ER 59.
5   See, for example, *Rae v Mars (UK) Ltd* [1990] 1 EGLR 161.

Trespassers

22.19   The Occupiers' Liability Act 1957 applies only to lawful visitors; hence, injuries to trespassers were governed by the common law, which had to deal with two separate problems. First, there is the trespasser who is injured by the very steps which the occupier has taken to keep him out. The position here seems to be that static deterrents, such as broken glass or spikes on top of a wall, are permissible;[1] concealed instruments of retribution (such as man-traps or spring-guns), on the other hand, are not allowed,[2] although a trespasser who enters with full knowledge of their presence may be held to have assumed the risk of injury.[3]

The second issue concerns the trespasser who is injured by the condition of the premises or by an activity which takes place on them. In such a case one might expect the law to strike a balance between the right of anybody, even a trespasser, to expect civilised behaviour from others, and the freedom of a landowner to use and enjoy his property as he wishes. For many years this balance was heavily weighted in favour of landowners, as is shown by the case of *R Addie & Sons (Collieries) Ltd v Dumbreck*.[4] A four-year-old trespasser there was killed when a haulage wheel on which he was playing was started up by colliery employees who, despite knowing that children often played on the wheel, did not bother to check that all was clear. The House of Lords, in holding that the colliery was not liable, said that a trespasser must take the land as he finds it, and that an occupier's duty is limited to not injuring the trespasser intentionally or recklessly. That this was a borderline decision was made clear within a year, when the House of Lords came to the opposite conclusion on rather similar facts. On this occasion the employees who started up machinery could, by merely turning round, have seen children on it, and they were held reckless for failing to take this simple step.[5]

The *Addie* rule, which drew no distinction between a vicious intruder and a playful four-year-old, was regarded by many judges as too harsh, and frequent attempts were made to evade it, for example by a strained finding of implied permission to enter the occupier's premises.[6]

1   *Deane v Clayton* (1817) 7 Taunt 489.
2   *Bird v Holbrook* (1828) 4 Bing 628.
3   *Ilott v Wilkes* (1820) 3 B & Ald 304.
4   [1929] AC 358, HL.
5   *Excelsior Wire Rope Co Ltd v Callan* [1930] AC 404, HL.
6   Para 22.8 above.

Common humanity

22.20   The legal position regarding injuries to trespassers underwent a radical change in *British Railways Board v Herrington*,[1] in which a six-year-old boy went on to an electrified railway line and suffered severe burns from the live rail. The line ran between two areas of National Trust land and it was clear, from gaps in the fences and a well-trodden path, that people were habitually taking a short cut across the line at this point. Children had indeed been seen on the track by employees of the defendants but, apart from informing the police, the defendants had taken no action to prevent further trespass. On these facts the Court of Appeal held that the defendants had been reckless and, while the House of Lords denied that the conduct could be described as reckless, they nevertheless decided that it fell short of the standard which the law would henceforth demand of an occupier in relation to trespassers. This standard, it was said, was considerably higher than that required by *Addie* (not to injure intentionally or recklessly), but was not as stringent as a duty of reasonable care; the occupier would be liable if he failed to act towards a trespasser with 'common humanity'.[2] In deciding whether or not the occupier had fulfilled this obligation, a fairly subjective test would be applied; no more would be demanded of the occupier than might reasonably be expected of a person with his knowledge, skill and resources.

1   [1972] AC 877, [1972] 1 All ER 749, HL.
2   However, this does not mean that an occupier could be positively compelled by injunction to fence children out from dangerous land: *Proffitt v BRB* [1985] CLY 2302, CA.

Occupiers' Liability Act 1984

22.21   Exactly what was meant by common humanity, and how it differed from reasonable care, are questions with which we need no longer concern ourselves. Fears that the new standard would prove vague and uncertain, and hence provoke much litigation, led to a recommendation from the Law Commission that the matter be governed by statute, and this was duly done with the enactment of the Occupiers' Liability Act 1984. It should be noted that this Act applies, not only to trespassers, but to all persons other than the occupier's visitors. It thus embraces persons entering under the National Parks and Access to the Countryside Act 1949[1] and also those using a private right of way, although persons using the public highway are specifically excluded. The result appears to be that, while *Greenhalgh v British Railways Board*[2] remains good law, the effect of *Holden v White*[3] is reversed.

1   See para 22.10 above.
2   [1969] 2 QB 286, [1969] 2 All ER 114, CA: para 22.11 above.
3   [1982] QB 679, [1982] 2 All ER 328, CA: para 22.11 above.

Scope of the duty

22.22   In attempting to strike the right balance between the interests of an occupier[1] of premises[2] and those of uninvited entrants, s 1(3) of the Act provides that the occupier shall only owe a duty to such a person if:

• he is aware of a danger or has reasonable grounds to believe that it exists;
• he knows or has reasonable grounds to believe that the other person is in the vicinity of the danger or that he may come into that vicinity;[3] and
• the risk is one against which he may reasonably be expected to offer the other person some protection.

The overall effect of this formulation appears to be that, while the occupier is not bound to inspect his property to see whether or not it is safe for trespasser and other uninvited entrants, he is assumed to be able to recognise a danger whenever what he actually knows should lead him to the conclusion that one exists.

It is important to note that the new statutory duty applies only to 'injury', which is defined to include death, disease and any impairment of physical or mental condition. The Act specifically provides that there is no liability for any loss of or damage to property (s 1(8)).

There have been few reported cases dealing with the Occupiers' Liability Act 1984. Those which have appeared provide little support for the suggestion that the courts will be eager to impose onerous obligations upon occupiers. In particular, judges have shown little sympathy for children who are injured after overcoming considerable obstacles in order to gain access to well fenced property.[4] However, the Court of Appeal did impose liability upon an allotment owner who fired a shotgun through a hole in the door of his shed an injured a trespasser who was attempting to break in.[5]

1   'Occupier' bears the same meaning as it does for the purpose of the Occupiers' Liability Act 1957; see paras 22.5–22.6 above.
2   'Premises' bears the same meaning as it does for the purposes of the Occupiers' Liability Act 1957; see para 22.7 above.
3   See *White v St Albans City and District Council* (1990) Times, 12 March, CA.
4   See *Adams v Southern Electricity Board* (1993) Times, 21 October; *Swain v Puri* [1996] PIQR P442, CA; *Platt v Liverpool City Council* [1997] 8 CL 540, CA.
5   *Revill v Newbery* [1996] 1 All ER 291, CA.

Defences

22.23   The 1984 Act provides an occupier with two defences against liability similar to those which are available under the 1957 Act. First, s 1(5) provides that the occupier's duty may be discharged by taking such steps as are reasonable 'to give warning of the danger concerned or to discourage persons from incurring the risk'.[1] Second, s 1(6) makes it clear that the defence of *volenti non fit injuria* is applicable.[2] Although it is not specifically mentioned, it seems likely that the defence of contributory negligence would also apply.[3]

1   See para 22.16 above.
2   See paras 21.2–21.10 and para 22.18 above.
3   See paras 21.11–21.16 above.

Exclusion of liability

22.24   We have already considered the extent to which an occupier may, by putting up a notice, exclude or restrict his liability to lawful visitors.[1] The 1984 Act gives no guidance whatever as to whether the rights of non-visitors may be similarly affected, and the arguments for and against seem fairly well balanced. On the one hand, since a trespasser has no permission to enter, it would be nonsensical to suggest that he enters subject to a condition that the occupier shall not be liable to him. Furthermore, there is the practical argument that a visitor is more likely than a trespasser actually to see a notice; after all, this will normally be placed at the entrance, while a trespasser may well climb over the fence. On the other hand, it would surely be odd if a lawful visitor were to be placed in a worse position, legally speaking, than a trespasser. A possible solution might be for the courts to hold that, while the rights of a lawful visitor may be excluded by an appropriate notice, the visitor would then be left with rights equivalent to those enjoyed by a trespasser under the 1984 Act, and that neither lawful visitor nor trespasser may suffer any further reduction of their rights.

1   Para 22.4 above.

Purchasers

Caveat emptor

22.25   By virtue of a legal doctrine known as *caveat emptor* or 'let the buyer beware', the rights of those who acquire land or buildings are more restricted than the rights of those who purchase goods, if what is acquired turns out to be defective. One consequence of this doctrine used to be that a vendor or lessor of real property owed no duty of care, either to his purchaser or tenant or to anyone else, to prevent any type of injury or damage resulting from defects in the property. In relation to injury resulting from defects which the vendor/lessor has not positively created, this (for the present time at least) remains the law. In *Rimmer v Liverpool City Council*[1] the Court of Appeal held, albeit reluctantly, that the vendor/lessor's immunity was based on authority of the House of Lords[2] and that it could only be changed by that court or by legislation.

At one time, the landowner's immunity even extended to dangerous defects which he had positively created; notwithstanding *Donoghue v Stevenson*,[3] an action in negligence for injuries could not succeed against an owner-builder,[4] nor against a landlord whose tampering made the premises dangerous before they were let.[5] However, in 1972 this anomalous position was affected by both judicial decision and legislation, as we now explain.

1   [1985] QB 1, [1984] 1 All ER 930, CA. Also see *McNerny v Lambeth LBC* [1989] 1 EGLR 81, CA.
2   *Cavalier v Pope* [1906] AC 428, HL.
3   [1932] AC 562, HL; para 18.5 above.
4   *Otto v Bolton and Norris* [1936] 2 KB 46, [1936] 1 All ER 960. By contrast, a builder who was not also the owner had no immunity: *Sharpe v ET Sweeting & Son Ltd* [1963] 2 All ER 455, [1963] 1 WLR 665.
5   *Davis v Foots* [1940] 1 KB 116, [1939] 4 All ER 4, CA.

Common law developments

22.26   In *Dutton v Bognor Regis UDC*,[1] the plaintiff was the second owner of a house which, a mere two years after being completed, developed alarming cracks in walls and ceilings. It was discovered that the house had been built on the site of an old rubbish tip and that, because of this, its foundations were inadequate. The plaintiff began an action for negligence against the owner-builder but was concerned that she might be defeated by the principle of caveat emptor.[2] She therefore settled this claim for a small sum, and instead sued the local authority, alleging that their building inspector had been guilty of negligence in passing the house's foundations as satisfactory. In holding the local authority liable to the plaintiff, a majority of the Court of Appeal took the opportunity to state their opinion that the builder would, if sued, also have been liable. This suggested reversal of the previous legal position received a good deal of criticism on various grounds, the most important of which was that the plaintiff's claim was one for pure economic loss.[3] However, it was unanimously approved by the House of Lords in the similar case of *Anns v Merton London Borough Council*.[4]

For some 10 years after 1978, the decision in *Anns v Merton* was used to justify the imposition of liability for negligence upon builders, sub-contractors, architects and other design consultants and, perhaps most importantly,[5] local authorities approving plans and inspecting buildings in the course of construction. However, a remarkable about-turn in the 1980s resulted in a series of decisions indicating that the House of Lords was extremely uneasy about this area of liability,[6] so far as it covered damage to the building itself.[7] Eventually, in *Murphy v Brentwood District Council*,[8] the House of Lords declared that *Dutton v Bognor Regis, Anns v Merton* and all the cases which had followed them must be regarded as having been wrongly decided.

1 [1972] 1 QB 373, [1972] 1 All ER 462, CA.
2 See para 22.25 above.
3 See para 18.22 above.
4 [1978] AC 728, [1977] 2 All ER 492, HL.
5 Since all the other potential defendants might well be insolvent and thus unable to pay any damages awarded.
6 The most important of these decisions was that in *D & F Estates Ltd v Church Comrs for England* [1988] 2 All ER 992, HL.
7 This type of damage was perceived as pure economic loss: see para 18.22 above.
8 [1990] 2 All ER 908, HL. The House of Lords immediately applied this ruling in *Department of the Environment v Thomas Bates & Son Ltd* [1990] 2 All ER 943, HL.

22.27 As a result of *Murphy v Brentwood District Council*, the ability of a purchaser or tenant of a defective building to recover damages in the tort of negligence from whoever is responsible has been drastically restricted. The present legal position is as follows:

- A negligent designer, contractor or sub-contractor will be liable if a dangerous defect for which he is responsible results in death, personal injury or physical damage to property other than the building itself (eg where a defective garage roof falls on a car). However, once such a defect is discovered, a decision by the occupier to continue using the building might break the chain of causation from the defendant's negligence,[1] or might be held to constitute contributory negligence by the occupier.[2]
- A local authority which is guilty of negligence in approving plans, or inspecting a building in the course of construction, is probably liable to the same extent as a designer or builder as regards personal injury or death. However, the local authority will not be liable for physical damage to other property, since its duty is limited to ensuring the health and safety of persons.[3]
- With two possible qualifications, there is no liability in negligence to a future owner in respect of damage to the building itself. This is perceived as pure economic loss and is therefore not recoverable. It makes no difference whether the building is merely defective or positively dangerous.

- The House of Lords in *Murphy v Brentwood District Council* suggested that, in two exceptional situations, a future owner might be able to recover damages in respect of damage to the building itself. Both of these have been recognised and applied in subsequent cases. The first is where the negligent work of one contractor or sub-contractor causes damage to other parts of the building which were not constructed by them (eg where a defective central heating boiler causes a fire); it appears that this may be treated as 'damage to other property', for which the negligent party would be liable.[4] Second, where a defective building constitutes a threat to adjoining property with the result that the owner is forced to incur the cost of repairing it, he may recover this cost from the person whose negligence caused the defect.[5]

1 See paras 20.7–20.14 above.
2 See *Targett v Torfaen Borough Council* [1992] 3 All ER 27, CA.
3 *Tesco Stores Ltd v Wards Construction (Investment) Ltd* (1995) 76 BLR 94.
4 *Jacobs v Morton ad Partners* (1994) 72 BLR 92.
5 *Morse v Barratt (Leeds) Ltd* (1992) 9 Const LJ 158.

Defective Premises Act 1972

22.28 Section 1 of this Act creates a legal remedy in respect of defects in dwellings (ie houses and flats, but not commercial property) which will run with the property for the benefit of purchasers or tenants. It provides that a person taking on work for or in connection with the provision of a dwelling (whether the dwelling is provided by the erection or by the conversion or enlargement of a building[1]) owes a duty:

a. if the dwelling is provided to the order of any person, to that person; and
b. without prejudice to paragraph a. above, to every person who acquires an interest (whether legal or equitable) in the dwelling,

to see that the work which he takes on is done in a workman-like or, as the case may be, professional manner, with proper materials and so that as regards that work the dwelling will be fit for habitation when completed.

This provision applies, not only to builders, but also to architects and other design consultants, sub-contractors, and the developer who arranges for someone else to do the work;[2] in short, to anyone who by his work contributes to the completed dwelling. However, it does not extend to a manufacturer or supplier of standard components, nor to a builder who works entirely to a specification which he is given.[3]

The duty imposed by s 1(1) is not a duty of care, but rather a statutory version of the warranty which the common law implies into contracts to build and sell a dwelling.[4] It applies to omissions as well as to positive acts[5] and cannot be contracted out of.[6] At one time it did not apply to any dwelling which was covered by the Buildmark scheme operated by the National House-Building Council, but that exclusion no longer operates. However, it has been held to apply only to defects which are sufficiently serious to render the dwelling unfit for habitation,[7] an interpretation which considerably limits the usefulness of this statutory provision. It may also be noted that claims under the Act are subject to a limitation period of six years from the date on which the dwelling is completed, which is shorter than the period for claims in negligence.[8]

1 This does not include works of mere rectification or refurbishment; there must be a new dwelling: *Jacobs v Morton and Partners* (1994) 72 BLR 92.
2 Section 1(4).
3 Section 1(2) and (3).
4 See *Hancock v B W Brazier (Anerley) Ltd* [1966] 2 All ER 901, [1966] 1 WLR 1317, CA; para 8.25 above.
5 *Andrews v Schooling* [1991] 3 All ER 723, CA.

6   Section 6(3).
7   *Thompson v Alexander* (1992) 59 BLR 77.
8   See paras 29.22 and 29.24 below.

Landlords

22.29   The law governing premises which are defective when disposed of applies to landlords just as it does to vendors. In respect of defects which arise after disposal, however, the position of the landlord requires separate treatment, since he may be under a continuing obligation to repair. At common law, the breach of a landlord's repairing obligation was actionable by the tenant alone;[1] a visitor who was injured could neither recover damages for breach of the landlord's contractual obligation to repair the demised premises, nor treat the landlord as 'occupier' of these premises.[2] This unsatisfactory state of affairs was remedied by the Defective Premises Act 1972, s 4[3], which provides: 'Where premises are let under a tenancy which puts on the landlord an obligation to the tenant for the maintenance or repair of the premises, the landlord owes to all persons who might reasonably be expected to be affected by defects in the state of the premises a duty to take such care as is reasonable in all the circumstances to see that they are reasonably safe from personal injury or from damage to their property caused by a [defect within the repairing obligation].'

The effect of s 4 is that an injured person (who may be a visitor, trespasser or even someone off the premises) may sue the landlord for injury or damage caused by a defect which the landlord is under an obligation (express or implied) to repair. Further, while the landlord might be able to answer a claim by the tenant on the ground that the latter had failed to notify him of the defect,[4] this will be no defence against a third party, provided that the landlord knew or ought to have known of the defect. It is important to note that s 4 also applies to the many cases where a landlord, although under no duty to repair the premises, nonetheless has an express or implied right to do so.[5]

1   *Cavalier v Pope* [1906] AC 428, HL; para 22.25 above.
2   Para 22.5 above.
3   Replacing the more limited provisions of the Occupiers' Liability Act 1957, s 4.
4   Paras 36.22 and 36.30 below.
5   See, for example, *Mint v Good* [1951] 1 KB 517, [1950] 2 All ER 1159. CA; *McAuley v Bristol City Council* [1992] 1 All ER 749, CA.

Chapter 23

Breach of statutory duty

23.1 Large areas of modern life are governed by legislative rules, in the form of either Acts of Parliament or (more commonly) regulations made under them. It frequently happens, therefore, that an act done by one person which causes injury or damage to another also constitutes a breach of some statutory obligation. This naturally renders the person concerned liable to whatever penalty is prescribed by the statute; but our present concern is with the effect, if any, which the statutory breach has upon his liability to pay damages to the plaintiff.

Many legal systems treat the fact that a defendant has or has not contravened a statutory rule as relevant only to the question whether or not he has acted negligently. By contrast, English law takes the view that a breach of statutory duty may be a tort in itself, quite independent of negligence on the part of the defendant, and with its own elements of liability and defences. However, it is not suggested that every statutory obligation gives rise to a civil action, for such is the bulk of modern legislation that the universal imposition of liability would, it is thought, be an unacceptably heavy burden. Thus, a preliminary task for a plaintiff who wishes to frame his action in this way (in order to recover damages without the need to prove negligence) is to satisfy the court that the rule or regulation in question is one for breach of which damages may be awarded.

In this chapter we examine the following issues:

- the way in which the courts decide whether Parliament intended to create a civil right of action for breach of a particular statutory provision;
- the circumstances in which the defendant's breach of a statutory rule may render him liable to pay compensation to anyone who is harmed by it;
- the matters on which an individual plaintiff must satisfy the court in order to succeed in an action for breach of statutory duty.

Existence of civil liability

23.2 In some (albeit too few) cases, a particular statute or regulation states clearly that it either does[1] or does not[2] give rise to civil liability. Usually, however, the point is not specifically mentioned, and the question is therefore left for the courts to determine by interpreting the relevant provision. In carrying out this task, the courts claim to be giving effect to the intention of Parliament, but it is probably sensible to recognise this as a fiction: in reality, the lack of express provision in the statute indicates that there is no Parliamentary intention, so that what the courts are doing is based on their view of policy.

In their search for the intention of Parliament, the courts sometimes claim to gain assistance from a consideration of what sanction, if any, has been laid down for a breach of the provision in question. In particular, if no sanction at all is mentioned, this points strongly to the existence of a civil action for damages, for, without it, the duty would be legally unenforceable.[3]

It has sometimes been said that statutes passed for the benefit of a particular class of persons give rise to a civil action, whereas those which benefit the public in general do not.[4] However, the House of Lords has emphasised[5] that the crucial question is not whether the plaintiff is in a 'protected class' but whether the legislature intended to create a civil right of action. Nor do the decided cases lend strong support to the 'class' theory. It has been held, for example, that no civil right of action arises under the Protection from Eviction Act 1977, s 1, which makes it a criminal offence to evict or harass a residential tenant;[6] nor for breach of the Prison Rules, which govern the conditions under which convicted prisoners are held;[7] nor for breach of the Prosecution of Offences (Custody Time Limits) Regulations 1987, which require the Crown Prosecution Service to bring an arrested person to court within a certain time;[8] nor for breach by a local authority of generally worded statutory duties to protect the welfare and educational interests of children within its area.[9] Furthermore, while a person who commits a criminal offence by making an unauthorised recording of a live performance may be liable in damages to the performer,[10] he is not liable to a recording company which has an exclusive right to record that performance.[11] Similarly, while the duty of a local authority to house a homeless person is one which carries a civil right of action for damages,[12] this only arises once the local authority has decided that he is homeless; no damages may be claimed for failure to decide that question properly.[13]

1   Eg the Nuclear Installations Act 1965 and the Consumer Safety Act 1978.
2   Eg the Guard Dogs Act 1975.
3   *Thornton v Kirklees Metropolitan Borough Council* [1979] QB 626, [1979] 2 All ER 349, CA.
4   See, for example, *Lonrho Ltd v Shell Petroleum Co Ltd (No 2)* [1982] AC 173 at 185, [1981] 2 All ER 456 at 461.
5   *R v Deputy Governor of Parkhurst Prison, ex p Hague; Weldon v Home Office* [1991] 3 All ER 733, HL.
6   *McCall v Abelesz* [1976] QB 585, [1976] 1 All ER 727, CA. An express right to damages in such cases has now been conferred by the Housing Act 1988, s 27.
7   *Hague v Deputy Governor of Parkhurst Prison; Weldon v Home Office* [1991] 3 All ER 733, HL.
8   *Olotu v Home Office* [1997] 1 All ER 385, CA.
9   *X v Bedfordshire County Council* [1995] 3 All ER 353, HL.
10 *Rickless v United Artists Corpn* [1987] 1 All ER 679, CA.
11 *RCA Corpn v Pollard* [1982] 3 All ER 771, CA.
12 *Thornton v Kirklees Metropolitan Borough Council* [1979] QB 626, [1979] 2 All ER 349, CA.
13 *R v Northavon District Council, ex p Palmer* [1996] 2 FCR 389, CA.

23.3   It seems from the case law that the courts are very reluctant to use this tort to create new types of civil right, by allowing an action where there is no common law duty of care.[1] In *Atkinson v Newcastle and Gateshead Waterworks Co*,[2] for instance, the defendants, in breach of a statutory rule for which they could be fined £10, failed to maintain the prescribed pressure of water in their mains. As a result, a fire in the plaintiff's property could not be extinguished. It was held by the Court of Appeal that Parliament could not have intended to make the defendants virtual insurers of every property in the city and that consequently no civil action lay for breach of this duty. A similar decision was reached by the House of Lords in *Cutler v Wandsworth Stadium Ltd*,[3] where an individual bookmaker unsuccessfully claimed damages from the defendants for breach of their statutory duty to make space available for bookmakers at their greyhound racing track. Again, the Court of Appeal in *F v Wirral Metropolitan*

Borough Council[4] held that a local authority in breach of a statutory code governing children in care could not be held liable in damages for 'interference with parental rights'.

It has been acknowledged by the House of Lords that 'directly applicable' legislation of the European Community[5] may confer upon individuals a right of action similar to that for breach of statutory duty.[6] In deciding whether or not this is the case, the courts do not, of course, refer to the intention of Parliament, but they nonetheless give attention to the criteria mentioned above. However, an important restriction upon this new form of civil liability lies in the fact that, even where a right of this kind is held to exist, it does not necessarily entitle a person aggrieved to recover damages; some other remedy may be appropriate.[7]

1   This is especially so where the plaintiff's 'injury' is not of a kind for which damages will normally be
     awarded: see *Pickering v Liverpool Daily Post and Echo Newspapers plc* [1991] 1 All ER 622, HL.
2   (1877) 2 Ex D 441, CA.
3   [1949] AC 398, [1949] 1 All ER 544, HL.
4   [1991] 2 All ER 648, CA.
5   See paras 3.37–3.38 above.
6   *Garden Cottage Foods Ltd v Milk Marketing Board* [1984] AC 130, [1983] 2 All ER 770, HL.
7   *Bourgoin SA v Ministry of Agriculture, Fisheries and Food* [1985] 3 All ER 585, CA; *An Bord Bainne
     Co-operative v Milk Marketing Board* [1988] 1 FTLR 145, CA.

23.4   It is difficult, if not impossible, to find any coherent principle by which to explain the intention of Parliament. However, the actual decisions reached by the courts on this issue fall with remarkable consistency into two groups. Industrial safety regulations are almost invariably interpreted as conferring a civil right of action for damages; outside the field of industrial safety, the attitude of the courts towards claims for breach of statutory duty has been one of considerable and increasing reluctance.

Two particular areas of law stand out as ones where, given a more robust judicial approach, breach of statutory duty could have been used to create a code of rights for an identifiable group. The first is road safety, where the wealth of statutes and regulations might have enabled many road accident victims to secure compensation for their injuries without having to establish negligence. However, this has not happened. In *Phillips v Britannia Hygienic Laundry Co Ltd*,[1] where an accident was caused by the defective condition of the defendants' van (albeit not due to any negligence on their part), the Court of Appeal rejected a claim based on the Motor Vehicles (Construction and Use) Regulations, which made the use of the vehicle in this condition an offence of strict liability. Likewise, in *Coote v Stone*,[2] it was held that no damages could be awarded in respect of a breach of parking regulations.

The second area, that of consumer protection, is also covered by a mass of detailed regulations. Again, however, the courts have declined the opportunity to use these in tort claims. In *Biddle v Truvox Engineering Co Ltd*,[3] for example, it was held that, while the seller of a dangerously unfenced machine was guilty of a criminal offence under the Factories Act, an injured workman was not entitled to recover damages for this breach.

1   [1923] 2 KB 832, CA.
2   [1971] 1 All ER 657, [1971] 1 WLR 279, CA.
3   [1952] 1 KB 101, [1951] 2 All ER 835.

Elements of liability
Class protected

23.5   As we have seen, the fact that a statute is passed for the protection of a defined class of persons does not necessarily mean that it creates a civil remedy in damages.

However, 'class-protection' is relevant in the important sense that, where it is held in principle that a statute gives rise to a civil action, this is available only to members of the class which it was intended to protect. A good illustration of this point is the case of *Hartley v Mayoh & Co*,[1] in which a fireman was killed by electrocution while fighting a fire at the defendants' factory. In an action by the fireman's widow it was held that the breach by the defendants of wiring regulations was irrelevant, since these were expressed to be for the benefit of persons employed at a factory, and this did not include the fireman.[2]

Even where a statute does not expressly define a 'protected class', a court may decide that Parliament intended to limit its protection. For example, it has been held that district auditors may be liable for breach of statutory duty to a local authority whose accounts they audit, but not to individual officers of that authority.[3] However, the courts are generally slow to impose limitations on the ambit of a statute in cases where Parliament has not done so. In *Westwood v Post Office*,[4] for example, a defective trapdoor, the condition of which constituted a breach of the Offices, Shops and Railway Premises Act 1963, led to the death of an employee at a telephone exchange. The trapdoor was in fact in a part of the premises which the deceased was not permitted to enter and it was argued by the defendants that, while the statute protected most employees, it did not cover trespassers. It was held by the House of Lords, however, that the employee's trespass did not deprive him of statutory protection.

1   [1954] 1 QB 383, [1954] 1 All ER 375, CA.
2   The plaintiff nevertheless succeeded in recovering damages on the ground of negligence.
3   *West Wiltshire District Council v Garland* [1995] 2 All ER 17, CA.
4   [1974] AC 1, [1973] 3 All ER 184, HL; para 22.9 above.

Type of injury
23.6   The plaintiff in an action for breach of statutory duty must show that the injury or damage which he has suffered is of a type which the statute is designed to prevent. The classic example of this principle is *Gorris v Scott*,[1] in which the absence of pens on the deck of the defendant's ship allowed the plaintiff's sheep to be swept overboard in a storm. Although pens were required by statute, this was held to be of no assistance to the plaintiff, for their purpose was merely to reduce the spread of disease among the animals. This principle also led to a rather harsh decision in *Close v Steel Co of Wales Ltd*,[2] where it was held that, since the purpose of a duty to fence dangerous machinery is to keep the operator out, it is of no relevance where the absence of a guard allows part of the machine to fly out and cause injury to the operator.

It is obvious that, the more precisely the purpose of a statute is interpreted by judges, the fewer cases will fall within it. The modern tendency, however, is to define the protected risk in fairly broad terms, an approach rather similar to that adopted towards the questions of how damage is caused in the tort of negligence.[3] Thus, in *Grant v National Coal Board*,[4] where a statutory breach allowed rock to fall from a mine roof, it was held that a miner could sue for injuries received when the bogie in which he was travelling was derailed by the fallen rock. So too, in *Donaghey v Boulton and Paul Ltd*,[5] the defendants failed in their statutory duty to supply an employee with crawling boards when he was working on a fragile asbestos roof. The employee fell, not through the asbestos, but through a hole in the roof adjacent to it. It was argued that this was outside the object of the statute, which was limited to fragile roofs, but the House of Lords rejected so narrow an interpretation and held that damages should be awarded.

It is noticeable that, in identifying the purpose of a statutory provision, the courts are usually reluctant to hold that it is intended to protect the plaintiff against pure economic loss.[6] This has even led to the rejection of a claim by a person whose house

345

suffered radioactive contamination from the discharge of nuclear waste, on the ground that the damage suffered was not physical damage, but rather the devaluation of the property.[7]

1   (1874) LR 9 Exch 125.
2   [1962] AC 367, [1961] 2 All ER 953, HL.
3   See *Hughes v Lord Advocate* [1963] AC 837, [1963] 1 All ER 705, HL; para 20.19 above.
4   [1956] AC 649, [1956] 1 All ER 682, HL.
5   [1968] AC 1, [1967] 2 All ER 1014, HL.
6   See *Wentworth v Wiltshire County Council* [1993] 2 All ER 256, CA.
7   *Merlin v British Nuclear Fuels plc* [1990] 3 All ER 711. Contrast *Blue Circle Industries plc v Ministry of Defence* (1996} 141 Sol Jo LB 11.

Breach by defendant

23.7   In those legal systems which treat a breach of statutory duty merely as evidence of a person's negligence, the fact that a person is almost infringing a regulation may also provide some (albeit less) evidence to the same effect. However, as we have seen, English law takes the view that breach of statutory duty is an entirely separate tort and, in consequence, only an actual breach is relevant. In *Chipchase v British Titan Products Co Ltd*,[1] the plaintiff fell from a working platform only 9 inches wide; had it been a few inches higher, statute would have required a width of 34 inches. On these facts the defendants were held not liable for either negligence or breach of statutory duty.

In deciding whether or not a particular obligation has been broken, it is important to realise that the standard of conduct required may vary, because of either the words used or their interpretation by the courts. For example, in *Ministry of Housing and Local Government v Sharp*,[2] the Court of Appeal differed as to whether the duty of a local land registrar in issuing certificates of search was absolute or, as the majority held, one of reasonable care. A duty qualified by such words as 'so far as is reasonably practicable' is, it appears, equivalent to one of reasonable care;[3] at the other extreme, an unqualified duty may be held to impose an absolute obligation. In *John Summers & Sons Ltd v Frost*,[4] for instance, it was held by the House of Lords that a grinding wheel could not be described as 'securely fenced', as required by statute, if any part of the wheel remained exposed, even though to cover it completely would render it unusable.

Between these two levels lies an obligation 'to take such steps as may be necessary'. In deciding what steps are necessary, the courts consider only such dangers as the defendant ought reasonably to have foreseen. If this test establishes that steps are necessary, however, the defendant's obligation to take those steps is an absolute one.[5]

1   [1956] 1 QB 545, [1956] All ER 613, CA.
2   [1970] 2 QB 223, [1970] All ER 1009, CA.
3   The onus of proof may well rest on the defendant: *Larner v British Steel plc* [1993] 4 All ER 102, CA.
4   [1955] AC 740, [1955] 1 All ER 970, HL.
5   *Brown v National Coal Board* [1962] AC 574, [1962] 1 All ER 81, HL.

Causation

23.8   As with any action in tort, the plaintiff must establish that the defendant's breach of duty was a legal cause of his injuries. With one exception the law on this matter, although complex, is no different from that which governs cases of negligence and which we have already considered.[1] The exception is where a statute is so drafted as to place identical duties on two parties (usually employer and employee) in such terms that an act or omission by one party constitutes a breach by both of them. In such a case, where a statute states simply that something 'shall be done', failure to do it puts both parties in breach, even though the moral blame may rest on only one of them. In

Ginty v Belmont Building Supplies Ltd,[2] for example, it was provided by statute that, when work was being done on fragile roofs, crawling boards 'shall be used'. The defendants supplied such boards, together with full instructions as to their use, to the plaintiff, an experienced workman whom they employed, but he decided not to use the boards and consequently fell through the roof. This breach of statutory duty was undoubtedly one for which both plaintiff and defendants could have been criminally liable. However, it was held that the plaintiff was not entitled to claim damages from defendants, for their breach of statutory duty consisted entirely of his own breach.

It is important to note that the decision in *Ginty* can only exonerate a defendant where the plaintiff is the sole cause of his own misfortune; if any kind of independent or extra fault can be attributed to the defendant, he will be liable, although the plaintiff is likely in such a case to lose a substantial proportion of his damages on the ground of contributory negligence. In *Boyle v Kodak Ltd*,[3] for instance, the House of Lords held the defendant employers two-thirds to blame for an accident at work, since they had failed to provide the plaintiff with adequate supervision or instruction in the relevant regulations. And, in *McMath v Rimmer Bros (Liverpool) Ltd*,[4] where the plaintiff fell from a ladder which no-one was 'footing', his employers were held liable for 50% of his damages, since the absence of anyone to foot the ladder was attributable to their fault.

1   Ch 20 above.
2   [1959] 1 All ER 414.
3   [1969] 2 All ER 439, [1969] 1 WLR 661, HL.
4   [1961] 3 All ER 1154, [1962] 1 WLR 1, CA.

Defences

23.9   In principle, the defence of *volenti non fit injuria*[1] is available in actions for breach of statutory duty. However, for reasons of public policy it has long been settled that an employer may not use it against his employee when the employer is personally in breach of his own statutory obligation.[2] In cases where the employer is not personally in breach, but is made vicariously liable for breach by his employees of statutory duties which are laid upon them, he may use the defence.[3]

There is no doubt that the defence of contributory negligence[4] is available (and it should be noted that the plaintiff's 'fault' for this purpose may itself consist of some breach of statutory duty). However, if too liberally used, this defence would deprive many employees of the benefit of regulations specifically designed for their protection. Consequently, in dealing with industrial accident cases, the courts are careful to make full allowance for problems of fatigue, repetition, boredom and the like.[5]

Where the defendant is personally under a statutory duty, it is no defence for him to show that he delegated its performance to the plaintiff. However, if the plaintiff's conduct is the sole cause of his injury, the defendant may avoid liability on the basis of the rule in *Ginty v Belmont Building Supplies Ltd*.[6]

1   Paras 21.2–21.10 above.
2   *Baddeley v Earl of Granville* (1887) 19 QBD 423, DC.
3   *Imperial Chemical Industries Ltd v Shatwell* [1965] AC 656, [1964] 2 All ER 999, HL; para 21.8 above.
4   Paras 21.11–21.16 above.
5   See *Caswell v Powell Duffryn Associated Collieries Ltd* [1940] AC 152, [1939] 3 All ER 722, HL; *Mullard v Ben Line Steamers Ltd* [1971] 2 All ER 424, [1970] 1 WLR 1414, CA.
6   [1959] 1 All ER 414; para 23.8 above.

Chapter 24

Trespass to land

24.1 This tort may be defined as a direct intrusion upon land in the possession of the plaintiff. Before expanding on this basic definition, a number of general points may be made. First, notwithstanding the multitude of notices proclaiming that 'Trespassers will be prosecuted', trespass in itself is not normally a criminal offence.[1] However, in civil law it is actionable per se, that is without any need to prove that damage has been done.[2] In this respect it differs from the tort of nuisance (in which the plaintiff must prove damage) and, since both torts may consist of causing objects to enter the plaintiff's land, it is important to appreciate the distinction between them. This lies in the fact that trespass applies only to direct invasions. Thus, the man who chops down a tree so that it falls into his neighbour's garden commits trespass; if he merely allows its roots or branches to grow across the boundary, he is guilty of nuisance.[3]

Where the intrusion of the defendant, or of some object propelled by him, is accidental, in the sense that he did not intend it and took reasonable steps to prevent it, he will be protected against liability by the defence of inevitable accident. Thus in *League Against Cruel Sports Ltd v Scott*,[4] it was held that the master of a hunt would only be liable for trespass by the hounds if he either intended them to enter the plaintiff's land or negligently failed to prevent them from so doing. On the other hand, if the defendant acts deliberately, it is no defence to show that he did not mean to trespass (eg because he was mistaken). Thus, in *Basely v Clarkson*,[5] a man was held liable in trespass when, in cutting his grass, he crossed an ill-defined boundary and cut some of the plaintiff's grass as well.

1   Except where statute so provides, eg on railway property (Railway Regulation Act 1840) or where the trespasser has an offensive weapon (Criminal Law Act 1977).
2   *Entick v Carrington* (1765) 19 State Tr 1029.
3   *Lemmon v Webb* [1894] 3 Ch 1, CA.
4   [1986] QB 240, [1985] 2 All ER 489.
5   (1681) 3 Lev 37.

24.2   In this chapter we examine the following issues:

- the extent to which trespass can be committed above and below the surface;
- the range of acts and activities which may amount in law to a trespass;
- the question of who is entitled to bring an action for trespass;
- the circumstances in which the law permits one person to enter land belonging to another;

• the remedies which are available to a person whose land is trespassed upon.

Land

24.3 In normal circumstances, possession of land carries with it possession of all underlying strata and of the airspace above, in which case the possessor may sue in trespass for intrusion at any level. Where, however, horizontal divisions are made, such as in a block of flats,[1] or on a sale of mineral rights, the possessor of the affected area is alone able to sue. Thus, for example, where X possesses land over which Y has rights of pasture, X may sue anyone who drives tent-pegs into the soil;[2] but only Y may take action against a person who merely rides across the grass.[3]

As far as the airspace above the land is concerned, it is clear that an unauthorised invasion of this is trespass, at least where it is not above the maximum height necessary for the occupier's ordinary use and enjoyment of his land and buildings. This may include, for example, a projecting advertisement[4] or the swinging jib of a crane.[5] In *Bernstein v Skyviews and General Ltd*,[6] however, the defendants were held not liable when they flew several hundred feet above the plaintiff's house to take unauthorised photographs of it, with a view to selling these to the plaintiff.

Over-flight is also subject to s 76 of the Civil Aviation Act 1982 which, broadly speaking, prevents the landowner from establishing a claim in either trespass or nuisance for the mere fact of the flight, provided that it takes place at a height which is reasonable, having regard to wind and weather. In *Bernstein*'s case, notwithstanding the purpose of their flight, the defendants were allowed to rely on this provision. However, the Act imposes strict liability in respect of any physical damage to the property below which results from an over-flight.

1   The tenant of a top floor flat is entitled to the air space above unless the lease defines an upper boundary: *Davies v Yadegar* [1990] 1 EGLR 71, CA.
2   *Cox v Glue* (1848) 5 CB 533.
3   *Cox v Mousley* (1848) 5 CB 533.
4   *Kelsen v Imperial Tobacco Co (of Great Britain and Ireland) Ltd* [1957] 2 QB 334, [1957] 2 All ER 343.
5   *Woollerton and Wilson Ltd v Richard Costain Ltd* [1970] 1 All ER 483, [1970] 1 WLR 411; *Anchor Brewhouse Developments Ltd v Berkley House (Docklands Developments) Ltd* (1987) 284 Estates Gazette 625.
6   [1978] QB 479, [1977] 2 All ER 902.

Intrusion

24.4 The most obvious form of trespass to land is entry by the defendant himself. The slightest crossing of the boundary, such as a hand across the threshold,[1] is sufficient but, in the absence of such a crossing (or at least some contact with the fabric of the property), there is no trespass. Thus, where a landlord cuts off mains services to a tenant's flat from a point outside the flat, he may be guilty of both a breach of contract and a criminal offence,[2] but his conduct does not constitute the tort of trespass.[3] At one time it was thought that this would prevent a tenant from claiming exemplary damages,[4] but such action by a landlord is likely to constitute the tort of nuisance, and the Court of Appeal has held that exemplary damages may be awarded where this is the case.[5] Moreover, ss 27 and 28 of the Housing Act 1988 have now provided a specific remedy, with a generous measure of damages, for unlawful eviction.

A common form of trespass consists of directly causing objects to enter the plaintiff's land, for example by erecting a building which straddles the boundary. The most trivial invasion will suffice, such as leaning a ladder against the plaintiff's wall.[6]

A person who is permitted or legally entitled to enter land may, if he exceeds or abuses his right of entry, become a trespasser.[7] This rule is especially important in relation to public or private rights of way, since these permit only reasonable passage; thus, in *Hickman v Maisey*,[8] the defendant, who had patrolled a 15-yard stretch of

highway across the plaintiff's land in order to spy on racehorse trials there, was held
to be a trespasser. In such cases, action may be taken by the owner of the subsoil, which
will in practice often be a highway authority.

Under an old doctrine known as *trespass ab initio*, a person who enters land under
some legal authority (not merely by permission of the owner) but who then abuses
that authority may be treated as having been a trespasser from the moment of entry.
The doctrine was originally devised to protect citizens against the abuse of power by
officials, but the Court of Appeal has expressed serious doubts as to its continued
usefulness.[9] The doctrine, which has the effect of inflating the damages awarded, does
not apply where the subsequent abuse consists of an omission,[10] nor where there remains
some justification for the entry, as where police seize some documents unlawfully and
others lawfully.[11]

1   *Franklin v Jeffries* (1985) Times, 11 March.
2   Protection from Eviction Act 1977, s 1.
3   *Perera v Vandiyar* [1953] 1 All ER 1109, [1953] 1 WLR 672, CA.
4   Para 29.2 below.
5   *Guppys (Bridport) Ltd v Brookling* (1983) 269 Estates Gazette 846, 942, CA.
6   *Westripp v Baldock* [1939] 1 All ER 279, CA.
7   Para 22.9 above.
8   [1900] 1 QB 752, CA.
9   *Chic Fashions (West Wales) Ltd v Jones* [1968] 2 QB 299, [1968] 1 All ER 229, CA.
10 Such as failure to pay for food ordered and consumed: *Six Carpenters' Case* (1610) 8 Co Rep 146a.
11 *Elias v Pasmore* [1934] 2 KB 164.

Possession

24.5   Trespass to land is a wrong to the plaintiff's possession rather than to his
ownership. As a result, where land is let, it is only the tenant who can take action against
a trespasser, unless permanent damage is done to the property, in which case the
landlord may sue.[1] For the same reason, a tenant who fails to quit the premises when
his lease expires is not thereby guilty of trespass, since the landlord is not in possession.[2]
Conversely, where land is occupied under licence, the licence normally[3] lacks the
exclusive possession of the property which is necessary to found an action in trespass;[4]
this remains in the hands of the licensor.

The common law's emphasis upon the protection of possession (based on its
historical concern with preserving the peace) is such that even someone whose
possession is wrongful may sue in trespass any other wrongdoer who disturbs him,[5]
and it is no defence for the latter to show that the true right to possession lies with a
third party. The only person who may override such wrongful possession is the true
owner, or someone acting on his behalf.[6]

The question of what constitutes possession in law receives different answers in
respect of different types of property. It is the occupation of a house which counts, but
the possession of open land may depend upon evidence of actual use, so that the mere
erection of a fence round an area of disputed land may not be enough.[7] If, as frequently
happens in trespass actions, possession is disputed,[8] the law presumes in favour of the
person with title[9] even if, on investigation, that title proves to be defective.[10]

A person who is not actually in possession of land, even if he has an immediate
right to possession, cannot sue for trespass. When such a person eventually enters upon
the land, however, he is deemed by the doctrine of 'trespass by relation' to have been
in possession from the moment his right accrued, and he is therefore entitled to claim
damages in respect of trespass committed in the interim.

1   *Jones v Llanrwst UDC* [1911] 1 Ch 393. If damage which is merely temporary causes financial loss to
    the landlord, he may claim in negligence: *Ehlmer v Hall* [1993] 1 EGLR 137, CA.
2   *Hey v Moorhouse* (1839) 6 Bing NC 52.

3   But see para 36.9 below .
4   *Hill v Tupper* (1863) 2 H & C 121.
5   *Nicholls v Ely Beet Sugar Factory* [1931] 2 Ch 84, CA.
6   *Delaney v T P Smith Ltd* [1946] KB 393, [1946] 2 All ER 23, CA.
7   See *Marsden v Miller* (1992) 64 P & CR 239, CA.
8   Especially where one party claims to have acquired title against the other by adverse possession: paras 32.19–32.31 below.
9   *Jones v Chapman* (1849) 2 Exch 803.
10 *Fowley Marine (Emsworth) Ltd v Gafford* [1968] 2 QB 618, [1968] 1 All ER 979, CA.

Defences

24.6   An entry cannot be a trespass if it is legally justified, and justification in this context may arise in various ways. Statutory powers of entry are conferred not only on the police, but also on a myriad of officials, such as inspectors of the Health and Safety Executive, trading standards officers and VAT inspectors. More generally, an access agreement or order made under the National Parks and Access to the Countryside Act 1949 entitles any person to enter the land concerned, provided that he complies with the specified conditions.

A person who exercises a public or private right of way over land is not of course guilty of trespass, unless he abuses or exceeds that right.[1] Moreover, the exercise of certain other rights over land (such as easements, profits à prendre and local customary rights[2]) may entitle a person to do what would otherwise be a trespass. Indeed, even a bare permission or licence will also have this effect. Once such a licence is validly revoked[3] any further intrusion is a trespass, although the licensee cannot be compelled to undo what he has done. Thus, in *Armstrong v Sheppard and Short Ltd*,[4] where the plaintiff withdrew the permission which he had given the defendants to lay and use a sewer under his land, it was held that further use of the sewer was a trespass, although the defendants could not be compelled to remove the sewer itself.

Where a person discovers that goods which belong to him are on someone else's land, he is entitled to enter that land to retake his goods, at least if the other person is wrongfully responsible for their presence there.[5] Further, apparent acts of trespass may be justified by necessity (defence of the realm or the preservation of life or property) provided that they are in reasonable proportion to the threatened harm and that the need to trespass is not brought about by the defendant's own negligence.[6] However, the defence of necessity is kept within strict limits; it does not entitle homeless persons to 'squat' in vacant premises,[7] nor does it permit a landowner to enter neighbouring land in order to repair his own property.[8]

1   Paras 22.9 and 24.4 above.
2   Ch 37, below.
3   For revocation of licences, see paras 30.37–30.40 and 32.8–32.16 below.
4   [1959] 2 QB 384, [1959] 2 All ER 651, CA.
5   *Patrick v Colerick* (1838) 3 M & W 483.
6   *Rigby v Chief Constable of Northamptonshire* [1985] 2 All ER 985, [1985] 1 WLR 1242.
7   *Southwark London Borough Council v Williams* [1971] Ch 734, [1971] 2 All ER 175, CA.
8   *John Trenberth Ltd v National Westminster Bank Ltd* (1979) 253 Estates Gazette 151. See, however, the Access to Neighbouring Land Act 1992; para 24.7 below.

Access to neighbouring land

24.7   Although, as noted above, a landowner's need to enter adjoining property in order to carry out repairs is not a defence to trespass at common law, there has been statutory intervention in this area. Under the Access to Neighbouring Land Act 1992, any person wishing to carry out works of preservation to his land for which access to adjoining land is necessary,[1] but who cannot obtain the necessary permission for entry to that land, may apply to the county court for an access order.[2] It is for the court to decide whether any proposed works are works of preservation for this purpose, but certain works are presumed to be so.[3] The Act does *not* permit entry for the carrying out of improvements, alterations, or demolition work, except where these are incidental to works of preservation.[4]

An order under the Act must specify the works which are to be carried out, the land which can be entered and the period during which entry is authorised.[5] The court can impose such terms and conditions as are reasonably necessary for limiting or avoiding loss, damage, inconvenience or loss of privacy to the respondent or any other person,[6] and may require the applicant to insure against specified risks.[7] An order will not be granted where the entry would cause either interference to the use or enjoyment of the servient land, or hardship to any person in occupation of that land, to a degree which would make it unreasonable to make the order.[8] Once the work has been completed all waste must be removed and the servient land must be made good; the applicant is not authorised to leave anything on the servient land such as cables, pipes or drains.[9]

An order under the Act may require the applicant to pay *compensation* for any loss, damage or injury, or any substantial loss of privacy or other substantial inconvenience which might be caused.[10] In addition, except in the case of works to residential land, the court may order the payment of *consideration* for the entry; this sum is to be based on the likely financial advantage of the order to the applicant and the degree of inconvenience to the respondent or any other person.[11]

1   Or which would be substantially more difficult to carry out without such access: s 1(2)(b).
2   Section 1(1). It may well be that the mere existence of the court's power will in future mean that parties are more prepared to negotiate access agreements.
3   These works, defined as 'basic preservation works', include such matters as the maintenance, repair or renewal of any part of a building, and the felling of trees or shrubs which are damaged or dangerous: s 1(4).
4   Section 1(5). The Act does not therefore solve the problem of tower cranes: see para 24.9 below.
5   Section 2(1).
6   Section 2(2).
7   Section 2(4)(b).
8   Section 1(3).
9   Section 3(3).
10   Section 2(4)(a).
11   Section 2(5). 'Likely financial advantage' is defined in s 2(6).

Remedies
Damages
24.8   Where actual damage is caused to the plaintiff's land, he is entitled to claim damages, and these will normally be assessed by reference to the amount by which the value of the property is diminished or, more commonly, the cost of reinstating it to its former condition.[1] Even where the land itself is not damaged, the plaintiff is entitled to claim for the loss of use of his property, and here the appropriate measure is its normal letting value,[2] whether or not it appears likely that the plaintiff could have let it.[3]

It should be noted that, where the defendant is guilty of a continuing trespass, for example by remaining in occupation of or leaving his goods on the plaintiff's land, he is liable to successive actions until he ceases the offence. Damages in each action will therefore be awarded for the effects of the trespass up to the date of judgment.[4] Where, however, the trespass consists of a single act, such as the digging of a hole in the plaintiff's land, that fact that its effects continue does not lead to the same result; here damages are awarded only once, and will therefore take into account both past and future effects of the trespass.[5]

1   Para 29.13 below.

2   *Whitwham v Westminster Brymbo Coal Co* [1896] 2 Ch 538, CA.
3   *Swordheath Properties Ltd v Tabet* [1979] 1 All ER 240, [1979] 1 WLR 285, CA; *Inverugie Investments Ltd v Hackett* [1985] 3 All ER 841, PC.
4   *Holmes v Wilson* (1839) 10 Ad & El 503.
5   *Clegg v Dearden* (1848) 12 QB 576.

Injunction

24.9   Where a trespass is continuous or repetitive, the plaintiff may seek an injunction to compel the defendant to cease the offending activity. Such an injunction will normally be granted as a matter of course, even though this may cause serious inconvenience or expense to the defendant. Thus, for example, the plaintiff can obtain an injunction ordering the demolition of an encroaching building[1] or the immediate cessation of oversailing by a tower crane.[2] In one case[3] the judge delayed the operation of such an injunction in order to allow the builders to complete a development, but this is generally regarded as incorrect.[4]

Although an injunction will normally be granted, it must be borne in mind that it is a discretionary remedy. It may accordingly be refused in special circumstances, such as where the court disapproves of the plaintiff's conduct.[5] Moreover, the court has a statutory discretion to award damages in lieu of an injunction in any case where it is felt to be appropriate.[6]

1   *Harrow London Borough Council v Donohue* [1993] NPC 49, CA.
2   *Anchor Brewhouse Developments Ltd v Berkley House (Docklands Developments) Ltd* [1987] 2 EGLR 173; *London and Manchester Assurance Co Ltd v O & H Construction Ltd* [1989] 2 EGLR 185.
3   *Woollerton and Wilson Ltd v Richard Costain Ltd* [1970] 1 All ER 483, [1970] WLR 411.
4   See *John Trenberth Ltd v National Westminster Bank Ltd* (1979) 253 Estates Gazette 151; *Patel v W H Smith (Eziot) Ltd* [1987] 2 All ER 569, CA.
5   *Tollemache and Cobbold Breweries Ltd v Reynolds* (1983) 268 Estates Gazette 52, CA.
6   See para 29.19 below.

Action of ejectment

24.10   This ancient action, more commonly known as the action for the recovery of land, enables the plaintiff to regain actual possession of his land.[1] It has often been said that, whereas a plaintiff seeking damages need only show that he was in possession of the land, one who seeks to recover the actual land must prove his title. However, in practice it seems that proof of prior possession by the plaintiff raises a presumption of title which the defendant, unless he himself is entitled to the land, will find almost impossible to rebut.[2] Whether proof that true title rests with a third party will suffice to defeat the plaintiff's claim is a matter of great controversy; even if it does, however, it is of no avail to a defendant whose possession is either wrongful as against the plaintiff or derives from the plaintiff.

A person who seeks to recover his land in this way frequently also claims for mesne profits, that is, any profit gained by the defendant from his wrongful occupation, together with damages for any harm done.

1   Under RSC Ord 113, a special summary procedure is available against persons who are unidentified, such as 'squatters' or 'sitters-in': see *Wiltshire County Council v Frazer* [1986] 1 All ER 65.
2   *Asher v Whitlock* (1865) LR 1 QB 1.

Self-redress

24.11   As an alternative to taking legal action, a person in possession of land is entitled to use a reasonable degree of force to eject a trespasser or to deny him entry.[1] Similarly, a person in possession of land may simply remove (or demolish) an encroaching object, but only in simple cases which do not justify the expense of legal proceedings or urgent cases which require an immediate remedy.[2] It has also been held that, so long as adequate notice is given, a person in possession of land may lawfully wheel clamp motor vehicles parked on that land without permission and charge the motorist a reasonable fee for releasing the vehicle.[3]

Where a person is wrongfully dispossessed of land, the use of reasonable force to recover that land will not amount to a tort. However, great care must be taken to avoid a breach of the criminal law. A residential tenant who refuses to quit, for example, cannot be evicted without a court order. Further, the Criminal Law Act 1977 makes it an offence for anyone except a 'displaced residential occupier' to use or threaten violence in order to secure entry to property.

1   *Hemmings v Stoke Poges Golf Club* [1920] 1 KB 720, CA.
2   *Burton v Winters* [1993] 3 All ER 847, CA.
3   *Arthur v Anker* [1996] 3 All ER 783, CA.

Chapter 25

Nuisance

25.1 The legal meaning of the word nuisance is surrounded by confusion. Its short definition, 'annoyance' or 'harm', tells one very little, although it does manage to convey the idea that this area of the law of tort is concerned more with the effect of something upon the plaintiff than with the conduct of the defendant. The truth is that the subject matter of nuisance is of enormous breadth, linking together such diverse activities as running a fish and chip shop or a brothel, digging a trench in the street and letting one's trees overhang a neighbour's garden. When it is further appreciated that liability is not based on any single standard of conduct, such as negligence, the complexity of nuisance is easy to envisage.

Part of the confusion surrounding nuisance arises because the term is used to describe several different areas of liability which have relatively little in common. First, and perhaps most important as far as the law of tort is concerned, a *private nuisance* consists of any unlawful interference with a person's land, or with his use and enjoyment of that land. Within this category there also falls any interference with a person's rights over land, such as easements or profits.[1] Second, and quite separate, a *public nuisance* is a criminal offence, consisting of an activity which endangers or inconveniences the public in general, or which obstructs people in the exercise of public rights. The relevance of this class of nuisance to the law of tort is that damages may be awarded to any individual who suffers loss or damage over and above that which is incurred by the general public. Third, and not within the law of tort at all, is a *statutory nuisance* under various Acts of Parliament, such as the Control of Pollution Act 1974, the aim of which is to protect the environment. Enforcement in respect of this type of nuisance is in the hands of public bodies such as local authorities.

In this chapter we examine the following issues:

- the range of activities which may amount to a private nuisance;
- the factors which will determine whether or not an interference is a nuisance in the legal sense;
- the persons who are protected against, and those who may be held liable for, the commission of a nuisance;
- the special defences which apply to the tort of private nuisance, and the range of remedies available to the plaintiff;
- the legal definition of a public nuisance, and the extent to which such a nuisance may found liability in tort.

1   Discussion of these rights belongs to land law; see ch 37 below.

Private nuisance

25.2 It has been said, and often repeated, that 'private nuisances, at least in the vast majority of cases, are interferences for a substantial length of time by owners or occupiers of property with the use of enjoyment of neighbouring land'.[1] The main function of the law is to balance the conflicting interests of neighbours, and to decide at what point an interference becomes intolerable and therefore actionable.

1   *Cunard v Antifyre Ltd* [1933] 1 KB 551 at 557.

Interference
Damage to land
25.3 A person who *directly* causes something to enter the plaintiff's land is, of course, guilty of the tort of trespass.[1] Where the element of directness is lacking, however, the appropriate tort is private nuisance. Thus, for example, while it would be trespass to plant a tree in the plaintiff's garden, it is nuisance when the roots or branches of trees which the defendant has planted on his own land grow across the boundary.[2] Similarly, to build a wall on the plaintiff's land is a trespass, but to allow one's own wall to become so dilapidated that it falls on to the plaintiff's land is a nuisance.[3] Indeed, an occupier of land may become liable for nuisances which exist on it in circumstances where he has not positively caused anything, even indirectly.[4]

The simplest case of this type arises where something tangible is allowed to enter the plaintiff's property. A defendant has been held liable, for example, for causing water to overflow on to neighbouring land, both by carrying out filling operations on his own land[5] and by merely allowing his drain to become blocked.[6] However, damage may also be caused intangibly, as when vibrations shake the foundations of the plaintiff's building,[7] or fumes from a factory kill his shrubs.[8] It is clear from these cases that nuisance protects crops and buildings as well as the land itself; in *Farrer v Nelson*,[9] for instance, a person who overstocked his land with pheasants was held liable for the effect which these had upon his neighbour's crops.

As we shall see, the tort of private nuisance protects only those with an interest in or exclusive possession of land, so that a mere visitor who is injured or whose goods are damaged cannot recover damages for this in nuisance. In contrast, the occupier may claim damages in respect of his goods, as in *Halsey v Esso Petroleum Co Ltd*,[10] where smuts from an oil depot damaged the plaintiff's lines of washing. However, even the occupier cannot recover damages in private nuisance for personal injury (for example where he is made ill by fumes which render his house an unhealthy place in which to live); unlike damage to goods, such injury is not regarded in law as consequential on the damage to the land.[11]

1   Ch 24 above.
2   *Lemmon v Webb* [1894] 3 Ch 1, CA.
3   *Brew Bros Ltd v Snax (Ross) Ltd* [1970] 1 QB 612, [1970] All ER 587, CA.
4   Para 25.15 below.
5   *Home Brewery Ltd v William Davis & Co (Leicester) Ltd* [1987] 1 All ER 637.
6   *Sedleigh-Denfield v O'Callaghan* [1940] AC 880, [1940] 3 All ER 349, HL.
7   *Hoare & Co v McAlpine* [1923] 1 Ch 167.
8   *St Helen's Smelting Co v Tipping* (1865) 11 HL Cas 642, HL.
9   (1885) 15 QBD 258.
10   [1961] 2 All ER 145, [1961] 1 WLR 683.
11   *Hunter v Canary Wharf Ltd* [1997] 2 All ER 426, HL.

Use and enjoyment
25.4 The feature of private nuisance which sets it apart from other torts is that it protects the amenity value of land, in the sense of the occupier's use and enjoyment of

the property. Even where no physical damage is done, an occupier is entitled to complain if his intended use of the property (be it residential, agricultural or commercial) is unreasonably curtailed by the activities of the defendant. It is on this basis that action in nuisance may be taken in respect of smoke from a factory chimney,[1] offensive smells from stables[2] or the periodic emptying of a neighbour's cess-pit,[3] the noise from a children's playground[4] or persistent offensive telephone calls.[5] Indeed, the law takes account of even more subtle attacks upon the plaintiff's enjoyment of his land, or upon its amenity. Thus, the picketing of a person's premises from the highway, if it does not fall within the statutory protection given to certain actions in furtherance of industrial disputes, may constitute a nuisance,[6] and the use of high-class residential premises for prostitution may be a nuisance to neighbours.[7]

In *Bridlington Relay Ltd v Yorkshire Electricity Board*[8] it was suggested that an action in private nuisance could not be brought in respect of interference with television reception, since this would be a purely recreational use of land. However, the House of Lords in *Hunter v Canary Wharf Ltd*[9] took the view that television reception would in principle attract protection under this tort. Even so, the action there failed because the actual cause of the interference (the erection of a very large building on the defendants' land which blocked signals from the television transmitter) was held to be something which the defendants were fully entitled to do.

1   *Crump v Lambert* (1867) LR 3 Eq 409.
2   *Rapier v London Tramways Co* [1893] 2 Ch 588, CA.
3   *Penn v Wilkins* (1974) 236 Estates Gazette 203.
4   *Dunton v Dover District Council* (1977) 76 LGR 87.
5   *Khorasandjian v Bush* [1993] 3 All ER 669, CA.
6   *Hubbard v Pitt* [1976] QB 142, [1975] 3 All ER 1, CA.
7   *Thompson-Schwab v Costaki* [1956] 1 All ER 652, [1956] 1 WLR 335, CA. See also *Laws v Florinplace Ltd* [1981] 1 All ER 659 (sex shop in predominantly residential area).
8   [1965] Ch 436, [1965] 1 All ER 264.
9   [1997] 2 All ER 426, HL.

Unlawfulness

25.5   Although private nuisance consists of an interference, not every interference constitutes a nuisance. It would be futile to demand absolute silence or absence of smell from neighbours; they must be allowed the occasional party or garden bonfire. The law seeks to apply the broad principle of 'give and take', or 'live and let live'; as Lord Wright put it in *Sedleigh-Denfield v O'Callaghan*:[1] 'A balance has to be maintained between the right of the occupier to do what he likes with his own, and the right of his neighbour not to be interfered with'.

The way in which the law seeks to balance the competing interests of neighbours may be seen from the case of *Home Brewery plc v William Davis & Co (Leicester) Ltd*.[2] The defendant property developers there filled in some disused clay pits on their land; this prevented the natural drainage of water from neighbouring land owned by the plaintiffs, which consequently flooded. It was held that, although the developers could not have sued the plaintiffs in respect of this natural drainage, they were not compelled meekly to receive the water. The developers were thus not liable for blocking the drainage, since this occurred when they were putting their own land to perfectly reasonable use.

In striking an appropriate balance, the courts will have regard to a number of factors, which we now consider.

1   [1940] AC 880 at 903, [1940] 3 All ER 349 at 364.
2   [1987] 1 All ER 637.

Degree of interference

25.6 One of the most important factors, and also the most obvious, is the seriousness of the interference in question. Where actual physical damage is caused, a fairly minor interference is sufficient to constitute nuisance but, where the plaintiff complains of interference with his use and enjoyment, rather more is required. It has been said that there must be 'an inconvenience materially interfering with the ordinary comfort physically of human existence, not merely according to elegant or dainty modes and habits of living, but according to plain and sober and simple notions among the English people'.[1] In accordance with this approach, the Court of Appeal held that fluctuating night time noise from the defendants' factory was not sufficient to constitute a nuisance, even though it exceeded the maximum level recommended by the World Health Organisation.[2]

The matter here is purely one of degree, as appears from the following two cases. In *Heath v Brighton Corpn*,[3] a buzzing noise from a power station, which disturbed a church congregation in a poor area, was held insufficient to be a nuisance. In *Haddon v Lynch*,[4] on the other hand, the persistent and early ringing of church bells on Sunday mornings was held to be actionable.

1   *Walter v Selfe* (1851) 4 De G & Sm 315 at 322.
2   *Murdoch v Glacier Metal Co Ltd* [1998] 07 LS Gaz R 3, CA.
3   (1908) 98 LT 718.
4   [1911] VLR 230.

Sensitivity

25.7 A person who is abnormally sensitive, or who puts his property to an abnormally sensitive use, is not thereby entitled to a greater freedom from interference than anyone else. This rule, which is really no more than an application of the general principle outlined in the previous paragraph, is illustrated by *Robinson v Kilvert*,[1] in which heat from the defendant's premises damaged the plaintiff's stocks of brown paper. The amount of heat was not unreasonable; the damage was only caused because the paper was unduly sensitive, and the defendant was accordingly not liable. So too, in *Bridlington Relay Ltd v Yorkshire Electricity Board*,[2] where the plaintiffs relayed television signals from their receiver to members of the public, they claimed to be entitled to a greater freedom from interference than the average domestic user, on the basis that, unless they could offer a superior signal, they would have no customers. Not surprisingly, this claim was rejected.

Although the law gives no extra protection to those who are particularly sensitive, it does not abandon them altogether. If an interference is sufficiently substantial to constitute nuisance by ordinary standards, the plaintiff may claim damages for the full effect which it has upon the extra-sensitive use which he makes of his property, such as the growing of delicate orchids.[3]

1   (1889) 41 Ch D 88, CA.
2   [1965] Ch 436, [1965] All ER 264.
3   *McKinnon Industries Ltd v Walker* [1951] 3 DLR 577 at 581.

Locality

25.8 In assessing the standard of comfort to which the plaintiff is legally entitled, the character of the neighbourhood is an important factor. In *Halsey v Esso Petroleum Co Ltd*,[1] for instance, where the plaintiff complained of the nightly noise of tankers driving in and out of the defendants' oil depot, the judge regarded it as crucial that the depot was situated in a quiet residential part of Fulham. This does not mean that a person in a noisy area is left without protection altogether. For example, in *Polsue and Alfieri Ltd v Rushmer*,[2] the plaintiff, who lived in Fleet Street, was held entitled to complain of the nightly noise from a new printing press which the defendants had installed.

In *Allen v Gulf Oil Refining Ltd*³ claims in nuisance were made where a massive oil refinery, constructed under the authority of an Act of Parliament, caused severe dislocation of the environment. It was pointed out by Lord Wilberforce that, even if these claims were not completely defeated by the defence of statutory authority,⁴ the appropriate standard of comfort for this locality was to be based on what Parliament had clearly authorised it to become, rather than on what it had been before the refinery was built. However, the mere fact that planning permission has been granted for an activity does not automatically provide a defence to an action in private nuisance; it will only do so where there has been a strategic planning decision affected by considerations of public interest.⁵

It should be noted that, where physical damage is caused to the plaintiffs property, the locality is irrelevant. Thus, in *St Helens Smelting Co v Tipping*,⁶ where the plaintiff's shrubs were killed by fumes from the defendants' smelting works, the House of Lords regarded it as no defence that the area was devoted to such industrial activity.

1   [1961] 2 All ER 145, [1961] 1 WLR 683.
2   [1907] AC 121, HL.
3   [1981] AC 1001, [1981] 1 All ER 353, HL.
4   Para 25.17 below.
5   *Wheeler v JJ Saunders Ltd* [1995] 2 All ER 697, CA.
6   (1865) 11 HL Cas 642, HL.

Continuity

25.9   In most cases of private nuisance, especially those in which the plaintiff's use and enjoyment of land are affected, there is an element of continuity or repetition in the interference of which he complains. This is hardly surprising, since the dust from building operations lasting years, or the noise from nightly revelries, may well be intolerable, whereas interference of a shorter or more sporadic nature might not be. This does not mean that an isolated incident can never be a basis for liability (though a court is less likely to grant an injunction in such cases);¹ where actual damage results, as where a dilapidated building falls on to the plaintiff's land, there is no need for a repetition before action can be taken.

Cases in which there is a single occurrence of damage are sometimes explained as resulting from a continuing state of affairs for which the defendant is responsible. Thus in *Spicer v Smee*,² where defective wiring in the defendant's bungalow caused a fire which spread to the plaintiff's property, the defendant was held liable in nuisance. In *British Celanese Ltd v A H Hunt (Capacitors) Ltd*,³ where light strips of metal foil, which were stored over a period of time on the defendants' land, blew on to adjoining property and caused damage, liability in nuisance was again imposed. In *SCM (UK) Ltd v W J Whittall & Son Ltd*,⁴ on the other hand, where a workman negligently severed a cable and thus cut off the electricity supply to the plaintiff's factory, it was held that the defendants could not be liable in nuisance. Here there was nothing which could be described as a state of affairs, but merely an isolated act of negligence.

1   *Swan v Great Northern Rly* (1864) 4 De GJ & SM 211.
2   [1946] 1 All ER 489.
3   [1969] 2 All ER 1252, [1969] WLR 959.
4   [1970] 2 All ER 417, [1970] 1 WLR 1017, CA.

Utility of the defendant's conduct

25.10   A frequent plea of defendants in nuisance actions is that the offending activity is being carried on for the benefit of the public. This can undoubtedly have some bearing on the degree of interference which the plaintiff can be expected to put up with (the noise and dust which usually accompanies demolition and rebuilding, for example, would certainly be actionable if caused for no good reason). However, it cannot be a complete defence, for the courts will not allow the public interest to ride roughshod over private rights. In *Adams v Ursell*,[1] for instance, the smell from a fried-fish shop was held to be a nuisance, notwithstanding its value in supplying good food in a poor neighbourhood. Even more striking is the case of *Shelfer v City of London Electric Lighting Co*,[2] in which vibrations from the building of a power station damaged the plaintiff's house. The Court of Appeal held that the plaintiff was entitled to an injunction to stop the work, even though the laudable purpose of the building was to bring electric light to the City of London.

It may be that modern courts are more willing than their predecessors to give weight to the public interest, at least to the extent of refusing to stop a beneficial activity altogether. In *Miller v Jackson*,[3] for example, the plaintiff bought a new house next to the ground on which the village team had played cricket for some 70 years. The Court of Appeal held, by a majority, that the danger from cricket balls constituted a nuisance; nevertheless, in view of the social value of the ground to the community, the plaintiff was denied an injunction and left to his remedy in damages. Likewise, in *Dunton v Dover District Council*,[4] where the plaintiff complained of the noise from a children's playground next to his hotel, the judge refused to order its closure, but restricted its opening times and the age-group of children permitted to use it. By contrast, the Court of Appeal in *Kennaway v Thompson*[5] granted an injunction which drastically curtailed the activities of a motor boat racing club, preferring to protect the interest of a neighbouring resident who complained about the noise.

1   [1913] 1 Ch 269.
2   [1895] 1 Ch 287, CA.
3   [1977] QB 966, [1977] 3 All ER 338, CA.
4   (1977) 76 LGR 87.
5   [1981] QB 88, [1980] 3 All 329, CA.

Order of events
25.11   Surprisingly, perhaps, it seems settled that a plaintiff is not precluded from complaining of a nuisance merely because he came to it with his eyes wide open. In *Sturges v Bridgman*,[1] a doctor was held entitled to complain of the noise from machinery used by the defendant on adjoining premises, even though this caused him no inconvenience until he chose to build a consulting room at the end of his garden.

1   (1879) 11 Ch D 852, CA.

The defendant's state of mind
25.12   The question whether liability in nuisance depends upon proof of any particular mental element on the part of the defendant is one of the most difficult and complex aspects of this tort. All that may safely be said is that the more unreasonable the defendant's conduct, the less likely it is that the plaintiff will be required to tolerate the interference in question. Thus, in *Christie v Davey*,[1] where the defendant banged a tray on the party wall in order to disrupt the plaintiff's music lessons, his malice was held to render this noise actionable as a nuisance, even though the volume itself might not have done so. Even clearer is *Hollywood Silver Fox Farm Ltd v Emmett*,[2] where the defendant fired guns near the boundary of his land for the specific purpose of disturbing the breeding season of the plaintiffs' silver foxes. This was held to be actionable, although it could hardly be said that the sound of gunfire would normally amount to a nuisance, unless unduly prolonged. However, it should be noted that malice

cannot make unlawful something which the defendant has an absolute right to do, such as the abstraction of percolating water from beneath his own land.[3]

Of less weight than malice, although still relevant to this question, is the possibility that the defendant has been negligent in failing to keep the interference to a minimum. If building operations cause more dust and noise than necessary,[4] or children in a day nursery are permitted to make excessive noise,[5] the defendant's lack of care may lead a court to the conclusion that the plaintiff cannot be expected to put up with the consequences.

Although malice and negligence may thus both be highly relevant to liability in nuisance, it seems that neither is essential. The courts have repeatedly stressed that, if the interference caused by an activity is substantial enough to be a nuisance, the defendant cannot evade liability merely by showing that he took all reasonable steps to reduce it. Defendants who have taken all reasonable care have nevertheless been held liable in respect of the smell from stables[6] or from a fried-fish shop[7] and the noise from a hotel kitchen.[8] The same principle applies where actual damage is caused; for example, where building works infringe a neighbour's right of support, it is no defence to show that the works were carried out without negligence.[9] In all these cases, however, the defendant was held liable as creator of the nuisance. As we shall see, where the defendant is sued as occupier of the land from which the nuisance emanates, proof that he has not taken reasonable care is normally essential to liability.[10]

The Privy Council in *The Wagon Mound (No 2)*[11] added to the confusion surrounding this issue by declaring that, while 'negligence in the narrow sense' might not always be needed for an action in nuisance, 'fault of some kind' is almost invariably necessary. What is meant by 'fault' in this context is far from clear. However, an important consequence of the decision is that, since fault involves foreseeability, the rules as to remoteness of damage in nuisance are identical to those in negligence.[12]

1   [1893] 1 Ch 316.
2   [1936] 2 KB 468, [1936] 1 All ER 825.
3   *Bradford Corpn v Pickles* [1895] AC 587, HL.
4   *Andreae v Selfridge & Co Ltd* [1938] Ch 1, [1937] 3 All ER 255, CA.
5   *Moy v Stoop* (1909) 25 TLR 262.
6   *Rapier v London Tramways Co* [1893] 2 Ch 588, CA.
7   *Adams v Ursell* [1913] 1 Ch 269.
8   *Vanderpant v Mayfair Hotel Co Ltd* [1930] 1 Ch 138.
9   *Brace v South-East Regional Housing Association Ltd* (1984) 270 Estates Gazette 1286, CA.
10 Para 25.15 below.
11 [1967] 1 AC 617, [1966] 2 All ER 709, PC.
12 *Cambridge Water Co Ltd v Eastern Counties Leather plc* [1994] 1 All ER 53 at 71–72, HL. We describe the relevant rules at paras 20.17–20.21 above.

Who is protected?

25.13   The tort of private nuisance is a means of protection for persons in possession or occupation of land.[1] This does not mean that only the freehold owner can sue; a limited interest, such as a weekly tenancy,[2] will suffice, although someone with such an interest is unlikely to be awarded an injunction except in very serious cases. In exceptional circumstances, a person who is in exclusive possession of land but who is unable to prove title to it may be entitled to sue in private nuisance,[3] as he can in trespass.[4] However, it is now settled that a person who has neither an interest in the land nor exclusive possession of it (such as a member of the occupier's family) is not entitled to maintain an action for private nuisance.[5]

The requirement that a plaintiff has possession of land serves to exclude actions by the landlord of property, at least in respect of temporary interference with its use and enjoyment, even if the effect of these is to reduce its letting value.[6] The landlord can, however, sue to protect his reversionary interest against either physical damage or such nuisances as may, by the doctrine of prescription,[7] operate to deprive him of rights or burden his land with obligations.[8]

Where, as frequently happens, a nuisance continues over a period, it is quite possible for its effects to be felt by successive owners or occupiers of the same property. The implications of this were considered in *Masters v Brent London Borough Council*,[9] where the roots of the defendants' lime tree encroached and damaged the foundations of a house. The plaintiff, having bought the house, paid for the necessary repairs and then sued the defendants for the cost. However, the defendants raised the defence that the damage had occurred during the ownership of the plaintiff's predecessor. Talbot J, having decided that some damage continued to occur during the plaintiff's ownership, held that this entitled him to claim for the losses he had actually suffered, which amounted to the full cost of repair.

1   This includes a permanently moored barge to which the plaintiff has a right of exclusive use and occupation: *Crown River Cruises Ltd v Kimbolton Fireworks Ltd* [1996] 2 Lloyd's Rep 533.
2   *Jones v Chappell* (1875) LR 20 Eq 539.
3   *Hunter v Canary Wharf Ltd* [1997] 2 All ER 426, HL, approving *Foster v Warblington UDC* [1906] 1 KB 648; CA; *Newcastle-under-Lyme Corpn v Wolstanton Ltd* [1947] Ch 427, [1947] 1 All ER 218, CA.
4   Para 24.5 above.
5   *Hunter v Canary Wharf Ltd* [1997] 2 All ER 426, HL, approving *Malone v Laskey* [1907] 2 KB 141, CA and overruling *Khorasandjian v Bush* [1993] 3 All ER 669, CA.
6   *Simpson v Savage* (1856) 1 CBNS 347.
7   Paras 37.33–37.44 below.
8   *Jones v Llanrwst UDC* [1911] 1 Ch 393.
9   [1978] QB 841, [1978] 2 All ER 664.

Who is liable?
Creator
25.14   In practice, most nuisance actions are brought against the occupier of the offending land. However, there seems no doubt that the person who actually creates a nuisance is always liable for it, whether he does this on his own land, someone else's land, or the public highway. This was certainly assumed to be the case in *Hall v Beckenham Corpn*,[1] where the plaintiff complained of noise from model aeroplanes in a public park, although the individual enthusiasts were not in fact sued in that case. Further, where a person creates a nuisance on his own land, he remains liable for it, even where he subsequently parts with possession of the property and so becomes unable to prevent its continuance.[2]

1   [1949] 1 KB 716, [1949] 1 All ER 423.
2   *Thompson v Gibson* (1841) 7 M & W 456.

Occupier
25.15   Quite apart from the possibility that he may actually create a nuisance, an occupier may be held responsible for any nuisance which exists upon his land, whether this arises from natural causes or from the actions of other persons. An extreme example of this is *Russell v London Borough Council of Barnet*,[1] in which a highway authority was held liable to a householder for damage caused by the spreading roots of trees which were growing in the street, notwithstanding that the trees actually belonged to the householder!

The general rule, in cases where the occupier is not personally responsible for the creation of the nuisance, is that he is only liable if, with knowledge or the means of knowledge of its existence, he fails to make reasonable steps to abate it. In *Sedleigh-Denfield v O'Callaghan*,[2] for example, a drainage pipe, which had been negligently laid in the defendants' ditch by trespassers, became blocked, with the result that water overflowed on to the plaintiff's land. The defendants were held liable, for they had known of the pipe for three years and should have appreciated the danger. In *St Anne's Well Brewery Co v Roberts*,[3] on the other hand, part of the city wall of Exeter which was owned by the defendant collapsed and demolished the plaintiffs' inn. The cause of this collapse was excavations which had been carried out by the defendant's predecessor. Since the defendant did not and could not know of these, he was held not liable.

The principle adopted in cases where nuisance is caused by the acts of others has also been applied to nuisances which arise naturally, such as fire caused by lightning striking a tall tree,[4] earth falling from a geological mound[5] or a landslip of cliff land occupied by the defendants which withdraws support from the plaintiff's property.[6] However, the courts in such cases have sought to avoid subjecting an 'innocent' occupier to too heavy a burden and have thus held that, in deciding whether the occupier has acted reasonably, regard should be had to his individual circumstances, such as his financial resources.

There is one anomalous exception to the general rule that an occupier's liability is based on negligence. It was laid down by the Court of Appeal, in the much-criticised case of *Wringe v Cohen*,[7] that, where premises abut upon a highway, the occupier (and landlord, if he is under a duty to repair) is strictly liable for damage resulting from disrepair, whether this is caused to neighbouring property or to the highway.[8] The extent of this liability is uncertain, since the court excluded cases in which the damage resulted from either the act of a trespasser or the secret and unobservable processes of nature.

The common thread which joins all these cases is that the nuisance is created neither by the occupier himself, nor by anyone for whom he is answerable. Where the nuisance arises out of the activities of a visitor, for example, it seems that the occupier will be liable, provided that this is a foreseeable consequence of what he has permitted the visitor to do. Thus in *A-G v Stone*,[9] the defendant, who had allowed gypsies to camp on his land, was held liable when the noise and insanitary conditions of their camp constituted a nuisance. The same principle applies where work carried out on the occupier's behalf by an independent contractor causes a nuisance; if this consequence is foreseeable from the nature of the work, as where support is withdrawn from neighbouring property,[10] the defendant will be liable. In *Matania v National Provincial Bank Ltd*,[11] for instance, building operations carried on by a contractor on behalf of the occupier of a building's first floor involved a clear risk of nuisance by noise and dust to the occupiers of higher floors. When this happened, the occupier was held liable for it.

1   (1984) 271 Estates Gazette 699. A highway authority is generally responsible for all trees, whether self-sown or planted before or after adoption of the highway: *Hurst v Hampshire CC* [1997] 2 EGLR 164, CA.
2   [1940] AC 880, [1940] 3 All ER 349, HL.
3   (1928) 140 LT 1, CA.
4   *Goldman v Hargrave* [1967] 1 AC 645, [1966] 2 All ER 989, PC.
5   *Leakey v National Trust for Places of Historic Interest or Natural Beauty* [1980] QB 485, [1980] 1 All ER 17, CA.
6   *Holbeck Hall Hotel Ltd v Scarborough Borough Council* [1997] 2 EGLR 213.
7   [1940] 1 KB 229, [1939] 4 All ER 241, CA.
8   In the latter case the occupier would be liable for public nuisance; para 25.25 below.
9   (1895) 12 TLR 76. See also *Page Motors Ltd v Epsom and Ewell Borough Council* (1981) 80 LGR 337.
10 *Bower v Peate* (1876) 1 QBD 321.
11 [1936] 2 All ER 633, CA.

Landlord
25.16   Where a nuisance arises from premises which are let, a plaintiff will normally take action against the tenant, who is the occupier. Whether or not the tenant is liable

for the nuisance depends upon the rules discussed in the previous paragraph. In certain circumstances, however, the landlord may also be liable, although it is important to realise that this will not exonerate the tenant; it will simply provide the plaintiff with an additional person to sue.

In the first place, the landlord is legally responsible whenever he can be said to have 'authorised' his tenant to commit nuisance. This will be so where the nuisance arises from the normal use of the land by the tenant for the very purpose for which it is let, as in *Harris v James*[1] (blasting and smoke from a lime quarry), *Sampson v Hodson-Pressinger*[2] (noise from tenants merely walking about in an insufficiently soundproofed top-floor flat) or *Tetley v Chitty*[3] (disturbance from a go-kart club which operated as tenants of the local authority). It should be emphasised, however, that it is authority, and not merely foreseeability, which must be established. Thus, in *Smith v Scott*,[4] where a local authority placed a problem family in the next house to that of the plaintiffs, it was held that the local authority were not liable for the foreseeable nuisances which ensued; having made their tenants covenant expressly not to commit nuisance, it could hardly be said that they had authorised them to do so.

Where nuisance arises not from the use to which the property is put, but from the state of repair in which it is let, the landlord is liable if he knows or ought to know of its state at the commencement of the tenancy.[5] Further, the landlord remains liable in this situation even though the tenant has covenanted to put the premises into repair; this is because a covenant between landlord and tenant cannot restrict the rights of third parties.[6]

In cases where the property falls into disrepair, and thus becomes a nuisance, during the currency of the lease, the landlord is only responsible if he has a duty to repair[7] or a right to enter and do repairs.[8] The common law on these points is somewhat uncertain, but s 4 of the Defective Premises Act 1972 contains similar principles which are rather more clearly expressed.[9]

The general rule is that a landlord, like an occupier, is only liable for nuisance by disrepair where he knows or ought to know of it. Once again, however, the case of *Wringe v Cohen*[10] lays down that, if the premises adjoin a highway, liability is strict.

1   (1876) 45 LJQB 545.
2   [1981] 3 All ER 710, CA.
3   [1986] 1 All ER 663.
4   [1973] Ch 314, [1972] 3 All ER 645.
5   *St Anne's Well Brewery Co v Roberts* (1928) 140 LT 1, CA.
6   *Brew Bros Ltd v Snax (Ross) Ltd* [1970] 1 QB 612, [1970] 1 All ER 587, CA.
7   This may be express or implied, eg under the Landlord and Tenant Act 1985, ss 11–14; para 36.22 below.
8   *Heap v Ind Coope and Allsopp Ltd* [1940] 2 KB 476, [1940] 3 All ER 634, CA. This may be implied, eg in a weekly tenancy: *Mint v Good* [1951] 1 KB 517, [1950] 2 All ER 1159, CA.
9   Para 22.29 above.
10 [1940] 1 KB 229, [1939] 4 All ER 241, CA.

Defences
Statutory authority
25.17   Many actions in private nuisance arise out of the activities of local authorities and other public or quasi-public bodies, which are carried on under the auspices of a statute. Such bodies may have a defence against liability where they can prove that the nuisance they have created is an inevitable consequence of what the statute ordered or empowered them to do, in the sense that it would occur despite the use of all reasonable care and skill, according to the state of scientific knowledge at the time.[1] However, the position may be further affected if, as frequently occurs, the statute in question contains a specific statement to the effect that liability for nuisance is, or is not, excluded.

The case law on statutory authority as a defence is complex, but an attempt was made to rationalise it in the case of *Department of Transport v North West Water Authority*,[2] where the following propositions, formulated by the trial judge, were endorsed by the House of Lords:

- In the absence of negligence, a body is not liable for a nuisance caused by its performance of a statutory *duty*.[3]
- This is so, even if the statute in question expressly imposes liability for nuisance.[4]
- In the absence of negligence, a body is not liable for a nuisance caused by its exercise of a statutory *power*, where the statute does not expressly impose liability upon it.[5]
- Even without negligence, a body is liable for a nuisance caused by its exercise of a statutory power, if the statute expressly imposes liability upon it.[6]
- In all cases, immunity depends upon proof that the work has been carried out, or the operation conducted, with all reasonable regard and care for the interests of other persons.[7]

In deciding whether or not a particular nuisance has been authorised by a statute, the terms of that statute must be interpreted, and it is important to appreciate that authority may be conferred either expressly or by implication. In the leading case of *Hammersmith and City Rly Co v Brand*,[8] for instance, where a railway company was expressly authorised to use railway engines, it was held by the House of Lords that no action in nuisance would lie against it in respect of damage caused by vibrations from passing trains. In *Allen v Gulf Oil Refining Ltd*,[9] the express authority of the defendants was limited to acquiring land and there *constructing* an oil refinery. A majority of the House of Lords, reversing the decision of the Court of Appeal, held that there was also implied authority to *operate* a refinery, so that no action in nuisance would lie in respect of the inevitable consequences (smell, noise, vibrations, etc) of its operation.

In the last two cases, the defendants were empowered to carry on the activity in question in a specific place. Frequently, however, this is not so, the defendants in question having a wide discretion under the statute as to the place and method of exercising their power. In such a case, a court is less likely to take the view that any nuisance arising from the exercise of the discretion is inevitable. Thus, in *Metropolitan Asylum District Managers v Hill*,[10] it was held that a general authority to build hospitals did not protect the defendants from liability when they chose to site a smallpox hospital in a residential area.

Where the statutory authority is to carry out not a specific undertaking, but such works of a particular kind as may from time to time be necessary, the courts have been somewhat reluctant to use private nuisance for the protection of private rights. This reflects the view that, if parliament has seen fit to confer an administrative discretion upon a public body, the bona fide exercise of that discretion should be challenged only through administrative channels and not through the ordinary courts of law.[11]

1   *Manchester Corpn v Farnworth* [1930] AC 171, HL.
2   [1984] AC 336, [1983] 3 All ER 273, HL.
3   *Hammond v St Pancras Vestry* (1874) LR 9 CP 316.
4   *Smeaton v Ilford Corpn* [1954] Ch 450, [1954] 1 All ER 923.
5   *Dunne v North Western Gas Board* [1964] 2 QB 806, [1963] 3 All ER 916, CA.
6   *Charing Cross West End and City Electric Supply Co v Hydraulic Power Co* [1914] 3 KB 772, CA.
7   *Allen v Gulf Oil Refining Ltd* [1981] AC 1001, [1981] 1 All ER 353, HL.
8   (1869) LR 4 HL 171, HL.
9   [1981] AC 1001, [1981] 1 All ER 353, HL.
10   (1881) 6 App Cas 193, HL.
11   *Marriage v East Norfolk Rivers Catchment Board* [1950] 1 KB 284, [1949] 2 All ER 1021, CA.

Prescription

25.18 It seems in principle that the right to commit certain private nuisances may be acquired by 20 years' use, under the doctrine of prescription. For this to be so, however, the right in question must be capable of forming the subject matter of an easement,[1] such as the right to send smoke through flues in a party wall.[2] It is generally thought that this requirement would exclude the possibility of prescription in respect of such variable nuisances as noise and smells, although cases on long-standing nuisances of this kind have all been decided on other grounds.[3]

1 Paras 37.2–37.10 below.
2 *Jones v Pritchard* [1908] 1 Ch 630.
3 See, for example, *Sturges v Bridgman* (1879) 11 Ch D 852, CA.

Other defences

25.19 The defences of *volenti non fit injuria* and contributory negligence, which we have already considered in relation to negligence,[1] are clearly capable of applying to nuisance, at least where the plaintiff sues in respect of a single incident which causes physical damage. Where, however, the gist of the plaintiff's complaint is the general effect upon him of the defendant's unreasonable use of land, these defences seem of little relevance. In particular, it is certainly no defence to prove that the plaintiff came to an existing nuisance,[2] nor that he could have reduced its effects, eg by shutting his windows against noise.

One line of argument which does not provide a defence to an action in private nuisance is that the defendant is merely one contributor to the plaintiff's discomfort,. Even if the interference is only sufficient to constitute a nuisance when combined with others, the defendant is fully liable as, indeed, are all guilty parties. In *Lambton v Mellish*,[3] for instance, where the plaintiff suffered from the combined effects of two rival fairground organs, it was held that he was entitled to an injunction, although neither organ was making sufficient noise to constitute a nuisance in itself.

1 Ch 21 above.
2 Para 25.11 above.
3 [1894] 3 Ch 163; *Pride of Derby and Derbyshire Angling Association Ltd v British Celanese Ltd* [1953] Ch 149, [1953] 1 All ER 179.

Remedies

Damages

25.20 Although private nuisance is in theory actionable only on proof that the plaintiff has suffered damage, the necessary damage will sometimes be presumed to exist. For example, the mere fact that the cornice of the defendant's house projects over the plaintiff's land is sufficient to found an action, without the need to prove that water falls from it.[1] So too, any interference with a proprietary right of the plaintiff is automatically actionable; this is important, since continued interference by the defendant might otherwise lead to the loss of the plaintiff's right altogether.[2]

Once it is established that the defendant is guilty of nuisance, the plaintiff is entitled to claim damages for consequential losses, provided that these are of a foreseeable kind.[3] As we have seen,[4] relevant losses include damage to goods and land,[5] together with the intangible 'use and enjoyment' of the plaintiff's property. The last category is obviously difficult to express in monetary terms; the courts have sometimes used the analogy of personal injury cases, so that damages for noise reflect those for deafness[6] and damages for smell reflect those awarded for loss of that sense.[7] However, the correctness of this approach was doubted in *Hunter v Canary Wharf Ltd*,[8] where it was stated that damages should be measured by the effect which the nuisance had on the value of the affected land.

1   *Fay v Prentice* (1845) 1 CB 828.
2   *Nicholls v Ely Beet Sugar Factory Ltd* [1936] Ch 343, CA.
3   *The Wagon Mound (No 2)* [1967] 1 AC 617 [1966] 2 All ER 709, PC.
4   Paras 25.3 and 25.4 above.
5   For what is included in damage to land, see *Midland Bank plc v Bardgrove Property Services Ltd* [1992] 2 EGLR 168, CA; para 37.50 n5 below.
6   *Chadwick v Keith Marshall* [1984] CLY 1037.
7   *Bone v Seale* [1975] 1 All ER 787, [1975] 1 WLR 979, CA.
8   [1997] 2 All ER 426 at 451, HL.

Injunction[1]

25.21   A commonly sought remedy in nuisance actions is that of injunction, whereby the plaintiff asks the court to order the termination of the offending activity. The award of this remedy lies in the discretion of the court, and it will seldom be granted in respect of injury which is trivial or temporary.[2] In more serious cases, however, the courts have displayed a notable tendency to grant an injunction even when the defendant's activity has public value,[3] which seems rather surprising in view of their statutory power to award damages in lieu of the injunction sought.[4]

1   Paras 29.17–29.19 below.
2   *A-G v Sheffield Gas Consumers Co* (1853) 3 De GM & G 304.
3   Para 25.10 above.
4   Para 29.19 below.

Abatement

25.22   The law has for centuries recognised the right of a person affected by a nuisance to take matters into his own hands and abate (ie remove) it. In a more sophisticated age, however, such self-help remedies are treated by the courts with suspicion and dislike, if for no other reason than that they may lead to a breach of the peace, and anyone claiming to exercise this right must therefore take great care not to exceed what the law permits. Where, for example, the defendant's tree overhangs the plaintiff's land, the plaintiff may lop off its branches;[1] he must not, however, keep the fruit.[2] Further, where abatement involves entry on to the defendant's land, notice must first be given, except in an emergency.[3] And the overall requirement that damage be kept to a minimum means that, where there are alternative methods of abating a nuisance, the less mischievous must be chosen.[4]

1   *Lemmon v Webb* [1895] AC 1, HL.
2   *Mills v Brooker* [1919] 1 KB 555.
3   *Jones v Williams* (1843) 11 M & W 176.
4   *Lagan Navigation Co v Lambeg Bleaching Co* [1927] AC 226, HL.

Public nuisance

25.23   Public nuisance covers an even wider area than private nuisance, partly because it is not limited to interference with land. Public nuisance falls into two broad categories. First, the kind of interference, such as noise or smoke, which is commonly a private nuisance, will also become a public nuisance if it affects a sufficiently substantial neighbourhood or section of the public. Whether or not this is so is a question of fact;[1] thus, in *R v Lloyd*,[2] where only three people complained of noise, the defendant was held not guilty of public nuisance. Second, public nuisance may consist of interference with the exercise of public rights, for instance by obstructing a highway or navigable river. Within these two classes, liability has been imposed on such diverse activities as blasting operations causing widespread vibrations, dust, splinters and noise,[3] organising a pop festival which causes noise, traffic congestion and general inconvenience,[4] and selling impure food[5] or water.[6]

It must be remembered that public nuisance is essentially a matter of criminal law.[7] However, as we shall see, a private individual may in some circumstances seek damages for the effect which a public nuisance has on him. Further, where the relevant criminal penalties are felt to be inadequate, the Attorney-General is empowered to bring what is called a relator action for an injunction to have the offending activity terminated.

1   *A-G v PYA Quarries Ltd* [1957] 2 QB 169, [1957] 1 All ER 894, CA.
2   (1802) 4 Esp 200.
3   *A-G v PYA Quarries Ltd* [1957] 2 QB 169, [1957] 1 All ER 894, CA.
4   *A-G for Ontario v Orange Productions Ltd* (1971) 21 DLR (3d) 257.
5   *Shillito v Thompson* (1875) 1 QBD 12.
6   *AB v South West Water Services Ltd* [1993] 1 All ER 609, CA.
7   A very important consequence of this is that a public nuisance can never be legalised by prescription.

25.24   Public nuisance, like private nuisance, involves the court in the task of balancing conflicting interests in accordance with the general idea of reasonableness. Therefore, a person is not automatically liable when queues form outside his shop and obstruct the highway, since these may be due to circumstances beyond his control, such as wartime shortages.[1] Liability will be imposed, however, on a theatre proprietor who takes no steps at all to reduce large nightly queues,[2] or on a shopkeeper who, by selling ice cream from a window, instead of inside the shop, positively increases the likelihood of obstruction.[3] The test is whether the defendant knows or ought to know that there is a real risk that nuisance of the kind which in fact occurs will be caused.[4]

Again, as with private nuisance, the court must apply the principle of 'give and take'. A builder may erect hoardings or scaffolding in the street,[5] vans may load and unload outside business premises[6] and vehicles may break down,[7] without liability arising in public nuisance. Indeed, where personal injury results from such an obstruction, as where the plaintiff collides at night with a parked vehicle, the modern tendency is to impose liability upon the defendant only where he has been negligent in causing the danger,[8] although it is not clear whether it is for the plaintiff to establish negligence or for the defendant to disprove it. Where, however, the obstruction is unreasonable in size or extent, as where a vehicle which has broken down is left for a long period in an unlighted or otherwise dangerous condition, the defendant will be liable in public nuisance.[9]

1   *Dwyer v Mansfield* [1946] KB 437, [1946] 2 All ER 247.
2   *Lyons, Sons & Co v Gulliver* [1914] 1 Ch 631, CA.
3   *Fabbri v Morris* [1947] 1 All ER 315, DC.
4   *R v Shorrock* [1993] 3 All ER 917, CA.
5   *Harper v GN Haden & Sons Ltd* [1933] Ch 298, CA.
6   *Trevett v Lee* [1955] 1 All ER 406, CA.
7   *Maitland v Raisbeck and AT and J Hewitt Ltd* [1944] KB 689, [1944] 2 All ER 272, CA.
8   *Dymond v Pearce* [1972] 1 QB 496, [1972] 1 All ER 1142, CA.
9   *Ware v Garston Haulage Co Ltd* [1944] 1 KB 30, [1943] 2 All ER 558, CA.

Highways
25.25   It is obvious from the previous paragraph that public nuisance frequently concerns the highway. In the first place, any obstruction, whether total or partial, of the highway is actionable, except where it can be justified on the broad ground of reasonableness. It has even been suggested[1] that it would be a public nuisance for pickets to harass workers in their use of the highway without actually obstructing it, but this has been doubted.[2]

Second, it is a public nuisance to carry on any activity, or to allow property to fall into a state, whereby users of the highway are endangered. This includes the creation of such obvious hazards as a pool of acid[3] or a pile of rubbish,[4] and the emission of large clouds of smoke from neighbouring premises[5] or defective vehicles[6] which obscure the vision of drivers. In *Castle v St Augustine's Links*,[7] liability was imposed upon a golf club which so sited one of its tees that golfers often sliced balls on to an adjoining public road. A person may be liable for public nuisance even where the danger which he has created is not technically on the highway at all, provided that a passer-by may be endangered without making a substantial detour. Thus, for example, an unfenced excavation at the very edge of the road, or sharp outward-pointing spikes on a boundary fence,[8] can constitute a public nuisance.

Where danger arises from work which is being done on or in the highway itself, such as excavations, it is important to note that the defendant is liable even where he is not negligent and, further, that he is responsible for any default of his independent contractor.[9]

The mere fact that a person's building or tree projects over the highway does not render him guilty of a public nuisance, unless it is such as to interfere with reasonable passage. Where, however, it falls and does damage, there may undoubtedly be liability, although the basis of this is disputed. It seems that, where trees are concerned, the occupier is not liable unless he had reason to suspect the danger;[10] nor is he responsible for the negligence of his independent contractor, eg in felling operations.[11] Where buildings collapse, liability appears to be strict, whether these project over[12] or merely adjoin[13] the highway.

As regards dangers arising from the condition of the highway itself, such as potholes or uneven flagstones, common law imposed no liability upon anyone for a mere failure to repair. In relation to highway authorities, this immunity was anomalous, and it was removed by statute in 1961. Under this provision (which is now contained in the Highways Act 1980), a highway authority may be liable in negligence, nuisance or breach of statutory duty for damage caused by its failure to maintain or repair a highway, subject to a statutory defence of proving that all reasonable care had been taken, by independent contractors or employees of the highway authority, to make the particular highway safe for the type and volume of traffic which might reasonably be expected to use it.

1   *Thomas v National Union of Mineworkers* [1985] 2 All ER 1.
2   *News Group Newspapers Ltd v Society of Graphical and Allied Trades 1982 (No 2)* [1987] ICR 181.
3   *Pope v Fraser and Southern Rolling and Wire Mills Ltd* (1938) 55 TLR 324.
4   *Almeroth v Chivers & Sons Ltd* [1948] 1 All ER 53, CA.
5   *Holling v Yorkshire Traction Co* [1948] 2 All ER 662.
6   *Tysoe v Davies* [1984] RTR 88.
7   (1922) 38 TLR 615.
8   *Fenna v Clare & Co* [1895] 1 QB 199, DC.
9   *Holliday v National Telephone Co* [1899] 2 QB 392, CA; see paras 28.26 and 28.29 below.
10 *Caminer v Northern and London Investment Trust Ltd* [1951] AC 88; [1950] 2 All ER 486, HL. See also *Quinn v Scott* [1965] 2 All ER 588, [1965] 1 WLR 1004.
11 *Salsbury v Woodland* [1970] 1 QB 324, [1969] 3 All ER 863, CA.
12 *Tarry v Ashton* (1876) 1 QBD 314.
13 *Wringe v Cohen* [1940] 1 KB 229, [1939] 4 All ER 241, CA.

Action for damages

25.26   The fact that a person is inconvenienced by a public nuisance does not of itself entitle him to recover damages in respect of it.[1] In order to claim damages, he must show that he has suffered some 'special' or 'particular' damage, over and above that which is sustained by the public in general. This requirement is obviously satisfied by personal injuries, and, in *Halsey v Esso Petroleum Co Ltd*,[2] it was held that the plaintiff was entitled to complain of smuts from the defendants' oil depot, since these had caused actual damage to the paintwork of his car, which was parked in the street outside his house. Similarly, where unlawful industrial picketing obstructs the highway, the costs incurred by an employer in 'bussing' in his workers and providing extra security for them are recoverable as damages for public nuisance.[3]

In all these cases, the damage to the plaintiff was of a different kind from that suffered by other persons, but it seems that a substantial difference in extent is also sufficient to found an action. In the Irish case of *Boyd v Great Northern Rly Co*,[4] for instance, a doctor with a busy practice recovered damages when he was delayed for 20 minutes at a level crossing, while in *Rose v Miles*,[5] where the defendant obstructed a creek and thus trapped the plaintiff's barges, the plaintiff was able to recover the considerable cost of unloading the cargo and transporting it by land. Again, in *Tate & Lyle Industries Ltd v Greater London Council*,[6] where the defendants caused serious siltation in navigable reaches of the River Thames, the plaintiffs recovered for losses caused by the inability of large vessels to load and unload at their sugar refinery.

The obstruction of streets not infrequently leads to complaints by neighbouring tradesmen of loss of custom. Where access to the plaintiff's premises is blocked, this certainly gives rise to an action for damages.[7] Where the obstruction is further away, the legal position is less clear, although the better view is that an affected tradesman can sue,[8] provided that the effect of the obstruction upon his business is foreseeable and therefore not too remote.[9]

1   *Winterbottom v Lord Derby* (1867) LR 2 Exch 316.
2   [1961] 2 All ER 145, [1961] 1 WLR 683.
3   *News Group Newspapers Ltd v Society of Graphical and Allied Trades 1982 (No 2)* [1987] ICR 181.
4   [1895] 2 IR 555.
5   (1815) 4 M & S 101.
6   [1983] 2 AC 509, [1983] 1 All ER 1159, HL.
7   *Fritz v Hobson* (1880) 14 Ch D 542.
8   *Wilkes v Hungerford Market Co* (1835) 2 Bing NC 281.
9   *The Wagon Mound (No 2)* [1967] 1 AC 617, [1966] 2 All ER 709, PC; paras 20.17–20.20 above.

Statutory nuisance

25.27   Although it falls outside the law of tort, an account of nuisance would be misleading without some reference to an impressive range of statutory provisions, the overall purpose of which is to minimise environmental damage. Unhealthy premises, provided that they affect persons outside,[1] noise, and the pollution of land, sea and air, are all covered by an elaborate system of administrative control, the enforcement of which is usually in the hands of local authorities and which is carried out by means of criminal prosecution. While some of these provisions give rise to an action for damages by any individual who is affected, the vast majority do not; nevertheless, a person aggrieved may, by complaining to the appropriate enforcement authority, achieve what he most wants, namely, the termination of the offending activity.

1   *National Coal Board v Neath Borough Council* [1976] 2 All ER 478.

Chapter 26

Strict liability

26.1 We pointed out in Chapter 17 that the basic function of the law of tort is to allocate responsibility for various kinds of loss or damage which result from human activity. We also noted that the common law normally leaves loss to lie where it has fallen (ie on the plaintiff), except where that loss has resulted from the defendant's fault, in the sense that he has caused it intentionally or negligently. What we shall consider in this and the next chapter are several situations in which liability may be imposed upon a defendant who is not guilty of any 'fault'.

It is important to emphasise that there is nothing either harsh or illogical in these departures from the normal requirement of fault. The law is in effect saying that, while it is quite permissible (and may indeed be in the public interest) to carry on certain high-risk activities, this can only be done on the basis that the losses which they are statistically bound to cause are borne by those who carry on the activities themselves, and not by innocent members of society on whom those losses happen to fall. Indeed, were this not so, the activity in question would in effect be subsidised, either by the unfortunate victims, or by the taxpayer, through state benefits paid to those victims.

If strict liability (ie liability without fault) has a legitimate place even in a system which is largely fault-based, the vital question becomes: to which activities should it be applied? From a purely logical point of view, there is much to be said for the view that all 'ultra-hazardous activities' should attract this form of liability. However, as will be seen, English law has never developed a general theory of strict liability; those parts of the law of tort in which liability is strict have grown up piecemeal both at common law and under statute.

In this chapter we examine the following issues:

- the scope of the principle of strict liability which was laid down in the famous case of *Rylands v Fletcher*;
- the special defences which are available in cases falling within that principle;
- the extent to which damage caused by fire attracts special treatment under the law of tort.

Rylands v Fletcher

26.2 The facts of this celebrated case were that the defendants employed reputable independent contractors to construct a reservoir on their land, for the purpose of supplying water to their mill. In the course of construction, the contractors discovered some disused mine shafts on the reservoir site but negligently failed to seal these properly, with the result that water flowed down the shafts and flooded the plaintiff's mine, which connected with the disused workings. No negligence was found against the defendants themselves and, at first instance, they were held not liable for the damage caused. On appeal, however, the plaintiff was successful, upon grounds stated by Blackburn J:[1]

> 'We think that the true rule of law is, that the person who for his own purposes brings on his lands and collects and keeps there anything likely to do mischief if it escapes, must keep it in at his peril, and, if he does not do so, is prima facie answerable for all the damage which is the natural consequence of its escape. He can excuse himself by showing that the escape was owing to the plaintiff's default; or perhaps that the escape was the consequence of *vis major,* or the act of God; but as nothing of this sort exists here, it is unnecessary to inquire what excuse would be sufficient.'

This decision, together with the reasoning on which it was based, was expressly approved and upheld by the House of Lords,[2] although Lord Cairns LC rather complicated matters by stressing the importance of the fact that the defendants were at the relevant time putting their land to a 'non-natural use'. This qualification has subsequently been treated as one of the main elements of liability under the rule in *Rylands v Fletcher,* and we shall deal with it as such. In addition, since Blackburn J clearly recognised that some defences were available against this form of strict liability, we shall consider a number which have proved successful in later cases.

1   (1866) LR 1 Exch 265 at 279.
2   (1868) LR 3 HL 330, HL.

Elements of liability
Land
26.3   An important part of the rule as laid down, and one which has helped to prevent it from developing to cover dangerous activities in general, is the requirement that the escaping object be something which the defendant has brought on to his land. This does not mean, however, that liability is imposed only upon the freehold owner, or even the occupier, of the land in question. If a licensee, for example, introduces a dangerous substance on to land which he is permitted to use, he may be liable under *Rylands v Fletcher* for its subsequent escape, provided that it is then still under his (ineffective) control.[1] In such a case, it seems that the owner who is not in occupation is only liable if he has expressly or impliedly authorised the accumulation.[2]

The requirement that the defendant be in occupation of land has been slightly relaxed, so as to bring within the rule those who have a right to lay pipes, cables etc under the land of others or under the public highway. Indeed, an escape in such circumstances may render the defendant liable, not only to neighbouring landowners,[3] but also to other public bodies with similar rights.[4]

Whether the rule is capable of any further expansion must be regarded as doubtful. However, it may possibly apply where a dangerous thing escapes from the highway on to which the defendant has brought it.[5] It has also been suggested that it might apply to accumulations of dangerous objects in a vessel moored on a river.[6]

1   *Rainham Chemical Works v Belvedere Fish Guano Co* [1921] 2 AC 465, HL.
2   *St Anne's Well Brewery Co v Roberts* (1928) 140 LT 1, CA.
3   *Northwestern Utilities Ltd v London Guarantee and Accident Co Ltd* [1936] AC 108, PC.
4   *Charing Cross West End and City Electric Supply Co v Hydraulic Power Co* [1914] 3 KB 772, CA.

5   *Rigby v Chief Constable of Northamptonshire* [1985] 2 All ER 985, [1985] 1 WLR 1242.
6   *Crown River Cruises Ltd v Kimbolton Fireworks Ltd* [1996] 2 Lloyd's Rep 533.

Accumulation

26.4   Blackburn J spoke of the person who 'for his own purposes brings on his lands and collects and keeps there' something which, if it escapes, will be dangerous. Subsequent cases support this idea that the defendant is strictly liable only for artificial accumulations, and not for either natural material, such as earth, or material which accumulates naturally, such as rainwater. For instance, in *Giles v Walker*,[1] an occupier who ploughed up forest land was held not liable for the subsequent spontaneous crop of thistles which spread to the plaintiff's land.[2] So too, in *Pontardawe RDC v Moore-Gwyn*,[3] it was held that *Rylands v Fletcher* had no application to a fall of rock from an outcrop due to the natural process of erosion. Again, where water is naturally on the defendant's land, the plaintiff cannot complain that the defendant's normal working of mines causes it to flow on to his land.[4]

Not surprisingly, an occupier who actively causes natural material to escape will be liable under *Rylands v Fletcher*.[5] For example, in *Miles v Forest Rock Granite Co (Leicestershire) Ltd*,[6] liability was imposed upon the defendants for damage done by the escape of rock caused by their blasting operations. A similar decision was reached in *Baird v Williamson*,[7] where the defendant pumped water which was naturally in his mine to a level from which it flowed into the plaintiff's mine.

Although strict liability can thus only apply to the artificial collection of material, or to artificially causing the escape of natural material, later decisions make it clear that a duty of *care* is placed upon an occupier whose land becomes a danger to his neighbour through natural causes. The occupier will be liable if, when he knows or ought to know of the damage, he fails to take reasonable steps to abate it.[8]

The requirement that the accumulation be for the defendant's own purposes should not be taken too literally, as restricting *Rylands v Fletcher* to cases where the defendant acquires some personal benefit. It has been held to apply, for example, to a local authority compelled by statute to receive sewage into its sewers,[9] although the liability of statutory undertakers was doubted by the Court of Appeal on precisely this ground in *Dunne v North Western Gas Board*.[10]

1   (1890) 24 QBD 656.
2   Contrast *Crowhurst v Amersham Burial Board* (1878) 4 Ex D 5, where the defendants actually planted a poisonous tree.
3   [1929] 1 Ch 656.
4   *Smith v Kenrick* (1849) 7 CB 515, approved in *Rylands v Fletcher*.
5   If his act is deliberate, the appropriate tort is trespass: *Rigby v Chief Constable of Northamptonshire* [1985] 2 All ER 985, [1985] 1 WLR 1242.
6   (1918) 34 TLR 500, CA.
7   (1863) 15 CBNS 376, again approved in *Rylands v Fletcher*.
8   Para 25.15 above.
9   *Smeaton v Ilford Corpn* [1954] Ch 450, [1954] 1 All ER 923.
10 [1964] 2 QB 806, [1963] 3 All ER 916, CA.

Dangerous things

26.5   As originally stated, the rule in *Rylands v Fletcher* applies only to something 'likely to do mischief if it escapes'. The difficulty with this is that almost anything is capable of causing damage in some circumstances; indeed, the very fact that the plaintiff is in court indicates that the object in question has caused damage. In practice, therefore, the courts appear largely to have ignored this part of the rule.

Among the many things which have given rise to strict liability are water in bulk,[1] gas,[2] electricity,[3] sparks,[4] acid smuts[5] and poisonous vegetation.[6] *Rylands v Fletcher* has also been held to apply to fire[7] and explosions,[8] notwithstanding that the thing which escapes in such cases is not necessarily the same as that which the defendant has accumulated. All these seem to fall fairly within the rule as originally laid down, but some other candidates for inclusion have stretched it more than a little. In *Firth v Bowling Iron Co*,[9] for example, the defendants were held liable for a rusty wire fence which flaked on to the plaintiff's land and poisoned his cattle, while, in *Hale v Jennings Bros*,[10] the principle was invoked where a chair from a fairground 'chair-o-plane' became detached from the roundabout and, complete with its occupant, flew off and injured the occupier of a nearby booth. Even a falling flagpole[11] has been held to come within *Rylands v Fletcher*, although its application to vibrations,[12] where the invasion is intangible, has been criticised. Most extreme of all is perhaps the case of *A-G v Corke*,[13] where the doctrine was applied to human beings so as to justify the grant of an injunction against a man who allowed caravan dwellers to use his field, when these committed various acts of nuisance in the neighbourhood. The dubious nature of this decision is emphasised by the fact that liability could in any case have been imposed on the simple ground of nuisance.[14]

1   *Ryland v Fletcher* itself.
2   *Northwestern Utilities Ltd v London Guarantee and Accident Co Ltd* [1936] AC 108, PC.
3   *National Telephone Co v Baker* [1893] 2 Ch 186.
4   *Jones v Festiniog Rly Co* (1868) LR 3 QB 733.
5   *Halsey v Esso Petroleum Co Ltd* [1961] 2 All ER 145, [1961] 1 WLR 683.
6   *Crowhurst v Amersham Burial Board* (1878) 4 Ex D 5.
7   *Mason v Levy Auto Parts of England Ltd* [1967] 2 QB 530, [1967] 2 All ER 62.
8   *Rainham Chemical Works v Belvedere Fish Guano Co* [1921] 2 AC 465, HL.
9   (1878) 3 CPD 254.
10 [1938] 1 All ER 579, CA.
11 *Shiffman v Hospital of the Order of St John of Jerusalem* [1936] 1 All ER 557.
12 *Hoare & Co v McAlpine* [1923] 1 Ch 167.
13 [1933] Ch 89.
14 *A-G v Stone* (1895) 12 TLR 76; para 25.15 above.

Escape

26.6   The decision in *Rylands v Fletcher* might have been used by subsequent courts as the basis for a general principle of liability for ultra-hazardous activities. That this has not happened is at least partly due to the courts' insistence that there must be an escape, in the sense that the damage complained of is suffered outside the land on which the defendant accumulates his dangerous things. In *Ponting v Noakes*,[1] for instance, the plaintiff was unable to recover damages when his horse reached over the boundary of the defendant's land, ate some poisonous vegetation which grew there, and died. This principle was unanimously endorsed by the House of Lords in *Read v J Lyons & Co Ltd*,[2] where the plaintiff, a munitions inspector, was injured by the explosion of a shell at the defendants' weapons factory. It was admitted that such shells were 'dangerous things'; nevertheless it was held that, in the absence of either negligence or an escape, the defendants were not liable.

In deciding whether there has been a sufficient 'escape' for this purpose, the courts are concerned, not with the niceties of land law, but with the simple question of fact whether something has travelled from a place where the defendant has control to a place where he has not. As a result, a landlord may be liable to his own tenant (or, possibly, his licensee) when something escapes from that part of the property which he has retained to that part which is in the occupation of the plaintiff.[3]

1   [1894] 2 QB 281.
2   [1947] AC 156, [1946] 2 All ER 471, HL.
3   *Hale v Jennings Bros* [1938] 1 All ER 579, CA.

Non-natural use

26.7 In laying down the rule in *Rylands v Fletcher*, Blackburn J stressed the importance of the fact that the defendants had brought on to their land something which was not naturally there. This element of liability, like all the others, was expressly approved by Lord Cairns LC, in the House of Lords, but the additional point was made that the defendant must be engaged in a 'non-natural' use of his land. This may have been meant simply as another way of expressing Blackburn J's point. However, subsequent courts have treated it as a separate issue. Thus, the simple question of fact whether the accumulation is natural or artificial is no longer sufficient; the judge must now also decide whether the use to which the defendant puts his land is natural or non-natural.

The effect of this requirement has been to introduce a great deal of flexibility into this area of law, because the courts are free not to impose strict liability upon a person whose use of land, although artificial, is an ordinary and usual one. The result of this discretion has been to tie *Rylands v Fletcher* more closely to the idea of exceptional risk, and it has been suggested that a non-natural use is one which brings with it increased danger to others and is not merely the ordinary use of the land or such a use as is proper for the general benefit of the community.[1]

It is difficult to predict how the courts will make what is in effect a value judgment, although decided cases offer some insight into judicial attitudes. Thus, while a domestic water supply,[1] or a house's electric wiring,[2] or a fire in a grate,[3] have all been held to be natural, similar utilities carried in bulk have not.[4] So too, trees, whether planted or self-sown, have been regarded as natural,[5] except where they are poisonous.[6] Such decisions do not necessarily mean that the dividing line lies between domestic or agricultural uses, on the one hand, and industrial uses, on the other. A number of modern cases have used the idea of natural use to avoid imposing strict liability on industrial activities which are regarded as for the public benefit,[7] even to the extent of suggesting that an armaments factory is a natural use of land in wartime.[8] However, in the recent case of *Cambridge Water Co Ltd v Eastern Counties Leather plc*,[9] the House of Lords regarded the storage of substantial quantities of chemicals on industrial premises as 'an almost classic case of non-natural use', even though the premises were in an industrial village and the defendants' activity created much-needed employment in the locality.

1   *Rickards v Lothian* [1913] AC 263 at 279, PC.
2   *Collingwood v Home and Colonial Stores Ltd* [1936] 3 All ER 200, CA.
3   *Sochacki v Sas* [1947] 1 All ER 344.
4   *Smeaton v Ilford Corpn* [1954] Ch 450, [1954] 1 All ER 923 (sewage).
5   *Noble v Harrison* [1926] 2 KB 332.
6   *Crowhurst v Amersham Burial Board* (1878) 4 Ex D 5.
7   Eg *Rouse v Gravelworks Ltd* [1940] 1 KB 489, [1940] 1 All ER 26, CA (working of mines and minerals); *British Celanese Ltd v A H Hunt (Capacitors) Ltd* [1969] 2 All ER 1252, [1969] 1 WLR 959 (light engineering factory on an industrial estate).
8   *Read v J Lyons & Co Ltd* [1947] AC 156 at 170, 174, 187, [1946] 2 All ER 471 at 475, 478, 484.
9   [1994] 1 All ER 53 at 79.

Damage

26.8 It was said in *Rylands v Fletcher* that a defendant would be liable for 'all the damage which is the natural consequence' of the escape. This formulation does not indicate the appropriate test for remoteness of damage, but it is now established that the defendant can only be liable for damage of a type which could have been reasonably foreseen, even though foreseeability is irrelevant to liability itself.[1]

As to the *kinds* of damage which are actionable, the major question is whether *Rylands v Fletcher* is like private nuisance in protecting only those persons with an interest in or exclusive possession of land.[2] Until recently, the balance of authority suggested that *Rylands v Fletcher* is not so limited; thus in *Halsey v Esso Petroleum Co Ltd*,[3] the plaintiff was able to claim for damage caused to the paintwork of his car, which was parked in the street, by acid smuts from the defendants' oil depot. So too, in *British Celanese Ltd v A H Hunt (Capacitors) Ltd*,[4] where strips of metal foil blew from the defendants' land on to an electricity sub-station, and the resulting power cut caused damage in the plaintiffs' factory, it was held to be no defence that nothing had 'escaped' on to the plaintiffs' land. However, these decisions may be open to doubt in the light of *Cambridge Water Co Ltd v Eastern Counties Leather plc*,[5] where the House of Lords placed great emphasis on the close relationship between *Rylands v Fletcher* and private nuisance.

It is uncertain whether damages may be recovered in respect of personal injuries, especially those suffered by a non-occupier. There is some authority in favour of such claims, whether by an occupier[6] or a non-occupier.[7] However, dicta in *Read v J Lyons & Co Ltd*[8] suggest that a claim for personal injury is always dependent on proof of negligence. Furthermore, the views expressed by the House of Lords in *Cambridge Water*, which were noted above, would appear hostile to such claims.

Whether or not it may accurately be described as a natural consequence, it is settled that no damages may be claimed under *Rylands v Fletcher* for pure economic loss.[9]

1   *Cambridge Water Co Ltd v Eastern Counties Leather plc* [1994] 1 All ER 53.
2   Para 25.13 above.
3   [1961] 2 All ER 145, [1961] 1 WLR 683.
4   [1969] 2 All ER 1252, [1969] WLR 959.
5   [1994] 1 All ER 53 at 69–71.
6   *Hale v Jennings Bros* [1938] 1 All ER 579, CA.
7   *Miles v Forest Rock Granite Co (Leicestershire) Ltd* (1918) 34 TLR 500, CA; *Shiffman v Hospital of the Order of St John of Jerusalem* [1936] 1 All ER 557; *Perry v Kendricks Transport Ltd* [1956] 1 All ER 154, [1956] 1 WLR 85, CA.
8   [1947] AC 156 at 174, 178, 180, [1946] 2 All ER 471 at 478, 480, 481.
9   *Cattle v Stockton Waterworks Co* (1875) LR 10 QB 453; *Weller & Co v Foot and Mouth Disease Research Institute* [1966] 1 QB 569; [1965] 3 All ER 560. See paras 18.18–18.20 above.

Defences
Consent of the plaintiff
26.9   The defence of *volenti non fit injuria*[1] means that, where the plaintiff consents to the presence of the source of danger, the defendant is not liable unless he is negligent. The plaintiff may consent expressly;[2] however, it is more commonly implied from the circumstances. As to when consent will be implied, the legal position is confused; many of the cases have concerned an escape of water from an upper floor to a lower floor, and these could have been decided on an alternative ground, namely, that the installation in question was a natural use of land.[3] Apart from this, two main threads emerge from the cases as reasons for holding that the plaintiff has consented. First, and despite its apparent conflict with the principle that 'coming to a nuisance' is no defence,[4] the plaintiff (at least where he is the defendant's tenant) cannot complain of the condition of his or the landlord's property at the commencement of the lease.[5] Second, consent to a dangerous installation will more easily be implied where it is maintained for the benefit of the plaintiff as well as the defendant.[6] This latter factor, however, is not conclusive, so that a consumer of gas is not precluded from suing the statutory undertakers by the fact that he benefits from the supply.[7]

It should be emphasised that the consent which is implied in these cases merely precludes the plaintiff from bringing an action under the rule in *Rylands v Fletcher*.

Where the defendant is guilty of negligence, he remains liable,[8] unless the circumstances are so extreme that the plaintiff can be said to have assumed the risk of this.

1 Paras 21.2–21.4 above.
2 As in *A-G v Cory Bros & Co Ltd* [1921] 1 AC 521, HL.
3 *Rickards v Lothian* [1913] AC 263, PC; para 26.7 above.
4 Para 25.11 above.
5 *Kiddle v City Business Properties Ltd* [1942] 1 KB 269, [1942] 2 All ER 216.
6 *Gill v Edouin* (1895) 72 LT 579, CA.
7 *Northwestern Utilities Ltd v London Guarantee and Accident Co Ltd* [1936] AC 108, PC.
8 *A Prosser & Son Ltd v Levy* [1955] 3 All ER 577, [1955] 1 WLR 1224, CA.

Default of the plaintiff and hypersensitivity

26.10 The doctrine of causation applies as much to *Rylands v Fletcher* as to any other tort. Thus, if the true legal cause of damage is some act or default of the plaintiff himself, no action will lie. In *Dunn v Birmingham Canal Navigation Co*,[1] for example, where a mine-owner, fully aware of the danger, worked his mine directly under the defendants' canal, he was held unable to sue in respect of the resulting flood. It also appears that, if the plaintiff is partly responsible for the damage, his damages may be reduced on the ground of contributory negligence.[2]

Where injury or damage results from the hypersensitivity of the plaintiff or his property, it seems, by analogy with nuisance,[3] that the defendant should not be liable. In *Eastern and South African Telegraph Co Ltd v Cape Town Tramways Companies Ltd*,[4] where the escape of minute electric currents from the defendants' tramway system interfered with the plaintiffs' submarine telegraph cable, the plaintiffs failed to recover damages. Where, however, the plaintiff is not actively responsible for his sensitivity, the position is less clear. For example, in *Hoare & Co v McAlpine*,[5] it was said to be no defence to an action for causing damage by vibrations that the plaintiffs' building was old and unstable.

1 (1872) LR 7 QB 244.
2 Paras 21.11–21.16 above.
3 Para 25.7 above.
4 [1902] AC 381, PC.
5 [1923] 1 Ch 167.

Act of God

26.11 The defendant is not exempted from liability merely because an escape was unforeseeable; if he were so exempted there would be no difference between *Rylands v Fletcher* and negligence. Nevertheless, the law recognises that there may be a natural catastrophe so overwhelming that even a system of strict liability should not hold the defendant responsible. Thus, where the escape is due to an operation of natural forces 'which no human foresight can provide against, and of which human prudence is not bound to recognise the possibility',[1] there is no liability. In *Nichols v Marsland*,[2] the defendant created artificial lakes on his land by damming a natural stream. A rainstorm of unprecedented violence broke down the banks which he had built, and the resulting flood swept away the plaintiff's bridges. The defendant was held not liable, on the basis that the storm constituted an act of God.

Nichols v Marsland appears to be the only reported English case in which the defence has succeeded, and even that decision has subsequently been heavily criticised. In *Greenock Corpn v Caledonian Rly Co*,[3] it was held by the House of Lords that, whatever the English position might be, an extraordinary rainfall in Scotland was no act of God!

1 *Tennent v Earl of Glasgow* (1864) 2 M 22 at 26.

2   (1876) 2 Ex D 1, CA.
3   [1917] AC 556, HL.

Act of a stranger

26.12   Although difficult to reconcile with the theory of strict liability, it is well established that a defendant is not liable under *Rylands v Fletcher* where the escape is due to the deliberate and unforeseeable intervention of a 'stranger', that is, someone over whom he has no control. This may be some unknown person who blocks up the waste-pipe of a washbasin and leaves the taps running,[1] a trespassing child who drops a lighted match into the petrol tank of a motor vehicle,[2] or even a neighbour who, by emptying his reservoir into the stream which feeds the defendant's reservoir, causes the latter to flood the plaintiff's land.[3] The defendant is responsible, however, for the acts of his employees, unless they go where they are expressly forbidden[4] and, of course, for his independent contractors.[5] Further, it appears that he may be liable for the actions of anyone lawfully on his land. For example, in *Hale v Jennings Bros*,[6] where a chair flew off a fairground 'chair-o-plane' and injured a stallholder, it was held to be no defence that this was due to tampering by the person who was riding in it.

A defendant is responsible, even for the intervention of a 'stranger', if he ought reasonably to have anticipated the danger and taken steps to prevent the accident. In *Northwestern Utilities Ltd v London Guarantee and Accident Co Ltd*,[7] for example, the plaintiffs' hotel was destroyed by fire after gas escaped from the defendants' mains and exploded. The mains had fractured when support was withdrawn from it during the construction of a sewer. The Privy Council held the defendants liable, for they were aware of the construction work and should have appreciated the very grave danger which this involved.

1   *Rickards v Lothian* [1913] AC 263, PC.
2   *Perry v Kendricks Transport Ltd* [1956] 1 All ER 154, [1956] 1 WLR 85, CA.
3   *Box v Jubb* (1879) 4 Ex D 76.
4   *Stevens v Woodward* (1881) 6 QBD 318, DC (employee caused a flood by leaving the taps running in a lavatory which he was not permitted to use).
5   *Rylands v Fletcher* itself.
6   [1938] 1 All ER 579, CA.
7   [1936] AC 108, PC.

Statutory authority

26.13   Where a person's activity is specifically authorised by statute, he is not liable under *Rylands v Fletcher* for any damage which it causes, although he will be liable if he is negligent.[1] Thus in *Pearson v North Western Gas Board*,[2] where an explosion of gas which had escaped from the defendants' mains seriously injured the plaintiff, killed her husband and destroyed her home, the defendants were not liable, since they had not been negligent.

Whether or not an activity is authorised depends upon the statute in question, and the principles of interpretation which are used by the courts are similar to those which apply in cases of nuisance.[3] In *Green v Chelsea Waterworks Co*,[4] for example, the defendants were under a statutory duty to maintain a certain pressure of water in their mains, and the statute, unlike many of its kind, did not expressly state that they would be liable for any nuisance caused.[5] When a mains burst, it was held that they were not liable in the absence of negligence. By contrast, in *Charing Cross West End and Electric Supply Co v Hydraulic Power Co*,[6] the defendants merely had a statutory power to carry water in mains, and they were specifically made liable for nuisance. It was held that the statute did not exempt them from strict liability under *Rylands v Fletcher* in respect of a burst main.

1   *Manchester Corpn v Farnworth* [1930] AC 171, HL.

2   [1968] 2 All ER 669.
3   Para 25.17 above.
4   (1894) 70 LT 547, CA.
5   Even if there had been such a provision, the defendants would probably not have been liable: *Department of Transport v North West Water Authority* [1984] AC 336, [1983] 3 All ER 273, HL.
6   [1914] 3 KB 772, CA.

Fire

26.14   Common law has for centuries imposed a form of strict liability upon anyone from whose property fire is allowed to spread and cause damage,[1] except where this is due to an act of God[2] or the intervention of a 'stranger'. The latter defence covers only those over whom the occupier has no control, so that liability has been imposed upon an occupier for the negligence of an employee who allowed a fire to spread,[3] an independent contractor who used a blowlamp to thaw frozen pipes and set fire to their lagging,[4] and even a golf club guest who dropped a lighted match.[5] In *H and N Emanuel Ltd v Greater London Council*,[6] a demolition contractor, on the defendants' land with their permission, lit a bonfire to burn rubbish; this was known to be his normal practice, although the contract specifically prohibited the lighting of fires on site. When sparks carried to the plaintiffs' property and caused damage, the defendants were held liable.

As we shall see, actions for the spread of fire are today usually governed by statute. Where this is not so, however, the common law rule still applies. Thus, for example, in *Mansel v Webb*,[7] the defendant was held strictly liable for the escape of sparks from his steam engine on the highway.

1   *Beaulieu v Finglam* (1401) YB 2 Hen 4, fo 18, pl 6.
2   *Turberville v Stamp* (1697) 1 Ld Raym 264.
3   *Musgrove v Pandelis* [1919] 2 KB 43, CA.
4   *Balfour v Barty-King* [1957] 1 QB 496, [1957] 1 All ER 156, CA.
5   *Boulcott Golf Club Inc v Engelbrecht* [1945] NZLR 556.
6   [1971] 2 All ER 835, CA.
7   (1918) 88 LJKB 323, CA.

26.15   The Fires Prevention (Metropolis) Act 1774, s 86 provides that no action shall be brought against any person in whose premises, or on whose estate, any fire shall accidentally begin. In view of the way in which this provision (which, in spite of its title, applies throughout the country) has subsequently been interpreted, the extent to which it modifies the common law rule is somewhat uncertain. In *Filliter v Phippard*,[1] 'accidentally' was said to refer only to a fire produced by mere chance or incapable of being traced to any cause. This rules out protection where the defendant negligently allows a fire to spread;[2] but it seems that a person may avoid liability, even for a fire which he has deliberately lit, provided that he is not guilty of any negligence. Thus in *Sochacki v Sas*,[3] a lodger who left his room for two or three hours with a fire burning was held not liable when a coal jumped out and set the house alight, since there was no evidence that the fire was too large for the grate. The operation of the statute is also shown by *Collingwood v Home and Colonial Stores Ltd*,[4] in which fire broke out at the defendants' shop as a result of defective electric wiring. In the absence of any negligence on the part of the defendants, they were held not liable.

It should be noted that, even where a fire is caused by an act of God or of a 'stranger', the defendant may still incur liability if, with knowledge of the danger on his land, he fails to take reasonable steps to abate it.[5]

1   (1847) 11 QB 347.
2   *Musgrove v Pandelis* [1919] 2 KB 43, CA.

3   [1947] 1 All ER 344.
4   [1936] 3 All ER 200, CA.
5   *Goldman v Hargrave* [1967] 1 AC 645, [1966] 2 All ER 989, PC.

26.16   Apart from the special rules outlined above, it is established that either fire itself,[1] or the combustible material on which it feeds,[2] may be treated as a dangerous thing for the purposes of the rule in *Rylands v Fletcher*. This might appear to be of great significance in view of the much-criticised decision of the Court of Appeal, in *Musgrove v Pandelis*,[3] that the Fires Prevention (Metropolis) Act 1774 provides no defence to such an action. In practice, however, the benefits to the plantiff may be more apparent than real. In the first place, either fire[4] or its cause[5] may be held to be a natural use of land, in which case *Rylands v Fletcher* does not apply. Second, where the defendant accumulates materials, it has been held that liability under *Rylands v Fletcher* requires proof both that they were likely to ignite and that the resulting fire was likely to spread.[6] If this is correct, liability in such cases appears no different from ordinary negligence.

1   *Jones v Festiniog Rly Co* (1868) LR 3 QB 733.
2   *Mason v Levy Auto Parts of England Ltd* [1967] 2 QB 530, [1967] 2 All ER 62.
3   [1919] 2 KB 43, CA.
4   *Sochacki v Sas* [1947] 1 All ER 344.
5   *Collingwood v Home and Colonial Stores Ltd* [1936] 3 All ER 200, CA (electric wiring).
6   *Mason v Levy Auto Parts of England Ltd* [1967] 2 QB 530, [1967] 2 All ER 62.

Statutory liability

26.17   One of the features of an industrialised urban society is that a single accident may disastrously affect an enormous number of people. A collapsing slag-heap, an explosion at a chemical plant or a crippled oil tanker, all may cause severe injury and damage over a wide area. In recent years, governments have sought by various statutes to provide for the possibility of certain of these incidents, and the provisions have often included the imposition of some form of strict liability for the consequences. Of special importance in this connection are the Nuclear Installations Act 1965 (liability of the licensee of a nuclear site for injury or damage resulting from the radioactive, toxic, explosive or otherwise hazardous properties of nuclear matter, or from radiations emitted from waste); the Merchant Shipping (Oil Pollution) Act 1971 (liability of shipowners for damage caused by the escape or discharge of persistent oil from a ship); and the Control of Pollution Act 1974 (liability for injury or damage caused by the deposit of poisonous, noxious or polluting waste on land). The forms of liability, and the defences available, vary from one statute to another, but they may all be regarded as strict, in the sense that the absence of negligence provides no defence.

Chapter 27

Animals

27.1 Considered merely as a kind of property, animals occupy no special place in the law of tort. A noisy farmyard is as much a nuisance as a noisy factory, and negligence applies to riding a horse as it does to driving a car. However, this is only part of the story; unlike other goods, animals have minds and instincts of their own, which may lead them to cause damage in various ways, from ravaging a turnip field to biting a postman's leg. Not surprisingly, therefore, the common law has for centuries adopted special rules of liability for harm done by animals, in addition to actions which may arise from the application of ordinary tort principles.

In modern times, there is perhaps less justification for subjecting animals to a special code. Society is more industrial and less agricultural; fences are more efficient; and transport systems are no longer reliant on the horse and the ox. Nevertheless, in 1967 a Law Commission Report on the common law rules governing liability for animals concluded that the basic forms of strict liability should be retained, although it recommended numerous changes of detail. Most of these changes were put into effect by the Animals Act 1971; unless otherwise specified, all statutory references in this chapter are to that Act.

In this chapter we examine the following issues:

- the extent to which the activities of animals may lead to a person becoming liable under the ordinary law of tort;
- the special statutory provisions governing liability for dangerous animals, straying livestock and the worrying of livestock by dogs.

Liability at common law

27.2 Most torts are capable of arising out of the acts of an animal, although some lend themselves more readily than others to this form of commission. It is, for example, an undoubted assault and battery to set one's dog on somebody, and there seems no reason why teaching a parrot to repeat slanderous material should not lead to liability in defamation. Of more practical importance, the action of fox hunters in riding across a farmer's land in spite of his protests has been held to constitute trespass[1] and, while direct authority is lacking, the application of *Rylands v Fletcher*[2] to both vegetation and human beings suggests that it could also be used in cases of escaping animals, subject to the question of non-natural user.[3]

The Dangerous Dogs Act 1991 was passed following a well-publicised spate of attacks on people by dogs bred specially for fighting (notably pit bull terriers and tosas). The Act inter alia imposes restrictions on the breeding, selling and control of such dogs; more generally, it imposes criminal liability where any dog is dangerously out of control in a public place, or where it injures or appears likely to injure any person in a place which is not a public place but where it is not permitted to be. The Act makes no express provision as to civil liability arising out of its breach, but it may well be that a person injured by a dog in consequence of a breach of the Act could recover damages in an action for breach of statutory duty.[4]

1 *Paul v Summerhayes* (1878) 4 QBD 9, DC. See also *League Against Cruel Sports Ltd v Scott* [1986] QB 240, [1985] 2 All ER 489; para 24.1 above.
2 Paras 26.2 to 26.13 above.
3 Para 26.7 above.
4 Ch 23 above.

Nuisance

27.3 The tort of nuisance is one in which animals frequently play a part. The smell of pigs[1] or the crowing of cockerels[2] may be actionable, while the obstruction of a highway by 24 cows has been held to be a public nuisance.[3] Where the gist of the complaint is the invasion of the plaintiff's land by numbers of wild animals, such as rats or rabbits, escaping from the defendant's property, liability has traditionally been dependent upon whether the defendant is in any way responsible for their accumulation. Thus, in *Farrer v Nelson*,[4] a defendant who overstocked his land with pheasants was held liable for damage to his neighbour's crops. On the other hand, there was no liability in *Seligman v Docker*,[5] where the increase in the pheasant population of the defendant's property was due simply to good weather. However, it should be noted that liability in the tort of nuisance may arise out of mere inaction where the defendant, with knowledge of the danger, fails to take reasonable steps to avert it.[6]

1 *Aldred's Case* (1610) 9 Co Rep 57b.
2 *Leeman v Montagu* [1936] 2 All ER 1677.
3 *Cunningham v Whelan* (1917) 52 ILT 67.
4 (1885) 15 QBD 258.
5 [1949] Ch 53, [1948] 2 All ER 887.
6 *Goldman v Hargrave* [1967] 1 AC 645, [1966] 2 All ER 989, PC.

Negligence

27.4 Damage done by animals, like other kinds of damage, is most likely to give rise to a claim in negligence.[1] There is no doubt that a person in charge of an animal is under a general duty of care to keep it from causing harm, and this can be of great assistance to a plaintiff who is unable to establish the necessary elements of strict liability under the Animals Act.[2] In *Gomberg v Smith*,[3] for example, a defendant who took his St Bernard for a walk in the street without a lead was held liable when it collided with and damaged the plaintiff's van. The dog in that case was merely clumsy, but the same principle may apply to a deliberate attack. For example, in *Aldham v United Dairies (London) Ltd*,[4] the defendants were held liable in negligence for leaving their pony unattended in the street for so long that it became restive and bit a passer-by. So too, in *Draper v Hodder*,[5] where a three-year-old child was attacked and seriously injured by a pack of Jack Russell terrier puppies, the defendant, a neighbouring breeder, was held negligent for allowing the dogs (which are known to be dangerous when in a pack) to wander both on his own property and on that of the plaintiff's family.

In a case of this nature, the plaintiff must show that there was a foreseeable risk of the type of injury suffered. This requirement proved fatal to two claims by persons injured when using public footpaths across fields. It has been held unforeseeable that a Limousin-cross cow with its calf would charge and butt a walker,[6] or that several horses would surround and push to the ground a person walking with his dog.[7]

There is no strict liability for livestock which stray from the highway,[8] but anyone who brings an animal on to the highway owes a duty of care to adjoining landowners. Thus in *Gayler and Pope Ltd v B Davies & Son Ltd*,[9] where the defendants left their pony and milk van unattended in the street they were held liable when it bolted and crashed through a draper's shop window. In *Tillett v Ward*,[10] by contrast, where an ox which was being driven along a street strayed into an ironmonger's shop, the defendant was found to have taken all reasonable care and was therefore not liable.

Common law recognised one exception to the general principle of liability for negligence in relation to animals, namely that an occupier of land owed no duty of care to highway users to fence his land or otherwise to prevent his domestic animals from straying and causing damage. Always regarded as anomalous, this rule attracted immense criticism when the invention of the internal combustion engine greatly increased the speed and volume of traffic on the roads. The immunity has now been abolished by the Animals Act 1971, s 8(1) so that here, as elsewhere, the tort of negligence prevails. It should be emphasised, however, that s 8(1) does not impose a universal obligation to fence; in areas such as the Welsh mountains, for example, motorists may be expected to look out for straying sheep, and the cost to farmers of fencing every roadside would be prohibitive. Section 8(2) attempts a compromise, by providing that a person is not to be regarded as negligent by reason *only* of placing animals on unfenced land if:

- the land is common land; or
- it is situated in an area where fencing is not customary; or
- it is a town or village green;

and he has a right (which includes permission from someone else who has a right[11]) to place the animals on that land.

This is not a return to the old immunity since, even in these areas, road and traffic conditions may be such that it is negligent to allow one's animals to stray.

1   An attack by an animal on a visitor to premises might also found a claim under the Occupier's Liability Act 1957: see *Hill v Lovett* 1992 SLT 994.
2   Para 27.7 below.
3   [1963] 1 QB 25, [1962] 1 All ER 725, CA.
4   [1940] 1 KB 507, [1939] 4 All ER 522, CA.
5   [1972] 2 All ER 210, CA.
6   *Ostle v Stapleton* [1996] CLY 4443.
7   *Miller v Duggan* [1996] CLY 4444.
8   Para 27.9 below.
9   [1924] 2 KB 75.
10 (1882) 10 QBD 17.
11 *Davies v Davies* [1975] QB 172, [1974] 3 All ER 817, CA.

Animals Act 1971

Dangerous animals
Classification of species
27.5   The Animals Act 1971, like the rules of common law which it replaced, makes the keeper of a dangerous animal strictly liable for all the damage it causes. The Act also follows the common law in treating two different kinds of animal as 'dangerous' for this purpose. First, certain species (lions, tigers etc) are regarded as so obviously

dangerous that all their members automatically attract strict liability. Second, members of other less dangerous species may attract strict liability as individuals by exhibiting dangerous tendencies, but only when their keepers are aware of these tendencies.

The classification of species is thus clearly of prime importance, and this is dealt with by s 6(2), which provides that a dangerous species is a species:[1]

- which is not commonly domesticated in the British Islands; and
- whose fully grown animals normally have such characteristics that they are likely, unless restrained, to cause severe damage or that any damage they may cause is likely to be severe.

The wording of this definition seems apt to include both animals which are normally fierce, such as bears, tigers and gorillas, and animals which, though normally docile, are likely to cause severe damage if they cause damage at all. An elephant, for instance, is unlikely to cause damage, but its sheer bulk makes it dangerous on the occasions when it does get out of control. It also appears that a species may be classified as dangerous on account of the threat which it poses to property; this could even include, for example, rabbits, squirrels and Colorado beetles, provided that the damage which they are likely to cause can be described as severe.

It is important to appreciate that, once a species is classified as dangerous, no allowance is made for the amiable nature of a particular individual. A circus elephant may be as tame as a cow and, because of its training, much easier to control; nevertheless, since the species satisfies s 6(2), the individual is dangerous in law.[2]

A species which does not satisfy the statutory definition contained in s 6(2) is automatically a non-dangerous species.

1 This includes sub-species and variety: s 11.
2 *Behrens v Bertram Mills Circus Ltd* [1957] 2 QB 1, [1957] 1 All ER 583.

Dangerous species

27.6 Section 2(1) provides that where any damage is caused by an animal which belongs to a dangerous species, any person who is a keeper of the animal is liable for the damage, except as otherwise provided by the Act. This wide form of strict liability is not limited to damage which results from the animal's dangerous characteristics, since it also includes, for example, injuries caused by the blunderings of a frightened elephant, or a disease transmitted by an infected rat. So too, a person who suffers nervous shock on being faced by an escaped tiger, or who falls and breaks his leg in running away from it, can recover damages under this provision. It has even been held applicable to someone falling from a swaying camel, although the plaintiff's claim under s 2(1) failed on the ground that she had voluntarily assumed the risk.[1]

Liability under s 2 is imposed upon the animal's keeper, defined in s 6(3) as someone who 'owns the animal or has it in his possession; or is the head of a household of which a member under the age of 16 owns the animal or has it in his possession'. That subsection further provides that a person who loses the ownership or possession of an animal continues to be its 'keeper' unless and until someone else fulfils the definition. Thus, if a person's pet fox escapes and reverts to the wild, he remains responsible for its activities. Where, however, a person takes possession of an animal merely to prevent it from causing damage or to return it to its owner, he does not thereby become its 'keeper'.[2]

1 *Tutin v Mary Chipperfield Promotions Ltd* (1980) 130 NLJ 807. The plaintiff recovered damages on the ground of negligence.
2 Section 6(4).

Non-dangerous species

27.7 The strict liability which attaches to dangerous species also encompasses other individual animals with known dangerous characteristics, although in such a case the keeper is liable, not for all the damage done, but only for that which results from those dangerous characteristics. This is laid down by s 2(2), which provides that where damage is caused by an animal which does not belong to a dangerous species, a keeper of the animal is liable for the damage, except as otherwise provided by the Act, if:

- the damage is of a kind which the animal, unless restrained, was likely to cause or which, if caused by the animal, was likely to be severe; and
- the likelihood of the damage or of its being severe was due to characteristics of the animal which are not normally found in animals of the same species (ie the particular breed of dog, rather than dogs generally[1]) or are not normally so found except at particular times or in particular circumstances; and
- those characteristics were known to the keeper or were at any time known to a person who at that time had charge of the animal as the keeper's servant or, where the keeper was the head of a household, were known to another keeper of the animal who was a member of that household and under the age of 16.

The essence of this provision is that strict liability is imposed on the keeper of an animal where he, or someone for whom he is responsible, knows of some abnormal characteristic which renders the animal dangerous. This abnormality (which applies to nervous unpredictable animals as well as vicious ones[2]) may be permanent or periodic, such as the tendency of certain breeds of dog to show unusual aggression when defending their territory[3] or that of a bitch to be aggressive towards humans when she has pups.[4] It may also be noted that the damage for which the keeper is liable may extend beyond the direct results of an attack; thus a person injured in a fall when his dog is attacked by the defendant's dog may recover damages under s 2(2), provided of course that the requirements of that provision are satisfied.[5] However, where horses were maliciously released from their field by an unidentified trespasser, their owner was held not liable for a traffic accident, since this was caused by the mere presence of the horses in the road rather than by any 'abnormal characteristic' which they possessed.[6]

A keeper is only liable under s 2(2) where he, or certain of his family or his employees, knows that the animal in question is dangerous. Such knowledge is usually gained as the result of a previous attack, but this is not the only possibility. For example, in *Worth v Gilling*[7] it was sufficient that the defendant's dog habitually ran at passers-by to the limit of its chain, barking and trying to bite them. A horse's tendency to bite other horses, however, is not necessarily evidence that it is dangerous to people.[8]

Where the conditions of s 2(2) are satisfied, reasonable care is no defence; the defendant keeps the animal at his peril. The question of negligence may, however, be highly relevant in cases where, for some reason, s 2(2) does not apply.[9]

1 *Hunt v Wallis* [1994] PIQR P128.
2 *Wallace v Newton* [1982] 2 All ER 106, [1982] 1 WLR 375.
3 *Curtis v Betts* [1990] 1 All ER 769, CA.
4 See *Barnes v Lucille Ltd* (1907) 96 LT 680.
5 *Smith v Ainger* (1990) Times, 5 June, CA.
6 *Jaundrill v Gillett* (1996) Times, 30 January, CA.
7 (1866) LR 2 CP 1.
8 *Glanville v Sutton & Co Ltd* [1928] 1 KB 571.
9 See *Draper v Hodder* [1972] 2 All ER 210, CA; para 27.4 above.

Defences

27.8 Liability under s 2 in respect of both dangerous and non-dangerous species is strict (ie independent of negligence). However, the liability is not absolute, since the Act expressly recognises four possible defences:

- Section 5(1) provides that a plaintiff cannot claim in respect of any damage which is due wholly to his own fault, as where he provokes a fierce dog, or reaches into a leopard's cage.
- A plaintiff who is partly responsible for his own injuries may suffer a reduction of his damages on the ground of contributory negligence.[1]
- The defence of *volenti non fit injuria*[2] is made applicable to actions under s 2 by s 5(2). This provision may be of great importance in practice, since the exclusion of this type of liability is not subject to the Unfair Contract Terms Act 1977.[3] The scope of this defence is, however, restricted by s 6(5), which provides that a keeper's employee is not to be treated as voluntarily accepting any risk which is incidental to his employment.
- Section 5(3) lays down special rules for injured trespassers by providing that, where damage is caused by 'an animal kept on any premises or structure to a person trespassing there', the keeper is not liable under s 2 provided either that the animal was not kept there for the protection of persons or property or that, if it was so kept, it was reasonable to keep it there. Thus, a trespasser injured by an animal in a zoo or a safari park would probably not succeed in a claim under s 2,[4] for the animal would not be kept for protection. As to animals which it is reasonable to keep for protection, this is in practice most likely to apply to dogs. The Guard Dogs Act 1975, which makes it a criminal offence to have a guard dog on premises unless it is either secured or under the control of a handler, does not give rise to civil liability. However, it is thought that a court would regard someone as unreasonable for the purpose of the Animals Act 1971, s 5(3) if he kept a dog in circumstances which contravened the Guard Dogs Act.

All the defences mentioned above were considered in the case of *Cummings v Granger*[5] where an untrained alsatian, kept by the defendant to guard his scrapyard, attacked the plaintiff who, despite seeing a large 'Beware of the Dog' notice and knowing that the dog was there, entered the yard as a trespasser. The trial judge held that keeping the dog in these circumstances was unreasonable and that the defendant was accordingly liable, although he reduced the plaintiff's damages on the ground of contributory negligence. The Court of Appeal, however, took a rather more robust view of the rights of Englishmen to defend their castles. While agreeing that the damage could not be treated as wholly due to the plaintiff's fault, the Court of Appeal held both that keeping the dog was reasonable[6] and that the plaintiff had in any case voluntarily accepted the risk of injury.

1 Section 10; paras 21.11–21.16 above.
2 Paras 21.2–21.10 above.
3 Paras 10.19–10.29 above.
4 An action might nevertheless lie under the Occupiers' Liability Act 1984; paras 22.21–22.24 above.
5 [1977] QB 397, [1977] 1 All ER 104, CA.
6 These events preceded the coming into force of the Guard Dogs Act 1975.

Straying livestock

27.9 Section 4(1) of the Act provides that where livestock belonging to any person strays on to land in the ownership or occupation of another and:

- damage is done by the livestock to the land or to any property on it which is in the ownership or possession of the other person; or
- any expenses are reasonably incurred by that other person in keeping the livestock while it cannot be restored to the person to whom it belongs or while it is detained in pursuance of s 7 of the Act, or in ascertaining to whom it belongs;

the person to whom the livestock belongs is liable for the damage or expenses, except as otherwise provided by the Act.

For the purpose of this provision, s 11 defines 'livestock' as 'cattle, horses, asses, mules, hinnies, sheep, pigs, goats and poultry [which means the domestic varieties of fowls, turkeys, geese, ducks, guinea-fowls, pigeons, peacocks and quails], and also deer not in the wild state'.

The right of action under s 4, which protects both owners and occupiers of land, but which imposes liability only upon a possessor of livestock, covers not only damage to the plaintiff's land and crops, but also damage to his goods, including other animals. As a result, the plaintiff is entitled to damages, not only where his own animals are attacked, but also for other consequences such as infection[1] or the serving of a thoroughbred heifer by a bull of low birth.[2]

Where livestock stray on to the highway, it seems that the owner or occupier of the land across which the highway passes may claim under s 4(3).[3] A mere user of the highway, however, has no such right and must, in order to recover damages (eg where straying livestock cause a road accident), establish negligence.[4] Further, where livestock which are lawfully on the highway[5] stray from it, liability again depends on negligence; s 4 is expressly excluded.[6]

1 *Theyer v Purnell* [1918] 2 KB 333.
2 *McLean v Brett* (1919) 49 DLR 162.
3 *Durrant v Child* (1611) 1 Bulst 157.
4 See Animals Act 1971, s 8; para 27.4 above.
5 But not those which have strayed on to it: *Matthews v Wicks* (1987) Times, 25 May, CA.
6 Section 5(5).

Defences

27.10 Liability under s 4 is strict, but certain defences are recognised by the Act. A plaintiff will fail altogether in his claim if the damage he suffers is wholly due to his own fault;[1] if it is partly due to his fault, his damages may be reduced on the ground of contributory negligence.[2]

The question of duties to fence is dealt with by s 5(6), which provides that a mere failure on the plaintiff's part to fence out the defendant's livestock does not amount to 'fault' on his part. However, the section goes on to provide that a defendant is nonetheless not liable where it is proved that the straying of the livestock on to the land would not have occurred but for a breach by any other person, being a person having an interest in the land, of a duty to fence. This, it should be noted, is not limited to the obvious case of the plaintiff who owes a fencing obligation to the defendant, since it also provides a defence where the plaintiff owes a legal duty to a third party, or where the duty is owed by a third party with an interest in the plaintiff's land, such as his landlord.

The defences of act of God, intervention by a 'stranger' and *volenti non fit injuria,* all of which previously applied at common law, are not available in an action under s 4.

1 Section 5(1).
2 Section 10; paras 21.11–21.16 above.

Detention and sale

27.11 In an attempt to provide a simple means of settling trivial disputes over straying animals without the need for legal action, s 7 creates a statutory power of detention and sale. Under this provision, an occupier may detain any livestock which strays on to his land and which is not under anyone's control, provided he gives notice within 48 hours to the police and to the possessor of the livestock, if known. He must also treat the livestock with reasonable care, which includes feeding and watering it. The person entitled to possession of the livestock may demand its return but, if the detainor has a claim under s 4 for damage done by straying cattle, or for expenses incurred, this must first be met. It has been held that a local authority on to whose land animals frequently strayed was justified in making standard charges to cover its costs, rather than working out the exact expense caused by each stray.[1]

Once livestock has been lawfully detained for 14 days, then, provided neither party has commenced legal proceedings, the detainor may sell it at a market or by public auction and keep the amount of his claim under s 4 out of the net proceeds of sale.

1 *Morris v Blaenau Gwent District Council* (1982) 80 LGR 793, CA.

Dogs worrying livestock
Liability for dogs

27.12 The worrying of livestock by dogs has long been a special problem and the Animals Act 1971, s 3, which deals with this, merely repeats with some modifications the rules laid down by earlier statutes. Section 3 provides that, where a dog causes damage by killing or injuring livestock, any person who is a keeper of the dog is liable for the damage, except as otherwise provided by the Act. For this purpose, 'livestock' includes the same animals as for the purpose of s 4,[1] but also includes pheasants, partridges and grouse in captivity; the meaning of 'keeper' is the same as it is under s 2.[2]

The effect of this provision, which makes a keeper liable without negligence and without any knowledge of his dog's dangerous characteristics, is to confer a greater degree of protection upon livestock than upon human beings! However, as with the other forms of strict liability under the Act, a plaintiff's claim may fail wholly under s 5(1),[3] where his loss results entirely from his own fault, or partly under the doctrine of contributory negligence. Section 5(4) also provides a defence where the attack takes place on land to which the livestock have strayed, so long as the presence of the dog there is authorised.

1 Para 27.9 above.
2 Para 27.6 above.
3 Para 27.8 above.

Protection of livestock

27.13 At common law, a person whose animals were under attack from another animal was not restricted to taking legal action against the owner of that animal; he could in certain circumstances act immediately in the defence of his property, even if this involved killing or injuring the attacker. The common law rules on this matter, which were laid down in the case of *Cresswell v Sirl*,[1] apply to all kinds of animal, both attacking and attacked, provided only that the latter belong to the person acting in their defence; there is therefore no right to shoot a dog which is attacking wild animals on the defendant's land.[2]

The common law rules remain in force but, in relation to a somewhat narrower area, namely the worrying[3] of livestock by dogs, the Animals Act 1971, s 9 confers even greater protection upon a person who takes matters into his own hands. According to this provision, it is a defence to an action for killing or injuring a dog that the defendant was entitled to act for the protection of livestock, that he did so act and that, within 48 hours of the incident, he notified the police.

A person is entitled to act for the protection of livestock if and only if either the livestock or the land on which it is belongs to him, or if he is acting with the authority of such a person. However, if the circumstances in which a dog attacks livestock are such that the dog's keeper would have a defence under s 5(4),[4] then s 9 does not permit anyone to act for the protection of the livestock by killing or injuring the dog. The conditions under which the defendant may otherwise act are clearly stated by s 9, with the proviso that the defendant is protected if he reasonably believes them to be satisfied. These conditions are that either:

* the dog is worrying or is about to worry the livestock and there are no other reasonable means of ending or preventing the worrying; or
* the dog has been worrying livestock, has not left the vicinity and is not under the control of any person and there are no practicable means of ascertaining to whom it belongs. The effect of this is that, in some cases, a stray dog may be shot even when it has ceased to be a danger to livestock, an innovation which represents the major difference between the statutory rules and those of common law.

1   [1948] 1 KB 241, [1947] 2 All ER 730, CA.
2   *Gott v Measures* [1948] 1 KB 234, [1947] 2 All ER 609, DC.
3   This probably includes not only an actual attack, but also chasing in such a way as is likely to cause injury.
4   Para 27.12 above.

Chapter 28

Vicarious liability

28.1   Vicarious liability, in the strict legal sense, arises when X is made answerable for a tort committed by Y, on the grounds that:

- there is a particular relationship between X and Y; and
- the tort is in some way connected to that relationship.

The only relationship which gives rise to a general presumption of vicarious liability is that of employer and employee; the employer will be held answerable for any tort committed 'within the course of employment'. Other relationships, such as those between principal and agent[1] and between partners,[2] may also create vicarious liability, albeit in more limited circumstances. Apart from these relationships, the law is slow to make X answerable for the tort of Y, as may be seen from the fact that a superior employee is not vicariously liable for the torts of his subordinate,[3] nor a parent for those of his child.

   Although, as stated above, the true basis of vicarious liability is that X is liable for a tort committed by Y, it is established that an employer may be vicariously liable even in circumstances where the employee himself would, if sued, have had a personal immunity.[4]

1   Paras 28.18–28.20 below.
2   For torts committed 'in the ordinary course of the business of the firm': Partnership Act 1890, s 10.
3   *Stone v Cartwright* (1795) 6 Term Rep 411.
4   *Broom v Morgan* [1953] 1 QB 597, [1953] 1 All ER 849, CA (employer liable for injury by employee to employee's wife, at a time when tort actions between spouses were not allowed).

28.2   In this chapter we examine the following issues:

- how the law defines the relationship of employer and employee for the purposes of vicarious liability;
- the scope of an employer's liability for the torts of his employee;
- the extent to which the employer may be held liable for prohibited acts or deliberate misconduct;
- the limited form of vicarious liability which exists between principal and agent;
- the extent to which damage caused by an independent contractor may result in liability for the client.

28.3 It should be noted that, quite apart from the doctrine of vicarious liability, there are other circumstances in which X may be responsible in tort for damage caused by Y:

- where X specifically authorises or incites Y to commit a tort;
- where Y without authority purports to act on behalf of X, and X, with full knowledge of all material facts, ratifies or accepts what Y has done;
- where X asks Y (who is not his employee) to carry out some task, but is then personally guilty of negligence in selecting, instructing or supervising Y;
- where X is under a duty of care to control Y.[1]

1   Para 18.17 above.

Employer and employee

28.4 As we have already seen, the relationship of employer and employee is the only one to which the law attaches a general principle of vicarious liability. It may be said that an employer is responsible for any tort which is committed by his employee in the course of his employment. This naturally raises two questions, which we consider below:

- who is an employee? and
- what is the course of employment?

Who is an employee?

28.5 Since an employer is not usually responsible for the torts of an independent contractor to whom he entrusts work, it is obvious that the distinction between an employee and an independent contractor is of paramount importance. Indeed, it is not only in relation to vicarious liability that this distinction is relevant; among other things, it may also serve to indicate whether the 'worker' (to use a neutral term) is protected under industrial safety legislation, and whether the duty to pay national insurance contributions falls upon the worker or upon the employer.

It is said that an employee works under a contract *of service,* while an independent contractor works under a contract *for services.* This, however, merely restates the problem in different words, for it gives no clue as to how these two kinds of contract are to be distinguished. Nor is the terminology of the contract itself decisive, though it is relevant; if the court decides that the relationship as a whole falls into one category, it will be treated as such, notwithstanding that the parties have called it by another name. Thus, for example, in *Ferguson v John Dawson & Partners (Contractors) Ltd,*[1] where a building worker was expressly described as a 'labour only sub-contractor', a majority of the Court of Appeal held that the relationship between the parties was in reality that of employer and employee.

It is perhaps worth stating at this point that, while the formulation of a precise yet simple test for distinguishing employees from independent contractors has caused serious problems, it is not usually difficult to see on which side of the line a particular case falls. As Lord Denning has said,[2] it is often easy to recognise a contract of service when you see it, but difficult to say wherein the distinction lies. A ship's master, a chauffeur and a reporter on the staff of a newspaper are all employed under a contract of service; but a ship's pilot, a taxi driver, and a newspaper contributor are employed under a contract for services.

Of the many attempts made by judges and writers to lay down some criteria by which a contract of service may be recognised, one of the best known is that of Lord Thankerton in *Short v J and W Henderson Ltd*:[4]

- the employer's power of selection of his employee;
- the payment of wages or other remuneration;
- the employer's right to control the method of doing the work; and
- the employer's right of suspension and dismissal.

It should always be borne in mind, however, not only that this list is far from exhaustive (one writer has identified no fewer than 15 relevant factors), but also that the feature which is in one case decisive may in the next be overwhelmed by other features which point to the opposite conclusion.

1 [1976] 3 All ER 817, [1976] 1 WLR 346, CA.
2 *Stevenson, Jordan and Harrison Ltd v Macdonald and Evans* [1952] 1 TLR 101 at 111.
3 (1946) 62 TLR 427 at 429.

Control and other criteria
28.6 The foregoing discussion serves to show that there is no single, simple test by which employees and independent contractors may be distinguished. It used at one time to be thought that such a test did exist, in the degree of control which the employer was entitled to exercise over each category. An independent contractor, it was said, could be told only what he was to do, whereas an employee was also subject to the command of his employer as to the *manner* in which he should do his work.[1] However, modern conditions, especially the widespread employment by corporations of highly skilled and qualified personnel, have shown up the inadequacy of this test. For example, it cannot be doubted that a ship's captain works under a contract of service, but it would be ludicrous to suggest that his employers are in a position to tell him exactly how to do his job. Indeed, many people today are employed for the precise reason that they possess some skill which their employer does not; in such circumstances the control test is clearly of little use.

If control alone cannot be regarded as decisive, the same applies even more strongly to the other criteria mentioned above. The employer's rights of appointment and dismissal, which were regarded as characteristic of a contract of service in *Short v Henderson*, seem equally applicable to independent contractors, while the type of remuneration paid, although helpful, is far from conclusive. After all, an employee is usually paid a wage based on time, but may be paid on the basis of work done. An independent contractor is more commonly paid for results, but may be on an hourly rate.

1 *Yewens v Noakes* (1880) 6 QBD 530 at 532.

Function of employee
28.7 It has been suggested that, instead of looking at the individual rights and duties which make up a contract of service or one for services, the courts should consider the *function* of the particular worker.[1] It is argued that, under a contract of service, a man is employed as part of the business, and his work is done as an integral part of the business; whereas under a contract for services, his work, although done for the business, is not integrated into it but is only accessory to it. This 'organisation' test certainly serves to explain a number of cases in which a contract of service has been held to exist despite the lack of any real control by the employer, especially those in which, contrary to earlier authority, hospitals were held liable for the negligence of

highly qualified staff.[2] However, in marginal cases, it seems merely to replace one difficult question: 'Is the person an employee?' with another: 'Is he part of the employer's organisation?'

Concentration upon the actual work which is done by a particular individual should not be allowed to obscure the fact that vicarious liability depends upon the existence of a contract of service. In *Watkins v Birmingham City Council*,[3] where a schoolteacher was injured due to the negligence of a 10-year-old milk monitor, the trial judge held the local authority vicariously liable on the ground that the boy was doing a job which would otherwise have been done by a paid employee. However, the Court of Appeal reversed this decision, holding that the boy was delivering the milk as a pupil and not as an employee.

1 *Stevenson, Jordan and Harrison Ltd v Macdonald and Evans* [1952] 1 TLR 101 at 111.
2 *Cassidy v Ministry of Health* [1951] 2 KB 343, [1951] 1 All ER 574, CA.
3 (1976) 126 NLJ 442, CA; para 19.6 above.

'Business' test

28.8 In a number of cases, the courts have adopted a slightly different approach to this problem, by considering whether it may fairly be said that the worker is in business on his own account.[1] Although this has links with the function test described above, it seems that the courts are concerned, not so much with the nature of the work done, but more with such questions as whether the person works on his own premises or with his own equipment, whether he hires his own helpers and can delegate the task to them, whether he works for a number of employers, what degree of financial risk he takes, what degree of responsibility he has for investment and management, and to what extent, if at all, he has an opportunity to profit from his own sound management.

Many of these factors were considered in *Ready-Mixed Concrete (South-East) Ltd v Minister of Pension and National Insurance*,[2] a case concerning the drivers of lorries designed for the delivery of concrete. The drivers bought their own vehicles, although they could not alter or sell them without the company's consent, and they were obliged to maintain them and to use them exclusively for the company. The company was responsible for obtaining orders and supplying concrete, and it paid the drivers a rate based on mileage. After a thorough review of the authorities, MacKenna J held that the drivers were not employees of the company, but independent contractors, so that the company was not responsible for the payment of their national insurance contributions.

1 *Market Investigations Ltd v Minister of Social Security* [1969] 2 QB 173, [1968] 3 All ER 732.
2 [1968] 2 QB 497, [1968] 1 All ER 433.

Borrowed employees

28.9 A particular problem may arise in cases where an individual employee is lent (or, more commonly, hired) by his general employer to a third party. If the employee commits a tort while working for the third party, the question is where the burden of vicarious liability is to fall. It might have been thought that both employers should be liable, but the law insists that the responsibility falls upon one alone.

In *Mersey Docks and Harbour Board v Coggins and Griffith (Liverpool) Ltd*,[1] a mobile crane, complete with its driver, was hired by the harbour board to a firm of stevedores. The driver was paid by the board but, for the period of hire, was subject to the detailed control of the stevedores. When the driver negligently injured a third party, the House of Lords held that vicarious responsibility must rest with the harbour board; this primary liability could, it was said, be transferred in an appropriate case, but the burden of proof upon a general employer would be a heavy one. This heavy burden is perhaps most likely to be satisfied in cases where the employee in question is an unskilled labourer, since it is then more realistic to treat control as having been passed on.

Where the contract of hire provides that any vicarious liability shall attach to the special employer, this cannot operate so as to deprive an injured third party of his rights against the general employer; its effect is merely to govern the position of the two employers.[3] Even to this extent, the provision may be subject to the test of reasonableness under the Unfair Contract Terms Act 1977.[4]

1   [1947] AC 1, [1946] 2 All ER 345, HL.
2   *White (Contractors) Ltd v Tarmac Civil Engineering Ltd* [1967] 3 All ER 586, [1967] 1 WLR 1508, HL.
3   See *Phillips Products Ltd v Hyland* [1987] 2 All ER 620, CA; *Thompson v T Lohan (Plant Hire) Ltd* [1987] 2 All ER 631, CA; paras 10.20, 10.23 and 10.29 above.

What is the course of employment?

28.10   The mere existence of an employer and employee relationship is not sufficient to create vicarious liability; it would, of course, be wholly unjust if the employer were to be made responsible for every wrongful act of his employees. On the other hand, to limit the employer's liability to those cases in which the employee is actually carrying out his instructions would be to deprive the law of an extremely useful doctrine, since the number of employers who specifically authorise the commission of torts is very small. What is needed is some intermediate limitation, and this is found in the rule that, for an employer to be liable, the employee must be shown to have committed the tort in the course of his employment. As to what is meant by this expression, the test which has often been judicially approved explains that an employer, as opposed to the client of an independent contractor, is liable even for acts which he has not authorised, provided they are so connected with acts which he has authorised that they may rightly be regarded as modes – although improper modes – of doing them. In other words, an employer is responsible not merely for what he authorises his employee to do, but also for the way in which the employee chooses to do it. On the other hand, if the unauthorised and wrongful act of the employee is not so connected with the authorised act as to be a mode of doing it, but is an independent act, the employer is not responsible: for in such a case the employee is not acting in the course of his employment, but has gone outside it.

Authorised acts

28.11   The idea that an unauthorised act may found vicarious liability if it can be treated as a mode of performing an authorised act means that a court, in seeking to determine the scope of an employee's employment, must first discover what acts are authorised and then consider what, if any, connection exists between an authorised act and the tort in question. The decision of the House of Lords in *Century Insurance Co Ltd v Northern Ireland Road Transport Board*[1] provides a good illustration of this approach in operation. The employee in that case was the driver of a petrol tanker who, while delivering petrol to a garage, lit a cigarette and dropped the match. The driver's employers sought to avoid liability for the resulting fire by claiming that they did not employ men to smoke. Not surprisingly, this argument was rejected for, given that the driver was specifically authorised to deliver petrol, it would be difficult to think of a more negligent mode of doing so. By contrast, in *General Engineering Services Ltd v Kingston and St Andrew Corpn*,[2] where firemen operating a 'go slow' policy in support of a pay claim took 17 minutes to reach a fire instead of the normal 3 or 4 minutes, it was held that their conduct was outside the course of their employment.

Their employers, the local authority responsible for the fire brigade, were thus not liable to the owners of property destroyed by the fire.

The need to find an authorised act, with which the unauthorised tort can be linked, may be illustrated by cases in which a vehicle owned by the employer is driven by an employee who has no specific authority to do so. In *Beard v London General Omnibus Co*,[3] where a conductor took it upon himself to turn a bus round for its return journey, it was held that his negligent driving which caused an accident was outside the scope of his employment, since he was not permitted to drive. His employers were therefore not vicariously liable. In *Ilkiw v Samuels*,[4] on the other hand, where a lorry driver allowed an incompetent person to drive it, it was held that the *lorry driver's* negligence fell within the course of his employment, for his job involved taking care of the vehicle. As a result, the lorry driver's employers were liable to a person injured in the ensuing accident.

There is no doubt that modern courts take a fairly liberal view of what can be regarded as authorised. Nevertheless, the decision in *Kay v ITW Ltd*[5] must be considered very close to the borderline. The employee there was a storekeeper whose duties included returning a fork-lift truck to a warehouse. Finding the warehouse door blocked by a five-ton lorry which belonged to another firm, the storekeeper attempted to move it and, in so doing, negligently injured the plaintiff. After some hesitation, the Court of Appeal came to the conclusion that the employers were vicariously liable, for this misguided act fell just within the course of the storekeeper's employment.

1   [1942] AC 509, [1942] 1 All ER 491, HL.
2   [1988] 3 All ER 867, PC.
3   [1900] 2 QB 530, CA.
4   [1963] 2 All ER 879, [1963] 1 WLR 991 CA.
5   [1968] 1 QB 140, [1967] 3 All ER 22, CA.

Implied authority

28.12   In considering exactly what acts of an employee may be regarded as authorised, it is important to realise that an employer's permission may be implied rather than express and, further, that this may well be so even in relation to acts which benefit the employee rather than the employer. To take a simple example, a person at work has implied authority to use lavatories, washbasins and so on. If he negligently leaves a tap running and thereby floods adjoining premises, his employer will be vicariously liable; he cannot argue that the employee was not in the course of his employment because he was not actually working at the time.[1] A similar principle applies to meals, tea breaks and the like, provided either that they are taken on the premises, or that the employee is travelling on the employer's business. For example, in *Harvey v RG O'Dell Ltd*,[2] an employee sent out on an all-day job was held to be within the course of his employment when riding his motor-cycle into a neighbouring town to have lunch.

As far as travel to and from one's place of work is concerned, the course of employment will normally include those parts of the journey which take place on the employer's premises[3] and also journeys off the premises which are undertaken on the employer's business and in the employer's time.[4] However, ordinary commuting journeys are excluded, so that in *Nottingham v Aldridge*,[5] for example, an apprentice was held to be outside the scope of his employment while driving to a GPO training establishment after a weekend at home, even though, by giving a lift to a fellow-apprentice, he qualified for a mileage allowance from his employers. Occasionally, this distinction is not maintained. In *Harrison v British Railways Board*,[6] for example, a station foreman who attempted to board a moving train in order to leave work before his shift officially ended was held not be acting within the course of his employment.

1   *Ruddiman & Co v Smith* (1889) 60 LT 708, DC.

2   [1958] 2 QB 78, [1958] 1 All ER 657.
3   *Staton v National Coal Board* [1957] 2 All ER 667, [1957] 1 WLR 893.
4   *Smith v Stages* [1989] 1 All ER 833, HL.
5   [1971] 2 QB 739, [1971] 2 All ER 751.
6   [1981] 3 All ER 679.

Ostensible authority

28.13   In certain circumstances an employer may incur vicarious liability where he has not expressly or even impliedly authorised his employee to commit a particular act. This is where the employer has given third parties the impression that the employee is authorised, and a third party relies upon this appearance of authority. In such circumstances the employer will in effect be estopped (prevented) from denying that authority exists. As a result, liability for a tort of the employee may be attributed to the employer, notwithstanding that it was committed purely for the employee's own benefit, or that it had been specifically prohibited by the employer.

The leading case on the subject of ostensible authority is *Lloyd v Grace, Smith & Co*,[1] in which the plaintiff, a widow, sought advice from a firm of solicitors about certain property which she had inherited. She dealt entirely with the solicitors' managing clerk, who fraudulently induced her to sign documents which transferred the property to him. The clerk then misappropriated it. It was held by the House of Lords that the solicitors were responsible for this fraud; having permitted their employee to deal unsupervised with clients, they were liable for any tort which he might commit in what appeared to be the course of his employment.

1   [1912] AC 716, HL.

Prohibitions

28.14   What, if any, is the effect upon an employer's vicarious liability of proof that he had forbidden his employee to do the thing which caused the damage? An instinctive reaction to this question might well be that such a prohibition must exclude the employer's liability, since the employee can hardly be said to be acting within the course of his employment when disobeying a specific instruction. A moment's reflection, however, will serve to show that such a conclusion would soon lead to the end of vicarious liability for all practical purposes, since every employer would simply insert a term into all contracts of employment forbidding the employee from committing any torts.

A prohibition, then, cannot be allowed automatically to exonerate the employer. In order to understand how this can be achieved, it is necessary to remember that vicarious liability applies not only to authorised acts, but also to unauthorised modes of performing authorised acts.[1] Therefore, the question which has to be asked is whether the employer has prohibited the act itself (in which case the employee cannot be within the course of his employment when performing it) or whether he has merely prohibited a particular mode of carrying it out. As was stated by Lord Dunedin, in *Plumb v Cobden Flour Mills Co Ltd*,[2] 'There are prohibitions which limit the sphere of employment, and prohibitions which only deal with conduct within the sphere of employment.'

Recognition that an employer may be legally responsible, even for conduct of his employee which he has banned, came as long ago as 1862, in the leading case of *Limpus v London General Omnibus Co*.[3] There, a bus driver, in attempting to obstruct a bus belonging to a rival company (a practice which his employers had expressly forbidden), caused an accident. Notwithstanding the prohibition, the employers were held vicariously liable, since the driver's negligence was undeniably committed in the course of performing an authorised act, namely, driving the bus. By contrast, where the prohibition is such as to remove all authority from the employee, he cannot then be said to act within the course of his employment. In *Kooragang Investments Pty Ltd v Richardson and Wrench Ltd*,[4] for example, a staff valuer was held to have gone outside the course of his employment in carrying out valuations for a client whom his employers had blacklisted. Likewise, in *Stevens v Woodward*,[5] an employee entered a washroom on the employer's premises, which he was not permitted to use, and, by leaving a tap running, caused a flood. The employer was held not liable because, if the employee's very presence in the washroom was forbidden, there was no authorised act in the course of which his tort could be committed. The effect of the prohibition in this case was to prevent any implication of authority.[6] However, it should be noted that ostensible authority cannot be removed by a prohibition unless the third party is aware of it.

The difference between prohibiting a class of acts, and prohibiting a mode of carrying out permitted acts, is simply one of degree. Much depends upon how precisely a court defines the scope of the employee's employment in the first place, and the modern tendency is to adopt a fairly liberal approach. In *LCC v Cattermoles (Garages) Ltd*,[7] for example, a garage hand was expressly forbidden to drive customers' vehicles, although he was allowed, and indeed expected, to push them around the premises. When he drove a customer's car and caused an accident, his employers argued that he was acting outside the course of his employment. The Court of Appeal, however, held the employers vicariously liable, on the ground that their employee was authorised to move cars; the prohibition applied only to the method which he used.

1 Para 28.10 above.
2 [1914] AC 62 at 67.
3 (1862) 1 H & C 526.
4 [1982] AC 462, [1981] 3 All ER 65, PC.
5 (1881) 6 QBD 318, DC.
6 Cf *Ruddiman & Co v Smith* (1889) 60 LT 708, DC, para 28.12 above.
7 [1953] 2 All ER 582, [1953] 1 WLR 977, CA.

28.15 Particular problems have been raised by cases in which a driver has negligently injured someone to whom he has given a lift contrary to his employer's instructions. Clearly the invitation is unauthorised, but the injury is actually caused by negligent driving, which is precisely what the man is employed to do. In *Twine v Bean's Express Ltd*,[1] the Court of Appeal held the employer not liable since, while the employee could be regarded as within the course of his employment vis-à-vis other road users, he must be treated as outside it vis-à-vis his unauthorised passenger. Once again, however, the modern approach seems to be a rather broader one. In *Rose v Plenty*,[2] a milk roundsman took a young boy on the float to help with deliveries, strictly against the instructions of his employers. When, due to the milkman's negligent driving, the boy was injured, a majority of the Court of Appeal held the employers liable on the ground that, in taking him on, the employee was doing in an unauthorised way what he was authorised to do, namely, deliver the milk.

1 (1946) 175 LT 131, CA.
2 [1976] 1 All ER 97, [1976] 1 WLR 141, CA.

Intentional wrongdoing
28.16 Given that prohibited conduct may still be held to fall within the course of an employee's employment, it should come as no surprise that the same is true of wrongs intentionally committed. Once again, the important question is whether the employee can be said to be doing wrongfully what he is employed to do lawfully. Thus, in *Moore v Metropolitan Rly Co*,[1] where a railway official arrested the plaintiff in the mistaken belief that he had not paid his fare, the railway company were held liable. In *Abrahams v Deakin*,[2] on the other hand, it was held that a barman had no implied authority to

give someone into custody on a mistaken charge of attempting to pass bad money. In taking this step, the barman was not protecting the interests of his employer, for the attempt to defraud him had failed; he was rather furthering the course of justice.

A similar distinction can be found in cases of assaults committed by employees. There may well be vicarious liability in respect of excessive corporal punishment administered by a schoolteacher;[3] a blow given by a driver to a boy whom he suspects of stealing sugar from a cart;[4] or an over-zealous ejection of a troublemaker by a dance-hall doorman.[5] On the other hand, the short-tempered petrol pump attendant[6] or bus conductor[7] who strikes a customer in the course of an argument will not normally render his employer responsible, even where the original cause of the dispute is connected with the employer's business.

The most difficult cases are those in which the employee has quite clearly acted (usually dishonestly) for his own benefit. While such conduct will normally be held to fall outside the scope of employment,[8] we have already seen from the case of *Lloyd v Grace, Smith & Co*,[9] that it will not always do so. Indeed, the *Lloyd* principle has been applied to torts other than deceit. In *Morris v C W Martin & Sons Ltd*,[10] the defendants, a firm of specialist cleaners, entrusted the plaintiff's mink coat to one of their employees. Instead of cleaning the garment, the employee stole it, and the defendants were held liable for this act of conversion. However, it should be noted that, had a third party or even another employee been guilty of the theft, the defendants would not have been liable; only in relation to the employee to whom the coat had actually been entrusted could it be said that he had done wrongfully what he was employed to do. Similar reasoning underlies the case of *Photo Production Ltd v Securicor Transport Ltd*,[11] where a patrolman employed by the defendants deliberately started a fire in one of the factories which it was his duty to visit. The House of Lords had no hesitation in holding that this tort was committed in the course of the patrolman's employment, so that his employers must in principle answer for it.[12]

1   (1872) LR 8 QB 36.
2   [1891] 1 QB 516, CA.
3   *Ryan v Fildes* [1938] 3 All ER 517.
4   *Poland v John Parr & Sons* [1927] 1 KB 236, CA.
5   *Daniels v Whetstone Entertainments Ltd* [1962] 2 Lloyd's Rep 1, CA; *Vasey v Surrey Free Inns* [1996] PIQR P373, CA.
6   *Warren v Henlys Ltd* [1948] 2 All ER 935.
7   *Keppel Bus Co Ltd v Sa'ad bin Ahmad* [1974] 2 All ER 700, [1974] 1 WLR 1082, PC.
8   *Heasmans v Clarity Cleaning Co* [1987] ICR 949, CA (office cleaning contractors not liable for their employee's unauthorised use of client's telephone); *Irving v Post Office* [1987] IRLR 289, CA (Post Office not liable for racist remarks written on mail by a sorter).
9   [1912] AC 716, HL; para 28.13 above.
10 [1966] 1 QB 716, [1965] 2 All ER 725, CA. See also *Nahhas v Pier House (Cheyne Walk) Management Ltd* (1984) 270 Estates Gazette 328.
11 [1980] AC 827, [1980] 1 All ER 556, HL.
12 On the facts, a term in the contract between the parties was effective to exclude the defendants' liability; see para 10.8 above.

Liability of employee

28.17   It is important to emphasise that the vicarious liability of an employer in no way displaces the employee's own legal responsibility for the tort which he has committed. In practice, of course, a victim will almost invariably choose to sue the employer, since this increases the chance that any damages awarded to him will actually be paid. Nevertheless, there is no doubt that, if sued, the employee will be personally liable.

Indeed, this does not represent the only danger to an employee who commits a tort in the course of his employment, since he may be legally liable to reimburse his employer for the damages which the latter has been forced to pay under vicarious liability. Such liability on the part of the employee may arise under the Civil Liability (Contribution) Act 1978, since employer and employee are joint tortfeasors.[1] Apart from this, however, it was laid down by the House of Lords in *Lister v Romford Ice and Cold Storage Co Ltd*[2] that the employer (or his insurers) can sue the employee on the basis of an implied term in his contract of employment that he will indemnify his employer against any liability incurred by the employee as a result of his wrongful acts.[3]

If employers were to make regular use of their right to seek indemnity from a negligent employee, vicarious liability as it operates today would be seriously undermined. However, this is unlikely to occur; faced with the threat that the *Lister* principle might be reversed by statute, employers' and insurers' organisations have undertaken to the government that they will not exercise their rights of indemnity against individual employees, except in cases of collusion or wilful misconduct.

1 Paras 29.15–29.16 below.
2 [1957] AC 555, [1957] All ER 125, HL.
3 See para 8.25 above.

Principal and agent

28.18 As stated at the beginning of this chapter, there is no general rule of law by which a principal is responsible for the torts of his agent, unless the relationship of employer and employee exists between them. Nevertheless, in two specific instances, and for widely differing reasons, the courts have imposed such liability.

Statements
28.19 From the legal point of view, the most important characteristic of an agent is that he is authorised to make contracts or dispose of property on behalf of his principal, and thereby to create obligations which the principal is bound to honour. Central to this function is the agent's role in making statements for his principal and, as a result, it has long been established that the principal is liable when these statements turn out to be false, even though the cause of action to which they give rise is tortious in nature rather than contractual.

The principle is well settled, but its extent is rather less clear. It has been used to make the landlord of a block of flats liable to an incoming tenant for the fraud of a managing agent who allowed a builder to deliberately cover up dry rot,[1] and to render an estate agent's client liable for a fraudulent statement made about his property to a prospective purchaser.[2] In *Gosling v Anderson*,[3] another estate agent's client had to pay damages in respect of a negligent statement. It may even be that a principal would be held liable for defamatory statements made by his agent.[4]

1 *Gordon v Selico Co Ltd* (1986) 278 Estates Gazette 53, CA.
2 *Mullens v Miller* (1882) 22 Ch D 194.
3 (1972) 223 Estates Gazette 1743, CA.
4 *Colonial Mutual Life Assurance Society Ltd v Producers and Citizens Assurance Co of Australia Ltd* (1931) 46 CLR 41.

Vehicles
28.20 In an attempt to ensure that the victims of road accidents do not go uncompensated for the lack of a defendant who is solvent or insured, English law treats the owner of a motor vehicle as vicariously liable for the negligence of anyone who is driving it with his consent and on his behalf.[1] Although the owner's presence in the

vehicle is not required, he will not be liable unless the so-called 'agent's' journey is undertaken both with the owner's consent and for his benefit. Thus, in *Morgans v Launchbury*,[2] where a husband, too drunk to drive home in his wife's car, asked a friend to drive it, it was held by the House of Lords that the wife was not liable to passengers who were injured for the friend's negligent driving.

The importance of this form of vicarious liability has been greatly reduced since the introduction of legislation making it compulsory for every driver to be insured against liability for causing injury or damage to other road users, including passengers. Provided that such insurance is in place, an accident victim can obtain compensation by suing the driver; there is no need to make the vehicle owner liable. Nevertheless, an action against the owner may still be of practical value in cases where an accident takes place off public roads, and the driver has no insurance to cover the consequences.

1   *Ormrod v Crosville Motor Services Ltd* [1953] 2 All ER 753, [1953] 1 WLR 1120, CA.
2   [1973] AC 127, [1972] 2 All ER 606, HL.

Independent contractors

General principle

28.21   As a general rule, a person (hereafter referred to as the client) who entrusts work to an independent contractor is not legally responsible for any torts committed by the contractor or the contractor's employees in the course of carrying out that work. Where, for example, the police arrange for an abandoned car to be towed away, and the car is damaged due to the negligence of the garage to whom the job is entrusted, the police cannot be held responsible; it is the garage alone which is liable.[1] Likewise, a local authority is not vicariously liable for injuries to a child caused by negligence on the part of foster-parents which it has selected.[2] The client will, of course, be liable for any tort which he authorises or ratifies, and he may also be liable if he has been personally negligent in selecting an incompetent contractor[3] or in giving him inadequate instructions.[4] Whether the client may be liable for failing to exercise reasonable supervision over the independent contractor depends on whether he owes any duty of care in this respect. Such a duty has been imposed upon an occupier of land in respect of work carried out there by a building contractor;[5] however, the House of Lords has held that a building contractor owes no duty of care in tort to a subsequent owner of the building to supervise the work of a sub-contractor.[6]

1   *Rivers v Cutting* [1982] 3 All ER 69, [1982] 1 WLR 1146, CA.
2   *S v Walsall Metropolitan Borough Council* [1985] 3 All ER 294, CA.
3   *Pratt v George J Hill Associates* (1987) 38 BLR 25, CA.
4   *Robinson v Beaconsfield RDC* [1911] 2 Ch 188, CA.
5   *AMF International Ltd v Magnet Bowling Ltd* [1968] 2 All ER 789, [1968] 1 WLR 1028; see para 22.17 above.
6   *D & F Estates Ltd v Church Comrs for England* [1988] 2 All ER 992, HL.

Non-delegable duties

28.22   Apart from these possibilities, there are a number of cases in which the law is prepared to say that the client owes a personal, non-delegable duty to third parties. In such cases the client, while entitled to delegate the performance of his duty to another, remains responsible for its due fulfilment. These exceptions to the general rule of non-liability for an independent contractor's torts do not appear to be based upon any coherent principle, but rather to have evolved to meet particular situations. Nevertheless, the main categories (which we describe in paras 28.23 to 28.28 below) are well established.[1]

It should be emphasised that the standard of liability which is imposed by these non-delegable duties is not entirely uniform. In some instances, such as the rule in *Rylands v Fletcher* and under many statutes, the client's duty is a strict one, in the sense that it can be broken even when there is no negligence on anyone's part. Other cases, such as the duty of a bailee of goods, depend upon proof that someone is negligent; the client here may be said to owe a duty that reasonable care be taken. The choice as to which standard is imposed by any particular duty does not appear to be based on any clear principle.

1   See *Alcock v Wraith* (1991) 59 BLR 20 at 23.

Statutory duties

28.23   Many, if not most, of the statutory duties which give rise to civil liability[1] are non-delegable. In *Gray v Pullen*,[2] for example, where the defendants were obliged by statute to reinstate the highway after laying a drain in it, they were held liable when their independent contractor failed to do so.

Furthermore, it seems that a person with a statutory power to do something which would otherwise be unlawful delegates the exercise of this at his peril. Thus, in *Darling v A-G*,[3] where the Ministry of Works employed a contractor to drill trial bore holes on the plaintiff's land, the Ministry was held liable for the contractor's negligence in leaving a pile of timber there which injured the plaintiff's horse.

1   Paras 23.2–23.4 above.
2   (1864) 5 B & S 970.
3   [1950] 2 All ER 793.

Withdrawal of support

28.24   Where a landowner has a right to have his land or buildings supported by those of his neighbour,[1] he may sue if that support is withdrawn by the neighbour himself or by his independent contractor. This principle, which was established in *Bower v Peate*,[2] was perhaps the first non-delegable duty to be recognised by common law. It extends to cases in which work on an adjoining property damages a party wall and, by analogy, to work negligently done on a roof above a party wall which permitted damp to penetrate the plaintiff's property.[3]

1   Para 37.50 below.
2   (1876) 1 QBD 321.
3   *Alcock v Wraith* (1991) 59 BLR 20, CA.

Strict liability

28.25   In chapters 26 and 27 we considered a number of areas in which the common law imposes strict liability, notably the rule in *Rylands v Fletcher*, the escape of fire and damage of various kinds caused by animals. In all these cases a client may be held responsible for the default of his independent contractor.

Operations on the highway

28.26   Where work is done by an independent contractor on or under the highway, the client is liable if the contractor negligently causes damage to a highway user, for example by leaving an unlighted heap of soil in the road,[1] or to the occupier of adjoining premises, for example by fracturing a gas main and thus causing an explosion.[2] This principle extends to the negligent repair by a contractor of an overhanging lamp which consequently falls on a passer-by;[3] it does not, however, cover the negligent felling of trees near a highway,[4] nor the obstruction of the highway by a contractor working on the client's property,[5] nor the negligent repair by a contractor of a motor vehicle which the employer then drives along the road.[6]

1   *Penny v Wimbledon UDC* [1899] 2 QB 72, CA.
2   *Hardaker v Idle District Council* [1896] 1 QB 335, CA.
3   *Tarry v Ashton* (1876) 1 QBD 314.
4   *Salsbury v Woodland* [1970] 1 QB 324, [1969] 3 All ER 863, CA.
5   *Rowe v Herman* [1997] 1 WLR 1390, CA.
6   *Phillips v Britannia Hygienic Laundry Co Ltd* [1923] 1 KB 539, DC.

Extra-hazardous acts

28.27   In *Honeywill and Stein Ltd v Larkin Bros Ltd*,[1] the defendants, a firm of photographers, were employed by the plaintiffs to take pictures inside a cinema owned by third parties. Due to the negligence of the defendants in the use of magnesium flares (which were then necessary for indoor photography), the premises were damaged by fire. It was held by the Court of Appeal that, since this was a 'dangerous operation', the plaintiffs' duty in respect of it was a non-delegable one, and they were accordingly liable. A similar line of thinking can be found in *Matania v National Provincial Bank Ltd*[2] where noise and dust from building works caused a nuisance; the builders' clients were held liable, since this was no mere ordinary building operation, but an extensive job involving a high risk of nuisance.

Such cases create confusion and uncertainty in the law by attaching important legal consequences to what is only a difference of degree. It is, after all, difficult to say precisely when an operation becomes 'dangerous' or an act 'extra-hazardous'. It is noticeable that the courts in subsequent cases have shown no great enthusiasm for this particular category.[3]

1   [1934] 1 KB 191, CA.
2   [1936] 2 All ER 633, CA.
3   See, for example, *Alcock v Wraith* (1991) 59 BLR 20, CA.

Other cases

28.28   Of the other situations in which courts have declared a person's duty to be non-delegable, so as to fix him with responsibility for the default of his independent contractor, three worthy of note are the duty of a contractual bailee to safeguard his bailor's goods;[1] the duty of every employer to take care for the safety of his employees;[2] and (probably) the duty of a hospital to look after its patients.[3] The emphasis in all these cases is on the relationship between the *client* and the victim, and it may well be that courts will be increasingly ready to find that a client has 'undertaken' a non-delegable duty, at least where he and the victim are parties to a contract.[4]

1   *British Road Services Ltd v Arthur V Crutchley & Co Ltd* [1968] 1 All ER 811, CA.
2   *McDermid v Nash Dredging and Reclamation Co Ltd* [1987] 2 All ER 878, HL.
3   *Cassidy v Ministry of Health* [1951] 2 KB 343, [1951] 1 All ER 574, CA.
4   See *Rogers v Night Riders* [1983] RTR 324, CA.

Collateral negligence

28.29   Even in circumstances where the law recognises a non-delegable duty, it is usually said that the client is not responsible for *casual* or *collateral* negligence of the independent contractor, but only for negligence in the very act which he is employed to carry out. Thus in *Padbury v Holliday and Greenwood Ltd*,[1] where a workman employed by sub-contractors negligently left an iron tool on a window-sill and it fell on to a passer-by, the clients of the sub-contractors were held not liable.

The difficulty of deciding when negligence is collateral in this sense is well illustrated by *Holliday v National Telephone Co*,[2] where the defendants, who were laying telephone wires under a street, employed a plumber to make certain connections. The plumber negligently dipped his blow-lamp into molten solder, and a passer-by was injured by the resulting explosion. The Divisional Court thought that this was about as typical a case of casual negligence as it was possible to imagine, but the Court of Appeal held that this was negligence in the very act which the contractor was engaged to perform!

1   (1912) 28 TLR 494, CA.
2   [1899] 2 QB 392, CA.

Chapter 29

Remedies

29.1 The foregoing chapters have concentrated on the elements of liability in a number of different torts, analysing what a plaintiff must establish in order to secure a verdict against the defendant. Here we are concerned rather with what it means in practical terms to have secured such a verdict.

In this chapter we examine the following issues:

- the extent to which an award of damages in tort may depart from the general aim of compensating the plaintiff for loss suffered;
- the way in which damages are assessed in cases of personal injury, death and damage to property;
- the statutory mechanism for allocating liability where responsibility for the plaintiff's loss is shared by more than one person;
- the availability of remedies other than an award of damages, especially that of injunction;
- the time limits within which actions in tort must be commenced if they are not to be statute-barred.

Damages

29.2 The availability of an action for damages is the hallmark of a tort; the absence of such a remedy is what serves to distinguish other civil wrongs, such as breach of trust. Moreover, it should be emphasised that damages are available even in respect of those torts which are actionable per se, that is without the need to prove that the plaintiff has suffered any actual loss. In such a case, the sum awarded may, but need not, be nominal. This is not so, however, where other torts are concerned; here the plaintiff is called upon to establish his loss and, having done so, he is entitled to be compensated for it.

Kinds of damages
29.3 As a general rule, the sole object of awarding damages to a plaintiff is to compensate him for the loss which he has suffered as a result of the defendant's tort. With a few minor exceptions, matters such as the punishment of the defendant, or the restoration of benefits which he has wrongfully obtained, have no place in the law of

tort. It should also be noted that, whereas damages for breach of contract generally endeavour to put the plaintiff, in monetary terms, into the position in which he would have been had the contract been performed,[1] and thus take into account any profit which he would have made from the bargain, damages for tort attempt to restore the plaintiff to his original position, as if the tort had not been committed at all.

In a number of instances, the courts may depart, or appear to depart, from the principle of compensation in assessing the amount of damages to be awarded to a successful plaintiff. For example, where the plaintiff has a bare legal claim, but the court feels that he is morally wrong to pursue it, he may be awarded *contemptuous* damages, usually the smallest coin of the realm. In such a case the plaintiff will probably be ordered to pay his own costs, which means that he will end up out of pocket to a considerable extent.

Not to be confused with contemptuous damages are *nominal* damages, which are awarded in respect of torts actionable per se to mark the infringement of the plaintiff's legal rights, in cases where no actual loss has been incurred. An award of, say, £2 for trespass in no way signifies that the court is critical of the plaintiff for bringing the case; on the contrary, such an award is frequently accompanied by an injunction restraining the defendant from committing further acts of trespass.

In torts such as trespass or assault, where damages are incapable of precise assessment in money terms, the manner in which the defendant commits the tort may be taken into account by the court; if this is such as to injure the plaintiff's dignity or pride, *aggravated* damages may be awarded. Indeed, even where the plaintiff has suffered a quantifiable financial loss, as where he has been defrauded by the defendant, he may receive an additional sum for injury to his feelings.[2] It should be noted that, while aggravated damages are in theory compensatory, they seek to give redress for something which would not be actionable if it stood alone. Thus, an insult itself cannot bring damages; but, if the defendant trespasses on the plaintiff's land in order to insult him, this may aggravate the damages which are awarded in respect of the trespass. However, a plaintiff cannot recover damages for his indignation at the high-handed attitude displayed by the defendant following the commission of a tort.[3]

Quite apart from any question of aggravation, there remains the possibility that, where the defendant's conduct is particularly outrageous, the court may order him to pay *exemplary* or *punitive* damages, over and above what is necessary to compensate the plaintiff, for the explicit purpose of punishing the defendant and of teaching him that tort does not pay. Such awards are open to criticism on the grounds that the defendant is being punished for something which is not a crime, and without the protection of a criminal trial. It might also be argued that what is in effect a fine should be paid to the state rather than to the plaintiff, since the latter has, after all, already received sufficient to compensate him for his loss. Nevertheless, the power to award exemplary damages is well established, although in *Rookes v Barnard*[4] the House of Lords laid down that it should only be exercised in three classes of case, and only in respect of torts for which such damages had already (in 1964) been awarded.[5]

The three situations in which exemplary damages can be awarded are:

- where statute authorises such an award;
- in cases of oppressive, arbitrary or unconstitutional acts by the servants of the government, such as assault or wrongful arrest by police officers, who are regarded for this purpose as the servants of the government;[6] or
- where the defendant has quite cold-bloodedly decided to infringe the plaintiff's rights after calculating that his profit in doing so will outweigh any compensation he may be ordered to pay. This has been held to include such cases as the publication of a book[7] or a newspaper[8] containing sensational libels in order to

boost sales, and the eviction of a protected tenant by a landlord[9] anxious to turn his flat to more profitable use.[10]

1   Para 12.3 above.
2   *Archer v Brown* [1984] 2 All ER 267, [1984] 3 WLR 350.
3   *AB v South West Water Services Ltd* [1993] 1 All ER 609, CA.
4   [1964] AC 1129, [1964] 1 All ER 367, HL.
5   This excludes public nuisance: *AB v South West Water Services Ltd* [1993] 1 All ER 609, CA.
6   Exemplary damages may be awarded for wrongful arrest, even where the behaviour is not 'oppressive': *Holden v Chief Constable of Lancashire* [1987] QB 380, [1986] 3 All ER 836, CA.
7   *Cassell & Co Ltd v Broome* [1972] AC 1027, [1972] 1 All ER 801, HL, in which it was held to be irrelevant that no profit was in fact made.
8   As to the assessment of exemplary damages where a newspaper article libels a group of plaintiffs, see *Riches v News Group Newspapers Ltd* [1986] QB 256, CA.
9   But not the landlord's agent, unless he stands to benefit personally from the eviction: *Daley v Ramdath* (1993) Times, 21 January, CA.
10 *Drane v Evangelou* [1978] 2 All ER 437, [1978] 1 WLR 455, CA (trespass); *Guppys (Bridport) Ltd v Brookling* (1983) 269 Estates Gazette 846, CA (nuisance). The Housing Act 1988, s 28 entitles an unlawfully evicted tenant to a measure of damages which effectively consists of the profit which the landlord makes from the eviction.

Personal injury

29.4   The rules which govern the assessment of damages for personal injury are complex and, in many respects, controversial; no more than an outline can be given here. One of the major problems is that the loss which flows from an injury falls into two very different categories. In the first place, the plaintiff may suffer monetary losses, such as medical expenses or loss of earnings; the guiding principle here is that he is entitled, so far as is possible, to full restitution of what he has lost. Secondly, however, there is non-monetary loss, which includes such matters as pain and suffering and loss of amenity. It is obviously impossible to place a precise value upon such things, and the law's aim here is simply to ensure that compensation should be fair and reasonable. This involves attempting to devise a scale of injuries (so that, for example, a lost leg is treated as worth more than a lost eye) and also maintaining some degree of consistency between the amounts awarded in similar cases. With these points, and especially these two categories, in mind we may now consider the various heads of damage under which personal injury awards are usually itemised.

Loss of amenity

29.5   The plaintiff is entitled to an award of damages in respect of the extent to which his injuries render him unable or less able to do what he previously enjoyed. Under this heading compensation may be awarded, for example, in respect of a lost limb or the impairment of senses or of sexual function. The seriousness of the deprivation, the plaintiff's degree of awareness of it, and the period for which he is likely to have to endure it, are all factors which influence the size of the award. In *Daly v General Steam Navigation Co Ltd*,[1] a woman whose injuries made it difficult and painful to keep house for her family recovered under this heading for the period preceding the trial; as to the future, she was held entitled to the estimated costs of employing a housekeeper, whether or not she in fact intended to employ one.

Although this category appears to be based on a person's lost enjoyment of life, it was laid down by the House of Lords, in *H West & Son Ltd v Shephard*,[2] that it represents an objective loss. Consequently, even someone rendered immediately and permanently unaware of his loss may be entitled to a considerable sum, a situation which has been criticised as being of benefit only to the plaintiff's dependants. Of course, a plaintiff who *is* aware of his loss may be compensated for this under the heading of 'pain and suffering'.[3]

1   [1980] 3 All ER 696, [1981] 1 WLR 120, CA.
2   [1964] AC 326, [1963] 2 All ER 625, HL.
3   Para 29.6 below.

Pain and suffering

29.6   This head of damage includes not only the physical pain of the injury and subsequent surgical operations, but also mental anguish arising out of disability or disfigurement. It cannot by definition apply to plaintiffs rendered permanently unconscious; nor, where a person is killed by a tort, can damages be awarded to the estate for that 'pain and suffering' which is really part of the death itself.[1]

As a general rule, the courts do not separate 'pain and suffering' from 'loss of amenity', but award a global sum to cover both categories. Where very severe injuries are involved, this can be a considerable amount.

1   *Hicks v Chief Constable of the South Yorkshire Police* [1992] 2 All ER 65, HL.

Loss of expectation of life

29.7   A plaintiff's entitlement to damages (usually a small 'conventional' sum) for the fact that his life expectancy has been reduced has now been abolished by the Administration of Justice Act 1982, s 1(1). However, this does not prevent him from claiming in respect of the suffering caused by his awareness of his reduced lifespan (s 1(1)(b)), nor for the money which he could have earned during the lost years (s 1(2)).

Medical and other expenses

29.8   The plaintiff is entitled to claim the cost, both past and future, of medical and nursing care including, where appropriate, the expense of living in a suitable institution or of adapting his own home to his needs. If he has to live in an institution, a sum representing his normal living expenses must be deducted from the damages awarded under this head, since these will no longer be incurred.[1] The plaintiff cannot recover damages for any expenses which ought reasonably to have been avoided, but it is not unreasonable to care for a severely injured person at home just because he could be catered for more cheaply than in an institution,[2] nor (more questionably) to seek private medical treatment rather than making use of the National Health Service facilities.[3]

Problems have arisen in the past where necessary nursing services have been rendered to a seriously disabled plaintiff by a close relative, as where a mother has given up a job in order to look after her crippled child. Notwithstanding that the plaintiff in such a case is under no legal obligation to pay for these services, it is now established that he can recover a reasonable sum in respect of them from the defendant.[4]

1   *Lim Poh Choo v Camden and Islington Area Health Authority* [1980] AC 174, [1979] 2 All ER 910, HL.
2   *Rialas v Mitchell* (1984) Times, 17 July, CA.
3   Law Reform (Personal Injuries) Act 1948, s 2(4).
4   *Donnelly v Joyce* [1974] QB 454, [1973] 3 All ER 475, CA. However, this does not apply where the defendant himself renders the services: *Hunt v Severs* [1994] 2 All ER 385, HL.

Loss of earnings

29.9   Earnings which the plaintiff has lost up to the date of the trial are relatively easy to measure, but loss of future earnings[1] must also be compensated, and here assessment is far less certain, especially where it appears that the plaintiff will never be able to work again. In such cases, the courts, having firmly refused to enter into detailed actuarial calculations,[2] simply multiply their prediction of the plaintiff's average annual income (net of income tax and national insurance contributions) by an appropriate multiplier. This is not simply the number of years' earnings which have been lost, but is discounted to reflect the chance of an earlier death and the benefit of having an immediate lump sum; it is not increased, however, to offset inflation,[3] nor to mitigate the effect which high rates of taxation will have upon the income produced by investing a large award of damages.[4]

Where a person's life expectancy is substantially reduced as a result of a tort, it is of course likely that he will thereby be deprived of the opportunity to earn money during the lost years. Under the Administration of Justice Act 1982, s 1(2), a living plaintiff[5] can recover for prospective earnings during the lost years, although a deduction must be made in respect of what he would have spent on his own support during that time. However, the courts will not make an award of this kind to a very young plaintiff on the grounds that his loss is too speculative.[6]

Much of the uncertainty which surrounds this particular head of damage arises from the fact that, since damages are paid as a lump sum, they must be assessed in advance. It has been suggested that the law should permit a court to award damages in the form of periodic payments, which could be reviewed in the event of a change of circumstances. This suggestion has not been implemented, although a more limited reform was introduced by the Administration of Justice Act 1982, s 6. This provides that, in cases where there is a chance that the plaintiff's condition will deteriorate at some time in the future, the court may make an initial award on the basis that this will not happen, the plaintiff being at liberty to seek additional damages if it does.[7]

1 Including loss or reduction of future pension rights: *Auty v National Coal Board* [1985] 1 All ER 930, CA.
2 *Mitchell v Mulholland (No 2)* [1972] 1 QB 65, [1971] 2 All ER 1205, CA.
3 *Cookson v Knowles* [1979] AC 556, [1978] 2 All ER 604, HL.
4 *Hodgson v Trapp* [1988] 3 All ER 870, HL.
5 The claim does not pass to the deceased's estate: see para 29.11 below.
6 *Croke v Wiseman* [1981] 3 All ER 852, [1982] 1 WLR 71, CA.
7 See *Willson v Ministry of Defence* [1991] 1 All ER 638.

Collateral benefits

29.10 A person who is injured in an accident may, as a result of this, receive sums of money from a wide variety of sources. It may be, for example, that he has insured himself against this contingency; he may receive sick pay or a pension from his employer; or he may be entitled to various social security benefits. To what extent, if at all, should this be regarded as relevant when the plaintiff comes to claim damages from the defendant in respect of his loss of earnings? Should the plaintiff be allowed to recover full damages and to keep his other benefit, and thereby be doubly compensated? Should damages be reduced, so that the defendant reaps the benefit of a payment designed to help the plaintiff? Or should the law seek to ensure that the money is in some way returned to the collateral fund?

To these questions, English law has no simple answers, largely because it has dealt with each type of collateral benefit as it has arisen, without attempting to lay down any general principles. Very broadly, the position now is that most state benefits received in the five years after the accident are deducted from the damages and then recouped from the defendant by the state.[1] Also deducted, but not recouped, are wages, sick pay,[2] redundancy payments[3] and the like to which the plaintiff is actually entitled, together with any saving on living costs where the plaintiff is maintained at public expense in an institution.[4] The product of private insurance,[5] or a charitable payment, on the other hand, is non-deductible.[6] On the very borderline is a pension; in *Parry v Cleaver*,[7] this was held by a bare majority of the House of Lords to be non-deductible, on the ground that it is not intended to be an equivalent of wages lost and cannot therefore be said to reduce the loss which the plaintiff has suffered.

1   Social Security Administration Act 1992, Part IV. After five years there is neither deduction nor recoupment.
2   *Hussain v New Taplow Paper Mills Ltd* [1988] 1 All ER 541, HL.
3   *Colledge v Bass Mitchells & Butlers* [1988] ICR 125, CA.
4   Administration of Justice Act 1982, s 5.
5   Even where paid for by the defendant employer: *McCamley v Cammell Laird Shipbuilders Ltd* [1990] 1 All ER 854, CA.
6   *Bradburn v Great Western Rly Co* (1874) LR 10 Exch 1.
7   [1970] AC 1, [1969] 1 All ER 555, HL; followed unanimously by the House of Lords in *Smoker v London Fire and Civil Defence Authority*; *Wood v British Coal Corporation* [1991] 2 All ER 449, HL.

Death

29.11   The Law Reform (Miscellaneous Provisions) Act 1934 provides that most tort actions survive for and against the estates of the parties.[1] However, the Administration of Justice Act 1982, s 4 provides that a deceased person's estate may not be awarded damages for bereavement,[2] exemplary damages[3] or damages for loss of earnings during the lost years.[4] Apart from this, where an action is brought on behalf of a deceased person, the damages awarded are such as he could have recovered if he had not died, which means that the headings considered above under 'personal injury' are again relevant, at least as regards the period between the tort and death.

1   Actions for defamation do not survive.
2   Para 29.12 below.
3   Para 29.3 above.
4   Para 29.9 above.

Fatal accidents

29.12   At common law, no tort action could be brought by A on the ground that the death of B had caused him loss. However, a statutory right of action for the dependants of a person who is killed by a tort has long been in existence and is currently governed by the Fatal Accidents Act 1976, as amended by the Administration of Justice Act 1982, s 3. Dependants for this purpose bears a wide meaning, including spouses, all ascendants and descendants, brothers and sisters, uncles and aunts and their issue, provided, of course, that they truly were dependent upon the deceased. Moreover, since 1982, the Act has extended to a former spouse or common law spouse of the deceased, although the amount of damages payable must reflect the fact that he or she had no legal right to financial support by the deceased.

The cause of action given by the Fatal Accidents Act is quite separate from that which may have survived for the benefit of the estate itself. Normal practice is for the action to be brought by the personal representative of the deceased, on behalf of all the dependants; the court will then assess the total liability of the defendant before apportioning the damages between the various dependants. Since the action is an independent one, it has its own limitation period of three years from the date of death. Further, it seems that where a dependant has through his own fault contributed to the causing of death, for example by negligent driving, his damages, though not those of other dependants, may be reduced on the ground of contributory negligence.

Although the action is thus separate, it is still subject to the principle that it can only be brought where the deceased himself could have sued if he had been injured rather than killed. As a result, if the deceased had already sued to judgment or settled his claim against the defendant, or if his action was barred by time or by an exemption clause, the dependants' rights are also defeated. So too, if the deceased was guilty of contributory negligence, damages awarded under the Fatal Accidents Act will suffer an appropriate reduction.

It is important to appreciate that the main purpose of this statutory cause of action is to compensate the dependants, not for their grief at losing a loved one, but for the loss of some benefit which has a monetary value (including, for example, services performed by a wife and mother[1] or unpaid help given by a son to his father's work[2]) and which would have come to the dependants because of their relationship with the deceased.[3] However, since 1982 there has been a limited exception to this principle, in that damages for bereavement (a fixed sum laid down by statutory instrument[4]) may be awarded to the widow(er) or, where the deceased is an unmarried minor at the date of death, to his parents.

In deciding how much to award for loss of dependency, the court must try to assess what the position would have been had the deceased lived and, in carrying out this task, the prospects of both the deceased and the dependants are of course relevant. However, the court is not to consider a widow's prospects of remarriage.

Section 4 of the 1976 Act provides that, in assessing damages, no account is to be taken of any benefits which accrue to the dependant in question as a result of the death, for example by way of inheritance or insurance policies.[5]

1   *Mehmet v Perry* [1977] 2 All ER 529, DC.
2   *Franklin v South Eastern Rly Co* (1858) 3 H & N 211.
3   Funeral expenses incurred by the dependants are also recoverable: Fatal Accidents Act 1976, s 3(3).
4   This is currently £7,500: Damages for Bereavement (Variation of Sum) (England and Wales) Order 1990.
5   See *Pidduck v Eastern Scottish Omnibuses Ltd* [1990] 2 All ER 69, CA.

Damage to property
Measure of damages
29.13   A person whose property (whether land or goods) is destroyed or damaged as a result of a tort is in principle entitled to full restitution in money terms of what he has lost. Where property is totally destroyed (which will hardly ever apply to land), the usual measure of damages is at least the full value to the plaintiff of that property at the time and place of its destruction. This value, in the case of a profit-earning chattel such as a ship, should take into account its profitability at the time, in the light of its current engagements.[1] However, if the plaintiff receives this sum he may yet be out of pocket, in that the acquisition of a suitable replacement may take time; in such a case, damages for loss of profit, or simply loss of use, may also be recovered.

Where the plaintiff's property is damaged by the defendant, the court has a choice of at least two possible measures[2] to award (which may or may not be the same): either the amount by which the value of the property has been reduced, or the cost of repairing it. In the case of goods, the courts have usually been prepared to award the cost of repair, unless this would be unreasonable. For example, the owner of a badly damaged car will not normally be allowed the cost of repair where this exceeds the write-off value of the vehicle.[3] A similar principle applies in respect of damage to land and buildings, so that the cost of reinstatement is usually appropriate, provided that the plaintiff's decision to repair is a reasonable one. Thus, in *Hollebone v Midhurst and Fernhurst Builders*,[4] where the plaintiff's house was damaged by fire, the judge held that the plaintiff was fully entitled to decide to rebuild what was in effect a unique property. That case also laid down that a plaintiff need not suffer any deduction from his damages in respect of 'betterment', ie the amount by which the value of the restored property exceeds its pre-accident value.

Where the plaintiff has no intention of repairing the building (as in *C A Taylor (Wholesale) Ltd v Hepworths Ltd*,[5] where fire damaged a disused billiards hall on a site which the plaintiffs had always intended to redevelop) damages should only reflect the diminution in value of the property. This is also true of cases where the cost of reinstatement would be out of all proportion to the loss suffered. In *Jones v Gooday*,[6] for example, where the defendant wrongfully removed soil from the plaintiff's field, the plaintiff was awarded only the amount by which the value of the field was reduced, and not the much greater cost of restoring it to its original condition. In *Heath v Keys*,[7] where the defendant wrongfully dumped spoil on a small area of woodland owned by the plaintiff, the award was something of a compromise; not the full cost of restoring the site to its original condition, but enough to pay the costs involved in removing most of the spoil and tidying the site, in addition to the diminution in value which would remain when this had been done.

Quite apart from the damages discussed above, a plaintiff is entitled to compensation for loss of profits or loss of use during the time taken to effect repairs, which may be assessed on the basis of the cost of hiring a reasonable substitute. What is reasonable is a question of fact, and may even include a prestige car.[8] It is important to note that the plaintiff is not required to show that he has actually suffered from the non-availability of his property. Consequently, in *The Mediana*,[9] where a damaged lightship was replaced for a time by a substitute which the plaintiffs kept for just such an emergency, they were nevertheless awarded substantial damages for loss of use.

It is worth noting that, where a purchaser brings an action for negligence against a surveyor on whose advice he relied in deciding to purchase, the basic measure of damages will be not the cost of repairing defects which the surveyor ought to have discovered, but the difference between what the purchaser has been led to pay for the property and its actual value. This is because the surveyor has not actually damaged the property; his offence consists of leading the purchaser to pay more than it is worth.[10]

1 *Liesbosch Dredger v SS Edison* [1933] AC 449, HL.
2 These are not the only possible measures; the court will select whatever is the most appropriate measure of compensation in all the circumstances. See *Dominion Mosaics and Tile Co Ltd v Trafalgar Trucking Co Ltd* [1990] 2 All ER 246, CA; *Farmer Giles Ltd v Wessex Water Authority* [1990] 1 EGLR 177, CA.
3 *Darbishire v Warran* [1963] 3 All ER 310, [1963] 1 WLR 1067, CA.
4 [1968] 1 Lloyd's Rep 38. Also see *Dominion Mosaics & Tile Co Ltd v Trafalgar Trucking Co Ltd* [1989] 16 EG 101.
5 [1977] 2 All ER 784, [1977] WLR 659.
6 (1841) 8 M & W 146.
7 (1984) Times, 28 May.
8 *Daily Office Cleaning Contractors v Shefford* [1977] RTR 361, DC.
9 [1900] AC 113, HL.
10 *Watts v Morrow* [1991] 4 All ER 937, CA.

Date of assessment
29.14 Times of rampant inflation have given rise to a particular problem in cases where damages are to be assessed on the basis of cost of repair. In *Dodd Properties (Kent) Ltd v Canterbury City Council*,[1] for example, the plaintiffs' garage was seriously damaged in 1968 by building works carried on by the defendants on adjoining property, in such circumstances that the defendants were clearly liable. The cost of repairing the garage in 1968 would have been £10,800. In 1970, which was the earliest possible date by which repairs could have been started, the cost would have been £11,300. By 1978, however, when the plaintiffs' action was tried, the cost had rocketed to £30,000! It was obviously of crucial importance to decide which date should be taken for the purpose of assessing damages. The Court of Appeal held that, while the basic rule in tort is that damages are to be assessed when they occur, this must not be allowed to penalise a plaintiff. In cost of repair cases, therefore, the appropriate date is that on which the plaintiff ought reasonably to have repaired the property. Here, the plaintiffs had chosen for financial reasons not to start repairs until they had recovered damages from the defendants and, despite the defendants' plea that lack of funds could not excuse the plaintiffs' failure to put the repairs in hand,[2] they were held to be entitled to the much higher sum which represented this cost at the time of the trial.

1   [1980] 1 All ER 928, [1980] 1 WLR 433, CA.
2   Based on *Liesbosch Dredger v SS Edison* [1933] AC 449, HL; paras 20.16 and 20.20 above.

Joint and several tortfeasors
29.15   Where the plaintiff is harmed by the tortious conduct of more than one person, the first question to be asked is whether each tortfeasor has caused a separately identifiable part of the plaintiff's overall damage. If this is so, then each is liable only for the part which he has caused. More commonly, however, the damage to the plaintiff will be indivisible; if so, the plaintiff is entitled to recover damages in full from any or all of the tortfeasors, subject to the proviso that he cannot recover more in total than he has lost. Thus, for example, if the plaintiff is injured by the combined negligence of A and B in such circumstances that the court regards A as three-quarters and B as one-quarter to blame, the plaintiff may nevertheless choose to sue B alone and may recover full damages. The importance of this principle is seen in cases where A is insolvent and uninsured; the loss then falls upon B, who is after all guilty of some fault, rather than upon the plaintiff who is completely innocent.

In practice, it is desirable that the plaintiff should bring all the defendants into court in one action. To encourage him to do so, the common law laid down the rule that judgment, even if unsatisfied, against one joint tortfeasor barred subsequent proceedings against the others. This rule has been abolished,[1] but the plaintiff is still unable to recover his costs in subsequent proceedings unless the court finds that there were reasonable grounds for bringing them.[2]

1   Civil Liability (Contribution) Act 1978, s 3.
2   Civil Liability (Contribution) Act 1978, s 4.

Contribution
29.16   At common law, if a plaintiff chose to sue one tortfeasor and not others, the loss lay where it fell; the others could not be ordered to make any contribution to the damages paid. This harsh rule was, however, abolished in relation to tort in 1935, and the availability of contribution orders was extended to other types of liability, such as breach of contract and breach of trust, by the Civil Liability (Contribution) Act 1978. According to s 1(1), any person liable in respect of any damage suffered by another person may recover contribution from any other person liable in respect of the same damage.[1]

Of course, no order for contribution can be made against a tortfeasor unless he is party to an action. As we have seen, the costs sanction encourages the plaintiff to join all defendants in the first place and, even where this is not done, one defendant can bring in others as third parties, in order that the liability of each may be determined in a single action.

The right of one defendant (D1) to claim contribution from another (D2) is independent of the plaintiff's right of action. Thus, the fact that the plaintiff's claim against D2 would have been barred by lapse of time[2] is irrelevant, provided that D1 himself brings his action for contribution within two years of the date on which his right arises (normally the date on which D1 pays compensation to the plaintiff).

In assessing the amount of contribution, the court is instructed to do what is just and equitable, and it seems that, in arriving at a fraction or percentage, it will rely on the same factors as in cases of contributory negligence.[3] However, it should be noted that D2 cannot be ordered to pay more to D1 than he would have had to pay the plaintiff (eg where his contract with the plaintiff contained a clause which limited his liability): nor does the Civil Liability (Contribution) Act prevail against a right of indemnity which is contained in a contract between the tortfeasors.

1   The phrase 'the same damage' requires both persons to be liable to the same third party: *Birse Construction Ltd v Haiste Ltd* [1996] 2 All ER 1, CA.
2   Paras 29.21–29.25 below.
3   Para 21.16 above.

Injunction

29.17   An injunction is a specific decree of the court which orders the defendant to do or, more commonly, not to do something. Like all equitable remedies it is not available as of right, but lies in the discretion of the court. As a result, it is unlikely to be granted where damages would be an adequate remedy, where the harm suffered by the plaintiff is of a very trivial or temporary nature,[1] or where the plaintiff has actually or apparently acquiesced in the defendant's tort. For example, in *Armstrong v Sheppard and Short Ltd*,[2] the plaintiff assented in principle to the laying of a sewer by the defendants under certain land near his house, unaware that he in fact owned it; upon discovering the truth, he sued the defendants in trespass. The Court of Appeal held that, since the defendants had been misled and the harm was trivial, the plaintiff was not entitled to an injunction but only to damages.

1   *A-G v Sheffield Gas Consumers Co* (1853) 3 De GM & G 304.
2   [1959] 2 QB 384, [1959] 2 All ER 651, CA.

Kinds of injunction

29.18   A *prohibitory* injunction, the most common kind, is an order to the defendant to stop certain conduct which represents a continuing or repetitive infringement of the plaintiff's legal rights (eg by the commission of trespass or nuisance). In the absence of special circumstances, the grant of such an injunction is almost automatic, though its operation may on occasion be suspended for a period to enable the defendant to make alternative arrangements.

By contrast, a *mandatory* injunction, which orders the defendant to take positive steps to repair the wrong he has done, is reserved for those few cases in which the plaintiff will suffer very serious harm unless the injunction is granted. Further, unless the defendant has acted in flagrant disregard of the plaintiff's rights, the court must weigh up what it will cost the defendant to comply with the order. Thus, in *Redland Bricks Ltd v Morris*,[1] where the defendants' excavations on their own land had caused subsidence of part of the plaintiff's land and danger to the rest, the House of Lords refused to order the defendants to restore support, since the cost of doing this would be greater than the total value of the plaintiff's land.

In matters of urgency, where the preservation of the status quo is important to save the plaintiff from further loss, the court may grant him an *interlocutory* injunction, a provisional order until a full trial takes place. Since the defendant may lose money because of this order, and then turn out to have been in the right all along, the plaintiff may be compelled to give an undertaking that in such circumstances he will pay compensation. The principles on which a court should exercise its discretion in relation to interlocutory injunctions were laid down by the House of Lords in the case of *American Cyanamid Co v Ethicon Ltd*.[2] Briefly, these are that, if there is a serious question to be tried, the court must consider all the circumstances, particularly whether the preservation of the status quo is important, and whether the defendant will be adequately protected by the plaintiff's undertaking to pay damages.

In rare cases, where the plaintiff's cause of action depends on proof of damage, the court may issue an injunction *quia timet* before such damage had actually occurred. In effect, this means that the defendant is liable before a complete tort has been committed; not surprisingly, therefore such an order is only granted where damage is almost certain to occur and where it is imminent.

1   [1970] AC 652, [1969] 2 All ER 576, HL.
2   [1975] AC 396, [1975] 1 All ER 504, HL.

Damages in lieu of injunction

29.19   In any case where an injunction is claimed, the court has a discretion to refuse the injunction and award damages in substitution for it. In effect, such an order allows the defendant to purchase the right to commit a tort against the plaintiff, and the discretion is consequently to be used sparingly. It has been suggested that the court should only act in this way where it is shown that the injury to the plaintiff is small, capable of estimation in money terms and adequately compensated by damages and that an injunction would cause great hardship to the defendant.[1]

In *Jaggard v Sawyer*,[2] the owners of a private road sought an injunction to prevent the occupiers of a new house from trespassing along the road. However, the Court of Appeal held that this was a case where damages should be awarded instead, since to award an injunction would in effect render the house uninhabitable. By contrast, in *Elliott v Islington London Borough Council*,[3] the Court of Appeal awarded an injunction compelling a local authority to cut down a tree which was encroaching on to the plaintiff's land, notwithstanding that the tree was an ancient horse chestnut which the local authority passionately wanted to preserve.

1   *Shelfer v City of London Electric Lighting Co* [1895] 1 Ch 287 at 322, CA.
2   [1995] 2 All ER 189, CA.
3   [1991] 1 EGLR 167, CA.

Other remedies

29.20   In the vast majority of tort cases which come to court, the plaintiff is seeking either damages or an injunction. However, in some circumstances other remedies may be of greater value, particularly an order for the specific restitution of goods or land.[1]

Although not popular with the courts, and therefore strictly controlled, a certain amount of self-help is tolerated, in the interest of avoiding unnecessary litigation. Examples of this principle, all of which we have considered at the appropriate place, are the ejection of a trespasser and re-entry on to land,[2] the abatement of a nuisance,[3] the detention of straying livestock[4] and the killing of a marauding dog.[5]

1   Para 24.10 above.
2   Para 24.11 above.
3   Para 25.22 above.
4   Para 27.11 above.
5   Para 27.13 above.

Limitation of actions

29.21   Any civil action will be barred by lapse of time unless the writ by which it commences is issued within the prescribed limitation period. The rules which govern this matter are entirely statutory, the relevant Act being the Limitation Act 1980, as amended by the Latent Damage Act 1986. For present purposes, the main limitation periods are 12 years (recovery of land and contracts made by deed); six years (breach of simple contracts and tort); and three years (actions for both tort and breach of contract in respect of personal injuries). Special periods apply to certain types of claim, for example those arising under the Defective Premises Act 1972.[1]

1 Para 22.28 above.

Commencement of limitation period

29.22 Whatever the period may be, the basic rule is that it starts on the day when the plaintiff's cause of action accrues. In contract cases, this is almost invariably the date of the defendant's breach, and the same is true of those torts which are actionable per se, such as trespass. On the other hand, where proof of damage forms part of the tort itself, as in cases of negligence or nuisance, the cause of action does not arise until the damage occurs and, accordingly, time does not start to run until that date.

Clearly, it may sometimes be to a plaintiff's advantage to be able to sue in tort rather than in contract, and this is what gives such importance to those decisions which have held professional men liable to their clients in the tort of negligence as well as for breach of contract.[1] However, the advantage of a tort action is not always as marked as might be supposed. For example, where a solicitor gives negligent advice to a client, as a result of which the client executes an imprudent mortgage of her property, it has been held that the damage is suffered as soon as the mortgage is executed, since the property is immediately rendered less valuable, rather than when the property is later seized by the mortgagee.[2] Similarly, where a surveyor negligently advises his client to purchase a badly constructed building, the client is regarded as having suffered loss at the date of purchase, rather than at the later date when the building itself suffers physical damage.[3] By contrast, where a mortgage lender sues the valuer on whose valuation he relied when deciding to lend, the lender's loss is deemed to occur at the first moment when the amount of the outstanding mortgage debt (including any accrued interest) exceeds the value of the property.[4]

Continuing torts, such as certain kinds of trespass[5] or nuisance, give rise to a fresh right of action every day until they are abated. The consequence of this is that a plaintiff is entitled to sue for everything which has occurred during the past six years, even if the tort was first committed outside that period or, indeed, before he acquired the property in question.[6]

1 Para 18.24 above.
2 *Forster v Outred & Co* [1982] 2 All ER 753, [1982] 1 WLR 86, CA.
3 *Secretary of State for the Environment v Essex, Goodman & Suggitt* [1986] 1 WLR 1432.
4 *Nykredit Mortgage Bank plc v Edward Erdman Group Ltd (No 2)* [1998] 1 All ER 305, HL.
5 Para 24.8 above.
6 See *Masters v Brent London Borough Council* [1978] QB 841, [1978] 2 All ER 664.

Personal injury

29.23 A particular problem may arise in cases where an injury, such as a progressive industrial disease, is not discovered (or, indeed, discoverable) by the plaintiff until some considerable time after it first occurs. It was held by the House of Lords in *Cartledge v E Jopling & Sons Ltd*,[1] a case concerning a lung disease contracted over a long period of time by workers in a particular industry, that the limitation period in such circumstances began to run as soon as the disease passed beyond the merely trivial, notwithstanding that this might mean that a victim's cause of action was barred by time before he could possibly have known that it existed.

The obvious harshness of this ruling in the context of personal injury cases led swiftly to its alleviation by statute. The Limitation Act 1980, s 11 now provides that the limitation period in cases of personal injury based on 'negligence, nuisance or breach of duty'[2] shall be three years and shall not begin until the plaintiff has knowledge of a number of material facts, of which the most important are the significance of his injury (that is, that it is serious enough to justify taking legal action) and its attributability to an identified defendant. The plaintiff's 'knowledge' for this purpose includes knowledge which he might reasonably have been expected to acquire from his own observations or from such expert advice as he ought reasonably to have sought, taking account of his age, background, intelligence and disabilities.[3]

1   [1963] AC 758, [1963] 1 All ER 341, HL.
2   This does not include trespass to the person: *Stubbings v Webb* [1993] 1 All ER 322, HL.
3   *Davis v City and Hackney Health Authority* [1989] 2 Med LR 366.

Latent damage

29.24   The problem of hidden damage is not confined to personal injury cases; negligence in building houses is another obvious example. In *Pirelli General Cable Works Ltd v Oscar Faber & Partners*,[1] the House of Lords laid down that, as with personal injuries before statute intervened, the correct starting-point is when the building actually suffers damage, not when it becomes visible. Indeed, it was said obiter that, if the building could be shown to have been 'doomed from the start',[2] then time would run from an even earlier moment, namely, that at which the building was completed.

Once again, the harshness of this rule led to statutory change. The Latent Damage Act 1986 effectively extends the limitation period for claims in tort for negligence,[3] other than in respect of personal injury.[4] It also permits an action for negligent damage to property[5] to be brought by a person who acquires that property after it has suffered damage but before the damage has become apparent.

The time limit on claims falling within the Latent Damage Act 1986 is either:

- six years from when the cause of action accrued;[6] or
- three years from when the plaintiff (or his predecessor in title, if property has changed hands) had both the right to bring an action and knowledge of material facts.[7]

However, the Act imposes an overriding time limit of 15 years from the defendant's breach of duty on which the action is based. After this, the action is barred whether or not the damage has become known or has even occurred.

1   [1983] 2 AC 1, [1983] 1 All ER 65, HL.
2   A possibility which subsequent courts have consistently rejected: see, for example, *Ketteman v Hansel Properties Ltd* [1987] AC 189, [1988] 1 All ER 38, HL.
3   The Act does not apply to claims based on a contractual duty of care: *Société Commerciale de Réassurance v ERAS (International)* [1992] 2 All ER 82n, CA.
4   Thus including both claims for both damage to property and pure financial loss.
5   But not for other types of claim, eg for negligent professional advice.
6   Ie when damage is suffered; see para 29.22 above.
7   'Knowledge' is defined in a similar way as for personal injury claims; see para 29.23 above. For the operation of the Act in respect of a negligent survey, see *Hamlin v Edwin Evans* [1996] 2 EGLR 106, CA.

Extension of time

29.25   It is provided by the Limitation Act 1980 that in certain circumstances the limitation period may either begin to run from a later date than normal or may simply be extended.

- Where there is fraud, concealment or mistake,[1] the limitation period does not begin to run until this has been or ought to have been discovered by the plaintiff. The question of concealment has arisen in a number of cases where defects in a building which are due to negligence by the builder have been covered up in the course of the construction work and have not come to light until many years later. It has been held that the mere fact that a builder continues with his work after something shoddy or inadequate has been done does not necessarily amount to concealment for this purpose.[2] The question is whether in all the circumstances it was unconscionable for the builder to proceed with the work so as to cover up the defect.[3]

- Where the plaintiff is a minor or is mentally ill, the limitation period does not begin to run until the removal of his disability or his death.[4] This provision has been held to apply where the plaintiff's unsoundness of mind is caused by the accident in respect of which he sues.[5]
- A sweeping change in the law governing limitation of actions was introduced by the Limitation Act 1980, s 33. This provision, which applies to all actions brought in respect of personal injuries, empowers the court simply to override the normal three-year period if it appears equitable to do so. In deciding how to exercise its discretion in this way, the court is instructed to have regard to all the circumstances of the case, and in particular to the extent to which each party would be prejudiced by an adverse decision, to the conduct of each party since the accident, and to the length and reasons for the delay.[6]

1   Para 12.37 above. 'Concealment' for this purpose may take place either when the cause of action first accrues or at any time thereafter: *Sheldon v RHM Outhwaite (Underwriting Agencies) Ltd* [1995] 2 All ER 558, HL.
2   *William Hill Organisation Ltd v Bernard Sunley & Sons Ltd* (1982) 22 BLR 8, CA.
3   *Applegate v Moss* [1971] 1 QB 406, [1971] 1 All ER 747, CA.
4   Limitation Act 1980, s 28.
5   *Kirby v Leather* [1965] 2 QB 367, [1965] 2 All ER 441, CA.
6   See *Thompson v Brown Construction (Ebbw Vale) Ltd* [1981] 2 All ER 296, [1981] 1 WLR 744, HL; *Hartley v Birmingham City District Council* [1992] 2 All ER 213, CA.

Injunctions

29.26   Injunctions are equitable remedies and their award, therefore, is not subject to the provisions of the Limitation Act. However, equity has its own rules concerning delay, and these we discussed in para 12.39 above.

Part IV

Land law

Chapter 30

Land, its ownership and use

30.1 The study of land law is the study of the law relating to the rights and interests (ie 'bundles of rights') which people may have in respect of land. It deals with the nature of these rights and interests and with how they are created, transferred to other people and enforced against them. When we speak of land being bought, sold or valued, we are not strictly referring to the physical entity itself, but rather to the abstract interests which people may have in the property. We would stress, however, that although land law can be viewed as essentially concerned with abstract rights and interests, its practical context of houses and flats, offices and shops, factories and farms should be borne in mind when studying its rules.

30.2 Rights to enter, use, occupy or own land can be infinitely variable in extent, ranging from a short-lived permission for a child to come into a neighbour's garden to retrieve a ball, to a right to stay in a hotel for a week, to a right to 'own' land either for a limited period or in perpetuity. Where all the elements of a contract are present[1], the law will enforce such rights as between the parties who created them. However, the doctrine of privity of contract[2] confines enforcement to the contracting parties. Such an approach is often unsatisfactory in the context of land since the effective use and enjoyment of land often needs to be supported by rights which remain permanently enforceable. So, for example, if the only access to Whitelands is across part of Blacklands, it is essential that the right of access does not cease to be enforceable once the owner of Blacklands who first conferred the right of access either dies or ceases to own Blacklands.

For this reason, the law has long recognised that certain rights to land are 'proprietary' in nature, with the result that they are legally capable of being enjoyed by, and being enforced against, not simply those parties who first created the rights in question, but also against future owners of the land to which they relate. It is with these proprietary rights that land law is largely concerned. However we shall also briefly discuss non-proprietary, that is 'personal', rights to use land[3]. Such a discussion helps to explain the distinction between proprietary and personal rights to land; it also demonstrates that personal rights to use land play an important practical role in the use and enjoyment of land.

1 See chs 4, 5, 6 and 7 above.
2 See ch 7 above.
3 See paras 30.36–30.41 below.

30.3 Proprietary interests in land may, broadly, be divided into two groups: those in respect of one's own land and those in respect of land belonging to another person. The former category we shall call 'ownership interests'; it may be further divided into that which in effect gives absolute ownership of the land,[1] popularly referred to as the freehold interest, and those which give rise to a more limited ownership, of which the main modern example is the leasehold interest. The two main ownership interests, then, are the freehold and the leasehold, though other forms exist, such as the life interest. These ownership interests may be enjoyed by a single owner or concurrently with other owners.[2]

As well as these ownership interests, a person may have interests in respect of land which is owned by another. Examples of such interests include a private right of way over neighbouring land (a species of easement[3]), a right to prevent a neighbour building on his land (an example of a restrictive covenant[4]), or a mortgage on land granted as security for a loan to its owner.[5]

1 For the notion that, as between rival claimants, ownership is not absolute but relative, see para 32 .20 below.
2 Chs 34 and 35 below.
3 Ch 37 below.
4 Ch 38 below.
5 Ch 39 below.

30.4 What makes land law a subject of some complexity, and what makes buying and selling interests in land potentially more complicated than buying and selling a car is that it is usual for a number of interests to exist simultaneously in respect of one piece of land. For example, A may have a life interest in the property, B may have the right to enjoy the freehold on A's death (a right of future enjoyment having a present market value)[1] and C may have a 21-year lease of the property. Meanwhile X, a neighbour, may have the benefit of a covenant restricting development on the property, Y may have a private right of way across it and Z may have a mortgage on C's leasehold interest. The rules of land law are concerned with the extent of the rights enjoyed by these various people and with the protection of those rights, particularly should the freehold of the land in question be sold.

1 Paras 33.6 and 33.7 below.

30.5 In this chapter we examine the following issues:

• the way in which the law defines 'land' and the physical limits of land ownership;
• how and why the law classifies proprietary rights to land as estates or interests;
• how the law treats personal rights to use land.

What is land?

Physical extent
30.6 Land, the thing in respect of which all these rights and interests can be enjoyed, includes more than just the surface of the earth.[1] This is expressed in the Latin maxim *cuius est solum, eius est usque ad coelum et ad inferos*, which may be translated as 'he who owns the surface also owns indefinitely upwards and downwards from the surface'. So, according to the case of *Mitchell v Mosley*,[1] 'the grant of land includes the surface and all that is [above] – houses, trees and the like – ... and all that is [below], ie mines, earth, clay, etc'. On this basis, in *Grigsby v Melville*,[2] where the conveyance to the plaintiff of his semi-detached house was of 'all that dwelling-house and premises

situate on the west side of Church Hill', it was held that the plaintiff acquired ownership of the cellar beneath his house, even though it could not be reached from the house but only from the adjoining property. He became owner of all the land above and below the surface.

The principle that ownership of land extends above and below its surface is, as we shall see, subject to important limitations[3]. Furthermore, it should not be taken to preclude an owner from expressly splitting up his land by means of horizontal boundaries[4], as may occur on the sale of flats or mineral rights. In *Davies v Yadegar*[5] it was held by the Court of Appeal that the tenant of a top floor flat was entitled to insert dormer windows into the roof above his flat. His lease, which had expressly included the roof and roof space, had not specified an upper boundary to his property and, consequently, he was a tenant not only of the flat but of the airspace above the flat, into which the windows could legitimately intrude.

In law, land in the extended sense just described, also includes physical things attached to it such as fixtures and things growing naturally on the land (which we consider in the following paragraphs): it also includes certain intangible ('incorporeal') rights to use or restrict the use of the land, such as easements (which we consider in later chapters).

1   *Mitchell v Mosley* [1914] 1 Ch 438, CA.
2   [1973] 3 All ER 455, [1974] 1 WLR 80, CA.
3   See paras 30.12–30.17 below.
4   Law of Property Act 1925, s 205.
5   [1990] 1 EGLR 71, CA.

Fixtures

30.7   It is sometimes said that whatever is attached to the land becomes part of the land, but the law is not as straightforward as this. Items brought onto land fall into one of three categories: they either become part and parcel of the land, or they are fixtures (in which case they are treated as part of the land), or they remain as chattels (goods)[1]. Whether or not something becomes part and parcel of the land is 'as much a matter of common sense as precise analysis'[2]. So, in *Elitestone Ltd v Morris*[3] the House of Lords decided that a wooden bungalow resting on, but not attached to, concrete pillars had become part of the land. As a dwelling house, which the evidence showed could not be removed and re-erected elsewhere without destroying it, it must, objectively, be regarded as having been intended to serve a permanent purpose. It did not matter that the bungalow was not physically attached to the land, nor was it relevant that the parties themselves believed that the bungalow was owned separately from the site on which it stood. By way of contrast, their Lordships made it quite clear that a building which is designed to be taken apart and re-assembled elsewhere would retain its character as a chattel.[4]

Whether or not something which is attached to the land is a fixture and thus treated as part of the land depends on all the circumstances, two of which are particularly important: the degree of annexation and the purpose of annexation[5] (or, in other words, how securely the thing is attached to the land and the reasons behind its being attached). The law appears to be that if something is fixed to the land it is presumed to be land, and the more firmly it is fixed the stronger this presumption becomes. However, this presumption may be rebutted by evidence that it was not the intention behind fixing the thing to the land that it should become a permanent part of the land. For example, a poster pinned to the wall of a student's room would not be intended to become a permanent part of the land, and would not be a 'fixture'. If an item is resting on land by its own weight it is presumed to retain its own independent character and not to become part of the land, although this may be rebutted by evidence of intention.

1   *Elitestone Ltd v Morris* [1997] 2 All ER 513, HL. In many instances there is no practical consequence of the distinction between an item that becomes part and parcel of the land and one that is a fixture. However, this is not always the case; for example, an item attached to property by a tenant which becomes part and parcel of the land cannot be removed. As we shall see in para 30.9 below, tenants, on leaving the property, are allowed to remove many of the fixtures which they have attached to the property during the course of the lease.
2   Lord Lloyd in *Elitestone Ltd v Morris* [1997] 2 All ER 513, HL.
3   [1997] 2 All ER 513, HL.
4   See *Potton Developments Ltd v Thompson* [1998] NPC 49 where it was held that portable units of bedroom accommodation erected at a public house had not become part of the land but remained chattels; the units had been put together off-site, transported by lorry and put in place by crane and could be removed in the same way.
5   *Holland v Hodgson* (1872) LR 7 CP 328.

30.8   Further illustrations of whether a chattel fixed to the land has retained its chattel nature or has become a fixture are provided by the following cases. *Leigh v Taylor*[1] concerned tapestries which were put on the walls of a house by being fixed to a framework of wood and canvas which was nailed to the walls, each tapestry then being surrounded by a moulding, itself attached to the wall. The House of Lords held that the tapestries did not become part of the land and thus pass with it as fixtures, but remained chattels, since the reason they were fixed to the wall was so that they might be better enjoyed as chattels. The case of *TSB Bank plc v Botham*[2] provided the court with a rare opportunity to consider whether a range of modern household items were fixtures or chattels. The Court of Appeal ruled that fitted kitchen units and bathroom fittings (taps, showerheads, towel rails etc) were fixtures; all were necessarily attached to the property to enable those rooms to be used for their respective purposes. On the other hand, the following items were all considered to be chattels: fitted carpets, curtains, light fittings which were not part of the electrical installation, gas and electric fires, a 'slot-in' electric cooker, a plumbed-in washing machine and a refrigerator. Although all of these were in some way attached to the property, they could all be detached or disconnected without doing any damage to the fabric of the building. Furthermore, the purpose for which they were attached to the property was to enable the items themselves to function.

In contrast, in *Reynolds v Ashby*[3] the House of Lords held that machines which were let into concrete beds in the floor of a factory and fixed by nuts and bolts, but which could be removed without difficulty, became fixtures, since the purpose of annexation was to complete and use the building as a factory. Similarly, in *Aircool Installations v British Telecommunications*[4] it had to be decided whether air-conditioning equipment had become a fixture. The internal units were bolted to the walls and were linked by pipework to external units which simply rested on their own weight; the system could have been removed and installed elsewhere. The court was nevertheless satisfied that the equipment had become a fixture. It was physically attached to the premises and the purpose of the annexation was manifestly for the better enjoyment of the building to which it was fixed.

1   [1902] AC 157, HL.
2   [1996] EGCS 149, CA.
3   [1904] AC 466, HL.
4   [1995] CLY 821

30.9   *Fixtures added by a tenant*   In principle it is immaterial who paid for or who previously owned items which have become fixtures. Accordingly, fixtures added by a tenant under a lease are treated as part of the land and are therefore regarded as belonging to the freeholder, who has absolute ownership of the land. However, in practice, the effect of this last rule is modified in many instances since it has long been recognised that it operates as a disincentive, particularly for tenants who use premises for commercial purposes. Accordingly, when leaving the premises at the end of a lease, a tenant is permitted[1] to remove any domestic or ornamental fixtures[2] that he has attached and which can be removed without substantial[3] damage to the fabric of the building, together with any fixtures[2] which he has attached for the purposes of his business.[4]

1　Unless the lease clearly and unequivocally excludes the right to remove fixtures: see *Lambourn v McLellan* [1903] 2 Ch 268, CA.
2　The right of removal attaches only to fixtures, not to items which have become part and parcel of the land: see para 30.7 above.
3　In *Young v Dalgety plc* [1987] 1 EGLR 116 it was held that light fittings could be removed by a tenant even though this would cause minor damage. Such minor damage as is caused must be made good so as to leave the premises in a reasonable condition: see *Mancetter Developments Ltd v Garmanson Ltd* [1986] 1 All ER 449, CA.
4　The common law did not allow farm tenants to remove agricultural (as opposed to trade) fixtures. The right of a tenant of an agricultural holding to remove agricultural fixtures is currently governed by the Agricultural Holdings Act 1986, s 10. The right of a tenant under a farm business tenancy to remove *any* fixture is governed by the Agricultural tenancies Act 1995, s 8.

Things growing on the land
30.10　Things which grow naturally on the land (such as grass) and plants and trees which, though they may need attention when first planted, do not need attention each year to produce a crop, such as apple trees, are known as *fructus naturales* and are regarded as part of the land. On the other hand, cultivated crops, such as wheat and potatoes, which are known as *fructus industriales*, are not regarded as part of the land.

Importance of definition of land
30.11　It is important to know whether something attached to, or growing on, land is regarded as being part of the land for a variety of reasons. For our purposes the most significant of these are as follows:

- a conveyance of land operates to pass to the purchaser all the vendor's land, including fixtures and *fructus naturales*, unless excluded by the contract for sale;[1]
- the expressly agreed terms of a contract for the sale of land, but not of one for the sale of goods, must be in writing;[2] and
- where land is mortgaged, the security includes all fixtures (unless specifically excluded)[3] and *fructus naturales*.

1　Law of Property Act 1925 (LPA), s 62.
2　Law of Property (Miscellaneous Provisions) Act 1989; para 32.2 below.
3　This was the issue in *TSB Bank plc v Botham* [1996] EGCS 149, CA: see para 30.8 above.

Limitations on the physical extent of a landowner's rights
30.12　We saw in para 30.6 above that land includes not only the surface but also what is above and what is below the surface and that, on the face of it, the rights of a landowner extend over all the land as so defined. However, the maxim *cuius est solum, eius est usque ad coelum et ad inferos* must not be regarded as containing a rigid legal definition of land but rather as being a somewhat imprecise expression of the rights of a landowner[1]. While the principle at least makes it clear that the rights of a landowner normally extend above and below the surface, it is obviously fanciful to treat it as meaning that the landowner's rights literally extend upwards to the heavens and downwards to the centre of the earth, a notion which would lead to the absurdity of a trespass at common law being committed every time a satellite passes over a suburban garden.[2] On the other hand, the limits which may realistically be put on the height and

depth to which the landowner's rights extend are not easy to determine. Those which can be identified will be dealt with briefly here.

1   *Railways Comr v Valuer- General* [1974] AC 328, [1973] 3 All ER 268, PC.
2   *Bernstein v Skyviews and General Ltd* [1977] 2 All ER 902 at 907.

Airspace
30.13   We have suggested in para 24.3 above, that, following *Bernstein v Skyviews and General Ltd*,[1] the rights of a landowner as regards the airspace above the surface of his land are restricted to such a height as is necessary for the ordinary use and enjoyment of the land and the structures on it. However, this begs the question of how high that is in any particular case. This means that whether or not a trespass to airspace has been committed in any particular instance depends on the facts of each case. However, it seems likely that, whenever the intrusion emanates from a structure on adjoining land such as a building or tower crane, as opposed to a flying object such as a hot air balloon, this will constitute a trespass.[2]

1   [1977] 2 All ER 902.
2   See, for example, *Anchor Brewhouse Developments Ltd v Berkley House (Docklands Developments) Ltd* [1987] 2 EGLR 173 in which it was held that a trespass occurred where the jib of a tower crane 'oversailed' neighbouring land.

Minerals
30.14   The conventional view is that the landowner's rights do indeed extend to the earth's core, and as mining techniques improve this may turn out to be of practical importance. It certainly constitutes a trespass to tunnel into adjoining land to exploit minerals.[1] Although the general rule is that the landowner is entitled to the minerals under his land, there are exceptions, of which the following are examples. All gold and silver in gold and silver mines belong to the Crown; therefore such a mine cannot be worked by an individual even on his own land without a licence from the Crown.[2] Oil and natural gas in underground strata belong to the Crown.[3] Coal is vested in the British Coal Corporation.[4]

1   See *Bulli Coal Mining Co v Osborne* [1899] AC 351, PC.
2   *A-G v Morgan* [1891] 1 Ch 432, CA.
3   Petroleum (Production) Act 1934.
4   Coal Act 1938; Coal Industry (Nationalisation) Act 1946; Coal Industry Act 1987.

Things found on or under the land
30.15   In the absence of evidence as to their true owner, the law presumes that the landowner, if he is in possession of the land, is entitled as against the finder to:

* things fixed or buried in the land[1];
* things on the land *where the landowner obviously intends to exercise control over the property and the things in it;*[2] and
* things on the land where the finder is a trespasser.[2]

However, finds of 'treasure'[3] belong to the Crown (or any franchisee of the Crown)[4] except where any rightful owner can be identified. Treasure may be returned to the landowner or finder;[5] this is likely to occur where the find is of little historical or archaeological significance. Where it is subsequently transferred by the Crown to a museum a reward may be payable to the finder, to the landowner on whose property the treasure was found, or may be shared between such persons.[6]

1   *Waverley Borough Council v Fletcher* [1995] 4 All ER 756, CA is modern authority confirming the important distinction between items found *in* the land, and those found *on* the land. In the former case

the landowner has the superior claim even in situations where he has no obvious intention to exercise control over the property and the things in it.

2   *Parker v British Airways Board* [1982] QB 1004, [1982] 1 All ER 834, CA; see para 28.17 above.
3   'Treasure' is widely defined in the Treasure Act 1996 (which came into force on 24 September 1997), s 1 with the aim of covering all finds of historical and archaeological importance; it is no longer confined to items of gold and silver, as was the case under the old law of treasure trove.
4   Treasure Act 1996, s 4.
5   Treasure Act 1996, s 6.
6   Treasure Act 1996, s 10. The Code of Practice drawn up under s 11 of the Act clearly envisages that finders who were trespassing at the time of their find may receive either no reward at all, or a reduced reward.

Wild animals

30.16   Animals which live wild on one's land cannot be owned but, once killed on the land, they become the property of the landowner,[1] whether killed by the landowner in the exercise of his common law right to kill and take wild animals found on his land[2], or by a trespasser such as a poacher.[3]

1   *R v Townley* (1871) LR 1 CCR 315.
2   Statute makes it an offence to kill certain wild animals: see, for example, Wildlife and Countryside Act 1981, s 9.
3   *Blades v Higgs* (1865) 11 HL Cas 621.

Water

30.17   Water standing on the land in a pond or lake is part of the land and belongs to the landowner. Water percolating in undefined channels or flowing in defined channels through or past his land cannot be the subject of ownership but, although the landowner does not own the water, he has certain rights in relation to it. The most important of these is the right of abstraction. The Water Resources Act 1991,[1] s 24 lays down the general rule that the landowner may only abstract water from a 'source of supply' in pursuance of a licence obtained from the National Rivers Authority (NRA). Rivers, streams and water in underground strata all constitute 'sources of supply', as do those lakes, ponds or reservoirs which discharge into rivers or streams. However, a licence is not required for certain limited purposes.[2]

Where no NRA licence is required, a landowner is quite at liberty to abstract water percolating in undefined channels through underground strata even if this prevents any reaching his neighbour's land.[3] There is no remedy for damage to neighbouring property caused by such abstraction.[4]

Where the owner of land contiguous with a river or stream (the riparian owner) needs no NRA licence for his proposed abstraction, he is nonetheless limited in what he may take by the common law. He is free to abstract what he needs for his domestic purposes and for his cattle without regard to the effect which his use will have on landowners downstream,[5] but abstraction for other purposes (which must be connected with the land) is subject to the requirement that the water is put back in substantially the same volume and quality. The reason for this limitation is that at common law each riparian owner has the right to the flow of the river or stream unaltered in quantity and quality, and may enforce this right against owners upstream by an action in nuisance.[6] If water is abstracted in pursuance of an NRA licence, the riparian owner has a defence to such an action.[7]

The riparian owner also has the right to fish in non-tidal waters, even where they are navigable rivers.[8]

1   Which re-enacts the rules previously laid down in the Water Resources Act 1963, as amended by the Water Act 1989.
2   Water Resources Act 1991, s 27.
3   *Bradford Corpn v Pickles* [1895] AC 587, HL; para 17.10 above.

4   *Langbrook Properties Ltd v Surrey County Council* [1969] 3 All ER 1424, [1970] 1 WLR 161; *Stephens v Anglian Water Authority* [1987] 3 All ER 379, [1987] 1 WLR 1381, CA.
5   *Miner v Gilmour* (1859) 12 Moo PCC 131.
6   *John Young & Co v Bankier Distillery Co* [1893] AC 691, HL; *Tate and Lyle Industries Ltd v Greater London Council* [1983] 2 AC 509, [1983] 1 All ER 1159, HL.
7   Water Resources Act 1991, s 48.
8   *Cooper v Phibbs* (1867) LR 2 HL 149; *Pearce v Scotcher* (1882) 9 QBD 162, DC.

Boundaries

The general law

30.18   Clearly it is important for a landowner to know the exact extent of his land, in order to know precisely what he has bought and can sell, or to prevent neighbours encroaching, or to know how much space is available for building. As a matter of law a boundary is simply an imaginary line which marks the confines or line of division of two contiguous parcels of land; in practice, the location of a boundary is often marked by some physical object such as a wall, hedge or fence. Unfortunately, despite the obvious importance of ensuring that the line of the boundary is clearly delineated in the conveyance or transfer of the property, this is frequently either not done at all or is left unclear, with the result that the question remains to be settled after the property has been transferred, often as a result of a boundary dispute between neighbours. As we shall see,[1] there are two separate systems of conveyancing in England and Wales; that which applies where title to the land is registered, and that which governs unregistered land. The legal rules governing the ascertainment of the exact line of a boundary depend in part on which of these systems applies.

1   Ch 31 below.

30.19   Where the title to the land is registered, the land to be transferred is generally described in the transfer deed merely as 'the land comprised in Title Number ... ', a form of words which thereby incorporates the description of the land in the Property Register of the register of title. However, this description normally gives only the address and refers to the Filed Plan, and since that plan, though an accurate Ordnance Survey Plan, is usually on a scale of 1:1250 and in any event does not purport to show the exact line of the legal boundary,[1] there remains much scope for uncertainty as to where the boundaries of the property lie.

1   Land Registration Rules (LRR), r 278.

30.20   In unregistered land, the determination of the boundaries depends upon what is stated in the conveyance. A clear verbal description in the 'parcels clause' of the conveyance will be conclusive (subject to what is said in para 30.25 below, concerning alteration of boundaries). If a verbal description is clear, but is inconsistent with a plan incorporated in the conveyance, the plan will normally only prevail where it is stated that the property is 'more particularly delineated' in the plan.[1] The verbal description will prevail where the plan is referred to 'for the purpose of identification only'.[2] Where, however, the verbal description is unclear or ambiguous, the court may have regard to a plan, however it is referred to,[3] in order to elucidate and supplement the verbal description, so long as it does not positively conflict with it.[4]

Any plan incorporated in a conveyance must be adequate to perform its intended function. In particular, if the plan is intended to prevail over any verbal description or is the sole means of identification, it is of the utmost importance that it is drawn to a sufficiently large scale to make it possible to represent the property and its boundaries in precise detail, giving dimensions and any other features which may be necessary to put beyond doubt the subject matter of the conveyance.[5]

Where the conveyance as a whole still leaves the matter of the boundaries unclear the court will have regard to extrinsic evidence, such as the contract itself,[6] auction particulars,[7] photographs and suveyors' oral evidence,[8] planning permission,[9] and any acts of ownership in relation to some boundary feature by one of the parties, such as the erection and maintenance of a boundary fence.

In a number of cases, where evidence is lacking as to the line of the boundary, the courts resort to certain rebuttable presumptions[10], which we consider in the following paragraphs.

1   *Eastwood v Ashton* [1915] AC 900, HL.
2   *Hopgood v Brown* [1955] 1 All ER 550, [1955] 1 WLR 213, CA.
3   And even if it is only annexed to the conveyance but not referred to in it: *Leachman v L & K Richardson Ltd* [1969] 3 All ER 20, [1969] 1 WLR 1129.
4   *Wigginton & Milner Ltd v Winster Engineering Ltd* [1978] 3 All ER 436, [1978] 1 WLR 1462, CA; *Scott v Martin* [1987] 2 All ER 813, [1987] 1 WLR 841, CA. In practice, a plan may more readily be resorted to where the property being conveyed is a newly created one (as with a first purchase of a house on a new development) since the verbal description of such a property (classically 'all that property known as Number 10 Acacias Avenue') may be of little assistance; see *Targett v Ferguson* (1996) 72 P & CR 106, CA.
5   *Scarfe v Adams* [1981] 1 All ER 843 at 852.
6   *Spall v Owen* (1981) 44 P & CR 36.
7   *Scarfe v Adams* [1981] 1 All ER 843, CA.
8   *Mayer v Hurr* (1983) 49 P & CR 56, CA.
9   *Stock v David Wilson Homes (Anglia)* [1993] NPC 83, CA.
10 Ie rules which apply only in the absence of evidence to the contrary; see para 1.13 above.

Presumptions

30.21   *Walls*   The outside of any external wall is presumed to be included in a sale or lease of the property[1], thus in one case[2] it was held to constitute trespass for a landlord to affix advertising hoardings to the outside wall of premises which he had let on the second floor of his property. As to where the legal boundary lies between two floors of a building, which have been separately let, it has been held that the ordinary expectation is that the lease entitles the tenant to occupy all the space between the floor of his flat and the underneath of the floor of the flat above.[3]

1   *Sturge v Hackett* [1962] 1 WLR 1257, CA.
2   *Re Webb's Lease* [1951] Ch 808
3   *Graystone Property Investments Ltd v Margulies* (1983) 47 P & CR 472, CA.

30.22   *Hedges and ditches*   Where parties are disputing[1] the exact line of a boundary along which runs a hedge or bank together with a ditch, the presumption of the law is that the boundary runs along the edge of the ditch furthest from the hedge or bank. This presumption derives from the quaint notion that the ditch was originally dug by the landowner at the furthest edge of his land and then, to avoid trespass, the resulting earth was thrown behind him onto his own land.[2] This presumption only applies where there is a hedge (or bank) and a ditch together. Where land bounded by a hedge is conveyed expressly by reference to the Ordnance Survey map, it appears that the court may, in the absence of other evidence, presume that the boundary lies down the middle of the hedge, following what has been the Ordnance Survey practice.[3] It does not follow that this latter presumption automatically applies to registered land transfers[4] because it is expressly stated that the plan does not purport to fix the legal boundary.[5]

1   The presumption only comes into play once there is an actual dispute. Hence, if at that time it is found that the line of the boundary has been fixed by an earlier conveyance, it cannot be argued that the presumption had determined the line of the boundary prior to that earlier conveyance: see *Alan Wibberley Building Ltd v Insley* [1998] 2 All ER 82, CA.
2   *Vowles v Miller* (1810) 3 Taunt 137. For a recent application of the presumption see *Hall v Dorling* (1997) 74 P & CR 400, CA.

3   *Fisher v Winch* [1939] 1 KB 666; *Davey v Harrow Corpn* [1958] 1 QB 60, [1957] 2 All ER 305, CA.
4   Para 30.19 above.
5   LRR, r 278.

30.23   *Highways*[1]   It is presumed that, wherever land is expressed in the conveyance to be bounded by a highway, the conveyance passes half of the road, so that the boundary line lies down the middle of the road.[2] This presumption, which applies only where there is no other evidence as to the boundary, is easily rebutted, for example in the case of a building estate where the developer might intend to retain ownership of the roads for construction purposes and for dedication to the public. We should add the important caveat that where the highway has been adopted by the highway authority,[3] there vests in that authority the surface and so much above and below the surface as is necessary for the carrying out of their duties as highway authority. Thus, where the highway is adopted, we are concerned only with ownership of the subsoil. In the case of registered land, it is not the practice of the Land Registry to show ownership of the subsoil where the highway is adopted.

1   Para 38.14 below.
2   *Central London Rly Co v City of London Land Tax Comrs* [1911] 1 Ch 467 at 474.
3   Highways Act 1980.

30.24   *Rivers, etc*   In the case of non-tidal rivers which form a boundary to land, it is presumed that the boundary runs down the middle of the river bed. The rights of fishing and abstraction, described in para 30.10 above, would therefore be divided midstream between opposite riparian owners. In the case of land bounded by a tidal river or by the seashore, the boundary lies at the medium high water mark, the foreshore being vested in the Crown. There appears to be no presumption to assist in determining the boundary where the land of several owners is bounded by a lake.

Alteration of boundaries

30.25   The line of a boundary may be altered by agreement of the parties. Since this will involve the transfer of land from one party to the other such an agreement should be by deed and completed by registration, so as to comply with the formalities required for the conveyance of an interest in land[1]. Where, as is often the case, such formalities are not complied with, the courts may be able to give effect to the agreement by the operation of the doctrine of estoppel.[2] The line of a boundary may also be changed by the effect of rectification of the title register where the Land Registration Act applies,[3] or by the operation of the Limitation Act (as where a landowner moves the boundary fence so as to incorporate some of his neighbour's land and remains in adverse possession for the requisite period).[4]

If a boundary dispute arises, it is possible that the parties may, informally, agree where the boundary between their properties lies. Such an agreement does not involve the transfer of any land and so it is not necessary for a deed to be used. However, it is likely that no consideration is provided with the result that the agreement has no contractual force. Nevertheless, the courts will strive to give effect to the parties' intentions, either by resorting to the doctrine of estoppel,[2] or by treating the agreement as evidence of where the boundary lies. So, in *Davey v Harrow Corpn*,[5] where adjoining landowners had agreed to the erection of a post and wire fence along the boundary, the Court of Appeal ruled that this rebutted any presumption which might otherwise have been relevant in determining the boundary line between the two properties, which were separated by a hedge and a ditch but had been conveyed by reference to the Ordnance Survey map.

1   See Ch 31 below.

2   As in *Hopgood v Brown* [1955] 1 All ER 550, CA. See further paras 32.11–32.15 below.
3   Para 35.36 below.
4   Paras 32.19–32.41 below.
5   [1958] 1 QB 60, [1957] 2 All ER 305, CA.

Boundary structures

30.26   Obviously any boundary structure exclusively on one side of the boundary belongs to the owner of that side, even though the neighbour may have the right that it be maintained.[1] It may be that the owner of land is unable to repair or maintain a boundary structure which belongs to him (or other parts of his property) without going onto adjoining land. As we have seen, at common law, there is no automatic right of access for such purposes so that in the absence of an express right of access, or a temporary permission from the neighbour, the landowner would be committing a trespass which can be restrained by an injunction.[2] This unsatisfactory state of affairs has been remedied by the Access to Neighbouring Land Act 1992.[3]

In practice many boundary structures straddle the line of the boundary. Irrespective of the nature of the structure it is known, in law, as a 'party wall'. In the ordinary case, party walls are regarded as being vertically severed, each side having the right to support from the other.[4] The Party Wall etc Act 1996[5] provides a scheme under which works can be carried out to party structures, and any disputes over such works resolved, without recourse to the courts.[6]

1   See para 37.50 below.
2   See para 24.9 above.
3   Discussed at para 24.7 above.
4   LPA, s 38.
5   Which came into force on 1 July 1997.
6   This effectively extends the scheme which used to be set out in Part VI of the London Building (Amendment) Act 1939 and which applied in London only to the whole of England and Wales.

Legal nature of proprietary rights to land

Ownership interests: estates and tenure

30.27   Having considered the legal nature of land and the physical extent of a landowner's rights, we now return to the nature of what we have called ownership interests in land. Under English law ownership of land is categorised according to the length of time for which it will last, a notion which finds expression in the doctrine of *estates*. Thus, rather than speaking of owning land in perpetuity or for life, we speak of owning a particular 'estate'[1] in the land which will last for ever, or for the lifetime of its owner. Furthermore, to be more accurate, we should speak not of *owning* land for a particular estate but of *holding* land for a particular estate. The reason for this is that, as a matter of legal theory – and it has almost no practical significance – all land is regarded as being 'owned' by the Crown, individual subjects of the Crown merely 'holding' particular estates from the Crown. This is the doctrine of tenure. We shall now briefly consider these two historical building blocks of English land law, the doctrine of *tenure* and the doctrine of *estates*.

1   The term is here used in its technical land law sense, rather than as a synonym for 'land'.

Tenure

30.28   Feudalism, in which tenure (from the Latin, *tenere*, to hold) was the basic element, formed the basis of society after the Norman Conquest. The social structure was based on grants of land by the king (to whom all land was regarded as belonging as the spoils of victory) to his followers, not as theirs to own, but to 'hold of' him (or 'have possession of' from him) as their superior lord in return for their performing certain services, such as furnishing the king with armed horsemen or with provisions. These 'tenants-in-chief' in their turn granted some of this land to other 'tenants' to hold of them as superior lords in return for services, and so on. Each tenant, then, held land in return for providing services to his lord. The theoretical possibility of creating an ever-increasing tenurial chain, with every grant of land involving the grantor and grantee in a tenurial relationship, was eventually cut short by the Statute *Quia Emptores* 1290. This statute, which is still law, had the effect that on every grant of freehold land, the grantee would step into the grantor's position on the feudal ladder and would not hold the land as tenant of the grantor as superior lord. *Quia Emptores* marked the beginning of the contraction of the tenurial system. Succeeding centuries saw a gradual decline in the practical significance of the system of tenure, with the benefits and obligations of tenure gradually disappearing, so that all that remains today is the legal theory that land is not owned outright but held of the Crown.

Estates

30.29 Although we referred in the last paragraph to the tenant holding land, it is more accurate to speak of the tenant holding the land for a particular estate, ie having possession of the land for an interest of a particular duration. The two most important estates are popularly referred to as the freehold and the leasehold. Historically, the law recognised other estates, in particular the fee tail and the life estate. The social importance of these has declined considerably over the years, and a change in the legal machinery for giving effect to them means that we shall postpone our discussion of them until chapter 33, concentrating here on the freehold and the leasehold.

30.30 *Freehold: the fee simple absolute in possession* The technical legal term for the freehold is the estate in fee simple absolute in possession.[1] The significance of this term is as follows. 'Fee' denoted, *historically*, an estate of inheritance, that is, an estate which, prior to the reforming property legislation of 1925, automatically passed on the death of the current owner to his legally designated heir. This type of fee was described as a fee 'simple' to distinguish it from the other variety of inheritable fee, the fee tail,[2] under which only the direct lineal descendants of the person originally granted the land (or that person and a particular spouse) could inherit it. The term 'absolute' distinguishes this type of fee simple from the rarely encountered, conditional and determinable fees simple, which we discuss later.[3] The words 'in possession' mean that the landowner must either be physically in possession of the land or in receipt of the rents and profits of the land,[4] and they distinguish a *present* ownership interest from future enjoyment of the land, a topic which we reserve until chapter 33.[5]

The owner of a fee simple absolute in possession is, in law, equivalent to an absolute owner. He has the complete freedom to dispose of his rights to the land either during his lifetime or under his will; in other words, he can transfer ownership of his property as he wishes. He can also carve lesser ownership interests out of his freehold, for example by granting a lease, and can grant rights over it (such as easements or mortgages) to others.

1   LPA, s 1.
2   Para 33.4 below.
3   At para 33.5 below.
4   LPA, s 205(1).
5   At paras 33.6 and 33.7 below.

30.31 *Leasehold: the term of years absolute*[1] The leasehold interest is the second of the two estates recognised at law. The terminology used in the Law of Property Act

1925 (LPA), s 1 for the leasehold interest is 'the term of years absolute'. This phrase need not detain us; it can be regarded as having no meaning other than to denote a leasehold interest. A person has a leasehold interest in land where another, the landlord or lessor, grants him exclusive possession of property, as tenant or lessee, for a definite or certain period.[2] The leasehold interest acquired by the tenant or lessee is known variously as a 'tenancy' – generally where it is of short duration, as in weekly, monthly or yearly tenancies – or as a 'lease', 'demise', 'term of years' or 'term certain' – generally where it is of longer, fixed, duration, perhaps of 21 or 99 years. Having granted a lease (or 'let', 'leased' or 'demised' the property) the lessor is said, somewhat inaccurately, to retain the 'reversion' on the lease,[3] on the basis that physical possession of the land will revert to him on the ending of the lease. In the eyes of the law, of course, he is still regarded as being in possession in that he is in receipt of the rents and profits of the land.[4]

1   Leaseholds interests are considered in more detail in ch 36, below.
2   See paras 36.3–36.7 below.
3   See also para 33.7 below.
4   LPA, s 205(1) (xix); paras 30.30 above and 33.6 below.

Third party rights: interests in land
30.32   We have already mentioned[1] that the law recognises not only ownership rights in respect of land, but also rights which one person may have over land which belongs to another, such as private rights of way. Where such rights fall within certain legally defined categories[2] they are regarded as interests in land. Interests in land, which are usually referred to, somewhat confusingly, as 'third party' rights, are 'proprietary' in nature. This means that they are capable of binding future owners of the land to which they relate, in other words that future owners can be obliged to recognise such rights.[3]

1   See para 30.3 above.
2   The most important of which are dealt with in chs 37–39 below.
3   The circumstances in which third party rights actually bind future owners are dealt with in ch 35 below.

Legal and equitable rights to land
30.33   The Law of Property Act 1925, s 1 distinguishes between legal estates and interests on the one hand, and equitable interests on the other. The freehold, or fee simple absolute in possession, and the leasehold, or term of years absolute, are now, by virtue of that section, the only estates that can exist at law. They are the two legal estates. Other forms of ownership, such as the life estate, which were formerly recognised by the law, today can only take effect as equitable interests.[1] The section also provides that only certain third party rights[2] can exist at law. The more important of these are easements[3] (rights of way, rights of support and the like) which have been granted for a period equivalent to a fee simple absolute in possession or term of years absolute, and charges by way of legal mortgage,[4] the most common device for mortgaging land. These are referred to as legal interests. Those third party rights which cannot take effect as legal interests now do so as equitable interests.

1   LPA, s 1(3); see ch 33 below.
2   Para 30.32 above.
3   Ch 37 below.
4   Para 39.6 below.

What is an equitable interest?
30.34   An equitable interest is either (as explained in the previous paragraph) an interest which, after 1925,[1] can no longer exist at law, or it is one which is derived from the rules of equity (ie those principles of law which originated in the decisions

of the former Court of Chancery [2]). As we shall see, apart from recognising rights for which the common law could find no place (such as restrictive covenants), equity was prepared to give effect to transactions which do not comply with the strict formalities demanded by the common law.[3] Whether a right is legal or equitable often makes little difference to its substance; however, the distinction can be crucial in determining its enforceability against future owners.[4]

1   As a result of LPA 1925, s 1.
2   Paras 1.9 and 1.10 above.
3   Ch 32 below.
4   Ch 35 below.

30.35   *The trust* One equitable concept which plays a particularly important part in the English law of property (both real and personal) is that of the 'trust'. The idea which lies behind the trust is that of separating the management of property from the enjoyment of its benefits, such as possession of it and income from it. The device is said to have originated in the practice of those going on crusades of transferring their land to trusted friends to hold for the benefit of their wives and children while they were away, and in the practice of granting land to be held for the benefit of Franciscan friars who, by the rules of their Order, could not themselves hold land. In the eyes of the common law, only those to whom the land had been conveyed had rights in respect of it; those for whose benefit the land was supposed to have been held were viewed as having no rights. The Court of Chancery, however, took a very different approach, and recognised that the persons to whom the land was conveyed (who are today known as trustees) were in conscience bound to observe the trust placed in them. This court obliged the trustees to deal with the land in accordance with the wishes of the person whom it was intended to benefit (whom we now call the beneficiary), and to permit him to use or take the income of the land. That the beneficiary had these rights against the trustees effectively meant that the trustees had only the bare legal ownership of the land, whilst the beneficial ownership lay with the beneficiary.

The trust has always been, and still is, used as a protective device under which the legal title and management responsibilities can be placed in the hands of an experienced and responsible trustee in order to guard the interests of a young and vulnerable (or, perhaps, not so young but irresponsible) beneficiary. However, it has always had other roles. From earliest times it was used as a pure conveyancing device. For example, it was possible to create a greater range of ownership rights in respect of the equitable interest in land than in the legal interest; further, it was possible to leave an equitable interest in land by will long before this was permitted at law. In more modern times, it became usual to create a trust of land where it was desired to give a number of different people ownership and other interests in the same piece of land, either in succession, or concurrently. In this way the legal title to the land, which would be vested in a limited number of trustees, could be kept relatively straightforward; the complex equitable interests being kept 'behind' the trust. This latter use of the trust was greatly extended by the 1925 property legislation and is a topic to which we return in chapters 33 and 34. Finally, equity has come to employ the trust as a means of compelling a common law owner of land, in appropriate circumstances, to hold 'his' land for the benefit of another. So, for example, as we shall see,[1] where land is conveyed to A alone but B has contributed to the purchase price, equity may insist that A holds the land on trust for himself and B.

1   See para 33.23 below. For other such uses of the trust, see paras 32.8–32.10 below.

Personal rights to use land: licences

30.36   An owner of land is free to confer on others a right to use his land which does not amount to an interest in land. Such rights, although infinitely variable in content, are collectively known as 'licences'. The classic definition of a licence relating to land states that a licence passes no interest in the land but only makes lawful what would otherwise be unlawful.[1] It would appear, then, that a licence to enter on, or to occupy, property is a personal arrangement between the licensor and the licensee under which the licensee acquires no interest in the property. If a licence creates no property interest but is dependent on the permission of the licensor, why is the topic of licences included in the study of land law? First, because occupation of land by virtue of a licence has been common as a substitute for occupation by virtue of a tenancy, as a means of avoiding legislation which protects the rights of tenants[2], so that the courts have frequently been called upon to draw the fine line between a licence (which is not a property interest) and a lease (which is).[3] Second, because the courts may, in certain circumstances, recognise certain types of use and occupation of land which are, on the face of it, enjoyed merely by licence as having proprietary characteristics, in particular that of being enforceable against subsequent owners of the land.[4]

Licences fall into one of the following categories

* gratuitous licences (sometimes referred to as 'bare' licences); or
* contractual licences; or
* licences coupled with an interest.

The characteristics and nature of these various types of licence will be discussed in the following paragraphs.

1   *Thomas v Sorrell* (1673) Vaugh 330 at 351.
2   Eg Rent Act 1977, Landlord and Tenant Act 1954.
3   See paras 36.9 and 36.10 below
4   Paras 32.8–32.18 below.

Gratuitous licences

30.37 A gratuitous licence is, in essence, a permission to be on land for which no consideration has been provided. The guest whom you invite to dinner has, when he comes to dinner, a gratuitous licence to be on your property. Your young neighbour, who with your permission enters your garden to retrieve his ball, is a gratuitous licensee. When a householder who lives in a dwelling-house which has a front garden garden in front and does not lock the gate of the garden, this amounts to an implied licence to any member of the public who has a lawful reason for doing so to proceed from the gate to the front door or back door, and to inquire whether he may be admitted to conduct his lawful business.[1] Although most gratuitous licences are of the relatively trivial variety just mentioned, it should be remembered that this category is a residual one; consequently any licence not falling within one of the other categories is a gratuitous licence.[2]

In each of the above examples the right of the licensee to be on the land is dependent entirely on the permission, express or implied, of the landowner/licensor. Without that permission, the licensee would be a trespasser. The licensee has no right to prevent the revocation of his licence and the landowner may revoke the permission to be on the land at any time. A withdrawal of permission does not mean that the licensee immediately becomes a trespasser. The law allows him a reasonable time to leave the premises; what is reasonable will vary according to the circumstances of the case.[1]

Clearly a gratuitous licence, being entirely dependent on the permission of the landowner, is neither assignable by the licensee nor, in the absence of additional factors, enforceable against successors of the licensor.[3]

1   *Robson v Hallett* [1967] 2 QB 939 at 953, 954, [1967] 2 All ER 407 at 414.

2   See, for example, *Horrocks v Forray* [1976] 1 All ER 737, [1976] 1 WLR 230; para 30.38 below.
3   Discussed at paras 32.8–32.18 below.

Contractual licences
Nature
30.38   A licence to enter land is a contractual licence if it is conferred by contract; hence, unless a deed is used, consideration must have been provided for the permission to be on the land. It is immaterial whether the right to enter the land is the primary purpose of the contract or is merely secondary.[1] An example of the former would be a contractual licence to hire a room for a function, or to occupy a room in a house as a lodger. (As we shall see,[2] in neither of these cases does the occupier have exclusive possession, hence there is no tenancy, merely a licence.) An example of a licence conferred as a secondary object of a contract is provided by *Hounslow London Borough Council v Twickenham Garden Developments Ltd*,[3] in which the primary object of the contract was that the defendants should build a housing estate for the plaintiffs; it was held that this necessarily conferred on the defendants a licence to enter the site.

Not surprisingly, in order for a contractual licence to be valid, it must be shown that the essential requirements of a contract are present. In certain cases where there has been no express agreement between the parties, the courts have been able to discern the presence of the requirements of a contract and thereby imply the existence of a contractual licence between the parties. In *Chandler v Kerley*,[4] the Court of Appeal was satisfied that an arrangement under which the defendant, a former co-owner of the property, agreed to sell it to the plaintiff for two-thirds of the asking price on the understanding that she and her children could continue to live there, amounted to a contractual licence. However, it is often impossible, particularly in a family context, to infer the necessary ingredients of a contract, notably any intention to create legal relations. So, in *Horrocks v Forray*,[5] the court was unable to treat an arrangement between a man and his mistress, whereby the former had for many years provided accommodation for the latter, as a contractual licence. In the absence of any additional factors[6] she was regarded as having only a bare licence and could not resist his executors' claim for possession of the house in which she lived.

1   *Hounslow London Borough Council v Twickenham Garden Developments Ltd* [1971] Ch 233 at 254, [1970] 3 All ER 326 at 343.
2   Para 36.8 below.
3   [1971] Ch 233, [1970] 3 All ER 326.
4   [1978] 2 All ER 942, [1978] 1 WLR 693, CA.
5   [1976] 1 All ER 737, [1976] 1 WLR 230, CA.
6   Paras 32.8–32.18 below.

Revocability
30.39   A contractual licence is not an entity distinct from the contract which brings it into being, but merely a provision of that contract.[1] Thus the extent to which the licensor is free to revoke the licence depends on the terms, express or implied, of the contract. It is a question of construction of the particular contract whether a purported revocation by the licensor is or is not in breach of contract.[2] In the absence of express terms there is no general rule as to the revocability of a contractual licence,[3] although (where there is no other evidence of the parties' intentions) it appears that the courts will readily imply a term that the licence is revocable on reasonable notice being given;[4] what is 'reasonable' depending on the circumstances of the case.

If the licensor purports to revoke the licence in breach of contract, what is the licensee to do? He has a contractual right to remain on the property despite the wrongful revocation by the licensor and cannot be treated as a trespasser[5] (and, if he is forcibly removed as a trespasser, he may sue for damages for assault).[6] If it is practicable for the licensee to seek the assistance of the court, he may obtain an injunction to prevent his being turned out or, in a case where the licensor refuses to let him enter in the first place, an order of specific performance.[7] However, these orders are available only at the discretion of the court, and, for example, the court will not specifically enforce an agreement for two people to live peaceably under the same roof.[8] A licensee who cannot obtain an order enforcing the contractual licence, either because in the circumstances it is not practicable for him to seek one[9] or because the licence is not regarded as specifically enforceable, must, unless he can otherwise secure peaceable entry to the property, accept the termination of the licence as a fait accompli and sue for damages for breach of contract.

1   *Hounslow London Borough Council v Twickenham Garden Developments Ltd* [1971] Ch 233 at 254, [1970] 3 All ER 326 at 343.
2   *Millennium Productions Ltd v Winter Garden Theatre (London) Ltd* [1946] 1 All ER 678, CA; rvsd sub nom *Winter Garden Theatre (London) Ltd v Millennium Productions Ltd* [1948] AC 173, [1947] 2 All ER 331, HL.
3   *Australian Blue Metal Ltd v Hughes* [1963] AC 74 at 99.
4   *Winter Garden Theatre (London) Ltd v Millennium Productions Ltd* [1948] AC 173, [1947] 2 All ER 331, HL; *Chandler v Kerley* [1978] 2 All ER 942, [1978] 1 WLR 693, CA.
5   *Winter Garden Theatre (London) Ltd v Millennium Productions Ltd* [1948] AC 173, [1947] 2 All ER 331, HL.
6   See *Hurst v Picture Theatres Ltd* [1915] 1 KB 1, CA.
7   *Verrall v Great Yarmouth Borough Council* [1981] QB 202, [1980] 1 All ER 839, CA.
8   *Thompson v Park* [1944] KB 408 at 409, [1944] 2 All ER 477 at 479.
9   As where a customer is threatened with eviction from a theatre performance, or from a restaurant.

Enforceability against third parties

30.40   In principle, the modern view that a contractual licence has no existence independent of the contract which creates it[1] means that the licensee cannot enforce his contractual right to remain on land against a successor of the licensor, for the arrangement between licensor and licensee is a personal contractual arrangement giving the licensee no interest in the land capable of binding the third party.[2] Thus, for example, the occupier of a university hall of residence room under a contractual licence could not insist on remaining in the hall were it sold by the university to a third party; his remedy would lie in damages against the licensor.[3] It follows that, although a person may enjoy under the terms of a contractual licence rights which appear to be very similar to a lease or easement, the contractual licence does not possess that most important characteristic of an interest in land, that of being capable of binding third parties. This is confirmed by the decision of the Court of Appeal in *Ashburn Anstalt v Arnold*,[4] where it was held that a mere contractual licence to occupy land is not binding on a purchaser of the land even though he has notice of the licence. In reaching this decision, the Court of Appeal held that its earlier decision in *Errington v Errington and Woods*,[5] in which the contrary view was taken, could not stand with the decisions of the Court of Appeal in *Clore v Theatrical Properties Ltd*[6] and of the House of Lords in *King v David Allen & Sons Billposting Ltd*.[7]

However, there are cases in which a person who occupies or uses property under a licence which may have been gratuitous or contractual at the outset is protected by equity from having his enjoyment of the property terminated by the licensor. In some instances the courts have even been prepared to enforce the licensee's rights against a subsequent purchaser.[8] The devices used include the doctrine of proprietary estoppel and the constructive trust. These are discussed more fully at paras 32.8–32.18, below.

1   Para 30.39 above.
2   *Clore v Theatrical Properties Ltd* [1936] 3 All ER 483, CA.
3   *King v David Allen & Sons Billposting Ltd* [1916] 2 AC 54, HL.
4   [1989] Ch 1, [1988] 2 All ER 147, CA.

5   [1952] 1 KB 290, [1952] 1 All ER 149, CA. It appears that in *Street v Mountford* (para 36.9 below) the
     House of Lords treated this ease as being concerned not with a licence at all but with an estate contract.
     The disapproval of *Errington v Errington and Woods* in *Ashburn Anstalt v Arnold* would appear to
     apply with equal force to another decision of the Court of Appeal, in *Midland Bank Ltd v Farmpride
     Hatcheries Ltd* (1980) 260 Estates Gazette 493.
6   [1936] 3 All ER 483.
7   [1916] 2 AC 54.
8   See, for example, *Inwards v Baker* [1965] 2 QB 29, [1965] 1 All ER 446, CA.

Licences coupled with an interest

30.41   These are licences which are linked to a recognised property interest. The
interest with which the licence is most commonly coupled is a *profit à prendre*,[1] such
as a right to take fish or game or crops from the land; the licence is to enter the land so
as to exercise the profit. Alternatively, the licence might be coupled with a chattel
interest; an example might be a licence to enter land to remove cut timber which one
has purchased.[2] So long as the proprietary interest exists, the licence cannot be revoked.
In fact, since a licence coupled with an interest exhibits all the characteristics of the
interest with which it is coupled, we consider that it is not strictly necessary to regard
the licence as legally separate from, rather than an integral part of, the proprietary
interest.

1   Paras 37.16–37.18 below.
2   *James Jones & Sons Ltd v Earl of Tankerville* [1909] 2 Ch 440.

Chapter 31

The formal acquisition of rights to land

31.1 The context in which most people experience the operation of land law is that of the transfer or creation of rights to land. The most commonly encountered transactions are the transfer of freehold ownership, the transfer (technically 'assignment') of the remainder of an existing lease, or the creation of a new lease. As part and parcel of any of these arrangements it will be usual for interests in land such as easements or mortgages to be transferred or created, although such interests can, of course, be created quite independently of any transfer.

Many land transactions can, legally speaking, be broken down into three stages:

- a binding agreement to carry out the agreed deal (the contract);
- the actual creation or transfer of the interest in land (the conveyance or transfer); and
- registration at the Land Registry.

As we shall see, the contract and the conveyance or transfer must *each* comply with *different* formal requirements; registration is applied for by the purchaser (or lessee or assignee where appropriate) and is effected by the Land Registry.

Not surprisingly, it is the common law which has always demanded that the actual disposition of interests in land should comply with strict formalities; these rules have long been enshrined in statutory provisions.[1] Furthermore, ever since the 17th century, legislation has dictated that contracts for the sale or other disposition of land should also satisfy formal requirements, albeit that these are different from those required for actual dispositions.[2] In practice, given the importance of such transactions to those involved, these formalities are normally observed, if only because it is usual for the parties to employ legal advisers. However, in those cases where these rules are not complied with, equity will sometimes intervene and give effect to the parties' intentions.[3] Furthermore, as we shall see, there are occasions where the common law is prepared to acknowledge that, even in the absence of any documentary evidence, freehold ownership[4] or an easement[5] has arisen on the basis of long unchallenged possession or use.

The rules governing the creation and transfer of interests in land are further complicated by the process of registration of title. As we shall see,[6] many titles to land are already entered on a central Land Register. Any dealings with such land not only must comply with the general law, but must also be carried out in accordance with the specific rules laid down for registered land. In cases where title is not yet registered, most transactions now trigger a requirement for the title to be registered so that compliance with registered land rules is also necessary. Hence it is only in respect of transactions relating to unregistered land which do not trigger registration of title, or the creation of titles to registered land which do not require registration (eg short leases) that the Land Registry procedures can be ignored.

In this chapter, we shall consider:

- the formalities with which contracts for the sale or other disposition of land must comply;
- the formalities with which the actual transfer or creation of legal or equitable rights to land must comply;
- the circumstances in which the transfer or creation of legal rights to land must be completed by registration at the Land Registry; and
- the typical process of negotiating and then transferring the ownership of land from one person to another.

1   Paras 31.6 and 31.7 below.
2   Paras 31.2 and 31.5 below.
3   Paras 32.2–32.18 below.
4   Paras 32.19–32.31 below.
5   Para 32.19 and paras 37.33–37.44 below.
6   Paras 31.8–31.10 below.
7   In 1998 the Land Registry estimated that some 16 million titles are registered, leaving some 6 million as yet unregistered.

Formal requirements governing contracts for the sale of land

The statutory requirements

31.2   A contract for the sale or other disposition of land is a legally binding agreement under which an owner of an interest in land becomes committed to transfer that interest to the purchaser. It is *not* the actual transfer of the interest in question; this takes place at the second and third stages of the transaction.[1] Such contracts must, of course, satisfy all the usual legal requirements relating to the formation of a contract.[2] In particular (and self-evidently), any agreement for the sale of land will fail to meet the contractual prerequisite for certainty unless it identifies the parties, the price or other consideration, and the property which is being sold. However, land contracts must also comply with additional rules governing the form in which they must be made. Prior to 27 September 1989 contracts for the sale or other disposition of any interest in land did not necessarily have to be in writing; an oral contract would be enforceable either if sufficiently *evidenced* by a written memorandum or, in equity, by an act of part performance.[3] However, since the Law of Property (Miscellaneous Provisions) Act 1989,[4] such[5]contracts[6] must now comply with the following requirements:

- the agreement must be in writing;
- all the terms expressly agreed by the parties must be incorporated in one document (or, where contracts are exchanged, in each document);
- the document or, in the case of an exchange, one of the documents (though not necessarily the same one) must be signed by or on behalf of each party;
- the expressly agreed terms may either be set out in the signed document or be incorporated by reference to some other document.

1   See para 31.6 below.
2   See chapters 5 and 6 above.

3   LPA, s 40 as bolstered by the equitable doctrine of part performance. Under this doctrine, a plaintiff who acted so as to alter his position in reliance on the contract, in circumstances which pointed to the existence of a contract with the defendant, might obtain specific performance of the contract despite the lack of writing.

4   Law of Property (Miscellaneous Provisions) Act 1989, s 2(1).

5   The Law of Property (Miscellaneous Provisions) Act 1989, s 2(5) provides that the following three types of land contract do not have to be in writing in order to be valid: contracts made in the course of a public auction; contracts to grant a lease not exceeding three years taking effect in possession at the best rent reasonably obtainable; and contracts regulated under the Financial Services Act 1986. Furthermore, the Act does not affect the creation of implied, resulting or constructive trusts. It should also be noted that a 'lock-out' agreement under which a vendor agrees not to negotiate with anyone else for a specified period (as to which see para 5.29 above) is not a contract for the disposal of an interest in land and does not, therefore, have to be in writing: see *Pitt v PHH Asset Management Ltd* [1993] 4 All ER 961, CA.

6   The same formal requirements also apply to the variation of an existing written contract: see *McAusland v Duncan Lawrie Ltd* [1996] 4 All ER 995, CA.

Amplification by the courts

31.3   In the vast majority of cases these statutory provisions give rise to no difficulties at all. Parties rarely embark on land transactions without professional advice and the procedures routinely followed[1] involve the signing and exchanging of standard-form, written documents which almost invariably meet the requirements of s 2. That said, and although the 1989 Act was intended to eliminate the uncertainties which had come to surround the previous law, the new legislation has spawned an unwelcome amount of litigation. This has clarified the following points.

The signature of all parties must appear on the same document, except where the standard conveyancing procedure of exchanging identical copies of the contract is followed, in which case the Act allows for each party to sign one copy. So, in *Commission for the New Towns v Cooper (Great Britain) Ltd,*[2] the Court of Appeal ruled that an exchange of letters each signed by one party did not amount to a contract. This decision appears[3] to rule out the possibility of a contract arising as a result of the exchange of correspondence. The requirement for a signature is not met by the mere insertion of the name of a party; each must write his name on the document in his own handwriting.[4] Where the terms of an agreement are to be found in more than one document, there will only be incorporation by reference where the document signed by both parties refers to the other document (which need not itself be signed[5]). So, in *Firstpost Homes Ltd v Johnson*[6] it was held that, where a vendor agreed in a letter addressed to the purchaser to sell land which it identified by reference to an enclosed plan and only the plan was signed, the letter and plan must be treated as two separate documents. Since the signed document did not refer to the letter, there was no incorporation by reference and thus no contract had come into being.

The courts have been rather more generous in their approach where parties to a contract for the sale or lease of land have entered into 'side' agreements which have not been referred to in the main contract. In the cases to date it has been held that these do not render the main contract invalid. Despite the argument that these 'side' agreements are, in reality, terms of the main contract which have not been included in the one document, the courts have ruled the 'side' agreements to be either collateral contracts,[5]entirely separate contracts,[7]or have ordered the main contract to be rectified so as to include the omitted terms.[8]

An important issue, which has yet to be litigated, is the position of a person who erroneously believes that he is party to a contract for the sale of land, but where the requirements of the 1989 Act have not been complied with. The Law Commission has suggested[9] that, where he has acted to his detriment in reliance on the agreement, the doctrines of promissory[10] and proprietary[11]estoppel might be relied on to overcome the lack of writing.[12]

1   See paras 31.12–31.27 below.
2   [1995] 2 All ER 929, CA.
3   An earlier ruling by the Court of Appeal in *Hooper v Sherman* [1994] NPC 153, CA that an exchange of letters did give rise to a contract was not followed in the *Cooper* case and can probably be safely ignored.
4   *Firstpost Homes Ltd v Johnson* [1995] 4 All ER 355.
5   *Record v Bell* [1991] 4 All ER 471.
6   [1995] 4 All ER 355.
7   *Tootal Clothing Ltd v Guinea Properties Management Ltd* (1992) 64 P & CR 452, [1992] 2 EGLR 80, CA.
8   *Wright v Robert Leonard (Developments) Ltd* [1994] NPC 49, CA.
9   Law Com No 164. Such an approach did not find favour in *Godden v Merthyr Tydfil Housing Association* [1997] NPC 1, CA, a decision which has been subsequently doubted in *Bankers Trust Co v Namdar* (1997) unreported, CA.
10   Paras 6.17–6.20 above.
11   Para 32.11–32.18 below.
12   If such an approach is adopted those who could previously have relied upon the doctrine of part performance (see para 31.2, footnote 3 above) may yet have a remedy, despite the effective abolition of that doctrine by the 1989 Act.

Options and rights of pre-emption

31.4   Two particular forms of land contract merit specific mention. An option to purchase a freehold or leasehold interest in land is traditionally viewed as a continuing offer to sell the land which the person to whom the option is granted has the right, if he so chooses, to convert into a contract for sale by notifying his acceptance of that offer.[1] While this analysis is not universally accepted,[2] it is clear that the initial grant of the option is itself a contract[3] to which s 2 of the 1989 Act applies. The difficulty is whether the exercise of an option also gives rise to a contract to which s 2 applies. This question came before the court in *Spiro v Glencrown Properties Ltd*[4] where it was held that it is *only* the initial grant which needs to satisfy s 2; the actual exercise of the option, which usually takes the form of a unilateral notice signed only by the grantee, is not caught by the Act.

A right of pre-emption, or right of first refusal, is rather different. Here the grantee does not have a *right* to require the land to be transferred to him; all that is required is that the potential vendor will not sell the land without first giving the holder of the right of pre-emption the opportunity to buy on the agreed terms. Although it has been held that a right of pre-emption confers no immediate rights to the land,[5] in the same case it was indicated that such rights do arise as soon as the prospective vendor takes some steps indicating a desire to sell; at this point the right of pre-emption effectively converts into an option. It would, therefore, appear that the initial grant of the right of pre-emption should, for all practical purposes, be viewed as falling within s 2 in the same way as an option does.

1   *Helby v Matthews* [1895] AC 471, HL. In order not to be void for uncertainty an option must be subject to an overall time limit and must either be at a fixed price or must contain a formula under which a price can be arrived at, eg open market value at the date of exercise.
2   Alternative views are that an option is a conditional contract which the grantee is entitled to convert into a concluded contract, or that an option comprises two contracts, the first a unilateral contract and the second a concluded contract of sale.
3   If the *initial grant* of the option is not supported by consideration as required under ordinary contractual principles it will need to take the form of a deed; see para 6.1 above. For the meaning of a deed, see para 31.6, below.
4   [1991] 1 All ER 600.
5   *Pritchard v Briggs* [1980] Ch 338, [1980] 1 All ER 294, CA.

Estate contract

31.5   Once a valid contract to convey or create a legal estate has been entered into, the purchaser has more than simple contractual rights. As we have seen,[1] the law regards every piece of land as unique, with the result that contracts for the sale or lease of land can normally be enforced by way of specific performance by either a purchaser or a vendor. For this reason the purchaser is regarded as having a right to the land from the moment the contract is entered into.[2] This equitable proprietary right is known as an estate contract. This means that if, for example, V contracts to sell to P[3] and then, in breach of that contract, conveys the land to X, P will usually[4] be able to compel X to convey the land to him rather than simply claim damages from V.

1   Para 12.29 above.
2   *Lysaght v Edwards* (1876) 2 Ch D 499.
3   Or grants either an option or a right of pre-emption to P.
4   For an explanation of the circumstances in which P's rights *will* bind X, see paras 33.11, 35.24 and 35.30, below.

Formal requirements governing the creation of legal and equitable interests

Legal estates and interests: the general law

31.6   In the preceding paragraphs we have dealt with the legal formalities governing the contract stage of a land transaction. We now turn to its second phase, that where the interest in question is created or transferred. The general rule governing the creation or transfer of legal estates and interests, which is laid down by the LPA, s 52(1), is that they must be created and conveyed by means of a deed. Traditionally, a deed was a document which was 'signed, sealed and delivered'. Many features of this old definition of a deed had long been unsatisfactory and, in 1989, reforms were enacted by s 1 of the Law of Property (Miscellaneous Provisions) Act. A deed is now defined as an instrument which makes it clear on its face that it is intended to be a deed (eg 'signed as a deed') and which is validly executed as a deed. The requirements of valid execution vary according to whether the deed is being entered into by an individual or by a company. A deed is validly executed by an individual provided it is both signed (in the presence of a witness who attests the signature) and delivered as a deed by him or a person authorised to do so on his behalf[1]. The term 'delivery' is misleading since no physical handing over of the document is necessary. Any act or words by the maker of the document showing an intention to be bound constitutes 'delivery' even though the document remains in the possession of the grantor.[2] There is no longer any need for an individual to seal a deed.

In the case of a deed entered into by a company, execution can be effected by the affixing to the document of the company seal.[3] Equally, it is now perfectly valid for a company to execute a deed without the use of a seal; in this case the document must be expressed to be executed by the company and must be signed by a director and the company secretary, or by two directors.[4] Once the deed has been executed, there is a presumption that it has been delivered unless a contrary intention is shown.[5]

1   A solicitor or licensed conveyancer acting in the course of a conveyancing transaction is conclusively presumed to have the necessary authority to deliver a deed, Law of Property (Miscellaneous Provisions) Act 1989, s 1(5).
2   *Vincent v Premo Enterprises (Voucher Sales) Ltd* [1969] 2 QB 609, [1969] 2 All ER 941, CA.
3   Companies Act 1985, s 36A(2).
4   Ibid, s 36A(4).
5   Ibid, s 36A(5).

Short lease exception

31.7   One important exception to the general rule that a deed must be used is that leases taking effect in possession[1] for a term not exceeding three years (for example, periodic leases such as yearly or weekly tenancies) may be created[2] orally or in writing so long as they are at the best rent reasonably obtainable and not for a lump sum payment. This is provided for by the LPA, s 54(2). Within this exception also falls the creation of a periodic tenancy by implication, arising from going into possession and paying rent which is accepted.[3] Another exception to the general rule relates to the acquisition of a legal estate in the land by virtue of adverse possession of the land for the statutory limitation period, a topic which we consider at paras 32.19–32.31 below.

1   Ie the lease must come into effect immediately. If it is to come into operation at a future date it will not
    fall within the exception and must be created by deed: see *Long v London Borough of Tower Hamlets*
    [1996] 2 All ER 683.
2   The transfer (assignment) of an existing lease of *any* length must be by deed: see *Crago v Julian* [1992]
    1 All ER 744, CA and para 36.23 below.
3   Para 36.13 below.

Legal estates and interests: registration of title

31.8   Prior to 1925 compliance with the rules laid down in the preceding two paragraphs would have ensured that the purchaser or lessee immediately acquired the relevant legal estate or interest. This is no longer always the case. In 1925 a system for registering the title[1] to land was introduced by the enactment of the Land Registration Act 1925 (hereafter the LRA).[2] The Act used only to apply to certain parts of England and Wales, known as areas of compulsory registration; it now applies to the whole country.[3] It is only the major legal *estates* in land, ie the freehold and leases for terms in excess of 21 years, to which title *can*[4] be registered; whether or not they *must* be registered depends on rules which we explain at para 31.10.

1   The registered system of conveyancing is usually known as the 'registered land' scheme; this is,
    however, something of a misnomer, for what is registered is not the land itself, but the title to the land,
    ie the evidence of the owner's right to the land.
2   The 1925 Act remains the main governing Act but it has been amended by subsequent statutes which
    are referred to where relevant. The Act itself is also augmented in important respects by the Land
    Registration Rules.
3   Registration of Title Order 1989, which came into effect on 1 December 1990.
4   LRA, ss 2, 4 and 8.

Title already registered

31.9   Once title to an estate in land has been registered all dealings in respect of it thereafter are governed by the LRA. Any subsequent transfer of the estate must be completed by registration, ie by the Registrar entering the transferee of the land on the register as proprietor.[1] Where a lease of more than 21 years is created out of a registered estate, the lessee should be registered as proprietor of the leasehold interest which is accorded its own separate title. The grant of such a lease will also be noted on the landlord's title register,[2] and this will be done automatically by the Registrar on the lessee's application for first registration. Thus, it is perfectly possible (and, indeed, commonplace) for one piece of land to be the subject of two or more registered titles; for example if A, the registered proprietor of the freehold title to Blacklands grants a 25-year lease of it to B, then B will also have to be registered as proprietor of a leasehold title to Blacklands; if B then grants a 22-year sublease of the property to C, C will also have to register his title.

Where a registered proprietor of either a freehold or leasehold estate creates a legal *interest* affecting his land, again it is not enough simply to use a deed; the disposition must be completed by registration if it is to be fully effective.[3] An interest is not accorded a separate title; completion by registration here means that the interest is noted on the titles of any properties to which it relates

Unless and until such dispositions are completed by registration, no legal estate or interest is created or transferred. The purchaser acquires only an equitable interest which is capable of being overridden if not protected under other provisions in the LRA.[4]

An important exception to the rule that the creation or transfer of legal estates and interests relating to registered land must be completed by registration arises where a registered proprietor grants a lease of 21 years or less. Such leases are neither capable of substantive registration nor are they noted in any other way on the register;[5] accordingly, exceptionally, they create a legal estate immediately on grant provided that the general law on formalities has been complied with.

1   LRA, ss 19(2) and 22(2).
2   Ibid.
3   Ibid.
4   LRA, s 101; para 35.21.
5   LRA, ss 19(2) and 22(2).

Title not yet registered

31.10   Where title to land has not yet been registered the following specified transactions[1] now always give rise to a requirement[2] for first registration of title:

- a disposition of freehold land by conveyance or assent;
- a grant of a lease or sub-lease of more than 21 years;
- an assignment of a lease having more than 21 years to run;
- the grant of a first legal mortgage.

Prior to 1 April 1998 conveyances of the freehold, and assignments of leases for more than 21 years, had to be 'on sale', with the result that gifts and bequests of such interests did not trigger a first registration of title. This is no longer the case. Neither the creation or transfer of leases not exceeding 21 years, nor the creation of legal interests (apart from a first legal mortgage) relating to unregistered land, lead to a requirement to register title.

Voluntary registration of title to freehold land, or leasehold land where the term has more than 21 years to run, is possible.[3] It is thus not necessary to wait until one of the transactions specified in s 123 occurs before first registration. This process is further encouraged by a provision[4], introduced by the 1997 Act, which allows for a reduced fee, or no fee at all, to be charged for voluntary registration.

Should a purchaser who is required by s 123 to register fail to apply for first registration within two months of completion, the transaction becomes void as to the passing of the legal estate[5] (unless the Registrar exercises his power to extend this period if sufficient cause for the delay is shown) and the legal estate reverts to the vendor who will hold it on trust for the purchaser. The latter will then have the right to require the legal estate to be conveyed to him again and this time he should have his title to it registered.

1   These 'triggering' events have recently been extended by the Land Registration Act 1997 which came into effect on 1 April 1998. The 1997 Act has, for this purpose, substituted a new version of s 123 (s 123 and s123A) into the LRA 1925.
2   LRA, s 123.
3   Ibid, ss 4 and 8.
4   LRA, s 145(3), (3A) as amended by the LRA 1997.
5   Ibid, s 123A. This part of the original LRA, s 123 has been reworded by the 1997 Act in order to clarify the position where a transaction is not in fact completed by registration.

Equitable interests

31.11   The LPA, s 53 states the general rule that equitable interests, although not

445

requiring the formality of a deed, must nevertheless be created or transferred by signed writing. Classically, s 53 applies to the express creation of trusts of land although, in practice, a deed is often employed. While s 53 must be complied with where equitable interests are deliberately created, as has already been indicated,[1] equity has traditionally given effect to some transactions which were intended to give rise to legal estates or interests but which failed to do so because the correct formalities[2] were not complied with. Here, as we shall see,[3] it is not necessary to comply with s 53. Equally there are other circumstances in which equitable interests can arise without the need to comply with s 53. The LPA specifically provides that the section does not affect the creation of resulting, implied or constructive trusts.[4] Furthermore, certain equitable interests may come into existence as a result of the operation of other equitable principles without any need for writing.[5]

1   See para 30.34 above.
2   See paras 31.6 and 31.7 above.
3   See paras 32.2–32.6 below.
4   LPA, s 53(2). See further para 32.8 below.
5   See paras 32.11–32.18 below.

A typical sale of land

31.12   In order to place the legal rules governing the creation, transfer and registration of estates and interests into their practical context, we propose to outline the steps involved in a typical sale of a freehold interest in land. The sale of a leasehold interest follows essentially the same path.

Initial negotiation
31.13   The typical sale by private treaty, rather than by auction, begins when the parties, introduced probably by an estate agent, discuss and agree on a price for the property. Although at this very early stage it might appear that vendor and purchaser are now parties to a binding contract, this is not the case. As we have seen, even if it were their intention to be legally bound at this stage, which is unlikely, a contract for the sale or lease of land must be in writing. It is normal practice for this written contract to come into existence by exchange of contracts.[2]

The period between the initial agreement and the exchange of contracts is one during which either side can withdraw. While such a withdrawal may be for perfectly legitimate reasons (eg an unsatisfactory survey, an unexpected lack of finance, or the loss of a purchaser for a party's existing property), one particularly irksome cause is where, in a rising market, a vendor backs out in order to achieve a higher price than that which has already been agreed with the present purchaser (although it should be noted that the reverse can occur in a falling market, ie the purchaser can back out in order to force a lower price than that which has been agreed). This practice—usually referred to as 'gazumping'—is one which is not only distressing to the innocent party; it can also cause the loss of any expenditure already incurred in the expectation that the deal would go through (notably solicitor's and surveyor's fees).

Where the risk of gazumping is high, for example because the market is volatile or because it is known that the period between initial agreement and exchange of contracts may become protracted, it is possible for the parties to enter into an option[3] or a 'lock-out' agreement.[4] The latter requires less formality[5] and is often the more realistic safeguard since the vendor merely agrees not to negotiate with anyone else for a specified period. While a lock-out agreement cannot be used to compel the vendor to exchange contracts,[6] its breach will give rise to a claim in damages; this, at least, compensates the innocent party for wasted expenditure. At the time of writing the Government is in the process of considering whether any changes to standard procedures could be introduced which would eliminate the problem. What is clear is that, under the present system, the risk of gazumping is greatly reduced by the simple expedient of exchanging contracts as soon as possible after the initial agreement is reached. There is little doubt that, in most cases, provided the parties themselves so wish, exchange within a matter of days can be achieved. The most usual stumbling block to this is not the legal procedures but rather the financing practices under-pinning the purchase of property, especially those in the domestic residential sector. A purchaser who already owns a house is rarely able to afford to purchase another until his existing property is sold. As a result, the sale of a residential property is seldom an isolated transaction but rather one in a chain of similar deals; if any one of these falls through, the chain breaks down so that the exchange of contracts on all the other dependent sales has to be delayed.

1   Law of Property (Miscellaneous Provisions) Act 1989, s 2; para 31.2 above.
2   Para 31.17 below.
3   See para 31.4 above.
4   See *Pitt v PHH Asset Management Ltd* [1993] 4 All ER 961, CA and para 5.29 above.
5   Unlike an option, a lock-out agreement is not a contract for the sale of land and thus does not need to comply with the Law of Property (Miscellaneous Provisions) Act 1989, s 2; see *Pitt v PHH Asset Management Ltd* [1993] 4 All ER 961, CA.
5   *Tye v House* [1997] 2 EGLR 171.

Enquiries and searches

31.14   Despite the disadvantages of the period between initial agreement and the exchange of contracts which we have alluded to in the previous paragraph, it does, in practice, provide an opportunity for the purchaser to take further steps, some of which ought to be completed to his satisfaction before it is sensible to become legally committed to the transaction. At this stage the wise purchaser will usually put matters in the hands of professional advisers: a surveyor to report to the purchaser on the structural state of the property and solicitors to carry out the transaction. Where, as is usually the case, the purchaser wishes to finance the purchase by means of a mortgage, this will need to be arranged. Apart from assessing the purchaser's personal credit-worthiness, the lender will require a valuation of the property to be carried out, at the purchaser's expense. The purchaser or his solicitor will also now institute the local searches' described in the following paragraph. In the case of non-domestic property the purchaser will send to the vendor a set of preliminary enquiries about the property, dealing with such matters as boundaries, the fixtures and fittings included in the sale, and asking whether the vendor is aware of any adverse interests affecting the property. Where the property is domestic, under the Law Society's National Conveyancing Protocol,[1] the vendor now provides the purchaser with a completed Property Information Form and Fixtures, Fittings and Contents Form which covers these matters.

1   3rd edn, 1994.

Local land charges and supplementary enquiries

31.15   A search of the local land charges register (not to be confused with the Land Register), maintained by the district council (or London borough council) under the provisions of the Local Land Charges Act 1975, will reveal such matters as revocations of planning permission, orders requiring the discontinuance of an existing use, building preservation notices, listings of buildings of special architectural or historical interest, and (charges of a private rather than a public character) light obstruction notices under the Rights of Light Act 1959.[1] Registrations of these matters are made against the land in question. A search may be personal or official (ie carried out by officials of the registry). By virtue of the Local Land Charges Act 1975, s 10 charges of a public character which are not registered nevertheless remain enforceable.[2] However, if a personal search fails to turn up the existence of a charge because it was not registered, or an official search fails to reveal an existing charge, the purchaser will be entitled to compensation for any losses he has thereby suffered.[3]

At the same time as an official search of the local land charges register is sought, a list of additional enquiries is also submitted to the district council.[4] While these supplementary enquiries form an essential adjunct to a search of the local land charges register, the procedure has no statutory basis. The district councils merely voluntarily answer the enquiries; nevertheless they may be liable to be sued for negligence in answering them. These enquiries cover such matters as whether the roadways abutting on the property are maintained at the public expense, whether it is proposed to construct any road or flyover close to the property, whether the property is drained to a sewer, whether the property is in a slum clearance area and other matters within the knowledge of the district council.

1   Para 37.48 below.
2   Unlike land charges governed by the Land Charges Act 1972; see para 35.12 below.
3   Local Land Charges Act 1975, s 10.
4   Or London borough council.

Draft contract

31.16   Meanwhile, the vendor or his solicitor will be preparing a draft contract of sale, usually based on the Standard Conditions of Sale.[1] At this stage of the transaction it has become normal, where title is already registered,[2] for the vendor to send to the purchaser, along with the draft contract, office copies of his register of title (ie those provided and authenticated by the Land Registry), title plan and any documents referred to on the register which are filed at the Registry; in the case of unregistered land, the abstract of title and Land Charges Search Certificate may be sent along with the draft. Thus, the vendor, in practice, takes the first step in fulfilling his contractual obligation to prove his title[3] before the contract is formally entered into.

1   3rd edn, 1995.
2   See further para 31.29 below.
3   Explained further in paras 31.29 and 31.33 below.

Contract
Exchange

31.17   Once both sides are ready to be legally committed to the transaction they will enter into a formal contract. As we have seen, since 1989 most contracts for the sale or disposition of an interest in land must be made in writing.[1]

It is almost invariable conveyancing practice for the contract to come into being by 'exchange of contracts', more accurately the exchange of identical copies of the contract signed by each party.

> 'When you are dealing with contracts for the sale of land, it is of the greatest importance to the vendor that he should have a document signed by the purchaser, and to the purchaser that he should have a document signed by the vendor ... that there should be no dispute whether a contract had or had not been made and that there should be no dispute as to the terms of it. This particular procedure of exchange ensures that none of these difficulties will arise.'[2]

In the past 'exchange' was effected in person but today it is usual practice to exchange by post or, increasingly, by telephone. Where exchange takes place through the post, it would seem that the contract is formed not when each party receives the other's copy of the contract, but when the second (vendor's) copy is posted.[3] In the case of sales of houses there is often a chain of transactions in which each purchaser needs to sell his property before he can buy the vendor's and each vendor needs to sell in order to buy another property. Here it is often vital that there be as near as possible simultaneous exchanges of contract in respect of each of these transactions. One method of achieving this object, sanctioned by the Court of Appeal[4] and regulated by the Law Society is the 'telephonic exchange'. In this case, either each solicitor holds his own client's signed part of the contract or one solicitor holds both parts, and they then, by telephone, deem the contracts to be exchanged, the date of exchange then being entered on each part.[5] Actual physical exchange by post follows.

1   Law of Property (Miscellaneous Provisions) Act 1989, s 2; para 31.2 above.
2   *Eccles v Bryant* [1948] Ch 93 at 99, [1947] 2 All ER 865 at 866, CA.
3   Para 5.16 above. The Standard Conditions of Sale explicitly provide that this shall be the case.
4   *Domb v Isoz* [1980] Ch 548, [1980] 1 All ER 942, CA.
5   In 1989 the Law Society authorised a more complex procedure which was specifically designed to deal with 'chain' transactions; this has not proved popular in practice, conveyancers preferring to use one or other of those described in the text.

Deposit
31.18   At exchange of contracts it is usual for the purchaser to pay a deposit. The purpose of this is that, in effect, it gives the vendor a remedy, which is available without bringing a court action, in the event of the purchaser failing to complete. This is because the vendor is normally entitled to keep the deposit where such a failure to complete amounts to a breach of contract. The court does, however, have an unqualified discretion to order the repayment of the whole deposit under the LPA, s 49(2).[1] It is usual for the contract to fix the amount of the deposit at 10% of the purchase price.

The deposit is normally paid not to the vendor but to his solicitor. The general rule is that the solicitor holds it as agent for the vendor[2] unless the contract provides that it should be held by the solicitor as stakeholder. In practice, except where the vendor is to be allowed to use the whole or part of the deposit towards the deposit on any property he is buying in a related transaction, it is usual for the contract to require it to be held by the vendor's solicitor as stakeholder.

1   *Universal Corpn v Five Ways Properties Ltd* [1979] 1 All ER 552, CA. Where, for no particular reason, an unusually large deposit has been paid this may be regarded as a penalty, in which case the court may order the repayment of the whole sum; see *Workers Trust and Merchant Bank Ltd v Dojap Investments Ltd* [1993] 2 All ER 370, PC. On penalties generally see paras 12.21–12.23 above.
2   *Ellis v Goulton* [1893] 1 QB 350, CA; *Tudor v Hamid* [1988] 1 EGLR 251, CA.

Terms
31.19   As we have said, the terms of the contract are largely based on those contained in the Standard Conditions of Sale, modified by any special conditions agreed to by the parties. So, for example, it is usual to specify a date for completion; any failure to meet that deadline would then be a breach of contract entitling the innocent party to damages.[1] He would only be entitled to terminate for breach where time is made of the essence;[2] it is normally provided that, while time is not automatically of the essence, either party can render it so by serving a notice to complete on the other party.

1   *Raineri v Miles* [1981] AC 1050, [1980] 2 All ER 145, HL.
2   Paras 9.8–9.11 above.

Vendor's liability for defects
31.20   It is said that an underlying rule in contracts for the sale of land is *caveat emptor,*

let the buyer beware; in other words, it is for the buyer to discover defects in the property he is buying, and not for the seller to warn him of them. However, this rule is subject to a number of important exceptions:

- The vendor may be liable for misrepresentation, which we discussed at paras 14.2 to 14.39 above.
- The vendor may be liable for breach of contract where the property is misdescribed; for example, if the contract describes his interest in the property or the size of the property as being greater than it is.
- The vendor is under an implied contractual duty to disclose all latent defects in his *title* to the property, ie defects which the purchaser could not discover on a reasonable inspection of the property. Thus, for example, the vendor is obliged to disclose that his title is dependent on adverse possession, or that the property is subject to restrictive covenants.

The vendor's liability under each of these three heads is likely to be modified by the terms of the contract. Under the Standard Conditions of Sale, for example, the vendor is to disclose to the purchaser all adverse interests of which he knew and the purchaser is to accept the property in the physical state it is in when the contract is made. Furthermore, albeit that property information will have been provided by the vendor, the contract provides that the onus remains on the purchaser to make all the searches, enquiries and inspections which a prudent buyer would make and that he buys the property subject to such defects as they would reveal. As to liability for misrepresentation, the Misrepresentation Act 1967, s 3[1] should be borne in mind when drafting any clause restricting or excluding liability.

It will be appreciated from this that the vendor is not normally liable to the purchaser for *physical* defects in the property.[2] To guard against these the purchaser needs to have a structural survey carried out before he enters into the contract.

1   Paras 14.37–14.39 above.
2   However, as we have seen, a vendor/builder may, in appropriate circumstances, be liable to his purchaser under the provisions of the Defective Premises Act 1972; see para 22.28 above.

Remedies
31.21   The contractual remedies of particular relevance to sales of land are of course applicable to contracts in general and little need be said here additional to our earlier discussion of these remedies.

31.22   *Rescission*   It is open to a purchaser to rescind the contract in the face of misrepresentation by the vendor,[1] although it should be remembered that he may be debarred from so doing after completion has taken place in a case where the property is purchased with the aid of a mortgage, for the mortgagee will be a purchaser of an interest in the property for value.[2]

1   Para 14.15 above.
2   Para 14.17 above.

31.23   *Termination of the contract for repudiatory breach*[1]   The injured party may not only accept the repudiatory breach of the defaulting party as terminating the contract but may also sue for damages for loss of the bargain or wasted expenditure and any other loss which is not too remote.[2]

1   Para 9.15 above.
2   Paras 12.2–12.18 above.

31.24 *Damages*   As in the general case, a breach of the contract for the sale of the land entitles the innocent party to sue for damages for loss of the bargain or for wasted expenditure, at his option, and any other loss which is not too remote. The date at which damages for loss of bargain are assessed is normally the date of breach though some other date may be chosen where otherwise injustice might be caused.[1]

A vendor who cannot show good title may have represented otherwise in answer to enquiries. Where there has been any misrepresentation by the vendor, the purchaser may choose to sue for damages for misrepresentation, rather than for breach of contract, a matter which we discussed in paras 14.19 to 14.30 above.

1   Para 12.6 above.

31.25 *Specific performance*   It will be remembered that the law regards every plot of land as unique, with the result that contracts for the sale or lease of land are always on the face of it specifically enforceable by both a purchaser and a vendor.[1] This does not mean that the remedy will always be granted, since it is discretionary. Where the court refuses to grant specific performance to either party, it has a discretion to order the repayment of the deposit,[2] wherever this is the fairest course between the parties.[3] Further, the court has a discretion to award damages in addition to, or in substitution for, specific performance. Where the innocent party obtains specific performance, but the order is not complied with by the party in breach, the innocent party, having elected to affirm the contract, cannot then unilaterally terminate for breach. He must return to the court, under whose supervision the performance of the contract now is, to seek enforcement of the order or dissolution of the order and termination of the contract.[4]

1   Paras 11.25 and 31.5 above.
2   LPA, s 49(2).
3   *Universal Corpn v Five Ways Properties Ltd* [1979] 1 All ER 552, CA; *Workers Trust and Merchant Bank Ltd v Dojap Investments* [1993] 2 All ER 370, PC. See para 31.19 above.
4   *GKN Distributors Ltd v Tyne Tees Fabrication Ltd* (1985) 50 P & CR 403.

Passing of the risk

31.26   As we have just seen, on the conclusion of a binding written contract, the purchaser becomes entitled to call for it to be specifically performed. Since equity looks on that as done which ought to be done this means that the purchaser is regarded as having an equitable interest in the property.[1] Accordingly, the vendor is henceforth regarded as a (constructive) trustee for the purchaser. Although the vendor is under an obligation to manage the property as a trustee, this is not an entirely straightforward trust since the vendor himself also retains a beneficial interest in the property until the purchase price is paid and until then is entitled to remain in occupation and receive the income of the property. The purchaser, however, is entitled to any capital appreciation in respect of the property.

On the other hand, under the general law, he must also bear any capital losses, which means that on exchange of contracts the risk passes to him. The purchaser should therefore on the conclusion of the contract insure the property against fire, flood etc. Although statute[2] provides that monies payable under any insurance policy held by the vendor in respect of damage or destruction to the property must be paid over to the purchaser on completion, it may be that the vendor has either not insured the property or has not maintained the policy. Where the parties employ the Standard Conditions of Sale, the onus is now placed on the vendor to transfer the property in the same physical state as it was at the date of the contract, which means that the vendor retains the risk until completion.

Despite this, the contract continues to provide that the vendor is under no obligation to insure the property. Although the contract provides that the purchaser may terminate for breach in the event of the property becoming unusable for its purpose, it is usual practice for the purchaser to continue to insure the property as in the past.

1   See para 31.5 above.
2   LPA, s 47.

Sale by auction

31.27   Where a sale is conducted by public auction there is a legally binding contract as soon as the property is knocked down[1] to the highest bidder, despite the absence of writing.[2] A person wishing to bid for a property may make pre-contract enquiries and searches before the auction but it is more usual either for the vendor to produce the relevant evidence at the auction, or for the contract to provide for the searches to be made after the auction, giving the purchaser the right to rescind if the searches produce adverse results. In *Rignall Developments Ltd v Halil*,[3] where the contract deemed the purchaser to have made the relevant searches and to have knowledge of what would thereby be disclosed, it was held that the vendor, who was aware of the defect in the title which the searches would disclose, could nonetheless not require the purchaser to complete the transaction since he had not made full and frank disclosure of the known defect.

1   See para 5.12 above.
2   Law of Property (Miscellaneous Provisions) Act 1989, s 2(5); para 31.2 note 5 above.
3   [1988] Ch 190, [1987] 3 All ER 170.

Conveyance or transfer stage

31.28   Up to exchange of contracts the procedure for transferring ownership of land is broadly the same whether the title to that land is registered or unregistered, and, indeed, to a considerable extent, whether it is freehold or long leasehold. However, after exchange of contracts, the procedures followed differ depending on whether the title to the land is registered or not. Where, as is now usual, the transaction itself is the occasion for first registration of title,[1] the procedure followed is that for unregistered land; title is then registered after completion.

1   See para 31.9 above.

Registered land

31.29   *Proving title*   During the period between contract and transfer it is for the vendor to carry out his contractual obligation to prove his title, ie to prove that he is in a position to sell what he has contracted to sell. It is increasingly the case that the first stage of this process will already have taken place in that the vendor will have furnished the purchaser with office copies of his register of title, etc.[1] These office copies can be relied on to the same extent as the originals[2] and do not need to be verified against them.

The vendor should also provide the purchaser with any available documentary evidence relating to any interests which do not appear on the register.[3] The purchaser's solicitor will inspect the office copies and any documents required to be furnished to ensure all is well. He may also raise requisitions on title, that is, make enquiries of the vendor for further particulars, for example as to adverse entries on the register, or, more likely, simply point them out and require their removal.[4] A failure by the vendor to answer a proper requisition on title may lead to the purchaser terminating the contract for breach or may lead to him applying to the court to require an answer under the summary procedure provided by the LPA, s 49(1).

At this stage, also, the purchaser's solicitor should draft the transfer of title, using the prescribed form.[5]

The next stage of the procedure is for the purchaser or his solicitor to request an official search of the register. This search is, in effect, to check for any further entries which may have been made since the date of the office copies already provided by the vendor.[6] The official certificate of search which results ensures that, provided the transaction is completed and the purchaser applies to be registered as proprietor within 30 working days[7], the purchaser will not take subject to entries made in the register during that time.[8]

Where a person suffers loss as a result of an error in an official search he is entitled to an indemnity.[9] He is still bound by any entry which the search fails to reveal.[10]

1 Para 31.16 above.
2 LRA, s 113.
3 Such as overriding interests; see para 35.21 below.
4 See *Re Stone and Saville's Contract* [1963] 1 All ER 353, [1963] 1 WLR 163, CA.
5 Land Registration Rules, r 98, Schedule, Form 19.
6 If any such entries are discovered, it may be necessary to raise further requisitions, for example requiring their removal.
7 Land Registration (Official Searches) Rules 1988.
8 See further para 35.34 below.
9 LRA, s 83(3); para 35.39 below.
10 *Parkash v Irani Finances Ltd* [1970] Ch 101, [1969] 1 All ER 930.

31.30 *Completion*   Completion now takes place. The transfer is executed and the purchase price paid. The transfer is in simple form but it must, of course, be validly executed as a deed.[1] On completion, the purchaser is entitled to the vendor's land certificate[2] relating to the property. If, however, as is quite likely, the property is subject to a mortgage in the form of a registered charge, the land certificate will already be lodged at the Registry.[3] In this case, assuming the mortgage is to be paid off, the vendor must obtain the charge certificate from the mortgagee together with a discharge of the mortgage.

1 Para 31.6 above.
2 As to which see para 31.44 below.
3 See paras 31.44 and 39.7 below.

31.31 *Registration*   As we have seen, the deed of transfer itself does not pass the legal estate in registered land to the purchaser. Only registration of the purchaser as proprietor vests in him the legal estate.[1] The purchaser should therefore apply to the Registry for registration as proprietor. His application should be accompanied by the vendor's land certificate, or where appropriate, the charge certificate; by the deed of transfer stamped with the correct stamp duty; where appropriate, by an application to register the discharge of the vendor's mortgage, and, again where appropriate, by an application to register the charge effecting the purchaser's mortgage. Following his registration as proprietor, the purchaser will be issued with his own land certificate unless he is purchasing with the aid of a mortgage, in which case this will be held by the Land Registry and the mortgagee will be issued with a charge certificate.

1 LRA, ss 19(1) and 22(1); para 31.9 above.

Unregistered land
31.32   As might be imagined, the procedure to be gone through on a conveyance of unregistered land is slightly more complex than that required for registered land.

31.33 *Proving title*   As with registered land, the vendor is required by the terms of his contract to show 'good' title. In the case of unregistered land, this means that he must show that he is in a position to pass the freehold, unencumbered, to the purchaser.

This involves him in tracing the course of dealings with the land, by means of the relevant documents, over the period commencing with a 'good root of title' at least 15 years old[1] and extending up to the time of the transaction. For reasons which we deal with later,[2] it is equally incumbent on the purchaser to check the title back to a good root.

A good root of title is a document in which the legal and beneficial ownership of the property to be sold is fully set out, the property is sufficiently identified, and no doubts are cast on the vendor's title.[3] The prime example of a good root of title is a previous conveyance on sale of the freehold. As it would be quite a coincidence to find a good root of title exactly 15 years old, it is likely to be necessary to go back to a good root which is more than 15 year's old.

The vendor fulfils his obligation to trace the links in the title from the root to the time of the current transaction by delivering to the purchaser an 'abstract of title'. This is a list of the relevant documents and events, together with photocopies of the documents, including official certificates of search of the Land Charges Registry.[4] As we have said, it is now common for the abstract to be delivered before exchange of contracts in order to speed up the conveyancing process.[5]

1   LPA, s 44(1), as amended by LPA 1969, s 23.
2   In order to avoid being regarded as having constructive notice: see para 35.6 below.
3   Williams *Vendor and Purchaser* (4th edn) p 124.
4   See paras 35.13 and 35.14 below.
5   Para 31.16 above.

31.34   The purchaser's solicitor will peruse the abstract of title and will raise requisitions on any defect or apparent defect.[1] Examples of such requisitions might be to require that the vendor produce evidence that a mortgage has been discharged, or to request production of land charges search certificates in respect of estate owners whose names do not appear in the abstracted documents.[2]

At this stage also, the purchaser's solicitor will draft the conveyance; where, as is now usually the case, the transaction is triggering a first registration of title[3] this will be by way of a standard Land Registry form, as if title were already registered. This should then be sent to the vendor for approval. Prior to completion the purchaser or his solicitor should request an official search of the Land Charges Register.[4]

1   Para 31.20 above.
2   Para 35.13 below.
3   Para 31.10 above.
4   The Land Charges Register should not be confused with the Land Register; see para 35.19 below.

31.35   *Completion*   Completion takes place when the conveyance is validly executed as a deed[1] and the purchase price is paid. The legal estate then passes to the purchaser. At this stage also the purchaser becomes entitled to the title deeds relating to the property, whether they have been held by the vendor or his mortgagee. However, since the transaction will now trigger the requirement to register title,[2] the purchaser must apply for first registration within two months. As we have seen,[3] should he fail to do so, the legal estate will revert to the vendor. Accordingly, the purchaser's solicitor will forward the title deeds (including his own purchase deed) to the Land Registry.

1   Para 31.6 above.
2   Para 31.10 above.
3   Para 31.10 above.

31.36   *First registration*   An application to the Registrar for first registration of title to land is made for one of three classes of title: absolute, good leasehold, and possessory.[1] A fourth class, qualified title, may be given where the Registrar is unable to grant the class of title originally applied for.

1   We defer discussion of possessory title until para 32.28 below since this only arises in circumstances where an applicant for first registration is unable to prove title by reference to title deeds either because these have been lost or destroyed, or where the claim to title is based on adverse possession.

31.37   Freehold.   Absolute title is applied for and granted in the vast majority of cases involving freehold land. Registration as proprietor of freehold land with absolute title vests in the proprietor the freehold estate together with all rights belonging to it (for example, easements such as rights of way) subject to:

- entries on the register; and
- overriding interests.[1]

Absolute title will be given where the applicant proves his title to the satisfaction of the Registrar. It is not quite accurate to say that registration with absolute title affords an absolute state guarantee of the registered proprietor's title, for there exists the possibility that the register may be rectified, ie amended if it does not show what should be the true state of affairs.[2] However, subject to this possibility, registration with absolute title effectively guarantees that the registered proprietor is entitled to the legal estate together with attached rights and subject only to overriding interests and interests entered on the register.[3]

1   LRA, s 5; see further paras 35.21–35.27 below.
2   Paras 35.36 and 35.37 below.
3   Cf effect of registration with other classes of title.

31.38   Leasehold.   It is possible for *absolute* title to be accorded in respect of leasehold interests, but this can only be done where the Registrar is satisfied not only as to title to the lease but also as to title to the freehold and any intermediate leasehold interests.[1] Only in such a case could the Registrar guarantee that the lease was validly granted. Although a lessee has no right to call for proof of his landlord's title,[2] it is increasing likely that he will have specifically contracted with his landlord for the production of the latter's title deeds. In such instances, the lessee will be in a position to satisfy the Registrar as to the landlord's title. Equally, where the freehold and any leasehold reversions are already registered, an application for registration with absolute title to a leasehold interest may be made, for the Registrar will then be in a position to satisfy himself as to these superior titles. Registration with absolute title vests in the proprietor the leasehold interest together with all rights belonging to it, subject to:

- covenants in the lease (express or implied);
- entries on the register; and
- overriding interests.[3]

1   LRA, s 8.
2   LPA, s 44.
3   LRA, s 9.

31.39   Good leasehold.   Where it is not possible for a proprietor of a leasehold interest to be registered with absolute title, because the Registrar cannot satisfy himself as to the landlord's title, application may be made for registration with good leasehold title. Registration with *good leasehold* title vests the leasehold interest in the proprietor subject to:

- entries on the register; and
- overriding interests;

but it does not guarantee that the lease was validly granted, for the interest is also subject to:

- rights or interests affecting the landlord's title to grant the lease.[1]

1   LRA, s 10.

31.40 Qualified.   In a few rare cases, the Registrar may decide that he is unable to grant the title applied for because of some specific defect in the title. In such a case, the applicant for registration may be registered with a qualified title. The effect of registration with a qualified title is the same as the effect of registration with absolute title except that in addition to entries on the register and overriding interests, the registered interest is also subject to a specified qualification stated in the register, for example any rights arising before a specified date or under a specified document.[1]

1   LRA, ss 7 and 12.

31.41 Upgrading of title.   It will be observed from what we have said so far that registration with a class of title other than absolute affords in some way less of a 'guarantee' of the proprietor's title than does absolute title. It is possible, however, for the class of title to be upgraded in certain cases to the more marketable absolute title. Thus, for example, a proprietor registered with good leasehold title may apply for registration with absolute leasehold title which the Registrar must grant if satisfied as to the freehold and any intermediate leasehold titles.

31.42 Cautions against first registration.   A person who has an interest in unregistered land which may be lost if another person is registered as proprietor may lodge a caution with the Registrar under the LRA, s 53. This entitles him to notice of any application that may be made for registration of an interest affecting his rights. He then has 14 days in which to oppose the registration if he wishes, otherwise registration will be effected.[1]

1   LRA, s 53(3); see also para 36.34 below.

31.43 *The register*   The register of each title is kept[1] at the appropriate District Land Registry. The register is open to public inspection.[2] Each register of title is divided into three parts: the Property Register, the Proprietorship Register and the Charges Register.[3]

- *Property Register* This part of the register contains a description of the land, states whether it is freehold or leasehold, and refers to a filed plan of the land.[4] Where the land is leasehold, brief particulars of the lease are set out. The Property Register also contains notes of any rights which benefit the land, such as easements.
  The filed plan is prepared from the plans and description of the land in the title deeds and is based on the Ordnance Map. It denotes the land comprised in the title by red edging. Boundaries shown in the filed plan are general, not fixed, boundaries; that is they do not purport to show the exact line of the legal boundary.[5]
- *Proprietorship Register* This part states the class of title with which the land is registered, the name and address of the registered proprietor, together with any cautions, inhibitions and restrictions[6] affecting the proprietor's right to deal with the land.[7]

• *Charges Register* This part contains entries and notices of rights and interests which adversely affect the title, such as restrictive covenants, easements, mortgages and registered leases.[8]

1 The Register was originally filed on a card index. Since 1988 all new titles have been computerised; existing titles are gradually being transferred onto this system.
2 LRA, s 112 as substituted by LRA 1988.
3 Land Registration Rules, r 2.
4 Ibid, r 3.
5 Ibid, r 278; para 30.19 above.
6 Paras 35.29–35.32 below.
7 Land Registration Rules, r 6.
8 Ibid, r 7.

31.44 *Land certificate* A copy of the register and filed plan, called the Land Certificate, is given to the registered proprietor.[1] Although this document affords some evidence of title,[2] it may not at all times correspond exactly with the register itself because some entries may be made on the register without the certificate being lodged at the registry for amendment;[3] accordingly, it is the register which is the proof of title. Where the registered property is mortgaged by means of a registered charge,[4] the Land Certificate is retained by the Registry and the mortgagee (lender) is issued with a Charge Certificate[5] which is likewise a copy of the register together with the deed of charge.

1 LRA, s 63.
2 Ibid, s 68.
3 See para 35.31 below.
4 Para 39.7 below.
5 LRA, s 65.

Chapter 32

The informal acquisition of rights to land

32.1   In the previous chapter we considered the formal rules which govern the creation and transfer of legal and equitable interests in land. As we have said, in practice the vast majority of land transactions satisfy those requirements. However, situations do arise, often in family or domestic situations, where parties do not act in accordance with strict legal niceties. Furthermore, landowners may exercise rights over their neighbour's land, or people use land as if it were their own, for very many years but without any proper documentary evidence of their legal right to do so. In this chapter, therefore, we deal with:

- the effect of transactions which ought to have been made by deed;
- the circumstances in which effect will be given to informal arrangements relating to land; and
- the operation of the statutory rules under which title to land can be acquired as a result of its use over a long period of time.

Informal transactions

32.2   Where parties make a positive attempt to create an estate or interest in land which fails in the eyes of the law because the formality of a deed is not gone through, their efforts may nonetheless give rise to an interest in the eyes of equity. The same principles apply whatever the type of estate or interest was intended to be created or transferred; hence, the same approach is taken to attempts to transfer a freehold, or to create a lease, an easement, or a mortgage. However, in order to demonstrate the application of these principles, we will take, by way of example, the case of an informal lease, ie a lease which has not been created in accordance with the formality required by law.

Informal leases
32.3   Suppose L grants to T a seven-year lease which is simply in writing (ie a document which falls short of the requirements of a deed).[1] Such a lease, not falling within the exception to the general rule for legal estates under the LPA, s 54(2),[2] should have been made by deed.[1] As a result, at common law, this transaction cannot create a seven-year lease. However, suppose further that, because the parties are not aware that they have failed to comply with the proper formalities, T goes into possession

and pays rent which L accepts. At common law, such an action gives rise to a periodic tenancy by implication.[3] Accordingly, the operation of the common law rules leaves T with a markedly inferior interest, a periodic tenancy (which can be terminated at any time by the landlord serving an appropriate notice to quit[4]), rather than the seven-year lease which the parties had meant to create.

Equity, however, regards the matter differently; it will, where possible, treat the purported lease as if it were a contract to create a lease.[5] So, if court proceedings were brought, equity would usually grant specific performance of the contract. This would have the effect of remedying the initial failure to comply with the formal rules, since the landlord would be compelled to draw up (or the tenant to accept) a proper deed granting a seven-year legal lease.

However, what is T's position if, as is likely, neither party goes to court to seek any remedy? (The parties' failure to use a deed may well have arisen from the fact that they did not appreciate that one was necessary, in which case they will have no cause to realise that they need a remedy because both will have acted as though a legal lease had been created.) In such circumstances equity applies one of its basic principles; ie it 'looks on that as done which ought to be done'. Since, in equity's view, the informal lease is treated as a contract to grant a lease, what ought to be done is that this contract should be performed. Equity therefore regards the situation *as if* the agreement had been complied with and a lease granted. Accordingly, in the eyes of equity, an informal lease is regarded from its inception as a lease.[6] But this lease is a creature of equity; thus T has an *equitable* seven-year lease, which, as we shall see, falls short of a legal lease in some respects.

1 Para 31.6 above.
2 Para 31.7 above.
3 Para 36.13 below.
4 See para 36.65 below. It may be that L's right to serve a notice to quit is restricted by statute (see paras 36.69–36.79 below), in which case the implied periodic tenancy may be less of a disadvantage to T.
5 Since this contract is one which creates an interest in land, it must be in writing sufficient to satisfy the requirements of the Law of Property (Miscellaneous Provisions) Act 1989, s 2 (see para 31.2 above). Accordingly, equity cannot be of assistance to T where the informal lease is oral since an oral agreement to create an interest in land cannot, since 1989, amount to a contract.
6 As we have seen, equity treats a 'genuine' agreement (ie a formal contract) to grant a lease in the same way; see para 31.5 above.

32.4 In the case of *Walsh v Lonsdale*,[1] the parties entered into an agreement that Lonsdale would grant Walsh a seven-year lease of a mill. The agreement provided that Walsh was to pay rent annually in advance. The required deed was never drawn up, but Walsh went into possession, paying rent quarterly in arrears. On the basis of the principles explained in the previous paragraph Walsh held two 'parallel' leases; at common law the absence of a deed meant that he was a periodic tenant, in equity he held a seven-year lease. The essential dispute in this case was whether Lonsdale was entitled to demand the payment of rent annually in advance (in accordance with the terms of the equitable lease) or whether Walsh could continue to pay rent in arrears (as was his right under the legal periodic tenancy). It was held that Lonsdale could demand the rent in advance since, where the rules of equity and law conflict, those of equity must prevail.[2] Accordingly, *as between the parties themselves*,[3] the terms of their equitable lease prevailed over the common law periodic tenancy. The principle of this decision, although adverse to Walsh on the facts, could have been of benefit to him (and to any tenant in his position) in other circumstances. If, for example, Lonsdale had been seeking to turn him out by notice appropriate to ending the periodic tenancy, this would not have been allowed. His seven-year equitable lease, which could not be terminated during its fixed term, would have prevailed over the periodic tenancy.[4]

1   (1882) 21 Ch D 9.
2   Supreme Court of Judicature Act 1873, s 25(11); now re-enacted in Supreme Court Act 1981, s 49(1).
3   As we shall see in para 32.5 and in ch 35, the equitable lease does not always prevail over a purchaser.
4   Para 36.65 below.

32.5   It has been said that, as a result of the decision in *Walsh v Lonsdale*,[1] a written agreement for a lease is as good as a lease. There are, however, some important differences between a legal lease and an equitable lease. First, equity will only look on the parties to an informal lease or an agreement for a lease as having a lease where it considers that specific performance ought to be granted. Specific performance is a discretionary remedy.[2] So, for example, should the tenant go into possession under the agreement and immediately break one of its terms, equity would refuse him specific performance of the agreement.[3] He would not then have a lease in the eyes of equity, although a legal periodic tenancy might have arisen through the payment and acceptance of rent.

Second, an informal lease, being regarded as a contract to grant a lease, constitutes 'a contract to convey or create a legal estate' which in turn, as we have seen,[4] constitutes a species of equitable interest known as an estate contract. As with all equitable interests, this means that an equitable lease, unlike a legal lease, is not necessarily binding on subsequent purchasers of the landlord's estate.[5] In particular, as we shall see, in some circumstances the tenant may need to register his lease.[6] Since the parties to an informal lease may well have been unaware of the legal requirement for creating a legal lease, they may also be unaware that an equitable lease should be registered as an estate contract. Thus, where a tenant is required to register his estate contract and fails to do so, and the landlord subsequently sells the freehold to a third party, the third party will not be bound by the tenant's equitable lease. The new landlord will be bound by any legal periodic tenancy which has arisen by implication, as this does not require registration; but, except where prevented by landlord and tenant legislation, this periodic tenancy can be terminated by notice.[7]

Further, informal and formal leases differ in that certain easements which may, by virtue of the LPA, s 62, be implied on the grant of a lease may not be implied where there is only an informal lease.[8]

Finally, it is sometimes not possible to enforce covenants contained in an informal lease against an assignee of the tenant.[9]

1   (1882) 21 Ch D 9, CA.
2   Para 12.30 above.
3   *Coatsworth v Johnson* (1885) 55 LJQB 220.
4   Para 31.5 above.
5   See generally ch 35 below.
6   Where appropriate under the Land Charges Act 1972, para 35.11 below, or as a minor interest under the Land Registration Act 1925, para 35.28 below.
7   This discussion is subject to the caveat that where the title to the freehold is registered under the Land Registration Act 1925 then, if the tenant is in occupation under the lease, his rights under the equitable lease will bind the purchaser as an overriding interest, see paras 35.21–35.27 below.
8   Para 37.27–37.32 below.
9   Para 36.47 below.

32.6   Finally, we should re-emphasise that the approach adopted by equity to informal transactions, which we have illustrated by reference to informal leases, applies equally to efforts to create any other legal estate or interest which fail for lack of a deed. Thus, for example, an attempt to create a legal mortgage or a legal easement without using a deed will often result in an equitable mortgage or an equitable easement.[1]

1   Provided that, as explained at para 32.3 above, the attempt takes the form of a written document which satisfies the requirements of the Law of Property (Miscellaneous Provisions) Act 1989, s 2.

Informal arrangements

32.7 In the foregoing paragraphs we have been explaining how equity may give effect to *positive* attempts to create interests in land, ie those which have, at the least, got to the stage of being formulated in a written document which satisfies the requirements of the Law of Property (Miscellaneous Provisions) Act 1989, s 2. We now turn to those situations where matters have never reached this point; the parties may merely have a spoken or unspoken understanding that one has, or will have, some right to property owned by the other, or the words or actions of the landowner may have given rise to an expectation that another has, or is to have, a right to his land. In such circumstances, equity may sometimes either

- accept that the parties intended a trust, or
- impose a trust, or
- order that either a legal, equitable or some personal interest in land be conferred.

In many of these cases the connecting thread is that the owner of the legal estate in land has acted in such a way that, in fairness, he should either be regarded as holding the land (either wholly or partially) in trust for another, or that he must formally grant an estate or interest in the land to that other.

Implied, resulting and constructive trusts

32.8 As we have seen,[1] s 53 of the LPA requires that equitable interests, including trusts, be created by a written and signed document. However, the section expressly provides that this rule does not apply to the creation or operation of resulting, implied or constructive trusts.[2] Accordingly, the courts have been able to use the implied trust (of which the resulting and constructive trust are now usually regarded as the two constituent species) as a mechanism for conferring an equitable interest in land even in the absence of any written evidence at all.

1 Para 31.11 above.
2 LPA, s 53(2).

Resulting trusts
32.9 Traditionally, a resulting trust arises where land is conveyed to A alone but where B has contributed either all or part of the purchase price. In such a situation it is presumed[1] that it was the intention that A should hold the land on trust for B to the extent of the latter's contribution.[2] Thus B will be regarded as either the sole or part owner in equity. So, in *Sekhon v Alissa*[3] a mother gave her daughter £22,500 (a sum representing most of the mother's savings) towards the purchase of a house which was conveyed into the daughter's name. Later, when the daughter wished to sell the property she claimed that the property was solely hers and that the mother's contribution had been a gift. It was held that, in the absence of any evidence that a gift had been intended, a resulting trust would be presumed; accordingly, the parties were entitled to share the proceeds of sale in proportion to their initial contributions.

Not surprisingly, the possibility of a resulting trust arises most commonly in the domestic situation where spouses or co-habitees make financial contributions to the purchase of a home which is conveyed or registered in the sole name of their partner. It is usual that, following the application of resulting trust principles, the parties are regarded as co-owners in equity; accordingly, this is a topic to which we shall return when dealing with co-ownership in chapter 33.[3]

1   Unless a contrary intention is proved. It may, for example, be shown that B was making a gift or a
    loan; see *Re Sharpe (a bankrupt)* [1980] 1 All ER 198, [1980] 1 WLR 219.
2   *Dyer v Dyer* (1788) 2 Cox Eq Cas 92.
3   [1989] 2 FLR 94.
4   At para 33.23 below.

Constructive trusts

32.10   Under the doctrine of constructive trusts, the courts may in certain
circumstances preclude a landowner from enjoying all or part of the beneficial interest
in his land by constructively treating him as trustee for another person. Although
modern courts sometimes use the terms 'resulting' and 'constructive' trust
indiscriminately, it would appear that, in order to establish a constructive trust the
following elements must be present:

*   an agreement, arrangement, understanding or common intention that a property
    right has been or will be created; and
*   detrimental reliance on that agreement, arrangement, understanding or intention.[1]

Again, the constructive trust is often used to confer equitable co-ownership in domestic
cases where a spouse or co-habitee, who is not named as a legal owner of the family
home, has not made direct financial contributions to the purchase price. Although
unable to establish a true resulting trust, the claimant may, in certain circumstances,
satisfy the requirements of a constructive trust. Again, we deal with this specific
application of the constructive trust later.[2]

However, the constructive trust has been employed in a very much wider context.
Thus, in *Bannister v Bannister*,[3] the defendant had conveyed the freehold of two
cottages to the plaintiff, her brother-in-law, at an under-value on the understanding
that she would be allowed to live in one of the cottages, rent-free, for the rest of her
life. When he sought to evict her, the Court of Appeal held that he was unable to do
so; he was a constructive trustee with his sister-in-law having an equitable life interest[4]
in the property. In *Lyus v Prowsa Developments Ltd*[5] it was held that a purchaser, by
expressly agreeing with the vendor to honour the plaintiff's existing contract to
purchase part of the land,[6] thereby became a constructive trustee and was obliged to
complete that contract. More controversially, it has been suggested that a purchaser
of land may find himself bound by a contractual licence by virtue of the imposition of
a constructive trust. In *Ashburn Anstalt v Arnold*[7] the Court of Appeal opined that, where
a purchaser expressly agrees to be bound by[8] an existing contractual licence, this
stipulation may independently give rise to a constructive trust under which the
purchaser must give continued effect to the rights of the licensee.[9]

1   See, in particular, *Lloyds Bank plc v Rosset* [1991] 1 AC 107, [1990] 1 All ER 1111, HL.
2   At para 33.23 below.
3   [1948] 2 All ER 133.
4   A conclusion which itself gave rise to legal problems which we discuss at para 34.4 below.
5   [1982] 1 WLR 1044.
6   Which was not otherwise binding on the purchaser because it had not been registered, see para 35.35
    below.
7   [1989] Ch 1.
8   The court made clear that merely taking with notice of a contractual licence is insufficient to give rise
    to a constructive trust. This, put alongside the court's ruling that a contractual licence does not, in itself,
    give rise to a proprietary right which can bind a purchaser, effectively overturns previous cases, such
    as *Midland Bank Ltd v Farmpride Hatcheries Ltd* (1980) 260 Estates Gazette 493, CA, in which it was
    held that a purchaser with notice was bound by a contractual licence.
9   Reasoning under which the much-maligned decision in *Binions v Evans* [1972] Ch 359 may still be
    regarded as correct.

Proprietary estoppel

32.11 An early statement of the equitable doctrine of proprietary estoppel is to be found in the judgment of Lord Kingsdown in *Ramsden v Dyson*:[1] 'If a man … under an expectation, created or encouraged by the land[owner], that he shall have a certain interest, takes possession of such land, with the consent of the land[owner], and upon the faith of such … expectation, with the knowledge of the land[owner], and without objection by him, lays out money upon the land, a court of equity will compel the land[owner] to give effect to such … expectation'. Whilst the development of this doctrine was greatly restricted for over a century by the very much stricter rules laid down in *Wilmott v Barber*,[2] it re-emerged following the decision in *Taylor's Fashions Ltd v Liverpool Victoria Trustees Co Ltd*.[3] There, Oliver J identified as the primary question for the court 'whether, in particular individual circumstances, it would be unconscionable for a party to be permitted to deny that which, knowingly or unknowingly, he has allowed or encouraged another to assume to his detriment'.[4] Having returned to its more broadly based roots the doctrine has, as we shall see, come to be used more widely.

However flexible the court's approach may have become, certain elements must be present if the doctrine is to be established in any given case. These we consider in the following paragraphs.

1   (1866) LR 1 HL 129 at 170.
2   (1880) 15 Ch D 96.
3   [1982] QB 133n.
4   See also *Habib Bank Ltd v Habib Bank AG Zurich* [1981] 2 All ER 650, [1981] 1 WLR 1265, CA. This approach has recently been endorsed by the Privy Council in *Lim Teng Huan v Ang Swee Chuan* [1992] 1 WLR 113.

Assurance

32.12 First, the landowner must have made a representation or created an expectation that the claimant has, or is to have, rights over the land in question. Whilst this will normally involve proof of some positive statement to such effect, the courts may infer the necessary assurance where the landowner has remained silent and allowed the claimant to incur expenditure.

Acts in reliance

32.13 Second, it must be shown that the claimant acted in reliance on that representation. While it has been suggested that, once it is proved that a representation has been made and that the claimant has acted to his detriment, there is a rebuttable presumption that those acts were in reliance on the representation,[1] the Privy Council has, more recently, expressed the view that such reliance must either be strictly proved, or that this must be a matter of 'inevitable inference'.[2] Thus, in the normal event, the claimant must show that his subsequent actions were induced or influenced by the landowner's assurance.

These acts often, in practice, constitute expenditure on, or improvements to, the land in question. So, in *Pascoe v Turner*,[3] the plaintiff, on leaving the defendant for another woman, represented to the defendant that the house in which they had been living as man and wife was hers. On the faith of this, the defendant spent money on repairs and decoration. When the plaintiff subsequently sought to determine what he alleged was a mere licence to occupy, the Court of Appeal held that he could not do so because the doctrine of proprietary estoppel gave rise to an 'equity' in favour of the defendant. In *Inwards v Baker*,[4] a father allowed his son to build a bungalow for himself on the father's land, which the son did, by his own labour, and sharing the expense with his father. The father had, by an old unrevoked will, left the land to someone else, and on his death his executors claimed possession of the land from the son. This the Court of Appeal refused, holding that the son, having spent money on the land in the expectation of being allowed to stay there, was entitled to remain on the property.

However, it is equally clear that other acts will suffice, for example, expenditure on one's own land in expectation of being granted some right over another's land. This is shown by the application of the doctrine in *ER Ives Investments Ltd v High*,[5] where the defendant had spent money constructing a garage on his own land in a position where it could be reached only across the yard of the neighbouring property. The neighbouring owners at that time (predecessors of the plaintiff) had stood by and, indeed, encouraged the defendant so to build his garage, knowing that he believed, as a result of prior transactions, that he had a right of way across the yard. The decision in *Crabb v Arun District Council*[6] demonstrates that the doctrine extends to the situation where the claimant merely acts to his detriment in reliance on the expectation encouraged by the landowner. Here, the plaintiff, believing himself entitled, as a result of negotiations with the defendant, to a right of way across the defendant's adjoining land, sold part of his land, leaving the remainder accessible only via this disputed right of way. The Court of Appeal held that the actions of the defendant, in encouraging the plaintiff so to act to his detriment, raised an 'equity' in favour of the plaintiff.

1   *Greasley v Cooke* [1980] 3 All ER 710, [1980] 1 WLR 1306, CA.
2   *Lim Teng Huan v Ang Swee Chuan* [1992] 1 WLR 113.
3   [1979] 2 All ER 945, [1979] 1 WLR 431, CA.
4   [1965] 2 QB 29, [1965] 1 All ER 446, CA.
5   [1967] 2 QB 379, [1967] 1 All ER 504, CA.
6   [1976] Ch 179, [1975] 3 All ER 865, CA.

Detriment

32.14   Finally, it is clear that, in order to found a claim based on proprietary estoppel, it must be shown that the claimant will suffer a detriment unless the court intervenes to offer protection. This detriment lies not in the acts that the claimant has carried out, but rather in the prejudice which he will suffer if the landowner is allowed to insist upon his strict legal rights and, thereby, to deny the expected rights. This means that the plaintiff must satisfy the court that 'the defendant, by setting up his right, is taking advantage of him in a way which is unconscionable, inequitable or unjust'.[1]

1   *Crabb v Arun District Council* [1976] Ch 179 at 195, [1975] 3 All ER 865, CA.

Effect of the doctrine

32.15   The doctrine of proprietary estoppel operates to prevent what the court regards as the true arrangement envisaged by the parties being frustrated by their being left to their rights and duties at law.[1] Its effect is to give rise to what is often referred to as an 'equity' in favour of the claimant, which the court satisfies by making an order appropriate to give effect to that arrangement. In the majority of the cases, the arrangement between the parties gives rise, at law, only to a gratuitous licence revocable at will. By virtue of proprietary estoppel, however, an equity arises in favour of the licensee which it seems the court may satisfy, according to the circumstances of the case, either positively, by conferring on the licensee a recognised proprietary interest in the land, or negatively, by holding the licensee to be protected from revocation. It is also possible that the court may conclude that, by the time the matter comes to court, the circumstances may be such that it is no longer equitable for the claimant's full expectations to be met, so that the owner is entitled to recover possession of the land free from any further claim.[2]

It is unusual for the court to order the outright transfer of the freehold, but it can happen. Thus, in *Pascoe v Turner*[3] the court decided that, in the circumstances, the equity could be satisfied only by declaring that the freehold of the property was vested in the defendant.[4] More likely is a declaration that the claimant is entitled to some lesser proprietary right such as a share in the ownership of the property,[5] or a right akin to an easement.[6]

However, the court may decide not to confer on the claimant a recognised proprietary right. For example, In *Dodsworth v Dodsworth*[7] the court merely protected the defendants' occupation until such time as they had been compensated by the plaintiff for their improvements to the property. A common course of action in the past has been for the courts to confer on the claimant an irrevocable licence for life.[8] While this has the attraction of representing fairly accurately the true arrangement envisaged by the parties, it does give rise to difficulties[9]. For this reason, the court will usually try to devise some alternative solution.[10]

1   *Chandler v Kerley* [1978] 2 All ER 942 at 946.
2   *Sledmore v Dalby* (1996) 72 P & CR 196, CA. Here, by the time of the hearing, the defendant had already occupied the property rent-free for 18 years and the plaintiff's need for the property was now very much greater than his. The court therefore decided that it was no longer equitable to fulfil the defendant's expectation that he would be allowed to remain in the property for the rest of his life, and the plaintiff was permitted to regain possession.
3   [1979] 2 All ER 945, [1979] 1 WLR 431, CA, para 32.13 above.
4   See also *Dillwyn v Llewelyn* (1862) 4 De GF & J 517; *Voyce v Voyce* (1991) 62 P & CR 290, CA.
5   *Lim Teng Huan v Ang Swee Chuan* [1992] 1 WLR 113.
6   *Crabb v Arun District Council* [1976] Ch 179, [1975] 3 All ER 865, CA; *ER Ives Investment Ltd v High* [1967] 2 QB 379, [1967] 1 All ER 504, CA.
7   (1973) 228 Estates Gazette 1115, CA. See also *Baker v Baker* (1993) 25 HLR 408, CA.
8   Eg *Inwards v Baker* [1965] 2 QB 29, [1965] 1 All ER 446, CA; *Greasley v Cooke* [1980] 3 All ER 710, [1980] 1 WLR 1306, CA.
9   See para 34.4 below.
10 In *Griffiths v Williams* (1977) 248 Estates Gazette 947, CA the court suggested that the parties should agree to the grant of a long lease, terminable on the death of the claimant, and subject to an absolute covenant against assignment.

Conveyancing problems

32.16   A number of potential conveyancing problems are created by the doctrine of proprietary estoppel. The first is that prior to any determination of the matter by a court the existence and extent of an 'equity' arising from proprietary estoppel is very difficult for a purchaser to detect. The equity arises from the estoppel and is not created by the court.[1] It thus dates from the moment when the landowner unconscionably sets up his own rights against the legitimate expectations of the claimant.[2] This equity was assumed to be capable of binding purchasers in *Ives v High*[3] and *Inwards v Baker*.[4] We shall leave until later[5] our discussion of the exact circumstances in which the equity *will* bind a purchaser.

Once a court has determined that the 'equity' arising from proprietary estoppel should be satisfied by the grant of a recognised property interest, further conveyancing problems should not arise. However, where the court decides to satisfy the equity negatively by holding merely that the claimant has an irrevocable licence, conveyancing difficulties remain. Where the irrevocable licence amounts to a right to occupy for life, such as was granted in *Inwards v Baker*,[6] there is an argument that this may give rise to a life interest; while this no longer gives rise to the same difficulties as previously, it may still result in the licensee having more extensive powers to deal with the property than might have been intended.[7]

There is clearly difficulty in fitting any licence protected by estoppel into the normal concepts of property law. It might also be noted that the right created in *Inwards v Baker* lacks the characteristic of property rights of being assignable to third parties. Certainly, a licence protected by estoppel falls rather short of the requisites of a property right suggested by Lord Wilberforce in *National Provincial Bank Ltd v Ainsworth*,[8] which are that it must be definable, identifiable by third parties, capable in its nature of assumption by third parties, and have some degree of permanence or stability. We would venture the opinion, however, that the doctrine of proprietary estoppel will continue to be used by the courts to give effect to recognised property rights arising from informal arrangements. However, now that the conveyancing problems are more widely appreciated, it seems likely that the courts, when deciding how to satisfy the equity, will adopt a solution which avoids these difficulties.[9]

1   *Re Sharpe (a bankrupt)* [1980] 1 All ER 198, [1980] 1 WLR 219.
2   *Lim Teng Huan v Ang Swee Chuan* [1992] 1 WLR 113 at 117.
3   [1967] 2 QB 379, [1967] 1 All ER 504, CA.
4   [1965] 2 QB 29, [1965] 1 All ER 446, CA.
5   Ch 35 below.
6   [1965] 2 QB 29, [1965] 1 All ER 446, CA.
7   See para 34.4 below. It was this result which the court was seeking to avoid in, for example, *Griffiths v Williams* (1977) 248 Estates Gazette 947, CA.
8   [1965] AC 1175 at 1248, [1965] 2 All ER 472 at 494, HL; compare *Plimmer v City of Wellington Corpn* (1884) 9 App Cas 699, PC and see also LPA, s 4(1).
9   As in *Griffiths v Williams* (1977) 248 EG 947, CA.

Proprietary estoppel and constructive trusts

32.17   It will be apparent from the foregoing paragraphs that there are strong similarities between the doctrine of proprietary estoppel and the constructive trust. Although the former doctrine has a quite distinct legal pedigree from the constructive trust and the two principles have developed separately without cross-fertilisation between them, it is clear that the two have come to bear a close resemblance, particularly when applied in the context of co-ownership.[1] That said, there remain important differences. Particularly in its more recent formulations,[2] the constructive trust appears to be based firmly on some sort of express or implied *agreement* between the parties. Proprietary estoppel is more firmly directed towards fulfilling *expectations* created by the landowner. It is also possible that, under the doctrine of proprietary estoppel, the courts may accept a wider range of acts in reliance[3] than is acceptable as a basis for imposing a constructive trust.[4] Finally, there is little doubt that the doctrine of proprietary estoppel affords the court a far wider range of remedies. As we have seen,[5] the court can confer a range of rights from a temporary licence through to full legal ownership. Where a constructive trust is imposed the almost invariable result is that the claimant has an equitable interest in the property which amounts either to sole or, more likely, a share in the beneficial ownership of the property.

1   As to which see para 33.23 below.
2   In *Lloyds Bank plc v Rosset* [1991] 1 AC 107, [1990] 1 All ER 1111, HL.
3   See, for example, *Greasley v Cooke* [1980] 3 All ER 710, [1980] 1 WLR 1306, CA and *Re Basham, decd* [1986] 1 WLR 1498 in both of which the continued contribution of domestic labour and services were held to be sufficient.
4   It remains highly unlikely that the courts will regard the performance of 'ordinary' domestic duties as sufficient; see further para 33.23 below.
5   Para 32.15 above.

The doctrine of benefit and burden

32.18   Further illustrating equity's flexibility in this area, other aspects of the case of *ER Ives Investment Ltd v High*[1] demonstrate how the doctrine of benefit and burden,[2] originally limited to those taking the benefit of a deed, may be pressed into service to protect rights arising from informal arrangements. High's original neighbour W built a block of flats on his land, the foundations of which encroached on High's land by about one foot. High and W agreed that the foundations could remain where they were and that in return High could have a right of way across the yard of W's flats to gain access to a side road. W subsequently sold his property to X. While X owned the flats, High, to X's knowledge, built a garage in such a way that it could only be reached across the yard, and also contributed to the cost of resurfacing the yard. Later X sold the flats to Ives Ltd, expressly subject to High's right to cross the yard. Ives Ltd brought this action to restrain High from crossing the yard. The Court of Appeal, in addition to upholding High's right on the basis of proprietary estoppel,[3] held that, on the principle that 'he who takes the benefit must accept the burden', so long as the owners of the blocks of flats had the benefit of having their foundations in High's land, they had to allow High and his successors to have access over their yard. The converse equally applies: so long as High took the benefit of access across the yard, he had to permit the foundations to remain. This would suggest then that should High, for example, decide to abandon using the access across the yard, he could demand that the foundations be removed from his land, no doubt necessitating the demolition of the flats. Thus, where the doctrine of benefit and burden does apply, it operates to render a licence irrevocable for so long as the corresponding benefit is enjoyed.

It has recently been made clear by the House of Lords in *Rhone v Stephens*[4] that the doctrine does not mean that any party deriving *any* benefit from a conveyance has to accept *any* burden imposed by that conveyance; the burden must be relevant to the exercise of the right. Accordingly, in that case, the defendant could not be required to repair a roof which overhung the adjoining cottage simply because she had the benefit of a right of support from that property.

1   [1967] 2 QB 379, [1967] 1 All ER 505, CA.
2   See also para 38.7 below; and see *Tito v Waddell (No 2)* [1977] Ch 106 at 289ff; [1977] 3 All ER 129.
3   Para 32.13 above.
4   [1994] 2 All ER 65, HL.

Adverse possession

32.19   Finally, we turn to the circumstances in which legal estates and interests may be acquired despite the absence of any formal grant, agreement or even an understanding between the parties. Here we are considering those situations in which, due to possession or user enjoyed by the claimant over a long period of time, the law is prepared to validate the claim to the estate or interest in question. The only legal rights to land which can be acquired in this way are a fee simple absolute (ie freehold ownership) and an easement (such as a right of way). Freehold ownership may be established by long use (or, more accurately, adverse possession) as a result of the application of the Limitation Acts. A claim to an easement is made under the rules relating to prescription. In this section we shall deal only with the acquisition of freehold title by way of adverse possession; prescription is more conveniently dealt with in chapter 37.

32.20   English law protects possession, a proposition reflected in the well-known maxim, 'possession is nine points of the law'. The right of a person who is in possession of land to that land is enforceable under English law against all-comers, except someone who can show a better legal right to possession.[1] Thus, as between A, the owner of land with the 'paper' title, and B, who takes possession of the land from him, A has the better right to possession. But were B subsequently to be himself dispossessed of the land by C, the latter could not in law say to B, 'you have no more title than I have, my possession is as good as yours', for B's possession constitutes good title against all but A.[1] As between the rival claimants A and B, or B and C, English law in effect regards 'ownership' as meaning 'having the better right to possession'.[2]

1   *Asher v Whitlock* (1865) LR 1 QB 1.
2   Megarry and Wade *The Law of Real Property* (5th edn) p 106.

32.21   Where a landowner's possession is interrupted he is entitled to take steps against the trespasser.[1] Where the trespasser takes possession, rather than simply intruding on a temporary basis, he is often referred to as a 'squatter' rather than just a trespasser; here the landowner will need to recover possession of the land rather than simply suing in trespass.[2] However, the law places a limit on the time within which he should take action to recover possession, for it is the policy of the law, first, to protect undisturbed possession and, second, that a person should pursue his lawful claims with diligence. This is the principle of 'limitation of actions'.[3]

The effect of the limitation principle is that a person who has the right to possess land may lose that right if someone else takes possession of the land in a way which is inconsistent with his possession, and remains in possession for the statutory 'limitation period', which is, generally, 12 years.[4] In such a case, the squatter puts an end not only to the original owner's right to take action to recover possession but also, thereby, puts an end to his title to the land.[5]

It should be appreciated that, while the limitation principle can sometimes operate to deprive a landowner of title to the whole of his land, its more usual application is far less dramatic (and rather more acceptable). Suppose, for example, that a boundary structure between A and B's properties is inadvertently erected in the wrong place so that A's garden now includes a strip of B's land. If this situation remains undisturbed for a period of 12 years, B's title to that strip will have been extinguished. In this way, minor boundary discrepancies are often resolved in a relatively straightforward manner.[6]

1   Ch 24 above.
2   Should he choose self-help rather than seeking a court order for possession he should take care to avoid transgressing the criminal law; see para 24.11 above.
3   Currently embodied in the Limitation Act 1980, as amended.
4   Ibid, s 15(1). This period may be extended in cases of fraud, concealment or acknowledgment; paras 12.36 to 12.39 above.
5   Ibid, s 17.
6   See para 30.25 above.

The operation of the Limitation Act
32.22   The Limitation Act 1980 provides[1] that no action may be brought to recover land after the expiration of 12 years from the date on which the right of action accrued. The right of action is deemed to accrue on the date on which the person in possession was dispossessed or discontinued possession and continues only so long as another person is in adverse possession of the land.[2] Hence, in order for time to start running it must be established that

•   the 'paper' owner has either been dispossessed or has discontinued possession; and
•   that the squatter has gone into adverse possession.

The adverse possession must continue, unbroken, for the full 12-year period. However, it is not essential that the same person is the squatter for the whole of that period.[3] So, if A (the 'paper' owner) is dispossessed by B for 5 years and then B is himself dispossessed by C, A's title will be extinguished once C has been in adverse possession for 7 years. However, C will remain vulnerable to an action for possession brought by B for a further 5 years; only at that point does C's title becomes secure. Equally, B could have voluntarily transferred his rights to the land to C; in that case C's title would become unimpeachable after 7 years.

1   Limitation Act 1980, s 15(1).
2   Ibid, Sch 1, paras 1 and 8. As we shall see in para 32.24 below, 'adverse' possession is very much more than simple trespass.
3   *Mount Carmel Investments Ltd v Peter Thurlow Ltd* [1988] 3 All ER 129, [1988] 1 WLR 1078, CA.

Discontinuance or dispossession

32.23   The Limitation Act 1980, Sch 1, para 1 requires that, for the limitation period to begin, the 'paper' owner must either be dispossessed or must discontinue his possession. Dispossession refers to a person coming in and putting another out of possession, while discontinuance refers to the case where the person in possession abandons possession and another takes it.[1] Abandonment of possession may be difficult to establish. The smallest act by the 'paper' owner will be sufficient to show that there was no discontinuance[2] since the owner with the right to possession will be readily assumed to have the requisite intention to possess.[3] Thus, the acts of the 'paper' owner, in *Leigh v Jack*[4] in repairing a fence on the land, and, in *Williams Bros Direct Supply Ltd v Raftery*[5] in measuring the land for development and depositing rubbish on it, were sufficient to show no discontinuance. However if, for example, the 'paper' owner erects a fence which prevents his own access to the disputed land, this will be strong evidence of abandonment, particularly in the case of urban property.[6]

The fact that there was no discontinuance or abandonment of possession by the 'paper' owner means only that the squatter's case must be based on his having dispossessed the 'paper' owner. However, time only starts to run if it is further proved that the squatter went into adverse possession. As we shall see, where it is possible to establish that the squatter's possession is adverse this will, necessarily, also serve to prove dispossession of the 'paper' owner.[7]

Contrary to the view taken in a number of earlier authorities,[8] it is not the case that a 'paper' owner, who plans to use the land for a particular purpose in the future (eg re-development) but has no present use for it, can only be dispossessed by a squatter whose acts are inconsistent with his future plans.[9] In most cases the courts have demonstrated that there is in any event no need for such a rule, as they are well able to frustrate the claims of would-be squatters by finding their acts were too trivial to amount to factual possession[10] or by finding that, particularly if the squatter is aware of the owner's plans, he has not demonstrated the requisite intention.[11] Nonetheless, as *Buckinghamshire County Council v Moran* shows, a squatter may occasionally succeed, despite the fact that his possession does not interfere with the 'paper' owner's future plans for the land.[12]

1   *Powell v McFarlane* (1977) 38 P & CR 452.
2   *Leigh v Jack* (1879) 5 Ex D 264, CA.
3   *Powell v McFarlane* (1977) 38 P & CR 452.
4   (1879) 5 Ex D 264, CA.
5   [1958] 1 QB 159, [1957] 3 All ER 593, CA.
6   *London Borough of Hounslow v Minchinton* (1997) 74 P & CR 221, CA.
7   *Treloar v Nute* [1977] 1 All ER 230, [1976] 1 WLR 1295, CA.
8   Commencing with a dictum of Bramwell LJ in *Leigh v Jack* (1879) 5 Ex D 264 at 273; see also, in particular, *Williams Bros Direct Supply Ltd v Raftery* [1958] 1 QB 159, [1957] 3 All ER 593, CA.
9   *Buckinghamshire County Council v Moran* [1990] Ch 623, [1989] 2 All ER 225, CA.
10 See, for example, *Boosey v Davis* (1987) 55 P & CR 83, CA.
11 See, for example, *Pulleyn v Hall Aggregates (Thames Valley)* (1992) 65 P & CR 276, CA, where it was held to be no adverse possession since the squatter's acts were consistent with the paper owner's present plans for the land.
12 A further device to frustrate the claims of squatters, the 'implied licence' theory invented by the Court of Appeal in *Wallis's Cayton Bay Holiday Camp Ltd v Shell-Mex and BP Ltd* [1975] QB 94, [1974] 3 All ER 575, CA, is statutorily overruled by the Limitation Act 1980, Sch 1, para 8(4).

Adverse possession

32.24   As we have said,[1] the limitation period does not start to run until adverse possession commences. The nature of adverse possession was considered by the Court of Appeal in *Buckinghamshire County Council v Moran*.[2] The Court, adopting the views of Slade J in *Powell v McFarlane*,[3] held that a person claiming to have been in adverse possession of land must show not only factual possession but also the necessary intention to possess the land (*animus possidendi*).

1   Para 32.22 above.
2   [1990] Ch 623, CA, [1989] 2 All ER 225.
3   (1977) 38 P & CR 452.

32.25   *Factual possession*   Whether a person has factual possession depends on the circumstances, particularly the nature of the land and the way in which land of that nature is commonly used or enjoyed. Basically, however, what is required is that the squatter's use of the land should amount to more than persistent trespass. He must have been exercising sufficient physical control over the land to amount to exclusive possession and must have dealt with the land in the same way as any occupying owner might have done. Clearly building on land, occupying and using a building,[1] or fencing[2] and then incorporating land into land already owned by the claimant[3] will amount to factual possession. Equally, acts falling short of such obvious control for example, rough shooting,[4] grazing and storage,[5] weeding, tending and putting a compost heap on land,[6] have all been regarded as sufficient to show factual possession, in the light of the nature of the land in question.

1   *Mount Carmel Investments Ltd v Peter Thurlow Ltd* [1988] 3 All ER 129, [1988] 1 WLR 1078, CA.
2   A claimant who fences the disputed land will almost always have done enough to demonstrate factual possession since this is viewed as 'the strongest possible evidence' (*Seddon v Smith* (1877) 36 LT 168). However, in some circumstances fencing will not provide proof of factual possession eg in *Boosey v Davis* (1988) 55 P & CR 83 (incomplete fence) and *Marsden v Miller* (1992) 64 P & CR 239 (fence in place for only 24 hours).
3   *Buckinghamshire County Council v Moran* [1990] Ch 623, CA, [1989] 2 All ER 225.
4   *Red House Farms (Thorndon) Ltd v Catchpole* (1977) 244 Estates Gazette 295.
5   *Treloar v Nute* [1976] 1 WLR 1295.
6   *London Borough of Hounslow v Minchinton* (1997) 74 P & CR 221, CA.

32.26   *Intention*   However, factual possession alone is not enough; the squatter must prove the requisite intention. *Animus possidendi* involves the intention, in one's own name and on one's own behalf, to exclude the world at large, including the owner with the paper title,[1] so far as is reasonably practicable and so far as the processes of the law will allow. What is required, according to *Buckinghamshire County Council v Moran*, is not that the squatter must intend to own or even to acquire ownership of the land but rather that he or she must intend to possess it for the time being. Thus the fact that Mr Moran's intention was to use land belonging to the council (which he had incorporated into his garden and access to which he had barred by a padlocked gate) only unless and until a proposed bypass was built on it did not preclude his having the requisite *animus*.

Evidence of the requisite intention is likely in most cases to be a matter of inference from the alleged squatter's acts. As in *Buckinghamshire County Council v Moran*, enclosure of the land by the squatter, for example by putting up a fence, is strong evidence not only of factual possession but also of the requisite *animus*. However, even fencing may be equivocal. It may, for example, be that, as in *Littledale v Liverpool College*,[2] it is done to protect a right of way enjoyed over the 'paper' owner's land from interference by the world at large, rather than to establish possession.[3] *Animus possidendi*, the intention to deal exclusively with the land, involves the intention to deal with it to the exclusion not only of the world at large but also of the true owner, even if only for the time being.[4]

1   It is not fatal that the squatter erroneously believes the land to be his own since the intention required is to *possess* rather than to *dispossess;* see *Hughes v Cork* [1994] EGCS 25, CA.
2   [1900] 1 Ch 19, CA.
3   See also *Fruin v Fruin* [1983] CA Transcript, where a claimant who had erected a fence to prevent an elderly member of the family wandering off was held not to have been in adverse possession.
4   As in *Buckinghamshire County Council v Moran*.

32.27   *Possession as of wrong.*   Possession is not adverse if it has a lawful basis. If therefore a person's use and occupation of land is with the permission of the 'paper' owner, it cannot be 'adverse'. There must be a genuine factual basis for any finding by the court that there is such a licence from the 'paper' owner. A licence is not to be implied just because the owner has not sought to recover his land because the squatter is not interfering with any plans he has for the land.[1] In *BP Properties Ltd v Buckler*[2] the 'paper' owner wrote to the squatter unilaterally permitting her to remain in the property; although the squatter ignored this letter, incorrectly believing she was entitled to remain as of right, it was held that her continued possession was attributable to the 'paper' owner's licence. This case suggests that the unilateral grant[3] to the squatter of a short-term licence to remain in the property is a speedy, cheap and effective way of stopping time running in the squatter's favour. By way of contrast, sending a letter which merely asserts the 'paper' owner's right to possession without more is ineffective to prevent the squatter acquiring title.[4]

1   Limitation Act 1980, Sch 1, para 8(4); para 32.23 above.
2   [1987] 2 EGLR 168, CA.
3   There must he an outright *grant* of permission; merely inviting the squatter to agree to a licence will not, where the squatter fails to respond, stop time running; see *Pavledes v Ryesbridge Properties* (1989) 58 P & CR 459.
4   *Mount Carmel Investments Ltd v Peter Thurlow Ltd* [1988] 3 All ER 129, [1988] 1 WLR 1078, CA.

The effect of the Limitation Act
Unregistered land
32.28   In the case of unregistered land, the title of the person entitled to bring an action for possession is extinguished on the expiration of the limitation period.[1] The effect of the Limitation Act 1980 is not to convey from one to another but to extinguish;[2] hence, the squatter does not acquire the title or estate of the owner whom he has dispossessed,[3] but acquires a new freehold title of his own. However, it is important to remember that the only rights extinguished for the benefit of the squatter are those of persons who might, during the statutory period, have brought, but did not in fact bring, an action to recover possession of the land.[4] Thus the squatter has no answer to the claim of a third party seeking to enforce, for example, an easement or a restrictive covenant over the land;[4] these rights continue to bind the land in accordance with normal principles.

1   Limitation Act 1980, s 17.
2   *Tichborne v Weir* (1892) 67 LT 735.
3   *Fairweather v St Marylebone Property Co Ltd* [1963] AC 510, [1962] 2 All ER 288, HL.
4   *Re Nisbet and Potts' Contract* [1906] 1 Ch 386 at 409.

Registered land
32.29   In the case of registered land, the LRA, s 75 provides that the Limitation Act applies to registered land in the same manner and to the same extent as to unregistered land except that, at the expiration of the statutory limitation period, the title of the

registered proprietor is not automatically extinguished. Instead, the registered proprietor is deemed to hold his estate on trust for the squatter. The latter may then apply to be registered as proprietor, such registration being treated as a first registration; when this occurs the title of the previously registered proprietor is closed.[1] A provision of this nature is necessary in applying the Limitation Act to registered land in order to deal with the fact that one only acquires title to registered land on being registered as proprietor.

Prior to his registration as proprietor, the squatter's rights constitute an overriding interest; this is irrespective of whether he has completed the full 12-year period of adverse possession or not.[2] This means that the rights of the squatter will bind anyone to whom the registered 'paper' proprietor transfers the land. Where the squatter has not yet been in adverse possession for 12 years, the transferee from the 'paper' owner will, of course, be able to take action to regain possession. However, he must do so prior to the elapse of those 12 years; he does not have the benefit of a fresh limitation period. Where the squatter has already been in adverse possession for the full 12 years, the new registered proprietor will, from the outset, hold his estate on trust for the squatter and so will never have acquired anything more than a 'paper' title.

1   Since, by definition, the squatter has no documents of title, he will normally, in the first instance, be registered with possessory title; this gives no guarantee as to the title prior to first registration.
2   Land Registration Act 1925, s 70(1)(f); as to overriding interests see para 35.21 below.

Limitation and leases
Adverse possession against a tenant
32.30   Where a person occupies land adversely to a tenant throughout the statutory limitation period, the tenant's title is extinguished.[1] There is no transfer of the tenant's lease to the adverse possessor since the title acquired by the latter is to a freehold estate. It follows that the squatter is not directly bound by covenants in the original lease[2] but, where (as is usual) there is a provision in the lease allowing the landlord to terminate in the event of any breach of covenant (known as a right of re-entry), this right is binding on the squatter.[3] Thus, unless the squatter complies with the covenants, the landlord will be able to re-enter the land and regain possession.[4]

1   Limitation Act 1980, s 17.
2   *Tichborne v Weir* (1892) 67 LT 735.
3   A right of re-entry in a lease is a legal interest binding on all-comers.
4   Paras 36.32–36.35 below.

The position of the landlord
32.31   Although adverse possession by a squatter will extinguish the tenant's title, time only begins to run against the landlord when the lease expires.[1] So, for example, where T, the tenant under a 20-year lease is dispossessed by S in the fifth year of the lease, T's title will be extinguished 12 years later (ie in the 17th year of the lease). Just over three years later, when the lease would have expired, the landlord becomes entitled to regain possession against S; only then does time start to run against the landlord. Accordingly, S is not secure against the landlord until he has been in adverse possession for a further 12 years.

Furthermore, it has been held, by the House of Lords in *Fairweather v St Marylebone Property Co Ltd*,[2] that where a tenant's title is extinguished as a result of 12 years' adverse possession, that title is only extinguished as against the squatter. As between the landlord and the tenant the lease remains on foot. Accordingly, in that case it was held that the tenant whose title had been extinguished could, nevertheless, surrender the lease to the landlord before the expiration of the term. This brought the lease to an end and enabled the landlord to take immediate action to recover the land from the squatter, since only then did time begin to run against the landlord.

There is a strong argument that the *Fairweather* case applies equally to registered land. While it is possible to suggest that the effect of the LRA, s 75 is that the squatter, when registered as proprietor acquires title to the 'paper' owner's (ie the tenant's) estate, this is inconsistent with the well-established principle that a squatter acquires title to a new *freehold* estate. Accordingly, when applying to be registered, a squatter should be accorded a qualified freehold title. This will prompt the closing of the dispossessed tenant's title and, where the freeholder's title is also registered, the closing of that title as well. Both will be informed by the Land Registry before this occurs which may well provoke an arrangement similar to that which took place in the *Fairweather* case. While this possibility was not considered by the court in *Spectrum Investment Co v Holmes*,[3] where it was held that, once the squatter is registered as proprietor, the original lessee cannot surrender the term, it appears that, in that case, the squatter had already been registered[4] with a *leasehold* title. If the latter had been registered with a freehold title the case could then have been dealt with in the same way as unregistered land.

1   Limitation Act 1980, Sch 1, para 4.
2   [1963] AC 510, [1962] 2 All ER 288, HL.
3   [1981] 1 All ER 6, [1981] 1 WLR 221.
4   Erroneously, it appears; see Pain *Adverse possession: a conveyancers guide*, p 85 and E Cooke 'Adverse possession – problems of title in registered land' (1994) 14 LS 1.

Tenants as squatters

32.32   A tenant cannot be in adverse possession of the land of which he is tenant until his lease comes to an end. In the case of a fixed term lease, this will be at its termination date. In the case of a periodic tenancy this will either be at the expiry of any notice to quit which has been served or, where no notice has been served, at the end of the period covered by the last rent payment.[1]

A lessee who takes possession of land which adjoins, or is in close proximity to, the land of which he is tenant is presumed only to acquire that land by adverse possession as tenant; this presumption applies whether the 'paper' owner of the additional land is the squatter's landlord or some other person. During the course of the lease the additional land is held by the squatting tenant on the same terms and conditions as are contained in the lease of his other land,[2] and, at the end of the lease, all of the land will revert to the landlord.

1   Limitation Act 1980, Sch 1, paras 4 and 5.
2   *Smirk v Lyndale Developments Ltd* [1975] Ch 317, [1975] 1 All ER 690, CA.

Chapter 33

Sharing ownership

33.1   So far, we have tended to speak of 'an' owner of land or an interest in land and we have discussed, in the main, only present freehold ownership. This over-simplistic view of land ownership must now be examined more closely. As we shall see, it is possible to carve up the ownership of land so that limited 'slices' of it are enjoyed successively, ie by one person after another. Equally, an ownership interest can be co-owned, ie enjoyed by two or more persons concurrently. The sharing of ownership in either of these different ways poses similar problems; notably how to balance the sometimes competing interests of the various owners, and how to facilitate the sale of the land in which a number of ownership interests exist. In this chapter we shall consider the following topics:

- the nature of limited ownership interests in land and of future enjoyment of land;
- the nature of concurrent ownership and the circumstances in which such ownership exists; and
- the potential problems posed where the ownership of land is shared, either successively or concurrently.

Successive ownership

Limited ownership interests
33.2   The two main forms of ownership interest in land are the freehold and the leasehold. The freehold interest is equivalent to absolute ownership of land, whereas the leasehold interest is a form of limited ownership. The leasehold interest has a certain duration (or a duration capable of being rendered certain). However, there are other forms of limited ownership interest, which differ from a leasehold interest in that they are of uncertain duration. These other limited ownership interests are not frequently encountered today; they are, primarily, the life interest and the entailed interest, and, equally rare, the conditional fee simple and the determinable fee simple. The nature of these interests will now briefly be considered, but their operation cannot fully be understood apart from the law relating to settlements.

The life interest

33.3 As its name makes clear, a life interest occurs where land is granted to someone for his life.[1] Such a person's rights of enjoyment of the land are more limited than those of a freeholder. Like a leaseholder he is subject to the doctrine of waste which provides for liability for substantially altering the premises where this is to the detriment of those who will succeed the 'life tenant', as he is known.[2] Should a life tenant sell his interest, he clearly cannot create a greater interest than his own; consequently, the purchaser will receive only an interest for the life of the grantor (an interest *pur autre vie*).

1　For leases for life, see para 36.6 below
2　Para 34.3 below.

The entailed interest

33.4 The entailed interest (known historically as the 'fee tail') is, like the fee simple absolute, an interest which can be inherited. However, unlike the fee simple which can be inherited by any heir, the entailed interest could only be inherited by a lineal descendant, and was often further limited to male descendants. The idea behind the entailed interest, then, was that it should forever pass from father to eldest son, thus keeping the land in the same family. No new entailed interests can now be created[1] and most existing entailed interests can[2] be converted into a fee simple absolute.

1　Trusts of Land and Appointment of Trustees Act 1996, s 2, Sch 1, para 5.
2　Not all entailed interests have been so converted; such interests are likely now to exist only among the old 'landed' families, where the pressure to preserve them remain strong.

Conditional and determinable fees

33.5 Both these interests are forms of fee simple, giving the owner the same rights to enjoy the land as the owner of a fee simple absolute. However, the determinable fee *automatically* comes to an end should some specified event occur (reverting to the grantor as a fee simple absolute), while a conditional fee *may be cut short by the grantor or his heirs exercising a right of entry*[1] should some condition specified for its exercise occur. For example, a conveyance of a building in fee simple *until* it ceases to be used as a hospice creates a determinable fee; a conveyance of a building in fee simple *on condition that* it is always used as a hospice creates a conditional fee. Determinable fees may be recognised by words, such as 'until' or 'as long as', which mark out time; conditional fees may be recognised by words, such as 'on condition that' or 'provided that', which lay down conditions.

1　Para 38.5 below.

Future enjoyment

33.6 The difference between the leasehold interest and the forms of limited ownership interest considered in the foregoing paragraphs is not only that the former is of a certain duration while the duration of the latter is always uncertain. If a landowner grants a lease, he is regarded as remaining in possession of the land throughout the duration of the lease by virtue of the fact that he receives the rents and profits of the land.[1] He thus has a *present* interest in the land despite the existence of the lease. However, if a landowner grants, for example, a life interest, then once that interest takes effect, the grantor's interest is no longer in possession; it is the life tenant who is entitled to the possession, income and profits of the land: only in the future, when the life interest ends, will the grantor enjoy possession of the land. The grantor is therefore regarded as having a *future* interest in the land.

1　LPA, s 205(1); para 30.31 above.

33.7 *Reversions and remainders* The right to future enjoyment of property may exist as a reversion or a remainder. Suppose X, the owner of Blacklands, grants a life interest in Blacklands to Y. When that life interest takes effect, X ceases to have a present interest in the land, having only a right to enjoyment of the land in the future. This interest in the land is known as a 'reversion'.[1] When Y dies, Blacklands will *revert* to X. If X grants a life interest in Blacklands to Y and the freehold to Z on Y's death, X will cease to have any interest in the land; Y will have a present life interest and Z a future freehold known as a 'remainder'. When Y dies, the land will *remain away* from the original grantor, X. A series of interests in the land may be granted in remainder (eg in the case of a grant by X 'to A for life, to B for life, to C in fee simple', B and C's interests are in remainder since on the ending of the previous interest the land remains away from the grantor); there can only be one reversion. A reversion is always in fee simple and always in favour of the original grantor of the limited interests. If a limited interest or a succession of limited interests is created out of land and the freehold is not expressly disposed of, then it automatically reverts to the grantor or his heirs on the ending of the limited interests.

1   Cf landlord's 'reversion', and reversionary leases; paras 30.31 above and 36.18 below.

Settlements

33.8 A 'settlement' is said to exist whenever limited (or successive) ownership interests in land are created. For example, if a landowner wishes to give his widow a life interest in his property after he dies, with remainder to his children, he creates a settlement.

Historically, settlements were usually established with one of two aims. One was to ensure that the family estates passed on to successive generations of the same family, as witness the common form of settlement in which the landowner 'settled' on himself a life interest followed by an entailed interest for his eldest son. Alternatively, a settlement of land could be set up in a way which allowed for it to be sold, with future generations provided for out of the investment income of the proceeds of sale.

Present-day conditions mean that settlements now have very little place. In particular the modern tax structure does not favour the creation of successive interests in land. Those who might otherwise create a settlement will, these days, be advised of the need to preserve the family wealth in a form which attracts as little taxation as possible. Although very few settlements may be created today, one may well be created accidentally. For example, a man who in a 'home-made' will leaves his house to his widow for the rest of her life then to his son after her death, creates a settlement; fortunately, recent changes to the law in this area[1] mean that this does not now create the complexities which used to arise.

1   Contained in the Trusts of Land and Appointment of Trustees Act 1996; see ch 34 below.

Concurrent ownership

33.9 As we have said, just as the law recognises successive ownership of land, so also does it allow for the concurrent ownership of interests in land, ie the simultaneous ownership of a freehold or leasehold estate in land by two or more people. However, in sharp contrast to successive ownership, modern social, political and economic conditions provide an environment in which the concurrent ownership of land thrives. It is now[1] usual for domestic residential property to be co-owned; equally, in the commercial sphere, where a business is run as a partnership, its property will be co-owned by the partners.

There are two forms of co-ownership: joint tenancy and tenancy in common. ('Tenancy' in this context effectively means 'ownership'.) Both forms may exist in relation to freehold or leasehold interests.

1   Whereas the 'family' home always used to be owned solely by the husband, the picture has changed dramatically in the last 30 or so years. The norm is now for a matrimonial home to be in the names of both husband and wife. This is increasingly the case where property is bought by those in other forms of relationship. Even where this is not so it is likely that, where any financial contribution is made to the purchase of property which is owned by another, the contributor will be accorded a share in its ownership; see para 33.23 below.

Joint tenancy

33.10   The essential characteristics of joint tenancy are:

*   the right of survivorship; and
*   the 'four unities'.

The right of survivorship

33.11   Where co-ownership takes the form of joint tenancy, a joint tenant's interest in the land passes automatically on his death to the surviving joint tenants (and so on, until there is one survivor who is then the sole owner of the land). This is the right of survivorship; the ultimate survivor takes all. Should a joint tenant try to leave his interest in the land by will, this disposition has no effect. Nor do the rules of intestacy, which apply where a person dies leaving no effective will, take precedence over the right of survivorship.

The four unities

33.12   The 'four unities' are the unities of possession, interest, title and time; if one of them is missing there cannot be a joint tenancy. Joint tenants share possession of the land, together having one interest in the land, deriving the one title to the property at the same time.

*   *Unity of possession*   Joint tenants enjoy unity of possession; each has the right to possession of all of the co-owned land. No one joint tenant can exclude the others from any part of the land. A co-owner cannot, by the very nature of co-ownership, point to one part of the land and say 'that is mine and no one else's'.
*   *Unity of interest*   Where there is joint tenancy, each co-owner is entitled jointly with the other joint tenants to the entire interest in the property. Each tenant's interest must, therefore, be the same and, necessarily, equal. There is one interest, freehold or leasehold, to which they are all entitled.
*   *Unity of title*   Joint tenants derive title to the property under the same document (or by simultaneously taking possession and acquiring it by adverse possession).
*   *Unity of time*   For a joint tenancy to exist the co-owners must not have interests commencing at different times.

Tenancy in common
No right of survivorship

33.13   If co-ownership takes the form of tenancy in common, the interest of each co-owner does not automatically pass to the surviving co-owners. The reason is that each tenant in common has a fixed share in the land which may or may not be equal. On his death this may be passed on, by his will, to whomsoever he chooses (or, in the event of his leaving no will, pass to the person(s) specified by the rules of intestacy). Although each tenant in common has a fixed share, the land is not, of course, physically divided to give effect to those shares; land subject to tenancy in common is referred to in the LPA as being held 'in undivided shares'.

Four unities not essential

33.14   Unity of possession is an essential characteristic of co-ownership, whatever form it takes, for there is clearly no co-ownership where a person possesses land to the exclusion of all others. However, the other unities are not essential to tenancy in common, although they are usually present.

How to recognise whether co-ownership is a joint tenancy or a tenancy in common
Express declaration

33.15   In most instances concurrent ownership is expressly created and the relevant documentation (ie the conveyance, transfer or will) will specify which form of co-ownership is intended by declaring that the co-owners are to hold as 'joint tenants' or as 'tenants in common'; in the case of tenancies in common, the size of the shares of the parties may also be stated.[1] In such cases this declaration is conclusive, in the absence of fraud or collusion[2] (except in those very rare cases where one of the 'unities' is missing, in which event the co-ownership can only be a tenancy in common).

It may be, however, that wording other than these technical terms is used. In these cases a different approach is necessary. Where wording other than 'joint tenancy' or 'tenancy in common' (or 'undivided share') is used the courts will have to decide on their meaning and effect. Any words which demonstrate that each co-owner is to take a particular share to the property, such as 'to A and B in equal shares' or 'to be divided amongst A and B' are known as 'words of severance'[3] and give rise to a tenancy in common. In *Re North, North v Cusden*[4] land was left in a will to two sons on condition that they paid to their mother the sum of ten shillings weekly 'in equal shares'. It was held that the sons should likewise hold the property 'in equal shares', ie as tenants in common. In addition, of course, words which confer unequal shares (eg 'two-thirds to A, one-third to B') create a tenancy in common.

1   Where, as is now almost invariable (see para31.8 above), the co-owners are subsequently registered as proprietors it should be appreciated that this declaration of trust is not entered on the Register; it should, therefore, be retained as evidence, should this ever prove necessary.
2   *Goodman v Gallant* [1986] Fam 106, [1986] 1 All ER 311, CA.
3   Since they destroy the essential unity which characterises a joint tenancy.
4   [1952] Ch 397, [1952] 1 All ER 609.

No declaration

33.16   Where the documentation merely makes clear that the parties are to be co-owners, but gives *no indication* as to the *form* of co-ownership, common law would always assume a joint tenancy.[1] In certain cases, however, equity infers the existence of a tenancy in common despite the presence of the four unities and the absence of words of severance. The rationale is that the right of survivorship, which benefits the co-owner who lives longest, might operate particularly unfairly in the following instances:

- where the purchase price for the land was provided by the co-owners in *unequal*[2] shares. The co-owners are then regarded as holding the land in undivided shares proportionate to their contributions;
- where the land was acquired by business partners as part of the assets of the partnership;
- where money is lent by co-mortgagees. As between themselves, co-mortgagees

are regarded as being tenants in common in relation to their interest in the land; The loan is repaid however into a joint account and the survivor can thus give a complete discharge for all money due;[3]

- where the co-owners hold the land for their separate individual business purposes.[4]

In each of these cases, equity presumes that each co-owner will wish to have the fullest ability to realise his investment. However, there is only a presumption of tenancy in common, which can be rebutted.

1   *Morley v Bird* (1798) 3 Ves 628.
2   Note that there is no equitable presumption of a tenancy in common where the contributions are *equal*.
3   LPA, s 111.
4   *Malayan Credit Ltd v Jack Chia-MPH Ltd* [1986] AC 549, [1986] 1 All ER 711, PC.

Severance

33.17   Severance is a mechanism whereby a joint tenant can convert his joint tenancy into a tenancy in common *during his lifetime*; he cannot sever *by will* since a will only comes into effect after his death, by which time the joint tenant's rights have already passed to his fellow joint tenant(s) under the right of survivorship.

As we shall see, co-ownership can now only exist in the form of a trust under which the trustees always hold the legal estate as joint tenants.[1] This legal joint tenancy can never be severed; the severance of a legal joint tenancy would create a legal tenancy in common, which cannot now exist.[2] Accordingly, severance affects only an *equitable* joint tenancy, converting it into an equitable tenancy in common.

The most important practical effect of severance is to defeat the right of survivorship since, once the joint tenant has become a tenant in common, his interest will, on his death, pass either under his will or under the rules of intestacy.

There are five methods of severing an equitable joint tenancy. In the first two methods, severance is effected by destroying one of the four unities.[3]

1   Paras 34.5 and 34.8 below.
2   LPA, s 1(6); para 34.11 below..
3   Para 33.12 above.

Acquiring a greater interest in the land

33.18   All the joint tenants have one identical interest in the land; if one acquires another interest, the unity of interest is destroyed. This is only of significance where the parties are joint tenants for life under a settlement.

By disposition of the equitable interest

33.19   A disposition of his equitable interest by the joint tenant during his lifetime effects a severance by destroying the unity of title, since the assignee derives title under a different document from the original co-owners. Thus, if A, a joint tenant with B and C, assigns his equitable interest in the land to X, X takes as tenant in common. As between themselves, B and C remain joint tenants, for between them the four unities remain. X becomes a tenant in common, having a one-third share, with B and C who are joint tenants of a two-thirds share. The disposition in question need not be an outright transfer; severance may result, for example, where a joint tenant mortgages his interest.[1]

1   *First National Securities Ltd v Hegerty* [1985] QB 850.

By mutual agreement to sever

33.20   Equitable joint tenants may by mutual agreement sever that joint tenancy. The agreement may be one to sever, or one to deal with the property in a way which involves severance, for example where joint tenants agree that one will sell his share to the other. The agreement itself converts the joint tenancy into a tenancy in common. It would appear that the agreement itself need not be in writing, nor be specifically enforceable since it is not necessary for it to *bind* the parties; it needs merely to demonstrate a mutual intention to sever.[1]

1   *Burgess v Rawnsley* [1975] Ch 429, [1975] 3 All ER 142, CA; see also *Hunter v Babbage* (1994) 69 P & CR 548.

By notice in writing

33.21   An equitable joint tenant may sever the joint tenancy by giving a notice in writing to that effect to the other joint tenant(s).[1] In practice this is by far the simplest method of severance; it does not require the agreement of the other joint tenant(s) but they are, by definition, informed of the position, which removes the possibility of subsequent disputes. Such a notice will readily be served by legal advisers where the relationship between joint tenants has broken down so that the right of survivorship has become inappropriate. That said, where a 'formal' notice has not been served, the question has often arisen as to whether documentation, which has been drawn up for other purposes, nevertheless also constitutes a notice of severance.

The case of *Re Draper's Conveyance, Nihan v Porter*[2] provides an illustration of the problem. Here, a husband and wife had been joint tenants of their home. After they were divorced, the wife issued a summons seeking a court order that the property be sold. The order was granted, but the husband remained in occupation and no sale was ever took place. The husband subsequently died intestate. The question for the court was whether the wife was beneficially entitled to the whole property. If the joint tenancy was still in existence, the operation of the rule of survivorship would mean that she was. If, however, her action in seeking a court order had severed the joint tenancy, a tenancy in common would now be in place, meaning that her deceased husband's share would pass under the rules of intestacy. The court held that the latter was the case; the wife was not solely entitled to the property. It was successfully argued for the husband's estate that severance had occurred because the issue of the summons constituted the giving of a written notice to sever, reasoning which was approved by the Court of Appeal in *Burgess v Rawnsley*.[3]

By way of contrast, in *Harris v Goddard*[4] it was held that a written notice which only expresses a desire to bring about severance at some time in the future will not suffice. Furthermore, the notice must exhibit a desire to *sever* – ie to separate off the share of the joint tenant. Hence the wife's application in a divorce petition for the court to exercise its powers under the Matrimonial Causes Act 1973[5] in respect of the house did not operate as a notice to sever since the court could have ordered a remedy which did not involve severance.

1   LPA, s 36(2).
2   [1969] 1 Ch 486, [1967] 3 All ER 853.
3   [1975] Ch 429, [1975] 3 All ER 142, CA.
4   [1983] 3 All ER 242, [1983] 1 WLR 1203, CA; see also *Gore and Snell v Carpenter* (1990) 60 P & CR 456 where a written *proposal* to sever was held not to be a notice in writing.
5   Para 34.26 below.

Course of dealings

33.22   In *Burgess v Rawnsley*[1] Lord Denning took the view that the negotiations which had taken place between the parties were a sufficient 'course of dealing' to bring about severance. The other members of the Court of Appeal thought, despite the unsatisfactory evidence, that there had been a mutual agreement to sever.[2] In that case, all were agreed that an uncommunicated declaration of an intention to sever, and realise one's share, is insufficient to bring about severance, but that a course of dealings between the parties sufficient to indicate a *shared* intention to sever will bring about severance.

1   [1975] Ch 429, [1975] 3 All ER 142, CA.
2   Para 33.20 above.

Co-ownership by implication

33.23   As we have seen,[1] in certain circumstances, where land is conveyed to one person alone, the courts may nevertheless imply that another has ownership rights. Much of the case law in this area has arisen in the context of the matrimonial home or the quasi-matrimonial home (by which we mean where a couple live together in a stable relationship): the property is conveyed in the name of one partner only (usually the man) but the other claims a share. There is no principle in English law of community of property or family assets whereby property belonging to either spouse is regarded as family property. Consequently, the claim to a share must, in general, be based on a claim to an interest arising under an implied trust.[2]

We have already discussed the basic principles governing resulting and constructive trusts.[1] Here we shall simply demonstrate how these principles are likely to be applied in the particular context of implied co-ownership cases. Where there have been *direct* financial contributions either to the initial purchase price or, more likely these days, to mortgage repayments, the principles of resulting trust will accord to the contributing party a share commensurate to that contribution unless it can be shown that no share in the property was intended.[3]

Where there have been no direct financial contributions to the acquisition of the property, or where it is desired to establish a share greater than that gained under ordinary resulting trust principles, resort must normally be had to the constructive trust. The operation of constructive trust principles was considered by the House of Lords in *Lloyds Bank plc v Rosset*.[4] It would appear that[5] there must at some time prior to the acquisition of the property (or exceptionally, at some later date) be evidence of an agreement, or arrangement or understanding reached between the parties that the property is to be shared beneficially. Once a finding to this effect is made, the partner asserting a claim to a beneficial interest against the partner entitled to the legal estate must show that he or she has acted to his or her detriment or significantly altered his or her position in reliance on the agreement in order to give rise to a trust.[6] The House pointed out that, in considering the claims of a partner to have acted to his or her detriment, the court must distinguish between reliance on an expectation of sharing the practical benefits of occupying the matrimonial home whoever owns it, and an expectation of sharing the beneficial interest in the property asset which the matrimonial home represents. Only in the latter case will a trust arise.

If there is no evidence to support a finding of an actual agreement or arrangement to share, the court must rely on the conduct of the parties both as the basis on which to infer a common intention to share the property beneficially and as the conduct relied on to give rise to a trust. In such a case only direct contributions to the purchase price by the partner who is not the legal owner, whether initially or by payment of mortgage instalments will readily justify the inference necessary to the creation of a constructive trust. It is extremely doubtful whether anything less will do; 'merely' keeping house and raising a family will not suffice to give a non-owner a share in the home.[7] In the case of *married* couples it is specifically provided, by the Matrimonial Proceedings and Property Act 1970, s 37, that, subject to any contrary agreement between the spouses, a substantial contribution in money or money's worth to the improvement of the property entitles a spouse to a share (or, as the case may be, an enlarged share) in the beneficial interest in the property.

In the *Rosset* case, Mrs Rosset alleged a constructive trust in her favour based on an express agreement with her sole proprietor husband that the property was to be jointly owned and detrimental reliance in the form of work undertaken in the course of renovation of the property. The court found no evidence of such an agreement and felt that any work of renovation was trifling. As Mrs Rosset had made no financial contribution to the acquisition of the property, there was no basis on which the court could infer a common intention to share the property. Accordingly she was not a beneficial co-owner of the house.

1   Paras 32.8,–32.10 above.
2   Occasionally such interests have arisen on the basis of proprietary estoppel; see para 33.13.
3   See para 32.8 above.
4   [1990] 1 All ER 1111.
5   Per Lord Bridge at 1118–1119.
6   See, for example, *Eves v Eves* [1975] 3 All ER 768, [1975] 1 WLR 1338, CA and *Grant v Edwards* [1986] Ch 638, [1986] 2 All ER 426, CA.
7   *Gissing v Gissing* [1971] AC 886, [1970] 2 All ER 780, HL; *Burns v Burns* [1984] Ch 317, [1984] 1 All ER 244, CA.

Quantifying the co-owners' beneficial shares

33.24   It is today commonly the case that where property is expressly transferred to co-owners there will be an express declaration as to what the share of each co-owner is to be. This declaration is conclusive as between the parties named therein as to their respective shares,[1] but it does not appear to preclude the implication of a trust in favour of further co-owners.[2]

Where there is no express declaration of this kind and, necessarily where co-ownership is implied, the question arises of quantifying the co-owners' shares. In identifying the shares of the co-owners, the court is simply seeking to give effect to the common intention of the parties.[3] Where a common intention as to what the shares should be has been expressed, effect should be given to that intention.[4] Where that intention is inferred from direct financial contributions to an outright purchase then the extent of their respective shares will depend on a more or less precise arithmetical calculation of the extent of their contributions. Where on the other hand, no intention as to the parties shares' has been expressed, then the court has to assess each of the parties' respective contributions in a broader sense and reflect these in the shares awarded.[5] Only when there is no evidence on which a court can reasonably draw an inference as to the respective shares intended by the parties should it fall back on the maxim 'equality is equity' and hold that the beneficial interest belongs to the parties equally.[6] Where the court implies co-ownership in unequal shares, the co-owners will, of course, be tenants in common. Otherwise, save in one of the cases referred to in para 33.16 above, equity follows the law and implies a joint tenancy.[7]

1   *Goodman v Gallant* [1986] Fam 106, [1986] 1 All ER 311, CA.
2   *City of London Building Society v Flegg* [1988] AC 54, [1987] 3 All ER 435, HL.
3   *Grant v Edwards* [1986] Ch 638, [1986] 2 All ER 426, CA.
4   *Clough v Killey* (1996) 72 P & CR D22, CA.
5   *Midland Bank plc v Cooke* [1995] 4 All ER 562, CA; *Drake v Whipp* [1996] 1 FLR 826, CA.
6   *Burns v Burns* [1984] 1 All ER 244 at 264–265.
7   *Walker v Hall* [1984] Fam Law 21, CA.

Ending co-ownership

33.25   Co-ownership may be ended by physical partition of the land or by union of the concurrent interests in a single co-owner.

Partition of the land destroys the unity of possession without which there can be no co-ownership. The parties agree to divide the land between them, the trustees conveying a part to each.[1] Sale may be ordered under the Trusts of Land and Appointment of Trustees Act 1996, s 14[2] as a substitute for partition and this will be particularly appropriate if partition is impractical, as where the property consists of a single house.

Union of the interests in the land in a sole tenant may occur by survivorship or by one tenant acquiring the interests of the others.

1   LPA, s 28.
2   Para 34.17 below.

Chapter 34

Trusts of land

34.1 In the previous chapter we examined the basis on which the ownership of land can be shared by more than one person, both successively (ie by way of a settlement) an concurrently (through co-ownership). We now turn to the legal mechanisms which are used as a framework for shared ownership. Over the past 200 years, land ownership has been reshaped by changing political, economic and social conditions. Land is no longer the major form of wealth, nor is it the basis of social position or political power. Hence its retention, in large tracts, for very lengthy periods of time in the hands of relatively few families has become a thing of the past. Like many other commodities, its exchangeability in the market place has become increasingly important and this, above all, has provoked changes which make the transfer of land in shared ownership much more straightforward. While these reforms started in the 19th century, the most recent, brought about by the Trusts of Land and Appointment of Trustees Act 1996 (TLA), came into effect on 1 January 1997.

In this chapter we shall

- outline the more important of the problems posed by shared ownership;
- indicate the approaches adopted in the past for the solution of these difficulties; and
- explain the 'trust of land' which provides the new machinery for both settlements and co-ownership, and any other trust of land.

The potential problems arising from shared ownership

Some of the problems
34.2 Where more than one person has ownership rights in the same property, either successively or concurrently, the potential for difficulties exists. Suppose, for example, that A, B and C concurrently own the freehold of Blacklands and that X wishes to buy the property. In theory X will have to investigate three different titles to Blacklands; equally, A, B and C may not be agreed as to its sale. These difficulties will rapidly multiply if A, B and C are tenants in common and A dies, leaving his share to his four children P, Q, R and S; there are now six titles to investigate and six people to agree to any sale.

Similar problems can arise if Whitelands is subject to a settlement (ie successive ownership), as where it is owned by D for life, then E for life and then F in fee simple, and Y wishes to buy Whitelands. In order to acquire a fee simple absolute *in possession*, Y must purchase the interests of D, E and F. The acquisition of D or E's interest will only give Y an interest *pur autre vie*,[1] which will come to an end on D or E's deaths; the acquisition of F's interest will not give a *present* fee simple because F's rights do not come into effect until the deaths of D and E.[2] This will mean that Y, too, will need to investigate three different titles. Again, it may be that D, E and F will not all agree to sell their interests, thus stultifying any sale of Whitelands. Settlements also pose management problems; the current owner (D, in the example given) has only a limited interest and so cannot act in a way which will affect the land after his death. So, the grant of long leases or mortgages may be either difficult or impossible. This hampered the management and full exploitation of the land.

1 See para 33.3 above.
2 See paras 33.6 and 33.7 above.

A summary of the old solutions
Settlements

34.3 By the nineteenth century the problems posed by settlements were well appreciated. Statutory reforms eventually required all settlements to take one of two forms, either the 'strict' settlement (which came to be governed by the Settled Land Act 1925), or the trust for sale (eventually controlled by the Law of Property Act 1925). At the same time the LPA, s 1 provided that the only estates which could henceforth exist at law were the fee simple absolute *in possession* (and the term of years). Thus limited ownership and rights to future enjoyment came to take effect only *in equity*; this meant that all settlements after 1925 had to take the form of a trust. The Settled Land Act provided a framework which resulted in the current owner (known as the 'tenant for life'—D in the above example) holding the freehold title and being able to sell all or part of the land (with the proceeds being invested by trustees of the settlement for the benefit of all the owners), and effectively to manage and raise loans where the land was retained, free from interference by subsequent owners (E and F above). The trust for sale effectively gave equivalent powers of sale and management to trustees acting on behalf of the limited owners (ie D, E and F above) who, instead of being legal owners, became beneficiaries under the trust. Again, if the land were sold (in this case by the trustees rather than the tenant for life),[1] the proceeds would be invested for the benefit of D, E and F.

1 It should be noted that, despite its name, land held under a trust for sale did not *have* to be sold provided all the trustees agreed to postpone any sale. In this way it could be an effective mechanism for *retaining* land.

34.4 While the strict settlement provided an elegant solution to the problems generated by successive ownership, in its detail it was complex and cumbersome. As a result it was only really suited to the large family estates for which it had been devised. As the 20th century progressed, a properly drafted trust for sale came to be regarded as far more appropriate in the increasingly rare situations where it was desired to create a settlement. Unfortunately, the 1925 legislation had been constructed so that the strict settlement was the 'default' form of settlement. This meant that, except where a trust for sale was *expressly* created, the creation of limited ownership interests (other than leases) necessarily brought the SLA into play, as did the transfer of land to a minor or subject to family charges.[1] A Settled Land Act settlement could also be created inadvertently under a home-made will, for example where a man simply leaves his house to his widow for life and thereafter to his children. Furthermore, as we have seen, it is clear that certain informal dealings with land could be viewed as giving rise to life interests in land.[2] There have been a number of cases in which this was held to result in a settlement governed by the Act, with the consequence that the person with the right to occupy for life had the extensive powers of sale and management accorded to a 'tenant for life'. It can, therefore, be seen that, in modern times, the strict settlement was never deliberately employed as a mechanism for creating a settlement; it merely operated as a trap for those acting without proper legal advice. This was a situation crying out for the further reform which has now taken place.

1   Two situations in which, despite the absence of any 'successive interest', a strict settlement would arise; Settled Land Act 1925, s 1.
2   See paras 32.15 and 32.16 above.

Concurrent ownership

34.5   The problems faced by co-owners were not tackled until 1925 (largely because co-ownership was nothing like as widespread as settlement at that time). Again, the trust for sale was the device used; this time as the sole mechanism for co-ownership. The Law of Property Act 1925 required all concurrent ownership to exist in the form of a trust for sale. If land was conveyed[1] to co-owners without the express use of a trust for sale, one was imposed by statute. Briefly, by requiring that, to revert to the example used in para 34.2 above, A, B and C must hold the legal estate, on a joint tenancy, as trustees on trust for sale for themselves as beneficiaries, the Act ensured that the legal title to the land was a single indivisible[2] one which could easily be investigated by any purchaser. In this way any sale of co-owned property was rendered more straightforward.

1   We have seen (at para 33.23 above) that co-ownership can arise by implication as a result of the operation of the doctrines of resulting or constructive trusts, or proprietary estoppel; where this occurred a trust for sale would also be imposed.
2   It will be remembered that a joint tenancy must have unity of title (see para 33.12 above), that the right of survivorship (see para 33.11 above) means that the number of joint tenants can only diminish, and that there can be no severance of a joint tenancy of the legal estate (see para 33.17 above).

34.6   However, the imposition of a trust for sale in the co-ownership context came to pose its own difficulties. In 1925 concurrent ownership was not widespread, especially in circumstances where the co-owned land was to be retained; at that time co-ownership was either a mechanism for sharing the income from property, or a temporary state of affairs pending its sale (eg where property was given, or bequeathed to children). In the early 20th century many family homes would have been leased rather than held in freehold ownership; in either event, it would have been owned by the husband alone. Co-ownership by husband and wife only started to become commonplace well after the Second World War and has only become standard practice in the last 40 or so years. The imposition of a trust *for sale* in the case of property which had been purchased for the purpose of occupation was not only confusing to purchasers who were buying a property in which to live, it gave rise to technical legal difficulties. The courts had to adopt some deft footwork in order to provide workable rules on rights to occupy co-owned property and on its sale where the co-owners were in dispute as to whether it should be kept or disposed of. As with settlements, reform of the mechanism for concurrent ownership has long been advocated.

Overreaching[1]

34.7   A fundamental feature of the reforms referred to in the paragraphs 34.3 and 33.5 above (and just as important to the new trust of land) is the concept of overreaching. Overreaching was an existing principle which applied where trustees of land exercised a power to sell that land. The statutory reforms of the 19th and 20th century merely extended and regulated its operation. Where either a tenant for life under a strict settlement, or the trustees under a trust for sale, actually sold the land then, provided the purchase money was paid to at least two trustees,[1] the interests of the beneficiaries ceased to relate to the land and attached henceforth to the proceeds of sale. In this way any purchaser who dealt with at least two trustees was certain to acquire the land free from the claims of either the owners of future interests in the land, or beneficial co-owners (ie B, C, D, E and F in the examples used above). The usefulness of this concept in freeing the title to land of equitable ownership interests is very clear and has been carried over into the new trust of land.

1   See further para 34.17 below.

Trusts of land

34.8   The Trusts of Land and Appointment of Trustees Act 1996 (TLA), which implemented proposals for reform made by the Law Commission in 1989,[1] came into effect on 1 January 1997. Broadly, the Act:

- leaves existing strict settlements untouched;[1]
- converts existing[2] trusts for sale (whether arising in the context of settlements or concurrent ownership) into 'trusts of land';
- ensures that settlements and concurrent ownership (and any other trust of land[3]) arising on or after 1 January 1997 take the form of 'trusts of land';[4] and
- allows for the express creation of a trust for sale but subjects such trusts to the same regime as the 'trust of land'.[5]

We now examine in a little more detail the machinery for creating successive and concurrent ownership.

1   TLA, ss 1 and 2. These, therefore, remain subject to the Settled Land Act 1925. Strict settlements are now so rarely encountered that we are treating them as beyond the scope of this book. For a detailed account see, for example, Kevin Gray *Elements of Land Law* (1993) ch 15.
2   TLA, s 1.
3   Such as a bare trust (ie a trust where there is a single, adult beneficiary); such trusts are rarely encountered but may, for example, be used as a device for transferring land to a nominee (the trustee) so that the identity of the real owner (the beneficiary) remains concealed. The Act also specifically applies to an implied, resulting or constructive trust: see TLA, s 1(2)(a).
4   TLA, ss 1,2 and 5 and Sch 2.
5   TLA, s 4. Hence, there will be little point, in practice, in creating an express trust for sale.

The imposition of a trust of land
Settlements
34.9   Prior to 1997 the following dispositions of land would, in the absence of an express trust for sale, have resulted in a strict settlement governed by the Settled Land Act 1925:

- the creation of a life interest;
- the creation of an entailed interest;
- the creation of a conditional[1] or determinable fee;
- the creation of a *future* fee simple absolute;
- the transfer of a legal estate to a minor;[1]
- the voluntary subjection of land to family charges.[1]

As we have already mentioned, no new entailed interests can be created after 1996.[2] In each of the other situations a trust of land will now come into being, governed not by the Settled Land Act 1925 but by the TLA 1996.[3] Where the settlement is created deliberately, the legal estate will be transferred to between two[4] and four[5] trustees who will hold it for the benefit of the (equitable) owners of the limited interests. Where the settlement is created inadvertently, eg by the informal creation of a life interest, or a purported transfer to a minor, the 'transaction' will render the current owner the trustee; he will hold the legal estate for the benefit of the intended recipient.

1   In none of these three situations is there any element of succession; nevertheless each was expressly brought within the definition of a strict settlement by the Settled Land Act 1925, s 1.
2   TLA s 2, Sch 1, para 5; see para 33.4 above.
3   TLA, ss 1 and 2.
4   Although it is perfectly legitimate for a trust of land to have only one trustee, any disposition by a single trustee cannot overreach (see para 34.7 above and para 34.16 below) the interests of the beneficiaries. Accordingly, any expressly created trust of land will ensure that there are at least two trustees.
5   There can never be more than four trustees of land (save in the case of trusts for charitable, ecclesiastical or public purposes); if land is conveyed to more than four trustees then only the first four named become the trustees, Trustee Act 1925, s 34.

Concurrent ownership

34.10   In cases of concurrent ownership a trust of land is imposed by the Law of Property Act 1925; the relevant provisions have been amended by the TLA so that what previously were references to a trust for sale are now references to a trust of land.[1] The LPA requires that, in all cases of co-ownership, a trust of land must be used. Where co-ownership arises expressly it is normal conveyancing practice to create an express trust. Where this is not done (and where co-ownership arises by implication) the LPA imposes a trust.[2] In the following paragraphs we explain the operation of the trust of land in the context of concurrent ownership.

1   TLA, s 5 and Sch 2, paras 3 and 4.
2   LPA, ss 34 and 36 (as amended by the TLA).

34.11   *Tenancy in common*   A tenancy in common cannot exist in relation to a legal estate;[1] consequently, it takes effect only in equity. If land is conveyed to a number of people as tenants in common, the LPA provides that the conveyance takes effect as if it were a conveyance of the legal estate to the co-owners (or, if there are more than four, to the first four named in the conveyance) *as joint tenants on trust* to give effect to the rights of the co-owners *as tenants in common in equity*.[2] Thus a tenancy in common can only exist behind a trust; it takes effect in relation to the beneficial, equitable interest in the land, but not the legal estate. It will be seen that the key to an understanding of the machinery of co-ownership is to consider separately the position of the co-owners in relation to the legal estate in the land (be it freehold or leasehold) and their position in relation to the equitable interests existing behind the curtain of the trust.

Thus, if land is granted to A, B and C in equal shares they will hold the legal estate as joint tenants and as trustees; the wording used[3] gives rise to a tenancy in common which will take effect in equity:

	A, B, C – legal JT (joint tenancy)
The 'curtain' of the trust	
	A, B, C – equitable TiC (tenancy in common)

Should C die, his individual share under the tenancy in common may pass under his will or on intestacy (say to X); but the right of survivorship operates in respect of the joint tenancy of the legal estate:

$$A, B - \text{legal JT}$$

$$A, B, X - \text{equitable TiC}$$

1   LPA, s 1(6).
2   Ibid, ss 34 and 35.
3   Being words of severance; see para 33.15 above.

34.12   *Joint tenancy.*   As in the case of tenancy in common there is a splitting of the legal and equitable ownership whenever a joint tenancy is created. The co-owners (or the first four of them) hold the legal estate as joint trustees for themselves as joint tenants in equity:[1]

$$A, B, C - \text{legal JT}$$

$$A, B, C - \text{equitable JT}$$

Should C die, the right of survivorship operates in respect of the joint tenancy both at law and in equity:

$$A, B - \text{legal JT}$$

$$A, B - \text{equitable JT}$$

1   LPA, s 36.

Intestacy

34.13   Where a person dies without making a will (ie intestate) statute used to impose a trust for sale on the deceased's property.[1] The TLA ensures that such trusts are now trusts of land.[2]

1   Administration of Estates Act 1925, s 33.
2   TLA, s 5, Sch 2, para 5.

The position of the trustees
Powers and duties

34.14   As we have seen[1] there will normally be between two and four trustees of a trust of land. In relation to the land, they have all the powers of an absolute owner of land.[2] This means that they can sell,[3] lease or mortgage the land. In doing so they must, under the general law of trusts, act in the best interests of the trust and have regard to the rights of the beneficiaries.[4] Where either the whole or part of the land is sold, or capital money is raised by the creation of other interests (eg the grant of an option or lease at a premium) the trustees must invest that money. They can do so by purchasing investments authorised by the Trustee Investment Act 1961. Equally, they are empowered to purchase other land as an investment, for occupation by a beneficiary, or for any other purpose.[5] Where all of the beneficiaries are of full age and capacity, the trustees can compel the beneficiaries to take a conveyance of the land irrespective of whether the beneficiaries wish this to happen.[6]

When exercising any of their functions relating to land[7] the trustees are under an obligation, so far as is practicable, to consult all the beneficiaries who are entitled to a present interest in the land. They should, in so far as is consistent with the best interests of the trust, give effect to the wishes of the majority of the beneficiaries.[8]

The trustees can choose[9] to delegate all or any of their functions relating to the land[10] to any beneficiary(ies) of full age who are entitled to an interest in possession in the land, either for a limited time, or indefinitely. Such a delegation must be made by way of power of attorney (ie formally by deed) which must be given by all of the trustees jointly. This power of attorney may be revoked by any one of the trustees, and will automatically be revoked by the appointment of a new trustee. Any beneficiary to whom the functions of a trustee have been delegated has the same duties and liabilities as regards the exercise of those functions as a trustee. The trustees are only liable for the acts or defaults of a beneficiary to whom they have delegated their functions where they were negligent in making their decision to delegate.[11]

1 See para 34.9 above.
2 TLA, s 6(1).
3 It should be noted that, in sharp contrast to the position of a trustee under the old trust for sale, there is merely a *power* to sell, not an obligation. Even if a trust of land contains an express provision *obliging* the trustees to sell, this can safely be ignored since the trustees always have a power to postpone sale for an indefinite period: TLA, s 4.
4 TLA, s 6(5) and (6).
5 TLA, s 6(3) and (4), s 17(1).
6 TLA, s 6(2). Where all the beneficiaries are of full age and capacity it has always been possible for the *beneficiaries* to compel the trustees to convey the land to them: *Saunders v Vautier* (1841) 10 LJ Ch 354. The TLA now allows the trustees the same freedom. Provided the beneficiaries *consent*, the trustees can, instead, partition the land between them: TLA, s 7.
7 The trustees' functions relating to land do not extend to their powers and duties in respect of capital monies, such as investment.
8 TLA, s 11.
9 Delegation is a matter of discretion for the trustees and, in deciding whether or not to delegate, they must bear in mind that they will become liable for the consequences of any negligent delegation. Any beneficiary to whom they refuse to delegate could apply to the court under TLA, s 14; see para 34.27 below.
10 Again (see note 7 above) the power to delegate does not extend to the trustees' powers and duties in respect of capital monies. So, for example, any capital monies received as a result of the sale of the trust property must be paid to the trustees.
11 TLA, s 9.

Restrictions on powers

34.15 In the case of an express trust of land (as opposed to one which is *imposed* by statute[1] or the courts[2]) certain of the trustees' power can either be expressly excluded,[3] or their exercise made subject to the consent of some person(s)[4] by the terms of the instrument creating the trust. The powers which can be restricted in this way are only those conferred by the TLA, ss 6 and 7. So, the all-important power to dispose of the land can be restricted, as can the power to require adult beneficiaries to take a conveyance of the land or the power to invest in other land. However, neither the other powers of investment, nor the power to delegate, can be excluded.

1 Such as is imposed by the LPA, ss 34 and 36 wherever co-ownership is created without the use of an express trust of land; see para 34.8 above.
2 Such as a resulting or constructive trust in the case of implied co-ownership.
3 TLA, s 8.
4 TLA, s 10.

The position of the beneficiaries

34.16 There can be any number of beneficiaries of a trust of land and, naturally, the interest of each one will be equitable. This may be limited, such as a life interest[1], or absolute such as a freehold or leasehold.[2] Any beneficiary who is entitled to a present interest in the land has the right to occupy the trust land provided that

- the purposes of the trust include the provision of land for the occupation of the beneficiary(ies); and
- the property is not unavailable or unsuitable for occupation.[3]

Where more than one beneficiary is entitled to occupation they can, of course, occupy the property together. Where joint occupation is not feasible, the trustees (and, if necessary, the courts) can resolve disputes over which of them should occupy.[4]

As we have seen,[5] any beneficiary of full age and capacity with a present interest in the land is entitled to be consulted when the trustees exercise any of their functions relating to the land. Where there is an express provision requiring their consent,[6] a beneficiary may be able to prevent the trustees exercising any of their functions relating to the land. Where delegation has taken place,[7] a beneficiary will be able to exercise all those functions which have been delegated to him, although in doing so he must act in the best interests of the trust.

The beneficiaries under a trust of land are not entitled to receive capital monies directly from a purchaser even where there has been full delegation of the trustees' functions.[8] Furthermore, they have no right to control[9] the trustees in the exercise of their functions relating to the investment of capital monies.

1   As where the trust arises in the context of successive ownership.
2   As where the trust arises in the context of concurrent ownership.
3   TLA, s 12.
4   TLA, ss 13 and 14. See para 34.29 below.
5   See para 34.14 above.
6   See para 34.15 above.
7   See para 34.14 above.
8   See para 34.14 above. It should be remembered that a purchaser would not wish to pay capital monies to anyone other than the trustees since this would prevent the overreaching of the beneficial interests under the trust: see paras 34.7 above and para 34.17 below.
9   Either by way of consultation, consent or delegation since all of these relate only to the trustees' functions in so far as they relate to the land.

The sale of trust land
The basic principles
34.17   One of the major purposes of using the trust to give effect to both successive and concurrent ownership is to avoid complexity in conveyancing. The ready marketability of land would be seriously inhibited if purchasers (and, in law[1], 'purchasers' include mortgagees[2] and lessees) could not be sure that the interest which they are acquiring is free from the claims of others (save where those claims are readily detectable and then either reflected in the price paid or otherwise dealt with to the satisfaction of the purchaser). We have seen[3] that, without the device of the trust, a purchaser of land which is owned either successively or concurrently would have a multiplicity of titles to investigate, and would take subject to the rights of any owner who would not co-operate in the sale or other transaction. The trust avoids these difficulties.

Trustees always hold an unfragmented legal estate, be it freehold or leasehold. They hold that estate as joint tenants; this means that there is unity of title, so that there is only one legal title (or register of title) for the purchaser to investigate.

Furthermore, a purchaser of land held on trust need not concern himself with the equitable ownership[4] interests behind the 'curtain' of the trust, no matter how many.[5] They are not part of the legal title to the property; they are 'off the title' and neither the existence of the trust nor its details are recorded in the Land Register.[6] A purchaser need only ensure that any purchase money (or loan or other capital monies) is paid to the trustees, who must be at least two in number (or a trust corporation)[7]; this ensures that the beneficial interests under the trust are overreached by the conveyance.[8] This does not mean that those beneficial interests are destroyed; it means that they cease to relate to the land and are transmuted into equivalent rights to the proceeds of sale. We shall illustrate this fundamental principle by way of three examples.

EXAMPLE 1

Suppose Blacklands is conveyed to H and W as joint tenants. This takes effect in the following way:

$$\frac{\text{H, W} - \text{legal JT}}{\text{H, W} - \text{equitable JT}}$$

On a sale of Blacklands a purchaser only needs to investigate the single legal title (or register of title) of H and W. He would not be concerned with their beneficial interests; he does not have to check whether H or W have, for example, severed the equitable joint tenancy and disposed of their interest to X, or whether Y has acquired a beneficial interest by way of financial contribution to the mortgage on Blacklands. By paying the purchase price to H and W *as trustees* any potential complexity in relation to the beneficial ownership of the land need not concern him, for the conveyance overreaches the beneficial interests. H and W's beneficial rights (and any rights which X and Y may have) are now rights to a share in the monies paid by the purchaser.

EXAMPLE 2

Suppose Whitelands is conveyed to A, B, C, D and E as tenants in common. This takes effect as follows:

$$\frac{\text{A, B, C, D} - \text{legal JT}}{\text{A, B, C, D, E} - \text{equitable TiC}}$$

Suppose A dies, leaving his interest in Whitelands to Z. The position now is:

$$\frac{\text{B, C, D} - \text{legal JT}}{\text{Z, B, C, D, E} - \text{equitable TiC}}$$

On a sale of Whitelands, a purchaser would only be concerned to investigate the single title of B, C and D. He would not be concerned with the beneficial interests in general or with what has happened to A's interest in the land, in particular. If he deals with and pays the purchase price to the trustees (B, C and D) the complexity in relation to the beneficial ownership of Whitelands need not concern him, for the conveyance overreaches the beneficial interests. The rights of Z, B, C, D and E are now rights to a share of the proceeds of sale.

EXAMPLE 3

Suppose that Pinklands is conveyed to P and Q to hold on trust for R for life and then S for life and then T in fee simple absolute. This takes effect as follows:

$$\frac{\text{P, Q–legal JT}}{\text{R–present life interest, S–future life interest, T–future fee simple absolute}}$$

As in the previous examples, a purchaser need only investigate the single title of P and Q. The beneficial interests of R, S and T are of no concern. So long as he pays the purchase price to P and Q the conveyance will overreach the interests of R, S and T. P and Q will, in this case, invest the proceeds of sale. Since R's interest in the land was only a *limited* one, he will receive only the *income* produced by the fund for his lifetime; on R's death S, too will receive only income; on S's death T, who would, at that point, have become entitled to the land absolutely will take the capital sum. (If T has died his rights, being inheritable and not merely 'for life' will have passed to his heirs and they will receive the capital.)

While the principle of overreaching is highly convenient for those purchasing, or lending on the security of land, it should be appreciated that it can operate unfairly to deprive beneficiaries of their right to occupy trust property. In cases where the trustees and beneficiaries are different persons, the trustees can sell or mortgage the property without the knowledge or consent of the beneficiaries; their interests are automatically overreached and while, in certain circumstances, the beneficiaries may be able to sue the trustees for breach of trust, they will certainly not regain their rights to the land. In 1989, the Law Commission proposed that the rights of adult beneficiaries who are occupying the property should not be overreached by transactions conducted without their consent,[9] but this suggestion has now been abandoned.[10]

1   LPA, s 205(xxi).
2   A mortgagee of land is a person who makes a loan on the security of land; he is a person *to whom* a mortgage is granted by the landowner/mortgagor.
3   See para 34.2 above.
4   A purchaser does, of course, need to be concerned about equitable interests which are *not* ownership interests, eg restrictive covenants, since these may can continue to affect the land (see generally ch 35 below).
5   LPA, s 27(1)
6   LRA, s 74. Any purchaser's lawyer checking title will, of course, realise that there is always a trust wherever there is more than one owner of the legal estate; however, the details of the trust is of no concern.
7   Overreaching also occurs where capital monies are not paid to the trustees at the time of the conveyance but later. In *State Bank of India v Sood* [1997] 1 All ER 169, CA the trustees executed a charge over trust property in favour of the bank, as security for present and future indebtedness on certain bank accounts. No loan was advanced at the time of the charge but the accounts became further overdrawn. When the bank wished to exercise its power of sale (as to which see para 39.35 below) it was held that it could do so free from the claims of the beneficiaries; their interests had been overreached at the time of the charge.
8   LPA, ss 2(ii) and 27(2).
9   In Law Com No 188 (1989), the sentiments of which were echoed by Peter Gibson LJ in *State Bank of India v Sood* [1997] 1 All ER 169, CA.
10   Press notice, 19 March 1998.

Problems over the sale of trust land

34.18   It may, of course, happen that a sale cannot proceed in the straightforward manner suggested by the examples given in the previous paragraph. The trustees may not agree that the land should be sold, or the beneficiaries may disagree with the trustees' decision to sell. In the typical co-ownership situation outlined in Example 1, it may be that H and W disagree as to whether a sale should take place, a state of affairs which completely rules out the possibility of overreaching since the purchaser would be unable to pay the money to at least two trustees. We defer until para 34.20 a discussion of how these difficulties may be resolved.

Furthermore, in the examples so far employed, the existence of the trust has been apparent on the title because each property was expressly conveyed to more than one person. What is the position where there is no indication on the title of the existence of any trust? This situation will arise when land has been conveyed in the name of one person only but where that person is regarded by equity as holding it on trust either wholly, or partly for another. The most commonly encountered example of this is where equity implies co-ownership.[1] As we have seen, there is no doubting the existence of a trust of land in such circumstances,[2] the problem is that a purchaser (or mortgagee) may unwittingly hand over purchase money or otherwise deal with someone who is in reality a *sole* trustee. This means that the purchaser is deprived of the protection of overreaching which only applies to dealings with *two* trustees. As we shall see,[3] in such circumstances the purchaser or mortgagee may be bound by the interests of the implied (co) owner (who is a 'hidden'[4] beneficiary under the trust) unless careful investigations are carried out.

1 See para 33.23 above.
2 See paras 34.8 and 34.10 above.
3 See para 35.18 and 35.26 below.
4 By 'hidden' we mean undetectable on the paper title; such beneficiaries are often, in practice, detectable since they are usually in occupation of the trust land. As we shall see in para 35.18 and 35.26 below, the purchaser's (and mortgagee's) best protection is the careful inspection of the property and the investigation of the property rights of anyone who is occupying the property either with, or instead of, the vendor/mortgagor.

Overview of the trust of land

34.19 The new trust of land is an infinitely flexible instrument capable of accommodating a wide range of different ownership requirements with the minimum of inconvenience to any purchaser or mortgagee should the land either be sold or used as security for a loan. Within a single framework, the 1996 Act provides devices which can be used to achieve widely differing objectives.

Sale or retention?

34.20 Perhaps surprisingly in this day and age,[1] the trust can be set up in a way which makes it impossible for the trustees to sell the property during the existence of the trust[2]: the trust instrument can expressly exclude the power of sale[3] and it seems most unlikely that this could be overridden by the court.[4] While it is not possible to ensure that the land is definitely sold,[5] the trustees will always have a power to sell which can only be blocked by the obtaining of a court order preventing sale.[6] Control over the sale of the land can be given to a particular beneficiary by requiring that they must consent to any sale[7]; such a requirement can only be overridden by a court order.[6]

1 Bearing in mind our earlier comments about the inappropriateness in modern times of the old form of settlement which tied land up in the family: see para 34.1 above.
2 It should be pointed out that, in the case of a trust of land of which the beneficiaries are natural persons, it must have a reasonably limited life. It has always been the policy of the law that land should not be tied up indefinitely into the future, a policy which is implemented by a complex set of common law and statutory rules known collectively as the 'rule against perpetuities'. This rule is well beyond the scope of this book; suffice to say that, for example, while a beneficial interest can be conferred on the unborn child of a living person (to A's son, where A does not as yet have a son), it cannot be conferred on the unborn child of an unborn child (to A's son's son where A does not as yet have a child).
3 TLA, s 8: see para 34.15 above.
4 As we shall see (para 34.27 below) the court can only control over the exercise of the trustees' functions; if the trust has specifically excluded the function of sale, there appears to be nothing for the court to control.
5 TLA, s 4; para 34.14, note 3 above.
6 TLA, s 14; para 34.28 below.
7 TLA, s 10; para 34.15 above.

Control: trustees or beneficiaries?

34.21 Day-to-day control of the land can rest with the trustees[1] or, by delegation, with one or more of the beneficiaries.[2] Where, as is often the case in co-ownership, the trustees and the beneficiaries are one and the same (see Example 1 in paragraph

34.17 above) the co-owners will, so long as they are agreed, have unrestricted powers of disposition and management. Where they are not agreed, the courts will resolve their disputes.[3]

1 TLA, s 6; para 34.14 above.
2 TLA, s 9; paras 34.14 and 34.16 above
3 TLA, s 14; paras 34.25–34.29 below.

Occupation: beneficiaries or others?

34.22 The trust may be set up with a view to the land being occupied by one or more of the beneficiaries, or its purpose may be that the property should be income-producing. In the former case, the beneficiaries have a right to occupy.[1] In the latter situation the land will be leased and the rental income distributed to those beneficiaries who are presently entitled. So, where the beneficiaries under the trust are A, B and C as co-owners, the income will be divided among them either equally, or according to their respective shares. Where the beneficiaries under the trust are A for life, then B for life and then C in fee simple, all of the income would be paid to A during his lifetime; on A's death all of the income would be paid to B; on B's death C, if of full age and capacity, would become entitled to bring the trust to an end. He could choose to continue to receive the income, or he could sell the land (subject to any lease) and receive its capital value.

1 TLA, s 12; para 34.16 above.

Property type: residential or commercial?

34.23 Although, when explaining the principles of the trust of land, we have often done so in terms of residential property, the trust is equally suitable for all types of premises. So, for example, a surveying partnership will own its office(s) through the medium of a trust. Up to four of the partners will hold the legal title as trustees; all of the partners will then be the co-owners in equity. It would be usual for the partnership agreement to dictate how partnership decisions are reached, a process which can readily apply to the trust of its land. (Obviously, where a business is set up as a company, there will not necessarily be any trust of its land; a company is a separate legal entity which will, in the normal event, be a sole owner of its property.)

Purchasers and mortgagees of trust land

34.24 Whatever the objective in setting up the trust, or whatever the reasons leading to the imposition of the trust, if and when the trust land is sold or mortgaged it is imperative that the purchaser or mortgagee can, by taking simple and straightforward steps, be confident that he takes the land free from the claims of any of the beneficiaries. Given that land is often subject to a trust, this is fundamental to the marketability of real property.

As we have seen, this is largely achieved by the process of overreaching.[1] However, there are also other provisions in the 1996 Act which are designed to protect purchasers and mortgagees from the need to make over-complex investigations when buying, or making loans on the security of, trust land. So, for example, a purchaser or mortgagee does not have to check whether the trustees, when selling, have had regard to the rights of the beneficiaries or have consulted the beneficiaries.[2] Where a sale or mortgage of unregistered land is in breach of an express restriction on those powers, it will not be invalidated unless the purchaser or mortgagee has actual notice of the restriction.[3] Where the trustees have delegated their powers of sale or mortgagee to a beneficiary, a purchaser or mortgagee acting in good faith can assume that the beneficiary is a person to whom those powers can be delegated.[4] Where a sale or mortgage requires the consent of more than two persons, the purchaser or mortgagee can safely proceed provided at least two consents have actually been obtained.[5]

1   Paras 34.7 and 34.17 above.
2   TLA, s 16.
3   TLA, s 16(3). Where the title is registered (as will usually be the case) any restriction will have been noted on the register; see para 35.29 below.
4   Ie is a person of full age and capacity and entitled to a present interest in the land.
5   TLA, s 10.

Disputes over trusts of land

34.25   Inevitably, there will be times when there are disputes over the operation of a trust of land. The trustees may disagree with each other over whether or not the land should be sold or retained, on whether (or which of) the beneficiaries should occupy the property, or on how it should be managed. The beneficiaries may be at odds with the trustees, or with each other.

These difficulties produce a total stalemate in the very common situation where the trustees and the beneficiaries are one and the same and where there are only two of them. Classically, this will occur where property is co-owned by a married couple or by co-habitees whose relationship has broken down. In practice, the legal title to their home will be vested in the two of them as trustees, and they will also be the only beneficiaries, holding either as joint tenants or tenants in common in equal shares (see Example 1 in paragraph 34.17 above). Obviously, they may be able to agree on what should happen to the property; for example that it should be sold and the proceeds divided between them, or that one should buy the other out. Often, however, they will be unable to reach agreement, if only because their respective interests will have become diametrically opposed. One may wish to remain in the house with any children; the other will need to realise their share in the property in order to fund the purchase of another home.

Matrimonial property

34.26   Where the dispute concerns matrimonial property (eg, where, in the scenario described in the previous paragraph are a married couple), it will be resolved by the courts under the Matrimonial Causes Act 1973,[1] as part of any divorce proceedings. The 1973 Act gives the court wide powers to make orders relating to what was matrimonial property; it can order that the property be sold, or retained (especially where there are young children still living at home) and it can adjust the parties' rights to the property. So, it can order that one party transfer their share to the other.

1   Matrimonial Causes Act 1973, ss 23–25.

Other trust property

34.27   Where disputes concern trust land which is not co-owned by a married couple, they must be resolved by the application of ordinary property principles. The TLA 1996 has sought to rationalise and improve the approach to differences arising in the context of trusts of land.[1] The courts have been given a wide jurisdiction to entertain applications from trustees or those with an interest in a trust of land.[2] They may make any order 'relating to the exercise by the trustees of any of their functions, including an order relieving them of any obligation to obtain the consent of, or to consult, any person in connection with the exercise of their functions'.[3] They may also make an order 'declaring the nature or extent of a person's interest' in the trust land.[4]

The Act sets out matters which the court should take into account when making *any* order;[5] there are also specific provisions dealing with a dispute as to which beneficiary(ies) should occupy the trust property.[6] Many of these principles are derived from the case law which was developed by the courts prior to 1997 so that, as we shall see, some pre-1997 cases provide an indication of how the courts are likely to apply these new statutory provisions.

In practice, most of the disputes concerning trust land concern one (or both) of two issues; whether the land should be sold or, which of the beneficiaries should occupy the trust property. We shall, therefore, address each of these in the following paragraphs.

1   It should be remembered that the provisions of the Act which we are about to deal with apply to *all* trusts of land. In practice, however, most of the disputes arise in connection with *co-owned* land.
2   TLA, s 14(1).
3   TLA, s 14(2)(a).
4   TLA, s 14(2)(b). It should be noted that, in sharp contrast to the position regarding *matrimonial property* (see para 34.26 above), the court has no power to *vary* the interests of the beneficiaries.
5   TLA, s 15.
6   TLA, ss 13 and 15(2).

34.28   *Sale*. Where there is an application to court under the TLA, s 14 because there is a dispute as to whether or not the trust land should be sold, it is clear that the court can

* order a sale; or
* order a sale but suspend the order for the time being; or
* refuse a sale; or
* refuse a sale and make an order as to the occupation of the property.

When making its decision the court is required to take into account:[1]

* the intentions of the person(s) creating the trust;
* the purposes for which the trust property is held;
* the welfare of any child who occupies or might reasonably be expected to occupy the trust property as his home;
* the interests of any secured creditor of any beneficiary; and
* the wishes (of the majority by value) of any beneficiaries of full age and capacity.

The following cases, albeit decided prior to the 1996 Act and, therefore, in the context of the old trust *for sale*, would, it is suggested still produce the same result since the reasoning used could, today, readily be framed by reference to the new statutory provisions. They do, therefore, give some indication of how these provisions will apply.

In *Re Buchanan-Wollaston's Conveyance*,[2] four neighbouring landowners purchased a plot of land which lay between their homes and the sea, in order to keep it free from development and so preserve their view. The documentation specifically provided that the land should be dealt with only in accordance with the wishes of the majority but (unwisely) did not deal with the quite predictable event which then occurred. One co-owner subsequently left the neighbourhood and, not unnaturally, wished to realise his share. Having failed to negotiate a solution, he sought a court order that the land should be sold. The court refused to order sale. Having regard to the circumstances, particularly the express agreement between the co-owners, it was not right and proper to order sale at that particular time.[3]

In *Re Evers's Trust, Papps v Evers*[4] a co-habiting couple had purchased a house as joint tenants. The court was satisfied that the property was bought as a family home. Even though their relationship had ended, that purpose remained, since the woman still needed a home for herself and the children. The man had no pressing need to realise his investment so the court refused to order sale, given that the woman was prepared to undertake to pay the mortgage and outgoings and to indemnify the man in respect of her occupation.

By way of contrast, in *Jones v Challenger*,[5] a married couple had purchased their home as joint tenants. Their marriage broke down and the wife left, leaving her husband living in the property alone. Here the court ordered a sale; the house had been bought as a home for the couple and was no longer required for that purpose. (Since the couple were *married* this case would now be dealt with under divorce legislation;[6] nevertheless, the case illustrates the approach which would be taken to an unmarried couple (or other co-owners) in a similar situation.)

In *Bernard v Josephs*,[7] where there were no children and the relationship had ended, an order for sale was made. However, the order was postponed because the parties agreed that the man, who wished to remain in occupation, would buy the woman out.

In *Dennis v McDonald*[8] sale was refused. Here the relationship had broken down and the woman had left because of the man's violence. However, the man, who remained in occupation of the house with some of the children, was ordered to pay the woman an 'occupation rent' as compensation for having excluded her from the property.[9]

Where an application under TLA, s14 is made by a trustee in bankruptcy, the above principles do not apply. So where, for example, one of the co-owners becomes bankrupt and their trustee in bankruptcy applies for an order of sale, it is the insolvency regime which applies.[10] Broadly, where the property is the home of the bankrupt or the bankrupt's spouse or former spouse, one year's grace following the bankruptcy is given; thereafter, on any application for sale by the trustee in bankruptcy the interests of the creditors are paramount so that, in practice, an order of sale will virtually always be made.[11]

1   TLA, s 15. The section makes it clear that what follows is not an exhaustive list, so that the court is free to take account of other matters as well.
2   [1939] 2 All ER 302, CA.
3   Since a refusal of sale effectively left the other co-owners in occupation of land from which the applicant could no longer gain any effective practical benefit, it is possible that, today, the court might order the others to pay some sort of rent under the TLA, s 13(3); see para 34.29 below.
4   [1980] 3 All ER 399, CA.
5   [1960] 1 All ER 785, CA.
6   See para 34.26 above.
7   [1982] 3 All ER 162, CA.
8   [1981] 2 All ER 632; varied [1982] 1 All ER 592, CA.
9   A similar result could today be achieved; see TLA, s 13(3) or (6) and para 34.29 below.
10   TLA, s 15(4).
11   Insolvency Act 1986, s 335A; *Re Citro* [1990] 3 All ER 952, CA.

34.29 *Occupation* As we have seen,[1] beneficiaries often have the right to occupy the trust property and, in the case of concurrent ownership where the property was purchased for joint occupation, this will invariably be the case. Where two or more beneficiaries are entitled to occupy at the same time, but do not wish to occupy the property together and cannot agree a solution, the trustees are given the power to decide which of them can occupy and on what terms.[2] If a beneficiary is dissatisfied with the trustees' decision, an application to court under the TLA, s 14 can, of course, be made. However, the more likely circumstance of an application to court will be where the trust arises as a result of co-ownership. Here, the trustees are usually the very same beneficiaries who no longer wish to share occupation and who cannot agree as to which of them should stay. Here, a court's intervention will be necessary. As can be seen from the cases considered in the previous paragraph, it may well be the case that the court considers the question of sale and occupation together.

The TLA, s 13 sets out the powers of the trustees and the circumstances which they must take into account when arriving at a decision about the occupation of trust property. If the matter goes to court it would appear that the court is not so constrained since, by virtue of s 14, it can make *any* order. That said, it seems likely that the matters set out in the Act will be particularly influential in any decision as to occupation, whether that decision is made by the trustees or by the court.

Section 13 provides that the trustees may exclude or restrict the right to occupy where it is reasonable to do so. Where this is done, the occupying beneficiary can be required to make payments to the excluded beneficiary.[3] Equally, the trustees can subject a beneficiary's occupation to reasonable conditions (such as, in particular, the payment of compensation to other beneficiaries and responsibility for any outgoings or expenses in respect of the land). In reaching any decision the trustees should have regard to the intentions of the person who created the trust, the purposes for which the land is held and the circumstances and wishes of the beneficiaries who are entitled to occupy.

In the previous paragraph we considered the cases of *Re Evers*, *Bernard v Josephs*, and *Dennis v McDonald*. It would seem that, if the circumstances of those cases were repeated today, the court would reach similar decisions as to the occupation of the property and the conditions attaching to that occupation.

1   See para 34.16 above.
2   TLA, s 13.
3   It is worth noting that where a co-owner *voluntarily* goes out of occupation, he is not entitled *as of right* (ie in the absence of an express agreement) to 'rent' or compensation from any other co-owners: see, for example, *Jones v Jones* [1977] 1 WLR 438.

Chapter 35

Enforceability of interests in land

35.1 We have already seen[1] that one of the essential features of any proprietary right to use and enjoy land is that it must be *capable* of binding, not just the landowner who created the right, but also subsequent purchasers of the land to which the right relates. Rights, such as licences, which cannot in themselves[2] bind a purchaser are, by definition, purely personal. The circumstances in which a proprietary right *will actually bind* a future owner is an issue which is of prime importance. The value, and indeed the very marketability, of land depends on a purchaser or lender[3] being able to discover exactly what rights relating to the land will continue to operate after the sale or mortgage since this can profoundly affect the decision to purchase or to lend (or the price to be paid or the amount of any loan). Equally, those who have the benefit of rights over land which belongs to another, wish to ensure that any transfer of that land will not result in the loss of their rights.

In this chapter we consider:

- in outline, the rules which governed the enforceability of proprietary rights prior to 1926;
- in outline, the current rules relating to the enforceability of proprietary rights affecting land the title to which is not yet registered; and
- the current rules governing the enforceability of proprietary rights relating to registered land.

1 Para 30.2 above.
2 Additional factors may persuade a court to invoke the constructive trust or the doctrine of proprietary estoppel as a means of protecting a licensee against a subsequent purchaser; see paras 30.40 and 32.15 above.
3 A 'purchaser' includes 'a lessee, mortgagee or other person who for valuable consideration acquires an interest in property…'; LPA, s 205(1)(xxi).

The original rules

35.2 The rules governing the enforceability of proprietary rights were changed quite significantly in 1925. The current rules, particularly those relating to unregistered land, have been grafted on to pre-existing principles and are impossible to grasp without some understanding of the historical position. Furthermore, there remain situations in which the pre-1926 rules themselves still apply.[1] Hence we start by outlining the old rules governing the enforceability of proprietary rights which were, in principle (rather than in their practical application), relatively straightforward; quite simply all depended on whether the right in question was *legal* or *equitable*.

1   See para 35.19 below.

Legal rights

35.3   It has always been a basic principle of English land law that legal rights to land 'bind the whole world'. Thus a legal right will always bind a purchaser irrespective of whether the purchaser knows of the right in question. So, for example, if A (a freeholder) grants a legal lease to B and then sells his freehold reversion to C, C will always be bound by the lease. The same would be true if, instead of selling the freehold, A had granted a legal mortgage to D; D would also be bound by B's lease. This rule rarely causes unfairness because it is easy for a purchaser to discover the existence of legal rights to land. As we have seen, common law usually requires rights to land to be created by deed[1] with the result that there will be documentary evidence of such rights which forms part of the title to the land.[2] In those instances where the common law recognises rights despite the absence of a deed,[3] the owner of those rights is either in occupation of the land, or is openly exercising his rights; accordingly they will be revealed by the physical inspection of the land which every prudent purchaser is assumed by the law to make.

1   Para 31.6 above.
2   This information will either form part of the title deeds to the property in the case of unregistered land (see para 31.33 above) or will be noted on the Land Register in the case of registered land (para 31.29 above).
3   Eg leases not exceeding three years (para 31.7 above), freehold ownership based on adverse possession (paras 32.19–32.31 above) and easements acquired by prescription (para 32.19 above and paras 37.33–37.44 below).

Equitable interests

35.4   We have seen that equity's first foray into English land law was when the Court of Chancery started enforcing the trust by requiring the trustees, the legal owners of the land, to abide by the terms of the trust, thus recognising that it was the beneficiary who was entitled to the benefits of the land.[1] However, the beneficiary's rights against the trustees would be of little avail if he could be deprived of these benefits should the trustees transfer their ownership of the land to someone else. Gradually, the Chancellor came to hold that there were others besides the original trustees who were in conscience bound to give effect to the rights of the beneficiary. Thus, these rights came to be enforceable against a trustee's heir, against someone to whom a trustee left the land by will, against someone to whom the trustees gave the land, and against someone who bought the land knowing that the beneficiary was entitled to the benefit of it. As the class of persons against whom the beneficiary could enforce his rights was extended the effect was that his equitable interest became almost as good as the legal estate which was held by the trustees. However, the Court of Chancery stopped short of enforcing the beneficiary's rights against the whole world; equitable rights came to be enforceable against the whole world *except* a 'bona fide purchaser of a legal estate for value without notice of the equitable interest'.

In addition to beneficial interests under a trust, equity had, over the years, come to recognise a number of rights in respect of land which were not recognised by the common law; for example the restrictive covenant.[2] Furthermore, as we have seen,[3] equity will sometimes give effect to rights despite the fact that they were created in ways which failed to comply with the formalities demanded by the common law and statute. The decision in *Pilcher v Rawlins*,[4] in 1872, made it clear that the rule that equitable rights were not enforceable against a bona fide purchaser of a legal estate without notice of their existence applied to all equitable interests, not just beneficial interests under a trust. Furthermore, it was established by the decision in *Wilkes v Spooner*[5] that, if the legal estate is acquired by a purchaser for value without notice, the equitable interest of which he has no notice is effectively destroyed. It cannot be enforced against a subsequent purchaser who, unlike the original bona fide purchaser, knows of the existence of the equitable interest.

1   Para 30.35 above.
2   Ch 38 below.
3   See paras 32.2–32.6 above.
4   (1872) 7 Ch App 259.
5   [1911] 2 KB 473, CA.

The bona fide purchaser of a legal estate for value

35.5   In order to appreciate the differences between the rules governing the enforceability of legal and equitable rights to land, we need to examine more closely the notion of the bona fide purchaser of a legal estate for value without notice. To fall within the exception and thus take free from prior equitable interests in the land, a purchaser must have acted bona fide, 'in good faith'; he must have acted honestly, and genuinely be without notice. As we have seen, the term 'purchaser' bears an extended meaning in law encompassing all those who acquire an interest in land[1] and includes a lessee and a mortgagee. However, the purchaser must acquire the legal estate 'for value', ie for valuable consideration[2] or in consideration of marriage. Thus, where a person acquires the legal estate as a gift or under a will or on an intestacy[3] he will be bound by any equitable interests, even if he has no notice of them.

The purchaser must acquire a 'legal estate', a concept which for this purpose includes both legal estates and legal interests. Where a purchaser acquires for value an equitable interest, for example where a beneficiary under a trust assigns his equitable interest to another, the latter will be bound by prior equitable interests affecting the equitable interest, such as an equitable mortgage,[4] whether or not he has notice of them. The rule here is that 'where the equities are equal the first in time prevails'.

1   Para 35.1 above.
2   See ch 6 above.
3   Ie where a person dies leaving no effective will.
4   Para 39.9 below.

The doctrine of notice

35.6   We now turn to the concept of notice itself, of which there are three varieties: actual notice, constructive notice and imputed notice. A purchaser has actual notice of rights of which he knows.

If actual notice were the only type of notice, a purchaser could avoid knowledge of an equitable interest, and thus take the land free from it, by refraining from inspecting the land he was buying or by failing to investigate the title to it. However, equity has long recognised that a purchaser has constructive notice of an equitable interest if its existence would have come to his knowledge if reasonable inquiries and inspections had been made. The onus is thus on the purchaser to make such reasonable inquiries and inspections as would be made by any prudent purchaser. We have already considered in chapter 31, above, the conveyancing procedures which ought to be followed and, where these are properly carried out, a purchaser will have done all that is required to escape being fixed with constructive notice of any equitable interests of which he remained unaware.

A further aspect of constructive notice is the doctrine of *Hunt v Luck*,[1] whereby a person's occupation of property (or, it may be, notice of a person's occupation of property[2]) constitutes constructive notice to others of his rights in respect of the property. Thus, a purchaser, on inspecting the property, should make inquiries of any person in occupation, other than his vendor, to establish whether that person has any rights in the property. Failure to do so will give him constructive notice of those rights.

Finally, we should mention imputed notice. For fairly obvious reasons, equity has taken the view that any notice, actual or constructive, which is acquired or deemed to be acquired by a solicitor or other agent acting for the purchaser in the transaction is imputed to the purchaser.

1   [1901] 1 Ch 45; affd [1902] 1 Ch 428, CA.
2   *Kingsnorth Trust Ltd v Tizard* [1986] 2 All ER 54, [1986] 1 WLR 783.

35.7   *The problems caused by the doctrine of notice*   The application of the fully developed doctrine of notice undoubtedly came to cause problems for both a purchaser of land and an owner of any equitable interest. A purchaser was at risk of being bound by an undiscovered equitable interest since he could be deemed to have notice unless he had made 'proper' pre-purchase inquiries. Furthermore, and conversely, an equitable interest in land could be lost if the legal estate was acquired for valuable consideration by someone without notice of its existence. If these difficulties were not seriously to hinder dealings in land (which were, of course, by the end of the 19th century starting to increase quite dramatically) changes in the law were necessary, and it is to these which we now turn.

The current rules

35.8   Two solutions were adopted in 1925 to ease the problems outlined in the previous paragraph. In the case of some equitable interests which might loosely be regarded as 'commercial',[1] the concept of registration was introduced. The essence of this is that if such interests are protected by being registered they will bind a purchaser; if they are not, they will not bind. A purchaser thus knows that, prior to his purchase, he must search the relevant register to discover the existence of those interests which will bind him; equally, the owner of the interest knows that, by registering his interest, they will be enforceable against all purchasers.

The second solution relates to those equitable interests of a 'family' nature, such as interests arising under a settlement or as a result of co-ownership.[2] We have already seen that, after 1925, all such interests are necessarily equitable and can now only exist behind a trust.[3] In the case of this type of equitable interest it was felt unnecessary that they should bind a purchaser at all, and undesirable that the legal estate should in perpetuity be encumbered with a string of beneficial interests. Consequently, the existing notion of 'overreaching' was extended. As we have seen[4] this is the process whereby, on the sale of the land, the beneficial interests under the trust cease to bind the land, and are satisfied thenceforth out of the proceeds of sale instead.

The detailed implementation of the policy of registering 'commercial' type proprietary rights was further complicated by the simultaneous introduction of the system of registration of *title*. While the introduction of a radically different system for the protection and enforcement of interests in land was a vital aspect of registration of title, the LRA 1925 had a much wider remit. As we have seen,[5] the Act put in place a scheme for the central registration of title to land which resulted in quite different procedures for the transfer and creation of rights to land once registration has taken place. For practical reasons which we have already explained, this had to be implemented on a gradual basis which, even now, is not yet complete. Accordingly, the legislators had to decide whether to leave unregistered land subject to the existing, unsatisfactory, rules on notice, or whether to introduce essentially temporary reforms, designed to apply until such time as the title to any particular piece of land is actually registered. In the event, the latter course was adopted with the result that we have two *quite separate and mutually exclusive* systems of registration. The first and far more limited scheme, is that which applies *only* to unregistered land and is contained in what is now the Land Charges Act 1972 (hereafter LCA). The second is that governed by the LRA. We have already dealt with the conveyancing aspects of the LRA;[5] in this chapter we concentrate on the rules governing the protection and enforceability of third party rights to registered land.

1   Eg estate contracts (para 31.5 above), restrictive covenants (ch 38 below) and mortgages (ch 39 below).
2   Ch 33 above.
3   Ch 34 above.
4   Paras 34.7 and 34.17 above.
5   Paras 31.8–31.10 above.

Unregistered land

35.9   We first consider, in outline only, the rules relating to the protection of interests in land where the LRA does not apply because the title to land has not yet been registered.[1] The key to understanding the rules governing the enforceability of rights in unregistered land lies in grasping the way in which such rights are classified. The rights of third parties will fall into one of two categories; they will either be registrable under the LCA or they will not be so registrable. This second category can itself be further divided into two groups; those rights which are legal and those which are equitable. Again this second group, ie equitable rights which are not registrable under the LCA, can be further divided into those which are overreachable and those which are not. The following diagram illustrates this classification:

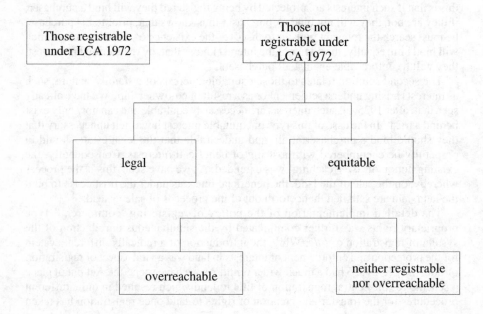

A different rule on enforceability applies to each category and we shall deal with each in turn.

1   Where the purchase in question actually triggers first registration of title (as to which see para 31.10 above) it is the rules governing *unregistered land* which determine by which rights this purchaser will be bound. It is only *after* this purchaser has become the first registered proprietor that the rules governing *registered land* apply.

Rights registrable under the Land Charges Act 1972

35.10   The policy of reducing the impact of the doctrine of notice, both to enable a purchaser more readily to discover interests affecting the land and to enable those entitled to those interests to fix the purchaser with notice of their existence, was given effect by the Land Charges Act 1925, now repealed and consolidated by the Land Charges Act 1972. The fundamental objective of this Act is to mechanise the doctrine of notice by requiring rights governed by the Act to be registered; as we shall see, such registration constitutes actual notice, while a failure to register renders the right void against most purchasers.[1]

The LCA obliges the Land Registry, in addition to operating the system of registration of title under the LRA, also to maintain a Land Charges department operating the Land Charges Act 1972. This department keeps on computer at Plymouth the Land Charges Register.

1   Para 35.15 below.

35.11   *Registrable land charges*   The LCA defines those rights which are registrable in the Land Charges Register by reference to six classes of charge or obligation affecting land, Classes A to F. With two exceptions, the rights which are registrable in the Land Charges Register are all equitable, in keeping with the notion that registration under the LCA constitutes actual notice. For our purposes the most important of the rights which are made registrable by the Land Charges Act 1972, s 2(4) are as follows:

- estate contracts (ie contracts for the sale or lease of land, including options and rights of pre-emption)[1]– Class C (iv);
- restrictive covenants[2] created after 1925– Class D (ii);
- puisne mortgages (ie legal mortgages under which the mortgagee does not hold the title deeds)[3]– Class C (i);
- general equitable charges (eg equitable mortgages under which the mortgagee does not hold the title deeds)–Class C (iii);
- certain equitable easements[4] created after 1925– Class D (iii);
- Spouses' rights of occupation under what is now the Family Law Act 1996[5]– Class F.

1   Para 31.5 above.
2   Ch 38 below.
3   Ch 39 below.
4   Ch 37 below.
5   In practice a Class F charge is only registered in the increasingly rare case of a spouse who has neither a legal nor equitable interest in the matrimonial home; even then a registration will only be made where the marriage has broken down because it is only at such a point that the spouse is likely to be advised of their rights.

Registration and failure to register

35.12   As we have said, the basic philosophy of the LCA is the mechanisation of the doctrine of notice; hence the registration of a land charge is deemed to constitute actual notice.[1] Broadly, a failure to register the right is void against most *purchasers*;[2] non-registration of a charge does not affect its enforceability against a donee, devisee (ie a beneficiary under a will) or squatter.

If a right is void as against a purchaser as a result of non-registration then the purchaser will not be affected by it even though he knows of its existence.[3] In *Midland Bank Trust Co Ltd v Green*,[4] a husband conveyed the legal estate in his farm, worth £40,000, to his wife, for £500, with the intention of defeating an option to purchase which he had earlier granted to his son but which his son had not registered.[5] The House of Lords held that the option was void against the wife for non-registration. She was a genuine 'purchaser'; the statute imposed no requirement that she should have acted in good faith. In any event, the House held, it was not fraud or a lack of good faith to take advantage of legal rights conferred by Act of Parliament.

However, there are some difficult cases where the purchaser not only knew of the unregistered charge, but also expressly agreed to take the land 'subject to' that charge. In *Hollington Bros Ltd v Rhodes*,[6] it was held that where land was acquired expressly subject to such tenancies 'as may affect' the premises the purchaser was not affected by an agreement for a lease since it had not been registered as a Class C (iv) land charge.[7] Harman J said that, although on the face of it, it might seem wrong that a purchaser who knows perfectly well of rights subject to which he is expressed to take should be able to ignore them, he did not see how something declared by statute to be void could be made valid again.

Nevertheless, it was held in *Lyus v Prowsa Developments Ltd*,[8] where a purchaser acquired land expressly subject to a specified unregistered estate contract (as opposed to 'subject to such rights as may affect the land', as in *Hollington v Rhodes*), that the purchaser became a constructive trustee[9] in favour of the person entitled under the estate contract; for to hold otherwise would be to permit the purchaser fraudulently to renege on the positive stipulation to give effect to the contract subject to which he acquired the land. Furthermore, certain cases[10] make it clear that, by regarding a right as arising under the doctrine of proprietary estoppel,[11] it can be taken outside the registration requirements altogether; in such instances a purchaser with notice will be bound.[12]

However, it should be noted that, because registration is merely a scheme governing the mechanics of enforceability, it does not confer validity on a right in respect of another's land which, for other reasons, is invalid. Similarly, a failure to register only affects the enforceability of the charge against a subsequent purchaser of the land affected; it does not affect its enforceability between the original parties. Thus, for example, the registration of a 'contract' for the sale of land which fails to comply with s 2 of the Law of Property (Miscellaneous Provisions) Act 1989[13] will not render the 'contract' binding on a subsequent purchaser of the land; there is, in law, no contract and registration cannot put that right. Equally, the failure to register a valid contract for the sale of land may make it unenforceable against a purchaser, but it does not prevent the aggrieved party suing the vendor for damages for breach of contract.

1   LPA, s 198(1).
2   Land Charges Act 1972, s 4(5) and (6). It should be remembered that the term 'purchaser' includes a lessee and a mortgagee; see Land Charges Act 1972, s 17.
3   LPA. s 199.
4   [1981] AC 513, [1981] 1 All ER 153, HL.
5   As an estate contract.
6   [1951] 2 All ER 578n.
7   Para 35.11 above.
8   [1982] 2 All ER 953, [1982] 1 WLR 1044; approved in *Ashburn Anstalt v Arnold* [1989] Ch 1, [1988] 2 All ER 147, CA.
9   Para 32.10 above.
10 See *ER Ives Investments Ltd v High* [1967] 2 QB 379, [1967] 1 All ER 504, CA; *Taylors Fashions Ltd v Liverpool Victoria Trustees Co Ltd* [1982] QB 133n, [1981] 1 All ER 897. However, note should also be made of *Lloyds Bank plc v Carrick* [1996] 4 All ER 630, CA. Here the court refused to side-

step the requirement to register and declined to treat what was, in truth, an unregistered estate contract as an arrangement giving rise to proprietory estoppel.

11   Paras 32.11–32.16 above.
12   Para 35.18 below.
13   Para 31.2 above.

The registration machinery

35.13   It is a fundamental defect of the system of registering interests in unregistered land that the registration is made, not against the land affected, but against the name of the owner of the legal estate.[1] Thus, a purchaser intending to buy 42 Acacia Avenue cannot look up 42 Acacia Avenue (or its reference number) in the Land Charges Register to discover, for example, whether it is affected by an option to purchase; instead, he must make a search against the names of all the owners of the legal estate of 42 Acacia Avenue since 1 January 1926.[2]

This problem is relieved as a matter of conveyancing practice by keeping copies of all official certificates of search of the register[3] received by purchasers in the past together with the title deeds, thus revealing the relevant names. However, should this practice break down in a particular case, the LPA 1969, s 25 provides that if a purchaser suffers loss by reason of the land being affected by a land charge of which he had no actual knowledge, which was registered against a name not discoverable from the relevant title, he is entitled to compensation payable by the Chief Land Registrar out of public funds.

1   Land Charges Act 1972, s 3(1).
2   When the Land Charges Act 1925 came into force.
3   Para 35.14 below.

35.14   *Searches*   A purchaser may make a search of the register in person[1] but it is usual to request an official search. The latter is the preferable course since it results in an official certificate of search which is conclusive in favour of the purchaser,[2] so that he takes free of any registered land charges which the certificate fails to disclose. Furthermore, an official search confers a priority period of 15 working days:[3] no charge registered within 15 working days of the issue of an official search certificate will bind the purchaser if he completes the purchase within that period.

1   Land Charges Act 1972, s 9.
2   Ibid, s 10.
3   Ibid, s 11.

Interests outside the Land Charges Act

35.15   As explained at the outset, the LCA system of registration was never intended to apply to all third party rights affecting unregistered land. In particular, it was always anticipated that virtually all *legal* interests, and those equitable interests to which the *overreaching* provisions apply, should not be registrable.

35.16   *Legal interests*   Subject to two exceptions[1] legal third party rights are not registrable under the LCA. For such rights the pre-1926 rules apply; namely that, as legal rights, they bind the whole world. Thus a purchaser is bound by such rights irrespective of whether he knows about them or not; as we have already explained, in practice, it is generally quite easy for a purchaser to discover the existence of legal rights.[2]

1   The puisne mortgage which is registrable as Class C (i) charge (see para 35.12 above) and the Inland Revenue charge for inheritance tax (registrable as a Class D (i) charge).
2   Para 35.3 above.

35.17 *Equitable interests which are overreachable* We have seen that certain equitable interests arising under trusts are overreachable. This means that, on a sale of the land, the rights of the beneficiaries do not bind a purchaser even where the purchaser is fully aware of them. It is important to realise that, in order for overreaching to take effect, the purchaser must pay the purchase money to trustees who must be at least two in number (or a trust corporation).[1] If this is not done,[2] no overreaching occurs; in such a situation whether or not the purchaser takes free from the rights of the beneficiaries depends on the doctrine of notice.[3]

1 Paras 34.7, 34.17 above and 35.18 below.
2 As already explained, this is most likely to occur in cases of implied co-ownership, where the title deeds often give the purchaser the impression that the property is solely owned so that he does not realise that any question of overreaching arises; see para 34.18 above.
3 Para 35.18 below.

35.18 *Equitable interests which are neither registrable nor overreachable* The LCA itself shows that there are equitable rights relating to unregistered land, namely pre-1926 equitable easements and restrictive covenants, and covenants in a lease, to which the registration system does not apply. Further, decisions of the courts such as *E R Ives Investments Ltd v High*[1] and *Shiloh Spinners Ltd v Harding*,[2] demonstrate that there are other equitable rights (in those cases a right arising by way of proprietary estoppel and an equitable right of re-entry) which are not within the Land Charges Act and which are not overreachable. In addition, as we have explained in the previous paragraph, there are circumstances in which an overreachable right is not in fact overreached. In each of these instances whether or not the purchaser is bound depends on the doctrine of notice.[3] Except in so far as the LPA has statutorily defined constructive and imputed notice,[4] the present doctrine is the same as the old equitable doctrine of notice.[5]

A good example of the modern operation of the doctrine of notice is provided by *Kingsnorth Finance Ltd v Tizard*.[6] Here the matrimonial home had been conveyed in the name of the husband only, although the wife had made a financial contribution and so was an implied co-owner in equity. Unknown to the wife the husband applied for a mortgage, indicating that he was not married; he arranged for the mortgagees' valuer to inspect the property at a time when she was not present. The valuer reported that the property appeared to be occupied only by the applicant and his two children and the loan was duly made. When the husband disappeared with the money the plaintiffs sought possession. The wife argued that the mortgagees were bound by her rights as a beneficiary under the statutory trust for sale; they had dealt with a single trustee when granting the mortgage so that no overreaching could have taken place and the doctrine of notice therefore applied. Since she was in occupation of the property they had constructive notice of her rights. The judge agreed and possession was refused. Thus, although the Land Charges Act has considerably reduced the importance of the doctrine of notice as the vehicle for the protection of equitable interests, it has not totally superseded it.

1 [1967] 2 QB 379, [1967] 1 All ER 504, CA; para 32.13 above.
2 [1973] AC 691, [1973] 1 All ER 90, HL.
3 *Caunce v Caunce* [1969] 1 All ER 722, [1969] 1 WLR 286.
4 LPA 1925, s 199(1)(ii).
5 Para 35.6 above.
6 [1986] 2 All ER 54, [1986] 1 WLR 783.

Registered land

35.19 As we have said[1] the introduction of a new system of registration of title by the LRA 1925 offered an opportunity to adopt a fresh approach to the question of the enforceability and protection of third party rights. In order to be covered by that Act at all a third party right must relate to or be parasitic on an interest to which title has been registered. So, for example, a restrictive covenant, a short lease or a mortgage, will only fall within the ambit of the LRA if the title to the freehold or long lease to which it relates has been registered. First registration of title[2] provides a chance for the Land Registry to check all the documentary evidence of rights affecting that property, to classify those rights and to record their existence by way of an entry in the register of title. By definition this initial investigation by the Land Registry will reveal, and result in the registration of, a far wider range of rights than are covered by the much more limited system of registration set up by the LCA. Since all dealings with the land thereafter should be completed by registration[3] the register can be kept up to date by the addition, where necessary, of fresh entries.

The classification of rights to land by the LRA is its own. Title can only be registered to either a freehold or leasehold estate; these are 'registrable interests'. Rights affecting any interest to which the title has been registered are either registered charges, overriding interests or minor interests. This can be illustrated by the following diagram:

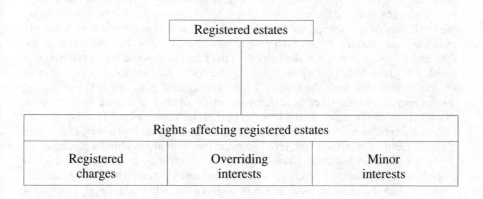

The enforceability against subsequent purchasers of rights affecting interests to which the title has been registered flows from the LRA classification and system of protection and not from whether the rights are legal or equitable.[4] Furthermore, the opportunity has been taken to eliminate the doctrine of notice from registered land.

1 Para 35.8 above.
2 Paras 31.10 and 31.36 above.
3 Para 31.9 above.
4 Although their initial classification may hinge on whether they are legal or equitable.

Registered charges
35.20 The most usual way of mortgaging registered land is by way of 'registered charge'. Because it must be created by a 'registered disposition'[1] and is not fully effective until the lender is registered as proprietor of the charge on the borrower's register of title,[2] the registered charge falls into a unique category. We deal with registered charges in more detail later.[3]

1 LRA 1925, ss 18(4) and 21(4).
2 LRA 1925 s 26(1).
3 Para 39.8 below.

Overriding interests

35.21 Overriding interests are rights and interests which do not appear on the register of title but are nevertheless binding on a purchaser of registered land. Consequently, a proprietor's register of title does not provide a complete picture of the rights affecting the title and so further inspection of the land and inquiries of the vendor will be necessary to discover the full picture. These rights are listed in the LRA, s 70(1); among the more important are:

- legal easements, and legal or equitable profits a prendre;[1]
- rights acquired or in the course of being acquired under the Limitation Act[2] (ie 'squatters' rights');
- the rights of every person in actual occupation of the land (or in receipt of the rents and profits thereof) except where inquiry is made of such person and the rights are not disclosed;[3]
- leases granted for a term not exceeding 21 years.[4]

The existence of the category of overriding interests, which bind the purchaser despite not being entered on the register, may appear surprising at first sight and clearly invalidates any idea that the registered land scheme ensures that all interests affecting the land should be discoverable from the state register. However, we have already examined the circumstances which give rise to this difficulty. For obvious reasons, the Land Registry can only make entries on the Land Register in respect of rights of which it is given documentary evidence. In chapter 33 we have examined a range of situations in which both the common law[5] and equity[6] give effect to events and transactions of which there is little or no written proof. It can be seen from an examination of the rights listed in s 70(1) that the policy of recognising certain informally created rights is carried over into the registered land system by classifying many of them as overriding and providing that they will always bind a purchaser.

Although the number and range of rights which may be overriding appear considerable, in practice a purchaser will find that many potential overriding interests are entered on the register since the Registrar has a discretion to note any overriding interests on the register.[7] Furthermore, as we shall see,[8] most adverse easements (such as rights of way across the registered land) are created by deed and so appear on the title at the time of first registration; in such cases they must be noted on the register of title.[9] Any express easements created thereafter by a registered proprietor must be completed by registration and will, again, be entered on the register.[10] Accordingly, the only easements which are almost invariably overriding are those arising by prescription (ie long use).[11] Once any overriding interest is in fact noted on the register it ceases to be overriding and takes its protection from the entry.[12]

1   LRA, s 70(1)(a). In *Celsteel Ltd v Alton House Holdings Ltd* [1985] 2 All ER 562, [1985] 1 WLR 204 it was held that the Land Registration Rules, r 258 extends the category of overriding interests to include equitable easements. This may not be correct, however, because the wording of this rule suggests that it was intended merely to include as overriding interests easements within the LPA, s 62 (as to which see paras 37.27–37.32 below). However, the *Celsteel* case has been treated as correctly decided in *Thatcher v Douglas* [1996] NLJR 282, CA.

2   Ibid, s 70(1)(f); paras 32.19–32.31 above.

3   Ibid, s 70(1)(g); paras 35.22–35.28 below.

4   Ibid, s 70(1)(k). In *City Permanent Building Society v Miller* [1952] Ch 840 at 853 it was made clear that para (k) applies only to legal leases; equitable leases are thus not overriding interests. Changes to the wording of para (k) by the LRA 1986, s 4(1) ensure that it now applies to all legal leases whether granted at a premium or at a full rent.

5   Eg by way of adverse possession or prescription; see para 32.19 above.

6   Eg by way of constructive trust or under the doctrine of proprietary estoppel; see paras 32.8–32.17 above.

7   LRA, s 70(3).
8   Paras 37.20–37.22 below.
9   LRA, s 70(2); *Re Dances Way, West Town, Hayling Island* [1962] Ch 490, [1962] 2 All ER 42.
10 Ibid, ss 19(2) and 22(2).
11 As to which see paras 37.33–37.44 below.
12 Ibid, s 3(xvi).

Rights of every person in actual occupation

35.22   This is potentially the most extensive category of overriding interest. Any proprietary right affecting registered land can fall within s 70(1)(g), provided only that its owner is in actual occupation of the land to which it relates. While, as we have mentioned,[1] the LRA seeks to eliminate the doctrine of notice, s 70(1)(g) may be regarded as affording very similar protection under the registered land system to that conferred by the doctrine in *Hunt v Luck*.[2] Indeed, s 70(1)(g) may be regarded as even more extensive since it protects not only the rights of those in physical occupation of the land, but also those of persons in receipt of rents and profits. Furthermore, while the doctrine of *Hunt v Luck* cannot save an interest in unregistered land which should have been registered under the LCA,[3] s 70(1)(g) can operate to protect a right which could have been entered on the Land Register;[4] it makes no difference that the right protected by occupation might also have been protected as a minor interest on the register.[5]

1   Para 35.14 above; see also para 35.35 below.
2   [1902] 1 Ch 428, CA. Ie whereby a purchaser has constructive notice of the rights of any person in occupation of land; para 35.6 above.
3   Land Charges Act 1972, s 4(5) and (6); see para 35.12 above.
4   *Webb v Pollmount* [1966] Ch 584, [1966] 1 All ER 481.
5   *Williams and Glyn's Bank Ltd v Boland* [1981] AC 487, [1980] 2 All ER 408, HL; see para 35.35 below.

35.23   *Rights with reference to land*   The only rights which can be protected by actual occupation under s 70(1)(g) are 'rights with reference to land which have the quality of being capable of enduring through different ownerships of the land according to normal conceptions of title to real property', in other words, recognised proprietary interests.[1] Examples include unregistered estate contracts (thus putting a tenant in occupation under an unregistered agreement for a lease in a better position in registered than in unregistered land[2]), interests under any trust of land,[3] and (possibly[4]) interests arising by way of proprietary estoppel. It is expressly provided that beneficial interests under an old strict settlement cannot constitute overriding interests,[5] nor can a spouse's rights of occupation under what is now the Family Law Act 1996;[6] these must be protected as minor interests by a positive entry on the register.[7]

1   *National Provincial Bank Ltd v Ainsworth* [1965] AC 1175 at 1226.
2   *Kling v Keston Properties Ltd* (1983) 49 P & CR 212; paras 32.5 and 35.12 above.
3   *Williams and Glyn's Bank Ltd v Boland* [1981] AC 487, [1980] 2 All ER 408, HL.
4   See *Habermann v Koehler* (1996) 72 P & CR D10, CA.
5   LRA s 86(2).
6   Family Law Act 1996, s 31(10)(b), replacing a similar provision in what was the Matrimonial Homes Act 1983.
7   As to which see para 35.28 below.

35.24   *Actual occupation*   Whether a person is in 'actual occupation' is a question of fact, depending on the circumstances including the nature and state of the property in question.[1] According to the House of Lords in *Abbey National Building Society v Cann*,[2] occupation is a concept which may have different connotations according to the nature and purpose of the property which is claimed to be occupied. It does not necessarily involve the personal presence of the person claiming to occupy. A caretaker or representative of a company can occupy on behalf of his employer. On the other hand, it does involve some degree of permanence and continuity which would rule out mere fleeting presence. A prospective tenant or purchaser who is allowed, as a matter of indulgence, to go into property in order to plan decorations or measure for furnishings would not, in ordinary parlance, be said to be occupying it, even though he might be there for hours at a time.[3] It is clear from *Williams and Glyn's Bank Ltd v Boland*,[4] that, contrary to what some had previously thought, a wife may be in actual occupation of property for the purposes of this provision even though her registered proprietor husband is also in occupation.

In *Abbey National Building Society v Cann*[5] the question also arose as to the relevant moment at which a person must be in actual occupation of property for their rights to bind a purchaser. Is it the time that the conveyance or mortgage is executed or is it sufficient that the person is in actual occupation by the time that the purchaser's or lender's interest is registered? The issue in that case was whether a person who goes into occupation after the creation of a mortgage, but prior to its substantive registration, had an overriding interest capable of binding the lender. The House of Lords held that the rights of such a person did not constitute an overriding interest since the relevant time to ascertain whether an interest in registered land is protected by actual occupation is when the purchaser's or lender's estate is transferred or created, not the date when it is registered.[6]

1 See *Williams and Glyn's Bank Ltd v Boland* [1980] 2 All ER 408 at 413.
2 [1990] 1 All ER 1085, HL.
3 Per Lord Oliver [1990] 1 All ER 1085 at 1101.
4 [1981] AC 487, [1980] 2 All ER 408, HL.
5 [1990] 1 All ER 1085, HL.
6 In any event, the House of Lords held that a purchaser who can only complete his purchase by borrowing money, for the security of which he is contractually bound to grant a mortgage to the lender at the moment of completion of the purchase, cannot grant an interest to a third party which has priority over the mortgage. See also *Paddington Building Society v Mendelsohn* (1985) 50 P & CR 244.

35.25 *Inquiry* A purchaser of registered land should inquire of all those who are or appear to be in actual occupation of the property as to whether they have any rights in the land; the vendor's word should not be accepted.[1] Furthermore, since the subsection protects the rights of those in receipt of rents and profits, the purchaser must also ask the occupier 'To whom do you pay your rent?'[2] If the answer to that question is someone other than the vendor, the purchaser must then inquire as to the rights of that person. Particular care needs to be taken where a spouse or co-habitee whose name is not on the register is in occupation; a prospective purchaser or lender should make inquiry of him or her. If as in *Williams and Glyn's Bank Ltd v Boland*,[3] the occupier has rights (in that case as a beneficial co-owner of the property[4]) and the purchaser or lender fails to make inquiry of him or her, the purchaser or lender takes subject to them.

1 *Hodgson v Marks* [1971] Ch 892 at 932.
2 *Strand Securities Ltd v Caswell* [1965] Ch 958, [1965] 1 All ER 820, CA.
3 [1981] AC 487, [1980] 2 All ER 408, HL.
4 Para 33.23 above.

35.26 *Overreaching* Many of the cases concerning s 70(1)(g) have involved the claims of implied co-owners. As we have seen[1] such rights give rise to a trust of land with the result that, in many instances, the person who appears to be a sole registered proprietor is in law a trustee holding the property on trust for himself and the implied co-owner. We have also seen that, where a purchaser deals with a sole trustee, the overreaching machinery is not triggered[2] so that the implied co-owner's rights may bind the purchaser. In unregistered land this will only be the case where the purchaser has *notice* of the rights of the co-owner;[3] in registered land those rights will bind a purchaser if they are registered as a minor interest[4] (which is unlikely) or if they rank as an overriding interest by virtue of s 70(1)(g). However, it has been made clear by the House of Lords in *City of London Building Society v Flegg*[5] that, where a purchaser (in that case a mortgagee) deals with the trustees who are at least two in number, the rights of any other implied co-owners will be overreached even where the latter are in actual occupation.[6]

1   Para 33.23 above.
2   Paras 34.7 and 34.17 above.
3   Para 35.18 above.
4   Para 35.28 below.
5   [1988] AC 54, [1987] 3 All ER 435, HL.
6   See also *State Bank of India v Sood* [1997] 1 All ER 169, CA.

35.27   *The operation of s 70(1)(g)*   The operation of s 70(1)(g) and the extent of the protection which it affords can be illustrated by looking at three cases. In *Hodgson v Marks*[1] Mrs Hodgson, the freehold owner of a house, transferred it, for nothing, to her lodger, Evans. This was not intended to be an outright gift, for the parties agreed that although Evans was to become the registered proprietor, the beneficial (equitable) ownership was to remain in Mrs Hodgson; in other words, Evans was to hold the land on (resulting) trust for Mrs Hodgson. The parties continued to live in the house as if nothing had changed: Mrs Hodgson as if owner and Evans as if lodger. Evans then sold the house to Marks who became registered proprietor. Marks was aware of Mrs Hodgson's presence in the house but not of any rights she might have in respect of it. Mrs Hodgson's interest under the trust could only bind Marks if either it was protected by an entry on the register, which it was not, or if it was an overriding interest by virtue of her occupation of the property. The Court of Appeal held that she was in actual occupation of the property and her rights under the trust constituted an overriding interest. The court held that simply because the vendor is, or appears to be, in occupation of the property does not mean that no one else can be in actual occupation.

In *Strand Securities Ltd v Caswell*[2] the defendant was the tenant under a sublease which, as the law then stood, was not required to have its title registered. He later allowed his stepdaughter and her family to live in the flat rent free. When his landlord's registered lease was later transferred to the plaintiffs the latter claimed to take free from the defendant's sublease. The Court of Appeal held that the defendant could not have an overriding interest under s 70(1)(g)[3] since, although he owned a right having reference to land (ie the sublease), he was not in actual occupation of the flat; he neither lived there nor was he in receipt of rent. Equally his stepdaughter did not have an overriding interest; although she was in actual occupation, she did not have a right with reference to land since she was only a licensee.[4]

In *Williams and Glyn's Bank Ltd v Boland*[5] Mrs Boland was, by virtue of her substantial contribution to its purchase price, an equitable tenant in common of the house which had been transferred into the sole name of her husband.[6] In order to raise money for his business, he later mortgaged the house to the bank which made no inquiries of Mrs Boland. On the husband defaulting, the bank started possession proceedings. It was held, however, that the wife had an interest with reference to land and was in actual occupation; she therefore had an overriding interest which had priority over the bank's mortgage and it could not therefore obtain possession against her.

1   [1971] Ch 892, [1971] 2 All ER 684, CA.
2   [1965] Ch 958, [1965] 1 All ER 820, CA.
3   The sublease did not meet the requirements of s 70(1)(k).

4   The court went on to hold that, for other reasons, the defendant's sublease bound the plaintiffs.
5   [1980] 2 All ER 408, HL.
6   Para 33.23 above.

Minor interests

35.28   Essentially, the category of minor interests includes all interests affecting an estate in land to which title has been registered, which are not overriding. In particular it includes:

- beneficial interests under a trust of land;
- rights which in unregistered land would be protected under the Land Charges Act 1972 or under the doctrine of notice;[1] and
- interests created by dispositions by a registered proprietor which have not been completed by registration as required by the Act.[2]

These minor interests must be protected by entry on the register; however, unlike under the LCA, the function of such an entry is not always to render the right binding on a purchaser. In some instances, notably entries in relation to the rights of beneficiaries under a trust of land, the purpose of the entry is to make any purchaser aware that the registered proprietors are trustees and that the overreaching machinery (ie payment of the purchase money to at least two trustees) needs to be complied with if the purchaser is to take free from the rights. In the other cases the function of the entry is indeed to inform the purchaser of rights which will bind him. There are four methods of protecting a minor interest by entry on the register; that used in any given case depends partly on the type of protection which is afforded and partly on whether or not the registered proprietor is prepared to co-operate in making the entry.

1   Paras 35.10–35.14 and 35.18 above.
2   LRA, s 101; para 31.9 above.

Methods of protecting minor interests

35.29   *Restriction* A restriction is entered in the Proprietorship Register of the register of title by, or with the consent of, the registered proprietor himself. Its object is to prevent dealings with the land unless a specified requirement has been complied with, such as the payment of the purchase money to trustees who must be at least two in number, or the obtaining of the consent of a particular person. Its main use is to protect beneficial (equitable) interests under a trust of land by ensuring that the overreaching provisions are complied with.[1]

1   LRA, s 58.

35.30   *Notice* A notice[1] is used to protect rights which in unregistered land would be protected under the Land Charges Act, eg an estate contract or a restrictive covenant. Also noted on the Register are adverse easements and leases subsisting at the time of first registration or created subsequently by registered disposition. For a notice to be entered the proprietor of the land affected must effectively consent to the entry since he is required to lodge his land certificate at the Registry.[2] However, if (as is often the case) the land is mortgaged by registered charge the land certificate will already be lodged at the Registry;[3] in such instances the proprietor will be given an opportunity to object to a notice being entered on the register, except in the case of notice of a non-owning spouse's rights under the Family Law Act. In practice the registered proprietor will co-operate in the registration unless he is disputing the validity of the right in question.

The effect of the entry of a notice is to render the right binding on a subsequent purchaser since a disposition by a registered proprietor takes effect subject to all rights protected by a notice;[4] however, it does not confer priority over an earlier, unregistered minor interest since, in such a situation, priority is governed by the order in which the interests are created.[5] As with the registration of a land charge under the Land Charges Act in unregistered land, the entry of a notice does not confer validity on an otherwise invalid interest.[6]

1   LRA, ss 48–52.
2   Ibid, s 64.
3   Ibid, s 65; para 39.11 above.
4   LRA, s 52.
5   *Barclays Bank Ltd v Taylor* [1974] Ch 137, [1973] 1 All ER 752, CA; *Mortgage Corpn Ltd v Nationwide Credit Corpn Ltd* [1993] 4 All ER 623, CA. See further paras 35.33 and 39.50 below.
6   Para 35.12 above.

35.31   *Caution*   There are two forms of caution. Cautions against first registration have already been considered;[1] the other form is known as a caution against dealings.[2] Such a caution is entered in the Proprietorship Register. Since there is no requirement that the land certificate be produced, the caution is often used where the registered proprietor is unwilling to co-operate in the entry of a notice; it may thus be described as a hostile entry on the register. A cautioner must have a claim to an enforceable right or interest in the land.[2] Entry of a caution entitles the cautioner to be notified of any proposed dealings with the land and to enter an appearance within 14 days to object.[3] If he fails to do so the caution is removed and the transaction can go ahead. Where the cautioner is able to substantiate his claim the Registrar has a wide discretion in giving effect to the cautioner's claim;[4] in practice he may well give the interest 'full' protection by entering a notice or a restriction.

It can be seen that a caution, in essence, affords temporary protection. It does not confer any priority over the rights of others; this is only given once the cautioner's rights have the benefit of the more substantial forms of protection.[5]

1   Para 31.42 above.
2   LRA, s 54.
3   LRA, s 55.
4   Land Registration Rules, r 220.
5   *Clark v Chief Land Registrar* [1994] 4 All ER 96,CA.

35.32   *Inhibition*   The use of inhibitions is very rare. An inhibition prevents all dealings with the land for a specified period.[1] The main use of inhibitions is in connection with bankruptcy. Once a bankruptcy order has been made a bankruptcy inhibition is automatically entered in the register prohibiting dealings until a trustee in bankruptcy is registered as proprietor.[2]

1   LRA, s 57.
2   LRA, s 61(3); Land Registration Rules, r 180.

Competing minor interests

35.33   As we have mentioned,[1] the entry of a notice or caution does not necessarily confer priority over other minor interests. Strangely, the LRA is silent on this question and the courts have taken the view that, since minor interests take effect in equity,[2] priority between competing minor interests follows the rule 'where the equities are equal the first in time prevails' and is thus determined by the order of creation, not of entry on the register.[3]

1   Paras 35.30 and 35.31 above.

2   LRA, s 2(1).
3   *Barclays Bank Ltd v Taylor* [1974] Ch 137, [1973] 1 All ER 752, CA; *Mortgage Corpn Ltd v Nationwide Credit Corpn Ltd* [1993] 4 All ER 623, CA.

The search procedure

35.34   As we have seen,[1] an intending purchaser (which, as always, includes a mortgagee) can request an official search of the register in order to discover the existence of protected minor interests.[2] Once in receipt of an official certificate of search the purchaser has the benefit of a 30-day priority period in which to complete his transaction and apply for registration; provided he does so, he will not be bound by any adverse entries made on the register during that period.

1   Para 31.29 above.
2   Land Registration (Official Search) Rules 1990.

Failure to register

35.35   The scheme of the LRA is designed to ensure that, in the case of minor interests, the state of the register is paramount and that the doctrine of notice has no application. All a purchaser has to do is consult the register; he will take free from any interest not entered on the register. To this, as we have seen, there is one exception, in that where the owner of an unregistered minor interest is in actual occupation of the land to which the right relates, that interest will be regarded as an overriding interest within s 70(1)(g). As such it will bind any purchaser.[1]

The intention that the enforceability of minor interests should hinge solely on an entry in the register is affirmed by a number of provisions in the LRA. Section 20 provides that the purchaser of registered land is bound by entries on the register and overriding interests but takes free from all other estates and interests whatsoever; s 59(6) provides that a purchaser is not bound by an unprotected minor interest even if he has notice of it; and s 74 provides that a person dealing with a registered estate is not to be affected by notice of any trust.

Nonetheless, there have been situations in which the courts have held that a purchaser was bound by an interest which was neither overriding nor entered on the register. This will be the case in clear instances of fraud.[2] In *Lyus v Prowsa Developments Ltd*[3] it was held that a purchaser of registered land who bought 'subject to' a specified estate contract which had not been protected by an entry on the register thereby became a constructive trustee and was obliged to give effect to it. It has subsequently been made clear that a constructive trust will only arise in such a situation where there is evidence that the purchaser was undertaking to honour the unprotected interest; merely purchasing with notice of the right is insufficient.[4] It also appears that, in appropriate circumstances, a registered proprietor may be prevented from denying that he is bound by an unprotected minor interest under the doctrine of proprietary estoppel.[5]

1   *Williams and Glyn's Bank Ltd v Boland* [1981] AC 487, [1980] 2 All ER 408, HL; see para 35.22 above.
2   *Jones v Lipman* [1962] 1 WLR 832. It should be appreciated that a purchaser will not be regarded as fraudulent simply because he knows of the unregistered minor interest; see *De Lusignan v Johnson* (1973) 230 Estates Gazette 499.
3   [1982] 2 All ER 953, [1982] 1 WLR 1044. See para 32.10 above.
4   *Ashburn Anstalt v Arnold* [1989] Ch 1, CA; para 32.10 above.
5   *Taylors Fashions Ltd v Liverpool Victoria Trustees Co* [1982] QB 133n, [1981] 1 All ER 897.

Rectification and indemnity

Rectification

35.36   It was pointed out earlier[1] that registration with absolute title does not, despite the name, absolutely guarantee the title, for there remains the possibility that the register of title may be rectified (either by court order or by the Registrar). Hence, just as a purchaser of registered land may find himself bound by overriding interests which do not appear on the register, so he may find that he is bound by an unregistered interest should the register be rectified against him. The LRA, s 82(1) lists eight cases in which the register may be rectified. Of these the most important are:

- where an entry on the register was obtained by fraud;
- where two or more persons are, by mistake, registered as proprietors of the same registered estate;
- where a legal estate has been registered in the name of a person who, if the land had not been registered, would not have been the estate owner; and
- in any other case where, by reason of any error or omission in the register, or by reason of any entry made under a mistake, it may be deemed just to rectify the register.

1   Para 31.37 above.

35.37   It follows that, on the face of it, there is a wide discretion to rectify the register. However, the LRA, s 82(3)[1] provides that this discretion cannot be exercised so as to affect a proprietor who is in possession,[2] except in four cases:

- to give effect to a court order (eg that another person is in fact entitled to the land);
- to give effect to an overriding interest;[3]
- where the proprietor has caused or substantially contributed to the error or omission by fraud or lack of proper care;
- where it would be unjust not to rectify.

1   As amended by the Administration of Justice Act 1977, s 24.
2   This expression includes being in actual receipt of rents and profits.
3   See *Epps v Esso Petroleum Co Ltd* [1973] 2 All ER 465, [1973] 1 WLR 1071.

Indemnity
35.38   In a sense it is the indemnity provisions of the LRA which give rise to registration being regarded as a state guarantee of title. Although registration does not absolutely guarantee the title, since there is always the possibility that the register will be rectified, anyone who suffers loss as a result of rectification of the register is entitled to an indemnity paid by the Registrar from moneys provided by parliament.[1] Likewise, anyone who suffers loss because the register is not rectified to remove some error or omission[2] is entitled to be indemnified, as is anyone suffering loss by reason of the loss or destruction of any document lodged at the Registry or by reason of an error in any official search of the register.[3]

The indemnity payable where the applicant has caused or substantially contributed to the loss by fraud or lack of proper care may be reduced to such extent as is just and equitable.[4] Nor, importantly, is an indemnity payable where the register is rectified to give effect to an overriding interest. This is because the registered proprietor's title has from the start been subject to the overriding interest; after rectification he is, strictly, in no worse position than he was in all along.[5] However logical, this limitation has been recognised as unfair by the Law Commission which has recommended that, in such an instance, an indemnity should be payable.[6]

1   LRA, s 83(1). The whole of LRA, s 83 has been redrafted and amended by the Land Registration Act 1997, s 2. The references in this paragraph are to the new s 83.
2   Ibid, s 83(2).

3   Ibid, s 83(3).
4   Ibid, s 83(6).
5   In *Re Chowood's Registered Land* [1933] Ch 574.
6   Law Com No 158 (1987).

Chapter 36

Landlord and tenant

36.1 We have, so far, given only passing consideration to leasehold ownership when dealing with the doctrine of estates[1] and the formal[2] and informal[3] creation of interests in land. This may have given a misleading impression for such ownership is widespread in England and Wales. The lease obviously provides a medium through which essentially short-term occupation of both residential and commercial property can be enjoyed without the need for a capital contribution to its purchase. However, the long-term lease (eg for 99 years or even 999 years) for which a capital sum (known as a 'premium') is normally paid is the usual mechanism for the occupation of a unit within a building (notably flats); this is because, as we shall see, obligations imposed under a lease are more readily enforceable against future owners of that lease than they would be if imposed on a freeholder.[4] Furthermore, the long lease has become, in the 20th century, a popular device for financing the development of land and for investing in land.

In this chapter we deal with:

- the essential features of leasehold ownership;
- the most commonly encountered of the obligations (ie covenants) imposed in a lease;
- the remedies available to both landlord and tenant in the event of a breach of covenant;
- the circumstances in which lease covenants are enforceable against those to whom either the lease or the landlord's interest (the reversion) may be transferred;
- the termination of leases; and
- an outline of the main forms of statutory protection afforded to tenants.

1 Para 30.31 above.
2 Paras 31.6 and 31.7 above.
3 Paras 32.3–32.5 above.
4 Para 38.4 below.

Characteristics of leasehold interests

36.2 In order for a lease to arise, exclusive possession of a defined area of land for a certain or ascertainable period of time must be conferred. Any occupation of land which fails to display these characteristics cannot be a lease and the occupier is a mere licensee.[1] While it is usual for rent to be paid this is not legally essential.[2] As will become apparent, the distinction between a lease and a licence has been fraught with difficulties because landowners have sought to devise agreements to occupy which do *not* amount to leases in order to avoid the statutory protection which is conferred on many tenants (but not on licensees).[3]

If a lease is to confer a legal estate it must comply with the required formalities; as we have seen, for leases in excess of three years a deed must be used, while those for three years or less may be created orally or in writing, provided that they take effect in possession[4] and are at the best rent reasonably obtainable.[5] Leases which fail to comply with these formal requirements may nevertheless take effect in equity.[6]

1   Paras 36.3–36.10 below.
2   *Ashburn Anstalt v Arnold* [1989] Ch 1, [1988] 2 All ER 147, CA.
3   The problem has diminished since the implementation of the Housing Act 1988; this Act has significantly reduced the protection given to residential tenants with the result that, since 1989, landowners have been happy to grant short-term tenancies of residential property.
4   A lease not exceeding three years which is to take effect on a future date must be created by deed; see *Long v London Borough of Tower Hamlets* [1996] 2 All ER 683 and para 31.7, note 1 above.
5   Paras 31.6 and 31.7 above.
6   Paras 32.3–32.5 above.

Certainty of term

36.3   The requirement that a lease must be of certain duration means that, at the outset, it must have a certain commencement date[1] and a certain or ascertainable maximum duration (often referred to as 'certainty of term'). These days most leases are for a fixed term, eg for five years, and no problems of certainty of term arise. However, from time to time cases arise where leases have been granted for a period measured by reference to an uncertain event. Periodic tenancies have also given rise to difficulties on the question of certainty. In addition, the LPA deals specifically with some unusual types of lease which might otherwise be regarded as uncertain, in order to bring them within the framework of modern leasehold ownership.

1   *Harvey v Pratt* [1965] 1 WLR 1025.

Fixed-term leases

36.4   A fixed-term lease is one which is granted for a predetermined period of time. It is not necessary for the term to be continuous; thus there is a valid lease where a holiday home is let on a 'time-share' basis for one week per year for 80 years.[1] A fixed-term lease cannot be certain if it is expressed to last until an event which either may or may not happen, or which will happen but at an unpredictable date. So for example, a lease which was expressed to last for the duration of the war was declared to be void by the Court of Appeal in *Lace v Chantler*.[2] This rule has recently been affirmed by the House of Lords in *Prudential Assurance Co v London Residuary Body*.[3] Here a lease granted until the land was required for road widening was held to be void for uncertainty.[4] Their Lordships emphatically rejected any suggestion[5] that a term can be certain where the event which is to bring about the termination of the lease is within the control of one of the parties.

Where a fixed-term lease is held to be void for uncertainty of term, the agreed 'lease' is of no effect but, provided the tenant has taken up occupation and paid rent, an implied periodic tenancy will arise.[6] This tenancy can be terminated by the service of an appropriate notice to quit. The courts will *not* imply that such a notice can only be served in the circumstances which would have brought about the end of the intended fixed term, since this would render the periodic tenancy uncertain. So, in the *Prudential* case, the tenants were held to be yearly tenants; the defendant landlords were entitled immediately to serve six months' notice to quit and were not obliged to wait until the land was required for road widening before serving such a notice.

1 *Cottage Holiday Associates Ltd v Customs and Excise Comrs* [1983] QB 735, [1983] 2 WLR 861.
2 [1944] KB 368, [1944] 1 All ER 305, CA.
3 [1992] 2 AC 386, [1992] 3 All ER 504, HL.
4 It is worth noting that the desired object can be achieved in such cases without offending the rule on certainty of term; for example, in *Prudential*, the parties could have expressed the lease to be for, say, 99 years determinable when the land was required for road widening.
5 See *Ashburn Anstalt v Arnold* [1989] Ch 1, [1988] 2 All ER 147, CA.
6 See para 36.13 below.

Periodic tenancies

36.5 Periodic tenancies – for example, weekly, monthly or yearly tenancies – do not determine (end) automatically at the end of the period, be it week or month or year, but continue from week to week, month to month, year to year, until ended by appropriate notice.[1] Thus, in one sense, at the outset of the tenancy its maximum duration is unknown and it has been said that the simple statement that the maximum duration of a term must be certainly known in advance of its taking effect does not directly apply to periodic tenancies.[2] However, this view has been rejected by the House of Lords in the *Prudential* case.[3] Here it was held that periodic tenancies are subject to the same rule on certainty as fixed terms. A periodic tenancy is normally sufficiently certain because each party has the right to terminate it at the end of any period of the tenancy. Equally, such a tenancy will be valid where, at the beginning of the tenancy, it is agreed that one side cannot serve a notice to quit until after a *certain* time limit has elapsed (eg that the landlord will not serve a notice to quit for at least one year).[4] However, any agreement preventing one side determining the tenancy for an *uncertain* period will render the tenancy void (eg that the landlord will only serve a notice to quit if he requires the property for his own personal use).[5] A provision purporting to prohibit absolutely the giving of notice by one party is repugnant to the nature of the tenancy and therefore invalid.[6]

1 Para 36.65 below, and note, in particular, paras 36.69–36.79 as to the statutory regulation of the termination of tenancies.
2 *Re Midland Rly Co's Agreement* [1971] Ch 725 at 732, [1971] 1 All ER 1007; see also *Ashburn Anstalt v Arnold* [1989] Ch 1, [1988] 2 All ER 147, CA.
3 *Prudential Assurance Co v London Residuary Body* [1992] 2 AC 386, [1992] 3 All ER 504, HL, overruling *Midland Rly Co's Agreement* [1971] Ch 725, [1971] 1 All ER 1007 and *Ashburn Anstalt v Arnold* [1989] Ch 1, [1988] 2 All ER 147, CA on this point.
4 *Prudential Assurance Co v London Residuary Body* [1992] 2 AC 386, [1992] 3 All ER 504, HL.
5 Ibid.
6 *Centaploy Ltd v Matlodge Ltd* [1974] Ch 1, [1973] 2 All ER 720.

Leases for life

36.6 Prior to 1926, it was possible to create a lease for life, despite the fact that such a term is far from certain. As a result of the LPA, s 149(6), an attempt to create such a lease, at a rent or for a premium, now results in the grant of a 90-year term which may be ended after the death of the lessee by one month's notice in writing given on one of the usual quarter days (25 March, 24 June, 29 September, and 25 December).[1] This same rule applies to leases determinable on the marriage of the lessee.

1 For a recent application of this provision see *Skipton Building Society v Clayton* (1993) 25 HLR 596, CA; here it was held that an arrangement whereby, in return for the grant of an option to purchase at one-third market value, a couple were to be given a right to occupy a property for their joint lives fell within s 149(6).

Perpetually renewable leases

36.7   Again, prior to 1926, it was permissible to grant a lease conferring on the lessee the right to have the lease renewed on the expiry of the existing term over and over again. Such leases were, by the Law of Property Act 1922, s 145 and Sch 15 converted into terms of 2,000 years commencing with the beginning of the then existing term. Any perpetually renewable lease granted since 1926 is likewise to take effect as a 2,000-year term. The term created by the statute is subject to the provision that the lessee may terminate the lease on 10 days' notice ending on a date on which it would have expired had it not been converted. It is, of course, highly unlikely that a landlord would deliberately create a perpetually renewable lease and the court leans against finding that a lease contains a perpetual right of renewal.[1] However, this may be the only possible conclusion, as is demonstrated by *Re Hopkin's Lease, Caerphilly Concrete Products Ltd v Owen*,[2] where a landlord granted a lease, for a term of five years at a rent of £10 per annum, containing a covenant to renew the lease at the same rent and subject to the same covenants, including the covenant to renew, with the result that the lease was perpetually renewable; the landlord had inadvertently created a 2,000-year term at a rent of £10 per annum.

1   *Marjorie Burnett v Barclay* (1980) 258 Estates Gazette 642.
2   [1972] 1 All ER 248, [1972] 1 WLR 372, CA.

Exclusive possession

36.8   For a person to be regarded as having a leasehold interest in property, it is essential that he should have exclusive possession of it. That is, he must have the right to exclude all others from the property, even the landlord himself. It is a fundamental principle that the landlord may only enter the property either with the permission of the tenant or under a right of entry[1] accorded to him by the lease. Without exclusive possession there can be no lease, only a licence. The latter confers only a personal permission to occupy property but does not give the occupier a stake in the property.[2]

1   Such a right is of a limited nature and allows entry only for specified purposes, eg to inspect for repairs.
2   *Marchant v Charters* [1977] 3 All ER 918, [1977] 1 WLR 1181, CA; para 30.36 above.

The distinction between a lease and a licence

36.9   The issue we are concerned with here is not simply an academic question of the difference between a personal right and a proprietary right, but also the practical question of whether in a given case a person is in occupation of property as a licensee or as a tenant. In some cases, particularly of shared occupation of residential premises, the grant of a licence to each occupier is more appropriate than the grant of a tenancy. However, the issue has more often arisen where a landowner has deliberately sought to 'dress up' a lease as a licence in order to prevent the occupier qualifying for the statutory protection which is conferred on many tenants. This used to be a particular problem in the residential sector because of the extremely beneficial nature of the protection conferred by the Rent Act 1977 and its precursors;[1] this legislation has now been supplanted[2] by the Housing Act 1988[3] and landlords are not now seeking to use residential licences to the same extent. Occasionally, also, landlords of commercial property will likewise seek to avoid the provisions of Pt II of the Landlord and Tenant Act 1954[4] by granting purported licences.

In considering whether a transaction constitutes a licence or a tenancy, the court is to have regard not to the label ('lease' or 'licence') which the parties give to the document but to the substance of the transaction.[5] As Lord Templeman pointed out in a now famous dictum in *Street v Mountford*,[6] 'The manufacture of a five-pronged implement for manual digging results in a fork even if the manufacturer … insists that he intended to make and has made a spade.'[7] In other words, if the parties' agreement has the hallmarks of a tenancy, it is a tenancy, even if the parties by their agreement 'intend' to enter into a licence.

The hallmarks of a tenancy are, according to the House of Lords, exclusive possession, for a fixed or periodic term, at a rent.[8] Since Mrs Mountford's agreement with Mr Street was admitted to give her exclusive possession of rooms owned by Mr Street at a rent for a term, she was a tenant even though she had signed an agreement under which she expressly accepted that it was only a licence which gave her no protection as a Rent Act tenant. Accordingly, subject to limited exceptions,[9] since *Street v Mountford*, the courts need only inquire whether or not an agreement to occupy confers exclusive possession (for a fixed or periodic term).

However, once it was made clear that the absence of exclusive possession precluded the grant of a tenancy, it became common for landlords wishing to avoid the provisions of protective legislation to make use of agreements which either stated that exclusive possession was not conferred, or which contained provisions which were designed to have the effect of taking away exclusive possession. So, for example, there might be included a term under which the owner was given the right to share the property with the occupier, or one which prevented the occupier from using the property during, say, the hours of 12 noon and 2 pm. Where a court is satisfied that terms of this kind do not truly represent the intentions of the parties (ie that they are 'sham' terms), they will be ignored and the occupier will be a tenant.[10] However, where, for example, the landlord provides attendance or services[11] which require the landlord or his employees to exercise unrestricted access to and use of the premises, or where access is genuinely needed in the particular circumstances,[12] the occupier will not have exclusive possession and will be a mere licensee.

1   See para 36.70 below.
2   The 1977 Act continues to apply to tenancies granted prior to 15 January 1989; accordingly the lease/licence distinction remains vital in such cases.
3   See para 36.71 below.
4   See para 36.76 below.
5   *Shell-Mex and BP Ltd v Manchester Garages Ltd* [1971] 1 All ER 841 and 845.
6   [1985] AC 809, [1985] 2 All ER 289, HL.
7   [1985] AC 809 at 819.
8   Ibid at 826. That is not to say that the payment of rent is an essential pre-requisite of a tenancy, but rather that if the three hallmarks are present there is a tenancy: *Ashburn Anstalt v Arnold* [1989] Ch 1, [1988] 2 All ER 147, CA. 'Rent' does not include a mere contribution to the household expenses (eg to gas and electricity bills) of the property owner: *Bostock v Bryant* (1990) 22 HLR 449, CA.
9   In *Street v Mountford* [1985] AC 809 it was acknowledged that there may be occasions when an occupier has exclusive possession yet is merely a licensee. Two situations referred to in that case were that of a service occupier (ie an employee who occupies his employer's premises in order better to perform his duties as an employee) and where occupation has been conferred as an act of friendship or generosity (which negatives any intention to enter into legal relations and hence negatives the existence of a tenancy).
10   See, for example, *Aslan v Murphy (Nos 1 and 2)* [1989] 3 All ER 130, CA.
11   Such as cleaning the room and changing the linen: *Marchant v Charters* [1977] 3 All ER 918, [1977] 1 WLR 1181, CA.
12   *Westminster City Council v Clarke* [1992] 2 AC 288, [1992] 1 All ER 695, HL.

36.10   *Sharers*   In one particular situation the courts faced further difficulties in determining whether or not an occupier enjoyed exclusive possession. Where the use of accommodation was to be shared, landowners commonly required each sharer to sign a separate (but often identical) agreement conferring a right to occupy the whole of the premises, subject to the rights of the other occupiers. In this way it could be argued that none of the sharers had exclusive possession; each destroyed the others' exclusive possession. Not surprisingly, this matter came before the House of Lords in 1988 when appeals in two cases, *AG Securities v Vaughan* and *Antoniades v Villiers* were heard together.[1] Here it was decided that, in such instances, the approach should be two-stage. First, it should be decided whether or not the signing of *separate* agreements was genuine. If so, each sharer would have an individual, but not exclusive, right to use the property and could only be a licensee. However, if the signing of separate agreements was itself a pretence, then the sharers should be regarded as having together signed a single agreement; if this agreement genuinely conferred exclusive possession the sharers would be joint tenants.

In *AG Securities* four individuals sharing a four-bedroomed flat in a London mansion block, signed separate licence agreements at different times on different terms. They had not known each other prior to moving in to the flat. In these circumstances there was no artificiality about the separate agreements; it was clear that the purpose and intention of both parties to each agreement was that it should confer an individual right on the licensee named. Each was individually liable for the amount of rent to which he had agreed which, in that case, differed from the amounts paid by the others. There had been no grant of exclusive possession of any identifiable part of the flat to any individual and so each was a licensee.[2]

By way of contrast, in the *Antoniades* case, the defendant and a woman friend each signed a separate agreement for the occupation of a small one-bedroomed flat. Each agreement provided that the licensee was to have the use of the flat 'in common with the licensor and such other licensees or invitees as the licensor may permit from time to time to use the rooms'. The House of Lords found that there was an air of total unreality about these 'separate' documents, given the fact that the appellants were together seeking a flat as a quasi-matrimonial home. The documents were a pretence designed to disguise the true character of the agreement which, their Lordships held, should be regarded as a single contract. As the parties' subsequent conduct indicated, there was never any intention on the part of the landlord to share possession (either by himself or by introducing others) with the couple, who together had exclusive possession and were, therefore, joint tenants.

1   [1990] 1 AC 417, [1988] 3 All ER 1058, HL.
2   See also *Stribling v Wickham* (1989) 21 HLR 381, CA.

Particular types of tenancy

36.11   The great majority of leases are created expressly and tend, these days, to be for a fixed term. That said, periodic tenancies remain common, particularly in the residential sector. While many of these are expressly created, they also often come into being by way of implication. In this section we also consider a number of anomalous forms of tenancy and, finally, we explain forms of lease under which the tenant does not necessarily take an immediate entitlement to physical occupation.

Fixed-term leases
36.12   This is the simplest and most common form of lease. It arises where the tenancy is granted for a pre-determined period, eg for six months, for five years or for 99 years. The law sets no minimum or maximum period for such leases; all that is required is that the period of time for which the lease is to last is certain or ascertainable at the outset.[1] When the term for which the lease has been granted expires, the lease comes to an end automatically without the need for notice.[2] A fixed term lease must, in principle, run its course; it can only be brought to an end before the end of the term:

- by the agreement of the parties (ie a surrender[3]);
- where the tenant is in breach, by the exercise by the landlord of a right of re-entry (ie forfeiture[4]); or
- by the exercise, where present, of an option to terminate (usually known as a 'break clause').

1 See para 36.4 above.
2 See para 36.64 below.
3 See para 36.62 below.
4 See paras 36.32–36.35 and 36.61 below.

Periodic tenancies

36.13 A periodic tenancy is one which continues automatically from period to period until terminated by either side serving an appropriate notice to quit.[1] It is not a series of renewed tenancies but one continuous term which will run until brought to an end.[2] The most commonly encountered periodic tenancies are weekly, monthly and yearly tenancies. Such tenancies must, by definition, have a minimum duration of the initial period; as we have seen,[3] its maximum duration remains unknown until a notice to quit is actually served.[4]

Periodic tenancies can be created expressly but, in practice, many arise by implication.[5] Where a person is allowed into occupation of property as a tenant, without any express agreement as to the duration of the tenancy, he will be treated initially as a tenant at will.[6] If rent is then paid and accepted, an implied periodic tenancy, based on the periods by reference to which that rent is calculated, may then arise. Thus if the rent is fixed at £1,000 per annum, a yearly tenancy arises even if the rent is paid at more frequent intervals; if rent is fixed at £20 per week, a weekly tenancy arises.[7] As the case of *Manfield & Sons Ltd v Botchin*[8] shows, there is no room for the implication of a periodic tenancy where the parties expressly provide that the tenancy should remain at will. Furthermore, modern cases stress that whether or not a periodic tenancy arises as a result of the payment of rent depends on the intention of the parties.[9] Such an intention is particularly difficult to establish where a tenant holds over on the determination of a previous tenancy; where he is entitled to do so by virtue of statutory protection it is now more usual for the court not to imply a periodic tenancy.[10]

1 For notices to quit see para 36.65 below.
2 *Hammersmith and Fulham London Borough Council v Monk* [1992] 1 AC 478, [1992] 1 All ER 1, HL.
3 Para 36.5 above.
4 However, the fact that either side can ascertain the maximum term by serving a notice to quit is sufficient to render periodic tenancies sufficiently certain; see para 36.5 above.
5 Periodic tenancies are almost invariably legal. Provided the period on which the tenancy is based does not itself exceed three years (which would be very unusual) no formalities are required; LPA s 54(2), para 31.7 above.
6 See para 36.14 below.
7 See *Ladies' Hosiery and Underwear Ltd v Parker* [1930] 1 Ch 304.
8 [1970] 2 QB 612, [1970] 3 All ER 143.
9 *Javad v Aqil* [1991] 1 All ER 243, [1991] 1 WLR 1007, CA.
10 *Harvey v Stagg* (1977) 247 Estates Gazette 463, CA; *Longrigg, Burrough and Trounson v Smith* (1979) 251 Estates Gazette 847, CA.

Tenancy at will

36.14 A tenancy at will occurs where a person is let into, or allowed to remain in, possession of property as a tenant by the landlord on the basis that either side may terminate the arrangement whenever he wishes. It may arise where a purchaser of the freehold is permitted to occupy the property prior to completion of the transaction or where a prospective lessee is allowed into occupation while the parties continue negotiating the detailed terms of the lease,[1] or where a fixed-term tenant is permitted to remain in occupation after the expiry of the term.[2] Consequently, it has been suggested by Scarman LJ in *Heslop v Burns*,[3] that it may be that the tenancy at will can now serve only one legal purpose, and that is to provide for occupation of property during a period of transition. It was certainly made clear in *Javad v Aqil*[4] that, in such a transitional situation, the court may conclude that the parties only intended a tenancy at will even though rent has been paid and accepted.[5] It will be noted that a tenancy at will does not satisfy the requirement of certainty of duration. It has thus been suggested that a tenancy at will does not constitute an estate in land at all but is merely a relationship of tenure,[6] which can be terminated forthwith by notifying the other party. Although a tenancy at will often arises by implication, such a tenancy may be expressly granted, as in *Manfield & Sons Ltd v Botchin*[7] where such a tenancy was granted pending the landlord's application for planning permission to develop the site. An express tenancy at will may provide for the payment of rent by the tenant, in which case there will be no implication of a periodic tenancy.[8] If no provision is made for rent to be paid, the landlord is entitled to compensation for the use and occupation of the property.

1   *Javad v Aqil* [1991] 1 All ER 243, [1991] 1 WLR 1007, CA.
2   Unless the tenant is staying in occupation by virtue of statutory protection; see paras 36.69–36.79 below.
3   [1974] 3 All ER 406 at 416.
4   [1991] 1 All ER 243, [1991] 1 WLR 1007, CA.
5   As opposed to a periodic tenancy; see para 36.13 above.
6   Paras 30.27 and 30.28 above.
7   [1970] 2 QB 612, [1970] 3 All ER 143.
8   Para 36.13 above.

Tenancy at sufferance

36.15   A tenant at sufferance is, at common law, someone who wrongfully remains in possession ('holds over') without the landlord's consent after his tenancy has come to an end. Such a person is in effect a trespasser. The landlord may at any time claim possession of the property. The tenant at sufferance is essentially in the position of a 'squatter',[1] though liable under statute[2] to pay either a payment calculated at double the rental value of the property or, in certain circumstances, double the rent which he paid under the lease, for holding over in the face of a notice to quit. In practice, many tenants who hold over after the end of their tenancies do so by virtue of statutory protection[3] and are not, therefore, tenants at sufferance.

1   Para 32.31 above.
2   Landlord and Tenant Act 1730; Distress for Rent Act 1737.
3   Paras 36.59–36.79 below.

Tenancy by estoppel

36.16   Where a person who has no power to do so purports to grant a lease or tenancy, he and his 'tenant' are estopped[1] from denying the validity of the 'lease'. Thus, as between the parties, a tenancy by estoppel has all the features of a valid tenancy; it will similarly bind assigns of the parties but will not bind third parties. A tenancy by estoppel could arise where a purchaser of land is allowed into possession prior to completion of the transaction and then purports to grant a lease, or where a mortgagor (borrower) purports to grant a lease where his power to do so has been excluded.[2] In the former case, the subsequent acquisition of the freehold estate by the purchaser is said to 'feed the estoppel' and confers on the tenant a valid tenancy.

1   Para 6.15, footnote 2 above.
2   Para 39.46 below.

Concurrent leases

36.17   A concurrent lease (sometimes called a 'side-by-side' lease, or a lease of the reversion) arises where a lease is granted which is to commence before the expiry of an existing lease of the same premises granted to another person. Accordingly the concurrent lessee becomes the landlord of the existing lessee. He is entitled to receive the rent and to enforce the tenant's covenants; equally he is obliged to honour the landlord's obligations under the existing lease. If the existing lease expires before the concurrent lease then the concurrent lessee becomes entitled, at that time, to physical possession of the property. If not, the concurrent lessee is only ever entitled to receive the income produced by the existing lease. The concurrent lease is thus a device by which income under an existing lease can be assigned for a fixed period of time, with or without any right to future physical occupation.

Reversionary leases

36.18   A reversionary lease is one which is granted now but which is to take effect at a future date, eg a lease for five years granted on 1 September 1998, to commence on 1 September 1999. A person may not create, or make a contract to create, a lease which is to take effect in possession more than 21 years after the date of the lease.[1] In order to create a legal estate, such a lease must always be made by deed.[2]

1   LPA, s 149(3).
2   The 'short lease' exception, whereby leases of three years or less can be created orally or in writing applies only to leases taking *immediate* effect; see *Long v London Borough of Tower Hamlets* [1996] 2 All ER 683 and para 31.7, note 1 above.

Rights and obligations of the parties to a lease

36.19   In practice a lease does much more than simply confer ownership for a limited period. Where it is of very short duration the landlord will wish to impose strict controls on the tenant, but will invariably have to accept responsibility for the upkeep of the property. Where a lease is relatively long and at a market rent, the landlord will wish to impose such restrictions as are necessary to protect the value of his investment. Even where a lease is granted at a premium for a very long term (and thus very similar in economic terms to a freehold), substantial obligations will still be imposed on the tenant; for example, a long lease of a flat will usually require the tenant to pay his share of the costs of repairs, maintenance and services.

The primary source of the rights and obligations of the landlord and the tenant is, of course, the lease itself. The terms of the lease are referred to as 'covenants', whether or not the lease was made by deed, even though, strictly speaking, that word is reserved for contractual terms contained in a deed.[1] It is possible, but increasingly less likely, that nothing will be expressly agreed by the parties to the lease, other than its duration and the rent. In such a case, only the most minimal terms will be implied by the law. It is therefore preferable that the parties should agree terms for themselves even where the tenancy is only to be of very short duration.

We consider first the position of the parties in the absence of express terms governing their rights and obligations.

1   Para 31.6 above.

Where no express terms
The landlord
36.20   *Implied covenant for quiet enjoyment*   This obligation on the part of the

527

landlord, implied in all leases as being a legal incident of the relationship,[1] is intended to secure for the tenant, not enjoyment of his tenancy free from the nuisance of noise, but enjoyment free from disturbance by adverse claimants to the property[2] and free from substantial physical interference with his enjoyment of the property by the landlord.[3] The implied covenant for quiet enjoyment extends only to the acts of the landlord and those claiming under him (such as other tenants of the same landlord). It does not apply to protect the tenant from any adverse rights arising from a title superior to the landlord's[4] or granted by the landlord's predecessor in title.[5]

The covenant will be breached if it emerges that the landlord has no right to grant the lease; it may also be broken where the landlord (or his agents) carry out excessively prolonged and intrusive works in the vicinity of the demised premises.[6] There are recent signs that the courts are extending the traditional ambit of the covenant by allowing a tenant to sue his landlord where the normal use of adjoining premises by other tenants is causing excessive disturbance; so, for example a landlord has been required to sound-proof flats where their normal use is causing sufficient disruption as to amount to a breach of the landlord's covenant of quiet enjoyment.[7]

A further use of this covenant is as a means of gaining compensation for unlawful eviction and harassment. Thus, the landlord was held liable in damages for breach of this covenant in *Perera v Vandiyar*[8] where, with the object of driving the tenant out, he cut off the electricity and gas supplies to the premises. It should be noted that a landlord of a residential occupier who indulges in such harassment will often be guilty also of a criminal offence under the Protection from Eviction Act 1977, s 1,[9] as will a landlord who unlawfully evicts a tenant. Furthermore, acts of harassment often also amount to a tort such as trespass or nuisance, in which case there may, in appropriate circumstances, be an award of exemplary damages.[10] However, such claims are diminishing because, under the Housing Act 1988, s 27, a residential occupier now has a statutory right to damages, based on the difference in value of the landlord's interest with and without the occupier being in occupation, where he is driven to give up occupation as a result of harassment or eviction. This section is being widely used and the cases indicate that it is producing awards of damages which far outstrip those gained for breach of the covenant of quiet enjoyment or in the tort of trespass or nuisance.[11]

1. Paras 7.22–7.23 above.
2. *Hudson v Cripps* [1896] 1 Ch 265.
3. See *Browne v Flower* [1911] 1 Ch 219 (landlord not in breach of this covenant where another tenant, with landlord's consent, erected an iron staircase outside the plaintiff tenant's window seriously affecting the plaintiff's privacy); contrast *Owen v Gadd* [1956] 2 QB 99, [1956] 2 All ER 28 (landlord in breach of this covenant where he erected scaffolding outside the entrance to tenant's shop).
4. *Jones v Lavington* [1903] 1 KB 253, CA.
5. *Celsteel Ltd v Alton House Holdings Ltd (No 2)* [1987] 2 All ER 240, [1987] 1 WLR 291, CA.
6. See *Mira v Aylmer Square Investments Ltd* [1990] 1 EGLR 45, CA.
7. *Sampson v Hodson-Pressinger* [1981] 3 All ER 710. CA; *Baxter v London Borough of Camden* [1997] EGCS 102, CA; *Southwark London Borough Council v Mills* [1998] 3 WLR 49. See also *Chartered Trust plc v Davies* [1997] 49 EG 135, CA. Note that if the disturbance to tenant A's property is caused by tenant B's *excessive* use of his property, tenant A will have to sue B in nuisance rather than their common landlord; see para 25.16 above.
8. [1953] 1 All ER 1109, [1953] 1 WLR 672, CA.
9. As amended by the Housing Act 1988. This does not, in itself give the tenant the right to any financial compensation.
10. See para 29.2 above.
11. See, for example, *Tagro v Cafane* [1991] 2 All ER 235, [1991] 1 WLR 378, CA where a monthly tenant was awarded damages of £31,000 under s 27.

36.21 *Non-derogation from grant*[1] A covenant is again implied in all leases that the landlord will not derogate from his grant. Indeed, it is a principle of general application that a grantor may not take away with one hand what he has given with the other.[2] Thus, if the landlord leases land to be used in a particular way, he must not so act in relation to land retained by him as to make the demised premises materially less fit for their intended use.[3] For example, a landlord, who leased to the tenant two floors of a block of flats for residential purposes and then leased the remainder to another tenant for business purposes, was held to have derogated from his grant to the first tenant in so doing.[4] It has also been held that a landlord who let retail premises was liable to the tenant under the principle of non-derogation where a neighbouring tenant of the same landlord used his premises in a way which amounted to a nuisance.[5]

1   Para 36.15 below.
2   *Birmingham, Dudley and District Banking Co v Ross* (1888) 38 Ch D 295 at 313.
3   *Aldin v Latimer Clark, Muirhead & Co* [1894] 2 Ch 437; *Browne v Flower* [1911] 1 Ch 219.
4   *Newman v Real Estate Debenture Corpn Ltd and Flower Decorations Ltd* [1940] 1 All ER 131. See also *Aldin v Latimer Clark, Muirhead & Co* [1894] 2 Ch 437, para 36.15 below.
5   *Chartered Trust plc v Davies* [1997] 49 EG 135, CA. It was of some significance that the landlord retained control of the common parts of the arcade in which both shops were located since this was why the court concluded that the landlord had a duty to act against the tenant whose activities were causing the problem.

36.22   *Fitness for habitation, and repair of premises*   The courts have not taken the step of implying, as a legal incident of the relationship of landlord and tenant, any covenant on the part of the landlord that the premises are and/or will remain fit for habitation.[1] There is one exception: where premises are let furnished, a condition is implied that they are fit for human habitation at the commencement of the tenancy.[2] Further, in one other situation, of little practical relevance because of ridiculously low rental limits and restrictive interpretation by the courts, a covenant is implied under statute.[3] It is worth noting that, under the Housing Act 1985, Part VI,[4] local authorities have power to require landlords to render their property fit for human habitation if this can be done at reasonable cost. A tenant may thus call upon the local authority to exercise its powers rather than rely on any covenant in the lease.

As to repairs, there is no generally implied covenant that the landlord shall carry out repairs. A statutory exception is contained in the Landlord and Tenant Act 1985, ss 11 to 14, which provide that where a dwelling-house is let for less than seven years, the landlord impliedly covenants:

*   to keep the structure and exterior in repair; and
*   to keep in repair and proper working order the installations in the house for the supply of water, gas and electricity, for sanitation, and for space- and water-heating.

The landlord is only liable for defects of which he has notice.[5] The landlord has the right, on giving 24 hours' written notice, to enter and view the premises at all reasonable times. The landlord's obligations under these provisions may, in the case of leases entered into on or after 15 January 1989, extend beyond the structure and exterior of the particular dwelling-house or the installations in it. Where the dwelling-house is a part only of a building, as in the case of a flat, then, in the case of breaches affecting the tenant's enjoyment of the dwelling-house or the common parts, the landlord's obligation to keep in repair the structure and exterior extends to any part of the structure and exterior of the building in which the landlord has an estate or interest, eg the common parts of a block of flats. Likewise, the obligation to keep in repair and proper working order the utility installations applies also to all those installations serving the flat or dwelling-house which the landlord owns or controls or which are in a part of the building in which the landlord has an estate or interest.[6]

In considering fitness for habitation, and repair, the following obligations of the landlord should also be noted. First, it was held in *Liverpool City Council v Irwin*[7] that where parts of a building (in this case, a high-rise block of flats) have been let to different tenants and the essential means of access, such as stairs and lifts, are retained by the landlord, a term may be implied that the landlord will take reasonable care to keep those parts reasonably safe and reasonably fit for use. Second, in *Rimmer v Liverpool City Council*[8] it was held that a landlord who designed and built the demised premises owed, in his capacity as designer and builder, a duty in the tort of negligence to the tenant (among others) to take reasonable care to ensure he would not suffer personal injury as a result of dangerous defects in the design and construction of the premises.[9] Third, the reader should note the obligations of a landlord under the Defective Premises Act 1972, s 4 which we discuss at para 22.31 above.

1 For the implication of a term in a particular case on grounds of business efficacy (for which see paras 7.24–7.25 above), see *Barrett v Lounova (1982) Ltd* [1990] 1 QB 348, [1989] 1 All ER 351, CA, although it now appears that this decision may be confined to its own particular facts: *Adami v Lincoln Grange Management Ltd* [1998] 17 EG 148, CA.
2 *Smith v Marrable* (1843) 11 M & W 5.
3 Under the Landlord and Tenant Act 1985, s 8, there is an implied condition in any letting of a dwelling-house at a rent not exceeding, in Greater London, £80 per annum, or elsewhere, £52, that the house is fit for human habitation both at the commencement of, and during, the tenancy. In *Quick v Taff-Ely Borough Council* [1986] QB 809, [1985] 2 All ER 321, the Court of Appeal remarked that this section must have remarkably little application.
4 As amended by the Local Government and Housing Act 1989, s 165 and Sch 9.
5 *O'Brien v Robinson* [1973] AC 912, [1973] 1 All ER 583, HL.
6 Landlord and Tenant Act 1985, s 11(1A),(1B), added by the Housing Act 1988. For leases entered into prior to 15 January 1989, the landlord's obligation is limited to the structure and exterior of the particular flat and the installations therein: *Campden Hill Towers Ltd v Gardner* [1977] QB 823, [1977] 1 All ER 739, CA, and see *Douglas-Scott v Scorgie* [1984] 1 All ER 1086, [1984] 1 WLR 716, CA.
7 [1977] AC 239, [1976] 2 All ER 39. See also *King v South Northamptonshire District Council* [1992] 1 EGLR 53, CA.
8 [1985] QB 1, [1984] 1 All ER 930, CA.
9 In *Targett v Torfaen Borough Council* [1992] 1 EGLR 275, CA it was expressly held that this liability has survived despite the House of Lords' decision in *Murphy v Brentwood District Council* [1991] 1 AC 398, [1990] 2 All ER 908; see para 22.27 above.

The tenant

36.23 A freeholder's rights of disposition and of enjoyment of his property are remarkably wide.[1] In the absence of an express covenant, a tenant is equally free to assign his interest, ie transfer his entire interest to another (the assignee) thus putting the latter in the position of tenant vis-à-vis the landlord,[2] or he may sub-let (ie carve a shorter lease out of his own, putting himself in the position of landlord to the sub-lessee).[3] However, these rights are almost invariably subject to restriction, absolute or qualified, by the express terms of the lease.[4] As to the tenant's use of the premises, in the absence of express covenants, there are two restrictions imposed by the law; he must not commit waste, and, in the case of periodic tenancies, he is bound by an implied covenant to use the premises in a tenant-like manner.

1 See para 30.30 above.
2 Note that assignment must be by deed (LPA, s 52(1)) even where the lease itself was not required to be created by deed (LPA, s 54(2)); see *Crago v Julian* [1992] 1 All ER 744, [1992] 1 WLR 372, CA.
3 A purported sub-lease which passes the residue of the term takes effect as an assignment.
4 Para 36.29 below.

36.24 *Waste* 'Waste' has been defined as 'any act which alters the nature of the land, whether for the better or for the worse'.[1] It is an ancient, tortious liability imposed on owners of limited interest in land in order to protect the interests of those with rights to the subsequent occupation of the property; those most likely to be affected are tenants for life under a settlement[2] and tenants under leases. It is rarely encountered in modern times, largely because both settlements and leases tend to contain express provisions which obviate the need to rely on the doctrine.[3]

Common law recognised two forms of waste, voluntary and permissive. Voluntary waste would be constituted by carrying out substantial alterations to the property, for example by pulling down a building, or, as in *Marsden v Edward Heyes Ltd*,[4] by gutting the ground floor of a building to convert the entire area into a shop. Permissive waste is damage caused by omission or neglect, as by letting the premises go to ruin. All tenants are liable for voluntary waste. A tenant holding under a periodic tenancy is not liable for permissive waste but the point is probably covered by his obligation to use and deliver up the premises in a tenant-like manner.

1   Megarry and Wade *The Law of Real Property* (5th edn) p 96.
2   See para 33.3 above.
3   That said, for various technical reasons, the doctrine was resorted to in *Mancetter Developments Ltd v Garmanson Ltd* [1986] QB 1212, [1986] 1 All ER 449, CA.
4   [1927] 2 KB 1.

36.25   *To use the premises in a tenant-like manner*   This covenant is implied in all periodic tenancies.[1] According to Denning LJ, as he then was, in *Warren v Keen*, 'The tenant must take proper care of the place … he must do the little jobs about the place which a reasonable tenant would do. In addition, he must, of course, not damage the house, wilfully or negligently, and he must see that his family and guests do not damage it, and if they do, he must repair it.'[2]

1   *Marsden v Edward Heyes Ltd* [1927] 2 KB 1; *Warren v Keen* [1954] 1 QB 15, [1953] 2 All ER 1118, CA.
2   [1954] 1 QB 15 at 20, [1953] 2 All ER 1118. For example, the covenant does not necessarily oblige the tenant to lag water pipes. This depends on the circumstances, including the severity of the cold and the length of contemplated absences from home (*Wycombe Health Authority v Barnett* (1982) 47 P & CR 394).

36.26   *Right to fixtures*   For the tenant's right to remove fixtures at the end of the lease, see para 30.9 above.

Express terms
36.27   Covenants commonly found in leases include:

•   a covenant to pay rent;
•   a covenant restricting assignment, sub-letting or parting with possession;
•   repairing covenants;
•   covenants restricting the use of the premises;
•   a covenant to insure. Either the landlord will covenant to insure the property on the basis that the tenant will pay the premiums, or the tenant will be required to insure the property, often with a named company, to its full value. Failure to keep the property insured constitutes a breach.[1]

We shall briefly consider these covenants in the ensuing paragraphs; for a more detailed treatment readers are advised to consult a specialist textbook on the law of landlord and tenant.[2]

1   *Penniall v Harborne* (1848) 11 QB 368.
2   See, for example, P F Smith *The Law of Landlord and Tenant* (5th edn).

Rent
36.28   The payment of rent, although a normal feature of leases, is not an essential legal requirement.[1] The rent payable by a tenant will generally take the form either of

a market rent or a ground rent. A market rent is sometimes described as a 'rack' rent. A ground rent, commonly paid in the case of long leases, is paid where the land has been leased partly in consideration of a lump sum payment (ie a premium) at the commencement of the lease, or in consideration of the tenant building on the land, this being reflected in the rent which is, in essence, a rent for the land only and not the buildings thereon. It is normally expressly provided that rent is payable in advance; if this is not done, rent is payable in arrears.

It is very common in the case of longer commercial leases to provide for the level of rent to be revised at prescribed intervals, for example every five years. The object of a rent review clause is to protect the landlord from the effects of increases in property values and falls in the value of money by increasing the rent payable in line with the market. A well-drafted rent review clause should contain both a formula for determining the revised rent and machinery for agreeing the rent and resolving disputes between the parties (generally by way of reference to a chartered surveyor acting as expert or arbitrator[2]).

1   *Ashburn Anstalt v Arnold* [1989] Ch 1, [1988] 2 All ER 147, CA.
2   See para 18.22 above.

Assignment, sub-letting, or parting with possession
36.29   An absolute covenant against assignment or sub-letting, etc is more usually found in short tenancies. In longer leases it is common to allow assignment or sub-letting provided that the tenant first obtains the landlord's consent which is not to be unreasonably withheld.[1] Should the landlord unreasonably refuse consent the tenant may go ahead with the proposed assignment or sub-lease, or may apply to court for a declaration that the refusal is unreasonable.

The Landlord and Tenant Act 1988 now imposes certain statutory duties on a landlord whose consent to an assignment or sub-letting is required. He must respond in writing, within a reasonable time, to the tenant's written application for consent, giving consent unless it is reasonable not to do so. Where his consent is conditional, he must specify those conditions (which must be reasonable). Where he is refusing consent he must give his reasons for that refusal (which must be reasonable). Breach of any of these duties gives rise to liability in tort for breach of statutory duty. This means that the tenant may now be able to obtain either damages or a mandatory injunction against a dilatory or unreasonable landlord.

In any case where the reasonableness of a landlord's refusal is in issue it is now[2] for the landlord to show that consent was reasonably withheld. In considering this question it is assumed that the purpose of such a covenant is to protect the lessor from having his premises used or occupied in an undesirable way or by an undesirable tenant or assignee. The court will take account of the purpose of the covenant and all the circumstances, including the statutory background, at the time when the consent is sought.

In the case of leases of commercial and industrial premises[3] entered into on or after 1 January 1996 the landlord is now permitted to specify in the lease any objectively verifiable circumstances[4] in which his consent to an *assignment*[5] will be withheld; where consent is later withheld, or subjected to conditions, in those circumstances the landlord's refusal (or any condition subject to which a consent has been given) is deemed to be reasonable.[6] A refusal of consent on a ground which has not been pre-specified in the lease can still be challenged as unreasonable. Although these provisions have only been in force for a relatively short period of time, it is clear that landlords are making full use of their new ability to control assignments more tightly; it is now standard practice to include in commercial and industrial leases a list of circumstances in which consent to an assignment can be refused, and conditions to which any consent may be subject.

An assignment or sub-letting in breach of covenant does not affect the validity of the assignment or sub-lease, but may expose the assignee or sub-lessee to the risk of forfeiture.[7]

1   Where a covenant requires the landlord's prior consent to any disposition, but does *not* expressly provide that this consent is not to be unreasonably withheld, the Landlord and Tenant Act 1927, s 19(1) operates to achieve this effect.
2   Landlord and Tenant Act 1988, ss 1(6) and 3(5).
3   The new law does not apply to residential or agricultural leases.
4   Ie circumstances which are essentially factual and which do not involve any value judgment, eg 'consent to an assignment to a company will not be given unless that company is a plc'.
5   The new law applies only to consent to *assignments*; it does not apply to sub-lettings and other types of disposition.
6   Landlord and Tenant Act 1927, s 19(1A), added by the Landlord and Tenant (Covenants) Act 1995, s 22.
7   *Old Grovebury Manor Farm Ltd v W Seymour Plant Sales & Hire Ltd (No 2)* [1979] 3 All ER 504, [1979] 1 WLR 1397, CA; and see paras 36.32–36.35 below.

Covenants to repair

36.30   A variety of covenants providing for the liability of landlord and tenant to repair the premises may be encountered. In the case of long leases of whole buildings, it is often provided that the full legal and financial responsibility for repairing the premises is placed on the tenant. Equally, the repairing obligations may be split between landlord and tenant, with the landlord being liable for repairs to the structure and exterior of the premises and the tenant being obliged to repair the interior. Also common, where premises are let to several tenants, are so-called 'clear leases', ie leases in which the landlord covenants to carry out all works of repair and maintenance to the building, but the tenants bear all the costs of these works (by way of service charges), so that the rent reaches the landlord clear of all expenses and overheads. In the case of shorter tenancies, the tenant's liability tends to be restricted to an obligation to keep, and deliver up at the end of the term, the interior of the premises in a good and tenantable state of repair, perhaps 'fair wear and tear excepted'. In the case of short residential tenancies, the landlord is always liable under the Landlord and Tenant Act 1985,[1] to keep in repair the structure and exterior and service installations.

Where the obligation imposed is to 'keep' in repair (which it usually is) this means that, where necessary, any *existing* disrepair must be remedied.[2] It is thus vital, where such a repairing obligation is being imposed on a tenant, that the property is structurally surveyed before the lease is entered into.

Whether or not the premises are, legally speaking, in disrepair is often a highly technical issue. 'Repair' connotes the idea of making good damage so as to leave the subject so far as possible as though it had not been damaged.[3] There can be no disrepair unless a part of the building to which the covenant relates has physically deteriorated since the date of its construction.[4] A covenant to repair may require renewal of subsidiary parts, but not of the whole.[5] Repair will, inevitably, involve some element of improvement, but it must not result in premises which are wholly different in character from those which were demised.[6] Within these limits, a covenant to repair will cover works necessitated by inherent defects in the premises.[7] It is always a question of fact and degree whether the work in question can properly be described as repair; in coming to any conclusion the court may well take account of the cost of the works compared to the value of the building.[8]

In any case where the landlord is under an obligation to repair the demised premise, his liability to the tenant does not arise until he has notice of the defect;[9] where the landlord is obliged to keep either his own adjoining premises, or common parts, in repair, his liability arises as soon as the disrepair occurs.[10]

1   Para 36.22 above.
2   *Proudfoot v Hart* (1890) 25 QBD 42, CA.
3   *Anstruther-Gough-Calthorpe v McOscar* [1924] 1 KB 716, CA.
4   *Quick v Taff-Ely Borough Council* [1986] QB 809, [1985] 3 All ER 321, CA. See also *Post Office v Aquarius Properties Ltd* [1987] 1 All ER 1055, CA.
5   *Lurcott v Wakely and Wheeler* [1911] 1 KB 905, CA.
6   *Ravenseft Properties Ltd v Davstone (Holdings) Ltd* [1980] QB 12, [1979] 1 All ER 929.
7   Ibid.
8   See, for example, *Brew Brothers v Snax (Ross) Ltd* [1970] 1 QB 612 and *Ravenseft Properties Ltd v Davstone (Holdings) Ltd* [1980] QB 12, [1979] 1 All ER 929.
9   *McCarrick v Liverpool Corpn* [1947] AC 219, [1946] 2 All ER 646, HL. Cf Defective Premises Act 1972, para 22.31 above.
10 *British Telecommunications plc v Sun Life Assurance Society plc* [1995] 4 All ER 44, CA.

Remedies for breach of covenant

For breach of covenants other than for payment of rent

36.31   For breach of covenants other than for payment of rent the injured party may sue for damages or seek an injunction to restrain the breach, or, in the case of the landlord, claim forfeiture of the lease. It should be noted that, where the breach is of the covenant to repair important variations to the basic rules sometimes apply.[1]

1   See para 36.36 below.

Forfeiture[1]

36.32   *The right to forfeit*   The landlord normally has a right to claim forfeiture of the lease because a proviso for re-entry in the event of a breach of covenant is invariably expressly included in the lease.[2] Such a right of re-entry is a proprietary right and as such enforceable not only against the tenant but also against assignees and sub-tenants (including mortgagees). In claiming forfeiture and exercising a right of re-entry the landlord is choosing to put an end to the tenant's interest in the property because of the breach.

1   It should be noted that the Law Commission has published a report incorporating a draft bill, which proposes sweeping changes to the law on forfeiture; see Termination of Tenancies Bill 1994 Law Com No 221.
2   In those rare cases where the lease does not contain an express right of re-entry for breach, the landlord can only forfeit for breaches of those covenants which are framed as conditions (eg by the use of wording such as 'on condition that').

36.33   *Waiver*   The landlord may lose his right to forfeit for a breach of covenant where he has expressly or impliedly waived his right to do so. Implied waiver can only occur where the lessor, knowing of the breach, does some unequivocal act which, considered objectively without regard to the landlord's motive or intention, is consistent only with the continued existence of the lease.[1] The onus is on the tenant to show that waiver has occurred. The act most commonly relied on as constituting waiver is the acceptance of future rent. The very fact of acceptance of rent,[2] even as a result of a clerical error, amounts, as a matter of law, to waiver of the right to forfeit.[3] Whether or not other acts amount to waiver is a question of fact.[4] If the breach is of a continuing nature, for example a failure to insure or to repair, continued breach after the waiver revives the right of re-entry. This type of waiver only deprives the landlord of his right to forfeit; he can still pursue other remedies for the breach.

1   *Matthews v Smallwood* [1910] 1 Ch 777 at 786; *Central Estates (Belgravia) Ltd v Woolgar (No 2)* [1972] 3 All ER 610, [1972] 1 WLR 1048, CA; *Expert Clothing Service and Sales Ltd v Hillgate House Ltd* [1986] Ch 340, [1985] 2 All ER 998, CA.
2   A demand for future rent is similarly treated as waiver as a matter of law; see *David Blackstone Ltd v Burnetts (West End) Ltd* [1973] 3 All ER 782, [1973] 1 WLR 1487.
3   *Central Estates (Belgravia) Ltd v Woolgar (No 2)* [1972] 3 All ER 610, [1972] 1 WLR 1048, CA.
4   *Expert Clothing Service and Sales Ltd v Hillgate House Ltd* [1986] Ch 340, [1985] 2 All ER 998, CA.

36.34   *Procedure*   The LPA, s 146 provides that a right of re-entry or forfeiture for breach of a covenant or condition *other than one for payment of rent* may not be enforced unless and until the lessor serves on the lessee a notice which is designed to give the tenant reasonable information about what, if anything, he has to do to avoid forfeiture. A s 146 notice must;

- specify the particular breach complained of;
- require the lessee to remedy it (if the breach is capable of remedy[1]); and
- if desired, require the lessee to make compensation in money for the breach.

Having served a s 146 notice, the landlord is compelled then to allow the tenant sufficient time to remedy the breach and to make reasonable compensation before he can take any further steps. Even where the breach is not capable of remedy, the tenant must still be given a short time in which to consider his position before the landlord proceeds to forfeiture.[2]

The landlord should normally forfeit by bringing a court action for possession. Although, theoretically, he may have the alternative of forfeiting by peaceably re-entering on the land, this is not to be recommended, for the following reasons. First, in the case of residential lettings, forfeiture must be effected by court proceedings while any person is lawfully residing in the premises.[3] Second, the landlord runs the risk of contravening the Criminal Law Act 1977, s 6 (which prohibits the use or threat of violence to secure entry) or some other provision of the criminal law. Third, forfeiting by way of peaceable re-entry does not give the landlord an unchallengeable right to possession since a tenant, sub-tenant or mortgagee may still be able to claim relief.[4]

It should also be noted that a landlord of residential premises is not entitled to re-enter[5] for non-payment of a service charge unless its amount has been admitted, agreed, or determined.[6] This is designed to prevent landlords threatening tenants (or their mortgagees) with the termination of their lease for non-payment of what might well be disputed service charge payments.

1   Certain breaches are, legally speaking, regarded as incapable of remedy. These include the breach of a covenant against immoral user (see *Rugby School (Governors) v Tannahill* [1935] 1 KB 87, CA) and that of a covenant against assignment or sub-letting (see *Scala House and District Property Co Ltd v Forbes* [1974] QB 575, [1973] 3 All ER 308, CA). See generally *Expert Clothing Service and Sales Ltd v Hillgate House Ltd* [1986] Ch 340, [1985] 2 All ER 998, CA and *Savva v Houssein* [1996] 47 EG 138, CA. Where a breach is incapable of remedy the landlord may proceed to forfeit more rapidly (see note 2 below); furthermore, the tenant is less likely to be given relief, see para 36.35 below.
2   *Horsey Estate Ltd v Steiger* [1899] 2 QB 79, CA. Fourteen days' notice has been held sufficient in such cases: *Civil Service Co-operative Society Ltd v McGrigor's Trustee* [1923] 2 Ch 347.
3   Protection from Eviction Act 1977, s 2.
4   *Billson v Residential Apartments Ltd* [1992] 1 AC 494, [1992] 1 All ER 141, HL; see para 36.35 below.
5   The landlord can serve a s 146 notice provided that this informs the tenant that the landlord cannot take the matter further (ie by actually re-entering) until the service charge amount is admitted, agreed or determined, Housing Act 1996, s 82.
6   Housing Act 1996, s 81.

36.35   *Relief*   At any time from the service of the s 146 notice until the landlord has recovered possession of the property under an unassailable court order,[1] the tenant may apply to the court for relief from forfeiture.[2] The court has a complete discretion as to whether or not to grant relief and on what terms, if any, it thinks fit,[3] although the tenant will, invariably, be required to remedy the breach.

Where a lease is terminated by forfeiture this necessarily destroys any sub-leases and mortgages granted by the lessee. This, of course, would involve considerable hardship to an innocent sub-lessee or mortgagee and so, under the LPA, s 146(4), they are entitled to apply to court for relief. This will normally only be given where the sub-tenant (or mortgagee) is prepared to remedy the tenant's breach. Where relief is given, a new lease, held direct of the landlord, will be vested in the applicant.

1   *Billson v Residential Apartments Ltd* [1992] 1 AC 494, [1992] 1 All ER 141, HL. This means that, should a landlord forfeit by way of peaceable re-entry, a tenant (and, presumably a sub-tenant or mortgagee) can still apply to court for relief. It is this which makes it unwise for a landlord to re-enter peaceably.
2   Under LPA, s 146(2).
3   Ibid.

For breach of repairing covenants

36.36   We have already mentioned that certain special rules apply in cases where the covenant which has been breached is that to repair. Where it is the *landlord* who is seeking a remedy the following restrictions apply.

First, he cannot normally obtain an *injunction* or *specific performance* in order to enforce a tenant's obligation to repair since damages will usually be an adequate remedy.[1]

Second, where a landlord is seeking *damages*, two special rules apply. In certain cases he cannot commence an action for damages without serving a s 146 notice[2] and, where the tenant so requires, without obtaining the leave of the court.[3] Even where he does obtain damages in any case, the measure of those damages is limited by statute; they can, in no event, exceed the amount by which the value of his reversion is diminished and, where the landlord is planning to demolish or re-develop the premises at the end of the lease, he cannot recover damages at all.[4]

Third, where a landlord is seeking to *forfeit* for breach of a repairing covenant a number of special rules apply. In certain instances[5] the s 146 notice must inform the tenant of his right to claim the benefit of the Leasehold Property (Repairs) Act 1938 by serving a counter-notice within 28 days. The landlord must prove that the tenant actually knows that the s 146 notice has been served.[6] Where the tenant does claim the benefit of the 1938 Act the landlord cannot proceed to forfeit without the leave of the court. This will not be given unless he proves that the tenant is in breach and that the case is covered by one of the 1938 Act grounds.[7]

Finally, where the s 146 notice relates to internal decorative repairs, the tenant may apply to court for relief from all liability for such repairs, which the court may grant if in all the circumstances it considers the notice unreasonable.[8]

Where it is the *tenant* who is seeking a remedy for the landlord's breach of his repairing obligations, not surprisingly, there are no special restrictions but, rather, additional rights. In the case of residential tenancies, there is no bar to the tenant being awarded specific performance,[9] and in any case the court has a general jurisdiction, which should be carefully exercised, to order a landlord to do some specific work pursuant to his covenant to repair.[10] It may also be noted at this point that the court has the power, at the suit of a tenant, to appoint a receiver to receive the rent and exercise the duties of the landlord,[11] a power which has been used where a landlord is in breach of a repairing covenant and has persistently failed to remedy the breach.[12] In the case of tenancies of flats, this general jurisdiction has been superseded by the right, given by Pt II of the Landlord and Tenant Act 1987, to apply to the county court for the appointment of a manager where the landlord is in breach of an obligation, such as a repairing covenant, which is likely to continue. Where this remedy does not solve the problem the tenants can apply for the compulsory acquisition of the landlord's interest under Pt III of the 1987 Act.

1   The first reported case in which an order for the specific performance of a repairing covenant has been made against a tenant has just occurred: *Rainbow Estates Ltd v Tokenhold Ltd* [1998]. Unusually, the lease contained neither a forfeiture provision, nor any right for the landlord to enter and carry out the repairs himself; in these circumstances it was clear that damages would not be an adequate remedy.
2   Ie all leases (except agricultural holdings) granted for a term of seven years or more, of which at least three years remain unexpired; Leasehold Property (Repairs) Act 1938, s 1(2). For s 146 notices, see para 36.4 above.
3   Where the tenant serves a counternotice within 28 days of receiving the s 146 notice the landlord must then obtain the leave of the court; ibid s 1(3).
4   Landlord and Tenant Act 1927, s 18.
5   Ie where the lease is covered by the Leasehold Property (Repairs) Act 1938; see note 2 above.
6   Landlord and Tenant Act 1927, s 18(2).
7   Leasehold Property (Repairs) Act 1938, s 1(5); see *Associated British Ports v CH Bailey plc* [1990] 1 All ER 929, HL.
8   LPA, s 147.
9   Landlord and Tenant Act 1985, s 17.
10 *Jeune v Queens Cross Properties Ltd* [1974] Ch 97, [1973] 3 All ER 97.
11 Supreme Court Act 1981, s 36.
12 See, for example, *Hart v Emelkirk* [1983] 1 WLR 1289; *Daiches v Bluelake Investments Ltd* [1985] 2 EGLR 67.

For non-payment of rent
36.37   In the event of non-payment of rent, the remedies available to the landlord are distress, an action to recover the rent, and forfeiture.

Distress[1]
36.38   This is an ancient remedy which the Law Commission has recommended should be abolished.[2] Its attraction to landlords is that it is available without recourse to the courts[3] and without prior notice to the tenant, thus making it extremely effective in practice. The landlord's right of distress entitles him, or rather his certificated bailiff, to enter the demised premises and impound goods found there[4] to provide security for the outstanding rent. Provided that notice is given to the tenant these goods may be sold after five days.

1   Distress for Rent Acts 1689 and 1737.
2   Landlord and Tenant: Distress for Rent (1991) Law Com No 194.
3   Save in relation to tenancies of dwelling-houses falling within the Rent Act 1977 or Housing Act 1988, where leave of the county court is required; Rent Act 1977, s 147, Housing Act 1988, s 19.
4   Subject to certain limited exceptions.

Forfeiture
36.39   The landlord may claim forfeiture of the lease for non-payment of rent where the lease contains an express proviso for re-entry.[1] At common law, the landlord cannot claim forfeiture without having first made a formal demand for the exact sum due, on the demised premises, between sunrise and sunset. The technicality of a formal demand is invariably dispensed with by an express provision in the lease.[2] A s 146 notice is not required in the case of forfeiture for non-payment of rent. (Thus, in theory at least, a landlord is usually able to forfeit for non-payment of rent without giving any prior warning to the tenant; in practice he is likely to have been chasing the tenant for payment for some time.) The law as to waiver and as to the exercise of the right of re-entry explained in paras 36.33 and 36.34 applies equally in cases of non-payment of rent.

Where the tenant owes at least half a year's rent, the landlord's action for forfeiture will be terminated if, before the date of judgment, the tenant pays into court the arrears together with the landlord's costs.[3] Otherwise the court has an equitable, and, hence, discretionary, jurisdiction to grant relief where the tenant pays the rent due and the landlord's expenses.[4] Unlike the case of forfeiture for breach of some other covenant,[5] relief may in this case be granted even after the landlord has obtained judgment for possession, at least within six months thereafter.[6] A sub-lessee or mortgagee equally may apply for relief under this general equitable jurisdiction or, before the landlord recovers possession under an unassailable court order,[7] under the terms of the LPA, s 146(4).

1   Where this is not the case, the landlord will still be able to forfeit if the covenant to pay rent is framed as a condition of the lease.
2   In any event, in cases where half a year's rent is in arrear and insufficient distrainable goods are available on the premises, there is no need for a formal demand: Common Law Procedure Act 1852, s 210. See also County Courts Act 1984, s 139(1), for actions brought in the county court.
3   Common Law Procedure Act 1852, s 212. Where the case is taken to the county court, even where six months' rent is *not* owing, the proceedings will be automatically terminated if the tenant pays off all the arrears and costs at least five days before the hearing date; County Courts Act 1984, s 138(2).
4   See also Supreme Court Act 1981, s 38.
5   Para 36.35 above.
6   Common Law Procedure Act 1852, s 210. In the case of county court proceedings, different provisions for relief apply. The court's order for possession must be suspended for not less than four weeks (subject to extension) to allow the tenant time to pay the arrears and costs. Where the lessor recovers possession at any time after the making of the order, the lessee has six months from that date to apply to the court for relief: County Courts Act 1984, s 138(9A).
7   Para 36.35 above. In the county court, sub-lessees or mortgagees may seek relief under the LPA, s 146(4) or under the provisions of the County Courts Act. In the latter instance relief must be applied for within the six months' time limit, *United Dominions Trust Ltd v Shellpoint Trustees Ltd* [1993] 4 All ER 310, CA.

Enforceability of covenants by and against assignees

36.40   We have indicated that, subject to any controls imposed by the lease,[1] a tenant may assign his lease to another, ie transfer the whole of the remainder of the term. The longer the lease the more likely this is to happen and, in practice, assignments are commonplace. Equally, during the continuance of a lease, the landlord is completely free to transfer his interest in the land. We now need to consider the effect which such transfers will have on the enforceability of the covenants contained in the lease. To what extent will a new landlord be able to enforce the lease covenants against either the original tenant, or an assignee of the lease? Can a new tenant insist that the original landlord, or an assignee of the reversion, perform the obligations imposed by the lease terms?

The law in this area has recently been radically overhauled by the Landlord and Tenant (Covenants) Act 1995 ('LTCA'). This introduces a new regime on the enforceability of leasehold covenants, but only for leases entered into on or after 1 January 1996 ('new' leases); the existing rules, with limited modifications, continue to apply to leases granted before that date ('old' leases). Since 'old' leases will remain in existence or very many years to come, those dealing with property need to be equally familiar with both regimes. We turn first to the enforceability of covenants contained in 'old' leases.

1   Paras 36.23 and 36.29 above.

Leases entered into before 1 January 1996

36.41 The rules relating to the enforceability of covenants in 'old' leases are essentially two-fold. First, and obviously, all covenants, whether imposing positive or negative obligations, are mutually enforceable between the original parties to the lease as a matter of basic contract law. Second, as we shall see, where there has been an assignment of the lease or the reversion, or both, all covenants which 'touch and concern' the land which is the subject of the lease are mutually enforceable between the persons who are now in the relationship of landlord and tenant. This relationship is known as privity of estate and is the very basis on which such covenants remain enforceable.

Touching and concerning

36.42 Before examining the operation of these two rules, we must first consider what is meant by the phrase 'touch and concern'. It means that the covenant should relate to either the demised land, or to the reversion; it must be reasonably incidental to the relationship of landlord and tenant rather than merely of personal advantage to the particular covenantee.

It was held that the House of Lords, in *P & A Swift Investments v Combined English Stores Group plc*,[1] that a covenant touches and concerns the land if:

- the covenant benefits only the owner for the time being and, if separated from the land, ceases to be of benefit to the covenantee;
- the covenant affects the nature, quality, mode of enjoyment or value of the land; and
- the covenant is not expressed to be personal.

Examples of covenants which have been held to touch and concern the property are a covenant to pay rent, a covenant to repair the property, a covenant not to assign, the landlord's covenant for quiet enjoyment, a covenant by a surety guaranteeing the rent and a covenant giving the tenant an option to renew the lease. It should be noted that, anomalously, to be enforceable against an assignee of the landlord this last covenant must be registered as an estate contract.[2]

Covenants which have been held not to touch and concern the land include a covenant not to open a public house within half a mile of the demised public house, a covenant to pay the tenant £500 unless the lease is renewed, a covenant to pay rates on other land, and a covenant giving the tenant an option to purchase the reversion.

1 [1989] AC 632, [1988] 2 All ER 885, HL.
2 *Phillips v Mobil Oil Co Ltd* [1989] 3 All ER 97, [1989] 1 WLR 888, CA.

Assignment of the lease

36.43 *A single assignment* We now turn to consider the operation of the two basic rules relating to the enforceability of covenants in 'old' leases.

We first consider the case where the tenant has assigned his entire leasehold interest:

Here, T has assigned his leasehold interest to A. L and A are now in the relationship of landlord and tenant. Therefore covenants in the lease which touch and concern the land are enforceable by L against A, and by A against L.[1] Thus, for example, A will be bound by a covenant to pay rent, L by the covenant for quiet enjoyment.

If A is in breach of a covenant touching and concerning the land, such as the covenant to pay rent, L could, and normally would, take action against A to remedy the breach.[2] However, it must be remembered that there is still a contract between L and T under which T remains liable on the covenants for the rest of the term. By virtue of the LPA, s 79, when originally entering into the relevant covenant, T is deemed to covenant not only that he will perform the covenant but also that his successors in title will do so. This means that, should a successor of the tenant fail to perform a covenant, the original tenant is in breach of his contractual obligation. So, instead of, or as well as,[3] suing A, L may also sue T in respect of A's breach of covenant.

It is to be noted that T will not be liable for the breach of any *new or changed* covenant inserted into the lease by L and A after the assignment from T to A.[4] However T is liable in respect of any changes which occur after the assignment but which are the result of the operation of the terms of the lease as they existed at the date of the assignment; this means that, in particular, T is liable for rent which has been increased after the assignment in accordance with a rent review clause which was already in the lease.[4]

If L does sue T, T may then sue A in an attempt to recover money paid to L, either in quasi-contract[5] or, if the assignment to A was for valuable consideration, for breach of a term implied by statute[6] that A and those deriving title from him will perform the covenant and, if they do not, will indemnify T.

In practice, L is only likely to sue T where A has failed to pay rent and is insolvent. However, during the recent recession, it became commonplace for landlords to utilise their rights against original tenants and it was the latter's complaints which eventually persuaded the government to implement a reform of this area of the law.

In the event, most of the provisions of the LTCA 1995 apply only to leases entered into after 1 January 1996, leaving tenants under existing leases to the rigours of the old law. However, two of the new measures introduced by the 1995 Act do apply to 'old' leases. First, in order to be able to recover a 'fixed charge'[7] from a former tenant, the landlord must serve on him a default notice within six months of those sums becoming due.[8] This notice must specify the sums due. Second, where a former tenant pays all the sums specified in a default notice, he is then entitled to require the landlord to grant him an overriding lease.[9] Broadly, this lease sits between the current tenant, A, and L; thus T becomes A's landlord and is able to take steps to enforce the covenants which A is breaking, and in particular, to forfeit A's lease. This at least means that T has the right either to occupy the premises, or to re-assign them to a more reliable assignee than A has proved to be.

1   *Spencer's Case* (1583) s Co Rep 16a.
2   Paras 36.31–36.39 above.
3   He may not recover twice in respect of the same loss.
4   *Friends Provident Life Office v British Railways Board* [1995] 48 EG 106, CA.
5   *Moule v Garrett* (1872) LR 7 Exch 101.
6   LPA, s 77(1)(c) and Sch 2.
7   Broadly, rent and service charge payments; LTCA 1995, s 17(6).
8   LTCA 1995, s 17(2), para 36.55 below.
9   LTCA 1995, s 19(1), para 36.56 below.

36.44   *A further assignment*

Here T has assigned his lease to A (as in the previous example) but A has then later assigned the lease to B. This allows us to demonstrate the fundamental difference between T's liability, which is based on privity of contract, and that of A, which is based on privity of estate. Once A assigns the lease he ceases to be in a relationship of landlord and tenant with L; since there is no longer any privity of estate between them, A cannot be made liable for any subsequent breaches committed by B.[1] However, T's liability remains unaltered; he is still bound by his original contract and can be sued in respect of breaches committed by B (or any subsequent assignee).

However, it should be noted that, particularly in the case of commercial leases, it has become the widespread practice for the basic rule concerning the liability of assignees to be varied by express agreement. It is usual for a landlord to require that an assignee enters into a direct contract with him under which the assignee agrees to be bound by the covenants contained in the lease for the remainder of the term; in this way the assignee accepts a contractual liability which is identical to that of an original tenant.[2] Thus, in our example, both A and B may have entered into a direct contract with L; if, and only if, this is the case, L can sue A in respect of breaches committed by B. If B assigns on, L can sue B in respect of subsequent breaches.

An assignee who remains liable to the landlord following a further assignment because of the imposition of a direct covenant is entitled to the limited benefits introduced by the LTCA. Accordingly, he must be served with a default notice and, if he has paid the sums specified in that notice, he is entitled to call for an overriding lease.[3]

1   *Onslow v Corrie* (1817) 2 Madd 330. For the same reason A is not liable for breaches which occur before he becomes the tenant, *Grescot v Green* (1700) 1 Salk 199.
2   *J Lyons & Co Ltd v Knowles* [1943] 1 KB 366, [1943] 1 All ER 477.
3   See para 36.43 above and paras 36.55 and 36.56 below..

Assignment of the reversion
36.45

In this case, the landlord has assigned his reversion to R. R and T are now in the relationship of landlord and tenant. Covenants which touch and concern the subject matter of the lease are mutually enforceable between R and T.[1] It has been held that the wording of s 141 (which passes the benefit of such covenants to a new landlord) is such that, once the reversion has been assigned, only R, and not L, can bring an action against T for breach of covenant, whether the breach occurred before or after the assignment.[2] Thus, if T owed rent prior to the assignment of the reversion, and L has not taken action to recover it, he loses the right to do so once he assigns his interest to R. Since R will be able to sue, it is usual for L and R to come to an appropriate arrangement in respect of existing breaches.

As with an original tenant, L remains contractually liable to T even after an assignment of the reversion.[3] However, since landlords do not, generally speaking, undertake obligations which are as onerous as those imposed on tenants, the continuing liability of landlords has not given rise to the same pressure for reform.[4]

1   LPA, s 141 provides that the *benefit* of such covenants passes to an assignee of the reversion; s 142 passes the *burden*.
2   *Re King, Robinson v Gray* [1963] Ch 459, [1963] 1 All ER 781, CA; *London and County (A & D) Ltd v Wilfred Sportsman Ltd* [1971] Ch 764, [1970] 2 All ER 600, CA.

3   *Stuart v Joy* [1904] 1 KB 362, CA.
4   Although, as we shall see in para 36.53 below, landlords under new leases can apply to be released from their obligations following an assignment of the reversion.

Assignment of both the lease and the reversion
36.46

Here both landlord and tenant have assigned their interest in the property. All covenants which touch and concern the land are mutually enforceable between R and A, the new landlord and tenant. Furthermore because of the effect of s 141, if the assignment T→A took place before the assignment L→R, R can nonetheless sue T for breaches of covenant occurring before R acquired the reversion even though there had never been any contract between the parties and they had never been in the relationship of landlord and tenant.[1] Equally, should A be in breach of a covenant which touches and concerns the land, R (and only R) may take action; either against A or, if need be, against T.

It should be noted that it is provided by s 3 of the Landlord and Tenant Act 1985 that in the case of leases of dwellings, on assignment of the reversion, L remains liable to the current tenant (T or, as the case may be, A) in respect of any breach of covenant (jointly and severally with R, where the covenant touches and concerns the land) until either he or R gives written notice of the assignment and of R's name and address to the current tenant.

1   *Arlesford Trading Co Ltd v Servansingh* [1971] 3 All ER 113, [1971] 1 WLR 1080, CA.

Equitable leases
36.47   The rules illustrated in the foregoing paragraphs apply equally to covenants in leases (within the LPA, s 54(2)[1]) not exceeding three years made in writing,[2] or, presumably, orally, though in the latter case an assignee may have difficulty ascertaining the details of some covenants. Where there is merely an agreement for a lease,[3] all covenants are mutually enforceable between the original parties to the agreement. In such a case, if the 'landlord' assigns his interest in the land, the effect of the LPA, ss 141, 142 and 154 is to make the benefit and burden of covenants in the agreement run with the land to the assignee,[4] subject to the caveat that, where necessary, the tenant has protected his lease by registration.[5] However, it would seem that, since under the law of contract the 'tenant' may assign only the benefit and not the burden of covenants in the agreement for a lease, an assignee of the 'tenant' will not be bound by any of the obligations contained in the agreement for a lease.[6] This rule is widely regarded as unsatisfactory, and does not apply in the case of new leases.[7] However, it should be noted that a landlord under an old lease will be able indirectly to enforce the covenants by using or threatening forfeiture since any right of re-entry contained in the original agreement will be binding on the assignee.

1   Para 31.7 above.
2   *Boyer v Warbey* [1953] 1 QB 234, [1952] 2 All ER 976, CA.
3   Or an informal lease; in either case the tenant is regarded as having an equitable lease; see paras 32.2–32.5 above.
4   *Rickett v Green* [1910] 1 KB 253.
5   This will normally only be necessary where title to the land is not registered; here an equitable lease must be registered as a Class C (iv) land charge under the LCA 1972; see para 35.11 above.
6   *Purchase v Lichfield Brewery Co* [1915] 1 KB 184.

7   The LTCA 1995, s 28(1) defines leases so as to include equitable leases; hence s 3 of that Act (which deals with the running of covenants in new leases–see para 36.49 below) ensures that tenant covenants in equitable leases do pass to an assignee.

Leases entered into on or after 1 January 1996
The broad effect of the LTCA 1995
36.48   The broad effect of the LTCA, which applies to all[1] leases entered into on or after 1 January 1996[2] is as follows:

- the requirement that covenants should 'touch and concern' the land is abolished;[3]
- all tenants, whether original tenants or assignees, are automatically released from future liability on an assignment of their lease;[4]
- however, a landlord can often require an assigning tenant to enter into an agreement guaranteeing that the assignee will perform the obligations imposed by the lease;[5]
- while landlords are not *automatically* released from future liability when transferring their reversion, they can seek release from the tenant or from the court;[6]
- where landlords are able to hold a former tenant liable for breaches committed by the current tenant, they must serve a default notice within six months of any sums becoming due and, where these sums are paid, must if required to do so by that former tenant, grant an overriding lease;[7] and
- landlords are given greater control over the assignment of leases. This aspect of the 1995 Act has already been dealt with.[8]

We now deal, in outline, with each of these changes.

1   The provisions of the Act cannot be avoided; any attempt to 'exclude, modify or otherwise frustrate the operation of any provision of this Act' is void; LTCA, s 25(1).
2   The major exception to this is where a lease is granted after 1 January 1996 as a result of the exercise of an option granted prior to that date; such leases are subject to the old rules.
3   See para 36.49 below.
4   See para 36.50 below.
5   See para 36.51 below.
6   See para 36.53 below.
7   See paras 36.54–36.56 below. As we have seen in paras 36.43 and 36.44 above, these provisions also apply to 'old' leases.
8   See para 36.29 above.

The transmission of covenants on assignment of the lease or the reversion
36.49   When either a lease or a reversion is assigned the benefit and burden of all landlord and tenant covenants passes to the assignee.[1] There is no longer any requirement that the covenants should 'touch and concern' the land, but covenants which are expressed to be personal will not pass.[2] A landlord or tenant covenant includes any term, condition or obligation, whether contained in the lease or in any collateral agreement entered into before or after the lease, which has to be complied with by either the landlord or tenant respectively.[3]

1   LTCA, s 3(1); the benefit of a landlord's right of re-entry also passes to the assignee of the reversion; LTCA, s 4.
2   LTCA, s 3(6)(a).
3   LTCA, s 28(1). Covenants which require third parties to discharge any function in respect of the demised premises (eg where a management company is required to carry out repairs, maintenance, etc) are treated as landlord or tenant covenants, as appropriate, and can, therefore, be enforced by assignees; LTCA, s 12.

Release of tenant on assignment of the lease
36.50   Where a tenant assigns a lease he is released from the tenant covenants from the date of the assignment.[1] The only circumstances in which this release does not occur

is where the assignment is 'excluded'; an assignment is excluded if it is made in breach of covenant (eg without consent where consent is required) or by operation of law (eg where a lease transfers automatically, on bankruptcy, to the tenant's trustee in bankruptcy).[2] As we shall see in the following paragraph, the practical benefits of this release are reduced where the landlord can, and does, require the assigning tenant to guarantee the obligations of the assignee.

1   LTCA, s 5 (2).
2   LTCA, s 11.

Authorised guarantee agreements

36.51   Although a tenant is released from the *tenant covenants* on assigning the lease, the Act expressly permits him to enter into an agreement under which he guarantees that his assignee will perform the tenant covenants.[1] This means that, if the assignee is in breach of those covenants, the former tenant can then be sued under the *guarantee*. Such agreements are known as 'authorised guarantee agreements' ('AGAs'). A crucial restriction on AGAs is that they cannot impose liability on a former tenant once his assignee has been released by a further, non-excluded, assignment.[2]

A landlord is entitled to require an assigning tenant to enter into an AGA in the following circumstances:[3]

- where the lease contains an absolute covenant against assignment (but the landlord is prepared to allow the assignment);
- where the landlord's consent is required in a lease of *commercial or industrial* premises and the lease contains an express requirement that, on assignment the tenant must enter into an AGA;[4] and
- in the case of any lease where the landlord's consent is required and a condition that the tenant enter into an AGA is *reasonable*.

In the period since the 1995 Act came into force, it has become clear that landlords of commercial and industrial premises are, as a matter of standard practice, including in their leases provisions which require their tenants to enter into an AGA as a condition of consent to any assignment; the *automatically* imposed AGA has therefore become a fact of life for such tenants. Accordingly, the normal pattern of liability following the assignment of a business lease is that the outgoing tenant is released from the tenant covenants but will remain liable (under the AGA) for any breaches committed by his own immediate assignee; only when that assignee further assigns will the original tenant be entirely free from any further obligation.

1   LTCA, s 16(1).
2   LTCA, s 16(4)(b).
3   LTCA, s 16(2) and (3).
4   As we have seen in para 36.29 above, the LTCA 1995, s 22 has inserted a new s 19(1A) into the Landlord and Tenant Act 1927; as a result it is now possible for landlords of commercial and industrial premises to specify in advance the conditions to which any consent to an assignment will be subject. Where this is done, any condition is deemed to be reasonable.

Illustrations

36.52   It may be helpful to illustrate the principles outlined in the previous two paragraphs by three examples.

EXAMPLE 1

T ⟶ A₁

Provided T's assignment to A₁ is not excluded, T is released from the tenant covenants. However, if he has entered into an AGA, he will be liable on that agreement if A₁ breaches any tenant covenant.

EXAMPLE 2

$$T \longrightarrow A_1 \longrightarrow A_2$$

Provided both assignments are not excluded, T is now free from any further liability. Any AGA which T entered into when assigning to A₁ cannot have any further effect after A₁'s assignment to A₂. A₁ will be released from the tenant covenants on assigning to A₂ but, if he entered into an AGA he will be responsible, under that AGA, for any breaches committed by A₂; A₁ will only be free from all liability when A₂ lawfully assigns.

EXAMPLE 3

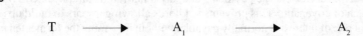

$$T \longrightarrow A_1 \longrightarrow A_2$$

Here let us assume that T's assignment to A₁ is excluded because he assigned without consent. This means that T is *not* released from the tenant covenants; should A₁ breach those covenants, T is *directly* liable to the landlord. If A₁ lawfully assigns to A₂, T is then released from the tenant covenants (as is A₁). However, T may be required to enter into an AGA guaranteeing A₂'s performance of the tenant covenants (as may A₁); in such a case T is not free from all liabilities until A₂ lawfully assigns.

Release of landlord on assignment of the reversion

36.53 A landlord is not automatically released from the landlord covenants when the reversion is assigned. Thus each successive landlord is, in principle, liable on the landlord covenants for the remainder of the lease.[1] It should be remembered that the continuing liability of a landlord is nothing like as onerous as that of a tenant; indeed, there has, as yet, been no reported decision in which a former landlord has been sued in respect of breaches committed by the current landlord.

That said, the 1995 Act does permit[1] a landlord who assigns the reversion to apply, in the first instance to the tenant, for release from the landlord covenants within four weeks of any assignment. Where the tenant objects to such a release, the landlord can apply to court.[2] Where a landlord fails to apply for a release, or fails to achieve a release, he can re-apply should his assignee further assign.[3]

This procedure is cumbersome and may, in itself provoke tenants into objecting to any release. It is clear that the parties are free simply to agree a release following an assignment by the landlord;[4] what is not clear is whether this allows a landlord to insert into a lease from the outset a provision under which the landlord *will* be released following any assignment.

1   LTCA, s 6(2). This differs from the position under an 'old' lease where only the original landlord
     continues to be liable following the assignment of the reversion; see para 36.45 above.
2   LTCA, s 8.
3   LTCA, s 7.
4   LTCA, s 26(1)(a).

Default notices and overriding leases

36.54 Despite the radical changes introduced by the 1995 Act, it is clear that the device of the AGA permits a former tenant to be liable for breaches committed by his immediate assignee; indeed, as we have seen, emerging practice suggests that in the case of commercial and industrial lease, this liability is turning out to be automatic.[1] However, the Act does contain provisions designed to alleviate the position of a former tenant who is being, or has been pursued, by the landlord. Landlords must now serve default notices wherever they wish to pursue a former tenant; furthermore, where a former tenant pays all the sums due under a default notice, he is entitled to require the grant of an overriding lease. As we have seen, these provisions apply not only to 'new' leases but also to 'old' leases to which the Act does not otherwise apply.[2]

1　See para 36.51 above.
2　See paras 36.43 and 36.44 above.

36.55 *Default notices*　No former tenant can be held liable for a 'fixed charge' unless, within six months of that charge becoming due the landlord serves on him a prescribed form of notice which informs him that the sum is now due, and the amount which is due, together with any interest thereon.[1] A 'fixed charge' is defined so as to cover rent, service charge payments and any other fixed sum payable in the event of a breach of covenant.[2] This prevents landlords allowing arrears to build up (on which a penal rate of interest is normally payable) without informing the former tenant. Where arrears continue to accrue the landlord must, of course, serve further default notices every six months in order to be able to pursue the former tenant.[3]

1　LTCA, s 17(2).
2　LTCA, s 17(6).
3　The service of regular default notices is a matter which will normally be left to a landlord's managing agent.

36.56 *Overriding leases*　A major defect in the law as it stood prior to 1995 was that a former tenant had no rights in respect of the demised premises. All original tenants, and any assignee who had signed a direct covenant,[1] could be held liable for all the obligations under the lease for the remainder of the lease, yet the current tenant could remain in occupation of the property.[2] The former tenants could sue the current tenant under their indemnity covenant (which would be worthless if the current tenant has no money) but could not regain the property. This has now been changed for all leases, 'old' and 'new'.

Where a former tenant pays all sums due under a default notice,[3] he is entitled to require the landlord to grant to him an overriding lease.[4] This overriding lease is, in effect, a concurrent lease (or lease of the reversion),[5] which sits between the landlord's reversion and the current tenant's lease; thus the former tenant becomes a direct tenant of the landlord and the landlord of the current tenant. This means that the former tenant can now take steps, as landlord, against the current tenant. In particular, he can forfeit the current tenant's lease and then either occupy the premises himself on the basis of the overriding lease, or assign the overriding lease to a reliable assignee who will thus take over its obligations.

1　See para 36.44 above.
2　Obviously the *landlord* can forfeit the lease, but may choose not to do so where there is a former tenant who is liable and able to meet all its obligations. This will particularly be the case where the premises are let on terms which are better than those which could now be achieved.
3　See para 36.55 above.
4　LTCA, s 19(1).
5　See para 36.17 above.

Sureties and sub-tenants
36.57　To conclude this section on the transmission of covenants we briefly consider the position of sureties and sub-tenants.

Sureties

36.58 For many years it has been the widespread practice of landlords to require a lease to be executed not just by the tenant but also by a surety (or guarantor). This does not make the surety a tenant, rather it commits the surety to the obligations imposed by the covenant of guarantee which is then included within the lease. The broad effect of such a covenant is to render the surety liable to the landlord in virtually[1] the same circumstances as the tenant would be liable; in other words the liability of the surety 'mirrors' that of the tenant he is guaranteeing. In particular this means that, where the tenant remains liable following the assignment of the lease, so does his surety. So, the surety of an original tenant under an 'old' lease will remain liable for the whole of the lease term, even after 'his' tenant has assigned. So far as 'new' leases are concerned, the 1995 Act has been drafted so as to ensure that sureties incur no greater liability than the tenant whom they are guaranteeing, and enjoy the same benefits. So, where a tenant is released from the tenant covenants, so is his surety;[2] where a former tenant is entitled to a default notice or an overriding lease, so is his surety.[3]

1   There are circumstances where a surety is released from liability where his principal is not, notably where, without his consent, the terms of the lease are varied in a material way.
2   LTCA, s 24(2).
3   LTCA, s 17(3), s 19(1). Note that these rights are accorded to sureties under 'old' leases as well.

Subtenants

36.59 The position where a tenant sub-lets is quite different from that where a tenant assigns:

Here T has created a sub-lease out of his own lease. In this case while there is a contract between L and T and a contract between T and S, there is no contract between L and S, nor are L and S in a relationship of landlord and tenant. Therefore enforcement between L and S of covenants contained in the head-lease (L–T) depends not on the foregoing rules but on the rules to be described in chapter 38.

Bringing leases to an end: the common law

36.60 At common law a lease may come to an end in a number of different ways. Those which we have not already dealt with, we outline in the following paragraphs. We consider how the common law concerning termination of leases has been altered by statute in paras 36.69 to 36.79 below.

Forfeiture

36.61 So long as there is an express provision within the lease (known as a right of re-entry) a landlord can terminate a lease where the tenant is in breach of covenant. We have already considered forfeiture in paras 36.32 to 36.35 and 36.39 above.

Surrender

36.62 A lease comes to an end where it is 'swallowed up' by the immediate landlord's reversion and is thus extinguished. Surrender of a leasehold interest may be effected by an express agreement[1] that the tenant is giving up his lease; this agreement should be in the form of a deed.[2] Surrender can also take place by operation of law. This will occur where the tenant gives up possession and the landlord accepts[1] this as surrender, or where the tenant takes a new lease from the landlord during the currency of the existing tenancy–this existing lease disappears.

1 It must be stressed that a surrender is *not* a unilateral act. A tenant cannot simply 'decide' that he no longer wishes to hold the lease; the landlord must agree that the lease is at an end.
2 LPA, s 52(1), see para 31.6 above.

Merger

36.63 This occurs where either the landlord's and the tenant's interests are acquired by a third party in the same capacity, or where the tenant acquires the landlord's reversion.

Expiry

36.64 At common law a lease for a fixed term of years comes to an end when that term expires without the need for notice from either party. The common law position is, however, much affected by statute.[1]

1 See paras 36.69–36.79 below.

Notice

36.65 A lease for a fixed term may not be determined by notice unless there is an express provision to that effect.[1] As we have seen,[2] periodic tenancies continue automatically until terminated by a notice to quit served by either party.[3] In the absence of any agreement to the contrary, a yearly tenancy may be determined by the service of no less than six months' notice expiring at the end of a period of the tenancy. In the case of other periodic tenancies, again in the absence of any agreement to the contrary, the minimum notice required at common law is equal to one full period of the tenancy; once again the notice must expire at the end of a period of the tenancy. So, a monthly tenancy can be terminated by the service of one month's notice expiring at the end of a month. These rules are subject to the overriding statutory requirement that, in the case of tenancies of residential premises, a notice to quit must be in writing[4] and must be for a minimum of four weeks.[5] Furthermore, the termination of leases by notice is also considerably affected in other respects by various statutes.[6]

1 Such options to terminate are known as break provisions; see para 36.12 above.
2 See para 36.13 above.
3 Where there are joint tenants or joint landlords, a notice to quit served by one only, without the knowledge or consent of the other(s), is effective to terminate the tenancy: *Hammersmith and Fulham London Borough Council v Monk* [1992] 1 AC 478, HL. It should be noted that this rule only applies where the notice is a valid notice to quit of the required length expiring at the end of a period of the tenancy. Any other notice will, in law, operate as a break notice; this requires the co-operation of all joint owners, *Hounslow London Borough Council v Pilling* (1993) 25 HLR 305, CA.
4 Protection from Eviction Act 1977, s 5(1)(a).
5 Ibid, s 5(1)(b). It should be noted that, as a result of an amendment introduced by the Housing Act 1988, s 5 no longer applies to tenancies where the tenant shares the home of the landlord or his immediate family.
6 See paras 36.69–36.79 below.

Enlargement

36.66 The LPA, s 153 provides that where a lease has been granted for a term of not less than 300 years, of which not less than 200 years are left unexpired, and either no rent or no rent having any money value is payable, the term of years may be enlarged into a fee simple (freehold) by the tenant executing a deed to that effect. Such a combination of circumstances is no doubt unlikely.

Frustration

36.67 A lease can be terminated as a result of the operation of the contractual doctrine of frustration, a matter which is discussed in para 11.9 above.

Disclaimer

36.68 Where a tenant becomes insolvent the tenant's trustee in bankruptcy or, in the case of a company tenant, liquidator (to whom the lease passes by operation of law) may disclaim it where the lease is not readily saleable.[1] This terminates the lease as against the insolvent tenant; however, the lease remains on foot for other purposes so that others, such as former tenants, or sureties will remain liable to the landlord.[2]

1 Insolvency Act 1986, ss 178, 315.
2 *Hindcastle Ltd v Barbara Attenborough Associates Ltd* [1996] 1 All ER 737, HL.

Statutory control of leases and tenancies

36.69 Our exposition of the law of landlord and tenant so far in this chapter deals with only half the story, for today the law relating to leases is much modified and qualified by statute. This statutory regulation is divided broadly into three areas: residential tenancies, business tenancies and agricultural tenancies. The nature of the regulation has been in two spheres in particular, rent control and security of tenure, though today the impact of legislation on the former is much reduced. A knowledge of this area of law is an important part of the study of estate management. However, we cannot, in a book of this nature, give more than the following brief reference to the statutory regulation of landlord and tenant.

Residential tenancies
Rent Act tenancies

36.70 The Rent Act 1977 applies to certain lettings of dwelling-houses, granted before 15 January 1989. Excluded from its application are, for example, houses with an annual rent above £25,000 or of £1,000 or less in Greater London (or £250 or less elsewhere),[1] tenancies where the rent includes an element for board or attendance, lettings to students by universities and colleges, and lettings where the landlord resides in another part of the same building (so long as this is not a purpose-built block of flats).

Such tenancies may terminate in accordance with the common law rules explained in the previous paragraph; however, on the termination of a protected contractual tenancy, provided the tenant is occupying the premises as his residence, there immediately arises a statutory tenancy,[2] on the same terms so far as consistent with the Act. This confers on the tenant, not an estate in the land, but a 'status of irremovability'.[3] The landlord under either a protected or statutory tenancy (known collectively as 'regulated tenancies') may not recover possession save by order of a county court which will only be granted in accordance with the provisions of the Rent Act 1977, s 98 and Sch 15. Possession will be granted where the court considers it reasonable to do so and either there is suitable alternative accommodation available to the tenant or the landlord makes out one of the discretionary cases for possession set out in the Act. The Act also provides for mandatory grounds for possession,[4] which, if made out, entitle the landlord as of right to regain possession. As regards rent control, the landlord or tenant may apply to the rent officer for the area for the determination and registration of a fair rent,[5] which must not thereafter be exceeded and which takes effect for two years. Either party can, after two years, apply for a re-registration of the rent; this is, in effect, the only means by which a landlord can achieve an increase in the rent.

1 Long tenancies (ie those in excess of 21 years) at a low rent fall within Pt I of the Landlord and Tenant Act 1954; tenants under such leases may also qualify for the rights conferred by the Leasehold Reform Act 1967 and the Leasehold Reform, Housing and Urban Development Act 1993, paras 36.55 and 36.56 below.
2 Rent Act 1977, s 2.
3 *Keeves v Dean* [1924] 1 KB 685 at 686.
4 These mandatory grounds usually only apply where the landlord has served notice to this effect on the tenant at the commencement of the tenancy.
5 The basis on which a 'fair rent' is to be ascertained is defined in the Rent Act, 1977, s 70. In particular, any element of scarcity must he ignored which means that fair rents are noticeably lower than market rents.

Housing Act tenancies

36.71 *Assured tenancies* Where a tenancy of a dwelling house is granted on or after 15 January 1989 and prior to 28 February 1997,[1] it will be an assured tenancy under the Housing Act 1988, so long as the tenant is an individual who occupies the property as his only or principal home.[2] As with the Rent Act, certain tenancies are excluded, such as those of dwelling-houses let at a rent above or below prescribed limits or let by educational institutions to students; also excluded are lettings by a resident landlord.[3] Where such a tenancy is entered into on or after 28 February 1997, it will only be an assured tenancy (as opposed to an assured shorthold tenancy[4]) where a notice to that effect is served on the tenant;[5] accordingly, most tenancies which satisfy the above criteria will henceforth be assured shorthold rather than assured tenancies.[4]

Where a fixed-term assured tenancy expires a statutory periodic tenancy arises (the periods of which are those in respect of which rent was payable under the fixed term).[6] A periodic assured tenancy, including one arising on the ending of a fixed term, cannot be terminated by the landlord serving a notice to quit.[7] To determine an assured tenancy, the landlord must serve on the tenant a statutory notice seeking possession in prescribed form specifying the ground(s) on which possession will be sought and stating that proceedings will commence within a specified period.[8] As with the Rent Act, the 1988 Act provides for discretionary and mandatory grounds for possession, though some of these grounds are new or differ in detail. Of particular note is the new mandatory ground based on two months' rent arrears; this provides the only opportunity for a landlord, whose tenant is in default, to recover possession as of right.

The Housing Act 1988 does not in any real sense impose rent control. Wherever an assured periodic tenancy does not contain its own provisions for rent review the Act provides a statutory mechanism under which a landlord can, by the service of a prescribed form of notice, seek to increase the rent; such a notice can be served every year.[9] A tenant who objects to the landlord's proposed rent may refer the notice to a rent assessment committee; where this is done the committee will determine the new rent by reference to open-market rental value.[10]

1 The date on which amendments to the Housing Act 1988, introduced by the Housing Act 1996, came into effect.
2 Housing Act 1988, s 1. In the case of joint tenants, each must be an individual, though only one need occupy the premises as his home.
3 Ibid, s 1 and Sch 1.
4 See para 36.72 below.
5 Housing Act 1988, s 19A, Sch 2A (inserted by Housing Act 1996, s 96).
6 Ibid, s 5.

7   Ibid, ss 5, 7.
8   Ibid, s 8. In *Mountain v Hastings* (1993) 25 HLR 427, CA it was held that, in order to be valid, the
    notice must identify all the elements which make up the statutory ground on which reliance is to be
    placed.
9   Ibid, s 13
10 Ibid, s 14.

36.72   *Assured shorthold tenancies*   The 1988 Act also allows for the creation of
assured shorthold tenancies.[1] For tenancies created on or after 15 January 1989 and
before 28 February 1997, these are assured tenancies which satisfy certain additional
criteria. These are that the tenancy is for a term of not less than six months, in respect
of which the landlord has, *before the commencement of the tenancy*, served on the
tenant a notice in prescribed form stating that the tenancy is an assured shorthold
tenancy[2], and which does not contain any provision (other than a forfeiture provision)
allowing the landlord to terminate the tenancy within six months.

As with an assured tenancy, once the initial fixed term expires, a statutory periodic
tenancy arises. This may be terminated by the landlord in accordance with the
provisions outlined in the previous paragraph. However, there is an important additional
means by which an assured shorthold, and any statutory periodic tenancy arising after
the expiry of an assured shorthold, may be brought to an end under the Act. If the
landlord serves at least two months' notice on the tenant stating that he requires
possession, which notice may be given either before or on the expiry of the fixed term
or to expire at the end of a period of the periodic tenancy, then the court *must* order
possession.[3]

A tenancy granted on or after 28 February 1997 which satisfies the basic
requirements of an assured tenancy outlined in the para 36.71, whether it be periodic
or for a fixed term of *any* length, will be an assured shorthold tenancy unless a notice
is served on the tenant stating that it is to be an assured tenancy.[4] Hence, in practice,
Housing Act tenancies created after this date will virtually always be assured shortholds.
This new style assured shorthold tenancy is terminable in the same way as the old style
shorthold; in particular, it can be brought to an end by the service of at least two months'
notice expiring no earlier than the end of a period of any periodic tenancy, or the end
of any fixed term. However, where such a notice expires *less than six months* after the
commencement of the tenancy and the tenant does not leave voluntarily, a court cannot
make an order for possession which will take effect before the end of that six-month
period.[5] This means that, irrespective of the fact that a shorter lease might have been
agreed, the landlord under an assured shorthold cannot be certain of regaining
possession within six months. Put another way, the tenant under such a tenancy has
security of tenure for at least six months.[6]

The relative ease with which possession may be obtained in the case of an assured
shorthold tenancy means that, as there is no maximum period for such a tenancy (despite
its name), landlords have always preferred to grant an assured shorthold tenancy rather
than an assured tenancy. The amendments introduced by the 1996 Act have made it
easier for landlords to achieve this objective by removing the additional criteria for
the creation of the shorthold.[7] The only theoretical drawback of an assured shorthold
tenancy for landlords is that a tenant is entitled to refer the *initial* rent to a rent
assessment committee; however, the committee's jurisdiction is limited and is designed
only to ensure that the landlord does not charge a rent which is *in excess* of market
rents and there is little evidence that such references are in fact made.[8]

1   Ibid, ss 20 –22.
2   The failure to serve such a notice, or the service of an invalid notice, will mean that the resulting
    tenancy cannot be an assured shorthold and the tenant will have the 'full' protection afforded to an
    assured tenant.

3   Housing Act 1988, s 21.
4   Housing Act 1988, s 19A inserted by the Housing Act 1996, s 96 and Sch 2A.
5   Housing Act 1988, s 21(5) inserted by the Housing Act 1996, s 99.
6   Where the tenancy is for longer than six months the tenant cannot, of course, be removed until the end
     of the agreed term, except where he is in breach of covenant.
7   The need for a *prior* notice was often overlooked by landlords with the result that many pre-1997 assured
     shortholds were in reality fully assured tenancies.
8   Ibid, s 22.

Secure tenancies in the public sector

36.73   The Housing Act 1985, Pt IV, confers security of tenure on public sector tenants
and licensees, for example, tenants of local authorities. Their 'secure tenancies' may
not be terminated save by a county court order for possession on specified grounds.[1]
There is no statutory control of rents; indeed, local authorities are now required to fix
rents in line with those in the private sector.[2] Certain public sector tenants do, however,
have a 'right to buy' at a price discounted in accordance with the length of time for
which they have been tenants.[3]

1   Housing Act 1985, s 82.
2   Ibid, s 24(3), (4).
3   Ibid, s 118.

Long residential tenancies

36.74   *Security of tenure* Tenants of residential premises let on leases in excess of
21 years at a low rent (ie an annual rent of £1,000 or less in Greater London, £250 or
less elsewhere) are given security of tenure at the expiry of the term, by virtue of Pt I
of the Landlord and Tenant Act 1954.[1] Their existing lease is automatically continued
on the same terms, including as to rent. The continued tenancy may be terminated by
the landlord giving to the tenant between six and twelve months' notice either offering
a statutory tenancy or, in the case of leases granted after 1 April 1990, an assured
tenancy, or stating that the landlord will seek a possession order from the court on
grounds stated in the Act, which are essentially the same as the discretionary grounds
provided for under the Rent Act (or Housing Act). This protection will now rarely be
necessary since such tenants will often, in practice, exercise the rights to enfranchise
or to extend their existing leases discussed in the next paragraph.

1   As amended by the Local Government and Housing Act 1989, s 186 and Sch 10 in respect of long
     tenancies granted on or after 1 April 1990.

36.75   *Enfranchisement*   Residential tenants under long leases of both houses and
flats now have extensive rights to enfranchise. By virtue of the Leasehold Reform Act
1967, as amended, where a tenant has occupied as his residence for three years a *house*
which was originally let for a fixed term of over 21 years at a low rent, he can, by
serving notice on the landlord, require that the freehold of the property be transferred
to him, or alternatively that he be granted a new lease in substitution for his existing
lease, for a term expiring 50 years from the end of the existing lease. This alternative
is rarely sought. The price or rent to be paid is to be determined in accordance with a
formula laid down in the Act.

Tenants under long leases of *flats* now have, in certain circumstances, a right,
together with other tenants in the same building, collectively to acquire the freehold
of that building.[1] Alternatively, a tenant may exercise an individual right to acquire an
extended lease; this takes the form of a new lease for 90 years plus the outstanding
period of the old lease.[2] Again, the price to be paid is prescribed by the Act.

1   Leasehold Reform, Housing and Urban Development Act 1993, s 1.
2   Ibid, s 35.

Business tenancies

36.76 Business tenancies[1] are regulated by Pt II of the Landlord and Tenant Act 1954. The term 'business' is very widely defined, to include a trade, profession or employment or any activity carried on by a body of persons.[2] The policy of the Act is to provide security of tenure for tenants who have established themselves in business in leasehold premises so that they can continue to carry on their business there. The Act provides that business tenancies do not come to an end by expiry or by common law notice. Save where the tenant ceases business occupation by the end of the term,[3] they are statutorily continued[4] until terminated in accordance with the Act.

The landlord can only terminate the lease by giving between six and twelve months' notice, in prescribed form, ending no sooner than the tenancy could or would have ended at common law.[5] Even where the landlord does give notice in this way, the tenant may apply to court, within strict time limits, for a new tenancy.[6] The landlord may only oppose such an application on certain statutory grounds: for example, because he intends to redevelop the property or intends to occupy the premises for the purposes of his business.[7]

Where the tenant wishes to initiate the procedures under the Act for obtaining a new tenancy, he can do so by serving a request for a new tenancy, giving between six and 12 months' notice, in prescribed form, expiring no sooner than the existing tenancy would have come to an end at common law.[8] Where this procedure is used, the tenant must still apply to court, within strict time limits, for the grant of a new tenancy. Again, the landlord has the right to oppose the grant of a new lease, but only on one of the statutory grounds. Where the tenant wishes to quit he may serve notice to that effect, at least three months before the end of the term where the lease is for a fixed term.[9] However, it appears that such a notice is not essential provided the tenant actually ceases business occupation by the end of the lease.[3] Once the tenancy has been continued under the Act, the tenant can then only terminate the lease by serving at least three months' notice expiring on a quarter day.[10]

The terms of any new tenancy granted may be such as agreed by the parties or, in default, as determined by the court.[11] Subject to certain statutory 'disregards', the rent under the new lease will be an open market rent.[12]

A high proportion of business leases in England and Wales are governed by the 1954 Act.[13] On the whole, the Act works well since landlords of this type of property are usually content for the existing tenant to remain in the premises so long as they are paying rent at current market levels (which is what, in principle, the legislation achieves).

1   Excluding, for example, mining leases, tenancies for a term not exceeding six months except where the tenant has been in occupation for more than 12 months, and leases 'contracted out' of the Act with the prior approval of the court.
2   Landlord and Tenant Act 1954, s 23.
3   *Esselte AB v Pearl Assurance plc* [1997] 2 All ER 41, CA.
4   Ibid, s 24.
5   Ibid, s 25.
6   Ibid, ss 24 and 29.
7   Ibid, s 30.
8   Ibid, s 26.
9   Ibid, s 27(1). A tenant under a periodic tenancy can terminate by serving an appropriate notice to quit; para 36.65 above.
10 Ibid, s 27(2).
11 Ibid, ss 33–35.
12 Ibid, s 34.
13 Despite the fact that it is possible to contract out of the Act; see note 1 above.

Agricultural tenancies

36.77   Most agricultural tenancies are regulated by one of two statutory schemes of protection. Those granted prior to 1 September 1995 are, where appropriate, governed by the Agricultural Holdings Act 1986. Those granted on or after that date are given very much more limited protection under the Agricultural Tenancies Act 1995.

Agricultural holdings

36.78   An agricultural holding is land (whether agricultural land or not), comprised in a contract for an agricultural tenancy. A contract for an agricultural tenancy is a contract of tenancy, other than one granted on or after 1 September 1995,[1] under which the whole of the land is let for use as agricultural land for the purposes of a trade or business. 'A contract of tenancy' is defined so as to include a lease or agreement for a lease for a term of years or from year to year; furthermore, it is provided that any letting of land less than a tenancy from year to year, or any licence to occupy such land, is to take effect as if it were an agreement for a tenancy from year to year.

A tenancy for a fixed term of two years or more[2] continues, on expiry, as a tenancy from year to year unless and until either party serves a notice to quit; this provision is modified where the tenant dies before the term expires and may be contracted out of, with approval of the minister.[3] As a general rule, an agricultural tenancy may only be terminated by a notice to quit of at least 12 months. On the service of such notice by the landlord, the tenant may serve a counter-notice, the effect of which is to prevent the notice to quit operating without the consent of the Agricultural Land Tribunal. The Tribunal is to withhold consent if satisfied that in all the circumstances a fair and reasonable landlord would not insist on possession, but subject to this it may consent to the notice operating if, for example, the landlord proposes to terminate the tenancy in the interest of good husbandry or the sound management of the estate.[4] In a number of cases the tenant may not serve a counter-notice and thus has no security, for example where the land is required for a non-agricultural use for which planning permission has been granted.[5] The 1986 Act confers some protection in respect of rent; either the landlord or the tenant may apply for the rent to be submitted to arbitration.[6] Such applications cannot be made more frequently than every three years.

1   Agricultural Tenancies Act 1995, s 4(1). This section does provide for the 1986 Act to apply in certain exceptional cases to tenancies granted on or after 1 September 1995.
2   It should be noted that, perhaps curiously, the scheme of the Act is such that a tenancy for a fixed term of at least 12 months but less than two years is a lease of an agricultural holding so that, for example, the other major statutory schemes of protection are excluded. However, it is *not* afforded any security of tenure under the 1986 Act since it is not made to continue, after expiry, as a tenancy from year to year. See *Gladstone v Bower* [1960] 2 QB 384, [1960] 3 All ER 353, CA. A recent attempt to challenge this decision has been rejected in *EWP Ltd v Moore* [1992] QB 460, [1992] 1 All ER 880, CA.
3   Agricultural Holdings Act 1986, ss 1–5.
4   Ibid, ss 25–27.
5   Ibid, Sch 3.
6   Ibid, ss 12, 84 and Sch 2.

Farm business tenancies

36.79   The Agricultural Tenancies Act 1995 applies to farm business tenancies granted on or after 1 September 1995. A farm business tenancy is one[1] under which all or part of the land comprised in the tenancy is farmed for the purposes of a business and has been so farmed since the beginning of the tenancy.[2] It is essential that the character of the tenancy is, at all times, primarily or wholly agricultural,[3] with the result that the tenancy can move in and out of the 1995 Act. At any time when it is outside that Act, ie when the tenancy is not primarily or wholly agricultural, it could, provided that there is business use of part, move into the protection of Pt II of the Landlord and

Tenant Act 1954.[4] This possibility can be avoided by each party giving notice to the other, at or before the beginning of the tenancy, that the tenancy is to be and to remain a farm business tenancy.[5]

A tenant under a farm business tenancy has only very limited statutory protection. Where the tenancy is a periodic tenancy other than a yearly tenancy, or where it is for a fixed term of two years or less, the tenancy comes to an end in accordance with the normal common law rules. Accordingly, it will either come to an end by effluxion of time,[6] or by means of a normal notice to quit served by either party.[7] A tenancy for a fixed term of more than two years, can only be brought to an end by one of the parties serving a notice to terminate in writing at least 12 months and less than 24 months before it is due to take effect; in the meantime the tenancy continues as a tenancy from year to year.[8] Similarly, a yearly tenancy can only be brought to an end by the service of a notice to quit, in writing, given at least 12 months and less than 24 months before the end of a year of the tenancy.[9] In neither case is there a need for there to be any grounds for the termination of the tenancy.

Part II of the 1995 Act sets out statutory provisions for rent review. These apply in all cases unless there is an express provision in a written lease which[10] either:

- states that the rent is not to be reviewed during the tenancy, or
- provides for the rent to be varied by a specified amount,[11] or
- provides for the rent to be varied in an upwards or downwards direction in accordance with a formula which does not require or permit the exercise by any person of any judgment or discretion in relation to the determination of the rent.[12]

1 Unlike the 1986 Act, the 1995 Act does not apply to licences; see Agricultural Tenancies Act 1995, s 38(1).
2 Ibid, s 1.
3 Ibid, s 1(3).
4 See para 36.76 above.
5 Ibid, s 1(4).
6 See para 36.64 above.
7 See para 36.65 above.
8 Ibid, s 5.
9 Ibid, s 6.
10 Ibid, s 9.
11 Eg a stepped rent.
12 Eg a rent which moves upwards or downwards in line with a specified index such as the Retail Price Index.

Chapter 37

Easements

37.1   We now turn our attention to one of the most important of the third party rights to land, the easement. As we shall see, there are a number of different types of easement (such as rights of way, rights of support, rights of drainage, rights of light) but they all share the same basic characteristics. Easements are irrevocable rights which one landowner enjoys in respect of his neighbour's land and, as such, they provide what is often an essential basis for the full enjoyment of land ownership. Many pieces of land or buildings or parts of buildings cannot be properly utilised without the existence of rights over adjoining property: for example, the tenant of a first floor flat will need a right of way over the ground floor of the premises; the owner of a semi-detached house needs support from the adjoining 'semi'.

In this chapter we consider:

- the essential legal characteristics of an easement;
- the methods by which easements can be created or acquired; and
- certain specific easements.

The nature of easement

37.2   An easement is a right which one landowner enjoys in respect of his neighbour's land; it may be legal or equitable.[1] Some idea of the nature of easements may be gathered from the following dictum of Lord Denning:[2] 'There are two kinds of easements known to the law: positive easements, such as a right of way, which give the owner of land *a right himself to do something* on or to his neighbour's land: and negative easements, such as a right of light, which give him *a right to stop his neighbour doing something* on his (the neighbour's) own land.'

The nature of an easement is best explained by reference to Cheshire's[3] four essential characteristics of an easement, approved by the Court of Appeal in *Re Ellenborough Park, Re Davies, Powell v Maddison*.[4] In this case, the Court held that the right to use a park or garden adjacent to a group of houses was an easement attaching to those houses. The Court reached its decision by considering whether the following four requirements were satisfied:

- there must be a dominant and a servient piece of land;

- the easement must 'accommodate' the dominant land;
- the dominant and servient owners must be different persons; and
- the right must be capable of forming the subject matter of a grant.

Each of these will now be considered.

1   Para 37.21 below.
2   *Phipps v Pears* [1965] 1 QB 76 at 82, [1964] 2 All ER 35 at 37.
3   *Modern Law of Real Property* (14th edn) pp 492–496.
4   [1956] Ch 131, [1955] 3 All ER 667, CA.

The essential characteristics of an easement
There must be a dominant and servient piece of land
37.3   This is another way of saying that there must be land which enjoys the right (the dominant land) and land which is subject to the right (the servient land). An easement takes effect for the benefit of *land*; it is annexed to that land and passes automatically on its transfer. An easement cannot exist independently of the ownership of land; it exists in respect of, and in amplification of, an owner's enjoyment of some estate or interest in a piece of land.[1] Thus there can be no grant of an easement at a time when the dominant land has not yet been identified, so that it is not possible to create easements in favour of land which has yet to be acquired.[2]

1   *Alfred F Beckett Ltd v Lyons* [1967] Ch 449 at 483, [1967] 1 All ER 833, CA.
2   *London and Blenheim Estates Ltd v Ladbroke Retail Parks Ltd* [1993] 4 All ER 157, CA. See also *Voice v Bell* (1993) 68 P & CR 441, CA.

The easement must 'accommodate' the dominant land
37.4   This means that an easement must be of benefit to the dominant land. There must be a clear connection between the enjoyment of the right and the enjoyment of the dominant land. In *Re Ellenborough Park*,[1] the court held that the park became a communal garden for the benefit and enjoyment of those whose houses adjoined it or were in its close proximity; it was the collective garden of the neighbouring houses. The necessary connection between the right and the land was thus shown. In contrast, a right given to the purchaser of a house to attend Lord's cricket ground without payment would not constitute an easement, for, although it would confer an advantage on the purchaser and doubtless would increase the value of the property, it would be wholly extraneous to, and independent of, the use of the house as a house.[2]

Similarly, in *Hill v Tupper*,[3] the tenant of premises on the bank of the Basingstoke Canal was given the 'sole and exclusive right' by the owners to put pleasure boats on the canal. He subsequently brought an action against the defendant, who had also started to hire out pleasure boats on the canal, alleging that the latter was interfering with his easement. This claim failed; the court held that the plaintiff merely had a contractual licence, giving him rights against the licensors (the owners of the canal) but not against the defendant. As this case was explained in *Re Ellenborough Park*,[4] the plaintiff was trying to set up, under the guise of an easement, a monopoly which had no normal connection with the ordinary use of his land but which was merely an independent business enterprise. So far from the right claimed accommodating the land, the land was but a convenient incident to the exercise of the right.

This is not to say that a right which primarily benefits a business may not also be held to accommodate the land from which that business is operated. Thus, in *Moody v Steggles*,[5] it was held that the right to affix an inn sign on adjoining property accommodated the plaintiff's public house. The question would seem to depend on whether the court is prepared to find an intimate connection between the land and the business carried on there.[6]

1   [1956] Ch 131, [1955] 3 All ER 667, CA.
2   Ibid, at 173.
3   (1863) 2 H & C 121.
4   [1956] Ch 131 at 175.
5   (1879) 12 Ch D 261. See also *William Hill (Southern) Ltd v Cabras Ltd* [1987] 1 EGLR 37, CA where the right to erect the name of a business on adjoining property was held to be an easement.
6   In *Clapman v Edwards* [1938] 2 All ER 507 a *general* right to advertise on adjoining premises was held not to be an easement since there was no connection with the land.

37.5   It may not be possible to demonstrate the necessary connection between enjoyment of the right and the dominant land where the dominant and servient properties are at some distance from each other: 'a right of way over land in Northumberland cannot accommodate land in Kent'.[1] On the other hand, it is not necessary that the properties be adjoining. In *Re Ellenborough Park*,[2] a few of the houses having the benefit of the use of the park were some 100 yards from it: nonetheless, the court held that the necessary connection between dominant and servient tenement existed. Again, in *Pugh v Savage*,[3] the owner of field C was held entitled to an easement of way across field A to reach the nearby highway despite the existence of field B, which he had a licence to cross, between the two properties.

1   *Bailey v Stephens* (1862) 12 CBNS 91; see also *Todrick v Western National Omnibus Co Ltd* [1934] Ch 561, CA.
2   [1956] Ch 131, [1955] 3 All ER 667, CA.
3   [1970] 2 QB 373, [1970] 2 All ER 353, CA.

The dominant and servient owners must be different persons
37.6   Clearly, as an easement is a right over another's land, one cannot have an easement over one's own land. However, the freehold owner of two plots may grant an easement over one plot to the tenant of the other, and a tenant may expressly or impliedly grant an easement to another tenant of the same landlord. Where the owner of two plots of land uses a way across one plot to reach the other, he is clearly doing so as owner rather than by virtue of an easement; nevertheless, it is sometimes said that he enjoys a 'quasi-easement'. We consider the relevance of quasi-easements in para 37.26 below.

The right must be capable of forming the subject matter of a grant, ie be capable of being granted
37.7   This requirement comprises a number of elements some of which are 'technical' and others of which are more policy based. So, the right claimed must be one which can be formulated in a deed of grant by a capable grantor to a capable grantee. For example, a tenant cannot grant an easement in fee simple, nor can an easement be granted to a fluctuating group of persons. However, the recognition of 'new' easements raises policy issues. Although there is no fixed list of easements, the courts do control the rights which will be recognised as easements. Easements are powerful rights which last for as long as the interest to which they are attached. So, an easement for the benefit of a freehold estate is, in reality, indefinite; an easement attached to a leasehold estate will continue for as long as the lease. Furthermore, as we shall see, easements do not always originate in an express agreement between neighbouring landowners; they can arise by implication or as a result of prescription (long use). For these reasons a court, when deciding whether a type of right, which has never previously been accepted as an easement, should be so recognised, will take into account three particular factors which are accepted as delimiting the nature of an easement.

37.8   *Sufficiently definite* The first factor is whether the right claimed is one which is of too wide and vague a character,[1] rendering it difficult to define in a deed of grant.

It is on this basis that the courts have refused to allow as an easement a claim to a general right of light for one's land;[2] such rights can only exist as an easement in respect of a defined aperture.[3] Similarly, the right to the general passage of air over one's land cannot exist as an easement,[4] but a right to air to a defined aperture can.[5] The extent of the right claimed can in the latter case be expressed with some precision. In *Phipps v Pears*,[6] the Court of Appeal had to decide whether the right to have one's property protected from the weather could exist as an easement. One of two houses, which were very close together but which did not actually support each other, was demolished, thereby exposing to the elements the wall of the other house, which had never been rendered or plastered. Reflecting the policy considerations which must always be present when a claim to a new type of easement is decided, the Court rejected the claim to an easement on the basis that this was a claim to a *negative* easement,[7] new examples of which the law was said to be chary of creating since they restrict the servient owner in the enjoyment of his own land and hamper legitimate development. We think that the court could instead have based its decision on the fact that the right claimed was of too wide and vague a character, since it could be said that all easements, whether positive or negative, restrict the servient owner in the enjoyment of his land to some degree.

1   *Re Ellenborough Park* [1956] Ch 131, [1955] 3 All ER 667, CA.
2   See *Roberts v Macord* (1832) 1 Mood & R 230.
3   Para 37.47 below.
4   *Webb v Bird* (1861) 10 CBNS 268.
5   *Bryant v Lefever* (1879) 4 CPD 172.
6   [1965] 1 QB 76, [1964] 2 All ER 35, CA.
7   Para 37.1 above.

37.9 *No joint possession* A second relevant factor in the decision whether to recognise a claim to an easement is that it must not amount to a claim to use and enjoy the servient land either exclusively, or jointly with the servient owner. An easement is a right which is compatible with the servient owner's right to exclusive possession of his own land. In *Copeland v Greenhalf*,[1] the defendant claimed that he was entitled to an easement to store vehicles awaiting and undergoing repair on a strip of land opposite his premises. Upjohn J rejected the claim as being virtually a claim to possession of the servient land, since it involved the defendant and his employees being able to carry out repair work on the land and involved the defendant leaving as many vehicles on the land as he wished, thereby effectively treating the land as his own.[2] Similarly, in *Grigsby v Melville*[3] it was held that an unlimited right to store items in an adjoining cellar could not amount to an easement.

It does not follow, however, that an easement to store articles on another's land cannot exist. The possibility was recognised in *A-G of Southern Nigeria v John Holt & Co (Liverpool) Ltd*,[4] and in *Wright v Macadam*[5] it was held, without argument on the point, that the right to store coal in a coal shed was clearly an easement. The question is, no doubt, one of degree. Thus, in *Miller v Emcer Products Ltd*,[6] a case demonstrating that the categories of easements are not closed, the Court of Appeal held that a right to use a neighbour's lavatory could exist as an easement. The Court pointed out that, although at the times when the dominant owner exercised his right the owner of the servient tenement would be excluded, this was a common feature to a greater or lesser extent of many easements, such as a right of way, and in any case this did not amount to so complete an ouster of the servient owner's rights as was held to be incompatible with an easement in *Copeland v Greenhalf*. In *London and Blenheim Estates Ltd v Ladbroke Retail Parks Ltd*[7] the view was expressed that a right to park a car anywhere within a defined area can be an easement; a right to park in a particular slot, to the exclusion of the servient owner, would not be.

1   [1952] Ch 488, [1952] 1 All ER 809.
2   Such facts might provide a basis for a claim to the *ownership* of the land under the principles of adverse possession: see paras 32.19–32.31 above.
3   [1973] 1 All ER 385, [1972] 1 WLR 1355.
4   [1915] AC 599, PC.
5   [1949] 2 KB 744, [1949] 2 All ER 565, CA.
6   [1956] Ch 304, [1956] 1 All ER 237, CA.
7   [1993] 1 All ER 307, affirmed by the Court of Appeal on another point.

37.10   *No expense for servient owner*   A third factor to be considered is that the easement claimed must not necessarily involve the servient owner in expenditure. An easement is either a right to do something or a right to prevent something. A right to have something done is not an easement, nor is it an incident of an easement.[1] Thus an agreement by a landlord to supply hot water and heating to the tenants of a block does not give rise to an easement;[2] rights such as these can only exist as express contracts or covenants. However, both a right to a supply of water[3], and a supply of electricity,[4] through meters located on the servient land and for payment of which the servient owner was responsible, have been analysed as easements for the passage of water and electricity respectively. In both instances the dominant owner would, by implication, be liable to reimburse the servient owner for the costs of the supply to the dominant tenement.

There is, furthermore, long-established authority that the owner of the servient tenement, though he must not act in such a way as to interfere with the enjoyment of the easement by the dominant owner, is not bound, in the absence of an express or implied contractual obligation,[5] to carry out any repairs necessary to ensure the enjoyment of the easement by the dominant owner; on the other hand, the grant of an easement does, ordinarily, confer on the dominant owner the right to enter the servient property to effect necessary repairs[6] and, where necessary to the enjoyment of the right by the dominant tenement, to make improvements (eg to a right of way).[7] It may now be the case, however, that the servient owner may be liable in negligence or nuisance if he fails to take reasonable steps to repair defects which he is aware or ought to have been aware threaten to interfere with the dominant owner's easement.[8]

An exception to the rule that the right claimed must not involve the servient owner in expenditure is provided by the easement, or 'spurious easement', of fencing. 'The right to have your neighbour keep up the fences is a right in the nature of an easement which is capable of being granted by law'.[9] The cases involve fencing against straying animals, but the principle would not appear to be so limited.

1   *Jones v Price* [1965] 2 QB 618 at 631, [1965] 2 All ER 625 at 628, CA.
2   *Regis Property Co Ltd v Redman* [1956] 2 QB 612, [1956] 2 All ER 335, CA.
3   *Rance v Elvin* (1985) 50 P & CR 9, CA.
4   *Duffy v Lamb* [1997] NPC 52, CA.
5   See *Liverpool City Council v Irwin* [1977] AC 239, [1976] 2 All ER 39, HL and *King v South Northamptonshire District Council* (1991) 64 P & CR 35, CA, two cases in which the courts were prepared to imply a contractual obligation on the part of a landlord to repair and maintain an essential means of access to the demised property; see para 36.22 above.
6   *Jones v Pritchard* [1908] 1 Ch 630.
7   The dominant owner may not, however, carry out works which amount to an improvement which increases the burden on the servient land where the right has been acquired by prescription (for which see paras 37.33–37.44 below). See *Mills v Silver* [1991] 1 All ER 449, CA where it was held that the dominant owner was not entitled to improve the surface of a right of way.
8   *Bradburn v Lindsay* [1983] 2 All ER 408; para 37.43 below.
9   *Crow v Wood* [1971] 1 QB 77 at 84–85, [1970] 3 All ER 425 at 429, CA.

Rights similar to easements

37.11   Under this heading we further explain the nature of easements by considering rights which are similar to easements and, in each case, what it is which differentiates them from easements.

Natural rights

37.12 Every landowner enjoys certain natural rights against neighbouring landowners. Unlike easements, these rights flow automatically from the ownership of land; they do not depend on any form of creation. Every landowner has the right to receive support for his land from that of his neighbour.[1] Further, as we have seen,[2] all landowners have certain limited right to water.

1 See further para 37.50 below.
2 Para 30.17 above.

Restrictive covenants[1]

37.13 A similarity between easements and restrictive covenants can be seen in that both require dominant and servient land.[2] Indeed, restrictive covenants were described by Sir George Jessel MR[3] as being an extension in equity of the doctrine of negative easements, such as the easements of light and of support. However, there are important differences. Restrictive covenants must be expressly created; as we shall see, easements may be implied, and can be acquired as a result of long use (ie by prescription).[4] Again, as we shall see, restrictive covenants are equitable only, whereas easements may be legal or equitable. Furthermore, it may be that the content of a restrictive covenant is not limited in the same way as that of easements. So, for example, while the right to a view is too vague to exist as an easement,[5] the same objective may be achieved by the imposition of a restrictive covenant preventing development which obstructs the view.[6] Certainly, save for the requirement that a restrictive covenant be negative,[7] the courts do not exercise control over the type of rights which can exist by way of restrictive covenant; as we have seen,[8] policy considerations do dictate the nature of rights which will be accepted as easements. Finally, as we shall see,[9] there are recognised circumstances in which both the common law and, more particularly, statute allows for restrictive covenants to be modified or discharged. There is no such provision for the removal of easements; indeed, once created, the law is most reluctant to extinguish an easement.[10]

1 Ch 38 below.
2 See para 38.10 below.
3 *London and South Western Rly Co v Gomm* (1882) 20 Ch D 562.
4 See paras 37.23–37.44 below.
5 *Aldred's Case* (1610) 9 Co Rep 57b.
6 *Wakeham v Wood* (1981) 43 P & CR 40, CA, para 39.27 below; and see *Gilbert v Spoor* [1983] Ch 27, [1982] 2 All ER 576, CA, para 38.39 below.
7 See para 38.9 below.
8 Paras 37.7–37.10 above.
9 See paras 38.28–38.41 below.
10 See para 37.45 below.

Licences[1]

37.14 The right to walk across another's field, for example, may exist either as an easement or a licence. The latter differs from the former in that it can, in general, be revoked. Moreover, a licence is a personal right not a proprietary right; it requires no dominant land and, unless supported by some equity, can only be enforced against the licensor, and not against any subsequent owner of the licensor's land.[2]

1 Paras 30.36–30.42 above.
2 See para 30.40 above.

Non-derogation from grant[1]

37.15 Where a person conveys or leases land *for a specific purpose*, he is under an obligation not to use the land retained by him in such a way as to render the land conveyed or leased unfit, or materially less fit, for the particular purpose for which the conveyance or lease was made.[2] *Aldin v Latimer Clark, Muirhead & Co*[3] illustrates how this principle may confer greater rights than may be conferred as an easement. Land was let to the plaintiff to enable him to carry on the business of a timber merchant. It was held that the landlord could not build on his retained land so as to interrupt the free passage of air to the plaintiff's timber-drying sheds. A general right to air such as this could not have existed as an easement; the easement to the free passage of air is limited to one through a defined aperture.[4]

1   Para 36.21 above.
2   *Browne v Flower* [1911] 1 Ch 219 at 226.
3   [1894] 2 Ch 437.
4   Para 37.8 above.

Profits à prendre

37.16 A profit à prendre is a right to take from another's land the natural produce of the land, minerals, or wild animals on the land. The most important modern day examples of profits are: the profit of pasture (ie a grazing right), whereby grass (a natural product of the land) is taken from the land by being eaten by the profit-owner's animals; the rights to take gravel and minerals from the land; the rights to catch fish and shoot game.

37.17 A profit may be legal or equitable.[1] In the case of registered land a profit which is not entered on the register is an overriding interest whether it is legal or equitable.[2]

A profit may be several or in common. A 'several' profit is owned by one person to the exclusion of others. A profit in common (or simply 'common') is owned in common with others. A common pasture is perhaps the most important type of profit in common. This is often encountered in hill-farming areas whereby a number of farms may enjoy the right to graze stock on the adjoining hills and mountains.

A profit may be appurtenant or in gross. If appurtenant, it is, like an easement, annexed to a dominant tenement. If so, the profit is limited to the needs of the dominant land. For example, an appurtenant profit of pasture will be limited to the number of cattle or sheep which the dominant land is capable of supporting. A profit in gross is owned independently of land and is unconnected with any dominant tenement. Nevertheless, it is still a right in land.

Profits are acquired in much the same way as easements,[3] with some variations as to detail. In particular, a profit in gross cannot be acquired by prescription.

1   The rules outlined in para 37.21 below apply also to profits.
2   Para 35.21 above.
3   Paras 37.20–37.44 below.

37.18 Under the Commons Registration Act 1965, any common right or common land (ie land subject to common rights) existing before 2 January 1970 must have been registered in the appropriate county council's register of commons before 31 July 1970, otherwise it ceased to be exerciseable. Should any new common land come into existence, registration under the Act is again required.

Customary rights

37.19 Customary rights are not public rights, available to the general public at large, but are confined to the inhabitants of a particular locality. They differ from easements in that there is no necessity for dominant land and in that they are not capable of forming the subject matter of a grant, since a fluctuating body of inhabitants is not a capable grantee. A customary right must be ancient, continuous, certain and reasonable.[1] Examples include the right of fishermen of a particular parish to dry their nets on private land[2] and the right of the inhabitants of a village to hold a fair on private land.[3]

1 Para 3.64 above.
2 *Mercer v Denne* [1905] 2 Ch 538, CA.
3 *Wyld v Silver* [1963] Ch 243, [1962] 3 All ER 309, CA.

Acquisition of easements

37.20 It is not sufficient for an easement to exist that a right exhibit the characteristics outlined above. It must also be created or acquired in a manner recognised by the law. In practice, most easements are created expressly by deed in the context of a sale or lease of part of the vendor's or lessor's land. However, it is important to note that easements can also be created by implication and as a result of prescription (ie long use).

We will now consider, in turn, the various methods by which an easement can be created.

Legal and equitable easements

37.21 An easement is legal if it is created in fee simple or for a term of years absolute,[1] and is made by deed.[2] Easements created by implication, or by prescription are also legal easements. This is because, in such cases, it is either implied or presumed that a deed has been used.

An easement is necessarily equitable if it is created for a lesser interest than a fee simple or term of years, eg for life. Furthermore, an easement in fee simple or for a term of years will, if not created by deed, be equitable if created by means of an agreement which satisfies the requirements of the Law of Property (Miscellaneous Provisions) Act 1989, s 2.[3]

Where a proprietor of registered land expressly grants an easement, the disposition must be completed by registration in order for the easement to exist as a legal interest. This means that the right will be entered in the property register of the dominant land (if title to that land is also registered) and a notice will be entered in the charges register of the servient land.[4] Any legal easement appearing on the title at the time of first registration must similarly be entered on the register.[5] A legal easement not required to be entered on the register (in practice, an easement arising by implication or as a result of prescription) takes effect as an overriding interest.[6]

An equitable easement is best protected by notice or caution on the title of the servient land;[7] however it has been held, in *Celsteel Ltd v Alton House Holdings Ltd*,[8] that openly exercised equitable easements constitute overriding interests. Although this decision has been criticised, it has been applied by the Court of Appeal in *Thatcher v Douglas*.[9]

In unregistered land, a legal easement binds all comers without the need for registration; an equitable easement must be protected by registration in the Land Charges Register.[10]

1 LPA, s 1(2).
2 LPA, s 52.
3 Para 32.6 above.
4 LRA, ss 19(2), 22(2).
5 LRA, s 70(2).

6   LRA, s 70(1)(a).
7   LRA, ss 54, 59(2).
8   [1985] 2 All ER 562, [1985] 1 WLR 204.
9   [1996] NLRJ 282, CA.
10 Land Charges Act 1972, s 2(4), (5).

Express grant or reservation

37.22   An easement may be created expressly, either on the transfer or lease by a landowner of part of his land or, independently of the transfer of land, by two neighbouring landowners. Furthermore, it was made clear by the Court of Appeal in *IDC Group Ltd v Clark*[1] that, even where a right displaying all the features of an easement has been expressly created, there will be no easement unless the parties *intended* to create an easement. Accordingly, in that case, a right to use a fire escape route across neighbouring land which had been created by deed, was held not to be an easement because it had been clearly described as a licence. This meant that the right was not intended to be proprietary and did not bind a purchaser of the 'servient' land.

An easement is said to be *granted* where the vendor or lessor confers an easement over the land he is retaining in favour of the land he is selling or leasing. An easement is *reserved* where the vendor or lessor of land reserves to himself a right over the land sold or leased in favour of his retained land. Any ambiguity in the terms of a grant will be resolved in favour of the purchaser/lessee and against the vendor/lessor; any ambiguity in the terms of a reservation is to be resolved in favour of the vendor/lessor, even though he will invariably have drafted the reservation.[2]

1   (1992) 65 P & CR 179, CA.
2   *St Edmundsbury and Ipswich Diocesan Board of Finance v Clark (No 2)* [1975] 1 All ER 772, [1975] 1 WLR 468, CA.

Implied grant or reservation

37.23   This method of creation is applicable only where a landowner is selling or leasing a part of his land and is retaining the remainder (or disposing of the whole in parcels), because only in such a case is there a transaction into which the grant or reservation of an easement can be implied.

The courts will imply the grant or reservation of easements of necessity and of intended easements, and will imply the grant (but not the reservation) of easements which, being necessary to the reasonable enjoyment of the property, are continuous and apparent, and enjoyed at the time of the grant by the owner of the whole of the land for the benefit of the part granted.[1] We consider each of these in turn.

1   Where an easement is implied into a deed, the easement will be legal rather than equitable.

Easements of necessity

37.24   Where a vendor sells or retains land which as a result is left without any legally enforceable means of access, ie which is 'landlocked', the law will imply from those circumstances that the parties intended a right of way of necessity to be granted or reserved.[1] It is for the vendor to select the route which must, however, provide convenient access. Such a right of way is limited to what was necessary in the circumstances of the transaction in which the implication that the parties intended a way of necessity is made. Thus, in *London Corpn v Riggs*,[2] the defendant retained a plot of land used for agriculture, which was completely surrounded by land which he had sold to the Corporation. The defendant thereby acquired a right of way of necessity, the conveyance containing no express mention of easements of way. He then put in hand plans to build refreshment rooms open to the public on the retained land.

The Corporation successfully sought to restrain him from using the right of way for any purposes other than those connected with the agricultural use of the retained land. Although the law is uncertain, we think that an easement of necessity does not come to an end when the need for it ceases. We consider, in para 37.21 below, another possible example of an easement of necessity.

1   *Nickerson v Barraclough* [1981] Ch 426, [1981] 2 All ER 369, CA. Such an intention cannot be implied where there is an alternative access by water; see *Manjang v Drammeh* (1990) 61 P & CR 194, PC.
2   (1880) 13 Ch D 798.

Intended easements

37.25   The law will readily imply the grant or reservation of easements in order to give effect to the common intention of the parties as to the purposes for which the land granted or some land retained by the grantor is to be used. However, it is essential that the parties intend that the land sold (or that retained by the grantor) should be used in some definite and particular manner.[1]

Where the *grant* of an easement is being sought on this basis, it is sufficient to establish the intended use on the balance of probabilities.[2] However, where a landlord or vendor is seeking to show the *reservation* of an intended easement the test may be rather stricter since he must show that the facts are not reasonably consistent with anything but a common intention. In *Re Webb's Lease, Sandom v Webb*,[3] where a landlord sought to show that he had the right to use the outside wall of demised premises for displaying advertisements, the court held that the mere fact that the tenant knew of the presence of the advertisements at the time of the lease was insufficient to show an intention common to both parties that the landlord was to have a reserved right to maintain the advertisements.

The categories of easements of necessity and intended easements overlap. For example, reciprocal easements of support will be implied on the sale by their owner of one of two adjoining properties. This may be regarded as an easement of necessity, although some regard it as an intended easement.[4] Conversely, the case of *Wong v Beaumont Property Trust Ltd*[5] was held to concern an implied easement of necessity, although it could equally well be regarded as concerning an intended easement. Here, cellar premises were let to a tenant who covenanted that he would carry on business as a restaurateur, would not cause any nuisance, and would control and eliminate all smells and odours in conformity with the health regulations. The tenant subsequently assigned to Wong. In order to comply with the health regulations, Wong sought the landlord's permission to affix a ventilation duct to the outside wall of the landlord's premises. The landlord refused but Wong obtained a declaration that he was entitled to attach the duct. The Court of Appeal held that, where a lease is granted which imposes a particular use on the tenant and it is impossible for the tenant so to use the premises legally unless an easement is granted, the law does imply such an easement as of necessity.

1   *Pwllbach Colliery Co Ltd v Woodman* [1915] AC 634, HL.
2   *Stafford v Lee* (1992) 65 P & CR 172, CA.
3   [1951] Ch 808, [1951] 2 All ER 131, CA.
4   *Jones v Pritchard* [1908] 1 Ch 630.
5   [1965] 1 QB 173, [1964] 2 All ER 119, CA.

Easements within the rule in Wheeldon v Burrows

37.26   In addition to the two bases of implication just discussed, there has evolved an extension of the doctrine of non-derogation from grant[1] known as the rule in *Wheeldon v Burrows*.[2] The rule states that where a landowner sells or leases part of his land, the *grant* (but *not* the reservation) of certain quasi-easements[3] will be implied into the conveyance (or into any contract to convey[4]). The quasi-easements which will pass to the purchaser or tenant as full easements are those which are 'continuous and apparent', necessary to the reasonable enjoyment of the property granted, and which have been and are at the time of the grant used by the owners of the entirety for the benefit of the part granted.[5] Thus, where, prior to the sale or leasing of part of his property, the owner has found that the exercise of some right over the part he is retaining is necessary to the reasonable enjoyment of the part he is selling, that right will pass to the purchaser or lessee as an easement, provided it is continuous and apparent.

It is said that, strictly, a 'continuous' easement is one that is enjoyed passively, without the need for action on the part of the dominant owner, such as the right of light.[6] Something is 'apparent' if it is discoverable on a careful inspection by a person ordinarily conversant with the subject.[7] Thus the presence of a window on the dominant tenement receiving light from the adjoining land suggests a continuous and apparent easement. However, the courts have extended the concept of what is 'continuous and apparent' beyond these narrow confines; the phrase is regarded as being 'directed to there being on the servient tenement a feature which would be seen on inspection and which is neither transitory nor intermittent'.[8] Thus, it is well established that a right of way over a made-up road or worn track can pass as an easement under the rule in *Wheeldon v Burrows*, provided it is necessary to the reasonable enjoyment of the property.[9] Similarly, a right to use drains running through the vendor's retained land may also be created as an easement under this rule.[10]

It is clear that the concept of an easement that is necessary to the reasonable enjoyment of the property granted is wider than easements of necessity.[11] In *Millman v Ellis*[12] it was held that the plaintiff, who had expressly been granted a right of way over part of a layby on the defendant's retained land which provided access to the road, was also entitled to an implied right of way over the remainder of the layby. The more extended right was reasonably necessary to the enjoyment of the plaintiff's property since, without it, access to the highway was dangerous. This can be compared with the decision in *Wheeler v JJ Saunders Ltd*[13] that a right of way over the defendant vendor's retained land would not be implied; given the presence of a perfectly adequate alternative access, this second access was not necessary to the reasonable enjoyment of the plaintiff's land.

1   Para 37.15 above.
2   (1879) 12 Ch D 31.
3   Para 37.6 above.
4   *Borman v Griffith* [1930] 1 Ch 493; *Sovmots Investments Ltd v Secretary of State for the Environment* [1977] QB 411, [1976] 1 All ER 178.
5   (1879) 12 Ch D 31 at 49.
6   Megarry & Wade *Law of Real Property* (5th edn) p 863.
7   *Pyer v Carter* (1857) 1 H & N 916 at 922.
8   *Ward v Kirkland* [1967] Ch 194 at 225, [1966] 1 All ER 609 at 616.
9   *Borman v Griffith* [1930] 1 Ch 493.
10   *Ward v Kirkland* [1967] Ch 194, [1966] 1 All ER 609.
11   Para 37.24 above.
12   (1995) 71 P & CR 158, CA.
13   [1995] 2 All ER 697, CA.

Creation of easements by the operation of the LPA, s 62

37.27 The creation of easements under the LPA, s 62 does not come about by implication in the conveyance; rather the words creating the easement are deemed by virtue of the section to have been expressed in the conveyance from the outset. However, it is convenient to treat s 62 here, because of the interrelation of the section and the rule in *Wheeldon v Burrows*.

The ambit of s 62

37.28 The section provides that a conveyance of land shall be deemed to include and shall by virtue of the Act operate to convey, with the land, all liberties, privileges, easements, rights and advantages, whatsoever, appertaining or reputed to appertain to the land or any part thereof, or, at the time of the conveyance, enjoyed with the land or any part thereof. This provision applies to dispositions of registered land by virtue of the LRA, ss 19(3) and 22(3).

Section 62 makes it clear that *existing* easements enjoyed with the land pass on a conveyance of the land. Furthermore, where part of the land conveyed originally had the benefit of an easement, the section enlarges the right so that, after the conveyance, it takes effect for the benefit of the whole. Thus, in *Graham v Philcox*,[1] where an easement of way was granted to the lessee of the first floor of a converted coach house, the easement passed under s 62 on the conveyance of the freehold of the whole, was for the benefit of the coach house as a whole. What matters for the purposes of s 62 is that the right was enjoyed with the land conveyed or at least part of it.

However, the section has a further most important effect, namely that it operates to convert mere privileges and advantages into *new* legal easements. In effect s 62 states that a conveyance of a piece of land operates to convey with that land all advantages appertaining to, or, at the time of the conveyance, enjoyed with the land, so as to convert such advantages into legally enforceable rights.[2] These rights and privileges must actually be enjoyed at the time of the grant with the land granted or a part of it.[3] Furthermore, they must have been enjoyed by an occupier of the land other than the grantor, over other land of the grantor.[4] It follows that, while the dominant and servient lands must have been in *common ownership* prior to the transaction creating the easement, they must have been in *separate occupation*.

It should be noted that the section does not operate to create easements out of rights not capable of existing as such; thus the right to protection from the weather,[5] or to the provision of hot water and heating,[6] cannot pass under s 62.

1 [1984] QB 747, [1984] 2 All ER 643, CA.
2 *Nickerson v Barraclough* [1981] 2 All ER 369 at 381–382.
3 *Payne v Inwood* (1996) 74 P & CR 42, CA. However, actual user must be judged not by reference simply to the moment of the conveyance, but rather in relation to a reasonable period leading up to that conveyance; see *Green v Ashco Horticulturist Ltd* [1966] 1 WLR 889. Furthermore, the operation of s 62 is *not* prevented where the use of the right has been *temporarily* interrupted at the date of the conveyance; see *Pretoria Warehousing Co Ltd v Shelton* [1993] NPC 98, CA.
4 *Sovmots Investments Ltd v Secretary of State for the Environment* [1979] AC 144, [1977] 2 All ER 385, HL; *Long v Gowlett* [1923] 2 Ch 177.
5 *Phipps v Pears* [1965] 1 QB 76, [1964] 2 All ER 35, CA.
6 *Regis Property Co Ltd v Redman* [1956] 2 QB 612, [1956] 2 All ER 335, CA.

The operation of s 62

37.29 The operation of s 62 is illustrated by *International Tea Stores Co v Hobbs*.[1] A tenant, with the landlord's permission, made use of a roadway on the landlord's property. Subsequently, the tenant acquired the freehold and it was held that the right to use the roadway passed to him as an easement under s 62. Similarly, in *Wright v Macadam*,[2] a tenant was given permission by the landlord to use a coal shed belonging to the landlord. The Court of Appeal held that on the renewal of the lease the right to use the coal shed passed as an easement, although previously depending on permission. These cases constitute a warning to landlords to revoke all licences granted to a tenant prior to renewing the lease or selling the reversion, or, preferably, positively to exclude the operation of s 62.[2]

1 [1903] 2 Ch 165.

2   [1949] 2 KB 744, [1949] 2 All ER 565, CA.
3   Para 37.32 below.

37.30   Another warning as to the possible effect of the section appears from *Goldberg v Edwards*.[1] Edwards leased an annexe at the rear of her house to Goldberg. This annexe could be reached by an outside passage at the side of the house. Goldberg was allowed into possession before the lease was executed and was given permission to use a passage through the landlord's house to reach the annexe. The lease was executed some time later. Edwards subsequently let her house to Miller, the second defendant, who barred the door to Goldberg. Goldberg claimed he was entitled to a right of way either under the rule in *Wheeldon v Burrows*[2] or under s 62.

The Court of Appeal held that the claimed right of way had not passed under *Wheeldon v Burrows* since it was not necessary for the reasonable enjoyment of the annexe, which could conveniently be reached via the outside passage. However, the right did pass as an easement under s 62 since, at the time of the conveyance (ie when the lease was finally executed), the privilege of going through the house was being enjoyed with the annexe and thus passed as an easement when the lease was executed.

1   [1950] Ch 247, CA.
2   Para 37.26 above.

37.31   Section 62 operates only in respect of a 'conveyance', ie the transfer or creation of a *legal* estate; accordingly it will not operate to pass easements in an equitable lease.[1] Just as *Goldberg v Edwards* illustrates how an easement may pass by virtue of s 62 where *Wheeldon v Burrows* is inapplicable, so *Borman v Griffith*[1] shows how easements within the rule in *Wheeldon v Burrows* may pass where s 62 is inappropriate. Borman occupied a house in the grounds of Wood Green Park under an agreement for a seven-year lease. He made use of the main drive of the park which ran past the front of his house although the agreement contained no reference to a right of way and despite the fact that his house could be reached by an unmade track at the rear. Borman claimed a right of way along the main drive in this action against the tenant of the remainder of the park who had prevented Borman's use of the drive. The court rejected the claim based on s 62 as Borman had only an equitable lease. However, the court in effect held that, just as easements within the rule in *Wheeldon v Burrows* will be implied in the grant of a legal estate, so continuous and apparent easements necessary for the reasonable enjoyment of the property will be implied in an agreement for such a grant,[2] and, since the drive was plainly visible and was necessary for the reasonable enjoyment of the property, a right of way over it passed to Borman.

1   *Borman v Griffith* [1930] 1 Ch 493. In this case the claimant occupied on the basis of a contract for a seven-year lease; as we have seen in para 32.3 above, this gives rise not to a legal lease but to an equitable one.
2   *Sovmots Investments Ltd v Secretary of State for the Environment* [1977] QB 411, [1976] 1 All ER 178.

Exclusion of s 62 and the rule in Wheeldon v Burrows

37.32   Neither the rule in *Wheeldon v Burrows* nor s 62 will apply in the face of a contrary intention and it is common for their operation to be expressly excluded by making it clear that rights which might otherwise pass are not intended to be conveyed.[1] Where there is no explicit exclusion, the courts may decide that other provisions in the conveyance necessarily exclude the implication of any easements. So, for example, it is possible that, where a purchaser covenants to erect a fence, this will prevent the implication of any access through that fence.[2] However, this will depend on the particular facts; in some circumstances it will be proper to treat the covenant to fence as permitting the inclusion of a gate, so that a right of access can still be implied.[3]

1   *Squarey v Harris-Smith* (1981) 42 P & CR 118, CA.
2   *Wheeler v JJ Saunders Ltd* [1995] 2 All ER 697, CA.
3   *Hillman v Rogers* [1997] NPC, 183, CA.

Prescription

37.33   Prescription is the method whereby the law confers legality on the long enjoyment of a right, by presuming it had a lawful origin in a grant. An easement acquired by prescription is, therefore, a legal easement. The law of prescription has been described as unsatisfactory, uncertain and out of date,[1] particularly because there exist side by side three methods by which a claim to have acquired an easement by prescription may be made: at common law, under the doctrine of lost modern grant, and under the Prescription Act 1832. Whichever method is being relied on as the basis of a claim (and it may be advisable to rely on more than one method) it must be shown that there has been:

* continuous enjoyment of the alleged right,
* in fee simple,
* as of right.

1   Law Reform Committee, 14th Report, Cmnd 3100 (1966).

Continuous enjoyment

37.34   This requirement does not mean that the right claimed must have been used ceaselessly day and night throughout the prescriptive period. What is continuous depends on the nature of the right being claimed and the circumstances of the case. In *Diment v NH Foot Ltd*,[1] the use of a path between six and 10 times a year was considered sufficient in regularity and extent to constitute continuous enjoyment. The claim to a right of way by prescription was, however, unsuccessful for other reasons.

1   [1974] 2 All ER 785, [1974] 1 WLR 1427.

In fee simple

37.35   An easement (other than one of light[1]) may only be acquired by prescription by a freehold owner against a freehold owner.[2] Hence prescription cannot be established during any period when the freeholds of the dominant and servient lands are in common ownership.

Where the *servient* land is held by a tenant under a lease throughout the period of enjoyment on which the dominant owner's claim to have acquired an easement is based, the claim will be unsuccessful. However, where the period of enjoyment began at a time when the servient land was held by the freeholder, the fact that subsequently the land became subject to a tenancy will not defeat the claim, unless the servient owner, the freeholder, can show that he had no knowledge that the enjoyment was continuing while the tenant was in possession.[3]

Long enjoyment of a right by a tenant of the *dominant* land will not enable the tenant to claim an easement by prescription, but his enjoyment of the right accrues to the freeholder; the easement is thus acquired by the freeholder. It follows from this, and from the fact that a person cannot have an easement over his own land, that a tenant cannot acquire a prescriptive right against his own landlord, nor can a tenant acquire an easement by prescription against another tenant of the same landlord.[4]

1   Para 37.48 below.
2   *Wheaton v Maple & Co* [1893] 3 Ch 48, CA.

3   *Pugh v Savage* [1970] 2 QB 373, [1970] 2 All ER 353, CA.
4   *Kilgour v Gaddes* [1904] 1 KB 457, CA.

As of right

37.36   A person claiming to have acquired an easement by prescription must show that he has thus far enjoyed the right on the basis that he was entitled to do so on a permanent basis. This he does by showing that his enjoyment was neither by force, nor secretly, nor by permission. Furthermore, the user on which a prescriptive claim is based must not be prohibited by statute.[1]

1   *Hanning v Top Deck Travel Group Ltd* (1993) 68 P & CR 14, CA.

37.37   *Without force*   There can be no claim to an easement by prescription where the alleged right has been exercised by force or in the face of open and continuous opposition from the servient owner.

37.38   *Without secrecy*   Where the servient owner has no knowledge, or means of knowledge,[1] of the enjoyment, that enjoyment cannot be said to be acquiesced in; it cannot be said to be as of right. Enjoyment 'as of right' cannot be secret but must be of such a character that an ordinary owner of the land, diligent in the protection of his interests, would have, or must be taken to have, a reasonable opportunity of becoming aware of that enjoyment.[2] Consequently, it was not possible to claim by prescription an easement in respect of the support of a dry dock where none of the supporting rods was visible on the alleged servient land.[2] Similarly, the intermittent discharge of borax at night into a sewer could not, even over a long period, ripen into an easement; the servient owner clearly would have no means of knowledge of the use.[3] Where long enjoyment is shown, knowledge on the part of the servient owner will be presumed, and it is for the servient owner to rebut the presumption.[4] The knowledge of a tenant or of the servient owner's agent will not be imputed to the servient owner.[5]

1   *Dalton v Angus* (1881) 6 App Cas 740 at 801, HL.
2   *Union Lighterage Co v London Graving Dock Co* [1902] 2 Ch 557 at 571, CA.
3   *Liverpool Corpn v H Coghill & Son* [1918] 1 Ch 307.
4   *Pugh v Savage* [1970] 2 QB 373, [1970] 2 All ER 353, CA.
5   *Diment v NH Foot Ltd* [1974] 2 All ER 785, [1974] 1 WLR 1427.

37.39   *Without permission*   To succeed in a claim to have acquired an easement by prescription, the dominant owner must show that the servient owner acquiesced in his enjoyment as if it were an established right, ie that the latter knew, or had the means of knowing, that the right was being exercised and stood by and allowed the use to continue.[1] However, if his enjoyment depended on obtaining the positive permission of the servient owner, or is subject to the control of the servient owner, this makes it clear that the latter did not regard the enjoyment as an established and irrevocable right, but merely as a licence which could be terminated at any time by the withdrawal of the permission.[2]

1   *Mills v Silver* [1991] 1 All ER 449, CA.
2   See *Goldsmith v Burrow Construction Co* (1987) Times, 31 July, CA: here the fact that the gate to a footpath was periodically locked by the alleged servient owner rendered the use of path permissive.

The three methods of prescription

37.40   *Common law*   Thus far we have said that a claim to have acquired an easement by prescription depends on showing long enjoyment as of right. Strictly, at common law, it is necessary to show enjoyment as of right since a time before 1189, which time, for historical reasons, is regarded as 'time immemorial'. Obviously, a need positively to prove continuous enjoyment since before 1189 would in most cases present insuperable hurdles; therefore it is *presumed* that enjoyment has been since time immemorial once it is positively proved that the right has been used in the required manner during living memory or even for a 20-year period. However, this presumption can easily be rebutted, and the claim will fail, if it is shown that at some time since 1189 the right either did not exist or could not have existed. So, for example, in the case of a claim to an easement of support, or an easement of light, there can be no prescription at common law if there was no building on the land in 1189. Equally, there can be no prescription at common law where it can be shown that the dominant and servient lands have been in common ownership at some time since 1189.

Because common law prescription is often impossible to establish, the doctrine of lost modern grant was developed.

37.41 *Lost modern grant* By this pretence, the court presumes that there was a comparatively recent deed granting the easement which has since been lost. In this way a lawful origin to long enjoyment is presumed without the need to show user since 1189. A lost modern grant will be presumed on evidence of 20 years' continuous use in fee simple[1] as of right, even where this period of user took place at some time in the past.[2] This presumption is a legal fiction; it cannot be rebutted by evidence that there was in fact no grant[3] nor by evidence that the parties mistakenly believed that a right already existed,[4] but only by evidence showing that a grant could not possibly have been made.[2]

1   Thus a tenant cannot acquire an easement under the doctrine of lost modern grant, nor can an easement be acquired on this basis by one tenant against a tenant of the same landlord: *Simmons v Dobson* (1991) 62 P & CR 485, CA; see para 37.31 above.
2   *Tehidy Minerals Ltd v Norman* [1971] 2 QB 528, [1971] 2 All ER 475, CA.
3   *Dalton v Angus* (1881) 6 App Cas 740.
4   *Bridle v Ruby* [1989] QB 169, [1988] 3 All ER 64, CA.

37.42 *Prescription Act 1832* 'The Prescription Act 1832 has no friends. It has long been criticised as one of the worst drafted Acts on the Statute Book'.[1] The Act was apparently drafted with the aim of avoiding the pitfalls involved in a claim at common law. In view of its complexity, the Act provides few advantages over the other two methods with which it co-exists. Nonetheless, it may, in fact, be of some utility to those claiming an easement by prescription. The Act provides for a claim to an easement other than light to be based either on 20 years' enjoyment as of right without interruption or on 40 years' such enjoyment; its provisions relating to easements of light will be considered separately in a later paragraph.[2]

1   Law Reform Committee, 14th Report, Cmnd 3100 (1966).
2   Para 37.48 below.

37.43 Where a claim under the Act is based on 20 years' enjoyment as of right without interruption, it cannot be defeated by evidence that enjoyment began later than 1189, although it may be defeated in any other way in which a claim at common law may be defeated.[1] Thus it is still necessary to show that enjoyment was continuous, in fee simple, and as of right.

The period of enjoyment must have *immediately preceded* a court action relating to the claim.[2] Proof of enjoyment for 20 years at some earlier time will not do. There must be some court action to confirm the embryonic right as an easement. This can take the form either of an action by the dominant owner for a declaration that he is entitled to the right, or an action by the servient owner to prevent continued enjoyment, in which the dominant owner relies on the Act as a defence. If there has been no enjoyment for some time prior to the court action, then even if there has been 20 years' enjoyment, a claim under the Act cannot, subject to what follows, succeed.[3]

Time during which the servient land is held by a person who is a minor, lunatic or tenant for life is to be excluded from the computation of the 20-year period, so that the claimant must show 20 years' enjoyment on top of that time.[4]

To constitute an interruption of the period of enjoyment an act must be submitted to, or acquiesced in, for one year after the party interrupted has had notice of both the interruption and the person making it.[5] So, if a landowner has enjoyed a right of way over his neighbour's land for 15 years and the neighbour then physically bars the way, this will constitute an interruption after the elapse of one year.[5] If the use of the way recommences thereafter, a fresh period of 20 years user will have to be established before an easement can be acquired. It also follows that, if that landowner had *already* enjoyed the right of way for 20 years before it was barred, he would still be able to claim an easement under the Act provided he brings an action to claim the right within one year of his becoming aware that the neighbour was obstructing the way.

1   Prescription Act 1832, s 2.
2   Ibid, s 4.
3   A claim can, however, be based on the doctrine of lost modern grant.
4   Ibid, s 7.
5   If the barring of the way ceases within one year it is of no effect, so that the claimant can continue to add to his 15 years of enjoyment.

37.44   A claim to an easement under the Act based on 40 years' enjoyment as of right without interruption is deemed to be absolute and indefeasible unless it is shown that the enjoyment depended on written consent.[1] Again, the 40-year period must immediately precede some court action. 'Interruption' has the same meaning as in relation to the 20-year period.

Although a claim based on 40 years' enjoyment will only be defeated by proof of written permission, the enjoyment must nevertheless be 'as of right'. Therefore, enjoyment which depends on regular permission (written or oral) – as in *Gardner v Hodgson's Kingston Brewery Co*[2] where an annual payment of 15 shillings had to be made for the use of a right of way – will not ripen into an easement even if the permission is oral and the enjoyment has continued for 40 years, because the enjoyment is permissive and not as of right.[3] Oral permission given at the outset and not renewed will not defeat a claim based on the 40-year period, though it will defeat a claim based on 20 years' enjoyment.

In computing the 40-year period, any time during which the servient land was held under a lease of more than three years is to be deducted, provided that the claim to the easement is resisted by the servient owner within three years of the ending of the lease.[4] Thus, providing the servient owner resists the claim within the time limit, the dominant owner must show that he has enjoyed 40 years' use over and above the period of the lease. If the dominant owner is unable to show this he may be able instead to base his claim on 20 years' enjoyment, for in that case the period of the lease is not deductible. However, the existence of the lease will then be relevant to the question of whether the 20 years' enjoyment was in fee simple.[5]

1   Prescription Act 1832, s 2.
2   [1903] AC 229, HL.
3   See also *Jones v Price and Morgan* (1992) 64 P & CR 404, CA.
4   Prescription Act 1832, s 8.
5   See *Palk v Shinner* (1852) 18 QB 568 and para 37.31 above.

Extinguishment of easements

37.45   Unlike the case of restrictive covenants, no provision exists for the modification or discharge of easements.[1] Easements may only be extinguished by being released, expressly or impliedly, by the dominant owner, or by ownership and possession of the dominant and servient properties falling into the same hands. In practice, implied release is extremely difficult to establish. It is not enough to show that the dominant owner is not using the right and has not used it over a long period,[2] or to prove that the obstruction of some aspects of the right has been acquiesced in.[3] It must be shown that the dominant owner intends to abandon the right, and abandonment of an easement can only be treated as having taken place where the person entitled to it has demonstrated a fixed intention never at any time thereafter to assert the right himself or to attempt to transmit it to anyone else.[4]

1   Paras 38.28–38.41 below.
2   See *Benn v Hardinge* (1992) 66 P & CR 246, CA where it was held that there was no abandonment of an easement simply because no one had occasion to use the right during the previous 175 years.
3   See *Snell & Prideaux Ltd v Dutton Mirrors Ltd* [1995] 1 EGLR 259, CA, where it was held that a right to use a passageway *both* as a right of way *and* for loading and unloading had not been abandoned simply because its use as a right of way had long been obstructed by the erection of a brick pillar.
4   *Tehidy Minerals Ltd v Norman* [1971] 2 QB 528 at 553, [1971] 2 All ER 475 at 492, CA.

Particular easements

Rights of way

37.46   A right of way may be limited, as to the times it may be used or as to the purposes for which it may be used (eg agricultural purposes only) or as to the modes of enjoyment (eg on foot only), or it may be unlimited.

The question may arise whether the extent to which the dominant owner is making use of the right is greater than his true entitlement. In answering this question, the method of creation of the easement is relevant. Where the easement was expressly granted or reserved, the question turns on the construction of the relevant deed in the light of the circumstances surrounding its making, in particular the nature of the road or track over which the right was granted.[1] However, in the absence of any special factors, the dominant owner is not confined to using the right of way for the purposes which existed at the date of grant but is entitled to use it for any lawful purposes to which the dominant tenement is later put.[2] Where the extent of the right granted is unclear, ambiguities in the deed are resolved in favour of the person having the benefit of the easement.[3] In the case of easements of way arising by implication, enjoyment is circumscribed by the situation prevailing at the time of the grant.[4]

The extent of enjoyment permitted in the case of an easement of way acquired by prescription is determined by the nature of the enjoyment during the prescriptive period,[5] though an increase in the frequency of use is unobjectionable unless it results from a change in the nature of the enjoyment.[6] For example, where a right of way had been acquired by prescription to a site used by a small number of caravans, the servient owner could not object to a considerable increase in the number of caravans using the site.[6]

Enlargement of the dominant tenement is not of itself sufficient to extinguish or affect entitlement to a right of way unless, as a consequence, the permitted extent of enjoyment would be exceeded.[7] Where a dominant owner is using a right of way in a manner or to an extent which exceeds that to which he is entitled, his action amounts to a nuisance and the servient owner may seek an injunction to limit the use to the permitted level.[8] However, where the express terms of a right of way permit a level of use which, in other circumstances, might amount to a nuisance the servient owner has no remedy.[9]

1   *Cannon v Villars* (1878) 8 Ch D 415; see also *Jelbert v David* [1968] 1 All ER 1182, [1968] 1 WLR 589, CA; *National Trust for Places of Historic Interest or National Beauty v White* [1987] 1 WLR 907.
2   *Alvis v Harrison* (1991) 62 P & CR 10, HL.
3   *St Edmundsbury and Ipswich Diocesan Board of Finance v Clark (No 2)* [1975] 1 All ER 772, [1975] 1 WLR 468, CA.
4   *London Corpn v Riggs* (1880) 13 Ch D 798.
5   *Mills v Silver* [1991] 1 All ER 449, CA.
6   *British Railways Board v Glass* [1965] Ch 538, [1964] 3 All ER 418, CA.
7   See *Graham v Philcox* [1984] QB 747, [1984] 2 All ER 643, CA where a right of access enjoyed in respect of a first floor flat was held to extend to the whole building when the tenant later acquired the freehold. However, note that in *Jobson v Record* [1997] NPC 56, CA it was held that a right of access granted in respect of the defendants' property could not be used as an access to adjoining land which they later acquired.
8   *Rosling v Pinnegar* (1986) 54 P & CR 124, CA.
9   *Hamble Parish Council v Haggard* [1992] 4 All ER 147, [1992] 1 WLR 122.

Rights of light
37.47   The right of light can exist only as an easement and then only in respect of a defined aperture, usually a window.[1]

1   See *Levet v Gas Light and Coke Co Ltd* [1919] 1 Ch 24.

Acquisition by prescription
37.48   Although a right to light can be created expressly or by implication, it is more usually acquired by prescription and is then sometimes referred to as 'ancient lights'. Ancient lights can be acquired by all three methods of prescription, though acquisition at common law is highly unlikely since it is often easy to prove that there was no building with windows on the site in 1189.[1]

Where reliance is placed on the Prescription Act 1832, special rules apply. Under the Act, a claim to an easement of light based on 20 years' enjoyment (immediately preceding a court action), without interruption, gives rise to an absolute and indefeasible right, unless the light was enjoyed by written consent.[2] There is no requirement that enjoyment be as of right, so the fact that the light was enjoyed by virtue of regular oral permission is no bar to a claim to have acquired a prescriptive right. Furthermore, since it is not necessary to show enjoyment in fee simple, a tenant may acquire an easement of light against his own landlord or against another tenant of the landlord.[3]

The existence of a right to light can severely restrict the servient owner's ability to build on his land so it is particularly important for owners of undeveloped land to be able to prevent their neighbours from acquiring rights to light. Enjoyment of the light could, of course, be interrupted[4] by the erection of a structure blocking the light to the particular window, and traditionally this was done by the erection of a hoarding. However, this method may now fall foul of the planning laws, and so, as an alternative, the servient owner may apply under the Rights of Light Act 1959 for registration in the local land charges registry[5] of a notice, which is treated as being equivalent to an actual obstruction of the light. The application for registration must state the size and position of the opaque structure which the notice is intended to represent.[6] Before such a notice can be registered, the Lands Tribunal must certify that all those likely to be affected by the registration have been notified.[7] Registration is effective for one year, which is sufficient to constitute an interruption; this means that, in order to acquire an easement of light, a further 20 years' enjoyment must be established which can, where necessary, be interrupted by a further registration of a right to light notice.

1 Para 37.40 above.
2 Prescription Act 1832, s 3.
3 *Morgan v Fear* [1907] AC 425, HL.
4 An act does not constitute an interruption for the purpose of the Act unless submitted to or acquiesced in for one year; Prescription Act 1832, s 4.
5 Para 31.15 above.
6 Rights of Light Act 1959, s 3.
7 Ibid, s 2.

Extent of right

37.49 An owner of a right to light is not necessarily entitled to maintain the level of light which he currently enjoys; generally speaking, he is entitled to sufficient light 'according to the ordinary notions of mankind' for the comfortable use and enjoyment of his house as a dwelling-house, if it is a dwelling-house, or for the beneficial use and occupation of the building if it is a warehouse, a shop, or other place of business.[1] Where there is a right of light, a dominant owner may only bring an action in respect of a reduction in the amount of light received where the reduction constitutes a nuisance; this will only be the case if the light received is reduced below what is sufficient according to the ordinary notions of mankind. In determining this question, the court may take into account the nature of the locality and may have regard to the fact that higher standards may be expected as time goes by.[2] A right of light exists in respect of a defined aperture in a building; the internal arrangement of the rooms in the building is not necessarily relevant to ascertaining the extent of the right.[3]

It is sometimes possible to have a right to a higher than usual level of light. In *Allen v Greenwood*,[4] the plaintiffs, who for at least 20 years had had a greenhouse in their garden, close to the boundary with the neighbouring property, sought an injunction restraining their neighbours from obstructing the light to the greenhouse. The obstruction was caused by a fence which the neighbours had erected and by the neighbours' caravan which was parked close to the greenhouse. Although the greenhouse still received enough light to read by, the Court of Appeal held that this was insufficient for the ordinary purposes of mankind for the use and enjoyment of a greenhouse as a greenhouse (which is regarded as a building with apertures). The question of the amount of light necessary for ordinary purposes is determined by the nature and use of the building, and thus a high degree of light may be necessary in a particular case. Alternatively, the Court held that it is possible to acquire a prescriptive right to a greater than ordinary amount of light. Just as the extent of enjoyment during the prescriptive period determines the extent of a prescriptive right of way, so it determines the extent of a right of light acquired by prescription. The greenhouse having enjoyed an extraordinary amount of light for 20 years, to the knowledge of the servient owner, a prescriptive right to that amount of light had been acquired.

1 *Colls v Home and Colonial Stores Ltd* [1904] AC 179 at 208,HL.
2 *Ough v King* [1967] 3 All ER 859, [1967] 1 WLR 1547, CA.
3 *Carr-Saunders v Dick McNeil Associates Ltd* [1986] 2 All ER 888, [1986] 1 WLR 922.
4 [1980] Ch 119, [1979] 1 All ER 819, CA.

Rights of support

37.50 All landowners automatically have a natural right of support[1] which means that they may bring an action in nuisance should the support to their *land* be removed. Equally, in certain circumstances at least, landowners can expect their neighbours to take reasonable steps to prevent the potential removal of support to their land.[2] For example, in *Redland Bricks Ltd v Morris*,[3] the plaintiff successfully sought damages and an injunction[4] when part of his market garden slipped into the defendants' land as a result of their digging for clay for their brickworks,[5] and, in *Lotus Ltd v British Soda Co Ltd*,[6] the plaintiff was held to be entitled to damages when the pumping of brine from boreholes on adjacent land resulted in withdrawal of support from and consequent subsidence of the plaintiff's land, with resultant damage to the buildings on it.

There is no natural right of support in respect of *buildings*. Such a right of support must be acquired as an easement. However, as *Lotus v British Soda* shows, damages may be claimed in respect of damage to buildings which results from infringement of the natural right of support to the land on which they stand.

An easement of support may be acquired expressly, by implication or by prescription. A servient owner who by an act of his own interferes with a right of support does so at his peril;[7] if he removes the support he must provide an equivalent. There is, however, established authority that he is under no obligation to repair that part of his building which provides support for his neighbour; he can let it fall into decay. On the other hand, the owner of the dominant tenement may enter and take the necessary steps to ensure the support continues by effecting the required repairs.[8] More recently though, it has been held that a servient owner who allows his property to fall into decay, in circumstances where he should reasonably have appreciated the risk to his neighbour's right of support, may be liable in negligence or nuisance for failing to take reasonable steps to prevent or minimise the risk.[9]

1   See para 37.12 above.
2   *Holbeck Hall Hotel Ltd v Scarborough Borough Council* [1997] 2 EGLR 213.
3   [1970] AC 652, [1969] 2 All ER 576, HL.
4   He failed to obtain a mandatory injunction: para 29.18 above.
5   Where the withdrawal of support causes no immediate collapse but merely the certainty of subsidence in the future, no action can be taken: *Midland Bank Ltd v Bardgrove Property Services Ltd* (1992) 65 P & CR 153, CA.
6   [1972] Ch 123, [1971] 1 All ER 265.
7   *Brace v South East Regional Housing Association Ltd* (1984) 270 Estates Gazette 1286, CA.
8   *Bond v Nottingham Corpn* [1940] Ch 429, [1940] 2 All ER 12, CA.
9   *Bradburn v Lindsay* [1983] 2 All ER 408.

Chapter 38

Restrictive covenants

38.1 As we have seen,[1] a covenant is a contractual agreement, usually occurring in a conveyance or a lease, in which one party, the *covenantor*, agrees to do or not to do something for the benefit of another, the *covenantee*. Typical covenants which might be entered into between the parties to a conveyance include covenants preventing building on the land conveyed, or preventing the building of more than one house, or requiring the building of a boundary wall. The parties to a lease may enter covenants requiring the payment of rent and the carrying out of repairs, or preventing sub-letting. All these covenants, being contractual agreements, are enforceable between the original parties according to the ordinary law of contract. However, a covenant may also be a right in land, which is enforceable not only between the original parties to it, but also by and against their successors in title to the property concerned.

In this chapter, we shall be considering the circumstances in which:

- covenants arise where there is no relationship of landlord and tenant;
- the burden of such covenants will pass to a successor in title of the covenantor;
- the benefit of such covenants will pass to a successor in title of the covenantee; and
- restrictive covenants will be discharged or modified.

1 Para 36.19 above.

Covenants where there is no relationship of landlord and tenant

38.2 We have already dealt with the circumstances in which covenants imposed between landlord and tenant will bind parties to whom the lease or reversion is transferred.[1] We now turn to the question of the extent to which the *benefit* of a covenant 'runs' (ie passes) with the land of the covenantee, and the extent to which the *burden* of it runs with the land of the covenantor where there is no relationship of landlord and tenant. Suppose that P purchases 100 acres of farmland from V and covenants with V that he will use the land for agricultural purposes only. If V then sells the remainder of his land to R, R will wish to know whether he can enforce the covenant entered into by V and P, ie whether the benefit of the covenant has run, with the land, to him. Were P subsequently to sell his land to A, A would wish to know if he was bound by P's covenant, ie whether the burden of the covenant has run with the land to him.

We are here dealing with the enforcement of covenants between persons who are not, either as original parties or as assignees, in the relationship of landlord and tenant. In other words, we are mainly concerned with the enforcement of covenants between freeholders, although it should be noted that these same rules apply should a landlord wish to enforce covenants against a sub-tenant since there is no direct relationship of landlord and tenant between such parties.[2]

In this area, common law and equity have separate rules. Both permit the benefit of a covenant to run with the land. Common law, however, does not allow the burden of a covenant to run, while equity allows the burden of negative covenants, which restrict the use of the land, to run. This means that the burden of positive covenants, which require the covenantor to do something in connection with the land, will not run with freehold land.

1 Paras 36.40–36.59 above.
2 Para 36.59 above.

38.3 Clearly, covenants entered into between freeholders, usually on the sale of part of his land by one to another, are mutually enforceable between the original parties on the basis of the contract between them. Furthermore, like other contractual rights, the benefit of a covenant may be assigned to a third party who may then enforce the benefit in his own right.[1] It should also be noted that in certain exceptional cases the LPA, s 56 allows a person to enforce a covenant relating to property as if he were a party to it, even though he is not named as a party to the covenant, so long as he is in existence at the time of the covenant, identified by it, and the covenant purports to be made *with* him.[2] Such a person is deemed to be a covenantee. Suppose X purchases land, and in the conveyance covenants 'with the vendor and also with his assigns, owners for the time being of land adjoining the land conveyed',[3] the persons who are owners for the time being of adjoining land purchased from the vendor are treated as covenantees along with the vendor. Although not naming them, the covenant identifies them and purports to be made with them. It should be noted that only those who, *at the time the covenant was made*, were owners of adjoining land are deemed to be covenantees by virtue of s 56.

1 See para 7.5 above.
2 *White v Bijou Mansions Ltd* [1937] Ch 610, [1937] 3 All ER 269.
3 See *Re Ecclesiastical Comrs Conveyance* [1936] Ch 430.

The running of the burden

Positive covenants
38.4 Where the parties are not in the relationship of landlord and tenant, the burden of a covenant does not run with the land at common law.[1] Since, as we shall see, equity allows the burden of restrictive (negative) covenants to run with the land of the covenantor, the practical effect of the common law rule is that the burden of positive covenants will not run with freehold land. This rule, 'the greatest and clearest deficiency' in the law of covenants,[2] is of considerable significance since it means that covenants which impose positive obligations, such as to keep premises in repair, to erect boundary walls, and to contribute to the maintenance of roads, cannot be enforced against successors of the original covenantor. Despite the criticisms of the rule, the House of Lords has recently declined to overrule it in *Rhone v Stephens*,[3]

expressing the view that such a significant departure from long-established principles should be implemented by legislation rather than by judicial decision.[4]

An inability to ensure compliance with positive obligations to repair or to contribute to the cost of maintenance and other services is a grave disadvantage in the case of certain types of property such as a block of flats, an estate with common facilities or a commercial building in multiple occupation. Indeed, the rule has, in the words of the Law Commission,[5] cast a blight on developments of freehold flats which for this reason (among others) are not considered to be a particularly good security for a mortgage. It has therefore become the usual practice for buildings in multiple occupation (such as blocks of flats) and estates with shared facilities to be sold leasehold, thus ensuring that positive covenants are enforceable.[6]

Not surprisingly, legal ingenuity has sought to devise methods of achieving the enforcement of positive obligations against successive freehold owners without transgressing the rule preventing the enforcement of positive covenants against successors of the covenantor. However, as the Law Commission has pointed out,[7] none of the devices used to achieve enforcement of positive obligations can be said to provide an effective general solution to the problem.

By virtue of the LPA, s 79, unless a contrary intention is expressed, a covenantor covenants that both he *and* his successors will abide by the covenant. Should a successor fail to do so, the covenantee may sue the original covenantor for breach of contract. The covenantor (and his successors likewise) should therefore ensure that purchasers from him undertake to indemnify him in the event of his being sued for their non-performance of an obligation. Such a chain of indemnity provides an indirect method of enforcing covenants, but like all chains it is only as strong as its weakest link.[8]

Of the other devices, we shall briefly consider the right of entry, the estate rentcharge, and the doctrine of benefit and burden. It will be noted that, while these could be useful in enabling a developer or management company to enforce positive obligations against successive residents of a housing estate or block of flats, they do not enable the individual residents to enforce such obligations against each other.

1   *Austerberry v Oldham Corpn* (1885) 29 Ch D 750, CA, approved *Rhone v Stephens* [1994] 2 All ER 65, HL. Section 33 of the Local Government (Miscellaneous Provisions) Act 1982 provides that local authorities may enforce positive covenants made by deed against successors of the covenantor.
2   Law Commission Report on the Law of Positive and Restrictive Covenants; Law Com No 127.
3   [1994] 2 All ER 65, HL.
4   For a discussion of proposals for reform see para 38.42 below.
5   Law Com No 127.
6   On the principles expounded in paras 36.40–36.59 above.
7   Law Com No 127.
8   Ibid.

Rights of entry

38.5   A right of entry may be used to secure compliance with positive covenants even though the covenants themselves are not enforceable as such.[1] A person having a right of entry has the right to enter property should certain conditions occur and take possession of it, thereby ending the interest of the person holding the land. For example, a vendor of property might insert in the conveyance a covenant requiring the purchaser and his successors to keep the property in repair and reserve to himself a right of entry should the property fall into disrepair. The threat that this right will be exercised will ensure that the purchaser and his successors comply with a positive covenant to repair. However, such a right of entry suffers two disadvantages: first, it is equitable, and in unregistered land depends for its enforceability against subsequent purchasers of the covenantor's land on the doctrine of notice, since it is not registrable in the Land Charges Register.[2] Second, it is subject to the rule against perpetuities; that is, there is a limit to how far in the future the right may be exercised.[3] To overcome these two disadvantages, it should be annexed to, ie incorporated with, an estate rentcharge, which we discuss in the next paragraph.

1   *Shiloh Spinners Ltd v Harding* [1973] AC 691, [1973] 1 All ER 90, HL.
2   *Shiloh Spinners Ltd v Harding* [1973] AC 691, [1973] 1 All ER 90, HL, para 35.18 above. In registered land it should be protected by a notice, see para 35.30 above.
3   Para 34.20, note 2 above.

Estate rentcharges

38.6   A rentcharge is any annual or other periodic sum charged on or issuing out of land, except rent reserved by a lease or tenancy or any sum payable by way of interest.[1] If it is perpetual or for a term of years it is a legal interest.[2] The Rentcharges Act 1977 prohibits the creation of rentcharges for the future, subject to the important exception of the estate rentcharge.

An estate rentcharge may be of two kinds. The first is one created for the purpose of making positive covenants enforceable by the person to whom the rentcharge is paid (the rent owner) against the owner for the time being of the land. Such a rentcharge must not be of more than a nominal amount.[3] This kind of estate rentcharge achieves its object of making positive covenants enforceable against successive landowners by having a right of entry annexed to it. A right of entry annexed to a rentcharge is a legal interest, and thus enforceable in unregistered land against all purchasers of the land affected, and is not subject to the rule against perpetuities.[4] Essentially, annexing a right of entry to this kind of estate rentcharge cures it of the defects which it suffers when not so annexed. Nonetheless, the remedy remains 'clumsy and draconian' and although the device of the estate rentcharge comes closest to providing a solution to the unenforceability of positive covenants, it is undoubtedly artificial and technical in the extreme.[5]

The Rentcharges Act 1977 provides for a second kind of estate rentcharge, defined as one created for the purpose of meeting, or contributing towards, the cost of the performance by the rent owner of covenants for the provision of services, or for the carrying out of maintenance or repairs, or for the effecting of insurance or the making of any payment by him for the benefit of the land affected by the rentcharge. Such a rentcharge must be reasonable in relation to the cost to the rent owner of performing the covenant.[6] Examples of this kind of rentcharge are where the developer of a housing estate reserves to himself a rentcharge from each purchaser to provide him with a fund to maintain the estate roads until adoption by the local authority; or where the management company of a block of flats reserves a rentcharge in respect of each flat to provide a fund for the maintenance of the common parts.

1   Rentcharges Act 1977, s 1. A legal rentcharge created out of registered land is noted together with the right of entry as an incumbrance in the Charges Register of the landowner's register of title, and the rent owner is substantively registered as the proprietor of a rentcharge and a rentcharge certificate issued to him: LRA, ss 2, 19(2) and 49(1); LRR, rr 50, 107 and 108.
2   LPA, s 1(2).
3   Rentcharges Act 1977, s 2.
4   LPA, ss 1(2) and 4(3).
5   Law Commission Report on the Law of Positive and Restrictive Covenants; Law Com No 127.
6   Rentcharges Act 1977, s 2.

Doctrine of benefit and burden

38.7   Another possible method of securing the enforcement of positive obligations against successive landowners is the doctrine of benefit and burden elaborated in the case of *Halsall v Brizell.*[1] Here, the developers of a private housing estate imposed a covenant on each purchaser, under which the latter covenanted to contribute towards the cost of maintaining the roads and footpaths of the estate, which were retained by the developer. Upjohn J held that as this covenant was positive it could not be enforced as such against successors of the original purchasers. However, by applying the doctrine that a person who takes the benefit of a deed is bound by any conditions in it, he held that if successors of the original purchasers wished to take advantage of the benefit of the roads and footpaths, which, of course, they had to do, they must also accept the burden of paying for their maintenance. It has recently been made clear that this doctrine does not mean that *any* condition can be rendered enforceable by attaching it to a right; the condition must be relevant to the right.[2] This doctrine is, therefore, only of utility where the obligation is linked to a corresponding benefit of which the successors wish to take advantage.

1   [1957] Ch 169, [1957] 1 All ER 371; para 33.16 above.
2   *Rhone v Stephens* [1994] 2 All ER 65, HL.

Restrictive covenants

38.8   The particular contribution of equity, originating in the case of *Tulk v Moxhay*,[1] is to allow the burden of restrictive covenants, those which restrict the uses to which the land may be put, to run with the land. Consequently, although a vendor may not ensure that successors of his purchaser act positively in relation to the land, he may ensure that they refrain from acting in particular ways: he may, for example, restrict building on the land or the carrying on of any trade. Equity will allow the burden of a covenant to run with the land of the covenantor if:

*   it is essentially negative;
*   the covenantee retains land capable of being benefited by the covenant;
*   the parties intend that the covenant should run with the land; and
*   the requirements of registration or of the doctrine of notice are complied with.

Each of these will now be considered in turn.

1   (1848) 18 LJ Ch 83.

The covenant must be essentially negative

38.9   The essence of the covenant, whether positively or negatively worded, must be negative or restrictive. The case of *Tulk v Moxhay*[1] provides an example. Tulk owned Leicester Square. He sold off the gardens in the centre and retained the surrounding land. The purchaser of the gardens covenanted that 'his heirs and assigns… would… at all times… keep and maintain the said piece of ground… in an open state'. This covenant was held to be binding on a successor of the purchaser. Although the covenant was phrased in terms of a positive obligation, 'keep and maintain in an open state', it was essentially negative, prohibiting building on the land. Conversely, a covenant 'not to let the premises fall into disrepair' is a positive covenant.

Why did equity confine its intervention to negative covenants? As we have seen,[2] equity does not override a common law rule, thus it could not compel positive compliance with a contractual obligation entered into by the current owner's predecessor. However, the court of equity could take the view that, where land is sold subject to a *restriction*, this means that the purchaser, and anyone who subsequently purchases the land with notice of that restriction, simply never acquires that right to use the land which he would otherwise have had.[3] If he tries to act in a way which contravenes the restriction, equity can restrain him by the issue of an injunction, a remedy which is particularly suitable for the enforcement of negative obligations, on the basis that he has no right to do so.

1   (1848) 18 LJ Ch 83.
2   Para 1.9 above.
3   See *Rhone v Stephens* [1994] 2 All ER 65 at p 68.

The covenantee must retain land capable of being benefited
38.10   The requirement that the covenant must have been imposed for the benefit of land retained by the covenantee is closely analogous to the necessity, in the law relating to easements, for dominant land.[1] It means that restrictive covenants are only enforceable as between neighbouring landowners. The rule was established in *LCC v Allen*,[2] where a developer covenanted with the London County Council (LCC) not to build on a plot which lay across the end of a proposed street. It was held that the LCC could not enforce this covenant against a successor of the developer since at no time did the council have any interest in any land capable of being benefited by the covenant.

It has been held that the reversion on a lease gives the landlord a sufficient retained interest in the land to enable him to enforce against a sub-tenant a restrictive covenant made by the tenant and contained in the head-lease.[3] Such a covenant may be enforced by the landlord against a sub-tenant having notice of it, despite the absence of a contract or privity of estate between a landlord and sub-tenant. A mortgagee's (lender's) interest has also been held sufficient to enable him to enforce restrictive covenants against successors of the mortgagor/covenantor.[4]

The courts will readily assume that the retained land is capable of being benefited by the covenant unless the defendant can show that the restriction cannot reasonably be said to be of value to the land.[5] Furthermore, the courts have been prepared to hold that a covenant restraining a purchaser from carrying on a business which competes with that carried on by the vendor on his retained land benefits the vendor's land. Both these points are illustrated in *Newton Abbott Co-operative Society Ltd v Williamson and Treadgold Ltd*[6] where a covenant imposed by the vendor prohibiting dealing in articles of ironmongery in the property sold was held to benefit the vendor's retained ironmonger's shop. Upjohn J stressed the enhanced price the vendor would realise on selling together the land and the business, as a result of the covenant.

The requirement that the covenantee must retain land which is benefited by the covenant is, in some circumstances, manifestly inconvenient. So, for example, statute expressly permits local authorities, local planning authorities, the National Trust and the Nature Conservancy Council to enforce restrictive covenants despite the absence of any retained land.[7]

1   Para 37.3 above.
2   [1914] 3 KB 642, CA.
3   *Hall v Ewin* (1887) 37 Ch D 74.
4   See *Regent Oil Co Ltd v J A Gregory (Hatch End) Ltd* [1966] Ch 402, [1965] 3 All ER 673, CA.
5   *Wrotham Park Estate Co v Parkside Homes Ltd* [1974] 2 All ER 321, [1974] 1 WLR 798. Contrast *Re Ballard's Conveyance* [1937] Ch 473, [1937] 2 All ER 691.
6   [1952] Ch 286, [1952] 1 All ER 279.
7   See Housing Act 1985, s 609, Town and Country Planning Act 1990, s 106(3), National Trust Act 1937, s 8 and Countryside Act 1968, s 15(4).

The parties must intend that the covenant should run
38.11   By the LPA, s 79, which applies unless a contrary intention is expressed,[1] the parties are deemed to intend that the covenant should run with the land, rather than being merely personal to the parties.

1   See *Re Royal Victoria Pavilion, Ramsgate* [1961] Ch 581, [1961] 3 All ER 83.

Registration and notice
38.12   In the case of unregistered land, covenants entered into prior to 1926 derive their protection from the doctrine of notice, under which a purchaser of a legal estate for value without notice is not bound,[1] while covenants entered into after 1925 must be registered as a land charge in the Register of Land Charges, otherwise the covenant will be void against most purchasers of the legal estate.[2]

In the case of registered land, the covenant must be protected by the entry of a notice in the Charges Register of the burdened land in order to bind the land of the covenantor.[3] The details of the covenant are set out in full on the register and land certificate of the burdened land, or a copy of it is attached to the certificate.

It should be noted that, both in registered and unregistered land, a restrictive covenant entered into between landlord and tenant cannot be registered. Consequently, enforcement of such a covenant by the landlord against a sub-tenant depends on notice in unregistered land; in registered land such a covenant is automatically binding where title to the headlease is registered;[4] where it is only title to the sub-lease which is registered, the doctrine of notice would appear to dictate whether or not restrictive covenants in the (unregistered) headlease bind the sub-tenant.[5]

1   Paras 35.6–35.7 and 35.18.
2   LCA 1972, s 4(6); para 35.11 above.
3   LRA, s 49; para 35.30 above.
4   LRA, s 23(1)(a).
5   In such circumstances the sub-lessee could only have been accorded a good leasehold title which does not guarantee that his landlord had the right to grant the lease free from incumbrances; see para 31.39 above and LRA, s 10.

The running of the benefit

38.13   As with the running of the burden, there are certain divergences between the rules of common law and of equity on this topic. To the extent that equitable rules differ from common law rules, they apply only to restrictive covenants. For our purposes therefore it is appropriate to retain the division of the subject matter into positive and restrictive covenants.

Positive covenants
38.14   At common law the benefit of a covenant will run with the land to a successor of the original covenantee if it is annexed to the land, that is incorporated with it so that on a transfer of the land the benefit automatically passes without the need for any mention being made of it. A covenant will be annexed and the benefit will run where the conditions set out in the following paragraphs are met.

The covenant must touch and concern the land of the covenantee
38.15   The covenant must either affect the way in which the land is occupied or it must be such that in itself, and not merely as a result of collateral circumstances, it affects the value of the land.[1]

In *Smith and Snipes Hall Farm Ltd v River Douglas Catchment Board*,[2] the Catchment Board covenanted with the owner of the land adjoining a brook that the Board would maintain the banks of the brook. The Court held that the covenant touched and concerned the adjoining land, in that it affected the value of the land by converting it from flooded meadows to land suitable for agriculture.

A difficulty can arise where the benefited land is large, with the result that it may successfully be argued that the whole of that land cannot be benefited from the imposition of a covenant relating to land which adjoins only part.[3] While it is possible to prove that the whole of a very large property does in fact benefit from the covenant,[4] the problem can be avoided altogether by the inclusion of an express provision that the covenant is imposed for the benefit of 'all or any part of' the covenantee's land.[5]

1   *Rogers v Hosegood* [1900] 2 Ch 388 at 395; see also *P & A Swift Investments v Combined English Stores Group plc* [1989] AC 632, [1988] 2 All ER 885, HL; para 36.42 above.
2   [1949] 2 KB 500, [1949] 2 All ER 179, CA.
3   As in *Re Ballard's Conveyance* [1937] Ch 473.
4   *Marten v Flight Refuelling Ltd* [1962] Ch 115.
5   *Marquess of Zetland v Driver* [1939] Ch 1, [1938] 2 All ER 158, CA.

It was intended that the benefit should run

38.16   In the *River Douglas Catchment Board* case, the Court of Appeal held that it was plain from the language of the covenant, under which the Board undertook to maintain the banks of the brook 'for all time', that it was intended to take effect for the benefit of successive owners of the land. While in this case evidence of intention was sought and found in the language of the document creating the covenant, we shall explain in para 38.23 below that this may no longer be necessary.

The land to be benefited should be identifiable

38.17   In the *River Douglas Catchment Board* case, the document creating the covenant referred only to 'certain land situate between the Leeds and Liverpool Canal and the River Douglas and adjoining the Eller Brook'. This was, however, regarded as sufficient; extrinsic evidence was admissible to prove the precise extent and situation of the relevant land.

The successor must acquire a legal estate

38.18   The common law used to require that the person seeking to enforce the covenant should have the same legal estate as the original covenantee. However, in *Smith and Snipes Hall Farm Ltd v River Douglas Catchment Board*, the Court of Appeal held that the covenant could be enforced against the Board not only by Smith who purchased the freehold from the original covenantee, but also by Snipes Hall Farm Ltd to whom Smith had leased the land. The Court held that the LPA, s 78 permits the benefit of a covenant to run to lessees and sub-lessees as well as to successors of the covenantee's legal estate. A further, more radical effect, of s 78 is considered in para 38.23 , below.

   It should be noted that it is not necessary that the covenant should have any connection with the land of the covenantor.

Restrictive covenants

38.19   As with the common law rules, the first requirement of the equitable rules, which apply to restrictive covenants, is that the covenant should touch and concern the land of the covenantee.[1] A successor in title of the original covenantee must then show that the benefit has passed to him either:

*   by annexation, or
*   by assignment, or
*   under a scheme of development.

1   See para 38.15 above.

Annexation

38.20   We have already considered the common law rules on annexation. In practice these are rarely encountered for the very good reason that they apply only where the burdened land has not yet changed hands. Once that has occurred, the assistance of equity must be sought for both the running of the burden and the running of the benefit. In truth, the equitable rules as to annexation are almost certainly a more fully developed version of the common law rules.

38.21 *Annexation by express words* Where a positive obligation is imposed, it is often clear from the circumstances that it is intended to benefit particular identifiable land. This is not always the case with obligations imposed by restrictive covenants. The original approach was, therefore, that in order to annex the benefit of a restrictive covenant in equity express wording must be used which clearly identifies the land and indicates the parties' intention that the covenant is for the benefit of that land; that is, words which demonstrate either that the covenant has been entered into for the benefit of identifiable land or that it was made with the covenantee in his capacity as owner of that land. As we shall see in the following paragraphs, it is now clear that it is not essential to use express words of annexation. Nevertheless, it is good conveyancing practice to put the matter beyond argument by formulating the covenant in a way which does itself achieve annexation.

There can be no express annexation if the covenant makes no reference to the land to be benefited, as where a covenant was expressed to be made with 'the vendors, their heirs ... and assigns'.[1] However, it is sufficient to state that the covenant is made 'with the vendor for the benefit of his property, Oaklands'. A fuller form of words, following the classic formula used in *Rogers v Hosegood*[2] is '...with intent that the covenant might take effect for the benefit of the vendors, their heirs and assigns and others claiming under them to all or any of their lands adjoining or near to the land conveyed'. The covenant is here expressed to be made with the covenantees in their capacity as owners of the property to be benefited.

This extended wording also makes it clear that the covenant is intended to benefit each and every part of the covenantee's property. This serves two purposes. First, as we have seen, it ensures that, where the land to be benefited is unusually large, there will be no argument over the question of whether the land is in fact benefited.[3] Second, it also means that, as well as the benefit of the covenant passing by annexation to subsequent owners of the entire benefited land, it will, if the benefited land is divided up rather than remaining as an entity, pass also to the purchasers of those parts. Certain decisions of the courts[4] have suggested that unless a form of words is used making it clear that the benefit is annexed to the whole and each and every part of the benefited land, the benefit will be presumed to be annexed only to the land as a unit. However, the decision of the Court of Appeal in *Federated Homes Ltd v Mill Lodge Properties Ltd*[5] is authority that the presumption is to the opposite effect. The Court held that, if the benefit of a covenant is annexed to the land, it is presumed to be annexed to every part of the land. This ruling may be viewed as unfortunate since a restrictive covenant which can be enforced by a purchaser of any part of the benefited land is clearly very much more onerous than one which can only be enforced by the owner of the whole land (and which will, therefore, cease to be enforceable should the benefited land be split up). If it is desired that the benefit of the covenant should pass only to successors to the whole of the benefited land this now needs to be made explicit.

1   *Renals v Cowlishaw* (1878) 9 Ch D 125; *Reid v Bickerstaff* [1909] 2 Ch 305.
2   [1900] 2 Ch 388, CA.
3   See *Marquess of Zetland v Driver* [1939] Ch 1, [1938] 2 All ER 158, CA and para 38.15 above.
4   *Russell v Archdale* [1964] Ch 38, [1962] 2 All ER 305; *Re Jeff's Transfer (No 2), Rogers v Astley* [1966] 1 All ER 937, [1966] 1 WLR 841.
5   [1980] 1 All ER 371, [1980] 1 WLR 594, CA.

38.22   *Annexation by implication* However desirable, it is clear that the use of express words is not essential to bring about the annexation of the benefit of a covenant. It is a question of construction of the particular covenant. There is authority that annexation can be implied where, from the document creating the covenant, the land intended to be benefited and an intention to benefit the land can be clearly established.[1] As we have explained, these two matters, together with evidence that the covenant touches and concerns the land, themselves establish annexation.

1   *Marten v Flight Refuelling* Ltd [1962] Ch 115; *Shropshire County Council v Edwards* (1982) 46 P & CR 270; *J Sainsbury plc v London Borough of Enfield* [1989] 2 All ER 817, [1989] 1 WLR 590.

38.23   *Annexation under LPA, s 78*   A more important erosion of any requirement for express wording is the ruling by the Court of Appeal in *Federated Homes Ltd v Mill Lodge Properties Ltd*[1] that the LPA, s 78 can cause the benefit of a covenant to be annexed, and hence to run with the land.

Section 78 provides that a covenant relating to any land of the covenantee shall be deemed to be made with the covenantee and his successors in title, including the owners and occupiers for the time being of the land of the covenantee intended to be benefited, and the persons deriving title under him or them, and shall have effect as if such successors and other persons were expressed.

Prior to the *Federated Homes* case, s 78 was regarded, like its mirror provision s 79, as merely a word saving provision with no substantive effect.[2] However, this view was rejected by the Court of Appeal which held that s 78 operates to annex the benefit of any post- 1925 covenant which touches and concerns (ie 'relates to') the land of the covenantee. It seems that it is not necessary for the covenant to express any positive intention that the benefit should run and it may not even be necessary for the covenant itself to identify the benefited land.[3] However, where the covenant makes it clear that there is no intention for the covenant to run, as where it provides that it should not take effect for the benefit of successors unless the benefit is expressly assigned to them, s 78 does not cause the benefit to be annexed.[4]

Although the decision in *Federated Homes* has been heavily criticised, it has now remained unchallenged for nearly twenty years. It radically simplifies the law relating to annexation which is of considerable assistance both to students learning the law and to those claiming the benefit of covenants. However, this simplification has its disadvantages; it is now much more difficult than hitherto for those ostensibly subject to the burden of covenants to escape liability on the grounds that there was no adequate annexation and thus no-one entitled to enforce the covenant.

1   [1980] 1 All ER 371, [1980] 1 WLR 594, CA.
2   A view which still prevails in relation to s 79; see *Tophams Ltd v Sefton* [1967] 1 AC 50, HL; *Rhone v Stephens* [1994] 2 All ER 65, HL.
3   The answer to this important question is left unclear in the judgment of Brightman LJ and was not alluded to at all by Megaw LJ who delivered the only other judgment.
4   *Roake v Chadha* [1983] 3 All ER 503, [1984] 1 WLR 40.

Assignment
38.24   The traditional view of the law was that if the benefit of a covenant was not originally annexed to the land by the use of appropriate wording, it was necessary for a successor of the covenantee to show that the benefit of it had been separately expressly assigned to him at the same time as the land was transferred to him. However, as we explained in the preceding paragraphs, it now appears to be the law that annexation may either be implied or be brought about by the LPA, s 78. Thus the circumstances in which it will be necessary to resort to the law of assignment are limited. In particular, where there is no express or implied annexation of a pre-1926 covenant, assignment

must be considered,[1] likewise where, as in *Roake v Chadha*,[2] annexation is expressly excluded. On one view of the *Federated Homes* decision, it may also be that assignment must be resorted to where the land to be benefited is not sufficiently identifiable from the document creating the covenant.

The rules as to the assignment of the benefit of a covenant are as follows. The assignment of the benefit of the covenant must be contemporaneous with the assignment of the land; once the covenantee has transferred the land he can no longer enforce the covenant[3] and he thus has no enforceable covenant to assign.[4] To be capable of assignment, a covenant must have been taken for the benefit of ascertainable land which is capable of being benefited by it. The existence and situation of the land to be benefited need not – and, since assignment is being resorted to in the absence of annexation, usually will not – be indicated in the terms of the covenant itself but it is sufficient that, on a broad and reasonable view, it can otherwise be shown with reasonable certainty.[5] In *Newton Abbott Co-operative Society Ltd v Williamson and Treadgold Ltd*,[6] a vendor, in 1923,[7] sold the shop opposite her own ironmonger's shop, imposing a covenant restraining the purchaser from using the shop for the sale of articles of ironmongery. Although the words of the covenant did not indicate an intention to benefit identifiable land, the court held that the attendant circumstances clearly showed that the covenant was taken for the benefit of the retained ironmonger's shop. Therefore, the covenant was assignable when that retained shop was later leased to a tenant.

The benefit of an assignable covenant may be assigned separately and at different times with parts of the benefited land.[8]

It was accepted without argument in *Re Pinewood Estate, Farnborough, New Ideal Homesteads Ltd v Levack*,[9] and decided at first instance in the *Federated Homes* case, that the rules as to assignment require a successor of the covenantee, who seeks to enforce a covenant not annexed to the land, to show a 'chain of assignments' from the original covenantee to himself; it is apparently not the law, despite academic opinions to the contrary, that once the benefit of a covenant has been assigned it thereafter and thereby becomes annexed to the land so that there is no need for any further assignment.

1   *J Sainsbury plc v London Borough of Enfield* [1989] 2 All ER 817, [1989] 1 WLR 590.
2   [1983] 3 All ER 503, [1984] 1 WLR 40; para 38.23 above.
3   *Chambers v Randall* [1923] 1 Ch 149.
4   *Re Union of London and Smith's Bank Ltd's Conveyance, Miles v Easter* [1933] Ch 611, CA.
5   *Marten v Flight Refuelling Ltd* [1962] Ch 115, [1961] 2 All ER 696.
6   [1952] Ch 286, [1952] 1 All ER 279.
7   Section 78 therefore was not relevant.
8   *Chambers v Randall* [1923] 1 Ch 149.
9   [1958] Ch 280, [1957] 2 All ER 517.

Scheme of development
38.25   Where a developer wishes to impose a set of mutually enforceable restrictions on a number of plots of land, the rules of annexation and assignment cannot achieve the desired result. This can be illustrated by the following example:

Plot 1	Plot 2	Plot 3	Plot 4
↓	↓	↓	↓
A	B	C	D

Elm Avenue

Plot 5	Plot 6	Plot 7	Plot 8

When the developer sells Plot 1 to A, subject to a number of restrictive covenants, the benefit of those covenants can be annexed to, or assigned with, the developer's retained land (ie Plots 2, 3 and 4); when Plot 2 is sold to B, subject to the same restrictions, these can only be annexed to, or assigned with the developer's retained land (ie Plots 3 and 4); the benefit of restrictions imposed on Plot 3 (sold to C) can only be for the benefit of Plot 4 and, by the time Plot 4 is sold to D, there is no longer any retained land to benefit. Hence it can be see that annexation and assignment do not allow the land of earlier purchasers to benefit from covenants imposed on land purchased later. So, in our example the restrictions imposed on A's land can be enforced by B, C and D, those imposed on B's land by C and D but not A, those on C's land by D but not A and B, and so on. This pattern would be extended by the sale of plots 5 to 8.

For this reason the rules relating to schemes of development were devised. A scheme of development exists where a landowner has disposed of his land in parcels, imposing, on each transfer of a parcel of land, restrictive covenants intended not simply for his advantage as owner of the land but for the advantage of each parcel purchased. Such schemes may be imposed to maintain the character of an area such as a housing estate. The scheme of covenants gives rise to what is in effect a local 'planning' law for the area of land disposed of, which is based on *reciprocal* rights and obligations.[1] However, the use of a scheme of development secures only the passing of the benefit of the covenants; in order to achieve the necessary reciprocity, it is essential that the restrictive covenants be properly registered[2] in order to ensure that they are mutually *binding*. If this is not done the whole scheme may collapse. As soon as the original vendor sells the first parcel of land, the scheme crystallises, and all the land within the area of the scheme (there must be a clearly defined area[3]) is bound, becoming subject to the 'local law'.[4]

Species of scheme of development which may be encountered include the building scheme, designed to provide for and regulate building development, and the letting scheme, under which a common set of restrictions is imposed on leasehold interests whether in relation to flats in a particular block or houses on an estate.

1   *Reid v Bickerstaff* [1909] 2 Ch 305 at 319, CA.
2   See Preston and Newsom *Restrictive Covenants Affecting Freehold Land* (7th edn, 1992). See para 38.26 below.
3   *Reid v Bickerstaff* [1909] 2 Ch 305, CA. The defined area of the scheme must be clear to both vendor and all the purchasers, see *Emile Elias & Co Ltd v Pine Groves Ltd* [1993] 1 WLR 305, PC.
4   *Brunner v Greenslade* [1971] Ch 993, [1970] 3 All ER 833.

38.26   In the case of *Elliston v Reacher*,[1] Parker J laid down four requirements of a scheme of development:

• both plaintiff and defendant in the action to enforce the particular covenant must derive title from the same vendor;
• this vendor must have laid out his estate, or a defined part of it, for sale in lots, subject to restrictions which were intended to be imposed on all the lots, and which are consistent only with some general scheme of development;
• these restrictions must have been intended to be, and be, for the benefit of all the lots; and
• the lots must have been purchased from the common vendor on the basis that the restrictions to which they were subject were to take effect for the benefit of all the other lots. This is an important requirement.

More recent cases have shown that this list does not constitute an inflexible definition. For example, in *Baxter v Four Oaks Properties Ltd*,[2] the estate was not laid out in lots by the original vendor, rather he sold the land in parcels of whatever size the particular purchasers required. Nonetheless the area was held to be the subject of a scheme. In *Re Dolphin's Conveyance, Birmingham Corpn v Boden*,[3] the original owners of an estate, having sold off part in lots, gave the rest to their nephew who continued the process of selling the estate off in lots, imposing the same restrictions. Again, there was held to be a scheme of development, despite the absence of a sole vendor. In these cases the intention to impose a scheme was evident in the conveyancing documents. Where such an intention is not evident, it is more necessary to consider whether Parker J's four requirements are complied with. Thus in *Emile Elias & Co Ltd v Pine Groves Ltd*,[4] where there was no evidence of a common intention to produce mutually enforceable covenants, the absence of a clearly defined area to which the alleged scheme applied and the lack of uniformity between the restrictions imposed on different plots, proved fatal to the existence of a scheme of development.

It must be remembered that a scheme of development is a scheme for the reciprocal enforcement of restrictive covenants and that to be enforceable restrictive covenants require protection by registration. Thus, every time a parcel is sold, the common vendor must register the covenants as land charges against the purchaser,[5] or have the covenants noted on the charges register of the purchaser's register of title,[6] as appropriate. Furthermore, since the nature of the scheme is such that the vendor is impliedly bound by the restrictions (even if he has not expressly covenanted), each purchaser should register the restrictions against the common vendor. Only if this is done can each purchaser enforce the restrictions against subsequent purchasers.

1   [1908] 2 Ch 374.
2   [1965] Ch 816, [1965] 1 All ER 906.
3   [1970] Ch 654, [1970] 2 All ER 664.
4   [1993] 1 WLR 305, PC.
5   Para 35.11 above.
6   Para 35.30 above.

Remedies

38.27   We mentioned earlier[1] that the equitable remedy of an injunction is particularly suitable for enforcing negative obligations such as restrictive covenants. Such a remedy achieves exactly what the plaintiff normally desires, namely the cessation of the activity which breaches the covenant, as opposed to mere compensation. Indeed, equitable remedies are, in principle, the only remedies available for the enforcement of restrictive covenants against a successor of the original covenantor. However, in such cases, the court has a discretion to award damages, as an alternative to granting an injunction.[2] A 'good working rule' for deciding whether to grant damages instead of an injunction was put forward in *Shelfer v City of London Electric Lighting Co.*[3] According to this an injunction will be granted unless:

- the injury to the plaintiff's legal rights is small;
- it is capable of being estimated in terms of money;
- it can adequately be compensated for by a small payment; and
- it would be oppressive to the defendant to grant an injunction.

It should be noted that this is only a good working rule and the court always retains its discretion to refuse an injunction.[4] In practice such a refusal is increasingly likely where the plaintiff fails to take immediate legal steps to protect his rights, eg by seeking an interlocutory injunction to stop any building in breach of covenant. Where damages are awarded on a discretionary basis, as an alternative to an injunction, they can be based on the profit which has accrued to the defendant as a result of the breach of covenant.[5]

Nonetheless, in the majority of cases an injunction is the remedy which is sought and that which is granted. In appropriate cases, a mandatory injunction will be granted; for example requiring the demolition of a building, as in *Wakeham v Wood*,[6] where the defendant erected a house blocking the plaintiff's sea view in flagrant disregard of a covenant prohibiting him so doing.

In the event of a breach by an original covenantor, damages at common law will be available as of right; unlike damages awarded as an alternative to an injunction, these cannot be based on the profit which has been gained as a result of the breach; accordingly, in the absence of actual loss by the plaintiff, damages will only be nominal.[7] Where the breach is of a positive covenant damages will normally be the appropriate remedy, though specific performance may be granted in certain circumstances.[8] Where the breach is of a restrictive covenant the plaintiff will normally seek, and be granted, an injunction.

1   Para 38.9 above.
2   Supreme Court Act 1981, s 50.
3   [1895] 1 Ch 287, [1891–4] All ER Rep 838.
4   See, for example, *Wrotham Park Estate Co v Parkside Homes Ltd* [1974] 2 All ER 321, [1974] 1 WLR 798.
5   *Wrotham Park Estate Co v Parkside Homes Ltd* [1974] 2 All ER 321, [1974] 1 WLR 798; *Surrey County Council v Bredero Homes Ltd* [1993] 3 All ER 705, CA; *Jaggard v Sawyer* [1995] 2 All ER 189, CA.
6   (1981) 43 P & CR 40, CA.
7   *Surrey County Council v Bredero Homes Ltd* [1993] 3 All ER 705, CA.
8   See, for example, *Jeune v Queens Cross Properties Ltd* [1974] Ch 97, [1973] 3 All ER 97; para 37.37 above.

Discharge of restrictive covenants

Development, planning law and restrictive covenants

38.28   Planning law and restrictive covenants exist side by side as a means of controlling development. 'From the individual's point of view, control by private covenant has obvious advantages over planning control, in that it can cover matters of important detail with which a planning authority would not be concerned and the procedure of enforcement is available to a person who is entitled to the benefit of a covenant and is aggrieved by a breach, instead of depending on the planning authority's decision to act'.[1] In the words of a leading textbook on the subject, 'one thing that is abundantly plain is that there is no prospect whatever that restrictive covenants will become unnecessary and that their place will be taken by the planning laws. For planning standards are still too often below the standards imposed by restrictive covenants'.[2] Another point is that, as the Law Commission says,[3] certain changes of use and certain building operations to which a neighbour might reasonably object do not require planning permission. It is important to realise that the fact that an individual has planning permission for a particular project in no way permits or excuses the breach of a restrictive covenant burdening his land, though the grant of planning permission may be relevant, but far from decisive, in relation to an application to the Lands Tribunal for the modification or discharge of the covenant.[4] However, as we shall see,[5] where land is acquired for planning or other statutory purposes, a restrictive covenant will not be allowed to impede those purposes.

1   Law Commission, Report on Restrictive Covenants No 11, para 8.
2   Preston and Newsom *Restrictive Covenants Affecting Freehold Land* (7th edn; 1982).

3   Report on Positive and Restrictive Covenants, Law Com No 127.
4   *Re Martin's Application* [1989] 1 EGLR 193, CA; para 38.29 below.
5   See para 38.34 below.

38.29   A purchaser or would-be purchaser of land, discovering that the land is apparently subject to some long-standing restriction preventing intended development, may make an application to the Chancery Division for a declaration as to whether or not the land is, or would in any given event be, affected by the restriction; or as to the nature and extent of the restriction and whether it is enforceable and if so by whom.[1] Such a declaration, which will only be made after due publicity of the proceedings has been circulated to all nearby owners who might have the benefit of the covenant,[2] is conclusive; anyone not named in the declaration will lose the benefit of the covenant. It should be noted also that it is possible to take out a 'relatively inexpensive'[3] insurance policy against one's plans being thwarted by the enforcement of a restrictive covenant.

1   LPA, s 84(2).
2   *Re Sunnyfield* [1932] 1 Ch 79; *Re Elm Avenue* [1984] 3 All ER 632.
3   Law Commission, Report on Positive and Restrictive Covenants, Law Com No 127.

38.30   There are various circumstances in which a person claiming the benefit of a restrictive covenant may be prevented from enforcing the covenant. At common law, there are four main possibilities:

- a change in the character of the neighbourhood;
- release of the covenant;
- unity of ownership; and
- acquisition for planning or statutory purposes.

Under statute, we consider applications to the Lands Tribunal to discharge or modify the covenant, and (briefly) applications under the Housing Act 1985.

Discharge at common law
Change in character of neighbourhood
38.31   In *Chatsworth Estates Co v Fewell*,[1] Fewell had opened a guest house contrary to a covenant that his house should be used as a private dwelling only. The estate company having the benefit of the covenant sought an injunction against him. Fewell claimed that the covenant was not enforceable on the ground that the character of the neighbourhood had completely changed since the covenant was made because some houses in the area were now used as guest houses, and some as schools. Farwell J rejected this argument holding that to succeed on this basis a defendant would have to show so complete a change in the character of the neighbourhood that there was no longer any value left in the covenant at all. This was clearly not so in this case.

1   [1931] 1 Ch 224.

Release of the covenant
38.32   Release may be express or implied. In *Chatsworth Estates Co v Fewell*, the defendant also argued that the estate company, by allowing others to open guest houses, etc had impliedly released the benefit of the covenants. This, said Farwell J, was a matter of degree, to be decided in this case by reference to the question, 'have the plaintiffs by their acts and omissions represented to the defendant that the covenants are no longer enforceable and that he is therefore entitled to use his house as a guest house?' Again, this was not so in this case.

Unity of ownership

38.33 If the burdened and benefited land come into the same ownership, any restrictive covenants are extinguished.[1] This follows from the fact that a person cannot have a third party right over his own land. Land subject to a scheme of development, however, forms an exception to this rule. Plots within the area of a scheme, which have fallen into common ownership, remain subject to the scheme and continue to do so if they are later sold off separately.[2] Thus, if the common vendor sells, subject to the scheme, a number of lots to a builder, who subsequently sells the lots to separate purchasers, the restrictions are enforceable between those purchasers even though their land had for a period been in common ownership.

1   *Re Tiltwood, Sussex, Barrett v Bond* [1978] Ch 269, [1978] 2 All ER 1091.
2   *Texaco Antilles Ltd v Kernochan* [1973] AC 609, [1973] 2 All ER 118, PC; *Brunner v Greenslade* [1971] Ch 993, [1970] 3 All ER 833.

Acquisition for planning or statutory purposes

38.34 Where land is acquired by a local authority for planning purposes, restrictive covenants will not be allowed to impede the carrying out of works in accordance with planning permission,[1] whether these works are carried out by the local authority or by someone to whom the local authority has later transferred the land.[2] Equally, restrictive covenants will not be allowed to prevent the use of land acquired by other bodies for statutory purposes.[3] It matters not whether the acquisition was made under compulsory powers, or by agreement.[3] It is usual for the person entitled to the benefit of the restriction to be entitled to the payment of compensation.[4]

Technically, the covenant remains in existence; it is merely the right to enforce which is taken away. However, the covenant will still be enforced where it does not directly prevent the statutorily authorised use. So, where a covenant prevented the carrying out of building works to a hospital without prior approval, it was held that such approval must be sought. Only if that approval was actually refused would the statutory powers (to operate a hospital) be impeded and the right to further enforce the covenant be denied.[5]

1   Town and Country Planning Act 1990, s 237.
2   *R v City of London Council, ex p Masters, Governors and Commonlity of the Mystery of the Barbers of London* [1996] 2 EGLR 128.
3   *Kirby v School Board of Harrogate* [1896] 1 Ch 437.
4   Usually under the Compulsory Purchase Act 1965, s 10.
5   *Cadogan v Royal Brompton Hospital National Health Trust* [1996] 2 EGLR 115.

Application to the Lands Tribunal

38.35 Under the LPA, s 84(1) the Lands Tribunal[1] has jurisdiction on certain grounds to discharge, wholly or partly, or to modify, restrictive covenants affecting freehold or leasehold land. In the case of leasehold land, the power is limited to where the term is of more than 40 years of which at least 25 years have expired.[2] The majority of applications made to the Tribunal under this section are to modify a covenant; for example, to enable the owner of the land affected to build at a higher density than that permitted in the covenant, or to carry out such projects as the conversion of a house into flats,[3] the building of a house in the garden of an existing house, or the erection of a public house. The fact that an applicant has planning permission for his intended development is in no way decisive of an application under s 84, although the Tribunal must take into account the development plan for the area and the pattern of grants and refusals of planning permission in the area.[4]

Provision is made for those having the benefit of the relevant covenant to lodge an objection to the application. If the applicant considers that any objector is not entitled to the benefit of the covenant the Tribunal may make a preliminary determination of the matter,[5] the onus being on the objector to prove his entitlement.[6]

There is no rule preventing the original covenantor making an application under s 84, nor preventing modification of a covenant which has only recently been imposed.[7] These are merely factors to be taken into account in the exercise of the Tribunal's discretion.

The Tribunal may, in modifying a covenant, add other reasonable restrictions which are acceptable to the applicant.[8]

The Tribunal may exercise its jurisdiction to discharge or modify a covenant on one or more of the grounds outlined in the following paragraphs.

1   Para 2.36 above.
2   LPA, s 84(12).
3   See also para 38.41 below.
4   LPA, s 84(1B).
5   Ibid, s 84(3A); Lands Tribunal Rules 1975, r 20.
6   *Re Edis's Application* (1972) 23 P & CR 421.
7   *Ridley v Taylor* [1965] 2 All ER 51, [1965] 1 WLR 611, CA; *Cresswell v Proctor* [1968] 2 All ER 682, [1968] 1 WLR 906, CA; *Jones v Rhys-Jones* (1974) 30 P & CR 451, CA.
8   LPA, s 84(1C).

Obsolescence

38.36   A restrictive covenant may be modified or discharged on the basis that it ought to be deemed obsolete by reason of changes in the character of the property or the neighbourhood, or other material circumstances.[1]

In *Re Truman, Hanbury, Buxton & Co Ltd's Application*[2] the applicant brewers applied on this ground to have a covenant modified to permit the erection of a public-house. The covenant was imposed under a scheme to preserve the character of an estate as a residential area. On appeal from the Lands Tribunal, the Court of Appeal held that only when the original purpose of a covenant can no longer be achieved can it be said to be obsolete. In this case it would be necessary to show that what was intended to be a residential area had become a commercial area, which was not the case. Furthermore, it was clear that the object of the covenant was still capable of fulfilment since the Lands Tribunal had expressly found that the proposed development would injure the objectors.

1   LPA, s 84(1)(a).
2   [1956] 1 QB 261, [1955] 3 All ER 559, CA.

Agreement

38.37   The second ground for modification or discharge is that the persons entitled to the benefit of the restriction have agreed either expressly or by implication, by their acts or omissions, to the discharge or modification.[1]

This ground is rarely relied on by an applicant at the outset for, if there is evidence of agreement to the discharge or modification, an application to the Tribunal is probably not worthwhile. However, an individual may amend his application to include this ground once it has become clear that those who are entitled to the benefit of the covenant have failed to object to the application or have withdrawn their objection. The application will then be granted, since the persons entitled to the benefit have shown by their acts or omissions that they agree to the proposals.[2]

1   LPA, s 84(1)(b).
2   *Re Dare's and Beck's Application* (1974) 28 P & CR 354.

No injury
38.38   A restrictive covenant can be discharged or modified where this will not injure the persons entitled to the benefit of the restriction.[1] This ground has been described as a long-stop against frivolous or vexatious objections,[2] and is limited to cases where there is no merit in the objections.

1   LPA, s 84(1)(c).
2   *Ridley v Taylor* [1965] 2 All ER 51 at 58.

Impedes reasonable use
38.39   The final and most widely used ground is where the restriction impedes some reasonable use of the land, and either:

• does not secure to persons entitled to the benefit of it any practical benefits of substantial value or advantage to them; or
• is contrary to the public interest;

provided that

• money will be an adequate compensation for the loss or disadvantage (if any) which any such person will suffer from the discharge or modification.[1]

The majority of successful applications are made on this ground. The leading case is *Re Bass Ltd's Application.*[2] The company wished to use a site, which was subject to a restriction limiting its use to dwelling-houses, as a loading area for articulated trucks. The site was zoned in the development plan for industrial use and planning permission had been granted. A large number of those having the benefit of the covenant, imposed under a scheme of development, objected. The Tribunal rejected the company's application, giving its decision in the form of answers to questions formulated by counsel. These have come to provide the usual approach to applications on this ground.

• *Is the proposed use which is impeded by the restriction reasonable?* This question is to be answered leaving aside for the moment the restrictions. Where planning permission has been granted it will be difficult to find the proposed use unreasonable.
• *Does impeding the proposed use secure practical benefits to the objectors?* The expression 'practical benefits' is very wide: the Tribunal is to consider the adverse effects of the applicant's proposal on a broad basis. Thus, in *Gilbert v Spoor*,[3] the preservation of a pleasant rural view enjoyed not from the benefited land but from a point a short distance away was held to be a practical benefit. The Tribunal in the *Bass* case answered this second question affirmatively, in view of the fact that the proposed development would give rise to increased noise, fumes, vibration, dirt and risk of accidents.
• *If yes, are the benefits of substantial value or advantage?* The Tribunal has stressed that the benefits are not to be assessed in terms only of financial value. In the *Bass* case the benefits were held to be of substantial advantage, as have been, in other cases, peace and quiet, an unobstructed view[4] and the advantage of not being overlooked.
• *Is impeding the proposed use contrary to the public interest?* Again, planning permission is relevant, but it must be remembered that planning permission does not necessarily imply that the proposed development is positively in the public interest. In the *Bass* case in view of the noise and amenity problem the development would cause, the economic interest of Bass Ltd could not be equated with the public

interest. It is worth noting that the Tribunal has normally interpreted the requirement of public interest strictly and has rejected claims that impeding particular development is contrary to the public interest because, for example, housing land is in short supply or government policy favours high density development.

* *If the restriction does not secure benefits of substantial value and/or the proposed use is not contrary to the public interest, would money be an adequate compensation?* This question was not relevant to the *Bass* case and so was not dealt with. It is clear that a restriction can be discharged or modified without the payment of any compensation where no loss or disadvantage is suffered.[5] By definition, even where a loss or disadvantage is suffered, the levels of compensation are likely to be modest since a restriction which secures substantial benefits will not be modified or discharged in the first place. Equally, there are cases where money is not adequate compensation, for example where the application is being opposed a local authority acting in the interest of the local community.[6]

1   LPA, s 84(1)(aa), (1A).
2   (1973) 26 P & CR 156.
3   [1983] Ch 27, [1982] 2 All ER 576, CA.
4   Ibid.
5   See LPA, s 84(1) and para 38.40 below.
6   *Re Martin's Application* [1989] 1 EGLR 193, but note *Re Willis' Application* [1997] 28 EG 137.

38.40   The Tribunal may order that the applicant pay to the objectors a sum by way of compensation intended either:

* to make up for any loss or disadvantage suffered in consequence of the discharge or modification of the restriction; or
* in an appropriate case to make up for any effect the restriction had, at the time when it was imposed, in reducing the price then received by the objector for the land affected by it.[1]

1   LPA, s 84(1).

Housing Act 1985, s 610

38.41   Application may be made under this section to a county court to vary a restrictive covenant to enable a house to be converted into two or more dwellings. The applicant must either have planning permission for the proposed conversion or prove to the court that (owing to changes in the character of the neighbourhood) the house cannot readily be let as a single dwelling but could if converted. The court must give interested parties an opportunity of being heard, and may vary the covenant (subject to such conditions and on such terms as it thinks just).

Proposals for reform

38.42   In 1984 the Law Commission produced a report and draft legislation[1] aimed at comprehensive reform of the law of covenants. The mainspring of their report was the need to deal with the unsatisfactory state of the law concerning positive covenants,[2] but they were equally unhappy with the complex and uncertain law relating to restrictive covenants. Their proposal was to introduce for the future a new interest in land, the land obligation.

However, it has just been announced that the report will not be implemented.[3] Nevertheless, the more ready enforcement of some positive obligations may yet come into effect by another route if the current proposals concerning commonhold find their way onto the statute book.[4] Briefly, the suggestion is that units of accommodation (either residential or commercial) may be declared a 'commonhold'. Individual units would be owned freehold, but the common parts would be owned by the commonhold association (which is made up of the unit owners). That association would be responsible for the maintenance of the common parts and for major expenditure; the positive obligation to contribute to the cost of such work would be enforceable against the original unit holders and anyone to whom they sell their unit.

1   The Law of Positive and Restrictive Covenants (1984) Law Com No 127.
2   Para 38.4 above.
3   Press Notice, 19 March 1998.
4   Commonhold Draft Bill, Commonhold Consultation Paper, July 1996.

Chapter 39

Mortgages

39.1 A mortgage of land is a transfer of an interest in the land as security for a debt. It enables the creditor, in the event of the debtor being unable or unwilling to pay off the debt, to enforce the debt against the land, for example by selling the land and recouping what he is owed. Mortgages are created most commonly where a building society or other institutional lender lends money towards the purchase of a home. A mortgage may, however, be granted by a landowner to secure (ie as security for) a bank loan, or a loan from a finance company, or to secure a current account, as well as, in the commercial sphere, to secure a loan to finance the purchase of property or the expansion of a business. The creditor, the lender of the money to whom the mortgage is granted, is called the mortgagee, the debtor or borrower is called the mortgagor.

39.2 Provisions in mortgages for the repayment of the debt, principal plus interest, vary considerably. In the traditional form of mortgage, in relation to which the law of mortgages developed, the principal is to be repaid in a lump sum, although provisions will normally be made for regular payments of interest in the interim. The endowment mortgage, now common in the case of house purchase, is a variety of this '*standing*' type of mortgage. Under this scheme, the mortgagor makes regular payments of interest to the mortgagee while at the same time paying premiums on an endowment assurance policy[1] which on maturity will provide a lump sum for the repayment of the principal.

Today, a very common form of mortgage is the instalment mortgage under which the principal is repayable in instalments. This may take one of two forms. It may be provided, as in a standing mortgage, that the entire principal be repaid at a fixed (early) date but subject to a proviso that so long as instalments of principal and interest are regularly paid, the provision for repayment of the whole sum will not be enforced. Alternatively, and this is now more usual, an instalment mortgage provides that the principal and interest are to be repaid over a period of years, subject to a proviso that the entire sum due shall become payable in the event of default.

In this chapter we consider:

- the ways in which mortgages can be created;
- the rights of the mortgagor;
- the right to possess the mortgaged property;
- the mortgagee's remedies; and
- the order in which mortgages will be paid off where the security proves to be insufficient.

1   The life assurance policy itself is mortgaged by way of assignment to the building society or other
     mortgagee as further security.

Creation of legal mortgages

Unregistered land

39.3 By virtue of the LPA, ss 85(1) and 86(1) legal mortgages of freeholds and
leaseholds may be created by one of two methods: the 'demise' or 'long lease' method
and the 'charge' method. The latter is now more usual; we begin, however, with the
demise method.

By demise

39.4 *Freehold*   A freeholder may mortgage his interest in the land by granting
(demising) to the mortgagee a long term of years subject to a provision for cesser on
redemption (that is, a provision that the lease shall come to an end when the mortgage
is redeemed by being paid off). The Act lays down no duration for the term of years,
but, by analogy with the provision next to be explained, 3,000 years is common.

Prior to the passing of the 1925 Act, the normal way for a freehold to be mortgaged
was for the mortgagor to assign his entire interest in the land to the mortgagee. (Such
rights as the mortgagor thereafter had in the land were protected by equity, in the form
of his 'equity of redemption'.[1]) Should a mortgagor today purport to mortgage his
freehold by conveying it to the mortgagee, the transaction is to take effect as a demise
of the land for a term of 3,000 years, subject to a provision for cesser on redemption.[2]

A freeholder may wish, providing his land offers sufficient security, to create a
second, or third mortgage. A second or subsequent mortgage by demise involves the
grant of a term one day longer than that vested in the preceding mortgagee.[2]

1   Para 39.13 below.
2   LPA, s 85(2).

39.5 *Leasehold*   A lessee may create a mortgage by sub-demise, ie by granting a
sub-lease of a term at least one day (in practice, 10 days) shorter than his own, again
subject to a provision for cesser on redemption. Should the lessee purport to mortgage
his interest simply by assigning his term to the mortgagee, the transaction takes effect
as a sub-demise for a term ten days less than the leasehold interest being mortgaged.[1]
Second or subsequent mortgages take effect as sub-demises for a term one day longer
than the term vested in the preceding mortgagee, where possible, and in any event at
least one day less than the mortgaged term.[2]

1   LPA, s 86; *Grangeside Properties Ltd v Collingwood Securities Ltd* [1964] 1 WLR 139.
2   LPA, s 86.

By charge

39.6 Both freeholds and leaseholds may be mortgaged by the mortgagor charging
his land, by a deed[1] expressed to be 'by way of legal mortgage', with the payment of
the mortgage debt.[2] The LPA, s 87(1) states that a mortgage by charge by deed
expressed to be by way of legal mortgage confers on the mortgagee 'the same
protection, powers and remedies' as if the mortgage had been created by demise.

The charge method is now the preferred one, and is particularly favoured by the
institutional lenders, as involving a shorter, simpler deed, under which both freehold
and leasehold land can be mortgaged together and which, to the layman, more obviously
creates a mortgage than does a document which by its terms leases the land for 3,000
years. A practical advantage in the case of leaseholds is that a mortgage by charge

does not constitute an infringement of a covenant, absolute or qualified, against sub-letting.[3]

We might mention here, as an aside, that a mortgagee of a leasehold by sub-demise or by charge may seek relief from forfeiture proceedings instituted by the head landlord in respect of a breach of covenant by the lessee.[4]

1   Para 31.6 above.
2   LPA, s 87(1).
3   Para 36.29 above.
4   LPA s 146(4); *Grand Junction Co Ltd v Bates* [1954] 2 QB 160, [1954] 2 All ER 385; *Abbey National Building Society v Maybeech Ltd* [1985] Ch 190, [1984] 3 All ER 262; para 36.35 above.

Registered land

39.7   A legal mortgage of registered land, freehold or leasehold, may be made in the same way as a mortgage of unregistered land.[1] However, the registered proprietor's power to mortgage is normally exercised by the creation, by deed, of a charge under the provisions of the LRA, s 25. Such a deed need not be expressed to be by way of legal mortgage for, unless it is expressed to take effect by demise or sub-demise, it is deemed to be a charge by way of legal mortgage.[2]

It is in fact common for institutional lenders to use the same form of charge by way of legal mortgage for both registered and unregistered land. A charge on registered land created under the LRA, s 25 must, of course, be completed by registration.[3] Details of the charge and its proprietor, ie the mortgagee, are entered in the charges register of the mortgagor's register of title; the mortgagor's land certificate must be retained by the registry,[4] and the mortgagee is issued with a charge certificate.[5]

1   LRA, s 106(1); LPA, ss 85(3) and 86(3).
2   LRA, s 27(1) and (2); *Cityland and Property (Holdings) Ltd v Dabrah* [1968] Ch 166, [1967] 2 All ER 639.
3   Ibid, s 26.
4   Ibid, s 65.
5   Ibid, s 63.

Creation of equitable mortgages

Unregistered land

39.8   An equitable interest in land, such as a beneficial interest under a trust of land may only be mortgaged in equity. The major category of equitable mortgage, however, is constituted by informal mortgages.[1]

1   See para 32.6 above.

Mortgages of equitable interests

39.9   The owner of an equitable interest may mortgage it by outright assignment in writing,[1] to the mortgagee, subject to a provision for reconveyance on redemption. Such a mortgage may be overreached on a conveyance of the legal estate.[2]

1   LPA, s 53(1)(c); para 31.11 above.
2   Paras 34.7 and 34.17 above.

Informal mortgages

39.10   A mortgage is constituted in equity:

*   where the mortgage is in writing so as to satisfy the requirements of LPA, s 53;[1] or

- where the mortgage is in writing rather than by deed as required at law;[2] or
- where the parties agree to create a legal mortgage, such agreement being in writing.[3]

An intended legal mortgage not made with the formality of a deed is regarded, as would be an informal lease,[4] as a contract to create a legal interest. Like an actual agreement to create a legal mortgage, it is regarded by equity as specifically enforceable provided it is in writing and gives rise to an immediate equitable interest. This equitable mortgage (unless protected by deposit of title deeds, mentioned below) requires protection by registration in the Land Charges Registry.[5]

The most common form of equitable mortgage used to arise where the mortgagor simply deposited his title deeds with the mortgagee as security for a loan. Such an arrangement was regarded in equity as giving rise to a contract to create a legal mortgage. This equitable mortgage, being protected by deposit of title deeds, would not be registrable in the Land Charges Registry. It is now clear that, as a result of the Law of Property (Miscellaneous Provisions) Act 1989, s 2, this form of informal mortgage can no longer exist.[6] It is now necessary for the deposit of title deeds to be accompanied by an agreement in writing (or by deed[7]) incorporating all the express terms of the mortgage and signed by or on behalf of the parties. An agreement in writing showing an intention to deposit title deeds as security constitutes an equitable mortgage even if the deeds are not in fact deposited, in which case, there being no deposit, the agreement should be registered under the Land Charges Act.

1   Para 31.11 above and see *Murray v Guinness* [1998] NPC 79.
2   LPA, ss 52 and 87; para 31.6 above.
3   Law of Property (Miscellaneous Provisions) Act 1989, s 2; para 31.2 above.
4   Paras 32.3 and 32.6 above.
5   Para 35.11 above.
6   *United Bank of Kuwait plc v Sahib* [1996] 3 All ER 215, CA.
7   The use of a deed has the advantage of making available to the mortgagee the statutory power of sale; see para 39.35 below.

Registered land

39.11   A proprietor of registered land may create an informal mortgage in the manner outlined in the previous paragraph since he is entitled to mortgage the land in any manner which would have been permissible if the land had not been registered. The LRA, s 66 confers power on the proprietor to deposit his land certificate as security for a loan. The mortgage so created may be protected by the mortgagee giving to the Registrar notice of the deposit, which operates as a caution under s 54,[1] or by the entry of a notice or caution[2] on the register of title. An equitable mortgage created in any other way should be protected by notice or caution,[3] unless accompanied by deposit of the land certificate, in which case it may be protected by notice of deposit.[4]

1   LRR, r 239.
2   Paras 35.30 and 35.31 above.
3   LRA, s 106(3).
4   *Re White Rose Cottage* [1965] Ch 940, [1965] 1 All ER 11, CA. As to the priority of mortgages of registered land, see para 39.50 below.

Mortgagor's right to redeem

Legal date of redemption

39.12   As we pointed out in para 39.4 above, prior to 1926 a legal mortgage of land was effected by an outright conveyance of the mortgagor's estate to the mortgagee, subject to a provision for reconveyance on payment of the moneys due. The mortgage would provide that redemption should take place on a fixed date. At common law, if the moneys due under the mortgage were not repaid on that date there could be no reconveyance. Further, the mortgagor, despite having lost the right to have his land reconveyed, remained liable to repay the money he owed.

The equitable right to redeem and the equity of redemption

39.13 This harsh common law rule was radically limited by equity. In equity, the essence of a mortgage was seen to be the provision of security for a debt and hence the mortgagee would be compelled to reconvey the land on payment of what was owed to him, ie the principal plus interest (and costs), even though the contractual (or legal) date for redemption had passed. Equity, recognising that the mortgagor still had rights in the land despite having conveyed the legal estate to the mortgagee, conferred on the mortgagor an interest in the land, known as his 'equity of redemption' which, in particular, gave him a continuing right to redeem the mortgage.

Once it was established that redemption was possible after the contractual date, that date came to be fixed at an early date, conventionally six months from the date of the mortgage. This clearly did not affect the mortgagor's equitable right to redeem, but enabled him to redeem at that early date if he wished. The contractual provision for redemption was not dispensed with, because – on the passing of the date fixed – the mortgage money was regarded as due and the mortgagee was thereafter in a position to exercise his remedies for non-payment.

We have seen that, today, a legal mortgage cannot be effected by an outright conveyance;[1] the mortgagor thus retains the legal estate. He is nevertheless regarded as also having an equity of redemption in respect of the land, giving him the right to redeem the mortgage despite the passing of the contractual date for redemption. In a standing mortgage and in certain instalment mortgages,[2] an early date for redemption is still fixed, commonly at six months from the date of the mortgage. Neither party intends that the mortgage should be redeemed at that date, the provision is inserted simply to bring into play the mortgagee's remedies, as the mortgage money is then due.

In those instalment mortgages which do not provide for an early contractual date but provide for payment of principal and interest over a number of years, perhaps 20 or 25, it is usual for the parties to provide that the entire mortgage moneys become due should the mortgagor default in respect of one or two instalments. Where the contractual date for redemption has passed, the mortgagor is entitled, subject to any express provision in the mortgage providing otherwise,[3] to redeem the mortgage by paying the principal plus interest on giving the mortgagee six months' notice or six months' interest in lieu of notice.[4]

1   Paras 39.4 and 39.5 above.
2   Para 39.2 above.
3   But see paras 39.18–39.20 below.
4   *Browne v Lockhart* (1840) 10 Sim 420; *Cromwell Property Investment Co Ltd v Western and Toovey* [1934] Ch 322.

Consolidation

39.14 It may briefly be noted at this point that where a mortgagor has separately mortgaged a number of properties to the same mortgagee, or those mortgages have been acquired by the same mortgagee, then provided the right has been expressly reserved in at least one of the mortgages, and the mortgage moneys are due in respect of each mortgage, the mortgagee will be entitled to consolidate the mortgages, treating them as one. In such a case the mortgagee may refuse to allow redemption of one mortgage unless all are redeemed.[1]

1   *Jennings v Jordan* (1881) 6 App Cas 698 at 700.

Discharge of the mortgage

39.15   On redemption, the mortgagee should, in the case of unregistered land, endorse on or annex to the mortgage deed a statutory receipt, stating the name of the person who paid the money, which operates as a discharge of the mortgage and puts an end to the mortgagee's interest. However, where the mortgage is redeemed not by the mortgagor but by, for example, a subsequent mortgagee, the effect is not to discharge the mortgage but to transfer it to the person redeeming.[1] An alternative form of statutory receipt may be used by building societies, but it cannot be used to effect a transfer of the mortgage since it does not name the person who paid the money. In the case of a registered charge under the LRA, discharge is effected by cancellation of the entry in the register on receipt of the prescribed form of discharge.[2]

1   LPA, s 115.
2   LRA, s 35.

Redemption by court proceedings

39.16   Redemption is normally a straightforward matter which does not require the intervention of the court. However, where the property is subject to more than one mortgage in favour of different mortgagees it is very occasionally necessary to bring an action for redemption in either the Chancery Division or the county court. Where such an action is brought by a second or subsequent mortgagee to redeem a prior mortgage, then not only must the prior mortgagee(s) be a party to the action, but also the mortgagor and any intervening and subsequent mortgagees. The reason is that in such actions the mortgagee seeking to redeem must 'redeem up, foreclose down'. For example, where M has mortgaged his property to A, B, C and D, C, in an action for redemption of A's mortgage, must also redeem B and seek foreclosure[1] in relation to D and M, thus giving each of these the opportunity to 'redeem up' or be foreclosed. The court may as an alternative order sale of the mortgaged property.[2]

1   Paras 39.42–39.45 below.
2   LPA, s 91; para 39.40 below.

Impediments to full redemption

39.17   Equity is careful to preserve the essential nature of a mortgage as a transaction involving the giving of security for a loan, a proposition reflected in the maxim, 'once a mortgage, always a mortgage'. In particular, it requires that there should be 'no clogs or fetters on the equity of redemption', that is, that the mortgage should not contain terms which impede the ability of the mortgagor to redeem his property free of the conditions of the mortgage. We shall see that the case law in the following paragraphs establishes that the court will declare void a provision in a mortgage which either is inconsistent with the mortgagor's right to redeem his property unfettered by any term of the mortgage, or is unfair and unconscionable. It should also be noted that, like any other contract, a mortgage transaction may be set aside on the basis of undue influence.[1] Many of the cases on this subject have involved mortgages, notably where a mortgagor has persuaded his spouse or co-habitee to participate in a mortgage; as we have seen, this may mean that the victim can have the mortgage set aside.[2]

1   Paras 14.47–14.55 above.
2   Para 14.55 above.

Provisions excluding redemption

39.18 It follows from what we said in the preceding paragraph that a provision excluding redemption in a mortgage granted by an individual[1] is of no effect.[2] Thus where the mortgage deed confers on the mortgagee an option to purchase[3] the mortgaged property, that provision is void[4] because, of course, at the option of the mortgagee, the mortgagor may be prevented from redeeming his property and be forced to sell. However, there is nothing to prevent the parties, by a separate transaction genuinely independent of the mortgage, agreeing that the mortgagee should have an option to purchase the property.[5]

A provision will be regarded as excluding the right to redeem where this is its real effect. Thus, in *Fairclough v Swan Brewery Co Ltd*,[6] F mortgaged his 17$\frac{1}{2}$-year lease to the brewery, the mortgage containing a clause prohibiting redemption until six weeks before the expiry of the lease. This clause was held to be void since, for all practical purposes, it rendered the mortgage irredeemable.

1 Under the provisions of the Companies Act 1985, s 193, a company may create an irredeemable mortgage.
2 *Re Wells, Swinburne-Hanham v Howard* [1933] Ch 29 at 53.
3 Para 31.4 above.
4 *Samuel v Jarrah Timber and Wood Paving Corpn Ltd* [1904] AC 323, HL; *Lewis v Frank Love Ltd* [1961] 1 All ER 446, [1961] 1 WLR 261.
5 *Reeve v Lisle* [1902] AC 461, HL.
6 [1912] AC 565, PC.

Oppressive or unconscionable terms

39.19 Equity has long regarded itself as having a broad jurisdiction to strike down any provision in a mortgage which impedes full redemption of the mortgaged property unfettered by the terms of the mortgage or which is unfair, oppressive or unconscionable. This is well illustrated by *Cityland and Property (Holdings) Ltd v Dabrah*[1] where the mortgage provided for the repayment by instalments over six years of a sum representing the capital sum advanced together with a premium of 57%. On the mortgagor's default, the court refused to permit the mortgagee to enforce payment of the stated sum, allowing him only the principal plus interest, which (in 1967) was fixed at 7%. In the circumstances, the provision for the payment of a premium was unconscionable, particularly as this was not a bargain between trading concerns but a case of house purchase by a mortgagor of limited means.

However, the limits of this general jurisdiction were explained in *Multiservice Bookbinding Ltd v Marden*.[2] Here the mortgage provided for the repayment by instalments of the capital sum plus interest at 2% above the bank rate payable on the whole sum throughout the term of the loan. Further, each instalment was subject to index-linking in the form of a 'Swiss franc uplift'; that is, the amount payable was then to be increased (or, theoretically, decreased) in proportion to the variation in the rate of exchange between the pound and the Swiss franc since September 1966. (Furthermore, the loan could not be called in, nor was the mortgage redeemable, for 10 years.) Browne Wilkinson J held that although the mortgage might be unreasonable this is not the relevant test; the question is whether any of the terms of the bargain are unfair and unconscionable which requires that the terms have been imposed in a morally reprehensible manner. In this case the parties were businessmen, who entered the agreement with their eyes open, with the benefit of independent legal advice and without any compelling necessity on the part of the company to accept the loan on these terms. The company was therefore bound to comply with the mortgage.

The general power to strike out unconscionable terms has been resorted to in two particular types of case which we consider in the following paragraphs.

1   [1968] Ch 166, [1967] 2 All ER 639.
2   [1979] Ch 84, [1978] 2 All ER 489.

39.20   *Provisions postponing redemption* We have seen that provisions which render a mortgage irredeemable will be struck out.[1] Terms which merely postpone the right to redeem are not automatically void; their validity depends on whether or not they are unfair or unconscionable. In *Knightsbridge Estates Trust Ltd v Byrne*,[2] the plaintiff company, wishing to pay off an existing debt, sought a loan of £310,000 from the friendly society of whom the defendants were trustees, at 5% interest repayable over 40 years. The society agreed and a mortgage was executed providing for repayment in half-yearly instalments over 40 years.

Five-and-a-half years later the plaintiff company brought an action claiming to be entitled to redeem the mortgage, on the basis that the postponement of redemption for 40 years was a clog on the right to redeem. The Court of Appeal rejected their claim, holding that equity is concerned to see only *two* things – one that the essential requirements of a mortgage transaction are observed and the other that oppressive or unconscionable terms are not enforced. Equity does not interfere with mortgage transactions merely because they are unreasonable, which, in any event, this transaction was not.

Instalment mortgages of the traditional building society repayment variety, although providing for repayment over 20 or 25 years, normally do not prevent early redemption; however, they often insist upon a period of notice or the payment of interest instead.

1   Para 39.18 above.
2   [1939] Ch 441, [1938] 4 All ER 618, CA; affd on other grounds [1940] AC 613, [1940] 2 All ER 401, HL.

39.21   *Provisions conferring collateral advantages* The parties may by their agreement confer on the mortgagee some advantage additional to repayment of the principal plus interest plus costs. Where such an additional advantage, such as an option to purchase, renders the mortgage irredeemable, it is clearly void, unless contained in some separate and independent transaction.[1] More complex are those cases in which mortgages impose some type of commercial tie such as that the mortgagor should only buy, and sell on the premises, beer or petrol supplied by the mortgagee. Originally the courts took the view that such provisions would be valid if limited to the period of the mortgage;[2] if designed to continue beyond redemption they would be invalid because they would then fetter the right to full redemption. Thus, in *Noakes & Co Ltd v Rice*,[3] a provision in a mortgage tying the mortgaged leasehold property to the mortgagee brewery not only for the duration of the mortgage but for the duration of the entire lease, was held void, for its effect would have been to permit the mortgagor, who mortgaged a free house, to redeem only a tied house thus fettering his right to redeem.

However, it is clear that the courts have become uncomfortable at the prospect of interfering with the terms of a bargain entered into by business people, often with the assistance of professional advice. Accordingly, various devices have been used to retreat from the position where the enforceability of a collateral adavantage hinges entirely on the technicality of whether or not they last beyond redemption. As with provisions excluding the right to redeem, in some cases the court may be able to construe a provision contained in a mortgage deed which confers some additional advantage on the mortgagee as in fact being a separate transaction even though it is contained in the same deed.[4] In this way the advantage will not be struck down as being inconsistent with, or a clog on, the right to redeem. Thus, in *Kreglinger v New Patagonia Meat and Cold Storage Co Ltd*,[5] the mortgage between the plaintiff woolbroker and the defendant meat packers provided that for a period of five years, whether or not the loan was paid off earlier, the defendants would give the plaintiff the right to buy all sheepskins. The mortgage was redeemed after two years and the defendants disputed the plaintiff's right thereafter to the sheepskins. The House of Lords held that the plaintiff remained entitled to the skins. The grant of the right to purchase sheepskins was in substance independent of the mortgage.

However, certain of the judgments in the *Kreglinger* case went rather further, suggesting that, in any event, an advantage collateral to the security will not be held void unless it is:

- unfair or unconscionable; or
- in the nature of a penalty clogging the equity of redemption; or
- inconsistent with or repugnant to the contractual and equitable right to redeem.[6]

If this wider approach is accepted, the validity of a collateral advantage may now quite simply depend on whether or not it is unfair, oppressive or unconscionable, rather than on the period for which it is imposed.[7]

1   Para 39.18 above.
2   *Biggs v Hoddinott* [1898] 2 Ch 307, CA.
3   [1902] AC 24, HL.
4   *Kreglinger v New Patagonia Meat and Cold Storage Co Ltd* [1914] AC 25, HL; *Re Petrol Filling Station, Vauxhall Bridge Road, London, Rosemex Service Station Ltd v Shell Mex and BP Ltd* (1968) 20 P & CR 1.
5   [1914] AC 25, HL.
6   Ibid at 61.
7   Subject to what is said in the following paragraph concerning the doctrine of unreasonable restraint of trade.

Restraint of trade

39.22   In *Esso Petroleum Co Ltd v Harper's Garage (Stourport) Ltd*[1] the House of Lords held that the restraint of trade doctrine, which we discuss in ch 15 above, applies to provisions in a mortgage. Thus collateral advantages contained in a mortgage, perhaps providing for a commercial tie, may not only be invalidated as preventing full redemption or as being unfair and unconscionable, but also as being in unreasonable restraint of trade.

1   [1968] AC 269, [1967] 1 All ER 699, HL.

Consumer Credit Act 1974

39.23   Under ss 137 to 139 of this Act, power is conferred on the county court to 're-open extortionate credit bargains' and to 'do justice between the parties' in consequence. Thus any mortgage where the mortgagor is an individual may be re-opened if it provides for the mortgagor to make 'grossly exorbitant' repayments or if it otherwise grossly contravenes ordinary principles of fair dealing. In determining whether the agreement is extortionate, the court is to take into account only the statutory criteria, without regard to any general principles of unconscionability;[1] these include interest rates prevailing at the time the agreement was made, the age, experience and business capacity of the mortgagor and the extent to which he was under financial pressure. In reopening the agreement, the court may, among other things, alter its terms or set aside the whole or part of any obligation imposed by it.

The Act further regulates mortgages granted to secure loans not exceeding £25,000, other than loans by banks, building societies, local authorities and certain bodies (including insurance companies and friendly societies) specified in subordinate legislation. The provisions of the Act relating to such mortgages (which, notably, cover second mortgages to finance companies), include that which provides for the prospective mortgagor to be given an opportunity to withdraw from the transaction, those providing for the form and content of the agreement, that which prevents a higher rate of interest being charged on default, and particularly (and to be borne in mind in relation to the mortgagee's remedies) that providing that a mortgage regulated by the Act may only be enforced by order of the court.

1 See *Davies v Directloans Ltd* [1986] 2 All ER 783, [1986] 1 WLR 823.

Possession of the mortgaged property

39.24 As a matter of legal theory, which has little relation to practical reality, it is not the mortgagor who has the legal right to possession of the mortgaged property. In the absence of agreement to the contrary, the mortgagee may go into possession before the ink is dry on the mortgage. He has this right because he has a legal term of years (or its statutory equivalent) in the property.[1] Thus the right of the mortgagee to possession has nothing to do with default on the part of the mortgagor. Furthermore, despite dicta to the contrary,[2] equity will not interfere to prevent the mortgagee from assuming possession save to adjourn the application for possession for a very short time in the unlikely event that there is a reasonable prospect of the mortgagor paying off the mortgage in full.[3] The rigour of this apparently harsh rule, that the mortgagee may have possession of the property at any time, is in fact mitigated in a number of respects, with the result that possession is almost invariably resorted to only as a remedy in the event of default and, even then, only as a preliminary step to an exercise of the power of sale, so that the sale may be made with vacant possession.

A legal mortgagee may take physical possession by peaceably entering on the property.[4] It is usual, however, in the case of a dwelling-house, to seek a possession order from a county court, requiring the delivery of vacant possession within a specified time. It is likely, but not absolutely certain, that possession of a dwelling-house can only be obtained by a court order.[5]

The mortgagee is also regarded as taking possession where he serves notice on the tenants of the mortgagor to pay rent to him.[6]

1 *Four-Maids Ltd v Dudley Marshall (Properties) Ltd* [1957] Ch 317 at 320, [1957] 2 All ER 35 at 36.
2 *Quennell v Maltby* [1979] 1 All ER 568 at 571.
3 *Birmingham Citizens Permanent Building Society v Caunt* [1962] Ch 883, [1962] 1 All ER 163.
4 For regulated credit agreements, see para 39.23 above.
5 A mortgagor who is in occupation of a dwelling may qualify for protection under the Protection from Eviction Act 1977, s 1. Furthermore, it has been suggested that, although the Administration of Justice Act 1970, s 36 (see para 39.30 below) does not explicitly require court proceedings to be taken in order to take possession of a dwelling, this requirement is implicit. Finally, anyone taking possession of premises, irrespective of their nature, needs to beware of falling foul of the Criminal Law Act 1977, s 6(1).
6 See *Davies v Law Mutual Building Society* (1971) 219 Estates Gazette 309, DC.

39.25 In contrast to the position of the legal mortgagee, it appears, though the matter is in some doubt, that an equitable mortgagee has no right to possession, in the absence of an expressly reserved right or a court order for possession.[1]

1 *Barclays Bank Ltd v Bird* [1954] Ch 274 at 280, [1954] 1 All ER 449 at 452.

Restrictions on the mortgagee's right to possession
39.26 The mortgagee's right to possession may be restricted in a number of ways. It may be limited

- by an express provision in the mortgage;

- by an implied provision in the mortgage;
- (indirectly) by the obligation to account strictly while in possession;
- (in the case of a dwelling) by the court.

Each of these will be examined in the following paragraphs.

Express restriction
39.27 The terms of the mortgage may expressly provide that the mortgagee may only go into possession in the event of default. This is increasingly the case in building society and similar mortgages.

Implied restriction
39.28 Although the legal mortgagee's right to possession should not be lightly treated as abrogated or restricted,[1] the court may find that the mortgagee has by implication contracted out of his right to possession. In particular, the court will be ready to find an implied term that the mortgagor may remain in possession until default in an instalment mortgage, but there must be something on which to hang such a conclusion other than the mere fact that it is an instalment mortgage,[2] for example where the mortgage speaks of the mortgagee having the power to eject the mortgagor in the event of default.[3]

1   *Western Bank Ltd v Schindler* [1977] Ch 1 at 9, [1976] 2 All ER 393 at 396.
2   *Esso Petroleum Co Ltd v Alstonbridge Properties Ltd* [1975] 3 All ER 358, [1975] 1 WLR 1474.
3   *Birmingham Citizens Permanent Building Society v Caunt* [1962] Ch 883, [1962] 1 All ER 163.

Duty to account strictly
39.29 A mortgagee who goes into possession is liable to account *strictly* to the mortgagor. This goes well beyond a natural requirement that he must account for any income which he has actually received since taking possession; the duty to account *strictly* means that he is also liable to the mortgagor for money which he ought to have received. Thus, where a mortgagee in possession (a brewery) leased[1] the mortgaged premises (a public-house) on the basis that it was tied to the brewery, the mortgagee was held liable to account to the mortgagor not only for the rent actually received but also for the (higher) rent which would have been received had the property been let as a free rather than a tied house.[2] While this duty to account strictly does not directly restrict a mortgagee's right to possession, any mortgagee who would have taken possession in order to receive the income of the mortgaged property so as to cover unpaid instalments is very much better advised not to do so and instead to appoint a receiver, a remedy which we consider at para 39.41 below.

1   For powers of leasing, see para 39.46 below.
2   *White v City of London Brewery Co* (1889) 42 Ch D 237, CA.

Possession of dwellings
39.30 *The basic jurisdiction* Where the mortgagee of a dwelling house is seeking possession the court has the power to delay any order for possession. By the Administration of Justice Act 1970, s 36 the court can adjourn the proceedings, or make an order but suspend its operation, or make an order postponing the date for possession, if it appears to the court that the mortgagor is likely within a reasonable period to pay any sums due under the mortgage or to remedy any other default under the mortgage.

39.31 *The problem of instalment mortgages* A problem which rapidly emerged out of the original drafting of s 36 concerned the usual provision in instalment mortgages that, in the event of default, the *entire sums* due under the mortgage become immediately payable. It was obviously not Parliament's intention to give the court the power to delay possession only where the mortgagor could pay off the *whole* mortgage debt within a reasonable period, but this was all the section achieved.[1] The Administration of Justice Act 1973, s 8 seeks to alleviate the problem. This provides that in the case of instalment mortgages, or other mortgages providing for deferred payment of the principal, which contain such a default clause, the sums due under the mortgage are to be regarded, for the purposes of s 36, as being the arrears of instalments or deferred payments. In such cases the court may exercise its power to delay possession where it appears likely that within a reasonable period the mortgagor will pay the *instalments* owing and that he will keep up with the *instalments.*

Unfortunately, the wording of s 8 is far from ideal and litigation has been necessary to establish exactly what types of deferred payment mortgages fall within its ambit. It is now settled that the section applies to endowment mortgages,[2] but not to mortgages which secure an overdraft repayable 'on demand'.[3]

1 *Halifax Building Society v Clark* [1973] Ch 307, [1973] 2 All ER 33.
2 *Bank of Scotland v Grimes* [1985] QB 1179, [1985] 2 All ER 254, CA.
3 *Habib Bank Ltd v Tailor* [1982] 3 All ER 561, [1982] 1 WLR 1218, CA.

39.32 *The court's discretion* Clearly the court will delay possession where there is a reasonable prospect of paying off the arrears within a reasonably short period. In practice, however, by the time proceedings are actually brought the mortgagor is often in substantial default. The decisions of the courts have been notoriously inconsistent and it is difficult to discern a principled approach. In *First National Bank plc v Syed*[1] the Court of Appeal ruled that, in order to justify a postponement, the mortgagor must have a realistic ability to make payments which will cover current instalments and make some inroads into the arrears. In this case the mortgagor was only able to afford payments which fell below the interest charges and a postponement was refused.

A crucial issue is often the period over which the repayment of the arrears can be made; in other words, what is the reasonable period within which payment of the sums owing must be made? Initially, the courts seemed to take the view that this would be no more than two to four years (and, often very much shorter).[2] However, the position was reviewed by the Court of Appeal in *Cheltenham and Gloucester Building Society v Norgan.*[3] Here, most importantly, the court has taken the view that, in principle, the outstanding period of the loan should be regarded as a reasonable period within which any arrears should be paid off, at least in a case where the property is still adequate security for the loan. Accordingly, it would now seem that, where the mortgagor can make payments which will cover current instalments and pay off the arrears by the end of the loan period (which can be anything up to 25 years), possession will be postponed.

The court may also delay possession in order to give the mortgagor an opportunity to sell the property himself (in order to produce the funds to pay off the debt), since such a sale will normally result in a better price than one earned out by the mortgagee;[4] the court will not adopt this approach unless there is a realistic prospect of a speedy sale.[5] Furthermore, where the proceeds of sale will not discharge the debt, and where the mortgagee is looking to conduct the sale itself, possession will not normally be postponed since the objective of the mortgagor in such a situation is not usually to obtain a better price but to hold up the eventual sale of the property.[6]

1 [1991] 2 All ER 250.
2 See the comments of Waite LJ in *Cheltenham and Gloucester Building Society v Norgan* [1996] 1 All ER 449, CA.
3 [1996] 1 All ER 449, CA.

4   *Target Home Loans Ltd v Clothier* [1994] 1 All ER 439, CA.
5   *Town & Country Building Society v Julien* (1991) 24 HLR 312, CA.
6   *Cheltenham and Gloucester plc v Krausz* [1997] 1 All ER 21, CA. The position will be rather different
     where the mortgagee is *not* wishing promptly to sell the property; see *Palk v Mortgage Services Funding
     plc* [1993] 2 All ER 481, CA which we consider at para 39.40 below.

Mortgagee's remedies

Action on the personal covenant

39.33   As we have intimated, the mortgagor's covenant to repay may take a number
of forms.[1] For example, he may covenant to repay the loan at a fixed date, and, until
repayment of the whole of the loan, to pay regular instalments of interest, or he may
covenant to repay by instalments of principal and interest over a period of years.
Whatever their precise form, should he default on his obligations, the mortgagor may
be sued for breach of covenant by the mortgagee. Where the mortgage provides for
repayment on a fixed contractual date, the mortgagee's right to sue arises in the event
of failure to pay on that date. Where the mortgage provides for repayment in
instalments, the mortgagee may sue for unpaid instalments. It is, however, usual to
include a default clause providing that the whole sum becomes due in the event of
failure to pay, perhaps, two instalments. Where the mortgage makes the whole sum
payable on demand, the right of action accrues at the start of the mortgage unless, as
is common, there is provision for notice to be given.[2] However, where a default clause
in an instalment mortgage provides for default to result in the mortgage money
becoming payable on demand, the demand must first be made before the right to sue
accrues.[3] If the mortgage is by deed, no action may be brought after 12 years from the
date on which the cause of action accrued.[3] If it is not, when it can only be equitable,
the limitation period is six years. As a general rule, not more than six years' arrears of
interest may be recovered.[4]

1   See para 39.2 above.
2   *Re Brown's Estate, Brown v Brown* [1893] 2 Ch 300.
3   *Esso Petroleum Co Ltd v Alstonbridge Properties Ltd* [1975] 3 All ER 358, [1975] 1 WLR 1474.
4   Limitation Act 1980, s 20.

Sale

39.34   Where the mortgagee brings an action against the defaulting mortgagor for
breach of his covenant to repay, he is clearly not relying on the fact that he is a secured
creditor. While such action may be worthwhile where the reason for default is the
reluctance of the mortgagor to pay, it is scarcely so where the reason is the mortgagor's
inability to pay. In such a case the mortgagee will wish to enforce his security, and he
will normally do this by exercising his power of sale. While it is possible to provide
expressly for a power of sale, it is usual to rely on the statutory power conferred by
the LPA, or that power as modified by the terms of the mortgage. The major attraction
of the statutory power is that there is no requirement for the mortgagee to obtain court
approval for its exercise, although it should be appreciated that, where the mortgaged
property is a dwelling-house, the mortgagee will, in practice, need to obtain a court
order for possession[1] in order to be able to sell with vacant possession.

1   Paras 39.30–39.32 above.

The power of sale

39.35   Where the mortgage is made by deed[1] and contains no expressed contrary
intention, the LPA, s 101 confers on the mortgagee the power to sell the mortgaged

property when the mortgage money has become due. The mortgage money becomes due when the contractual date for redemption has passed, if such a date is fixed, or, in the case of mortgages providing for repayment in instalments of principal and interest, when an instalment is due and unpaid.[2] The contractual date of six months or earlier usually fixed in standing mortgages is incorporated therefore, not with the object that the mortgage should be redeemed at that time, but in order that the remedy of sale and other remedies for enforcing the security should become available at an early opportunity. As to mortgages providing for repayment by instalments of principal and interest, the mortgagee may only exercise his power of sale to enforce his security in respect of instalments in arrear,[2] unless, as is normal, it is provided that failure to pay one or more instalments causes the entire sum to become due. In endowment mortgages it is likewise usual for a default clause to provide that failure to pay instalments of interest makes the entire sum, principal and interest, due.

Although the mortgagee's power to sell *arises* when the mortgage money has become due, he may not, by virtue of the LPA, s 103, *exercise* the power, unless and until:

- notice (in writing) requiring payment of the mortgage money has been served on the mortgagor, and he has not, within three months thereafter, paid the sums due; or
- some interest under the mortgage is in arrear and unpaid for two months after becoming due; or
- there has been a breach of some provision contained in the mortgage deed or in the LPA other than the covenant for repayment.

The provisions of the mortgage deed itself may, and commonly do, vary or extend the statutory provisions,[3] for example by providing that the power of sale should be exerciseable as soon as it arises.

1 Ie legal mortgages and equitable mortgages by deposit where the agreement for deposit is executed as a deed; see paras 39.10 above and 39.39 below.
2 *Payne v Cardiff RDC* [1932] 1 KB 241.
3 LPA, s 101(3).

Exercise of the power

39.36 The power of sale is exercised, and the mortgagor's right to redeem thus barred, as soon as the mortgagee enters into a binding contract to sell.[1] The mortgagee may not purport to sell the land to himself.[2] There is, however, no hard and fast rule that a mortgagee may not sell to a company in which he is interested. Where he does so, the mortgagee and the company seeking to uphold the transaction must show that the sale was in good faith and that the mortgagee took reasonable precautions to obtain the best price reasonably obtainable at the time.[3]

Although the mortgagee has only a term of years or equivalent charge in respect of the land, he has full power to convey the mortgaged freehold or leasehold together with fixtures attached to the land, the mortgage term or charge and any subsequent terms or charges being merged in the estate conveyed or extinguished, as the case may be.[4]

The purchaser takes the estate subject to rights having priority to the mortgage, but freed from subsequent rights. The Act provides that the purchaser's title may not be challenged on the ground that the mortgagee's power was not, in fact, exerciseable, or due notice was not given, or the power was otherwise improperly or irregularly exercised. The Act further provides that the purchaser is not concerned to inquire as to these matters.[5] It would thus appear that, unless the power of sale has not even arisen (in which case the purported sale takes effect as a transfer of the mortgage) the purchaser takes a valid legal title to the mortgaged land. However, it has been suggested that, if the purchaser becomes aware of any facts showing that the power is not exerciseable, or that there is some impropriety in the sale, he does not get a good title.[6] In any event a person affected by an improper or irregular exercise of the power of sale has a remedy in damages against the mortgagee.[5]

1   *Property and Bloodstock Ltd v Emerton* [1968] Ch 94, [1967] 3 All ER 321, CA.
2   *Farrar v Farrars Ltd* (1888) 40 Ch D 395 at 409; *Williams v Wellingborough Borough Council* [1975] 3 All ER 462, [1975] 1 WLR 1327, CA.
3   *Tse Kwong Lam v Wong Chit Sen* [1983] 3 All ER 54, [1983] 1 WLR 1349, PC; see para 39.37 below.
4   LPA, ss 88 and 89, and see LRA, s 34; for the powers of an equitable mortgagee, see para 39.39 below.
5   LPA, s 104.
6   *Lord Waring v London and Manchester Assurance Co Ltd* [1935] Ch 310 at 318.

39.37   *Price* In exercising its power of sale, a building society is under a statutory duty to take reasonable care to ensure that the price at which the property is sold is the best price which can reasonably be obtained.[1] In any event it was established in *Cuckmere Brick Co Ltd v Mutual Finance Ltd*[2] that all mortgagees are under a duty to the mortgagor to take reasonable care to obtain 'a proper price' or 'the true market value'. In that case the duty was framed as one in the tort of negligence; this suggested that a mortgagee's professional adviser could owe a similar duty[3] and that a mortgagee could owe such a duty to third parties, such as guarantors.[4] However, later cases have made it clear that the duty is one imposed by equity on the mortgagee alone, and is owed only to the mortgagor.[5]

Case law indicates that sale by auction does not necessarily show that reasonable care has been taken to obtain the proper price.[6] A mortgagee proposing to sell should consult professional advisors such as estate agents as to the method of sale and the measures which should be taken in order to secure the best price. However, this does not mean that the mortgagee must exercise his power of sale as a trustee would. On the contrary, he is entitled to exercise it for his own purposes whenever he chooses. It matters not that the moment may be unpropitious and that, by waiting, a higher price could be obtained.[7] However, and by way of example, should the mortgagee, in advertising the property for sale, negligently fail to mention that it has the benefit of planning permission, he will be liable to account to the mortgagor for the difference between the price obtained and 'a proper price' or 'the true market value'.[2] A purchaser in such a case would appear to be protected by the LPA, s 104,[8] unless, perhaps, he was aware of the irregularity.

1   Building Societies Act 1986, Sch 4, para 1.
2   [1971] Ch 949, [1971] 2 All ER 633, CA; see also *Predeth v Castle Phillips Finance Co Ltd* [1986] 2 EGLR 144, CA.
3   See remarks in *Cuckmere Brick Co Ltd v Mutual Finance Ltd* [1971] Ch 949, [1971] 2 All ER 633, CA.
4   *Standard Chartered Bank Ltd v Walker* [1982] 3 All ER 938, CA.
5   *China & South Sea Bank Ltd v Tan* [1989] 3 All ER 839, PC; *Parker-Tweedale v Dunbar Bank plc* [1990] 2 All ER 577, CA.
6   *Tse Kwong Lam v Wong Chit Sen* [1983] 3 All ER 54, [1983] 1 WLR 1349, PC.
7   *Bank of Cyprus (London) Ltd v Gill* [1980] 2 Lloyds Rep 51.
8   Para 39.36 above.

39.38   *Proceeds* The LPA, s 105 provides that, first, any prior mortgages to which the sale was not made subject must be discharged. Then the proceeds are held by the selling mortgagee in trust:

*   to pay the costs and expenses of the sale;

- to pay off the principal plus interest and costs due under the mortgage;
- to pay the surplus to any subsequent mortgagee of whom he has notice (he should therefore search the Land Charge Register or register of title as appropriate), or, if there is no subsequent mortgagee, to the mortgagor.

Equitable mortgages

39.39 Unless an equitable mortgage, or a memorandum of deposit, is effected by deed, the mortgagee may not sell, save by order of the court.[1] Where the mortgage is made by deed, the statutory power under s 101 is available; however, there is some doubt as to whether it enables an equitable mortgagee to sell the legal estate or simply his own equitable interest.[2] Although this latter would seem unlikely, to avoid any doubt it is usual for the memorandum to confer on the mortgagee a power of attorney to vest the legal estate in a purchaser on a sale. Alternatively (or as well) the memorandum may contain a declaration that the mortgagor holds the legal estate on trust for the mortgagee, conferring on the latter the right to appoint himself as trustee in place of the mortgagor and thus enabling the mortgagee to acquire, and vest in a purchaser, the legal estate.

1   LPA, s 91(2); para 39.40 below.
2   *Re Hodson and Howes' Contract* (1887) 35 Ch D 668; *Re White Rose Cottage* [1965] Ch 940, [1965] 1 All ER 11, CA.

Court's power to order sale

39.40 It will be appreciated from the foregoing paragraphs that the mortgagee's statutory *power* to sell is almost invariably more than adequate to allow the realisation of the security once the mortgagor is in default. However, as we have seen in the previous paragraph, there may be situations in which the mortgagee does not have a statutory power to sell because the mortgage is not by deed; in such a situation, a mortgagee wishing to sell will need to seek a court *order* of sale.[1] Further, as we shall see, where a mortgagee is seeking to foreclose,[2] the court may well choose to order a sale instead.[3]

In addition, there have been recent illustrations of applicants asking the court to exercise its jurisdiction to order a sale, despite the existence of a statutory power to sell. In *Arab Bank plc v Merchantile Holdings Ltd*[4] the mortgagee had already negotiated a sale which was the best that could be hoped for in the light of the fall in the property market. It asked the court to order a sale rather than rely on its statutory power because of strong evidence that the mortgagor would try, unjustifiably, to prevent the transaction going ahead. The court agreed to do so, especially given that the sale might well fall through unless the purchasers were confident that it could not be challenged.

Palk v Mortgage Services Funding plc[5] was a case in which, most unusually, it was the *mortgagor* asking the court to order a sale. Here, again, the value of the mortgaged property had fallen dramatically. The mortgagors wished to sell, albeit at a price well below their outstanding debt, in order to reduce the amount of capital owed and so to stem the ever-increasing interest charges. The mortgagee was refusing to co-operate,[6] taking the view that it would be better to let the property (even though the rent would not meet the interest payments) and wait for the market to improve. In these exceptional circumstances the Court of Appeal was prepared to order a sale. However, it has recently been made clear that the court will not allow the mortgagor to conduct a sale where it is clear that the mortgagee does wish to exercise its statutory power of sale (which was not the case in *Palk*); in such a situation, the mortgagor's motive is normally to delay the sale for as long as possible.[7]

1 Under LPA, s 91(2).
2 See paras 39.42–39.45 below.
3 See para 39.44 below.
4 [1994] 2 All ER 74.
5 [1993] 2 All ER 481, CA.
6 A sale by the mortgagor could not, in practice, go ahead without the mortgagee undertaking to discharge the mortgage; see para 31.30 above.
7 *Cheltenham and Gloucester plc v Krausz* [1997] 1 All ER 21, CA and para 39.32 above.

Appointment of a receiver

39.41 In the case of commercial or tenanted properties, the mortgagee may wish to secure payment of any instalment due to him without taking action to realise his security, by appointing a receiver to manage the property and receive its income or rents. The statutory power to appoint a receiver arises and is exerciseable on the same conditions as the power of sale,[1] again subject to any extension or variation in the mortgage deed. The appointment and removal of the receiver must be in writing. A receiver appointed under the statutory power is deemed to be the agent of the mortgagor.[2] The mortgagee will be liable to account to the mortgagor only for what he receives from the receiver, and not for what, without wilful default, might have been received.[3] The receiver has power to demand and recover rents due but may not himself grant leases unless he has the sanction of the court[4] or the mortgagee has delegated his power of leasing to him. The receiver is to apply money received by him in the following order:

* in discharge of all outgoings affecting the mortgaged property;
* in making payments under prior mortgages;
* in payment of his own commission, of insurance premiums payable under the mortgage, and of the cost of carrying out repairs required by the mortgagee;
* in payment of interest due under the mortgage;
* in or towards paying off the principal if required by the mortgagee; and
* in paying the residue to the mortgagor.[5]

1 LPA, ss 101 and 109; para 39.35 above.
2 LPA, s 109.
3 See para 39.29 above.
4 *Re Cripps* [1946] Ch 265, CA.
5 LPA, s 109.

Foreclosure

39.42 As soon as the mortgage money is due,[1] or in the event of a condition of the mortgage being broken,[2] the mortgagee may apply to the court for foreclosure. A mortgage is foreclosed when a court order of foreclosure is granted to the mortgagee which has the effect of putting an end to the mortgagor's right to redeem and vests the mortgaged property in the mortgagee, subject to any prior mortgages but freed from any subsequent ones. On the face of it, this is, from the point of view of the mortgagor and any subsequent mortgagees, a harsh remedy because their rights in the property are extinguished. For this reason both the mortgagor and any subsequent mortgagees must be made parties to the foreclosure action.

Because of the severity of the remedy it is in fact made subject to a number of restrictions which have had the effect that foreclosure is rarely sought, mortgagees preferring to enforce their security by seeking vacant possession of, and subsequently selling, the mortgaged property. An application for foreclosure remains of utility in certain cases, particularly where there is no statutory power of sale, for example in the case of equitable mortgages of a legal estate not made by deed.[4]

1 Para 39.33 above.
2 Eg a covenant to pay instalments of interest: *Twentieth Century Banking Corpn Ltd v Wilkinson* [1977] Ch 99, [1976] 3 All ER 361.
3 LPA, s 88(2); LRA, s 34(3).
4 Para 39.39 above.

39.43 On an application for foreclosure, the court will first grant an order nisi. This requires accounts to be taken of what is due to the mortgagee in respect of principal, interest and costs, and orders the mortgagor, within (usually) six months thereafter, to pay the sums due or be foreclosed in default. In the event of non-payment an order absolute for foreclosure may be made. Where there are subsequent mortgagees, they too have the opportunity to redeem but in default will be foreclosed.[1]

The court has a discretion to extend the period given for repayment of the sums due or even to 'open the foreclosure' after an order absolute has been made. Relevant factors in the exercise of this latter discretion include whether the mortgagor made his application within a reasonable time, whether he was prevented from redeeming only by some accident, the value of the mortgaged property as compared to the sums due (for the courts are reluctant to allow the mortgagee a windfall profit), and any special value the property had for the mortgagor.[2] A foreclosure order has even been reopened after the mortgagee had sold the property to a third party, but only where the sale took place immediately after the foreclosure and the third party had notice of the facts which gave rise to the order being re-opened.[2]

Furthermore, in cases of instalment (or other deferred payment) mortgages of dwelling-houses, power is conferred on the court by the Administration of Justice Act 1973, s 8 to adjourn the proceedings or suspend its order, where it appears likely that the mortgagor will pay the instalments owing and keep up with future instalments.[3]

1 Para 39.16 above.
2 *Campbell v Holyland* (1877) 7 Ch D 166.
3 Paras 39.30–39.32 above.

39.44 Perhaps more influential than the foregoing in reducing the importance of foreclosure as a remedy is the fact that, under the LPA, s 91(2), the court has power on the application of any interested party to order sale of the property instead of foreclosure.[1] Clearly, the court will be particularly willing to exercise this power where it is shown that the value of the property exceeds the amount due under the mortgage since, otherwise, the mortgagee reaps a windfall profit. Sale may be ordered on such terms as the court thinks fit; for example, it may even require that the mortgagor pay into court a sum sufficient to protect the mortgagee against loss. While it may order immediate sale, it may equally provide time for redemption of the mortgage. Conduct of the sale will usually be given to the mortgagor since he will be most concerned to realise the highest price for the property. A reserve price will be fixed, and the purchase money must be paid into court.

Given that sale of the mortgaged property is highly likely as a result of an application for foreclosure, it will be preferable for the mortgagee to exercise his power of sale to realise his security. However, that power must have arisen and must be exerciseable.[2]

In *Twentieth Century Banking Corpn Ltd v Wilkinson*,[3] the mortgage provided that, for the purposes of the LPA, the mortgage money was not due until the end of the mortgage term. The mortgagor defaulted on his obligation in the meantime to pay instalments of interest and the mortgagee sought an order for sale or foreclosure. The court held that the mortgagee's statutory power of sale would not arise until the mortgage money became due, but that the mortgagee was entitled to seek foreclosure because the mortgagor was in breach of a condition of the mortgage. Since the mortgagee was entitled to foreclosure the court had a discretion to order sale instead, which it did.

1 Para 39.40 above.
2 Para 39.35 above.
3 [1977] Ch 99, [1976] 3 All ER 361.

Registered land

39.45 The proprietor of a registered charge has all the powers of a legal mortgagee. Sale of the mortgaged property and an order of foreclosure must be completed by registration respectively of the purchaser or mortgagee as proprietor of the land and by cancellation of the charge.[1]

1 LRA, s 34.

Leasing

39.46 Both the mortgagor, while in possession, and the mortgagee, if he has taken possession or has appointed a receiver,[1] are empowered by the LPA, s 99[2] to grant leases in accordance with that section. The leases authorised by the section are agricultural or occupation leases for a term not exceeding 50 years, and building leases for a term not exceeding 999 years. Such leases must take effect in possession not later than 12 months from their date, must reserve the best rent reasonably obtainable, and must contain a covenant for payment of rent and a condition of re-entry in the event of breach.[3] The lessee must execute a counterpart of the lease. If in good faith a lease is granted which does not comply with these requirements, it takes effect in equity as a contract to grant an equivalent lease in accordance with the statutory power.[4]

Save in relation to mortgages of agricultural land[5] and the grant of new tenancies of business premises under the Landlord and Tenant Act 1954, Part II,[6] the statutory power applies only to the extent that it is not excluded by the parties. In fact it is normal practice to exclude the mortgagor's statutory power of leasing altogether. In this way the mortgagor is prevented from creating (without the positive consent of the mortgagee), for example, an assured tenancy within the Housing Act 1988,[7] which would devalue the mortgagee's security. Where the mortgage terms exclude the power to create any tenancy, any breach is commonly expressed to give rise to the mortgage money becoming due, and hence to the mortgage's remedies becoming available. Where the mortgagor's power of leasing is so excluded then any purported tenancy granted by the mortgagor is binding on the parties to it by estoppel[8] but does not bind the mortgagee.[9]

1 To whom the power of leasing may be delegated.
2 See also LRA, s 34.
3 Further conditions are imposed in respect of building leases.
4 LPA, s 152(1).
5 Agricultural Holdings Act 1986, Sch 14, para 12.
6 Para 36.76 above.
7 Para 36.71 above.
8 Para 36.16 above.
9 *Iron Trades Employers Insurance Association v Union of House and Land Investors Ltd* [1937] Ch 313, [1937] 1 All ER 481; *Dudley and District Benefit Building Society v Emerson* [1949] Ch 707, [1949] 2 All ER 252, CA; *Britannia Building Society v Earl* [1990] 2 All ER 469, CA; and see *Quennell v Maltby* [1979] 1 All ER 568, CA.

Insurance

39.47 The mortgagee is empowered by the LPA, s 101 to insure the mortgaged property against loss or damage by fire up to the amount specified in the deed or up to two thirds of the amount which would be required to reinstate the property in the event of total destruction.[1] The premiums become part of the mortgage debt. It is common expressly to provide that the mortgagor shall insure the property for a specified sum or the full value of the property or, particularly in building society mortgages, that the society will effect the insurance for a specified sum but the premiums will be payable by the mortgagor.

The mortgagee may require that all moneys received under an insurance of the mortgaged property effected under the terms of the Act or the mortgage deed be applied by the mortgagor in making good the loss or damage or be applied in or towards the discharge of the mortgage money.[1] Should the mortgagor independently of any obligation in the mortgage insure the property the mortgagee is not entitled to any money received, but where the money is payable in the event of fire he can require that it be used towards reinstatement,[2] and in any event it is common to exclude the mortgagor's power independently to insure the property.

1   LPA, s 108.
2   Fires Prevention (Metropolis) Act 1774, s 83.

Priorities

39.48 The issue of priorities between competing mortgagees arises where the value of the mortgaged property is insufficient to provide security for all the mortgages to which the property is subject. The incidence of this problem is rare in times of rapidly increasing property values, so long as mortgagees act with care. However, as the property recession of the early 1990s has shown, should the value of property decline the difficulty may well arise. In such a case, if the property is sold to realise the security, the various mortgagees do not share in the proceeds equally or rateably in proportion to the size of their mortgage; the mortgagee having priority is paid in full before any money is passed to the second in priority, and so on. The rules for determining the priorities differ according to whether the mortgaged property is subject to the Land Registration Act or not.

Unregistered land
39.49 As regards legal and equitable mortgages of a legal estate, we must distinguish between those protected by deposit of title deeds and those not so protected. A first legal mortgagee is entitled to hold the title deeds to the mortgaged property[1] and this confers on him priority over all subsequent mortgagees[2] unless he is by his conduct estopped from asserting his priority, or guilty of fraud or gross negligence in relation to the title deeds, as by, for example, releasing them to the mortgagor to enable the latter to grant another mortgagee by representing himself as the owner of an unencumbered legal estate.[3] A first equitable mortgagee by deposit will enjoy similar priority unless guilty of fraud or gross negligence. He will also lose priority where a subsequent legal mortgagee has no notice of the prior equitable mortgage, although this is somewhat unlikely given the absence of the mortgagor's title deeds.

Any mortgage, whether legal or equitable, which is not protected by the deposit of title deeds (usually second and subsequent mortgages) must be registered under the

Land Charges Act 1972.[4] Such mortgages rank for priority according to date of registration.[5]

Failure to register such mortgages renders them void against a purchaser for value of any interest in the land, including subsequent mortgagees, legal or equitable.[6] Failure to register does not affect the enforceability between mortgagor and mortgagee, but postpones the unregistered mortgage to the subsequently created one.

Mortgages of equitable interests[7] have priority in accordance with the order in which notice in writing of the mortgage is received by the trustees.[8]

1   LPA, ss 85(1) and 86(1).
2   LPA, s 13.
3   *Walker v Linom* [1907] 2 Ch 104; *Northern Counties of England Fire Insurance Co v Whipp* (1884) 26 Ch D 482; *Perry-Herrick v Attwood* (1857) 2 De G & J 21.
4   Para 35.11 above.
5   LPA, s 97.
6   Land Charges Act 1972, s 4(5).
7   Paras 35.12 and 39.9 and 39.11 above.
8   *Dearle v Hall* (1823) 3 Russ 1; affd (1828) 3 Russ 1 at 48; LPA, s 137.

Registered land

39.50   Registered charges[1] rank for priority as between themselves in order of registration.[2] Mortgages created off the register[3] take effect as minor interests in equity[4] and may be protected by the entry of a notice[5] or caution.[6] Since the LRA makes no provision for the priority of minor interests, the courts have applied the basic rule of equity that the first in time prevails;[7] thus, as between themselves, they rank in order of creation, irrespective of the order in which any entry on the register was made.[8] However, where any subsequent mortgage is by registered charge, this will override any prior mortgage which is merely protected by the entry of a caution;[9] a registered charge will *not* override a prior mortgage protected by the entry of a notice.[10] A mortgage which is not protected by any entry at all will be overridden by a subsequent registered charge but, being the first in time, it will take priority over all other subsequent mortgages, even where these are protected by the entry of either a notice or a caution.[11]

As in unregistered land, mortgages of equitable interests, such as a life interest, rank in order of notice being received by the trustees of the settlement, in accordance with the rule in *Dearle v Hall*.[12]

1   Para 39.7 above.
2   LRA, s 29.
3   Para 39.7 above.
4   LRA, s 66.
5   See para 35.30 above.
6   Para 35.31 above. Mortgages by deposit of the land certificate (see para 39.12 above) may be protected by the entry of a notice of deposit; this has the same legal effect as a caution, LRA, s 106(3)(b), LRR, r 239(4).
7   See para 35.33 above.
8   See *Re White Rose Cottage* [1965] Ch 940, [1965] 1 All ER 11, CA; *Barclays Bank Ltd v Taylor* [1974] Ch 137, [1973] 1 All ER 752, CA; *Mortgage Corpn Ltd v Nationwide Credit Corpn* [1993] 4 All ER 623, CA.
9   *Clark v Chief Land Registrar* [1994] 4 All ER 96, CA. It should be noted that it will be rare for a registered charge to override a prior mortgage in this way since the cautioner, on being informed of the impending registered charge, will normally take steps to protect his position. In the *Clark* case the Land Registry failed to warn the cautioner as it should have done; although the latter was held to be deferred to the subsequent registered charge, he was entitled to an indemnity from the Land Registry.
10 *Mortgage Corpn Ltd v Nationwide Credit Corpn* [1993] 4 All ER 623, CA.
11 Ibid.
12 (1823) 3 Russ 1; LPA, s 137; LRA 1986, s 5.

Tacking of further advances
Unregistered land

39.51   Where a mortgagee makes a further loan, or advance, to the mortgagor, in certain circumstances it may be 'tacked on' to the original mortgage so as to enjoy the priority of that mortgage. Tacking of further advances is particularly important where a person mortgages property to a bank to secure his overdrawn current account. The overdraft at the time of the mortgage represents the original debt for which the mortgage is security: each subsequently honoured cheque represents a further advance. The bank will, of course, wish to ensure that it does not lose priority in respect of these further advances to any intervening mortgage of the property created by the debtor.

The circumstances in which tacking is permitted are:

* if an arrangement has been made to that effect with the subsequent mortgagees; or
* if the mortgagee had no notice of such subsequent mortgages when he made the further advances; or
* where the mortgage imposes an obligation to make further advances, in which case it matters not that the mortgagee had notice of subsequent mortgages.[1]

In one particular type of case, registration of a subsequent mortgage in the Land Charges Register does not constitute notice. This is where the mortgage is expressly made as security both for the original loan and any further advances (as in the case of building society mortgages and mortgages to secure overdrafts). In such a case, the original mortgagee therefore need not search the Land Charges Register before making each further advance.

1   LRA, s 94.

Registered land

39.52   Where a registered charge is made for securing advances, that fact will be noted on the register of title. Any further advances will have the priority of the original charge unless and until the mortgagee receives (or ought in due course of post to have received) a notice from the Registrar of an entry on the register which prejudicially affects the priority of further advances. Further advances made under a registered charge imposing an obligation on the mortgagee have the priority of the original charge, the obligation being noted on the register to warn prospective mortgagees.[1]

1   LRA, s 30.

Index